DOCUMENTS OF SOCIAL HISTORY

Editor: Anthony Adams

THE SHEFFIELD OUTRAGES

THE SHEFFIELD OUTRAGES

REPORT PRESENTED TO
THE TRADES UNIONS COMMISSIONERS IN 1867
WITH AN INTRODUCTION BY

SIDNEY POLLARD
Professor of Economic History, University of Sheffield

AUGUSTUS M. KELLY · PUBLISHERS
NEW YORK 1971

Published in the United States by
Augustus M. Kelly · Publishers
New York, New York 10001
SBN 678 07766 5
Library of Congress Catalogue Card No. 72-108850
Printed in Great Britain by Redwood Press Limited,
Trowbridge & London

INTRODUCTION

The Minutes of Evidence taken by the Commissioners enquiring into the Sheffield Outrages in 1867, which are republished here together with their Report, form a mid-Victorian social document of wide and absorbing interest. They contain a verbatim account of a quasi-judicial examination in which several men, prominent in their city and in their trade, were gradually forced to admit in public to having repeatedly broken the law and to having committed some major crimes. This will naturally hold the attention of any reader acquainted with modern crime fiction, especially that which puts its climaxes into the Court Room. Such a reader may be allowed to find his own satisfaction from the personal drama of the pages which follow, irrespective of any historical interest, and he will not be disappointed. He should, perhaps, be advised to begin with the evidence of George Shaw, and then go on to that of James Hallam, Samuel Crooks and William Broadhead. But for those who would also derive some knowledge of a corner of nineteenth-century England from this volume, these introductory paragraphs may offer a guide through the maze of social and industrial relationships existing in Sheffield in the 1860's covered by the Inquiry.

The industries with which the Inquiry was mainly concerned, the making of tools and knives in the town of Sheffield, do not belong to those factory trades which caught the eye of contemporaries, and which were admired by foreign visitors, praised by politicians, described in detail by such as Karl Marx, and generally held to be responsible for the prosperity of Britain, the 'workshop of the world'. Yet they were representative of mid-Victorian England for all that. For it is often forgotten how much of British industry and prosperity, even as late as 1867, depended on the manual skill of workmen working with primitive tools but with exquisite craftsmanship, not in large manufactories but in small and intimate workshops. Cotton cloth and iron rails, steam engines and beer were, it is true, mainly produced in huge establishments. But printers and furniture-makers, tailors and cobblers, hat-makers and bakers and numerous others, were still earning their living at the workshop and outwork stage of industrial organization.

Among them were the Sheffield cutlers, the saw- and tool-makers who speak to us out of the pages which follow. Lacking the limelight of the large unit, their history and experience have been unduly obscured. They are worthy of rescue from oblivion for at least two reasons. First, because of their own significant role in Victorian society, where their splendid but underpaid skill encouraged the solidity and the over-ornamentation which characterized the typical products of that age. But secondly, because they are a survival from an earlier period, from the eighteenth century and centuries beyond, of which we cannot now directly learn the intimate details and the flavour of their lives, but to which the men of 1867 may give us some limited access.

There are, to be sure, numerous descriptions of the craftsman's world of the pre-factory age. We know of his apprenticeship, his wages, his methods of work, and much else besides. But we seldom hear him speak with his own voice: the information comes to us through other eyes and other mouths. But in the evidence given in Sheffield in the summer of 1867 we get a direct and immediate sense of the self-confidence, the pride of skill, the assured place in society, the facility for making decisions, which the man who works with his hands once possessed, but has now lost with the machine, and which survived in Sheffield to spill over into the crowded room in the Town Hall in which the Commissioners heard their evidence.

The claim must not be driven too far. Many things had changed in the past century, and Sheffield in 1867 was no exact replica of pre-industrial conditions. If for no other reason, this was because the workmen of Sheffield knew that their industries were at the centre of a world commercial network, that technical progress was potentially very powerful, and that elsewhere in England wage-earners worked under very different conditions. But it is impossible to follow again the evidence given in 1867 (particularly if read against the background of contemporary press comment) without being conscious that here was an encounter between the nineteenth century and the eighteenth, a clash between the ethos of industrial capitalism and that of pre-capitalist industry. At times, the learned Commissioners, good, solid middle-class citizens, do not even speak the same language as the grinders and forgers who appear before them, and communication all but breaks down. But there are other times when those among the questioners who know Sheffield well catch the tone of the men, and then it is we who are in danger of losing touch with them, for we have all been conditioned by a very different ethos, by a very different concept of economic reality and therefore of right and wrong. At such points we have to listen very carefully, so as to be sure to hear what they are saying, rather than what we expect them to say.

* * *

On 8 October 1866, in the early hours of the morning, a can of gunpowder was thrown into the cellar of a dwelling in New Hereford Street off the Moor in Sheffield, the house of Thomas Fearnehough, a saw-grinder. Its explosion caused much damage to the house, though no one was hurt. Sheffield was not greatly agitated about this attack at first, for it was known that Fearnehough was at loggerheads with his 'trade', and in such cases Sheffield trade unions were liable to resort to violent means to bring the defaulter into line. Indeed, compared with other cases of explosions and actual killings and maimings, this was a relatively mild affair, and the men in the trade might have been forgiven for thinking that in this case, as in so many others, the role of the trade union would be suspected, but nothing would ever be proved against anyone, and the matter would be allowed to drop into oblivion, as being an internal issue between Fearnehough and his fellow saw-grinders.

In this, however, they would have been wrong. The 'Hereford Street outrage' was not allowed to be passed over. An outcry arose, first among Sheffield manufacturers and then quickly taken up by the national press. The local manufacturers offered a reward of £1,000 for information leading to conviction, and the local trade unions, protesting their innocence, offered £100. But as the ripples of the affair spread outward from the town, its scope was progressively increased. First, there arose a clamour for an official inquiry, to prove that the trade unions were responsible for this outrage and other similar ones, and to see that the perpetrators were brought to justice. Before long, the activities of the Sheffield unions were submerged in the question of the survival of trade unions as such, not just in Sheffield, but in the country as a whole.

How was it that single canister of gunpowder proved capable of setting off a whole minefield? The reason is to be sought in the fact that trade unions had been propelled into public consciousness in the mid-1860s and were to find themselves very quickly at a most critical turning point of their career. For the first time, large national amalgamated societies had arisen which were solid enough to survive trade depressions, or defeat in disputes, without breaking up, and with their strength almost unimpaired. One of them, the carpenters' and joiners' union, had defied the powerful London master builders' lock-out in 1859 and had gone from strength to strength after that. At the same time the more traditional unions in coal mining and iron-working, in cotton and in building also showed signs of greater maturity and cohesiveness. Moreover, the amalgamated societies with their full-time secretaries, centred on London, proved to possess an ominous ability to put pressure on Members of Parliament and to influence other centres of traditional middle-class power.

Beyond the organization of their own trades, workmen had also shown an increasing effectiveness in combining the forces of many different trades. In one town after another, local trades councils had been established in the late 1850s and the 1860s. The International Workingmen's Association, set up in 1864, emphasized the growing political involvement of the trade unions by offering the spectacle of an alliance between British trade unionists and Continental revolutionaries like Marx and Bakunin. In 1864 also, the Glasgow trades council had called a national conference in London, attended by leading unionists, in order to initiate a reform of the one-sided Master and Servant Acts. This was followed by another national conference, in July 1866, this time in Sheffield, called by the Sheffield trades council. It was attended by 138 delegates, representing nominally some 200,000 members, including most of the trades unions of the north and the Midlands, though the amalgamated societies were at best lukewarm towards it. As was customary at that time, the officers of the local association were elected to the offices of the national body; George Austin, of the Sheffield railway spring-makers, became chairman, William Dronfield, of the

Sheffield typographers, secretary, and William Broadhead, of the saw-grinders (later proved to be the chief instigator of the outrages), was treasurer.

The chief object of the Sheffield conference was to form a defensive alliance against lock-outs, and it arose out of a large file trade lock-out in Sheffield lasting sixteen weeks, earlier in the year. On that occasion, the normal practice of the other local trades to support any locked-out men could not be put into operation, for the filesmiths, much the largest of the local unions, were too numerous and proved too heavy a burden, so that the local men were driven to look for national support. But there was also a second reason. In the previous October, the Social Science Association had met in Sheffield, and had discussed trade unionism. In its report, the bitterly anti-union paper by a local Liberal working-man, John Wilson, was reprinted, and so was a summary of the discussion, but the pro-union paper, read by Dronfield, was omitted. It was Dronfield's hope that the national trade union conference would become a forum for hearing papers and a counterweight to the biased middle-class propagandist body which had treated him so shabbily.

At first sight this might seem a trivial matter, right outside the mainstream of trade union development since, after all, the T.U.C., which arose out of these conferences, has never become a forum for learned papers. But the incident is not without significance. We find Dronfield, a working man, claiming the same rights as middle-class and professional people or their spokesmen—a claim which could not have been seriously put forward in any city outside Sheffield and, perhaps, Birmingham. At the same time, things were changing in London, too, and there also, but on quite a different basis, leading trade unions were becoming 'respectable' and were claiming political and social rights. It was these claims which lay behind the general uneasiness, and the public interest, over trade-union affairs. It was also these claims which coloured much of the activity of the first International. Here, then, was an issue bridging in some way the gap between Sheffield and London, between the old and dying system, and the new, rising organizations.

The permanent organization founded by the Sheffield meeting, the United Kingdom Alliance of Organized Trades, petered out after two further meetings in 1867, in Manchester and Preston, but it became the direct forerunner of the Trades Union Congress, officially dated from the next national meeting, held in Manchester in 1868. It also had its obvious links with the national meetings called in 1867 to deal with the threats to the trade union movement provoked by the Sheffield outrages themselves, and the Royal Commission of 1867 on the Trade Unions.

Behind the apparent newly-found powers of the trade unions which were thus agitating the organs of public opinion, lay yet another threat, perhaps felt as the most serious of all: the growing certainty, as the year 1866 drew to a close, that the skilled working-men of the towns would soon be given the vote, as indeed they were in the following year by the second Reform Act. There was fear, in any case, of what these newly enfranchised voters would do with their power, and whether they would use it, as the other classes had done, to shape legislation in their own narrow class interest. More precisely, there was the fear, frequently rekindled by the sporadic excursions of the trade unions into politics, that the trade unions might become an alternative focus of political allegiance and draw off working-class votes from the two established parties. Even the most Radical of the electoral reformers were unwilling to contemplate a working-class party to challenge the party game in Westminster which had kept Victorian society intact.

If the middle classes feared the new self-confidence of the unions and if many of them wished to use the Sheffield outrages to discredit them, the trade unions were not without fears and grievances themselves. We have already noted their efforts to combat the gross inequalities of the Master and Servant Acts. A more immediate threat was posed to them by a judicial decision of the Court of Queen's Bench in the case of *Hornby* v. *Close* in January, 1867. According to this, trade unions could not sue their defaulting officers for embezzlement of funds, since, as the Lord Chief Justice declared, the unions, while they were no longer criminal, were in restraint of trade and therefore illegal. This decision, one of many in legal history in which the British courts have undone years and decades of trade-union progress, was rightly seen as an invitation extended by the judiciary to officials to destroy unionism by theft, and was accompanied by several other legal decisions, including the notorious

R. v. *Druitt* case (1867), which made virtually all normal trade-union actions liable to prosecution for criminal conspiracy. Together they removed what shaky legal foundation there had been for trade unionism since the Act of 1825.

Thus it was that trade unionists, anxious to repudiate the accusations that unions as such were responsible for the outrages, and at the same time in desperate need to re-establish their legal rights which had suddenly been taken from them, joined the clamour for a Commission of Inquiry and for new legislation. Defence Committees were formed in London and in Sheffield, public meetings were complemented by pressure behind the scenes, and the Government bowed before the storm of the forces hostile as well as those favourable to trade unionism. In February 1867, a strong Royal Commission was appointed to enquire into trade union affairs as a whole; and a separate Sub-Commission was set up to enquire into the trade outrages. A minor inquiry was mounted into some violence committed in Manchester, but the major investigation was concerned with the acts of violence reported from Sheffield, and it is this Commission whose minutes of evidence and official report are herewith reprinted.

* * *

There were three Commissioners, headed by William Overend. Overend, a Queen's Counsel, was a local man who had won some distinction as Chief Commissioner of the tribunal set up after the Sheffield flood of 1864 to determine compensation for the victims. The other two, Thomas Irwin Berstow and George Chance, also had legal training, and both the manufacturers and the unions were legally represented. Behind the scenes, the manufacturer's association and the police had collected details of some 209 cases of violence, including 20 major outrages, and had some confessions and convictions to serve as a base, though none for a major crime. The Town Hall Council Chamber, and the Mayor's Parlour, were put at their disposal.

Two features of the Commission's terms of reference deserve special mention. One was their limitation to the past ten years, which tended unwittingly to convey the impression that 'rattenings' and other illegal actions were a recent development. The evidence, on the contrary, made it quite clear that these practices to enforce trade union rules can be understood only by seeing them as long-established traditions, accepted as such both by perpetrators and by victims and, indeed, by the town as a whole. 'My impression is', said Broadhead, 'that rattening has existed in every trade before any of this assembly here were born.'[1] The Commissioners, to give them credit, noted this in their report and stated further that violence had tended to decline somewhat from its high point in *c.*1859–1861.[2]

The other is of much greater significance. This was the power given to the Commissioners to grant certificates of indemnity to any of the lawbreakers who were judged to have made a full and truthful confession. The grant of such powers overriding the laws of the land, which was almost unique in British legal history, caused grave misgivings in the House of Lords, in the House of Commons and in legal circles generally when it was put forward by the Government, on advice from Sheffield. It was held by some that this emphasis on the criminal element was designed to prejudice the general investigation into trade-union affairs. Others noted that it ensured that criminals, as individuals, got off scot free while their victims, many of whom had sustained much serious damage, had no redress. As such, it violated every concept of justice. It did, however, emphasize that where the basic relationships of classes are at stake, individual interests soon go by the board in favour of the major issue, which was in this case to prove that the crimes were squarely to be laid at the door of the trade unions. There can be no doubt that without that quite extraordinary power the Commissioners would have been as unable as the police had been before them to lay bare the sources of the violence. Even as it was, the breakthrough to the sequence of startling confessions was made only by holding Hallam, clearly the weakest link among the saw-grinders, overnight at Sheffield with doubtful legality (instead of sending him to Wakefield to face a charge of contempt of court) and subjecting him to the fear that others had talked and had incriminated him, during his confinement.

[1] Q. 13234. All numbers in the subsequent notes refer to the questions and answers in the evidence to the Commission.

[2] Also see *Sheffield Independent*, 25 May 1867.

Other witnesses were found covering up under hours of hostile questioning until one or other had made his confession and claimed his exemption, and even then they made sure that all concerned would get their freedom before they talked. Moreover, they clearly kept back information on which the Commissioners had not yet had a lead, despite the rewards offered and despite the grave danger in which each witness put himself by a confession which could later be proved to have been partial only.

With the help of this power, and by insistent and intelligent questioning, the Commissioners did succeed in uncovering a complex system of trade-union intimidation, a private legal code almost, operating in the Sheffield trades. At the centre of the more violent outrages, the shootings and the cans of gunpowder, was William Broadhead, Secretary of the saw-grinders, who employed Samuel Crooks for the more daring attacks, but instigated and paid for many others. Some violent action was also brought home to other grinders, and indeed there were few among the dozen or so grinding trades which did not admit at least to rattening at some time or other in the past.

These disclosures appeared to be all the more damaging to the trade-union case since Broadhead was by no means an obscure trade unionist, but on the contrary one of the leading officials in the town, treasurer both to the local trades council and the United Kingdom Alliance of Organized Trades, a frequent spokesman and one of those who had protested most loudly that the unions were being unjustly implicated in the outrages, before his self-incrimination. Yet, in a curious way, the Sheffield Commission, like the national one sitting in London, served rather to strengthen the unions' case and their legal position, than to undermine it.

In the case of the (national) Royal Commission, the parent body of the present Sheffield Inquiry, the story has often been told how the leaders of the amalgamated societies presented their evidence skilfully to persuade the Commissioners that they were members of peaceful, respectable and worthy bodies whose main function was to act as friendly societies. As a result of their efforts before the Commission and outside, the Master and Servant Acts were indeed amended in 1867, trade union funds were given some protection in 1868, and in 1871 and 1875 major Statutes were passed which freed the trade unions from most of their shackles.

But in the case of the Sheffield Inquiry also, despite the opprobrium heaped on individual witnesses, the overall impression tended to favour in some way the trade union point of view. After all, it was mainly the unionists who were called to give evidence, while there were but few anti-unionists, and they, with few exceptions, not the most engaging witnesses. Thus statements assuming that unions kept up wages, or that non-unionists as a rule were incompetent workmen and drunkards, or that employers would be oppressive without the countervailing power of the unions, remained uncontradicted and were enmeshed even in the hostile examination, though of course the Commissioners did not accept rattening or other illegalities as legitimate means of enforcing the unions' claims.

The Commissioners, on the other hand, went out of their way to praise those Sheffield unions, about four-fifths of the total number, which were not involved in violent acts. It is even more intriguing to see the Commissioners taking the side of the 'poor workmen' who are at risk of being defrauded, whenever they come upon an example of a slipshod audit of a union's books,[1] at a time when the High Court had incited all union officers to defraud their members, by deliberately removing all means of redress for such depredations. All this becomes more astonishing still when it is remembered that elsewhere, in most towns and most industries, unions were not accepted at all as legitimate, and most employers refused even to recognize their existence. Thus the powerful builders' unions still had to fight for recognition, and many engineers were still faced with the 'document', asking them to renounce union membership before they could be employed, though these two were among the best organized trades. Coal miners and railwaymen, among others, would not have their unions universally recognized until fifty years later. Most organs of public opinion, and most orthodox economic doctrine, still held unions to be either pointless or mischievous. Yet in Sheffield the unions not only took their own existence for granted, but even claimed extended statutory powers for themselves.

* * *

[1] E.g. 14481 *passim*, 17885.

The most astonishing claim made by the Sheffield unionists in their evidence was the demand for legal powers, including powers of distraint, in regard to the collection of union dues from their members. As early as 1863, the Sheffield Organized Trades had petitioned Palmerston, who was then visiting the town, to give favourable consideration to 'legislating for trades unions so as to give powers for compelling payments in the county courts by defaulting members',[1] and the theme constantly recurred, for example in the local press, long before the Commission began its hearings.

Is it not a fact that we all have to surrender our independence and obey the laws of the land, often contrary to our ideas of right or wrong? If we do not obey, we are rattened—instead of our goods being stolen, they are taken away and sold, and our bodies confined . . . If the law on this point is just, is it not equally a moral obligation on the part of individual members of a trade to subscribe to laws made by themselves for the general good?[2]

No state of society that I ever heard of could exist together without regulations, and more or less of coercion made use of to enforce them; and trades' unions need them in particular . . . (it is said) if a member will not pay nor comply, shut him out from the benefits of the society; in our case, Sir, that is not possible, for . . . you cannot deprive him of the benefit of the protection of his labour . . . therefore, I say honestly that I would use a certain amount of force to make him comply in a reasonable manner.[3]

Before the Commission, the same point was made again and again, not least by Broadhead himelf:

I had a right to take these courses in the absence of the law, and that the end would justify the means . . . If the law would give (the trades) some power, if there were a law created to give them such power to receive contributions without having recourse to such measures there would be no more heard of them . . . if a legislative measure was adopted to meet these things it would destroy these acts that have taken place and which placed me in this painful position.[4]

Samuel Stacey, of the edge-tool grinders, who considered rattening 'no sin', cheerfully went even further:

16679. Did you ever do anything else in that way, except authorizing a man's bands or nuts to be taken?—Certainly, we would take his sofa if we could.

16680. You would steal anything if you could, under those circumstances?—We would be bailiffs if we could.

The view that the law was basically at fault, and that if such powers had been given to the unions, rattening would never have survived, was held by a large number of witnesses,[5] though they had to admit that this concession would not deal with men who offended the unions in other ways, for example by taking too many apprentices.

This demand by the traditional Sheffield unions must have struck trade unionists elsewhere, who were still fighting for their very existence even on a basis of strict voluntarism, as something akin to lunacy. Indeed even today, when trade unions have achieved many of the aims they set themselves in the nineteenth century, nothing like such powers has ever been granted or even requested. The demand, in fact, was looking backward rather than forward, and in order to understand its basis we must look more closely at the organization of the local industries of Sheffield.

In the Sheffield industries little complex machinery was used, and there was therefore little to be gained by bringing the men under one roof under the control of the manufacturers. Instead, the men hired their own rooms, including power for turning the stones if they were grinders, and they mostly worked 'out', i.e. not on the premises of the firm from whom they received their orders. Most, in fact, were independent contractors rather than workmen, who took on jobs at contract prices, and decided for themselves what hours they would work and how many helpers, if any, they would employ. The contract prices in all well-organized trades were fixed in a price statement, or wage list, though with the ups and downs of the trade cycle and other circumstances, actual wages might differ by a given percentage from the list prices. Within this general framework the system was infinitely flexible. Thus men might work for, i.e. accept orders from, one master or many, they might in turn sub-contract with others to take on part of their orders, or become sub-contractors

1 15369-71.

2 Letter by "Both Sides", *Sheffield Independent*, 14 October 1866.

3 Letter by Henry Cutts, the respectable secretary of the file smiths, *Sheffield Independent*, 8 April 1862.

4 12970, 13241, 13243.

5 E.g. 12204, 15372, 16698, 18051.

themselves, and any man might thus be a journeyman and a 'little mester' in quick succession.

In at least one case, that of the saw-grinders, the union itself owned some tools, hired room and power, and took on contracts, at which they set their unemployed members to work.[1] In principle this was not much different from the normal practice of keeping a list of unemployed members and supplying it to masters who needed labour.

The Sheffield unionist in the local trades is therefore much nearer to his master, much more like him and much less in awe of him, than the typical unionist elsewhere. He takes him to court much more frequently in disputes over contracts or payments, and often defeats him there. Many masters, indeed, are in the union and at least one, Hoole, in whose works there arose the dispute which led to the Acorn Street outrage in which an innocent person was killed, had been a prominent official of the trades council itself.[2] We also find the witnesses, on the whole, to be undaunted by the Committee, and to be well able to look after themselves,[3] though they found themselves very much in the public eye, with many representatives of the press in attendance, and in front of a crowd buzzing with excitement at the latest revelations and thirsting for more.

The basis of this power, this independence and, incidentally, the relatively high wages earned in the Sheffield cutlery and tools trades, was the exceptional skills involved in most of them. In turn, these were based on minute subdivisions of trades. Thus there were not only separate skills and apprenticeships for the makers of saws, of edge tools, of files or of table knives, among others, but among the makers of each article there was a further subdivision as to process. Usually there were forgers or smiths; grinders; and assemblers, hafters or handle-makers, besides possibly others. In total, therefore, there might be some 40–50 separate skills and trades, though they would not all be 'in union' at any one time, i.e. have an active trade organization. Conversely, the average numbers for each trade were small, in many cases small enough to be able to assemble in a single room, and in such a trade, every member was likely to know every other member.[4] Since their skill, moreover, was unmatched over most of the Western world, they had little to fear from foreign competition, and they knew it.[5] Thus they had a very clear consciousness of 'the trade' as almost a physical entity within which they worked.

It was within their 'trade' that they were apprenticed, that they spent their working lives, that their wages and their work load was settled, and that their welfare provisions, in case of sickness or unemployment, death or legal costs, were met—or, if the trade was 'out of union', failed to be met. One could not escape one's trade, not even by leaving the union, and it was this that the Commissioners failed to grasp, and that caused some of the most persistent misunderstandings in their examination. Repeatedly they questioned the unionists about men who had left the union by failing to keep up with their weekly subscriptions, and repeatedly they were at cross-purposes with witnesses who appeared to give them unclear or shuffling answers. What the unionists were trying to explain, and what the Commissioners genuinely failed to see, was that one did not cease to be a member of one's trade simply by not paying up; one would fall out of benefit, but the workmen in Sheffield, both those who continued to pay, and those who had stopped paying, knew better than to imagine that one could thereby sever one's connection with the economic reality of the 'trade'.[6] In at least one case, the union lent its members who had fallen out of benefit by not paying, sufficient money to make them 'financial' again, i.e. entitled to benefit just before calling a strike,[7] and such action was clearly unintelligible to men who thought of unions as clubs which one could join or leave at will.

Similarly, it was hard for the Commissioners to believe that rattening, i.e. the removal of the bands which drove the grinders' stones or the nuts which secured them,

[1] 4219, 9639–40, 10683 *passim*.

[2] 21205–8.

[3] They were also not without humour, e.g. 7479–82, 7506–9, 17884.

[4] 13435.

[5] Eg. 21708.

[6] 3525–37, 14895, 16113.

[7] 16137–9.

until such time as the man was straight again with the union, was undertaken without official orders by the union. Yet normally such action would be taken entirely at the initiative of individuals, who only afterwards might or might not use the good offices of their union secretary to secure a payment, nominally called 'expenses' but in reality constituting a fine, for their trouble. Broadhead was obviously not believed when he stated, quite truthfully, that

> The way that (this ancient custom of rattening) has been adopted has been . . . not by rule or regulation of the society, but members, as a matter of course, when others have been in arrear have taken upon themselves to roll up their bands until the payment was made, and there have been payments made to them for the expense of it; and as a rule the parties rattened have had to pay those expenses. The society themselves as a rule have not given orders but it has simply been an understanding.[1]

Typically, indeed, it was members in the same room, or in the same building, who tended to ratten defaulters. In at least one case one man rattened his father, and there was even a case of a man being asked to ratten himself; but such cases are rare, and are possible only among such trades as the saw-grinders, who were strong enough to insist that the bands belonged to the masters, and not the grinders. It was also necessary that these should be occasions in which the defaulters were not among the grinders, but among the smiths or handle-makers, who could not be so easily attacked as the grinders. Then the grinders' bands would be taken, the works would come to a halt, and it would be the smiths' (or handlemakers') union, which had initiated the proceedings, that would be expected to pay out-of-work benefit to the grinders, until their own defaulting men had paid up.[2]

In any case, there were no formal rules and no formal resolutions. Opinion in the trade was usually pretty unanimous and as one observer put it, the union was held to be 'the authorized expression of public opinion in the trade'.[3] In one case, when a rattened man had to spend an extended period in the Royal Infirmary, the union decided that the hospital should not be burdened with the cost, and voted it £10 out of its funds.[4] Unions like the saw-grinders' still had monthly meetings at which attendance was compulsory, at which all members' names were called over, and those absent were fined. In the case of members who had fallen into arrears and who perhaps tacitly wanted to leave the union, fines were added to the arrears and might amount to very large sums in total; and it was at the calling over that all members would be made aware of the names of the defaulters, if gossip in the trade had not noticed them before.[5]

There was a rough and ready justice in the workshops and a code of conduct reminiscent of that of medieval guilds. A man was expected to pay his share of the drinks, to take no more than his share of the well-paid work, and not to encroach on the work of other trades. He was also expected to keep to the apprenticeship rules and not overstock the trade with boys, and to pay his subscriptions. As it was universally accepted that everyone's wages went up substantially when the trade was organized, or 'in union',[6] he benefited by the union's very existence and was therefore expected to pay his share of the upkeep. Perhaps the most hated man was he who drew unemployment benefit from the union for weeks on end, but the moment he found work again, ceased paying subscriptions to maintain those who were still out of work.

There was also a sense of fairness in other respects. The fork makers, for example, stinted themselves to a reduced number of hours of work per day in slack times to make the work go round. The fork grinders decided to work for ten named masters only, in order to end the encroachment of knife manufacturers and others upon their trade. Since there were such small numbers involved, the men knew quickly when the trade had become overstocked. There was usually a substantial contribution paid by the union to those who were willing to emigrate, while newcomers who wanted to enter the trade without formal apprenticeship would be charged a high entrance fee, or would not be accepted at any price, for it seemed clear that they, or an

[1] 13239.
[2] 6321–2, 9430–1, 12198, 12365, 12529, 14144, 14300, 14910, 16171, 16644, 17418.
[3] P. H. Rathbone, 'Moral of the Sheffield Outrages', in *National Association for the Promotion of the Social Sciences, Report*, 1867, p. 693.
[4] 13124.
[5] 3311–3, 3383–5, 12227.
[6] Eg. 16951.

equivalent number, would be permanently added to those on the box thereafter.[1]

Consider the position of the following unions, picked at random from the evidence submitted to the Commissioners:[2]

	Number of Men		
	In the Union	Outside	'On the box', i.e. drawing relief pay
Joiners' Tool Makers	160	?	12
Fork Grinders	130	30	30–40
Patent Scythe Makers	60	12	3
Fork Makers	134	40	17
Scissor Workboard Hands	190	40	6–12
Edge Tool Forgers	370	30	8
Table Blade Grinders	450	150	50

The summer of 1867, when these figures were taken, was by no means a period of bad trade for most of these groups. Bearing in mind that they all tried to pay adequate relief scales,[3] usually 8s to 10s for a man, 2s or 2s 6d for his wife and 1s or 1s 6d for each child (at a time when most unskilled workers were glad to earn 15s a week), the typical unionist might have to pay up to 5–10 per cent of his wage, or more, merely to maintain his comrades on the box, quite apart from any other union expenses. This proportion would be materially affected by the numbers in the trade who were currently not contributing, and the grinders, it will be noted, were usually the worst off in this respect.

* * *

So far, most trade unionists, then and now, would have agreed with the Sheffield unionists. But granted all this, why and how did the violence originate?

Some of it was a relic of the handicraft and guild days, of the horseplay associated with apprenticeship and *compannonage*, the physical games and rough justice found among all men who work with their hands. 'Rattening' was technically an easy trick to play in the working condition of the town, in the isolated workshops and 'public' building let out to any workman who came. 'Rattening is a matter I am quite prepared to make a clean breast of', Broadhead admitted from the start. 'I do not look upon it as a matter of any interest at all'. All grinding trades were more or less subject to this practice. Even William Overend, questioning one witness, agreed that it was 'a common thing, and which is hardly considered a crime at all in this town apparently'.[4] Judging by the evidence, it also seems to have been remarkably effective in most cases.

Not many, even among the grinders' trades, went further towards more serious attacks on property and ultimately on persons. Conditions and personalities both had to be ripe for it. But bearing in mind the mode of work and the long-standing self-determination and independence of local men, the frequent accidents and high death-rates caused by the grinders' diseases, the very recent elevation of Sheffield to the status of a Borough with its own police force and a modicum of self-government, such progression is not altogether surprising.

What weighed particularly heavily in the local consciousness was the example of the Cutlers' Company, the local guild which, almost within the memory of those appearing before the Commissioners in 1867, had had precisely those legal powers which the unions then claimed. It could exclude legally any men from working in the trades concerned in Hallamshire who were not freemen; it could levy fines and have them legally enforced; and it was the self-governing spokesman for the trade. It had, of course, always been a masters' organization and when, by the end of the eighteenth century, it came to be in the interest of the masters to abolish apprenticeship and other restrictions, they secured their abolition. In 1814, after a series of local struggles fought when the unions were at a particular disadvantage owing to the Combination

[1] Eg. 12545, 16973–4, 17224–5, 18160, 19854, 21655 *passim*, 21704–7.

[2] 16725, 16953–4, 16957–62, 16997–9, 17157–60, 17236–9, 18027.

[3] E.g. 11238, 16129.

[4] 1690–3, 1456–60, 2027, 12198, 12213, 14208, 16633, 18362–4.

Acts, these powers of the Cutlers' Company were repealed: any man could now legally enter the local trades, could take as many journeymen or apprentices as he liked, and could spread from his own specialism into as many other branches as he cared to do.

The unions never accepted this decision. Again and again they tried to recombine with their masters in a guild-like association. Again and again they declared themselves to be the rightful heirs of the guild's powers, and even in 1867, before the Commissioners, there were still men who talked of union members as 'freemen'.[1] The doctrine held generally in the rest of the country, that masters have rights which the law would not dream of extending to workmen, and that there could be no equality before the law between those two groups, was simply not accepted in Sheffield where men had the vote, and where the distinction between a 'master' and a 'man' was often impossible to draw. Sheffield men, as indeed all men at that time, were surprisingly ignorant about conditions elsewhere, and merely looked to the framework of their own past. Within it, they held it to be an injustice, and one which would be rectified if only enough pressure were applied, that the masters, as long as they wanted them, used to have legal powers which were now being denied to the journeymen. Meanwhile, however, they felt they had a right to take these powers into their own hands. The moral position, given the views of the rest of English society, was of course ambiguous, and Sheffield men knew that no other class would support them. Also, the legal position was known to be adverse, and therefore called for secrecy and conspiracy. But those who felt strongly enough about an issue, and had the courage, ventured further on the road to violence and generally had the tacit support of the whole trade for their action.

The dilemma can best be demonstrated in the case of the saw grinders, who were proved to have committed much the largest number both of the more violent outrages and the rattenings. They were among the last to have come in from the country waterwheels around Sheffield, with their wild freedom, into the steam-powered 'wheels', or buildings, in the town. Saw grinding needed a great deal of physical strength, and the men in the trade were of better build, healthier, and less affected by silicosis, than most other grinder's branches. For this and other reasons they were among the most self-confident and the most independent; they were also among the highest paid by far. Wages of £4–5 a week, or more than double those of skilled engineers, were not unknown.[2] These high wages made the saw-grinders extremely vulnerable, not only to machine grinding, but also to the encroachments of other trades. There are echoes of demarcation disputes with the so-called 'Jobbing Grinders' men who ground machine knives but who could also tackle saws, and had recently formed a rival union which attracted those saw-grinders who wished to have the high pay but not the high contributions of the 'old' saw-grinders' society.[3] There are also some examples of outsiders gatecrashing the trade, and some committed the worse offence of taking in large numbers of apprentices to gain the short-term advantages of their output, but creating the permanent threat of overstocking the trade. The two worst offenders in this regard were the two victims of the more violent outrages, Thomas Fearnehough and James Linley.

Under Broadhead's able leadership, the saw-grinders had decided in 1859 to take these men and their boys into the trade, rather than risk the undercutting of rates if they stayed outside.[4] In the short term, this proved to be a wise policy, for it paid the men to keep their high wages and divert a small proportion of them to maintain the rest on the box. The working members, explained Broadhead,

> thought it well worth their while to bring their labour out of the market. . . . This is the vital part: it regulated the supply of labour in the market according to its demand. If masters had to come to the union for labour, and choose from a list, 'the object obtained is this, that surplus labour is not seen in the market until it is required'. If the union did not keep the idlers and ruffians off the market, these men would still have to live, and 'they would offer themselves to work at such prices as they could get. It would be an inducement to an employer to take them, and they could got (sic) into situations by that means'.[5]

[1] 343–6.
[2] 4001–6, 9235, 9259.
[3] 3274 *passim*, 4213, 4243, 4485, 9792, 9979, 18298.
[4] 5737–42, 10568.
[5] 12519, 12521, 12527.

But in the long run the position was highly precarious. With only about 190 members, of whom up to 50–80[1] were kept out of the labour market by the rest, by being maintained on the box at a fairly generous rate (otherwise they might have preferred to seek work), it was inevitable that very high weekly subscriptions, up to 4s 2d in the £ of earnings, were payable.[2] There were three dangers in this: some members would leave rather than pay such subscriptions, increasing the burden on the remaining ones still further; the trade would continue to attract interlopers, who would all ultimately come on the box; and the men on the box, some of whom were young men who spent from six to eight years after being loosed from their apprenticeship without a job, were troublesome and were potential undercutters—but they were also ready-made ratteners. Nearly all the major criminals who came before the commission as having committed violence on behalf of the saw-grinders were the apprentices of the two main victims, Fearnehough and Linley.[3] As the saw-grinders' union paid out some £5,000 in benefits in the previous five years, or over £5 per member p.a., it could keep that whole structure going only by some 100 or more cases of rattening.[4] But where rattening proved ineffective in stopping the wilful actions of a few which would severely damage the livelihood of many, measures stronger than rattening could be justified in the narrow atmosphere of a Sheffield trade, though few, if any, would sanction murder: indeed, it did not appear that either of the two killings had been intentional.

One of the most perceptive accounts of the saw-grinders' dilemma came from the pen of James Greenwood, a journalist who passed through Sheffield and interviewed a scissor-grinder and his wife who happened to live near Broadhead's public-house. The account first appeared in the *Morning Star* and was reprinted by the *Sheffield Independent* on 18 September 1867. It will bear re-printing in part. Here are the scissor-grinder's views on James Linley, the man whom two of his former apprentices, Crooks and Hallam, followed about for five or six weeks carrying a shotgun before they found the opportunity of shooting him.

He is dead and gone, but Linley wasn't a pleasant sort of man, poor fellow. Not a just man by a long way. He might have done well—as well as I am doing. But he was kind of greedy, you see, and thought that he might be getting something out of somebody else's labour as well as his own. This was to be done by his taking unlawful apprentices. Now comes the grievance. You must know that more can be got out of lads that work at saw-grinding than at scissor-grinding, so what does Linley do but throw over his own good trade and somehow or another take up that of the saw grinder, and took boys to work for him—all of course against the laws of that trade. As I said before, no man can hold up his hand in favour of downright killing; but when a man brought up amongst us turns round and uses such means to take the bread out of another man's mouth—not because he himself wants bread, but because he's got a tooth for lazy roast meat— . . . He worked when he was compelled, and never else. It was this way, you see, Sir. If a body of men go in for a statement they must stick to it through thick and thin, or it's no good. . . . The 'statement' is the pay scale; all regularly settled and agreed on between master and man. The statement is what we've got to uphold—it's the keystone of our trade's prosperity. Well, such a man as Linley and his illegal lads, goes dead against the statement; laughs at it; puts it in his pipe and smokes it . . . He's gone now, poor fellow, and I've nothing to say against him; but certainly he was aggravating. The sort of man, you see, Sir, that is fond of parading his idleness at working hours; a man loud at the drinking bar; with a habit of jingling what money he had in his pockets.

But how do you account for his apprentices turning against him?

Enough to turn 'em when they found themselves lugged into a trade and only half taught it, and so pushed about from post to pillar. How could they like a man such as he was? D'ye recollect, Matilda, how they used to duck him on Monday morning? . . . The 'prentices in our line have their spending money—a sort of pocket money—on Monday mornings, and oftentimes, if Linley got out on Saturdays, there'd be no money for 'em. But they would have it—young Crooks and Hallam and the rest of 'em. They'd wait on him and haul him into the water-trough, and there hold him till he promised to get their spending money somehow. Ah, they were devils, those lads of his!

Who, bearing in mind the reality of conditions in the Sheffield trades, would be quite sure that the ruling laissez-faire philosophy, which would have made a hero of Linley, was right, and that the Sheffield craftsman's philosophy, which made him into a villain deserving punishment, was wrong and criminal?

No other union was quite as vulnerable as the saw-grinders, though some, like

[1] 12512–4.

[2] 3105–10, 3601–2, 3829–30, 8231, 8291, 9910, 10391, 10396, 11125, 11691, 12390–2, 12517.

[3] 5722–34, 6204–6, 7130, 8050, 8184, 11351, 12070, *et seq.*

[4] 12165.

the sheep-shear and edge-tool grinders with their weekly wages of £3–4 came near it,[1] and no other union found a secretary of quite the same determination as William Broadhead. But altogether, some 13 out of about 60 Sheffield unions were found to be implicated, all, with the exception of the brickmakers, being in the traditional Sheffield industries. By the time the Commission rose, it had received details of 166 rattenings, 20 outrages, 22 threatening letters and 12 cases of intimidation, relating to the past ten years.[2]

* * *

The immediate impact of the revelations contained in the Report and Minutes of Evidence which follow was less than might have been expected. The outrages were, of course, cited voluminously by all those who had always held unions to be vicious and violent conspiracies and they were, equally predictably, repudiated by trade unionists. But the country at large was more impressed with the evidence presented to the main Commission sitting in London, in which the leaders of the London amalgamated societies, often called the 'Junta', had skilfully diverted attention from the bargaining functions of trade unions to their role as self-help organizations and as friendly societies that did much good by keeping their members off the poor rates.

Perhaps the most significant consequences were felt within the trade union movement rather than outside it. Before the events of 1867, the union world had been divided on many basic issues, between the Junta on the one hand, and George Potter, editor of the *Beehive*, on the other, acting as the spokesman of a number of more militant unionists in the London Working Men's Association, and attempting, not without success, to rally most of the provincial trade unions behind his concept of the role of working-class organizations. When the need arose to present a picture of respectability which would impress the middle-class members of the Royal Commission, the Junta easily pushed Potter and his friends into the background, and the Sheffield events completed Potter's discomfiture.

As soon as Broadhead had admitted to having instigated a large number of rattenings and outrages as part of his trade union policy, the leaders of the London Trades Council called a mass meeting for the purpose of showing their abhorrence of his actions and of emphasizing the difference between their own and his concept of trade unionism. The meeting took place in Exeter Hall on 2 July 1867, and one trade union leader after another rose to condemn in the strongest language the practices of the Sheffield saw-grinders. At the end, Professor E. S. Beesly was asked to speak. He was a Positivist and an old friend of the trade-union cause, and he also had been depressed and made insecure by the Sheffield revelations; but having listened to the other speeches of the evening, he could sense danger also in the swing of the pendulum too far into the opposite direction. The gist of his speech was to be quoted many times in the following five weeks:

> Murder was a great crime. They were all agreed about that. But after all it must not be forgotten that a trades' union murder was neither better nor worse than any other murder. The wealthy classes of this country, in whose eyes unionism itself was a crime, naturally considered that any crime connected with unionism was doubly criminal. But clearly that was a doctrine which this meeting could not admit. . . . He was no apologist for murder. During the last twelve months he had subscribed his money and given what other assistance he could to bring a greater murderer to justice[3]—a murderer whose hands were red with blood not of two or three victims, but of more than four hundred. That murderer had committed his crimes in the interests of employers, just as Broadhead had committed his crimes in the interest of workmen.
>
> The wealthy class of this country had been called on to express their opinion on the crimes committed by wealthy men in Jamaica just as the poorer classes in London were now called upon to express their opinion on the crimes committed by poor men in Sheffield. And what opinions did they express? Did they summon a meeting in Exeter Hall and proclaim aloud that they abhorred the crime, and that though they wished to protect property and wealth they repudiated such means of protecting it as Governor Eyre had adopted? (Cries of 'Question' from one or two individuals which was immediately drowned by a roar of applause.) Did they do so? No! But they offered him banquets; they loaded him

[1] 9772.

[2] 22464–8.

[3] The allusion is to Governor Eyre, Governor of Jamaica 1862–6, who had suppressed a riot in a savage manner, killing 586 negroes, and who had become the target of much working class and Radical hostility, particularly when he was lionized for his exploits on his return to England.

with honours; they made his deed their own.

That murderer was now at large in England, not because he had a certificate of indemnity like Broadhead, but because a bench of magistrates of his own class had refused to send him before a jury. London workmen acted differently. It was not their class to which the stigma of encouraging murder attached. He did not see that they need take the blame or shame to themselves for what had been done at Sheffield. He did not see why they should hold their heads less high or recede one inch from the claims they were making on the legislature. The middle classes would go on talking about the Sheffield outrages for a long time, and they would be glad to keep workmen talking of them in order to divert their attention from the state of law as affecting unionism. It had aready been pointed out tonight by more than one speaker that the law refused protection to union funds. Thus the middle class invited thieves to do what they were afraid to do themselves. They set thieves to steal the union funds just as Broadhead set on his agents to steal bands. In short, the only difference between rattening as practised by trades' unions and rattening as practised against trades' unions was that the law punished the one and encouraged the other.[1]

Beesly's speech, and particularly the phrase at the beginning of this extract, led to a furore in the press, and sustained efforts were made to deprive him of his chair of history at University College, London, and expel him from the Reform Club. But meanwhile his stand had helped to put some backbone again into the current efforts of the national unions to fight for an improved legal status.

In Sheffield on the other hand, sentiments such as those expressed by Beesly were quite common. The sense of revulsion was more immediate and perhaps greater for a time, and the trade union defence committee under Dronfield and Austin at once expelled Broadhead and the saw-grinders.[2] But there were more voices to hint that here they had to do at least as much with a clash of loyalty and of moral codes, as with a simple series of crimes.

The saw-grinders' union, indeed, met and passed a resolution to the effect that Broadhead was not to be victimised since, after all, what he had done had been undertaken in the interests of the trade, and that the law did not protect them otherwise. When an outcry greeted this resolution and pressure was exerted by other unions, they met again (having meanwhile amalgamated with their old rivals, the jobbing grinders) to rescind it, but voted by 73:71 votes in favour of keeping Broadhead in membership, and by 106:39 for keeping Crooks. Other implicated leaders, like Skidmore, Smith and Thompson, also received much continued support from their respective unions even after the revelations.

Samuel Crooks was allowed to keep his old job. Broadhead, it is true, who like most trade union secretaries kept a public house, did not have his licence renewed, but he accepted this decision only under protest. He retained considerable influence in some important sections of the trade-union world of Sheffield, and his influence waned in the end largely because his notoriety did, too, and not because of any deliberate ostracism.

Most significantly of all, rattening went on for at least another ten years, though on a much diminished scale. If it ceased in the end, it was only in part because of the work of the Commission; it was largely because the conditions which gave rise to it had also changed. The modern world was at last beginning to catch up with the traditional industries of Sheffield.

[1] *Report of Proceedings*, reprinted in part in James B. Jefferys: *Labour's Formative Years 1849–1879* (1948), pp. 101–3.

[2] 11621.

Glossary of Terms

BAND	Leather strap connecting the grinder's stones to the pulleys of the driving shafts from which they got their power
BOX, ON THE BOX	Being maintained from the union's funds
CLERK, TO CLERK	To check the declared weekly earnings of grinders at times when union contributions were a proportion of earnings
HULL	A room in a 'wheel', containing several grinders' workplaces
KNOBSTICK	Blackleg, strike breaker
MAN IN THE MOON MARY ANN NATHAN	Signatures used in threatening letters
NATTY MONEY, NATTY BRASS	Weekly union subscription
RATTENING	The taking away of bands or nuts, as punishment for breaking union rules. This would normally stop the man from working for the time being
SCALE, DRAWING SCALE	Obtaining the weekly benefits from the union's funds
'SMITE-EM'	Nickname of William Broadhead
SHY MAIDEN SWEEP TANTIA TOPEE TIDD PRATT	Signatures used in threatening letters
TROUGH, TROW	The grinder's workplace
WEB	A saw
WHEEL	A building containing motive power, either a steam engine or a water wheel, and divided into hulls and troughs rented by grinders and some other workmen.

Bibliography of Further Reading

ARMYTAGE, W. H. G. 'William Dronfield', in *Notes and Queries*, Vol. 193, (1948)

BEESLY, E. S. *The Sheffield Outrages* (1867)

CONGREVE, R. *Mr Broadhead and the Anonymous Press* (1867)

FROW, E. and KATANKA, M. *1868, The Year of the Unions*. A Documentary Survey (1968)

HARRISON, R. J. *Before the Socialists*. Studies in Labour and Politics, 1861–1881 (1965)

LLOYD, G. I. H. *The Cutlery Trades* (1913, repr. 1968)

MCCREADY, H. W. 'British Labour and the Royal Commission on Trade Unions 1867–69,' in *University of Toronto Quarterly*, 24 (1955)

MUSSON, A. E. *The Congress of 1868*. The Origins and Establishment of the Trades Union Congress (1955)

'OWD SMEETOM' *The Sheffield Outrages*. Reprinted in 1895 and 1896 from *The Anarchist*, vol. 2/23, Nov. 1895.

POLLARD, S. *A History of Labour in Sheffield* (1959)

POLLARD, S. 'The Ethics of the Sheffield Outrages', in *Hunter Society Transactions* 7/3 (1954)

RATHBONE, P. H. 'Moral of the Sheffield Outrages', in Report of the National Association for the Promotion of the Social Sciences (1867)

READE, C. *Put Yourself in His Place* (Repr. 1922)

REPORT of the Conference of Trades' Delegates of the United Kingdom, held in Sheffield on 17 July 1866 and four following days (1866)

WEBB, S. and B. *The History of Trade Unionism* (1902 ed.)

TRADES UNIONS COMMISSION: SHEFFIELD OUTRAGES INQUIRY.

(TRADES UNION COMMISSION ACT, 30 VICT. c. 8.)

REPORT

PRESENTED TO

THE TRADES UNIONS COMMISSIONERS

BY

THE EXAMINERS

APPOINTED TO INQUIRE INTO

ACTS OF INTIMIDATION, OUTRAGE, OR WRONG ALLEGED TO HAVE BEEN PROMOTED, ENCOURAGED, OR CONNIVED AT BY TRADES UNIONS

IN THE

TOWN OF SHEFFIELD.

VOL. I.—REPORT.

Presented to both Houses of Parliament by Command of Her Majesty.

LONDON:
PRINTED BY GEORGE EDWARD EYRE AND WILLIAM SPOTTISWOODE,
PRINTERS TO THE QUEEN'S MOST EXCELLENT MAJESTY.
FOR HER MAJESTY'S STATIONERY OFFICE.

1867

[*Price 2d.*]

CONTENTS.

COMMISSION.

VICTORIA R.

Victoria, by the Grace of God, of the United Kingdom of Great Britain and Ireland, Queen, Defender of the Faith.

To Our right trusty and well-beloved Councillor Sir William Erle, Knight; Our right trusty and right well-beloved Cousin Thomas George Earl of Lichfield; Our trusty and well-beloved Francis Charteris, Esquire (commonly called Lord Elcho); Our right trusty and well-beloved Councillor Sir Edmund Walker Head, Baronet, Knight Commander of Our most Honourable Order of the Bath; Our trusty and well-beloved Sir Daniel Gooch, Baronet; Our trusty and well-beloved Herman Merivale, Esquire, Companion of Our most Honourable Order of the Bath; Our trusty and well-beloved James Booth, Esquire, Companion of Our most Honourable Order of the Bath; Our trusty and well-beloved John Arthur Roebuck, Esquire, one of Our Counsel learned in the Law; Our trusty and well-beloved Thomas Hughes, Esquire, and Frederic Harrison, Esquire, Barristers at Law; and Our trusty and well-beloved William Mathews, Esquire, greeting.

Whereas it has been represented unto Us that it is expedient that inquiry should be made into the several matters herein-after mentioned.

Now Know Ye, that We, reposing great trust and confidence in your ability and discretion, have nominated, constituted, and appointed, and do by these Presents nominate, constitute, and appoint, you, the said Sir William Erle, Thomas George Earl of Lichfield, Francis Charteris, Esquire (commonly called Lord Elcho), Sir Edmund Walker Head, Sir Daniel Gooch, Herman Merivale, James Booth, John Arthur Roebuck, Thomas Hughes, Frederic Harrison, and William Mathews, to be Our Commissioners for the purposes of the said inquiry.

And We do hereby enjoin you, or any Four of you, to inquire into and report on the Organization and Rules of Trades Unions and other Associations, whether of Workmen or Employers, and to inquire into and report on the effect produced by such Trades Unions and Associations on the Workmen and Employers respectively, and on the Relations between Workmen and Employers, and on the Trade and Industry of the Country; with power to investigate any recent acts of intimidation, outrage, or wrong alleged to have been promoted, encouraged, or connived at by such Trades Unions or other Associations, and also to suggest any improvements to be made in the law with respect to the matters aforesaid, or with respect to the relations between Workmen and their Employers, for the mutual benefit of both parties.

And for the better discovery of the truth in the premises, We do by these Presents give and grant unto you, or any Four of you, full power and authority to call before you, or any Four of you, such persons as you shall judge necessary, by whom you may be better informed of the truth in the premises, and to inquire of the premises and every part thereof by all other lawful ways and means whatsoever.

And Our further Will and Pleasure is that you, Our said Commissioners, do, with as little delay as may be consistent with a due discharge of the duties hereby imposed upon you, certify unto Us from time to time, under your hands and seals, your several proceedings in the premises.

And We do further will and command, and by these Presents ordain, that this Our Commission shall continue in full force and virtue, and that you, our said Commissioners, or any Four of you, shall and may from time to time proceed in the execution thereof, and of every matter or thing therein contained, although the same be not continued from time to time by adjournment.

And for your assistance in the execution of these Presents We do hereby authorize and empower you to appoint a Secretary to this Our Commission, to attend you, whose services and assistance We require you to use from time to time as occasion may require.

Given at Our Court at St. James, the Twelfth day of February 1867, in the Thirtieth Year of Our Reign.

By Her Majesty's Command.

S. H. WALPOLE.

WARRANT.

Whereas by an Act passed in the present Year of Her Majesty's Reign, entituled " An Act for facilitating in certain cases the proceedings of the Commissioners appointed " to make Inquiry respecting Trades Unions and other Associations of Employers or " Workmen," it is, amongst other things, enacted that " the Commissioners or such one " or more of them as they may, with the concurrence of the Chairman for that purpose " appoint, or such number of Persons not exceeding Three, and qualified in manner " herein-after mentioned, as one of Her Majesty's Principal Secretaries of State, may, " upon the application of the Chairman of the said Commission, appoint, may, in " pursuance of this Act, inquire into any acts of Intimidation, Outrage, or Wrong, " alleged to have been promoted, encouraged, or connived at by Trades Unions or Asso- " ciations, whether of Workmen or Employers, in the Town of Sheffield or its immediate " Neighbourhood, and as to the causes of such acts and the complicity therein of " such Trades Unions or Associations, subject to the following restrictions:

" (1.) That no Inquiry in exercise of the Powers of this Act shall be held elsewhere " than at Sheffield or its immediate Neighbourhood.

" (2.) That no Inquiry in exercise of the Powers of this Act shall be made into any " case of Intimidation, Outrage, or Wrong which has occurred more than Ten Years " before the passing of this Act, without the written sanction of one of Her Majesty's " Principal Secretaries of State to be given at the written request of the Chairman of the " Commission :

" Provided that no Person shall be appointed by the said Secretary of State in pur- " suance of this Section to conduct such Inquiry under this Act unless he is a Member " of the said Commission, or a Barrister of not less than Ten Years' standing."

And whereas an application was made on the Fifteenth day of April last past, to the Right Honourable Spencer Horatio Walpole, then one of Her Majesty's Principal Secretaries of State, by the Right Honourable Sir William Erle, Chairman of the said Commission, to appoint Three Persons to make inquiry accordingly.

Now know Ye, that I, Gathorne Hardy, one of Her Majesty's Principal Secretaries of State, do hereby, upon such application, in pursuance of the powers vested in me by the said Act, appoint you, William Overend, Esquire, one of Her Majesty's Counsel learned in the Law, Thomas Irwin Barstow, Esquire, and George Chance, Esquire, all being Barristers-at-Law of not less than Ten Years' standing, to conduct the Inquiry into the several matters set forth in the said recited Act, with all the Powers, Rights, and Privileges thereby conferred.

I do also appoint John Edward Barker, Esquire, Barrister-at-Law, to be a Secretary to the Trades Union Commissioners to act specially in the Inquiry hereby entrusted to you, whose services and assistance you are to use from time to time as occasion may require.

Given under my Hand and Seal at Whitehall, this Twenty-third day of May 1867.

GATHORNE HARDY. (L.S.)

R E P O R T.

Sir William Erle, My Lords and Gentlemen,

We received our appointment as Examiners under the "Trades Union Commission Act, 1867", on the 23rd day of May 1867. We at once caused advertisements to be inserted in the Sheffield papers and placards to be posted throughout the town, notifying our appointment, and requesting all persons who could give information on the subject of our inquiry to communicate with Mr. J. E. Barker, our secretary, and to receive his instructions. We have much pleasure in expressing our perfect satisfaction with the manner in which that gentleman discharged his duties. We have derived great assistance from him during the whole of our inquiry.

The Mayor and Corporation of Sheffield kindly offered the use of their Council Hall, and there we commenced our inquiry on the 3rd June 1867, and continued it, with a few short adjournments, until its close on the 7th July. We wish to express our thanks to the Watch Committee for having placed at our disposal a body of policemen, who were of great service in maintaining order and in serving our summonses. We also desire to acknowledge the great aid we received from Mr. Jackson, the Chief Constable of the borough of Sheffield, to whom we are in no small degree indebted for whatever success has attended our inquiry.

With a view to our inquiry, an association of masters had been formed, and we found on our arrival in Sheffield that Mr. John Chambers, who acted on their behalf, had collected a number of cases for our investigation. A "Defence Committee," to protect the interests of the unions, had also been formed, and Mr. Sugg, solicitor, appeared for them. We examined all the witnesses ourselves, and at the close of our examination we put to each of them any questions suggested to us either by Mr. Chambers or Mr. Sugg.

The first subject which engaged our attention was that of "rattening." Rattening is a mode of enforcing payment of contributions to and compliance with the rules of the union The wheel-bands, tools, and other materials of a workman are taken and held in pledge until he has satisfied the society by payment of his arrears, or by submitting to the rules which he has infringed. At first it was denied that the unions connived at this practice, but we had not proceeded far with our investigation, before it was admitted on all hands that rattening had been for a long time prevalent in the grinding trades, and in all trades connected with them.

It is fair to the unions to say, that in the majority of cases where the demands of the union have been complied with, and a payment of a small sum for the expenses of rattening has been made, the property taken has been restored.

Rattening is always done in the interests of the union, and very commonly by the direction of the secretary, who negotiates with the party rattened for the restitution of his property. In some cases a member of the union, without express authority, rattens another member who is known to have incurred the displeasure of the society, and takes his chance of having his act adopted by the union.

Recourse is seldom had to the police to recover property so taken away, but application is almost always made to the secretary of the union immediately upon the loss of tools, &c., being discovered.

The practice of rattening is well known to be illegal, and persons detected in illegally taking away property have frequently been convicted and punished. The excuse offered by the unions for this system is, that, in the absence of legal powers, rattening affords the most ready means of enforcing payment of contributions and obedience to the rules of the union.

Many articles of Sheffield manufacture require for their completion the labour of various classes of workmen. For example, the manufacture of a saw requires the work of the saw grinders, the saw makers, and the saw handle makers. All these workmen form separate branches of the saw trade and are in separate unions. These unions are, however, all amalgamated together for mutual support. In case of default by any member of any of the branches, or in case of a dispute with the masters, as the grinders' tools are the most easily abstracted, and as stopping the grinding stops the whole saw trade, the course commonly adopted is to ratten the grinders, although the dispute may be with the saw makers or saw handle makers, and on the matter being arranged, the other branches indemnify the grinders for their loss of time and for the expenses incurred. An attempt is often successfully made to saddle the whole cost of the rattening, as well as the cost of supporting the men while out of employment, upon the master, even where he is no party to the dispute, on the ground that he ought to have compelled his workmen to comply with the rules of the union.

The system of rattening has generally proved successful in effecting its object. If, however, the person rattened continues refractory, he commonly receives an anonymous letter warning him of the consequences of his obstinacy. If this warning is disregarded, recourse has been had to acts of outrage, the nature of which will be understood from a perusal of the cases actually investigated by us.

The following cases, as they affect each union, are taken in the order of time of their occurrence.

THE SAW GRINDERS' UNION.

1853. (30 Vict. c.8. s. 2.) The earliest case is that of *Elisha Parker*, into which we inquired with the written sanction of Her Majesty's Principal Secretary of State for the Home Department.

Elisha Parker is a saw grinder living at Dore, about five miles from Sheffield. In the year 1853 Parker was working for Messrs. Newbould, who employed two non-union men, and he was repeatedly required by the union to discontinue working for Messrs. Newbould; this he refused to do.

In July of the same year a horse of Parker's was found hamstrung in a field where it had been grazing, and it had to be killed. Broadhead, the secretary of the Saw Grinders' Union, confessed that he had hired three members of the Saw Grinders' Union (Elijah Smith, John Taylor, and Phineas Dean) to commit this outrage.

1854, March. Some gunpowder was laid in the night time at Parker's door and exploded, but the explosion did but little damage. A few minutes later there was an explosion of gunpowder in the house of another man, one Bishop, a saw maker, who lived at a little distance from Parker, and who had apprenticed a son to the saw handle makers' trade. The evidence was not satisfactory as to who did these acts, but we have no doubt they arose from trade disputes.

1854, Whit Sunday. About 11 o'clock at night, Parker was roused by the noise of stones being thrown on the roof of his house. He took a double-barrelled gun, which he kept for his protection, and went out. Immediately on getting outside his door, a gun was fired at him from a plantation on the opposite side of the road about 20 yards off. He advanced a little into the road, when a second shot was fired, and Parker was wounded with small shot in the left arm and neck. A third shot was then fired which hit Parker's right arm and knocked him down. The right arm has been disabled up to the present time. At least two men were engaged in this outrage. One of them, John Hall, was hired to do it by one George Peace, a member of the Saw Grinders' Union, at the instigation of Broadhead, who found the money out of the funds of the union. Peace was a neighbour of Parker's, and had no quarrel with him, and described himself as being at the time a farmer, saw grinder, and colliery master.

Hall was sent to America soon after the occurrence, the funds for his voyage being provided by Broadhead.

1857, November 12th. *James Linley*, who formerly had been a scissor grinder, had shortly before this period become a saw grinder, and kept a number of apprentices, in defiance of the rules of the Saw Grinders' Union.

He was shot by Samuel Crookes with an air gun on November 12th 1857, at the instigation of Broadhead, in a house in Nursery Street, and was slightly wounded.

1859, January 11th. *James Linley* was lodging with his brother-in-law Samuel Poole, a butcher, whose wife and family were living in the same house. Crookes, at the instigation of Broadhead, threw into Poole's house a can of gunpowder, which exploded and did some damage to the shop, but hurt no one.

1859, August 1st. Crookes and Hallam tracked Linley from house to house nearly every day for five or six weeks, intending to shoot him. On the 1st August they found him sitting in a public-house in Scotland Street, in a room full of people, the windows of which opened into a back yard, and from that yard Crookes shot Linley with an air gun. The shot struck him on the side of the head, and he died from the effects of the injury in the following February. Crookes and Hallam were hired by Broadhead to shoot Linley.

1859, May 24th. *Samuel Baxter*, of Loxley, was a saw grinder, but "kept aloof from the trade." Crookes and Needham, at the instigation of Broadhead, put down the chimney of his house a can of gunpowder, which they exploded; no one was hurt by the explosion.

Joseph Helliwell was not a member of the union, and had not been brought up to the trade of a saw grinder. On the 18th October 1859, he was working at saw grinding for Joseph Wilson (who refused to employ union men), and he was blown up by the explosion of gunpowder, which was ignited by the sparks from his glazier when he began to work. Broadhead gave three cans of gunpowder to Dennis Clark to blow up Helliwell, and Clark and Shaw placed half a can of powder in Helliwell's trough. Helliwell was blind for nearly a fortnight, and it was a month before he was able to resume work. 1859, October 18th.

Joseph Wilson, master of the above-named Joseph Helliwell, had "set the trade at defiance," and had determined not to employ any one connected with the union. 1859, November 24th

On the night of the 24th November 1859 Wilson's house, in which his wife and family were asleep, was blown up by the explosion of a can (containing a quart of gunpowder) in the cellar, under the children's room; no one was hurt, but great injury was done to the house and furniture. Broadhead employed Crookes to commit this outrage.

Shortly after this time, but the exact date was not proved, an unsuccessful attempt was made by Crookes, at the instigation of Broadhead, to blow down a chimney of Messrs. Firths. Messrs. Firths had at the time two non-union men in their employment named John Helliwell and Samuel Baxter.

John Helliwell had left the union and took discounts, *i.e.* worked for less than the scale of prices regulated by the union, and had more apprentices than were allowed by their rules. 1859, December.

Crookes and Hallam, at the instigation of Broadhead, watched for Helliwell on several occasions, on the Midland Railway, in order to shoot him while at his work at Messrs. Firths. They were, however, misinformed as to the place where he worked and failed to find him. Before they had succeeded in their object they were requested by Broadhead to let Helliwell alone for the present, as there was "a job to be done" at Messrs. Wheatman and Smith's which was of a more pressing character.

Messrs. Wheatman and Smith had introduced machinery for grinding saws, to the detriment, as Broadhead conceived, of hand labour. Broadhead gave Crookes 2*l.* to purchase gunpowder, in order to blow down Messrs. Wheatman and Smith's chimney. Crookes and Hallam bought 24 pounds of powder, placed it in a can strengthened by a lash line wound tightly round it, and attached a fuse to it. They at first intended to place it in the chimney, and went on several nights to find an opportunity, but owing sometimes to the workmen being about, and at other times to the chimney being too hot, they were unable to do so. Ultimately they placed the powder in a drain in the neighbourhood of the chimney, and exploded it, and the explosion caused considerable damage. 1860, January 17th.

Harry Holdsworth did not acknowledge the union, and refused to discharge one Jonathan Crapper, a saw grinder, who had a dispute with the union, and employed some jobbing grinders who did not contribute to the union. In October and November 1861 he received several threatening letters. On the night of December 1st 1861, a can of gunpowder was exploded in the cellar under his warehouse, which did damage to the building to the amount of 100*l.* 1861, December 1st.

In the year 1861 the Jobbing Grinders' Union was associated with the other three branches of the saw trade, and Joseph Hoyle was their secretary. Broadhead applied to him to compel the non-union jobbing grinders to join the union, and Hoyle consented to their being rattened, and agreed to bear his share of the expense, which he stated he believed would be about 10*s.* The men were not rattened, but Holdsworth's warehouse was blown up, and after the committal of this outrage Broadhead applied to Hoyle for 6*l.* as his share of the expense. Hoyle obtained the 6*l.* from the committee of the union, but denied that he had authorized the blowing up, and he stated that in consequence of this circumstance his own union had withdrawn from the amalgamation on the first convenient opportunity. Their secession from the amalgamation, however, did not occur till three years afterwards, and we report that this outrage was promoted and encouraged by the Saw Grinders' and Jobbing Grinders' Unions.

Messrs. Reaney were the owners of a wheel in the Park, and Thomas Fearnehough, who was obnoxious to the trade, was working there; Crookes, at the instigation of Broadhead, attempted to blow up this wheel and failed. 1863, June 7th.

Thomas Fearnehough, a saw grinder, had long been obnoxious to the union. Having been a member of the union, he left it eight years ago, and shortly after joined again from fear of bodily harm. In 1865 he left the union a second time, and never rejoined it. He had been in the habit of working on his own tools instead of his master's (which was against the rules of the union), and at the time of this outrage he was working for 1866, October 8th.

Messrs. Slack, Sellars, and Co., who had a dispute with the saw handle makers. The saw grinders had in consequence been withdrawn, but Fearnehough had, notwithstanding the withdrawal of the grinders, persisted in working for the firm. Messrs. Slack, Sellars, and Co., aware of the danger which Fearnehough incurred by working for them, took power for him at Messrs. Butchers' wheel, to which there was no access except through a covered gateway which was carefully guarded. Fearnehough was therefore safe from being rattened.

Two or three months before October 1866, Henry Skidmore, secretary of the Saw Makers' Society, and Joseph Barker, secretary of the Saw Handle Makers' Society, called on Broadhead, and represented to him that Fearnehough was working for Slack, Sellars, and Co., and thereby injuring the trade, and asked him "if something could not be done at him to stop his working." They were aware that he could not be rattened at Butchers' wheel, but no plan was laid down by them by which Fearnehough was to be coerced, although they agreed to bear their share of the expense of compelling him to submit to the union. On the 8th October 1866 a can of gunpowder was exploded in the cellar under Fearnehough's house in New Hereford Street, in which he was then living with his family, consisting of two sons and a daughter. No one was hurt, but great damage was done to the house. Samuel Crookes was hired by Broadhead to commit this outrage, and was assisted by Joseph Copley, a member of the Saw Grinders' Union. A day or two after this occurrence, Barker and Skidmore, with the knowledge of Thomas Smith, secretary of the Saw Makers' Union, paid Broadhead 7*l.* 10*s.*, the share of each union for the expense of committing the outrage. Joseph Barker found the money (the Saw Handle Makers' Union being then 18*l.* in debt to the Saw Makers' Union), and Smith credited Barker with the amount in the books of the Saw Makers' Union. The entry of this amount was passed over by the auditors without inquiry in the December following; this could not have been done if the audit had been carefully and honestly conducted.

A reward of 1,100*l.* offered for the detection of the perpetrators failed to elicit any information.

The fact of these outrages having been done in the interest of the trade was well known to the union, and although in one or two instances individual members had protested against them, yet nothing like an investigation had been demanded, nor had there been any general vote of condemnation of these acts until the case of Fearnehough occurred, when public indignation was aroused, and then the outrage was denounced, and a reward was offered by the union for the detection of the offenders. The whole of the above offences were directed by Broadhead, and sums amounting to nearly 200*l.* had been taken by him out of the funds of the union to pay the parties who committed them. Although these acts were not proved to have been directly authorized by the union, there must have been a knowledge, or at all events a well-grounded belief, amongst its members that they were done, not only in the interests of their society, but through the agency of some one or more of their governing body, and we report that all the above outrages were promoted, encouraged, and connived at by the Saw Grinders' Union; and that the "Hereford Street outrage" was promoted and encouraged by the Saw Grinders', Saw Makers', and Saw Handle Makers' Unions.

The following members of the Saw Grinders' Union have been engaged in the concerting or perpetration of outrages :—

Broadhead, William.	Hallam, James.
Clark, Dennis.	Peace, George.
Copley, Joseph.	Shaw, George.
Crookes, Samuel.	Smith, Elijah (dead).
Dean, Phineas (dead).	Taylor, John (dead).

The File Grinders' Union.

1857, April 25th. *George Gillott*, a file grinder, had ceased to pay to the union, and had more apprentices than were allowed by the trade. He was working at the Tower wheel, where it was almost impossible that he could be rattened. On the night of April 25th 1857, while he and his wife, two children, and two apprentices, were in bed, a can of gunpowder was thrown into the cellar of the house and exploded. No one was hurt, but one wall of the house was blown down, and great damage was done to the building and to the furniture. There was entire absence of any private cause for this act, and though the perpetrators are undiscovered, and we have no evidence directly implicating the union, we do not hesitate to report that this was a trade outrage.

William Torr, a file manufacturer, had a dispute with the union on account of his paying his men less than the union scale of prices. The union men in his employment were drawn out by the union; his factory was picketed, his warehouse broken into, a cistern containing a preparation for hardening files was tapped three times, his bellows were cut, and the books of his trade were taken away and never restored. The offenders are undiscovered, but the circumstances of the case, and the admission made by Cutts and Holland, joint secretaries of the File Smiths' Union, that these acts had certainly the appearance of being society matters, draw us to the conclusion that these outrages were encouraged and connived at by the File Grinders' Union. 1864, November.

The Sickle Grinders' Union.

Christopher Rotherham had been a sickle manufacturer for nearly 50 years, at Dronfield, five miles from Sheffield. Shortly before 1860 his men refused to pay to the union, and he thereupon received several threatening letters to the effect that his premises would be blown up if he did not compel them. 1860, July 26th.

About the year 1860 his boiler was blown up, and shortly after a can of gunpowder was thrown, at night, into a house belonging to him at Troway (inhabited by two of his nephews, who worked for him, and were not members of the union), and exploded. No one was hurt, but great damage was done to the house. He has had at different times nine pairs of bellows cut, twelve bands cut to pieces, and his anvils thrown into his dam.

In 1865 a two-gallon bottle, filled with gunpowder, with a lighted fuse attached, was placed in the night time in his warehouse. The fire of the fuse from some cause became extinguished before it reached the powder. Adjoining the warehouse were sleeping rooms, which, at the time the bottle was placed in the warehouse, were occupied by a mother, three sons, and a daughter. This he said "beat him," and he forced his men to join the union, adding that since that time "they had been as quiet as bees." 1865.

George Castles, the secretary of the Sickle and Reaping Hook Grinders' Association, told us that in the September of last year he saw a cash book of the union, containing entries of payments made at the time some of these outrages occurred, burnt in the committee room, and also that leaves had been torn out of other books of the union which might have implicated the union.

We have to report that these outrages were promoted and encouraged by the Sickle Grinders' Union.

The Fork Grinders' Union.

In this year a resolution had been passed by the union, that no fork grinder should work except for one of ten specified masters who were sanctioned by the union. 1859, February 17th.

William Mason, *Thomas Roebuck*, and *Samuel Gunson* were non-union men, and were working for masters not sanctioned by the trade. One night Mason was assaulted by about 30 union men, five of whom were summoned before the magistrates, and of these two were fined. Three weeks after this assault, namely, on 17th February 1859, gunpowder was placed in the troughs of Mason, Roebuck, and Gunson.

In Mason's case the powder exploded immediately Mason began working, and burnt his arm, face, and neck; he was wearing spectacles, and these saved his sight. Roebuck fortunately perceived the powder before he began work, and he found about 1 lb. of gunpowder in his trough.

Gunson being in America we have not been able to ascertain the particulars of his case.

The books of the union applicable to this period were not produced before us. They were said to have been destroyed, for the purpose, as stated by the secretary, of hiding their contents. The secretary of the union said that he believed these outrages were trade affairs; and we report that they were encouraged and promoted by the Fork Grinders' Union.

The Brickmakers' Union.

James Robinson, a master brickmaker, had had disputes with the union before 1857, and in this year he had in his employment four non-union men who had been seven years in his service At the latter end of the year 1857 four men came to Robinson, saying that they were sent by the committee of the union to take the places of the four non-union men. Robinson refused to turn off his old hands. The union ordered the union men to leave, which they refused to do. In the following summer 17,000 bricks were trampled upon and destroyed. This was done by four or five men at the least. 1857.

1859. One of Robinson's cows was found stabbed while grazing in a field adjoining his brick-yard, and had to be killed.

1859, October. On the day of October 1859, at 3 a.m. an attempt was made to blow up the house in which Robinson, his wife, his son, and four daughters were living. Three gingerbeer bottles, filled with gunpowder and nails, with lighted fuzes attached, were thrown at a chamber window of Robinson's house. Two struck below the window sill and fell outside the house. One was thrown through the window and was broken against the wall of the room, by which means the powder escaped and exploded harmlessly.

1860, November. An unsuccessful attempt was made to burn a haystack, worth 150*l.*, situated 10 yards from his house, and close to a stable in which were his cows and horses. A length of calico saturated with naphtha and turpentine had been pegged round the stack; the ends of the calico were carried down so as to touch 11 boxes of lucifer matches, and a roll of paper, to act as a fuze, was extended along the ground. The paper had been lighted and had burnt about a yard, but owing to the dampness of the atmosphere, or some other cause, the light had gone out.

1861. One of his horses was found dead in his field. During the night it had been stabbed in the side by a pointed instrument.

The perpetrators of these outrages have never been discovered, although active steps were taken by the police at the time. The secretary stated to us that he believed these outrages were done by the union.

1861, April 21st. *Henry Bridges*, formerly a master brickmaker, was not in 1861 a member of the union.

On the Saturday before the 21st April 1861 one of his men, named Thomas Poole, had a quarrel with John Baxter, a member of the committee, in reference to the payment of what is called "outworking money."

On the night of 21st April between 40,000 and 50,000 bricks, five or six barrows, and a pressing machine, the property of Bridges, of the value of 40*l.*, were destroyed. This must have been the work of five or six men.

Bridges applied to Baxter as to the cause of his bricks being spoiled, and Baxter said it was because he (Baxter) had been insulted by one of Bridges' men.

The books of the Brickmakers' Society, containing their transactions for the whole of the year 1861, were destroyed, and William Hy. Owen, a former secretary, admitted that if they had been produced, they would have shown that money was paid by the union for the commission of these outrages.

We report that these outrages were promoted and encouraged by the Brickmakers' Union.

The Fender Grinders' Union.

1861, November 5th. *John Sibray* was foreman to Mr. H. E. Hoole, stove, grate, and fender manufacturer, in the spring of 1861. At that time Mr. Hoole's "heavy" grinders having absented themselves from work for more than a week, Mr. Hoole desired Sibray to endeavour to procure other men. Sibray engaged Charles Taylor, a non-union man When the union men returned and found Charles Taylor at work they quitted the works in a body, taking the "light" grinders with them. Their places were filled by Rd. White, George White, W. Hulse, George Wastnidge, and others. On the next day Mr. Hoole received a threatening letter; this was followed by several others, and deputations from the union saw Mr. Hoole on the subject of his employing non-union men.

On the 5th November Sibray was assaulted in the street by two men, and about the same time Richard White, George White, and William Hulse, three of the non-union men, were assaulted and beaten, and one of the Whites was left for dead.

1861, November 23rd. *George Wastnidge*, one of the above-named non-union men, lived in Acorn Street, with his wife, child, and a lodger named Bridget O'Rourke. Wastnidge, his wife, and child, slept in the garret, and Mrs. O'Rourke in the chamber below fronting the street. About 1 o'clock in the morning of the 23d November, a can of gunpowder was thrown through the chamber window. Mrs. Wastnidge hearing a noise, ran down into Mrs. O'Rourke's room and found her holding in her hand a parcel emitting sparks. She seized it in order to throw it through the window, and it exploded in her hands, setting fire to her night dress and seriously injuring her. She ran upstairs, her husband stripped off her burning clothes, and in her fear she threw herself through the garret window into the street. Wastnidge dropped his little boy to persons who were below in the street, and by means of a ladder which was brought escaped from the house. Mrs. O'Rourke was found in the cellar shockingly burnt.

Mrs. Wastnidge was taken to the infirmary in a state of insensibility, where she remained five or six weeks. She has not recovered from the injuries she received. Mrs. O'Rourke was also taken to the infirmary, where she died a fortnight after. A person of the name of Thompson was tried at York, at the spring assizes, 1862, for the murder of Mrs. O'Rourke, and was acquitted.

Robert Renshaw confessed before us that he threw the can of gunpowder into Wastnidge's house, and that he was hired to do so on the promise of 6*l.* by William Bayles and Samuel Cutler, both members of the Fender Grinders' Union, and he stated that it was done because Wastnidge was not right with the trade.

James Robertson, now secretary, and at that time acting secretary of the Fender Grinders' Union, stated that he paid to William Bayles 6*l.* which he had received from Kenworthy, the then secretary of the union, and that he had falsified the books of the union in order that that payment should not be discovered.

We report that all the above outrages were promoted and encouraged by the Fender Grinders' Union.

The Pen and Pocket Blade Grinders' Union.

Samuel Sutcliffe was a surgical instrument maker. There was a strike in this trade in 1861. 1861, and Sutcliffe had "gone in when the others were out." Broomhead (now dead), secretary of the union, and one Braithwaite, in the same trade, hired Hallam "to make him so that he could not work for a week or two." Hallman and Crookes waylaid him at his own door and beat him on the head with life preservers, and hurt him so severely that he was confined to his bed for a week. Broomhead paid Hallam 5*l.* for the job, remarking at the time that 5*l.* was as much as the committee would allow him to pay him. The books of the union for this period have been destroyed.

We report that this outrage was encouraged and promoted by the Pen and Pocket Blade Grinders' Union.

The Scissor Forgers' Union.

George Gill, scissor manufacturer, had in his employment a man named Joseph Hague, 1865, February 22nd. who was not in the union. Joseph Hague had frequently been solicited by Joseph Thompson, the secretary, to join the union, and a deputation from the union called upon him and told him, that if he did not join, they would do something for him. Three weeks after this a pair of bellows on which Hague was working, but which belonged to Mr. Gill, were cut.

Robert Winter, scissor forger, refused to join the union, and had in his employment 1865, August. some men who had also refused. The bellows of the men who had refused to join the union were cut, whilst those of the union men were not injured. William Fearnly, a member of the union, confessed to having committed these outrages in consequence of the men not paying to the union, but he denied that he cut the bellows by the authority of the union.

In the early part of this year *Messrs. Darwin*, scissor manufacturers, had employed non-union men at a scale of prices less than that sanctioned by the union. Joseph Thompson, secretary of the Scissor Forgers' Union, admitted that he employed John Clarke to take 1863. away their tools and hide them. Clarke, however, was examined by us, and stated that he was employed by Thompson to take their tools and cut their bellows, and we believe his statement. Clarke was tried for this offence at Leeds, and convicted and sentenced to nine months' imprisonment. Thompson paid Mrs. Clarke 6*s.* a week during the time her husband was in prison, and although Thompson said that he had embezzled the funds and falsified the accounts of the union in order to conceal this payment, and although he had in consequence tendered his resignation, the society passed a resolution to the effect that the money had been taken and paid for services rendered to the union. The books of this union, as we have already stated, were mutilated and falsely kept by the secretary, and they were never subjected to any careful audit.

We report that all these outrages were encouraged and promoted by the Scissor Forgers' Union.

The Scissor Grinders' Union.

Edwin Sykes, a scissor manufacturer, had, when a master grinder, refused to pay to the 1866, December. trade; for this he was threatened by Holmshaw, president of this union, and subsequently he was rattened. In December 1866 he had in his employment a man, named Pryor, who was not a member of the union, and who had never been apprenticed to the trade. Holmshaw had told him that Pryor must not work for him, and on his refusal to dismiss

Pryor, had threatened to "serve him out." On the 26th of the same month his wheel was broken into and damage done to the amount of 24*l.*; a large quantity of tools were damaged, and the remainder thrown into the dam.

We report that this outrage was encouraged and connived at by the Scissor Grinders' Union.

The Edge-Tool Forgers' Union.

1864 *Mr. David Ward*, of the firm of Ward and Payne, edge-tool manufacturers, had frequently been requested by their customers to obtain a first-rate carving tool forger. They brought to Sheffield *James Addis*, a London workman, who had received prize medals for carving tools at the Exhibitions both of 1851 and 1862. At this time, tools of the kind made by Addis were not manufactured in Sheffield. Addis offered to pay to the union an entrance fee of 15*l.* in addition to the usual contributions, and undertook not to claim any benefit from the union for two years. The committee, however, refused to accept him, and Addis returned to London. Some time afterwards Mr. Ward sent for Addis again and set him to work. Deputations from the union called upon Mr. Ward, withdrew the union men from work, and would consent to no terms except the dismissal of Addis, and a payment by Mr. Ward of 30*l.* to the union, to cover the expenses of the men whom the union had withdrawn from his employment.

Mr. Ward paid the 30*l.* and dismissed Addis. In order to secure the carving tools made by Addis, Mr. Ward was obliged to advance the money requisite to set Addis up as a small manufacturer on his own account. He thereby ceased to be a workman, and now, instead of forging only, he is obliged also to grind and finish his tools, so as to bring them in a complete state to Mr. Ward's warehouse. This is both expensive and inconvenient.

Addis, with the assistance of an apprentice, could earn 7*l.* a week, and has earned as much as 10*l.* a week. Whilst Addis was at work for Mr. Ward, and before the payment of the 30*l.*, he was standing one day at the bar of a public-house, when four men, members of the union, fastened the door and asked him, "How many trades union meetings have we had through you?" and then kicked him and inflicted two serious wounds on his head. The parties were summoned before the magistrates and three were fined 5*l.* each, and one 3*l.* 10*s.* Although this outrage was done by members of the Edge-Tool Forgers' Union, we have no evidence to show that it was an outrage promoted or encouraged by that union.

The Edge-Tool Grinders' Union.

John Hague, sheep-shear and edge-tool grinder, was never apprenticed, but as a boy worked for his father, who belonged to the trade. He had offered to pay 20*l.* to be allowed to join the union. Whilst working for a person called Greaves, 13 axletrees and glaziers, six wheelbands, and 12 pulleys, belonging to Hague, were taken away from the wheel and were found to be so much burnt as to be rendered useless, a shank stone was broken, and his horsing chopped into firewood. Whenever he appeared amongst union men he was called a "knobstick." Although the circumstances of the outrage would indicate that it was done in the interests of the trade, yet there was no evidence before us to show that this was an outrage promoted or encouraged by the Edge-Tool Grinders' Union.

There is no ground to doubt the correctness of Hague's statement. We think it right, however, to observe that Hague was a very disreputable witness, having been several times convicted, and once transported for seven years.

The Scythe Grinders' Union.

1858. *Messrs. Tyzack and Sons*, scythe, saw, file, and steel manufacturers, employ 250 men, and are brought into communication with several unions. They have had continual disputes with the unions, in the course of which they have received several threatening letters, and have had considerable damage done to their property.

1858. Three pairs of bellows were destroyed at their works at Abbey Dale, in consequence, as was stated, of the scythe finishers in their employment not paying their contributions.

1859, July. Thirteen scythe grinders' bands were taken because they had engaged a man without the consent of the union.

1863 and 1865. Several shops were broken open and tools taken away in consequence of some of the men being in arrear with their contributions.

A man called Needham, who had been convicted of a trade outrage, had when in prison made a statement to Mr. Joshua Tyzack, affecting Michael Thompson, the secretary of the Scythe Grinders' Union. On Needham's coming out of prison, and shortly before November 1862, Mr. Joshua Tyzack made frequent inquiries for him in order to get his evidence against Thompson. 1862, November.

In the month of November 1862, Mr. Joshua Tyzack was returning in his gig from Sheffield, according to his usual habit, at about 8.30 p.m.; he had proceeded three-quarters of a mile from Sheffield, when passing a plantation he heard a shot fired, and then a second one in quick succession; he looked round and saw the flash of a third shot about 15 or 20 yards off, and at the same instant a bullet passed through his hair and the brim of his hat. He became unconscious for a moment and sank down in the gig, and in so doing stopped his horse. He almost instantly recovered himself, and as he rose to whip the horse two more shots were fired at him from the same place. Mr. Tyzack stated that in his opinion this attempt to shoot him was made in consequence of the inquiries which he had set on foot respecting Needham, but we are unable to satisfy ourselves from the evidence before us that this was an outrage promoted or encouraged by any trade union.

The Nail Makers' Union.

This union has its head-quarters at Belper, in Derbyshire, but the persons on whose property the following outrages were committed lived and worked at Thorpe Hesley, within the district to which the present inquiry is limited. In this union there is no regular weekly contribution, but when a strike occurs a levy is made to support the men who are out. 1861, December.

In December 1861 the nailmakers in the employment of Mr. Favell, of Rotherham, were on strike, but *John Hattersley* and *Charles Butcher*, who carried on their trade at their own shops at Thorpe Hesley, persisted in working for Mr. Favell. Hattersley was subjected to many acts of annoyance, and Butcher, on going to his work, discovered one morning, in the chimney above his hearth, a can full of gunpowder suspended by a rope from the top, which would have exploded immediately the fire was lighted.

On the 21st December 1861 the shops of these men were blown up by a can of powder suspended by a rope in the chimney of each shop, and exploded by a fuse. Isaac Emanuel Watson, Joseph Tomlinson, and Samuel Proctor committed these outrages, and were paid for doing them out of the funds of the union (by order of the committee) by Charles Webster, a member of the committee, the money being handed to him by James Beighton, the chairman, for that purpose. 1861, December 21st.

Watson, Tomlinson, and a brother of Watson, were tried for these outrages at the York Spring Assizes, 1862, and found guilty, and sentenced to 14 years' transportation. Upon strong representations being made of their innocence, they were pardoned and released. The men were defended by the union, and their defence cost the union 40*l*. or 50*l*.

We report that these outrages were promoted and encouraged by the Nail Makers' Union.

The Ironworkers' Union.

In consequence of the reduction of wages in the early part of this year, a large number of the workmen of *Messrs. J. Brown and Co.* (*Limited*), steel manufacturers, went out on strike. The firm made great exertions to get new hands. This was strenuously opposed by the union. For three weeks the works were watched by policemen specially appointed, and the new men were lodged and fed within the walls of the establishment James Dunhill and Edmund Higgins, two non-union men working for Brown and Co., were found in a public-house by seven or eight union men and assaulted, and on leaving the public-house, they were followed into the street and again assaulted. Dunhill and Higgins summoned the men before the magistrates, and they were bound over to keep the peace. 1867, February and March.

We have not sufficient evidence before us to justify our reporting that these outrages were promoted or encouraged by the Ironworkers' Union.

We have now given an outline of all the cases of importance which were submitted to us for investigation. Mr. Thomas Thorpe, managing clerk to Mr. Albert Smith, clerk to the magistrates acting for the Petty Sessional Division and borough of Sheffield, prepared for us a list of cases supposed to be connected with trade unions, and which had been brought before the justices within the last ten years; it comprised, in addition to the outrages mentioned in this report, 166 cases of rattening and 21 cases of sending threatening letters. A very small proportion, however, of the persons rattened give information either to the police or to the justices.

Most of the outrages we have investigated were brought before the justices, and although in several cases large rewards had been offered for the detection of the perpetrators, the offenders have with two or three exceptions remained unknown up to the period of this inquiry.

We believe that there are about 60 trades unions in Sheffield, of which 12 have promoted or encouraged outrages within the meaning of the Trades Union Commission Act, 1867.

We have to report that there has not occurred within the last ten years any act of intimidation, outrage, or wrong promoted, encouraged, or connived at by any association of employers.

We point to the year 1859 as the one in which outrage was most rife, and we notice with pleasure that it has diminished since that time.

During the course of our investigation, matters connected with trades unions (such as the number of apprentices allowed to each workmen, and the class from which they may be taken, the remuneration of labour, the restraints exercised upon voluntary action, and the rules and general policy of trades unions) have frequently been brought before our notice. These, however, are questions for the consideration of the Royal Commission sitting in London, and we purposely avoid making any observations upon them.

At the commencement of our inquiry, and frequently during the course of it, we explained the provisions of the Trades Union Commission Act, 1867, with regard to the powers conferred on us of granting certificates of indemnity to witnesses who should by their evidence inculpate themselves. We are convinced that the most material disclosures made to us were so made in reliance on our promise of indemnity made in conformity with the Act of Parliament. Had no such indemnity been offered, we are satisfied, that we should never have obtained any clear and conclusive evidence touching the most important subjects of our inquiry, and that the system of crime which has now been disclosed, as well as the perpetrators, would have remained undiscovered; we have therefore granted certificates to all witnesses whom we believe to have made a full and true disclosure of all offences in which they have been implicated.

WILLIAM OVEREND.
THOMAS I. BARSTOW.
GEORGE CHANCE.

Dated this 2nd of August 1867.

TRADES UNIONS COMMISSION: SHEFFIELD OUTRAGES INQUIRY.

(TRADES UNION COMMISSION ACT, 30 VICT. c. 8.)

REPORT

PRESENTED TO

THE TRADES UNIONS COMMISSIONERS

BY

THE EXAMINERS

APPOINTED TO INQUIRE INTO

ACTS OF INTIMIDATION, OUTRAGE, OR WRONG ALLEGED TO HAVE BEEN PROMOTED, ENCOURAGED, OR CONNIVED AT BY TRADES UNIONS

IN THE

TOWN OF SHEFFIELD.

VOL. II.—MINUTES OF EVIDENCE.

Presented to both Houses of Parliament by Command of Her Majesty.

LONDON:
PRINTED BY GEORGE EDWARD EYRE AND WILLIAM SPOTTISWOODE,
PRINTERS TO THE QUEEN'S MOST EXCELLENT MAJESTY.
FOR HER MAJESTY'S STATIONERY OFFICE.

1867.

CONTENTS.

MINUTES OF EVIDENCE

TAKEN BEFORE

THE EXAMINERS

APPOINTED TO INQUIRE INTO

TRADE OUTRAGES AT SHEFFIELD

UNDER

"THE TRADES UNION COMMISSION ACT, 1867."

FIRST DAY.

Council Hall, Sheffield, Monday, 3rd June 1867.

PRESENT:

William Overend, Esq., Q.C.
Thomas Irwin Barstow, Esq.
George Chance, Esq.
J. E. Barker, Esq., Secretary.

WILLIAM OVEREND, Esq., Q.C., in the Chair.

FIRST DAY.

3 June 1867.

(*Chairman.*) We are very much obliged to the gentlemen present for the mode in which they have received us, but perhaps they will excuse my making this observation, that it is very undesirable that there should be any expression either of applause or of dissent as regards any of the proceedings which may take place here ; therefore I shall feel obliged to all present if they will not express their approbation or disapprobation.

I think that before we open this inquiry it is my duty to state in a few words what its object is, and what we have come down here to do. My friends Mr. Barstow and Mr. Chance have been appointed, with myself, to make inquiry into certain acts of intimidation, outrage, and wrong which have been perpetrated at Sheffield, within a period of ten years before this time, and we are instructed by Her Majesty's Secretary of State to make an inquiry into those outrages for the purpose of ascertaining whether they have been either promoted, encouraged, or connived at by the trades' unions or associations of Sheffield, be they the trades' unions or associations, either of the workmen or of the masters, of this town. We have great pleasure in coming down to do this, for this reason : we believe that it is done at the invitation as well of the masters as of the men, that the men desire it as well as the masters, and therefore we expect that we shall obtain as well from the masters as from the men the most perfect and cordial co-operation in the objects of our inquiry.

Now our duty is not so much to investigate what outrages have been committed, or who have committed them ; but our duty is to inquire whether those things have been done with the connivance of, and have been encouraged by those trades' unions or associations either of masters or of men, and to see whether there is any connexion between the two, and if there is, what has been that connexion, and how it is, and what circumstances there have been which have given rise to the interference of the trades' unions.

We have by this Act of Parliament a power of asking for the attendance, and compelling the attendance of witnesses before us ; and witnesses when they do come before us will be sworn, and when they are sworn they will differ in this respect from ordinary witnesses : they will be compelled to answer whatever lawful questions we put to them, and if they refuse to answer, we can immediately send them to prison for refusing to answer the questions which we may put. Now in an ordinary case there might be hardship in that, but in this case there is no hardship, because the Act of Parliament which enables us to compel the attendance of witnesses, and to compel them to give answers to questions put to them, also authorizes us to give to the persons who shall come as witnesses and make full disclosures of all the circumstances connected with these matters which are within their knowledge a certificate of the fact that they have made such disclosures ; and thereupon they are indemnified against all consequences. Neither the Government nor a private person nor anyone can proceed against them. They cannot be proceeded against criminally for any act which they may have committed, and they cannot be proceeded against civilly for any injury which they may have caused. Therefore there is no hardship in a man being asked to tell all he knows ; he cannot say, "If "I do I shall be criminally prosecuted, or some person "will bring an action against me," because in every case, if he only makes a full and fair disclosure of all the facts within his knowledge, immediately he produces our certificate, by virtue of the Act of Parliament he is cleared of all consequences. Therefore we shall of course feel it our duty (and I hope there will be no difficulty about it) to put all those questions to the witnessses who come before us which will have a tendency to throw light upon this inquiry, and we shall press them and urge them to give all the information they possess, and the witnesses will do so at the peril of being sent to prison if they decline.

There is another thing which I should state. The public are protected against any false statement that a witness may make, because although we may grant persons certificates of indemnity against a civil or criminal prosecution, yet if a man should make any false statement before us upon oath, he would still be

FIRST DAY.

3 June 1867.

liable to be prosecuted for perjury. Our certificate would be no protection to him. Of course we should not grant him it, if we thought he was committing perjury, but if a man states before us what is false he is liable to be prosecuted for perjury in a court of law. These are our powers for compelling the attendance of witnesses and for compelling them to answer questions; and this is the security which the public have against their telling that which is untrue. I hope we shall none of us have any reason to use any of those powers which are granted to us. We trust persons will come fairly before us and fairly and candidly tell us all that they know. If they do they will be acting in accordance with their own suggestion to the Government, that they wished this inquiry to be instituted, and they will be doing this, they will be throwing light upon a transaction which has now interested not only England but Europe and America, namely, the relation of capital to labour, and also the question of the real position of trades unions throughout the world; and they will be giving information to the Commission in London and to the Legislature, and enabling them to pass such Acts of Parliament as in the result may be beneficial both to masters and men.

With these observations, stating what really the nature of our duty is, we propose to enter at once upon those duties by calling the witnesses whom we have, examining them and trying to elucidate as far as we can those matters which form the subject of our inquiry, namely, as to the supposed connexion that exists between the outrages, which no doubt have occurred within the last ten years, and the various trades unions, whether they be of masters or of men in this town.

Mr. J. Platts.

Mr. John Platts sworn and examined.

1. (*Chairman.*) What are you?—I am a scissor grinder and manufacturer.

2. Where do you live? ?—At Mitchell Street works, Brook Hill.

3. How long have you been a manufacturer?—About 9 or 10 years.

4. Before that what were you?—Journeyman grinder.

5. A scissor grinder?—Yes.

6. Did you serve any apprenticeship to the trade?—Yes.

7. Are you now a member of any union at all?—No, I have ceased to pay.

8. Have you ever been so?—Yes.

9. When were you a member of a union?—Up to 1863 I believe I paid.

10. What was the union of which you were a member?—The scissor grinders.

11. And for how many years were you a member of that union?—Altogether, I should think, I have paid to that union for perhaps about 17 or 18 years. Of course the trade has not been together all that time, but when it has been together I have paid to that trade.

12. Then you were for 17 or 18 years a member?—Yes.

13. What was the union composed of?—A president, secretary, and a committee.

14. Who is its president now?—Robert Holmshaw.

15. Who is its secretary?—Joseph Gale.

16. Do you know who are its committee?—I know several of them; there is Enoch Holland, he is one, and Joseph Thompson. There are about half a dozen that I know, but I cannot call them to mind at this moment. There is a man of the name of Samuel Lee.

17. And several others you say?—Yes; they are composed of about 12 altogether.

18. Do you know whether they have any rules?—I never saw any printed rules.

19. Have they any unwritten rules which are promulgated amongst the members?—They have reference to taking in apprentices, and all that sort of thing.

20. What are the rules about taking apprentices?—I believe that they now prohibit any boy coming into the trade, unless he be a freeman's son. There is another rule in reference to manufacturers; there is a rule that they shall contribute weekly 1*s.* 6*d.* to the trade, but they are never allowed to receive any scale from the fund.

21. When you speak of manufacturers, do you mean master grinders?—Yes; they pay 1*s.* 6*d.* per week, which they call "natty money."

22. Does that mean subscription money?—Yes.

23. You used the word "scale." What does that mean?—It is relief from the trade.

24. Do you know what are the objects of the union; are they a friendly society as well as a trade society?—Yes; there is a sick and funeral society connected with it.

25. Are they separate or are they together?—I think they are one and the same.

26. You say that they must subscribe 1*s.* 6*d.* a week to that?—1*s.* 6*d.* includes the sick money, 4*d.* per week, and in the event of death there is 6*d.* extra put on to meet that expense.

27. How much do the masters subscribe a week?—1*s.* 6*d.* a week.

28. And you say that that includes 4*d.* for sick money; that is to say, in the event of his being sick he will receive a contribution from the funds of the society?—A journeyman will do so.

29. Is the 1*s.* 6*d.* then which the master subscribes a subscription for himself and for his journeymen?—It is for himself.

30. But supposing a master subscribes 1*s.* 6*d.* a week, what benefit does he get from the union in the event of he himself becoming sick?—He gets no benefit; they will not allow him any benefit.

31. In case of his death what do his representatives get?—They get nothing. I never heard tell of anybody getting anything.

32. Then what benefit does the master get by this subscription of 1*s.* 6*d.* a week?—He gets no benefit at all.

33. If that is so I do not see the object that the master has in subscribing to this union. Why should he subscribe to the union if he gets no benefit from it?—Because he is compelled to do so.

34. Has a master grinder in the scissor trade any apprentices or journeymen?—No; of course he can have journeymen. There are cases in which a man has journeymen.

35. Supposing that a man has journeymen, does a journeyman subscribe to this fund?—The journeyman subscribes 1*s.* 6*d.* a week, but the case is different there. He receives when sick 6*s.* a week sick money.

36. For how long?—I suppose it is for the time that he remains sick.

37. Does his wife get anything in case he dies?—I think it is either 3*l.* or 6*l.*, I am not certain which, but I think that it is 6*l.*

38. Is there any subscription in respect of the apprentices?—There is a box allowance.

39. But do you subscribe anything in respect of apprentices?—I do not.

40. What is the subscription?—9*d.* a week is subscribed for apprentices.

41. If an apprentice becomes ill does he get anything?—I think not, but I am not certain; I never heard about it.

42. Do you know whether, if he dies, anything is given to bury him?—I have never heard of anything of the sort.

43. You do not say that it is not so, either one way or the other?—I am not aware that it is so; I do not know anything about it.

44. Those allowances are in the nature of a provision by a friendly society?—Yes.

45. Is there any other object which you are aware of for which the union is formed besides paying in case of illness or in case of death to the family of the man?—They combine of course to get their price

for their labour, and in case that a manufacturer refuses, of course they take out his men in order to prevent his business going forward. If there is any dispute with the grinders, then they draw out the shop-board hands, that is the forgers and filers.

46. Are those scissor grinders' unions in connexion with any other unions, or are they amalgamated with any other unions ?—They are not amalgamated, but there is this understanding between them : supposing the grinders have a disagreement with the manufacturers they would go to the scissor forgers' union and get them to take out the scissor forgers, and the grinders would pay the expenses of the scissor forgers.

47. And so they stop the concern ?—Yes.

48. That is in case of dispute ?—Yes.

49. What are the disputes that you are aware of which arise between the union men and the masters ?—Perhaps I had better relate my own case. Up to 1863 I did journey work ; of course I was what was called a journeyman grinder. I paid to the union up to the time that I did journey work. When I ceased to do journey work of course I ceased to pay to the union. I thought as a manufacturer not doing journey work I had no right to pay to that union, and the consequence of my ceasing to pay was that one morning all the bands were gone.

50. What was the date of that ?—I can give you the date ; that would be February the 28th, 1863.

51. Will you tell us what happened on that day ?—The bands were gone.

52. How many bands did you lose ?—Six bands.

53. Were they taken away ?—Yes.

54. Where were you working then ?—At the Union Grinding Wheel.

55. What kind of a place is the Union Wheel ; is it a place where persons rent "troughs" ?—Yes.

56. How many persons are there working in the same wheel ?—I had three journeymen working with me at the time.

57. And how many other men were there working in the same place with you ?—None ; it was a three-trough wheel, and I had it to myself.

58. Then you were the sole occupant of that room ?—Yes.

59. Was it locked or unlocked at night ?—It was locked.

60. You say that on the 28th of February those bands were taken away ; what time of the day or night was it ?—It would be from Saturday night to Monday morning.

61. Did you notice whether any damage had been done to the property itself ?—None.

62. Then how could any person have got into the premises to destroy the apparatus ?—It is the usual practice with grinders at most of the wheels where there are more than one working in a place that there is a certain place where the key is to be left, and the door was shut but not locked.

63. Was that known to other men about besides your own men ?—Most of the wheelers would know. It is a regular practice amongst grinders to do so.

64. In other parts of the wheel were there other rooms which were let off to other men ?—Yes.

65. You have said that this was done in consequence of some quarrel with the union ; why did you say that ?—My refusal to pay to the union.

66. How long before the 28th of February had you refused to pay to the union ?—I scarcely know, but at that time the contribution to the union was 2*d.* for a boy and 4*d.* for a man. My arrears had run up to 11*s.* 6*d.*, at 4*d.* a week. I had a boy at the time, and I always paid his contribution. Of course I considered by having this boy I had a privilege.

67. What privilege had you ?—By having an apprentice boy at the time.

68. But why should you pay to the union for that ?—There was no privilege beyond having the boy.

69. Having the permission to have the boy ?—That was the only privilege.

70. You paid 2*d.* a week for the boy ?—I paid 2*d.* a week for the boy,

71. But supposing you had not paid 2*d.* a week ? Do you mean to say that you paid it to the union for being allowed to have a boy as an apprentice ?—Yes.

72. Could that boy, in case he was ill, get the benefit you talk of ?—No. There was no sick society then ; that was just the forming of the union, the old union had just broken up.

73. Then, as I understand you, the only thing that you paid the 2*d.* a week for was the privilege of taking an apprentice ?—Yes.

74. And if there were no unions in the world you would have had no 2*d.* to pay, you would have taken your apprentice in the ordinary course ?—Yes.

75. But there being a union they said, "If you take an apprentice you must pay us 2*d.*" ?—Yes.

76. You say you had paid your 2*d.* and your arrears had got up to 11*s.* 6*d.* ?—Yes. I did not pay it myself.

77. You being a master did not pay ?—Yes.

78. But you having an apprentice did pay the 2*d.* ?—Yes.

79. Is what you call "a boy" an apprentice ?—Yes.

80. It is the same thing ?—Yes.

81. Now then, how do you connect the taking away of your bands with the union ?—I went down to the secretary, at least to the collector.

82. What is his name ?—His name is Thomas Robinson.

83. When did you do that ?—On the morning when the bands were gone.

84. On the 28th of February ?—Yes.

85. He was the collector ?—He was the collector of the "natty money." I asked him the reason that my bands were gone.

86. They had not gone then, had they ?—They had.

87. I thought they went between the Saturday and Monday ?—I went to him on the Monday.

88. What did you say to him ?—I asked him the reason that my bands were gone ; he said of course that he knew nothing at all about it.

89. Is Thomas Robinson alive ?—Yes.

90. Where does he live ?—I think it is No. 30, Wartery Street.

91. What did you say to him and he to you ?—He denied all knowledge of it, and he said I had better see Mr. Holmshaw, that was the president.

92. Is Mr. Holmshaw alive ?—Yes, he is the president now.

93. What is his christian name ?—Robert ; and Holmshaw referred me to the committee.

94. You saw Holmshaw ?—Yes, but he referred me to the committee.

95. Do you know where Holmshaw lives ?—It is in Arthur Street, I think. He referred me to the committee, and I went to the committee on the Monday night about this affair.

96. Where did the committee meet ?—They met in Bridge Street at that time, at the "Bowl Inn," or some place of the kind. It is a smith's public-house.

97. Did you see them ?—Yes, and of course at the first they denied all knowledge of the affair.

98. Did you tell them that the bands were gone ?—Yes.

99. Who were present at that meeting ?—There was Robert Holmshaw and Joseph Gale, that is the secretary.

100. Who besides ?—John Willey ; he was one of the committee-men at that time.

101. Where does Willey live ?—He lives somewhere down Broomhall Street, but I do not rightly know.

102. Who besides ?—There would be several others, but I quite distinctly remember those three.

103. Then you say that at first they said that they knew nothing at all about it ?—Yes, of course. We got into conversation, and I said, "If you had let me "have notice stating what you wanted I should have "known what was to be done in the case, but you

159. If you were not to receive any benefit from this contribution of 4*d.* a week, what was the reason that you subscribed that 4*d.* ?—Because I was compelled to do so.

160. How were you compelled to do so ?—Because if I had not done so I should have lost my bands as at first.

161. Then it was out of fear of losing your bands that you contributed ?—Yes.

162. Then am I to understand that you would not have been a member of that union but for the fear of having your property taken away from you ?—I would not.

163. And you did not wish to belong to a union at all ?—No.

164. Had you no benefit of any sort from your payment ?—No.

165. Except this immunity from having your bands taken ?—No.

166. You derive no benefit in case of illness, death, or bad work ?—No benefit in any shape or form.

167. And no prospects ?—No prospects.

168. How long did you continue to pay these contributions of 2*d.* and 4*d.* You say that it was without any benefit to yourself, but merely to protect your property ?—About a year after those bands went my health failed me, and then I gave up grinding.

169. Then you contributed for a year ?—Somewhere about a year. I paid up to the time that I ceased to grind, then I ceased paying.

170. When was your last payment ?—It will be in that book. The contributions have been raised since then. It was May the 16th, 1864.

171. And you contributed till May the 16th ?—I see that I am wrong ; I see that I have payments here till 1865.

172. How long did you contribute in this way before your health failed ?—I daresay that it would be

as far as you understood, the same as they were before ; that is to say, were you to receive any benefit for that 1*s.* ?—No ; they passed a resolution that no master should receive anything from the fund. The journeymen grinders do so.

191. The master gained nothing ?—Nothing.

192. Neither for death nor anything ?—Neither for sickness nor anything.

193. Was that an old resolution or had they passed a new one ?—They passed this resolution, I believe, not many months back. I do not know how long. Of course the masters are never allowed to attend the grinders' meetings.

194. You say that they passed this resolution. Before this resolution was passed were the masters entitled to anything ?—Yes. I believe formerly the masters used to receive scale.

195. Formerly. Up to what time did the masters receive scale ?—I do not know ; perhaps nine months ago.

196. But I have understood you to say that up to this time you were never entitled to 6*d.*, and you said, "I paid 6*d.* a week, 2*d.* for a boy and 4*d.* for myself. "I was not entitled to any scale. I did not wish to "belong to the union. I had no prospect of any "benefit." Is that right or not, because we must not have it wrong on our notes ? Were you, before this resolution was come to, entitled to receive any benefit from that contribution ?—I never gave any notice till about 13 weeks back.

197. You do not understand me. When you made your first payments before you were ill, was a master entitled to receive any payment in case of illness or of death by right of the contribution which he paid ?—There was not a sick society formed at that time.

198. Was there a sick society when you began to pay in the second case ?—Yes, there was then, but not very soon after. I am not certain about the ex[illegible]

FIRST DAY.

Mr. J. Platts.

4 June 1867.

"have taken advantage of my being away and nobody "knows what to do."

104. What did they say to that?—Then Gale, the secretary, made answer and said, "Well pay your money and they will be back to-morrow;" and I said, "But how can you give me a guarantee that they "will be back to-morrow if you do not know anything "at all about them?"

105. What did he say to that?—He said, "Well you know as well as I know." Then I asked him of course what the arrears were, and he said they would be about 1*l*. 10*s*. or 1*l*. 12*s*., I forget which. I asked him how it had got to be so much, and he said, "Well "you owe so-and-so, and your two or three journey-"men owe so much."

106. How much would that be?—I should owe 11*s*. 6*d*.

107. And the remainder is owed by your journeymen?—Yes, by the journeymen. I asked if he thought there was any reason why I should pay other men's debts, and he said he thought I should not object to it; and I said, "I do object to it; I shall pay my own but nobody elses." I paid the money to the committee on the Monday night.

108. What did you pay?—11*s*. 6*d*. I had not this book with me (*producing it*) when I went down, but I took it with me on Tuesday morning when I paid the money to have it entered in this book.

109. What is that book?—That is the contribution book.

110. "Scissors Mutual Aid Fund Contribution "Book, held at the Punch Bowl. Law 15. That any "member owing one month's and under three months' "contributions must pay the said contributions on or "before Monday night or he cannot receive any "benefits; and any member owing more than three "months' contribution shall stand two weeks." What do you mean by "standing two weeks"?—Without relief from the fund.

111. Was this a book supplied you by the union itself?—Yes.

112. And in it there is the date of the month, I see, and of the contributions?—Yes.

113. And February 23rd is marked as having been your day?—Yes, that was the time the bands went.

wheel with you?—At the same wheel, but not in the same room, and he was with me when I got the note.

123. What did you do?—Of course we went to the works and we had to get a ladder in order to get up to this place; it was a decent height up, but when we got into the place there the bands were.

124. How high was it?—It would be on the top of the workshop. The cistern is a great height up in the Union Wheel yard. We could not get in without a ladder. It was an old lumber room that they were thrown into.

125. Under the cistern as described?—Yes.

126. And there you found your bands?—Yes.

127. Were they damaged?—No.

128. The bands which you have mentioned are the bands by which you connect your grinding wheel, I suppose, with the power?—Yes.

129. Communicating with the main drum, the driving wheel?—Yes.

130. You got your bands, I suppose, and started working?—Yes.

131. And you say you were in arrear at the time as they said, and that you applied to them and they told you that you were in arrear, and that you might get the things in a certain way, and one of the men delivered you a letter, and thereupon you went and found them?—Yes.

132. That is your case, is it?—There is a good deal more connected with it, that is not half.

133. Was Colley a member of that union or not at that time?—Yes; his band was taken for the contribution, and of course he had to pay the same as I had.

134. There is no "of course" in this matter. Do you know that Colley was a member of the same union that you were?—Yes.

135. Do you know whether he was in arrear as well as you?—Yes; his bands would not have gone if he had not been.

136. Our business is to ascertain whether this has been done by the authority of the union, and you may have your opinion about it, but we must not come to a rash conclusion. How do you know that he was in arrear as well as you?—Because he had his arrears to pay of his own, and 2*s*. besides for the "Sweep."

137. What does that expression "for the sweep" [illegible]

IRST DAY.

Ir. J. Platts.

June 1867.

benefit from the sick society?—Nor from the trade funds either.

201. What do you mean by the trade funds?—It was what we call the "box scale."

202. What do you mean by the "box scale?—They allow for anyone out of work 8*s*. a week.

203. For how long? as long as he is unemployed?—Yes.

204. Is that in case of a man being out of employment by reason of a strike, or by reason of there not being work?—Both.

205. Supposing trade was bad in Sheffield, and a man was out of employment, would he have a right to go to the union and to say, "I have con-"tributed to your union for so many months or weeks, "and you must give me 8*s*. a week"?—Yes.

206. In case of bad trade or otherwise?—Yes.

207. But you say that about nine months ago they passed a resolution; was it in writing do you know?—I do not know.

208. Was it communicated to you?—Yes.

209. Who told you of it?—I was told by the president when I went down for the box scale.

210. What was his name?—Robert Holmshaw. Of course I got it directly from him.

211. When did he tell you?—I gave notice for the scale about 13 weeks ago. We had not a stroke of work, we had no orders in the place.

212. When you say that you gave notice for the scale, that means, that you gave notice that you were out of employment and wanted your allowance of 8*s*. a week?—Yes.

213. And what did he say to you?—He said, "Well, but you are a manufacturer." I said, "Well, "but don't I pay to the trade; do I owe any con-"tribution?" He said, "No, but the masters pay and do not receive."

214. Was that the first notice which you had that the masters paid but did not receive?—No, I had heard it before.

215. But still you paid?—I still paid.

216. If you had heard before that there was a resolution that the masters had to pay and were to derive no benefit, that the masters paid but did not receive, what was your object in contributing to the union after that?—From fear of the bands and things being destroyed. The notice was expired because he told me that I was a manufacturer but could not receive; and he said that I had better see the committee on the Tuesday night.

217. Who were the committee?—There was Enoch Holland. I think that you have those names.

218. Were they the same people?—Yes; I do not remember all the names, but you had two or three of the names. They thought that being a manufacturer, I was not entitled to any relief from that fund.

219. Who told you that?—Both Gale and Robert Holmshaw; of course he told me before.

220. Both Gale and Holmshaw said that they thought that as a manufacturer you were not entitled to any of the fund?—Yes. They had no objection, they said to giving me that week's scale provided I would pay the arrears back for the time I was not grinding.

221. What do you mean by the time that you were not grinding?—The two years that I was not grinding at all.

222. And they wanted you to pay as if you had been grinding?—Yes; and then I could have that week's scale.

223. Do you know what the arrears would have come to?—Yes. I asked what the arrears were, and the secretary ran through the book and he put the

226. And they offered to pay you how much?—The whole of the scale; that is 8*s*. for myself, 4*s*. for a woman, and 1*s*. for children, and I should have 16*s*. if I had paid 7*l*. 2*s*. 10*d*.

227. If you had paid 7*l*. 2*s*. 10*d*. you would have got 16*s*.?—Yes.

228. What then?—I said, "Do you consider I am insane or something worse?" They said that unless I paid it I could not receive anything, and I said I would not pay 1*d*. The week but one following that, 11th of February, Robert Holmshaw called again to see if I was going to pay. I told him that I considered he had a good deal of brass in his face to come to ask for anything more, and he asked me what I meant. I said, "I simply mean what I say." He said, "Well, "but you must not consider that we are lumps of wood "that you can do just as you have a mind with.' "Well," I said, "now don't you bother yourself, you "have been once and I will put you where you ought "to have been then." I was referring then to that note about the bands. He said, "Well, but I did not give you the note." I said, "No, but your collector "did, and you are the president, and of course you "will have to answer for it." His reply to that was, "Well, but we shall not do it in that way this time, we shall do it in some other way." I said, "Well, it "makes no difference so long as you do it, so that it is "but done it will be all the same."

229. You say this was the week but one following the 11th of February, that would bring it to about the 25th of February that this occurred?—Yes.

230. Then nothing happened to you at all, although you ceased to pay from the 11th of February up to the 27th April?—No.

231. Had more than one application been made to you to pay your contribution money before the 27th of April?—Yes; he kept coming for the men's money and he expected that mine would be paid as well, but I would not pay.

232. He applied to you from time to time?—Yes.

233. And you refused each time?—Yes.

234. How many applications do you think he made between the 11th of February and the 27th of April?—I was not always there of course.

235. But he came every week?—Yes, he generally came once a week, but if the men were not there of course he comes till he finds them.

236. From the 11th of February up to this time, had you journeymen working on the premises?—Yes, one had been on the box until the 9th of February, and then he commenced working, until the 2nd of May I think it was.

237. Was that the journeyman?—Yes, he worked up to the 9th of March from the 9th of February.

238. What was that journeyman's name?—Robert Booth.

239. Where does he live?—He lives in Brightmoor Street, Saint Phillip's Road.

240. Is he working with you now?—No, he has not been working, he is on the box, and I sent for him on the 26th of March. I had work for him.

241. Then from the 9th of February to the 9th of March he worked?—Yes.

242. Therefore they did not interfere with his working?—No.

243. Then what happened on the 9th of March again?—I had no work again, and of course he had to go upon the box.

244. Did they pay him?—Yes.

245. He had paid to the union?—Yes.

246. Then he had paid independently of you?—Yes; of course I had nothing to do with him.

an ill temper, and all that sort of thing, and he never opened his mouth. On the 28th of March Robert Holmshaw called to see if I had got any work for them. I said, "Yes, I have some for Robert Booth, but I have none for the others."

249. What others?—Hadley the journeyman. There was one on the box, and one had not paid his money, and he was walking about; he had no scale. "Well," he said, "are you going to pay" and I said, "No, not unless I can receive."

250. What did he say to that?—He said, "All right," and turned round and went out of the place. The men did not come to work, and I was without grinders for about eight or nine weeks, and what grinding was done I did myself, and when I thought I had plenty I sent off for some other men.

251. Had you applied for workmen to work for you?—I had sent for Booth. I had work from the 26th of March up to now for him.

252. Has he worked for you from that time?—No.

253. Have you had any quarrel with Booth?—No.

254. Have you any reason to suppose that Booth was willing to come if he had been allowed?—Yes, I believe he would.

255. What reason have you to believe that?—Because I think he would rather have plenty of work than receive 8*s.* a week from the box.

256. Has he been on the box all this time?—Yes, he is on now.

257. If he had come to you what could he have earned?—He gets such a thing as 30*s.* or 2*l.* a week.

258. You have had work, you say, for Booth; as he would not come, did you apply for other workmen?—No.

259. Why not?—It is no use applying to them, they would laugh in your face unless you do all they say and comply with all they say. You cannot have any men.

260. Are there not non-union men who could have done your work?—I have set on three now, about three weeks ago.

261. But during all this time why should you have gone to Robert Booth, if Robert Booth did not like to come for any reason of his own, or because the union did not like him to come? Why did you not get other men?—I did not wish to make any quarrels. If they would let me alone I would never trouble them, and if he had come to his work on the 26th of March I should have put him on, but I shall never receive him again certainly.

262. That is another thing. But why did you not get other men?—If I had made strict inquiries no doubt I could have got some other men.

263. But your object was to be all right with Booth?—Yes. I said, "Do not misunderstand me; I do not "want your money, but if you want mine I shall have "yours."

264. Then you insisted upon being upon the scale if you were to contribute?—Yes, certainly.

265. You did not look for non-union men because in point of fact you say you did not want to quarrel with the union?—Yes.

266. Will you proceed with your narrative. We have now got to the 28th of March, and you said you had work for Robert Booth but not for the others. What was the next thing?—Things went on; nothing occurred. He said, "All right," and turned round and went out of the place, and Booth did not come to his work; and from the 27th to the 29th of April I had five dozen of 11-inch paper scissors, and there was one pair short.

267. Where were they?—They were given out to a man of the name of James Prior. This is a class of work which, if Booth had been working, he would not have done. There are two separate branches in the scissors trade, the shot scissors and the steel scissors. Those paper scissors are what we call the shot scissors, and this man that I gave them out to has ground for me by shot work for nearly 10 years past, and he works at Trafalgar wheel.

268. That was not the wheel where you worked, was it?—No.

269. But you had given them to Prior?—Yes.

270. And they were taken from James Prior?—Yes.

271. But what reason have you to say that they were taken from James Prior in connexion at all with you?—I had a detective to make inquiries about those scissors.

272. What was his name?—Jackson, I believe.

273. Do you mean the chief constable?—No, Jackson, the detective. I think his name is Jackson. He went to look round the wheel and made inquiries as to the way in which they fastened the other door, and they of course, the same as the rest, leave the key hung up in a certain place, so that the men can find it in the morning, and after looking round and searching we could not find them.

274. Were you with him?—Yes. He asked one of the men if he had noticed anybody about the wheel that was a stranger and did not work in the place, and he said, "Yes, Robert Booth came into our room last "Thursday and asked if we could tell him where "James Prior worked."

275. What was the man's name that told you that?—Samuel Jubb.

276. Where does he live?—I do not know where he lives. He works at Trafalgar wheel.

277. He told you that Booth had been to the wheel and inquired where Prior worked?—Yes; and of course he told him where Prior worked.

278. Jubb told Booth where Prior worked?—Yes. Booth went into the hull in which Prior works, but Prior was not in; he had just gone out, and he did not see him. Those scissors were stolen from Saturday night to Monday morning.

279. Who is this Prior?—He is a man who has ground for our shot work ever since I commenced business.

280. How long is that, these 18 or 20 years?—No, he has worked for me about eight or ten years. I am not certain; but ever since I have commenced business, at all events, he has had the shot work to do.

281. Did Booth know that he was grinder for you?—Yes.

282. Are you aware whether Prior had had any dispute with the union?—No; he says that he had not.

283. You had no reason to believe that he had any quarrel at all with the union?—No, not any at all.

284. Is he a union man?—Yes.

285. And you had no reason to believe that he was in dispute with them either about his apprentices or his contributions, or anything of the sort?—No; I had no reason to believe anything of the sort.

286. You say that those scissors were missing. Can you suggest to us who has taken them?—Of course I have my opinion about it.

287. You say that Jubb told you that Prior went to look at the hull?—I said Jackson.

288. But Booth went to the hull where Prior worked, and he saw Jubb and asked Jubb where Prior worked, and you say that Jubb pointed it out to him; when was that?—You understand that that was two or three days perhaps before the scissors were missing.

289. Did you make any complaints at all to the union about those things being taken away? had you any reason to suppose that the union had anything at all to do with it?—It occurred to me at once. When I referred to that note, that they should not do it in that way but in some other way, it occurred to my mind at once that this was the other way.

290. But the only difference in the ways was that they were taken away in both cases?—Yes; only the one is bands and the other is scissors.

291. One is taking away part of the machinery and the other is taking away the goods that you work on?—Yes.

292. Did you go to the union and make any complaints about them?—I have been a time or two, but I can get no reason out of it.

FIRST DAY.

Mr. J. Platts.

3 June 1867.

293. But have you charged them with taking those scissors?—I charged Booth with being one of the parties.

294. Did you charge him with having done this act?—Yes.

295. When?—It would be about the day after we missed them; we missed them on the Monday, and it must have been on the Tuesday or the Wednesday; it would be on the Tuesday, I think.

296. What did you say to Booth?—I said that I had every reason to believe that he was one of the parties that had taken them; I gave my reasons for that.

297. What did he say to that?—He began laughing, and that was all that I could get out of him, laughing and sneering and that sort of thing.

298. When you charged him with having stolen this property, do you mean to say that he merely laughed and said nothing about it?—He did not deny it; he laughed, but he said nothing of any moment; he tried to laugh it off, as if it were as a joke that it was done.

299. But, however, you made the serious charge against him of having stolen this property?—Yes.

300. Why did you not give him into custody? Did you go and take steps about his being taken into custody?—Yes.

301. To whom did you go?—To Mr. Jackson.

302. To the chief of the police, the chief constable?—Yes.

303. And did you tell him what suspicions you had?—Yes.

304. I suppose that you had no proofs at all?—I did not see him take it.

305. It was mere suspicion, and therefore you could take no steps. Did you tell Mr. Jackson in substance what you have told us?—Yes.

306. Are you quite sure about that?—Yes.

307. Are you quite sure that immediately when you found out that those scissors were gone you went to the chief constable and told him all those facts that you have told us this morning?—Yes; I went the same morning, but I did not get to see him till night, because he was engaged.

308. You saw him the same night?—Yes.

309. And you told him all these facts?—Yes.

310. But there was no evidence to convict him and no steps were taken?—No. I was going on to say that the reason I suspected him was this: the week previous to their being taken he was up and down the works and had hold of those scissors and examined them.

311. When was that?—The week before Easter. He took them off the stick and examined them very minutely, and turned over the bows and shanks, and examined them.

312. Did you see him at the wheel doing that?—Yes, Booth did that.

313. How long was that before they were taken?—It would be about three or four days perhaps; four days, I daresay.

314. And you saw him examining them minutely as you say?—Yes, those scissors of mine were picked out of a lot more. The man that had those scissors to grind had some other scissors of the same class to grind for Mr. Gibbons. My five dozen were all picked out. My scissors were with some scissors belonging to Mr. Gibbons, the same class of scissors; but Mr. Gibbons's scissors were left, and mine were taken.

315. What was the difference between Mr. Gibbons's scissors and yours?—There is always a slight difference in the making of them, a very slight difference.

316. And a skilled workman like Booth would now the difference, would he?—He would know mine by examining them, as there is one maker who has made for me ever since I commenced business, and he knows the class of scissors he makes.

317. A skilled workman you say would have known that; this man had worked for you before, had he not?—Yes.

318. Would a man who was not a skilled workman be able to distinguish the difference?—Oh no!

319. How long had Booth been in this branch of the trade?—He was apprenticed to it. He has had work from me about six years.

320. Was he a skilled workman or not?—Yes.

321. Is there anything else you know about this matter?—I think this is about the end of what we know in this affair.

322. Have you ever paid up your contribution?—I have not paid from the time that I gave notice of the scale, and I never shall again.

323. You have never paid since the 11th of February?—The week before that; I have not paid since that.

324. And you will never pay again?—No.

325. Have you got back those scissors?—No; I never heard anything more about them.

326. Have you any knowledge of where they are at all?—Not in the least.

327. They have in point of fact been stolen from you?—Yes.

328. Have you had to make them good?—Oh yes.

329. What is the value of them?—11*s.* 6*d.* per dozen they cost up to the stage that they had got to, that would be 2*l.* 17*s.* 6*d.* I went to Prior about them, and he wanted me to go down with him to the committee about them, and I said that I would not go an inch towards the committee. I had been before and I would not do it again. I gave him a note of the cost of them; he has been ill of rheumatics himself and could not get down, but he sent it by the secretary, and he said that all he did they laughed at, and that he seen the president since then, and he told the president that I should make him pay for them, and the president said that Prior must say that he was not to take any notice of me if I claimed to be paid for them. Since those scissors were stolen, Robert Holmshaw has been to Joseph Thompson, the secretary of the forgers.

330. How do you know that?—The secretary him self told me.

331. Where does Joseph Thompson live?—He lives in Allen Street, at the "Corner Pin" public-house.

332. What do you say he has been going about?—To see how many forgers I employ and what their average wages were. He said that they wanted to take the men out in order to compel me to comply with their wishes.

333. How do you know this; has Thompson told you so?—Thompson has told it in my own house. He said he understood that there had been unpleasantness with the grinders. I said, "I am not aware that "there has been any unpleasantness, any more than he "has made himself," and I said, "What did he say?" He said, "I did not ask him." Of course I simply told him how things stood, as I have told you already; and he seemed quite amused at the idea of taking the other men out in order to meet a case of that sort, and compelling me to pay to the union from which I could never receive any benefit. Of course I told him that any objection he had he must take the consequence of, and that is as far as I could get in the affair.

334. With regard to the rules. May you, according to your rules, have any quantity of apprentices you please?—I cannot have any.

335. You can have apprentices, can you not?—No, we cannot. I can have my own sons if I happen to have any, but I cannot have anybody else's.

336. How many apprentices can you have?—If I had half a dozen sons I could put them all on the wheel.

337–8. But if a boy loses his father what becomes of the boy?—There is a case of that kind now. The boy's father was in the trade as a scissor grinder for many years to my knowledge, and his father has died, and of course he could not get to work on grinding just then, but he went out into a rolling mill, and he was out about a year and a half or two years, and now they will not allow him to come into the trade, but

FIRST DAY.

Mr. J. Platts.

3 June 1867.

his brother works for me, and has brought this boy along with himself at the present time.

339. You say that you can employ any quantity of your own sons as apprentices; but supposing you were to die leaving five sons behind you, and they all wanted to become apprentices in the grinding trade, what would they do?—The committee would put them to anybody they thought proper.

340. They do put them out?—In some cases they have done it, I believe. I am not sure of it, but I believe they have in some cases.

341. But supposing that you saw a nice clever lad and you wanted to take him as your apprentice, and his father were quite willing that he should come into your business to learn the trade, he being no relation of yours, is there any rule against that?—Yes.

342. You could not do such a thing?—I could not do such a thing.

343. You made use of some expression about the son of a "freeman." What is the meaning of a "freeman?"—That is the same as my son.

344. But what does a "freeman" mean?—It means the head of a family. I can bring in my own son but nobody else's.

345. What you mean by the word "freeman" is that it must be your own son, in fact?—Yes.

346. But you cannot take a strange lad as an apprentice?—No.

347. What are the rules with respect to the number of journeymen? what number of journeymen can a a master take?—I am not aware that there is any restriction about that.

348. Do you know whether there is any rule in your trade with respect to the wages which the men are to receive?—There is a certain price.

349. I am speaking now of a journeyman. What are a journeyman's wages? do you pay him by the piece or by the day, or how do you pay your journeymen in Sheffield?—A journeyman now has about 30*s.* a week.

350. Is he paid by the amount of work which he does?—He is paid so much a day; 5*s.* a day, some more and some less, according to their abilities, of course.

351. Are they all paid alike?—No.

352. Then can a good workman get more money than an inferior workman?—Not in all cases.

353. Do the union put down a scale and say you shall not pay a journeyman less than 5*s.*, or that you should pay them all alike, or do they make any rule upon the subject?—No; before the trade was together the prices were very low. Supposing that I paid a journeyman working for me 20 per cent. or 40 per cent.

354. What do you mean by 40 per cent.?—By the state of the price. We have a statement of price for the work at so much per dozen for grinding. Supposing that we say that those scissors are 1*l.* a dozen, I take off 30 per cent. discount; that leaves it 14*s.* Then there are advances of prices so that they are at 20*s.*; if I had an inferior workman working for me I should be compelled to give the inferior workman 10 per cent. as well as the superior one, because they reason in this way: "He has served "you for such a time, and of course he has a right to "an advance if the trade is good."

355. Is there any rule in the trade by which you are compelled to pay an inferior workman at the same rate as a superior workman?—Yes, in some cases. If I had an inferior workman and a superior one who supplied me at 30 per cent. before the advances, the superior one would get so much and no more than the inferior one in advance.

356. Supposing that one journeyman is getting 5*s.* a day, and another is getting 4*s.* a day, and there is an advance of say 1*s.* a day, or 10*d.* or 6*d.* on each, what you complain of is that the superior workman gets 5*s.* 6*d.*, and the inferior workman gets 4*s.* 6*d.*; why should not the inferior workman get the benefit of the advance as well as the superior workman?—Because they want to make one price round. He only gets 10 per cent. raised upon what he has.

357. The union says that there is a rise of 10 per cent. Why should one class of men get it more than another—bad and good workmen all get the benefit of the rise—he only gets 10 per cent. whether he is a good or a bad workman, and what is the harm of that?—They are not paid after that rate. There is a misunderstanding.

358. This is our first day, and we are going a little into the question of how these rules are viewed by a person who is opposed to the union?—I am not opposed in the least to them, if they will use me fairly and give me the same privileges which they ask for themselves.

359. You are a complainant in a certain sense, you know; we will hear their case afterwards. But is there anything of which you complain with reference to the advance of the wages of journeymen?—There are different prices in all branches, and superior workmen will not work at inferior work, that is certain. An inferior workman cannot do superior work. The reason is that there are two different prices; the inferior workman who does the inferior work gets a less price, but the superior man at superior work gets a better price. A strike takes place for 10 per cent. all round, the inferior one is raised 10 per cent. and the superior one gets the same.

360. What harm is there in that?—I do not complain of any harm.

361. Then all that they say that they want is an increase of wages?—Yes.

362. That is a common case of strike?—Yes.

363. Therefore there is no equality of payment?—No.

364. (*Mr. Chance.*) Is there an inequality of wages for work of the same kind? You say that the superior workman gets a higher wage for the superior workmanship, but then the superior workman, generally speaking, works on things which require superior work, does he not?—Yes.

365. Supposing a superior workman works at that branch of the trade which is, generally speaking, taken up by inferior workmen, would he then receive the same wages as the inferior workman?—Just so, for the same class of work.

366. (*Mr. Barstow.*) What do you consider the superior work, the very top work in your trade?—It depends upon a man's abilities.

367. But do you consider scissor grinding or polishing, or what branch of your trade is the best paid?—To tell the truth, I believe that the men who get the most money are the metal grinders.

368. Are all the metal grinders paid alike?—I could not say. I am not in the branch, but I think they are not.

369. But in your trade?—There are various prices; some allow 40 per cent., some 20 per cent., some 10 per cent., and some 15 per cent. It depends entirely upon what prices they had before the advance took place. They merely get the advantage of those rates.

370. (*Mr. Chance.*) Supposing that there are two men working in an inferior branch and one man does his portion far better than the other man in that branch, does he still receive the same wages?—Just the same.

371. However well he does his work in that branch, if it is of an inferior kind, he will always then receive the same wages?—The same wages.

372. (*Mr. Barstow.*) How does that come to be so; is it by any rule of the union, or by your own doing?—It is the rule of the union.

373. (*Chairman.*) What is the rule of the union?—Supposing I employ two men both at the same price, I pay them 40 per cent., say for the same class of work; one is superior in ability; he does his work considerably better. In case of a strike they say, "We want 10 per cent. advance," and I am compelled, although the superior workman is worth perhaps 10 or 15 per cent. more than the other man, to give the inferior workman the same price as the other.

FIRST DAY.

Mr. J. Platts.

3 June 1867.

374. (*Mr. Chance.*) Supposing you were to pay this better workman higher wages, what would be the result?—It would rob the man.

375. (*Mr. Barstow.*) You are supposing that you originally pay those two men the same price?—Yes.

376. But how did it come that you originally paid them the same price before the rise?—It is a question how many men there are. Sometimes, in case there is no union, you can choose your man, but where there is a union you must have what the committee will supply.

377. (*Chairman.*) As I understand it, where the union declare a strike they say, "We want a rise of 10 per cent," that is, a rise upon the prices then being given, whatever they are?—Yes.

378. Therefore all round you must advance your prices 10 per cent.; is not that so?—No; in the first instance, when the trade has been broken up, they cannot support the union. Suppose they break up to-day, next week lots of the men may be working at any price. Then the master will say, "I will pay this man "according to his capabilities; what his work is worth "I will give him." Then in a fortnight's time the union have got together, and there comes a strike, and all work is to be at 40 per cent. That brings them all level for a time, and not long after that there comes a rise of 10 per cent., so that it brings an inferior workman into the same position as a superior one.

379. (*Mr. Chance.*) Then the result of this is that there is no inducement to a man to improve his work to a superior class?—No.

380. If he is only to be paid the same amount as the inferior workman there is no inducement to him to make his work better?—Not a bit. I have invariably heard of this complaint, that if a man can work well he will always get a good price, and, generally speaking, those men who are getting a good price where there is a strike do not advance. I always paid Prior 30 per cent. for his work. There have been two or three advances, and all that he has ever got is 10 per cent. Some of his men are getting 5*s.* or 6*s.* a week extra wages. Those are superior workmen.

381. (*Chairman.*) Is there any rule with respect to machinery that you are aware of which prevents masters from introducing into their establishment machinery to supersede the use of manual labour?—It does not affect our trade at all.

382. You know nothing about it?—No. Of course it will affect other trades, but not ours.

383. Have they any rule for compelling subscriptions that are in arrear except by the destruction of machinery that you are aware of?—I do not know that they have.

384. Are there no penalties or rules of that kind?—I am not aware of any.

385. Has your society at all amalgamated with any other society?—I think not.

386. In case any other society were to be on strike, do you contribute from your society to the other society?—Yes.

387. How is that?—They make them a grant of so much to keep them in the struggle.

388. Do you know that?—I have been told so.

389. Did you contribute at all towards a strike at any time?—I have been paying 1*s.* 6*d.* a week; that 6*d.* extra was put on at the time that the file trade was on strike and it has never been taken off since; we were paying 1*s.* a week up to that time, but 6*d.* a week was put on to meet that strike.

390. The file trade is perfectly distinct from your business?—Oh, yes.

391. Do you believe that was as a matter of charity as sympathizing with them in the struggle, or was it a rule of the union that they should help one another?—As a rule they do it.

392. But do you know as a fact that there is a rule to that effect?—I do not know that there is a printed rule, but I know that it is done.

393. I want to know whether you can tell us whether the file trade, when they were on strike, would as a matter of right call upon your scissors union to help them?—Yes, they did do so.

394. As a matter of right?—I do not know as a matter of right, but of course as a matter of sympathy. Of course they would if they had been amalgamated, but they are not; they are separate and distinct. I know that the parties representing the file trade had meetings along with the scissors trade, and in the general meeting it was decided to give them so much, and this 6*d.* a week was put on to meet that emergency in this strike. I do not know that they could claim it as a matter of right.

395. Is there anything that occurs to your mind which can further aid us in this inquiry?—I think not.

396. (*Mr. Barstow.*) Were you ever a member of the scissor grinders' union when you were a journeyman?—Yes.

397. Then you contributed of course?—Yes.

398. Were you yourself ever a member of the committee?—Yes, several times.

399. You attended meetings, I suppose?—Yes.

400. Can you tell us what was the business transacted at those meetings?—I hardly can; there is a good deal occurs in connexion with committees that everybody on the committee does not know.

401. During the time that you were on the committee did anyone come to you with respect to there being any rattening?—I do not remember that they did.

402. Do you happen to know of how many members your scissor grinders' union now consists?—About 200, I think; somewhere about that.

403. How were the accounts kept when you were on the committee?—I do not know.

404. That never came before you when you were on the committee?—No; Gates and Holmshaw, I believe, had principally to do with the accounts.

405. Nobody, you think, but them?—No.

406. Is there an auditor of the accounts?—No, I never heard of an auditor.

407. Do they keep any books?—Yes.

408. How do you know that?—I have seen them.

409. When you say that you have seen them, in what sense have you seen them; have you looked through them?—No, I have seen them on the table.

410. But you have never looked into them?—No.

411. (*Chairman.*) Are they open to the committee?—Any member of the committee can look at the books at once.

412. (*Mr. Barstow.*) How did you become a member of the committe?—It is customary at a general meeting to elect the committee.

413. (*Chairman.*) Who elects them?—They are elected by the trade at the general meeting.

414. (*Mr. Barstow.*) Is it part of the president's business to find work for journeymen?—Yes.

415. When a man is out of work he is on the box as you say?—Yes.

416. That is, he receives a contribution from the funds of the union?—Yes.

417. Is he entitled to receive that as long as he is out of work?—Yes.

418. Supposing that he was out of work and you, for instance, or any other manufacturer, were to apply for a workman, would the president tell him of that and put him on the work?—Yes.

419. And then perhaps after that he would cease to receive if he did not take the work?—No.

420. He might object to take it?—Yes.

421. And still go on receiving from the box?—Yes.

422. (*Chairman.*) Do you mean to say that if the committee told a man he must go and work for so-and-so they would allow him the option, and if he did not choose to go they would still pay him the 8s. a week.—Yes, they did so in this case of mine.

423. (*Mr. Barstow.*) Then for all I can see he may remain on the box as long as he lives?—In that case he may. I know one case of a man who has been on the box ever since the 18th of March, and they offered

him a place as a journeyman under another man, and he refused to take the place.

424. At how much per week?—30*s*.

425. (*Chairman.*) What is that man's name?—Robert Booth; and the name of the man they wanted to send him to is George Marshall.

426. When your bands were first taken did you apply to the police?—No, I did not go to the police.

427. Why was that?—I dared not.

428. Why dared you not?—In consequence of being worse off if I had. I should either have been done again, or have been done myself very likely.

429. (*Chairman.*) That was your belief?—Yes, that is the reason that kept me away. I would have done it now, but I was younger then.

430. Will you be more explicit: what do you mean by "being done yourself?"—The same as other men have been done, disabled in some shape or form.

431. Do you mean that you would have suffered personal violence in some way?—I think so; that is my impression.

432. That was the reason that you did not apply to the police?—Yes.

433. (*Mr. Barstow.*) How came Prior to work for you when, as I understand, the union had drawn off their men from you?—He had always done my shot work. It is not much shot work that I get up, but whatever shot work I have he always grinds it. I am in the smaller branch of the steel line; it is not a class of work which they would have done if they had been at work, but I rather anticipated that there would be some bother, and before I sent those scissors to Prior I sent my boy to Prior and asked him if he could do them, and he said he could.

434. (*Chairman.*) He was not working for you alone?—No.

435. (*Mr. Barstow.*) It was a mere job?—Yes.

436. I suppose that the union could have prevented him from working then if they had chosen?—Yes; it was a class of work which he had to grind.

437. How does a man become a journeyman in this scissor grinding trade?—He has to serve an apprenticeship till he is 21.

438. And then he is a journeyman?—Yes.

439. Then are all the present journeymen the sons of people who have been journeymen?—No; it is getting on for two years I daresay now; they will not take any more into the trade, only freemen's sons.

440. Then of course it follows that for the future no man can be a journeyman scissor grinder who is not the son of a freeman who has been a journeyman scissor grinder before?—Yes, it is all in the family.

441. You said early in your examination that though a master got no benefit from contributing to the union he is compelled to subscribe?—Yes.

442. What do you mean by his being oompelled; in what way would he be compelled?—He must either subscribe, or he is constantly in danger of his bands or something being missing.

The witness withdrew.

Mr. James Prior sworn and examined.

Mr. J. Prior.

443. (*Mr. Barstow.*) Are you a scissor grinder?—Yes.

444. Where do you live?—At Clarence Street, Broomhill.

445. Are you a member of the scissor grinders' union?—Yes.

446. How long have you been a member?—Since the commencement.

447. When was that?—Two or three years since.

448. Were you ever a member of a union before that?—Yes.

449. Was that a scissor grinders' union?—Yes.

450. How long have you been a member of the union altogether?—The union has been broken up once or twice.

451. When were you first a member of a union?—When I was 21 years of age.

452. How old are you now?—44.

453. That was 23 years ago?—Yes.

454. That is the same union of which the last witness was a member; it is the same of which Holmshaw is treasurer?—Yes.

455. Do you do work for the last witness?—Yes.

456. Occasionally?—Yes.

457. How long have you worked for him?—About two years.

458. Do you remember some time ago having some scissors to work for him, I believe it was on the 27th of April?—Yes.

459. Did you miss them before they were finished?—Yes.

460. At what wheel were they finished?—They were sent to the Trafalgar wheel.

461. Have you a trough there?—Yes, I have three troughs there.

462. What sort of scissors were they?—They were 11-inch paper scissors.

463. Were they just like other 11-inch paper scissors?—There are the bodkin paper scissors and the roll-blade paper scissors; these were roll-blade paper scissors.

464. One sort of roll-blade paper scissors is very much like another sort of roll-blade paper scissors?——Yes.

465. Has Gibbons sent you any?—I had some work from Gibbons of the same description at the same time when these scissors were missing.

466. At the same time that you had the scissors from Platts had you any scissors from anybody else besides Gibbons?—I had some also from Newbold.

467. Could a man who is not a skilled workman tell the difference between Platts' scissors and the other two?—I should think not.

468. Could a skilled workman tell the difference?—I should think he could not.

469. (*Chairman.*) Were the scissors that you got from Gibbons roll-blade scissors?—Yes, they were the same sort of scissors.

470. Still a skilled workman could tell the difference between the one and the other?—I should think not.

471. Could not you tell the difference?—I could tell the difference, knowing that the one belonged to Gibbons and the other to Platts.

472. Was there nothing in the shape or look of them by which a man could tell the one from the other?—There might be a difference in the shape.

473. (*Mr. Barstow.*) There was some difference?—There might be some difference.

474. How did you keep these scissors; where were they?—On the side of the place where we were going to grind them, by the side of the trough.

475. Had you them all together?—Yes; they were all together.

476. What do you mean by saying that they were all together?—They were put together; Newbold's, Gibbons' and Platts' were at the side.

477. Were they in separate parcels?—Yes, they were all in separate lots.

478. Were they of different quantities, different numbers of dozens; you had five dozens of Platts?—We had five dozen with the exception of a pair.

479. How many had you of Gibbons?—Half a dozen of Gibbons, that is seven pairs, what we call half a dozen.

480. They were lots of different sizes?—Yes, they were lots of different sizes.

481. (*Chairman.*) How many had you of Newbold's?—Three or four dozens of Newbold's, but they were a different kind of scissors.

482. (*Mr. Barstow.*) Newbold's were a different kind of scissors?—Yes.

483. (*Chairman.*) How many had you of Platts?—Five dozen with the exception of a pair.

484. (*Mr. Barstow.*) Had you done any work to

FIRST DAY.

Mr. J. Prior.

3 June 1867.

Platt's stock of scissors?—No, we had not commenced working them.

485. When did you miss them?—I missed them on Monday morning.

486. How did you find the place; did you yourself go into your shop on Monday morning?—I was not in there myself first, the person who works for me was there; that is Edward Hackworth, he was there first.

487. Did you go afterwards?—Yes; he says, "Where is Platts' scissors; they have gone."

488. (*Chairman.*) Did you ascertain that they were gone?—Yes. I could soon see they were gone.

489. Did you look to see whether you had Newbold's and Gibbons' scissors?—Yes.

490. (*Mr. Barstow.*) Was anything else to be seen about the room except that Platts' scissors were gone?—No. I did not see anything else wrong.

491. When you missed them what did you do?—I sent to Mr. Platts and told him that the scissors were missing.

492. Do you know a man named Booth?—I cannot say. I recollect him; I do not know him.

493. Robert Booth?—I do not know him.

494. (*Chairman.*) Had you been at work before the Saturday?—I had been working on the Saturday.

495. Had you been doing any of that work?—Yes.

496. Had you seen a man named Robert Booth about your wheel?—I cannot say he was there. I was not at the wheel when he came.

497. (*Mr. Barstow.*) Who told you he was there?—I forget who told me.

498. Have you a man in your employment named Jubb?—No.

499. Do you know a person called Samuel Jubb?—Yes.

500. Did he tell you he had seen Booth?—I believe he had seen Booth.

501. (*Chairman.*) Did he tell you so? Do you believe that Samuel Jubb told you he had seen Booth?—I cannot swear.

502. Do you believe so?—I believe so; I cannot swear that.

503. (*Mr. Barstow.*) When did he tell you?—It was when Mr. Platts came down to the wheel.

504. What did Jubb tell you about Booth?—He told me Booth had been round the wheel.

505. What time did he say Booth had been there?—I do not remember that.

506. Are you quite sure?—I am quite sure.

507. You inquired how these things came to be missed?—I did not know whether it was Jubb or who told me. I believe I heard somebody say that Booth had been about the place.

508. Cannot you tell us about what time you were told he had been about the place?—No, I cannot.

509. When did you hear that Booth had been about the place, before the scissors were missed or after they were missed?—I cannot exactly swear.

510. You know whether it was before or not?—I do not know whether it was before Platts was at the wheel or after.

511. Was it before the things were gone or after they were taken?—After they had been gone.

512. (*Chairman.*) I understand you that after the things were gone and you were inquiring about who took them, somebody, whom you believe to be Jubb, told you that Booth had been about the place?—That will be it.

513. (*Mr. Barstow.*) Did you go anywhere with Platts?—I sent out to Platts, and I was told I was to go myself to Platts.

514. What then?—I was told they were missing, and he said he would come down to the wheel either that afternoon or the next morning.

515. Did he come down?—He came down the next morning, I think.

516. Did Platts go down with you?—No, he came down to the wheel where I was working.

517. After you had seen Platts what did you do?—Then I went to my work.

518. Did Platts go back with you or not?—No, not at the time.

519. When did you see him next after you left his house?—He came down to our wheel.

520. When was that?—The next morning; he came down that afternoon, and then came the next day with the detective.

521. A person named Jackson?—Yes.

522. Did he come down the same day?—He came down the same day to the wheel, himself and his son.

523. Did you make any search for these scissors?—Yes.

524. You did not find them?—No.

525. You have never found them?—No.

526. Did you go and see anybody about them?—I made it known to Holmshaw.

527. (*Chairman.*) You made it known to Holmshaw?—Yes.

528. (*Mr. Barstow.*) Was he the first person you went to?—I believe he was.

529. Was anyone with him?—No.

530. What made you go to Holmshaw?—I went to Holmshaw to know whether he knew anything about the scissors.

531. You might as well have gone to the town crier. Why did you go to Holmshaw?—I went to try to ascertain anything about it.

532. (*Chairman.*) Why did you go to Holmshaw?—Because I thought I might get to know something about it.

533. Why would Holmshaw know anything about it?—Because the scissors were missing.

534. Why did you go to Holmshaw if the scissors were missing, if Holmshaw did not work at your wheel?—I went to ascertain if I could learn anything about the scissors.

535. Why did you go; what was your reason for going to Holsmshaw before anybody else?—Because the scissors were missing.

536. We know that the scissors were missing, but why did you go to him?—To try and ascertain whether he knew anything about it.

537. (*Mr. Barstow.*) Why should Holmshaw know anything about them?—I do not know.

538. On your oath, you do not know?—No.

539. Why should you go to him?—I thought there was a possibility of his knowing something about them.

540. Why should there be a possibility of Holmshaw knowing anything about them?—I went to several places.

541. You told us that Holmshaw was the first person you went to?—Yes.

542. Why did you go direct to Holmshaw?—I went to see whether it was likely or unlikely.

543. But did you think him likely or unlikely; you would not go to an unlikely person to tell. On your oath, did not you think him a likely person to tell you?—I thought there might be a possibility of getting to know.

544. Upon your oath, did not you consider Holmshaw a likely person to tell you?—Of course I naturally did think so.

545. Why did you think he was a likely person to tell you?—There might be some grievance between my employer and the trade.

546. (*Chairman.*) You say you went to Holmshaw because you thought there might be some grievance between your employer and the trade; why should that induce you to go to Holmshaw?—If there was a grievance between the trade and him, it was just possible that they might have gone by the trade.

547. It is just possible that the scissors might have gone by the trade?—Yes.

548. (*Mr. Barstow.*) By the trade you mean the union?—Yes.

549. What made you think it just possible that the scissors might have gone by the trade?—If there is any grievance between them and the employers, it is possible there might be something of that sort done; that was my reason for going.

550. That they were taken by the union?—I did not know that they were taken by the union.

551. What you thought was, that if there had been a grievance between the union and Platts, probably the union had taken these things away to punish Platts?—Yes.

552. That was your notion?—Yes.

553. What did Holmshaw say to you?—He said he knew nothing about the affair at all.

554. You then left him?—Yes.

555. Was that all that he said at that time?—That was all that transpired between him and me.

556. When did you see Holmshaw again after this?—I believe the Monday after.

557. That would be just a week?—Yes.

558. (*Chairman.*) The 27th of April was the day they were missed?—Yes.

559. (*Mr. Barstow.*) It would be the week after that; about the 4th of May?—Yes.

560. How did you come to see him at that time?—He collects the contribution.

561. He came to you for your contribution?—Yes.

562. Had you any conversation then about these scissors?—No, not that I know of. I do not know that there was any conversation at all after the first time I saw him. I do not know that I said anything about the scissors then.

563. Did you say nothing to him at that time?—No, not respecting the scissors.

564. Nothing at all about the scissors?—No.

565. Are you quite sure?—Yes.

566. Did he say anything to you about Platts?—No.

567. Did you ask whether there was any difference between Platts and the trade?—No.

568. You said nothing on the subject?—No.

569. You were in no difficulty with the union at all?—No.

570. Why did not you say anything to Holmshaw when he came the second time?—I thought it was useless saying anything to him when I did not learn anything on the first onset.

571. You were liable for the loss of them?—I believe he then held me good for the loss of the scissors.

572. Why did not you try again; you said you thought it possible that Holmshaw might know about them?—It was no use asking him when he told me at the first that he knew nothing about the affair at all. I thought it was useless asking again.

573. When Holmshaw came the second time, that is to say on the Monday, did not you at that time know that there was a difference between Platts and the union?—I knew very shortly after I missed the scissors that there was a difference between them.

574. Holmshaw was the president of the union?—Yes.

575. Do you mean to tell us that you did not, after you knew that there was a difference, speak to Holmshaw again?—I did not speak to Holmshaw again respecting the scissors at all.

576. Why was that?—I think it was the middle of the week when I saw Holmshaw the first time, and I asked him if he knew anything about these scissors.

577. I am speaking of the second time?—It would be on the Monday when he came for the contribution.

578. But the second time you knew that there was a difference between Platts and the union?—Yes.

579. Why did not you then speak to Holmshaw about it?—I thought it was useless when I could not ascertain it the first time.

580. Holmshaw might have ascertained in the meantime?—It is just possible, but I never asked him any question about the scissors after.

581. (*Mr. Chance.*) Did you ask anybody else besides Holmshaw about these scissors?—No. I believe when Platts came down it was named to Gale, and Gale denied knowing anything about them.

582. Did you hear anything said to Gale about it? when Platts came down were you present?—Yes.

583. Was Gale present at the same time?—We went into Gale's room with Jackson.

584. Was anything said to Gale about losing the scissors?—I believe it was said to Gale that he knew something about the scissors.

585. Who said so?—I believe Platts did.

586. Platts then said to Gale that he (Gale) knew something about the scissors?—Yes.

587. Did Gale say anything upon that?—Gale objected to it, and said he knew nothing about the scissors at all. I believe it was said if he did not mind he would have to be called up over them.

588. Who said so?—Platts said so to Gale, that was what passed between us.

589. After Platts said that to Gale; did he make any observation about the scissors?—No; that was what passed between them.

590. Just think over it and try to recollect?—That was all that passed between them then.

591. Did you at any other time have any conversation, or hear any conversation with Gale about the scissors?—Not the slightest.

592. Or any other person besides Gale and Holmshaw?—No, I never heard anything said about the scissors at all.

593. Are you certain?—With the exception of Platts coming down last week, when he asked whether I knew anything about the scissors, and I told him I did not.

594. (*Chairman.*) I want to know whether the scissors were in parcels of paper or open?—They were open; they were on scissor sticks.

595. Those of Gibbons and Newbold were left?—Yes.

596. How had you left them the night before?—I reckoned to put every man's work by itself, but they were the whole of them down one side. I put Platts' here (*describing the same*), Gibbons' here, and Newbold's here, in separate lots.

597. In quite distinct and separate lots?—Yes.

598. Those belonging to Platts were taken out and the others remained?—Yes.

599. These were stolen?—They must have been stolen; they disappeared.

600. Did you go and lay an information before the magistrates?—No, I went to Platts first.

601. Did you go before the magistrates?—No.

602. Why did not you do that?—I went to my employer.

603. Your place had been robbed; why did not you go to the police and give information?—I thought it was the best policy to go to my employer.

604. Supposing your house is robbed you would go and give information to the police; why did not you give information to the police in this case?—I thought it the best policy to go to him.

605. Why did not you go to the police?—I thought my employer's was the first place to go to. I could not see any other.

606. Supposing a man broke into your house, would you go to anybody but the police?—I should go to the police.

607. Why did not you go to the police in this case?—I do not know.

608. Be cautious. Do you mean to tell us that you do not know the reason why you did not go to the police?—I do not know the reason. I went to my employer.

609. What is the reason that you did not go to the police?—Very likely it might have been the best step I could have taken.

610. If a person came in and robbed you of your watch or bed or anything else you would have gone to the police, therefore why in this case did not you go to the police?—I do not know.

611. Yes, you do: why did not you go?—I had no idea of going to the police. I thought when the scissors were gone it was my duty to go to my employer and tell him.

612. I ask you, upon your oath, was it any fear of the union that caused you not to go to the police?—No, it was not.

613. Was it any fear of the union that prevented

FIRST DAY.

Mr. J. Prior.

3 June 1867.

you going and making a charge to the police?—It was not.

614. You swear that?—Yes.

615. You are quite clear about it?—Yes.

616. You never made a charge to the police?—No, I never made a charge to the police.

617. You never went to the police?—No.

618. You had no quarrel with the union yourself?—Not the slightest.

619. Who bore the loss?—I believe my employer sent me a paper about it.

620. Have you had to pay for it, or who has borne the loss?—If he does not find the scissors I shall have to pay for them; he says he will hold me good for them.

621. That is Platts will hold you good?—Yes.

622. You have not paid for them yet?—No.

(*Chairman.*) I am afraid we shall have to adjourn this question until we get further information about it.

The witness withdrew.

Mr. R. T. Eadon.

Mr. Robert Thomas Eadon sworn and examined.

623. (*Mr. Chance.*) Are you a member of the firm of Moses Eadon and Sons?—Yes.

624. What are you?—We are steel, saw and file manufacturers.

625. You have been in that manufacture for a long time?—Yes.

626. How many years?—I have been in the trade ever since I went to business.

627. How long is that?—30 years.

628. Was there a man of the name of Staniforth working for you at any time?—Yes.

629. When was it that he was working for you?—He has been working for us these six or eight years.

630. That is for six or eight years up to the present time?—Yes.

631. He is still working for you?—Yes.

632. What is his christian name?—John, I think.

633. Are there two Staniforths working for you?—I think not; only one.

634. Was this John Staniforth ever secretary for a union?—Yes, I think he was.

635. You are sure that there were not two men of that name working for you?—Yes, I am quite sure of that.

636. Was John Staniforth ever a secretary to one of the unions?—I believe so; but not during the time he was in our employ.

637. It was previously?—Yes.

638. He was once secretary to a union?—Yes, to the saw grinders' union.

639. Is that the union to which Broadhead is now the secretary?—Yes.

640. Staniforth was secretary prior to him?—Yes, I believe so.

641. Have you at any time had any of your implements taken from your works?—Yes.

642. What was the first occasion on which anything was taken from your works?—We had them taken before this inquiry; before the 10 years.

643. Then you have had them taken from you previously to 10 years from this time?—Yes.

644. We will not go into that, but can you give any instances where you have lost any of your property during the last 10 years?—Yes, about eight years ago we were rattened.

645. What do you mean by "rattened"?—Our bands were taken.

646. You mean by rattening simply the fact that the bands are taken without relation to who has done it?—Yes.

647. It does not involve the fact that they were taken by anybody, but that they were taken, you do not know by whom?—It is understood in the trade of the town that a person who has been rattened has lost something.

648. Supposing you lose something and do not know how the loss is occasioned you call that, as a matter of course, rattening?—As connected with trade affairs we call it rattening.

649. Supposing your bands were injured and you had reason to suppose that it was not a trade affair, you would not call it rattening?—No.

650. It would be larceny?—Yes.

651. If connected with the trade it would be rattening?—Yes.

652. It is a taking away by some person in connexion with the trade; it is a trade business?—That is our belief.

653. It is a short way of expressing your belief that the loss or taking away was connected with the trade?—Yes.

654. You say that eight years ago your bands were rattened?—Yes.

655. How many bands?—I could not give the number, but there would be more than one.

656. (*Chairman.*) Are you a member of any union?—No.

657. Not of any union?—No.

658. And were not then?—No, we are simply employers.

659. Are there several employers who are members of unions?—Yes, of the class of Mr. Platts, who is a sort of middle man between workmen and masters, that is where there is combination.

660. They are sometimes members of a union?—Yes.

661. But men in your position, the larger employers of labour, are not members of unions?—Certainly not.

662. The persons who are members of unions are men who employ fewer hands than you do, that is, only a journeyman and an apprentice; is that so?—Yes.

663. It is confined to them?—Yes.

664. (*Mr. Chance.*) You have never been called upon to pay any money to the union?—No.

665. Do you belong to any union at all connected with the employers?—Yes.

666. (*Chairman.*) Were you eight years ago a member of an union?—No, I was not.

667. (*Mr. Chance.*) We are referring to the rattening which you say took place some eight years ago. At that time had there been any dispute arising between your workmen and the union to cause the rattening? Can you give any reason why you were rattened upon that occasion?—We had certain men working for us who had not paid their natty money, or contribution to the trade.

668. At that time do you recollect any man who was a defaulter?—Yes, I believe Henry Taylor and a person of the name of Henry Bollington.

669. They had not paid their natty money?—No.

670. Were there any men besides those two?—There might be.

671. Those were the only two men that you remember?—Yes.

672. Do you know where they live now?—They are both in our employ and can be found.

673. They are still in your employ?—Yes.

674. Can you tell us what their addresses are at the present time?—They are still at our works.

675. You say you believe that at that time they had not paid their natty money?—No.

676. Had you any further reason than that to induce you to suppose that the rattening took place because they had not paid their natty money?—Yes.

677. What was the reason?—The reason why we supposed that it was a trade affair was that our men went at once to Broadhead, the secretary.

678. Broadhead at that time was secretary to the union?—Yes.

679. How do you know that the men went to Broadhead?—They told us so.

680. Did they tell you what they went to Broadhead for?—Yes, to make arrangements with him for the bands to come back.

681. Did they say anything about the arrangements they were to make with him?—Yes, they said that they had to pay their natty and arrears and certain expenses for the bands being taken.

682. (*Chairman.*) Who told you that?—The men in our employ.

683. The same men, Taylor and Bollington?—I believe they are the same men.

684. What did they tell you?—They told me that they were to pay the natty and expenses.

685. The natty money was the arrears?—The contributions.

686. What are the expenses?—I suppose the expenses of fetching the bands.

687. Do you mean the expense of taking away the bands?—Yes.

688. (*Mr. Chance.*) Can you explain it a little more; I do not quite understand what you mean by the expenses of taking away the bands?—The men not having paid the natty, and being rattened, had to go to Broadhead. They did go to Broadhead, and before a note was given to them, or before a note was found enabling them to find the bands, they had not only to pay the natty, but certain expenses which, I understood, were the expenses incurred in doing the rattening.

689. Money was paid to certain persons for doing the rattening, and they would have to pay that money back?—Yes.

690. Did they pay the arrears and expenses?—Yes.

691. Did they pay them themselves or come upon you to pay them?—They paid them themselves.

692. Did you afterwards get the bands back?—Yes.

693. Was that after the men went to Broadhead?—Yes.

694. How long after the men went to Broadhead did you get the bands back again?—In the course of a day or two.

695. How were they brought back?—A note was sent or given to one of the men, and they were found in a drain.

696. (*Chairman.*) How do you know that; did you see the note?—I believe I saw the note.

697. (*Mr. Chance.*) Was the note sent to you, or how did you see it?—The men I believe showed me the note.

698. I am speaking of the rattening that took place eight years ago?—Yes.

699. What became of the note?—I do not know.

700. Did you see what was contained in the note?—I believe I saw the note; I am satisfied I saw the note; it contained information that the bands would be found on a certain portion of our premises hid in a drain pipe.

701. Did you then search or cause search to be made in the place indicated by the note?—The men did.

702. And there they found the bands?—Yes.

703. Did you ever take any further proceedings upon that case of rattening?—No.

704. Did you ever speak to Broadhead about it, or any member of the union?—I might have done. I do not remember that I did.

705. Do you know who formed the committee of the union at that time?—I do not know the committee, I know that Broadhead was the secretary.

706. (*Chairman.*) Were those your goods?—They were all our goods.

707. (*Mr. Chance.*) Who was president of the committee?—Mr. Broadhead is secretary and presidant I believe.

708. Did you take any further proceedings afterwards; did you make any application to the police?—No.

709. Why not?—Because the police in my opinion would have been useless in the matter.

710. Why would they have been useless?—I do not think they would have got our bands back so easily as the men would by going to Broadhead; it was simply a trade dispute, they had no dispute with us.

711. Was the reason why you did not go to the police the fear of what the union might do?—No, not any personal fear.

712. Simply to get back your bands?—The men went for them to the place.

713. The reason why you did not take any further proceedings was simply on the ground of expediency, believing the best mode was to go to Broadhead?—I did not go to Broadhead; we left the men to arrange the matter between themselves, knowing it was a trade dispute.

714. I speak of the men; you did it more as a matter of expediency than anything else?—Yes.

715. You thought that it was useless going to the police to get back your bands?—Yes.

716. That case of rattening took place eight years ago?—Yes.

717. Are there any other cases of rattening in your recollection that have taken place since that?—Yes.

718. When was the next?—In 1860.

719. What was the nature of the rattening on that occasion?—The same cause, men in arrears.

720. What was taken away or damaged then?—They took a band or bands.

721. Do you know the date of that?—About 1860.

722. Can you give the month in 1860?—No.

723. Tell us the reason why the bands were taken at that time?—I believe the men were owing arrears.

724. Who were the men?—I think Challenger was in arrears.

725. Do you know his christian name?—Charles.

726. What other man was in arrear at the same time?—In this case they made a mistake; they rattened the wrong man, they took a band belonging to a man of the name of Christopher Taylor.

727. (*Chairman.*) Challenger was in arrear?—I think he was in arrear.

728. (*Mr. Chance.*) They took the bands of Christopher Taylor?—Yes.

729. He is also in your employ?—Yes.

730. And it was Challenger who was in arrear?—Yes, I believe Challenger was the man.

731. (*Chairman.*) How do you know that they had taken the bands of the wrong man?—Our man told me so.

732. What man?—Christopher Taylor.

733. (*Mr. Chance.*) Christopher Taylor told you that he was not in arrear?—Yes.

734. And did Challenger admit that he was in arrear?—The man admitted it.

735. Was it from the circumstance of one man telling you that he was in arrear, and the other man that he was not in arrear, that you supposed the bands of the wrong man had been taken?—Yes.

736. You concluded that the bands of the man in arrear ought to have been taken and not the other?—According to the trades notion the man who was in arrear ought to have had his bands taken.

737. You came to the conclusion that the mere fact of one of the workmen being in arrear was the reason why the bands were taken?—Yes.

738. Upon that what was done by you or your workman?—I saw Broadhead myself.

739. What did you say to Broadhead?—I told Broadhead I thought it very wrong indeed that our property should be taken for a thing that we had nothing at all to do with.

740. What did Broadhead say to that?—He denied all knowledge of the matter.

741. Did the conversation stop then?—No, I told him it had cost us 2*s.* 6*d.* to have the door repaired which they had broken through, and I should expect him to repay the 2*s.* 6*d.*

742. What did Broadhead say to that?—He said, well, he did not want any unpleasantness; but his paying the 2*s.* 6*d.* must not be construed into the fact of the trade knowing anything at all about it.

743. Did he pay the 2*s.* 6*d.*?—I received 2*s.* 6*d.* from Christopher Taylor who is now in my employ, and he said Broadhead had given it to him to bring to me to pay for the door mending.

FIRST DAY.

Mr. R. T. Eadon.

3 June 1867.

744. After your interview with Broadhead did you get your band back?—Yes.

745. Did you get your band back before Challenger had paid up his arrears, or did he pay his arrears first?—They did not take Challenger's band, they took the man's who was not in arrear; they took Taylor's band.

746. Challenger was in arrear?—I believe Challenger was in arrear.

747. Can you tell me whether Challenger did, in fact, pay up his arrears before the band of Taylor's was restored?—I cannot answer that question; we got it back.

748. Was that soon after your interview with Broadhead?—Yes.

749. How soon after?—A few days.

750. Where did you find the band, was it brought to you or was it found in any particular place?—I should say that the men went to Broadhead, and while they were there Broadhead called their attention to a note that was in his fender, and that note contained the information where the band would be found. I do not know where the band was found.

751. (*Chairman.*) Who were the men?—I think Staniforth was one.

752. He was in your employ then?—Yes.

753. John Staniforth?—Yes, I believe he was one of the men.

754. He went to whom?—To Broadhead, who keeps the "Royal George" Hotel, and while there Broadhead pointed to a note that was in the fender. He said, "What have we here?"

755. Broadhead is here?—Yes, he is here. This note contained the information they sought.

756. (*Mr. Chance.*) One of them picked it up?—Yes.

757. (*Chairman.*) It informed them where they were to find the bands?—Yes.

758. (*Mr. Chance.*) They acted upon the information they found there?—Yes.

759. Do you know how many of your workmen besides Staniforth went to Broadhead upon that occasion?—More than one.

760. You do not remember the names?—No. I have no doubt they will tell you when they come.

761. That took place in 1860?—Yes.

762. Is there any case of rattening which has happened to you since that time?—Yes.

763. What was the next time?—We were rattened in November 1864.

764. What were the circumstances of that rattening?—Similar circumstances; I suppose the men were in arrear.

765. (*Chairman.*) Do you know as a fact that they were in arrear?—Yes, the men said they were in arrear, and expected their coming.

766. Who were in arrear?—Taylor and Bollington and some others.

767. There was more than one man in arrear?—Yes.

768. The reason why we press you for their names is that your evidence is merely hearsay, and if we can we should like to call the men themselves and ask them about it?—Henry Taylor was one, and Joshua Barton and Henry Bollington, I believe, were the others. It would be some of those.

769. (*Mr. Chance.*) Two of those are men who were in arrears on the first occasion?—Yes.

770. What was taken upon that occasion, the bands as before?—Two bands were taken, and a policeman captured a man with one. His name is Bradshaw.

771. Do you know the policeman's name?—No; Mr. Jackson would know his name.

772. (*Chairman.*) The policeman caught Bradshaw taking them away?—Yes.

773. (*Mr. Chance.*) Had he possession of the whole bands that were taken on that occasion?—Two bands were taken, and he had them in his possession.

774. What was afterwards done with him?—He was taken to the Town Hall and remanded to the sessions. We prosecuted, and he got six months.

775. (*Chairman.*) Do you know who Bradshaw was?—A saw grinder, I believe.

776. (*Mr. Chance.*) Was he a member of any union?—Yes.

777. He was a member of the saw grinders' union?—Yes.

778. You received back your bands from the policeman?—Yes, at the Town Hall.

779. And no application was made to the union on that occasion?—I was told by Cristopher Taylor that when it was found out that Bradshaw had been apprehended Broadhead told Taylor that if he would go and get a new band they would pay for it.

780. Broadhead told Taylor that; who told you?—Christopher Taylor.

781. Christopher Taylor told you if he would go and get a new band Broadhead would pay for it?—Yes.

782. Was the new band obtained?—No.

783. Had you at any time any interview or conversation with Broadhead in reference to the taking of this band?—No.

784. Or any member of this trade union?—None except our own men.

785. (*Chairman.*) Why was it a rattening case, and why was not Bradshaw a common thief; you speak of it as a rattening case?—I cannot tell, but Mr. Stuart Wortley, who was the chairman, drew a legal distinction, and so did Campbell Foster, but I cannot tell why it is not burglary.

786. Why did you say that Bradshaw took it as a supporter of the union rather than on his own independent account for his own benefit?—I did not think that he took it on his own account. I supposed it a case of rattening.

787. Bradshaw got the bands; why did you suppose that he took them as a case of rattening instigated by the trades' union rather than to dispose of them on his own account?—Because they are not articles they are likely to dispose of very readily, they would lead to detection.

788. They could not dispose of a band?—No.

789. Was the whole band taken?—There were two bands.

790. Is that the only reason, because they could not dispose of them?—I believe it would be contrary to anything I know if the bands had been taken for anything but trade purposes.

791. You form your opinion also from the fact of your men being in arrears?—Yes.

792. And also from the experience you have had of similar transactions?—Yes.

793. You mentioned the conversation that took place and the offer that you were told had been made by Broadhead to replace the bands?—To replace Taylor's bands.

794. (*Mr. Chance.*) Are there any other cases of rattening that have happened to you since that time?—Yes.

795. What is the next in order of date?—November 1865.

796. (*Chairman.*) Just a year after?—Yes.

797. (*Mr. Chance.*) What was done then?—The bands were again taken.

798. Do you know whether any of your workmen were in arrear then?—Yes.

799. Who were they?—I believe they were all in arrear but Christopher Taylor.

800. All the saw grinders were in arrear?—Yes.

801. How many saw grinders had you in your employ at that time?—I believe eight; Christopher Taylor, Henry Taylor, young Christopher Taylor, that is three Taylors, Henry Bollington, Jacob Barton, Charles Challenger, and Staniforth.

802. Then there was one man who was not in arrear?—Christopher Taylor I understand was not in arrear.

803. You say they were taken; do you attribute the rattening to the same cause?—We have power on our own premises, and an accident having occurred to

FIRST DAY.

Mr. R. T. Eadon.

3 June 1867.

the engine, we were compelled to have temporary power and to take other wheels in the town; it was temporary power.

804. Where was that?—At Mr. Jackson's, Sheaf Island works, the other was Marsden Brothers in Bridge Street; we were rattened twice while at Jackson's and once in Bridge Street.

805. During what period was that?—In November 1865.

806. Both in the same month?—Yes, both at the same time or nearly so.

807. What was taken on that occasion?—Bands.

808. The bands were taken on all three occasions?—Yes, and a nut was taken off the end of the axle that carries the stone.

809. (*Chairman.*) The rattening that occurred at the Sheaf Island works and the rattening that occurred at Bridge Street took place within what time of each other?—Within a few days of each other.

810. (*Mr. Chance.*) And you say the cause was to be attributed on those occasions also to your men being in arrear?—Yes.

811. Some of those eight men whom you mentioned?—Yes.

812. Do you know whom they were?—I daresay seven of them would be in arrear.

813. What proceedings did you take on that occasion?—I went to Mr. Jackson, the chief constable, and made an arrangement with him to send a policeman to stay from the time the wheel ceased to work till the next morning.

814. Where was that?—At Jackson's wheel.

815. (*Chairman.*) That is Sheaf Island?—Yes.

816. (*Mr. Chance.*) What was your object in sending the police to watch the premises?—To watch the premises and to detect the people.

817. That was to prevent any further rattening?—Yes.

818. Did you take any measures to recover the bands that had already been taken and the nut?—We did not personally, our men did.

819. Can you state what was done?—Our men went to see Mr. Broadhead again.

820. They went to see Mr. Broadhead again?—Yes, certainly.

821. Did they make any arrangement with Mr. Broadhead?—Yes; the men that were rattened went and paid him 20*s.* for arrears and 5*s.* for expenses.

822. (*Chairman.*) 20*s.* each?—I do not know whether it was 20*s.* each or not.

823. That is, the expense of doing the rattening?—Yes.

824. (*Mr. Chance.*) Upon that were the bands recovered?—We were rattened twice.

825. Twice and once?—Yes.

826. Within the course of a few days?—Yes. I would not have anything to do with Mr. Broadhead; I sent them to get a new band and began working again. They rattened us a second time, and they had to pay twice. There was 10*s.* charged.

827. You were rattened a second time besides the three occasions?—No, after the first time.

828. (*Chairman.*) You then got new ones, and directly you got new ones they came again?—Yes.

829. (*Mr. Chance.*) The arrears were paid up at last?—Yes.

830. The arrears were paid after the three rattenings?—Yes, all the arrears were paid up to the last.

831. The second and third rattenings were done because the arrears were not paid up?—Yes.

832. The arrears were paid up and the bands were recovered?—Yes.

833. In what way were they got back; do you know yourself?—I do not.

834. You know the fact simply that they came back?—Yes.

835. You took no further proceedings upon any of those occasions?—I employed the police in the hope of catching them.

836. Did they succeed in getting any information?—No; they succeeded in rattening us after the police were engaged.

837. (*Chairman.*) After you had got a man watching the premises?—No. I made arrangements that the police were to come from the time the wheel stopped to the time of commencing, and, by some means or other, they rattened before the policeman came, between the time of the men going and the policeman coming.

838. (*Mr. Chance.*) Were you rattened on any occasion after that?—Yes, we were rattened on the 9th of September 1866.

839. Were the bands taken as before?—They took seven bands from our place.

840. Was that from the same cause as before, the nonpayment of arrears?—Yes.

841. Whose bands were taken?—Our bands.

842. Belonging to what workmen?—They belonged to us.

843. What workmen were working at the bands?—They would be the men named.

844. Can you give us the names of the men who were working on that occasion?—Staniforth, Bollington, Taylor, and so on.

845. The same men?—Yes.

846. Probably the whole of those except Christopher Taylor?—They might have taken his bands on this occasion. I believe they took them all.

847. Did you make any application again to Mr. Broadhead?—No; the bands were found secreted in some coke ovens and taken to the Town Hall, where we recovered them.

848. What coke ovens?—They belonged to a pit near the canal.

849. Is that some distance from your works?—A distance of half a mile.

850. How soon after you lost them were they found there?—I believe they were taken from our works on the Saturday and discovered on the Sunday by some men.

851. Can you give the names of those who discovered them?—I could not give them now. I can give you them after; the bands were taken to the Town Hall.

852. Were all the bands found there that you lost on that occasion?—Yes.

853. (*Chairman.*) The coke ovens were not burning?—No; they secreted them there.

854. (*Mr. Chance.*) Then you got the bands back on that occasion without the arrears being paid up?—Yes.

855. Upon that, having got the bands back, did you have any communication with Mr. Broadhead?—No; we took no further notice.

856. Was there any occasion subsequent to that?—No, that was the last.

857. Is it a matter of considerable loss when the bands are taken?—Necessarily it is an interference with the business, and if the bands are not discovered it would be a loss. I do not think the trade have any complaint with us.

858. You were made to suffer for the fault of your workmen?—Yes.

859. If it can be called a fault; if the workmen did not pay up the arrears to the union the fault would be visited upon you?—They prevent the men working by taking the bands which belong to us.

860. (*Chairman.*) Is that the last case?—That is the last case of rattening.

861. Have you had any acts of intimidation at all towards you?—No, not recently.

862. Have you at any time?—We had a person call on us of the name of Machin, a saw grinder, intimating that some manufacturers induced the men to pay their natty money. I told him we had nothing to do with that.

863. Who was Machin?—A saw grinder.

864. Do you know whether he is connected with any union?—He was connected with the saw grinders' union at that time.

865. Do you know whether he held any office under

FIRST DAY.

Mr. R. T. Eadon.

3 June 1867.

the union ?—No ; I suppose he would be requested by the union to call upon me.

866. That is a mere guess ?—Yes, of course.

867. When you told him you had nothing to do with it what did he say to that ?—He took it very mild indeed.

868. He did nothing ?—I wanted to know what he meant.

869. He came to tell you that some manufacturers induced their men to pay natty money, and you said, "What do you mean by that ?"—He said he meant nothing, it was to avoid trouble.

870. What did he say ?—He said his object in coming was not to dictate but to prevent trouble, or avoid trouble.

871. When did this occur ?—It would be the latter end of 1865 or the beginning of 1866 ; I could not say. I have been trying to get the date.

872. What did you say to that when he said that he did not want to dictate but to avoid trouble ?—I told him we should take no steps in the matter.

873. What did he say to that ?—He went away.

874. Did anything happen in consequence of this that you know of ?—I have no doubt that if we had collected the natty money this subsequent affair would not have happened.

875. How long was it before this last rattening happened ?—I cannot say whether it was in the earlier part or the last part, but we have been rattened since.

876. We have now got November 1864, and November 1865, and in September 1866 this took place ; how long before the rattening occurred was it that this interview took place with Machin ?—I cannot speak positively; I have been trying to find out by referring to my diary, but I cannot find the date.

877. What is the impression upon your mind as to the date ?—I have tried to fix it, but I cannot fix it. I know he did come, and I know what passed between us.

878. You cannot tell me how long before ?—No.

879. Do you find the tools for your workmen ?—Yes ; a man is not allowed to have his own tools in our trade.

880. Do you find the wheel ?—Yes, we find the wheel.

881. The men are not allowed to have their own tools ?—No. Here are our rules upon that subject which I have here.

(*The witness handed the book of rules to the Chairman.*)

882. I see here, "No member holding a situation "shall find his own tools." What is the object of such a rule as this, by which a member of the union is not at liberty to find his own tools ?—I suppose the object of the union is to prevent men who have tools, in the event of trade becoming bad, competing for work by employing their tools.

883. A man who had tools of his own and worked would be in a certain sense independent of the union ?—Yes.

884. If he worked with his own tools ?—Yes.

885. Supposing a man has not tools he would have to come to you for the tools ; who would supply him with the tools ?—We must supply the tools.

886. You supply the men with tools ?—Yes.

887. If he is a member of the union you supply him with tools ?—Yes.

888. Why is it that the man is not allowed to find his own tools ?—I suppose one reason for preventing a man having his own tools is this, that where men have had their own tools it has reduced the cost of the work done ; 40 per cent. ought to be allowed for tools. Supposing a man earns 3*l*. a week, he ought to have 24*s*. to pay for the tools ; as a matter of course, if a man was a tenant and had tools of his own he would be anxious to employ them, and I suppose he would employ them if possible at a reduced price so as to prevent them competing with him ; so that they made a rule preventing them having tools at all.

889. Do you know of any other object than that which you suggest ? Supposing I were a journeyman saw grinder, and I happened to have tools for grinding, and I have paid my natty money regularly to the union, why should not I be at liberty to have my own tools ?—I cannot say why it is so, but you would not be allowed to have them according to the rules.

890. Can you furnish me with any explanation on the subject except the desire to prevent them being competitors ?—That is all. I can see no other reason.

891. Supposing a man does not find his own tools but they are found by the master, who finds both rent and tools; in the event of a strike all the loss falls upon the master ?—Certainly.

892. He has the tools and the rent to find, so that if there is a strike and there is no employment the whole of the loss falls upon the master ?—Just so.

893. Therefore they would have a much greater control over the master by this kind of rule than by allowing the workmen to have their own tools ?—It would be so I imagine.

894. Do you know whether in the trade, notwithstanding this rule, there are outsiders who work upon their own tools ; are there non-union men in Sheffield who work upon their own tools ?—I do not know whether there are or not at the present time.

895. Have you known of any such case ?—The trade themselves have tools.

896. You mean the trade union ?—Yes, they have their own tools now, or had.

897. Do you mean the union supplies tools ?—No ; the union will do the work for small or large manufacturers on tools that belong to the union.

898. Then the union have tools ?—The union have tools, but they do not belong to any individual man, they are their own property.

899. The union have tools of their own ?—Yes ; they had, if they have not now.

900. The union have tools of their own and do work with their own tools ?—Yes.

901. Do they let them out to the men ?—No.

902. How do they manage ?—I suppose they pay the men the same rate of wages as we pay the men, and they take the profit if any arises from the tools.

903. Are there any persons whom you have known who have been working with tools of their own ?—I do not know of any.

904. You do not know of a single case ?—I believe Fearnehough.

905. Why do you say Fearnehough; was he a man who worked with his own tools ?—I believe he found tools.

906. Fearnehough is the man in whose case there has been a reward offered ?—Yes.

907. Do you believe Fearnehough worked on his own tools ?—I believe he did.

908. Do you know whether Fearnehough was a member of the union or an outsider ?—I do not know anything about Fearnehough.

909. If a man has got his tools of course he cannot afford to be idle, he must work ?—Yes, he must work, or it would ruin him soon.

910. Therefore a man has a greater temptation to offer his work for a smaller sum if he has tools on his hands than if he were working for the trade ?—I suppose it would have that effect.

911. Do you know a person of the name of Linley ?—No.

912. Do you know whether he worked on his own tools or not ?—I cannot say of my own knowledge.

913. Do you know whether Fearnehough worked on his own tools at the time this outrage was committed ?—I believe he worked in George Street, but I only know that from the newspapers.

914. (*Mr. Chance.*) Do you employ all union men, or ordinary men as well ?—We have non-unionists as well.

915. You are not prevented ?—No.

916. (*Chairman.*) Will union men employ non-union men ?—They do sometimes, I believe.

917. There is no rule that you are aware of in the union to prevent them working with non-union men ?—They would not a short time ago have allowed a

FIRST DAY.

Mr. R. T. Eadon.

3 June 1867.

man who did pay to the union and a man who did not pay to the union to work together.

918. Will they now?—I believe none of our men are paying to the old union at present.

919. They are all getting into arrear?—No. I believe they have formed a new union independently of the old saw grinders' union which was under the presidency of Mr. Broadhead.

920. Is the saw grinders' union amalgamated with other unions?—They have some sort of amalgamation.

921. (*Mr. Chance.*) You never had a case of rattening in consequence of employing non-union men?—No.

922. (*Mr. Barstow.*) How does taking your bands put a pressure upon the men?—Because without the bands they cannot work, and without work they cannot live.

923. You do not pay them wages?—We do not pay them wages when the bands are gone.

924. What is the cost of the band?—It depends upon the length, the strength, the width, and the weight of leather on it; an ordinary band costs 50*s*.

925. (*Chairman.*) It is not so much the value of the band as stopping the work?—No.

926. (*Mr. Barstow.*) Is it a heavy thing?—The saw grinders' band, I should imagine, which we have would weigh about half a hundredweight.

927. (*Chairman.*) How many men would it take to carry one off?—Not many to carry 56 lbs.

928. (*Mr. Barstow.*) You said five or six bands were taken away on one occasion?—Seven.

929. It would take more than one man to carry those away?—Yes.

930. It would be a large bulky parcel?—Yes, one was carried away in a large hamper.

931. In a large hamper?—Yes.

932. That must have been carried through the streets of Sheffield some distance?—Yes, unless taken in a cart.

933. It must have been conveyed?—Yes.

934. (*Chairman.*) You mentioned a person of the name of Bradshaw?—Yes.

935. He was convicted of rattening you?—Yes.

936. When was that?—In November 1864. I have got it here; a policeman captured a man named Bradshaw with two bands.

937. Are you aware whether that is the same William Bradshaw who had been convicted of the same offence against a person named Worrell in 1860?—No.

938. (*Mr. Barstow.*) I suppose when you miss bands you know at once it is a trades' union affair?—We do not know for certain.

939. You act as if it was?—We instinctively believe it is a matter that refers to trade or some dispute with our men.

940. Have you ever been made answerable for your men's arrears?—No.

941. And never had to pay for them?—No.

942. (*Chairman.*) And you never would pay?—No.

943. (*Mr. Barstow.*) When you missed your bands how did you come to know it was a trades' dispute?—Our men had been expecting them to come before we had known of it.

944. You knew they were coming?—No, we expected they were coming.

945. If you expected them did not you do something to receive them?—Yes, we have paid for policemen standing waiting for them.

946. Is that on all occasions?—Not on all occasions; we have had a policeman there; Mr. Jackson has sent us one down.

947. (*Chairman.*) On occasions when you have not been rattened?—Yes.

948. And you believe you have put them off in that way?—Yes, we put them off while the policeman was there.

949. (*Mr. Barstow.*) What caused you to expect them on these occasions?—Because our men told us themselves that there was a disagreement with the trade, and they took extra precautions.

950. And upon that you took precautions?—Yes.

951. Has that happened pretty often?—No.

952. It has happened?—Yes.

953. How often?—You see how often we have been rattened.

954. How often have the men given you reason to expect you would be rattened, in consequence of which you took precautions?—I cannot say.

955. More than once?—Yes.

956. Half a dozen times?—Perhaps half a dozen times.

957. Within the last 10 years?—Yes.

958. Would you say half a dozen is the greatest number of times that your men have told you that they have had a difference with the trade, and that in consequence of that you have taken precautions?—They have told me that they have been in arrear.

959. That is not what you told us at first?—I said that we expected them.

960. Yes, so I understood?—That is so certainly.

961. How often has that happened in these last 10 years?—You mean how often have they been in arrear.

962. I ask how often in consequence of your expecting some outrage at your works have you taken precautions?—We have taken precautions repeatedly by locking the place up, and so on.

963. That is not what you told us. I ask how often have you taken precautions by sending for police?—I have called at the town hall.

964. (*Chairman.*) How often have you called at the town hall?—Once. I have been twice for them, once for Jackson's and once for our own place.

965. What is your own place?—The place that belongs to us. We occupied power at Jackson's wheel temporarily during an accident to our own engine.

966. How many times have you been to the police to take precautions?—Twice altogether.

967. Are those the two occasions you have mentioned already; was one of the occasions that on which they got your bands before the policeman came?—Yes.

968. Do you count that occasion as one?—Yes.

969. And there was another one besides?—Yes; once at our own place and once at Jackson's.

970. Did you expect them at any other time?—No.

The witness withdrew.

Adjourned to to-morrow at 11 o'clock.

SECOND DAY.

Tuesday, 4th June 1867.

PRESENT :

WILLIAM OVEREND, Esq., Q.C.	GEORGE CHANCE, Esq.
THOMAS IRWIN BARSTOW, Esq.	J. E. BARKER, Esq., Secretary.

WILLIAM OVEREND, ESQ., Q.C., IN THE CHAIR.

SECOND DAY.

Mr. J. Platts.

4 June 1867.

Mr. JOHN PLATTS recalled.

The Chairman informed Mr. Sugg (who appeared for the Trades Unions) that if he desired to put any questions to this witness he might do so through the Commissioners.

Mr. Sugg replied that he should prefer to produce rebutting evidence.

The witness withdrew.

R. Booth.

ROBERT BOOTH sworn and examined.

971. (*Chairman.*) You are a scissor grinder at Brightside Street, Sheffield ?—Yes.

972. Do you belong to any union ?—Yes.

973. To which ?—The Scissor Grinders' Union.

974. Were you brought up as an apprentice to the trade ?—Yes.

975. Were you afterwards a journeyman ?—Yes.

976. And are you now a journeyman or a master ? —I do my own out ; that is, working for myself, not journey work.

977. You have been both an apprentice and a journeyman, and now you work for yourself ?—Yes.

978. Have you worked for John Platts ?—Yes.

979. When was it that you worked for him ?—It is about 11 or 12 weeks since.

980. How long did you work for him ?—About five years.

981. Up to within 12 weeks ?—Within 11 or 12 weeks.

982. Did you work in a hull there ?—Yes.

983. A hull is the same thing as a room, is it not ? —Yes.

984. And in that room there are troughs or places where the wheel goes round where you work ?—Yes.

985. And a trough is a place where a man works before a stone ?—Yes.

986. Then you worked at a trough in a hull which he rented ?—We had them between us. The master was booked for the room, and we divided in equal shares on the Saturday night. It was put down in a sum and reckoned up, and we each paid half. Platts stopped it out of the wages on Saturday night.

987. You each paid half the rent ?—Yes, he took it out of the wages on Saturday night.

988. Do you recollect whether, on the 9th of March in the present year, you were on the box ?—I believe so.

989. What does being on the box mean ?—It is drawing scale if you have nothing to do.

990. Drawing scale is getting funds from the union ?—Yes.

991. How long were you on the box ?—The first time, I think, I was on about a week or a fortnight.

992. On the 26th of March did Platts send to you to come to work ?—Yes.

993. Did he tell you that he had work for you to do ?—No, he did not.

994. What did he tell you ?—Of course he told me there was work for me to do, but when I got there there was none. He sent word that there was work, but when I went there was none.

995. Did you speak to him about the work ?—Yes, I went into the hulls, and I said, "Now, is all this "work ready ?" and I looked round. He says, "You must go up to the borers' and hardeners' shop ;" and I went up there, and there was not any. That was on the Thursday morning, and I said, "This is "a latish hour this week, and I shall not begin till "Monday morning."

996. Did you go to the borers' and hardeners' shop ?—Yes, and he said that there would be a whole lot ready for me, but when I got there (to the borers' and hardeners') there was not any.

997. Who was the borer that told you so ?—James Parkins.

998. Then what did you do ?—I said, "Very well, "if there is not any work ready I will not stop now ; "you may get some ready by Monday, and I will "start fair on Monday."

999. What day was this ?—Thursday.

1000. You went away then ?—Yes, I went away from the warehouse, and went on the Monday following, and told him that I thought it was not reasonable and right that I should have all the work before he started working, and that when he started working he should have all the best work, and I should have only the best he thought fit to give me ; and that he should take the best and give me the worst, I thought it was not right.

1001. On the Monday did you go to him, and did he tell you that he would have work for you, but not for the others ?—No, he did not. I told him that I thought it was not right that he should take the best work, and leave me the worst.

1002. What kind of work did he take ?—There are many kinds.

1003. But what was it in this case ?—It is what comes to the most money which you can earn in the least time. Perhaps you can earn as much in an hour at one kind of work as you could in two or three hours at others.

1004. And you complained that he took that work which enabled him to earn more money in a shorter time than you ?—Yes, and I had always been used to having it.

1005. What did he say to that ?—He said if I could not come and get to work again he would get somebody else ; he would not bother with me. I went down to the trade, and asked them if they thought it reasonable and right.

1006. Whom did you ask ?—I went to the fund.

1007. Whom did you see ?—I saw the committee.

1008. Who were they ?—There were many of them ; I do not know their names, I am sure.

1009. You went down to the trade committee ?—Yes.

1010. Where did you go to ?—To the "Star Inn."

SECOND DAY.

R. Booth.

4 June 1867

1011. Where is that?—Gibraltar.

1012. Did you go in the afternoon or in the evening, or when?—It would be at night.

1013. Was the committee sitting?—Yes.

1014. Who was there?—There may be a few that I should not know.

1015. I do not ask you whom you did not know, but whom you did know; who was there?—Holmshaw and Gale were there. That is about all I know.

1016. How many besides?—There were perhaps about a dozen of them altogether.

1017. What did you say to them?—I asked them if they would support me while I stopped on. If he shared work equally with me I said I would go in, and if not, I would not work at all.

1018. You asked them if they would support you in this?—Yes.

1019. What did they say to that?—They said they would do so if I thought well to stand out, whilst he should give me equal shares, I could do so and they would support me.

1020. Then you have stood out?—Yes.

1021. Was that all that passed?—Yes.

1022. Is that all your story about it?—Yes.

1023. You have nothing more to tell us, have you?—No.

1024. Did you go at all to the wheel?—Yes, I went to the wheel.

1025. When was that?—Perhaps six or seven weeks ago. I cannot tell exactly.

1026. Did you go round?—Yes, I went into our hull.

1027. Your hull or your room is closed with a key, is it not? Did you put the key outside?—Not that I am aware of.

1028. How do you close the door?—I went in when the master was in.

1029. But before that how did you get in?—We locked the hull and left the key in the house in the yard.

1030. Who keeps that house?—It is Johnson's name at the house.

1031. You went there; what did you go there for if you were on strike?—I went to look at my things.

1032. What things?—The tools; part of the tools in the hull are mine.

1033. Did you see any scissors there?—I saw that master was glazing some, that was all.

1034. Whose were they?—Platts'.

1035. Did you examine them?—No.

1036. Did you have them in your hand?—No.

1037. Now mind what you are about—had you those scissors in your hand, on your oath?—Of course master was glazing some, and I looked at what master was glazing.

1038. Then did you have them in your hand?—Yes.

1039. Then why did you say you had not? Then you did take up the scissors and examine them?—Yes, those that master was doing.

1040. What kind of scissors were they? They were about 6-inch scissors.

1041. What kind of scissors were they?—What we call square shanks and blades.

1042. Were they shot?—Yes.

1043. You are quite sure about that?—Yes.

1044. How long were you examining them?—I stood on the hearth; and many a time when we go into our hull the master might come and look at us.

1045. But how long were you examining them?—I should not have it half a second. I just looked at it and put it down again.

1046. Do you know a person of the name of Pryor?—Yes.

1047. Do you know that Pryor worked for Platts?—He did jobs now and then, but not continuously.

1048. You know that?—Yes.

1049. Where did Pryor work; in the Trafalgar Wheel?—Yes, in Melbourne Street.

1050. Did you go to the Trafalgar Wheel?—Yes.

1051. When was that?—It would be somewhere about six weeks ago, as nearly as I can remember.

1052. How long was it after you had been to the wheel where Platts works?—I have not been to Platts' wheel since he ordered me out with policemen.

1053. You told us just now that you went to the wheel six or seven weeks ago?—To Well's wheel, but not at Platts'; they do not work all at one wheel.

1054. But you told me just now that you went to Platts'; you said, "I went into our hull, and we "leave the key at Johnson's in the yard;" and you said, "I went to look at my things," and that that was six or seven weeks ago. How long after that was it that you went to the Trafalgar Wheel?—About six or seven weeks; but when I went to our wheel and the master ordered me out, and said I was to book up my scissors, was more than six or seven weeks ago.

1055. Then you say that when you went to the Trafalgar Wheel was before you went to your wheel; did you go to look at those scissors and examine those scissors, and then afterwards did you go to the Trafalgar Wheel?—No, I did not examine those shot scissors.

1056. But you did examine some scissors which he had been at work upon, did you not?—Not at Trafalgar Wheel.

1057. But at your own wheel where Platts was working?—Yes.

1058. When was it that you went to Platts' wheel, and saw him at work upon some scissors?—It would be about seven or eight weeks, as nearly as I can tell.

1059. Did you after that go to the Trafalgar Wheel?—Yes, I believe I did.

1060. How long was it after you had been to your own wheel that you went to the Trafalgar Wheel?—It might be about a week or three or four days.

1061. Had you anything to do at the Trafalgar Wheel?—No.

1062. You know that Pryor worked there?—I knew that he worked at the wheel, but I did not know which hull he worked in.

1063. But you had nothing to do with the Trafalgar Wheel; why did you go there?—When we are out of work perhaps there are a dozen wheels we go to. We might have a little job of hanging a stone, or something of that sort.

1064. But why did you go to the Trafalgar Wheel?—I was passing by and I thought that I would call in.

1065. Did you go in and ask for work?—No.

1066. Did you see anybody there?—Yes.

1067. Whom did you see there?—I got into Jubb's hull first, I believe.

1068. When you went to the wheel did you inquire where Pryor worked?—Yes, I asked which hull Pryor worked in.

1069. What did you do that for?—I simply asked which hull Pryor did work in.

1070. What was your reason for asking which was the hull in which Pryor was working?—I do not know I am sure.

1071. You cannot give us a reason. You know you need not be afraid, no consequences can happen to you at all. You are perfectly protected if you tell the whole truth. Now what was your reason for asking for Pryor?—I merely asked which hull he worked in. I asked for Jubb's hull first.

1072. I know you did, but I asked you why you asked for Pryor?—I wanted to see Pryor.

1073. But what did you want to see him about?—He has been in the habit of making fanners, I had made two or three fanners myself, and I wanted to ask him what he reckoned to charge for fanners that we use in a grinder's wheel to take the dust away.

1074. Did you ask him that?—He was not there.

1075. Did you tell anybody for what reason you wanted to see him?—No.

1076. Did they point out to you where he worked?—No.

1077. Did not Jubb know where he worked?—He told me at which hull he worked. It was not at Jubb's hull where Pryor worked.

SECOND DAY.

R. Booth.

4 June 1867.

1078. Did he tell you where Pryor worked?—He showed me the hull.

1079. Did you ascertain from him that Pryor was not there before you went to his hull?—No.

1080. Did Jubb tell you before he went to Pryor's hull that Pryor was not there?—I am sure I do not know. I do not remember his telling me.

1081. Will you swear that he did not tell you that Pryor was not about?—I cannot swear.

1082. Did not you say, "But which is his hull?"—I asked Jubb which hull it was, and I went and saw it.

1083. But before that time had he not told you that Pryor was not about?—I do not remember that he did.

1084. Will you swear that he did not?—I do not remember that he did.

1085. Will you swear that he did not tell you that he was not there?—I will not take an oath that he did not.

1086. Did you go into his hull?—Yes.

1087. Did you see what he was working at?—I saw the scissors.

1088. Did you see what Pryor was working at?—No.

1089. Was he working at scissors?—He was not working at all.

1090. But did you see the scissors there that he would have been working at if he had been at work?—Yes.

1091. What kind of scissors were they?—There were big ones and little ones.

1092. But what kind of scissors were they?—There are metal scissors and steel scissors and shot board.

1093. Where they 11-inch paper scissors?—I am sure I cannot say.

1094. You are a man in the trade and you know what you saw; did you see in that hull a lot of 11-inch paper scissors?—There were a many both big and little.

1095. That is no answer; were they 11-inch paper scissors which you saw?—I did not see any scissors or take hold of any scissors in Pryor's.

1096. I ask you if you saw some 11-inch paper scissors?—Perhaps they would be 11-inch.

1097. Were there paper scissors there?—I do not know, I am sure whether they were paper scissors or what they were. They were big scissors.

1098. Were they 11-inch paper scissors?—I did not see any 11-inch paper scissors. I saw scissors, I do not know what they were.

1099. Although you have been brought up to the trade as an apprentice and as a journeyman, you mean to tell me that you would not know what 11-inch paper scissors were?—I should if I had seen them.

1100. You having seen what were there, were what you saw there 11-inch paper scissors—you know that you need not be frightened, if you tell the truth you shall be perfectly protected?—I believe they were.

1101. Why did you hesitate before to tell us that they were paper scissors, and now you tell us at last that you believe they were, why have you been fencing all the while with this, and objecting to tell the truth?—Of course from not being confident.

1102. Now then on your oath did you not see amongst the scissors which you saw at the wheel of John Platts' where you worked with him the same kind of scissors which you saw at Pryor's?—No.

1103. You never saw the same kind?—No.

1104. What sort of scissors did you see at John Platts'?—Six-inch scissors, what you call square shank.

1105. You never saw anything but six-inch scissors?—No.

1106. What quantity of six-inch scissors did you see at Platts'?—Platts had about a dozen on his board.

1107. That is all you saw?—Yes.

1108. Now did you see Platts after he had missed the scissors?—Yes; I was at the hull; I went to the hull, I believe, the day but one afterwards.

1109. Did Platts charge you with having taken them?—Yes.

1110. Did he tell you that you had been to his hull and seeing what scissors he was making and then that you had gone on to Pryor's and seen what scissors Pryor was grinding?—Yes.

1111. And what did you say to that?—I told him that it was false.

1112. Did you laugh?—Yes.

1113. What did you laugh about?—Because I thought that he was not without impudence to tell me so.

1114. For a person to tell you that you had committed a theft you think is a laughing matter—you laughed at being accused of having stolen this man's scissors—did you laugh at the accusation and think it a joke or how was it?—I thought that it was his nonsense.

1115. Did you not believe that he had been robbed?—I did not believe that because I did not know.

1116. Then what did you laugh at?—I did not know what he was meaning when he said so.

1117. When you went to the committee and saw Holmshaw, did Holmshaw give you any kind of instruction as to what you were to do?—No.

1118. Did Gale?—No.

1119. Nor any of the committee?—No.

1120. Did you receive instructions from anyone to take away those scissors?—No.

1121. Have you ever told Holmshaw or Gale that you took away those scissors?—No.

1122. Nor anyone?—No.

1123. Did you take them away?—No, I did not.

1124. On your oath you did not?—I will take my oath I did not.

1125. That you never took them away?—I never took them away.

1126. Do you know who took them away?—No.

1127. Do you believe it to be a trade business, or what do you believe it to be?—I do not know, I am sure, what it is.

1128. And you neither took them yourself nor know who did take them?—No, I do not.

1129. Are you still on the box?—Yes.

1130. You are still what they call on strike?—Yes.

1131. Is there plenty of work for you if you would go on?—I went one day, and he said that he would not have me at any price, that day that he fetched a policeman to me.

1132. Is there plenty of work for you now if you like to go?—Not now; he denied me his employment any more.

1133. Do you work elsewhere?—I have not a place at present.

1134. Are you receiving wages from the committee?—I am receiving funds.

1135. What are you receiving from the committee?—I have been receiving about 14*s.* 6*d.*

1136. For how long?—For about 12 weeks.

1137. What can you earn at your trade if there is a fair amount of work?—It depends—perhaps 30*s.*, and sometimes one can get a deal more than at others.

1138. But what is a fair average amount of work?—I daresay we might get 28*s.* to 30*s.* a week on an average, and we might get more some weeks; that would make a lot of difference.

1139. So you say that the only ground of your not working was because Platts did the superior work and left you the inferior work?—Yes.

1140. Do you know that other persons in your hull have not paid up their subscription?—No.

1141. Were there any other persons who worked with you who contributed to the Union?—I had a man working with me a bit, and of course he paid to the Union.

1142. Was his "natty money" paid up?—I do not know.

1143. You do not know the fact?—No.

1144. Did the collector come round and ask for the

SECOND DAY.

R. Booth.

4 June 1867.

money from the other people ?—He came round and asked me for my "natty," and asked Mr. Platts for his "natty."

1145. Did you hear Mr. Platts say to him that he was not going to pay, and that he would not pay without he was going to receive ?—Yes.

1146. How long was that before you went on strike ?—That would be about 11 or 12 weeks ; that would be about the first onset, I think.

1147. When you first went out ?—Yes.

1148. You went out almost immediately after that, did you not ?—I believe it was about a week after.

1149. It was a week after Platts told the collector that he would not pay without he was going to receive that you struck ?—Yes.

1150. Now upon your oath were you not told to go out on strike on the ground that Platts had not paid his contribution ?—No, I was not.

1151. Was nothing said to you about his not paying his contribution ?—No.

1152. By no one ?—No.

1153. Was it a matter of talk in the hull ?—No.

1154. (*Mr. Barstow.*) How many weeks have you been altogether on the box ?—About 11 or 12 weeks altogether as near as I can guess.

1155. Have you applied anywhere for work during that time ?—No.

1156. Are you in ill health ?—Yes.

1157. Why have you not applied for work ?—Because we are charged not to find ourselves work. The committee finds us a place when we want any.

1158 Have you applied to the committee to find you a place ?—No.

1159. You say that Platts had some tools of yours ?—Yes.

1160. And I think I understood you to say that he has them now ?—Yes.

1161. What tools are they ?—There is a fan, and old materials, that is pipes, bands, and pulleys. There are about two bands, and little oddments besides.

1162. He has them now you say ?—Yes.

1163. Does he pay you anything for the use of them ?—No.

1164. Have you applied to him for them ?—Yes ; and that day when I went for them he fetched a policeman.

1165. Why did you not take them from him, they were yours, you know ?—He said he would see me far enough before I should have a halfpenny of them, and of course I am not in circumstances to go to a higher court with it.

1166. Do you owe Platts anything ?—He says I owe him 3*l.* for tools ; but if I owe him these 3*l.* I shall want the whole of the new things which he is getting mended and repaired lately.

1167. You told us that Platts proposed to give you inferior work ; what did he say to you then ?—He told me that if I came there to be master he would do the other work himself, he would not be bothered with me.

1168. But what kind of work did he ask you to do ?—It is what we call the worst work.

1169. What kind work ?—There are many kinds of work in scissors.

1170. But that is what I want to know ; what work did he offer you ?—He did not offer me anything ; it was a kind of agreement.

1171. What was the work that he offered to you ?—When I went in to him on Monday morning——

1172. That was after the Thursday ?—Yes, I went into the hull and said "Can I be equal, or are you "bound to hold the best and give me what you think "well. Before we start let us have an understanding," and he said, "If you are not satisfied I will get "someone else," and I said, "Very well, if I cannot "get equal shares and have the best work I will get "work where I can."

1173. But you had no work then, had you ?—Yes, we had work.

1174. But you had none ; you were going to stop ?—I told him that if he would share it equally I would stop on.

1175. You told us that on the first occasion you shared equally ?—I have had it all to myself about three years, and he has only lately started working.

1176. You told us that the place was in Platts' name, that you paid half the rent, and that you shared equally on Saturday ?—Yes.

1177. That was when you worked for him at first ?—No, this has lately started ; I had it on my own bottom about three years, and now we have begun it afresh. Mr. Platts did not work at all for about three years, and I did all the work, and of course he started working again, and that has altered the case altogether. I was booked for the room about three years, and his tools were in my possession, and then we went to another wheel about Christmas and he was booked for them there. Of course that was just about when we started working, and he got booked for the room, and he bought all the working stuff in and reckoned it up and put it as so much apiece and took it out of my wages.

1178. But now you have not told us what this inferior work was ?—What we call polished work ; fine work ; fluting.

1179. (*Chairman.*) You cannot get so much by the polished work as by the other ?—No.

1180. And he took the other work and left you the polished work ?—Yes ; he took the glazed work and all the big ones, and left me the little ones.

1181. (*Mr. Barstow.*) When was this that he took the glazed work and left you the polished work ?—He has been taking it all the time since first we started.

1182. Did you complain to him ; Yes.

1183. When did you complain to him about it ?—Of course, I have told him on Saturday nights that it was not reasonable that he should take all the best work and leave me the worst, and he said he did not know that he was taking it all.

1184. And he denied doing so ?—Yes.

1185. Did you receive as much money as he did on the Saturday night ?—No ; I had not so much work, because he had plenty to go on with, and I had to have what he could not do. I had not as much as I could do.

1186. (*Mr. Chance.*) Are the fans used by you in your work ?—Yes.

1187. Then when you went to Pryor you say you went to see him because you wanted to make use of fans ?—Yes, merely to ask him the price, he being a man who had made a many. I had made about three ; one for myself, one for my brother, and one for another fellow ; and so long as I was out of work I thought I might as well get a job or two as not.

1188. But you were not at work then ?—No.

1189. Then what did you want the fans for then ?—To make them for other grinders.

1190. But you say you wanted to know for what Pryor would make them for you ?—No, to know what Pryor charged for making them, so that I might have an idea what to charge for mine.

1191. When you went to the Trafalgar Wheel you saw Jubb ?—Yes.

1192. Was Jubb in the same hull with Pryor ?—No.

1193. Who was in the hull besides Pryor ?—I believe there were about two or three.

1194. At what distance would they be working from each other ? Do you mean to say that two or three were working in the same hull with Pryor ?—No, they were not working, they were on the hull hearth, what we call the fire-place.

1195. Could you see the place at which they would work as soon as you entered the room ?—Yes.

1196. Then you could see at once that Pryor was not there ?—Yes.

1197. Then if you knew that Pryor was not there why did you go to the place where he worked ? you

SECOND DAY.

R. Booth.

4 June 1867.

went up to where Pryor was working, did you not?—I went into the hull, of course.

1198. But you went up to where he was working?—Yes.

1199. Why did you go up to where he was working when you found that he was not in?—When I saw that he was not in I came out again. I was not in but a minute.

1200. But you would have seen at once that he was not in, why did you not go at once?—As soon as I saw that he was not in I went out at once.

1201. But did you not look at the scissors?—I did not look at the scissors there.

1202. (*Chairman.*) You told us that you saw at Pryor's hull a lot of scissors, and I asked you if they were paper scissors, and you said they were.

1203. (*Mr. Chance.*) You told us just now that you had seen those scissors, and you told us that they were 11-inch paper scissors?—I told you that I had seen scissors at Platt's.

1204. We were speaking of two different times; at one time you examined the scissors at Platt's and you told us that those were 6-inch blade and shank scissors?—Yes.

1205. And you also told us that the scissors at which you saw Pryor was working were 11-inch paper scissors; why was it that as soon as you knew that Pryor was not in the hull you did not leave at once?—I did do so.

1206. You told us just now that you saw the scissors?—Of course, going in one can see all round.

1207. How far is the place where the scissors were from the door of the hull?—You might come into the hull and see them anywhere.

1208. But how far were the scissors on which Pryor was working from the door at which you entered?—About as far as this (*describing the same*).

1209. I want to ascertain from you whether you are telling the truth. Now tell me the distance at which Pryor was working from where you entered the hull?—I was not any farther than from here to there (*describing the same*).

1210. Do you mean the end of that desk?—I mean the end of that desk.

1211. Then how could you tell at that distance whether those were 11-inch paper scissors or not?—I said that they were big scissors, and that they might be paper scissors.

1212. You said that they were paper scissors after plenty of time had been given you to consider.

1213. (*Chairman.*) Will you swear that you did not go into the hull?—No, I will not swear that I did not go into the hull.

1214. (*Mr. Chance.*) How far did you go?—You may go as it might be up here (*describing the same*), and I went in at the door and went up to the fireplace.

1215. Did you stand by the fireplace?—I stood perhaps half a minute or a second.

1216. You stood by the fireplace; how does the fireplace stand with reference to the scissors where Pryor was working?—Perhaps the scissors were three or four yards off.

1217. And you did not go up to the scissors?—No.

1218. Upon your oath you did not?—No.

1219. And you could perceive from the distance where you were whether they were 11-inch scissors or not?—I said that they were big scissors; they might be paper scissors.

The witness withdrew.

G. Colley.

GEORGE COLLEY sworn and examined.

1220. (*Mr. Barstow.*) You are a scissor grinder?—Yes.

1221. Where do you live?—I live in Allen Street.

1222. Have you been an apprentice to the trade?—Yes.

1223. And are you now a journeyman?—Yes.

1224. How long have you been a journeyman?—Since 1855; 11 or 12 years.

1225. Are you a member of any Union?—Yes.

1226. What Union is that?—The Scissor Grinders' Union.

1227. How long have you been a member of the Union?—About five years.

1228. Are you a member of the committee?—No, not now.

1229. You have been?—I have been on the committee.

1230. Do you know John Platts?—I know him, and that is about all.

1231. Have you ever worked with him?—No.

1232. Do you take power at the same wheel?—I did once, about five years since.

1233. (*Chairman.*) Was that in February, 1863?—Yes; not with him, but at the same wheel.

1234. (*Mr. Barstow.*) Were you at that time a member of the Union?—Yes.

1235. At that time were you in any arrear with your natty money?—I daresay a trifle, but not a deal.

1236. You were, in fact, in arrear?—Yes, a little.

1237. Do you remember on the 28th of February losing your bands?—I do remember once having them taken.

1238. (*Chairman.*) On this occasion?—I never had them taken but once, and that would be the time.

1239. Were there two or three, or how many bands taken?—Three of mine.

1240 (*Mr. Barstow.*) They were your own?—Yes.

1241. What was the value of them?—Perhaps 1*l.* or 1*l.* 5*s.*

1242. Do you know whether Platts' were removed at the same time as yours?—Yes.

1243. Did you go with Platts anywhere in consequence?—No, with the exception of his coming to me and telling me where they were.

1244. When your bands were gone what steps did you take?—I did not take any steps at all about them.

1245. You did nothing?—No.

1246. Did you know why they were taken?—No, not at all. Platts came and told me.

1247. Did you know why they were taken?—I did not know; he came and told me where they were.

1248. Did you know why your bands were taken?—I do not know why they were taken, unless it was owing this trifle of money. I expect perhaps that would be it, but I do not know.

1249. Have you ever heard of persons in the trade losing their bands before when they were at all in arrear?—I do not know that they have lost them.

1250. (*Chairman.*) But they have had them taken away and they have been rattened as it is called?—Yes, I have known them taken away at different times.

1251. When persons have been in arrears?—Yes, when persons have been in arrears.

1252. (*Mr. Barstow.*) How often have you known that?—Some few times. I cannot say how many.

1253. Can you say about how many times?—I cannot say. I know two or three cases at the Union Wheel.

1254. (*Chairman.*) I suppose that rattening is a thing which is understood very well in Sheffield, is it not?—Grinders understand it well enough.

1255. And they understand that rattening is when their bands are taken away, because they have done something against the Union; that is what they mean, is it not?—I believe so.

1256. That is how it is understood in the town, is it?—Grinders understand it so.

SECOND DAY.

G. Colley.

4 June 1867.

1257. And it often happens amongst grinders when they do anything against the Union that they find their bands are gone?—I have known it to be the case.

1258. How often have you known it to be the case? —I have known it once.

1259. Yourself?—Yes, some five or six years since for owing 12*s*.

1260. (*Mr. Barstow.*) What did you do when you lost your bands?—I did not do anything at all about them.

1261. You did nothing?—No; I did not see anybody about them. I did not bother about them.

1262. Did you go to the committee about them?—I went to the committee about them.

1263. (*Chairman.*) You did not go to the police I suppose?—No, I did not.

1264. (*Mr. Barstow.*) Whom did you see?—I do not know who was secretary.

1265. (*Chairman.*) Did you see the secretary?—Yes.

1266. (*Mr. Barstow.*) Do you know his name?—Gale was secretary.

1267. Was that the man you saw?—Yes.

1268. Did you see anyone else?—A few more.

1269. (*Chairman.*) Did you see Holmshaw, the president?—I think that he was not president at that time.

1270. You are mistaken about that. Holmshaw was president then, and Gale was there. Did you see the president?—I do not think that he was there at that time.

1271. (*Mr. Barstow.*) Whom did you see besides Gale?—There were some few on the committee; I do not know who they were personally I am sure.

1272. Whom do you think they were?—I am sure I could not recollect any particular party. We used to change the committee every three months during that time.

1273. What did you say to Gale?—I asked him where my bands were.

1274. And what did he say?—He said that he did not know anything at all about them.

1275. Did you ask him why they had been taken? —He said that he did not know anything about them.

1276. But did you ask him if he knew why they were taken?—No, I did not ask him if he knew why they were taken.

1277. (*Chairman*). What more passed?—There was not anything particular passed only that.

1278. Did you ask him how you could get them back?—No, I did not say anything at all about getting them back.

1279. Did he tell you how you could get them back?—No.

1280. Did anybody tell you how you could get them back?—No.

1281. Was anything been said about your being in arrear at all at that interview?—No.

1282. Did you tell him that this was too bad, that you were only 11*s*. 6*d*., or whatever it was in arrears, and ask why they took your band?—I did not think they had any right to take it for a sum like that.

1283. Then you did tell them so. You said you thought that it was not right that they should take them away when you were only 11*s*. 6*d*. in arrear?—I did not think that they took them themselves; I went there because all other grinders go there, to see what I could make of them, and to see whether they knew anything about it.

1284. (*Mr. Barstow.*) I suppose you did not go to the police?—No.

1285. Grinders never go to the police when they lose their bands, do they?—I have never been, and I have never known of such a case.

1286. Did you see Platts with the committee?—No.

1287. You were not there with him at all?—No.

1288. Did you get any note?—No.

1289. Did you get any note signed "Sweep?"—No.

1290. Did you never see one?—No, I never did.

1291. You are quite sure that Platts never showed you one?—Never.

1292. Did you get your bands back again?—Platts came and told me where they were.

1293. And where were they?—In a place over the engine house.

1294. (*Chairman.*) Platts told you where they were, and you got a ladder and went up and got them? —Yes.

1295. Did you pay your subscription?—No.

1296. You were 11*s*. 6*d*. in arrears, were you not? —But I had not to pay; I do not think that they took them for that.

1297. But have you ever paid up these arrears?—I am not stopped now.

1298. Did you pay your arrears?—I did not pay any at that time.

1299. Have you paid them since?—I have paid some since that has been running on at different times since I have been working.

1300. But before he told you where your bands were had you paid the money which was due from you?—No, I did not pay anything.

1301. Have you never paid anything?—Yes; I have paid since at different times my weekly contributions.

1302. Your bands and Platts's bands were both in the same spot, were they not?—Yes, they were.

1303. (*Mr. Chance.*) You say that you heard of two or three cases of bands being taken; supposing members of any Union are in arrear and do not pay, should you not be rather surprised if they were not rattened under those circumstances?—I do not understand you.

1304. Supposing that a man is in arrear and does not pay the money that he owes to the Union, should you not be rather surprised at the man's bands not being taken away?—I do not know anything at all about that.

1305. (*Chairman.*) When a man does not pay are not his bands always taken?—They are not always taken, that I know of.

1306. But occasionally?—I have known cases where they have been taken.

1307. (*Mr. Chance.*) And when they are taken you say you always go to the committee?—Yes, they generally go to the committee to see if the committee know anything about it.

1308. You say that the committee did not take them?—They did not take them.

1309. When you lose your bands, why do you and all the scissor-grinders go to the committee to get them back?—They think that they have taken them.

1310. Did you think that they had taken them?—No; I was in arrears, but I had not done anything to make them do anything to me.

1311. You tell us that you and all the scissor-grinders go to the committee when you lose your bands; you must have some reason for that; if you suppose that they do not take them, do you suppose that they have any influence over any person who has taken them?—I do not know.

1312. Then why do you go to the committee?—They go down on purpose to see if they can hear about them.

1313. (*Chairman.*) You think that they know where they are, and they can get them for you if they like?—I do not know.

1314. (*Mr. Barston.*) As a matter of fact you do go to the committee and you do get back your bands? —I went to Platts', and I got them back that time.

The witness withdrew.

SECOND DAY.

J. Thompson.

4 June 1867.

JOSEPH THOMPSON sworn and examined.

1315. (*Mr. Chance.*) Where do you live?—No. 80 Allen Street.

1316. And what are you?—I am the secretary to the Scissor Forgers' Society.

1317. What are you by trade?—I am a scissor forger by trade.

1318. How long have you been a scissor forger?—I served my apprenticeship to it.

1319. Is it a Union?—It is really a Union but that is the name we give it, the Scissor Forgers' Provident Society.

1320. You say you served your apprenticeship?—Yes.

1321. And then you became a journeyman?—Yes.

1322. And then did you progress from a journeyman to become a master, or are you still a journeyman?—I was a journeyman until the trade took me from the shop to devote the whole of my time as secretary to the trade.

1323. Then now as I understand you, you are simply and purely secretary to the Scissor Forgers' Society?—Exactly,

1324. Then how long have you been secretary to the Scissor Forgers' Society?—From the commencement of the Society, I think it was in March 1864—I beg your pardon I was not the secretary for the first three months.

1325. Would it be for three months after March then?—Yes.

1326. You say you call the Society a Provident Society; is it a Sick Society as well as a Trade Society?—It is.

1327. (*Chairman.*) Have you any written rules?—Yes.

1328. (*Mr. Chance.*) Are they contained in a book?—Yes.

1329. Are they written or printed?—Printed.

1330. Have you that book with you?—Yes.

1331. Will you let us look at it?—Yes (*producing a book*).

1332. Before going into that I will just ask you a question in reference to something else. Did you know John Platts who gave evidence here?—I do.

1333. Do you remember any scissors having been taken away belonging to Mr. Platts and Mr. Pryor?—I heard speak of the affair.

1334. That was somewhere towards the latter end of April was it not?—I should think so.

1335. Do you remember a conversation taking place about the loss of the scissors?—I remember the conversation.

1336. Did you have any conversation with Platts at all about it?—Not at all, only that when I waited upon him a week or two since he mentioned the affair to me.

1337. And that is the only conversation you ever had with him about it?—Yes.

1338. Did you ever have any conversation with Mr. Holmshaw about the loss of those scissors?—No.

1339. Do you mean to say you never had any conversation with Holmshaw at all about the scissors?—Not about the scissors.

1340. Nor about the loss of the scissors?—Nor about the loss of the scissors.

1341. Nor in reference to the scissors?—Nor in reference to the scissors.

1342. Did you have any conversation with Holmshaw in reference to the bands that had been taken from Platts?—I had not.

1343. You say you had not any conversation with Holmshaw about the bands?—I had not.

1344. Did you have any conversation with Holmshaw about any case of bands having been taken?—Not about bands.

1345. Nor about anything in reference to what we call rattening of any of Platts' property?—No, I have not.

1346. I must put this question to you. Did Holmshaw ever come to you to ascertain how many forger you employed?—I met him in the street and he asked me that question.

1347. When was that?—I have no note of that.

1348. But about what time was it?—Say a fortnight or three weeks from this time, I am not exactly sure.

1349. You met Holmshaw in the street about three weeks ago?—Yes.

1350. And what conversation took place between you then?—I think the first question that he asked was this, "How many forgers has Mr. Platts?" and I told him.

1351. (*Chairman.*) How many did you tell him?—One works in the place, and two or three work out, some belong to the society and some do not.

1352. (*Mr. Chance.*) Was this question put abruptly to you, or was it led up to by any other conversation?—It was not led to by any other conversation. I spoke simply of trade, "Do you find things "dull," or something to that effect.

1353. And then he asked you this question?—Yes.

1354. And you said you had one in and two out; what further passed then?—He told me there was some little difference between Platts and their society, and asked me if I should make it in my way to call upon Mr. Platts soon; and I told him I should have occasion to go there during the week. He said if I saw Mr. Platts would I bring round in conversation the unpleasantness that they had. I understood from him that Mr. Platts had refused to pay his contribution; and there is a rule or understanding between their society and ours, that supposing we wish to take out the grinders for a certain purpose, the men are supposed to lay down by our paying their expenses. If the grinders wish to obtain an object, and they can do so by stopping the forgers, of course they have the forgers to pay when they are not working; and the same rule applies to the grinders.

1355. (*Chairman.*) It is a kind of amalgamation in that way?—Yes.

1356. You back one another out?—We back one another out, but not to raise the price; it is simply to get in the contribution.

1357. (*Mr. Chance.*) That is to say, if there are arrears of the grinders' society they go to the forgers for the purpose of supporting the men on strike?—Yes.

1358. And conversely the grinders support the forgers?—Yes.

1359. So that there is mutual support between the two societies?—Yes, to get in the contribution.

1360. But there is no amalgamation between the societies?—No; there is no further amalgamation.

1361. What further conversation took place between you and Holmshaw upon this matter; you said he wanted to settle the differences between his Union and Platts?—Yes; I promised him that I would use my influence to that effect.

1362. Was that all that took place then?—That was the sum and substance of it. I cannot say every word that passed.

1363. (*Chairman.*) It is a common thing you say to take men out in order to compel them to pay their contribution?—I say it is a common thing, because we have a rule to that effect, although the rule has not been acted upon in many cases.

1364. (*Mr. Barstow.*) The threat to take the men out induces compliance with your rule?—We do not use the threat.

1365. (*Chairman.*) But you tell them that if they do not pay you will have to take the men out?—We do not go so far as to say that much.

1366. Then do you take them out without telling them a word?—It is usual for Mr. Holmshaw and myself if we have a dispute with the employers to go together, and we remind the employers that we have a certain rule that the grinders would come out if the forgers wanted it.

SECOND DAY.

J. Thompson.

4 June 1867.

1367. You remind them?—We just remind them to that effect.

1368. Has that in many cases the effect of inducing the masters to comply with your rules?—I cannot say that it has in many cases the effect upon the masters, but it has upon the men, and sometimes we go to the masters and sometimes to the men. Usually we go to the men first.

1369. You go to the men first?—We go to the men first.

1370. (*Mr. Chance.*) Then if the men do not pay their arrears what do you say to the men? What is the form of the reminder?—I will give you a case. I asked Mr. Holmshaw to go with me to a certain factory, and we had two men there that are in arrears.

1371. That is in your society?—Yes.

1372. Then you see the men, I suppose?—Yes.

1373. What do you say?—In that case Mr. Holmshaw would begin the conversation. He would represent the case that I had made application to their society to take out the grinders on account of the forgers there being in arrears.

1374. Would you go to those two men that are in arrears?—Yes.

1375. Then you would go to those two men who are in an arrear who are scissor forgers?—Yes.

1376. And what would Holmshaw say? — He would see what grinders were working there, and whether they would be likely to lay down if requested. Probably he would wrap up the conversation in his nice sort of way by saying, "We do not want " our men to come out. Why cannot you pay up " your contribution, and save us this trouble? We " do not want the forgers to take our men out," that is, the grinders. Generally that is sufficient.

1377. Then what I understand is this. The men understand from that that if they do not pay the forgers will take out all the men?—All the grinders, and they will understand that unless they pay the forgers may take out the grinders. They do not take them out in all cases.

1378. But they would understand that unless they paid the forgers would take out the grinders? — Probably.

1379. They might?—Yes.

1380. And in that case the grinders would be kept at the expense of the forgers?—Exactly.

1381. While they were on strike?—Yes.

1382. (*Mr. Chance.*) You say that they might be taken out?—Yes.

1383. But you say that it does not very often happen that the reminder or threat is put into execution?—Very seldom.

1384. But supposing that they do not consent, what is the course which you adopt with reference to the men?—We should probably wait a second time upon the employer.

1385. That is, after going to the men you go to the employer?—Yes.

1386. What would you say to the employer?—We would kindly ask him to use his influence with the forgers to cause them to pay. Sometimes the employer would say that he would have nothing to do with it.

1387. But we are speaking of the grinders now. You go to the grinders to ask them to pay, and therefore you go to the employers of the grinders to ask them to use their influence with the grinders to pay?—Yes.

1388. You are rather altering the term; it is the grinders?—Yes; I was simply giving you a case, and Holmshaw would do the same for me that I should do for him if requested.

1389. Then supposing that the masters are unsuccessful in inducing the grinders to pay, what is the course which you would next adopt?—Sometimes we should let the matter drop.

1390. On what occasions would you let the matter drop?—If we saw that it would cost us more money than the case was worth we should not enter into it.

1391. That is from motives of expediency; as far as the society was concerned you would let the matter drop?—Yes.

1392. But, supposing it would not cost you too much money, you would take other steps—what would you do then?—We have had a case where we have actually taken out the grinders.

1393. And you supported them while they were out?—Just so.

1394. But would it not be the case in all those instances, that when you think it worth while, if you do not get the contributions which you are seeking, you would take the grinders out?—I cannot say that in all cases that would be so. In many cases it would be so, but really I think we have only taken out two cases during the whole time that the society has been in existence, as far as my recollection serves me.

1395. How long has the society been in existence? —Since March 1864.

1396. But has that been for the reason which has been given by you that it would not be expedient to carry the threat into execution?—Yes, as a rule.

1397. Then you advocate a principle as I understand of using this threat over both men and employers for the purpose of getting your contributions?—I beg your pardon sir, we do not threaten.

1398. But you remind men that certain things will take place unless they do certain other things; is not that a threat?—It is generally wrapped up in a kind sort of way.

1399. (*Chairman.*) You know that the Act of Parliament will not allow you to threaten?—Just so.

1400. (*Mr. Chance.*) You say that it has not been carried out in more than two cases from motives of expediency?—Yes.

1401. So that after having applied to the men and not getting due contributions, and after applying to the employers then you draw out the grinders?—Yes, we have done so.

1402. And you would do so unless it were expedient for you to act in a contrary manner?—Just so.

1403. On this occasion to which I am referring, did Mr. Holmshaw say that he wanted to take Platts' men out in order to make Platts comply with the wishes of the Union?—He did not.

1404. He did not say so upon the occasion referred to?—No.

1405. Did he say so at any other time?—No.

1406. (*Chairman.*) He has never said that you were to take them out?—No.

1407. I see, so far as I have looked at these rules, which you were kind enough to give me, that one of your rules is to demand a fair remunerative price for scissor forging?—Yes.

1408. One of the objects of your society is to control the prices which are given?—Exactly.

1409. And the number of apprentices also you control?—Yes.

1410. That is to say you do not allow a man to have more than a certain number?—Just so.

1411. How many apprentices do you allow a man to have?—At present we do not allow a man to have any apprentice in the forging unless he is a journeyman's son or another forger's son.

1412. Supposing a man were to take a clever boy whom he met with who was not either his own son or another forger's son, he would be acting hostilely to your Union, and you would take steps against him?—We have not taken any steps.

1413. But it would be against the rules?—Exactly.

1414. Then I see that your society is for the purpose of maintaining the unemployed members, and also for decent interment at death?—Yes.

1415. As to the price for scissor forging, what is your rule about that?—There is a list price.

1416. Have you that list price with you?—I have not one with me.

SECOND DAY.

J. Thompson.

4 June 1867.

1417. Can you give me a notion of what it is?—Yes, it is a small book containing the prices of all the different kinds of scissors, and the different sizes of the patterns.

1418. Now, for instance, give me a size, how much must a man be paid for five-inch scissors?—One shilling and twopence a dozen.

1419. Are all forgers equally good?—No.

1420 There are good forgers and bad forgers?—Yes, very bad.

1421. I am not speaking of their moral character, but of their qualities for working?—Just so.

1422. There are bad workmen and good workmen?—Yes.

1423. In your price of 1*s.* 2*d.*, are all men according to your regulation entitled to have the same price?—Exactly.

1424. Whether they are good workmen or bad workmen?—Yes.

1425. What is the principal house in the scissors' trade in Sheffield?—Mr. Hobson's.

1426. If Mr. Hobson were to find a very good workman, and if it was worth his while to employ the workmen, and give him 1*s.* 2*d.* a dozen?—I am speaking now of a common pattern.

1427. I only want it as an illustration, it is a dozen is it not?—Yes, 14 pairs.

1428. Supposing that Mr. Hobson met with a very clever fellow indeed, a first rate workman, and instead of 1*s.* 2*d.*, it was worth his while to pay 1*s.* 4*d.*, and he said to the man, "I will give you 1*s.* 4*d.* a dozen for "all the dozens which you make for me," could he do it?—Yes, 1*s* 6*d.* if he thought proper.

1429. Then what do you mean by fixing the rate at 1*s.* 2*d.*?—We mean that we do not expect a man to make them for less than 1*s.* 2*d.*

1430. He might give them you say as much as 1*s.* 6*d.* if he liked?—Just so.

1431. Now, then, we will take the other case, you supply the workmen do you not?—Yes.

1432. Supposing Mr. Hobson takes a man in your Union, and supposing that a man in your Union was a very bad workman, or not a very good workman, and he finds that with regard to that workman, instead of it being worth his while to give him 1*s.* 2*d.*, it is not worth his while to give him more than 1*s.* a dozen, and Mr. Hobson says, "I will not give you more than "1*s.* a dozen." Will your Union stand that?—If Mr. Hobson will give the man a proper month's notice; after that he would have the preference of all men who wish to change their place of employment, or of such men as might be on the box at the time.

1433. If he were not satisfied with the man, you would not allow them to give less than 1*s.* 2*d.*?—No.

1434. But you would say, "Discharge the man by a "month's notice, and then you shall have the pick of "the men who are now on the box?"—Yes, or any man who wishes to change his place of work.

1435. But who is to select the man, are you to select the man, or is Mr. Hobson to select him?—I am supposing that there is a list of men who wish to change their places, and likewise of all men who are out of employment. Supposing that a manufacturer wants a man, it is usual for him to send for me, I should wait upon him, and I should ask him what kind of man he wanted, and what class of work, and generally I should be able to send a man, or recommend a man to his notice better than he could himself.

1436. I daresay you would; but do you impose upon him such a man as you select, or do you allow him to select a man for himself?—We allow him to choose a man for himself.

1437. Supposing that he knows a man on the box, and that he selects him, do you allow the master to select him, or do you say, "You must have this other man"?—No; we allow the master to have the preference, and he takes the man he thinks proper.

1438. From the list?—From the list.

1439. Now I am supposing that Mr. Hobson (about whom I know nothing. I am merely taking him as an instance) has got a lot of your Union men at work, and that he has discharged one of those men because he is a bad workman, and that you bring him a list of workmen from which to choose, he says, "I do not "like any of your men, but I know a non-union man "who will do my business a deal better than the men "in your list." What do you say to that?—We should object to it.

1440. If he employed him, what would be the result?—Probably the other men would cease work.

1441. You would tell them to cease work?—In many cases they would not want telling.

1442. But that is the rule of the society?—Just so.

1443. We must not finesse; it is known as well as possible, you know. It is an understanding amongst you, is it not, that the men go out if a master takes a non-union man?—Yes.

1444. I would carry the case further. Supposing that you are all of a mind, both the union men and the committee, and that all are agreed that it is the interest of the working men that that should be the course pursued; but supposing that one of the union men had said, "I do not agree to this; I shall still "hold with Mr. Hobson, and I shall work for him "notwithstanding the other men go out," what would happen to that man?—In some cases the other men would leave, and take no notice of him.

1445. How do you mean take no notice of him, send him to Coventry?—No, allow him to do the best he could for himself.

1446. And he would be allowed to remain?—Yes.

1447. He would be acting in opposition to you?—Yes.

1448. As a committee, what course should you adopt with reference to that man? Would he pay his contributions then, and continue a member or how would he be?—If he thought well to pay his contribution, we should receive it.

1449. And supposing he were to be ill, or anything of that kind, would you allow him the benefit of it or not?—We should.

1450. Then can a man go in opposition to the Union without any consequences happening to him?—Not in all cases.

1451. Supposing that a man goes in opposition to the Union, and the Union wants to compel him to comply with their rules, what is their course of proceeding?—I do not exactly understand you.

1452. I will take a case of the non-payment of money. Supposing a union man does not pay his money, or supposing a man does not obey the rules of the society. In law, you know, if a man does not fulfil his contract, there is a certain mode of compelling him by process of law; but you have no process of law at all. How do you act, supposing a man does not pay his "natty money," for example, to compel him to pay it?—If we take out the other forgers, or the other forgers come out, the manufacturer must of necessity have other men, so that he would very likely say to the man that was in, "Well now, you "must either pay this money, or you must leave my "service."

1453. And if he does not pay you take out the other men?—Yes.

1454. But supposing you did not think it worth your while, do you at all interfere with the man himself?—No. I may say that we have gone to very extreme cases.

1455. I know you have, and I believe you are inclined to tell us all about it. I will put it as fairly as possible. You know what rattening is?—Yes.

1456. It is a well understood thing in the trade, is it not?—It is. I do not exactly understand what you wish me to answer.

1457. I wish you to answer whether that is in accordance with the practice of the town?—Yes.

1458. And you know that it prevails to a very great extent?—It does.

1459. Will you describe to me what your notion of rattening is?—I think it is a very arbitrary mode of enforcing law, but at the same time it is the best way that we have got.

SECOND DAY.

J. Thompson.

4 June 1867.

1460. How do you mean that it is the best way you have got?—Because we could not summon the man for his contribution.

1461. As you find you cannot summon a man for his contribution, you say rattening is the only way of enforcing the payment of contributions?—I am speaking of trades generally.

1462. I am speaking of rattening; is it done by the trade?—Rattening in our trade is not recognized under any circumstances.

1463. Do you mean to say that rattening has never taken place in any case of scissor forgers?—I do not mean to say that, but I expect afterwards to be examined upon that point.

1464. I daresay you will, presently, but I want to come to the gist of the thing. Have you seen the "Independent" of this morning?—Yes.

1465. I saw in it a statement this morning; it seems a very clever and well-written article, and I daresay the gentleman who has written it knows a great deal about trade. I want to know your opinion upon this. They say that "rattening is the coercive power "which unions use to enforce compliance with their "rules by neglectful or refractory members."—Yes.

1466. Then the rattening is used by the trades generally?—Certainly.

1467. You know that as a matter of knowledge? we may take it as a matter of course we all know Mr. Leader, and I suppose he is the person who has written this. He knows trades, I suppose, as well as you do, and he tells us that it is known in the town that rattening is resorted to by the trade?—Yes; I believe it is an old established law in Sheffield and the neighbourhood.

1468. How do you mean an old established law?—I have read that before Unions were in force to anything like the extent they are at the present day, supposing that a man refused to comply with the rules of a factory, they would take away his tools.

1469. Where have you read that?—I think it was in one of our local papers.

1470. That is some years ago?—Yes; many years ago. I did not read it many years ago, I read it in a paper a short time since. It was speaking of rattening generally, and it laid it down as being an old established, and, in fact, an ancient custom.

1471. This is very useful, because if your mode of enforcing the penalties is not right, we hope to have law to enable you to enforce your penalties in some other and more desirable way, and if this is wrong it can be put an end to?—That is what we desire.

1472. Quite so. I knew I was speaking to an intelligent man. You say that this rattening is the ancient system. It is a bad mode of enforcing your rules, but it is the only mode you have got?—Quite so.

1473. Supposing that a man is a defaulter, what course do you pursue?—Are you speaking of my own trade?

1474. I am speaking of any trade you know of?—We take away his tools and hide them.

1475. You say that in your Union you do not know that it is being done?—Just so; will you ask me the question again, if you please, and then I shall understand?

1476. Has it never been done in your own Forgers' Union?—It has been done, but it has never been recognized by the committee.

1477. What was the instance in which it was done in your Union?—In the case of Mr. Darwin.

1478. Who is Mr. Darwin?—I think that he has a case to bring here.

1479. Who is Mr. Darwin?—He is a scissors manufacturer.

1480. Can you tell me how he had offended the Union?—I am rather afraid that we are drifting out of the argument, although you should know better than myself.

1481. I only want to know how this rattening is used; what had Mr. Darwin done?—I have a statement to make which will implicate my own conduct, if you think well that you should have it now.

1482. If you please. It may save us a great deal of trouble. If there is misconduct, we will give you, if you make a clear statement, a certificate directly which will protect you?—Mr. Darwin, scissors manufacturer, in Snow Lane, had in his employment as a forger, a person named Hague. He worked in the factory on Mr. Darwin's tools, I believe. He left, not Mr. Darwin's employment, but the firm.

1483. How is that; I do not quite understand that?—We have in our trade in-workers and out-workers. If a man works in he is supposed to work on the manufacturer's own tools, if he works out he works on his own tools, a journeyman's tools. By working out he would receive a little extra for his work.

1484. Then you mean that he left the factory and became an out-worker?—Just so; in order that a brother of his (Hague's) might come from the workboard branch, and commence forging, having served no apprenticehip. I waited upon him several times and asked him to commence contributing to our society, and to become a member of it. He rather objected, and said that he would see me again on the matter. As he became more efficient in his workmanship the consequence was, that instead of there being, I may say, three men working for the firm, there were four, on account of his coming in, and it had a tendency to cause one of the men to become short of employment. Mr. Darwin then took the advantage, and said, "Now "I am very short of work, but I will find you work if "you will do it at something less." I believe the man lowered the price of his labour 10 per cent., through Mr. Darwin's influence. Mr. Darwin said, "I will give you so much less," and he paid them 10 per cent. less.

1485. (*Mr. Barstow.*) All the men?—The one that I will mention named Clarke.

1486. (*Chairman.*) That was less than your list prices?—Yes; I believe then that the other men settled the price of labour at 10 per cent.

1487. You are not quite clear about that?—I am not quite clear about it. Mr. Darwin then appealed to Clarke to settle another 10 per cent., and Clarke refused to allow the 20 per cent., and the consequence was he turned him without work. He must then come on the box. Clarke was exasperated at the trade allowing the young man to come in without contributing. He appealed to me and said that we ought to do something. I said, "What can we do?" He said, "Here you have so many men on the box, why "not set them to work?" I understood what he meant—to commit some outrage. In order to draw him into conversation, I said, "What can thou do?" He replied that if I would give him permission he would rip open Hague's bellows, which really belonged to Mr. Darwin, and take away all the tools that he could carry. The smaller tools are supposed to belong to the journeymen.

1488. Then he could damage Mr. Darwin by cutting up the bellows?—Yes.

1489. And he could damage the journeymen by taking away their tools?—Yes. I replied, "If there "is one thing above another that I detest it is this "knife business," meaning cutting and destroying bellows. The conversation that followed I could not repeat exactly, but we came to the agreement that he should carry away the smaller tools.

1490. Did you tell him that he was to cut the things or not?—I distinctly told him not to do any such work.

1491. But you told him that he was to take away the tools?—Yes; at the same time I made this observation, that by destroying the tools we should cause enemies in the employers. By destroying the bellows Mr. Darwin would naturally be an enemy to our society, but by carrying away the smaller tools and hiding them we might return them when the men had commenced paying. For this piece of business I was to give him a sovereign. The result was that he went in the night and he took away the smaller tools and destroyed the bellows likewise. He was taken into custody and brought before the magistrates, and after

SECOND DAY.

J. Thompson.

4 June 1867.

being remanded once he was sent to Leeds assizes. I had then, at the time that he was taken, an impression that unless I furnished funds for the defence of this man, he would implicate me. Mr. Chambers was for his defence here at Sheffield, and he could have had the work, as I may term it, at Leeds, but he very modestly wanted to charge us 20*l.* This money I had to find at the time from my own purse. He was sentenced to nine months' imprisonment.

1492. He never disclosed your complicity at all?—No, there is that much credit due to him. I was further informed——

1493. By whom were you informed?—I cannot say a colleague, but an acquaintance of his.

1494. What is his name?—I would rather not disclose the name.

1495. Of what did he further inform you?—That unless I saw that his wife was maintained during his absence, if he should be committed,——

1496. That was before he was committed?—Yes.

1497. Was he in custody at that time?—Yes; he said that he would divulge the secret and bring me in custody.

1498. So that he put a rattening process upon you?—Yes, I have felt it ever since.

1499. No man is safe from it?—No. I agreed to give his wife 6*s.* per week, and she received that sum during the whole nine months of his absence. He is now returned.

1500. Did that come out of your own pocket?—It had to come out of my own pocket at first. The fact of his being taken in custody appeared to create strange enemies in the trade. No doubt had he done the work nicely without being caught they would have applauded him. It simply resolves itself into this: had he not been caught they would have said that some clever man had done it, but that being such a fool as to be caught it served him right, and so they turned round upon him. This practice was not recognized at all by the committee. I had simply taken it upon myself. I found myself in a dilemma, with very few friends. I knew from the feeling in the trade that I could receive nothing from the trade.

1501. Do you mean by the trade your own Union?—Yes; therefore all the money that I have received I have had to receive unknown to anyone. It cost me about 28*l.*

1502. From beginning to end?—Yes.

1503. Then you were saved the fee to Mr. Chambers of 20*l.*?—Yes, by going to Leeds we employed another gentleman much cheaper; I do not know whether he was a knobstick or not. I have received at different times, or at least I have taken at different times, from the funds of the society about 10*l.* 6*s.* 6*d.*

1504. On this account?—Yes, and that was during the first three months of his imprisonment. Whilst Clarke's wife was receiving this 6*s.* a week it appears that she could not hold her tongue; it was noised abroad and got to the manufacturers.

1505. What was noised abroad?—That the Scissor Forgers' Society was paying this woman (different rumours stated different sums) from 4*s.* to 10*s.* per week. When he had been there three months the committee was changed.

1506. Will you be kind enough to tell me the names of the committee during the past three months?—I could not just now, I have not the list with me.

1507. Could not you recollect, it is a short time ago?—It is nearly 12 months ago, and we change them every three months.

1508. Do you not recollect who was chairman during that time?—I do not recollect who was chairman; I know who was treasurer.

1509. Who?—Ashforth.

1510. Do you remember any other persons who were members of the committee during those three months?—I think, though I am not certain, that there was one Drakeford, one Fernley, and one Sorby, but I could not be so confident of the others.

1511. You say after the three months had passed the committee was changed?—Yes. One Gillott was appointed president, and Habbigham treasurer. At the very first sitting of the new committee I was asked by the new president, Gillott, what the trade was allowing Clarke's wife. I said, "Nothing." He told us that he had been called into a warehouse and informed by his employer——

1512. For whom did he work?—Messrs. Nowell's. He was informed by his employer that we were positively maintaining this woman. Of course, the new portion of the committee were equally inquisitive. I told thom that if they would leave it in my hands for a week I would give them sufficient proof that the society was not giving her maintenance. I felt my own welfare more at stake at that time than I do just now. I thought that if it was known that the trade was allowing, or that even I was allowing this woman anything, I might still be brought before a court of justice. I have not much of that fear just now. I got this wife of Clarke's to give her mark to a document which I think I have here stating that she was receiving no weekly maintenance from the Scissor Forgers' Society.

1513. Would you mind giving me that document?—No (*handing in the same*).

1514. "In consequence of reports having been " circulated to the effect that I, Ann, wife of John " Clarke, am in receipt of a certain weekly main- " tenance from the Scissor Forgers' Society, I beg " most emphatically to deny that I am receiving any " such maintenance; and further state that all such " reports are false.—ANN CLARKE—Her mark." Did you write that?—Yes.

1515. Would you mind my keeping it?—You are welcome to it. That had the desired effect.

1516. You showed this to the committee?—Yes; and I proposed to have some sheets printed and circulated among the employers, but the committee ruled that that was quite sufficient without having any printed. They, at least, were satisfied whether the employers were or were not.

1517. They were satisfied that the trade paid nothing?—Just so. I stated just now that I have received certain sums, altogether 10*l.* 6*s.* 6*d.*

1518. What is that sum?—I had to take that unknown to the committee during the first three months on account of the rumours being circulated and new committee-men taking office. I think that I was more narrowly watched afterwards. You will bear in mind that we pay scale out on Saturday evening at 6 o'clock. The whole of the committee are not supposed to be there, but they are supposed to meet on the Monday evening. It has sometimes happened that the treasurer and myself were there alone.

1519. During the time you were taking out that 10*l.* 6*s.* 6*d.*?—Yes; the treasurer even did not know that I had taken it. This was the way I got it, supposing I had received during the week in contributions (I collect the whole of it), 7*l.*—we had at that time men on the box who lived in the country, and we are permitted to pay those men before coming down to the meeting-house, and I obtained the money in sums varying from 9*s.* to 1*l.* by inserting men's names in the scale-book as having been paid by me, and I never have paid it. I do not know whether the treasurer suspected me or not, but at any rate he said nothing. I can only add that the act was my own folly and the trade had really nothing to do with it; and I here beg Mr. Darwin's pardon for having consented to so vile an act, but at the same time I hope that from this better days will appear.

After an interval.

1520. (*Chairman.*) Have you anything further to state?—No, Sir, I think not.

1521. That is the whole of your communication?—Yes.

1522. This is an act of rattening you say?—Yes.

1523. Done by your orders and not by the committee?—Yes.

1524. Have any scissor forgers been rattened during that time except in this case. Have there been

SECOND DAY.

J. Thompson.

4 June 1867.

any other rattenings at all during the time you were secretary ?—Yes.

1525. What other rattenings ?—There was one at Mr. Winter's, scissors manufacturer, Copper Street. I do not know how long it is since, perhaps nearly two years.

1526. Without going into particulars what was it for ?—I do not know.

1527. Was there a man who owed natty money working for Mr. Winter ?—If I remember correctly there were two or three forgers in the firm that belonged to the society, and one or two that did not.

1528. You say there might have been five working men, three union men and two non-union men ?—Yes, probably.

1529. Was that in August 1865 ?—I could not say.

1530. Now we are in 1867, this was about two years ago ?—It might be so.

1531. What was there wrong about this ?—I am not aware that there was anything particularly wrong; we had at different times waited upon the men that were not paying, and I do not know but that the men were comfortably situated together, the union and the non-union men. I do not know that there was anything particular in the matter.

1532. You have waited upon them to ask the non-union men to contribute ?—Yes, just so.

1533. Have the non-union men refused to contribute ?—Yes.

1534. Have you gone yourself ?—Yes ; I have also gone with a deputation from the committee.

1535. Who were they ?—I could not say.

1536. You recollect who went with you ?—I think that one would be Ball, that was then president. I am not certain upon the matter, but I think so.

1537. Who besides ?—I have gone with one George Straw.

1538. How many were there in the deputation ?—At that time we had deputations nearly weekly.

1539. How many were they composed of ?—It was left to me sometimes, and sometimes the committee would appoint a person to go with me, or two.

1540. You say they had refused to contribute. After their refusal did you hear of anything having been done to them ?—I heard that one pair of bellows had been destroyed. I am not sure whether there was one or two ; I cannot say just now.

1541. When was that ; how long after you had been to Mr. Winter's place ?—I do not know that I ever waited upon Mr. Winter personally. I had occasion to go every week.

1542. Had you been there a day or two before this happened ?—I could not say upon what day of the week it did happen, but I should be there on the Monday to collect the contributions from the men that were paying.

1543. You were there on the Monday to collect the money ?—Yes, every Monday.

1544. Do you recollect how soon after you were there on the last Monday you heard that the bellows had been cut ?—I was there the Monday after they were cut.

1545. And then you knew the fact ?—Yes.

1546. Had you heard of it before you went to Mr. Winter's premises ?—Yes.

1547. From whom did you hear it ? — I could not say who told me ; it was a rumour, the account going from ear to ear.

1548. It was a rumour ?—Yes, that Mr. Winter's shop had been rattened.

1549. Did you know before this cutting took place that they were going to ratten ?—I did not.

1550. You knew it was done on account of the trade ?—No, I did not.

1551. On what account was it done, if not on account of the trade ?—I am not in a position to say who did it or on what account it was done.

1552. I do not ask that. Did you at that time know it was done on account of the trade ?—When you speak of the trade, do you speak of the trade officially, or of any workman in the trade ?

1553. Whatever you like. Tell me what you knew about it ? whether you knew that it was done by men connected with the trade or the trade officially ?—My own impression is that neither the committee, nor the president, nor the treasurer of the committee, nor myself, knew anything of the matter.

1554. And what else have you to say ?—But I heard it was done.

1555. Who was to do it ?—I had no idea.

1556. You had no idea ?—No.

1557. Who had an interest in its being done except the trade ?—It might be through personal malice.

1558. Anything else ?—Or it might be that some person in the trade would feel himself aggrieved by the men not contributing to the society.

1559. And such person who felt himself aggrieved might have done it ?—Yes.

1560. But in doing this the damage was done to Mr. Winter and not to the men ?—The damage, so far as the bellows cutting went, was Mr. Winter's loss.

1561. And he is not a member of the Union at all ?—No.

1562. Unless it were the trade, it must have been some person who had a personal malice to Mr. Winter ?—If my memory serves me well, at the same time there were some tools missing which would belong to the men.

1563. Does your memory serve you as to whether there were two bellows cut or only one ?—I could not say.

1564. You recollect that there were certainly one pair of bellows cut and tools taken away ?—Yes.

1565. Upon that what do you say about it ?—On the following Monday I went to Mr. Winter's firm as usual. He very calmly asked me who I had sent to cut his bellows ? I emphatically told him that I had sent no one to cut his bellows. He said that he believed that he knew who had done it, but he had no proof. I told him if I was in his place, and knew who had done it, I should certainly enter an action. He then said he was not sure, because he had no proof.

1566. Had you any belief at that time as to who had done it ?—No.

1567. How many workmen were there on the union working at Mr. Winter's at that time ?—Belonging to the society, do you mean ?

1568. Yes ?—Two or three ; I think three.

1569. Then the only persons, if it were a trade matter, who were interested in this, were either the trade as a body or the two or three men who were working with Mr. Winter ?—The only persons who would be interested in it ?

1570. Yes ?—I do not know what personal malice any other one might have had.

1571. I am putting it as a trade matter. If it were a trade matter it would either have been done by the trade itself, or, as you suggest, by one of the men working there ?—Yes, if it was a trade matter.

1572. Upon which Mr. Winter charged you as being the organ of the trade for having it done ?—As far as asking me who I had sent.

1573. Were the men who were working on the box or off the box at the time ?—I believe, though I am not certain, that at that time we had one man on the box that had previously been in Mr. Winter's employment.

1574. Did he continue on the box ?—By the way I believe I am wrong, because I know one of the men that worked there had to leave Mr. Winter's employment at the time at which we struck for an advance of wages, so that I think the probabilities are that we had not had the man on the box—at that time he would be in his employment.

1575. Did you make any inquiry of the men as to whether they had been parties to this ?—I spoke to the men on the matter.

1576. Whom did you speak to ?—I spoke to Smith, who is now in America.

1577. What did you speak to him for, did you think that he had done it ?—No ; I had no reason to believe that the man had done it.

SECOND DAY.

J. Thompson.

4 June 1867.

1578. Why did you speak to him?—Simply in conversation.

1579. What did you ask him?—I could not exactly tell what questions I did put to the man, probably how many tools had been missing.

1580. Only to know the fact, not to charge him at all?—No.

1581. Did the committee, as a committee, take any steps to ascertain who had done it?—I believe there was no resolution passed on it, but it was canvassed over in the committee.

1582. It is a singular feature in this that, although you did not instigate it at all, it is exactly like the one that you did instigate?—Yes.

1583. Then in the one, which you say you did instigate, you caused the bellows to be cut?—I beg pardon, I did not.

1584. Then the bellows were cut; I know you make that distinction?—Yes.

1585. The tools were taken away?—Yes.

1586. In this case the bellows were cut, and the tools taken away?—Yes.

1587. Upon your oath did not you authorize that to be done?—Upon my oath I did not; such outrages were committed before our society was in existence.

1588. Tell us distinctly about this what you have told us about the other?—I will.

1589. I suppose you are aware that Mr. Winter had told you distinctly that he had no proof in this case?—Yes.

1590. He told you that?—Yes.

1591. You have made a statement with respect to Mr. Darwin, were you aware that Mr. Darwin was coming to make a statement before us?—I did hear that Mr. Darwin had received a summons to appear before this Commission.

1592. Have you ever heard of any other case of rattening that you can tell us about in your Union?—Since the Union has been together?

1593. Since you have been the secretary?—Yes.

1594. How many cases of rattening of scissor forgers are you acquainted with?—There was one about five years since.

1595. Where was that?—At Mr. Hunter's.

1596. Mr. Edwin Hunter's?—Yes, before our society was established; he had two pairs of bellows cut, and I think some small tools taken away.

1597. Do you know what that was for?—I do not.

1598. You do not know what it was for?—No; I could say what the rumour was.

1599. What was the rumour?—At that time there was a new process of scissor forging just coming into operation. I need not describe the process.

1600. No; was it by machinery?—No; I believe that the workman that had adopted the new principle was working in one of the hearths, I think so from what I have heard, and that his bellows were cut, and another pair in the same shop.

1601. Did the new process interfere with the price of wages?—No.

1602. How would the trade be affected by it?—I cannot see that the trade is in any way affected by it, in fact, I think of the two, that when a person is thoroughly acquainted with the new process it is rather a saving to the men than otherwise.

1603. It threw the men out of work who did not adopt it?—It could not make them much quicker.

1604. Was it believed at the time that it would interfere with the work?—Yes, by some.

1605. Can you tell me of another case?—About two and a half years since there was one, Abraham Parker, he was not a member of our society.

1606. Was he a member of any society?—No.

1607. A non-unionist?—Yes.

1608. What is he?—A scissor forger, he was proved to have entered a shop, and taken away scissors belonging to a non-unionist, and to have left in the fire the scissors belonging to a unionist.

1609. Was he tried?—Yes.

1610. Where?—At Sheffield, and sentenced to twelve months.

1611. For what was he convicted?—For stealing scissors; there was this particular feature in that, that he knew whose scissors were in the fire, he took away the scissors of a man not paying, and left in the fire the scissors of the man that was paying, thereby making it appear at once that it must be a trades' union outrage, because the scissors of the man that was paying were left there.

1612. He took the scissors of the non-payer?—Yes.

1613. This was a non-unionist who was in default to the club?—Yes.

1614. He was a unionist who had not paid up his natty money?—I believe at that time that the person whose scissors were stolen had never entered a society.

1615. Do you know whether the person whose scissors were taken was a member of a Union or not?—He was not in a Union.

1616. Did he intend to destroy them by putting them in the fire?—After we have forged them we have to put them under a large coke of clean coal and let the fire die out on them, so that in the morning they would be soft and the men may work on them afterwards; and the young man had moved away the fire and taken out what he wanted, and nicely covered up again those that he did not want.

1617. He had stolen a certain quantity?—Yes.

1618. Are those all the cases that you know?—I believe there is another.

1619. What is the other?—One Needham who worked at Mr. Hall's—it used to be Hall and Collis—had some tools stolen.

1620. What next?—I do not know that they were ever returned to him.

1621. Was he in default to the Union?—I believe at that time he had never joined it, or if he had he must have paid very little indeed.

1622. Was he in default?—Yes, he was in default.

1623. He must have joined the Union if he was in default?—Yes.

1624. Did he owe money to the Union?—Yes.

1625. He had not paid up his arrears of natty money?—No.

1626. When was Needham's case?—It would be the last winter but one, perhaps 18 months since.

1627. You were secretary then?—Yes.

1628. Was there anything else but his tools taken?—No.

1629. Do you know any other case connected with your Union?—No; I believe that is the whole.

1630. In those cases do you know the persons who committed the offences?—I do not.

1631. Have you reason to believe that they were done and things taken in consequence of trades' disputes?—I can scarcely say that I have reason to believe so.

1632. You said just now that you thought they were in consequence of trades' disputes, say what you believe now; do you believe that those are the result of trade dispute?—I do not know.

1633. You very frankly told me that it is the mode, oppressive if you like, of enforcing the payment of the money; what reason have you to doubt that these are things that come within this class?—Why should I suspect any one?

1634. What is your belief about it. You are a part of the Sheffield public. We are told in the Sheffield newspaper that that is the mode of enforcing the rules of the clubs and societies, that is in one of your papers. You say it is correct?—Yes.

1635. Have you any reason to doubt that these came within the same class?—I do not wish to be too hard upon our unionists.

1636. What is your belief about it?—Probably they were.

1637. Can you at all tell me what is the kind of machinery that is adopted when they resort to this kind of expedient of enforcing their rules. When the trade finds that a man will not pay his natty money what is the course of proceeding that they adopt?—I do not think that I can give you that

SECOND DAY.

J. Thompson.

4 June 1867.

information that some of our secretaries could. I have heard it said that two men shall be in a beer house and by conversation it becomes known that one of them owes money to the society without any one further knowing of it.

1638. Do they talk together?—We will suppose three men. Supposing three men were in a beer-house, and began to talk of trade matters, and in conversation it is found that one of the three owes money to the society, trades' unionists as a rule would not be surprised to hear of that man's tools being taken without the interference of any official or any one further than the three.

1639. If it is the practice to enforce it by taking away their bands and so on, of course people would not be surprised, but I want to know what is the course of proceeding that they adopt. They meet together, there are two men, do they bring the third man in and talk, or how is it done?—I have scarcely had the experience that you will require in this matter.

1640. You will give us as much as you know?—Yes.

1641. What is the course?—Although these heavy charges are generally laid to the officials, it is my firm opinion that in many cases the officials of trades unions have nothing whatever to do in the matter.

1642. It is only in some?—Yes, just so.

1643. When the officials have nothing to do with them, how is it done?—I could not tell.

1644. You have said now here are three men come into a public-house, let us have the public-house named?—Take my public-house.

1645. You keep a public-house?—Yes, the "Corner Pin," Allen Street.

1646. We will suppose they came into your public-house?—Yes.

1647. Is there anybody present besides the two persons?—The three.

1648. No one else is present?—No.

1649. Who are the three, there is the man who is in default, who are the other two?—Brown and Robinson.

1650. Who are they?—Two men that may or may not belong to the society.

1651. How do they get to talk upon this matter, have they been sent there?—No; suppose they have not been sent there, they have happened to meet.

1652. Then how is that, the man who is a defaulter happens to meet the two other men, and when they are in your public-house they talk, and he says, "I "owe the Union 10*s*., and I will not pay them it," is that the sort of conversation?—Yes.

1653. Then you are not surprised to hear if he makes such a statement as that, that his goods are rattened?—No, because the other two men would look upon it as being a crime.

1654. They would do it as a sort of moral obligation?—Yes.

1655. Their morality would be affected by this, and they would think it their bounden duty to go and steal his bands?—Yes.

1656. That is their sense of morality?—Yes; there are such men to be found in all trade societies, and it requires the firm hand of an official to keep some such characters down.

1657. Have you found that it required your firm hand to keep them down?—Yes.

1658. Have you exercised a firm hand upon them?—Yes.

1659. Often?—Yes, when men have hinted to me that such and such deeds ought to be done, I have repeatedly said this to them, "If ever you do such "and such acts, you must not tell me, because I will "tell no lies."

1660. What have they asked you to be permitted to do, who has asked you for instance?—Do you wish me to name anybody?

1661. Yes; you are here to make full disclosures. Who has asked you to be permitted to do anything?—Does it really come upon me to tell you that?

1662. Yes, who has asked you to be permitted to do any such crime. You come here to make full disclosures?—There was a person named Smith that worked on my tools.

1663. What did he tell you that he wanted to do?—I do not say that any man ever told me he wanted to do anything.

1664. What did Smith tell you?—Speaking of the men that would not pay, he said that they ought to be rattened.

1665. Whom did he say ought to be rattened?—I could not find out any particular man.

1666. Smith came and told you that you were to be a party to something?—I am supposing a case.

1667. You said that there were bad men at that time in every union, and it required a strong hand to keep them down, and you used your strong hand to keep the men down?—Yes.

1668. Who are the men that you used your strong hand to keep down?—I spoke of Smith.

1669. Is he the man you used a strong hand to keep down?—Yes.

1670. When did he want to do anything wrong?—During the time he worked in my shop, that would be 18 months since.

1671. What did he want to do 18 months ago?—I did not say he wanted to do anything.

1672. What did you put the strong hand upon him for?—I have not a very good memory for names, there is one Hague.

1673. What about Hague?—Hague and Smith were acquainted with each other, and were speaking of Hague not paying his contribution.

1674. Who is Hague?—A person in our works, at Mr. Cousins's—he was a neighbour of Smith's.

1675. He works for Cousins now?—Yes.

1676. Where did he work then?—I think he went to work on Shales Moor.

1677. For whom?—I think he would work out at that time for Cousins, he works in Cousins' factory now.

1678. Now what as to Hague?—I told him that Hague was not paying, and he used some such expression as this. I could not exactly say the words, that a bit of night business would do him good. I told him that I did not like night business.

1679. What next?—And if ever any of our men took it on themselves to go in the night for another man's tools they must not tell me, because if brought to justice I should tell no lies. I think that would have the desired effect.

1680. You think that would have the desired effect?—Yes, with that man.

1681. You think that would have, or did have, the desired effect?—Did have.

1682. What do you call the desired effect?—Simply that he did not go in the night.

1683. Was Hague rattened?—No.

1684. Never?—No.

1685. Is that the only person that you used the strong hand to?—That is the only person that I could mention as pointing out a direct case; but still it has always been my impression that any official wanting a deed doing would not need to go far to get it done.

SECOND DAY.

J. Thompson.

4 June 1867.

1686. By any official you mean supposing you should want it to be done you would have had no difficulty in getting a man that would do it ?—Yes.

1687. That has always been your opinion ?—Yes.

1688. Has it been your opinion also, that officials have got men to do it ?—In some cases.

1689. Do you know of any case in which officials have done so ?—No.

1690. Then why do you say so ; from what have you drawn the inference, and in what case have you drawn the inference that an official has done so ?—Because, as I said a short time since, that it is looked upon as being an ancient law.

1691. There is no crime in it at all ?—No.

1692. It is not thought a crime ?—It is simply the best law that they have got.

1693. If you do not think it a crime amongst your officials, you talk about it ; and if a man hired another man to go and ratten anybody you tell one another ?—No, we do not.

1694. Why not ?—Officials, as a rule, do not communicate this to each other. I speak from my own knowledge. I do not know that ever any official came to me and said he had hired a man to do a certain deed.

1695. Has he not ?—No.

1696. Have you never heard from any one at all ?—I do not know that I have.

1697. You have gone a long way and you must go further ?—I should think you would not wish me to go farther than the truth.

1698. Tell the whole truth ?—I say decidedly that according to my own memory at present I do not know of any official that ever told me that he had hired a man to do any act of darkness.

1699. Will you swear that no official connected with any Union in the town has ever told you that he has ever instigated any act of what you call " darkness " ?—I will swear I do not remember any.

1700. Will you swear none has ?—I will.

1701. You will swear that ?—I will.

1702. I caution you about this, because we have a good deal of private information ; I want to know upon your oath, have you never received any information from any one of the officials ?—I never have.

1703. Have you ever been informed by any official in the trade that he had known who had done an act of darkness, we will call it rattening, I will not put it further?—Will you ask me the question again.

1704. Has any official ever told you of his own knowing of a person who had committed an act of rattening ?—No.

1705. You mean to say that no one has ever told you that he knew So-and-so had been rattened, and that John Smith had rattened him ?—I never heard such a thing.

1706. How is it, if it is not thought a crime, and these things are constantly happening, and that you a prominent person in the trade have not heard about it ?—Because the law of the land has its strong hand upon it.

1707. And you never heard of anybody ?—No, I never heard any one tell us that he had hired a man to do this.

1708. Two men come into a room and they hear a man say he has not contributed to the Union, and they ratten him out of their sense of justice ?—I think I made the observation that I was then speaking from what I had heard, not from what had come under my own observation.

1709. Have you never heard of the case of a man's name being selected out of a hat ?—The most I have heard of such things I read in the "Daily Telegraph."

1710. Is this a thing known in trade matters ; is it customary amongst Unions to draw in a hat for the person who shall do any act of rattening ?—The most I know of it is in that some of our townsmen have written to local papers who say they do know it.

1711. Can you tell me of any person who knows it ; has any person told you he knew it ?—No.

1712. Have you heard of any person who said he knew it ?—You do not mean what I have read, but what I have heard.

1713. Yes ?—I have not heard.

1714. Have you read ?—I think a letter in one of our local papers, mentioned a person being on a committee when the hat business was introduced.

1715. Will you describe what the hat business is. That was an anonymous letter ?—Yes.

1716. What kind of business is the hat business ?—He described it as having small balls in a hat and each member of the committee drawing one ; one of the balls was marked. Each person took his own ball, put it in his pocket and walked away with it, and the one that had the marked ball was supposed either to do some act of rattening or to get it done.

1717. Have you ever known of the system being adopted ?—Never.

1718. Have you ever in your communications with your committees heard that it was adopted by them ?—Never.

1719. But it was stated in public print anonymously, that that is the course adopted ?—Yes.

1720. In that case no man would know who did anything ?—Just so.

1721. No one would know as long as the man kept his own counsel ?—Nobody would know.

1722. It would be known to the committee that there was something to be done, the thing would be done, but by whom nobody would know ?—Yes, if the hat business was introduced to the committee it would be so.

1723. Have you ever heard of any mode of suggesting to a person to do this kind of thing by the committee, or is it done ; you say you have not known of the hat business, how have you heard that it is done ?—I do not know that I have heard.

1724. You are a member of an influential body in Sheffield, you are the secretary of a society ?—Yes, but I have not mixed up with the secretaries as much as some have.

1725. You believe it to be done sometimes you say by the Trades Unions, sometimes by individual members of Trades Unions, and sometimes by men having malice and so on ; do you know when it is done by Trades Unions, in what way it is done ; do they hire a man and pay him ?—I do not know.

1726. You do not know at all ?—No.

1727. You can give no information upon the subject ?—Only the information that I have given of myself.

1728. As to yourself, were you aware at the time you made this statement to us that Mr. Darwin had been already in communication with us ?—Yes.

1729. You did know it ?—Yes.

1730. You did not know what he had told us ?—No.

1731. And did not you, after hearing that Mr. Darwin had been with us, address a letter to our secretary telling him that you were anxious to make a communication ?—Yes ; the detective that brought the summons took that letter back.

1732. But you had at that time heard that Mr. Darwin had been with us ?—Yes.

1733. Shall I read the letter ? "Mr. Barker, Sir—

SECOND DAY.

J. Thompson.

4 June 1867.

" I am willing to give information respecting the " destruction of small tools on the premises of Mr. " Darwin, scissors manufacturer, Snow Lane, which " took place ten months ago. Yours truly, Joseph " Thomson, Secretary to the Scissor Forgers' " Society."—Yes.

1734. You wrote that letter ?—Yes.

1735. Had you up to the time of this letter ever told your society anything about it ?—No.

1736. Your society learn now for the first time that you were the instigator of that act of rattening ?—Yes.

1737. They knew nothing till now ?—They knew nothing till now; the only few words I said last night were simply this to our committee. We met last night, and I told them that to day I should surprise them, but I would tell them nothing further at present.

1738. I suppose they had, up to this time, considered you as an honest man ?—Yes.

1739. And as far as you believe, up to this time they have no knowledge at all that you have been dishonestly abstracting their money ?—None, and I feel the sense of shame very much.

1740. And from the earnings of the working men of this Union you have, for your own purposes, and to cover your own misdeeds, appropriated the sum of 10*l.* 6*s.* 6*d.* ?—Yes.

1741. And the men from whom you had taken it would have been all liable to be called upon unless you had made this revelation to pay up arrears in consequence of your having taken it ?—No, it does not alter the men's arrears.

1742. Have you an auditor ?—Yes.

1743. Who is he ?—We have two auditors appointed once a quarter.

1744. Who was the auditor during the time you took away from the society the 10*l.* 6*s.* 6*d.* ?—I think John Hernshaw.

1745. Who was the other ?—William Habbigham.

1746. What were their duties ?—To look through the amount of contributions received and the expenditure.

1747. And they had to see that the balance was all right every week ?—No, once a quarter.

1748. And I understand you to say that the money which was due from persons living in the country appeared not to be paid when in point of fact they had paid it ?—No, it was not in the income ; but I wrote down a person's name as having received 10*s.*, and at the same time the man had not received the 10*s.*

1749. Have you got your books here ?—Yes.

1750. Bring the books and show me where it is in the books. (*The witness explained the same to the Chairman.*)

1751. September the 3rd; what year is this, the year does not appear ?—No.

1752. On September the 3rd you say there is an entry made by you having paid to George Hall 15*s.* ?—Yes.

1753. Where does George Hall live ?—He works at Mr. Platts'.

1754. Where does he live ?—At Brightmoor Street.

1755. You say you have put down having paid him 15*s.*, whereas you never did pay him ?—Yes.

1756. Whom else have you put down ; September 10th, William Fernley, junior, 15*s.* ?—Yes.

1757. You never did pay him ?—No.

1758. Where does Fernley live ?—Furness Hill.

1759. When did you make that entry ?—About a fortnight since.

1760. What do you call this ?—My pocket book.

1761. I see you have made mention of entries here: September 3rd, 15*s.* ; September 10th, 15*s.* ; September 17th, 15*s.* ; September 24th, 1*l.* ; October 1st, 1*l.* ; October 8th, 12*s.* ; October 15th, 19*s.* ; October 22nd, 11*s.* ; November 5th, 11*s.*; November 12th, 18*s.*; November 19th, 12*s.* ; November 26th, 9*s.* ; December 3rd, 16*s.* 6*d.* ; December 10th, 13*s.*; Total, 10*l.* 6*s.* 6*d.* ?—Yes.

1762. I see on the opposite page there is put 17*l.* and 11*l.* ; what is that ?—That is as near as I can recollect money paid for the defence of Clark ; 11*l.* would be the money his wife received.

1763. 17*l.* and 11*l.* so paid and so received are the total sums that you have paid on his account ?—Yes, as near as I can tell.

1764. When did you make these entries ?—A fortnight since.

1765. What did you make them for ?—For the purpose of bringing them here.

1766. Did you do it for the purpose of getting a certificate if you made the disclosures, and protecting yourself from the consequences of your misconduct ?—I have had it on my mind ever since the act was committed. I did not give that man the permission or authority to destroy the bellows. I did give him permission to take away small tools. For that I was to give him 1*l.*, he, unfortunately for me as well as for himself, was taken into custody, and for fear of being brought up before the justices, I had the money to pay out of my own pocket.

1767. What were these men that you paid 15*s.* and 18*s.* and 1*l.* ?—Men that sometimes were on the box.

1768. How does the auditor know whether a man is on the box or not ; have you a list, or what check have they upon the men being really on the box ?—There is a committee or a portion of the committee that ought to come and see the money given out. At present one half of the committee meet to see the money paid.

1769. Then, according to this, on these days of September the 3rd, first, was there a person present at the committee to see the money paid ?—I daresay there was.

1770. On the occasion when you put this September 3rd down as having paid it to George Hill. George Hill would be known to the committee men ?—Yes.

1771. How was it that it was possible for you to put George Hill's name in, unless he were a man on the box ?—Suppose I had received 7*l.* in contribution, in handing over the money to the treasurer, I say the contribution is 7*l.*, my wages is 7*l.* There are the committee expenses so much. I have already paid George Hill, and any other person that I might have paid. I give him the difference.

1772. But they know whether Hill is on the box or not ?—At that time the committee did not attend as they do now.

1773. But the committee now know everybody who is on the box ?—Yes.

1774. Have you any book which shows what persons are on the box or not ?—I keep a list.

1775. Have you the list now that you kept for September the 3rd ?—No, I have not.

1776. Can you produce the list that you kept at the time ?—When a man is on the box he does not pay his contribution.

1777. Show the list that you kept for September the 3rd, you kept a list you say ?—I have not got the list.

1778. Where is the list of any time from September the 3rd to December the 10th ?—I have not the list.

1779. What has become of them ?—When I said I kept a list, I should have said that that is a portion of my duty.

1780. You had the committee sitting all that time ?—Yes.

1781. Was it a portion of the committee's duty to look over the list, and see who was on the box or not ?—No ; I do not know that it has ever been done.

1782. Not to see who was on the box ?—No. On the committee night, which is Monday night, I would say, " We have such a man come on the box to-day, " or we have such a man gone off." The men meet me the first three days in the week at dinner time,

SECOND DAY.

J. Thompson.

4 June 1867.

and on Saturday night they come for their scale, and their scale is paid to them. If a man was to come who was not on the box at the time, I should tell the society that he had no right to his scale.

1783. But you say that you have kept lists, do you keep them in a book or a detached list?—I ought to say that I ought to have kept lists.

1784. Have you ever kept lists?—Yes.

1785. Where are they; just show me any lists?—I have not them here.

1786. You must produce them, you were summoned to produce everything you have; why have not you brought the list?—At the commencement of the society, when I was not so conversant with the names of the men, I did keep a list; but since I have known the men more intimately I have not put myself to that trouble.

1787. How long is it since you ceased to keep lists?—I have an old book with pencil lists in.

1788. Why did not you bring it to-day?—It was an old book that belonged to the old society, and the only use I had for it was simply to scribble in pencil.

1789. If there were no lists, how was the auditor to know whether these sums had been paid or not?—Such a question has never been asked.

1790. You have got the funds of the union men who are subscribing and contributing to you, and they think they have got regular officers who look after their funds, and see that they are properly applied; they ought to see that they are properly applied, and they ought to see that a man is on the list if you put him down as having had money paid to him?—The committee are supposed to be responsible.

1791. And they look upon you as the secretary, to whom they pay wages of 1*l.* a week, as keeping lists by which the auditor shall be able to check your conduct?—Admitting that my conduct is faulty, I think you will not crush me more than necessary.

1792. I want to know where the list is?—I have not kept a list, only at the commencement of the society when the names of the men were not so familiar to me, at that time I did keep a list of all the men's names, and I made a rule every dinner time of calling over the men's names; but since then I have not done it.

1793. I cannot understand how the auditor can audit this account, unless he has something to audit it by. Supposing you were to tell him you had paid me 20*l.* for the week ending September the 3rd, and you never paid me 6*d.*, how is the auditor, who sits there for the protection of the union men who have sent in their natty money, to know whether it is truly paid or not; how is the auditor to know whether you have been doing right or not?—It is taken for granted that I am honest.

1794. If the auditor is to take it for granted that you are honest, what is the use of the auditor?—I might have said that he has taken it for granted that the committee have attended to their duty.

1795. Then he would know that the committee in attending to their duty would have a list of the persons who are on the box?—That is a list.

1796. These are the entries of the money that you have paid?—That is the list.

1797. You keep a list of the men who are on the box?—If an employer applies to me next week for the men I look at that book; there are the whole of the men that there would be employed or out of employment.

1798. Then in point of fact this is a list that you do not keep?—The reason I give that answer is this, that when the society was first formed I kept another list, and called over that list every day.

1799. When was it that you gave up that list?—I think I kept the list the first two quarters.

1800. When you were the secretary?—After we began to pay scale.

1801. You then gave it up?—I believe so.

1802. Are there any other men's names put down here as having received money who have not done so?—The money that is there put down and not really paid is not all down to one man.

1803. Who were they; there is Hill and Fernley, and who besides?—William Caldwell.

1804. Who besides?—Henry Gillott.

1805. Who besides?—I believe Charles Ward.

1806. They are all mentioned in this little book of the dates?—Yes.

1807. You are the treasurer?—No; the secretary.

1808. What are the duties of the treasurer?—To receive the money and to pay out scale; to keep the money in his own possession in sums less than 10*l.*

1809. Therefore as secretary you would go round, or a collector would collect these monies, and when he had more than 10*l.* he would pay it over to the treasurer?—I pay the money over every week to the treasurer.

1810. Then it is no part of your duty to pay this money, it is the treasurer's business?—Yes.

1811. It is your duty to keep a list of the persons that are on the box?—Yes.

1812. But it is part of the treasurer's duty to put down the money which is paid, because he pays it?—No; the treasurer sits with the money and gives Hill 15*s.*, or whoever it may be; the treasurer pays the money and I put it down in a book.

1813. Then the treasurer was by when you wrote it?—Yes; when I wrote that, but not the name of Hill.

1814. The treasurer would be present when you wrote this?—Am I to understand the whole of the names there?

1815. I ask you the question, it is the treasurer's duty to pay the money, and it is your duty to supply him with a list of the persons on the box?—Yes.

1816. Does he put down the figures that are there?—I put down the figures.

1817. Are these your figures or his?—Mine.

1818. He was present when you put down these figures?—No; I put down my own wages, the committee's expenses, and the name of the person whoever he might be whom I wished to receive the money when I had not paid it. I put down the names and the figures, and when I came to the treasurer I said, "The contribution is so much, and I have already "paid this."

1819. You told him that you had paid this?—Yes.

1820. Is that the usual thing. I find that you have paid as much in one week as 11*l.* 1*s.*, 10*l.* 16*s.*, 10*l.* 4*s.*, 9*l.* 16*s.* 2*d.*, 10*l.* 6*s.* 8*d.* Is it customary for you, the secretary, to pay this money and not ask the treasurer to pay it?—The treasurer does pay it.

1821. You say you told him that you paid this on account?—Suppose that I had received 7*l.* during the week, instead of handing over the 7*l.* I say, "Pay me "my wages and the committee expenses that I have "already paid." I say that I have received 7*l.*, and I have already paid this much, my wages, committee expenses, and such a person as I may have paid the scale to.

1822. If you had only received 7*l.* for the week?—Yes.

1823. Was not this all written at the same time?—Yes; this book up to December was written all at one time; you notice that the names of Hill and of the different men I have pointed out who have received money are some in the middle and some at the bottom, but in the other book which I have destroyed—

1824. We never heard of the book that is destroyed. I want to see how it is that your auditors should pass it over. I should have thought that if the treasurer paid the money it would come in in different figures, and not have been written at one time; this has all been written at once; this is not the real book then, there is another book?—There was another book.

SECOND DAY.

J. Thompson.

4 June 1867.

1825. Up to what time did you keep that book ?—Up to last Christmas.

1826. Did it contain entries of monies received and paid by you ?—Monies paid.

1827. The monies paid by you up to the end of December ?—Yes.

1828. On behalf of the trade ?—Yes.

1829. What has become of that book ?—I burnt it.

1830. When did you burn it ?—It would be at Christmas, at the time I took a copy of it.

1831. Was it a book like this ?—Yes.

1832. Was it full or empty, or how, or like that ?—Like that up to Christmas.

1833. Is this a copy of it ?—Exactly. When I say that is a copy of it I do not say that every name is inserted in rotation as they are there, but the names and the sums of money received are the same.

1834. Why are they not in the same rotation ?—simply that they may not be detected.

1835. That was to avoid detection ?—Yes.

1836. What was your object in destroying the book ? was that with the same object also, to avoid suspicion ?—Yes.

1837. You swear that you have destroyed that book ?—I do swear.

1838. Where did you destroy it ?—In my own kitchen fire.

1839. Was anybody present at the time you destroyed it ?—There might have been my own little children.

1840. Did anybody see you destroy it ?—I do not think they did ; I believe not.

1841. You had kept that book up to December ?—Up to December.

1842. Had you passed your accounts with that before the auditor ?—I am not sure whether the December account was passed in it.

1843. Were the other accounts passed for September, October, and so on ?—We passed the accounts quarterly ; I mean the quarter ending December.

1844. If you knew that that book contained entries, and you were so afraid of detection that you burnt the book, and then altered the rotation in which the monies were paid, do you mean to come and say that you do not know whether that book had been passed by the auditor or not ?—I believe that that was the book that the auditor passed for the December quarter.

1845. It cannot be a question of belief, you must know it quite well ; if you were standing in jeopardy about this matter you know whether you destroyed that book before the auditor examined it or whether it was done afterwards ?—I believe that that would be the book, but I do not wish to state everything on my oath.

1846. But you must. Will you swear that it was this book or the other book that the auditor passed ?—That book.

1847. You will swear that the auditor passed this book, and not the other ?—Yes, the quarterly meeting that should have been held on the first Monday in January, was held on the second Monday.

1848. How much of this book was written at the same time ?—I cannot say because I wrote it upon different evenings. I copied it from the other one.

1849. How much did you do at a time ; just show me how much you did at a time ?—I could not say, sometimes I would write two or three pages, sometimes five or six.

1850. When was it you made this alteration, did you write this January account before the meeting passed the December account, and up to what time did you copy ?—I began in December.

1851. That is a copy of another book up to a certain point, up to what point is it a copy, it is a copy from a certain point to a certain point ?—From September the 3rd this is an exact copy of the other one.

1852. After September the 3rd what is it ?—An exact copy of the other book with the exception of the men's names being placed in the middle in some cases, when they should have been placed at the top.

1853. Up to how long did you keep making a copy of the other book ?—Up to Christmas. Am I to show you the last entry in this book, which was only copied from the other book.

1854. How much of it contains a copy, and how much contains original writing ?—The other book would be written up to December 24th, since then there was nothing written in the other book but in this.

1855. Up to December 24th ?—Yes.

1856. Now look at this entry, on your oath was not it written all at the same time ?—No, I am speaking from memory, and not from the writing.

1857. Look at the writing of the month of January, and tell me whether that was not all written at the same time ?—I believe not.

1858. Will you swear it was not ?—If I swear, it will be upon my own recollection.

1859. Of course it will ?—Upon my own recollection I swear that was not all written at the same time.

1860. Look at the page again ?—I could not swear by the writing. I swear by my own recollection.

1861. You wrote it ?—Yes.

1862. I ask you on your oath was not it all written at the same time ?—I have already stated upon my oath according to my own recollection.

1863. You must not get out of it that way. I ask you upon your oath was not it all written at the same time ?—I say it was not.

1864. How was the other book bound ?—Very similar to that one.

1865. Was it the same size ?—Nearly.

1866. Was it an old book or a new book ?—It was bought a new book.

1867. Was this ?—Yes ; and the other one too.

1868. Was this the book that the treasurer had to deal with ?—The treasurer could see me write in it.

1869. Had you to hand it over to the treasurer ?—No, only when he paid out the money, I would then give him the book to reckon it up and see whether it corresponded with his cash on the table.

1870. The treasurer would be so far familiar with the old book that he would see it on all these previous weeks, from August of the year before, he would see it every week would he not ?—Yes.

1871. What was the name of the treasurer of December ?—The treasurer at that time was Alfred Ashforth.

1872. Did he notice that you had got a new book ?—He never told me about it, he never hinted such a thing.

1873. If he had been in the habit of dealing with this book for something like a year and a half, for the entries that he had had to pass himself every week, when you produced the new book, spick and span, and written out in this way, does not it occur to you that it is curious that he did not say, "You have got a new "book here ?"—There must be a new page every week as I turn over.

1874. Was not it curious that he did not say, "You have got a new book here" ?—No, I did not think it curious.

1875. He never made any observation ?—No.

1876. Was the other book larger, or about the same size as this ?—About the same size.

1877. Are these entries made at the time you pay money, or are they made at one time ?—At the time we pay the money.

1878. Always ?—Yes.

1879. At the time you pay the money ?—Yes.

1880. And since December these entries have all been made at the time you paid the money ?—Exactly.

1881. As the payments occurred ?—Yes.

1882. Where did you make the entries ? at the place you paid the money, or at your own house ?—On the table at the meeting room.

SECOND DAY.

Thompson.

June 1867.

1883. Were they always paid the same night ?—Yes.

1884. You never paid except on the Monday night ?—On the Saturday night ; but sometimes when a man has not fetched his scale on the Saturday night, the committee order it to be paid on the Monday, and I should stop the money out of the next week's contribution.

1885. When do you enter it ?—On Saturday night.

1886. Find me in this book any one case of an entry that appears to have been made at a different time from the rest ?—I am not aware that there are any entries in this book made except those made on Saturday night.

1887. Then they are, apparently, made at the same time ?—Yes.

1888. I thought so ; that is the reason I wanted it explained. You say you destroyed the book and altered the rotation of the men ; now, on your oath, did not that book you have destroyed contain entries of payments to these men for rattening ?—It did not.

1889. Have you not destroyed it to conceal all that ?—No, upon my oath I have not.

1890. A man who comes here and makes the statements you have done, and makes books which are evidently false, must be asked these questions ?—I have spoken nothing but the truth, although I knew when I was coming that I was going to make a statement against my own character ; at the same time I am taking a great weight off my own mind.

1891. When I find facts like these, I must ask about them, although it is very painful to me ?—When I got this new book I did not know you were coming here.

1892. Then the treasurer, unless he relied upon your statement was as much guilty of breach of faith as any one else ?—Just so ; but I believe he did rely upon my statement.

1893. The treasurer and auditor and you are all equally to blame in this matter, is that so ?—I think I am to blame the most.

1894. There is another thing which I should like to ask you about ; do you know a person of the name of Edwin Hunter in Eyre Street ?—Yes.

1895. Had he some men who were once on strike ?—Yes.

1896. Did you tell him you would not allow the men to commence work again till he had paid you a fine of 5*l.*—Yes.

1897. When was that, somewhere about August 1865 ?—Yes, I dare say it was.

1898. They would not pay their natty money ?—The forgers would not.

1899. Because they would not pay the natty money you said you would compel Mr. Hunter to pay a fine of 5*l.* before you would allow them to come back to work ?—Yes.

1900. Had you before that time compelled Mr. Hunter to pay the arrears of the men ?—He paid them at the same time.

1901. You compelled him not only to pay the arrears of the men due to you but also to pay a fine of 5*l.* to the club ?—Yes.

1902. He did not belong to your Union ?—No.

1903. On what principle did you think it right to make a master pay the natty money or contributions of his man, and also to pay a fine before you would allow the men to work ?—Do you ask me my own opinion, or to express the opinion of my trade ?

1904. I ask it any way you like ?—I will give the opinion of my trade.

1905. In your judgment do you think that is right ?—No ; in my own judgment it was wrong.

1906. Now what was the principle upon which the trade acted ?—We have a rule that sets forth that " Any member or workman causing expense to our " society "——

1907. Just point it out to me ?—The 15th rule.

1908. At page 5 we have the rule, and it is this : " Any forger or master causing expense to this society " shall pay such fine as a general meeting may deter- " mine ; " that being the rule what do you say upon it ?—A portion of the men in Mr. Hunter's employment had refused to pay the contribution, and we formed an alliance with the grinders to assist each other in such a case. Mr. Hunter had repeatedly used his influence to cause the men not to pay.

1909. How do you mean that he had used his influence ?—By threatening that any one joining our society should be expelled his service. We believe it was on account of the master's influence that the men refused to pay. Another circumstance that caused the trade to form that opinion was this, that he had ordered me from the premises.

1910. Did not he tell you that he would not allow the natty money or contributions to be collected in his works ?—Yes, just so.

1911. What next ?—We asked the grinders in his employment how much they would each cease work for, and we satisfied every man, and at a given hour they ceased to work for him.

1912. They stated the amount and you gave it them ?—Yes.

1913. And they left his employment ?—Yes ; we kept the grinders I think two weeks, and on account of the men not grinding the scissors of course he could finish none.

1914. How much did you pay the grinders ?—12*l.* a week.

1915. You paid 24*l.* altogether ?—I think it was 26*l.* with all the expenses.

1916. How much was it to each man ?—We gave the men according to their average earnings ; I am sure I forget what each man received.

1917. No man was a sufferer by leaving ?—No.

1918. Do you know what number of grinders there were ?—There would be nine or ten and two or three boys. At length Mr. Hunter or Mr. Holmshaw sent to or called upon me and we waited upon Mr. Hunter together, and told him the decision the trade had come to.

1919. It was that he should pay the 26*l.* ?—No ; that he should cause the men to pay their contributions and 5*l.* for having caused our society an unnecessary expense.

1920. And you fined him accordingly ?—Yes.

1921. And he paid you the money ?—Yes.

1922. What date was this ; was it in August 1865 ?—I daresay it was.

1923. Have you got the book of 1865, showing the entry and payment of that money ?—Yes.

1924. Where is it ?—Here (*producing the same*).

1925. "Mr. Hunter 5*l.*, August 4th." Have you a meeting of your committee every week ?—Yes.

1926. Have you monthly meetings ?—We used to have a general meeting once a month ; at present we have them once a quarter.

1927. Formerly they were once a month ?—Yes.

1928. When did you alter the rule about holding general meetings ?—Perhaps about 18 months since.

1929. Was that before August 1865 ?—We altered it since.

1930. Formerly you held a general meeting once a month ?—Yes.

1931. I see by your rule that nobody can order a master to pay except the general meeting ; how was it that you and Mr. Holmshaw made him pay the fine ?—On account of the decision of the trade.

1932. How ?—The trade had come to a decision that when he gave in we should fine him 5*l.*

1933. Was that done at a general meeting ?—I believe it was.

1934. You are the secretary, was there a general meeting at which they had decided to fine him 5*l.* ?—I believe it was at a monthly meeting.

1935. There had been a monthly meeting ?—Yes.

1936. You have told me about your list, you say this is a list merely of persons you have paid ?—Just so.

1937. Do you know the 18th rule of your society,

SECOND DAY.

J. Thompson.

4 June 1867.

" That the secretary keep a list of names of all forgers " on the box, or in part employment, and such as are " desirous of changing their places, and any manu- " facturer wanting a man may have preference by " making application to the committee or secretary ?" —Yes.

1938. Have you made such a list as that ?—I should refer to the list you have there.

1939. That is the only one ?—It is.

1940. Although there was an actual rule that you were to keep a list of all the forgers on the box or in part employment ?—Those men are on the box or in part employment.

1941. That is the only list you kept ?—Yes ; if a man does not earn his scale we make it up to him.

1942. Has the book been made up all at the same time ?—No.

1943. Was it made up at different times as the cases occurred ?—Yes.

1944. What do you call this book ?—I call it the cash book ; the treasurer has one just the same.

1945. And this you say has entries of payments made and put down as they are made ?—Yes, on Saturdays.

1946. Therefore, if you paid a man 1*l*. you put it down ?—Yes, I should put the sum total down in that book.

1947. Where would you put the other sum ?—In the scale book.

1948. Which is the scale book ?—The list that you refer to.

1949. I see that you have entries in this book, is this written at the same time ?—This has been written at different times.

1950. Have those entries been written at different times ?—They have been written one one Saturday and another another Saturday.

1951. Do you pledge your word to it ?—Yes.

1952. That those have been written on different Saturdays ?—Yes.

1953. 26*l*. 6*s*. 4*d*. was for Hunter's grinders ?— —Yes.

1954. When a man is paid 1*l*. you enter, or ought to enter it. I see here John Richards, 1*l*., and 31st July, Hunter's men, 26*l*. 6*s*. 4*d*., which are the particular entries ?—This is the first week of our paying scale, previous to that date we had no man on the box.

1955. Where are the entries of the particular amounts ?—Hunter's grinders, 11*l*. 18*s*. 3*d*. ; ditto for second week, 11*l*. 18*s*. 3*d*. ; here is the sum for lost time, for committee expenses, and that makes the total expenditure for that week.

1956. The first entry in this book is the entry of Hunter's accounts ?—Yes.

1957. That you had paid Hunter's grinders 11*l*. 18*s*. 3*d*. the first week ?—Yes.

1958. Is it enough to say " Hunter's grinders " without saying the names of the persons whom you paid, is this the way you keep your accounts ?—The grinders' committee paid the money, and we handed the sum total over to the grinders' committee.

1959. Therefore you handed over to the grinders' committee 11*l*. 18*s*. 3*d*. ?—Yes.

1960. I understand it now, if you paid it over to the grinders' committee they would keep an account of the men, you paid it over to the grinders' committee ?—Yes.

1961. You are a very important witness in this inquiry, and, although it does not occur to me that I have anything more to ask you, I wish that you would attend to morrow morning, and if anything should occur to me during the night I will ask you then, perhaps you will be in attendance ?—I would ask you whether you are satisfied with the explanations I have given.

1962. (*Chairman.*) I cannot say anything of that kind at present.

The witness withdrew.

Adjourned to to-morrow at 11 o'clock.

THIRD DAY.

Council Hall, Sheffield, Wednesday, 5th June 1867.

PRESENT:

William Overend, Esq., Q.C.
Thomas Irwin Barstow, Esq.
George Chance, Esq.
J. E. Barker, Esq., Secretary.

WILLIAM OVEREND, Esq., Q.C., in the Chair.

THIRD DAY.

J. Thompson.

5 June 1867.

Joseph Thompson recalled and further examined.

1963. (*Chairman.*) You told us yesterday that you thought you had mentioned to us all the cases of rattening, and all the cases which may be considered to be illegal with which you have been concerned as secretary?—Yes.

1964. Have you on reflection thought of any more? No, I have not.

1965. And you believe that you have told us everything?—I believe so.

1966. Was your society formed somewhere about the month of September 1864?—It was.

1967. Do you know a person of the name of George Gill, a manufacturer in Lambert Street?—Yes.

1968. Do you recollect writing a letter to Mr. Gill asking him to compel his men to attend your meeting?—I do.

1969. Can you at all give me the substance of what the letter was, and in what mode it was addressed?—I will try. I informed Mr. Gill that the workmen in his employment were not paying to our society, and that our society did not consider that they were doing him justice, inasmuch as through the influence of our society the price of labour in small manufactories had been raised considerably, thereby enabling him to go into the market much better than he used to do, because the prices were more uniform. You will bear in mind, please, that before the formation of our society——

1970. But I want to know what was the nature of your letter to Mr. Gill, not about the benefits to him, but about compelling him to force his men to attend your meetings?—I am not aware that I did use any such language; but I asked him as a favour if he would use his influence with the men.

1971 It was only to use his influence?—Yes.

1972. Are you aware the letter was handed to the men?—I believe so.

1973. And I believe that afterwards some of the men attended your union?—They did.

1974. Others did not, I believe?—They did not at the time.

1975. Do you know a person of the name of Joseph Hague?—Yes.

1976. Did he refuse to attend?—I am not aware that he refused to contribute, but he has frequently refused to attend the meetings.

1977. Have you talked to him on the subject of his not attending the meetings?—Yes.

1978. What have you told him—have you told him that if he did not attend the meetings he would be made to do so?—Oh, no.

1979. What have you told him?—I have told him that inasmuch as the general meeting had the making of all the rules by which he was supposed to be governed (if I may use the term), he ought at least to be there to have a voice in framing the rules, and I begged him to come.

1980. But have you ever used anything like a threat towards him of what consequences would happen to him if he did not attend?—No.

1981. Have you requested any of the men connected with your union to speak to him upon the subject?—I have requested at times the men to go with me; I believe to him as well as to others. I believe deputations have waited upon him upon the subject.

1982. Do you know any persons who have been with you to call upon Joseph Hague?—Yes, I believe Sorby.

1983. James or George Sorby?—Joseph.

1984. And you did not remind him that persons who did not attend would be rattened?—I did not.

1985. And you used nothing like any language from which he might infer that if he did not attend it would be worse for him?—No, I did not.

1986. Not Sorby?—Not that I am aware of.

1987. Can you speak with confidence as to Sorby?—I can speak with confidence that he never did in my hearing.

1988. He never did it by your authority or with your connivance?—No.

1989. You never instructed him to tell Hague that if he did not attend there was a mode of compelling his attendance?—I never did.

1990. He did not attend the meetings, I believe?—I do not think that he has attended two meetings the whole of the time.

1991. On the 24th of February, after your meeting, were his bellows cut?—I remember a pair of bellows being cut that he worked on.

1992. That was about February, I believe?—Probably.

1993. How long was that after you had been talking to him about attending?—I believe that I should see the man every week.

1994. And you were importuning him to come?—Yes.

1995. He did not come, and his bellows were cut?—Yes.

1996. Did you give any kind of instruction to any person to cut those bellows?—Never.

1997. Are you aware who cut them?—I am not.

1998. Have you no suspicion?—I have not.

1999. I suppose that nobody would be benefited by cutting his bellows but persons connected with the trade?—I am not aware that they would.

2000. Was it not your belief at the time that they were cut in consequence of his not attending your meeting?—It was not my belief.

2001. What was your belief about the cause of his bellows being cut?—I cannot say that I formed an opinion as to the subject.

2002. Have you any doubt that they were cut in consequence of his not coming to your meeting?—They may have been cut by some one in the trade or even some one in the factory.

2003. But what is your belief about it?—I cannot say that I can form an opinion.

2004. But private malice or his not complying with the rules of the trade are the only motives by which you can explain why his bellows were cut?—One of the two.

2005. Do you know where the bellows were which were cut?—Yes.

2006. You do not know that there was in the same room another pair of bellows belonging to one of your men who was a union man?—He was not a union man.

2007. The other man?—The other man was not, neither was Hague.

2008. Who was the other man whose bellows were not cut?—His name was Peace.

2009. They were in the same shop with him, were

THIRD DAY.

J. Thompson.

5 June 1867.

they not?—In the same shop. The man's name was Oswald Peace.

2010. Was he or was he not a man who attended your meetings?—He never did attend the meetings that I know of up to the present time.

2011. Did he ever contribute to your funds?—I should think that during the whole of the time he has contributed about 5*s*.

2012. But why did he contribute if he did not belong to your union?—He thought that inasmuch as he was a man of delicate health it would be no benefit to him.

2013. But you say he was not a union man, but still he did contribute 5*s*. Why does he contribute who does not belong to a union?—Since that time he did agree to pay half contribution and receive half benefit.

2014. He was in point of fact a member of your union only deriving one half of the advantages?—I believe not at that time.

2015. Are you satisfied about it; have you a list of your members?—Yes.

2016. Will you be kind enough to refer to it and see whether in February 1865 he would be on the list of your members?—I did not know that our books were required. I thought that you had done with me and I left my books at home with the exception of one. I know that from nearly the commencement of the society Oswald Peace's name has been in the books.

2017. How long do you recollect that it continued? As far as my memory serves me he would pay two or three times, something to that effect.

2018. But not afterwords?—Not afterwards. The payments would be made very irregularly.

2019. In the early period he was a member?—He had entered.

2020. Did Hague call upon you after his bellows were cut?—No, Mr. Gill sent the bill of the bellows mending to me.

2021. That cost about a guinea, did it not?—I think so.

2022. You declined paying it, I believe?—Just so.

2023. You said that you had nothing to do with it?—Yes.

2024. I thought that you would be anxious to give an explanation as regards this which we did not have yesterday?—Quite so, it slipped my memory.

2025. I am requested to ask you this question; have you ever heard, and do you know, of any cases of intimidation or outrage or wrong committed by a master upon any man or men whether of the trades unionists or otherwise? Do you know of anything with which you wish to charge a master, because we have to inquire as well into intimidations by masters as by men?—I cannot bring any charge of intimidation against masters, but I can bring this charge, that in the absence of trades unions prices in our trade are reduced something like 40 or 50 per cent.

2026. That is I am afraid not within the scope of our inquiry, that is for the inquiry in London, and I should not wonder if gentlemen connected with the trade will be asked to give evidence on that question in London; but our business is to trace, if we can, any intimidation that has been made use of, or any outrage or wrong that has been committed by any person either to a combination of masters or of men, and our inquiry is limited to that. If you can tell us of any case, where a master has committed an outrage or wrong on a servant, that we will inquire into, and see if we can trace it to a combination of masters, and not to a single master?—I am not prepared at present to enter into that.

The witness withdrew.

ROBERT HOLMSHAW sworn and examined.

R. Holmshaw.

2027. (*Mr. Barstow.*) Where do you live?—15, Arthur Street, Addy Street, Upperthorpe.

2028. What are you by trade? — A scissor grinder.

2029. How long have you been a grinder?—Something like 40 years.

2030. We hear that you are the president of the Scissor Grinders Union?—Yes.

2031. How long have you been the president?—About four years altogether.

2032. Did you hold any office in the union before that?—I have been on the committees at several times.

2033. Have you been secretary or treasurer?—I have been treasurer.

2034. Of the same union?—Yes.

2035. How long were you treasurer?—About the same time, four years.

2036. Was that immediately before you were elected president?—It is all one in our trade.

2037. You were president and treasurer at the same time?—Yes.

2038. I believe your union is not amalgamated with any other?—We have alliance between the forgers and shop board hands and grinders.

2039. What do you mean by shop board hands?—They are composed of the filers, borers, and hardeners (or you might say drillers and hardeners; they drill the holes to put the rivet in), and putters together.

2040. Are the filers persons who make files?—No, they file scissors. It is divided into branches in that kind of way.

2041. When you say in alliance you mean there is an understanding with one another to promote your objects?—Yes, to get a fair price for our labour.

2042. Have you a copy of the rules of your association here?—I have not them, but our secretary has.

2043. Perhaps you will have the goodness to hand up a copy. What are the objects of your society?—The reason why we began to league together was because prices were so low that we could not live. Our objects were to obtain better remuneration for our labour.

2044. (*Chairman.*) To obtain a fair price for your labour?—Just so. (*The rules were handed up.*)

2045. (*Chairman.*) You have no printed rules?—No.

2046. (*Mr. Barstow.*) And is that the only object; you have a sick society?—Yes, we pay 6*s*. a week in the sick and funeral society.

2047. That is to say, it is a benefit society as well?—Yes.

2048. I suppose you levy some contributions?—Yes, 1*s*. 6*d*. a week for a man and 9*d*. for a boy.

2049. How do you enforce the payment of those contributions?—We try to advise them to pay; we talk to them nicely.

2050. I suppose the great bulk is paid willingly?—Yes.

2051. (*Chairman.*) You talk to them nicely?—Yes, certainly we do, knowing that it is their interest to pay.

2052. (*Mr. Barstow.*) I suppose from what you say that it sometimes happens that people will not be advised?—We have those characters that will not be advised unfortunately, and it is generally the drunken characters that will not.

2053. Those you seem to say are not the best class of workmen?—They invariably are the indifferent class of workmen, and they are the intemperate men generally speaking. They want all the money for another purpose.

2054. I suppose very frequently they fall into arrear?—Oh, yes; they are sure to do that if they spend it in drink.

2055. Do you take any steps to collect the arrears?—I invariably go to the employers when the men are really so obstinate, and ask them if they will be so kind as to use their influence with the men.

THIRD DAY.

R. Holmshaw.

5 June 1867.

2056. Now, supposing that the employer's influence should fail, what then?—Then we apply to the other branches and see what the other men say about it.

2057. By the other branches you mean the scissor forgers, and the shop-board hands?—Yes, we hold a consultation and see what those men think about being in arrears.

2058. Where do you hold those consultations?—It is just as it happens; we have no particular place for them. Sometimes it might occur in one place and sometimes in another; in the street; it is not particular, it is just as it happens. Suppose a factory was at one side of the town, we should be in that neighbourhood, and if it was in another side of the town, we should be in that neighbourhood.

2059. I understand you that you go and talk yourself with those other men, the shop-board hands and forgers, and ask them their opinion?—Just so.

2060. It is not done at a formal meeting?—No; there is no necessity to call a public meeting on that question.

2061. And you take their opinions?—Yes, every man's opinion is asked on the question that is connected with that place.

2062. Those opinions, of course, vary in different cases?—Just so; they vary this way, some man may say, "It will be very unfortunate for us to be punished for this man;" and some men say, "Well, I won't "work if that man doesn't pay his contribution as "well as me."

2063. (*Chairman.*) You are aware that you have no legal mode of enforcing the payments?—We are very well satisfied of that; we know that. We know we are left in the back ground, and everybody else is protected.

2064. And I suppose this is the reason you wanted this inquiry, in order to show that although you are carrying on all these meetings, you have no power at all of enforcing the payment of your contributions?—No, we have not. I wish we had the same power as you gentlemen have.

2065. As I understand, the unions want the Legislature to give them some assistance?—They do, and they require it.

2066. Now the Legislature cannot help you unless you tell them how you are placed. You say you have no legal power at all to enforce payment of your contributions, and we want to know what you are driven to by being placed in that situation?—We are driven to work for anything they like to give us.

2067. You know you cannot enforce it by law; that is your hardship; and I believe that it is felt in the country, that if these unions are good things, you are placed in a very false position?—They never know when to stop, and you are never all they wish. They are trying now to reduce us every day.

2068. But what do you do in consequence of not having a legal power to enforce your contributions? Do you strike, or what do you do?—We take no other means; only by withdrawing all men, and going and asking them if they will give up work, whilst those other parties pay.

2069. (*Mr. Barstow.*) Does that mean that you withdraw your hands from a shop where one of those men works, and will not pay?—Just so.

2070. Do you say that that is the only means which you take to enforce payment?—Yes.

2071. You have been in this employment 40 years. Have you never heard of any other means being taken to enforce payment?—Oh yes. We had a case this week where a man has lost his bands who belongs to a union; at least one band was stolen by somebody. There had been lots of bands and glazers stolen at different towns in the county; it is a continual occurrence.

2072. (*Chairman.*) Stealing bands is a continual occurrence?—Stealing bands is a continual occurrence. It is both in the union and out of the union; it makes no difference. We are always having cases; proprietors take them and all.

2073. (*Mr. Barstow.*) For what purposes are those bands and glazers taken?—For various purposes; perhaps out of spite, or any thing of that sort; one man spiting another. One man goes and takes another's work, and will do it privately. There is not a doubt about it. It is a very serious thing for a man to have a family and another man to go and take his bit of work when things are slack, and leave him without a bit to eat on Saturday night.

2074. Do you mean to tell us that they are never taken to enforce the payment of their contribution?—We never do so.

2075. That is not the question; do you mean to say that these bands and glazers are never taken to en force the payment of natty money?—We do not take that means.

2076. I do not suppose that you do, but within your knowledge are they ever taken?—I assure you that if they ever did they have not informed me of it.

2077. Can you tell us whether they are not so taken?—I cannot.

2078. You cannot tell us that they are ever taken to enforce the payment of natty money, that is the question I asked you?—I say distinctly that I do not know.

2079. That is the answer that you give us, that you do not know whether in Sheffield bands and glazers and tools are ever taken to enforce the payment of natty money?—I do not know; I do not knowany thing at all about it.

2080. You have never heard of such a thing?—Oh yes, I have heard it talked about very oft, because if it were taken for anything else it would be the trade. They always lay the charge to the trade no matter who has done it.

2081. In your union do you ever make the masters responsible for the arrears of the men?—No.

2082. You yourself have never made a demand upon a master to pay the arrears of his men?—No, I have gone and named the circumstance to him, that he had men that were not contributing as I should like them, and I believe that in one instance one employer once paid me a sovereign, I have never received any other money.

2083. You never made any demand upon a master for payment of workmen's arrears?—No, no further than that I went and told him how the man was fixed, and told him what he had to pay, and he paid it, but he was not obliged to, he did it spontaneously.

2084. Have you any masters contributing to your union?—Yes.

2085. How many?—I should think there will be perhaps about 12.

2086. Could you mention their names?—William Darwin, William Whiteley, George Platts, Thomas Lillyman, John Newton, John Parkin; and there are two that have got too old, and we have allowed them to withdraw. There is William Hattersley.

2087. Have you a book there?—Yes, it is the collecting book, which I go round with to collect the contributions.

2088. We will not trouble you to give us any more names. I suppose that those are generally small employers are they not?—Yes they are small employers.

2089. Perhaps not much removed from the condition of a journeyman?—No, everyone has to guide himself, otherwise he would not have to contribute to us.

2090. Are they people who are likely to suffer from slack times?—Yes, they have to suffer as well as all the others in slack times; generally they do not suffer so much, I daresay, as the other employers.

2091. When an employer is out of work, is he entitled to the benefit of the society?—Yes.

2092. (*Chairman.*) One of the gentlemen who came here on Monday said that he had refused to pay because he did not receive?—Yes, I should think he would. I should like to know any gentleman that would like to receive when he had paid 7*l.* less than another man's contribution.

2093. But I want to know what benefit a master has by contributing to your society?—If he is within

THIRD DAY.

R. Holmshaw.

5 June 1867.

a certain limit he gets relief if he is sick, and he gets relief if he is out of work.

2094. How do you mean within a certain limit?—If he is within four weeks contribution.

2095. (*Mr. Barstow.*) Do you mean that if he has contributed to you for four weeks he is entitled to relief?—No; if he owes no more than four weeks contribution he gets relief.

2096. (*Chairman.*) Is he different to the men?—Not at all, only he has this privilege, if he thinks well to contribute when he is working, and when not working not to contribute, he can be in that way. He has the benefit the other way when he is working, and we are in union, and he will get a better price for his labour.

2097. But I want to know what Platts meant when he said that the masters got nothing, that they were obliged to contribute, and that they got no benefit but that the men did; does the master get any benefit in the case of illness, just like the men?—Just the same.

2098. How do you understand what Platts means by that?—Mr. Platts came to us and wanted to have scale when he owed 7*l.* 2*s.* 10*d.* contribution. The other men receiving scale had paid that amount of money more into the funds than he had.

2099. But he had not been working?—No, but he and I had a conversation upon the matter, and it was understood between us that when he contributed he was to receive, and not to receive when he did not contribute. He knew that perfectly well, but he did this out of a bit of aggravation, so that he could do all the work that was there, and if there was none go on the box.

2100. But do I understand you to say that the masters get as much benefit as the men from your union?—Just so, if they are within the limit of four weeks.

2101. Then it is the same thing with both masters and men?—The same thing with both.

2102. Then the masters get the same benefit as the men?—The same benefit.

2103. Then I understand that the masters are on exactly the same footing as the men?—On the same footing as the men in every sense of the word.

2104. (*Mr. Barstow.*) In every respect?—In every respect.

2105. You mentioned something about having 1*l.* from an employer for the arrears of his man, what was that?—It was simply that I went and told him that the man was not contributing.

2106. Who was the employer?—It was Mr. Mozley, a very nice gentleman and all he is —.

2107. How came that about?—I simply asked him, in fact the man asked me to go to him and ask him if the master would lend him a sovereign to pay.

2108. (*Chairman.*) Who was the man?—They call him George Redfern.

2109. And he was in arrears?—Yes.

2110. He worked with Mr. Mozley, and he said, "Go to Mr. Mozley and ask him if he will lend me a sovereign?"—Yes.

2111. That is your story?—Yes, and the correct one.

2112. (*Mr. Barstow.*) Have you any rule in your society about apprentices?—Yes, we are oliged to have.

2113. Will you explain what is your rule?—We have a rule that no one shall take an apprentice without he is a member's son.

2114. No one can be apprenticed in your trade except he is the son of a member of the trade?—No.

2115. Have you any other rule on the subject of apprentices?—Yes, we have another rule, that no boy shall begin to work in our trade till he is 13 years of age.

2116. Have you any rule with reference to the number of apprentices to be employed?—No, a man can take all his own sons.

2117. Can a master take as many apprentices as he wishes?—Not without they are members sons.

2118. Then I understand that, provided that his apprentices are the sons of member's he may have as many apprentices as he chooses?—It would not be reasonable to allow them all to go to one man, because he would not be able to manage them.

2119. But have you any rule upon the subject?—If a member dies in the trade, and he has any sons, and the widow wishes to put them in the trade, then we look out for an employer for them; to get them as good an employer as we can possibly find them.

2120. Quite so, but that is not an answer to my question at all. Supposing an employer limits himself to the sons of men in the trade, can he have as many apprentices as he chooses?—No.

2121. (*Chairman.*) How many do you let him have?—That would depend upon circumstances.

2122. You exercise a control over it, and you say, "You shall have two or three or four," just as you think right, is that so?—Very likely.

2123. Answer the question, yes or no?—You had better let me give it you in my own way, and then you will perhaps understand it. It is simply this, as I told you before, if there was a member's son and he did not want him himself, or the member was dead and the widow applied to us or to anybody else, if she had a preference for any man in the trade, we should very likely let him go to that man. I do not suppose that we should put any obstacles in the way.

2124. Supposing I am in the trade, and I want to take four apprentices, and you think it a very unreasonable thing and say that I cannot manage them, as you say; would you say, "You shall not have the four?"—I do not know that we should go so far as that, but we should tell him that he was very unkind and very unreasonable if he did take them.

2125. But that is all sentiment. I want to know whether you would prevent a man taking any number of apprentices he pleased, assuming that they are the proper sort. Do you exercise control over the men, and say, "You shall have a certain number of apprentices, and no more?"—I do not know which way to begin to answer you, because I do not know that we have a rule to that effect as to members' sons. That is a question which would have to come before the general meeting. We have no rule to that effect.

2126. (*Mr. Chance.*) Has the difficulty ever arisen?—No, not respecting members' sons.

2127. (*Chairman.*) You limit them to members' sons?—Just so.

2128. But as to the amount of members' sons that question has not arisen?—No.

2129. (*Mr. Barstow.*) Then I suppose I may say that you have no rule with respect to the number of apprentices which any employer may have, provided they are members' sons?—No.

2130. (*Chairman.*) May a man take an apprentice at any age?—No.

2131. At what age may he take an apprentice?—28 years of age.

2132. Then if a man is a master from 21 years of age, up to 28 you would not allow him to have an apprentice?—Not till he was 28 years of age.

2133. (*Mr. Barstow.*) Supposing one of those men under 28 years of age was to take an apprentice, what would you do?—We should tell him that we thought he had done wrong.

2134. (*Chairman.*) And he would say, "I do not care for what you tell me; I shall go on?"—Very likely he would, if he is a stupid man.

2135. Supposing that he is a stupid man, and did this, what should you do?—We should use all the moral influence which we had to try to persuade him different.

2136. Would you stop at moral influence?—We might go to his employer.

2137. And tell his employer to exercise his influence?—Yes.

2138. Supposing the master says, "I will not?"—Then I should apply to the other two branches.

2139. And then you would say to the other two branches, "Here is this man taking an apprentice "contrary to our rule. I have gone to him, and he

THIRD DAY.

R. Holmshaw.

5 June 1867.

"will not listen to me. I have gone to his master, "and his master will not interfere; what is to be "done?" Now, what would be done if you were going to put the screw on?—We do not put the screw on; we generally do it in a kinder way than that.

2140. What would you do?—The men would say that it was wrong.

2141. But assuming that it was wrong, what would you do?—The men would very likely in that case do what they would do in case he omitted to pay the contribution.

2142. (*Chairman.*) What would that be?—They would give up work while the boy was sent away.

2143. (*Mr. Barstow.*) In short they would strike in that case?—Yes.

2144. (*Chairman.*) Is there a good deal of angry feeling displayed amongst the men when there is anything like resistance to the rules?—No. Generally speaking, in our trade the men are of a pretty even temperament; they appear to take things pretty easy.

2145. Then they are not very angry if people break your rules?—No, they try to settle it with kindness.

2146. But supposing they cannot settle it with kindness, what then?—They simply give over working till it is settled.

2147. Have you ever known a case of their giving over working, and beside that of there being the accident of a man having his bands cut?—I cannot recollect anything of the sort.

2148. Not in any case of a man violating your rules with respect to apprentices?—I have heard of men having their bands cut, and I have heard of their having them taken away.

2149. But in those cases where the men have struck, and still the man has held on violating your rule, have you heard after that of the bands being taken away?—Yes, I believe such cases have occurred, but I know nothing at all about them.

2150. (*Mr. Barstow.*) Has nobody ever come to you and told you that his bands were taken away?—If all the trade was to lose a band each to-morrow they would come to me.

2151. (*Chairman.*) They would come to you first, would they?—I do not know about their coming to me first. Very likely they would go to the Town Hall first.

2152. But they would certainly come to you?—They would be sure to come to me, going about the trade as I am; they would want to make it known.

2153. Why would they come to you?—Merely to make it known in the trade, and to ask any party if they saw anything to inform them of it.

2154. If a man loses his band, you are the man they come to?—No. I should think invariably they see all the men about their own place first.

2155. Do they come and ask you what you have done with the band?—I should think not.

2156. You never knew such a case?—No.

2157. (*Mr. Barstow.*) Do you mean to say they have never asked you what you have done with the bands?—I do not recollect any man ever asking me such a question.

2158. Have they ever asked you if you knew where they were?—No.

2159. (*Chairman.*) In no case?—No, I do not know that a man ever asked me such a question. They might have done, but I cannot think of it.

2160. (*Mr. Barstow.*) Have you ever been the means of a man's bands being returned to him?—No, because I never had any.

2161. Then, though people have very frequently applied to you about their bands, you have never been able to give them any information?—No.

2162. And you never have given them any information directly or indirectly?—No.

2163. Do you know of your own knowledge how bands that have been taken have been returned?—I have heard tell of Mr. Platt's stating a case here how they were returned.

2164. That we know about already. Is there any other case?—I am sure I could not recollect.

2165. Has it ever come to your knowledge at all how lost bands have been returned to their owners?—We have had bands on our wheel many a time belonging to different parties.

2166. Will you answer the question?—I have no idea which way the men get the bands back.

2167. That was not the question. Do you know how those lost bands have come to be returned to the owners?—I do not.

2168. In no case?—No. I never had such a job to do and I do not know.

2169. Not only bands but any other tools that may happen to have been taken away?—No.

2170. (*Chairman.*) You have never known of any tools?—No.

2171. (*Mr. Barstow.*) Have you ever endeavoured to give any assistance to persons who have lost their bands or tools?—If I were to hear tell of any man in our trade losing any bands I should give him all the assistance I possibly could.

2172. That is not an answer to my question. Did you ever give any person assistance to recover his lost bands or lost tools?—Do you mean pecuniarily?

2173. Not pecuniarily; have you ever given any person assistance to recover his lost bands or tools?—Do you mean, have I gone with him to assist him?

2174. (*Chairman.*) Have you given him any help in getting back his tools?—You mean simply in searching for them?

2175. It is much better to answer the question, because we shall presently hear more about it. Can you tell us whether you have or have not given any such assistance?—No, I have not.

2176. You have never given any assistance?—No, I have not.

2177. (*Mr. Barstow.*) When those innumerable people who you say have gone to you to complain of lost bands or tools have come to you what have you said to them?—I have said that it was a bad job.

2178. Is that all you have said?—I am sure I could not tell. Very likely there would be a lot of conversation arising in respect of men losing things.

2179. That is what you generally say; that it is a bad job?—Yes.

2180. Is that all you say?—Well, I could not tell just at this moment what conversation might occur in such like cases.

2181. You seem to say that it is a thing that has happened very often and that they always apply to you; you told us so just now?—Did I say that they all applied to me? I said that they invariably apply to me.

2182. Those are much the same things?—I was not aware of that.

2183. What do you do when you are applied to?—I cannot do anything further than say that it is a bad job.

2184. That is all you say?—That is all I can do in it; I might merely say this, that I would make inquiry and see if I could ascertain anything in respect to them in the trade as I went round collecting.

2185. You say that you sometimes offer to make inquiries for them?—Certainly, in all cases I should, no matter whether in our trade or not. A razor grinder told me about missing a lap, and I promised I would make inquiries through the trade, and see if it could be found, and if anybody had seen it.

2186. I suppose you keep your promise and do make inquiry?—Yes.

2187. Has your inquiry ever resulted in the recovery of the lost property; have you ever got the lost property back for the man who asked you about it?—I know that men have had their bands taken and had them restored, but I am not aware whether it is through me or from anything on their own account.

2188. Has any man who has asked you to assist him in recovering his lost bands or tools had them returned?—Not that I am aware of; not from me.

2189. That is your answer?—Yes.

2190. Your inquiries have in every instance been unsuccessful?—For anything I know they have.

THIRD DAY.

R. Holmshaw.

5 June 1867.

2191. When you say for anything you know, what do you mean ?—I could not recollect a case.

2192. You do not recollect any case in which a person applying to you who has lost his bands has had them returned ?—I do not recollect.

2193. When a person has applied to you for his bands, have you ever referred him to the committee ?—Yes.

2194. (*Chairman.*) To your own committee ?—Yes.

2195. (*Mr. Barstow.*) To the committee of which you are president ?—Yes.

2196. Would that be in the case of a man being in arrear of natty money ?—It would be simply for him to go there and state his case to them.

2197. (*Chairman.*) Was that man in arrear who had lost his bands ?—I do not know whether he was or not. You have not named any particular man.

2198. But before we get to the man, we want to know whether in the case of a person having lost his bands and being in arrear to the society you have on those occasions ever referred him to your committee ?—Yes.

2199. You have done so ?—Yes.

2200. (*Mr. Barstow.*) What was your object in referring him to the committee ?—To ask the committee simply if they could give him any assistance in any shape or form about the bands ; to make it publicly known throughout the trade, or take what steps they thought well in the matter.

2201. (*Chairman.*) The circumstance of a man having lost his bands is public enough, that could not be your object ; what was your object in referring him to the committee ?—In some cases we might offer a reward for them.

2202. Have you ever done so ?—We have never done so.

2203. Then why should you say that you offer a reward ?—In serious cases we should do so, but if it is only a little bit of a band that is lost we should not.

2204. (*Mr. Barstow.*) Have any of those persons in those cases applied to the committee ?—Yes.

2205. Have you been present when they made the application ?—Yes.

2206. Can you tell us what has taken place at the committee on such occasions ?—I cannot exactly. I could not tell you all the conversation that took place in the committee.

2207. In any case ?—I do not remember a single case where I could give you any information in respect to the conversation which really took place.

2208. (*Chairman.*) Have you ever in any case heard the committee say, or any member of the committee say, "Pay your subscription and you will get back your bands" ?—No.

2209. You never have ?—No.

2210. In no single instance ?—No.

2211. In no single instance has it ever been said by one of your committee, "If you pay your arrears of subscription you will get your bands" ?—No, I do not recollect that it ever has.

2212. Will you swear that in your presence it has never been said to a man, "If you pay your subscrip-" tions which are now in arrear you will get back your " bands," or words to that effect ?—No I will swear that I never did.

2213. (*Mr. Barstow.*) Have you ever heard of anyone applying to the committee and asking why his bands had been taken ?—I am sure I cannot tell. I could not think of all the circumstances.

2214. (*Chairman.*) You need not think of all the circumstances, but you are asked if you can think of this circumstance ; have the committee been asked by a man in your presence, " What is the reason my bands have been taken " ?—It might have occurred.

2215. (*Mr. Barstow.*) Did it or did it not occur ?—I am sure I could not give a correct answer on the matter.

2216. Now speaking before this crowd of people, do you mean to tell us that you do not know that ; do you know or do you not know whether a man has ever asked if the committee knew why his bands have been taken ?—I have not the least doubt but that they might have asked, but I could not recollect.

2217. (*Chairman.*) Do you not know that they have many times come and asked the committee why their bands had been taken ?—I could not recollect the circumstance.

2218. But answer the question. Do you not recollect that it has been done many times in your hearing ?—I have not the least doubt that it has been done, only I cannot recollect.

2219. (*Mr. Barstow.*) Can you recollect what answer has been made to that question on those occasions ?—Well I should think that they would say they did not know, I should think so.

2220. Is that the answer that is invariably made, that they do not know ?—I should think it would be. They might say to the man simply this, "You are in arrears so-and-so." I do not suppose that they would say anything else. I am not aware that they would. It would not matter what question he came on, they would tell him about his arrears if he owed any.

2221. Have you ever known a person to whom that answer was made offer to pay his arrears ?—I have not.

2222. Never ?—I have not. I could not give any single instance. I never keep any account of such things as those.

2223. But you have been president of the society, and a very active man, have you never on such occasions when you have been told that a man was in arrears for so-and-so heard him say, " If I pay up my arrears shall I get back my bands," or anything of that sort ?—I do not recollect that ever a man said so.

2224. (*Chairman.*) Will you swear that he did not ?—I will swear that he did not, not to my recollection.

2225. But will you swear that he did not ; that is trifling with us ?—I do not think it is.

2226. But we think it is, and we are the judges ?—Very well.

2227. Will you swear that he did not ?—I think if I was to ask anyone here if they could remember all the conversation that had occurred throughout, they would have a bad case in hand.

2228. We do not want to use strong measures, but we desire to go on very peaceably and quietly with you, but you must answer the questions. Do you mean to tell Mr. Barstow that no person has gone there and said to you, " If I pay my arrears shall I get my bands back " ?—They might have said so. I do not recollect whether they have or not.

2229. Do you believe that they have ?—I do not recollect it.

2230. Do you swear that ?—I do.

2231. Will you swear that it has not occurred ?—I will not swear that it has not occurred ; that is not possible ; I do not want to.

2232. (*Mr. Barstow.*) Have you ever known them to use words to that effect ? Have you ever known them ask whether if they paid their money they would get back their bands, or words to that effect ?—I think it is just possible that they might do such things. I think that it is just possible that it might occur. I think it is natural to occur that men would ask those questions. If a man has lost his bands he is sure to ask questions about them.

2233. Have you ever known the man pay his money ?—Yes.

2234. I understand that you have known a man, who has inquired for his bands, and was told that they were taken because he was in arrear, pay his arrears ?—Yes, I have known men come up and pay their arrears when they have lost their bands.

2235. Have you ever known the bands returned after such payment ?—Yes, I have heard speak of them being returned.

2236. Have you known yourself that they have

THIRD DAY.

R. Holmshaw.

5 June 1867.

been returned?—I have seen them after they have been returned.

2237. Do you know why they were returned?—No.

2238. Have you no belief upon the subject?—Yes, probably it might occur in this way, that some party might have taken the bands to force him to pay the parties themselves; that has been done times and times again.

2239. (*Chairman.*) That is not an answer. Have you any belief why those bands were returned? Was it because the money was paid?—Very likely it was.

2240. (*Mr. Barstow.*) Have you any doubt that the bands were taken to enforce the payment of the money?—No, I do not think that I have.

2241. And that the taking of the bands did in fact enforce the payment of the money?—Yes, I daresay it would.

2242. Have you any doubt that this has been very extensively practised?—I think that you have asked me that question before, haven't you, if you will refer to your book?

2243. (*Chairman.*) But we did not get a distinct answer. Do you not know that that has been done very frequently in the trade. We find in the "Independent" that that is a very common mode of compelling a man to pay his subscription, do you agree with that, is that your view?—It is.

2244. Everybody says so, and I expected from you that you would have come manfully forward, and said, "We have no legal mode of compelling the "payment, and we are obliged to resort to this "mode." You are protected from any consequences, and why not come and give that information if it is so. Now, do I clearly understand that that has been the practice which unfortunately has prevailed in this town, that when there have been arrears of subscriptions you have resorted to the practice of taking away bands to enforce payment?—I believe that it has been done generally in most trades.

2245. Has it also been done not only in the case where money has been in arrear, but where the laws of the trade have been violated in some way?—Yes.

2246. Do you know whether they have also gone as far as to cause the bellows of people to be cut for the same reason?—No, we never go to that extreme I should think, and no trades do I should think.

2247. All that you do as a trade is to take away the bands?—Yes.

2248. Now, as a trade, what is the course that you adopt when you want to take the bands; when a man will not pay his subscriptions what does the trade do; do they go to a man and say, "We want you to take away the bands?"—I do not know that we interfere in respect to taking away bands. I know the thing is done with parties, but we have nothing at all to do with it.

2249. Do the parties tell you they have done it?—No, they never bother us about it.

2250. But does the trade connive at its being done? What do they do?—Our system of getting it, as I told you at the beginning, was to get the contribution by withdrawing the men.

2251. But we have passed far beyond the withdrawing of the men, that is not enough, and you are obliged to resort to some severer process, and the severer process is taking away the bands, and you say that the trade adopt that process of taking away the bands; what course do they pursue, do they say to the men, "Here is a man who will not contribute, go "and take away his bands, and we will keep them "till he does pay"?—I should not think of doing so.

2252. But how is it done?—I cannot tell you; I was never in a case of that sort, so I do not know.

2253. But you know that it is done?—It is done by some party or other.

2254. Things cannot be done unless they are done by some party, you know?—Certainly not.

2255. But supposing that it is done by a man for the benefit of the trade, do you protect him?—No, we do not protect him.

2256. Do you not know who has done it?—No.

2257. Never?—No.

2258. Do you mean to say that you have never known a case where you have known the man who has taken away the bands?—I do not know.

2259. We do not want to treat you as a hostile witness; we wish you to come here to tell us the truth without any cross-examination at all. Have you never known a case of a man taking away bands?—I have never known a case of an individual who has gone and done so.

2260. Have you ever paid money in respect of its having been done?—No.

2261. Not by yourself, but have you ever known a case of the trade having paid it?—Not in my recollection.

2262. Will you swear that in your time it never has been paid?—Yes.

2263. Taking away a man's bands is a kind of security or pledge; you lay hold of them, and if he complies with your terms he gets them back again. You do not steal them, you merely take them and return them if he complies with your terms. Have you ever known a case where a man was paid for doing that?—I do not recollect any case where a man has been paid for doing that.

2264. Will you swear that?—Yes.

2265. Have you ever known a case where the bands were restored, and where a man has been given a sum of money to pay for the expenses?—No.

2266. Have you known of any other society but your own which has done it?—No, I have nothing at all to do with other societies.

2267. You know you need not be alarmed; if you have done anything that is wrong you are perfectly protected; we shall give you a certificate?—I do not know of anything to tell you.

2268. I only tell you that this is not an ordinary inquiry. In an ordinary case a man may say, "I "decline to tell you anything about it because it may "put me in peril;" but if you tell us all about it you are not in peril at all?—I do not know; Mr. Butcher would not answer the questions; you could not get him to answer.

2269. I did not ask Mr. Butcher anything. Mr. Butcher has not been before us. If you wish it I will ask him any questions which are reasonable when he comes, but it is for you to answer these questions. I only tell you that for your own satisfaction, but if you have done anything that will otherwise imperil you, tell us all?—I do not know that I have done anything wrong to any man.

2270. (*Mr. Barstow.*) You know John Platts, I believe?—Yes.

2271. Can you remember as far back as the 28th of February 1863?—I should think I should.

2272. Do you remember about that time hearing that Platts had lost six bands?—Yes, I think I recollect the case,

2273. Did Platts himself apply to you on the subject?—I believe he did.

2274. What did you say to him?—I told him I did not know anything at all about them.

2275. Did you refer him to the committee?—Yes, I think I did. I think I told him to go to the committee.

2276. (*Chairman.*) He was in arrears then, was he not?—I think he was.

2277. (*Mr. Barstow.*) Were you present when Platts went to the committee?—Yes.

2278. Was Gale there?—Yes.

2279. Do you remember whether there was a man named John Willey was there?—I am sure I could not recollect. I would not be certain on that.

2280. Do you recollect Platts' letter to the committee?—I could not think of the exact conversation that took place upon the matter. He came asking something in respect to his bands.

2281. What answer did they make?—They told him that they did not know anything at all about it.

2282. Did Platts say to the committee, "If you

THIRD DAY.

R. Holmshaw.

5 June 1867.

" had left me a note I should have known what to " do" ?—I am not aware that he did.

2283. (*Chairman.*) Will you swear that he did not ?—I should not like to take an oath of it—it is so long ago.

2284. He may have said so ?—He may have said so or he may not. I should not like to take an oath upon that question, it is so long ago.

2285. (*Mr. Barstow.*) Do you recollect whether Gale made him any answer ?—I am not aware that he did.

2286. Do you recollect whether Gale said, " Pay " your money and you will have it back to-morrow " ?—I should not think he did.

2287. That is not an answer to the question.—Well, I will swear that he never did.

2288. Did Platts then say, " How can you tell me " they will be back to-morrow if you know nothing " about them " ?—I am sure I cannot say whether he did say so or not.

2289. Will you swear that he did not say so ?—I will not.

2290. Did Gale say to Platts, " You know as well " as I know " ?—I could not answer to be correct.

2291. Will you swear that he did not say so ? You were present at the meeting were you not ?—Yes, I was.

2292. And no doubt you attended to all that took place ?—Yes.

2293. Can you remember it ?—I told you a little time ago that I could not. It is four or five years ago. You could not, I think, tell all the conversation that took place.

2294. (*Chairman.*) But you can recollect quite well whether he said " You know as well as I know how it is " ?—He might have said so. Do you mean Gale or Platts ?

2295. Gale.—I should think that he never would say so.

2296. Will you swear that he did not ?—I should not really like to take an oath of it. In my private opinion I do not suppose that he would.

2297. (*Mr. Barstow.*) Your attention has been called to these things since. Did Platts ask what the arrears amounted to ?—Yes.

2298. Did Gale tell him 1*l.* 10*s.* or 1*l.* 12*s.* ?—I am sure I forget what the amount was.

2299. Did Gale mention some sum to which the arrears amounted ?—I should think that he would. If any man was to come and ask what his arrears were he would tell him.

2300. (*Chairman.*) Did he tell him the amounts ?—It is very likely that he would.

2301. But do you know that he did ?—It is a customary thing if a man comes to ask to say so.

2302. But did Gale tell him ?—You want me to answer questions as to which I am not certain whether or not.

2303. But you can say yes or no ?—Well, not that I can recollect.

2304. He asked what the arrears amounted to; what did Gale tell him ?—He would tell him the amount, certainly, the same as I should. I do not see that it needs a question upon it.

2305. (*Mr. Barstow.*) Did Platts ask how it came to be so much ?—I should think there is no need to ask such a question as to how it was.

2306. (*Chairman.*) But we are asking you what the facts were ?—I am not aware that he asked such a question.

2307. (*Mr. Barstow.*) Did Platts ask, " How does it come to be so much ? " and did Gale say to him " You owe so much, 11*s.* 4*d.*, and your journeymen so much " ?—I thought you said 26*s.* in the first onset.

2308. (*Chairman.*) Platts said 30*s.* or 32*s.*, and he said part of it was for himself and the remainder was for his journeymen.—I understood you that it was 1*l.* 10*s.*, and I thought that was more than had been paid.

2309. However, the amount was stated ?—Yes, the amount was sure to be named.

2310. And he would say part of it was for himself and part was for his journeymen ?—Yes, certainly he would.

2311. (*Mr. Barstow.*) Did you hear Platts ask if there was any reason that he should pay other men's debts ?—No, I cannot recollect that he did.

2312. Will you swear that he did not ?—I should not like to take an oath of it. It is just possible that he might or he might not. I know that it has never been thought of in our trade to make one man pay another man's debts.

2313. Did Platts then say that he should not object to pay his own ?—I am sure I do not recollect.

2314. You do not recollect whether he said so ?—I am sure that I cannot. I really could not be certain upon it at all.

2315. Did Platts then pay his arrears ?—Yes. It is down in our book, and so he must have paid them.

2316. Did you make any entry in the book with reference to it ?—No.

2317. (*Chairman.*) Do you know whether Colley's bands were taken at the same time ?—According to what Colley says, they were, or else I am sure I did not recollect it till it was named.

2318. But Colley's bands were taken at the same time ?—I believe they were.

2319. (*Mr. Barstow.*) Do you recollect Colley taking a note to you ?—No.

2320. (*Chairman.*) Were you ever shown a note addressed to Platts or Colley, in these words : " Sir, " You will find your bands in the storeroom under " the cistern. Yours respectfully, SWEEP. "—I never saw that note any further than I believe once John Platts held it in his fingers like that (*holding up his hand*), but it was a bit of paper and that was all I could distinguish from it.

2321. But he told you what was in it ?—I do not recollect that he did.

2322. Will you swear that he did not ?—He said that he was speaking in respect of his bands. He has named it more than once to me, I think.

2323. (*Mr. Barstow.*) At the same time, did Platts ask you for the wages that he had lost by reason of his bands having been taken away ?—No.

2324. (*Chairman.*) Will you swear that he did not ?—I cannot swear that he did not, if I cannot recollect these things I do not wish to swear any way.

2325. (*Mr. Barstow.*) But that was a remarkable thing to ask you, you must recollect whether he asked you or not ?—I am sure I could not recollect it. I should not like to take an oath of it.

2326. Did you ask him where he got the note ?—No, I do not think that I ever did.

2327. Did you or did you not ?—No I did not.

2328. When he held it up did you not say " What is that ?"—No.

2329. Do you mean to say that he did nothing but hold the note up ?—He held the note up and never allowed me to see it further than that.

2330. (*Chairman.*) You never asked where he got it ?—As far as I recollect, I never did.

2331. Did you ask where he got the note ?—No, I never did.

2332. (*Mr. Barstow.*) Do you mean that all that passed was, that he held up the note ?—That was all.

2333. Did you never say, " What do you do that for ?"—I do not know that there was any need to say so.

2334. Did you make no remark ?—He held up the note and said it was about his bands. I did not know what the note contained till I saw it in the paper.

2335. Did you say nothing when he said that it was about his bands ?—I do not know that I did.

2336. Did you not really say something ?—I do not recollect that ever I did.

2337. Did he say that Robinson had given him the note ?—I believe he said that he had found it in Robinson's window. I believe that I recollect that he said that some party had put it through the window.

THIRD DAY.

R. Holmshaw.

5 June 1867.

2338. Did you make any remark at all about Robinson ?—Not at all.

2339. Did you say, "He is a soft ———, we must be shut of him at any rate ?—Such language I never used.

2349. (*Chairman.*) Did you tell him that you must get rid of Robinson ?—No.

2341. Not at the time ?—No, I never said such a thing.

2342. (*Mr. Barstow.*) Was Robinson, in fact, got rid of not long after that ?—I do not know; I am sure I do not recollect.

2343. You were president ; did Robinson cease to be collector shortly after this occurrence ?—I am not aware.

2344. (*Chairman.*) You went to America ?—Yes. You are asking me questions that I do not know anything about.

2345. (*Mr. Barstow.*) At the time we have been speaking of was it a sick society or only a trade society ?—Only a trade society at that time.

2346. Do you remember at what time it became a sick society as well ?—I am sure I could not tell the date ; our secretary will have it I daresay.

2347. Do you remember Platts making application to you for scale ?—Yes.

2348. Did you say to him, "You are a manufacturer ?"—No ; I told him distinctly that he could not have it on account of his being in arrear with his contribution.

2349. You did not say to him that he was a manufacturer ?—No, I could not do it, because we had not a rule in any shape or form to prohibit his receiving if he was not in arrear of his contribution.

2350. (*Chairman.*) But it was not a sick club then, was it ?—Yes, I think it was then. Yes, certainly, when he applied for his scale it was a sick club at the same time.

2351. (*Mr. Barstow.*) Did Platts say, "I pay to the trade" ?—Yes.

2352. Did Platts, in fact, get any relief ?—No.

2353. You refused him ?—Yes, as any other member would have been refused.

2354. (*Chairman.*) Did you offer to give Platts 16*s.* if he would pay 7*l.* 2*s.* 10*d.* ?—No.

2355. (*Mr. Barstow.*) Did you see Joseph Gale give Platts a piece of paper ?—Yes.

2356. There were the arrears I suppose ?—Yes.

2357. (*Chairman.*) That is the 7*l.* 2*s.* 10*d.* ?—Yes.

2358. You saw him give him that ?—Yes.

2359. (*Mr. Barstow*). Did Platts say, "What do you consider me ?"—I think he said something to that effect.

2360. Did he also say, "I will not pay 7*d.*" ?—Yes.

2361. And then, in the following week, did you call upon him ?—I do not know whether it would be the following week or not.

2362. Shortly after that did you call upon him ?—I called upon him to see whether he had any work for Booth.

2363. That is another occasion. Did you call upon him to ask him to pay ?—I did not call upon him till Booth had commenced work ; he had commenced work previous to Booth.

2364. Did you ever "dun" him for his natty ?—Yes, on one occasion I asked him if he was going to contribute.

2365. Did he say that you had a good deal of brass in your face to come and ask him for anything more ? —Yes, he did.

2366. Did you say to him, "You must not consider "that we are lumps of wood, and that you can do just as "you have a mind ?"—No, I am not aware that I did.

2367. (*Chairman.*) Will you swear that you did not ?—Yes.

2368. Nothing of that kind ?—No, he had all the conversation to himself or nearly so.

2369. (*Mr. Barstow.*) Did Platts say, "Don't you "bother yourself, you have been here often before, if "you come again I will put you where you ought to "have been then "?—He never said such a thing.

2370. That you swear ?—That I swear.

2371. (*Chairman.*) I understand you to say, he did not say that to you ?—Yes.

2372. Have you heard him say that he did ?—I saw it in the papers.

2373. He has sworn that you said this to him ?—And I swear that I did not.

2374. That is a point blank contradiction ?—Yes.

2375. (*Mr. Barstow.*) Did you say, "I need not "give you the note "?—I am sure I do not recollect, I might have said so.

2376. Will you swear that you did not say so ?—I might have said so. I recollect his naming the note, and I believe I said I had nothing at all to do with the note.

2377. Did Platts say, "No, but your collector did, "and you will have to answer for it " ?—I do not recollect such a conversation.

2378. (*Chairman.*) Will you say he did not ?—I will say he did not.

2379. He never said that your collector had given it him and that you would be responsible for it ?—I will not swear that he did.

2380. Will you swear that he did not, because it is a very serious accusation? Did he charge you with that or not, it is no use your saying you do not recollect ? —I think he did not.

2381. Will you swear he did not ?—I will swear he did not.

2382. Why not say that he did not at first ?—Because I do not want to swear anything of which I am not really certain.

2383. You are not really certain ?—No, but to satisfy you I will say he did not.

2384. But it does not satisfy us, personally we have no interest in this matter. A man comes and makes a charge against a person holding a responsible situation like you do in the union, and he says, "I went and "charged him with having been a party to taking "away my property. I told him a note had been given "me by one of his members, and that I should hold "him responsible for it ;" and nothing was said against it. What a wrong thing it would be to you not to allow you to come and say, "Well that is false." Therefore in kindness to you, if it did occur to you, you can contradict it.

(*Mr. Barstow.*) You know this was a conversation charging you with felony, you must remember something about it ?—It is not an uncommon thing for men to fly into passions on even the most frivolous affairs, even in asking for contributions, when they are in a pet, and Platts being an irritable sort of man flies into a passion almost if you look at him.

2385. (*Chairman.*) But we ask you, did he tell you that Robinson, or you had given it to him, and that he would hold you responsible for it ?—I do not believe he did.

2386. Will you swear that he did not ?—I will swear that he did not.

2387. (*Mr. Barstow.*) Did you say to him, "Well, "but we shall not do it in that way this time, we "shall do it in some other way " ?—No.

2388. You swear that ?—Yes.

2389. Did he say, "It makes no difference how you "do it so long as it is but done ?"—He never said that in my hearing.

2390. Do you remember applying to Platts on the 27th of April ?—On what question ?

2391. For his arrears ?—I never applied to him at all for his arrears, because I understood that he was to pay when he worked and to receive nothing, and when he did not work he was not to pay ; so I had no necessity to apply to him for his arrears.

2392. I ask you the question, did you on the 27th of April apply to Platts for his arrears ?—I asked him one day for his contribution, and that is all I said to him.

2393. Then it is not true that you kept applying to

THIRD DAY.

R. Holmshaw.

5 June 1867.

him from time to time ?—It was only his week's contribution, and not the arrears.

2394. (*Chairman.*) You asked him once only ?—Yes.

2395. Did you ever ask him for his arrears ?—I never asked him for his arrears.

2396. (*Mr. Barstow.*) Did you go to him from week to week for his contribution ?—No. Having to go to the place to the other men, on one occasion, I believe, I asked him if he was going to contribute.

2397. (*Chairman.*) That is the only time ?—That is the only time that I recollect.

2398. You know Platts says that you have gone to him from week to week ?—I have had occasion to go to other men.

2399. But Platts said that you had applied to him for contributions from week to week, is that true ?—It is not.

2400. (*Mr. Barstow.*) When you have been to the men have you said such a thing as this, "Now, Platts, " are you going to pay ?" except on one occasion ?—That is the only occasion that I can recollect.

2401. And you never did so but that one time ?—Never, that I am aware of.

2402. Do you know a man named Robert Booth ?—Yes.

2403. Did you ever call upon Platts to ask if he had any work ?—Yes.

2404. Was that on the 28th March of this year, or about that time ?—I could not give you the date.

2405. (*Chairman.*) But was it about that time ?—Yes, I suppose it would be.

2406. (*Mr. Barstow.*) Did Platts say to you, "I " have work for Robert Booth but not for the others"?—I think he did.

2407. Did you then ask him to pay ?—No.

2408. You are sure you did not ?—I am sure I did not.

2409. Then Platts at that time was not a member of the union ?—No. He had withdrawn himself.

2410. And Booth was a union man ?—Yes.

2411. Did not you say that before you could send Booth he must pay, or something of that sort ?—No.

2412. You are sure that you did not ?—I will swear that I did not.

2413. Do you remember the circumstance of some scissors belonging to Platts being taken from Pryor's hull ?—I recollect hearing the circumstance.

2414. Did Pryor say anything to you about it ?—Yes. I believe Pryor named it to me.

2415. Did you tell Pryor that he was not to take any notice of Platts ; if Platts claimed that he was to pay for them ?—No.

2416. You swear that you never said anything of the sort ?—Yes.

2417. Had you ever any conversation with Booth about those scissors ?—No, not further than casual conversation in respect to them ; that is all.

2418. You had a conversation with him ?—The thing has been named, certainly. Those things are necessary to name.

2419. Did you ever directly or indirectly advise or prompt Booth to take these scissors ?—Never.

2420. That you swear ?—That I swear.

2421. Do you know who did ?—No.

2422. Do you know if anyone did ?— I suppose some one must have taken them.

2423. But do you know if anyone spoke to Booth on the subject ?—Not that I am aware of.

2424. Now, on your oath, do you know who took those scissors ?—No, I do not.

2425. Do you know where they are now ?—No.

2426. (*Mr. Chance.*) You say that employers of the kind of which you have been speaking were not expected to contribute, but that when they did contribute they were to receive scale and the benefits of the union generally ?—Yes, if they contributed the same as the men.

2427. Then they receive scale in the same way as the men ?—Yes. We paid one of our employers scale on Saturday night last.

2428. Was it not the fact that some time ago a resolution was passed by your society that masters were not to receive any benefit from the sick fund ?—No.

2429. When you pass resolutions do you enter them in a book ?—Yes.

2430. Have you the book into which you put your resolutions ?—I think you had it a little time ago.

2431. I suppose that if a resolution were passed it would appear in the book ?—Yes.

2432. And you say that it was not passed ?—It was not passed.

2433. Then you say that there was no resolution of that kind ?—None whatsoever.

2434. And on all occasions where employers do pay their contributions they then receive all the benefits just the same as the journeymen ?—Just the same.

2435. You made a distinction a short time ago between employers who work at the wheel and other employers ; is that the distinction that where an employer works at the wheel then you expect him to pay contribution in the same way as if he were a journeyman ?—Yes, just so.

2436. But that where an employer does not work at the wheel then you do not expect him to pay contributions ?—No.

2437. Now, you tell us that those union men who are, generally speaking, members of your trades unions are the best workmen and the most sober men ?—Yes.

2438. Do you mean to say that there are no non-union men who are good workmen and sober men ?—There are some individuals.

2439. But do you mean to say that there are very few ?—Very few, comparatively speaking with the others.

2440. Can you give me any notion in round numbers of the number of non-union men in comparison with union men in your trade ?—There might be perhaps about a dozen who are what we might term steady men who do not join us.

2441. My question was this : can you tell me at all the proportion in your trades between non-union men and union men ?—I should think we should have in the trade such a thing, perhaps, as 30 non-union men.

2442. About how many union men do you suppose that there would be ?—I should think there would be 230.

2443. Do you mean to say that those 30 non-union men are men who are remarkable for drunkenness, or for being bad workmen ?—No, there are some few that are good workmen and there are some of them that are very bad workmen, and there are good workmen that are very intemperate men.

2444. Are there no men amongst your union men who are bad workmen or given to drunkenness ?—Oh yes. I wish there was not.

2445. Then it is not necessarily a rule that a union man is a good workman or a sober man ; it does not follow as a necessary consequence ?—No ; but we invariably find that those men that are in the habit of losing their time for drink cannot contribute as they ought to the trade and still they may be good union men in the heart.

2446. You say that you never make the masters responsible for the arrears of the men ; is that so ?—Never.

2447. But supposing men do not pay up their contricutions, if your application to them is unsuccessful, then you apply to the employers ?—Yes.

2448. And if the application to the employers is not successful, other means are then taken ?—We apply to the other two branches.

2449. And then if the application to the other two branches is not successful you endeavour to draw off the men ?—Yes.

2450. If then the employer, I suppose, pays the arrears of the men you let the men go back again ?—If the employer thought fit to do so, certainly.

2451. Is not that rather putting a pressure upon the employer to pay the arrears of the men ?—It is

THIRD DAY.

R. Holmshaw.

5 June 1867.

not a greater pressure than he puts upon us when he wants to lower us.

2452. But never mind that; is not that rather a pressure put upon the master?—I should think that it is a pressure put upon him.

2453. (*Chairman.*) If after you have gone to a man and he will not pay, you go to his master, and his master says, "I cannot pay for other men's debts, but "I wish my men would pay, and I will go to my men "and say, 'Now, union men, let us have no bother "'about it; go to Mr. Holmshaw and pay what you "'owe him,'" and they will not, and you withdraw the men; is not that a very great hardship upon the masters?—There is not a doubt but they consider it very hard.

2454. (*Mr. Chance.*) But is it not a very hard case?—Well, I think it is, and I sympathize with an employer under those circumstances. We must acknowledge that.

2455. The master does very often pay the men's arrears, does he not, in order to prevent your taking them away?—I told you before that I only recollect one instance.

2456. You gave us an instance where one of the employers paid a sovereign?—I recollect two cases. There was one just came across my mind. There was Mr. Gill; but it is simply a man saying to me, "Go to our master and ask him to give you so much money."

2457. And he gave it?—He did; the same as in the other case.

2458. (*Chairman.*) Mr. Gill paid for the men?—Only for one man.

2459. Who would not pay?—He was willing to pay, only he told me to go and ask the employer to lend him the money.

2460. But is it not the fact that the masters sometimes pay you when the men have refused to pay you?—They have never done so in our case that I can recollect.

2461. Are you aware that it never has occurred that a master has paid in order to prevent your taking his men away?—I am not aware that he ever has done so in our case.

2462. Are you aware whether the master in order to keep his men has paid what is due from them; is not that the case?—Not in our branch of the trade.

2463. Has it never occurred?—No.

2464. This will be published in the papers and if any man hears it who knows it not to be true he will come and contradict it. I daresay that you are quite right, but if you are inaccurate you will be contradicted?—Very well, and that might bring it to one's memory.

2465. (*Mr. Chance.*) You say that there are two circumstances under which an employer may be induced to pay; first of all it may be that he believes that the men are about to be taken off. Have you ever known an instance in which an employer has paid money in order to prevent his men being taken away?—Not in our branch of the trade.

2466. Nor in the other two branches, the scissor grinders and the shop board hands, which you have spoken of?—I do not know how they regulate all their business.

2467. Then I will confine my question to the scissor grinders; do you know any instance where an employer has paid money for the purpose of preventing the men being drawn off?—No, I do not know a single case.

2468. Do you know whether an employer has ever paid arrears of contributions for the purpose of getting the men back again?—Not in our branch of the trade that I am aware of.

2469. (*Chairman.*) Have you ever known it in other branches?—Yes, one which Mr. Thompson named.

2470. What is the case?—Hunter's.

2471. (*Mr. Chance.*) Is that the only case you know of?—That is the only case I know of. There might be others but I cannot recollect them.

2472. (*Chairman.*) I think you told my friend Mr. Barstow that you have in no case told a man that the rattening had been done by reason of his arrears not being paid up?—I do not ever recollect telling a man to that effect.

2473. You know whether you told him or not?—I never did.

2474. You have also said that you have in no case asked for the payment of money for the doing the rattening?—No.

2475. You have said that?—Yes.

2476. Is that true?—Yes.

2477. And that in no case have you ever restored goods that have been taken away?—I do not recollect that ever I did.

2478. Have you ever restored tools or bands, or anything which has been taken away?—Never.

2479. You never have?—No.

2480. You have never caused them to be restored?—No.

2481. You are not taken by surprise. I have cautioned you. Do you know a man called George Platts in Talbot Place Park, a scissors manufacturer?—Yes.

2482. You do know such a person?—Yes.

2483. Do you recollect when your union was first formed an application being made to him to join which he declined to do?—I do not recollect the application any further than by the collector that went round, who asked him to contribute.

2484. Do you recollect that he did not become a member of your union?—I think it was sometime before he paid.

2485. I believe he had not contributed up to May 1863?—I could not give you the date.

2486. Before he had contributed do you recollect hearing that his shop had been broken open and that his bands had been taken away?—I recollect him naming to me about his bands being taken away.

2487. At that time he had not contributed?—I cannot say whether he had commenced paying or not.

2488. Is not your belief that he had not; he says he had not?—He might be correct. I am sure I could not say.

2489. He did tell you that he had had his bands taken away from his shop?—Yes, he did.

2490. Did your committee ever meet at the "Punch Bowl," in Bridge Street?—Yes, at the commencement of our union.

2491. Did you tell him he had better go to the committee?—Yes. When he applied to me I should be sure to tell him to go to the committee.

2492. He applied to you about his bands, and you told him to go to the committee?—Yes, I should be sure to tell him that.

2493. Were you at the committee at the "Punch Bowl" on the following day when he came?—I recollect him coming, but I could not tell you the day.

2494. You recollect his coming to the committee room?—Yes, I recollect him coming; it is a long while ago.

2495. At that time what office did you hold; were you the treasurer?—Yes.

2496. And was the subject of his having lost his bands brought before the committee?—Yes, he came for that purpose.

2497. Did not he ask you why his bands had been taken away?—I do not know whether he did, but very likely he would. They are simple questions in themselves, which a man would ask under some circumstances I suppose.

2498. Did you say to him it was for back arrears?—No, sir.

2499. Now, mind; did you say to him it was for back arrears, or anything to that effect?—Not that I am aware of.

2500. Did you say to him it was for back arrears, or something to that effect,—that was in 1863?—It is a long time to recollect.

2501. But you know whether you told him it was for back arrears. When a man asks why his goods have been taken away you know whether you told him it was for back arrears or not. Did you tell him it was for back arrears?—No, I never did.

2502. There is no mistake about it, because this is very serious. Did you tell him it was for back arrears or not; speak boldly, if you did tell him so?—I feel almost certain that I did not.

2503. Will you swear you did not tell him it was for back arrears?—Would you really want me to swear a thing I am not certain of?

2504. I want you to tell the truth and nothing but the truth?—I am not sure whether I did say so or not.

2505. Are you aware whether you did or not? I do not want you to be responsible for this, because you may hear of it if it is not true?—You would not wish me to say a thing that is not true?

2506. I give you a caution?—You do not want me to say—

2507. You recollect when a man asked you why his bands were stolen whether you told him it was for back arrears or not. Did you say that?—I cannot be certain on it.

2508. You cannot be certain whether you did say so or not?—I might have said so, or I might not. I should not like to swear either way.

2509. If you might have said so, how was it that a moment ago you swore you never did say so?—Because you forced me into these things.

2510. Do not say that?—If I tell you I cannot recollect, you force me into saying a thing; you make me swear whether I can recollect or not.

2511. Is it so or not? You will not swear that you may have told him so?—I cannot possibly recollect.

2512. Did he ask you what you intended doing?—You must bear in mind—

2513. You must answer my question?—You must bear in mind it is a thing I could not say; it is so long ago that it is almost impossible for a man to recollect every word stated on that occasion.

2514. Here is a man charging you with stealing his property, and you are not going to tell me you do not recollect what the man said to you about it. Did not he ask you what you were going to do?—I do not recollect he ever asked me what I was going to do.

2515. Will you say he did not ask you?—I should not like to swear either way.

2516. Did you say to him that he must pay 1*l.* 13*s.*?—We might tell him his arrears were that amount.

2517. Did you tell him that his arrears were 1*l.* 13*s.*?—I could not tell you what amount he really did pay.

2518. Did you tell him that his arrears were 1*l.* 13*s.*?—Not that I am aware of.

2519. Will you swear you did not?—I should not like.

2520. You would not like to say you did not say that?—I should not like to swear either way.

2521. Did he ask you what the 1*l.* 13*s.* was for?—I think it is very likely he would do so.

2522. Did you say it was for arrears and expenses?—No, I do not recollect ever saying such a thing.

2523. Will you swear you did not?—I will swear I did not.

2524. You will swear you did not?—Yes.

2525. You swear you did not say it was for arrears and expenses?—Yes.

2526. You know what expenses mean?—There are expenses of many things.

2527. You do not know what I mean by expenses. Did you say arrears and expenses?—No, I did not.

2528. Did he tell you he would not pay it?—Yes, I think he did.

2529. Now, a night or two after this, did you and Gale go and see him?—I believe he sent word to me that he wanted to see me.

2530. Did you go to see him?—I went to see him because he sent for me.

2531. Did you meet him in Sheaf Street?—Yes, I think I did.

2532. Did you tell him you had come to see what arrangement could be made about the bands?—No.

2533. Did you say to him that if he would pay 1*l.* the bands should be given up?—I believe he named that circumstance himself.

2534. Did you say if he paid 1*l.* the bands should be given up?—No; he said he would pay 1*l.* himself.

2535. Did you say if he paid 1*l.* the bands should be given up?—No, sir.

2536. He said he would pay 1*l.*?—Yes.

2537. You did not say he should pay 1*l.* if the bands were given up?—No.

2538. Did Gale in your hearing?—I am not certain whether Gale was there.

2539. You are not certain whether Gale was there?—No.

2540. I am speaking of Sheaf Street?—Yes.

2541. Did anyone in your presence say the bands would be given up if he paid 1*l.*?—I am not aware.

2542. You are aware whether somebody did or did not, you know whether a person said to the man "If you pay 1*l.* the bands will be given up"?—I think the conversation was between him and me.

2543. Was anything of that kind said when you met him? Now you must answer that; did you tell him if he would pay 1*l.* the bands should be given up?—I say distinctly, no.

2544. Was it said in your presence?—I do not recollect it.

2545. Did he say, "If I pay 1*l.* will the bands be given up"?—No. I do not recollect him saying that.

2546. Will you swear he did not?—I should not like to swear so when I cannot recollect it.

2547. He said he would pay 1*l.*, what for?—The arrear of contribution.

2548. Would that get his bands back?—No, it was to become a member of the trade.

2549. Did you tell him that 13*s.* of the 1*l.* 13*s.* was for the "Sweep"?—No.

2550. What do you mean by the "sweep?"—It is a new term to me.

2551. You never heard it before?—I never heard it any further than what is talked about in the town.

2552. What does "sweep" mean as talked of in the town?—It is a term like "Mary Ann." I think "rattening" has generally been the name.

2553. "Sweep" as talked of in the town means the man who rattens?—I suppose it has the same meaning.

2554. "Sweep" means a man who rattens?—Yes, I should think that is the meaning, and the term is generally "rattening."

2555. What does "Mary Ann" mean, is that the man who rattens too?—Yes, I suppose they are all one term.

2556. Is "Nathan" the same thing too?—Yes.

2557. These names are usually put at the bottom of letters are they not, sometimes they write the signature "Mary Ann," sometimes "Nathan," and sometimes "Sweep"?—I should think they do. I never had any writing of a letter.

2558. But letters are written?—I never saw one signed that way in my life, except the one Platt's held up in his fingers.

2559. That was signed "Sweep" according to what he says?—Yes.

2560. You never saw such a letter?—No.

2561. You have heard of one very often?—Yes.

2562. A great many people in the town have received such letters?—I am not aware of any.

2563. Do you mean to say it is not a thing of common knowledge in the town that these letters are sent about?—I am sure I have no knowledge of anyone receiving one.

2564. How do you know then about "Mary Ann"?—The first account I ever heard of "Mary Ann" was what I saw in the newspapers.

2565. When was that?—Some little time ago.

2566. Did you see a letter in the newspapers signed "Mary Ann"?—Yes.

2567. It is known in the trade that "Mary Ann"

THIRD DAY.

R. Holmshaw.

5 June 1867.

means a man who rattens ?—I never heard the term till I saw it in the newspaper.

2568. You have heard it since ?—Yes.

2569. It is known in the trade as a man who rattens ; if a man gets a letter signed " Mary Ann " he knows pretty well what it means ?—Yes, I daresay he would.

2570. And he would look out for his tools ?—It depends.

2571. Having called your attention to the word " sweep," and what it means, did not you tell Platts that the 1*l.* was for the arrears and the 13*s.* was for the sweep ?—Not that I am aware of; I never recollect telling him so.

2572. You may have told him that the 13*s.* was for the sweep ?—I should say distinctly no that I never did.

2573. You say you cannot recollect telling him ?—If I never did I could not recollect.

2574. May you have told him ?—No.

2575. You may not ?—I never have.

2576. You swear that you never told him ?—I swear that I never have.

2577. Did he pay you 1*l.* ?—Yes, for arrears of contributions, and became a member of the trade.

2578. At the time you took the 1*l.* did you tell him that the bands would be forthcoming and that there should be no more bother ?—No.

2579. Do you know that the next morning his bands were taken to his yard ?—I do not know ; I know that he got his bands back, but I do not know when he got them back.

2580. The next day after he had paid you did not he get them back ?—Not that I am aware of; I do not know when it was. I know that he did get his bands back I have heard him say so.

2581. If Mr. Platts comes and contradicts you on all these points, you must recollect I have given you ample opportunity for giving all the information about it, and it is our duty, having got private information about different things, to ask you about them ?—I speak to the best of my recollection ; I hope you do not want me or any other man to answer questions that I cannot recollect.

2582. There is no danger if you make a full disclosure ?—If I could recollect having said so I would not deny it for a moment, but I cannot recollect any conversation of that description having taken place ; with respect to what he states it is another thing.

2583. I want your attention to a simple question. In no case have you given instructions to the men to do any rattening ?—Never.

2584. Have you been told by a person that he had done rattening ?—No, never.

2585. Have you ever caused bands to be returned that had been rattened ?—No.

2586. Have you received money in order to get bands returned ?—I have received money as contributions.

2587. But never to get bands returned ?—No.

The witness withdrew.

J. Gale.

JOE GALE sworn and examined.

2588. (*Mr. Chance.*) What are you ?—A scissor grinder.

2589. How long have you been in the trade ?—I was apprenticed in the year 1850.

2590. When did you become a journeyman ?—In 1858, nine years ago.

2591. Are you a journeyman now ?—No, a scissor grinder ; as a rule we are master grinders, though you might term us journeymen. I am employed for a scissors manufacturer in the town.

2592. You employ journeymen ?—Sometimes.

2593. And you also work yourself ?—It is the rule in the town that scissor grinders are master grinders because they find their own tools and pay for power, and can leave at a moment's notice.

2594. You sometimes employ journeymen and sometimes not ?—Yes.

2595. Then you work for yourself, and are at the same time an employer, and also a scissor grinder ?—Yes, and also a journeyman.

2596. You are secretary, are you not, to the Scissor Grinders Union ?—Yes.

2597. When did you become secretary to the union ?—This is a new minute book (*producing the same*), and it is an abstract of the other book.

2598. You have the other book with you ?—Yes.

2599. Refer to it, and tell us when you became secretary ?—March 24th, 1862.

2600. You have been secretary since March 1862 ?—Yes.

2601. What are your duties as secretary ?—To keep the books. I think you will find in the rules that my duties are defined.

2602. What are the duties of the secretary, to keep the books, and what else ?—The treasurer's duties are to collect contributions and wait on manufacturers and men when there is any difference, and to find men to work for the manufacturers when they require them, and in collecting money, attending meetings, and paying monies out. My duties are to book the contributions that are paid, and keep a correct account of all monies paid and received, and all minutes of the committee and general meetings.

2603. You keep a book of the contributions, and keep an account of what takes place ?—Yes.

2604. Is it your duty to enter those in your book ?—Yes.

2605. (*Chairman.*) Have you your book containing your disbursements ?—Yes.

2606. Will you allow me to see them ?—Yes ; here is the sick book, here is the unemployed, and here are the expenses every week.

2607. Have you any balance sheet ?—It is in the book.

2608. (*Mr. Chance.*) Does this book commence from the time that you commenced being secretary ?—Yes.

2609. Does it go back any time before that?—Yes, two unions before this one and a portion of another.

2610. Is it your duty at all to pay money ?—No, I never handle money, unless it is anything like postage. If I have any letters to write I get the postage stamps.

2611. That is the only sum that you pay out ?—Yes, it comes out of the treasurer's hands.

2612. You do not handle any money ?—Except when a member gives me contributions ; the treasurer receives the contributions.

2613. But you sometimes receive the contributions for the treasurer ?—Sometimes for the men that work at our wheel ; a man in the town will say, " Will you " take my contribution ? I shall not see the treasurer " this week."

2614. If paid to you it is not as the secretary but as a matter of convenience, and you pay it over to the treasurer ?—Yes.

2615. What are the objects of your society ?—The object of the society when first formed was to obtain and maintain a fair and equitable price for our labour, and resist the tyranny of our employers ; that was the object of the trade society.

2616. Was it a trade society or a sick society ?—A trade society only.

2617. Has it become a sick and funeral society ?—Yes.

2618. It was to obtain a fair price for your labour ?—Yes.

2619. (*Chairman.*) And protect yourselves against the arbitrary usage of your masters ?—Yes.

2620. (*Mr. Chance.*) The expression you used was, to protect yourselves against the tyranny of your employers ?—Yes, and not without occasion.

2621. When did you form the sick society ?—The first sick money we paid was October 14th, 1865, so

THIRD DAY.

J. Gale.

5 June 1867.

I think we had formed it about three weeks before that.

2622. Before it became a sick society all the contributions that you received were for the purposes of your trade?—Yes.

2623. Up to 1865 you received no contributions except such as were for the purposes of your trade?—No, until a few weeks before October 14th.

2624. Who were the members of the trade that had to pay contributions to you; they were the members of the society?—All men working as scissor grinders.

2625. When you say men working as scissor grinders, you do not mean that all men working as scissor grinders were members of your union?—No, some held back for a long time.

2626. But all that became members paid the contribution?—Yes.

2627. How much did they pay?—4*d.* a week for a length of time.

2628. Then I suppose sometimes these contributions fell into arrear?—Yes.

2629. Was 4*d.* a week the sum paid till it became a sick society?—No, it was advanced up to 8*d.* about March 9th, 1864.

2630. Still being a trade society?—Yes. We got an advance at that time in wages of 10 per cent.

2631. You got an advance of wages from the masters?—Yes, and we doubled the contribution to 8*d.*

The witness withdrew.

G. Platts.

GEORGE PLATTS sworn and examined.

2632. (*Chairman.*) Are you a scissors manufacturer in Talbot Place, Park?—Yes.

2633. You commenced manufacturing about 10 years ago?—Yes.

2634. About five years ago there was an attempt to form a scissor grinders union?—Yes, I believe it was about 1862.

2635. Were you called upon by a person named Nott, a collector, to join the union?—Yes, repeatedly.

2636. Did you refuse?—I refused several times to comply.

2637. Did you ultimately pay something?—Yes, I commenced paying 4*d.* a man and 2*d.* a boy. I paid 8*d.* a week, that was my amount.

2638. Did you go on paying?—Yes, I went on paying something like four or five months, and I thought it was all right; however, one Monday evening when I left work I saw the shop secure.

2639. What year was that?—In 1863, the latter part of May. I left my shop secure; on the morning following between 7 and 8 my apprentice came up to my house and said the bands were stolen.

2640. Did you go down?—I went down at once.

2641. In what state did you find your shop?—I found the partition board had been broken open and six wheel bands stolen.

2642. Is that the partition board that separated it from another grinding hull?—Yes.

2643. What was the value of them?—About 50*s.* as near as I can name; from that to 3*l.*

2644. What did you do?—I went to the committee the same evening.

2645. The committee of what union?—The Scissor Grinders Union at the "Punch Bowl," in Bridge Street.

2646. Whom did you see there?—I saw Mr. Holmshaw, Mr. Gale, Mr. William Sadler, and Mr. Bishop, and there were some that I did not know the names of.

2647. When you got there what did you say?—I said, "I have come to see about my bands. What "was your motive for taking them; I am paying "regularly"? I had not missed for four or five months, but paid every week.

2648. Who answered?—Mr. Holmshaw.

2649. What did he say?—He says, "Ah, some-"times you pay and sometimes you do not;" and I ascertained afterwards that the collector had appropriated some of those sums to his own use.

2650. He said "You sometimes pay and sometimes you do not?"—Yes.

2651. Did he give you any information as to why your bands were gone?—I believe Gale had to fetch his books.

2652. What was told you?—There seemed to be a deal of cavilling. Mr. Holmshaw told me that my contribution (I did not commence at the outset, it was back contribution) and arrears would be 1*l.* 13*s.* I declined at once to pay the amount, because I knew it was not so much.

2653. Did you say so?—Yes; I told them distinctly that they could not make it so much in contribution.

2654. What did Holmshaw say to that?—I had to withdraw, and when they called me in, Holmshaw told me I must pay the whole. I had not the amount with me; I had some 15*s.*; I offered them that and they declined to take it. I was very grossly insulted by William Sadler, in fact he was beastly drunk; he got hold of my necktie and disarranged it, and used very vile epithets too.

2655. Did they tell you how the 1*l.* 13*s.* was made up?—Merely contribution and expenses.

2656. Are you quite sure that they made use of the word "expenses," that the 1*l.* 13*s.* was for arrears and expenses?—Decidedly; I am quite certain.

2657. There is no mistake about the word "expenses?"—No mistake whatever.

2658. Who said it was for arrears and expenses?—Holmshaw said so.

2659. Were there any expenses at all due?—I was not aware of it, but I supposed what they meant by expenses at once. I supposed they meant the "Mary Ann."

2660. You understood it to be the expenses of rattening then?—Of course.

2661. You have used the word "Mary Ann," is that a common word in the trade?—Repeatedly—it is a common phrase in Sheffield.

2662. It is a common thing—everybody knows it?—Yes.

2663. Is "Sweep" also a thing known in Sheffield?—It is synonymous of Mary Ann.

2664. Is it well known?—Yes, and the "Man in the Moon," and so forth.

2665. They are well known?—Yes.

2666. If Mr. Holmshaw says he never heard of them till lately that is not what you say?—No, I have repeatedly heard of them.

2667. Have you ever seen letters with the name of "Mary Ann" or "Sweep," or anything of that kind attached to them?—I think I have seen them in the press, but not any real document.

2668. You say that it was for arrears and expenses—did you agree to pay them?—I consented to pay a pound.

2669. At that time you offered to pay a pound?—Yes, and I offered them 15*s.* down.

2670. And then you offered to pay them a pound?—Yes. I knew that was about my arrears.

2671. Did they agree to take that or refuse?—They refused.

2672. Did you thereupon go and give information to the police?—I went straight from there to Mr. Jackson and reported the case.

2673. (*Mr. Barstow.*) He is the chief constable?—Yes.

2674. (*Chairman.*) I believe that was on Tuesday?—On a Tuesday.

2675. On the Thursday following did you meet Gale and Holmshaw?—Yes, in fact they were waiting for me.

2676. Where?—In Sheaf Street, opposite the Queen's Hotel. They were standing there on the footpath. Holmshaw stopped me and said, "Now "then let us make an end and this here little bother."

THIRD DAY.

G. Platts.

5 June 1867.

I said, "Why did not you make an end of it on Tuesday "night when I offered you very fairly to pay a pound, "which I know is as much as I owe."

2677. What did he say?—He says, "Well pay a "pound now and there will be no more about it." I paid the pound forthwith.

2678. Did he say anything about the 13*s.*?—No, he did not name it; then I said, "How about those "bands, there are five of us idle." I had two journeymen, two apprentices, and myself. "I am very busy," I said, "When can I have them?" and he says, "All right, you will have them to-morrow."

2679. Well, what else?—This was on the Friday morning. I went down to the works pretty early, about a quarter past 6, the engine tenter was there; he said, "The bands have come back." I said, "In-"deed, where are they?" He said, "Under the "gateway."

2680. Were they there?—Yes, and some more bands of another man named Henry Leigh at the same time all mixed together.

2681. And you looked under the gateway?—They were in the gateway, there were nine or 10 bands. I had to sort my bands from Leigh's bands.

2682. Then Henry Leigh lost his bands?—Yes, from the same wheel at the same time.

2683. What wheel was it?—The Old Park grinding wheel, Sheaf Street.

2684. Would you have paid this pound had you not been sure of getting back your bands?—Decidedly not.

2685. Have you been a member of the union since? —I have paid regularly ever since.

2686. And have never been rattened since?—Never since.

2687. Do you recollect whether Holmshaw in your conversation with him mentioned the name of "sweep" to you?—Never.

2688. Not in talking about expenses?—He never mentioned the name of "sweep" to me.

2689. But he told you that 13*s.* was for the expenses?—Yes.

The witness withdrew.

J. Gale.

JOE GALE recalled and further examined.

2690. (*Mr. Chance.*) You were telling me just now that the first contribution was 4*d.* a week, and then after the wages had been raised the contribution was raised to 8*d.* a week?—Yes, 8*d.* per man and 4*d.* per boy; before it was 4*d.* per man and 2*d.* per boy.

2691. You say the prices had been raised, was there any particular reason why the prices were raised?—Yes, the men asked for an advance and obtained it.

2692. Was there any difficulty in obtaining the advance?—No, none at all, with the exception of a few tailors scissor grinders, shot scissor grinders, they asked a little more advance than the other branches, and there were some few men thrown on the box.

2693. Do you consider the prices were raised in consequence of the union?—Yes, we should never have got the advance if we had not got the union; the others got it without costing a single penny.

2694. Did the tailors scissor grinders get an advance of wages afterwards?—Yes, ultimately they got it without any man being on the box.

2695. From time to time the contributions of the members fell into arrears?—Yes.

2696. When the men are in arrears what is the course generally adopted by the union?—I can make an addition to what Mr. Holmshaw said; when men fall into arrears it is a weapon then in the masters hands, with not having a legal remedy the men fall out of benefit of which the masters take advantage and reduce the prices.

2697. When they are in arrears, why is it a weapon in the masters hands?—Because the men cannot receive any scale when they have no work, the masters can withhold the work, and the men cannot receive out of our funds, and consequently the price gets settled in some cases.

2698. The fact of their being in arrear arises from their being members of the union?—Yes.

2699. Therefore the weapon in the masters hands arises from the existence of the union?—Yes.

2700. Therefore if the union did not exist the weapon in the masters hands would not exist either? —Yes, to a far greater extent. Before the union was formed we never knew what price we were going to have till we got to the warehouse.

2701. As far as that particular weapon is concerned you say that when the men are in arrear of contribution that is a weapon in the masters hands?—Yes.

2702. The fact of their being in arrear is a weapon? —Yes.

2703. Therefore, supposing there were no arrears, there would be no weapon that the masters could use?—No, there would not.

2704. So far as that particular weapon is concerned it does arise from the existence of the union?—Yes, certainly.

2705. Supposing a man is in arrear, what are the steps taken by the union for the purpose of enforcing the payment?—I can only repeat what Mr. Holmshaw said.

2706. And not having any legal mode of enforcing the contribution, you, as a trade, are obliged to resort to other modes?—I will not go so far as that; that has been done, but not with the authority or sanction of the trade or committee. I will not say individual members have not done it.

2707. Individual members may have adopted some other mode than a legal one to obtain the arrears?—Yes, without the sanction of the trade or the committee.

2708. What is the first step, is it as Holmshaw told us, that when there are arrears you apply to the men to pay them?—He applies to the men and reasons with them, and shows the advantage of the union.

2709. It is his duty as president and treasurer to apply to them?—He is collector, president, and treasurer of the committee.

2710. Then when there are arrears it is his duty to apply to the men for payment?—Yes.

2711. Then if you do not get it from the men you apply to the masters?—Yes, as Mr. Holmshaw has said.

2712. If you do not get it from the masters then you draw off the men on strike?—It is his duty to see the men in the other branch of the trade, and see what they say of it.

2713. If you cannot by any of those measures obtain the arrears of the contribution, you then draw off the men on strike?—We never have done, though we might do if we saw a necessity for it.

2714. You never yet have drawn men off on strike to obtain the contribution?—No, never.

2715. Not during the whole course of time this trade union has been established?—No, not drawn the men off for this purpose.

2716. (*Chairman.*) Have you ever drawn any men out?—No, to the best of my recollection I do not think we have ever drawn any men out for any purpose of trade.

2717. For any purposes at all?—Not for any purposes whatever.

2718. You have not drawn any men away?—No.

2719. (*Mr. Chance.*) You now confine your observation to the particular union of which you are a member?—Yes.

2720. That is since 1862?—Yes.

THIRD DAY.

J. Gale.

5 June 1867.

2721. As a fact, you never, for any purpose whatever, have ever drawn any men off work?—No.

2722. Having stated that generally, what do you mean by drawing the men off work?—You want me to suppose a case?

2723. Yes.—We will suppose that all the grinders where I work were in arrear; if Mr. Holmshaw sees that the men will not pay he goes to the employer and asks him to use his influence; he either refuses or says he cannot do any good; then in conjunction with the secretary of other branches he calls the men in the other branches together and asks their opinion, and if it was worth their while they would cease work and stop the factory.

2724. (*Chairman.*) But there never has been a case yet?—No, not in the grinders branch.

2725. (*Mr. Chance.*) You would support each other?—The trade requiring assistance would be supported at once.

2726. You say such a case never has arisen?—No, we never had an occasion to go so far as that; we generally obtained our object by the masters assistance.

2727. Has it ever occurred when you applied to the masters that the masters have paid the money which has been in arrear?—Mr. Holmshaw can answer that question best, because I never applied to the masters myself; he mentioned two cases, and they are the only two I ever heard speak of.

2728. Have you ever heard of any occasion that a master when it was represented that the contributions were in arrear has paid up the contributions, or any part of them?—Only in these two cases.

2729. Do you know of any other cases?—No.

2730. I suppose if a master were to pay up, supposing you had drawn the men off on strike, they would go back to their work as before?—We have not had a case of that kind. I cannot answer that question.

2731. You know very well that these cases called rattening do take place in the trade?—Yes, I am perfectly well aware of that to my sorrow.

2732. (*Chairman.*) Who does them?—If a man in the trade was to ask me me that question I should ask him what he was saying.

2733. I ask you who does it?—I do not know. I never did know, and if I had an opportunity of knowing, I never would know.

2734. You mean you would not let a party tell you anything about it if he wanted?—No.

2735. (*Mr. Chance.*) I suppose you can tell us pretty well how the thing is done?—I can say how some cases were done at the Union wheel. I believe Mr. Platts was done by the same men; it is only what a drunken man said in company, and he took it to himself; there is no harm to be done in telling, for the man is dead.

2736. About what time was this?—We had a general meeting on September 11th, 1862; at that meeting a resolution was passed, "That all that are in "arrear shall pay double contribution till they are "straight with the others, those that are straight to "pay the usual contributions." The general meeting sanctioned it unanimously. For about six months we had lives like dogs, myself and Holmshaw; we had men applying to us every week, saying, "Where are my bands?"

2737. Men were constantly applying to you to know what became of their bands?—Yes, bands were missing continually.

2738. How was it that these applications were constantly made to you?—Because the bands were going constantly about the Union grinding wheel, and the Soho grinding wheel, commonly called the Crofts.

2739. How many persons do you suppose in the trade at that time applied to you about their bands?—I cannot give you any idea.

2740. (*Chairman.*) Fifty?—No, not so many as that.

2741. Forty?—You might put them down at 40 during that time, Mr. Holmshaw among the number.

2742. (*Mr. Chance.*) Did Mr. Holmshaw apply to you?—Mr. Holmshaw lost his bands amongst the number.

2743. What was the value of Mr. Holmshaw's bands?—I do not know.

2744. Did you get them back again?—Yes.

2745. (*Mr. Chance.*) When they applied to you for these bands what did you do?—What could we do; we told them we knew nothing at all about them; some said they would pay their arrears off, and some said they would not pay; they said they must have gone through "natty."

2746. What did you tell these men when they came to you for these bands?—They did not come to us for the bands, they knew it was of no use; no man with sense would ask where the bands were.

2747. They came to you?—They applied to us for what they owed, and they told us their bands were missing; it was my duty to tell them what amount there was in arrears.

2748. (*Chairman.*) You say they told you that the bands were missing, and it was your duty to tell them what amount of arrears they owed?—They asked the amount of their arrears, and I told them.

2749. When you told them did they pay?—Some did, and some did not.

2750. (*Mr. Chance.*) Where did they, generally speaking, come to you to inquire about their bands?—To the committee.

2751. When did the committee meet?—We met then on Monday nights.

2752. Every Monday night?—Every Monday night at that time.

2753. Then were the arrears paid up?—Some of them were paid.

2754. Some were and some were not?—Yes.

2755. Do you know whether the bands were restored to them?—I do not know that there was any party who had the bands taken at that time that had not received them back again either sooner or later.

2756. (*Chairman.*) When the people did not pay their arrears?—They all came back.

2757. Were they given back when they did not pay?—They came back.

2758. You make use of that expression, "they came back?"—They found them in the wheel yard as a rule.

2759. After they had paid you?—Some without paying.

2760. You are before your townsmen. You say they came to you and asked what their arrears were and you told them, and their bands came back the next day. Do you mean to tell us and the public that the whole thing was not a trade business?—I mean to say that the trade had no connivance with it—neither myself individually, the committee, nor Mr. Holmshaw.

2761. How was it brought about?—As I said at first, this is what the man said when he was fresh, and it has been corroborated by others who had seen the bands that he took them himself, and was determined to make the men straight and to get a better price.

2762. (*Mr. Chance.*) Who was that man?—Joseph Parrott.

2763. (*Mr. Barstow.*) How did Parrott come to know that the men were in arrears?—He could very easily know; he could look over my book.

2764. Was Parrott a member of the committee?—No.

2765. (*Chairman.*) He was a union man?—Yes.

2766. In point of fact, did Parrott come to know of it by looking over your book?—I do not know that he did.

2767. You said he might do so?—He might look over my shoulder at my book or over the collector's book.

2768. (*Mr. Chance.*) When any man asks you for your book do you allow him to look at it?—No; when the collector is coming round to collect contributions the arrears are brought forward every month. Supposing you are paying the money, and the collector is putting it down here, you can see on the same page

THIRD DAY.

J. Gale.

5 June 1867.

who is in arrear. That is the way I suppose it has been done. I know nothing any further.

2769. Do you never hold the book so that he can see it?—I was not a collector.

2770. If a man comes to the committee, does the committee tell him who is in arrears or not?—No.

2771. Supposing he asks the committee, would the committee tell him?—We should tell him to mind his own business and settle his own account.

(*Chairman.*) That is not the way it is done at all; you do not tell him anything; that is not the way you would do it.

2772. (*Mr. Chance.*) You say it was never connived at or encouraged by the trade?—No.

2773. Have you done anything to discourage it?—Yes; I worked very hard to form a sick and funeral fund, so as to get men to pay, to avoid rattening in future.

2774. (*Chairman.*) Then that was in order to avoid rattening in future?—Yes.

2775. I do not understand that. You say you worked very hard to form a sick and funeral fund, do you give me to understand that it was because men had not paid that the rattening took place?—I say it had; I have in this case that I have stated.

2776. And it was in consequence of their not having paid?—In my opinion.

2777. You say you worked to avoid rattening in future?—I wanted to remove the cause.

2778. The cause was non-payment and you wanted to remove the cause by getting the men to pay?—Yes.

2779. (*Mr. Chance.*) Did you succeed in forming a sick and funeral society?—Yes.

2780. It was mooted you say several times; when did you succeed in forming it?—It would be September or October 1865 when we first commenced paying to the sick society.

2781. Did you find that the result was that after you established that society rattening became less frequent?—Yes.

2782. Supposing contributions are in arrears, now what course is adopted for the purpose of obtaining these arrears?—At present we are taking no steps; men have to suffer and they are suffering fearfully, many of them on account of trade being so bad; they are suffering from shortness of work.

2783. In what way would the formation of such a society as this prevent rattening?—Because the men have a double benefit; for a small trifle we can afford to pay the sick and funeral expenses.

2784. The men have a double benefit?—Yes.

2785. But they have to pay a larger contribution in consequence?—4*d*. per man.

2786. Fourpence per man, is that to the sick fund?—Yes.

2787. How much do they pay besides the 4*d*.?—1*s*. 2*d*., making the total contribution 1*s*. 6*d*. per week per man.

2788. Still if the contributions in respect of trade are in arrears, is there not the same temptation to ratten as there was before?—I leave you to put your own construction upon that.

2789. You say a society was formed for the purpose of diminishing rattening. I want to know how it would succeed in that way?—It caused many men to become financial that were not financial before.

2790. Do you mean by "financial" becoming improvident?—Men that were not able to receive relief since the sick and funeral fund was formed have become able to receive.

2791. (*Chairman.*) Directly a man pays his money and contributes he gets the benefit of his club?—Yes.

2792. (*Mr. Chance.*) You mean by being "financial" having the benefit of a club?—Yes.

2793. Do you know a man named John Platts?—Yes.

2794. Do you remember in the year 1863 Platts losing his bands?—Yes.

2795. About the 28th of February?—It would not be that date.

2796. Have you a memorandum of it there?—Yes, I made a memorandum of it on the committee night, and I see in the contribution book that when this money was booked was February 23rd, 1863.

2797. Platts was a member of the union at that time?—Yes.

2798. Do you remember at the committee meeting Platts coming to the committee?—Yes.

2799. Do you remember what he came for?—Of course he said his bands were missing, and he wanted to know what he owed.

2800. That was on Monday night?—Yes, we only met on Monday nights then.

2801. Who were present at the committee that night?—I can tell you every man. Henry Braithwaite, Henry Burke, William Burke, John Malkin, Daniel Hemmings, Thomas Nott, William Lomas, William Rogers, William Sadler, Henry Thomson, William Sanderson, John Willy, Robert Holmshaw, Joe Gale, and Joseph Smith.

2802. Are those all?—Yes.

2803. All those members of the committee were present on that night?—Yes, on that evening.

2804. When John Platts' came to the committee about his bands?—Yes.

2805. How did he introduce the matter?—I think you might form an opinion after seeing his performance here last Monday in his usual roaring tearing style.

2806. Did he inquire after his bands?—He always comes the same as a maniac when he has to face the trade, as he always does when he comes before the committee.

2807. Did he say, "If you had sent me a note "stating what you wanted I should have known what "to do"?—I cannot remember the conversation; he might have said that or he might not; he said many things; he was there I should think from about 8 to 11 o'clock.

2808. What he said was in reference to the loss of his bands?—Yes.

2809. (*Chairman.*) And he was charging you with having been the cause of it?—Yes.

2810. (*Mr. Chance.*) Did you say, "Pay your money, and they will be back to-morrow"?—I should have more sense than to say a thing of that sort.

2811. Did you say so?—No, nor would any other man with any reason at all about him.

2812. Did he say to you, "How can you guarantee "they shall be back if you do not know anything "about them"?—He might have said so. I should never guarantee him his bands when I know nothing about them.

2813. Was the effect of that his telling you that you knew about them?—He wanted to imply that we knew about them.

2814. (*Chairman.*) He was three hours in the room charging you with being the cause of taking the bands away?—That and conversation.

2815. (*Mr. Chance.*) Did he ask you what his arrears were?—Yes.

2816. Did you tell him?—Yes.

2817. What were his arrears?—He said on Monday that I said 1*l*. 10*s*. 0*d*. or 1*l*. 12*s*. 0*d*. I find on looking at the book that the arrears were what he said 11*s*. 6*d*.; he paid that and I booked it; if I coupled his man with him it is unknown to me.

2818. You say if you coupled his man with him it is unknown to you?—It is unknown to me at the present time.

2819. Do you remember his asking whether it was reasonable that he should have to pay another man's debts?—No, I cannot remember anything of the conversation.

2820. (*Chairman.*) You would not like to be certain upon that?—No.

2821. (*Mr. Chance.*) He was charging you with taking his bands?—Yes.

2822. It was an important matter to be charged

THIRD DAY.

J. Gale.

5 June 1867.

upon?—A man like that I do not care what he says. I take very little notice of what he does say, because he is qualified to say anything.

2823. Did he pay the arrears?—Yes, I had them booked for that date.

2824. Do you remember that he got his bands back?—I heard the Monday following that he had received them back.

2825. (*Chairman.*) After he had paid you the money?—Yes, it was a week after that that I heard he had received his bands during the week.

2826. Can you give me any notion of how it was that he happened to lose his bands and get them back again?—I was not there when they went.

2827. Have you got any opinion about the matter? —As I said before this Parrott he had pulled the prices down to a very low figure himself, and he got other men to work at the same figure, and he could not do it any longer. He said he was determined to make the men straight, and he owned doing it. He was a very good-natured fellow, and fond of working for nothing, for he never charged a single halfpenny for his trouble.

2828. You did not charge anything for his expenses?—He never made any application.

2829. I understand you that you believe this rattening that took place was done by a man who was a member of your union who wanted to increase the price of wages?—Yes.

2830. That it was not done by order of the trade. Your belief is that it was done by a man connected with the union, but that he was not ordered to do it by the committee or anybody else?—It was done on his own responsibility.

2831. In the first place how did he know that there were arrears?—I have explained the reason.

2832. That he might have looked over the men's books?—Yes, and also from this, that the assent of a meeting was asked for somewhere about the time they knew the men were getting into arrears, and they asked for all their names to be called over and the amount every man owed.

2833. That was done?—Yes, at the general meeting.

2834. All these men who were in arrears had their names called out at the general meeting?—Yes.

2835. If a man wanted to do a mischief he could do so?—He could get to know what they owed.

2836. Who ordered these names to be called out? —It was a motion at the general meeting. There was a proposal made and carried unanimously.

2837. You say that if a man would tell you he had done it you would not hear it?—No.

2838. You would say that you would have nothing to do with it?—Yes, I would.

2839. You would not connive at it?—No, I would simply be *non est.*

2840. (*Mr. Barstow.*) Did the men in arrears attend the general meeting?—Yes.

2841. Did they consent that their names should be called over?—Yes; it was put and carried unanimously.

2842. You have a minute of that?—Yes, I daresay I shall find it.

2843. (*Chairman.*) You say the man would know who were in arrears because you passed a resolution that the names should be publicly announced of those who were in arrear?—All the names were called over, what they owed, and whether they were straight.

2844. I am supposing that Parrott was the man who did it. Parrott took the things, and then Parrott, after the money had been paid by these men, restored the bands?—I suppose he did. They came back.

2845. How was Parrott to know that the money had been paid except from you?—It would be talked of by the committee; the money was paid to the committee.

2846. You say that the names had been called out at the general meeting, and then after the money was paid that was proclaimed by the committee?—They would naturally say so-and-so had been and paid his money.

2847. Parrott was not a member of the committee but he was a union man?—Yes, he paid his contributions to the trade.

2848. He is dead?—Yes; and a bad thing for his wife and family.

2849. (*Mr. Chance.*) Do you remember Platt's coming again about his bands a second time complaining that they were not given back again?—No, he never complained to me.

2850. You were not present when he came into the office?—No, I worked at this end of the town.

2851. Do you remember sometime after that on some Tuesday night, you being with Holmshaw, that Platts applying to you for payment of scale?—Yes, John Platts applied for payment.

2852. (*Chairman.*) I want to ask you about the committee's statement; when did the committee state that the persons had been and paid their contribution? —How should I know?

2853. How was it done?—I do not know, they would tell anybody they met.

2854. How was it stated by the committee, you say the committee stated when the persons had paid their money; how would it be done?—In ordinary conversation when they met the members of the trade.

2855. The arrears being paid they deemed it their duty to tell who had paid?—Yes, they would tell everybody in order to get his bands back.

2856. The committee, when the money was paid, deemed it their duty to tell everybody that the men had paid their money?—Yes; and then if anybody knew anything about the bands they would return them.

2857. You did that because you thought some person had taken them in consequence of this money not being paid?—Certainly that is the case.

2858. (*Mr. Chance.*) Do you remember Platts applying for payment of scale money?—Yes.

2859. Were you and Holmshaw together then?—Yes, we were in the committee room.

2860. Did you tell him that he was not entitled to any of the fund?—Yes, I referred him to the rule.

2861. Why was not he entitled to the fund?—Because he had not paid contribution the same as any other member.

2862. At that time he was a master employer?—Yes, a master grinder, an employer of labour.

2863. Did you offer to pay him scale if he paid his contribution?—We told him that if he would pay contribution like another man we would.

2864. He was not liable to pay contribution when not grinding?—It was a proposal made by the master grinders that when they were working that they would pay, and if they wanted to receive benefits they must pay contributions for every week whether they were working in the wheel or not, and Platts agreed on his own accord to pay when he was in the wheel, simply because he was taking away the work of another man when he was working, and we had the man to support.

2865. Unless he paid contributions while he was not grinding he would not receive any benefit?—No.

2866. Was a resolution passed by your trade that masters were not to receive any benefit from the sick fund?—No, we have not such a resolution on the books—the same rule applies to masters as to grinders.

2867. Were you with Holmshaw when he called upon Platts sometime afterwards?—No.

2868. Do you know George Platts?—Yes.

2869. Is he any relation to John Platts?—I believe he is a brother.

2870. Do you remember in May 1863 George Platts losing some bands?—I cannot remember the time, but I believe that he did once come down to the committee and say his bands were gone.

2871. Have you an entry in your book about it?—It will be in the contribution book what he has paid.

2872. You can find it in the book?—I have not the contribution book here.

THIRD DAY.

J. Gale.

5 June 1867.

2873. You have a book where the entries of the meetings of the committee are put down ?—Yes.

2874. Will not it be in that book ?—No, there would not be a resolution upon that subject.

2875. Did not George Platts attend the committee ? —Yes, he attended one night and said the bands were gone.

2876. Have you a note of it in the book ?—No, only when the resolution was passed ; we put down in the book all resolutions when the committee meet.

2877. Do not you make the entries in the book of the meetings of the committee ?—No, it shows the attendance of the committee.

2878. Do not you put down what takes place upon these occasions ?—No, except when a resolution is come to.

2879. There are no minutes of what takes place when the committee meets ?—No ; unless there is a resolution passed, then it is put down. If a man comes and says, "I want to pay my arrears" that is the ordinary course of things.

2880. You gave the place of the entry when John Platts attended before the committee ?—That was about the number of the committee men.

2881. Was any resolution passed then ?—No ; that was the committee attendance book.

2882. Are these the entries of the various meetings of the committee ?—Yes.

2883. Does each page represent a meeting of the committee ?—Yes.

2884. Would there be a meeting of the committee on this occasion ?—Yes.

2885. Just find me that, it is about May 1863 ?—I have the 4th and 11th of May here.

2886. You have no minute in that book as to what took place ?—No, we do not make minutes unless there is a resolution passed.

2887. Did they meet then as before ?—Yes, they meet every Monday night.

2888. Do you remember George Platts coming to one of these committee meetings ?—Yes.

2889. Do you remember who were present then ?—No; I could tell you if you know the exact date.

2890. You remember the fact of his coming ?—Yes.

2891. Would Holmshaw be there ?—Yes.

2892. Were Sadler and Bishop there ?—They were on the committee at the same time.

2893. Do you remember what he came about ?—Yes, he said his bands had been taken.

2894. Did Holmshaw say anything to him about paying his contributions ?—I should be the man they would apply to ; he would ask what he owed and I should look in the book and tell him the amount.

2895. Did you fetch your books to see what was in arrear ?—He said it was Tuesday night ; we meet on a Monday ; if it was Tuesday it would be a special meeting. We meet downstairs ; I should have to go upstairs to get the book then.

2896. Did Holmshaw say that the contributions and arrears were 1*l.* 13*s.* ?—I cannot say.

2897. Did Platts say he declined to pay ?—I do not remember the conversation sufficiently ; he was pretty stormy.

2898. Is George Platts as stormy as the other Platts ?—I think he is a little better ; but it is enough to make a man storm when his work is stopped.

2899. Did he say, "You could not make it as much in contribution ?"—I could not say.

2900. Just think ?—I have been thinking it over since Mr. Platts was up here, and I cannot call to recollection any conversation.

2901. (*Chairman.*) You are not prepared to say that what he says is not true ?—No, not what transpired that night.

2902. (*Mr. Chance.*) Do you remember the circumstance of George Platts withdrawing from the committee? —Yes ; every man when he makes a proposition to the committee has to retire till the committee have consulted.

2903. Do you remember the fact that he did on this occasion retire ?—No, but it is customary to do so.

2904. You do not remember his being called in again ?—I do not remember anything connected with it.

2905. Do you remember his offering to pay 15*s.* ?—No, I do not remember anything that transpired.

2906. He might have done so ?—Yes.

2907. You say that Sadler was in the committee room that night ?—No, I could not be certain about it.

2908. Do you remember an occasion on which Sadler was very violent ?—Sadler was often very violent when he came down ; he is in the habit of getting drunk, and he is then very noisy.

2909. He might have been drunk on that occasion ? —Yes.

2910. Do you remember whether he was drunk or not ?—I do not remember whether he was there or sober, or drunk.

2911. Do you remember him taking hold of Platts by the necktie ?—I do not remember that.

2912. Do you remember that ?—No, I do not remember seeing a case of violence with George Platts in the committee room.

2913. Can you say that it did not occur ?—No. It might have or might not have occurred ; I could not say.

2914. Might Holmshaw have said that that 1*l.* 13*s.* was for contribution and expenses ?—I should think from what I have seen of Holmshaw that he did not say so. I cannot say that I ever heard him say such a thing.

2915. May he have said so ?—I would sooner say that he had not.

2916. Will you say that he did not ?—I will not be confident either way, but to the best of my knowledge he did not say so.

2917. (*Chairman.*) You will not swear that he did not ?—No.

2918. (*Mr. Chance.*) Do you remember the Thursday following the Tuesday being with Holmshaw, and meeting Platts in Sheaf Street ?—I think Mr. Platts was wrong there. I think it would be the day following.

2919. Did you meet Platts the day following in Sheaf Street ?—Yes. I met Holmshaw, and he said, "We will see him together."

2920. Did you meet Platts in Sheaf Street ?—Yes.

2921. Did Holmshaw say to Platts, "Let us make an end of this here little bother" ?—No, Platts said he wanted to be friends with the union, he wanted to be comfortable altogether.

2922. What did you say to that ?—We said we did not want anything else but to be comfortable.

2923. Did Holmshaw say to him, "Pay the pound now and there will be no more about it" ?—No.

2924. Will you swear that he did not say so ?—No.

2925. Did he pay the pound ?—Yes, he paid a sovereign.

2926. (*Chairman.*) You will swear he did not say, "If you will pay a sovereign there will be no more about it" ?—It was Platts' proposition.

2927. Did Holmshaw say, "If you pay a sovereign there will be no more about it ?"—No.

2928. You swear that ?—Yes.

2929. (*Mr. Chance.*) Did Platts say, "Now, what about the bands ?"—He might have said some such thing ; he paid the sovereign and then went into conversation.

2930. Did he say, "I and my three or four men have been standing idle for two or three days," and did Holmshaw say, "Oh, they will be all right, you "will have them to-morrow" ?—No.

2931. (*Chairman.*) You swear he did not say so ?— I will swear he did not.

2932. Why did not you say so at once ?—Because it would be contrary to reason.

2933. (*Mr. Chance.*) Do you know when he got the bands back ?—I believe he got them back during the week.

2934. Do you know whether Henry Lee had lost his bands at the same time?—Yes.

2935. De you know anything about them?—It was at the same wheel.

2936. Was he in arrears of contribution?—Yes.

2937. And after he had paid his arrears he found the bands?—The bands came back the same as the others, and he said it was a friend of his that did it which got him into benefits that he otherwise would not have got, and he is very thankful to him for doing it.

2938. (*Chairman.*) You say you believe in this case that it was Parrott who did all these things?—I do at the union (Croft's) wheel.

2939. How many do you think Parrott did?—I could not say the number.

2940. Thirty to forty?—Yes, I think about that.

2941. How many of those do you think were persons who were in arrears?—Ten or a dozen there would be that were not in arrear.

2942. The rest were all in arrear?—Yes.

2943. You say if Parrott had come to you and offered to tell you that he had taken them away you would have refused to have heard from him at all?—I should.

2944. Since that time how many have been rattened? —I have no idea.

2945. Are you aware that in the course of the last 10 years there have been as many as nearly 200 persons rattened in the town of Sheffield?—I should say there have.

2946. More?—I do not know. I should think there have. There are many trades' unions in the town, and it will be 200 persons in 10 years.

2947. You think that is nothing for trades' unions? —I think it is nothing, considering what trades unions have had to suffer.

2948. You lay it all to trades' unions?—No, some.

2949. What do you lay to trades' unions?—I mean if these had not been formed this in our trade would not have occurred.

2950. You attribute all things to trades' unions. You do not believe it is done by the committee, but by members of the union?—These last I speak of.

2951. Is it all done in the same way?—I do not know of any other.

2952. Am I to understand that in these cases the committee, although they do not order them, would not make themselves acquainted from the person who did it how it was doue, or anything about it?—I would not.

2953. Was that a plan laid down by the committee to keep clear?—No, it was my own intention not to connive at them in any shape.

2954. It was the best way of conniving by refusing to hear anything about it. If a man had offered to tell you you would not have heard it?—No.

2955. Has any person called to tell you whom you have refused to hear?—Parrott told me, and I listened to his tale.

2956. When did Parrott tell you?—Shortly before his death.

2957. How long was it after he had done it?—I cannot remember exactly the time when he died.

2958. When did Parrott die?—I have no recollection.

2959. You know whether it was one, two, or three years ago. How long is it since Parrott died?—He has a brother in the court, he knows.

2960. Is it a year or two years?—It may be about two years.

2961. And a short time before his death he told you this and you would not listen to him?—Yes, I did listen to him.

2962. If he had come to you at that time you would not have listened to it?—No.

2963. If any other man were to come to you and tell you he had been rattening a man, you would say, "Go away, I will not listen to your story"?—I should say, "If you tell me I shall tell somebody else."

2964. Would you listen to him?—Not if he went away.

2965. Supposing a man came to you and wanted to tell you about a rattening job, if he gave you to understand he was the person doing it would you allow him to tell you or not?—I should say, "I want to know nothing about it; if you tell me I shall keep no secrets."

2966. And as a matter of course he would not tell you?—He would be a fool if he did.

2967. Has anybody been damaged in the scissors trade in their persons during the last 10 years?—I am not aware of any outrage on person or property except the bands, except the one that occurred last week.

2968. What was that?—It was a grinder at the Soho wheel; his bands were cut to pieces last Tuesday or Friday night.

2969. What is his name?—George Shackley.

2970. Has any person been blown up?—They have not the pluck to blow them up in our trade.

2971. Has it occurred in the town of Sheffield?—Yes, to the disgrace of Sheffield.

2972. But persons' houses have been blown up and they have been shot at and other things done to them; has anything of that kind occurred in your trade?—No.

2973. Nothing of the kind has occurred?—No, nothing of the kind.

2974. Nothing has ever occurred to any man in the scissors trade. No one has ever been shot at or had any gunpowder blown into his house, or anything of that kind?—No.

2975. The only thing that has occurred to members of your union is that they have been rattened?—Yes.

2976. (*Mr. Barstow.*) You said that your union was formed to protect you from the tyranny of the employers; do you mean anything else but an employer taking advantage of a journeyman to lower his wages?—No. I think that is sufficient; that was my meaning, lowering the wages and detaining the work and punishing the men.

2977. That was what you meant when you used the word "tyranny?"—Yes.

2978. Do you know of any act of intimidation, outrage, or wrong on the part of the masters towards the men; I speak of your own trade?—I cannot answer that at present.

2979. Do you know of any?—I am not aware of any at present.

2980. You know the question of wages is out of the scope of this inquiry?—Yes.

2981. You do not know any with reference to the employers?—No.

2982. I will ask you a question which I omitted to ask Holmshaw. Is it the rule in your trade that no apprentices shall be taken except they are the sons of freemen?—Yes.

2983. How does an employer know what sons of freemen are willing to be apprenticed?—We have never had any yet for them to take; we have never had a vacancy as yet.

2984. Then during the last two years there has not been a single apprentice entered in the scissor grinders' trade?—That is about the time; there has not been a single apprentice except the scissor grinder's own sons.

2985. I thought you said that no apprentice had been taken at all?—I understood you apprentice of a freeman's son.

2986. Supposing A is a freeman, and B is a freeman, and A does not want to take his son, but he must take the son of somebody in the trade, has there been a case of that sort?—Yes.

2987. That has been so?—Yes.

2988. How does a man know what freemen's sons are willing to be apprenticed; would he apply to you? —If we had one we should make it known; if there was a widow or a man that could not employ his son in the trade, if he wanted his son employed in the trade, and they made it known to the committee, we should make it known to the trade, applications would come in and we should decide.

2989. Applications would come in through the

THIRD DAY.

J. Gale.

5 June 1867.

parents of the children, is that so?—Yes; if parents made application to the committee the treasurer would spread it up and down the trade, and the men that wanted one would make an application for him.

2990. After the application has been made to you from the employer then you would let it be noised abroad that such and such a one would want an apprentice?—No, we never have had a lad yet that wanted a situation, but what they have found one themselves without applying to the committee, and we have sanctioned it.

2991. Must every apprentice have his apprenticeship sanctioned by the committee; in the case of a scissor grinder wanting an apprentice must he come to you for your sanction to take one?—If it is a member's son and not his own he will come down to the commttee for our sanction.

2992. Even if it is a member's son?—Yes.

2993. (*Chairman.*) If he were a stranger you would not allow it?—No.

2994. (*Mr. Barstow.*) I thought from your rule that he was at liberty to take any freeman's son?—That is with the consent of the committee, but we never had a case yet. I think there have only been one or two freemen's sons bound to another man, not their father, that I know of.

2995. (*Chairman.*) Your rule is that you are to have the control of it, and if you do not like it you would not let him?—Yes, I believe it would be the case.

2996. (*Mr. Barstow.*) If there was a particularly sharp and handy lad, not the son of a freeman, the employer could not have him at all?—No, our rules forbid it.

2997. And he must take an inferior lad as an apprentice or go without?—No, it is contrary to our rules.

2998. We have heard of outworkers, is there any regulation in your trade about outworkers?—No, they can either work in or out; a great majority of the trade are outworkers; there are only one or two cases where a master finds wheel power, and they have to pay for it.

2999. You said that the institution of the sick fund had diminished the rattening very much?—Yes. I do not know when we had a case; it is long since, except cases similar to the one of last week and the one the night before last.

3000. The cases of rattening have much diminished since that time?—Yes.

3001. That you attribute to your exertions in getting up a sick fund?—Yes.

3002. The payments since the institution of the sick fund are considerably larger than they were before?—Yes, 4*d.* per week more.

3003. And the men have also to pay the 4*d.* per week more?—Yes, because they have increased advantages.

3004. Does not that induce you to think that they appreciate the benefit portion of your society more than the trade portion?—I never took it into consideration.

The witness withdrew.

Adjourned to to-morrow at 11 o'clock.

FOURTH DAY.

Thursday, 6th June 1867.

PRESENT:

William Overend, Esq., Q.C.
Thomas Irwin Barstow, Esq.
George Chance, Esq.
J. E. Barker, Esq., Secretary.

William Overend, Esq., Q.C., in the Chair.

FOURTH DAY.

J. Staniforth.

6 June 1867.

John Staniforth sworn and examined.

3005. (*Chairman.*) I believe you are a saw grinder? —Yes.

3006. And you work at Hill Foot, near Sheffield? —At Moses Eadon and Company's.

3007. Where is their place?—In Saville Street East.

3008. How long have you worked with them?—Betwixt six and seven years.

3009. In what capacity do you work?—As a journeyman saw grinder.

3010. Were you brought up to the trade as an apprentice and so on, and afterwards as a journeyman? —I was with my father; he was a saw grinder.

3011. You were brought up to it in the regular way?—Yes.

3012. Were you ever a member of any saw grinders' Union?—Yes.

3013. When was that?—About 18 months since I joined one saw grinder's Union.

3014. Were you ever an officer in any of the saw grinders' Unions?—I have been secretary.

3015. Of which Union was that?—In what they call the Original Saw Grinders' Union.

3016. When was that?—21 years since, in 1845 and 1846.

3017. Was that the same Union as the Union to which you now belong?—No.

3018. Is it a different one?—Yes.

3019. What do you call that Union?—The Little Grinders' Union.

3020. But what did they call the first one to which you belonged?—That was called the Old Original Saw Grinders' Union.

3021. You were secretary?—Yes.

3022. Did you resign?—I resigned.

3023. When?—About the beginning of March, 1846.

3024. Did you still continue a member?—Yes.

3025. Up to what time?—18 months back from this time.

3026. Then what did you do?—I joined what they call the Little Grinders, the jobbing grinders.

3027. Can you tell me what is the difference between the two Unions? Is there any difference at all; are they associated together or not?—I was not satisfied with the proceedings of the original Union.

3028. Before going to what dissatisfied you, can you tell me who has succeeded you as secretary?—I believe a person named Joel Yellott.

3029. Do you know how long he remained?—I cannot say to a month or two, but it was a very short time.

3030. Who succeeded him?—Mr. William Broadhead.

3031. Then is William Broadhead secretary now? —Yes.

3032. He has been secretary for a good while then? —Ever since.

3033. Since 1846 or 1847?—I should say since 1847, as nearly as I can guess.

3034. You say that you were dissatisfied with the proceedings of the first Union and left it, what was it which caused you to be dissatisfied?—I did not like one man holding two or three situations.

3035. I do not quite understand what you mean—how was that?—The secretary was both secretary and treasurer, that is my meaning.

3036. You objected to Broadhead being both secretary and treasurer?—Yes.

3037. What was your objection to that?—I did not think he was doing his duty; he had plenty of of work in one situation without holding two.

3038. Whose duty was it to receive the contributions; was it the secretary's?—The secretary did receive them.

3039. And who paid them out?—The secretary.

3040. Then he was everything?—Yes; he was the treasurer.

3041. Who was there to overhaul his accounts?—They were chosen out of the trade.

3042. You had auditors?—Yes, of the sort they were of.

3043. Then was it on the question of finance that you left them, because you were not satisfied with the mode in which their accounts were kept, or what was it?—That is right.

3044. You objected to the mode in which their accounts were kept?—Yes.

3045. Now, were you satisfied with the auditors? —The auditors have nothing to do, only just simply as a school boy would do; if you set him a sum he will add up; that was the auditors' business, and nothing more. They did not know how the money was laid out, and they did not know how it was brought in.

3046. Do you know whether they had vouchers before them, that is to say, had they receipts produced for money paid, or anything of that kind?—No.

3047. How do you know all this; are you speaking of your own knowledge?—As to the receipts, all they have would be the scale book or the contribution book.

3048. Do you mean to say that they were obliged to take his word for every thing in that way?—Yes.

3049. Then according to that a secretary could have misappropriated funds in any way if there were no vouchers. Is that what you mean that you objected to?—I do not say that he did so.

3050. But he had the means of doing it?—He had the means of doing it in the way the accounts were kept.

3051. During the time you were a member of that Union did you complain of this system of keeping accounts?—Yes.

3052. To whom did you complain; did you complain to Broadhead?—To the whole body at a general meeting.

3053. And what answer did you receive to your complaints?—I had no chance of being heard; I was clamoured down.

3054. Could you fix a date about when you made that complaint?—I should say it would be three years back.

3055. What was the reason of your making this complaint; had you any suspicion that anything was wrong, or was it merely because it was a bad system? —I had suspicions that things were wrong.

3056. Had there been any events in the town which had called your attention to this mode of keeping accounts?—No; I cannot say there had.

FOURTH DAY.

J. Staniforth.

6 June 1867.

3057. There had not been anything in the town?—No.

3058. Can you tell me whether rattenings had been prevailing at that time before this complaint was made?—They might have.

3059. Do you know it?—I cannot speak to them.

3060. It was not in consequence then of any rattening at all?—I think not.

3061. Had there been any outrages at that time?—Not to my knowledge; not that I can call to memory.

3062. Had you before three years ago complained at all? Have you more than once complained?—I have complained several times more or less.

3063. I should like to know what you said?—The accounts used to be read over perhaps every two months, and when he read the accounts over he read the receipts and disbursements.

3064. That was Broadhead?—That was Broadhead; and in general the disbursements overran the receipts. There were more disbursements than there were receipts.

3065. So that you were in debt then?—Yes.

3066. Well what did you say to that?—I did not know how that was done.

3067. What answer did Broadhead give to that?—He gave no answer. He went on reading the books over, and when he came to "miscellaneous," that was a thing that I objected to very much.

3068. Did you express your objection to it at the meeting?—I wished to know how those "miscellaneous" disbursements were put in the book, and what was their form.

3069. Can you give us any notion of what was the amount?—It would vary. Sometimes it would be 7*l.* and 10*l.*, and from that to 14*l.* I have known it as high as 14*l.*

3070. Incurred within the previous two months?—Yes.

3071. Were they put under any head at all, or was it put "miscellaneous?"—Yes.

3072. And you wanted to know what that consisted of?—I wanted to know what it consisted of.

3073. And did you address that to Broadhead?—Yes.

3074. What did he say to that?—He said nothing. He gave me no answer.

3075. Did you press it upon the meeting?—I pressed it upon them to know how it was, but nobody could give me an answer what it was.

3076. What was the society of which you were a member. Was it a trades' society, or a sick society, or what kind of society was it?—You mean this society that Broadhead was secretary of?

3077. Yes?—It is a sick society.

3078. How long has it been a sick society?—I should think 18 years to my knowledge.

3079. Then has it been both a trade society and a sick society for 18 years?—Yes, and you may term it a funeral society as well.

3080. You are acquainted with the trade and the Union. Have you any notion at all how it could arise that there should be this kind of miscellaneous payments?—I could call to mind how they had done it, that is the reason I asked the question, but I could not get an answer.

3081. You have been secretary yourself have you not?—Yes.

3082. In your time had you payments of this description or not?—We had a committee at that time when I had the office, and that committee took the money. It was my place only to book it. The committee took the money and paid the money out.

3083. But had you in your books at that time any entry of large sums like 7*l.*, 13*l.*, or 14*l.* without any items at all?—No.

3084. Never?—No.

3085. You had accounts of the items set out?—Yes.

3086. How soon after you ceased to be secretary was it that you first observed in the accounts those miscellaneous sums?—That has not occurred farther back than these last seven years or nine years I should say.

3087. Have you from three years ago to the time that you left the society repeated your objection to those miscellaneous sums?—Yes; I have been dissatisfied with them.

3088. Had you expressed your dissatisfaction?—Yes, I have been dissatisfied with them. If I have not expressed my dissatisfaction at any meeting I have told parties belonging to the Union.

3089. Whom have you told?—I have told several people. I cannot speak as to the number.

3090. You say you were put down on one occasion by clamour?—Yes.

3091. Has any answer or explanation ever been given to you?—Not the least; not as to the miscellaneous account. I never could get to know how it was.

3092. And have you the slightest notion now what it was?—I have not.

3093. You do not know what it was?—No.

3094. Have you any suspicion as to what it was?—I cannot say. I should not like to say a thing unless I knew it to be a fact. I have in my own mind a suspicion as to what it is, but it is no use my saying without I know it for a fact.

3095. What were your suspicions that caused you to leave them—what did you suspect those miscellaneous items were?—I thought they were appropriated for some other purpose after paying the scale.

3096. Can you tell me what other purpose you suspected they were appropriated to?—I cannot say positively, and so I should not like to answer the question.

3097. But what did you believe they were appropriated to?—I cannot say for certain what they were appropriated to. If I knew for a fact I would bring it out.

3098. Did you ever mention what you thought they were appropriated to?—I did not.

3099. Never to anybody?—No.

3100. Have you never stated to anybody that you thought they were appropriated to improper purposes?—No.

3101. Do you believe they were appropriated to improper purposes?—I believe so.

3102. To what improper purposes?—I believe they were appropriated to other purposes than what they ought to have been, that is, paying men their scale.

3103. You paid your contribution I suppose?—Yes.

3104. What contributions did you pay?—It varied; it was sometimes more and sometimes less. We have paid poundage.

3105. What is your mode of payment in that Union?—It was half-a-crown in the pound; at one time it was 3*s.* 4*d.* and 4*s.* 2*d.* at another time.

3106. On your wages?—Yes.

3107. Supposing your weeks wages was a pound, you would have to give this sum?—Yes, half-a-crown, or 3*s.* 4*d.* or 4*s.* 2*d.*

3108. Do you mean to say you have paid as much as 4*s.* 2*d.* a week out of every pound that you have earned?—Yes.

3109. Will you be good enough to tell us what you could earn in the course of a week?—Taking an average, 2*l.* a week if I had work.

3110. Then have you paid to the Union as much as 8*s.* 4*d.* a week?—That has been the amount that has been levied upon us if we have not paid it.

3111. That was the claim by the Union?—Yes.

3112. And is that amount paid by certain members of the Union?—It has been paid by members of the Union.

3113. How much have you paid?—I have paid, sometimes when I could, as much as that, but I do not say every week.

FOURTH DAY.

J. Staniforth.

6 June 1867.

3114. You have paid it, but not always ?—I have paid it.

3115. Are their rules printed ?—No ; I believe not.

3116. Are they written ?—Yes ; I believe they are.

3117. I will not ask you about the rules until the book is brought ; they will speak for themselves. Were you a defaulter in your natty money ; did you not pay up your subscription regularly ?—No.

3118. When did you begin to be a defaulter and cease to contribute to the Union according to the scale of the Union ?—I believe I have paid twice these 18 months back.

3119. But I am speaking of the time before you joined the last society and when you were in the former society, Broadhead's society ?—That is the one I mean.

3120. How often were you a defaulter there ?—I cannot tell.

3121. But were you during the latter part of your time always in arrear ?—Yes.

3122. For how long before you left were you in arrear ?—I cannot say.

3123. About how long ?—Broadhead says he has sent for the books and that will tell.

3124. But cannot you give me a notion ; was it about a year or two years or how long ?—I cannot say to what amount.

3125. But for how many years were you a defaulter ? —I cannot say as to that.

3126. Do you recollect about what time you first began to be in arrear ?—I cannot say.

3127. Was it 1862, 1863, or 1861, or any other time ?—It might be that time.

3128. But it is rather important to me to know exactly ?—I cannot speak as to that.

3129. Have you ever been rattened ?—Yes.

3130. When was that ?—In 1862 ; that was the first time.

3131. That is just the very point that I wish to call your attention to. Have you a check contribution book ?—I have not. I destroyed them when I ceased to belong to William Broadhead's Union.

3132. Knowing when you were rattened that it was in 1862, can you tell me whether at that time you were a defaulter or not ?—I was a defaulter.

3133. Have you ever been rattened since ?—Yes.

3134. When ?—In 1863.

3135. What did they take from you in 1862 ?—There were four bands taken, and mine was amongst them.

3136. How many were yours ?—One.

3137. Whose were the others ?—Henry Bollington, George Bradshaw, and Abraham Green.

3138. Did they work all at the same place ?—Yes.

3139. Do you know whether they were in arrear also ?—Yes, they were.

3140. Now then, when was the next occasion that you were rattened ?—In 1863.

3141. Can you give us the month at all ?—It would be somewhere about May or June.

3142. On both occasions ?—Yes ; it was summer time I know.

3143. Were you still a defaulter in 1863 ?—Yes.

3144. What did they do to you then ?—Four bands went again.

3145. Whose were they ?—The same parties.

3146. Can you tell me whether on those occasions those same parties were also in arrear ?—Yes, they were in arrear the same.

3147. When was the next time that you were rattened ?—In 1866.

3148. Was that in June or May, or when ?—The 7th and 8th of September.

3149. What happened to you then ?—There were eight bands taken then.

3150. Whose were they ?—Christopher Taylor, senior, was one, Henry Taylor, Christopher Taylor, junior, Samuel Dungworth, Henry Bollington, Joshua Barton, Charles Challenger, and myself.

3151. Were they all workmen at Mr. Eadon's works ?—Yes.

3152. Do you know whether they were in arrear or not ?—I do not know whether they were all in arrear or not, but all their bands went.

3153. Were you ever rattened again ?—No, I believe that closed our career.

3154. And had you left at that time in 1866 ?—Yes, I had left the Union.

3155. At that time you had left the Union ?— Yes.

3156. When you had lost your bands in 1862, what course did you adopt ?—We made a search for them and we found the four bands.

3157. Where did you find them ?—They were found in a drain.

3158. Where was the drain ?—It was about 150 yards from where they were taken from ; from the wheel.

3159. It was from Saville Street that they were taken, was it not ?—Yes.

3160. Whereabouts was this drain where you found them ?—It would be close by the railway bridge, across the railway, about 150 yards from the place where they were taken.

3161. Was it a public drain, or what was it ?—No ; it was a drain that runs by the side of the railway.

3162. Was it a railway drain ?—I cannot say who it belongs to.

3163. Was it near the road or in a field, or how was it ?—It was at the bridge end, at the foot of the bridge.

3164. What induced you to go to look for it there ? —I do not know ; we thought that we might find them if we looked about ; there had been bands found in a similar way—and we found them there.

3165. You had no intimation given you that you would find them there ; but it was by reason of your searching places in the neighbourhood ?—Yes.

3166. Did you apply to the Union in 1862 ?—Not upon that occasion.

3167. Have you ever made any complaints to the Union with reference to those bands in 1862 ?—No ; we fetched them back to our works and commenced working as if nothing had happened.

3168. You were allowed to work ?—Yes, and we did work.

3169. Now what happened in 1863 ?—The same bands were taken as the first time.

3170. What became of the bands in 1863 ; did you get those back ?—We were not so successful that time.

3171. You did not find them ?—No.

3172. What did you do ?—We had no other alternative but to go to Broadhead.

3173. What did you say to Broadhead ?—I enquired for him at his own house and I told him that we had lost our bands.

3174. What did he say to that ?—He smiled and he said "indeed."

3175. Why did you go to Broadhead ?—That was the only alternative we had to get our bands back.

3176. Had you had anything to say to him before the rattening at all ?—He had been there frequently for contributions and did not get any.

3177. And he said "indeed," what next ?—I asked him how I was to get them back again ; he said, no doubt I was aware how they would come back by paying my contribution.

3178. Who said that ?—Broadhead.

3179. Did he say "by paying contribution ;" were those the words he used ?—"By paying contribution."

3180. What did you say to that ?—I said, "Well, what is it we have to pay ?"

3181. What did he say to that ?—He went into a room and he brought the contribution book and he looked our names over, and he found we had paid nothing. I asked him what we should have to pay. He said we should have one sovereign to pay as contribution and 5*s*. for Mary Ann.

FOURTH DAY.

J. Staniforth.

6 June 1867.

3182. Are you quite sure that he said that?—Yes, we had not got the money to pay just at that time.

3183. When you say "we" who were you?—The persons who were with me who had lost their bands.

3184. What were their names?—Abraham Green, Henry Bollington and George Bradshaw.

3185. And did they hear him tell you that you were to have your bands back again if you paid 1*l.* for your contribution, and 5*s.* for "Mary Ann?"—I do not think they heard him; it was by our two selves when we were looking the contribution book over.

3186. What did you say to that?—I said that we had not got the money. We promised to bring it in the course of the day, which we did.

3187. Although you say that these men, as you think, did not bear what Broadhead told you, immediately after you had heard this from Broadhead did you go to the men and tell them what Broadhead had said?—Yes, they were in another room.

3188. Did you go to them from Broadhead and say to them that they were not only to pay their 1*l.* for their contribution, but that they were to pay 5*s.* for "Mary Ann"?—Yes that was for the expenses.

3189. And you told them that he had said so?—Yes.

3190. Then did you get your 1*l.* 5*s.* a-piece and pay it?—We went and got the money and we went to Broadhead's again at night with the money.

3191. All of you?—Yes, the four of us.

3192. Where did you get the money from?—I got mine from Mr. Eadon, I believe.

3193. He lent you the money?—Yes; Abraham Green got his money from Mr. Eadon too I believe.

3194. When you came to Broadhead what took place on that interview?—We went into the taproom.

3195. Where was it?—At the "Royal George" in Carver Street.

3196. Does he keep that public-house?—Yes; we inquired for Broadhead and were informed that he had gone to the theatre—that would be about 7 o'clock at night. Therefore, we could not see him to give him the money. We did not leave the money, and we concluded to go the next morning, we went the next morning.

3197. All four of you?—Yes, and saw Broadhead, I told him that we had brought the money to redeem our bands, and I believe that the words he used were either "Very good" or "Very well" I will not be quite sure but I believe it was "Very well." We paid him the money 1*l.* 5*s.* each.

3198. When he produced the book and showed you that you had paid nothing did you see whether the amount due from you was 1*l.* or not?—No I did not take that notice.

3199. But you paid the 1*l.* 5*s.*?—Yes.

3200. You were all in the same room together were you?—Yes.

3201. During the payment of the 1*l.* 5*s.*?—Yes.

3202. Now what did you say to him?—I told him we should want a note where to find our bands, but he did not give any answer direct then whether we should have one or not and I said we would give a little grace, we would take a walk and perhaps it would come to his recollection.

3203. Did he say anything to that?—No; we went away from his house about a quarter of an hour.

3205. Why was it that you asked him for a note?—That is the way that the bands are redeemed in general. A note must be placed somewhere or other.

3205. Have you known of that being done before?—Yes.

3206. By whom?—I cannot tell who has placed the note.

3207. But have you known of notes being placed?—Yes.

3208. How many times?—I cannot say how many times.

3209. But a good many times?—Yes.

3210. Was it after a man had been rattened?—Yes.

3211. What did the note contain?—It informed you where to find your bands.

3212. You took your walk?—Yes we took a walk for about a quarter of an hour.

3213. And returned to his house?—Yes.

3214. Was he there?—Yes.

3215. What happened?—We went in to the taproom and called for a quart of beer.

3216. For each one or for the four?—No for the four of us.

3217. Was the taproom the same room that you had been in before?—Yes.

3218. Were there any other customers in the room besides yourselves?—No.

3219. And there had not been? on the first occasion it was an entirely an unoccupied room?—It was between 9 and 10 o'clock in the morning.

3220. It was an unoccupied room?—It was an unoccupied room.

3221. You called for your beer and it was brought?—Yes.

3222. Did you sit down and drink?—Yes, we sat waiting with patience for "Mary Ann."

3223. But where was he?—He was in the kitchen, washing himself. While we were sitting down in his room, Broadhead came up with a cloth in his hand, wiping himself. He had been washing himself in the kitchen. I told him it was of no use his stopping there, we wanted some information with respect to our bands. I was sitting next to the fire-place; there was no fire in the fire-place. Broadhead pointed to a note, and he says "by-the-bye, what is that inside the fender;" I said "this is the identical note that we have been waiting for."

3224. Did you say that before you took it up or after you took it up?—When I picked it up.

3225. You looked at it?—I looked at it.

3226. And then you found that it was the note you wanted?—Yes.

3227. And what did the note contain; have you got it?—No, my wheel mate Abraham Green—

3228. What has become of it?—I believe it has been destroyed in some way.

3229. What did it contain?—It gave information where to find our bands.

3230. What did it say?—It was written in the Sheffield dialect; it said "go up Hallcar Lane till you come to a high wall; go down the side of that wall about 100 yards; then get over 'Mary Ann,'" that was get over the wall. We got over the wall and found our bands.

3231. And then it was signed "Mary Ann"?—Yes.

3232. Then you went away and left Broadhead's?—Yes.

3233. You said "this is the identical thing we have been waiting for," and so on, and then you left him?—Yes.

3234. When you said "this is the identical note we have been waiting for," what did Broadhead say?—He said nothing.

3235. Did you say anything besides that?—No, we drank up our beer and said "good morning." That was what we said.

3236. Having got your note, did you go according to this note that you had along Hallcar Lane till you came to this high wall, and did you go along that wall for about 100 yards, and did you get over the wall?—Yes.

3237. And did you there find your bands?—Yes.

3238. After this did you see Broadhead at all about them and tell him that you had got them, or anything of that kind?—No; we took them to our place, and then we commenced working.

3239. You have told us that you were rattened in 1863; you also tell us that you were rattened in 1866?—Yes.

3240. In 1866, what did you do when you found your bands had gone?—They were taken I believe

FOURTH DAY.

J. Staniforth.

6 June 1867.

on the 7th or 8th of September. That would be on the Friday night or the Saturday morning. We did not know they were gone while Monday morning. On the Monday morning when we got to the works we were informed that all our bands were gone; eight of them.

3241. Who told you?—The timekeeper. Information came down to the works in the course of the forenoon on Monday that they had been found.

3242. Where did you hear that they had been found?—In the coke ovens near the canal, some old coke ovens that there were there.

3243. Do you know who had found them?—Some boys found them as they were playing on the Sunday. They drew the attention of the police to them, and the police took them to the Town Hall, Sheffield.

3244. Did you go the Town Hall and get them?—No; they were identified by the brand mark that there was on them; they were marked "M. Eadon."

3245. Whose bands were they, were they Mr. Eadon's or were they yours?—They were Mr. Eadon's.

3246. Then it was Mr. Eadon's property that they had been taking?—Yes.

3247. Had Mr. Eadon anything to do with the Union?—Not to my knowledge.

3248. They had taken his bands for your misconduct?—Yes.

3249. Now what took place next?—Mr. Eadon sent a cart for them down to the place, and on Tuesday morning we commenced working as usual.

3250. Had you any conversation with Broadhead in reference to those bands having been taken away?—Not a word.

3251. Before their being taken away in this month of September 1866, you say you were a defaulter; had you seen Broadhead at all?—No.

3252. Had Broadhead been to you to ask for contributions, or anything of that kind?—No.

3253. Had you been asked for contributions by anybody?—No.

3254. How much were you in arrears?—When I left the Union I cannot say how much.

3255. At that time had you left the Union?—Yes.

3256. How long before had you left it?—Twelve months.

3257. Do you know whether the other men whose bands were taken had been asked for contribution?—I do not know.

3258. Were they members of the old Union or had they joined the new one?—They were members of the old Union; two of those parties are since dead.

3259. What are their names?—Abraham Green and George Bradshaw.

3260. You say that you had left the Union about twelve months?—Yes, as near as I can guess.

3261. Had you given them notice to leave, or how was it you left?—I ceased paying.

3262. Was that all you did?—Yes.

3263. You declined to contribute?—Yes.

3264. How are the rules as to that; can a man leave the Union when he pleases or not?—Yes, he can leave the Union by ceasing paying to it.

3265. Is that according to the rules of the Union?—I do not know whether the rules express that or not; but if a man ceases paying he ceases to be a member.

3266. No notice is required to be taken off the books?—No.

3267. But a man might say, "I cease to be a "member," and get out of his contributions; a man may not pay his contributions and be in arrears, and then cease to be a member?—I ceased paying.

3268. Did you tell Broadhead or the collector or anybody that you wished no longer to be a contributor to or a member of that Union?—No.

3269. You never gave any notice at all?—No.

3270. Did they ever ask you on the subject?—No.

3271. You never attended their meetings afterwards?—No.

3272. With regard to this other Union, is it at all in opposition to the old one?—Not that I know of.

3273. What is the difference between the two Unions?—The payments every week are not so much.

3274. Do you know how the second Union happened to be got up?—It is an old established Union, it is what they call the jobbing grinders, but the other is what they call the Old Original Union. The saw grinders commenced joining it, and they have commenced joining a new Union. We term it a new Union.

3275. Are they considered as rivals? Is there any hostile feeling between them, or have they friendly relations?—They are a Union to themselves. There is a distinction between a jobbing grinder and a saw grinder.

3276. What is the difference between a jobbing grinder and a saw grinder?—A jobbing grinder grinds small saws and saw backs.

3277. A saw grinder grinds large saws and everything?—Yes; that is the distinction.

3278. Are you a jobbing grinder?—No.

3279. You ought not to belong to that Union then, ought you, according to your work; you are a saw grinder?—Yes.

3280. You are not a jobbing grinder?—No.

3281. Is that Union confined to jobbing grinders, or does it admit into its Union any saw grinder that likes to join?—Any saw grinder that wishes to join it.

3282. Although it is a jobbing grinders' Union?—Yes, although it is a jobbing grinders' Union.

3283. They will admit any person who is a saw grinder?—Yes.

3284. Is there any jealousy on the part of the old Union of persons going and joining the other Union?—Yes; they have been dissatisfied, the same as I was.

3285. Persons have left the old Union on being dissatisfied, and joined the other?—Yes.

3286. Do you know any case besides your own of persons leaving from dissatisfaction and joining the other Union?—There are cases, but I cannot say.

3287. Can you mention the name of any person who has left for the same reason as you did?—Yes, there are; I could mention some of their names.

3288. Tell me them, if you please?—There is John Crapper.

3289. Did he leave for the same reason as you did?—Through being dissatisfied.

3290. But was he dissatisfied on the same ground?—Yes.

3291. When did he leave?—I cannot say.

3292. Before you or after you?—Before me.

3293. Did you and Crapper talk together over the way in which they kept their accounts?—Yes, we have had conversations upon that subject.

3294. Upon the question of their keeping those miscellaneous accounts?—Yes.

3295. Do you know of any other person who has left besides Crapper?—William Ashworth.

3296. Do you know what he left for?—I do not.

3297. But he formerly belonged to the old Union and joined the jobbing grinders' Union?—Yes.

3298. But you do not know for what reason?—I do not.

3299. When was it that he joined?—I cannot say.

3300. You have been rattened yourself three times. In the time when you were secretary of this old Union was there any rattening going on?—Yes.

3301. Do you know how it was done?—I cannot say how it was done.

3302. But you were the secretary and had the funds, had you not?—Yes.

3303. How was the rattening done in that time?—The bands were taken.

3304. Had you anything to do with that?—I had a knowledge of it.

FOURTH DAY.

J. Staniforth.

6 June 1867.

3305. Will you be good enough to tell me how it was done in your time ?—If a person did not pay his contribution his bands were taken, the same as they are at the present time.

3306. How were they taken ?—They were rolled up and put by.

3307. Who did it ?—I cannot mention the names at present ; it is 21 years back.

3308. You cannot recollect the persons, but were they employed by the trade ?—I cannot say they were employed by the trade.

3309. You say you had a knowledge of it ?—Yes.

3310. Supposing a man owed your Union a sum of money, and he would not pay, and refused to pay altogether, did you go to a man and ask him to go and take the other man's bands, or how did you do it ?—There are the names of persons in arrear in a book, and they are called over ; that would be in the contribution book.

3311. Where was it that they were called over ?—At the meeting house.

3312. At the public meeting ?—Yes.

3313. Their names were called over as defaulters ?—Yes ; they were known and picked out for the job, but when a person took their bands then the secretary was informed that the bands were gone.

3314. Who informed the secretary ?—The parties that took the bands.

3315. Then the man came and said, "I have taken "the bands," and he would of course tell the secretary where the bands were ?—He would say that so-and-so's bands were gone ; that would be the parties who had lost their bands.

3316. What next ?—He would be in the same position as I have been fixed, and would go to the secretary and redeem them back.

3317. You say that the secretary was informed by the man who took the bands that the bands were gone. He would also tell him, I suppose, where he had placed them ?—He might do that.

3318. The secretary could not give them information without he knew ?—That is right.

3319. Therefore the man must tell him where he had put them ?—Yes.

3320. And then the parties came to the secretary, and the secretary told them where the bands were, and then they were redeemed ?—He would give them a note where they were ; he would not tell them where they were. There would be a note found in some shape.

3321. The secretary would give a note, or a note would be given to tell them where the things were to be found ; that being so, the man who did it would of course be paid ?—Of course.

3322. Did the secretary pay them ?—Pay whom ?

3323. Pay the men who took away those bands ?—Yes.

3324. Did he pay them before the bands were redeemed, or after they were redeemed ?—I cannot say when he would have to pay them. I should think when he got the money.

3325. Had you any scale in your time as to the amount of payment ? How much did they give for a band, 5*s.* or 3*s.* ?—No, there was no scale of prices upon it.

3326. What was the kin   sum that you paid a man for taking a person's bands away ?—Sometimes a man will think that he ought to have more than another.

3327. Can you give us any notion of what was the price which was paid for taking away a man's bands ?—No, I cannot say ; I think 5*s.* would be about the price of it.

3328. For each band ?—For each band.

3329. Have you paid men then for taking bands yourself ?—Yes.

3330. How often ?—I cannot say how often ; I was only in office about a year and nine months.

3331. During that time how many times do you think you paid for bands being taken ?—I cannot say I am sure.

3332. Twenty times ?—No.

3333. Ten ?—Not a fourth of 20.

3334. That is five times ?—Not five. I do not know about the number I am sure ; it might be more, or it might be less.

3335. In your time, when you could not get the persons to contribute, had you any regard as to whether the bands belonged to the masters or to the men ; or did you take them indiscriminately ?—I was aware that they belonged to the masters.

3336. And in cases where the masters did not belong to the Union you still took their bands ?—No ; they were taken on account of the men.

3337. Did you speak to the men before they took them, or after they had taken them ?—Do you mean the parties that were rattened ?

3338. No ; the parties who took them ?—When they took the bands they used to come to me to state where they were.

3339. That was all ?—That was all.

3340. Did the same man often do the same job ?—I cannot say that he did.

3341. But you recollect in your time about the rattening ; was it one man or two men, or was it always the same person, or who was it ?—I can hardly say who the party was at present.

3342. I do not ask who the party was, but I want to know whether in your time it was the same man ?—I cannot say I am certain.

3343. Just think ?—I cannot.

3344. I think you might tell us if you recollected ?—I cannot.

3345. What is your belief about that ; was it the the same person ?—I am certain I cannot say whether it was the same person or not.

3346. What is your belief about it ?—I cannot say I am certain what man it was.

3347. But what is your belief about its being the same person who always did the same thing ?—It might be, but I will not be sure.

3348. What is your belief about it ?—I believe that it was not.

3349. How many persons do you think did it in your time ?—I cannot say.

3350. Can you say whether it was more than one ?—I cannot.

3351. I will not ask you who the man was, if you recollect him, I do not think that it is within our province to enquire that, I only wanted to know the particulars ; you say that the mode in which it was done was by reading over names ; when you read over the names I suppose you did it with the view that this rattening should take place ?—No, I did not.

3352. Did you do it on purpose that something should be done in order to compel the parties to pay up their arrears ?—It was done in order to expose the parties that were in arrear before the meeting.

3353. But I suppose when you did that you knew from the practice which prevailed in the trade that the probabilities were that after that had been read over the men would be rattened ?—I cannot say that that was my intention ; they were generally read over at the general meeting.

3354. It was not your intention, but was it not your belief that after having read over a man's name in that way he would be rattened ?—They were read over at every general meeting in that way.

3355. And with that view ?—I cannot say with that view ; there might be no rattenings for three months after that.

3356. They were read over every month ?—They were read over every month.

3357. Did you not anticipate that after being exposed in that way some steps would be taken ?—I cannot say that that was my meaning.

3358. But it did so happen that after the names were read over the men were rattened ?—Yes.

3359. Now in your time how many do you suppose were in arrear that were read over at a meeting ?—I am sure I do not know.

3360. Would it be 10 or a dozen ?—Yes, there would be above 20 I should say.

3361. That is an average list?—Yes.

3362. But if in your time the list was 20 and only five were rattened, how was it that the person who did it made his selection?—I do not know.

3363. You do not know how he made his selection? —I do not.

3364. Who read over the list?—I read over the names from the contribution book.

3365. If there was any dissatisfaction on the part of the meeting at a man having got much into arrear or having done anything particularly wrong, was there disapprobation or anything of that kind manifested by the meeting?—I cannot say that there was.

3366. Was there any hooting or groans?—I cannot say that there was.

3367. Was there no expression of feeling?—No, I cannot say that there was.

3368. Was there any expression by you?—No.

3369. Was there any kind of suggestion that this man had been a long time a defaulter?—I did not refer to any individual person, I read over the names simply to let them see who was in arrear.

3370. And was that all that was done?—Yes.

3371. Did you read those men's names over in a louder voice than others?—No I read so that they all might hear what I said.

3372. Was there any hint or suggestion as distinguishing one particular man from another?—No.

3373. Nor in the crowd at all?—No.

3374. Then when it came out that a person came to you and said "I have rattened such a man or have "got his bands" how was the selection made?—He never was selected, he did it voluntarily himself, the man was never selected to fetch the man's bands.

3375. But how did it come about that this man went and took his bands?—He might by hearing the names read over select the man himself.

3376. But was it a matter of choice simply for himself, had he nothing to guide him?—I cannot say what his motive was, he might take them because he considered it a trade affair.

3377. Although you did not tell him to do it, yet when he had done it you paid him for doing it?—I paid him for doing it.

3378. Was the list of defaulters as many as 20 or were there as many as 20 persons present at the meeting?—I cannot say how many there would be but it has been calculated that there would be about 20.

3379. If there were only 10, do not let us put it at 20?—21 years back is a long while back to remember.

3380 (*Mr. Chance.*) Were you speaking of 20 persons being present at the meeting, or did the number of the names read over amount to 20?—All the names were read over belonging to the Union. There was no distinction between a man being in arrears and not. When his name was called over he answered to it and when I came to his name it was said that he owed so much.

3381. (*Chairman.*) You did not say how many were in arrear?—No.

3382. Of how many is the Union composed?—At that time I should think that there would be about 126. The Union would be that strong.

3383. How many persons were there present at the meeting when you have had this read over?—I cannot say. There would be a fine for anyone that was absent.

3384. But how many did your meetings consist of as a rule?—I cannot tell I am sure.

3385. Would there be 60, 50, 40, or 30?—More than that; there would be above 100 I should say.

3386. Let us suppose that in your time the course was this; supposing a man had been in arrear and had been rattened, and a man had come to you and said, "I have rattened such a man and I have taken two "bands, and I want 10*s*. for it," and you paid him? —Not then, I should not.

3387. But when you got the money, did that entry appear in your books?—No.

3388. Why not?—That was for expenses.

3389. For "Mary Ann"?—It had nothing to do with the contribution, it was for "Mary Ann."

3390. In your book I suppose you entered nothing for expenses?—No.

3391. Did you put expenses at all in your book?—No.

3392. And therefore if a man did this you waited till the person came who claimed his bands and then you said, "You will have to pay not only your arrears "but the expenses;" and supposing that there were two bands, "You will have to pay 10*s*."—Yes.

3393. And the man paid you the 10*s*.?—Yes.

3394. And you paid the 10*s*. over to the man who had done the job?—Yes.

3395. And, therefore, a man examining your books could not ascertain whether the job had been done or not?—No; he could not tell that.

3396. In your time, did you ever know a case of a man having his bellows cut?—No.

3397. Not in your time?—No.

3398. Did you ever in your time know of any personal damage being done to any individual?—No.

3399. Do you know of any case in your time of a man being blown up by a can of gunpowder or by gunpowder being thrown into his house in a can or a bottle, or anything of that sort?—Not in my time.

3400. You have heard of it since?—I have heard of it since.

3401. In your time when you were secretary, were all the things which were done in this way confined simply to taking a man's bands?—Yes.

3402. I suppose that you were not able to get your money by law, and that was the only means you had of enforcing payment?—There is no law for that, and I suppose that is the only remedy there was.

3403. I suppose that your object was to restore the things if the man would pay?—Yes.

3404. And if he did not pay what became of his bands?—The master was generally applied to and they would be got back in some way or another. The master generally paid the money sooner than have the work stopped.

3405. But suppose that the master would not pay the money, what then?—The parties who had taken the bands had to find the money.

3406. If they did not find the money the bands would be destroyed I suppose?—The bands would be retained. I do not know that they would be destroyed.

3407. I have been reminded of one thing which I have not asked you. In your time were any tools damaged?—I cannot say that there were.

3408. Were any bands cut?—I cannot say that there were.

3409. But can you say that there were not?—I can say that to my knowledge there were not.

3410. In your time did it often occur in the trade, that not only were men's bands taken and restored when the money was paid, but that men's bands were cut?—I cannot remember anything of the kind.

3411. Or bellows being cut?—No, that was not in my trade.

3412. What you have addressed yourself to up to this time is this, arrear of contribution money, supposing a man infringed your rules what happened; did you allow a person to have apprentices?—I cannot say that there were any apprentices taken then except their own sons.

3413. Supposing a man broke that rule, did you ratten him then?—I believe he would be rattened on that occasion.

3414. Who was that?—I cannot say the person, but I believe there have been instances of that being done.

3415. Was rattening done for any other thing than taking apprentices contrary to rule. Have you known it done for working at under prices?—It has been done on that occasion.

3416. Has rattening been done for employing men not belonging to the Union?—I never heard tell of that.

FOURTH DAY.

J. Staniforth.

6 June 1867.

3417. In the case of a man not paying his contribution, if you took his bands, directly he paid his contribution you could restore them?—Yes.

3418. But supposing that you took a man's bands for working at under price he could not put you right for that. How did you do then?—I cannot remember that as being done in my time.

3419. You said rattening was done for working at under prices. I want to know what happened in that case; had he to make up by money for the price which was lost to the trade, or how was it, because that would not be laying hold of his property as a pledge until he had complied with the rules, because he had violated the rules, and there was no redeeming thing?—I do not know that I can remember a case of that kind.

3420. What was the mode of proceeding in those rattenings for apprentice; how did they do it?—They would take their bands whilst they turned the apprentice boy away, if he was not a freeman's son; if he did not belong to a saw grinder.

3421. How would the man who did this rattening know about the apprentices.—He would be informed upon it.

3422. Who would tell him?—He would be informed by the secretary that he was taking an apprentice boy against the rules.

3423. The man who did the rattening would be told that?—Yes, that would be perhaps before he was rattened.

3424. I am speaking of the man who did the rattening. How would he know that a man had to be rattened?—He would know that he was not doing right according to the rules of the trade.

3425. How would he know that?—He would know that he was taking an apprentice boy illegally.

3426. Would the secretary tell him that?—No, he would know it by his experience.

3427. I am speaking now of the question of the case of an apprentice. How was it that the men who had to do this rattening knew that the man had to be rattened for having an apprentice improperly?—He would know, but the man that was rattened would not know that he was to be rattened for having a boy.

3428. No, but the man who had to ratten him would know it?—Yes, he would know it.

3429. How would he know it?—By his own experience.

3430. By his being a member of the Union and its being talked of in the trade I suppose?—Yes.

3431. In your experience have the men who have done those rattenings been members of the same Union or non-union men employed by the Union?—I should say they would be members of the same Union,

3432. As far as your experience goes?—Yes.

3433. Have you known a case when you were in office at all of a man having been detected and taken up and brought up for stealing the bands?—

3434. We have heard of a case of a man who was employed by the secretary on his own account, as he says, to do rattening, and he was taken up and the poor man was sent to prison for nine months?—No. Not in my time. I do not know a case of that kind.

3435. You did not know a case in your time of a man being taken up and tried as if for stealing?—No.

3436. Do you know whether in case a man has been taken up, a society has contributed to his maintenance or defence?—There was a case at my works.

3437. When was that?—That was in 1864. I believe you have the person in court now who will be able to give you information about that. It was not in connection with bands.

3438. What are the names of the persons?—Christopher Taylor and Henry Bollington.

3439. Will you give us an outline of what that case was?—That was band taking. The man that took the bands in 1864 was apprehended with them on him in his possession, and he was taken to the Town Hall and brought before the magistrates and committed for the sessions, and he was tried at the sessions and received six months' imprisonment.

3440. What was the name of the man?—Joseph Bradshaw.

3441. Is that man dead?—No; that is George Bradshaw that is dead.

3442. Do you know who defended him on that occasion? Do you know whether the Union defended him?—I do not know.

3443. You have spoken of what occurred in your time?—Yes.

3444. Can you give us any kind of information as to whether the same course of proceeding has been adopted since your time or not?—I cannot say; I have had nothing to do with any committees for the last six years. I should say if I knew anything about them.

3445. But have you had, up to six years ago, any connection with committees?—I have attended upon committees; I have been chosen on committees.

3446. Up to six years ago?—I daresay I have.

3447. And up to that time was the same proceeding adopted of which you have spoken?—Yes.

3448. Up to six years ago?—Yes.

3449. Then have you been on the same committee with Broadhead?—I have been on committees at Broadhead's house since he was secretary.

3450. Are you aware of any instance besides the one about which you have given us information of your own case where Broadhead has paid money to a man for having done rattening?—No; I cannot say.

3451. Then how do you say that the same system has prevailed up to six years ago?—As I made remark with respect to my case, it was that Broadhead received the money, and I suppose it was the same way with other people for getting their bands back by paying money to Broadhead.

3452. Is it your belief that that is the common course?—Yes.

3453. Is it your belief that this system of going to the secretary and asking for bands, and his furnishing information, and so on, is confined to that Union alone, or does it extend to various Unions in the town?—I should say it is in the various Unions in the town the same. It says so, but I do not know.

3454. How many cases have you known of persons having been rattened and having paid their money and having got back their bands?—I cannot say.

3455. Can you tell me about how often in the year in the town of Sheffield a rattening is going on?—I cannot.

3456. I want to know how often it prevails in the trade generally?—I am sure I do not know.

3457. Would it be an uncommon thing to happen once a week?—I cannot say; there might be instances take place whilst I am at my work and I never hear of them.

3458. I believe it is a very common thing, unfortunately?—No doubt it is.

3459. I want to get a figure if I can. At all events once a week a rattening would be done?—I cannot give you that information.

3460. Is it so common a thing that if you heard of a man being rattened you would take no notice of it?—I cannot say that I have heard of one for this long while. My own case was the last I heard of; that was in September, 1866, and I cannot say that I have heard tell of one since.

3461. Supposing one man had rattened another, can you conceive any way in which a man could be paid for his work except through the secretary?—He might be paid by another person.

3462. By what person?—By the person that is in the room.

3463. How do you mean in the room?—Another person might receive the money for the secretary if he is not there.

3464. I do not quite understand you. The difficulty is this: supposing a man goes on his own account and rattens a man, and has got away his bands; this man has to redeem them. He will not go and tell the man, that he has rattened him, because if he did the man would immediately go to the police and have him taken up; there must be a third man somewhere?—That is the secretary.

3465. (*Mr. Chance.*) Do you know as a fact how many times in your experience masters have had to pay money to pay the arrears of the contributions of their men?—I do not.

3466. In your experience have more cases than one happened where the master has had to pay the contributions of the men in order to get back the bands? —Yes, they have given the men the money to pay when they have not money themselves.

3467. Has more than one case occurred in your experience of that kind?—I cannot say. I was speaking of my own case then. I asked Mr. Eadon to find me 1*l.* 5*s.*, and he did.

3468. Is this (*showing a book to the witness*) the kind of book which was read over to you, and with which you were dissatisfied? What is the kind of account with which you were dissatisfied?—We had nothing of this sort when I was secretary.

3469. You told me that you had left this society because you were dissatisfied with the mode in which they kept their accounts, and that there were miscellanies put down there of which you had no items, which were the accounts which gave you dissatisfaction?—I did not look those accounts over. They were audited and found correct. Broadhead added up the figuring, and all the auditor has to do is to add up the columns and see if those tally. It is like setting a schoolboy to add them up.

3470. What did you say about "miscellanies"?—I said that amounted to a good deal of money, and I do not know that ever I heard him say what those "miscellanies" were for, unless there are other things that he has not mentioned, if he brings them forward there.

3471. They are put forward in the sum total here at the end of 20*l.* 17*s.* 11*d.*, but if you refer to these particulars you see the details of them, so that you are not quite correct in what you state.

3472. (*Mr. Chance.*) Were those "miscellanies" or "sundries" read over to you at the general meeting?—They might be; I will not dispute it.

3473. (*Chairman.*) You will not dispute it?—I will not dispute it; it does not look as if they had been written recently.

3474. I do not quite understand what your real objection to those accounts was?—If you see them there you will see the figures have been altered in some shape or other.

3475. That may be the casting. Did you object to the alteration of the figures?—Yes; I did not like to see the figures altered in that shape.

3476. There are certainly many figures altered here, but that may be from bad casting?—You will see that those figures have been altered in very many places.

3477. No doubt, in almost every page there are alterations. You cannot explain how those alterations occurred?—No. I am dissatisfied because scores of figures have been altered in that book, and I do not know what for. You will see that.

3478. I do see a great many alterations. However, you took an objection both to the alteration of the figures and to the "miscellanies" as not containing a detailed account?—Yes.

3479. And that is the ground of your objection?—Yes, the biggest part.

3480. Now then, there is another question, which is this,—In your trade, the saw trade, who finds the bands?—The manufacturers; the masters.

3481. Does the Union find bands?—No, the masters.

3482. The saw grinders?—The saw manufacturers find bands for the saw grinders.

3483. Are there any persons who find their own? —I do not know of any at present. There are tools belonging to the Saw Grinders' Union; they are their property.

3484. Are those bands?—Tools altogether; complete.

3485. Do the Union let them out and charge for them?—They charge so much in the pound upon work done.

3486. For tools?—Yes.

3487. Then those are irrespective of the master, the master has not them?—No. I should like just to refer to that former subject, and I will point it out, and then you will understand it.

(*The witness explained entries in the book to the Commissioners.*)

3488. I understand you that they earned by their tools 38*l.* in one month?—Yes; that is to say, it is for work done. The amount clear is for the work done by those two sets of tools belonging to the Union.

3489. Then the 38*l.* was what they have received? —It had been done on that wheel room. The totals would be so much on the pound upon that money that was earned for tools.

3490. Is it an advantage or disadvantage that a man should have his own tools?—It was taken for an advantage both to the manufacturers——

3491. Is it a matter with which the Unions interfere; do they allow men work on their own tools?—Yes, the Union men work on their own tools.

3492. The Unions allow men to work on their own tools, not on the Union's tools?—On the Union's tools, but that belongs to the Union.

3493. The Union men work on the Union tools? —Yes.

3494. And the Union gets the profit?—The Union get the profit.

3495. But supposing a man says, "No, I will not work on your tools, I will work on my own;" what would the Union say to that?—I do not know that I ever heard that case mentioned.

3496. I will put a case to you. Do you know a man of the name of Fearnehough?—Yes.

3497. His house was blown up was it not?—Yes.

3498. Do you know whether he worked on his own tools or not?—He used to do so.

3499. Do you know whether any notice had been served on him that they would not allow him to work on his own tools?—I do not know whether he had any notice to that effect.

3500. But do you know whether it is allowed in the trade for a man to work on his own tools as distinguished from those of the Union?—I believe in the list of prices it is mentioned that masters must find their own tools.

3501. If the masters find their own tools the Union does not find them?—If a man finds his own tools it is not the master that finds them.

3502. Then they do not object to the masters finding the tools, but they object to the men finding them?—Yes; they object to his working on his own tools.

3503. The master must find them?—Yes; it is in the book with the list of prices.

3504. It is a stipulation that the master is to do it, and not the men?—That is stated in the list of prices.

3505. Did you hear the ground of complaint which there was against Farnehough at the time his house was blown up?—I did not.

3506. Do you know whether he had given any dissatisfaction at all to the Union?—No; I was not a member of that Union then.

3507. Have you ever heard it talked of in the trade, as to what it was which was the cause of that blowing up?—I have not.

3508. Have you heard of any blowings up or any damage done to houses in the town?—No, I have heard of them to be sure, but I thought you meant, did I know. I have heard of them.

3509. Have you ever heard of any cause of offence

FOURTH DAY.

J. Staniforth.

6 June 1867.

given by the parties whose houses were damaged?—No.

3510. Have you not known why it was?—No.

3511. Not whether they had taken apprentices contrary to the rules or had violated the rules of the Union or anything of that kind?—No.

3512. You have never heard it?—No.

3513. (*Mr. Barstow.*) You have told us that you were a member of the committee about six years ago; are those books open to the inspection of any member of the committee?—Yes.

3514. Did you take the trouble to look and see whether the items under the head "Miscellanies" were set out?—I took it for granted when I saw "Miscellanies," as Broadhead said "They are now "minuted down," and the alteration of figures I did not like.

3515. Did you look at the minutes?—I cannot say that I did.

3516. (*Chairman.*) Is there any rule about outsiders being employed in the trade?—No.

3517. Can any master employ any person he pleases, could he get a man down from London for example, would that be allowed?—I do not think it would.

3518. Is there any rule against it?—I do not know that there is.

3519. Have you known any case where a man has brought from a strange town any workmen of his own selection and has been prevented from employing them?—Not in the saw grinding.

3520. Have you known it in any other branches of the Sheffield trade?—I cannot say that I have.

3521. (*Mr. Barstow.*) Do you know whether the saw grinding trade is carried on in any other town besides Sheffield?—I never was in any other town besides Sheffield.

3522. (*Chairman.*) They carry on the business at Wolverhampton?—I do not know.

3523. (*Mr. Chance.*) Suppose a master were to hear of a very first rate workman in some other part of the country and bring him into Sheffield would he be allowed to give him work?—I cannot say, I believe the Chairman has got the rules and they will explain that matter, I do not know of any rule to that effect.

3524. The rule is "No member holding a situation "shall find his own tools"?—Yes.

3525. (*Mr. Chance.*) You stated in the course of your evidence that no notice is necessary when a member wishes to cease to be a member of a Union, is that so?—That is so.

3526. No notice is necessary?—No.

3527. Supposing you do not pay at the end of the week you are still a member of the Union?—I am a member of the Union.

3528. Does your not paying your contribution cause you to cease to be a member of the Union?—No.

3529. Suppose you go on for several weeks, are you still a member of the Union, though you have not paid?—Yes.

3530. And unless some notice is given you would be a member of the Union and liable to contribution?—Yes.

3531. You would be liable to contribution unless you had given them notice or determined your membership in some way or other; how do you cease to be a member of the Union?—By giving up paying the contribution.

3532. In what length of time will that cause you to cease your membership?—I cannot say.

3533. Is there no rule as to any notice being necessary?—No; the secretary would find it out himself if he comes to visit you for contributions, and you pay him nothing, and he comes often to you and you pay nothing at all, he thinks you have ceased to be a member.

3534. (*Chairman.*) Why, do not you say "I have "not paid because I do not mean to belong to the "Union any longer?"—That is not customary. I do not know that there is any rule to that effect as to giving notice.

3535. (*Mr. Chance.*) It appears to me that it may be unreasonable for a man to refuse to pay his contributions unless he has given some notice to the Union that he does not wish to be a member any longer?—I give up paying.

3536. The ceasing to pay does not necessarily determine your membership?—It is the case.

3537. But in no particular time?—No.

3538. That is left very much to the discretion of the secretary?—It is left to his opinion in one sense whether he is a member or not; if he ceases going to him for his contribution he considers he has ceased to join the Union.

3539. (*Chairman.*) You say you have paid as much as a per-centage on 2*l.* a week; are they the average earnings of your trade?—I can speak for myself, some people get more money than others, it depends upon the work and liabilities.

3540. Are you a fair average workman or a better class workman?—I do not want to appreciate myself, I shall be content with 2*l.* a week, taking one week with another.

3541. You do not work on Monday, I suppose; nobody works on a Monday at Sheffield?—I believe it must be the rule.

3542. You do not work on a Monday?—Not every Monday.

3543. You seldom work any Monday?—I do work on a Monday very often.

3544. When you speak of earning 2*l.* a week, you can do it without working on a Monday?—I might do it.

3545. Would you work on a Saturday?—Yes.

3546. How much?—I cannot say.

3547. Half a day?—It might be half a day.

3548. That would be about four days and a half you would work for 2*l.*; can a man earn in four days and a half 2*l.*?—I must work on a Monday if I do that, take it as an average.

3549. Can an average saw grinder earn 2*l.* a week at Sheffield?—I should think he can, taking it on the average.

3550. Do you employ apprentices?—No.

3551. Nor journeymen?—No.

3552. It is your own sole work?—Yes.

3553. You speak of what you with your own hands and head can do; you can earn 2*l.* a week on the average?—Yes; but I must work on a Monday and must not play on Saturday half a day.

3554. You must work six days?—Yes.

3555. (*Chairman.*) How much have you paid to the new society since you joined it?—I cannot say.

3556. Have you paid contributions weekly?—No, I have not.

3557. Have you paid anything to the new society?—Yes.

3558. What have you paid; have you paid it several weeks?—I have not paid it several weeks back; I have had very little work.

3559. You have had very little work?—Yes.

3560. At the time you were in work did you contribute to your new society?—I suppose I am in work yet.

3561. Did you contribute to the society as long as you were in work?—I am in work now.

3562. How long have you ceased to pay; how many weeks?—I cannot say.

3563. About how many?—I cannot say how many weeks.

3564. Can you tell me about how many weeks?—Perhaps three months.

3565. You have not paid for three months?—No.

3566. And before that time had you paid?—Yes, I think so.

3567. Had you paid regularly up to three months?—I will not be sure.

3568. How much have you paid in a week?—I cannot say how much; I cannot say how long it is since I did pay.

3569. You say you were secretary of the old Union?—Yes.

3570. Did they turn you out as secretary?—No.

3571. How did you cease to be secretary?—I gave it up.

3572. You resigned?—Yes.

3573. You were not turned out?—No.

3574. Were you on the committee after you ceased to be secretary?—I might be afterwards, I was on the committee afterwards; I do not know how long since.

3575. Are the committee of your Union elected by the trade?—Yes.

3576. You were elected in the ordinary way?—In the ordinary way.

3577. How much per week is the largest sum you have paid to the new society?—I have paid as much as 5*s.*; that has been to fetch up certain weeks that had been missed.

3578. What is the rate of the charge?—1*s.* 6*d.* per week.

3579. That is a fixed sum not a poundage?—1*s.* 6*d.* per week net.

3580. In the old Union it was poundage money?—Yes.

3581. (*Mr. Chance.*) You have stated that you paid as much as 8*s.* 2*d.* in the course of the week poundage?—Yes.

3582. (*Chairman.*) You say that you were not turned out, and that you resigned your secretaryship?—Yes.

3583. What was the ground of your resigning?—I did not like the office.

3584. Was any objection made to you by any person in the society before yon resigned?—I do not know that there was.

3585. No fault found with you by anybody?—I think not.

3586. Upon your oath had there not been some information given you then that they were dissatisfied with the mode in which you conducted the affairs as secretary?—No; I gave up the very day that a person told me that they were dissatisfied, I gave it up that very day.

3587. The day you left you were informed that they were dissatisfied with you?—That was not the meaning of it; they did not say that.

3588. What did they say?—I told them that I was not satisfied with the office for this reason; it was so unpleasant, parties must do as some people wished, and you were not right this side, and you were not right that side, and therefore I said, "You "can take the job from me if you think proper." It was at the general meeting that I told them I should resign, and at the time they put it whether I should resign or not; it was carried that I should resign, and I resigned on that account; but there was nothing said about being dissatisfied with my accounts at all.

3589. Not only dissatisfied with the accounts, but was anything said about your having done anything wrong in your office?—I had not done anything wrong.

3590. Did they say so?—No.

3591. Were you told that if you did not resign you would be turned out?—No.

3592. It was a purely voluntary act of yours?—I gave it up purely on that account; I did not like the office, I was not satisfied with it.

The witness withdrew.

CHRISTOPHER TAYLOR sworn and examined.

C. Taylor.

3593. (*Mr. Barstow.*) Were do you live?—In Verdon Street.

3594. You are a saw grinder?—Yes.

3595. You work for Mr. Eadon?—Yes.

3596. Are you a member of any Union?—I belong to the Saw Grinders' Union.

3597. Which of them?—The Saw Grinders' Union, the old one.

3598. How long have you been a saw grinder?—Ever since I was 16; I am 50 years old now.

3599. How long have you been a member of the Saw Grinders' Union?—Every since I was 21.

3600. What is your contribution to the Union?—5*s.* a week now.

3601. How is it ascertained what you have to pay?—It is 5*s.* a week, whether we earn little or more.

3602. (*Chairman.*) Every man pays 5*s.* a week?—Yes.

3603. (*Mr. Barstow.*) Has that always been the way in which the contribution has been ascertained?—No.

3604. What was it formerly?—It has been 8*s.* a month.

3605. You were a fellow workmen of John Staniforth's?—Yes.

3606. Do you remember early in the summer of 1862 that you and he were in arrear to the Union, in May or June 1862?—I was in the Union.

3607. (*Chairman.*) Were you ever rattened?—Yes.

3608. When?—In 1863.

3609. (*Mr. Barstow.*) Were you rattened in 1862?—I cannot remember being rattened in 1862.

3610. At that time were you in arrear to the Saw Grinder's Union?—No, not in 1862.

3611. However, you were rattened then?—Yes, in 1863.

3612. What was done to you, did you lose your bands?—Yes, I lost mine and another man lost his; a man named Bollington.

3613. Did not Staniforth lose his?—No, not at that time; in 1864 I was rattened again.

3614. Your bands were taken in 1864?—Yes.

3615. In 1863 you and Bollington lost your bands?—Yes, they were found by a watchman; a man had them in his possession named Bradshaw.

3616. (*Chairman.*) Was that in 1863 or 1864?—In 1863.

3617. (*Mr. Barstow.*) Did you appear against him at the Town Hall?—It was in 1864 when Bradshaw took them; 1863 and 1864.

3618. You were rattened in both years?—Yes.

3619. We will go on now with 1864; a man named Bradshaw had them in his possession, did you appear against Bradshaw at the Town Hall?—Yes.

3620. I believe Bradshaw was sent to the Quarter Sessions for trial?—Yes, he was committed at Sheffield.

3621. He was tried at the Quarter Sessions?—Yes.

3622. Now what happened in 1863?—My bands were taken, and others besides mine.

3623. How many?—I believe there would be about six or seven bands taken.

3624. (*Chairman.*) Tell us the names of the persons?—Henry Taylor, Charles Challenger, John Staniforth, Henry Bollington, and Abraham Green.

3625. (*Mr. Barstow.*) At that time did you owe anything to the Union?—No, not at that time I did not.

3626. Do you know whether any of these other men did?—Yes, I believe the other men did.

3627. Had anyone been there before the bands were taken asking for contributions?—Yes.

3628. Who was it?—Our secretary, William Broadhead.

3629. When you missed your bands, what did you do?—Our other men found them.

3630. Did you go anywhere with Staniforth?—No, I did not go with him.

3631. When did you get them back again?—The day after they were found.

3632. Do you know how they were found?—Yes, they were found in a wood called Hallcar Wood.

FOURTH DAY.

C. Taylor.

6 June 1867.

3633. Were you ever rattened after that?—Yes, after 1864 there was a party's bands taken, but not mine. In 1865 I went and took wheel room at Screw Mill and Sheaf Island, the bands were taken then, but my bands were not there.

3634. What men were rattened at your wheel?—Our wheel was lame, and we took some room at Screw Mill and Sheaf Island Works; mine were not taken.

3635. Were you rattened in 1866?—No.

The witness withdrew.

JOSHUA BARTON sworn and examined.

J. Barton.

3636. (*Mr. Chance.*) What are you?—A saw grinder.

3637. Do you work for Messrs. Eadon?—Yes.

3638. How long have you been a saw grinder?—About 45 years.

3639. Did you serve your apprenticeship?—Yes.

3640. You are a journeyman saw grinder?—Yes.

3641. Are you a member of the Saw Grinders' Union?—Yes, and have been so many years.

3642. Was your Union (that you are a member of) the one which has existed for a long time? Are you a member of the old or the new Union?—The old one.

3643. Have you always been a member of the old Union?—Yes, up to a late date. I have not been a member for two years or so.

3644. When did you cease to be a member?—The latter end of 1864.

3645. You were a member up to the latter end of 1864?—Yes.

3646. Did you cease to become a member by not paying subscriptions, or did you give any notice?—I did not pay my subscriptions.

3647. Have they continued to make application to you for your contributions?—Not of late.

3648. How long have they ceased to make application to you to contribute?—Two years.

3649. (*Chairman.*) They never asked you to pay?—No.

3650. (*Mr. Chance.*) For two years you have not been asked to pay?—No.

3651. How long have you been in the employ of Mr. Eadon?—Near upon 13 years.

3652. During that time have you been rattened at all?—Yes.

3653. How many times have you been rattened?—The last time was in 1864.

3654. How many times have you been rattened before 1864?—I think I was not rattened before 1864, not personally.

3655. When you say "personally," you mean to say you have not lost anything personally?—No.

3656. Have you been rattened since 1864?—In November 1864.

3657. Was that the first case of rattening which you remember?—Not at our place, but on my account it was.

3658. That was the first time you were rattened on your own account. Do you think that that was for not paying contributions?—Yes.

3659. Were you rattened previously to that, although not upon your own account?—I believe mine went along with the others.

3660. Your bands were taken with other bands?—Yes.

3661. When was that?—That was before 1864, but I have no memorandum to go by.

3662. Whose bands were taken at the same time that yours were taken at the same time as yours were taken?—At one time they all went.

3663. You mean all the men's bands who were working with you?—Yes.

3664. Do you remember the names of those who were working with you at that time?—Yes.

3665. Give me the names?—Christopher Taylor, Henry Taylor, Henry Bollington, and George Bradshaw.

3666. Who else, was there a man named Green?—Yes, Abraham Green.

3667. Was a man named Dungworth's bands taken too?—I believe Dungworth would not be working there then.

3668. Were there any other men working who lost their bands at that time?—There was Charles Challenger.

3669. Any other?—I think not; and Staniforth I have not mentioned.

3670. Was it before 1864 or after 1864?—It was after 1864 when they all went.

3671. You say that you were rattened on your own account in 1864?—Yes.

3672. My question just now was, were you rattened before 1864?—No, I think not.

3673. I want you to speak to the best of your recollection; but upon consideration have you come to the conclusion that you were not rattened before 1864?—No.

3674. Now we come to 1864, when you say you were rattened on your own account; on what account were you rattened?—For not paying my contributions.

3675. How much were you in arrear at that time?—I am not able to say.

3676. Did any one come to you about your contributions?—No, not particularly. It was brought by one of the men who said I had not paid my contribution.

3677. Some man came to you?—No, one of our own members told me, one of our workmen.

3678. Did any one come to you from the Union to say that you had not paid your contribution?—No.

3679. (*Chairman.*) Did not the collector come round every week and ask you for your money?—Yes.

3680. (*Mr. Chance.*) Who was the collector at that time?—Broadhead.

3681. Broadhead applied to you for your contribution?—Yes.

3682. Did he apply to you for your contribution more than once?—Yes.

3683 (*Chairman.*) Every week he came round I suppose?—Yes.

3684. (*Mr. Chance.*) Were your bands taken then?—Yes.

3685. Whose other bands were taken, if any, at the same time that yours were taken?—I think not any one's at that time.

3686. Yours only?—Yes.

3687. After you lost your bands what did you do?—I sent some money to pay what their demands were.

3688. Who did you send it by?—One of our men. I do not recollect who it was now, but I sent it and ceased to have any interest in the affair. I never have had any interference with the trade for 25 or 30 years.

3689. You say you sent some money by a workman?—Yes.

3690. What workman did you send the money by?—I cannot say who it was, but I did send it.

3691. Did you send the money in consequence of having lost your bands?—Yes.

3692. Did you suppose that your bands had been taken because you had not paid your money?—I believe it was so.

3693. Therefore you sent the money by this workman to the Union?—Yes.

3694. Did you tell him to take it to the collector Broadhead?—I sent it to him.

3695. And then did you get your bands?—Yes.

3696. How did you get your bands back?—Mine were brought into the place.

3697. Not the place where you were working?—Into the yard.

FOURTH DAY.

J. Barton.

6 June 1867.

3698. Were the bands given to you ?—No; I was told where to find them.

3699. Do you remember who told you where to find them ?—I do not know that.

3700. Are you sure of that ?—Yes.

3701. Where did you find them ?—They were in the yard quite openly when I got there in the morning.

3702. Did you ever say anything to Broadhead about them ?—No.

3703. Did you take any more notice of them then ?—No.

3704. Then you say you were rattened again in 1866 ?—Yes.

3705. That was not on your own account ?—No; I was taken with all the rest in 1866.

3706. Were the men that lost their bands on that occasion in arrears of contributions ?—I should say they were.

3707. Do you know as a fact whether they had paid up their contributions to the Union ?—I do not think they had.

3708. Do you suppose that was the reason why they were rattened ?—I have not the least doubt of it.

3709. You have no doubt that was the reason why they were rattened ?—No.

3710. Did you take any steps then to recover the bands taken from you ?—Not at all.

3711. Were you in arrears at that time ?—Yes, I believe I was.

3712. And you suppose your bands were taken because your contribution was not paid ?—I have not the least doubt of it.

3713. Did you pay up your contributions ?—No, I have not paid anything since.

3714. After the arrears had been paid up by the other men did you get your bands back ?—They were found.

3715. (*Chairman.*) They were found in the coke ovens ?—Yes.

3716. (*Mr. Chance.*) Did you have any communication with Mr. Broadhead about them ?—No, I never heard a word.

3717. (*Chairman.*) Now as to 1864. You say you were rattened in 1864 ?—I think it was in 1864.

3718. In 1864 you were rattened, were not you ?—I believe we were.

3719. Who was rattened besides you ?—I am not able to say at this moment.

3720. Yes, you are ?—I cannot call it to mind.

3721. I can make you call it to mind. Who was rattened in 1864 besides yourself ?—I am sure if you were to commit me I could not say.

3722. I am speaking of 1864 ?—Since 1866 I happened to receive a very bad misfortune. I broke my wrist, and it gave a shock to my system, and my memory has failed me very much.

3723. You must tell all you know ?—I am quite open and willing to do it, but I hope you will not require me to say more than I am able to do.

3724. In 1866 you say you were rattened ?—Yes.

3725. When was the time before that that you were rattened ?—I am sure I have no fixed date.

3726. Was it the year before ?—No, I think it was not.

3727. Were you in arrears at the time you were rattened ?—Yes, I dare say I was.

3728. You were in arrears, and they rattened you ?—Yes.

3729. Before that time had they been applying to you to pay your money ?—I always have been a member.

3730. Did Broadhead come to you week by week to ask you to pay ?—Yes.

3731. Had you refused to pay ?—No; sometimes it was out of my power.

3732. Did you find your bands gone at night or in the morning on that occasion, the last but one ?—It would very likely be in the morning.

3733. They were lost in the morning ?—Yes.

3734. What did you do about those bands when you found they had gone in the morning ?—I did not do anything that day.

3735. What did you do the next day ?—I applied to Broadhead for my bands.

3736. What did you say to him ?—I asked him what my bands had gone for, and he did not know anything about it.

3737. What did you say to him ?—I told him they were gone.

3738. What did he say to that ?—He did not say anything more at present, but I said, "Well, but what "am I in arrears."

3739. What did he tell you ?—He told me so much.

3740. The sum that you were in arrear ?—Yes.

3741. What did you say to that ?—I did not say anything more at present. I paid him the money.

3742. Did he tell you anything was due for expenses ?—I will not answer that question.

3743. Yes you will.—I have forgot that.

3744. Did he tell you anything was due for expenses or not ? You will answer me that.—It might be so.

3745. It might be he told you something about expenses. What did he tell you about expenses ?—I forget now what the expenses were.

3746. About how much was it he told you ?—Perhaps 5*s*.

3747. You know it was 5*s*. ?—I am speaking offhand; I have no criterion to go by.

3748. Do not you believe that it was 5*s*. ?—We will say 5*s*.

3749. Did you pay him the 5*s*. ?—Yes.

3750. Then you paid him for your contribution whatever was in arrear, and 5*s*. for "Mary Ann" ?—I have not the least doubt of it.

3751. Your memory is better than you thought it was ?—It is not very good.

3752. Did you get a receipt for your money ?—No.

3753. After you paid your money and paid for "Mary Ann," did you get your bands ?—Yes sir, they were forthcoming.

3754. Did he tell you they would be forthcoming ?—No; I did not ask him that question.

3755. You were satisfied, having paid your money ?—I felt quite satisfied when I found the bands back again.

3756. The next morning as you had paid the money and paid for "Mary Ann," you went into the yard and there found your bands ?—Yes.

The witness withdrew.

HENRY BOLLINGTON sworn and examined.

H. Bollington.

3757. (*Chairman.*) You have worked at Mr. Eadon's I believe ?—Yes.

3758. Are you a member of either of the Unions ?—Not now I am not.

3759. Have you been ?—Yes.

3760. Which of them ?—The old one.

3761. Up to what time were you a member of the old one ?—Last Christmas but one.

3762. Then that was till Christmas 1865 ?—Yes.

3763. How did you cease to be a member ? did you cease to pay your contributions or give notice that you intended to leave ?—I gave no notice.

3764. But you did not pay ?—No.

3765. Were you rattened after this ?—Yes; the bands were taken.

3766. Was that in 1866 ?—Yes.

3767. I believe there were a good many others as well; there was Christopher Taylor, Henry Taylor, and Dungworth, Barton and others rattened at the same time ?—They all went.

3768. On that occasion, did you go to Broadhead's at all ?—No.

3769. What did you do ?—They were found.

FOURTH DAY.

H. Bollington.

6 June 1867.

3770. Some lads found them, and they brought them to the police ?—Yes.

3771. Before, in 1866, had you been rattened ?—Yes.

3772. When had you been rattened before ?—I do not know what year it was.

3773. Was it in the year 1863; about three years before that? How long before 1866 were you rattened; two years before ?—I did not keep it in my mind.

3774. From two to three years before were you rattened ?—I think twice before that.

3775. How many years ago is it since you were first rattened ?—In 1862 or 1863; I do not know which.

3776. Give us an account of the first time they took your bands. Did you get them back ?—Yes.

3777. How did you get them back ?—We had a note, and we had to go and find them.

3778. When you found they were gone what did you do ? did you go to Broadhead ?—Yes, I went to Broadhead.

3779. Did you go with Staniforth ?—Four or five of us went.

3780. Did you complain to Broadhead that you had lost your things ?—We told him the bands were gone.

3781. What did he say to you ?—He said he knew nothing about it.

3782. What happened next ?—We got a note next day where to find them.

3783. Did you go again to him ?—No.

3784. How did you get the note ?—One of us got a note.

3785. Who got the note ?—Staniforth I believe got the note.

3786. Were you with him when he got the note ?—No.

3787. Did you see the note ?—Yes.

3788. What was in the note ?—He said we were to go to Hallcar Lane and look over the wall.

3789. Before you got the note had you to pay any money ?—I think we paid either 1*l.* or 1*l.* 5*s.* apiece.

3790. Which do you believe it was ?—I think 25*s.*

3791. Do you recollect Staniforth coming out of the room where he had a conversation with Broadhead and telling you what was the sum you had to pay ?—No; I saw the note the next day.

3792. I do not speak of the note, but do you recollect Staniforth coming out of the room where he had been with Broadhead, and saying you would have to pay 25*s.* ?—No.

3793. Did not he tell you 1*l.* was for your contribution and 5*s.* was for "Mary Ann" ?—We had all 25*s.* to pay.

3794. Did not he tell you that 5*s.* of it was for "Mary Ann" ?—He said we should have 25*s.* to pay and we paid it.

3795. How much did you owe for contributions ?—More than that.

3796. Did he tell you whether anything was paid for doing the job ?—No.

3797. Did Staniforth ?—No; they never said nought to me about it, but they said I had 25*s.* to pay before I could have my bands.

3798. And you thereupon paid 25*s.* ?—Yes.

3799. Where did you get the money ?—I got it of our master.

3800. Mr. Eadon lent it you ?—Yes.

3801. And you then got the note the next day ?—One of them brought the note and showed where we were to find the bands.

3802. And you went up and found the bands ?—Yes.

3803. Then you went together ?—Yes.

3804. Did you all go to an inn together and get some beer; in Carver Street ?—There was me and Joseph Barton went together.

3805. Was Broadhead gone to the theatre when you went the first time ?—I never asked whether he was gone to the theatre or not.

3806. Was he at home the first time you went at night ?—I think not.

3807. Then you went the next morning ?—Yes.

3808. Was it the next morning that you got the note ?—No; it would be after that that we got the note.

3809. Are you quite sure it was the next day, the day after, or the next day. Do you recollect taking a walk, going down to the public house and having some beer and then taking a walk and coming back again ?—There was some went back, but I do not think I went back; I went to look after the money.

3810. You told us that the first time you were rattened you paid all 25*s.*, and you got a note and got the bands ?—Yes.

3811. When was the next time ?—They were taken again by a chap called George Bradshaw; they were found, they were found in the sough.

3812. How long was it after the first time ? was it a year after ? what was his name, George Bradshaw ?—Yes.

3813. Were you a member of the committee at the time Bradshaw was committed ?—Yes; I was one of the committee.

3814. And of course you knew nothing about your bands being taken ?—No.

3815. They never come to the committee and tell them when the rattening is done ?—Never when I had been there.

3816. How many is the committee composed of ?—Six.

The witness withdrew.

THOMAS CHAPMAN sworn and examined.

T. Chapman.

3817. (*Mr. Barstow.*) You work for Mr. Parkin ?—Yes.

3818. Are you a saw-grinder ?—Yes.

3819. How long have you been a saw-grinder ?—Nearly 20 years.

3820. You are not now a member of the Saw Grinders' Union ?—No.

3821. When did you cease to be a member ?—I cannot say exactly.

3822. Two years ago ?—Yes; I was a member up to last June.

3823. Did you cease to be a member of the Union in June last ?—I cannot exactly say the time; I was a member of the Union then.

3824. I suppose you did not pay your contributions ?—Yes; I paid in June.

3825. Was that the last time you paid ?—I cannot say.

3826. What was the amount of your contribution to the Saw Grinders' Union ?—5*s.* a week then.

3827. Was it always 5*s.* a week ?—No, not always 5*s.* a week; it was then.

3828. What used it to be ?—It used to be poundage sometimes.

3829. What was the poundage ?—It has been 2*s.* 6*d.* in the pound; it has been 4*s.* 2*d.* and 4*s.* 6*d.* I believe.

3830. 2*s.* 6*d.* and as much as 4*s.* 2*d.* and 4*s.* 6*d* ?—Yes, I believe that is right.

3831. Have you ever been rattened ?—Yes.

3832. When was the first time ?—I cannot say.

3833. How many times have you been rattened ?—I cannot say.

3834. Very often ?—No, I have never been rattened very often.

3835. Have you been rattened half-a-dozen times ?—No, I do not think I have.

3836. Five times ?—I cannot say.

3837. Do you believe you have been rattened five or six times? or do you know how many times you have been rattened ?—I do not know how many times I have been rattened.

3838. It is not such a very common thing with you, is it ?—They lie a long way apart, and I never take any notice of them.

3839. Rattening means taking your bands and throwing men out of work?—Yes.

3840. You remember how many times it has happened to you, surely?—No, I do not.

3841. Have you been rattened three times?—I should think I have been rattened three times. I cannot say for a fact how many times I have been rattened.

3842. Have you been rattened more than once?—Yes.

3843. Now when was the last time you were rattened?—In June last year.

3844. Just a year ago?—Thereabouts.

3845. Were you at that time a member of the Saw Grinders Union?—Yes.

3846. Were you in arrear?—Yes.

8347. Had any applications been made to you to pay up your arrears?—I was called on every week.

3848. Who called on you?—Broadhead.

3849. What happened to you in the way of being rattened?—Two grinding bands went and two axle nuts.

3850. How would the taking the axle nuts affect you?—We fasten on the pulleys by the nuts, and when the nuts are not there we cannot work.

3851. Then it has just the same effect as taking away the bands?—It has a double effect then.

3852. How?—If you take either we cannot work.

3853. (*Chairman.*) If you take either the bands or nuts away it would stop work?—Yes.

3854. (*Mr. Barstow.*) When you missed these first what did you do?—I went to Mr. Parkins' foreman.

3855. Who is that?—His name is Heslop.

3856. What did you say to him?—I did not need to say anything; he knew my bands were gone, and he gave me another band to go on working with.

3857. Did you make any inquiry about your old bands?—Yes, that night.

3858. Whom did you inquire of?—I went to Broadhead, the secretary.

3859. (*Chairman.*) To his own house?—Yes.

3860. (*Mr. Barstow.*) What did you say to him?—He said he did not know anything about them.

3861. What did you say to him?—I asked him whether he knew anything about my bands. He said he did not know anything about them.

3862. What then?—I asked him if he thought it was for my contributions not being paid up.

3863. What did he say to that?—He said he should suppose it was. He did not know, but he should suppose so.

3864. Did you ask him anything further; did you ask him how much was due?—Yes; I asked him how much was due.

3865. What did he do?—I cannot say exactly.

3866. Did he tell you?—Yes, he told me.

3867. Did he say anything else besides what was due?—Yes; he said there would be so much arrears and expenses.

3868. Do you recollect what the arrears were?—There were some back reckonings, but the arrears were when reckoned up right 1*l.* 17*s.* 5*d.*

3869. What did he tell you were your arrears?—1*l.* 17*s.* 5*d.*

3870. And how much of expenses?—I left him 10*s.* on account.

3871. (*Chairman.*) How much did he say the expenses would be?—He did not say; he did not know

3872. (*Mr. Barstow.*) You inquired, of course, what the arrears were?—Yes.

3873. What did he say the arrears were by themselves?—1*l.* 17*s.* 5*d.*

3874. Did he tell you what the expenses were?—No, he did not.

3875. Did you ask him if there would be any expenses?—I am not aware of that.

3876. Did you as a matter of fact ask him what the expenses were?—Well, sir, I left him 10*s.*

3877. (*Chairman.*) What was the 10*s.* for?—For the expenses.

3878. (*Mr. Barstow.*) What did you understand by expenses?—The expenses of the bands being taken away.

3879. Did you ask him whether you would get your bands?—No, I have never got my bands.

3880. Did you never get them?—We have got the nuts back, but not the bands.

3881. How did you get the nuts back?—Two little boys found them in the river.

3882. (*Chairman.*) How did the boys find them there?—They were washing some wood and they saw them.

3883. (*Mr. Barstow.*) Who are the little boys?—I do not know their names.

3884. Was it accident?—It was accident on their part finding them.

3885. What is the size of the nut?—Five inches in diameter; a very long size.

3886. If you had made no inquiry of Mr. Broadhead where to get your bands, what was the use of paying 1*l.* 17*s.* 5*d.* and the expenses?—I did not pay it on that night; not the 1*l.* 17*s.* 5*d.*

3887. You did pay it some time or other?—Yes; but I did not pay it then.

3888. What was the condition upon which you paid that money?—I paid the 1*l.* 17*s.* 5*d.*, and when I paid it he hinted to me that the expenses would want paying.

3889. You tell me that you did pay 10*s.* on account of the expenses?—Yes; but not at the same time that I paid the 1*l.* 17*s.* 5*d.*

3890. It does not matter; you did pay it?—I had two or three different interviews with him; the first time I never paid any. I had so many interviews that I cannot say when it was that I paid the separate money.

3891. What did you pay first, the 10*s.* or the 1*l.* 17*s.* 5*d.*?—The 1*l.* 17*s.* 5*d.*

3892. (*Chairman.*) You paid up all your contributions; you paid the money, and that made you right?—I was right on the book when I had paid it.

3893. You were straight on the book?—Yes.

3894. (*Mr. Barstow.*) How many interviews had you had with Mr. Broadhead before you paid the 1*l.* 17*s.* 5*d.*?—I cannot say, I am sure, but I think only one.

3895. The second time you went to him you got straight in the book?—I think it was the second time that I paid the 1*l.* 17*s.* 5*d.*

3896. Did you then ask him for your bands?—When I paid the 1*l.* 17*s.* 5*d.*?

3897. Yes?—He hinted when I paid the 1*l.* 17*s.* 5*d.* that the expenses would want paying.

3898. You do not answer my question. Did you ask him for your bands?—No; I knew if I paid the money they would come back. I never asked him for them.

3899. (*Chairman.*) You say that he hinted to you about the expenses; what did he say to you?—He says, "The expenses will want paying."

3900. (*Mr. Barstow.*) What did you say to that when he said that the expenses would want paying?—I asked him what it would be.

3901. What did he say to that?—He said that he did not know.

3902. What did you do upon that?—Then I gave him 10*s.*

3903. What did he say to that?—He said that if 10*s.* was not sufficient he would hold himself responsible and return it me back.

3904. What then?—He would return me that money if it was not sufficient.

3905. Do you know whether it was sufficient?—No.

3906. Have you ever seen him again about it?—After that he called upon me.

3907. Was that at Mr. Parkins'—Yes.

3908. What did he say to you?—He said that he had received a letter from the post.

3909. Did he show you the letter?—Yes.

3910. Did he give you the letter?—No.

3911. Did he read the contents of it?—It said as

FOURTH DAY.

T. Chapman.

6 June 1867.

far as I can remember it that I must pay 10*s.* for the former rattening, and 5*s.* each for the two bands, and 5*s.* for two nuts, making altogether 1*l.* 5*s.*

3912. Did you say anything about it ?—I told him that I should not pay it.

3913. What did he say to you ?—I believe he waited on me.

3914. (*Chairman.*) What did he say when you said that you would not pay it ?—He went away and never said anything.

3915. (*Mr. Barstow.*) Did you make any application to him after that. Did you see him again ?—I do not know whether I went to him next time or whether he called upon me the next time. I saw him several times.

3916. What about this money ?—He gave me the 10*s.* back. I asked him for that 10*s.* and he gave it me back again.

3917. (*Chairman.*) He gave it you back. What did he say when he gave it you back ? Did he say that it was not enough or that the people were not satisfied, or what did he say as to why he gave it back ?—I believe I told him that I should fetch a summons for him, and he said "very well, I can go on with my work."

3918. What did he say to that ?—He said "very well, he did not mind that," or something to that effect.

3919. Did you fetch a summons ?—No.

3920. Have you ever seen him again about it ?—Yes, I saw him after that.

3921. When was that ?—I cannot say the day that I saw him, but the next time I saw him in conversation I offered to pay 15*s.* and he said that was not sufficient ; I should have 1*l.* 5*s.* to pay.

3922. He said that was not sufficient ?—Yes.

3923. That you must pay 1*l.* 5*s.* ?—Yes.

3924. What next ?—I saw him after that and he said that I could have my bands back for 15*s.* He had had information that I could have my bands back for 15*s.*

3925. What did you say ?—I left him there.

3926. You never paid the 15*s.* ?—No, I never paid the 15*s.*

3927. (*Chairman.*) Did you say whether you would or would not pay it ?—I cannot say whether I did or not.

3928. (*Mr. Barstow.*) In fact you never paid and you never got your bands ?—No.

3929. Is that all that you can tell us about that rattening ?—Yes, that is all that I know about it.

3930. You have not seen him since upon the subject ?—No ; I do not think that I have seen him above four times since that.

3931. Have you had any conversation about it ?—No.

3932. You said that you had to pay 10*s.* for the former rattening ?—Yes, they said I had to pay 10*s.* for a former rattening.

3933. (*Chairman.*) When were you rattened before that ?—I think it was a year before ; it might be.

3934. What did they take that time ?—They took two bands.

3935. (*Mr. Barstow.*) Had you been in arrear to the Union at the time these bands were taken ?—Yes.

3936. Where were they taken from ?—The same place as before.

3937. What did you do when you missed them ?—I began to search about for them and found them.

3938. Where were they ?—They were in the next yard buried in the ash heap.

3939. You fitted them to your wheel and went to work again ?—Yes.

3940. Did you make any inquiry why this was done ?—Yes, I went to Broadhead's.

3941. Did you see him ?—Yes.

3942. Did you tell him ?—I asked him the reason of my bands going.

3943. What did he say ?—He said he did not know

3944. Did you say anything to him then ?—Yes, I told him I had got my bands, but before that I asked him what my arrears were.

3945. You knew why your bands were gone ?—I had an idea. I was in arrear.

3946. What did he say to that. Do you remember what Broadhead said. Did he tell you what you were in arrear ?—I cannot exactly remember what he said my arrear was, but I believe it was 2*l.* 5*s.*

3947. He told you so ?—Yes.

3948. What did you say to that ?—I said I should not pay the 2*l.* 5*s.* and I told him that I had got my bands.

3949. Did he say anything to that ?—No, he did not say anything, not that I am aware of.

3950. Had you any other interview with him about these bands ?—No, I had no other interview with him about the bands.

3951. 2*l.* 5*s.* is a considerable sum ; what was your contribution at this time ?—I do not know whether we had been paying poundage.

3952. (*Chairman.*) Do you know yourself how much you owed at that time ; was 2*l.* 5*s.* the right sum for contribution ?—I cannot say whether it was or not.

3953. What is your belief about that. Do you believe that you owed as much as 2*l.* 5*s.* ?—I cannot say.

3954. (*Mr. Barstow.*) Did Broadhead at this time that you are now speaking of ask you to pay anything for expenses ?—No ; I believe expenses were never named at that time.

3955. Have you lost anything at any other time besides these ?—Yes.

3956. When was it ?—I cannot say.

3957. (*Chairman.*) How long before the time that you were talking of ?—I have no idea.

3958. Six months or a year ?—More than that.

3959. (*Mr. Barstow.*) Two years ?—I cannot say the exact time.

3960. However, you did lose something before ?—Yes.

3961. Was it the same sort of thing as this ? Were you in arrear ?—I do not know.

3962. Did you lose bands ?—Yes.

3963. Anything besides bands ?—No.

3964. Was it from the same place ?—Yes.

3965. Did you apply to Mr. Broadhead upon that occasion ?—Yes, I believe I did.

3966. At his own house ?—Yes ; I believe I went to Carver Street as usual.

3967. Did you ask him if he knew why they had gone ?—I cannot say.

3968. Did you ask him about them ?—Probably I should ask him about them.

3969. (*Chairman.*) You went for that purpose, did not you ?—Yes, of course I asked him, but I cannot remember it.

3970. (*Mr. Barstow.*) You did ask him ?—I should think I did.

3971. What did he say to you ?—I should expect that he said the same as he did before, that he knew nothing about them.

3972. Did you ask him what you were in arrear then ? did the same kind of thing happen as before ?—I do not know whether I did or not.

3973. Did you pay him anything ?—No, I do not know that I did.

3974. You must remember something about that, you went to his house, what did you do when you went to his house, we have this much that you went to his house about having lost your bands ?—Yes.

3975. (*Chairman.*) How many bands had you lost ?—I do not know how many went at that time.

3976. (*Mr. Barstow.*) Can you remember nothing about it ?—Very little about it.

3977. Can you remember whether you paid him anything at all ?—I cannot.

3978. Can you or cannot you remember whether you paid him anything at all ?—I do not remember whether I paid him anything at all.

FOURTH DAY.

T. Chapman.

6 June 1867.

3979. You only remember that you lost bands and went to Broadhead's?—I could not tell within five years when that time was except by my being at the place a certain time.

3980. (*Chairman.*) Did you get your bands back again?—Yes.

3981. How did you get them back?—We had a note left.

3982. Who left the note?—I do not know.

3983. Do you mean to say that you had not paid the money if you got the note?—They did not always go on our own account.

3984. Did other persons have their bands taken at the same time as yours were?—No.

3985. Then yours were the only person's bands taken on that occasion?—Yes.

3986. Then you say you got a note?—Yes, saying where they were.

3987. When did you get the note, how long after you lost them?—Two or three days, I cannot say exactly.

3988. In the meantime had you seen Broadhead?—Yes.

3989. And upon your oath had you not paid the money before you got that note?—No I believe I had not.

3990. You had not?—No.

3991. How was it that you came to get the note?—I believe it was not on my account that they went.

3992. You say that there had been a rattening and they had taken the wrong man's bands?—No there are other Union men of other societies who worked for Mr. Parkin besides me, and by stopping me it prevented them working.

3993. You were not in default on that occasion but they stopped you in order to stop another man?—Yes.

3994. Where did you find the note?—It was found by the gates.

3995. Where did they tell you the bands were?—I believe, if I remember right, that they were in the next yard.

3996. And, as before, in the ash heap?—No.

3997. Where?—I believe it was the adjoining yard to that.

3998. (*Mr. Barstow.*) Have you ever been rattened except on these three occasions you have told us of? is there any other?—Yes, they had gone before, but I cannot recollect, I do not think they had gone on my account before, it was something similar, and I did not take any notice of them.

3999. What were you earning a day at this time?—I cannot say exactly.

4000. (*Chairman.*) What do you earn now?—Sometimes more and sometimes less.

4001. In good employ will a saw grinder like you make 2*l.* to 3*l.* a week?—If I was single handed I should be satisfied with 2*l.* a week.

4002. (*Mr. Barstow.*) Is that a fair average?—Yes that is a fair average, some men might get more.

4003. Do you suppose you were earning that about this time?—I might be getting more than that, I employed a boy.

4004. What do you think as a matter of fact you were earning about that time?—Myself.

4005. Of course you cannot say to a shilling, but tell us what you think you were earning?—Do you mean what I earnt on the average a week?

4006. (*Chairman.*) Yes, at the time when you employed that boy, what can a man earn with a boy in that way?—3*l.* or 3*l.* 10*s.* a week if there is plenty of work.

4007. Then you had the expense of keeping the boy?—Yes.

4008. (*Mr. Barstow.*) How many days were you thrown out of work by the loss of these bands?—I cannot say.

4009. (*Chairman.*) How long were you before you found your bands, you lost your bands and they were found in an adjoining yard, how long were you without them?—Perhaps two or three days.

4010. Did they make you compensation?—No.

4011. You did not receive anything for it?—No.

4012. (*Mr. Barstow.*) You lost two days' wage, and received nothing for it?—No.

4013. Although you had no difference with the Union?—No.

4014. (*Chairman.*) It was only to stop another man who was in arrear?—Yes.

4015. (*Mr. Barstow.*) Have you been rattened at any other time, either on your own account or any other person's account?—Not that I am aware of.

4016. Never besides the three times?—Not that I can call to memory. I have never been rattened but twice on my own account.

4017. Twice on your own account and once on another man's account?—Yes.

4018. (*Chairman.*) Have you ever been stopped because Mr. Parkin would not pay the contribution money of his men. Do they ever call upon masters to pay the contribution of the men?—No, not that I am aware of.

4019. (*Mr. Barstow.*) With respect to the bands that you lost in June 1866, have you ever said that you yourself had found the buckles of the bands in a house?—Yes, I have said so to Broadhead. I did find them.

4020. You did in fact find them?—Yes, and a small piece of a band with them. I found the buckles of my bands on Kelham Island in some old houses.

4021. You say you found a bit of a band with the buckles?—Yes, there was a tab. We have to make them longer and shorter with the tab.

4022. Did you infer from that that the bands have been destroyed?—I cannot say.

4023. (*Chairman.*) Had they been cut?—No, not that I could ascertain.

4024. (*Mr. Barstow.*) You yourself looked for the bands?—Yes.

4025. And you found the buckles of them?—Yes.

4026. Did anybody live in this house?—No, it was an empty house.

4027. With reference to these bands that you lost in 1866, do you remember having any conversation with Broadhead, and Broadhead saying to you that if you would pay back the 10*s.* which you have mentioned that he repaid to you, that the committee themselves would pay the sum of 15*s.* to the man who did the rattening? Did not Broadhead say to you, out of consideration of your being out of work, if you would return the 10*s.* that the committee would pay 15*s.* to the man who rattened you?—I do not understand you.

4028. (*Chairman.*) Was there any conversation at all about their paying 15*s.* and you giving your 10*s.*?—Not that I recollect.

4029. (*Mr. Barstow.*) Do you recollect Broadhead saying that the committee would be willing to pay 15*s.* towards the expense of the rattening?—On the last occasion that I saw him he said 15*s.* would do for me; that is all that I recollect. That is the last conversation that I had with him.

4030. Did he say anything about anybody else contributing?—No, not to me.

4031. (*Chairman.*) Do you recollect whether Mr. Broadhead did not say to you that to show their kindness to you, and how much they wished to be kind to you for the loss of time that you had incurred, that they themselves would pay 15*s.* towards the expenses that had been incurred in rattening you?—15*s.* towards the expense of my being rattened?

4032. Yes, did not he say so to you?—No.

4033. Not the committee?—I do not recollect that he ever said any such words.

4034. (*Mr. Barstow.*) Do you remember saying to Broadhead that the bands were old bands, and were not worth anything?—No; I do not know that I said any such words, because I knew they were worth money.

FOURTH DAY.

T. Chapman.

6 June 1867.

4035. (*Chairman.*) I have no doubt that Mr. Sugg has good reason for wishing this question put, and I should like an answer?—If such a thing did occur, and I could not recollect it, you would not have me say I could?

4036. No, of course not.

The witness withdrew.

Mr. JOSEPH RAGG sworn and examined.

Mr. J. Ragg.

4037. (*Mr. Chance.*) Are you the manager of Messrs. Slack, Sellars, and Company?—I am.

4038. What are they?—Saw manufacturers.

4039. When you say saw manufacturers, do they complete the saw?—Yes.

4040. How long have you been manager to them? —Nine years, I think.

4041. Do they employ any grinders?—Yes.

4042. And saw handle makers, and saw smiths?—Yes.

4043. Are those the three different kinds of men employed in saw making, or are there others also?—No, those complete the three branches.

4044. Are you a member of any Union?—No.

4045. Have you ever been a member of any Union? Not that I am aware of.

4046. I suppose you would know if you had been? —I am only speaking in my own time.

4047. Have you ever been a journeyman in any of these branches?—Never.

4048. How many men have Messrs. Slack, Sellars, and Company in their employ?—About 20.

4049. That is including the three branches?—Yes.

4050. Are the men they employ Union men?—They are all non-Union men at the present time.

4051. How long is it that they have been all non-Union men?—I think the last Union man we had gave us notice to leave on the 14th of July 1866.

4052. Before that time had there been working with you Union men and non-Union men?—Yes.

4053. Why did the Union men give you notice to leave?—About November 1865, we were assured by our saw handle makers that the majority of the master manufacturers of Sheffield were giving an advance of 10 per cent.; I said I would make inquiries if this statement was correct, and in few instances only I found it correct; nevertheless, we said that whatever any person in the trade did we would do the same, and we gave them an advance of 10 per cent. upon that; perhaps a fortnight after this advance I discovered in our wages book a further advance of 15 per cent. on one class of handles which had been surreptitiously made without our knowledge.

4054. How could it occur?—Simply from not having a statement beside you at the time these wages were entered, and perhaps not being conversant with the prices of everything without reference, but generally on Monday morning reference is made to the book to see that the prices have been correctly entered by the men.

4055. Who kept the book?—I keep it. I make it up first from the men; they had made a mis-statement of the thing, and given it me as the actual price.

4056. (*Chairman.*) You are not right in saying "surreptitiously," but they had given you a false account of what was the proper amount to be paid? —Yes.

4057. (*Mr. Chance.*) You had made the entries in the book of 15 per cent. upon the statement made by the men?—Yes.

4058. Who were they?—The saw handle makers.

4059. (*Chairman.*) Then you were charged 15 per cent. too high?—Yes.

4060. (*Mr. Chance.*) Then, when you discovered that there was this incorrect statement in the book, what occurred?—I went to the shop and asked the men if there was not some mistake.

4061. (*Chairman.*) Is it 15 per cent. too high?—15 per cent. in addition to the 10 per cent. that we had already given.

4062. (*Mr. Chance.*) Had they stated to you that the master manufacturers were giving the 15 per cent. in addition to the 10?—No, this was only upon one class of handles.

4063. (*Chairman.*) In giving in the prices they had put on 15 per cent. too high?—They said there was no mistake whatever; they said that was the price that they had agreed amongst themselves to have. I said "Then you do not think it necessary to consult us "about the advance of price."

4064. What did they say to that?—They said no, they should have it, and we might as well pay it in peace and quietness, as otherwise they said we could not get a handle maker in the town if were to give 50*l.* for one.

4065. What did you say to that?—I said "perhaps "you will allow us to try?"

4066. Did that end the interview?—Yes; we told them it left us no margin, and that we could not pay the advanced price and we would not pay it.

4067. Upon saying that did they go on working?—Yes, with this understanding that the foreman says, "You must work at the usual things." In this department of the business it is not necessary to give a man an order out every week, so long as he keeps a given stock of goods to execute orders; we never interfere with the man, and if the man makes handles of one class it is not quite so good a work; when he has had four and a half days working he makes a better class of work to eke out the business; they thought this class was not so good, but they said "You "must go on making handles as usual, but of this "class you must make none."

4068. The foreman of the saw handle makers said, "You may make any other class, but none of this?" —Yes.

4069. What do you call a foreman?—The man who selects the woods and marks the handles out, and so on.

4070. He is your foreman?—No, the foreman amongst the men.

4071. He said, "You may make any class of saw "handles but these?"—Yes.

4072. That particular class which they might not make was of a better description than the other?—No; it was a class that we wanted made.

4073. How did they know that?—Because we had orders in the place at the time that they knew of.

4074. They knew the amount of orders that you gave out from time to time?—Yes.

4075. What took place upon that?—They said they should not make any, and I said I should give them an order out with a fair proportion of this class of handles for every man's work, and unless they made them they would be paid for nothing else. They then gave us a month's notice to leave.

4076. The whole lot of the saw handle makers did so?—Yes.

4077. At that time was any notice given you by any of your other workers?—No.

4078. Upon their giving a month's notice to leave what did you do?—We advertised for handle makers.

4079. (*Chairman.*) They had the right to give notice if they liked?—Yes.

4080. (*Mr. Chance.*) This is still in July?—No, it was in July when the saw smiths went. They went on the 6th of January 1866. They gave notice in December 1865.

4081. You advertised in January 1866?—Yes.

4082. What was the result of your advertisement? —We got some handle makers.

4083. From Sheffield?—Yes.

4084. How many did you get?—We got two in-workers and several out-workers.

4085. Were they members of the Union?—No; non-Union men.

4086. What happened then?—Nothing happened at that time. We continued to work on in our usual course.

4087. Did they go on working until the 23rd of June of that year ?—Yes.

4088. (*Chairman.*) That is the fresh men, the two in-workers and several out-workers ?—Yes.

4089. (*Mr. Chance.*) Up to this time had there been any difficulty with any of the other branches ?—No.

4090. In June what occurred ?—On Saturday afternoon the 23rd of June I received an anonymous note, wishing to see me at the "Warm Hearthstone" Inn, just above our house.

4091. Have you that note with you ?—I think it is in the hands of the solicitor, but it was an anonymous note ; there was no signature to it ; it was written on a little scrap of paper.

4092. Was there any date upon it ?—No, I think it was simply a statement, "Will you be kind enough to "slip up to the 'Warm Hearthstone' immediately after "you have ceased business ?".

4093. Did you go up ?—Yes.

4094. You went up the same day ?—Yes.

4095. Whom did you see ?—I saw two persons who represented themselves as a deputation from the Handle Makers' Society. I believe one was the secretary, Barker, and another person.

4096. Do you know the name of the other person ?—No, I do not.

4097. They represented themselves as a deputation from the Saw Handle Society ?—Yes.

4098. Had you ever seen either of these two persons before ?—Never.

4099. (*Chairman.*) Do you know who the other man was ?—I do not.

4100. (*Mr. Chance.*) What occurred ? What did they state to you ? Who spoke, Barker or the other man ?—Barker, or both. They said they wished to send us two men to take the situations of the two men we had working in. I said the situation was not open. They said that they were better workmen than the two that we had, and they would suit us better. I told them that we did not want two better men, that we were satisfied with the men, and that when we did want two men we would feel obliged if they would send us two. They said if the two did not suit us they would send some more till we were suited. I said it was extremely kind, and that we would apply to them when we wanted any men. I said the man that we employ is a non-Union man, and they said that they knew it, and he is obnoxious to the trade.

4101. What further conversation took place ?—I told them he was our servant, and not the servant of the trade, and if he was not obnoxious to us we should keep him.

4102. Did that end the interview ?—No ; they said they were determined they would have him out of the trade. I said that it was all nonsense to talk about taking a man out of the trade who was upwards of 50 years of age, who had served his apprenticeship, and worked at it all the days of his life.

4103. Was it the case with the man that he was a man who had been apprenticed to it, and brought up to it, and had worked at it up to 50 years of age ?—Yes.

4104. What did they say to that ?—I said, "Moreover he will pay to your funds for peace and quietness." They said they did not believe that. I said, "He has promised to pay you 4*s.* per week towards "your Union, 3*s.* for arrears and 1*s.* of contribution."

4105. Was that arrears for the time he had been in your employ ?—While he was out of the Union. They said the man would not conform to them. I said we would pay them on the Monday morning ourselves, would that be satisfactory.

4106. Was that intended as a promise to pay every Monday morning ?—Yes, because we should receive it from the man and pay them.

4107. What did they say to that ?—They said they would not allow it, that they would have him out of the trade. I said, "Do you wish to make a "common highwayman or garotter of him, or what "do you want to make of him." I said the man must live. They said they had nothing to do with that. I told them that they had, and society at large had. I said, "Now would it not be much better to "receive this man's money, and make him a good "member of your society, than to try to drive him "out of the trade." "Oh !" they said, "He was a "bad one, and they would have him out." I told them we should neither aid nor assist them in such a wicked undertaking, and I left them.

4108. (*Chairman.*) What kind of a man was he whom they wanted to drive out of the trade ; is he a respectable man ?—For anything I know to the contrary ; he is one of the most obliging men that we have about our place at the present time.

4109. Is he a well conducted man ?—Yes, a steady man.

4110. And a good workman ?—Yes.

4111. Do you know any reason why they should drive him out of the trade ?—Simply because he is a non-Union man.

4112. Is that the only reason that you are aware of ?—I am not aware of any other.

4113. (*Mr. Chance.*) That was the whole of the transaction so far as you have told us ?—Yes.

4114. Soon after that did anything occur to the manufactory ?—At our grinding wheel something occurred.

4115. How soon after ?—This was on the Saturday afternoon that I have been talking of ; our wheel bands and nuts were stolen on the Monday following.

4116. (*Chairman.*) You found them gone on the Monday morning ?—No, we found them gone on the Tuesday morning ; we received a letter by post on the Tuesday morning.

4117. (*Mr. Chance.*) You missed them on the Tuesday ?—Our grinding wheel was some distance from our warehouse ; it is not always on Monday that saw grinders are working.

4118. When had you discovered them missing ?—On Tuesday night we received a note.

4119. On Tuesday you missed them, not Monday ?—We ourselves missed them then. Our grinders had been working on the Monday, but they did not tell us. On Monday morning, from half-past 12 to 2 o'clock, these nuts and bands were stolen.

4120. I ask what you can tell us of your own knowledge. You know as a fact that they were taken between 12 and 2 on Monday ?—Yes.

4121. How many were taken ?—Three bands and two nuts.

4122. Between 12 and 2 is the time when the men go to dinner ?—Yes.

4123. The next morning, Tuesday, you got a note ?—Yes.

4124. That was the first information you had of the matter ?—Yes ; the note said "attend to the saw-handle "makers. Yours, Mary."

4125. (*Chairman.*) The next morning you got that note ?—Yes.

4126. How did you get it ?—By post.

4127. Was it addressed to you, or was it addressed to Slack, Sellars, and Company ?—Slack, Sellars, and Company. During the morning our grinders came to the place, and they brought us a scrap of paper with the same sentence upon it, written on a piece of common wrapping-up paper in a large pencil hand, "attend to the handle makers."

4128. Did they say where they got it from ?—It was left on the horsing.

4129. You made enquiries and found these had been missing between 12 and 2 ?—Yes, the grinders told us so ; they came up shortly after the receipt of the letter by me.

4130. (*Mr. Chance.*) What did you do after you received that letter ? Did you make any search after the missing bands ?—Yes ; but prior to making search I went to the secretary of the saw grinders, Mr. Broadhead.

FOURTH DAY.

Mr. J. Ragg.

6 June 1867.

4131. Was that the same day ?—Yes, on the Tuesday morning.

4132. Where did you go to to Broadhead ?—The Royal George, in Carver Street.

4133. To his house ?—Yes.

4134. Did you find him there ?—Yes, I said to Broadhead, " Our bands are stolen," I asked him the reason. He said he did not know. I said " Are your men in arrear ?" He said " No." I said " Have you any " grievance against us ?" He said " No." He said he had no knowledge whatever about it. I told him of the dispute between us and the handle makers, I said " Now Mr. Broadhead you have tools belonging to the Union and men on the box, we will find you employment both for the tools and the men."

4135. What did he say to that ?—He said I must really see him again, I promised to see him in the afternoon, he said under the circumstances he could not accept the offer.

4136. Did you go in the afternoon ?—Yes, I did.

4137. You went and saw him, and he said that under the circumstances he could not accept the offer ? —Yes.

4138. Did he say anything else ?—Yes, he said the handle makers would ratten them if they did.

4139. What did you say to that ?—I told him their tools might as well be in the committee room of the Handle Makers Union as standing idle at their grinding wheel.

4140. What did he say to that ?—He said he was sorry he could not help me, but he could not interfere in the matter, I left Mr. Broadhead, and there the interview ended.

4141. (*Mr. Chance.*) Did you see Broadhead again upon the matter ?—No.

4142. You never saw him again upon this subject ? —No.

4143. Did you get your bands and nuts back ?— No.

4144. You have never seen them from that time ?— No.

4145. Did you lose any other articles from the factory ?—Not that we are aware of.

4146. Do you remember Jackson the detective assisting you to search for the tools ?—Yes.

4147. Was that soon after ?—It would be during the week.

4148. It was the same week ?—Yes, this was during the time that the engine was running so that they gave us no opportunity of going underneath the drums and various other secret places where we thought we should have an opportunity of finding them, so we left the place until the engine was set down, that was on Saturday afternoon.

4149. At the end of the week on Saturday when the machine came to a standstill where did you search? —Underneath the drums and in various places.

4150. Did you make any inquiry from the men in charge of the engine ?—Yes, from the engine tenter.

4151. Did you ask him ?—Yes we asked whether he had seen any strange people about.

4152. What did he say to that ?—" No."

4153. Did you say anything further to him about them ?—Jackson said to him " If you can give this " gentleman any information respecting these bands " you can have a 10*l*. note."

4154. (*Chairman.*) That was to the tenter, the engine driver ?—Yes.

4155. (*Mr. Chance.*) What did the engine tenter say to that ?—He hesitated and said " Well, if I know I dare not tell if you gave me 100*l*."

4156. Did he say anything more ?—I said " Why ? " He said " Because I should expect my engine being blown up."

4157. What is the name of the engine tenter ?—It was Jackson, Newton, and Company's engine tenter, Sheaf Island Works. He said " My engine would be blown up or some gunpowder laid for me."

4158. Was that all that took place on that occasion ? —Yes.

4159. Do you remember getting another threatening letter ?—Yes.

4160. Was it in November ?—I am sure I cannot say.

4161. (*Chairman.*) Was it before or after this ?— After this.

4162. December was the last transaction and then January ; how long after would this be ?—We have been so accustomed to receive threatening letters, and they have not been very interesting, that I do not remember.

4163. How many times have you seen threatening letters ?—Many times.

4164. Give us a notion ?—Five or six years ago we had some.

4165. Within five or six years how many have you received ?—I am sure I cannot say.

4166. Cannot you give us some kind of a notion ? —Three or four.

4167. Three or four within five or six years ?— Yes.

4168. Two of them were last year ?—Yes ; but had we been aware that such an inquiry as this would have taken place we should have taken great care of these things, but they were consigned to the waste basket.

4169. (*Mr. Chance.*) You say you have received so many that you can hardly remember the dates of them ?—Yes.

4170. What was the tenour of them ? Did they appear to come from the same branch of the trade, the saw handlers ?—No ; it was chiefly the grinders.

4171. (*Chairman.*) These threatening letters were chiefly purporting to come from the grinders ?—Yes.

4172. (*Mr. Chance.*) Was any particular signature attached to them ?—Yes.

4173. What was it ?—" Tantia Topee."

4174. There is no particular meaning to be attached to that ?—No.

4175. Was any well known signature attached to them ?—" Mary Ann " and the like.

4176. Have you been rattened on any other occasion beside the one of which you told us ?— Yes.

4177. How many times have you been rattened as far as you can remember ?—I am sure I cannot say ; three or four times.

4178. Within what period would that be ?—It would extend over your limits, but we have been rattened three times within eight years.

4179. And two or three times beyond that period ? —Yes.

4180. Have those rattenings to which you refer been the taking away of your tools and bands ?—Yes, and they have thrown our saws into the river as well.

4181. They were destroying them ?—They knew where they could find them when the wheel dam was run off ; they would not take any harm if they were under the water all the time.

4182. They were to be taken out at some convenient season ?—Yes.

4183. What were those rattenings for as far as you can remember ?—I think it was not a grievance so much with us, as a little rivalry between the Jobbing Grinders' Society and the Saw Grinders' Society.

4184. (*Chairman.*) It was the new company against the old ?—They were not the new and old company at that time ; they were two distinct bodies, the Saw Grinders' Union and the Jobbing Grinders' Union.

4185. (*Mr. Chance.*) What was the nature of the rivalry that existed between the two societies ?—It would be a long explanation.

The witness withdrew.

Adjourned to to-morrow at 11 o'clock.

FIFTH DAY.

Council Hall, Sheffield, Friday, 7th June 1867.

PRESENT:

WILLIAM OVEREND, Esq., Q.C.
THOMAS IRWIN BARSTOW, Esq.
GEORGE CHANCE, Esq.
J. E. BARKER, Esq., Secretary.

WILLIAM OVEREND, Esq., Q.C., in the Chair.

FIFTH DAY.

JOSEPH THOMPSON re-called, and further examined.

J. Thompson.

7 June 1867.

4186. (*Chairman.*) I find in the "Independent" of this morning a notice of a meeting of your union; that is so, is it not?—Yes.

4187. Who was present at it?—Nearly, I should say, three parts of the trade.

4188. Who was the chairman?—Thomas Gillott.

4189. Who was the secretary?—I called the meeting to tender my resignation.

4190. And did you tender your resignation?—Yes.

4191. Was it accepted?—Yes.

4192. And who was appointed in your place?—John Hearnshaw as secretary.

4193. Did you tell them about the money which you had taken from the funds?—There was nothing further stated than I stated here.

4194. You stated what you have stated here?—Oh yes.

4195. And I suppose that the proceedings which took place when you were a witness were known to the meeting?—Exactly.

4196. Did they pass a resolution to the following effect "That this meeting is of opinion that the "monies taken by the secretary were not embezzled, "inasmuch as they were taken and paid for services "rendered to the trade"?—Yes.

4197. Were you reprimanded for your conduct?—I was reprimanded inasmuch as I had taken it upon myself without acquainting the committee.

4198. That was all?—As I had before stated it here, and in that statement damaged my own character, they considered that at least they ought to justify me inasmuch as the money which I had taken was not for my own use.

4199. That is the resolution?—Yes.

4200. What is the name of the person who did this thing for you?—John Clark.

4201. Where is he now?—He was at our meeting last night.

4202. Do you know his residence?—It is either Bedford Street or Cross Bedford Street.

4203. Who moved the resolution?—I do not know just now, but I will ascertain. The resolution I wrote out myself.

4204. At whose suggestion?—My own. I wrote it out before I went to the meeting.

4205. Had you consulted with anybody previous to writing it out?—No.

4206. And it was adopted unanimously I believe? I am not aware that there was a dissenting voice.

4207. Yo do not know who read the resolution to the meeting, do you?—The president.

4208. Gillott?—Yes.

4209. Do you know who seconded it?—I do not just now.

4210. You will tell us perhaps afterwards?—I will.

4211. You have been asking for your certificate?—Yes.

4212. I do not think we should grant certificates to anybody until the inquiry has advanced very much further than this. I do not say that we shall not grant it to you at all, but it will not be prudent to give a certificate until the inquiry has gone very much further; perhaps until it has terminated. We do not know what persons may come forward, and say, and as long as the inquiry is open we are bound to hold our hands. You will be safe from any proceedings in the meantime; if any person brings an action against you, or proceeds criminally against you, come to us, and we will decide what course to adopt?—Thank you.

The witness withdrew.

Mr. JOSEPH RAGG re-called, and further examined.

Mr. J. Ragg.

4213. (*Mr. Chance.*) You were proceeding last night to give us an account of rattening which took place in consequence of the rivalry existing between the saw grinders and the jobbing grinders?—Yes.

4214. Will you continue that statement if you please?—I cannot speak exactly as to the date, but as to the facts I shall be perfectly correct.

4215. Do you know what year it was in?—It is certainly within the jurisdiction that you have.

4216. Within what time?—I should think within eight or nine years. We were exceedingly busy at that time, and we had a large order for machine chaff knives. Having considerably more work than our saw grinders could do we sent them to the jobbing grinders; in consequence of that our hands were removed, and some of the knives were thrown into the wheel dam.

4217. What was the reason of that?—Well, I must say, in the first place, I went to see Mr. Broadhead, the secretary.

4218. Was he secretary to the Saw Grinders Union then?—He was. He could not say—he had no idea.

4219. (*Chairman.*) He could not tell who had done it?—No; he had no idea. In conversation he told me that they had men on the box, and tools of their own, and that it was our duty to send them to their grinding wheel.

4220. When he said this, had you mentioned to him the fact of your having sent these chaff knives to the jobbers?—He knew it; there was no necessity to tell him. That closed the conversation, and we got our bands back in the usual way by paying.

4221. But what course did you pursue?—We made an arrangement with our grinders, and they paid "Mary Ann" or "Nathan" or any person.

4222. You say that the grinders paid him?—Yes.

4223. What did they pay?—I am sure I cannot say without referring back to our cash book.

4224. Do you know to whom it would be paid?—It would be paid to the secretary.

4225. Do you know that as a fact yourself?—I know it as a fact so far as this, that I find on reference to our books that there was one knife which could not be found, and I find an entry in our cash book "Received from Mr. W. Broadhead 3*s.* for a chaff knife." Of course that was paid by our grinders and entered in Broadhead's name. He said that he had received it from Mr. Broadhead

FIFTH DAY.

Mr. J. Ragg.

7 June 1867.

4226. Who was the man?—John Oates.

4227. (*Mr. Chance.*) Who is John Oates; is he alive now?—He is alive, but he ran away from Sheffield and is in America now; but it is the same John Oates whose signature was to Mr. Broadhead's book yesterday.

4228. (*Chairman.*) The signature to what book?—The auditor's.

4229. He was actually the auditor of the books of the union?—Yes.

4230. He was the man who received the money, you say, from Mr. Broadhead?—He told us so.

4231. And paid it to you?—Yes.

4232. Do you know anything about the expenses, the money for rattening, being paid on that occasion?—I do not.

4233. Do you know whether money was paid for the expense of rattening you?—I cannot swear to that because I think the expenses were paid betwixt themselves. It was a strife between the two bodies of grinders, the jobbing grinders and the general saw grinders.

4234. It was an arrangement between them?—I think that was it.

4235. (*Mr. Chance.*) Nothing more took place upon that occasion?—No.

4236. Do you remember a case of rattening when you were rattened by mistake?—Yes; but that is beyond your jurisdiction.

4237. (*Chairman.*) Do you know a man of the name of Fearnehough?—I do. But, if you will allow me, I would relate another case of rattening.

4238. A case which has occurred within 10 years?—Yes.

4239. When did that occur?—It would be perhaps about a year after the other rattening.

4240. About seven years ago?—Yes. I cannot say to a year or two; they are things that I do not keep in my memory.

4241. Can you state the circumstances of that case?—Yes; I went to see Mr. Broadhead and asked him the reasons.

4242. What was taken on that occasion?—The bands were taken. He said he did not know anything at all about it. In the course of our conversation he said that it must have been from some violation of their laws. He said that the jobbing grinders had become an important branch in the business, and that they had taken them in by amalgamation, and that they ought to have a share of the machine chaff knives or straw knives.

4243. Who ought?—The jobbing grinders. I said: "It is very strange—you ratten us for giving " them to the jobbing grinders, and then you ratten us " for not giving them to the jobbing grinders; how is " that?"—I said "What do you mean by a share?" he says, "Well, that we have not defined."

4244. (*Mr. Chance.*) Do you mean the amount of share?—No; the share of the numbers.

4245. (*Chairman.*) They have not defined that?—They have not defined that. I said "Why do you make a " resolution if you do not define a thing? We may be " still in error. Under the circumstances, if we give " too many to the jobbing grinders we are rattened " by the saw grinders, and if we give too many to " the saw grinders the jobbing grinders ratten us." So I said "Give us the right number, and then we " shall steer clear." He said he could not do that. I told him we should give them as we thought fit, and take the course into our own hands. He said that we could please ourselves as to what we did about that, and that we ought to know best. I went down to the Town Hall, and I asked Mr. Jackson if he would kindly put a detective on to our grinding well; he said that he would with pleasure, but he thought it was out of his district, and that it was in Colonel Cobbe's district; and he said, if I would write a note, or he would write a note, to Colonel Cobbe, at Wadsley Bridge, it should be attended to.

4246. Did you get a detective?—Yes; we got two.

4247. One was in the borough and one was in the county?—Yes; but it really was in the borough.

4248. (*Mr. Chance.*) How long did those detectives remain with you?—They remained during such time as we got the order that we had on hand executed; some four or five days, or perhaps a week.

4249. Did you lose anything during the time that they were there?—No.

4250. Did you ever get your bands back that you lost upon those occasions?—Oh yes.

4251. When did you get them back?—They were brought back almost immediately after we had arranged with the grinders; at least they made the arrangement for themselves.

4252. Was anything paid by you?—Nothing that I am aware of.

4253. (*Chairman.*) Were the bands that were taken yours or the mens?—They were ours; the men do not find anything.

4254. You do not know whether they paid anything for the rattening?—No.

4255. (*Mr. Chance.*) Have you had any other rattening at your works of which you can give us an account?—Yes; the last rattening, that I gave you the evidence of last evening.

4256. But is there any other, besides those which you have already related to us, of which you can give us an account?—No.

4257. (*Chairman.*) In all the cases in which you have had dealings, either with Mr. Broadhead or the union, when they have bargained, have they always stuck to their bargain, and returned you your things?—Well, I think generally they have kept their word. If you will allow me to explain——

4258. There was a certain amount of honour about them, and when they made a bargain to return your things they returned them?—Yes. I spoke last night about the old union and the new union. At that time there were two distinct unions, the saw grinders and the jobbing grinders, so that this little difficulty arose between the two, the one trenching on the other's privileges, or supposed privileges. Then after this affair this book was published; we had no knowledge whatever upon it; and I find there is a list of articles claimed by the saw grinders and a list of articles claimed by the jobbing grinders.

4259. (*Chairman.*) When was that?—That was a list printed in 1859.

4260. By whom?—The Society of Saw Grinders I presume.

4261. What is that book called?—"List of prices for grinding and glazing saws, &c.," to come into operation July 25, 1859.

4262. (*Mr. Chance.*) You do not know by whom that is published?—Yes; the saw grinders. Mr. Broadhead furnished you with a copy of the same thing yesterday; that is precisely the same.

4263. (*Chairman.*) Was this furnished to you by Mr. Broadhead?—It was furnished to us by our grinders, and Mr. Broadhead gave it to them.

4264. What does the list say?—It gives a list of the articles claimed by the Society of Saw Grinders, by virtue of an agreement made by a committee composed of and on behalf of the two respective societies of saw grinders and jobbing grinders, the jobbing grinders, by virtue of this agreement, being pledged not to interfere with any of the under-mentioned articles. Then the articles are enumerated. Then another classof articles are claimed by the jobbing grinders.

4265. Therefore, as I understand, one list contains things to be done by the saw grinders?—Yes.

4266. And another list contains things to be done by the jobbing grinders?—Yes.

4267. And the saw grinders are not to do what is contained in the list of the jobbing grinders?—No.

4268. And the jobbing grinders are not to do what is contained in the list of the saw grinders?—Yes.

4269. Therefore they knew, according to the rules of the societies, what kinds of goods were to go to each class?—No; I beg your pardon; that is where we were at fault. I will read it to you. It says here: "A list of articles claimed by the members of "the Society of Saw Grinders, and the members "belonging to the Society of Jobbing Grinders, at all "places where they have been accustomed to do "them up to the date of this list. The members of "each of the respective societies make this claim by "virtue of agreement mutually entered into by a "committee composed of and on behalf of the two "respective societies of saw grinders and jobbing "grinders. The members of each society, by virtue "of this agreement, being furthermore pledged not to "interfere with the foregoing articles," and so on. The arrangement was a verbal one with us. They said, "Wherever a jobbing grinder has ever ground "any of those things he must have a share; wherever "a jobbing grinder has had the whole of them he "must have the whole of them; and where a jobbing "grinder never had ground any he must not have "one." So that you see, as I said, when we were in a prosperous state of trade, with no more than our grinders could do (because a jobbing grinder is virtually not our man, he is anybody's man, he can grind for anyone), we give them all to our men; but if we give them to a jobbing grinder we have to pay a per-centage for ware room and tools, and it is not to be supposed that we should do that with our own standing idle.

4270. Have you jobbing grinders of your own?—Generally we have jobbing grinders of our own.

4271. According to that rule, supposing you have jobbing grinders of your own at the work, and you have an immense quantity to give them, you would not be at liberty to give them to your own men, but must send them to members of the union?—We give them a share, but what that share is we do not know yet.

4272. At all events you could not give them to your own men alone?—Not exclusively, nor to jobbing grinders exclusively.

4273. Then, although the men have plenty of work, might you have your own men standing idle in order to comply with that rule?—Yes.

4274. (*Mr. Chance.*) You do not know, you say, what amount of share would be sufficient to enable you to have complied with the rules?—No, I cannot say; but I may just say here that after this had taken place our jobbing grinders and our saw grinders came to the warehouse and mutually arranged the matter betwixt them. We talked the matter over with them, and we showed them the inconsistency of doing this sort of thing, and so they went away with this understanding, that we would take our own course, but to do as fairly as possible. The reply was, "When we "are not pressed for business we will give you a "moderate share, but when we are pressed we shall "give them such a share as would be fair between "the parties."

4275. (*Chairman.*) Was that the union?—Not the union, but our men who are in the union.

4276. But you have never had a representative from the union?—None whatever.

4277. Have you carried out that arrangement?—We carried it out up to the time of this rattening that I am speaking of.

4278. And, therefore, if the rattening were done by the union it would appear that the union have not assented to that arrangement?—Of course.

4279. Was the rattening done in consequence of that mode of carrying on business by you?—No.

4280. How do you known then for what reason the rattening was done?—I think if we go to that other case we shall get to that.

4281. But has there been any rattening in consequence, as you believe, of your having adopted this resolution and carried it out?—Not that I am aware of. I believe not.

4282. (*Mr. Chance.*) Then you have no complaint against the union?—Not at all.

4283. (*Chairman.*) There is no ground of complain at all against the union?—Not at all.

4284. (*Mr. Chance.*) Have you any other case of rattening besides those of which you have already told us?—No.

4285. I asked you just now whether you knew a man of the name of Fearnehough?—I do.

4286. Did he ever work for you?—Yes.

4287. When?—He works for us now.

4288. And when did he first commence working?—I am sure I cannot exactly say, but it was immediately after our bands were stolen that I waited upon him; that would be upon the 25th of June. It would be some time in the commencement of July 1866, I think, that he commenced to work.

4289. In what capacity did he work?—He worked as a general grinder for the trade in his room and on his own tools.

4290. Was working on his own tools a violation of any of the rules of the union?—Yes, "No member holding a situation shall find his own tools."

4291. (*Mr. Barstow.*) What is the number of that rule?—It has no number; it is at page 33 of the list of prices.

4292. (*Chairman.*) But he was not a member, was he?—He was not.

4293. Then that is not a violation of that rule?—He had been a member. It may not be a violation of that rule.

4294. (*Mr. Chance.*) You say that at one time he was a member; do you remember when he was a member?—I do not. I was not acquainted with the man at all until I engaged him.

4295. (*Chairman.*) Did he hold a situation?—Not particularly; he worked for any small manufacturer, or any person.

4296. Then he did not hold any situation?—No, not any permanent situation.

4297. (*Mr. Chance.*) What does holding a situation mean?—A man whom you regularly engage, and who expects a month's notice to be given or taken.

4298. (*Chairman.*) He did not come within that rule as far as I understand you?—No.

4299. (*Mr. Chance.*) He worked for you but he was not in your employ as holding a situation?—No.

4300. (*Chairman.*) Before we go into the history of this, what is the benefit which the union derived from no member being allowed to find his own tools?—If they have any grievance they can get at the master immediately by getting at his tools and destroying his property.

4301. It is a means of coercion upon the masters? By taking his tools they can coerce him?—Yes.

4302. That is the object of the rule, as you understand it?—Yes; that is my idea of what it is.

4303. (*Mr. Chance.*) Did you take power for Fearnehough?—No, not at that time. If you will allow me to explain, my little explanation will lead you to it. Fearnehough was employed at that time by two or three small manufacturers. I offered him work. He accepted it. We had considerably more work for him than he could do to continue with his smaller employers. I pressed him to do for us as much work as he could. He said that he should like to retain the masters that he had because it might be giving up a certainty for an uncertainty. I said, "Serve us and we will serve you." He said, "I will." We then thought where we could get power, where we should be safe from rattening. I negotiated with Messrs. W. and S. Butcher in Hare Lane for a room which we could have in five or six weeks. We took that room. I saw Fearnehough, and told him that we were in a position to offer him a permanent situation, and he accepted it. He had then I think about five weeks to remain in his old grinding wheel, and to make himself secure and ourselves and the owners of the grinding wheel I put a night watchman upon the place.

4304. (*Chairman.*) What did you pay him?—Five guineas, I think it was, to the Watch Committee. We

FIFTH DAY.

Mr. J. Ragg.

7 June 1867.

then removed to Hare Lane, and permanently engaged Fearnehough.

4305. You set him to work?—We set him to work.

4306. Was he a good workman?—Yes, he is an excellent workman.

4307. Is he a sober man, a good steady man?—For anything that I know to the contrary; but we had a very fearful character with him. I suppose they did not want us to have him; but he has been very attentive to his business while with us and we have no cause to complain.

4308. (*Mr. Chance.*) From whom did you have that character?—There are tales going about. I cannot particularize anybody.

4309. (*Chairman.*) But as far as you have seen him he is a well-conducted man?—Oh yes; we have no cause to complain.

4310. (*Mr. Chance.*) Had you known anything of him before the time that he came to work for you?—Only by hearsay.

4311. (*Chairman.*) You heard from the trade that he was a very bad character?—Yes.

4312. What did they say of him?—They said that he was drunken. That we know is not an exception.

4313. What did they say besides?—That he would not serve us; that he would go off drinking when we wanted our work; and various other things to that effect.

4314. Who told you this?—It was general conversation throughout the shops amongst the men.

4315. Union men, or non-union men?—Union men.

4316. How long had you employed him?—I am not quite certain as to the time.

4317. About how long?—It would be somewhere about July, I should say.

4318. Have you employed him ever since?—Ever since.

4319. Since then have you found him to be a steady workman? I want to know whether those stories were founded on fact, or whether they were merely false representations as to his character?—We have heard on several occasions that he has had one or two days drinking; but that, as I said before, was no exception.

4320. But, on the whole, was he what they represented him to be?—He was not what they represented by any means.

4321. You say that he has been off occasionally, for one or two days, drinking?—We are not aware of it, but we have heard as much.

4322. But never so as to interfere with your work?—No. He has two sons working with him, and perhaps when the father is off they do a little extra to make up.

4323. But you do not find that his drinking has interfered with your work?—No.

4324. (*Mr. Chance.*) From whom have you heard this?—From people in our work, who say they have occasionally seen him in the town dressed up in his best clothes I suppose.

4325. (*Chairman.*) You say that you put a night watchman on, and paid him five guineas?—Yes.

4326. (*Mr. Chance.*) Will you proceed with your narrative?—I think that the best way would be to go back to about July. I think, a few days prior to July the 14th, our saw smiths went down the yard.

4327. (*Chairman.*) What yard?—Our shop. Our warehouses and shops are at the top of a yard. I inquired what they had been out for, and they said the secretary of the Saw Makers Society had sent for them.

4328. Who was he?—I believe his name is Smith.

4329. The Saw Makers Society?—Yes, what we call anvil men—men who smith.

4330. Do you know what his name is besides Smith?—Thomas Smith, I think it is. On July the 14th, the Saturday following, they all gave us notice to leave.

4331. Had Fearnehough got to work then?—Yes, working regularly.

4332. Did they know of it?—Yes, they were working on his grinding. When they came in to reckon on the Saturday afternoon, each man left us a notice of this form, simply saying, "I have to leave you that." That is one of them (*handing a paper to the Commissioners*).

4333. "July 14th, 1866,—To Messrs. Slack, "Sellars, and Company.—Please to take notice that "I, William Turner, will leave your employment one "month from the date thereof." That was a month's notice?—Yes.

4334. And each man gave you a corresponding notice to that?—Yes, a corresponding notice to that.

4335. (*Chairman.*) Do you happen to know in whose handwriting the notice is?—No.

4336. Did you try to find out who wrote this?—Some of the notices were sent in by men who could not write, so that by whom they were written I do not know.

4337. (*Mr. Barstow.*) Were they all in the same handwriting?—No.

4338. (*Chairman.*) There was no signature or mark, or anything of that kind?—No.

4339. Had the persons who could not write signed their mark, or how did they do?—I believe not.

4343. It is merely "please to take notice that I, William Turner, will leave your employment one month from the date thereof" and there was no signature to it?—Nothing beyond that. I cannot swear to that being William Turner's writing; I never saw him write.

4341. Will you be kind enough to leave this with us?—To be sure.

4342. Have you any other notices of the same kind?—I had, but I have not them here.

4343. Will you be kind enough to supply us with the whole of those notices which you have?—I will do so. I thought they were all put in the waste paper basket.

4344. (*Mr. Chance.*) Each of your men gave you that notice?—Yes.

4345. What took place after that?—They left us after the usual month's notice. We then tried to fill their places by non-society men or non-union men. We engaged a many at one time or another, and a many of them came and perhaps worked for a day or two days and we saw no more of them; some never came at all; one stayed an hour, and he left and we saw no more of him, and others stayed with us.

4346 (*Chairman.*) Can you give the proportions at all of how many stayed with you?—We have six who stayed with us.

4347. And how many went away in this way?—Perhaps a dozen; I beg your pardon, I should think about the same number, perhaps six.

4348. About six stayed with you and about six went away?—Yes.

4349. (*Mr. Chance.*) Did those who went away give you any reason why they went?—I have had a reason, since some of them came back, why they went.

4350. What was that?—The report was, prior to this reason, that the union said they would take them upon their box, and allow them scale, conditionally that they did not work for us. If they would cease to work for us they would make them straight with their natty money, and wipe off the arrears of the contribution. That was the condition.

4351. (*Chairman.*) Was that the Saw Grinders Union?—No; the Saw Makers Union.

4352. (*Mr. Chance.*) Was this reason assigned to you by many of those men?—Yes.

4353. By themselves?—Yes.

4354. They have told you that since?—Yes.

4355. (*Chairman.*) Who was the secretary of the Saw Makers Union?—Thomas Smith.

4356. (*Mr. Chance.*) Then you say six stayed with you, and six went away?—Yes.

4357. What took place after the six non-union men came to work in your employment?—If you will allow me I will substantiate that; it is simply hearsay; but I can substantiate it if you will allow me.

Frederick Gray and Charles Lee applied for work. We engaged them, and they never came.

4358. (*Chairman.*) What wages did you offer them?—Anything that they could earn, regular statement prices. This Frederick Gray we have in our employ at the present time, and he tells me that the secretary sent for them and offered to allow them 8*s*. per week from the box, conditionally that they did not come and work for us.

4359. And they were non-union men?—Non-union men. They said that they should engage at Slacks, that is the usual term that they give our place. He said it would be a bad job for them if they did. They did not come to work; but the secretary found them some little quantity of work, I suppose as outworkers; and in lieu of this 8*s*. the first week the secretary gave them 5*s*.

4360. He found them work, you say?—Yes; but they were to have 8*s*. a week, besides the little work that he could find them. The second week he gave them 2*s*., and the third week nothing. The secretary asked them if they did not feel ashamed of themselves to come to him to ask for money knowing what they already had to pay.

4361. How do you mean?—To keep our men out. You must understand that the whole of the saw makers men that gave us notice to leave had not got situations; they were on the box, living on the funds of the society some six or seven weeks after this time.

4362. Were you without work those six or seven weeks?—No, we were at work all that time. We had no difficulty about it, only they were non-union men. Six or seven weeks after this time Mr. Smith, the secretary, called upon us; he said that he had a proposition to make peace. After some conversation we asked him what proposition he had to make. The proposition was that we should take all the old men back again, and that bygones should be bygones; but this was conditional that every man took his situation again, and of course that we should turn the new men out of their situations to make room for them. We said that the new men had served us well, and we should retain them, and that when we wanted our old men back again we would send for them. I think that is all now.

4363. (*Mr. Chance.*) What did he say to that?—He said it was no use his waiting any longer, if that was our decision, and he left us.

4364. And then you went on with your non-union men as before?—Yes.

4365. (*Chairman.*) And you have done so ever since?—Yes; but will you allow me to say that the man came in a courteous way and conducted himself with very great propriety, and everything passed off agreeably. I simply say that to give the man credit, because some people run away with the notion that the men sometimes do these things in a very off-hand way.

4366. (*Mr. Chance.*) That is all that you have to say with reference to the union men leaving and the non-union men coming to work with you?—Yes. I spoke to you last evening about their threatening letters (*handing in papers*). "The saw handlers and "saw makers. Mary." "Attend to the saw handlers."

4367. Where was that found?—That was found on the seat that the saw handlers sit upon.

4368. (*Chairman.*) Is this the envelope that the letter was enclosed in?—Yes.

4369. (*Mr. Chance.*) What is that which you have in your hand now?—This is a threatening letter.

4370. That has no reference to this?—No.

4371. Was that which the saw grinders brought up to you as having been found upon the seat brought up about the same time?—Yes, about the same time; that would be on the Tuesday morning.

4372. Would that be before or after Fearnehough came to work for you?—It would be after Fearnehough came to work for us. At this time we employed a person of the name of Edward Gray, a brother to the Frederick Gray that I have spoken of.

4373. (*Chairman.*) At what time was that?—It was in November 1866. It was prior to this time that we engaged him; perhaps sometime in November 1866 we engaged him.

4374. You are calling our attention now to some facts which occurred in November 1866?—Yes.

4375. What was he, a union man or a non-union man?—A non-union man.

4376. (*Mr. Chance.*) Was he a saw-handle maker?—A saw maker. During his employment we received this note (*producing a paper*). The note was brought by post, but being directed with a black lead pencil and in a very suspicious looking hand, it was refused. It was not postage paid. It was refused by Mr. Slack. I went to the Post Office and fetched it, and paid for it.

4377. Was that soon after you learnt that it had been refused?—Yes, immediately after (*handing in the letter*).

4378. (*Chairman.*) "Messrs. Slack and Sellars, "Saw Makers, Town Head Street, Sheffield, No-"vember the 2d." At this time, were Fearnehough and Gray in yeur employment?—Yes.

4379. "Sir, we write to inform you that if you do "not turn Ted Gray away there will be another "blow up, a damned sight worse than the last. We "know where you live so look out, for if you don't "turn all the men away you have got and taken the "old ones back it will be the worse for you, for we "have another can ready full of gunpowder. I finish "with telling you to beware of me; beware of all "such devils as you." Had there been any can of gunpowder before this?—Yes.

4380. Where was the can of gunpowder?—It was in New Hereford Street, Fearnehough's case.

4381. How long before had that occurred?—On the 8th of October 1866.

4382. We have heard generally of the case, but can you tell us what occurred to Fearnehough?—I believe that none of the family were injured.

4383. But what was done to Fearnehough?—Nothing had been done to him that I am aware of.

4384. But had anything been done to his house?—Yes, it had blown the window out.

4385. What had blown the window out?—This combustible matter which was put in. I do not know what it was. Those that did it probably know what was.

4386. Will you tell us what happened to Fearnehough as far as you know?—On Monday morning the 8th October 1866 I heard that Fearnehough's house had been blown up. When I visited the house I found that the window had been blown out, and the door and partition wall knocked down into a passage, the staircase wall rent almost from top to bottom, and flags removed in the floor of the house. It was a stone floored house.

4387. (*Chairman.*) How do you mean removed?—Blown out of their situation. The front of the house was partially blown out, perhaps to the extent of an inch from the ceiling, and the partition wall next to where Fearnehough's bed had stood was everything but knocked down. In fact a child could oscillate it. It had removed it from the ceiling, and left it so that it would oscillate backwards and forwards from its foundation, and everything in the place presented the appearance of complete desolation.

4388. Where was this?—In New Hereford Street.

4389. Did you ascertain when this had been done? Yes.

4390. When?—On Monday morning the 8th of October.

4391. Was it in the night or in the day time?—It was supposed to be about 5 o'clock in the morning.

4392. Did you ascertain how it had been done?—By removing the cellar grating and throwing the gunpowder into the cellar.

4393. Do you know whether any can or anything of that kind was found?—I do not.

4394. Was that what the letter, as you understood it, alluded to?—Yes.

4395. I believe Fearnehough was not injured; no

FIFTH DAY.

Mr. J. Ragg.

7 June 1867.

one in the house was injured ?—I believe not, beyond a shaking of the nervous system.

4396. No bodily injury was sustained ?—No bodily injury.

4397. And you understood that that letter when speaking of a previous blowing up applied to that tragedy ?—Just so.

4398. Had there been any other blowing up that you are aware of in the town antecedent to this and shortly before this, except in Hereford Street ?—Do you mean blowings up generally or in our particular trade ?

4399. Was there anything else that it could refer to, except that, that you are aware of ?—There had been nothing that it could refer to except that at that time that I am aware of.

4400. I do not want a full history of that case now. I merely want to show that this was a thing to which it might refer ?—I do not know any complaints whatever that took place that that letter could have any reference to except Fearnehough's case.

4401. There had been a reward offered in Fearnehough's case, I believe ?—There has.

4402. How much ?—1,000*l.* was offered by the Manufacturers Association, and 100*l.* by the organized trades.

4403. What do you call the organized trades ?—Every trade in Sheffield. They are in a state of organization.

4404. You mean the workmen ?—Yes.

4405. All the unions combined ?—It is a combination of the unions.

4406. And what besides ?—I am not quite sure, but I think Mr. Broadhead offered a reward of 50*l.* himself.

4407. Had this been offered at the time when you got that letter ?—This blowing up ?

4408. No; at the time when you received this letter on the 2nd of November had those offers of sums of money been made by the manufacturers, and so on ?—I am not quite certain whether the reward had been offered.

4409. It might or it might not have been offered ?—It might or might not.

4410. You are not quite sure about it ?—I am not quite sure.

4411. (*Mr. Chance.*) The letter was dated November the 2nd, I believe ?—Yes.

4412. Was the reward offered within a month after the blowing up occurred ?—I believe it was within a month.

4413. (*Chairman.*) Have you any notion at all who wrote that letter ?—Not the most remote.

4414. You do not know the handwriting in any way ?—No, not at all.

4415. We must carry it a little further, I think. Did you keep Ted Gray or not ?—We have him now; we kept him.

4416. And you have never been blown up ?—No.

4417. Has anything followed upon that letter at all ?—Nothing.

4418. Has anything happened to you since the date of that letter ?—No, nothing.

4419. Have you had any police at all to protect your premises ?—No.

4420. Fearnehough has still continued to work for you ?—Yes.

4421. And Gray too ?—Yes.

4422. Have you been aware whether there have been other blowings up besides the case of Fearnehough in the town ?—I believe there have.

4423. Are you acquainted with any ?—No ; except through the medium of our local journals.

4424. On receiving this letter did you take any steps ?—None.

4425. Have you received any other letters besides the letters which you have brought before our notice ; the letter of the 2nd of November and those letters which were deposited on July the 25th ?—Oh ! yes, on several occasions.

4426. Are they to the same effect ?—Yes, similar things.

4427. Have you ever been threatened to be blown up before ?—I am not quite certain whether we have or not.

4428. You cannot speak to that ?—I cannot speak to that.

4429. Have you ever been blown up ?—No, never.

4430. Have you ever found any combustible on your premises at any time ?—No.

4431. Nothing of that kind ?—No, never.

4432. And the only injury as I understand has been in the way of rattening ?—Yes.

4433. Have you bellows ?—Yes.

4434. Have you had them cut ?—No, we have had nuts stolen.

4435. How often have the nuts been stolen ?—There were a couple of nuts stolen on the 3rd of July ; they are unrestored yet. The other nuts have been returned ; the bands are unreturned.

4436. Have you had any injury done to you in any way besides being deprived of your bands, which have been restored ?—No.

4437. And I believe in point of fact you have not absolutely lost any bands ?—No, except the last three that I am speaking of that were lost on the 25th of June. We have not heard anything about them since.

4438. The nuts work the pulley drums, do they not ?—They are to hold the pulley on to the axletree.

4439. And if you remove the nuts you cannot work ?—You cannot work ; you might as well be without the bands as without the nuts.

4440. Does it require a good deal of trouble to remove them, or is it easily done ?—It is easily done ; it is immediately under the spanners, and in half a minute you can remove both nuts.

4441. What is the price of them ?—We had two new ones made, and they were 12*s.*

4442. 12*s.* apiece ?—No, 12*s.* a pair.

4443. But there would be no difficulty I suppose in getting another at once ; they would not stop you long ?—We would have to send an engineer to see the exact size of the screw that the nuts must go upon. It must fit exactly.

4444. How long would it stop you ?—It was above a week before we got the nuts made ; they did on that occasion, but on our old wheel we should never have attempted to grind because we had no security.

4445. When you saw the system prevailing you gave it up ?—Yes.

4446. Was anything done at Butcher's Place to Fearnehough that you know of ?—Not that I am aware of. They would have some difficulty in doing anything there.

The witness withdrew.

J. Hazlewood.

JONATHAN HAZLEWOOD sworn and examined.

4447. (*Chairman.*) You are a saw grinder living in Hanover Street, are you not ?—Yes.

4448. Have you received any threatening letters ?—Yes.

4449. When was the first ?—I cannot say to a year or two.

4450. But about when was it ?—Eight or nine years since.

4451. Have you got it ?—No, I did not take any care of them.

4452. Did you destroy it ?—I kept them in my pocket while they wore away.

4453. And they do not exist ?—I do not know whether there is any of them now.

4454. Will you tell me what the first threatening

letter was about, as near as you can say ?—I cannot, I am sure.

4455. But what was the object of it ?—It was something about getting shut of an apprentice lad that I had, I believe.

4456. Had you an apprentice lad in your employment at that time ?—Yes.

4457. What was his name ?—Thomas Hallam.

4458. Did the note tell you what was to be the consequence, if you did not get quit of Thomas Hallam ?—Something to that effect.

4459. What did it tell you ?—I do not know what it said, I am sure. I have forgotten it.

4460. Have you had any application made to you before that to get rid of Hallam ?—Not that I particularly recollect ; I am not aware that I had.

4461. Was he a person who was employed by you according to the rules of the union, or was he at variance with the rules of the union ?—I took him against the rules of the union.

4462. Were you in the union ?—Yes, at that time.

4463. And did you continue to employ the boy, or did you get rid of him ?—He stopped with me while he was 21.

4464. What age was he at the time when you got that letter ?—The lad came to me when he was about 17, and stopped while he was 21.

4465. How long had you had him when you got that letter ?—Not a long while.

4466. He stayed three years after you had got that letter ?—It would be four years nearly.

4467. After you got the letter did anything happen to you in consequence of your retaining Hallam ?—I do not know for a certainty, but I lost my grinding bands soon after.

4368. Do you know that it was for that ? You lost your grinding bands at any rate ?—Yes.

4469. What did you do when your lost your bands ?—I bought some more.

4470. What became of them ?—I used them while they were worn out.

4471. They were not taken ?—No, I have never lost any more since.

4472. Have those bands which you lost been restored to you ?—Never.

4273. Had you any conversation with the union people with reference to those bands being taken away ?—No ; I never went and made any complaint to any one about them. I went and bought some more.

4474. That was after the first threatening letter ? Have you had any other threatening letters ?—I do not know to one or two, but I should think four or five, or it might be six altogether, that I have had.

4475. What had they been about ?—The first one or two, I dare say, were about the boy ; they might be more, I cannot say for certainty.

4476. Then what was the third ?—Perhaps the third and fourth were about my grinding machine knives.

4477. Have you those letters, or have you lost them ?—I did not take care of any of them.

4478. What did the letters say about grinding machine knives ?—Something to the effect that I was to mind my own work, and let the machine knives alone. It was something to that effect, but I do not know that those would be the exact words.

4479. Did the note purport to be signed at all by anybody ?—I cannot recollect, but I think one or two of them would be signed "Mary Ann," as usual, and some of the others.

4480. Did they come by post, or were they delivered, or how did you get them ?—One I recollect was left on the horseing where the men generally sit, and the others, I dare say, generally came by post.

4481. Were they written in pencil or in ink ?—I could not say positively at this distance of time, but I have some impression that one if not two would be written in pencil, and the rest in ink ; but I could not be certain.

4482. With regard to these machine knives, had you been grinding some machine knives ?—I had been grinding machine knives then for some four or five years.

4483. Was that a part of your business, or was it something which was not recognised by the trade ?—It was part of the business which I had been taught when I was an apprentice.

4484. In the Sheffield trade is it customary to grind machine knives as you did them ?—Yes.

4485. Then what was the complaint ? was your business something different from grinding machine knives ?—You will have to understand that there are three or four different unions of grinders that grind these machine knives,—edge tool grinders, saw grinders and scythe grinders,—and the scythe grinders had taken into consideration that they ought to grind them for this particular place that I was working for, seemingly. They thought so.

4486. At what place was it ?—For Messrs. William Tysack and Sons, Rockingham Street, and Abbey Dale Works.

4487. Had they told you so before this ?—Who ?

4488. Had you heard from the scythe grinders or the union of the scythe grinders ?—Yes.

4489. Had you been informed that that was their determination or opinion ?—Oh no.

4490. You say that the scythe grinders had taken it into consideration that they ought to grind them ; who told you so ?—Because I knew nobody else would object to my grinding. My own trade would not object.

4491. How do you know it then ?—Because some time after they took 13 or 14 scythe grinders away from Mr. Tysack, and kept them away.

4492. At that time you were working for Messrs. Tysack and Sons ?—Yes.

4493. Did Messrs. Tysack and Sons deliver out to you machine knives to grind ?—Yes.

4494. Then what you were grinding were not your knives, they were Messrs. Tysack's ?—Yes.

4495. What did you say that they had done about Messrs. Tysack's men ?—They never applied to me personally, only by this letter,—that I was to give over grinding those machine knives ; but in the course of a month or two after I had no intentions of giving over, 13 or 14 of Mr. Tysack's scythe grinders left their employ without giving any notice, and they could not have them back again until they promised to let them have those machine knives for the future.

4496. And what was done? Were the machine knives taken from you and given to some of those scythe grinders to grind ?—Yes.

4497. And that was all in reference to that ; you lost the trade ?—Yes.

4498. According to your belief were you able to grind them as well as other people ?—Mr. Tysack thought so ; he would rather have employed me than them if he had not been forced.

4499. You say that was about those machine knives ; have you had another threatening letter ?—Not since that time, which will be some eight or nine years since.

4500. Do you know that letter (*handing a letter to the witness*) ?—Yes ; this looks like one of the envelopes that I received.

4501. Is that the letter ?—That will be one.

4502. That had reference to the apprentice, had it ?—Yes.

4503. It bears the Sheffield post mark of January 3rd, 1853 ; is it 1853 or 1863 ?—It will not be 1863, and I should think that it would be a long while after 1853.

4504. It is 1858. "Your bands will come back if " you give up that lad, and if not you will not see " them again. I thank you to know what we want " without this trouble. We do not want to come " again, if we do we shall not spare you as before. " If you comply with this, come and show your face " to a proper quarter. Signed by those who will " come again if occasion requires, at a time, in such " a way, as was as little expected as before." Was

FIFTH DAY.

J. Hazlewood.

7 June 1867.

that the letter that you received about the apprentice?—Yes; I believe it is.

4505. You have received no letter since this last one that you have given us as to the machine knives?—About the machine knives?

4506. Have you ever been rattened at all, except that once?—Only that once.

4507. Has your person ever at all been interfered with?—No.

4508. There has been no interference with you or with the conduct of your business?—Not that I am aware of.

4509. What was the date of that scythe grinders disturbance?—I do not know; I have not preserved any of the letters.

4510. Do you recollect how many years ago it was?—It would take place directly after that. I should think that I received them all within three or four months.

4511. Do you pay to any union?—Yes; at present.

4512. To what union do you pay?—To the Saw Grinders Union. It was called "The Small Saw and Jobbing Grinders Union."

4513. You are in the Jobbing Grinders Union?—I took that portion. That was the reason of my grinding machine knives. I left the saw department. I preferred the machine knives.

4514. Are you aware that the difference between Messrs. Tysack and the union was satisfactorily settled, and that Messrs. Tysack gave 10*l.* to the union towards their expenses?—No. I did not hear of anything of that. I expected there would be something of the kind most likely, but I never heard of it.

The witness withdrew.

T. Davenport.

THOMAS DAVENPORT sworn and examined.

4515. (*Chairman.*) Are you a saw manufacturer in Rockingham Street, Sheffield?—A grinding wheel proprietor.

4516. Where do you carry on your business?—In Rockingham Street.

4517. Do you remember on the 15th of January 1858 receiving a letter?—Yes.

4518. Have you the letter with you?—No.

4519. What has become of it?—I took it down to the Town Hall at the time.

4520. Is that the letter (*handing a letter to the witness*)?—This is the letter.

4521. The post mark is January 15th, 1858, "Sir, "When we paid a visit to your wheel we forebore to "injure your property, but if Jonty does not turn the "lad up we will visit you again, and let you try all "you know to protect your premises, nothing shall "deter us from accomplishing our object. N.B.—"This is not the first time you have been warned "about it. Yours, &c., Hack Hammock." Who was meant by Jonty?—Jonathan Hazlewood, the last witness.

4522. Are you aware whether he had an apprentice at that time?—Yes; I believe he had.

4523. Do you know whether he had him against the rules of the union or not?—I do not.

4524. Whom did you understand the lad to mean?—I did not know.

4525. What did you do with that letter?—I took it to the Town Hall to Mr. Raynor, the chief constable.

4526. And I believe that by Mr. Raynor's advice you put a detective on?—Yes.

4527. How long did you keep him?—Perhaps a fortnight.

4528. Did he protect your premises?—No.

4529. Were they entered?—Yes.

4530. Was any damage done?—Some little.

4531. How soon was this after that letter?—I can scarcely tell you; I do not remember how long.

4532. Was it a week, or a fortnight, or a month?—It would be shortly after the letter.

4533. (*Mr. Barstow.*) What was the amount of damage that they did?—It would be under the amount of 5*l.*, I think.

4534. What did they do?—They broke open several doors and windows.

4535. Did they remove any bands?—Yes; I believe they did.

4536. What did you do when your bands were removed?—Well, I do not know that they were removed.

4537. Were they hidden away?—No; I believe not.

4538. (*Chairman.*) Were the bands restored? Did they not take them away?—They took them away, I believe.

4539. Do you know what became of them?—I do not know.

4540. Were the bands your own, or were they the men's?—They were the men's.

4541. The wheel was yours?—Yes.

4542. Then the breaking open of doors and windows, and so on, caused damage to you?—Yes.

4543. What was the amount of your damage?—It would not be very considerable.

4544. About how much?—About a couple of pounds perhaps.

4545. Have you ever been recompensed for them at all? Had you any money given to you for the damage which was done to you?—No.

4546. Has it been an absolute loss to you?—Yes.

4547. You had to repair the damage, and did not receive compensation from anybody?—No.

4548. Did you at all apply to the union with respect to that?—No.

4549. Have you had any communication with anybody about it?—No.

4550. Have you no means of knowing who did it?—No.

4551. Have you no suspicion attaching to anybody?—No.

4552. Do you know who wrote this letter?—I do not.

4553. You took it to the Town Hall, and there was an inquiry about it, but nothing came of it?—No.

The witness withdrew.

Mr. D. Ward.

Mr. DAVID WARD sworn and examined.

4554. Are you a member of the firm of Ward and Payne, edge-tool and sheep-shear manufacturers?—Yes.

4555. I believe your business has been carried on since the year 1800?—Since 1800.

4556. And you have a great reputation, I believe, as edge-tool makers?—As edge-tool makers.

4557. Do you know a person of the name of Addis?—I do.

4558. Whence did he originally come?—From London.

4559. What was he?—He was a carving-tool manufacturer.

4560. Are there many carving-tool manufacturers in Sheffield?—Not a great number.

4561. Do you know whether this Addis, in consequence of his being so good a workman, had obtained a prize at the Exhibition?—He had obtained a prize for carving-tool making in 1851. I believe that he got the only prize which was awarded simply for carving-tools.

4562. I believe that he had never been a member of any union ?—No.

4563. In consequence of what he had done, and his reputation as a workman, were you recommended to employ him, and to get him to come down to Sheffield ?—He came down in the autumn of 1864.

4564. At your suggestion, or of his own accord ?—On his own account. He applied to me for a situation. Knowing that he was not connected with the trades union, I requested him to make application to the committee.

4565. To what union was it that he was to apply ?—He was to apply to the Edge-tool Forgers' Union.

4566. Do you know who are the officers of that union ?—James Reaney is the secretary. The committee are selected at various times, I believe.

4567. Is there a man of the name of Stacey connected with it ?—He is secretary of the Grinders' Union.

4568. Reaney is the secretary of the Forgers' Union ?—He is the secretary of the forgers. Addis made application the same day. The committee were then assembled. Being desirous to work peaceably with the union men he offered to give them a premium of 15*l*. to be accepted a member, to contribute the usual weekly instalment, and to abide by their rules in every respect. The committee declined to accept him as one of their members, upon which he went back to London.

4569. You could not engage him ?—I could not engage him at the time. In the course of some short time afterwards I received one or two letters from some London customers, stating that they were sorry to hear that I had omitted having the services of so good a workman, that carving tools as made in Sheffield were of very little use for the London trade, and that it required a man who knew the use of the tool to make it. That party was prepared to give me considerable orders in the event of my employing Addis, but if the tools were made by a Sheffield workman he could not give me any orders whatever. I thereupon wrote up to Addis, requesting him to come down, and stating that I would find him employment in a part of the town away from the union men, in order that they might not be dissatisfied with his society. He commenced to work for me.

4570. Where did he work ?—In Rockingham Street ; and his work was found to be so superior to that which I had made on my premises, that one of the grinders who ground the work informed me that they could do much more of it, in the same time, than of the union men's work. It appearing to give dissatisfaction to the edge tool union that this man should be working for me——

4571. How did that appear ?—I had interviews with the secretary. He waited upon me upon various occasions.

4572. With James Reaney ?—With James Reaney.

4573. Will you tell me what he said ?—He came in anything but a gentlemanly way, and informed me that I must ged rid of Addis at once ; that Addis was simply come to ascertain how to forge in Sheffield, and that when he had learned the art he intended to go back to London, and to take the trade with him. I informed him that my experience was that his work was much superior, and in fact essential to the success of my trade in that department. It happened that I had at that time 16 troughs at Messrs. Marsden Brothers, my own wheel being fully occupied. During the first six months that Addis was working for me, several interviews had taken place with the trade, and one day, on the last occasion, the committee of the edge tool grinders and the edge tool forgers met me in the office, and I endeavoured to persuade them to settle the dispute by taking the man into their union. The interview lasted about half an hour, and they consented to reconsider the subject, and let me know their final decision. Instead, however, of seeing me again upon the matter, one morning the nuts from 16 troughs that I occupied at Marston Brothers disappeared.

4574. Would it be 16, or the double number ?—The double number, I believe.

4575. Sixteen troughs were stopped working by the nuts being taken away ?—Yes. At the first onset I had no idea that it was anything in connexion with Addis, and I took no further steps ; but one of my workmen informed me in the course of a day or so that it was on account of Addis's working for me that they were taken.

4576. What was the name of the workman who told you ?—I really at the present moment do not recollect. Being at that time very busy in work, and seeing that there was no probability of the dispute ending, I sent for James Reaney and Samuel Stacey, and asked them if the matter could not be brought to a conclusion.

4577.—Did they come ?—They came. I told them that it was most unreasonable that a manufacturer's work should be stopped, especially by the taking of the manufacturer's tools ; and they informed me that that was one of those things which they were compelled to do, to make manufacturers comply with their demands.

4578. Who told you that ?—James Reaney.

4579. Who was present at the time when he told you ?—Samuel Stacey, and one George Fox, and one James Higginbottom.

4580. Who is Stacey ? — The secretary of the Grinders Union. One Henry Mitchell was also present.

4581. What is Fox ?—The secretary of the Sheep-shear Forgers Union, at that identical time a foreman in my employ.

4582. What was Higginbottom ? — I believe an edge-tool grinder.

4583. Do you know whether he was in office ?—I think he would be, but I am not certain.

4584. What was Mitchell ?—An edge-tool forger in my employ, and likewise an important man, I think, with the trade.

4585. They were all present, you say ?—Yes.

4586. When those parties came, did they come as a deputation ?—Yes, just so.

4587. Did they hear what Reaney said with respect to this particular thing that they were compelled to do to make manufactures comply with their demands ?—I believe they heard every word.

4588. All of them ?—I believe they did.

4589. Was any expression of dissent manifested by any of them to such a proposition as that ?—No, I believe not.

4590. No one dissented from that doctrine.

4591. What did you say to that ?—I replied that it was very unjust ; but as my orders were all standing still I had no alternative but to consent to discharge the man, James Reaney informing me that that was the only means of the work being allowed to be recommenced. He thereupon stated that there was one other matter that would require settling, namely, that I should pay 30*l*. expenses for the men being out of work for a week. Of course I protested against that.

4592. What did you say ?—I protested against that line of conduct.

4593. Did you say you would pay it, or not ?—I protested against it, and paid the money.

4594. To whom did you pay it ?—I paid it to James Reaney ; a cheque upon the Sheffield Banking Company ; and I hold James Reaney's receipt for it.

4595. Is it in your book ?—Yes.

4596. It is a stamped receipt for 30*l*. James Reaney, that is the signature (*showing the same to the witness*) ?—That is his signature. Not being able to do without these men's work, I told the committee that I should be compelled to set him up as a small manufacturer on his own account, and that in lieu of simply forging the work he would likewise grind it, and bring it in in a finished state. He continues to do so to this day.

4597. And you did do so ?—Yes.

4598. Was that at any expense to you?—At a great expense to me.

FIFTH DAY.

Mr. D. Ward.

7 June 1867.

4599. How do you mean you set him up?—I agreed to pay the rent of a little room that he had occupied elsewhere, and to find him with steel; and he invoiced the goods back to me every week, and I charged him with the steel.

4600. Was it a matter of inconvenience to you or of convenience in setting him up in this way?—A matter of very great inconvenience, but it was the only manner I could adopt to get his work.

4601. You have set him up, and he works for you on those terms now?—Just so. As a proof that it was a matter of quality, and not the employing a man at a reduced price, he gets a higher price for the work that he does for me than what the union men could get. I pay him a higher price for the work he does for me than what the union men in my employ would receive for the like work.

4602. Are you aware of any union man in the town getting as high a price as that?—There are no Union men getting as high a price for that class of work.

4603. In your judgment is he the the best man in the trade?—He is the best man in the trade.

4604. In your judgment, is it a matter of great importance to the town of Sheffield that they should have workmen of that description if they can get them?—I think they should, especially where manufacturers are determined to send out a first-class article.

4605. Do you compete in this with foreign countries? —Yes.

4606. What countries compete with you in carving tools?—Russia and Germany.

4607. They all compete with you?—Yes, and in the London market especially.

4608. Do they make them in London in a way that is better than Sheffield, or that competes with Sheffield?—They are made in London by several small manufacturers who know exactly the requirements of the trade, and of those who use them. A Sheffield workman does not know what is required, therefore he simply makes them to pattern.

4609. You think it is of great importance to import into Sheffield men who have this particular knowledge?—Men who know what is wanted by the people who use these particular articles, which this man knows.

4610. Have you anything further to say?—No, I think that is all I have to state.

4611. (*Mr. Barstow.*) Are we to understand that it is not in the power of a Sheffield manufacturer to bring a workman from any other town, and employ him here in the trade?—Not without the consent of the union.

4612. That consent is very difficult to procure?—Very difficult.

4613. Do you think it operates injuriously to the trade of the town?—Most decidedly so.

4614. If you were to do so in defiance of the decrees of the union, would you be subjected to losing your articles in the way you have told us?—I think on every occasion I should.

4615. This man was a forger?—Yes.

4616. He prepares the work for the grinder; the grinder is the next stage?—No; the hardening and step tempering is the next stage; after forging then comes the grinding.

4617. Are the grinders paid by the day or are they paid by the piece?—They are paid piece work.

4618. You told us that one of your grinders told you that he could do a great deal more of Addis's work than the other men?—Yes.

4619. It would be of great advantage therefore to the grinders to work on Addis's work?—Yes.

4620. They would earn more per day?—Yes.

4621. They have that advantage, of course?—Yes, they have that advantage.

4622. That advantage is being destroyed by the union?—Yes. As to the 30*l.* which I paid, a letter appeared afterwards in the paper, to state that it was given towards charities; but I know too well that when workmen are out of employ on trade union purposes the money is divided amongst them.

4623. (*Chairman.*) That is a mere suspicion, of course?—Yes.

4624. Is there any pretence for saying that he came to learn to forge and then go to London?—No pretence whatever.

4625. Did he know how to forge?—Yes; he had forged for a great many years.

4626. Did you believe that was a real substantial objection to him, or merely a pretence?—It was only a pretence, that they would not have a man in Sheffield, because he had not been brought up to the trade in Sheffield.

4627. (*Mr. Barstow.*) What harm would there be if he had learnt the trade, and taken his knowledge to London; they do not forge in London, do they?—Yes, they do. I do not know that there would be any harm, except that some small branch might have less to do in Sheffield, perhaps.

The witness withdrew.

J. B. Addis.

JAMES BACON ADDIS sworn and examined.

4628. (*Chairman.*) You come from London?—Yes.

4629. And have been brought up to the trade of carving-tool forger?—Yes.

4630. I understand you came down to Sheffield? —Yes.

4631. Did you apply in 1864 to Mr. Reaney, to be allowed to go and engage yourself with Messrs. Ward and Payne?—Yes.

4632. What did Mr. Reaney tell you?—That he could not do with me at all. I offered two years clear, and to pay 15*l.* down.

4633. What do you mean by two years clear?—I should not receive any benefit from the society.

4634. Mr. Reaney said what?—They did not want me; there were men on the premises could do my work.

4635. The result of it was that you had to go back to London?—Yes.

4636. After that did you receive a letter from Mr. Ward, asking you to come down to Sheffield?—Yes.

4637. And did you come down?—Yes.

4638. Then I believe he engaged you?—Just so.

4639. Then you set up working at your employment for him?—Just so.

4640. After that do you recollect some troughs being interfered with?—Yes.

4641. Had you any communication, after you began work, with Mr. Reaney?—No; at one time I got knocked about very much by two or three of the union men.

4642. When was that?—I cannot say when it was.

4643. How long after you came to Mr. Ward?—Some three or four months. I do not swear it is three or four months.

4644. Some short time after you came, you were knocked about?—Yes.

4645. How were you treated?—My wife and children went to London on one of the 5*s.* trips.

4646. By an excursion train?—Yes. Mr. Scamadine, keeping a public-house nearly opposite my house, went up with my wife to some hospital. He was very ill. I went over to see if he had returned. I was at the bar, and one of the men named Jephson said, "Here is a bloody Irishman wants to insult me; come and take my part."

4647. Who said that?—A man named Jephson said, "Here is a bloody Irishman wants to insult me; come and take my part."

4648. Whom did he say that to?—To me. I called

for three glasses of beer, and when I got my glass I said to this man who insulted me, "Drink with me, and let us be comfortable together," and they made the room up, and there were four of them knocked me about and kicked my head in with heavy boots, and I took them to the town hall, and they had to pay 22*l.* for the assault.

4649. They knocked you about with their boots and kicked your head?—Yes.

4650. What other damage did they do to you; had you any wounds?—Two wounds.

4651. Where?—On my head, two or three inches in length.

4652. Were you bruised otherwise?—Yes; all over my body.

4653. Who was the person who did this?—One was Jephson, and the other three parties I really forget their names; it was some time back.

4654. Who were they? Were they men belonging to the union, or not?—Yes, I believe they were. They were working for Messrs. Ward and Payne at the time.

4655. Was this a public-house row or not? Had you any quarrel with them, or what was it?—I had not any words with them. They said, "How many "trades union meetings have we had through you, "you bloody cockney?"

4656. What did you say to that?—I said, "I have "nothing to do with what your business is. I came "here to enquire if my wife had arrived at London "all safe." I think it was 20 minutes to 11 at-night; it was raining very heavy.

4657. When you said that, what did they say?—They made the door up, and knocked me down and kicked my head. I was bleeding very much.

4658. How many were there of them, do you say?—Four of them.

4659. You say you applied for a warrant against them?—Just so.

4660. They were apprehended, and brought before the magistrate?—Yes.

4661. And what became of them?—Three of them were fined 5*l.* each. I spoke on behalf of Jephson, who was the instigator in getting me into the quarrel, for which he was fined 3*l.* 10*s.* and costs. The judge cautioned me, and said, "This is the man who got "you into the bother, and yet you speak for him." It was because I belonged to a club that he belonged to. I did not think he owed me any spite. Since then I have found he was the worst; but that was the case at the time. He was fined 3*l.* 10*s.* and costs, and the others were fined 5*l.* each.

4662. Is that the only time when you have been interfered with at all?—Three of the other parties threatened to fight me since; Jephson and another man; I forget his name.

4663. What do you mean by threatening to fight you?—I had been drinking in front of the bar; it is very seldom I sit down in a room.

4664. What did they do?—He said, "Now, you "bloody cockney, you have made me pay this fine;" and he said, "If you want to fight come and take it "out of me. I am ready to fight you whenever you "are ready." I treated it with contempt, and went away. I was in the house of Mr. Webster on Saturday afternoon, and these parties were in there, and another party, I forget his name, challenged me to fight for 3d. I treated it with contempt.

4665. Have you ever been assaulted, or has anything been done to you?—No, not since that, because I have threatened them that I have a protection.

4666. Have any threats been held out to you if you continued your work by any person?—No; there has not.

4667. Has anything been done to your house at all?—No.

4668. (*Mr. Chance*). You were invited to come down from London?—Yes.

4669. Should you have remained in London if you had not been asked to come down here?—I think I should.

4670. Were you earning good wages in London?—Yes.

4671. (*Chairman.*) What wages can you make here?—I could earn 6*l.*, or 8*l.* or 10*l.* a week. I have done so here.

4672. (*Mr. Barstow*). Do you mean that you have actually earned as much as 10*l.* a week?—Yes; here at Messrs. Ward and Payne's.

4673. Often?—Not very often.

4674. (*Mr. Chance.*) You do not take a Monday half holiday, then?—No; of course I should have to work extra.

4675. Would you work extra hours to earn that amount?—Yes.

4676. (*Chairman.*) Working usual hours as an ordinary workman, 10 hours a day, what could you make?—7*l.* a week.

4677. Are you paid by the quality of your work or the quantity of your work or both?—Both.

4678. You make carving tools?—Yes.

4679. How are you paid? What is the mode of payment; so much a dozen?—So much a dozen.

4680. Is there any trade price or any regulation price in the union?—Yes.

4681. What is the trade price?—There are many branches. I begin and finish.

4682. Therefore you get the whole, whatever it is, of the profit upon it?—I think I get more than the statement price, because I make a better article; at least they say so.

4683. And you believe so?—Yes.

4684. (*Mr. Chance.*) Do you do the whole of the work yourself?—The forging, hardening, and finishing.

4685. There is no division of labour in your case, you do the whole it?—Yes.

4686. Generally speaking, one party does the forging and another does the grinding; you do the whole?—I do the whole of it.

4687. (*Mr. Barstow.*) You have apprentices or some one who assists you?—Yes.

4688. (*Chairman.*) You say you earn 7*l.* a week?—Yes; 10 hours per day.

4689. Does that include your strikers as well?—Yes; an apprentice—a mere lad.

4690. You are obliged to have a lad?—Yes.

4691. The lad you have to keep?—Yes.

4692. How much out of that would you pay the lad? Does the apprentice pay you for learning his trade?—No; I took him for nothing.

4693. You keep him?—Yes.

4694. Do you give him any money weekly?—I give him 1*s.* 6*d.* a week pocket money.

4695. Out of the 7*l.* you would have to deduct his keep and 1*s.* 6*d.* a week pocket money?—Yes.

4696. Do you find him clothes?—Yes.

4697. The rest is all for yourself and family?—Just so. If a man has a superior knowledge he is not going to throw it away. I cannot help being a good workman.

4698. No person will pay you if you do not earn it?—No.

4699. (*Mr Barstow.*) Do you earn that amount all weeks, or only for a certain time?—Trade has been very bad.

4700. (*Chairman.*) What are your average wages?—4*l.* a week.

4701. Your average earnings are what?—Now that trade has been bad I get 4*l.* a week.

4702. (*Mr. Chance.*) Do you attribute the excellence of your work in some respects to the knowledge of the use of the tools that you have to make?—Yes.

4073. You are a carver yourself?—I am not a practical carver, but I can carve. I understand thoroughly every part of the branch.

4704. And therefore you know how best to make those tools?—I received the prize medal in the Exhibition of 1851 and also the prize medal in 1862.

4705. You consider it an important thing for a man who is the maker of carving tools that he should understand the use of them?—Yes.

4706. And he should have some practical knowledge

FIFTH DAY.

J. B. Addis.

7 June 1867.

of the use of them ?—Yes; he must have some practical knowledge of these things. I have from my infancy.

4707. What age are you ?—37.

4708. Your father and grandfather were in the same business ?—My grandfather was the original inventor of carving tools.

4709. Where did he live ?—At Deptford in Kent.

4710. (*Chairman.*) By working, if you were allowed to work fairly in the town, could you communicate your knowledge to other workmen, so as to improve the style of work in the town ?—I should think so.

The witness withdrew.

W. Oxley.

WILLIAM OXLEY sworn and examined.

4711. (*Mr. Barstow.*) Are you manager to Messrs. J. and J. Barber, Broad Lane, cutlery manufacturers ?—Yes.

4712. Do you remember your men being out on strike ?—Yes.

4713. About what time was that ?—The notice was up the day that the flood took place; the 12th of March.

4714. Do you remember giving out some knives to a man named John Thompson ?—Yes.

4715. What did you give him out ? — About 17 dozen, but I cannot particularise the quality of them.

4716. What was he to do with them ?—Polish them.

4717. Where did he work ?—He said he worked at Butcher's wheel.

4718. Did you see him the day after ?—Yes.

4719. What did he tell you ?—He told us that the knives were stolen. Mrs. Barber answered, "Why "you told us that Mr. Butcher's place was as safe "as a bank, and I told you you would be responsible "for them." He says, "Yes; but Mr. Butcher's "wheel was lame, and I took them down to the "union wheel."

4720. Do you know Mr. Butcher's wheel ?—Yes.

4721. Has Mr. Butcher's wheel been built to make it more secure than others ?—There are wheels that are built as secure, but then there was a watchman at the door always.

4722. Is that a circumstance that makes it more secure than other wheels ?—No; I do not know that it is.

4723. Has it the reputation of being more difficult to get into than other wheels ?—I dare say there is more difficulty than what there is in many wheels in Sheffield.

4724. Do you know whether it was so or not ?—No.

4725. I believe you obtained a warrant on this occasion ?—Yes.

4726. Against whom ?—John Thompson.

4727. That is the man you gave the knives to ?—Yes, that was the man I gave the knives out to.

4728. What occurred after that ?—He came on the Thursday morning, to the best of my recollection, to the warehouse.

4729. Did he bring back the knives ?—Yes; but allow me just to speak on that point. He came on Thursday, and told Mrs. Barber that the goods were stolen. Now you have got down to the time that he brought the goods back.

4730. Tell your own story in your own way ?—We got the warrant out for him on the Wednesday. It was to be heard on the Saturday, on account of Mrs. Barber going to Birmingham. We told him to bring the goods back, which he did on the Saturday.

4731. He brought them back on the Saturday ?—Yes.

4732. (*Chairman.*) Did you see him ?—Yes.

4733. What did he say to you ?—He told me that he had brought the goods.

4734. (*Mr. Barstow.*) You refused to withdraw the warrant. Did he ask you to withdraw the warrant ?—The warrant should have been heard on the Saturday, and we had seen him there. There was no appearance.

4735. Did he ask you to withdraw the warrant ?—No.

4736. Did you withdraw the warrant ?—We did not appear.

4737. When he brought back the goods, what passed ?—He was going away, and I wished him to wait. He said that these goods would be finished in three hours' time.

4738. Did you say anything else ?—I told him to wait while I looked the goods over. I looked the goods over, and told him he had made a promise that the work would be finished in three hours' time. "Now" (I says), "you told us this work would be "finished in three hours' time." "Nay, nay, mister," (He says,) "I did not say so." I said, "Only state "your own time, that is all I care for." "Well," (he says,) "Six hours." I looked at the work; that work cost 12*s*. to finish it off after.

4739. Did you see any one on the following Monday ?—I met the secretary in Broom Hill Street.

4740. Who was he ?—His name was Broomhead.

4741. Of what union is he secretary ?—Secretary of the Spring Blade Grinders.

4742. He is dead ?—Yes. He told me that he had been and settled the affair with Mrs. Barber. He was very glad of that, he said.

4743. Did he mention to you how he had settled it ?—He told me that he had paid all the money but 6*s*.

4744. What was that for ?—The warrant, and Mr. Fredson's bill.

4745. Did he say so ?—He had said what we had charged him; Mr. Fretson's costs, the summons, and 2*s*., which, I believe, that I had paid for the goods going rusty. He said he had called and paid Mrs. Barber, and he was glad he had done with it.

4746. He had paid the expenses of the summons and warrant ?—Yes.

4747. (*Chairman.*) And the attorney's bill whom you employed ?—Yes.

4748. Was Mr. Fretson employed by you ?—Yes.

4749. (*Mr. Barstow.*) Can you give us any other instance of interference with your business ?—No.

4750. That is the only one ?—We did not know anything more particular about that case.

4751. But about any other case ?—No.

4752. You never had any hands taken ?—I have never had anything of the sort. I had been connected with the union long before I got there.

4753. Are you a member of the union now ?—No. I never knew a case in our line of business; that is the table-knife line.

4754. (*Chairman.*) You were a table-knife grinder ?—I was apprenticed to that, but I am now in Mrs. Barber's warehouse.

4755. What are Messrs. Barber ?—Spring-knife cutlers.

4756. Do you know what kind of knives these were that were taken ?—Yes.

4757. What were they ?—What we call 4-inch stag, and $3\frac{3}{4}$-inch buck.

4758. Were those spring knives ?—Yes.

4759. The person that you saw was the secretary, who is dead, Mr. Broomhead; he was the secretary of the Spring Knife Union ?—The Spring Blade Grinders' secretary.

4760. He paid all the expenses ?—Yes; excepting 6*s*.

4761. Do you know how he happened to pay it ?—I do not know anything about it.

4762. All that you know is that your things were taken away, and the man afterwards brought them back to you, and then the secretary of the Union said that he had paid, in respect of the Union, for all your expenses ?—Yes.

FIFTH DAY.

W. Oxley.

7 June 1867.

4763. Mrs. Barber is alive ?—Yes. Mrs. Barber is here. The greatest wonder in the concern is how the thing should turn up ; how the men should turn out when I think I could come up to this day and show from the books that no man has ever been settled a fraction from that price for 20 years.

4764. (*Mr. Chance.*) How long have you left the Union ?—It is 10 years since.

The witness withdrew.

Mrs. HARRIETT BARBER sworn and examined.

Mrs. H. Barber.

4765. (*Mr. Barstow.*) Do you remember one Sunday in March 1865 some large knives being missing ? —Yes.

4766. You do not know on what day it was ?—I cannot tell the date.

4767. Did you know a man named Broomhead at that time ?—Yes.

4768. Do you know what he was ?—He was the secretary to the Spring-knife Grinders Union.

4769. On the Monday following did you see him ? —No ; I think I left on Monday.

4770. (*Chairman.*) When did you see him ?—They turned out for an advance, and it was a month before I saw any of them ; they sent me a letter on the Monday morning.

4771. Who did ?—It came from Mr. Broomhead.

4772. (*Mr. Barstow.*) Have you got that letter ?—No ; it got lost.

4773. (*Chairman.*) What were the contents ?—They wanted an advance.

4774. After you lost your tools what happened ?—They wanted that advance of course. They were out a month.

4775. (*Mr. Barstow.*) Did Mr. Broomhead ever pay you any money ?—Yes.

4776. When was that ?—It would be sometime in September, but I cannot say the date.

4777. How long was it after your things were taken ?—Perhaps, three months.

4778. Did he say what it was for ?—Yes ; one of the men told me that Mr. Broomhead had been, and then he sent one of the men the day after to me.

4779. (*Chairman.*) Did Mr. Broomhead pay you any money ?—Yes.

4780. How much did he pay you ?—I believe it was 16*s.* 6*d.*

4781. Did he tell you what it was for ?—He said that it was for Mr. Fretson's expenses and the summons.

The witness withdrew.

Mr. JOHN HAGUE sworn and examined.

Mr. J. Hague.

4782. (*Mr. Chance.*) Are you a member of the firm of Hague, Clegg, and Barton ?—Yes.

4783. Saw and file manufacturers ?—Yes.

4784. And machine-knife makers ?—Yes.

4785. How long have you carried on that business ? —Since 1859.

4786. You began in 1859 ?—Yes, as near as I can remember.

4787. Where is your business carried on ?—In Silvester Lane and Arundel Street.

4788. Does the wheel at Arundel Street belong toyou or Mr. Allen ?—The building belongs to Mr. Allen.

4789. And the troughs belong to you ?—Yes.

4790. Did you employ a man named Fearnehough ? —Yes.

4791. When was that ?—We employed him about May the 12th, 1863.

4792. In what part of the business did you employ him ?—As a saw grinder.

4793. You took him off the box, I believe ?—Yes.

4794. How long did you employ him ?—It would be about May 1865, when he left us.

4795. At that time was he working upon your tools ?—Yes.

4796. (*Chairman.*) That was one of the rules of the Union ?—Yes.

4797. (*Mr. Chance.*) He was a member of the Union before that time ?—Most of the time ; but at the time we engaged him he was on the box, and we sent to the secretary of the Union for a list of the men on the box, and he sent us a partial list, not a whole list.

4798. Who was the secretary at that time ?—Broadhead.

4799. You say that Fearnehough's name was not in the list ?—No ; Fearnehough's name was not in the list ; I sent back for a complete list.

4800. How did you know that it was not a complete list ?—Because I knew there were a great many more men on the box at the time.

4801. You sent the list back to Broadhead and sent for a fuller list ?—Yes.

4802. Did he send you a full list ?—He added a few more names ; but Fearnehough's name was not down, although he was on the box.

4803. Do you know how that was ?—We wanted to employ the man ; but we had not made it known to any man.

4804. (*Chairman.*) Do you know why his name did not appear ?—His name did not appear on the list because Broadhead said that we had given him the previous engagement and he was not eligible.

4805. That because you had engaged Fearnebough previously, and therefere he was not eligible ?—Yes.

4806. Was it because you had not complied with the rules of the Union ?—It is the rule of the Union that we shall not engage with a man, but send to the secretary of the Union.

4807. You had engaged him without having applied to the Union first ?—We had not done so, we had named it to him that we should want a man ; but we complied with the rules of the Union, and took him off the list.

4808. That is, Broadhead said that he was not eligible because you had made an engagement with him before ?—Yes.

4809. Why does the fact of your having made an engagement with him before render him not eligible ? Was it because it was contrary to the rules of the Union ?—Yes, it was contrary to the rules of the Union.

4810. (*Chairman.*) Just mention how it was ?—According to the rules of the Union you must send to the secretary or to the society for the list, and you can pick any of the names that are placed on the list. Fearnehough's name not being on the list, and we, knowing that he was on the box—this was the man that we wanted to engage, because he was a man who was very proficient in the kind of work. He said that he was not on the list.

4811. You saw the secretary ?—Yes, I went to him.

4812. And asked why Fearnehough's name was not on the list ?—Yes.

4813. What did he say ?—He said that we had engaged him previously.

4814. What did you say to that ?—I said that we had named it to him, but not engaged him.

4815. What did he say to that ?—He said he was not eligible on that account ; he believed he was previously engaged.

4816. (*Mr. Chance.*) You had not in fact engaged him, but he thought you had ?—Yes, I asked him how he knew it.

4817. What did he say to that ?—He said it did not matter how he knew it, but he believed it was so. I asked him if we might engage this man, and he said "No"; he said I might engage him.

4818. What took place upon that ?—He said, of course he had nothing to do with the engagement ;

FIFTH DAY.

Mr. J. Hague.

7 June 1867.

but he was no longer a member of the trade if he engaged with us.

4819. Fearnehough would be no longer a member of the trade if he engaged with you?—Yes. I told him I would engage him, and take the consequences if he would engage with us.

4820. Did any more conversation take place then? —There was no more conversation; but I saw Fearnehough, and he said he would engage with us.

4821. Did you engage him?—Yes; and he said he would stand by us if we would stand by him; at that time we were about taking troughs at the Park Wheel or Kenyons.

4822. You were about taking them at that time? —Yes; Fearnehough said that part would not be safe as it was too much exposed to the ratteners; so we took other troughs for him in the Park at Rayner's wheel.

4823. Is that in the Park also?—Yes; and about November 1864 the handle-makers in our employ were not paying to the trade.

4824. What was Fearnehough?— A saw-grinder. Fearnehough came to us; he said that our handle-makers were not paying to the trade, and there would be some trouble about them; he had had Broadhead to see him. There was something about it that I can scarcely clear up; I did not remember him mentioning anything to me at the time, though he says he did; but since the blow-up at his house he says, that Broadhead offered him money to take away our bands.

4825. Do you recollect him telling you so?—I do not recollect him telling me so. I was naming the circumstance to him the other day, and he said he told me so; I do not remember it.

4826. (*Chairman.*) Fearnehough told you that he had told you that Broadhead had offered him money to take the bands?—Yes.

4827. Did he name the sum?—I believe it was *5s.*

4828. You say you do not recollect that conversation?—I do not. I remember hearing something said by him about Broadhead, but I do not remember what it was.

4829. About this time was that?—Yes, about this time.

4830. Are you prepared to say that Fearnehough's story is not true, or that you cannot recollect it?—I believe it is true.

4831. You believe it is true, but you do not recollect it?—I do not recollect it.

4832. You believe it is true what Fearnehough says that he told you?—Yes.

4833. I do not ask whether it is true that Broadhead did apply to him, but you say he told you, Broadhead offered him *5s.* to take away the things, but you do not recollect it; do you believe when Fearnehough makes a statement, and says, he told you, that it is true that he did tell you?—I do not remember the circumstances at all, though I remember him saying something about Broadhead.

4834. Do you know enough to say that it is untrue?—No; I do not.

4835. If a man had told you that a person had offered him *5s.* to take away your bands, it is very odd you should have forgotten it; it strikes me as curious? —I think somehow that he did not name that circumstance to me, but he might have named it in some other way; he might have intended to name the circumstance to me, but named it in some other way.

4836. How do you mean that he named it in some other way?—He said, that Broadhead had been to him, and said, that he must come and give notice, or something would be done.

4837. He never in express terms told you that he had been offered *5s.* to ratten you?—No.

4838. (*Mr. Chance.*) Do you remember any conversation taking place, after the explosion, about Broadhead?—No.

4839. (*Chairman.*) How soon after the explosion was it that Fearnehough reminded you of this conversation?—A fortnight after he mentioned it to Mr. Clegg.

4840. How soon after the blowing up was it?—It may be about a fortnight.

4841. (*Chairman.*) When was Fearnehough blown up?—I do not remember the date.

4842. It is a notorious fact. When was the date of the explosion? I am told it was the 8th of October; you say you had a conversation with Fearnehough in which Broadhead's name was mentioned.—Yes.

4843. Was it before or after the 8th of October?— It would be at the time he came down; it might be the same day that he had had the conversation with Broadhead. I dare say it would be the same day.

4844. Was it before the outrage?—Yes; long before.

4845. How long before?—It would be perhaps in November 1864.

4846. The conversation you had with Fearnehough, in which Broadhead's name was mentioned, was in November 1864?—Yes.

4847. Was it in 1865 or 1866 that the explosion took place?—I should think it was 1866.

4848. What you have spoken of is in November 1866; when was it that Fearnehough reminded you of the conversation that he had with you?—It would be about a month or six weeks after the blow up.

4849. Therefore he told you in November 1866. Just tell me how it happened that he spoke to you, and what he said to you.—I stopped him on account of my partner telling me that he had been naming this circumstance to him.

4850. What did you say to him?—I asked him if it were true.

4851. What did you ask him?—I asked him if it were true that Broadhead had offered him *5s.* to take away bands, and he said it was.

4852. Did he tell you that he had told you so before?—Yes, he did.

4853. What did you say to him?—I said, I did not remember it.

4854. Did he tell you when he had told you this?— He said, that it was when he came down to our place to give us notice; he gave us a month's notice on account of it.

4855. He told you that he had told you this when he gave you notice, about a year or a year and a half before?—Yes; that was in 1864.

4856. You said to him "I do not recollect your telling me"?—Yes.

4857. (*Mr. Chance.*) At that time Fearnehough was working for you?—Yes.

4858. Do you remember his working for you at the Arundel wheel?—Yes.

4859. While he was working for you at the Arundel wheel, were you rattened?—Yes.

4860. When was that?—It would be at the beginning of May 1865.

4861. Where was he working for you?—At the wheel in Arundel Street.

4862. (*Chairman.*) What did you lose?—One wheel band; the others had been taken away; they were removed because we had notice that they were coming to take them.

4863. Who had given you notice?—A person of the name of William Woodhead; he was working for us at the time.

4864. When did he give you notice?—The evening of the night they took the bands.

4865. Had you done anything, except having Fearnehough, to cause you to be rattened?—Nothing.

4866. (*Mr. Chance.*) Was anything said to you by any of the men who were working with you, or was any hint given to Fearnehough?—Yes; Woodhead told him.

4867. Did he tell you that they gave him the office; that he must turn out?—Woodhead told him the night before "You had better look out, for you have "not a minute to call your own." We had some conversation when Fearnehough told us this.

4868. (*Chairman.*) Fearnehough told you this?— Yes, he told us this the same evening.

FIFTH DAY.

Mr. J. Hague.

7 June 1867.

4869. Was it in consequence of that that you took away the bands ?—Yes, we took away the bands and nuts and all the moveable things ; that day we had made a road out of one shop into another, and there was no one in the place that we can remember except Shaw and Woodhead, besides Fearnehough and his sons.

4870. When was this ?—It would be in the evening when we got the notes that the ratteners were coming.

4871. There was no stranger in the place ?—No, the ratteners when they came broke through the file shops.

4872. Why did you leave any band at all ?—I do not know why it was left; it was forgotten.

4873. It was overlooked ?—Yes, it was overlooked.

4874. One band was left which was overlooked ?—Yes.

4875. The next morning you went in ?—Yes.

4876. Did you go there ?—Yes.

4877. In what state did you find the place ?—I found the window shutter and frame and the window altogether pulled out or prized out by something, and we found the glazier was cut.

4878. And a band was taken away ?—Yes.

4879. Can you use the glazier again after it is cut ?—We have to re-cover it ; that is all the circumstance connected with that.

4880. (*Mr. Chance.*) Did you go the next morning to Broadhead ?—Yes ; the next morning we went to Broadhead and I asked Broadhead what had become of our band, and he said he did not know anything at all about it ; "had we lost any ? " And we had other conversation. I cannot particularly call to mind the words that he used at the time ; but, however, we ascertained that Fearnehough had got three or four weeks in arrear.

4881. Who told you that ?—Broadhead.

4882. Broadhead told you that Fearnehough was three or four weeks in arrear ?—Yes ; we said that it was a trade affair and he must know something about it.

4883. What did he say to that ?—He said he had no doubt it was a trade affair, but he knew nothing at all about it.

4884. Was Mr. Clegg with you at that time ?—He was with me. Mr. Clegg told him he believed that he knew all about it, and the sooner he made up the damage the better it would be for him.

4885. What did he say to that ?—He said he should make good nothing, he knew nothing at all about it, and had nothing to do with it. At that time Mr. Clegg went to Mr. Jackson the chief constable, and he sent down two inspectors with me, and Wynn and Whiteley came down to the place. I went on a journey the next day, so I know nothing more about it.

4886. Did you ever get your band back ?—No.

4887. Did you continue to employ Fearnehough ?—He became too much afraid ; the place was not safe for him ; he became too much afraid to remain in the same place.

4888. In point of fact, how long did he stay with you ?—Till the end of 1865 I think it would be ; I think it would be about that time.

4889. Did you see anything done to Fearnehough by anybody ?—No.

4890. Did you ever hear any threats directed to him ?—No, but I have heard of some being made. We had a smith working for us, and there was a man, I think his name was Shaw, I have heard him say that he had heard a man say that he would blow the place up any time if he would only just say the thing. A smith of the name of James Thomas has said that he had heard a grinder say that he would blow the place up any time if they would only say so.

4891. What was the name of the person ?—I think it was Shaw.

4892. Is James Thomas here ?—No.

4893. Where is James Thomas ?—He is living at the bottom of Arundel Street.

4894. And he is a man who told you ?—Yes.

4895. A man of the name of Shaw had said what ?—That he would blow the place up.

4896. That he, Shaw, would blow the place up ?—Yes.

4897. If they would give the word ?—Yes, if they would give the word.

4898. If who would give the word ?—I suppose it meant the committee or secretary of the Saw Grinders Union.

4899. Do you know who this Shaw was that you speak about ?—No, I do not know him at all ; I do not know his name in fact.

4900. Was Shaw a man who worked for you ?—No ; he is a person that I do not know

4901. Is Thomas in your employ now ? — Not permanently, but partially.

4902. Does he work in Arundel Street ?—He works in Jessop Street.

4903. Could we find him now ?—Yes, I should think so.

4904. Did you communicate the fact to the police which Thomas told you ?—No ; we took no more notice of him.

4905. It is a pity you did not ?—There was a good deal of trouble about this Woodhead, and we were told that we could not compel Woodhead to state where he got his news from.

4906. Woodhead told you of the bands going ?—Yes.

4907. Who is Woodhead ?—He is a saw grinder ; at that time he was working for us.

4908. Where is he working now ?—I do not know.

4909. He was a saw grinder working for you at that time, but he is not working for you now ?—No.

4910. You say you did not know whether you could compel him to tell ?—Yes ; we were told we could not do so by some one ; that was when I was away.

4911. You were told you could not compel Woodhead to tell you who had told him who was coming to ratten you ?—Yes.

4912. Did you communicate that fact to the police also about Woodhead ?—Yes ; and he was seen. Mr. Barton and Mr. Payne went up to the Park ; he was working at the Park Wheel at the time.

4913. You told the police about Woodhead, and the police saw him ?—Yes, they saw Woodhead.

4914. Are those police still in the force ?—Yes, I think so.

4915. Give me their names ?—Wynn was one and Whiteley the other.

4916. Do you know whether Woodhead gave them any information about where he got his knowledge ?—I think he did not. I think he would say nothing, though they tried many ways to get information from him, but he would say nothing to throw any light upon it.

4917. You say there were no strangers in the place; can you tell me the names of the workmen who were in the place the evening when you got the information that you were going to be rattened ?—I think Shaw and Woodhead, Fearnehough and his son.

4918. Who besides ?—I do not remember any more than that; but I believe they were there; but he would take him aside to tell him that.

4919. Who ? — When he communicated it to Fearnehough he would take him on one side.

4920. I only want to know who were on the premises ?—I have told you.

4921. Had you any threatening note.—No.

The witness withdrew.

FIFTH DAY.

W. Bradshaw.

7 June 1867.

William Bradshaw sworn and examined.

4922. (*Chairman.*) Are you a butcher's blade grinder?—Yes.

4923. At 21, Blue Boy Street?—Yes.

4924. Have you been a member of the Table Knife Grinders Union for a number of years?—I have been a member, but not for many years.

4925. How long?—Perhaps six or seven years.

4926. Are you a member still?—No.

4927. When did you cease to be one?—Perhaps two years since; I gave up paying.

4928. You ceased two years ago to be a member?—Yes.

4929. What is the reason that you ceased to pay, or what is the reason you ceased to be a member?—We had a little bother about the price of the work at the place where we were working for; it was about some men belonging to the trade.

4930. And you left?—Yes.

4931. About four years ago did you work for Messrs. Martin Brothers?—I worked at their wheel.

4932. Was that about four years ago?—Yes.

4933. About that time were you in arrears of your contribution to the Union?—Yes.

4934. Did the secretary call upon you?—Yes; he calls every week.

4935. What was his name?—Jonathan Ragg.

4936. He called upon you several times you say?—Yes.

4937. Asking you to pay?—Asking me if I had any money. I had to tell him "No."

4938. While you were in arrear in this way did anything happen to your bands or tools?—Yes; I had some bands taken and the nuts from the axle-tree.

4939. How many bands?—I think there were two.

4940. How many nuts?—One.

4941. How much were you in arrear?—I do not know how much I was in arrear; it was agreed that I should pay 18*s*.

4942. About how much were you in arrear?—I was a good bit in arrear.

4943. A couple of pounds?—A good bit; it might be a couple of pounds.

4944. You said something was arranged?—Yes; that I should pay 18*s*.

4945. When you lost your bands where were they taken from?—From the grinding wheel.

4946. What grinding wheel?—From Martin Brothers.

4947. Did you rent troughs there?—Yes.

4948. When you went on the morning after they were taken did you find that the place had been broken into, or how was it?—I did not go there first; I did not know whether the place had been broken into or not; but the bands were gone.

4949. When you found that your bands were gone what did you do?—I went to the Town Hall and sent a charge in there, then I went to the Moseley's Arms.

4950. Where is the Moseley's Arms?—In West Bar.

4951. Whom is it kept by?—I believe they called him Levi Everson, but he is dead.

4952. What did you go there for?—To see the secretary.

4953. Who was the secretary?—Jonathan Ragg and Robert Law.

4954. Did you see them?—Yes.

4955. What did you say to them?—I told them the band was gone, and asked whether they knew anything about it, and they said "No," and they commenced talking then about what I was to pay to get them back.

4956. Who did that?—We all three of us talked about that.

4957. Tell us what they said to you?—They said they did not know anything about it, but they thought that they could get to know, and it was arranged that I should see them again at dinner time.

4958. Did you go?—Yes, I went to them, and it was arranged that I should pay 18*s*., and to go again at 7 o'clock at night to see them.

4959. Whom were you to pay that to?—To them I suppose; I did pay it to them.

4960. And what were you to do?—Go again at 7 o'clock at night, and they would let me know something about them.

4961. Did you go?—If they could not let me know anything about my own they would recompense me with new ones.

4962. Did you pay the 18*s*.?—Yes; they would replace them.

4963. Or if not, they would recompense you for them?—Yes.

4964. What was their value?—The bands would be valued at about 24*s*. I do not know what the value of the nut was. I went again at 7 o'clock at night; I did not see them. I asked the landlord whether they were there, and he said "No." I received a letter from the landlord to tell me where they were.

4965. Have you got the letter?—No, I took it to the Town Hall and gave it to one of the inspectors.

4966. What did it say?—To tell me where they were. I went the next morning to the place where the letter stated, and I found them there.

4967. About the 18*s*., what was the 18*s*. for, was it to pay off your arrears, or what was it for?—I understood that it was to pay off my arrears.

4968. You say that you owed as much as 2*l*.?—Yes, that was to straighten me if I paid on afterwards.

4969. Was anything said about the expense of rattening you?—No.

4970. Nothing of that kind?—No.

4971. Nothing about "Mary Ann"?—No.

4972. The 18*s*. was to settle all disputes between you?—Yes.

4973. Have you ever been rattened since?—I have not been what we call "rattened." I have had some tools damaged, but I do not think they had anything at all to do with that.

4974. When was that?—As near as I can guess it might be six months after.

4975. What tools were they?—I had one buff.

4976. Where was it?—At the grinding wheel when I went away at night; I found it in the trough with the leather off.

4977. What damage was done to it; what did it cost to put it right again?—It would not be only cost but labour as well, and then when I put it on again and got it as I thought ready for working it never was worth anything. It wanted quite a new leather, and that leather cost about 8*s*.

4978. How long did that stop your work?—I borrowed one while I got it agate again.

4979. There was no difficulty about borrowing one?—No.

4980. It would not stop your work much?—No.

4981. The expense was how much? Do you say 8*s*.?—The buff leather cost about 8*s*. to clean.

4982. You do not think that that was a trade business?—No; I think it might be a bit of private malice, or something of that kind.

4983. Why do you think it was private malice?—Sometimes we have words with the different people at the wheel.

4984. Had you any quarrel at that time with any person in the wheel?—I cannot say that I had, but there might have been.

4985. Were you in arrear at all to the Union?—I am sure I cannot speak to that.

4986. You know whether you were in arrear or not; you do know that?—I might be a small trifle, but I cannot say.

4987. What do you call a small trifle; how many weeks were you in arrear?—I cannot say.

4988. About?—I cannot speak about it.

4989. Oh, yes you can; come, you know how many weeks you were in arrear?—It might be six and it might be 12. I cannot say.

4990. Several weeks?—Yes.

FIFTH DAY.

W. Bradshaw.

7 June 1867.

4991. Had you been applied to for this by the secretary?—He used to call the same as usual. He never used to say anything to me when I said that I had not got it.

4992. Had he not pressed you for payment?—No; if I told him I had nothing he used to go away.

4993. How much was your contribution?—3*s*. a week at that time for myself and furnace boy.

4994. Before this injury to your buff, had anything been said to you by anybody about being in arrear?—No.

4995. Had there been any complaint by the trade of your workmen?—No.

4996. Had you ever been to any meeting of the union?—No.

4997. Do you know whether your name had been read over in the book as being a defaulter?—I do not know whether they did at all.

4998. Have you ever attended a meeting of the union?—Not these many years.

4999. Have you never been to a general committee meeting of the union?—No.

5000. Have you any suspicion who injured your buff?—No, I have not.

5001. Has anybody else in your wheel been rattened?—Not that I am aware of.

The witness withdrew.

JAMES THOMAS sworn and examined.

J. Thomas.

5002. (*Chairman.*) In the year 1865, that is now about two years ago, were you working for Hague, Clegg, and Barton?—Yes.

5003. What are you?—A smith and engineer.

5004. Had you a fellow workman of the name of Shaw with you then?—A saw-grinder.

5005. Yes?—There was another man came to help, Fearnehough.

5006. What was his name?—It was Thomas Fearnehough; he was helping.

5007. What did they call Shaw; George Shaw, or what?—I think it is William Shaw.

5008. Where does he live?—I do not know.

5009. When did you see him last?—It was a long time since.

5010. Where was he working when you last saw him?—I do not know. It is a man I had very little to do with; he only came there on a job.

5011. Do you know where he lived then?—No, I do not.

5012. Do you know whom he worked for before he came there?—No; he came there a stranger, and was only there a week; he was helping Fearnehough when I saw him.

5013. You say that you do not know where he worked before?—No.

5014. Or where he worked afterwards?—No.

5015. Nor where he lived then?—No.

5016. Was he a married man?—I cannot say, but I think not.

5017. Was he a Sheffield man?—I think he is. I could not be certain.

5018. You can tell by his talk?—Yes; he talked like a Sheffield man.

5019. What was he by trade?—A saw-grinder.

5020. Did you ever have any talk with him?—I think not much.

5021. Did he tell you that he was a member of the Union?—Yes; I heard him say that he was a member of the Union; he was a box-man when he came.

5022. Did he tell you how long he had been a member of the Union?—No.

5023. You say he came to help Fearnehough?—Yes, he came to help him.

5024. How did he happen to come to help Fearnehough?—Fearnehough had some heavy work, and I believe the secretary forced them all to earn their scale.

5025. Was he a man that had been sent by the secretary?—I think so.

5016. Are you in any Union?—No.

5027. He helped Fearnehough for a week?—Yes, somewhere about a week.

5028. During the time that he was helping Fearnehough was there any trouble with Fearnehough and the Union?—There had been trouble a good while.

5029. At that time there had been a good deal of trouble between Fearnehough and the Union?—Yes.

5030. That was the Saw-grinders' Union?—Yes, the Saw-grinders' Union.

5031. During that time had you any conversation with Shaw about Fearnehough?—No, not at all.

5032. Or about this dispute?—No. I had very little to say to him at all.

5033. You never talked to him about this dispute?—Very little at all about anything.

5034. Did you talk to him about this dispute with the Union?—I do not know that I did; not that I am aware of.

5035. Will you swear that you did not talk to him about the dispute between Fearnehough and the Union?—Yes; not that I am aware of.

5036. Will you swear that you had not any conversation with him about Fearnehough's quarrel with the Union?—I could not say to be positive; perhaps I might say a word to him and forget.

5037. Did he say anything to you about the dispute between Fearnehough and the Union?—While he was working for him?

5038. Yes?—No, I do not think he did.

5039. Will you swear that he did not?—Not at that time.

5040. Did he at any time?—Yes; he once told me about the trade outrage.

5041. What did Shaw tell you about the trade outrage?—He said that there was a party wanted to blow the place up.

5042. Wanted whom?—Wanted one of the saw-grinders to blow it up.

5043. To blow what up?—Hague's place up; the grinding wheel where Fearnehough was at work.

5044. Who did he say was the party?—He did not say who was the party.

5045. What did he say to you? Give the words that he used?—There was a man wanted to blow it up for 5*l*., and Broadhead would not sanction it.

5046. Shaw told you that there was a man wanted to blow up Hague's place for 5*l*., but Broadhead would not sanction it?—Yes.

5047. When did Shaw tell you this?—A long time after he had left. He was telling Charles Staniforth this.

5048. Where?—In the wheel yard.

5049. In whose yard?—In Hague and Barton's yard.

5050. When was this?—Some time after he had worked with Fearnehough.

5051. How long was it after he had ceased to work for Fearnehough?—It might be four or five months, perhaps it would be.

5052. You must tell me exactly?—I cannot.

5053. Was it a week after?—It would be more than a week a good deal.

5054. How long was it after? Was it a month after?—I will tell you as near as I can. It would be above a month; it would be two or three months after.

5055. Who is Charles Staniforth?—He was a man who worked for Hague and Barton, then a saw-grinder when Fearnehough left.

5056. Was anybody else present besides Charles Staniforth?—No.

5057. At that time had Fearnehough's house been blown up?—No; it was before his house was blown up a long while.

5058. Have you ever told this to anybody?—I told it to Mr. Clegg.

5059. When did you tell it him?—I told him soon after I heard it.

5060. Was not it during the time that Fearnehough was in their employment?—No; it was after, because Fearnehough had left, and Charles Staniforth took his situation.

FIFTH DAY.

J. Thomas.

7 June 1867.

5061. Did not you tell Mr. Hayne that you had heard Shaw say that he would blow up the place if they would give the word?—No. I told him that there was a man who wanted to blow it up if Mr. Broadhead gave the word. That was what I told him.

5062. You told Mr. Hague?—Yes.

5063. You told Mr Hague and Mr. Clegg that Shaw said that he himself would blow up the place? —No; Shaw did not say so.

5064. Did not you tell Mr. Clegg and Mr. Hague that Shaw had said that he would blow up the place if they would only give the word?—No. I told him that I heard Shaw tell Staniforth that if Broadhead gave the word he would blow it up for 5*l.*

5065. The place where this took place was Hague's works?—Yes.

5066. You heard him say so?—Yes.

5067. Mr. Hague has been here and told us what you told him. Now I call your attention to it again. Was not that at the time when Fearnehough was in their employ?—No. Charles Staniforth was in the yard, and he was telling him.

5068. Are you sure Fearnehough had left at the time you heard Shaw say this?—Yes; he had not left long when he said that.

5069. Fearnehough had not left long. How long do you believe he had left when this was told to Staniforth?—I do not think more than a week.

5070. How soon did you tell Mr. Clegg or Mr. Hague after you had heard it?—It would not be long; it may be two or three days or a week; I cannot say exactly as to the day.

5071. Why did not you tell him before?—I told him the first time I could think of it when I saw him. It might be two or three days, or it might be the same day.

5072. Do you know whether it was the same day or two or three days afterwards?—I cannot say.

5073. If you heard a man say that he knew a person who was willing to blow up their place for a five pound note, did not you think it your duty to tell Mr. Clegg about it?—I did tell him.

5074. You waited for a week. They have very little to thank you for. How long was it before you told him?—I cannot be certain as to that; it was not a week.

5075. Upon your oath was not it at the time Fearnehough was in their employ?—No, I am certain of that.

5076. Upon your oath did not Shaw himself say that he was the man who was willing to blow it up?—No.

5077. Did not you say so to Mr. Clegg?—No, I did not, upon my oath; I did not hear it said.

5078. You never said that Shaw had said that he was the man?—No, Shaw did not say so. He said there was a man who wanted to do it if Mr. Broadhead would give the sanction; he said it would be blown to atoms if he would.

5079. Did Shaw mention the name of the man who was willing to blow it up?—No.

5080. Are you sure he did not?—I am certain he did not.

5081. Did not you ask him?—No.

5082. Do you mean to say that if you heard a man say that he knew a man who was ready to blow it up for 5*l.* if he would only give the word, you would not ask him who it was?—He said this man had been several times to ask for a job.

5083. Did he tell you who he was?—No; I expected he was a Trades' Union man.

5084. Did he say he was a Trades' Union man?—No.

5085. Did he say when he had been there?—He said he had been to Broadhead several times.

5086. What did Charles Staniforth say to him?—He did not say anything particular that I know of. I had to look after the engines.

5087. And Charles Staniforth said nothing?—I do not know that he did.

5088. Did not he say this was a dreadful thing?—He was not a man who said much.

5089. Where is Charles Staniforth now?—I do not know. I saw him in Arundel Street the last time I saw him.

5090. When was that?—Four or five months since.

5091. Who does he work for?—I do not know. He was out of work then; he had been working in Manchester.

5092. Do you think he is in Sheffield now?—I do not know; I have not seen him since I saw him in the street.

5093. Did he say anything about how it was to be done?—No, not at all.

5094. Did he say whether he had offered to blow it up with a can of gunpowder or not?—No; that was all I heard.

5095. How did you happen to be present?—He was at the engine door where the grinding wheel was, and I was just going forth, and they were talking.

5096. Was Shaw at that time in the employ of Messrs. Hague or not?—No; he was not in their employ at all.

5097. What was Shaw doing there?—He merely called to see Staniforth; I think that was all.

5098. Had Shaw quarrelled with Fearnehough before he left?—No.

5099. Were Shaw and Fearnehough on good terms? —Yes.

5100. You swear that?—Shaw told me that Fearnehough had paid him capital well for what he had done for him; that he was very well satisfied.

5101. As I understand you, Shaw had no business at all there at that time?—No; only when they are on the box they often come to those that are working.

5102. If they are on the box they cannot work without being sent in by the Union?—I do not know about that.

5103. If he had no business there, what had he come there for? I ask you again solemnly, did not Shaw say, "If they will only give the word I will "blow up the place"?—No, he did not.

5104. You swear it was not Shaw?—Yes; I swear Shaw did not say anything of the kind.

5105. How long did Shaw stay on the spot?—I do not know; I went into another shop, and had to look after the engine, and just in going past I saw him, and then I went about my own business again.

5106. What is the age of Shaw?—He will be about 26 or 27, as near as I can guess.

5107. How long had you known him before this took place?—I did not know him till he came to work with Fearnehough.

5108. You do not know where he works?—No, I do not. They call him "Putty Shaw," but I think his name is William.

5109. What does "putty" mean? Is "putty" the name of a man; is it given him for anything he does? —It is a nick name.

5110. Is it a nickname for anything he does, or what?—They have almost all bye-names.

5111. What do you call a man "putty" for?—I do not know what the reason is.

5112. What is the meaning of "putty"?—I do not know.

5113. What does it mean?—There used to be a white washer, and they called him "Putty Shaw." We did not know his other name.

5114. Is it any name in Sheffield acceptation? If a man is called "putty," what do you mean by it?—I do not know. There are very few but what have a bye-name where many work.

5115. The origin of the bye-name is something; you do not get a bye-name without doing something?—I do not know; they are called very frivolous names sometimes.

5116. Had you any row with the Union?—No, I have had no row with them.

The witness withdrew.

Adjourned to to-morrow at 10 o'clock.

SIXTH DAY.

Council Hall, Sheffield, Saturday, 8th June 1867.

PRESENT:

WILLIAM OVEREND, Esq., Q.C.
THOMAS IRWIN BARSTOW, Esq.
GEORGE CHANCE, Esq.
J. E. BARKER, Esq., Secretary.

WILLIAM OVEREND, Esq., Q.C., in the Chair.

CHARLES STANIFORTH sworn and examined.

5117. (*Chairman.*) What are you?—A saw grinder.

5118. Did you work for Messrs. Hague, Clegg, and Barton at any time?—Yes.

5119. Was that at the same time that Fearnehough was at work there?—I left about the 24th of last June, as near as I can remember to a day or two.

5120. Were you there about two years ago when Fearnehough was at work with them?—I never was in the yard while Fearnehough was working there.

5121. Were you there before Fearnehough's house was blown up?—Yes.

5122. How long before his house was blown up were you there?—I was in Manchester at that time. I went to Manchester in June, the same month as I left Hague's. There was a meeting the same day that I went, about reform. I left the Saturday before.

5123. Do you recollect Fearnehough being at work at Hague, Clegg, and Barton's?—I never saw him work there.

5124. Do you know when he left?—I went that morning that he left, and helped him to load some of his tools. Of course, we were on good terms.

5125. Do you remember a man of the name of Shaw coming to the place while you were there?—He came several times.

5126. They call him "Putty Shaw" do they not?—"Putty Shaw."

5127. He came several times you say. How soon was that after you got there?—I do not know, it happened on the day after he came to see if Fearnehough was there. I think he helped him some time. I never saw him help him, but I think he did.

5128. Do you recollect any conversation which you had with him about blowing up the place?—I had none with him about blowing up.

5129. Did Shaw tell you anything about any person wishing to blow up the place?—No, he did not tell me distinctly. I have heard him talking to Jimmy.

5130. Who is Jimmy?—Jimmy Thomas. It did not much matter to him.

5131. Did you upon one occasion hear him say anything about blowing up the place?—No, I heard Jimmy say it could be done, or something of that sort.

5132. Tell us what he said?—I do not know anything more than that he said it could be done. "Putty" said it could be done. I did not know what he meant by "could be done." There is rattening a man and taking his bands, and there is giving him a good hiding, that is another way.

5133. Did "Putty" say to Jimmy that it could be done?—He said "Putty" told him so.

5134. Did you hear him say so?—No.

5135. To whom did he say it?—I suppose Jimmy told me that "Putty" told him.

5136. He says that he heard him tell you that it could be done?—No.

5137.—But you say that Thomas told you that "Putty" told him?—The conversation often went on as I have said, but I remember naught else.

5138. Did Shaw not tell you in Hague's yard that there was a man who wanted to blow up Hague's place for 5*l.*, but that Broadhead would not sanction it?—No, he did not.

5139. Has Thomas ever told you that Shaw told him so?—Give him 5*l.*?

5140. No. Has Thomas ever told you that Shaw said there was a man that wanted to blow up the place for 5*l.*, but Broadhead would not sanction it?—He said it could be done; he did not say anything about any man.

5141. Jimmy Thomas said so?—He said Shaw told him so; I never went to Shaw; I knew better.

5142. Upon your oath did not Shaw tell you the same thing?—No.

5143. Nothing of the kind?—No.

5144. Then if Thomas has told us this, he is not accurate about it?—The conversation ended. I never went to him since. If I was in the yard I would not go him.

5145. Why would you not go to him?—I never worked with him, and Mr. Hague always grumbled to see men coming there.

5146. Had Shaw any business there?—No.

5147. What did he come about?—It is a practice that people do look in to see one another. It is a thing that I do not do myself. I did not encourage it one way or another; Mr. Hague did not approve of it, and in fact they did not allow it, so I never encouraged anybody.

5148. Did Shaw say anything to you about this?—I never had any conversation with him about it.

5149. Did he ever tell you anything about it?—No.

5150. Was anything said about a can of gunpowder?—No.

5151. Did you ever hear anything about a 5*l.* note?—No.

5152. Nor 5*l.*?—No.

5153. Nothing of the kind?—No.

5154. And Shaw never told you anything of the kind?—Never.

5155. And you swear that?—Yes; I never do tell stories.

5156. I ask you again, did Thomas ever tell you anything of the kind?—He said as I have told you before, that it could be done, but by whom I do not know.

5157. How did he happen to tell you that it could be done?—They had been consulting together. Thomas said, "Well, Putty, it could be done to Fearnehough."

5158. Did he not tell you how it could be done?—No.

5159. What did he mean by "being done"?—I do not know what he meant.

5160. Come, you know what he meant?—There are four, or five, or a dozen different ways of doing it.

5161. Of doing whom?—I suppose he meant Tom. I do not know what he might do; he might take his bands, or give him a good hiding, or do anything.

5162. But what do you mean by "doing him"?—That is doing him: fetching his bands was doing him; giving him a good hiding was doing him.

5163. Was anything said about blowing him up?—No, there was not, not to me.

5164. Did he say anything about a good hiding?—No, not to me. I did not enter into conversation with him.

5165. Did Thomas tell you anything about that?—Not farther than that.

5166. Did Shaw say anything about his deserving a good hiding?—Not to me.

SIXTH DAY.

C. Staniforth.

8 June 1867.

5167. Did he say it to Thomas in your hearing?—I did not go to them.

5168. But did you hear him say anything to Thomas about doing it?—No, when I saw him I was about as far off as I am from you.

5169. Then you could hear what he said?—No, when the wheel is at work you cannot hear what a man says close to you, much more when you are three or four yards off.

5170. What had you been saying before his saying it could be done?—Nothing.

5171. A man comes up and says, "Shaw says Fearnehough could be done," that is nonsense you know; how did it arise?—I do not know how it arose. I did not arise it.

5172. But how did it arise?—I told you he came into the yard and came straight to Thomas, he did not come to me.

5173. But how did it happen that he told you that it could be done?—He told me when Putty was gone, if you call him Putty.

5174. What did he say?—He told me after Shaw was gone that he had said that Old Tom could be done.

5175. "Old Tom" is Fearnehough?—Yes.

5176. What did you say to that?—I made no answer to it.

5177. What did you understand by his saying, "Old Tom could be done"?—I have told you.

5178. What is that?—Giving him a good hiding, or fetching his bands, or anything else.

5179. But what did you understand by "being done;" you know whether or not they meant taking his bands?—They could not take his bands where he had gone to, a stranger could not.

5180. What was their only chance of doing it?—The men working beside him can do it.

5181. You must not equivocate, you must tell us why should anything more be done to Fearnehough?—He did not please them very likely. I know what he did not please them in, he did not do as he agreed to do.

5182. Whom did he not please?—All of us.

5183. He did not please you?—We were on good terms, but when he has work he pays no money, and when he is out of work he gets his money.

5184. Where you out of work at that time?—No, I was in Manchester.

5185. Had you any conversation with Jimmy Thomas about "Old Tom" not doing right and behaving badly to the club?—I said that he ought to pay the same as the rest, no more than that. Of course if a man makes a rule he ought to stick to it, and he ought to pay the same as others.

5186. Was it after you said that Shaw made the statement that Thomas said he could be "done"?—Oh, yes, after that.

5187. Was it when you were talking about not doing as he ought to to the club that Thomas said he could be "done"?—It would be after that, because Thomas said it the same day that I left.

5188. But how was it that it came about that anything was said about its being done? was it after the conversation when you said he was not doing right in not paying to the club?—Yes, he came regularly once or twice a week for a short time, oftener than we wanted him.

5189. For a short time after Fearnehough left?—Yes.

5190. Was it while Fearnehough was there, or after he had gone?—It was when I was there.

5191. Did you never talk at all to Shaw?—No, we were never on very good terms, and I think never shall be.

5192. On your oath did you not talk to Shaw on those occasions when he came to the works?—Never on those occasions.

5193. You never spoke to him after the first week after Fearnehough left?—No, he used to ask me if he should help me to grind big saws, and I did not want him. I had two sons of my own, and I am sorry to say I had not enough work for them.

5194. Then I understand you to say that you never had any conversation with him during the week after Fearnehough left, about Fearnehough not doing right with the union?—He said, "Old Tom is gone to Butcher's, and they cannot get into Butcher's." I looked up and said, "Butcher's? No one can get in except those that work there."

5195. Was it not in answer to that that Shaw said, "Notwithstanding he has gone to Butcher's, and you "cannot get into Butcher's without you work there, "it can be done."—No, he did not, not to me.

5196. Did Thomas tell you he had said so to him?—He told me that Old Tom could be done. He did not say where, or when, or how, or anything more.

5197. But was it after he said Old Tom had gone to Butcher's where they could not get in, and where they were locked up?—Yes, of course.

5198. It was in reference to his being at Butcher's where they could not get in?—Yes.

5199. It was in reference to that, that he said that, notwithstanding that, it could be done?—Yes, he went for protection, and I suppose he got it.

5200. Did Thomas say he had gone there for protection?—No.

5201. Did Shaw say so?—No.

5202. Did neither of them say he had gone to Butcher's for protection?—They need not tell me, I knew he had.

5203. Did you talk to him about his having gone there for protection?—To whom?

5204. To Jimmy Thomas?—No, he was making tools for Tom; we were working both in one shop with a bit of division between us.

5205. Jimmy Thomas was making tools for Fearnehough?—Yes, he had a shop of his own, and worked there nights and mornings and days when he had nothing else to do.

5206. Were you at Sheffield at the time when his house was blown up?—No. I came back last 12th of January, a very snowy day I believe.

5207. Were you in Manchester then?—Yes.

5208. Do you know what month you left for Manchester?—I left that very day they had that meeting in the square, last June. I left Hague's on Saturday, and I went there on Monday.

5209. And he was blown up in October?—Yes.

5210. Did you ever come to Sheffield between June and October?—No.

5211. Did you ever see Broadhead at the place?—Which place?

5212. At Hague's?—He came a time or two to me, but very seldom. I used to take the money which I had to take, or else send it; he did not often come to me, I took it to him.

5213. Did you ever hear Broadhead speak about Fearnehough when he came to Hague's?—No.

5214. Did he never mention it?—He said Tom had left. It was his business to tell me and nobody else, Hague went and told him and he told me, and then I went down to Hague's.

5215. Did Broadhead tell you why Tom had left?—He said he had not seen him. In some parts of his work there had been some complaints.

5216. Who complained of him?—The masters I suppose, they told me they complained of me as well as him.

5217. Do you mean to tell me that Fearnehough left that place because Hague was dissatisfied with him?—Yes, and Hague told me so.

5218. I thought you said he had gone to Butcher's for the purpose of protection?—Yes, he did not take Hague's work with him.

5219. But was it for the purpose of protection, or because he had quarrelled with Messrs. Hague?—He had to leave Hague's, and he dare not go anywhere.

5220. Why not?—For fear of their rolling him up, that is the only plan.

5221. What do you mean by "rolling him up"?—Rolling his band up.

5222. Has Fearnehough ever expressed to you at any time his fear of injury being done to himself?—

No, he told me he would not pay any more while Broadhead was Secretary, and that he would see him at hell first. It is not very good language, but I tell you what he said. That was on one occasion.

5223. When was it that he told you that ?—I met him in the street one morning, and then I met him another time again, and he said he would pay again if Broadhead would get booked.

5224. Was that the week after he left ?—He was coming up to Butcher's, and I was going down. It was the week or the week but one after he left.

5225. And you told this to Broadhead ?—I told Broadhead that he would pay if he would get booked.

5226. What did Broadhead say to that ?—He said it would be worth while to get booked, and let him pay.

5227. That he would cease to be secretary in order to let him pay ?—Yes.

5228. It would be so good a thing then, would it ? —It would, and I said I thought so too. I like to see them pay when they agree to it.

5229. Then you were all very angry with Fearnehough, were you ?—Yes, we did not like his not paying and our paying.

5230. Have you ever been at any meeting of the committee where Fearnehough's conduct has been mentioned ?—It was mentioned when he got drunk; we often mentioned his conduct.

5231. I did not ask you that; I asked you whether you had been at any meeting where Fearnehough's conduct was mentioned ?—I have never been to a committee meeting for 10 or 12 years.

5232. At a general meeting ?—Yes, I have been at general meetings better than 12 months since ; I imagine that it is 12 months since.

5233. How long before you went away was it that this general meeting to which you went took place ?— I do not know when this last meeting was, I am sure.

5234. Was it at a meeting held in June or July ?— No, it was not near July.

5235. Was it in June ?—I am sure I cannot tell you the truth without the book.

5236. Was it in May or June ?—I was there, I say, the last meeting before I went away. I cannot tell without looking at the books ; I have not looked at any of them. I did not know that I was coming.

5237. At that meeting was Fearnehough's conduct mentioned as not having contributed to the funds ?—I believe nobody mentioned it.

5238. Did they read over his name ?—They called us all over.

5239. They did not call any names over except of those who did not pay ?—They called us all over ; it does not go by paying.

5240. Did they call over the arrears ?—No, they did not call them over there. All the names are in a book, and you have to answer "Aye" or "No." He will say, "Staniforth, Charles," "Here," and if you are not there, he will put down an "A."

5241. But do they put down the names of those persons who are there and those who are not there, and read over the names of those who are in arrear ? —No, they do not do it there.

5242. You were there the last meeting before you left ?—I think I was there, but I would not be sure.

5243. Was Jimmy Thomas there ?—No, he is not a saw grinder.

5244. Is Shaw a saw grinder ?—Yes, they say he is. He is a saw glazer, I think ; that amounts to the same thing.

5245. Was he at the meeting ?—I cannot tell you, because when you get a room with about 200 people in it you cannot pick them all out.

5246. But I want information, you know. Was he there ?—I do not know that I saw him.

5247. He was a member of the union, you say, but you do not know whether he was at that meeting ?— I do not know ; not to speak to, at all events.

5248. Have you heard Broadhead say anything about Fearnehough's misconduct, or about his not paying up ?—To me ?

5249. Yes ?—No.

5250. Have you ever said anything to him about it ?—No, but I like to see them pay the same as I do. I kept right with them while I went away.

5251. Have you heard any other member of the union complain of Fearnehough ?—They complained of one another ; there was naught else.

5252. Did you hear many complaints about Fearnehough ?—No, I do not know that I did. I do not go among them much myself.

5253. But did the men at the union complain much about Fearnehough ?—If you get at one end you do not hear what they say at another.

5254. Did they call him "knobstick" ?—Yes, and they called him worse than that sometimes.

5255. What else did they call him ?—I do not know what they called him—a damned thief.

5256. Whom have you heard call him a damned thief ?—The box-men, several of them ; they cannot call him a good name.

5257. Have you called him a damned thief ?—I might call him so. He has called me so many a time. I have worked with him many a time.

5258. Have you called him a damned thief and a "knobstick" ?—No.

5259. Will you swear that you never called him a "knobstick" ?—Not to his face.

5260. Behind his back, have you never called him a "knobstick" and a damned thief, or anything of that kind ?—No, I called him that when I was at Manchester. I said that he should do as other men did. They said, "Why ?" I said that he would get folks to pay his-sen ; and they said, "Sarved him right," if he did not pay. I said he would put a horse in the shafts, but he would not pull his-sen.

5261. Was this after he was blown up, or before ? —It was at Manchester. Of course, when he was blown up, they sent me a paper with it in, and they said what they were going to do.

5262. What who was going to do ?—They said they were going to find out who had done it, but I did not think they were. The papers said so.

5263. Why do you say that you did not think they would ?—Because I do not think they would.

5264. But why not ; who do you think had done it ?—I do not know.

5265. Then why did you think they would not find it out ?—Because I did not think they could.

5266. We will see if we cannot find it out now ?— I wish you could.

5267. But why did you say that you thought that they could not find it out ?—I did not think so.

5268. But you must have had a reason ?—I thought they could not ; I cannot tell you any more.

5269. Did you think it had been done so secretly ? —No.

5270. Then why do you think that they could not find it out ?—Because they have never found out anything of the sort, and I believe they never will do.

5271. It was because it was done so secretly ?—I think so myself ; I was not in the town at the time, but I saw that they offered 1,000*l.*, and this, and that, and to'ther. I think if they had offered 10,000*l.* or 1,000,000*l.*, they would not find it out ; it is naught but thinking, but I think not.

5272. Why did you think that money would not find it out ?—I do not know. I think there are not two folks that know aught about it. If there were two, I doubt it almost. I think not.

5273. It is a mere matter of opinion all this ?—I form my opinion the same as many. Where there are three or four in a party it gets blown you understand. I have often seen that where there are three or four in a party it is too many.

5274. Had you heard any person threaten Fearnehough ?—No.

5275. Have you ever heard any person say that he would do anything to him if he would not pay his contribution ?—No. When they came they said, "Old Tom" did not pay. They have come upon me as bad as upon him, and they turned their back when he gave them his hand. They go round.

SIXTH DAY.

C. Staniforth.

8 June 1867.

5276. Who goes round?—The man.

5277. Are there certain men who go about?—I have given many a one 6*d*.

5278. What did you give them 6*d*. for?—To get their dinners with when they had naught to do.

5279. Were the men doing nothing when they come round to the wheel?—Yes, but at some places they do not like them. They did naught to me round there, because I was friendly with them all, Tom and all, and master and all. I had no words with them when I left; he sent a boy with the money and he came.

5280. Will you swear that you never had any conversation with Shaw about Fearnehough?—I will. I have no fear or anything of that sort either.

5281. I do not think you had anything to do with that?—Nor would not have. They may all do as they like for me.

5282. (*Mr. Barstow.*) Have you ever been in arrear yourself?—Yes.

5283. Has anything ever happened to you?—I have had my bands rolled up.

5284. When were you in arrear?—Sometime back now.

5285. Many times?—When I left I had some arrears to draw.

5286. Were not your bands taken upon another occasion?—Yes, I believe once they went; I think they took them all at once.

5287. Do you know what that was for?—Arrears I believe. It was another man's bands which went instead of mine, but however they did go, but I was not in arrear when it was done.

5288. What did you do when you missed your bands?—I went up for them. I did not go, but I wanted information and I would not go after it.

5289. Who were they?—The other grinders that worked with me.

5290. What were their names?—They call one Charley Dams.

5291. Was there anyone else?—I am sure I cannot tell you whose bands went that time. It is some years ago.

5292. To whom did they go?—I think they were found in the yard somewhere.

5293. But to whom did those men go?—I suppose they went for information to Broadhead.

5294. They went to him for information?—I guess so, I did not go myself. They knew where to go always.

5295. What makes you think they went to Broadhead?—Because they generally go to that team you know. They generally go there and pay their money, and then they come back.

5296. Did those men tell you anything about what they said to Broadhead?—No, we had a word Dams and me. He said they took his bands, and I said they took mine, and we said they could not be far wrong if they took them both; they took them both and they would not be wrong then. But then you see it made two 5*s*., and that made it better.

5297. (*Chairman.*) What do you mean by saying that two 5*s*. made it better?—For expenses.

5298. They charge 5*s*. for rolling up a band, do they?—Yes, and little enough it is they say.

5299. (*Mr. Barstow.*) Were they charged this 5*s*. for rolling up the bands?—I do not know who charged it, nor who got it.

5300. (*Chairman.*) To whom did they pay it?—They paid it to Broadhead, I guess.

5301. Have you paid Broadhead?—No, and I have seen nobody else pay him, but I believe they go there and make it right.

5302. (*Mr. Barstow.*) Had he told you that they had paid it?—I have heard them say that they had been to Broadhead and made it right. Nearly all the men in the trade have been to Broadhead at one time or another. They all do it more or less.

5303. Then you got you bands back?—Yes.

5304. Did you pay anything?—No, my boy went up and paid a week's arrears and my bands came back.

5305. (*Chairman.*) Had you to pay anything for expenses?—I never paid anything myself.

5306. What were the week's arrears?—I cannot say whether it 3*s*. 4*d*. or what.

5307. Was there anything paid to get back your bands besides the arrears which were due?—You have to pay for their being fetched.

5308. And you paid for them too?—My wife did, I daresay, but I did not.

5309. (*Mr. Barstow.*) Your wife paid 5*s*.?—She used to send up when she went past.

5310. To whom did she pay that?—Perhaps she paid it to Broadhead. I do not know who she paid it to.

5311. (*Chairman.*) We must send for her you know if you do not tell us all about it?—Well, she paid it to Broadhead of course.

5312. (*Mr. Barstow.*) Have you ever been rattened at any other time?—At Wheatman and Smith's a time or two.

5313. On those occasions did you pay the expenses?—No, I found them myself the next day in the next yard.

5314. Then you had nothing to pay?—No, I and master went as far as Broadhead's and he knew nothing about it, and then I came back and turned some wood over and I found them.

5315. What were they taken for?—Because they said I had not the price, and then we had to pay you know.

5316. But you had the price?—I went to the committee and proved that I had it.

5317. Where did you go to? where was this committee?—It was down Shales Moor or Gibraltar. They kept the "Dog" there.

5318. Where was this committee?—At the "Greyhound," down in Gibraltar we will say.

5319. What is the name of the landlord? Broadhead.

5320. How long ago was this?—It is a good many years since now, it is eight or 10 years ago.

5321. What passed when you were before the committee? what did you say?—I said that I had it, and I stuck to it that I had it. What could I say anymore than to say that I had it, and stick to it if I have it? If you tell them two things they will know you are wrong.

5322. Was Broadhead there?—Yes.

5323. Was it to him that you spoke?—It was not to so many as that (*pointing to the reporter's table*), but it was something like seven or nine.

5324. Was Broadhead sitting at the end of the table?—I do not know whether it was the end or the middle; he was there.

5325. He heard all you said?—Yes.

5326. And what did he say to you?—He gave me credit of course, and all the committee did.

5327. And they said it should not happen again, did they?—No they did not, they could not say that and speak the truth.

5328. Well did it ever happen again? were your bands ever taken again?—Not there I think.

5329. Where else?—I have told you about the next time they went.

5330. Are those the only times that they have been rolled up?—Sometimes, but longer sin' a good deal.

5331. Have you ever rolled anybody's bands up yourself?—Aye to be sure.

5332. (*Chairman.*) Have you rolled anybody's bands up?—Well I do not know that I have.

5333. We can send you to prison if you do not tell us the truth you know?—I am not bound to say I have when I have not.

5334. Have you ever rolled anyone's bands up?—Never.

5335. Never?—Never; I have taken my own nut.

5336. You have never taken any other persons?—No.

5337. Will you swear that you never have done so?—Yes.

SIXTH DAY.

C. Staniforth.

8 June 1867.

5338. Why did you say that you had?—I did not say it.

5339. When you were asked whether you had ever taken anybody's bands, you said, "Aye, to be sure." Do you swear that you have never taken anybody's bands?—No, I do not go taking people's bands.

5340. You never did take anybody's bands?—No.

5341. (*Mr. Barstow.*) If we should find out from any other witness that you have taken any bands it will be the worse for you?—I will risk that you do not.

5342. (*Mr. Chance.*) You need not be afraid if you have?—No, but it is no use saying that I have, if I have not. I never went to a man's wheel and rolled his stuff up in my life; I have rolled my own up to protect it.

5343. Have you ever known any person who did go and roll up another man's stuff?—No, I do not know for truth who saw them do it.

5344. Has anybody ever told you that he has had 5*s.* for doing it?—No.

5345. Just think?—I may have helped to spend it, but I have not known at the time.

5346. (*Chairman.*) But have you known afterwards?—No.

5347. (*Mr. Chance.*) They have told you sometimes that they have had 5*s.* for rolling up a man's band?—No they have not, they know better than that; I never asked them any questions where they got it.

5348. But have they not told you without asking them?—No, they did not.

5349. Sometimes they have told you that they have had 5*s.* for rolling up Thomson's bands, or some other man's bands, have they not?—No.

5350. (*Mr. Barstow.*) You told us that 5*s.* was little enough for rolling up bands?—Yes, I would not do it for 5*s.* for the risk of being catched, and happens it might cost you 20*s.* to get out or perhaps more then that,

5351. (*Mr. Chance.*) Has anyone ever told you that they thought 5*s.* very little?— I say it is little enough to risk.

5352. Are you a member of the union now?—No, not since I went to Manchester. I never joined one since.

5353. Are you going to join them again?—There are two societies now, and you do not know which is which hardly.

5354. Are you going to join them again?—I have said that I would not, but I do not know but I may do.

5355. Do you wish to join the union?—I would as lief have the scale as work hard. If you get a good scale it is better than having to work hard as some people do for nothing almost.

5356. You would sooner have scale than work hard would you not?—I would, to speak the truth.

5357. When you were a member of the union before were you forced into it against your will?—Into the union?

5358. Yes?—Nobody is, we are willing to join it, and we are yet. We will all have a good try if we can get it.

5359. (*Mr. Barstow.*) I am asking you this question at the request of Mr. Sugg; do you happen to know whether Mr. Hague gave Fearnehough notice to leave his employment?—Yes, I knew before I went. I was told he gave him notice.

5360. Who told you?—Broadhead told me. I expect either Hague, or Clegg, or Barton told him. I do not know which of them it was.

5361. Did Hague ever tell you so?—He said they had given him notice. When I went Hague told me that they would give him notice when I was sent there.

5362. That they would give Fearnehough notice?—They had given him notice.

5363. Did he tell you for what reason he gave him notice?—Clegg said he did not suit them by a long chalk, that is in his work. "A long chalk" was a new expression to me. I did not understand it before.

5364. (*Chairman.*) Do you know whether Fearnehough was a drunken man or a sober man?—He would get drunk for two or three weeks together sometimes, not drunk but drinking.

5365. (*Mr. Barstow.*) You said that you had drunk part of the money that was paid?—No. I say I may have supped some of it sometimes, but I do not know.

5366. Do the people whose bands have been taken, and those who have taken them drink together afterwards?—I do not know whether they drink together. I expect the money they get they spend together sometimes. I do not know who pays them, and who does not pay them.

5367. The man who gets the 5*s.* treats those whose bands have been taken?—I do not know whether he does or not; it depends upon whether they are good friends or not.

5368. But is it a common thing for the man who gets the 5*s.* to spend it with those whose bands he has rolled up?—Very likely he would spend it.

5369. But with those whose bands had been rolled up?—On some occasions they might do so. They might work next door to each other and they might be friendly, and they will do so sometimes.

5370. (*Chairman.*) Is there such a person as William Fearnehough as well as Tom Fearnehough?—Yes.

5371. Who is William Fearnehough? — He is Tom's son. I have not now seen him for nearly two years.

5372. Have you ever known saws thrown into a pond or dam?—I have not seen any.

5373. Do you know of it?—I have heard of it.

5374. Have you ever had any of your own thrown in?—No.

5375. Have any of the men with whom you have been working?—Yes.

5376. (*Mr. Barstow.*) Mr. Sugg desires me to ask whether you have ever rattened yourself?—No.

5377. On any occasion?—Yes.

5378. And have you ever rolled up your own bands?—Yes, I have put them on one side a time or two, for fear someone else should.

5379. Was that for protection?—I thought they would come, but they did not, seemingly, but they would have taken the bands if they had come.

The witness withdrew.

GEORGE SHAW sworn and examined.

G. Shaw.

5380. (*Chairman.*) Do you go by the name of Putty Shaw sometimes?—Yes, my father was a plasterer.

5381. Did you work for Fearnehough?—Yes.

5382. While he was at Hague's?—Yes, I jobbed a little with him.

5383. Were you a member of the union then?—Yes.

5384. Was he in arrear at that time?—I know nothing about him.

5385. You do not know whether he was in arrear at all?—No, he never told me.

5386. Do you know whether he had any dispute at that time with the union?—No, he never told me.

5387. I did not ask you that. You were a member of the union, and I ask you whether at that time you knew whether there was a dispute between him and the union?—No.

5388. You swear that you do not know?—No.

5389. And did you not know?—No.

5390. After he left, did you not know?—No.

5391. Now mind what you are about. You know

SIXTH DAY.

G. Shaw.

8 June 1867.

what we can do with you if you do not tell us the truth ?—Yes.

5392. If you tell us all that you know you need not be in fear of any consequences at all. If you make a full disclosure we will give you a certificate and you will be perfectly free from any consequences, but if you do not tell the truth very serious consequences may happen ?—I shall speak the truth.

5393. Now I ask you if you did not know at the time you were working for Fearnehough that there was a dispute between him and the union ?—No. I was sent there on trial to see what my workmanship was. I worked by the side of Fearnehough.

5394. I am asking you whether there was a dispute between the club and Fearnehough ?—Yes.

5395. You swear that you do not know ?—Yes.

5396. Do you know Staniforth, the last witness ?—Yes.

5397. Have you ever talked to him about Fearnehough not being right with the club, and not paying his contributions ?—Not to my recollection.

5398. Will you swear that you never talked to him about his not paying his contributions ?—No. I have been to him and asked him about his work.

5399. Have you talked to Staniforth about Fearnehough not paying him the contribution ?—Not to my recollections.

5400. You shall not get out of it in that way. You must answer me. Have you or have you not ?—No.

5401. You have never talked about it to Staniforth ?—No.

5402. Nor about his being in arrear ?—No.

5403. Or not behaving well to the union ?—No.

5404. Do you know James Thomas ?—Not by name.

5405. Do you know Jimmy Thomas ?—No, not by name.

5406. He is an engineer who worked for Hague, Clegg, and Barton ?—Yes, I know him.

5407. Did you ever speak to Jimmy Thomas about Fearnehough ?—Well, we might talk in conversation, but not to my recollections.

5408. But did you ever have any conversation with Thomas about Fearnehough not paying his arrear ?—No.

5409. Or not contributing to the box ?—No.

5410. Did you go frequently to Hague's place after Fearnehough left ?—I used to call when I was coming from my place, as I came backwards and forwards with work.

5411. Do you know any person who ever wanted to do an injury to Fearnehough ?—No.

5412. Did anybody ever tell you that he was disposed to do it ?—No.

5413. Did you ever know of any person who wanted to blow Hague's place up ?—No.

5414. Or who said that he would do it for 5*l.* ?—No.

5415. Have you ever known that any person had applied to Broadhead for permission to blow up the place, and that Broadhead would not consent ?—No.

5416. Now, mind how you answer me. Did you ever tell this same man, James Thomas, that there was a man who wanted to blow up Hague's place for 5*l.*, but Broadhead would not sanction it ?—No.

5417. Did you ever say anything of that kind ? Did you ever speak about a man blowing Hague up ? —No, I never had any occasion.

5418. Will you swear you never mentioned anything about his being blown up ?—Yes.

5419. I do not say it was you, but I want to know if you did not say that you knew a man who wanted to do it ?—No, not to my recollection. I never mentioned it at all.

5420. May you have forgotten it ?—Perhaps I might, but it is not in my recollection at all

5421. Then it is possible you may have said so and may have forgotten it ?—I cannot recollect anything of the sort.

5422. Is it possible that you may have said it and have forgotten it now ?—When people are talking they very often say things and forget all about them.

5423. Is it possible that you may have said it and forgotten it ?—No. He and I used to talk. I used to ask him to get their master to get me employment.

5424. That is idle talk, you know. I ask you whether you may have told him this, and may have forgotten it ?—No.

5425. Then why did you say you might have forgotten it, because if you might have forgotten it you must have said it ?—No, I have not said it.

5426. You have never said it ?—No.

5427. Have you heard what Thomas has said. I will remind you that Thomas has been here, and has been sworn. I will tell you what he says, and I caution you—he swears that you told him that there was a man who wanted to blow Hague's place up for 5*l.*, but that Broadhead would not sanction it. Now, I remind you that Thomas said that you told him so, and I ask you again if you did ?—No.

5428. You say that is false ?—Yes.

5429. Do you still persist in it ?—Yes.

5430. Did you ever allude to anything of the kind ? —Not at all.

5431. Then this is entirely an invention of Thomas's ?—Yes.

5432. Did you ever hear anybody talk about blowing up Hague's place ?—No.

5433. Never anything of the kind ?—No.

5434. Did you ever talk to Broadhead about Hague's place being blown up ?—No, never in my life.

5435. Did you have any conversation about what Thomas said of you last night ?—No. I did not know while about an hour and a half that I was coming here.

5436. Who told you ?—The policeman came to our place.

5437. Had you never heard of it till the policeman came ?—No. I was working while 9 o'clock at night, and I went at 3 this morning.

5438. And you never had heard till the policeman told you that Staniforth had said that you had mentioned that you knew a man who wanted to blow Hague's place up ?—No.

5439. What age are you ?—I think it is 28 next birthday.

5440. Are you a member of the union ?—No.

5441. Were you then ?—Yes. I worked for Messrs. Davenport in Jessop Street then.

5442. Were you in the habit of going to Broadhead's public-house ?—I went when I had to pay my contributions on Saturday nights. Sometimes he fetched it; on Tuesdays I think it was.

5443. Have you ever rolled up any bands ?—No, not one in my life.

5444. Do you know of anybody who ever has ?—No. I have had my nuts fetched once.

5445. When was that ?—When I worked for Messrs. Pagden, about five years since.

5446. Were you in arrear at the time ?—I think I owed 7*s.*

5447. Did you get them back again ?—Yes.

5448. How did you get them back ?—I paid my contribution what I owed.

5449. And what besides ?—I forget now what it was, but it was 14*s.* I think.

5450. You owed 7*s.*, and you got your nuts back by paying 14*s.* ?—Yes. I forget exactly now, it is a long time since.

5451. Whom did you pay the money to ?—I paid my contribution to Mr. Broadhead.

5452. That was the 7*s.* a week. Did you pay the other 7*s.* too ?—I paid the 14*s.* to Mr. Broadhead.

5453. You paid the whole 14*s.* to him ?—Yes.

5454. The other 7*s.* were for the expenses ?—Yes.

5455. Is that the only time that you have been rattened ?—Yes.

5456. You say you have never had any conversation at all about Fearnehough ?—No. Fearnehough and I were always on very good terms.

5457. I asked you whether you knew Fearnehough was at all in disgrace with the union ?—No.

5458. Do you know that he went to Butcher's?—Yes. I helped him to get the stones on the dray.

5459. What did he go to Butcher's for?—I suppose he went to work. I did not know who he was working for.

5460. I did not ask you that. Did you know why he went to Butcher's?—No, not then.

5461. Do you know Charles Staniforth?—Yes.

5462. Did you ever tell him he went there for protection?—No.

5463. Did you ever talk to Staniforth about his being in arrear?—No.

5464. Did you ever talk to Staniforth about "Old Tom"?—Yes, when I used to call; when I used to go to our place for work.

5465. Did you not ask him about paying his contribution?—No. I talked to him about grinding; that is all that has passed between him and me.

5466. Did you never talk about his going to Butcher's for protection?—No; only what Stamforth told me.

5467. Did Staniforth tell you that there was some person who had offered to blow him up?—No.

5468. Then protection for what?—He had gone there for protection, I suppose, for protection for his bands and nuts going.

5469. Did Staniforth tell you that he had been threatened; that some person was willing to blow up the place, or something of that kind?—No.

5470. Then what did he say?—He said Old Tom had gone to Butcher's.

5471. You said he told you he had gone there for protection?—Of course he would be right there. Of course they could not take his bands there. I could hardly tell what he said.

5472. How did you happen to be talking about their not being able to get his nuts and bands there?—I used to know Fearnehough a bit. I was apprenticed by the side of him.

5473. Did you know he was in fear of losing his nuts and bands?—No.

5474. I thought you told me just now you did not know he was in arrear at all?—I did say so.

5475. Then you never lose your nuts and bands unless it is to pay up your money, do you?—No.

5476. Then why did you say he was going there for protection?—I did not say so.

5477. You say Staniforth said so?—He said he was gone to Butcher's.

5478. You said he was gone for protection?—He might say something of the sort.

5479. Why should he go for protection if he was not in arrear?—I do not know. That is best known between him and the trade.

5480. And you still swear, although you have been told by Staniforth that he had gone there for protection, that you did not know he was in arrear?—No; I did not look at the books.

5481. Did you go to the meeting?—Yes.

5482. Was his name called over?—No.

5483. Was his name alluded to as being a person in arrear?—No, they never call over the names except in another room.

5484. What other room?—A backroom where they go into to pay their additional arrears of so much a week.

5485. Where is that; is it at Broadhead's house?—Yes.

5486. There is a room in Broadhead's house where the persons who are in arrear are called in?—Yes. They sit in a parlour, four or five men.

5487. Who sits in the room when they are called in?—I do not know the men that sit there.

5488. Have you ever been called in there?—Never in my life.

5489. Have you ever seen men called in?—I have seen men go in there, and heard from them when they came out what they had to pay, so much a week.

5490. Is any list kept of the persons who are in arrear at your club?—I have not seen the list.

5491. I did not ask you that. Is there any list kept?—Not to my knowledge.

5492. Have you ever heard from the men who went into the room who were the committee?—No.

5493. Was Broadhead one of them?—No, Broadhead was upstairs at the meeting.

5494. How were they called into the room?—Separately, I suppose.

5495. Were they called out of the meeting?—No, they stood down stairs, waiting to go in.

5496. Who stopped them down stairs?—Of course they stopped themselves; they knew they owed something.

5497. And were they not allowed to go in to the general meeting, or how was it?—Yes, they were taken as they came. There were, perhaps, 20.

5498. But when they were in arrear, they had to go first to this small room?—Yes, they went upstairs and waited while it was their turn to go in.

5499. Have you seen Mr. Broadhead on this matter?—No.

5500. Have you talked to Mr. Broadhead this morning?—No.

5501. Have you seen him this morning?—No, I see him now yonder.

5502. Have you spoken to him about your evidence?—No.

5503. You have had no communication with him at all?—No, I have not spoken to Mr. Broadhead three times since Christmas.

5504. Have you spoken to him this morning?—No.

5505. Have you spoken to anybody connected with the union?—Only my friend that came with me.

5506. What is his name?—Woodhead.

5507. Did he tell you what evidence had been given yesterday?—No.

5508. Will you swear that you have had no communication from the committee at all?—No, I have never been to the committee since I left them.

5509. Have you seen any member of the committee?—No, we are all out men where I work.

5510. Have you had any letters?—No.

5511. When did you receive your summons to come here?—The policeman here brought it not so long since.

5512. Have you ever had any communication with anybody upon the subject of your coming here?—No, I have been working 16 hours a day this week.

5513. But have you spoken to anybody on this subject?—Only to the policeman and that man that came into the room.

5514. Did you ever see Fearnehough go into this room?—No.

5515. Did Fearnehough attend the meetings?—Sometimes.

5516. (*Mr. Chance.*) Did you ever say that you knew how "Old Tom" could be "done"?—No.

5517. Nothing about that?—Not to my recollections.

5518. But might you have said it and forgotten it?—I might have said it when we were talking together and jesting, but not to my recollections.

5519. Are you likely to have ever said, in a jesting way, how "Old Tom" could be "done"?—Perhaps I might. There are many men that, in talking together, might say small items and forget all about it.

5520. But that is not a small matter?—No. I and Fearnehough have never had a word in our lives. I have been to their house many a time.

5521. You say you remember Fearnehough going to Butchers?—Yes.

5522. Did you say at that time that he could be got at when he was there?—No.

5523. Are you sure of that?—Yes, because I went and asked him to lend me his tools.

5524. Then, if Staniforth says that you said that you knew how "Old Tom" could be "done," he is not speaking the truth?—No.

5525. But you might have said it in jest?—Yes.

5526. Then why should you say it in jest if there

SIXTH DAY.

G. Shaw.

8 June 1867.

was no reason why you should say it; because you said just now that you did not know that "Old Tom" was in arrear?—I did not say so.

5527. But you said just now that you might have said it in jest?—It is very hard for a man to look back three years ago.

5528. But some things remain in the memory?—Not in my memory.

5529. You are on your oath, you know?—Yes.

5530. You say that you might have said it, but it was in jest?—Yes.

The witness withdrew.

Mr. A. C. Branson.

Mr. ANTHONY CLARK BRANSON sworn and examined.

5531. (*Mr. Chance.*) You are an attorney living in Sheffield, are you not?—I am.

5532. Do you know a man of the name of Henry Trippass?—Yes.

5533. And another man of the name of William Manifield?—Yes.

5534. What was Trippass?—He was, I believe, secretary to the Table-knife hafters Union.

5535. And what was William Manifield?—He was a table-knife hafter.

5536. Do you remember an information being laid against Trippass?—I do.

5537. That was under the 6th of George the 4th?—Yes.

5538. For what was that?—For intimidation; to compel Manifield to pay to the union.

5539. (*Chairman.*) Against whom was it laid?—Against Henry Trippass, by William Manfield.

5540. (*Mr. Chance.*) For intimidation, or threats?—For both.

5541. When was that?—The case was heard on the 27th of September, last year, by Mr. Dunn and Mr. Wilkinson, and a conviction took place, and Trippass was sentenced to a month's imprisonment. Mr. Whitfield, the solicitor, of Rotherham, appeared for him.

5542. Will you give us the particulars of the information, as far as you can recollect them?—Trippass called upon Manifield at his work and asked him if he intended to pay his natty, as he was in arrears for several weeks. It was on the 24th of September that he called. Manifield replied, "I do not intend to pay." Trippass then went to Frank Bartholemew who was a workman in the same shop, and asked him the same. Bartholomew replied that he was not going to pay. Trippass then said that it would be better for him to pay to the trade, or else they would soon be working at the old prices. They both replied that they had made up their minds not to pay to the trade again. Trippass said then, "Then we will make you pay, and before long," and left. On the following morning, on going to his work, Manifield found that the workshop had been broken open, and that all his work was gone.

5543. It was upon that that the information was laid?—Yes.

5544. You told us that he was convicted and sent to prison?—Yes.

5545. Do you remember on the 6th of October following Manifield calling upon you?—Yes.

5546. (*Chairman.*) Then it was Manifield against Trippass?—It was. I should say that verbal notice of appeal was given by Mr. Whitfield at the time. Sureties were named, to one of whom I objected without making inquiry about him, but ultimately the recognizances required by the statute were entered into, and an appeal was entered for the Doncaster Sessions.

5547. That was before the sessions came on?—On the same day the appeal would be entered.

5548. But on what day of the month were the Doncaster Sessions?—On Friday, the 19th of October.

5549. Therefore the 6th of October would be before the case came on?—Certainly. Manifield called at my office on the 6th.

5550. (*Mr. Chance.*) What did he say to you?—He asked me how much money I should require for carrying the case forward, they were poor men, and could not afford much. I said, "Well, you must pay "me six guineas on account before the sessions, and "if the conviction be affirmed no doubt costs will be "ordered to be paid by the defendant; if not, you "will have the difference to pay, the rest of my costs." "Well," he said, "I will gladly pay that amount; when will you want it?" and they paid the amount two or three days before the 19th.

5551. Was that all that took place on that occasion?—Upon that occasion I think it was all that took place.

5552. Did Manifield call upon you again upon the 13th of October?—On the 13th of October Manifield and his witness, Bartholemew, called upon me and asked me if he might settle the matter, as there had been an offer made by the then secretary to pay all the expenses, and something besides, if he would make it up and make an end of it.

5553. Do you know who was the secretary whom he named?—I think that he mentioned the name of James.

5554. The secretary of what union?—The then secretary of the same union. I told him that I could not give my consent, nor did I think that it would be right. Then he said, "Then we will not make it up," and left.

5555. And that was the end of the interview?—Yes.

5556. Did he call again upon you on the 15th of October?—Yes, he called again on the 15th of October with Bartholemew, and I believe Mr. James. I was then again asked.

5557. (*Chairman.*) Was that in the hearing of all?—In the hearing of all. I was asked whether Trippass and Bartholemew might make it up.

5558. Was it Manifield who asked you?—Manifield asked me, and Mr. James said so also. I said that I could not consent, and then left. On the 17th or 18th I sent a messenger to Manifield saying that I wanted to see him and his witness, and that they would have to go to Doncaster by the first train on the following Friday morning, the 19th. He disregarded my message, and I did not see him. He never came.

5559. Manifield was to go with you?—No, not with me, but I wanted to see him at my office.

5560. You wanted to see what he would say?—To go over the brief again. I sent the brief over on the Thursday night to Mr. Waddy, and on the Friday morning I went and saw the defendant and his sureties, but not my client or his witnesses. The appeal being entered, was called on. An objection was taken that notice had not been given in compliance with the practice of the quarter sessions. It was held to be a good objection, and the appeal was dismissed.

5561. The objection was taken by the respondent?—Certainly, and after argument by Mr. Hannay for the appellant and Mr. Waddy for the respondent, the court decided that the appeal could not be heard.

5562. Then the conviction was confirmed?—Certainly. At all events the appeal was dismissed. That is what we are going up to London about now. The court refused to make any order about costs.

5563. And you saw nothing of the respondent upon that occasion?—No.

5564. (*Mr. Chance.*) Did anything take place between that time and the 24th of December?—I sent my bill to them.

5565. You sent in your bill to Manifield?—Yes.

5566. (*Chairman.*) How much was it?—The balance was 14*l*.

SIXTH DAY.

Mr. A. C. Branson.

8 June 1867

5567. The balance after they had paid the six guineas ?—Yes.

5568. It was not paid I suppose ?—No. On the 24th of December James, the present secretary, called upon me and said, "You have sent your bill in to Manifield." I said, "Yes I have." He said, "If you will send it in to Bartholemew it will be paid." I said that I did not understand him, that Bartholemew was no client of mine, he was only a witness. He said, "Well, but the indictment says, that it is for using threats to Manifield and others." I said that I could not take any notice of that, and that I should not send it to Bartholemew, and he left. Before he left he said, "I suppose you know he has got the money."

5569. Who did he say had got the money ?—Manifield.

5570. (*Mr. Chance.*) Who said that ?—James said that.

5571. What did you say ?—I said that I did not know that, I had some idea.

5572. What did he say ?—He left then.

5573. Did anything further take place upon it? No, nothing of importance.

5574. (*Chairman.*) You have not been paid ?—No.

5575. Have you applied to Manifield for it ?—I think once my clerk went, but he said that he could not pay that amount, that was the reply.

5576. As I understand Trippass was never sent to prison ?—No.

5577. How was it that if the conviction was affirmed he did not go to prison ?—I think that you had better not inquire into that point. We are going to move the Court of Queen's Bench to compel the magistrates to issue a warrant of committal.

5578. There is a point reserved is there ?—None at all, not the slightest.

5579. Are you going to London about it to-morrow ? —No, I am not going to London to-morrow about it.

5580. Is the case left undecided in any way ?—Not the slightest, I have applied for a warrant of committal. The magistrates' clerk thinks that the magistrates have not the power, but I am advised that they have the power, and I am going to apply for a mandamus to the magistrates to issue a warrant.

5581. But for whom could you appear ?—I appear for Manifield.

5582. Have you his authority for going on ?—I have not seen him.

5583. But do you think that you are right ?—I think that I am right, I am advised that I am.

5584. You are going to apply for a mandamus ? —Yes.

5585. You do not act upon the instruction of Manifield ?—No.

5586. Then upon what motion do you take it, as representing the public ?—Certainly, to carry out the magistrate's decision.

5587. Are you instructed by any manufacturer or association of manufacturers ?—I decline answering the question.

5588. I beg your pardon, you must answer all questions. Are you instructed by any manufacturers ? —You will take my objection if you please ?

5589. Nobody can object to any question here, I will grant you a certificate if you want a certificate ? —I think that as a professional man I am not compelled to answer.

5590. I cannot admit that objection, we are not allowed to receive any objections to questions ?—Of course I cannot argue with you.

5591. You know that the Act of Parliament is a very peculiar one ?—I know it is, I have seen it and I am protected I know.

5592. Are you instructed by any person to proceed with this matter ?—By no client.

5593. But are you instructed by any person ?—I cannot call it instruction, I am pressed to do it, I am pressed by some of the public, and I should not like to disclose my clients' names ; I have been pressed by one of the magistrates who sat and heard the appeal, over and over again.

5594. Who is the magistrate ?—Mr. Rodgers.

5595. But at whose instance are you going up to London to apply for a mandamus ?—It is of my own motion, pressed as I am by Mr. Rodgers, and being told by him that one of the convicting justices thinks that there has been an obstruction to justice and a failure of it.

5596. But is it only upon that suggestion that you are going ?—That is all.

5597. You say that you were pressed by some of the public ; how do you mean that you are pressed by some of the public ?—I am asked why I do not proceed with it.

5598. I put it to you because I have no doubt that it is suggested on the other side that it may be an association of masters, and we are bound to ask that question. Is it an association of masters who are pressing you to proceed in this matter ?—None whatever. I do not consider the matter completed until I have exhausted all.

5599. Is there any union at all of any sort which is urging you to do this ?—None whatever. They never alluded to it. I may say that I do not conceive that I have completed my business until I have exhausted the matter.

5600. We are bound to inquire whether there is any association ?—Not the slightest.

5601. The men may say that there is tyranny towards them, and therefore I put the question to you whether there is any association of masters which is setting you in motion ?—Neither an association of masters nor a master.

The witness withdrew.

William Woodhead sworn and examined.

W. Woodhead.

5602. (*Mr. Barstow.*) What are you ?—A saw grinder.

5603. Are you a member of the saw grinders union? —Yes.

5604. Were you so in May 1865 ?—Yes.

5605. All that time I believe you were in the employment of Mr. Hague ?—Never.

5606. Were you never in the employment of Mr. Hague ?—Never ; I have helped in stones and glazed a few saws, but I have never been in his employment.

5607. Were you at Mr. Hague's works at that time ?—Yes, but never employed by him.

5608. Who did employ you then ?—Fearnehough.

5609. And you were working in Mr. Hague's works employed by Fearnehough ?—Yes.

5610. Did you say anything to Mr. Hague to the effect that they might expect to be rattened ?—No, never.

5611. Nor to anyone ?—To Fearnehough ; if I did once make the suggestion it was one night between five and six o'clock. I called in at the place, Hague and Clegg's works, and he was standing at the wheel door, and we sat in a wheelbarrow, and a boy, one of his sons, was rolling a band. I said, "You are rolling them up, are you frightened of anyone else rolling them up ? " and I believe the very night I made the suggestion they happened to go, but I never knew, it was a mere suggestion thrown out.

5612. You did not mean to throw out notice that he might expect to be rattened ?—No, it was thrown out as a mere suggestion as we sat in the barrow together.

5613. What made you throw out that suggestion ? —It was seeing the boy rolling it up.

5614. Would it be a common thing that the boy should roll up the band ?—No, it is a very uncommon thing.

5615. What was he rolling it up for ?—I do not know.

SIXTH DAY.

W. Woodhead.

8 June 1867.

5616. Why did you say it then?—It was just a mere suggestion as I sat.

5617. What made you suggest it?—Seeing the boy rolling it up.

5618. I ask you again, what was the boy rolling it up for?—I do not know.

5619. What put it into your head to say anything to him?—It was just seeing him.

5620. That is all the answer you can give us?—Yes, I know no more.

5621. Seeing him roll up the band did you say, "What, do you expect to be rattened"?—No. I never did say so. I said, "Well," in this way, "You are saving somebody else the trouble," or something like that.

5622. Did you tell Mr. Hague anything?—Never.

5623. Did you not speak to Fearnehough himself? —Yes, we were sitting together.

5624. What did you say to him?—I said what I have just repeated, no more nor less.

5625. Did you not tell him he had better look out? —Never.

5626. Did you not use those words, "You had "better look out, you have not a minute to call your "own"?—Never.

5627. Will you swear you never used those words? —Yes, I will swear it.

5628. Who were there when you said this?—No one, only myself and Fearnehough, and his son. His son was working. We were sitting together in the barrow as I represented before.

5629. Do you know whether that night the place was entered?—Yes, I went the next morning.

5630. Do you know what was done?—When I got there I saw Mr. Clegg, and he told me the premises had been opened by a party, and asked me if I knew anything about it, and I said I did not.

5631. Did you know at this time that Fearnehough was in arrear?—No.

5632. Did you know that he was in any difficulty with the union?—No.

5633. You were a member of the same union were you not?—Yes.

5634. Do you now know for a fact that he was at that time in difficulties with the union?—Now I know that he was, but I did not know then.

5635. (*Chairman.*) Can you wish to make us believe that it was not a well known thing in the whole town, that Fearnehough was an object of very great dislike by the union at that time, and that all the union was complaining of his conduct?—No. I cannot say.

5636. You can say, and you know quite well, and it was a well known fact in the town that Fearnehough at that time was causing great dissatisfaction to the union?—I do not know it.

5637. (*Mr. Barstow.*) Do you mean to say that you never heard anyone complain of Fearnehough's conduct at that time?—No; of course we have happened to speak, being together, a few words as friends. We have met when I was just working a little, and said, "Well, Fearnehough," and so on.

5638. What did they say about Fearnehough being so and so?—They said about his being in arrear.

5639. Then did you know that he was in arrear?—Not till the time I was working with him.

5640. Do you mean to say you did not know he was in arrear while you were working with him?—Not while I was working with him.

5641. You never heard anyone say that he was in arrear during the time you were working with him? —Never.

5642. Nor before that time?—Never.

5643. Did you never hear anybody say he was a damned thief?—Never.

5644. You never heard expressions of abuse used towards him?—Never.

5645. Did nobody ever say to you, "Why do you work with Fearnehough?"—Never.

5646. Did no one ever endeavour to induce you to leave his employ?—I was discharged from the premises.

5647. Who discharged you?—Clegg.

5648. What for?—When the window was broken open and the glazer cut, something of that kind.

5649. Why should Clegg discharge you for that?—He had a little suspicion on me, and thought I was the man, I suppose that did it.

5650. When Mr. Clegg dismissed you from the premises, did he not tell you that you had mentioned the night before that the premises would be entered? —I and Thomas.

5651. Answer the question?—It was a suggestion thrown out.

5652. Answer that question; when Mr. Clegg dismissed you, did he tell you that you had mentioned the evening before that his premises would be entered? —Yes, he told me so.

5653. What did you say to that?—I told him that I did not say so. It was only a mere suggestion.

5654. What did he say to you when you said that it was only a mere suggestion?—He said, I must know something about it by suggesting such a thing, or something like that. I cannot say exactly the words.

5655. What did you say?—I told him I did not know anything about it.

5656. However, he dismissed you for it?—I was discharged from going in the yard, and I never went into it afterwards.

5657. On your oath, had you received any information from anyone that the premises would be entered? —No.

5658. How come you to make the suggestion?—I naturally made it, seeing the boy wrap the bands up.

5659. You guessed that the premises would be entered, and they were entered?—They were entered the same night that I made the suggestion.

5660. (*Chairman.*) Do you mean to tell us, on your oath, that you threw that matter out hap-hazard, and that it took place without your having some knowledge of it?—I do, and I knew nothing about it.

5661. Had not somebody given you notice that probably they would be rattened that night?—Never.

5662. (*Mr. Barstow.*) Do you mean to say that at that time you did not know that Fearnehough was in a difficulty with the union?—Not at that time.

5663. How soon afterwards did you know it?—Some three months perhaps.

5664. Do not you know that it was a matter of common talk among the members of the union that Fearnehough was misbehaving towards it?—No. I never went into company much, and I never heard much about it.

5665. Did you usually attend the meetings of the union?—Not always.

5666. You were fined if you did not?—Yes.

5667. I suppose you generally attended?—In a general way I did.

5668. Did you hear Fearnehough's name read out? —I have heard his name called out the same as we all were.

5669. Did you ever hear that he was a defaulter? —Not in the meeting.

5670. When were you summoned to come here?—I had a summons yesterday.

5671. Who came with you here this morning?—I came by myself this morning.

5672. (*Chairman.*) You came by yourself this morning, did you?—Yes. I came up the road, and I turned down here. I came with Broadhead this morning. I was at his house, and came along with him.

5673. You came by yourself this morning with Broadhead?—I was not thinking nothing about that.

5674. Was Broadhead the only person with you?—Yes.

5675. Nobody else?—No.

5676. Was George Shaw in your company?—I saw him once this morning.

SIXTH DAY.

W. Woodhead.

8 June 1867.

5677. Did Shaw come along with you ?—No, he left me at Broadhead's.

5678. Then he went with you to Broadhead's ?—No, I went by myself; he was there when I went in.

5679. Shaw was at Broadhead's ?—Yes.

5680. Where did you see Shaw ?—At Broadhead's.

5681. Where was he ? in what part of the house ?—He was in the tap-room.

5682. Where was Broadhead ?—He was in with him.

5683. Who was with Shaw when you saw him at Broadhead's ?—No one, only Broadhead himself.

5684. Was any policeman there ?—No.

5685. Why did you go to Broadhead's ?—I went to see whether he knew anything about this affair that I had come here for.

5686. Have you talked the matter over with Broadhead ?—Yes. I talked of it at a time before.

5687. Have you talked the matter over with Shaw?—Never with Shaw.

5688. Where did you first meet with Shaw ?—At Broadhead's.

5689. And how long did you remain in his company?—Perhaps five minutes, something like that.

The witness withdrew.

George Shaw, recalled and further examined.

G. Shaw.

5690. (*Chairman.*) I understood you to say that you were at work very early this morning ?—Yes.

5691. And that you never heard of what you were coming for till the policeman came for you ?—Yes.

5692. And that you came on with the policeman here, and that that was all you knew about the matter ?—Yes.

5693. And you never saw Broadhead at all ?—I saw him in here.

5694. You never saw him till then ?—Yes, I did.

5695. You have told us that you came with the policeman from your work to this Court ?—No, I did not.

5696. I beg your pardon, you did, you told us that you had never seen Broadhead ?—I left the policeman, I was above 20 minutes away from the policeman.

5697. You never told us about that, you said you came on with the policeman, and that you had not seen Broadhead or talked to him about this matter, is that true or is it false ?—I told him I knew nothing what I was fetched up for.

5698. Is it true that you have seen Broadhead this morning ?—Yes.

5699. Why did not you tell me that when you were here before ?—I did not know that you asked me that.

5700. Yes, I did, why did you say before that you came on direct with the policeman ?—I did not say that.

5701. Is it true that you came on with the policeman ?—No.

5702. Is it true that you went to Broadhead ?—Yes.

5703. What did you go to Broadhead for ?—I asked him what they had sent me a note like this for. I could not read, and I asked him to read it.

5704. You talked the matter over with him ?—No ; he read me what there was in it. He told me there was something in the paper about me.

5705. I asked you if you had seen Broadhead about this business, and you said, No, you had not, you had only seen him three times since Christmas. What do you mean by telling me that, if you went to consult him about this business ?—I went to ask him about it.

5706. I want to know how you dare tell me this morning that you had never spoken to Broadhead and had only seen him three times since Christmas ?—I had not.

5707. Why did you say that you had never consulted him about the matter when you went to ask him about the summons that you received ? how do you explain that ?—I do not remember your asking me that.

5708. Then you did go to consult him this morning ?—I asked him what it was.

5709. Are you in work ?—Yes.

5710. What do you work at ?—I am a saw grinder.

5711. Whom do you work for ?—Mr. Peace.

5712. How long have you worked for him ?—Since a month after Christmas.

5713. And you say that you have never seen Broadhead except three times since ?—That is all.

5714. Since when ?—Since Christmas. (*The following passages from the witness' previous evidence were read.*) " Q. Have you talked to Mr. Broadhead " this morning ?—*A.* No. *Q.* Have you seen him " this morning ?—*A.* No ; I see him now yonder. " *Q.* Have you spoken to him about your evidence? " —*A.* No. *Q.* You have had no communication " with him at all ?—*A.* No, I have not spoken to Mr. " Broadhead three times since Christmas. *Q.* Have " you spoken to him this morning ?—*A.* No. *Q.* Have " you spoken to anybody connected with the union ?— " *A.* Only my friend that came with me. *Q.* What " is his name ?—*A.* Woodhead. *Q.* Did he tell you " what evidence had been given yesterday ?—*A.* No. " *Q.* Will you swear that you have had no communi- " cation from the committee at all ?—*A.* No. I have " never been to the committee since I left them. *Q.* " Have you seen any member of the committee ?— " *A.* No, we are all out-men where I work. *Q.* Have " you had any letter ?—*A.* No. *Q.* When did you " receive your summons to come here ?—*A.* The po- " liceman here brought it not so long since. *Q.* Have " you ever had any communication with anybody upon " the subject of your coming here ?—*A.* No. I have " been working 16 hours a day this week. *Q.* But " have you spoken to anybody on this subject ?—*A.* " Only to the policeman and that man that came into " the room."

5715. (*Chairman.*) You told me that you had not seen Mr. Broadhead this morning ?—I said I had seen him.

5716. You did not; here are the words as they are taken down; how dare you come here and tell me that ? Mr. Chance has a note of it, and we have sent for the shorthand writer's notes, which confirm him. Do you know what you are liable to be done with for this ?—No.

5717. I will not tell you what I will do with you ; it is a very serious case. You have committed as gross perjury this morning as a man could do. It makes one think that you are guilty of things a great deal worse. I am much surprised that Mr. Broadhead should be in the room without getting up and contradicting you.

(*Mr. Broadhead.*) I was not to speak till called for. You will find explanations in that book that I have placed in your hands.

5718. (*Chairman to Mr. Broadhead.*) You let the witness make that statement and you did not contradict him.

(*Mr. Sugg.*) Mr. Broadhead told me this morning that the man had been to him.

5719. (*Chairman to the witness.*) We will consult together as to what we shall do with you.

Adjourned to Thursday next, at 11 o'clock.

SEVENTH DAY.

Thursday, 13th June 1867.

PRESENT:

WILLIAM OVEREND, Esq., Q.C.
THOMAS IRWIN BARSTOW, Esq.
GEORGE CHANCE, Esq.
J. E. BARKER, Esq., Secretary.

WILLIAM OVEREND, Esq., Q.C., in the Chair.

GEORGE SHAW re-called and further examined.

SEVENTH DAY.

G. Shaw.

13 June 1867.

5720. (*Chairman.*) I have mentioned the circumstances of your very gross perjury to the authorities in London, and I have consulted with my colleagues here, under the advice of gentlemen in London, as to what course is to be pursued with you. We have made up our minds as to what that course shall be, and if it should be one which is very serious indeed to you, you can have no ground whatever of complaint, because, before you gave your evidence when we last met, you were told distinctly that if you made a full and candid disclosure of all the circumstances within your knowledge you would be entitled to have a certificate which would free you from any kind of penalty, either civil or criminal; and, notwithstanding that you committed as gross perjury as I ever heard committed upon any inquiry in my life; now, that is a most serious offence; I told you that I did not know what course I should pursue then. We none of us could make up our minds what was our duty, but we have made up our minds now, and we think it our duty, serious as the consequences would be to you, at all events to give you another chance before doing anything at all or taking any steps in the matter. We are prepared to give you a chance, and if you like to come now and reveal all that you know, either on that matter or any other matter which is within your knowledge, it is the only means that you have of saving yourself from the consequences to which you are liable. How old are you?—I think that I am either 28 or 29 next birthday.

5721. Were you apprenticed? did you enter the trade of a saw grinder as an apprentice?—I entered the trade when I was taken in as a man; when I was 29 years of age.

5722. You never were apprenticed then?—Yes, I was apprenticed to James Linley, but we were outlaws, and I joined the trade when I was 20.

5723. Who was James Linley?—He was a saw grinder.

5724. Was he the same man who was afterwards shot?—Yes.

5725. Do you know when he was shot?—I can scarcely think how long it is.

5726. But about when was it?—Just a few months before we went into the trade.

5727. Can you not give me some notion of when it was that you went into the trade? how many years have you been in the Union?—Rather better than eight years I think it is, as nearly as I can recollect.

5728. It is about eight years ago then?—Yes.

5729. You say that you were an outlaw?—Yes.

5730. And he was an outlaw?—Yes.

5731. What do you mean by being an outlaw?—He was not in the Union.

5732. But what do you mean by not being in the Union. I am not in the Union, but I am not an outlaw?—He did not pay to the trade.

5733. Did he refuse to pay?—Yes, he did not pay. He had seven or eight of us apprentices.

5734. And you paid nothing to the trade as an apprentice?—No.

5735. Then seven or eight years ago you became a member of the Saw Grinder's Union?—Yes; when I was 20 years of age.

5736. Who was secretary at that time?—Mr. Broadhead.

5737. Do you know whether Linley became a member of the trade or not?—Yes.

5738. At the same time?—Yes.

5739. Anybody else?—Yes; there was a man at the time joined, Fearnehough and many others.

5740. Can you mention the names of the persons who joined with you?—Well, there was Joseph Copley, Dennis Clarke, Matthew Woollen, William Wood, and Thomas Fearnehough.

5741. Are there two Fearnehoughs, Thomas and William?—Yes; his son William and all joined. There was Henry Garfitt and Henry Bradshaw.

5742. And some others?—Yes; there was a many joined at the same time.

5743. What was Dennis Clarke; for whom did he work?—He was apprenticed with Linley.

5744. And did he work for Linley after he joined the Union?—No.

5745. Whom did he work for?—I think his first situation was with Mr. Taylor.

5746. Who is Mr. Taylor?—Mr. Taylor, Adelaide Works, Harvest Lane.

5747. Did you work for Linley?—No; no one worked for him after he joined the trade.

5748. For whom did you work?—I worked for Mr. Marshall after he went into the trade.

5749. What Marshall was that?—He is a bankrupt now; his place was formerly at the top of Cornhill.

5750. Did you go to the meetings of the Society?—Yes.

5751. Did you see Mr. Broadhead there?—Yes.

5752. Has he any particular name by which he is known?—Yes; "Smite 'em."

5753. What does that mean?—I do not know; that is his bye-name.

5754. Do you know what "Smite 'em" means at all?—No, I do not.

5755. Had you ever any occasion to speak to him or in company with anyone else about any matters at all?—Yes; I went to him a few weeks back about a matter.

5756. But shortly after, taking things in the order of time, what had you to do with Broadhead first?—I was once in his house, one night, and Clarke came to me and and asked me if I would do a job.

5757. You say that was about a fortnight after you had been in the Union?—Yes; Clarke asked me if we would blow "Old Topsey" up.

5758. What did you say to that?—I said, "Yes."

5759. Who is "Topsey"?—A man named Helliwell.

5760. Where did he work?—At the Tower Wheel.

5761. Did you know anything about Helliwell?—He was not in the Union.

5762. Did Clarke suggest to you why you should go and blow up Halliwell?—Yes; he said that we could have 3*l.* for it. He brought three cans of gunpowder.

5763. Where was that?—At Broadhead's house.

5764. Where did he get it?—He went upstairs to see "Old Smite 'em." We took the powder.

5765. Did he come down again?—Yes; with the powder.

SEVENTH DAY.

C. Shaw.

13 June 1867.

5766. In how long a time ?—Perhaps five minutes.

5767. With what did he come down ?—With three kegs of powder. I took this powder to my mother's.

5768. Then he gave the powder to you ?—Yes; I put it under my slop. I took it upstairs and put it between the bed and the matrass.

5769. Up stairs at your mother's house ?—Yes.

5770. All the three kegs ?—Yes.

5771. In whose bed did you place it ?—My bed; we did not use them all; we put smithy-slack in instead of powder.

5772. What became of those three cans ?—I sold two and a half of them to a man named Simmonite.

5773. Who is Simmonite ?—He is a man who goes shooting at pigeons when they escape at Hyde Park.

5774. Where does he live ?—Cricket Road.

5775. How long had you had the powder before you sold it to Simmonite ?—Perhaps two days.

5776. Were you alone when you sold it, or was anybody with you ?—Clark was with me.

5777. Where did you sell it ?—In Simmonite's open yard against his shop.

5778. What did he give you for it ?—I can hardly scarcely recollect what it is; we spent it in ale and "pig-hock."

5779. Where did you get your ale ?—At the "Green Man" at the bottom of Westbar.

5780. Who keeps the "Green Man" ?—Mr. Humphrey keeps it now.

5781. Who kept it then ?—Mr. Bradley or Bramley, I think that is his name.

5782. Did you get several shillings for this powder ?—Yes.

5783. How long did you stay at the "Green Man" drinking this beer ?—We did not stop there long.

5784. Was there anybody in the house when you were at the "Green Man" ?—No, it was on the Friday when Clarke and me was in.

5785. Did you know Bradley ?—Yes.

5786. Did he know you ?—No, he knew my father, and that was how I knew him.

5787. Did he know Clarke ?—Not to my knowledge.

5788. Was there anybody in the house who knew any of you ?—No, not that I am aware of.

5789. Who served you with ale ?—A woman.

5790. Do you know her name ?—No.

5791. Is Bradley alive now ?—Yes.

5792. Where does he live ?—I do not know.

5793. Have you ever seen him since ?—Yes.

5794. When did you see him ?—I have seen him many times.

5795. Have you ever spoken to him since ?—No.

5796. You say you had spent part of it at the "Green Man" ?—Yes.

5797. What time of the day was it that you were at Simmonite's ?—In the afternoon.

5798. About what time was it that you got to the "Green Man" ?—It was in the middle of the afternoon sometime.

5799. After this where did you go to ?—I think we went to the next place, the "Corner Pin."

5800. How long did you stay there ?—Well, I can scarcely recollect.

5801. But up to about what time ?—I cannot tell.

5802. What did you do there ?—We had some ale.

5803. Who was there ?—There was the place full.

5804. And did you and Clarke go together ?—Yes.

5805. Were there any persons there whom you knew ?—Yes, there were Birmingham people; I only knew them by sight.

5806. What were Birmingham people doing there then ?—It is a noted house for the Birmingham people.

5807. But was there anybody there that night whom you knew ?—Yes.

5808. Who was that ?—I knew these Birmingham people well by sight.

5809. Was there any person who knew you ?—Yes, by sight they knew me.

5810. Who was there that knew you ?—I do not know their names.

5811. Did the landlord know you ?—No.

5812. Be accurate about this; was there nobody there that knew you ?—We used to go there very often when we were working as apprentices.

5813. Then if you went there often they would know you ?—They would know us to speak to.

5814. Now do not be inaccurate; was there anybody there that night that knew you ?—Mr. Rose that kept it knew us both well.

5815. Is Mr. Rose alive ?—No, I think he is dead now.

5816. Did you see his wife ?—No.

5817. Nor any maid or young woman who served you ?—No.

5818. And up to what time did you stay at the "Corner Pin" ?—I think we got drunk there.

5819. And after you had got drunk what became of you ?—I went home.

5820. Had you a father at home, or a mother, or whom ?—My father has been dead 17 years.

5821. Then you live with your mother ?—Yes.

5822. Was she the only person who lived in the house ?—My sister.

5823. Is your mother alive ?—Yes.

5824. Is your sister alive ?—Yes.

5825. Where is your mother ?—She is in the adjoining room.

5826. Your mother is here, is she ?—Yes.

5827. Where is your sister ?—She is working.

5828. Where ?—I am sure I do not know where the place is; she is working at a place at this end of the town.

5829. Is she a married woman ?—No.

5830. Does she live with your mother still ?—Yes.

5831. You went home drunk you say ?—Yes.

5832. Then you had sold two and a half cans of powder ?—Yes.

5833. And you had half a can left ?—Yes; we put it into the trough then.

5834. Was the powder sold to Simmonite in the can or sold loose ? how did you sell it ?—We sold him some in a paper and some in two cans.

5835. And what did you do with the remainder of the powder ?—We put it in Helliwell's trough, it and the smithy slack.

5836. You are speaking of Friday ?—Yes, that was on Friday morning.

5837. The remainder you say you put in Halliwell's trough ?—Yes, on Friday morning, and then we sold the remainder afterwards.

5838. You had already put half a can of powder in Helliwell's trough ? How did you put it into his trough ?—I spread it about.

5839. Did you put it in loose ?—Yes.

5840. Did you put it in yourself ?—Yes; Clarke stood beside me.

5841. But a person going into a trough would see at once whether there was powder there or not. How did you disguise it ?—We threw it in as it was, amongst the emery.

5842. Was it in such a state that a person going in would notice it, or would the emery conceal it ?—No, there would not be as much as would be seen amongst the emery.

5843. Then you mean to say you put it on the bottom of the place where the man worked, and he stood upon the horsing above ?—When he glazed he stood at the side.

5844. Did he stand with his feet on the place where you put the powder ?—The powder was in front of him in the trough, and when you are glazing it scatters sparks, and they make a bit of a fuzz like about.

SEVENTH DAY.

G. Shaw.

13 June 1867.

5845. And these sparks in the course of work would fall upon the spot where you placed the powder ?—Yes.

5846. Now, what time in the morning was this ?—A little before noon. The wheel was down. It started on Saturday morning, the day following.

5847. At this time the wheel was lame ?—Yes.

5848. Was there anybody in the wheel at the time ?—No, not that I saw. There were men jobbing about the wheel, but I took no notice of them.

5849. Did anybody that you are aware of see you in company with Clarke the morning that you put that powder down ?—There might be some.

5850. Do you recollect noticing anybody particularly ?—Not particularly.

5851. Is there anybody that you saw in the course of that day that you recollect who can speak to seeing you in the company of Clarke ?—Yes, there is one man, named Yellatt, that saw me; a grinder, named Yellatt.

5852. What is his name ?—Joey Yellatt.

5853. Is that the only person ?—There was another man and him together—George Allen—he might take notice of me.

5854. Did not a person of the name of Copley see you together ?—There would be a lot knocking about there, holing stones, and such as that.

5855. Were you not seen in company with this man Clarke when you saw Copley ?—Perhaps he might be there, but not to my knowledge.

5856. Do you know Copley ?—Yes, we were apprenticed together.

5857. Do you know where Copley was working ?—He used to work for Mr. Wilson, but he was not working at all then.

5858. Do you recollect having met him on that day when you were in company with Clark ?—Not to my knowledge.

5859. How long did it take you to put this powder down ?—Two or three seconds. I threw it in, that was all.

5860. And then you left it ?—Yes.

5861. And you came away from the wheel ?—Yes.

5862. And afterwards went to the public house, to Simmonite's ?—We went to our house first, and then to Simmonite's.

5863. Did you notice whether Clarke had any powder before he went up stairs ?—No.

5864. And you saw it in his hand when he came down ?—No; I was not up stairs.

5865. He told you when he came down stairs from whom he had got the powder ?—Yes, "Old Smite 'em."

5866. Immediately he came down he told you that "Smite' em" had given it to him; did he ?—Yes.

5867. Did anybody ever see you in possession of that powder from the time you got up to the "Green Man" to the time you sold it to Simmonite ?—My mother found it under the bed.

5868. Had you any conversation with her in reference to this powder ?—She asked me what I was going to do with it, and I said I should harm nobody with it.

5869. And when was that ?—That was when it had been up stairs about a day; she found it when she was making the bed.

5870. How long was the time between your getting it at the "Green Man" and your selling it to Simmonite ?—We did not get it at the "Green Man," we got it at the "Greyhound Dog," Shales Moor.

5871. Where is that ?—On Gibraltar.

5872. He does not live there now, I believe ?—No.

5873. But he lived there then ?—Yes.

5874. When did you get it at the "Greyhound Dog ?"—We got it on the Wednesday.

5875. When was it that you sold it ?—We sold it on Friday afternoon ?

5876. What became of it after your mother had shewn you this ? Where were you when she showed it to you ?—She did not shew it me; she asked me what it was and I told her; I told her it was powder.

5877. Did your mother tell you who had given it to you ?—I said that it had come from "Old Smite 'em's."

5878. Had you said anything about what you were to do with it ?—I told her I should do no one any harm with it.

2879. But did you tell her for what purpose you had got it from Smite 'em's ?—No.

5880. Did you say anything about any money for it ?—No; I said we had got three "quid."

5881. But at the time that your mother asked you about the powder you told her that it had come from "old Smite 'em" ?—Yes.

5882. Did you tell her anything about any directions that "Smite 'em" had given you at all ?—No; I said that we should not harm anybody with it.

5883. Has Clarke any bye-name ?—We call him "Tucker."

5884. Denis Clarke goes by the name of "Tucker" does he ?—Yes.

5885. Then we take it that according to your story you left the powder in the trough ?—Yes.

5886. What happened next ?—It exploded the next morning, towards dinner time I think it was.

5887. On the Saturday ?—Yes.

5888. Was any damage done to Helliwell ?—It just made him a black colour, that was all; it frightened him.

5889. Do you know whether he was blind in consequence for some time ?—No, I do not.

5890. Do you know how long he was kept from his work by it ?—Well, I have heard say two or three weeks.

5891. Now, after it had exploded as you say in this way, did you see Clarke at all ?—Yes.

5892. When did you see him after the explosion ?—I saw him when he was drawing his scale on Saturday.

5893. That would be the same day then ?—Yes.

5894. When he was drawing his scale where ?—At Mr. Broadhead's.

5895. (*To Mr. Broadhead.*) Have you the book containing the money payments to your members ?—The scale ?

5896. Yes ?—For what year ?

5897. For the year 1859 ?—I do not think we have that.

5898. Why not ?—It is so many years since, and we do not keep books to that time. I think we have not that book.

5899. Will you be kind enough to search for it ?—I will look over again, but I think that we have not it.

5900. Can you tell me for how far back you can furnish me with the scale books ?—We have some books that go back for 14 or 15 years; that is, such as "bill books," but it is the same book that we have had in use ever since then. It is not full then, and we have other books varying from periods of time also.

5901. Do you mind sending for your books this morning ?—No.

5902. I wish you would be kind enough to send for your books this morning.

Mr. Sugg submitted that as these were charges brought against Mr. Broadhead, it was fair that he should hear all that was said against him, and promised that the books should be produced at the proper time.

The Chairman stated that the Commissioners were the best judges of what was the proper time, and insisted upon the books being produced at once.

A policeman was accordingly sent with Mr. Broadhead's messenger to bring all the books connected with the Union.

5903. (*Chairman to the witness.*) Do you recollect the month when you joined the Union ?—No.

SEVENTH DAY.

G. Shaw.

13 June 1867.

5904. Nor the year?—No.

5905. You saw Clarke, you say, on the same day when he was drawing his scale at Broadhead's?—Yes.

5906. Did anything pass with reference to Helliwell between you on that occasion?—Yes; he said we should get paid in the middle of the next week.

5907. Did you see him after that?—I saw him when we went to get paid.

5908. When was that?—In the middle of the week following. I was in the "Clock" public-house waiting for him to come out of the "Dog." I asked him if he had got it. He said that he had got three quid.

5909. That is three sovereigns, I suppose?—Yes, "three quid" he said. I got 30*s*. of it.

5910. During this time had you any conversation at all with Broadhead, or did you see Broadhead on the matter?—No.

5911. You never saw Broadhead?—No.

5912. And all the reason why you had a notion that it came from Broadhead was the statement of Clarke?—Yes.

5913. But you went to his house, and Clarke went in and came out with 3*l*. and gave you 30*s*.?—Yes.

5914. And did he say from whom he had got it?—"Old Smite 'em."

5915. Did you go with him to fetch it?—No; I went into the "Clock" while he came to me.

5916. But did he leave you at the "Clock"?—Yes.

5917. And he went to Broadhead's, as you say, and came back again and said "Old Smite 'em" had given him three "quid"?—Yes.

5918. Did you see him go, or did you not?—I stopped in the dram shop while he came back.

5919. Then you did not see whether he went there or not?—No.

5920. Have you ever talked to Broadhead about this matter?—Well, I was in a public-house about eight weeks since, as near as is in my recollection, the "King William"——

5921. Where is the "King William" public-house?—In Spring-street, I think it is. Clarke was there boasting about what we did.

5922. To whom did he boast?—The whole company.

5923. Who was the company?—There was a many men in, saw grinders;

5924. Who were they?—One Crapper was there.

5925. What is his Christian name?—Jonathan Crapper.

5926. Who besides?—One Woodhead was there.

5927. What is his name?—John Woodhead.

5928. Who besides?—There was the room full.

5929. But mention any names to us that you recollect. It does not convey any notion to us by merely saying "a room full."—There was a many others besides, but I do not know their names.

5930. Can you mention none others besides Crapper and Woodhead?—Yes; I think there was one James Hallam there.

5931. What did Clarke say?—He said if I would give the word he could lag "Old Smite 'em."

5932. What does "lagging" mean?—Transporting.

5933. He said that if you gave the word he could "lag," "Old Smite 'em"?—Yes.

5934. What passed besides?—I told him I thought he had better mind his own business. This was on Thursday, and I went up to Mr. Broadhead's on the Saturday night.

5935. What did the company say when he said that if you gave the word he could "lag" "Old Smite 'em"?—I came away disgusted. I left him.

5936. Did they say anything at all when he said that he could "lag" "Old Smite 'em"? Did they say nothing?—No.

5937. Did the company say nothing?—No.

5938. Did you say nothing more than that?—I came away. We had got agate a-fighting.

5939. But if you had nearly got agate fighting something must have passed. What did you say?—He was going to thrash the man that worked with me, Woodhead.

5940. What was he going to thrash Woodhead for?—Woodhead told him to mind his own business.

5941. When was it that he told him to mind his own business?—That very time.

5942. But was it after he had said that he could "lag" "Old Smite 'em"?—Yes, when we were rowing.

5943. What took place at the row?—It was over this talking and boasting.

5944. What did he say?—He said he could lag "Old Smite 'em" if I gave the word.

5945. What besides?—I told him to shut up.

5946. And what besides?—Then he and Woodhead began falling out.

5947. What did they say?—I did not scarcely take any notice what they were saying.

5948. But was anything more said about "Old "Smite 'em"?—No.

5949. Nothing more?—No.

5950. Are you quite sure that nothing was said more than this—that if you gave the word he could "lag Old Smite 'em"?—Yes.

5951. And you said, "Oh! Slinkeys"?—Yes; I went and communicated to Mr. Broadhead on the Saturday night what he had said.

5952. You are quite sure then that Crapper heard this?—Yes.

5953. And Woodhead heard this?—Yes.

5254. And Hallam heard it?—Yes.

5955. What did Broadhead say to you?—He said I had done perfectly right in telling him.

5956. Where was it that you told Broadhead?—At his house door.

5957. On Saturday?—On Saturday night.

5958. At what time?—Betwixt eight and nine o'clock.

5959. Did anybody see you there?—Yes, Joseph Copley saw me there. He was standing by the side making mortar.

5960. Now, at that time were you receiving scale?—No; I was outlawing at that time.

5961. Then you had no business there?—No.

5962. And you say Copley saw you?—Yes, I had a pint of beer with him in the dram shop.

5963. Did Copley see you talk to Broadhead?—Yes.

5964. So he told you that you had done perfectly right?—Yes.

5965. Did anything else pass between you and him?—Between me and Broadhead?

5966. Yes?—Well, I saw him on Green Lane a week last Thursday.

5967. Where is Green Lane?—It is against the Ebenezer Chapel.

5968. In the open street?—Yes.

5969. (*To Mr. Broadhead.*) Are those your books (*referring to some books which had been brought in*)?—Part of them are.

5970. Can you find us the scale book for 1858 or 1859?—We have not it.

4971. Have you looked for it?—These are all I can find, the scale book going back to May the 28th 1864. I do not find any more, but I will look again.

4972. I have no hostile feeling to you, it is simply in the discharge of my duty to do it, but your greatest protection would have been to produce this book to prove that this man is telling falsehoods?—I have not been able to find it at the present time, but I have sought everywhere for it.

4973. (*To the Witness.*) You saw Broadhead in Green Lane, against the Ebenezer Chapel? What did he say to you?—I asked him what he had been reading that compact up for in the meetings.

5974. What did he say to that?—He said that he had not been reading it.

5975. What did you say to that?—I asked him what he read it up at the meetings for? and he said he had not read it up, and I said, I had heard he had. People heard us shouting in Green Lane, talking very hard.

5976. What people?—Women that were walking about in their houses.

SEVENTH DAY.

G. Shaw.

13 June 1867.

5977. Do you know anybody who heard you?—Hallam came to me and asked what Broadhead and I had been rowing for in Green Lane; I told him nothing much. I left Mr. Broadhead then with a gentlemen and went down——

5978. Then did Broadhead see Hallam?—No; those women came and asked what we had been rowing about.

5979. Hallam had heard from the women?—Yes. Well I never saw Mr. Broadhead after that, while I called at his house, and asked him where this place was on Saturday morning.

5980. Now did you ever hear of Clarke being at Alvey's public house?—Yes.

5981. When did you hear that?—I heard that a week last Thursday.

5982. Who told you?—A saw grinder.

5983. What saw grinder?—One Lee, and another Yellatt.

5984. What did they tell you?—They fetched me out of our place into the "Woolpack" just facing.

5285. What did they tell you?—They said it was hot for me; they said Clarke had got 20 crowns from the Commissioners to give evidence against Broadhead and me.

5986. Did they tell you how they knew that?—They said a man in a cart had stopped them in the Wicker. Clarke said Yellatt had stopped him in the Wicker and had squared him.

5987. But how did this man Yellatt and Lee know that he got the 20 crowns from the Commissioners?—I suppose they had been all drinking together at Alvey's the day previous.

5988. But did you hear them say that they had heard it from Clarke or anything of that kind?—Yes.

5989. They said that Clarke had told them that?—Yes.

5990. When you heard this what did you do?—I left them and went away directly.

5991. Did you see Broadhead about it?—I saw Broadhead when I was going down Green Lane, that was the day.

5992. When you had this conversation with Broadhead about the compact, did you tell him that you heard Clarke boasting that he had got some money from the Commissioners?—We had a great many words, I might have said it to him but I do not scarcely recollect whether I said so or not.

5993. Are you quite sure you did not tell him what you had heard?—We had a good many words, I cannot scarcely recollect what I said to him.

5994. Do you recollect whether he made any observation about Clarke, and your being safe from him or anything of that kind?—I asked him about the compact and he said I had nothing to fear.

3995. Now what do you mean by "compact"?—Well, about eight or nine weeks before Christmas to the best of my knowledge, I had to go to warn Elijah Parker to come to a meeting.

5996. Who told you to warn him?—I got a note which one of the men had given to him, and he would not go, and then he gave it to me.

5997. What man?—One of the grinders, it was in the taproom one Saturday, there were different districts to warn, and 1*s*. a district was paid for warning them.

5998. Whom did the note come from?—Mr. Broadhead.

5999. Do you know Mr. Broadhead's handwriting?—Yes.

6000. Have you got the note?—No, I gave it him when I came back.

6001. (*To Mr. Broadhead.*) Have you got that note?—No.

6002. (*To Witness.*) Mr. Broadhead issued a note to a saw grinder?—Yes.

6003. Who was that saw grinder?—That was Stephen Green, I think they call him.

6004. To warn a district?—Yes.

6005. And he would not go?—No, he said it was out of his way.

6006. And he gave the note to you as I understand?—Yes.

6007. What did you do?—I went and warned him. Then I had to call at the "Little London" to warn one George Peace. While I was there Peace asked me if I wanted something to do. I said I should be very glad to earn a few shillings. I holed him a stone or two and hanged it in for him, and earned a few shillings besides. Well, from that time I was tracked all up and down by a man named Martin.

6008. What is his Christian name?—They call him Joseph Martin. He goes by the name of "Currant."

6009. And Martin, you say, tracked you?—Yes.

6010. Who is this Martin?—He is a saw grinder. He has gone to America.

6011. How did he track you?—He watched me wherever I went to.

6012. For how long?—For perhaps a week or a fortnight. When I was coming up the moor on Saturday I had had a couple of pints of beer with Peace. He came out of a shop with two rabbits and dabbed me in the face with them. I told him he had better not do that again, and we got a-fighting. He tracked me then up to Broadhead's when I was going for my scale.

6013. Therefore you were on the box then?—Yes, I went up stairs for my scale and he followed me.

6014. Was the committee sitting?—There were the three men that pay the money and Broadhead.

6015. Who were the three men?—I think one was Marsden and the other Haigh, and the other Machin. I was sitting in a chair like this that I am sitting upon now, when he ordered Broadhead not to pay me my scale.

6016. Who did?—Martin. Well we got agate a-wrangling and we got agate a-fighting.

6017. In the committee room?—Yes; he tried to gouge my eyes out. He tore all my face and tried to pull my throat out. I went up the following Monday morning to see Broadhead.

6018. Martin ordered Broadhead not to pay your scale you say; did you get your scale?—No.

6019. Was anything done to you besides your having this fight?—No; not when I went on the Monday.

6020. On the Monday you went to Broadhead's again?—Yes; Broadhead said, "Come sober and "quiet," and he had no doubt but what I should get my scale.

6021. When did he say that?—On the Monday morning. I went on Tuesday night for my scale before the committee. Mr. Broadhead had drawn up a paper for me to sign.

6022. This was eight weeks before Christmas, you say?—Yes.

6023. What year?—This last year; just before Christmas time it was; just before the winter fair.

6024. When is Sheffield fair held?—It is held in November sometime. I signed the paper.

6025. What was in the paper?—It was to say that I knew nothing about Mr. Broadhead.

6026. How do you mean that you knew nothing about Mr. Broadhead?—Well, it is best for him to explain it.

6027. But what became of this paper that you saw?—He kept it; he had either six or seven of the committee to sign it.

6028. And it was signed by you and signed by them?—Yes.

6029. And what became of it?—I had two reasons for signing it.

6030. Never mind about that; what became of the paper?—Mr. Broadhead has it in his possession now.

6031. (*To Mr. Broadhead.*) Have you that paper?—Yes.

SEVENTH DAY.

G. Shaw.

13 June 1867.

6032. Do you mind producing it?

Mr Sugg stated that the paper would be produced in cross-examination.

The Chairman stated that the Commissioners would not allow Mr. Broadhead to be compromised without giving him an opportunity of answering any charges against him, and requested that the document might be handed in.

The document was handed in to the Court.

6033. (*Chairman, to the Witness.*) Is that the document (*showing him a paper*)?—Yes.

6034. Is that your handwriting?—That is my name.

6035. Is that the one that was signed by the committee?—It looks like it.

6036. Do you believe it is the same?—I believe so.

6037. I will read it:—"Saw Grinders' Committee Room, Royal George Hotel, Carver Street, Sheffield, November 27th, 1866. George Shaw being present. William Broadhead states he had heard a report, that George Shaw had been circulating, to the effect that he, Broadhead, had several years ago employed and paid Shaw to force his way through the wheel race at the Castle Mills, Blonk Street, to commit an outrage with gunpowder upon a person named Joseph Helliwell. Broadhead in the presence of the committee interrogates Shaw upon it. Now Shaw declares he never had been employed for any such purpose and he therefore willingly signs the following statement:—I hereby declare that I never at any time was either employed or paid by William Broadhead, to commit any such outrage as above described, nor did Broadhead ever make such offer to me. (Signed) George Shaw, witness, James Coldwell, Samuel Baxter, Matthew Frith, Henry Garfitt, Alexander Ellis (his mark), W. Broadhead."

The Chairman inquired of Mr. Sugg whether he might keep the document.

Mr. Sugg replied that he should like to retain the original for Mr. Broadhead's protection, but that he would furnish the Court with a copy.

6038. (*Chairman to the Witness.*) I see that the charge alleged against you is that you had been stating that several years ago Broadhead had employed and paid you to force your way through the cog wheel race at the Castle Mills, Blonk Street?—The "Tower."

6039. Here it is called the "Castle Mills, Blonk Street?"—Yes, but it is commonly called the "Tower."

6040. Had he ever employed you to force your way through the cog wheel race?—No, he means that affair with Clarke.

6041. That is another thing, but had he ever employed you to force your way through the cog wheel race?—No.

6042. To commit an outrage with gunpowder upon a person named Halliwell; you say you never were employed to do it?—Not by Broadhead.

6043. Were you ever employed to do it by anybody else?—By Clarke, by Denis Clarke.

6044. But it was not to force your way as I understand through the wheel race. What you did was, as I understand, to go in to the Tower Wheel and finding no person there to put the gunpowder into the trough?—Yes.

6045. But as far as you have described there is nothing about your forcing your way through a cog-wheel race?—No; I had no way to force.

5046. You deny in this paper that you ever were employed by him to force your way through a cog wheel race?—No, of course I never was employed by Broadhead.

6047. And what you mean to say is that in giving this notice although you were employed to commit an outrage upon Halliwell it was not by Broadhead but by Clarke?—No; I was employed by Clarke who said it was Old Smite 'em.

6048. Before you signed this did Mr. Broadhead tell you any reason that he had why he wanted you except that he heard you had been talking about it?—No.

6049. Had you been circulating a report to that effect?—Not to my knowledge.

6050. You know whether you had or not?—Well I had not.

6051. You never told anybody that you had been so employed?—When Clarke boasted so.

6052. But had you yourself been spreading a report to that effect?—Not about Mr. Broadhead employing me.

6053. Had you circulated a report that Clarke had employed you?—Yes.

6054. To whom?—To Mr. Broadhead.

6055. Had you told him so?—Yes.

6056. When have you told him?—Many a time when I have heard tell of Clarke talking in public houses.

6057. And what did Broadhead say to you when you told him that you had heard those reports that Clarke had been talking about this in the public houses?—He said he thought Clarke was not right.

6058. How many times do you think you have told Broadhead this?—Several times.

6059. How many?—I can scarcely say how many.

6060. About how many?—Pephaps I may have told him half a dozen times or more.

6061. When was the first time that you can recollect that you told him; how long ago did you first tell him that Clarke had been saying that he was employed by Broadhead to blow up Halliwell?—Soon after.

6062. Was anything done by Broadhead in consequence of your telling him this that you know of?—No, he said I had no occasion to fear.

6063. Has any person been present at any time when you have told him this?—No.

6064. Can you recollect any particular occasion when you have been present with him and told him this?—Yes, I told him about eight weeks since on Saturday night. That is the last time I did tell him about it.

6065. And how long before that had you been telling him?—At various times.

6066. Had a year elapsed?—No.

6067. How long?—It might be sometimes three or four months, at different times.

6068. What was your object in telling him this?—Well, of course, I knew I had done it and Clarke had employed me; and of course I went to tell him.

6069. But he knew it too, if it is true?—Well, I expect he did know it.

6070. But why did you tell him from time to time?—Because Clarke told me that he would have "old "Smite'em" and me run in and have us lagged.

6071. Have you heard Clarke say so?—Yes; he said it at the "King William."

6072. When?—About eight weeks since, when I communicated Broadhead with it.

6073. That was just before?—Yes.

6074. How long after was it that this note was drawn up?—That was drawn up before Christmas. It is about eight weeks since I heard him talking about it. When I had signed that note I went back to hear the decision of the committee.

6075. You say that you told him this; upon any occasion when you have mentioned those facts to him, that you had heard that Clarke was saying that he would have you and him transported or "lagged," as you call it, has Broadhead taken any steps to bring Clarke up?—No; he never said a word that I have heard of.

6076. Did you ever tell Broadhead that you had done it in this way under the direction of Clarke?—Yes.

6077. What did Broadhead say to this?—He said nothing; he said "H'm, h'm."

6078. You told him all the particulars?—Yes; I had told him I was in the mess.

6079. What did he say to that?—He said nothing, but only hummed and ha'd.

SEVENTH DAY.

G. Shaw.

13 June 1867.

6080. Except upon that occasion, eight weeks ago, have you ever heard that Clarke has said that he would have you "lagged"?—Yes; he was talking in Alvey's public-house, and saying that he had got squared with the commissioners and that he would have us lagged. That was a week since, a week last Thursday.

6081. I forget who you say was present in Alvey's public house?—There was a many grinders.

6082. Have you mentioned their names?—There was one Lee there. Yellatt and Lee fetched me out.

6083. Was that at Alvey's public house?—They had been there.

6084. And they fetched you into the "Woolpack"?—Yes; to tell me what a critical position I was in.

6085. A week last Thursday?—Yes; a fortnight since to-day.

6086. Now you say in this document something about forcing your way through a cog-wheel race; Mr. Wilson is a saw manufacturer, is he not?—He employs troughs there.

6087. At this place was there a kind of box covering the cog-wheels?—Yes.

6088. And was there through this box a way of getting into the hull?—A straight way; it wanted only the top lifting off.

6089. Was that the way in which you got in?—Yes.

6090. By lifting the box which covers the cog-wheel?—Yes.

6091. Were you at this wheel before the explosion?—I was apprenticed at the wheel.

6092. Were you there, and did you speak to Helliwell before you blew him up?—No.

6093. Now, in the presence of Mr. Wilson, did you not a day or two before this, or some short time before this, say to Helliwell, "If you do not join the Union "you will have your head knocked off?"—No; he had been fighting with a fellow wheelmate. I might have been chaffing him as regards that, but I said nought to him to my knowledge.

6094. Now mind what you are about. I ask you, in the presence of Mr. Wilson, you did not tell him that if he did not join the Union he would have his head knocked off?—They would not have him in the Union.

6095. I did not ask you that. Did you tell Helliwell in the presence of Mr. Wilson that if he did not join the Union he would have his head knocked off?—Not to my recollection.

6096. Will you swear that you did not?—I did not to my recollection; I might have said so.

6097. Did you threaten him at all?—Not to my recollection.

6098. You must know—did you threaten him at all before you blew him up?—He and I were going to fight a bit before. I might have threatened him as we were falling out for ought I know.

6099. Have you fought with him?—No; my fellow mate did.

6100. What is his name?—Garfitt.

6101. About what had they fought?—I am sure I do not know what it was about.

6102. Was it about his not joining the Union?—They were fighting about the work. I think Garfitt told him to go home and that he was worth nought.

6103. That he was a bad workman?—Yes; he told him he thought he had better stop at home, or something of that kind.

6104. Was Helliwell a bad workman?—It was reported so.

6105. Then you will not swear that you did not threaten him yourself?—No; I might have done it and forgotten it.

6106. You say that you got into the wheel, and were forcing open this covering to the cog-wheel?—Yes.

6107. Did Clarke ever get in?—No; he stood waiting for me to get out.

6108. Where did he stand?—By the side of the cogs. There were two hulls joining one another, and you could go from one into another hull

6109. Clarke never came into the hull, but remained in the adjoining hull, and could see through?—Yes.

6110. And he could see you do it?—Yes.

6111. You talked about Helliwell having his hair singed, and so on. Do you not know that he was fearfully burnt?—No.

6112. Do you not know that all the windows were blown out?—No, they were not, not that I know of. There was nothing put in to blow the windows out.

6113. Were the windows blown out? Mind, you are on ticklish ground?—Not to my recollection.

6114. You make a much less story of it than some persons coming after you will do. Were the windows blown out?—Not to my recollection.

6115. Did you go to see the place afterwards?—No. I was jobbing about the town. I might walk past the wheel, but I cannot recollect whether I did or not.

6116. A can of powder contains about a pound of powder, does it not?—Yes.

6117. Do you know whether Helliwell went to Broadhead to be admitted into the Union afterwards?—No.

6118. You had nothing to do with him?—No.

6119. And you say that you never were at the wheel after the explosion?—Yes. I have been at the wheel many a score times since the explosion.

6120. Now, I ask you if you were not there just after the explosion, and if you did not see Mr. Joseph Wilson there?—Mr. Wilson used to go there regularly.

6121. That is not an answer. Did you not see Mr. Joseph Wilson there just after the explosion?—I used to be holing stones and things there.

6122. Did not the engine tenter show the box and the door through which anybody could get into the hull to Mr. Wilson, in your presence?—Not to my knowledge.

6123. Now, be careful what you are about. Your only chance is by telling the truth. Did not you, in the presence of Mr. Wilson, when he found out the place where the man had got in, shake your fist in his face, and threaten the engine tenter?—No, not me.

6124. Did you not fight, and did not Mr. Wilson part you?—No; Mr. Wilson never saw me fight in his life.

6125. Had you ever any fight with the engine tenter?—No, never in my life.

6126. What was his name?—Bill Wright was the engine tenter, and I forget the other man's name.

6127. You swear that you did not, in the presence of Mr. Wilson, shake your fist in the engine tenter's face, and threaten him?—No. I am sure to my recollection I never threatened him at all. We never had any words, the engine tenter and me.

6128. Was there any person who pointed out to Wilson, in your presence, the way in which the person had got in, to put in the powder, and did you thereupon put your fist up to that man, whoever he was, and threaten him?—It is so long that, supposing I did, I cannot think of it.

6129. You will not swear one way or the other?—No.

6130. But if you fought with him you would recollect it?—Yes.

6131. If what you say is true, if you went and laid powder and blew a man up, and a man pointed out the way in which it was done, I think you would recollect afterwards, the thing would be upon your mind immediately. Now, did you do so or not?—Well, not to my knowledge.

6132. That will not do. You recollect very well whether a man pointed it out to Mr. Wilson in your presence?—I do not.

6133. You would recollect quite well whether you threatened him, and whether you fought?—No. I have not fought with anybody here.

6134. Mr. Wilson is here?—Very well, it does not matter.

6135. It does matter, you know?—He has never seen me fight in his life, not to my knowledge.

6136. You have told us about this. How was it that you signed this compact that you have talked

SEVENTH DAY.

G. Shaw.

13 June 1867.

about, although you say that you were never employed by Mr. Broadhead to do this? That is a mere quibble. You said that you had done it, and that you believed that it was done as you told us, at the instigation of Mr. Broadhead. How was it, if you thought that you had been set on by Clarke, and that Clarke had been set on by Broadhead, you came to sign that document?—Because they stopped my scale; that was the reason I signed it. I signed it on purpose to get my scale.

6137.—Then, though perhaps not in words, yet in substance, you told a lie, in order to get your scale?—Yes.

6138.—Was there any other inducement except that of getting your scale which caused you to sign that document?—No.

6139. Now, upon your oath, were you employed by Clarke?—Yes.

6140. Did you not do it yourself without any interference by Clarke?—No.

6141. Now, I ask you solemnly again. Is it true that you talked to Broadhead about this, and told him all about it in the way you have mentioned?—Yes. Broadhead has a letter, if he will publish it, which I sent to him after I had signed that paper.

6142. (*To Mr. Broadhead.*) Have you got such a letter?—I leave the case entirely in the hands of my legal adviser.

Mr. Sugg stated that he had no such letter.

6143. (*To the Witness.*) Did you send him such a letter?—Yes.

The *Chairman* inquired whether Mr. Sugg produced the letter.

Mr. Sugg replied that he did not.

Chairman (*to the Witness*). Have you seen it in Mr. Broadhead's possession?—Not since I sent it him. He read it out publicly at the meeting.

6144. Did you hear him?—No, but all the whole body told me.

6145. Have you ever heard from Mr. Broadhead himself that he got your letter?—Yes.

WILLIAM BROADHEAD sworn and examined.

W. Broadhead.

Chairman: Did you get that letter?—I got the letter.

6146. Have you it now?—I have not it here.

6147. Will you send for it?—I must go for it myself.

6148. Go with a policeman and get it.

Mr. Broadhead left the Court to fetch the letter.

GEORGE SHAW recalled and further examined.

G. Shaw.

6151. (*Chairman.*) The letter which has been referred to is addressed to Mr. Broadhead, "Royal George," Carver Street, Sheffield; the post mark is November 27th, 1866?—I believe, if it is the letter which I indited, that it is to the editor of the "Telegraph."

6152. A part of the envelope is torn off?—That is the part I wrote.

6153. You wrote on the envelope, "This will suit "the editor of the 'Telegraph'"?—Yes; I meant it to be forwarded to him if they opened it at the Post Office.

6154. If not taken in by Mr. Broadhead, and if it was opened at the Post Office, it was to be sent to the "Telegraph"?—Yes.

6155. The postage was not paid?—No, I wanted it to get forwarded there.

6156. The letter is as follows:—"Sir, Mr. Broad-"head—I sined Your Document but I have you "because I have the Man that Bought three Parts of "the Powder—You thaught We blew him up With—"We sold It for 5*s*.—and I have A Nother Witness "that saw and saw mee Put it under My bed, and "went with Me to sell it, and know one that has to "Do With you know Mr. B i have found You a "Traitor I shall be Like to be one to so the Publick "at large Will know the Honest Sectary—Remember "Mr. B that if ever My Strings Disapere i shall by a "set of Tools—i shall be on your Track if I do not "let the Public know before That Man That evi-"dence can be that empoys men—You understand i "shall Have a gift for informing about it Mr. B. I shall "fetch a summond for Martin to Morrow and go into "Business at once for prouncing up one wen com for "my bit of a scale—Whe will see what we cane do "for the royal George—i thing I make Royal like "me Poor George for sticking to my Trade. Mr. "B. I sined Your Because I Thaught be Treating "With having my Life Taken if I Did not sine "same as on Saturday when I came for my scale. I "went to the Town Hall and Told Them what I "Received on Saturday Look out we Did knot blow "im up as you thaught—Rember What an informer "Can Do Long henry St Sheffield Park"?—That is the letter.

6157. What about Martin? You signed that document, as I understand, on November 27th?—I wrote that letter the same night when I got home.

6158. That was on November 27th?—Yes, I wrote it the same night when I got home.

6159. It bears exactly the same date. This is the letter you wrote the very same night when you got home?—Yes, the very night after I signed this compact.

6160. In that letter you talk about Martin employing a man; what do you mean by that?—When I was caught earning a few shillings at Little London, Martin tracked me up and down. I was going to work there on a very dark and very rainy night. I had an umbrella, and was wrapped up so that I thought no one could recognize me; but just before I got to Heely Bar I heard some one say, "He is coming." It was a fearful dark night. I had my topcoat and rug on, so that thought nobody would know me. I recognized Martin's voice. I had a dark avenue to come down, and instead of going forward I crossed and went under the railway bridge, and then doubled across the shuttle and got to the wheel by a back way. I told the men there that I dared not work there alone, as there was a trap set for me; I was sure there was some one about. I was ready to work if they would have worked with me; but having to work close to the shuttle I dared not stay there, expecting that if I did I should be shot while at my work; but they would not stay. I told Mr. Peace's son that I dared not stop to work by myself, and I went home. The following night I went to work and heard the same voice at the same spot say, "He is coming," and I took my old way. I did not go underneath the bridge. After that we had not been working but a few minutes when our candles went out. I asked why we had not some more, and they said that they had sent for a replenish. I said, "You must go and borrow some," and they went to an adjoining house to borrow some candles, and when the messenger came back he said, "By Jove, "George, you must be on your guard; they are out "yonder." I said, "Where are they?" He said, "In "an old out-building." He then said, "Let us ferret "them out; if we are to die, we may as well die "game, and have a struggle for it." I got a bar of iron, and I asked a young fellow to carry the candles, and he did; and young Peace seized another bar and said, "Where you go I will go; if they take your life "they shall take mine." We got into the ruinous old place, but they were gone, and I thought I saw something at the top of some steps. I went up the steps

SEVENTH DAY.

G. Shaw.

13 June 1867.

and Peace followed me, and we saw some shadows running up the river side. We followed them, but as it was raining my working clogs got clogged up and I slipped backwards and forwards, and I could not get on; but I did not stop till I was completely exhausted with running, and they escaped us. I then came back to the place. Martin after that repeatedly told me that he intended having my life, if I had come underneath the bridge that night.

6161. Martin told you that he determined that he would have your life?—Yes.

6162. What has that to do with employing men which you mention in your letter?—Martin said that he defended the trade with his blood; he played all sorts of games to get what he could for the benefit of the trade.

6163. What do you mean by saying in the letter that Mr. Broadhead employed men?—I took it from what Martin said; Martin tracked me up and down.

6164. How do you say that Broadhead had anything to do with that?—Because he was Broadhead's head man; he said "We will stop his scale." He ordered Broadhead to stop my scale, that was in the meeting, when I went for it on the Saturday.

6165. Martin said that on the Saturday to Broadhead?—Yes.

6166. And you say that was the reason why you alluded to employing him?—He said he defended the trade by his blood, that was my reason for thinking so.

6167. Did you tell Broadhead that he had said so?—No. Broadhead had stopped Martin's scale and he had to face the trade for it. He said they had used him bad and came and begged and prayed of me that what had passed and gone should be forgotten. I gave the man a few words when he was going away.

6168. When did he go to America?—He had gone a week or two before. I knew naught about it, he went seven or eight weeks back.

6169. You say in the letter "You know Mr. B. "I found you a traitor"?—Yes.

6170. How was that?—As soon as ever I had signed the contract there was no scale for me. I found him to be two-faced.

6171. You said "I shall fetch a summons for "Martin to morrow," what did you mean by that?—I thought of fetching him up for what he had done with me.

6172. What had he done to you? — He nearly gouged my eyes out, my nostrils were pulled open. I have the scars on me now.

6173. "I signed the paper because I thought to be "threatened with having my life taken if I did not "sign"?—Yes.

6174. You signed the paper because you thought you would be threatened with having your life taken if you did not sign?—Yes.

6175. What did you mean by that? — Because Martin was such a dangerous man.

6176. What did you mean by that; did you mean that you signed because you thought your life was in danger?—Yes, of course.

6177. You say in this letter that the reason you signed was because you thought your life was threatened?—Yes.

6178. How does that agree with what you told us to day, that the reason you signed was to get the scale?—Of course that was it, and all.

6179. You never said a word about it?—No; I was going to tell you it when I had the chance.

6180. You said you wanted to get scale, but you also signed because you thought your life was in danger?—Yes.

6181. And then you go on to say "I went to the "Town Hall and I told them what I received on "Saturday"?—No, I meant me and Crapper got towards the Town Hall, and I told him I did not like to fetch any one up. I thought he might have given me my scale if I told him I was going to the Town Hall.

6182. You said you went to the Town Hall and told them what you received on Saturday?—Crapper told Mr. Jackson.

6183. Did you go to the Town Hall?—No; I got close by it.

6184. You went to the Town Hall and did not tell them what you received. Then it was false what was contained in this letter?—Yes.

6185. You put it in to see if he would give you your scale?—Yes.

6186. I do not follow you; if you told him you would tell them at the Town Hall, it would be one thing, but if you had already told them at the Town Hall he would not care for you; how was it you told him that? If you had told it, then there was an end of the matter, he had nothing to get by paying the scale; but if you told him that you would tell, he would have every inducement. What do you mean by saying you went to the Town Hall and told them what you received on Saturday?—I was trying to see whether he would give me the scale.

6187. That was quite false?—Yes.

6188. "We did not blow him up as you thought," what do you mean by that?—That Clarke had told me that Smite 'em had sent us to it and we sold the stuff instead of blowing him up.

6189. You meant by "We did not blow him up as "you thought," that you had only used part of the powder?—We only put a small portion in.

6190. Then you say "Remember what an informer "can do," and sign it "Long Henry Street, Shef- "field"?—Yes.

6191. You never sign your name as far as I can see?—No.

6192. Is there any person but yourself connected with the Union who lives in Long Henry Street?—There is one at the far end, 150 yards from our house, they call him "Woollen."

6193. The only other person in your street connected with the Union is Joseph Woollen?—Yes; I was apprenticed underneath him.

6194. Was he at that time in any dispute with the Union?—No, not at the time I wrote the letter.

6195. Was this written the same night that you signed the document?—Yes; under half an hour after, as soon as I got home.

6196. They had refused to give you the scale before you wrote that letter?—Yes, that made me defy them. I told them I must have a living.

6197. Did you ever see Broadhead after you wrote that letter?—Yes, I have seen him several times since.

6198. Has he spoken to you about it?—No; he publicly read it up to the whole assemblage.

6199. Have you told him that you had heard he had publicly read it up?—I told him the other day in the Green Lane that I had heard he had read my letter at the public meeting.

6200. At the public meeting?—Yes; my compact, letter, and all.

6201. What did he say to that?—He said it was false.

6202. You say that Martin has gone to America?—Yes.

6203. What did Martin do? What was he? Was he a man that worked?—A saw grinder; sometimes he worked.

6204. You told us that he went seven or eight weeks ago?—Yes, to my recollection.

6204. What did he do, did he work at his trade or not?—Sometimes I expect, I have not known him work since he was apprenticed; he was apprenticed to the same master as me; he was just out of his time when I went there.

6206. It was the same master?—Yes.

6207. Who was it?—Thomas Lindley.

6208. That was the man who was shot?—Yes.

6209. He was apprenticed with Thomas Lindley as well as you?—Yes.

6210. Did Martin ever do any work at all? Did he follow his trade?—He went to Mr. Marsden's wheel in Love Street, and the master would not have him about the premises because he was such a character. A few weeks before he went to America that was.

SEVENTH DAY.

G. Shaw.

13 June 1867.

6211. At the time you are talking of, when he tracked you up and down, was he in work or not?—No.

6212. Have you often seen him at Mr. Broadhead's house?—Yes, when I have gone he was always there when I was in the trade.

6213. You have now told us a great deal that you did not tell us when you were examined before. Now I will call you back to some questions that I put to you when you were previously examined. You have now told us a great deal more, and if it were not for the protection which this statute gives, you would be in very great peril indeed?—I have told you nothing but the truth.

6214. We have not heard what is said on the other side yet?—No.

6215. It may be that you have told us what is entirely false or what is entirely true. I cannot give an opinion at present, but I call your attention to the fact that you have told us something which is very much contradicted by a person who apparently is a respectable man, and that is James Thomas. James Thomas has told us that you told him that there was a man wanted to blow Hague's place up for 5*l.*, but Broadhead would not sanction it. Now you said that that was not so. Having thought over that and considered your position, I ask you again, did not you tell James Thomas so?—No, not to my recollection.

6216. Will you swear that you did not?—Yes.

6217. You persist in that?—Yes. I went a many times to Fearnehough's place, we might in jest talk of it, but not to my recollection did I say anything to him.

6318. To the best of your recollection you never said anything of the kind?—No. I never did.

6219. Did you know a man who was ready to blow him up?—No.

6220. Have you ever said to anybody that you knew any such a man?—No, not to my recollection.

6221. Have you ever said to anybody that you knew a man that wanted to blow up Hague's place, but that Broadhead would not sanction it?—No.

6222. To no one?—No.

6223. You never have said so?—No.

6224. You swear that?—Yes.

6225. Do you know a man called Hallam?—Yes.

6226. Did you ever say that Hallam was ready to blow it up?—No.

6227. Have you never said that Hallam was ready to blow it up?—No.

6228. Did Hallam ever tell you that he was?—No.

6229. Did Broadhead ever tell you that Hallam was?—No.

6230. You never heard it?—No.

6231. Was there ever any conversation between you and anybody else about the blowing up Hague's place?—No; I used to go there very often.

6232. Was there any conversation between you and anybody else about blowing up Hague's place?— Not to my knowledge.

6233. You do not talk about blowing up a man's house without recollecting it?—I do not recollect it.

6234. You swear that you did not?—Yes.

6235. You recollect his house being blown up?—Whose house?

6236. Fearnehough's?—Yes.

6237. Do you recollect a person talking about it before it happened?—No.

6238. Or after it happened?—No.

6239. You do not know anybody who suggested to you who did it?—No, I read it myself in the paper.

6240. You have nothing at all from which you could draw any inference who had done it?—No; not a suggestion in the world.

6241. Do you know when it was first talked of in Sheffield that there was to be a Commission down here?—No. I have only gone by what was in the paper.

6242. When was it first talked of that there should be an inquiry into the Trades' outrages?—It did not bother me.

6243. But when was it first talked of in Sheffield?—I have never taken any notice of it except the last few weeks.

6244. Had you heard of it before you wrote this letter?—No. I never took any notice of it.

6245. Had you heard of a possibility of some persons being sent down by Government to inquire into the Trade outrages at the time you wrote this letter?—It was rumoured that there was to be an inquiry.

6246. At that time it had been already reported that there was to be an inquiry?—Yes.

6247. I must caution you again, it does not stand upon the statement of Thomas, who said that he heard you say so, and that he went and told Mr. Hague that very night what you had told him?—What was it?

6248. That you knew a person who was ready to blow up Hague's premises for 5*l.* if Broadhead would only give the word?—It is entirely false. I never said such a word in my life.

6249. There is no doubt you went to Mr. Clegg and told him so?—It must be his own imagination, it was not me.

6250. It does not stand upon him alone, there is another man; Staniforth said "He would tell me after "Shaw was gone how 'Old Tom' could be done."—I never said such a word to Staniforth.

6251. You did not?—No.

6252. At the time of this blowing up that you talk of, were you on the box or not?—I was taken in when I was 20 years of age.

6253. Were you in employment or out of employment?—I had nothing to do.

6254. When you blew up Helliwell you had nothing to do?—The only work I did when I was taken in the trade, was working about three days on the trade's tools.

6255. Were you short of money at that time?—I had not a father, and being apprenticed I had nothing but my scale.

6256. Were you apprenticed at the time you blew up Helliwell?—I was taken on as a man and had 5*l.* to pay by instalments when I was 20 years of age.

6257. That was for fine?—No; the fee for entrance to the trade.

6258. And what else?—I worked three days on the trades' tools; that was all the work I had. Staniforth took my place who works for Moses Eadon.

6259. At that time you had no money?—No; I was 20 years of age.

6260. 20 years of age without work and without means?—I used to pick a shilling or two up any way; he was officiated by the trade to take my place, and I had to go on the box.

6261. How much did you get?—I had 8s. a week, but they stopped it by a shilling or two (I can scarcely tell what it was now) till the 5*l.* was paid.

6262. How did you happen to be turned on to the box in this way?—Because I said I would not serve my term out with anybody else.

6263. You said you would serve your time out with Linley?—Yes, he was taken on the box, he was unemployed, he had no situation.

6264. Therefore he did no work?—No.

Chairman (*to Mr. Sugg*).—I can quite understand that these are very important communications which this man has made; how far they are true I do not know; but I do not think that it is right to call upon you to cross-examine him now. If you wish for time to consider the matter you can have it. Anything we can do either to investigate this matter or get at the real truth we will do, and every assistance that can be given to Mr. Broadhead to meet the case shall be given. We will try to get at the bottom of it, and therefore whatever course you propose we will accede to at once. What do you ask for?

Mr. Sugg.—For an adjournment till Monday morning.

The witness withdrew.

SEVENTH DAY.

J. Hallam.

13 June 1867.

JAMES HALLAM sworn and examined.

6265. (*Chairman*).—You have been summoned to come here this morning?—Yes.

6266. You know the last witness I believe?—Yes.

6267. How long have you known him?—About 10 or 11 years.

6268. Were you brought up as a saw grinder?—Yes.

6269. Were you apprenticed?—Yes.

6270. To whom were you apprenticed?—My father.

6271. When did you join the Union?—When I was 21 years of age.

6272. How old are you now?—29 years.

6273. Have you been in the Saw Grinders' Union ever since?—No.

6274. How long did you continue in the Union?—Till last August or September.

6275. How did you happen to leave it?—I cannot rightly answer that.

6276. Did you give notice to leave or cease to pay? I ceased to pay.

6277. You have known Broadhead I suppose?—Yes.

6278. Ever since you were in the Union he has been there?—Yes.

6279. Has he ever applied to you at any time to do any business for him?—No.

6280. Have you ever done any business for him. It may be wrong, but supposing I am right do not be afraid —speak the truth; the law is strong enough to protect you even from violence, and you shall be protected; and if the consequences should be, that you might be proceeded against civilly or punished criminally, you will be protected if you will tell the truth. You must make a full disclosure of all you know, and you will have ample protection. Now I ask you, has Broadhead ever employed you to do anything connected with the trade?—I have asked him.

6281. When did you ask him, and what did you ask him?—I have asked him if there was anything to do.

6282. When was it that you first asked him?—I could not say that.

6283. About how long ago?—Four or five years perhaps.

6284. What did he say to that?—He told me there was nothing.

6285. Do you know a person of the name of Joseph Taylor?—Yes.

6286. Is he a saw manufacturer in Mowbray Street? —Yes.

6287. Do you know whether a person of the name of Samuel Hallam was in arrear who worked upon his tools at any time?—Yes.

6288. Do you know a person of the name of Matthew Broadhead?—Yes.

6289. Do you know whether he was in arrear?—Yes, he was.

6290. Did they both work for Taylor?—Yes.

6291. Did you do anything to them?—Yes, once.

6292. What was it you did to them?—I took their nuts.

6293. When you had taken them what did you do with them? where did you put them?—I forget the place where I put them now.

6294. Do not be frightened; there is nothing to be afraid about; do not you recollect where you put those nuts?—I cannot speak to a certainty.

6295. It is seven years ago—we speak of Samuel Hallam and Matthew Broadhead—you say they were in arrears, and you took their nuts; did they pay up their arrears after you had taken their nuts?—I do not know.

6296. What became of the nuts? — They were found, I believe.

6297. But before they were found did you do anything at all? You had them, what did you do with them? you do not recollect where you put them?—I did nothing.

6298. How were they found; was any note sent? —Yes, I believe there was a note sent.

6299. Who wrote the note?—I wrote the note.

6300. What did you do with it?—I sent it to the firm, I believe.

6301. To Mr. Taylor's firm?—Yes.

6302. How did you send it, by post or by hand?—I sent it by post.

6303. Did you mention in that note any place where the nuts were to be found?—Yes.

6304. Did you place them where you stated in the note?—Yes.

6305. After that the nuts came back?—Yes.

6306. After they had gone back did you see Broadhead about it?—No.

6307. Did Broadhead see you about it?—No.

6308. Are you sure about that?—Yes.

6309. You are quite sure about that?—Yes.

6310. Did you ever get any money for doing that? —Yes, I got some money.

6311. How much?—*25s.*

6312. Who paid you that?—Another man paid me the money.

6313. It was another man who paid you the money? —Yes.

6314. What was his name?—I cannot tell you his name.

6315. Did that man assist you in taking away those nuts, or did you do it alone?—He assisted me.

6316. Did he show you the money he had got?—No.

6317. You got *25s.*?—Yes.

6318. Was that for the half, or was it for the full? —I do not know. I suppose it was for the half.

6319. Where was it that you got the money; at what place were you paid the *25s.*?—John Woollen's dram-shop.

6320. Was anybody present when you were paid? —Nobody that I know.

6321. Whose nuts were they that you took, Samuel Hallam's?—Yes.

6322. Who was Samuel Hallam; was he your own father?—He was my father.

6323. You say you got *25s.*; did you ever talk to Mr. Broadhead about the money that you had got?—No.

6324. Now I ask you did you talk to Mr. Broadhead about having done this thing?—No, not to the best of my recollection. I believe I never did.

6325. Who paid the money for that?—The other man paid me.

6326. Who paid him?—I do not know.

6327. Upon your oath, did not you see the money paid over to that other man? You know we have private information from other sources; mind what you are about; did not you see that money paid over to that other man?—I cannot answer that question.

6328. Yes you can. I have reason to know that you can answer it. Did you see that money paid over to the other man, yes or no?—I really cannot answer that question.

6329. Yes you can. I caution you. You know where you saw that other man; you say you do not know his name; you know whether you saw that other man receive the money or not; did you see him receive it?—No.

6330. On your oath do you mean to say you did not see him receive it?—On my oath I did not.

6331. Did you ever talk to Broadhead about the money ever having been paid?—Not to my recollection.

6332. Were you present when the man was paid? —I might be.

6323. Do you believe you were present when the money was paid?—I believe not.

6334. Will you swear you were not present when he was paid?—Yes; I was not present.

SEVENTH DAY.

J. Hallam.

13 June 1867.

6335. You were not present when he was paid?—No; I cannot tell you any more.

6336. Did you hear Broadhead at any time talk to this man?—No.

6337. Did you hear him talk to Broadhead?—No.

6338. Now upon your oath have you never said that you saw him paid?—I might say many things.

6339. Have you ever said that?—I might have said so.

6340. Have you said so?—I cannot swear to it.

6341. Will you swear to the contrary, that you never have said so?—No.

6342. Then you may have said so?—Yes.

6343. Was it true?—No.

6344. Did you say so?—I cannot swear that I ever have.

6345. Will you swear you did not?—No.

6346. If you did and it was untrue, why did you say it? You say you cannot say whether you said it or not, and you will not swear you did not say it; if you did say it, why did you say it if it was untrue?—I do not know.

6347. Have you ever said that Broadhead gave him the money?—I might have said so.

6348. Do not you believe you have? If you believe you have, there is no reason to be nervous about it; do you believe that you have said so?—I cannot say.

6349. You can say if you like; have you said so or not? Is it possible that you may have said that you saw Broadhead pay him?—It is possible.

6350. It is possible that you may have said that you saw Broadhead pay him; if it is possible that you may have said so perhaps you recollect now that you did say so?—I cannot say that.

6351. You are not prepared to say that you did not?—No.

6352. Why should you say that you saw Broadhead pay him? I do not say you did say so, but you say you may have said so; how might you have said so if you never saw him?—I cannot answer that.

6353. Did you ever say so?—I do not know that I have not for a certainty.

6354.—Do not you recollect quite well seeing him paid?—No.

6355. You do not recollect it?—No.

6356. Will you swear that Broadhead did not pay the money over to that other man?—I do not know.

6357. You do not know whether Broadhead did pay him or not? are you quite sure that Broadhead did not pay it in the same room in which you were standing with him? are you not quite sure that he paid him in the same room where you were?—No; I am not sure.

6358. Do you believe he did?—No.

6359. Do you believe he did not?—I do not know.

6360. Have you ever told Broadhead that he paid him?—No.

6361. Has Broadhead ever told you?—No.

6362. You mean to say you never had any conversation with Broadhead about that payment of money?—No, I believe not.

6363. You know you did the job and that you got paid for it; where did the money come from that you got?—It came to me; I do not know where it came from.

6364. You mean to tell us that you do not know where it came from?—No.

6365. You know the consequences if you tell what is false. I do not want to tell you anything to act upon your fears; I must caution you, you must know where the money came from. Did not you say that you saw Broadhead pay the other man, and that he gave you half; have you not said that? mind what may happen to you if you tell a falsehood. Have not you said that you saw Mr. Broadhead pay the money to the other man and that that other man gave you half?—I might have said so.

6366. Do not you believe you did?—No.

6367. Will you swear that you did not?—No, I will not swear.

6368. Why will not you swear that you did not say so?—Because I am not certain about it.

6369. But if you did not see him, how could it enter into your head that you could say that? If you never saw it, why should you have a doubt about it, because if you did not see it how could you say so?—I cannot answer that question.

6370. In point of fact did not you see Broadhead pay the money?—I cannot answer that.

6371. Yes you can; you know quite well whether you saw Broadhead pay the money or not; it is trifling with us to say that you do not know whether you saw a man pay money for doing a job of this kind; you must know it?—The other man paid me.

6372. I ask you whether you did not then see Broadhead pay the money to the other man?—I did not see it, I believe.

6373. It will not do for you to trifle with us in this way; if you trifle with us I must deal very differently with you; you are brought here because you cannot help yourself, you are summoned here and cannot help coming, and you must tell all you know, now you are here, or else take the consequences. You say you believe you never saw him pay it; will you swear that you did not see it?—Yes.

6374. Now mind, it is not without warning that this is done. Did you know from whom the money came?—No.

6375. Do you mean to say that you have no knowledge where the money came from that this other man had?—I did not ask him; he paid me.

6376. Would you rather not mention his name, or do not you know his name; which do you say?—I cannot mention his name.

6377. Is it because you do not know it?—No.

6378. You do know it?—Yes.

6379. What is that man's name?—I cannot tell you that.

6380. You can. You say you know his name but that you cannot tell what is his name, I know that you know it; a man does not go to do a deed like this with a person whose name he does not know; it is nonsense to trifle with us in that way, you must tell us?—I will not tell you that.

6381. Will not you?—No.

6382. We will leave that case; I have pressed you without success. Have you ever been engaged in any other mischief?—Only what I have engaged myself in.

6383. You have never been engaged in any other mischief but what you have engaged yourself in? do you know some works called Marsden's Works in Coulson Crofts?—I do not know where that is.

6384. You do not know Coulson Crofts?—No.

6385. Do you know Marsden's Works?—I do not know where you mean.

6386. Do you know a person of the name of Pacey?—Yes.

6387. Do you know Bridge Street?—Yes.

6388. Do you recollect Pacey working in Bridge Street?—No.

6389. You do not recollect that?—No.

6390. Do you recollect that he had some tools there?—Yes.

6391. Do you recollect a person of the name of Charles Damms?—Yes.

6392. Was he in arrear?—Yes, I believe he was.

6393. Do you know Joseph Copley and John Woodhead?—Yes.

6394. And Dennis Clarke?—Yes.

6395. Do you recollect any conversation with them at the "Blue Pig"?—Yes.

6396. What was it?—I cannot say particularly.

6397. Yes you can; you say you recollect; do you recollect saying anything about taking his bands?—No.

6398. Do you recollect Clarke saying that he had got the order to do Damms, and that he should do him?—Yes, that is true.

6399. Clarke said that he had got the order?—Yes.

6400. Did you slip out and take his pulley?—No.

SEVENTH DAY.

J. Hallam.

13 June 1867.

6401. Did you take anything? did you take his nut?—Yes.

6402. What did you do with it?—Put it in my pocket.

6403. After you had got it in your pocket did you show it to Broadhead?—No.

6404. Did he give you 5*s*. for doing it?—Not me.

6405. Not you?—No.

6406. What do you mean?—He did not give me 5*s*.

6407. He did not give you 5*s*.?—No.

6408. Did you get 5*s*. for doing it?—No.

6409. But did you get anything?—I got some ale for it.

6410. Who gave it to you?—Joseph Copley paid for it.

6411. Did you get any money for it?—He must have got some or he could not have paid for the ale.

6412. Who paid him for it?—I do not know.

6413. Did you see him paid for it?—No.

6414. Upon your oath did not Broadhead pay you 5*s*., and did not you and Copley divide the money?—No.

6415. Did you see the money paid to Copley?—No.

6416. I ask you again on this subject, have you ever said that at that place, the "Blue Pig," Clarke got the order to do Damms, and that he should do him, and then you thought this so shabby that you thought you would do Clarke; so whilst they were drinking in the "Blue Pig" you stepped out and took the pulley nut yourself; did you say that?—Yes.

6417. Did not you say that you showed it to Broadhead, and that Broadhead paid you 5*s*.?—No.

6418. You never have said so?—No.

6419. To no one?—No (*after a pause*).

6420. Why did you pause so long as that, because if it is not true, you never could have said it. Why did you wait so long before you answered the question? were you in doubt about it?—Which question?

6421. Whether you said that you had shown it to Broadhead and that he had paid you 5*s*., were you in doubt whether you had said that or not?—Yes.

6422. You said that you were in doubt whether you had ever said that Broadhead paid you 5*s*.?—Yes.

6423. Then you may have said so?—Yes.

6424. Why?—I do not know.

6425. You do not know?—No.

6426. Do you mean to say that you said of Mr. Broadhead, if he had never done it, that he had paid you 5*s*. for doing a rattening, would you do such a wicked thing as that, to say that a man had offered you 5*s*. if he never did?—He never did offer me 5*s*.

6427. I thought you said you did not know whether you said so or not?—I might have said so.

6428. You might have said of an innocent man that he had given you 5*s*. to do a rattening, have you said that?—I do not know whether I said so.

6429. Will you swear that you did not?—Yes.

6430. To no one?—Yes, to no one.

6431. You never said so to any one?—No.

6432. Now then I will ask you another question. Do you know a firm called Wheatman and Smith?—Yes.

6433. Was there a man there called John Helliwell?—No.

6434. Do you know a man of the name of Helliwell, a saw grinder of the Wicker?—Yes.

6435. Do you know whether Broadhead was on good terms with him or not?—He never did join the trade, I think.

6436. Do you know whether he was obnoxious to the trade; whether the trade were discontented with him?—I do not know.

6437. Did they disapprove of him in his conduct?—I do not know.

6438. Do you know whether Helliwell ever worked with Firths in Saville Street?—I think so.

6439. Had Wheatman and Smith a kind of machine that interfered with the trade?—Not that I know of.

6440. Were you ever set to watch Helliwell?—No.

6441. Did you ever watch him?—I never saw him.

6442. You never looked after him?—I never saw him.

6443. And never looked after him?—No.

6444. Did you ever try to blow up Wheatman's premises?—No.

6445. Were you ever solicited to blow them up?—No.

6446. Did you buy a quantity of gunpowder? Did you buy 28 lbs. of gunpowder?—No.

6447. Did you get any gunpowder at any time?—No.

6448. Never?—No.

6449. Were you ever paid 15*l*. to do business at Wheatman's, to blow them up?—No.

6450. Nor any sum of money?—No.

6451. Did you ever buy some powder and put it in the quarry near Bole Hill, Crookes?—No.

6452. Did you ever buy a fuse at Twibell's, at Snig Hill?—No.

6453. Did you ever try to put any powder at the bottom of the chimney at Wheatman's, the engine chimney bottom?—No.

6454. Is there a large sough or drain that runs out of Wheatman's yard into the river?—No.

6455. You do not know that there is one?—No.

6456. Did you ever put up the drain a quantity of powder with a fuse to it?—No.

6457. Did you ever stand on Rutland Bridge and see it go off?—No.

6458. Did you go on the Saturday following to Broadhead, and did he pay you 15*l*. in sovereigns for having done it?—No.

6459. I suppose you are aware that if you commit perjury, besides the penalty for not telling the truth, you can be punished for what you have done?—I am perfectly aware of that.

6460. Have you never said that you were set to watch John Helliwell?—No.

6461. Have you never said that you were hired or engaged to blow up Wheatman's premises?—No.

6462. You never said that you had bought some gunpowder and put it in Bole Hill, Crookes?—No.

6463. Have you never said that you bought a fuse at Twibell's in Snig Hill?—No.

6464. Have you never said that you went to the bottom of the engine house chimney, and that it was so hot that you could not put it in?—I never said nothing about it.

6465. Did not you say that you had put a quantity of powder with a fuse up the drain, and that you then went to Rutland Bridge and saw it explode?—No.

6466. And that on the following Saturday you went to Broadhead and that he paid you 15*l*.?—No.

6467. I have given you every caution that a man can do; if you have told anybody (I do not say whom) that you had blown up this place, you can be indicted for it to-morrow?—I cannot help that.

6468. You can be indicted for it to-morrow if you have told anybody, and if you have told us a falsehood, about having told anybody you can also be indicted for perjury. Now mind, I ask you again, have you told anybody?—No.

6469. You still persist in that?—Yes.

6470. I will remind you again I do not wish to take severe measures; have you ever been at Mr. Fretson's house?—Yes.

6471. Was Mr. Jackson, the chief constable, there?—Yes.

6472. In Mr. Fretson's presence did you make a statement?—No.

6473. Was anything that you said taken down by Mr. Fretson?—No.

6474. Did you say it in the presence of Mr. Jackson, the chief constable?—What I did say I said before him.

6475. Did you say, "The first job I did for Broad-"head was a rattening on Joseph Taylor's tools, a "saw manufacturer in Mowbray Street, because

" Samuel Hallam, a saw grinder, was in arrear, and " he worked upon those tools ? "—To save you the trouble of reading all that, it is false what I did say.

6476. You will save me the trouble of reading all that because what you said there was false ?—Yes.

6477. Then you did say something there ?—Yes.

6478. Was what you said taken down in writing ?—It was a false statement that I made altogether.

6479. Did you tell them this : " The next job was " Wheatman and Smith's. There was a man named " John Helliwell, of the Wicker, a saw grinder, who " had several apprentices, and had been obnoxious to " the trade ? "—It is a false statement all through.

6480. But you told them so ?—Yes.

6481. " I and another man were looking after " Helliwell, who worked at Firth's in Saville Street, " in the best way we could, and who was several " times attempted to be blown up." Did you tell them that ?—Yes, I dare say I did.

6482. Did you tell them, " Before we could get an " opportunity of doing anything, Wheatman's case " turned up, and was thought to be more urgent." Did you tell them that ?—Yes.

6483. Did you say, " So Broadhead told us on the " Saturday night we must do Wheatman first, as we " had several times tried to get into Firth's, but could " not on account of the difficulty of entering, as we " had to cross the railway." Did you tell them that ? Yes.

6484. Did you tell them, " He told me and Sam " —who was Sam ?—Sam Nicks.

6485. You said Sam something. What did you say just now ?—I do not know.

6486. Yes you do know. Did you say Sam Nicks or Sam Nixon ? What did you say just now ?—Nicks.

6487. " He told me and Sam Wheatman's must be " done at once." Did you tell them that ?—You have it down there.

6488. Did you tell them so ?—Yes.

6489. " He gave me a sovereign to buy gunpowder " with ; he also gave Sam one." Did you tell them that ?—No.

6490. You did not tell them that ?—No ; not exactly that.

6491. What did you tell them ?—I do not know.

6492. Then how do you know that you did not tell them that ? What did you tell them ? Did you tell them that he gave you a sovereign and Sam a sovereign ?—No, I think not.

6493. Did you tell them, " We were to buy 28 lbs. " of powder, and with the remainder get implements " to defend ourselves if attacked " ?—It is a false statement altogether.

6494. I know; but did you tell Mr. Jackson and Mr. Fretson that ?—I dare say I did.

6495. Did not you tell them that you were to have 15*l*. for the job, clear ?—I dare say I did.

6496. Did not you tell them that you looked round Wheatman's place outside as well as you could, and that you purchased all the powder ? Did you tell them that ?—Yes.

6497. Did you tell them that the first time you bought 4 lbs. at Milner's in Fargate ?—All you have down there I told them.

6498. " And 2 lbs. at a grocer's shop at the bottom of " Pinstone Street " ?—Yes.

6499. Did you say, " The night but one after that I " bought 8 lbs. at Milner's. I afterwards bought the " remainder in small quantities at both places, making " 28 lbs. altogether " ?—Yes.

6500. Did you say, " I bought the bottle at " Milner's " ?—Yes.

6501. Did you say, " A strong tin milk bottle, a two-" gallon bottle " ?—Yes.

6502. And " I gave 4*s*. 6*d*. for it ? "—Yes.

6503. Did you tell them, " We had all the powder " put by in a quarry as we bought it at Bole Hill, " Crookes " ?—Yes.

6504. Did you tell them, " I bought a sash line such " as they hang clothes on to wrap the bottle in to make " it stronger " ?—Yes.

6505. Did you tell them that you bought it at a shop in Division Street ?—Yes.

6506. Did you say that you bought the fuse at Twibell's in Snig Hill ?—Yes.

6507. Did you say that you forgot what you gave ? —Yes.

6508. Did you say that you and Sam put the powder into the bottle, and wrapped it with the cord ?—Yes.

6509. Did you say that you went with the bottle on the Saturday night to Wheatman's, but that they were working late, and that you hid the bottle in a spare place near ?—Yes.

6510. On the Sunday night was Sam ill ?—Yes.

6511. And he could not go ?—Yes.

6512. And you then went yourself, but they were working on the Sunday night. Did you tell them that ?—Yes.

6513. Did you tell them, " I did not disturb anything, " and went and told Sam ; and he said it was perhaps " better put off a bit " ? Did you tell them that ?—Yes.

6514. Did you tell him that if he was not ready to go on Monday, the next night, you should go and do it yourself ?—All that you have down there I said.

6515. Did you say, " We at first intended to put it " in the engine chimney bottom, to blow it down " ?—Yes.

6516. Did you say, " We had got into the works on " the Saturday evening, but found the chimney bottom " too hot " ?—Yes.

6517. And that you heard the men walking about finishing the machine. Did you tell them that ?—Yes.

6518. Did you tell them that on the Monday night Sam was still ill, so that you went by yourself ?—Yes.

6519. Did you tell them that you found you could not get inside the works and were about to give the job up, when you found that there was a large sough or drain which ran out of the yard into the river ?—Yes.

6520. Did you tell them there was a timber yard near ?—Yes.

6521. And that you went and fetched a long pole to see how far the sough went ?—Yes.

6522. Did you tell them that you went and fetched the bottle ?—Yes.

6523. Did you say that at that time the drain was dry, and that you put the fuse in and forced it up with a long pole as far as you could ?—Yes.

6524. Did you tell them that the fuse would be five or six yards long, and that then you made up the end of the sough as well as you could with stones out of the river ?—Yes.

6525. And that you waited some time to see if the men would go ?—Yes.

6526. Did you tell that it was about eleven o'clock at night, and that when you found there was no likelihood of the men going you resolved to fire it and take the consequence ?—Yes.

6527. You told them that ?—Yes.

6528. Did you tell them that it was a very cold, bitter night, and that you had to keep running up and down to keep your feet warm ?—Ah! it wur an all.

6529. Then you were there, were you ? You said, Ah ! it wur an' all. You said that it was a very cold night, when you were there ?—I did not say I was there.

6530. Well was it a cold night ?—That night it was done ?

6531. You did not mean to say that you intended to say that you were there ?—No. I was not there.

6532. You told them that it was a very cold bitter night, and that you had to run up and down to keep your feet warm ?—Yes.

6533. Did you say that you had to cross the river ? —Yes.

6534. And that at length you fired the fuse and recrossed the river ?—Yes.

6535. Did you say you stood on Rutland Bridge, and in about a minute or so it went off ?—Yes.

6536. Did you say that you went to Crookes and told Sam that you had done it ? did Sam live at Crooke's ?—No.

SEVENTH DAY.

J. Hallam.

13 June 1867.

6537. Where did he live?—I do not know.

6538. Did you tell them that the day after, you saw placards on the wall describing the damage and that when you found how little had been done you were dissatisfied with yourself?—Yes.

6539. Did you say that you did not work that day, and did you say that you went to Broadhead and that he told you that he was not prepared to pay you that day, but would do so on Saturday, but that he lent you 10*s*.; did you tell them that?—I might do.

6540. Did you or not?—I cannot remember everything; you have it down there.

6541. Did you tell them that? — I cannot say whether I did or not.

6542. Do you mean to say that you cannot tell me that?—I cannot remember it.

6543. You made up the story?—Yes.

6544. Did Broadhead tell you that although you had not done so much damage as was expected it would answer the end, and that he was very well satisfied; did you tell them that Broadhead said that to you?—Very likely I did.

6545. Did you tell them that you were then working at Spear and Jackson's?—Yes.

6546. That was true?—Yes.

6547. Did you tell them that on the Saturday you went to Broadhead, and that he paid you 15*l*. in sovereigns?—Yes, I dare say I did.

6548. Did you tell them that no one was present? —Yes.

6549. And did you say that you paid him the 10*s*. back that he had lent you?—Yes.

6550. Did you say that you were a little in arrear on the books and you told him that he ought to set you straight?—Yes.

6551. Did you tell them that he said "No, a bargain is a bargain;" did you tell them that.—Yes.

6552. And you told them a great deal more?—Yes, I filled them another paper.

6553. And you say that all that you told them was false?—Yes.

6554. Before you saw Mr. Fretson had you previously seen Mr. Jackson?—Yes.

6555. Had you told Mr. Jackson substantially the same story?—Yes.

6556. Now I ask you what was your object, if this was untrue, in going first to Mr. Jackson to tell him this wilful set of lies and afterwards going to Mr. Fretson; what was your object in going to Mr. Jackson?—I cannot answer that.

6557. What was your object in going to Mr. Fretson?—I cannot answer that.

6558. On your oath was not it all true?—No.

6559. Who put it into your head to invent such a story?—Nobody.

6560. Then why did you go?—I do not know.

6561. Yes you do; you must answer that. Why did you go?—I cannot answer you.

6562. Did you tell Mr. Jackson that you were afraid of your life, and dared not tell the truth?—I dare say I did.

6563. Is it from fear of being personally injured that you do not tell the truth now, is that what you are afraid of? Are you afraid of speaking out now? —I would rather go on as we are doing.

6564. Is it fear of the consequences, not lawsuits, but fear of personal violence that prevents you telling more about it? is that it?—I would rather you took it as it is down here.

6565. Is it fear of personal violence that prevents you telling all about it?—I cannot answer that question.

6566. But you must answer that question? — I cannot answer it.

6567. I will let you off that. You have told us before that you joined with some person in taking Joseph Taylor's tools?—Yes.

6568. That is true?—Yes.

6569. And you said you did it with another man? —Yes.

6570. Now tell me the name of that other man?— I cannot.

6571. If you do not I will send you to prison.—I would rather go there than tell you.

6572. Why would you rather go there than tell me? —I do not like implicating another man.

6573. A man who has rattened his own father I should have thought would have had very little scruple about that; tell me the name of that other man?—I cannot.

6574. If you do not I will send you to prison; if you do not tell me the name of that other man you shall forthwith go to prison.—I will not tell you.

6575. You will not?—No.

6576. You know his name but you will not implicate him?—Yes.

6577. Although you know the name of the man, you refuse to tell us his name?—Yes.

6578. Now again I tell you that you are screened from all consequences if you tell me. Tell the truth, and do not let me driven into sending you to prison or taking extreme steps, for I put before you all these consequences: you refuse to answer questions, and I may send you to prison. If you are proved to have committed perjury, you will be indicted for perjury, and upon your own confession you will be convicted for blowing up these works. Now that is the situation in which you stand. Now think of your position, and before any steps are taken there is one chance more, and only one: what was the name of that man?—I cannot tell you.

(*Chairman.*) I shall call a policeman to take you into custody.

After consultation with the members of the Commission:

(*Chairman.*) James Hallam, we have come to the conclusion that it is our duty to send you to the Wakefield House of Correction for the period of six weeks for contempt of Court in not answering legal questions which in our judgment you are bound to answer. You have refused to give the name of the person who was with you, not because you do not know the name, but because you say that you are unwilling to implicate an associate. For that refusal we order you to go to the Wakefield House of Correction and be there kept for the period of six weeks from this time. With respect to your being indicted for perjury and your prosecution for these offences which you have confessed to both Mr. Jackson and Mr. Fretson, we at present make no order. All that we send you to Wakefield House of Correction for is a contempt of Court for refusing to answer a question that you are bound by law to answer.

The witness was then removed in custody.

Mrs. S. Shaw.

Mrs. Sarah Shaw sworn and examined.

6579. (*Mr. Barstow.*) Are you the mother of George Shaw?—Yes.

6580. Was he apprenticed to a man named Linley? —Yes.

6580. Is that the same man that was shot?—Yes.

6582. Do you remember the time he gave up working for Linley?—Not exactly.

6583. You do not remember that?—No.

6584. He did give up working for Linley?—Yes.

6585. What did he do when he gave up working for Linley?—He was ostler to his uncle.

6586. Do you remember some time in the end of the year 1859 finding some gunpowder in his bed?— Underneath it.

6587. Did you say anything to him about it?— Yes.

6588. What did you say?—I hoped he was not going to do any harm with it.

SEVENTH DAY.

Mrs. S. Shaw.

13 June 1867.

6589. What did he tell you ?—He told me he would not; I had no occasion to bother myself; he would not; he would never feel easy if he did.

6590. What did you mean when you said you hoped that he was not going to do any mischief with it ?—I hoped he was not.

6591. What did you mean by "mischief" ?—I was afraid he was going to do something that he ought not to do.

6592. What were you afraid of ?—I did not know what he might be going to do with it.

6593. What did you think he might possibly do that you were afraid of ?—I did not know what he might do.

6594. What did you think he might do ?—That was what he said to me.

6595. What made you say that to him ?—I was afraid that he was going to do something that he ought not to do.

6596. What did you mean by the word "mischief"? —I was afraid he was going to do mischief.

6597. What did you mean by "mischief," what kind of mischief ?—I did not know what he might be going to do with it; I said "doing any harm."

6598. You know what you meant by "mischief;" what was it ?—I did not want him to do any harm or mischief with it.

6599. What harm was he likely to do ?—I do not know.

6600. Hundreds of people have gunpowder without doing mischief with it ?—I knew he had no right with it.

6601. What mischief was he going to do ?—He did not tell me exactly what they were going to do with it. Mr. Broadhead would give them *5l.* for doing it, but he did not tell me what he was going to do with it; he and Tucker were to have half each for doing it.

6602. For doing what ?—He did not say what.

6603. Did not you ask him ?—He would not tell me.

6604. What did he mean by doing it? did he mean doing something with the powder ?—Yes.

6605. Did not you ask him what it was ?—He would not tell me.

6606. You did ask him ?—Yes; it was at the same time when he said it had no occasion to bother me; he would not do any harm with it.

6607. Did he say anything more at that time ?—No.

6608. That was all ?—Yes.

6609. You were contented with his assurance that he would not do any harm ?—Yes.

6610. Did he leave the powder there ?—Yes, at that time he did.

6611. Do you know what became of it ?—He told me he had sold it when I missed it.

6612. When you missed it did you ask him what had become of it ?—Yes.

6613. How soon after was it that you missed it ?—That day, or the day following.

6614. Then you asked him what he had done with it ?—Yes.

6615. What did he tell you then ?—Sold it.

6616. Is that all you know about it ?—Yes, he told me he had sold it to Simmonite.

6617. Did you hear anything some days after this about any blowing up ?—No.

6618. You never did ?—No.

6619. Did you know a man named Helliwell ?—No.

6620. You have never heard of him ?—No.

6621. Did you hear nothing in the town about his being blown up ?—I might.

6622. But did you ?—I cannot say whether I did or not.

6623. Can you say now whether you did or not ?—I cannot say whether I did or not.

6624. Have you quite forgotten all about it ?—Yes I have; he eased my mind by saying he would do no harm with it, and I did not bother myself.

6625. You might have heard that there was some mischief done in the town, but you cannot remember ? —No, I have plenty of trouble of my own without that.

6626. You can try and recollect whether you did not hear that something had gone wrong in the town ?—I might, but I did not take much notice of it.

6627. Might you hear that there was some accident with gunpowder ?—Yes, several accidents.

6628. But there were several accidents just about that time ?—Yes.

6629. Of what nature were those accidents ?—In different parts.

6630. What was the nature of the accidents ?—I cannot say; it is just as I have been told. I never went out of my own house to hear it.

6631. Cannot you say what the nature of them was ?—I cannot.

6632. What do you mean by accidents ?—I knew they were nothing concerning me, so I did not let them bother me.

6633. Though they did not concern you, you might inquire ?—I did not. I am not one who interferes with other people's affairs.

6634. If a man is blown up you will not ask how it happened ?—I did not.

6635. You heard about the accidents but you did not inquire about them ?—No.

6636. Did your son never tell you about accidents ? —No.

6637. Did he never mention to you that he had blown up Helliwell ?—No.

6638. Did he give you any money about that time ? —No.

6639. He did not ?—No.

6640. (*Mr. Chance.*) How much powder did you find ?—Three tin cans.

6641. Did you say just now that your son told you that Broadhead had given *5l.*, or would give *5l.* ?—That he would give *5l.*

6642. Was your daughter living in the house at the same time ?—Yes.

6643. (*Mr. Barstow.*) Does Simmonite live near you ?—No, at the top of the hill.

6644. Are you quite sure that your son did not tell you what he got the powder for ?—No, he did not.

6645. Did he tell you where he got it ?—He did not receive it from Broadhead, they sent it to him.

6646. Did he tell you what he got for doing it ?—No.

6647. He never mentioned any sum to you ?—No.

6648. What did he say about money at the time the powder was found ?—When I found the powder ?

6649. Yes ?—That they were to have *5l.*

6650. Are you quite certain of what your son said at the time you found the powder about the money he got for it ?—He did not say what money he got for it.

6651. (*Chairman.*) Your son says that he told you that he had got three quid, or three sovereigns, is that true ?—No; he did not tell me that he had got three sovereigns.

6652. He told you that they were to have five sovereigns ?—Yes.

6653. He did not tell you they had got three ?—No.

6654. (*Mr. Barstow.*) Where did you find the powder ?—Between the bed and mattress.

The witness withdrew.

SEVENTH DAY.

T. Simmonite.

13 June 1867.

THOMAS SIMMONITE sworn and examined.

6655. (*Mr. Chance.*) Where do you live?—At Cricket Lane.

6656. What are you?—A table blade forger.

6657. (*Chairman.*) Do you know Hyde Park?—Yes.

6658. Do you stand outside the park when a pigeon match is going on to shoot the outside birds?—Yes.

6659. (*Mr. Chance.*) Do you remember the occasion of there being a blowing up at Helliwell's?—No.

6660. Did you ever know a man of the name of Helliwell?—No.

6661. Do you mean to say that you never heard of any blowing up taking place at Helliwell's some seven years ago?—No.

6662. Did you never read any account of it anywhere?—No; I cannot read.

6663. I suppose that the paper is sometimes read to you?—No.

6664. Have you heard of it since?—No.

6665. Nor of the troughs in Helliwell's works being blown up?—No.

6666. Do you know a man of the name of George Shaw?—Yes.

6667. How long have you known him?—Ever since he was little.

6668. Have you never said anything to Shaw, or has Shaw never said anything to you, about Helliwell?—No.

6669. Did Shaw ever sell any powder to you?—No, never in his life.

6670. Are you sure of that?—Yes.

6671. Do not you remember Shaw once coming to you when you were shooting pigeons outside the park?—No.

6672. Shaw never sold you the powder?—No.

6673. Just think whether some years ago, seven or eight years ago, Shaw did not sell you some powder?—No, he never did.

6674. Some powder in two cans?—No; I never bought any powder from him in my life.

6675. Never bought any powder?—No, nor nothing else.

6676. I believe you have known him some years?—Yes, I have.

6677. Who do you buy your powder from?—At Cannon's.

6678. You cannot have forgotten it?—I never had anything to do with him.

6679. You have known him a great many years?—Yes.

6680. But you never had anything to do with him?—Nothing to do with him in my life.

6681. Have you never kept company with Shaw?—Not a day.

6682. You do sometimes?—No, I have not these many years.

6683. Where does Shaw live?—I do not know.

6684. Do you often see him?—No, I have not seen him for many a week.

6685. Are you a member of the Union?—No; I have not been for a long while; I do not pay to the Union.

6686. Have you ever paid to the Union?—Yes.

6687. How long?—Three years.

6688. Were you ever a member of the same union as Shaw?—No.

6689. You say you never bought any powder?—No, never in my life.

6690. Do you know a man named Dennis Clarke known by the name of Tucker?—Yes.

6691. Have you ever seen him and Shaw together?—No, I have not.

6692. You are sure of that?—Yes.

6693. Has Clarke ever sold you any powder?—No.

6694. I am speaking now of some years ago?—No. I never had to do with Clarke in my life.

6695. How long have you known Clarke?—Many years; we were nearly brought up together.

6696. You have not seen Shaw and Clarke together at any time?—No.

6697. You still persist in telling me you never heard of Helliwell's being blown up?—No.

6698. Have you never heard of it since at any time?—No.

6699. Not up to the present time?—No, I have not heard anything about it.

6700. You never heard of his being blown up, up to the present time?—No.

6701. You have known both Clarke and Shaw?—Yes, a long while.

6702. Did you live near one another?—Not that I know of.

6703. Do you know where they did live?—No.

6704. They were both in the same trade?—I do not know what trade they are.

6705. Although you know them very well you do not know what trade they follow?—No.

6706. You do not know what trade Shaw followed?—No, I do not.

6707. You do not know, although you have known him from a baby, what trade he followed?—No, I do not.

6708. Whom do you work for?—For Mr. Crossland.

6709. What is he?—A table blade manufacturer.

6710. Where?—He did live in the Park, he lives now down the Moor.

6711. How long since did you work for him?—A month since.

6712. What do you do for your livelihood?—I grind a bit now.

6713. Are you a gardener?—I can do it a bit.

6714. How do you mean garden?—Set things.

6715. Do you set them for yourself or other people?—Other people.

6716. Is that the way you get your livelihood?—No. I work at my own trade when I have it to do.

6717. Why are you not working at it now?—There is no work.

6718. Do you mean to say that there are no table forgers doing any work at present?—No, not in my line.

6719. What is your line?—I make very big blades.

6720. And there is no work for them?—No.

6721. When was it that you were first applied to to give any evidence on this matter?—On Saturday.

6722. Who applied to you?—Two gentlemen came on Saturday night.

6723. What were their names?—I do not know.

6724. Do you know them now?—I know one of them.

6725. Is that the gentleman, Mr. Sugg?—No.

6726. Which is the gentleman, have you seen him this morning, what kind of man was he?—A stoutish fellow.

6727. Did he tell you who he was?—No.

(*Chairman to Mr. Chambers.*) I am told by the secretary that he believes that your clerk went to him on Saturday.

(*Mr. Chambers.*) I am not aware of it.

(*Mr. Sugg.*) He was called at my request.

6728. (*Chairman.*) You say that these gentlemen came to you. Did they speak to you?—Yes.

6729. They talked to you?—Yes.

6730. Did they ask you whether you had bought any powder?—Yes, from Shaw and Tucker.

6731. They asked you if Shaw and Tucker had sold you some powder?—Yes, and they went away.

6732. What did you tell them?—I told them that they never had.

6733. Was Shaw one of the persons who was there?—No.

6734. They were two persons whom you did not know?—I know one of them.

6735. What is his name?—I do not know; he is a detective.

SEVENTH DAY.

T. Simmonite,

13 June 1867.

6736. You know the detective; you told them that they never had sold you any, and then they went away?—Yes.

6737. How did you happen to be a witness here?—I do not know.

6738. When did you receive any notice to appear here?—On Monday.

6739. Had you a summons on the Monday?—Yes; Shaw and one of them came again.

6740. Did Shaw talk to you on that occasion?—Yes.

6741. Did Shaw tell you that he had sold you the powder?—Yes; he said, "I want you to go and say "that I sold you some powder."

6742. What did you say to that?—I said I should do nothing of the sort.

6743. What did he say to that?—He came on Sunday morning when I was in bed.

6744. I thought you said it was on Monday?—He came on Sunday morning, and said, "I want you; I "have a good job for you, as you have nought to do."

6745. Go on?—He says, "You will get 5*s.* a day "or 7*s.* 6*d.* a day if you go and say I have sold you "some powder, and it won't do you any harm."

6746. What did you say?—I said, "No, I shall have "nought to do with it."

6747. You told him that?—Yes.

6748. And Shaw knew this when he came and gave his evidence this morning? He knew that you were going to contradict him?—Yes; I said I should not do anything of the sort.

6749. Was he alone then?—He went away then and left me.

6750. Have you seen him since?—I have seen him to-day, and I saw him on Monday.

6751. What happened then?—I said nought to him any more; the same gentleman and him went away.

6752. Who is this gentleman?—I do not know I could tell if I saw him.

6753. What coloured hair had he?—I did not take any notice of him.

6754. He and this gentleman went away?—Yes.

6755. Did they speak to you?—Yes; they asked me whether I would sign my hand to a paper saying that I had bought some powder.

6756. What did you say?—I said I should do nothing of the sort.

6757. And they went away?—Yes.

6758. Have you seen him since?—I saw him to-day.

6759. Where?—Upstairs here.

6760. Have you talked to him?—No; I never spoke to him.

6761. Have you had any communication with Mr. Sugg?—No.

6762. Have you never spoken to him?—No.

6763. Nor to Mr. Broadhead?—Not that I know of.

6764. You do not know him?—I know him if I see him.

6765. Is that Mr. Broadhead (*pointing him out*)?—I do not know; I never saw him.

6766. Have you had any communication on the matter with any person at all except this gentleman who came with Shaw?—No.

6767. With nobody else?—No.

6768. Then you had not told anybody connected with the Trades' Unions that this was all false?—No.

6769. You never mentioned the fact until to-day when you came here?—No.

6770. You never talked to anybody about it, you kept it quite a secret till you came here, either that Shaw had applied to you or that he had asked you to do this or anything of the kind?—No.

6771. You never told them anything about the powder at all?—No.

6772. How did they think you knew it? I was asked to call you for the purpose of contradicting this man. How did they know it?—I do not know, I am sure.

6773. Was it a guess do you suppose? You do not know how they could have imagined this?—No.

6774. You never told it to anybody?—No.

6775. Then it was a mere guess on their part?—It must have been.

6776. Upon your oath, have you not been communicating with the Trades' Union people, and telling them this?—I know nothing about it.

6777. Will you swear that nobody had been to you to talk with you on this matter?—No.

6778. Not at all?—No.

6779. You were called here on our summons to give evidence in support of Shaw's story?—Yes.

6780. The other side call you, and still for all that they do not know what you are going to say?—No.

(*Chairman.*) I should like you to certify and fix upon the person who was present when Shaw came.

6781. (*Mr. Barstow.*) Did anybody, besides the gentleman you do not know, see you and Shaw talking together?—No.

The witness withdrew.

George Shaw recalled and further examined.

G. Shaw.

6782. (*Chairman.*) Did you go to Simmonite's on the Saturday?—On the Friday afternoon.

6783. Who was with you?—Dennis Clarke.

6784. Had you seen Simmonite since you sold him the powder?—Yes; I went to him on Sunday morning.

6785. Had you been to him before that?—No.

6786. Were you there on the Saturday?—No.

6787. On the Sunday were you alone or in company with some other person?—I was alone.

6788. Did you tell him, "I want you; I have a good "job for you, you have nothing to do"?—No, I told him I wanted him to speak about buying the powder, and he said that a policeman came and told him on Saturday night that me and Clarke was in the Town Hall; he said he did not want to have anything to do with it.

6789. Did he say that he had not bought the powder of you?—He would not say anything.

6790. Did he say that he had not bought it?—No, he would not say anything then. I told him it would not harm him. I went up again on Monday in company with Mr. Lewis Brammer.

6791. Who is Mr. Brammer? Is he Mr. Chambers' clerk?—Yes; he promised to give us an answer to night. Mr. Brammer went down in the night to the Falstaff in the Wicker, where he promised to come to. I met Simmonite against the market place, and I asked him if he had been to see Mr. Brammer according to appointment, he said, "no," he had not had time, he had been to the new ground, the "Queen's Hotel" ground. Well, sir, he went away and left me and I have not spoken to him since.

6792. Did you tell him this on the Sunday, "I want "you, I have a good job for you, you have nothing to "do, and you will have 5*s.* or 7*s.* 6*d.* a day if you "will say you bought some powder of me"?—No, I told him he would get his day's wages if he came here and spoke the truth.

6793. Did he say "I shall have nothing to do with "you?"—He said he should have nothing to do with it.

6794. Did he say at any time to you that he had not bought the powder from you?—No.

6725. Simmonite says now that he never did buy the powder from you; do you still persist in the story that he did?—Yes.

The witness withdrew.

Adjourned to to-morrow at 11 o'clock.

EIGHTH DAY.

Council Hall, Sheffield, Friday, 14th June 1867.

PRESENT:

WILLIAM OVEREND, Esq., Q.C.
THOMAS IRWIN BARSTOW, Esq.
GEORGE CHANCE, Esq.
J. E. BARKER, Esq., Secretary.

WILLIAM OVEREND, ESQ., Q.C., IN THE CHAIR.

EIGHTH DAY.

Mr. L. Brammer.

14 June 1867.

Mr. LEWIS BRAMMER sworn and examined.

6796. (*Mr. Barstow.*) Are you clerk to Mr. Chambers?—I am.

6797. Did you go on Sunday last with George Shaw to Simmonite's?—On Monday.

6798. (*Chairman.*) Which day of the month was that?—The 10th, I think.

6799. (*Mr. Barstow.*) Was that to take Simmonite's evidence for the purpose of this inquiry?—It was.

6800. Did you see Simmonite?—I did.

6801. Was that at his own house?—At his brother-in-law's.

6802. (*Chairman.*) What is his name?—Chadwick, I think. It is a beerhouse there.

6803. (*Mr. Barstow.*) What did you say to him?—I told him that I had come for the purpose of asking him a question about some powder which was supposed to have been purchased by him from Shaw.

6804. What answer did he make to you?—He wanted to have nothing to do with it.

6805. (*Chairman.*) What did he say?—"I want "to have nothing to do with it."

6806. (*Mr. Barstow.*) Did you say anything to him upon that?—I did; I told him that I wanted the truth, and nothing but the truth.

6807. What did he say to that?—I then continued, "If you did purchase the powder, say so; if you did "not, deny it." He then said, "I did not buy any "powder of him."

6808. What was said upon that?—Shaw then wanted to interfere.

6809. (*Chairman.*) How do you mean that Shaw wanted to interfere?—He wanted to say something to him. I told Shaw to wait. Simmonite again said that he had not bought any powder. I said then, "Recollect what I told you on Saturday with respect "to a statement which had been made by Shaw." I said, "Do you still persist in saying that you did not "purchase any powder?" He said, "Yes." I then said to him, "Did you purchase any from Clarke?" He said, "That he had not, and that he knew nothing "about it." I then served him with a summons. Shaw then said, that he knew that he had purchased it, and that he had better say so: "Thou "knows thou did, and thou had better speak to it." That was how he put it. "Me and Tucker Clarke "were together," that was what Shaw said, "and "we spent the money together at the 'Green Man' "at the bottom of the park. We had not stole it. "Thou will come to no harm, only thou must speak "truth." I then explained to him that he would have to appear here yesterday morning, and that he would be expected to speak the truth and nothing but the truth. Simmonite then said that he must be going; he had to go to the new ground to see a race, and he asked me whether he could not see me another time. I said, "Yes; but recollect if there is any nonsense "about it, you will get into trouble."

6810. (*Mr. Barstow.*) Then, I suppose, you left him?—No; he then asked me when he could see me. I then said, "Anywhere; fix your own place." He then suggested to meet me at his uncle's at the "Falstaff," in the Wicker, at eight o'clock, and said that he would then give me his final reply.

6811. Did you then go to him?—I went there, but he did not come.

6812. You went at eight o'clock?—I went at eight o'clock.

6813. On Monday evening?—Yes.

6814. You had had some interview with him previously to this?—I had, on Saturday.

6815. (*Chairman.*) What took place then?—I then had a detective officer with me.

6816. Had you gone to his house?—To the same house where I found him.

6817. With what detective?—Battersby, I think it was. I then explained to him my object in calling upon him.

6818. What did you say?—I told him that I had called upon him for the purpose of seeing him about some powder which it was supposed that he had purchased from Shaw. He then asked me, "What Shaw?" and I told him "Putty Shaw." He denied having purchased any. I then told him that he had better wait before he said anything. I then read him over the statement which had been made by Shaw.

6819. Have you that statement?—I have not; I have handed it in.

6820. Was that a document from which he was examined yesterday?—I am sure I do not know.

6821. Do you recollect what the statement was?—It was a statement made by Shaw, that he had been employed by Mr. Broadhead, through the medium of Clarke, to put some powder in the trough of a man named Helliwell, who worked at the Tower wheel. That they had not done that. That they had got three canisters of powder, and two and a half they had sold to this man Thomas Simmonite, who was a table-blade forger. I then asked Simmonite, after reading that over to him, if he still said that he had not purchased the powder. He said that he had not. I then said, "You know best. I have merely come for the "purpose of getting at the truth, but you will cer- "tainly be summoned; and whoever is denying the "truth will get punished." I then left him.

6822. Did Shaw say, "I want you to say that I sold you some powder?"—Certainly not; he told me he had sold him some, and he knew he had, and he must speak the truth.

6823. (*Mr. Barstow.*) Did Shaw in your presence tell him he would get any money for coming here?—Certainly not; he only said he would get paid his wages.

6824. He did say that?—He said that.

6825. Did he say, "I have a good job for you as "you have nought to do?"—No.

6826. Did Shaw say, "I have sold you some "powder; it will not do you any harm?"—Yes, he told him, and he said that Clark and he were both together when they sold it to Simmonite.

6827. Did he offer him any paper to sign?—Certainly not.

6828. Did you ask him to sign his name to a paper about the powder?—Certainly not.

6829. (*Chairman.*) It never was done while you were there?—Oh no, certainly not. There is one thing that just slipped my memory, and I forgot to tell you, that is this—that Shaw told him in my

EIGHTH DAY

Mr. L. Brammer.

14 June 1867.

presence on the Monday, that he knew he acknowledged on the Sunday morning, that he had purchased it. He said "Thou knows when thou saw me yesterday thou acknowledged thou had bought it."

6830. What did Simmonite say to that?—He shook his head, but he made no reply.

6831. (*Mr. Barstow.*) Did Simmonite make no reply to that at all?—No; he shook his head.

6832. And did you press him at all about it?—No, certainly not; I let it remain where it was.

The witness withdrew.

R. Helliwell.

REBECCA HELLIWELL sworn and examined.

6833. (*Mr. Chance.*) You are living in Scotland Street, are you not?—Yes.

6834. Are you the widow of Joseph Helliwell?—No, I am not a widow.

6835. You are living apart from your husband, Joseph Helliwell, are you not?—Yes.

6836. Was your husband a saw-grinder?—Yes.

6837. Did he work at the Tower wheel?—Yes.

6838. And he worked for Mr. James Linley?—One of the name of James Linley and Joseph Wilson.

6839. And they I believe were saw manufacturers?—Yes; Mr. Wilson was a saw manufacturer.

6840. About how long ago was that?—Eight or nine years ago.

6841. Do you remember about that time his receiving any letters?—Three.

6842. He received three letters?—Yes.

6843. Have you those letters with you?—No, I have not.

6844. What has become of them?—I cannot tell, we have lost all, everything is gone.

6845. Do you remember what the character of those letters was?—Yes, one particularly. I cannot say for the other two, for I am no scholar, and I never read them.

6846. Were they all received at once, or at different times?—At different times.

6847. And at what interval of time would they be received?—Perhaps a week or two, or three weeks, or something of that kind. I cannot say now for certain.

6848. Can you call to mind what were the contents of the first letters that you received?—I know one of the letters was, that if he did not give up working for "Bulldog" Wilson, he might expect what would follow.

6849. Was that all the letter contained, or was there anything more?—There might be more, but I cannot say for certain. Perhaps I might know what it was, but it is so long since that I cannot think of it.

6850. That you say was one of them, but can you tell which?—I will not say for certain, but it was one of them.

6851. Was there any signature to the letter?—There was no name.

6852. No name at all?—No name; it was signed by no one. There was no name.

6853. And there was no signature of any kind?—No.

6854. Do you remember the contents of any other letters that you received then?—No, I do not.

6855. Were they letters of the same character?—It was for the same purpose, if he did not give up work.

6856. Were they letters of a threatening character?—Oh yes, but I do not know. I cannot say what was in them.

6857. But you are quite sure they were threatening letters?—Yes, they were threatening letters.

6858. Do you remember one Saturday morning taking your husband's breakfast to him?—It was one morning, but I do not know the morning.

6859. Was that about the same time?—The letter came before that time.

6860. It would be not long after the letters that you remember taking his breakfast to him one morning?—Yes.

6861. Where was that?—I lived in the Wicker, and it was to the Tower wheel that I went with the breakfast.

6862. Did he say anything about bringing his dinner?—Yes; I asked him if I might bring his dinner, and in a few minutes he came home black all over. In a short time, perhaps ten minutes or so afterwards, he came home with his hair singed off, and his face and his bosom burnt; and blind too he was.

6863. When he came home did he make any remark?—"They have done me at last."

6864. Whom did he mean by "they"?—I suppose the company that was with him that made the remark in the letters, and that sent the letters.

6865. Look at this letter (*handing a letter to the witness*)?—I cannot read. I am no scholar.

6866. Are those similar to the letters which you received?—I cannot say.

6867. Should you remember them if they were to be read over to you?—I cannot read at all. I am no scholar.

6868. Were the threatening letters read over to you when they were received?—My husband read them over to me.

6869. If the same letters were to be read over to you, should you remember what the contents were?—Well, I perhaps might know something. I do not know, I am sure.

6870. "To Messrs. Firth and Sons, saw grinders. "Gentlemen. The game works merrily, and we "brush away all obstacles before us. If we appear "to be rather long about it, you see we are none the "less sure. It is your turn next, and the man that "hangs back will be the first to get out; and if I but "move my finger you are sent to eternity as sure as "fate. Be advised, and take the hint in time." Do you recollect anything about that?—Yes, I can. "The "hint in time," and "they would advise him to get "away as quick as possible," that I do remember.

6871. (*Chairman.*) Do you know what became of that letter? was it given to the police?—No; we had three sergeants came, but I do not know what my husband did with them, and I do not know who the inspectors were that came.

6872. (*Mr. Chance.*) As far as your recollection goes, do you think that that was one of the letters which was received?—There was a great deal that I could not tell in the letters, but there was something in those words, but I cannot say what now.

6873. But you say you remember about the "hint "in time"?—Yes.

6874. Now listen to this one: "So you have had "an accidental fire, John. Singular; but did no "one ever acquaint you that they would drop on you "sooner or later if you persisted in certain conduct "that I think I need not name. You see all that I "promised has come to pass. I have kept my word "to the very letter, as I have never failed to do in "matters of this kind, cause lads, John! and I shall "visit you again in due time with a stronger dose if "you do not take notice and mind certain conduct, "which you understand. I never give up, John. I "fight for years, aye, aye, until death, if it is neces- "sary; and, like you, with all kinds of craft and "duplicity. Rely, I shall do again what I promise "if you do not take the hint. (Signed) TANTIA "TOPEE." Do you recollect that?—Not to my husband, excuse me.

6875. To whom was it written?—To John Helliwell, my husband's brother.

6876. (*Chairman.*) Was he blown up?—Never. I think the trap was laid, but he was not blown up.

EIGHTH DAY.

R. Helliwell.

14 June 1867.

6877. But do you recollect hearing that letter read?—Yes.

6878. When was that? Was it after your husband was blown up or not?—Before he lived in the Wicker, I believe. I cannot say whether he lived in the Wicker, or in the "Twelve o'Clock."

6879. But when was it that you heard that letter read; was it after your husband was blown up? He talks about there having been an accidental fire. Was your husband's name John?—I will tell you about how many years. It is not above three years. It is between three and four years, I think.

6880. What was three or four years?—Since the fire was. Since I heard that letter read.

6881. John Helliwell was your husband's brother?—Yes.

6882. He worked at Wheatman and Smith's?—I do not know whether he worked at Wheatman and Smith's, but the last place he worked at was Firth's.

6883. What was your husband's name?—Joseph.

6884. Do you recollect your brother-in-law reading that letter to you?—My brother's wife.

6885. (*Mr. Chance.*) One of the letters, I think you said, mentioned the name of Wilson?—Yes; if he did not give up working for "Bulldog" Wilson.

6886. After your husband came home so much injured, how long did he remain at home?—A fortnight, blinded.

6887. And how long was it before he was able to go to work again?—He was a month before he could go to work, but he was a long time before he could work his full time.

6888. Have you been with your husband to see Mr. Broadhead?—Yes.

6889. When was that?—Ten years ago.

6890. I mean with regard to this blowing up. Was it after the blowing up?—No; it was before the blowing up, I believe.

6891. For what did you go to Broadhead?—I did not see Mr. Broadhead myself, but I went with my husband, and stood outside the door while my husband went to him to see if he would allow him to enter the trade for 5*l.* When he came back to me he says, "No, "they will not take me." My husband told me they would not take him in under 10*l.* Well, we came home, and we went again with 8*l.*, to see if they would take him in then.

6892. Where did you go?—To his house.

6893. (*Chairman.*) You went to Broadhead's did you?—Yes, and he came down to me again outside, and he said they would still not take him in for 8*l.*, not under 10*l.*; and we went again with the 10*l.*, we got the 10*l.*, and he told him that he would not have him in at any price. That was all.

6894. Then you went home again?—Oh, yes! we went home again.

6895. How long was that before the blowing up?—Well, it will be about 10 years since as near as I can think on now; 10 or 11 years since.

6896. That will be between one and two years before the blowing up, would it not?—I think it would not be so long as that.

6897. Do you remember going to see Mr. Broadhead after your husband had been blown up?—No; we did not go after he was blown up.

6898. Did you not go to Mr. Broadhead to see if you could get some work for your husband?—I remember seeing Mr. Broadhead's wife on some occasion, but I am sure I do not know when.

6899. But did you not go to see Mr. Broadhead after your husband had been injured, for the purpose of getting some work for him?—I remember going to Mrs. Broadhead's for something, but not to Mr. Broadhead, and on what occasion I went to Mrs. Broadhead I do not know.

6900. (*Chairman.*) Are you a friend of Mrs. Broadhead's?—I am not a friend, but I have known her ever since she was a little girl living near her mother's. I do not know anything further about her.

6901. (*Mr. Chance.*) Then you do not remember going to Mr. Broadhead's except on these occasions?—Only those three occasions.

6902. Are you sure that the time you went to see Mr. Broadhead was before your husband was injured or after?—Before.

6903. Are you quite certain of that?—I will not be quite certain; but the reason was that I was afraid of this blowing up, and I told him that he had better go.

6904. But did you not go to see Mr. Broadhead to get work for your husband in consequence of his having beeu injured?—I did not go myself, only with my husband, and stood outside at the door.

6905. But did you ever go with your husband or without your husband to Mr. Broadhead in order to get him work after he was injured?—I cannot say; I was always anxious for him to work because he had not work.

6906. Your husband was out of work you say for a month, in consequence of the injuries which he received?—Yes.

6907. You did not go to Broadhead to get work for him in consequence of the injuries which he received?—The last time I was in Mr. Broadhead's house was seven years ago; but I cannot say what I went for, whether I went for work or no. I used to carry the work up and down for him. I did a great deal that I really cannot think of now.

6908. Can you not recollect?—I have been to his house on three different occasions.

6909. For what purpose did you go?—I went one time to see if they knew anything about my husband, and another time I went for the same purpose.

6910. In what way do you mean?—With him going away and leaving me for one thing; at least if he had come back. I had been told that he had come back again and was in Sheffield, and I thought that he would perhaps be likely to know; but I never got any information at all.

6911. Do you not remember having been to see Mr. Broadhead, in order to get work for your husband after he was injured?—I cannot tell whether it was before or afterwards, to speak the truth.

6912. You have told us that you went before he was blown up, in order to get him into the trade?—Yes; I went with him three times.

6913. Did you not go to see, after he was blown up, if you could get work for him in consequence of his having received injuries, you must remember that?—I cannot.

6914. Were you anxious to get work for him after he had been idle for a month in consequence of the injuries which he had received?—Oh, yes.

6915. Did you make any attempts to get work for him?—Yes.

6916. What attempts did you make to get work for him?—I went to Mr. Wilson's to see if I could get work for him.

6917. Did you go anywhere else?—I used to go to Hill Foot to a man that he worked for. I know for a certainty that I went to Mr. Linley and asked him if he would employ him, because we were wanting bread, and I went to Linley for employment; but as to going to Mr. Broadhead I cannot say for certain.

6918. I think that you will be able to remember if you reflect for a moment. Did you not go at the same time that you went to this gentleman to ask Mr. Broadhead if he could not assist your husband to work?—I know another time.

6919. (*Chairman.*) It will not do to go off in this way; we shall be severe with you if you do not answer the question?—I cannot answer for I really do not know.

6920. (*Mr. Chance.*) Do you recollect going to Broadhead before the blowing up?—Yes; I cannot say whether I went to him before or afterwards for employment.

6921. Then you did go to him for employment?—I think I did, but I will not be certain.

6922. (*Chairman.*) Then you did go to Broadhead?—I think I did, but I would not be certain.

EIGHTH DAY.

R. Helliwell.

14 June 1867.

6923. Then why did you not say so before?—I cannot say; I will not be certain.

6924. When was it that you went to Mr. Broadhead to get your husband employment?—It will be seven and a half years since. It would be after the blowing up.

6925. Then you did go to Mr. Broadhead?—The blowing up is seven and a half years since. It would be after the blowing up.

6926. Then you did go to Mr. Broadhead?—But I did not see Mr. Broadhead. I only saw his wife, and I told his wife what I wanted.

6927. Did you go by yourself, or with your husband?—I went by myself one morning.

6928. You saw Mrs. Broadhead?—Yes.

6929. What did you say to her?—I asked her to name it to her husband about my husband's not having work.

6930. Did you ever go again to see Mrs. Broadhead?—I have never been twice since that time.

6931. (*Chairman.*) Have you not said that you went to Mr. Broadhead because you thought that your husband's life was in danger?—I was afraid of the blowing up. I said that.

6932. Answer my question. Have you not said that you went after he was blown up to Mr. Broadhead because you thought his life was in danger?—Not after he was blown up; after I was afraid. What made me want him to join the trade was that I was afraid of this blowing up.

6933. And after he was blown up, did you not yourself go to Mr. Broadhead?—It is seven and a half years since.

6934. After he was blown up, did you not go to Mr. Broadhead?—Yes; after he was blown up.

6935. Did you, or did you not? Answer the question.—Yes, I did. I went to Mr. Broadhead's wife.

6936. Did you see Mr. Broadhead?—No, I did not.

6937. Did you not tell Mr. Brammer that you had been to see Mr. Broadhead after your husband was blown up?—Before.

6938. I was asking you after, and not before?—I never went.

6939. Did you not tell Mr. Brammer so?—I am not certain.

6940. You will not say so. Did you, or did you not, tell Mr. Brammer that after your husband was blown up you went to see Mr. Broadhead about it?—I cannot say, to tell truth, whether I went after he was blown up, or if I went before he was blown up.

6941. But did you not a few days ago tell Mr. Brammer that you went to see Mr. Broadhead after your husband had been blown up?—I cannot answer that.

6942. I am not saying whether it is true or not; but did you not tell Mr. Brammer so, and that you saw Broadhead, and not his wife?—I never was in ——

6943. Did you tell Mr. Brammer that?—I cannot say that I did.

6944. Will you swear you did not?—No, I will not swear. I cannot swear to anything that I have not my mind on.

6945. Then you will not swear that you did not tell him?—I should not like to swear anything that I do not know.

6946. Did you see Mr. Broadhead after your husband was blown up at any time?—I did not about the blowing-up.

6947. Did you see him at all about anything?—Not after he was blown up.

6948. You never saw Broadhead after your husband was blown up?—Not that I am aware of.

6949. Did you see him about anything after your husband was blown up?—No, not about that affair.

6950. I did not ask you about any affair. Did you see Broadhead after your husband was blown up?—At the time?

6951. Shortly after your husband was blown up?—No.

6952. You swear you did not?—It is seven and a half years ago.

6953. I know as well as you when it was; but did you see Broadhead after your husband was blown up?—Not about that affair, that I am aware of.

6954. But you must know. If your husband was blown up it is a very serious matter, and you know very well whether you saw him about it or not. You had gone to him before, because you thought your husband would be blown up?—Yes, before.

6955. Will you swear you did not go to him after your husband had been blown up?—How can I swear to things I do not know.

6956. You have no occasion to do so. Will you swear you did not go to Broadhead after your husband had been blown up?—No. I never had any interview with him.

6957. You never saw him?—No; I have only seen him in his own house.

6958. Did you see him in his own house?—Not about this.

6959. What did you see him about?—To see if he knew anything about my husband.

6960. But while your husband was living with you?—I never went then. I went three times before he was blown up; and I never saw him afterwards till after my husband had left me.

6961. You went to see him afterwards, and saw his wife?—I only saw his wife.

6962. But you went to see him?—I went to see him, but I only saw his wife.

6963. (*Mr. Chance.*) But are you sure that when you went about getting him into the trade that was not after your husband was blown up?—No; I think it was before.

6964. Did you not tell Mr. Brammer, that it was after your husband was blown up that you went to Broadhead?—We went twice to Mr. Broadhead before the outrage was, and once afterwards; and it was on the Wednesday night, I believe, we went the last time. It was the committee night, let it be what night it might.

6965. And the time you went after the blowing up did you see Broadhead?—No; my husband did, and that was saying they would not take him at any price, and then he went to work for Mr. Wilson.

6966. You did see him afterwards?—Once afterwards and twice before.

6967. (*Chairman.*) You did not see him yourself; your husband only saw him, and what you tell us is what your husband told you?—I did not see him at all then.

6968. (*Mr. Chance.*) Do you know a man of the name of Dennis Clarke?—One of the name of "Tucker."

6969. Have you seen him within the last day or two?—I picked him out this morning. I had not seen him for four years before.

6970. Do you remember whether he ever used any threatening words to your husband?—Yes, he did.

6971. (*Chairman*). Did you hear him?—Yes.

6972. What did you hear him say?—I heard him say, "I will do thee yet."

6973. (*Mr. Chance.*) When was that?—Before the blowing up.

6974. Do you remember how long before the blowing up it was?—Not long.

6975. Where was it that you heard him say it?—At the "Corner Pin" in the Wicker.

6976. Do you remember what further took place then; what did your husband say when Clarke said, "I will do thee yet"?—He passed on and went home with me and took no notice; and I turned myself round and said, "They will do thee, without "thee minds."

6977. (*Chairman.*) Did Clarke hear you say that?—No; we walked along.

6978. You had left them?—We were passing by when that was said.

6979. Then you did not say that in the hearing of Clarke?—No.

EIGHTH DAY.

R. Helliwell.

14 June 1867.

6980. Who was present when Clarke said that?—I have found out that Shaw was one that was present.

6981. Who besides?—I do not know his name but I saw him here yesterday. They were all three together.

6982. Could you point him out if you saw him?—Yes; I think I could. I have never seen the man since before yesterday.

6983. Was he a witness?—I do not know I am sure.

6984. Did either Shaw or the other man say anything when Clarke said, "I will do thee yet"?—Not in my hearing.

6985. They did not say anything?—No.

6986. (*Mr. Chance.*) Do you remember Clarke joining the trade?—No; I do not.

6987. You do not recollect when that was?—No.

6988. (*Chairman*). Was the man you saw yesterday a small bow-legged man?—Yes; he was.

6989. (*Mr. Chance.*) Was it about this time that your husband had had a quarrel with the Union when you heard the threatening words used by Clarke?—They had words and fighting about the time that he was blown up. They were fighting in the wheels. They were always tricking him in some way or other, and they had been doing it then.

6990. What do you mean by "tricking him"?—Taking his things away; taking little oddments and that away from him that he had to work with.

6991. (*Chairman.*) Taking his tools away?—Yes.

6992. (*Mr. Chance.*) Do you know who were the men at that time who were tricking him?—Yes; this crooked-legged man and Shaw was in the wheel, and Tucker and all I believe was in the wheel when he was fighting.

6993. (*Chairman.*) Who fought?—This crooked-legged man.

6994. (*Mr. Chance.*) Were there any other men working in the wheel at that time whose names you can remember?—No; I think the four were all there were.

The witness withdrew.

Mr. L. Brammer.

LEWIS BRAMMER recalled and further examined.

6995. (*Chairman.*) Is this the paper which you read over to us?—Yes.

6996. "George Shaw says that about eight years " ago he was employed by Broadhead, together with " Dennis Clarke, to blow up Joseph Helliwell at " Tower wheel. He, Broadhead, gave the powder " to Clarke who gave it to me at Broadhead's house. " I sold it to Thomas Simmonite. I and Clarke put " smithy slack into the trough instead of powder. " I got about 30*s.* from Clarke; Dennis Clarke, saw " grinder at Royal Standard, Nursery Street, works, " at 'Taylor's' Harvest Lane." Was that what you read to him?—Yes.

The witness withdrew.

J. Copley.

JOSEPH COPLEY sworn and examined.

6997. (*Chairman.*) What are you?—A saw grinder.

6998. Where do you work?—At Mr. Taylor's.

6999. Where is Taylor's?—In Mowbray Street.

7000. How long have you worked for him?—About four years off and on.

7001. Are you a member of the Union?—Yes.

7002. How long have you been so?—About seven or eight years, I dare say.

7003. Did you know "Putty" Shaw?—Yes.

7004. Did you know Joseph Helliwell?—Yes.

7005. Did you ever work with him?—No.

7006. Were you ever in the wheel with him when he was there?—No.

7007. Do you know a person called Garfitt?—Yes.

7008. Is his name Henry Garfitt?—Yes.

7009. Is he your brother-in-law?—Yes.

7010. Where you ever in the wheel where Helliwell worked, the Tower wheel?—I might have been.

7011. Have you seen him there?—Yes.

7012. Have you seen any person fighting with him?—I believe I have.

7013. Whom did you see?—Henry Garfitt.

7014. How old is Henry Garfitt?—He is rather older than me.

7015. How old are you?—I think I shall be 31 next birthday.

7016. And he is older than you, is he?—Yes.

7017. Is he much older than you?—I cannot say; perhaps about six months, perhaps something of that sort.

7018. They tell me that he is a low crooked-legged man; is that so?—Yes.

7019. Is he a strong built man?—Middling.

7020. How old was Helliwell?—I do not know.

7021. But you knew him; about what age was he?—I cannot say.

7022. But about what age was he; was he 30?—I should think he would be older than I was.

7023. What kind of man was he?—Rather bigger than Garfitt, but he was straight legged.

7024. Who won in that fight?—I do not know; it was a toss up between them.

7025. Was it not decided at all?—I think Garfitt had the best of him.

7026. Do you know what it was about?—Well, I cannot say.

7027. Do you mean to say that you saw two men fighting and did not know what they were fighting about?—I cannot say.

7028. Did not Garfitt complain of him for something that he had done in his trade?—Not to my knowledge.

7029. What were they fighting about? you must know that?—I am sure I cannot say now; it is so long since.

7030. How long is it since?—I should think that it is about six or seven years since.

7031. Do you mean to tell me that you saw two men fighting and did not know what they were fighting about, one of them being your own brother-in-law?—I do now, what they were fighting about.

7032. Do you mean to tell me that now?—Yes; it was a dispute, or something about work, or something of that sort.

7033. Then you did know, you see, quite well; what was the dispute?—I cannot say.

7034. Yes you can, you have recollected already; what was it?—It might be over some saws; perhaps he might get more saws than the other did; they toss up for which gets the biggest share.

7035. But what did they quarrel about?—They tossed up which should get the biggest share of work, don't you see?

7036. But what was that dispute about; what did Garfitt say that he had done?—That Helliwell got more work than him.

7037. Is that what it was?—Yes, something of that sort.

7038. Do not talk to me about something of that sort; what was it?—That Helliwell got more work than him.

7039. Did Garfitt say so?—Yes.

7040. To whom did he say so?—To me.

7041. Was that all that they fought about?—Yes.

7042. And that you swear?—Yes.

EIGHTH DAY.

J. Copley.

14 June 1867.

7043. Have you ever seen them fight upon any other occasion?—No.

7044. Have you ever seen any other person fighting with Garfitt?—No.

7045. Did you ever see any person take his tools away from him?—No.

7046. Nothing of that kind?—No.

7047. Have you ever heard him complain of a person having taken his tools from him?—No.

7048. Have you ever seen Shaw in company with Helliwell?—Not to my knowledge.

7049. Did you know that he was blown up?—Yes.

7050. Did you ever hear that he was to be blown up before he was blown up?—No.

7051. Nobody has told you?—No.

7052. Did you ever talk to him about it?—No.

7053. Did you ever tell him that he was to be blown up?—No.

7054. You never alluded to it?—No.

7055. Did you ever tell him after he was blown up?—No.

7056. Did you ever see Shaw at the wheel?—Shaw was apprenticed at the wheel where I was.

7057. Did you see Shaw at that wheel where Helliwell was?—Yes.

7058. Was he in company with a man called Tucker Clarke?—We were all apprenticed together.

7059. But do you recollect ever seeing him at Helliwell's wheel where Helliwell worked? did you ever see "Putty Shaw" in company with Tucker Clarke?—Yes, they were always in company together.

7060. How long before Helliwell was blown up did you see "Putty" Shaw and Tucker Clarke at that wheel?—Many years.

7061. But how soon before he was blown up? the day before, or the day but one before?—I cannot say.

7062. Do you believe that you saw him there the day before?—I should say he was there; we were all hanging stones when we joined the trade.

7063. How shortly after you joined the trade was Helliwell blown up?—I cannot say; it might be two or three days afterwards, perhaps.

7064. You used to go to Broadhead's, did you not?—Sometimes.

7065. Do you ever recollect seeing Shaw at Broadhead's?—Yes, I have seen Shaw at Broadhead's when he has come for his scale.

7066. Do you recollect his coming on the Saturday, after Helliwell was blown up, to Broadhead's?—Not to my knowledge.

7067. Will you swear that he was not there and that you were not then also on the Saturday after the blow up?—I cannot say.

7068. Did you go to Broadhead's and find Shaw there?—I cannot say.

7069. Now I will remind you; did not you on that night go into a dram shop and have something to drink with him?—With "Putty" Shaw?

7070. Yes.—No, never.

7071. Did you never go into a dram shop with "Putty" Shaw?—Not lately.

7072. But when was this blow up? seven or eight years ago?—Yes.

7073. And at that time you say you were fellow apprentices; did you never go into a dram shop with "Putty" Shaw?—I never amalgamated with "Putty" Shaw at all.

7074. But did you never go into a dram shop with him?—Not to my knowledge.

7075. Is there a dram shop opposite where Broadhead used to live, opposite the "Greyhound"?—No, there is not; there is a Lancastrian school; there is the "Clock," which is very gain.

7076. Did you ever go to the "Clock"?—No.

7077. Will you swear that you did not?—Not to my knowledge.

7078. Will you swear that you have never been in the "Clock" in your life?—I have been in the "Clock" many times; but not with "Putty" Shaw.

7079. Then you have been in the "Clock"?—Yes, but not with "Putty" Shaw.

7080. Did you ever go there on a Saturday night?—I have been several times, both Saturday nights and Mondays.

7081. Were you there on the Saturday night after the blowing up of Helliwell?—Not to my knowledge.

7082. Can you say one way or the other?—No.

7083. You do not know?—No.

7084. You may have been there?—I cannot say.

7085. You will not swear that you were not there?—No.

7086. Can you swear whether Shaw was in the "Clock" that night?—I cannot.

7087. He may have been there?—He may have been there for what I can tell.

7088. Have you ever drunk there with him?—No, not to my knowledge.

7089. Will you swear that you never drank with him?—No.

7090. Be cautious; did you never drink with "Putty" Shaw in that public house?—Not to my knowledge.

7091. Will you swear that you never drank in the "Clock" with "Putty" Shaw?—I do.

7092. You never did?—No.

7093. Never in your life?—Not to my knowledge.

7094. Do not talk about your knowledge; you know it one way or the other. Will you swear that you never drank in that dram shop with "Putty" Shaw?—I cannot say that ever I did.

7095. But are you positive that you never did?—I cannot say that I ever did, to my knowledge; I never amalgamated with him.

7096. But I want to know whether you did on any night at all take any drink with him at the "Clock;" may you have done so?—Not to my knowledge.

7097. Will you swear that you never did on any one night?—If I swear I shall not say an untruth; I do not think I ever did.

7098. You will not go any further than that?—No, I never amalgamated with a man like him.

7099. The only reason that you say this is because you never "amalgamated" with him?—No.

7100. You know you need not "amalgamate" with him although you might drink some beer with him once?—No.

7101. Will you pledge your word that you never drank with him once in that beershop?—I did not.

7102. You never did?—No.

7103. Never in your life?—No; there is nobody can say so.

7104. You have never drunk anything with him there?—Nothing to my knowledge.

7105. That to "my knowledge" will not save you, because you must know it?—I cannot say it.

7106. You cannot say it one way or another?—I might have been once perhaps, I cannot tell; it is a many years since.

7107. You cannot tell; is that so?—I do not think that I have ever been with "Putty" Shaw, in my life, on the spree, you know.

7108. But have you ever drunk with him upon any occasion?—Not to my knowledge.

7109. But would you swear that you have not?—I durst swear I did not.

7110. Will you swear so?—Yes.

7111. Do you swear that you have never done so on any occasion?—Not to my knowledge.

7112. I was yesterday forced to take a very extreme course with a man; I do not want to do the same with you; but it is quite clear that you must know this fact, whether you did or not, and you must answer the question?—Well, I never did.

7113. And that is your deliberate answer?—Yes.

7114. If you know that you never drank with Shaw at the "Clock" what is the reason that you have been keeping me back with all those answers to my questions put in various ways all this time?—It is so long since that I cannot remember.

EIGHTH DAY.

J. Copley.

14 June 1867.

7115. Is that the statement which you make now, that you cannot remember?—I do not think ever I have; I am sure I have not.

7116. Then if you knew it all this while, why did not you say so at first? what is the reason that you have been fencing with me all this while?—I ought to have said so before.

7117. You have known it all the while, have you?—Yes.

7118. Then why have you been answering in this way if you have known it all the while?—I do not know.

The witness withdrew.

Mr. J. Wilson.

MR. JOSEPH WILSON sworn and examined.

7119. (*Mr. Barstow.*) I believe you are a saw manufacturer in Milton Street?—Yes.

7120. How long have you been in business?—About 22 or 23 years.

7121. About seven or eight years ago had you a hull at the Tower wheel?—Yes.

7122. Who worked there?—I had a person of the name of Dennis Clarke.

7123. Who else?—And I had a person of the name of Henry Garfitt.

7124. Was Matthew Woollen in your employment?—Yes, he was then; he worked for me.

7125. George Shaw?—I cannot say for George Shaw; he did work a bit for me, but not a deal.

7126. Is he in your employment off and on at this time?—Yes, off and on.

7127. Was Joseph Helliwell in your employment?—Those men left to join the Union, and so I was out of a man then; and then I employed Helliwell.

7128. (*Chairman.*) Clarke, Garfitt, Woollen, and Shaw left?—Yes, to go to the Union.

7129. And then you employed Helliwell?—Yes.

7130. (*Mr. Barstow.*) Had all those men except Helliwell been apprentices to James Linley?—Yes, except Woollen, and he had been apprenticed to Fearnehough.

7131. Garfitt, Clarke, and Shaw had been apprentices to Linley?—Yes.

7132. And Woollen to Fearnebough?—Yes.

7133. Is Linley the same man who was blown up so many times, and who was subsequently shot?—Yes.

7134. And this Thomas Fearnehough was the saw grinder whose house was blown up last year?—Yes; his house was blown up not long ago.

7135. Those three men left you to join the Union, you say?—Yes.

7136. And then you took on Helliwell?—Yes.

7137. Did those men come back to your employment afterwards?—No. They used to come in the yard to help to hang stones, or do anything about the place. They used chiefly to spend their time in the wheel-yard. They used to hang the stones, or do any other jobs about the place.

7138. Had they access to the place where Helliwell worked?—In the daytime they went in. It was locked up at night-time; and we hung the key in the time-house on the premises.

7139. Did you ever see those men in the place where Helliwell worked?—Yes. I have frequently seen them in and out and about the place.

7140. (*Chairman.*) While he was at work?—Yes.

7141. (*Mr. Barstow.*) Do you know how they behaved to him?—They behaved to him very badly. They called him all kinds of names, and insulted him.

7142. You have heard them?—Yes.

7143. What used they to call him?—"Topsey."

7144. Did you ever hear them say anything to him about joining the Union?—No. I heard a person of the name of Shaw ask him if he meant going on working for me, and he said, "Yes, I do." And he said, "Well, if thou dost go on thou wilt get thy head "knocked off."

7145. Had you any objection to employing Union men?—Yes. Well, I did not want to be tyrannised over by them. That was the only objection that I had.

7146. Then you had an objection?—Yes.

7147. Was your objection well known to those men?—Yes.

7148. Some few days after this observation which you spoke of, of Shaw's, do you remember anything happening in that hull?—Yes.

7149. What was that?—Helliwell's wife came up to my place at the works, and said they had blown her husband up.

7150. Can you fix the date when this happened?—I cannot fix the date without the newspapers.

7151. (*Chairman.*) Have you a newspaper?—No.

7152. (*Mr. Barstow.*) Do you know what year it was in?—I do not know what year it was in.

7153. (*Chairman.*) Do you think it was about October 1859?—I could not tell you the date. I never thought of being asked these questions. I saw it in the papers afterwards.

7154. Did you communicate with the police about it?—I did.

7155. Do you believe it was about October 1859?—Yes, I believe it was about then.

7156. (*Mr. Barstow.*) Did you go and see Helliwell?—Yes; I went down directly, when she said so, to the wheel.

7157. In what state was the hull?—When I got to the wheel door, there was what we call "Putty" Shaw (I do not recollect his other name) standing at the bottom. He had a little bundle under his arm, and was dressed in his Sunday clothes; and when I got down he said, "Mr. Wilson, what is amiss?" I said, "Thou scoundrel, thou know'st all about it." He said, "Nay, I do not; I went out of town on "Saturday night, and I have only just now come back."

7158. (*Chairman.*) What day of the week was this?—On Monday morning. I think it was Monday morning.

7159. When had the wheel been seen right?—On Saturday. It was his place to lock it up, and to go and hang the key up in the time-house.

7160. Whose duty was that?—Helliwell's; and he always took care to have it safe.

7161. (*Mr. Barstow.*) Was this all that passed between you and Shaw?—No. Then I went upstairs into the wheel, and I saw a glazer blown out, and all the things scattered about as if there had been an explosion.

7162. (*Chairman.*) How was the window?—Generally, in grinding wheels, the windows are all out. They generally break them. They get pretty well of air.

7163. But did you notice whether anything had been done to the window?—No; I could not speak to that. While I was in the wheel the man that lives in the time-house came in, and he said, "If you will "just come round here into Jimmy Linley's hull, I "will show you how it has been done." And Putty Shaw, when I went up, followed me all over. He would not leave me; so he went into the hull with us. There are what we call cogs in a large box; one runs in the other and drives our wheel and Jimmy Linley's wheel.

7164. The same cog-wheel drives both?—Yes, one and the t'other. He took hold of a piece of boarding that was very loose, and said, "Here; they have gone "through here into your hull." So then this Shaw put his fist into the man's face and threatened to knock him over for showing me which way they had gone. And I thought they would have had a

EIGHTH DAY

Mr. J. Wilson

14 June 1867.

fight; but I interfered between them, and asked Shaw what he had to do with it; and then I interfered betwixt them, and told him that if he did it would be a deal the worse for him; and then we all three came out again. Then I went down to Helliwell's house, and he was not in. He had gone on to the Infirmary. Then I went again, and he was in, and two detectives also; and he said, "You see they have done me at last." And I asked him then what he was going to do; whether he meant working on for me after he did get better or not.

7165. Then you had a conversation with him about what he was going to do afterwards?—Yes.

7166. Was Dennis Clarke there at that time?—Yes.

7167. Was he at the wheel when the conversation took place as to how they got in?—No; nobody but this Shaw and the time-house man and myself. Three of us were all that were there.

7168. Are you quite sure that it was Shaw that said he would knock his head off, and asked why he did not mind his business?—Yes.

7169. And it was not Dennis Clarke?—No.

7170. You are quite sure it was not Clarke?—Yes; I could see him now in my imagination.

7171. You know Clarke?—Yes; most decidedly.

7172. And you are quite sure it was not Clarke?—Yes; most decidedly.

7173. And you are sure it was Shaw?—There is no question about it.

7174. (*Mr. Barstow.*) Now some time after this, do you remember anything taking place at your own house?—Yes.

7175. How long after?—I cannot say; but it was not so very long after.

7176. Give us a notion; was it weeks, or months, or what?—Happens, it might be six months.

7177. What time of the day?—About six o'clock in the morning; about the 24th of November.

7178. (*Chairman.*) What happened?—Well, I was afraid that they would come to me next; under the bedroom where I sleep there is a cellar grate, and I put some old cans and old pots in there so that if they took up this grate they would all fall down and make a noise.

7179. When had you done this?—I dare say it had been put down about a week and then I heard them fall down. Then I opened the window and saw somebody run round the corner.

7180. Do you know who that person was?—No; I do not know who he was.

7181. Have you a suspicion who he was?—No; I could only see him just turning round the corner?

7182. Could not you see enough of him to come to any belief as to who he was?—No; I could not swear to him.

7183. Have you any belief about him?—No; not exactly. I could not tell who he was, to swear to the man.

7184. What kind of man was he?—He seemed to be about my size; about five feet seven inches.

7185. What age?—He was a youngish man; a young man.

7186. How was he dressed?—I could not exactly say, he had a dark coat on, but I could not tell whether it was a frock coat or a tail coat.

7187. Did he wear a cap or a hat?—A cap.

7188. What else?—I could not tell you.

7189. Are you five feet seven inches?—Five feet seven or eight inches. Then I dressed myself and got up and went down stairs into the cellar and made the cellar grate fast. I made it fast because I thought he would come back again.

7190. What became of the pots and pans?—They all fell down, and it aroused me.

7191. What was the effect if they raised up the grate? how by raising up the grate did they make them fall down?—On the cellar grate there is an iron about a yard long which we have for fastening it to the wall, and I had not fastened that. I had put a bit of stick across to hold those pots on, so that when they pulled this amongst them this stick would break and they would all tumble down.

7192. So they had tumbled down?—Yes; when I got up I went up and fastened the cellar grate.

7193. (*Mr. Barstow.*) Did anything happen at that same time?—No; nothing happened.

7194. (*Chairman.*) Then your belief was that if there were any bad intentions they were put off by hearing the things fall?—Yes.

7195. (*Mr. Barstow.*) But did not something happen some time after that?—Yes.

7196. What next?—I forgot to fasten the cellar grate under where the children lay; three little ones I had in bed.

7197. (*Chairman.*) Not the grate?—Yes; we generally in Sheffield call it the grate.

7198. (*Mr. Barstow.*) Was that the same grate?—No; the one above. There were two boys and a girl there.

7199. (*Chairman.*) How long was that after the other affair?—About a week.

7200. (*Mr. Barstow.*) Did you hear anything?—Yes; there was a loud explosion, and the children came running to me in bed. I was just getting out.

7201. (*Chairman.*) What time of the day was this?—At six o'clock in the morning. I was getting out of bed when the children came in.

7202. You were getting up?—No, I was not getting up. I was wakened by the explosion, and I was getting up to go and see what was amiss, and they said, "Father; oh! what is that? It has blown us out "of bed." So I said to my wife, "Come, you had "better go into the other place in the office." It is a place adjoining. And I said, "It is old Tucker, "and Putty Shaw and Clarke, I am sure."

7203. That was your suspicion?—Yes.

7203*a*. What did you do?—I got up and went down stairs.

7204. You never saw anybody?—No.

7205. Now describe what you found?—There was a many people in the street.

7206. Was it a very loud explosing?—Yes.

7207. It would be dark at that time I suppose?—Yes it was dark. Then I tried to go into this room under where they had put it.

7208. You say that it was a cellar under the room where your children slept?—Yes.

7209. Was there a room between their bedroom and the cellar?—Yes; a living room.

7210. And did you try to go into that living room?—Yes.

7211. You wanted to go into that living room which was between the cellar and the place where your children were?—Yes; I could not open the door, and so I went into the street; and there was a many people standing about the cellar grate. There was a man of the name of Hill, but he has not anything to do with it; he was a friend of mine, one of the neighbours; and while we stood there, looking down this grate, there struck up in the cellar a light.

7212. Who struck a light?—I do not know. There was a light. It struck up as if something had been burning and the smoke going away and the air getting to it had set it on a blaze. It was a rag or something of that kind, and a part of them ran on one side of the road expecting it would be another. I did not care whether it was or not. I went down the grate into the cellar. I thought it might be another. This was burning, and I thought I would make haste down the grate to put it out, and I went and found it was a piece of rag or touch, or something which had come off the other in the former explosion and I put it out.

7213. In what state was the cellar?—It was all of a ruck, and I found in the cellar a tin can which would hold about three pints or a quart.

7214. In what state was the tin can?—It was blown open; and I found also in the cellar some clothes' line.

7215. Was there any smell about it or blackening?—Yes.

EIGHTH DAY.

Mr. J. Wilson.

14 June 1867.

7216. What was the smell?—As if it had contained gunpowder.

7217. You found a clothes' line you say?—Yes; blown to pieces as if it had been tied round the can to keep it tight. Then when I came out of the cellar I went up to Mr. Jackson and told him all about it.

7218. Was the cellar damaged at all?—Yes; it had blown a part of the flooring up in each of the cellars. We had two large cellars, and it had broken the furniture over the cellars where it went off in.

7219. And what had it done to the room where your children were sleeping?—It all cracked right round it; it had cracked and given way as if it had a good shake. There was four or five inches between the wall and the joist of the flooring as if it had tried to give that a lift.

7220. As if the floor had been raised up?—Yes.

7221. None of your family were hurt, I believe?—No; the powder or something had got in the little boy's eye, and he had a bad eye for a long time after. Whether it was from the smell or what we do not know, but he had a bad eye.

7222. Will you continue your narrative?—After I saw I had put it all out and all was safe, I then ran up to Mr. Jackson, the chief constable, and I waited while he got up, and he came down to our house with me.

7223. And there was nothing discovered, I believe, was there?—No; I found out who made this rope, and I found out who made the can.

7224. Who made the can?—Mr. Smith.

7225. What Smith?—Just below here, next door; he is a brazier. He swore he made the can.

7226. Who made the rope?—Mr. Brady, just down here.

7227. Baker's Hill?—Yes, Baker's Hill. I went to him and he said, "We have made that rope."

7228. Is that all that you have to say about this, that you are aware of?—Yes.

7229. Have you been at all able to ascertain who was the party who did this to you?—I went up with Inspector Sills to Putty Shaw's house; he lived up at the park, and we asked if he was in, and his mother said, "He is not." I asked her if he had been out all night, and she said he had, and so Inspector Sills said, I had better say no more and come away.

7230. Have you any reason to believe that any person in particular has done this?—I believe it was Putty Shaw and Dennis Clarke.

7231. Why do you believe it was Putty Shaw and Denis Clarke?—Because Dennis Clarke was working for me previous to his going into the Union, and this Putty Shaw was working for Linley on the back of us. I went down to the wheel, and Dennis Clarke was on grinding, and it is not often when I go down early that he is on. I said to him, "How is this "that you are on so soon?"

7232. When was this?—That was before I was blown up.

7233. How much before?—I should think 12 months before, it might be, I could not say exactly. While I stood with him, this Shaw came running into the wheel with his shirt neck collar turned down and a smock on and a thick rope round his neck hanging down about a yard. I said to this Dennis Clarke: "What is he after?" "Why," said he, "they have "been and shot Jimmy Linley."

7234. Who said that?—Dennis Clarke said: "They have been and shot Jimmey Linley;" and then I said, "He will be getting himself in a mess." When he saw me in the wheel as soon as ever he came in he went out again; but he had this rope hanging about him and was shaking it about, and I did not see him afterwards; I went away.

7235. That is a year you say before you were blown up?—I dare say it was; I could not speak to it.

7236. But why should your having seen him running about with a rope hanging round his neck a yard long cause you to think that he had done this deed?—He was capable of anything.

7237. From his bad character?—Yes, and from my seeing his ways and going there every day I got intermixed with them and knew all their movements, and knew what they were.

7238. But I want to know what ground you had for suspecting Clarke and Shaw of having done this, excepting Shaw's bad character?—He was always into some trouble or other, and I suspected him of it from his blowing Helliwell up and doing all those jobs.

7239. But how did you know that he had blown Helliwell up?—I knew him to be a very bad character.

7240. Had you any quarrel with him?—No, I cannot say that I had.

7241. What about Dennis Clarke; what reason had you to suspect him?—They were always together, and when Dennis Clarke went to join the Union he afterwards saw an apprentice I had, "Well, he says, "Jack, how are you going on?" "Oh," he says, "we are going on all right enough." He said, "Well thou won't say nothing, but thou will hear "of summat."

7242. What is the name of that apprentice?—His name is John Hall; he is dead now.

7243. Did John Hall tell you that?—Yes.

7244. Did John Hall tell you that before the blowing up? did you speak to Dennis Clarke about it?—No.

7245. Have you ever charged Dennis Clarke or Shaw with having done this?—Yes.

7246. When did you do that?—I took a detective and went and searched Dennis Clarke's house.

7247. When was that?—After the blowing up.

7248. How long after?—Perhaps two or three days; we could not find where he lived; we had something to do to find out where he lived.

7249. You did find it at last?—Yes.

7250. Where did he live?—He lived up in the park with his brother-in-law, I think.

7251. What is his name?—I do not know, I am sure.

7252. Is that the man who has been examined this morning?—I do not know.

7253. Was his name Copley?—No.

7254. Who was it then?—I do not know his name.

7255. He lived in the Park with his brother-in-law?—Yes. Mr. Brady said that they had not tied all the rope round this can, and that the man that had it had some more rope. We went to try to find the other rope, and some more powder, but we did not. We got up to his mother's house below, and she would not know where he did live, and would not know anything of him. She pretended she did not know; so when we went the day afterwards and found him out, of course he had time to make it right.

7256. Did you find anything?—No; we did not find anything.

7257. Then all that comes to nothing. Now what is the reason why you suspected him, except from his bad character?—Nothing but what he has said to this apprentice, that he would hear something.

7258. Are these your only grounds of suspicion?—Yes.

7259. Did you ever charge Clarke with having done it?—We charged him so far as this: we went up with this policeman and searched the house.

7260. But did you tell him that you suspected him?—Yes.

7261. What did he say to that?—He said he would make me pay for coming to search his house. He did not say that he had not done it.

7262. Did he say anything more?—No. He sat himself down in the chair and seemed overdone, and he wanted some water.

7263. Did you take out a search warrant then?—No; I do not know.

7264. Has he ever made you pay?—No.

7265. Has he ever taken any steps against you for doing it?—No. I have often seen him afterwards in

EIGHTH DAY

Mr. J. Wilson

14 June 1867.

the street, and he always wanted to speak to me, but I would not have anything to say to him.

7266. Have you seen him in company with Shaw since that ?—I cannot say.

7267. But before that time were they often in company ?—Yes ; they were always together almost.

7268. Have you charged Shaw with this ?—Yes ; I went up to his house, as I told you a bit since, and the first time I saw him after it was on the hull in this wheel. He said, "Mr. Wilson, what have you been " up to our house with a policeman for ? "

7269. What did you say ?—I told him we had been up to see whether he was at home that night.

7270. What did he say ?—He said if I did not hold my noise, and mind how I went on, I should get more than I had done. He was oiling a stone then. I had to go past him to go into the wheel. It was then when he stopped me, and asked me that ; so I took no further notice, and I went away. He seemed getting angry, and so I thought I had better leave him.

7271. Have you ever told him at any time since that you suspected that he was one of the men ?—He has been two or three times to my place to see whether I would have him and give him work, and I have always shown him out of the yard, and called him a rascal, and told him that if he came again I would send for a policeman, and still he will keep coming.

7272. Is that all which you have to tell us ?—It is all I can think on. One's memory gets jogged as one goes on. Previous to that I received several threatening letters, and I have been trying to find them all, but I cannot ; they have been destroyed.

7273. How many have you received ?—I should think a dozen or so, but I could not tell because I did not take a deal of notice of them. I did take notice of the first and the last, and so I kept them, and the others I put amongst some papers. The first is the long one.

7274. " Dear sir. Seeing you are plunging about " and endeavouring to extricate yourself from the " meshes which you have been placed in, and as all " your efforts will be futile, let me advise you to give " up your opposition, for to this it must come at last, " and depend upon it it will be the worst. You " erroneously conceive the society to be your " enemy. They only wish to place you on the same " conditions as other houses, and this they have both " means to do and will accomplish. So let me " advise you to make peace, and take men according " to rule, which I am sure once being done you will " be much more comfortable and satisfied with than " being as you are, for instead of being compelled to " employ the most disreputable of characters (which " is no benefit to you in the end) you will have the " opportunity of employing some steady, industrious, " honest men, such as you was wont to employ when " you employed Union men, and which you know you " was much more comfortable with. I am aware " that in these times of competition discounts and " under prices are very tempting to an employer " when he can squeeze them out of a workman's " necessities, under the cry and guise of each man " being free to make his own bargains, and which " said necessities are not unfrequently brought about " by the men's unsteady, intemperate, and general " bad character. Having broken faith with all whom " he has had dealings with, his necessities make him " a fitting instrument for such an object. But a man " of this kind I should think your past experience " has taught you is dear at any price, as if he breaks " faith with others he will break faith with you. I " am quite aware you will answer by saying, I do " not object to pay the price, as I am willing to pay " the price to any man who will leave the society " and work for me ; but you know it was price that " caused your disagreement with the society in the " first place, and hence your opposition to the society. " But men know full well if you were to pay it now, " and they had not the protection of the Union, you " would reduce them the very first chance you had. " Consequently I believe it is useless to expect to " get any one in any other way than that according " to the rules of the Union. I believe the Union has " no ill-feeling towards you, and I have no doubt " (as I have before stated) will be quite willing and " glad to treat you on the same terms as other em- " ployers. So let me advise you to do with a good " grace what you may depend upon you cannot avoid. " Believe me, dear sir, no enemy of yours, but your " best adviser." The next is, " To Mr. Joseph Wilson : " Dear sir. I take this opportunity of just reminding " you that you are trying on a dangerous game. You " are taking the place of another,—the person whose " name I need not mention —— " ?—He means James Linley, that was shot in the Wicker.

7275. " —by running about to decoy boys to grind " for you. It will save your life if you do not succeed, " as it would cause you to come the next game, and " in that case it is fifty to one upon your days being " numbered. You may treat this lightly, and toss it " into the fire, if you will, but so sure as you are a " doomed man ; and bear in mind I have hitherto " always done all that I have promised in this way " to the fullest measure. (Signed) TANTIA TOPEE." Now, as to the intermediate ones which you received, what was the character ?—They were more like the last one. They threatened me.

7276. They threatened your life ?—Yes.

7277. And now many had you of those ?—I had about a dozen of them. I could not say I did not take a deal of notice of them.

7278. (*Mr. Barstow.*) What sort of a workman was Helliwell ?—He was a very hard-working man. I should think he was as hard-working a man as any man in Sheffield.

7279. Was he a good workman ?—Yes, a good workman ; but a harder working man I think there is not.

7280. I believe he is now in America ?—I do not know where he is ; he left to go to Manchester. The last time I heard of him he was in Manchester.

7281. How long ago did he leave the town ?—I do not know ; some years since. I could not speak to that.

7282. Do you remember his going ?—Yes.

7283. (*Chairman.*) Did not the complaint, or what you call the tyranny of the Union, consist in this, that they objected to your employing an unlimited number of apprentices ?—No ; for I had not any in the saw-grinding.

7284. Have you any apprentices ?—Not in the saw-grinding, nor have I had any.

7285. Have you any other apprentices ?—Yes, I have others.

7286. What had you ?—I had about five of them, I dare say, as near as I can guess.

7287. What were they ?—They were saw-makers.

7288. All of them ?—I think they were all saw-makers.

7289. Was that according to the rules of the Union ?—No.

7290. Was it in violation of the rules of the Union ? —Yes, in violation of the rules.

7291. How many apprentices were you allowed to have, by the rules of the Union ?—By the rules of the Union, two to four journeymen. I had a letter. I gave it to Mr. Brammer.

7292. It appears that you are allowed to have a number of apprentices no larger than in the proportion of one apprentice to every four men ; is that so ? —I never took any notice of it. I cannot speak to it.

7293. But how were you with respect to men ? You say you had five apprentices ?—Yes.

7294. How many journeymen had you at the time when you had those five apprentices ?—Perhaps three or four ; I could not say.

7295. Then in point of fact you had more apprentices than journeymen ?—Yes,

7296. You say you had three journeymen at the time ?—I had.

7297. Did the Union complain of this ?—No.

EIGHTH DAY.

Mr. J. Wilson.

14 June 1867.

7298. Did they never make complaints to you about it ?—No.

7299. You had no complaint from the Union of having too many apprentices ?—No.

7300. Then what was the tyranny of which you did complain ? you say it was not the complaint about their interfering with your having an unlimited number of apprentices ?—It was the employing of this Helliwell.

7301. Then they interfered with your employing Helliwell ?—Yes.

7302. Was that the tyranny of which you complained ?—Yes ; they wanted me to turn him off, to get those men back.

7303. You say they wanted you to turn him off ; who wanted you to turn him off?—Dennis Clarke and those men.

7304. But how do you connect Dennis Clarke with the Union ?—They left me to go and join the Union, as I have said.

7305. What for ?—He had been apprenticed with Linley, and he never had joined.

7306. But the fact of his joining the Union would not show that the Union wanted you to part with Helliwell ?—No ; and then I had not a man for about two weeks. Then I went about to seek them, and then I met with Helliwell. Then while I was seeking them I received that letter ; the first letter ; somewhere there about.

7307. And is it from that that you believe that that is the tyranny of the Union ?—Yes.

7308. It is from that letter that you believe that ? —Yes.

7309. Have you had any complaint on the part of the parents of your apprentices as to your conduct to apprentices ?—No.

7310. Never ?—No, not that I know of.

7311. Have the fathers or mothers or relations of your apprentices complained of your misconduct to apprentices ?—I have had two or three cases of them at the Town Hall, where they have absconded for two or three months.

7312. But you made the charge then ?—Yes.

7313. I am not speaking of your charging the apprentices. I am asking you if the fathers or mothers, the parents of the children who were under your care, have not complained of your misconduct to the apprentices ?—No ; I do not know that they have.

7314. They never have complained ?—I do not know that they have. I had a case a few months ago.

7315. What was that ? who complained ?—I think the boy's father.

7316. What is his name :—Fearnehough.

7317. Fearnehough complained of what ?—That I did not teach his son his trade.

7318. Was he your apprentice at that time ?—Yes.

7319. What about that ?—It was a person of the name of Fernell. Mr. Fernell asked me to have this lad as apprentice, and he said he was a very good one, and I had a case at the town hall ; Mr. Fernell had pleaded for me about making too much smoke.

7320. Fearnehough complained that you did not teach him his trade ? Did he summon you before the magistrates ?—Yes.

7321. What became of the summons ; where you fined, or what became of it ?—I had to pay the costs.

7322. Did you pay anything else besides the costs ? —No.

7323. Did the boy go back into your service ?—Yes, he came back ; and then Mr. Fernell came to me. This lad's father is Mr. Fernell's gamekeeper up in Dore, and Mr. Fernell came to me, and advised me to break the lad's indentures. He said, " The lad will " never do you any good. Let me advise you as a " friend to break his indentures." I said, " Why should I break them ?" and he said, " The lad does " not like the trade ; he wants to be the same trade " as his father." I said, " I never did break a lad's " indentures, and I have had a great many in my time."

7324. Did you ultimately agree to break the lad's indentures ?—No. A fortnight after the father summoned me up again for not teaching his son his trade.

7325. What became of that summons ?–Mr. Fernell wanted it tried before Mr. Atkinson.

7326. But what became of it ?—Then I objected to its being tried before him. I said, I had rather have it tried before the mayor, who tried it about a fortnight since.

7327. But what became of it ?—Then Mr. Atkinson came on to the bench with the mayor, and advised me to break the indentures.

7328. And they broke the indentures ?—Yes.

7329. Then the boy left you ?—Yes.

7330. Is that the only time in which a father or a parent has complained of your conduct to his son ?— Yes. I think that is about the only time.

7331. Are you quite sure that it is the only time that you have been brought before the magistrates for misconduct to an apprentice ?—I think it is. I cannot exactly say.

7332. Will you swear that it is ?—I cannot swear that is it, exactly. I have been with my apprentices, and we have been several times before the magistrates.

7333. What has it been for ?—Absconding. I had one apprentice up ; he had been absent about six or eight weeks.

7334. But is there no case where the apprentice had you up ?—I do not think any has had me up, except for not teaching him the trade.

7335. Has an apprentice ever had you up before the magistrates except on those two occasions that you spoke of ?—No.

7336. Have you ever been taken up for cruelty to your apprentices ?—I cannot say that I have.

7337. But you must know ; will you swear you have not ?—No ; I cannot say that I have.

7338. Have you ever been brought up before the magistrates for misconduct to your apprentices on any occasion except those two that you have spoken of ?— No, I cannot say that I have.

7339. But recollect. Have you ever on any other occasion, besides those two, been brought before the magistrates ?—I cannot say that I have.

7340. Can you say you are sure you have not ?— I cannot say I am sure.

7341. Do you recollect any such case ?—I do not recollect any.

7342. Can you say there never was any other occasion ?—No. I have had apprentices many years.

7343. I am requested to ask you this. Has no other apprentice besides Fearnehough brought you up ?—I cannot recollect.

7344. Will you swear none has ?—No, I cannot swear any has.

7345. But can you swear that none has ?—No, I cannot say.

7346. May another have brought you up ?—I do not know.

7347. Cannot you put it clearer than that ?—No ; if I could I would. All I want to speak is what I know of, and what I remember.

7348. Have you yourself ever been brought up before the magistrates for any offence against the laws ?—No, I do not think I have.

7349. Have you ever been convicted of any offence ? —No.

7350. You say you have been so far convicted that they have broken the indentures and dismissed the apprentice ?—Yes.

7351. And you think that only occurred on one occasion ?—Yes.

7352. Have the boys complained that you are not able to teach them their trade ?—No.

7353. Are you a man who is acquainted with the business ?—Yes.

7354. How long have you been in it ?—I was put an apprentice to the trade, and when I was a boy I was reckoned as good a workman as any in Sheffield. When I was a man I went to work for Mr. Roberts,

EIGHTH DAY.

Mr. J. Wilson.

14 June 1867.

and he said I was one of the best workmen that he had; and I believe now I can get an old tool to say that when I was a journeyman I was reckoned as good a workman as any in Sheffield, and I believe that is my character yet, and I shall be very glad if you can bring any one to show that I am not.

7355. Have you at this moment any apprentices besides saw makers?—No.

7356. Have you saw-grinders apprentices?—No.

7356*a*. Have you none but saw makers?—No; I have only two saw makers.

7257. But no saw grinders?—No.

The witness withdrew.

Mr. C. Battersby.

Mr. Charles Battersby sworn and examined.

7358. (*Chairman.*) You are a detective officer?—I am.

7359. On Saturday the 8th did you go to Chadwick?—I did; I went with Brammer to Chadwick.

7360. Did you see Simmonite?—I did.

7361. Did you tell him that you had called about some powder?—Brammer did.

7362. Which he was supposed to have purchased from Shaw?—Yes.

7363. What did he say to that?—He said he had never purchased any powder from Shaw.

7364. Did Brammer say anything to him upon that?—He said, "Did you buy any of Clarke." He said, "No never."

7365. Did Brammer say anything to him upon that?—He said, "I will repeat it another way." He says, "Did you ever receive any powder from any one "else, that came from Shaw?" and he says, "No never."

7366. Was anything said about his waiting; that he had better wait before he said anything?—Yes.

7367. What?—He said, "You had better consider. "I will ask you in another way. Was there ever any powder left for you at any place by Shaw?" and he says, "No."

7368. Was a statement read to him which Shaw had made?—There was.

7369. Was he then asked if he still persisted in saying that he had not purchased the powder?—He said he never did.

7370. Was anything said to him, that they wanted him to come and give evidence, and that if he did he would get 7*s.* 6*d.* a day or any sum from the Commissioners?—Not in my presence.

7371. Was anything said like this, that he had got a good job for him, as he had nothing to do, and that he had better come down and tell it; was anything of that kind said?—No; I never heard anything of that kind.

7372. Was he asked to sign a paper about the powder in your presence?—He was not.

7373. Did you see Simmonite again?—I saw him at Hyde Park.

7374. Was anything said about your coming again to see him?—There was not in my presence.

7375. You saw him at Hyde Park?—Yes.

7376. Did you speak to him at Hyde Park about this?—I did.

7377. What hid he say?—He said, "I suppose I "shall have to go to-morrow." I said, "Yes, you "will." That is all he said, and that is all I know.

The witness withdrew.

H. Garfit.

Henry Garfit sworn and examined.

7378. (*Chairman.*) What are you?—A saw grinder.

7379. Where were you apprenticed?—At the Tower Wheel.

7380. With whom?—Linley.

7381. When you were out of your apprenticeship what became of you?—I went to work for Joseph Wilson.

7382. How long did you work for him?—Twelve months.

7383. What did you do next?—I worked for Constantine, Hollis Croft.

7384. How did you happen to leave Wilson's?—He said he had nought to do.

7385. Was that the reason that you left Wilson?—Yes.

7386. Did you get into work immediately you left Wilson?—Yes; a week after.

7387. For Constantine?—Yes.

7388. How long did you remain with Constantine?—I am sure I do not know; a couple of years, I dare say; perhaps more.

7389. Did you work at Wilson's at the time that Helliwell was there?—Yes.

7390. Did you leave him there?—Yes.

7391. Were you on good terms with Helliwell when you where there?—Yes; we were when I left.

7392. During the time that you were working with him, were you on good terms with him?—All but once.

7393. What was that once?—We quarrelled once; him and me.

7394. What about?—About work.

7395. What about it?—He wanted to get more work than me, and I would not stand it.

7396. Did you fight with him?—Yes.

7397. Did he beat you?—No; I beat him.

7398. Did you ever call him him names?—No.

7399. Have you never called him bad names?—No.

7400. Have you ever threatened him?—No.

7401. Have you ever threatened him? I ask you again?—No; never. I never quarrelled with him in my life before that time.

7402. Have you quarrelled with him since?—No, never.

7403. Were you at that time working with him?—Yes.

7404. You were working together?—Yes.

7405. Did you ever insult him?—Never.

7406. Did you ever object to his working for Mr. Wilson?—Never.

7407. Where you and Shaw great friends?—Yes, always.

7408. Is Dennis Clarke a friend of yours too?—Yes.

7409. Were you apprentices together?—Yes.

7410. Have you ever heard Shaw insult him?—Not to my knowledge.

7411. They called him Topsey, did not they?—I believe they did.

7412. You know whether they did or not? Did they call him so or not?—Yes, they did, sometimes.

7413. Do you know what "Topsey" means particularly?—Not to my knowledge.

7414. Have you heard Shaw ask him if he intended going on working for Mr. Wilson?—Never.

7415. Have your ever heard Shaw tell him that if he did go on working he would get his head knocked off?—Never.

7416. Have you ever said anything of that kind?—Never.

7417. Never to Helliwell?—No.

7418. You never told Helliwell that if he went on working for Wilson he would get his head knocked off, or any damage done to him?—No, never.

7419. Never?—No, never.

7420. Have you ever threatened him, or told him that it would be worse for him if he went on working?—Never.

EIGHTH DAY.

H. Garfit.

14 June 1867.

7421. Do you recollect the time of Helliwell being blown up?—I remember something about it, but I was not working there then.

7422. Do you mean to say that a man whom you were working with was blown up in his wheel, and you did not hear of it?—No; not for a day after.

7423. Did you hear of it the day after?—Yes.

7424. Do you recollect being at the "Corner Pin" in the Wicker a short time before he was blown up?—No; I was not there.

7425. You never were?—No.

Mrs. Rebecca Helliwell recalled.

R. Helliwell.

7426. (*Chairman.*) Look at that man (*the witness*), and tell me if you know him?—Yes; it is the man.

7427. Where did you see him?—At the "Corner Pin."

7428. That is the man you saw at the "Corner Pin"?—Yes.

The witness withdrew.

H. Garfit.

7429. (*Chairman.*) (*to Henry Garfit.*) You have heard what Mrs. Helliwell has said. I ask you now were you in the "Corner Pin" in the Wicker a short time before Helliwell was blown up?—No.

7430. Were you ever at the "Corner Pin"?—Never. I have been many times; but I was not there then.

7431. You have been many a time at the "Corner Pin"?—Yes, sir.

7432. Have you been at the "Corner Pin" with "Putty" Shaw and "Tucker" Clarke?—Yes.

7433. Again I put it to you. Were you there at the "Corner Pin" on a Saturday night, a short time before Helliwell was blown up?—No.

7434. Did you hear Clarke say to Helliwell at any time, "I will do thee yet"?—No, never.

7435. A short time before he was blown up?—Never.

7436. Did you ever hear Shaw say that?—Never.

7437. You never heard Shaw or Clarke say so?—No.

7438. You did not hear them say to Helliwell "I will do thee yet"?—No, never.

7439. Did you ever see Helliwell there when his wife was there?—No; I have never seen his wife in my life.

7440. You never saw Mrs. Helliwell before to-day?—I have never seen Helliwell and his wife together. I have seen his Missus many a time.

7441. You never saw them at the "Corner Pin"?—No, never.

7442. And you never said at the "Corner Pin" that you would do for him?—No.

7443. You never said that?—No.

7444. And you never heard Shaw nor Clarke say so?—No.

7445. And when Mrs. Helliwell comes, and says that you were there, and she heard Clarke say that, you do not agree with her?—Mrs. Helliwell is false; I will swear that.

7446. You will swear that?—I will swear it.

7447. Did you ever take Helliwell's tools away from him?—Never. We was always on good terms, except that once.

7448. Did you ever know any other apprentices take tools from him?—No, not to my knowledge.

7449. You never heard Clarke say he did it?—No.

7450. You never heard Helliwell complain that his tools were gone?—No.

7451. You never heard him complain that he had lost any?—No; I was not working there then.

7452. Have you kept company with Clarke and Shaw up to this time?—No.

7453. When did you cease to keep company with Shaw?—It is a long while since I kept company with Shaw.

7454. How long?—I cannot tell you.

7455. But you can tell me? When did you cease to keep company with Shaw?—He has not been a companion with me for many years.

7456. Have you been in his company lately?—Yes, several times.

7457. Within the last two or three years?—Yes.

7458. Were you present when Shaw signed a paper which he gave to Mr. Broadhead?—Yes.

7459. Do you know when that was?—No; I cannot tell what day it was.

7460. How long ago is it?—It might be 10 weeks, perhaps more.

7461. How did you happen to be there?—I was on the Committee.

7462. Is your name appended to it? is your name there as one of the persons who saw it signed?—Yes.

7463. Were you one of the committee-men?—I was that night.

7464. You were on the committee that night. Do you mean to say that your committees alter from night to night? or how was it?—No; they do not alter from night to night.

7465. Were you on the committee for a single night?—No.

7466. How long were you a committee-man?—I was on 16 weeks.

7467. When did you begin to be a committee-man? I cannot tell you; I am no scholar.

7468. Do you think that is an answer?—I cannot tell you. I am no scholar.

7469. How long had you been a committee-man before that paper was written?—I am sure I do not know how many weeks I had been on then.

7470. Had you been several weeks?—Yes.

7471. You are no scholar?—No.

7472. Do you mean to say that you cannot write? I can write my own name, but that is all.

7473. "Henry Garfit;" that is your signature?—Yes.

7474. Who produced this document?—I am sure I do not know.

7475. One half of the committee changed every eight weeks?—Yes.

7476. What are the duties of the committee-men?—I do not know exactly.

7477. You must have been a very useful committee-man. What are the duties of the committee-men?—I do not know rightly.

7478. You do not know?— No, not rightly.

7479. What were you doing on the committee?—I sat still the same as a good many more that goes.

7480. Then you were a dummy?—Yes.

7481. You did nothing but sit still?—And supped some ale.

7482. Did you pay for your own ale, or did the committee find it?—They found me some, and some I paid for.

1483. How long have you been thus useful to the Union?—I have been about eight or nine years.

7484. You were there not only to sit still and drink ale, but to write your name that night—Yes, I put my name there that night.

7485. You do not know who produced that document?—No.

7486. You are not a good committee-man; you have a bad memory?—Yes.

7487. You do not know who produced it?—No.

7488. Do you know how it happened to get signed?—I put my name to it, that is all I know.

7489. Why you put it, or how you put it, you do not know?—That is all I know. I put my name down.

7490. How did you happen to put your name down ?—It was given to me.

7491. Who gave it to you ?—I do not know who gave it to me now, I am sure.

7492. You do not know who gave you that paper ?—No ; it was put on a table and I signed it.

7493. Who put it on the table ?—I do not know.

7494. Did Mr. Broadhead put it on the table ?—I do not know ; there were eight of us there; I do not know who put it on the table.

7495. Who were the eight ?—Broadhead, one ; me, two ; Matthew Frith, three ; Caldwell, four ; Alexander Ellis, five ; Baxter, six. I forget the others now.

7496. Who was there besides ?—I forget now ; it is so long. I forget who were the other ones.

7497. Why did not they sign their names ?—They have done, have not they ?

7498. No ?—I think they have. I think they all signed.

7499. There is Alexander Ellis and William Broadhead. Do you know that man ?—He was there.

7500. Was anybody else ?—Those that I have given you ; that is all.

7501. You say you were asked to sign it. They put it down for you to sign ?—Yes.

7502. Was anything said before you signed it ?—No ; not to me.

7503. You were on the committee. You were a committee man ?—Yes.

7504. You know whether there was some reason for this, you being on the committee acting for the Union. The Union is managed by such people as you ?—I was downstairs that night a good deal.

7505. What do the people do upstairs ?—I am sure I do not know ; many different things.

7506. What do the committee do upstairs ?—I do not know rightly.

7507. You do not know what they did ?—Not rightly.

7508. Have you attended the committees and do you not know what they do ?—Yes.

7509. What do they do downstairs ?—Sup ale.

7510. You were on the committee 16 weeks only ?—Yes.

7511. Not nine years ?—No ; 16 weeks.

7512. Were you on the committee they call the investigating committee ?—No, never.

7513. You have such a committee ?—There was once, but there is not know.

7514. What has become of it ?—It is done away with now.

7515. When did you do away with it ?—A long while since.

7516. How long ago ?—Two or three years ago. A couple of years perhaps, or more.

7517. How long is it since you gave up the investigating committee ?—I was never on it.

7518. How long has it been given up ?—Perhaps a couple of years.

7519. I do not know what "perhaps" means ?—That is to my knowledge.

7520. Your belief is that it was given up two years ago ?—Perhaps it might be.

7521. How long had it existed ?—I am sure I do not know.

7522. To your knowledge how long has it existed ?—I do not know.

7523. Did it exist a year ?—I cannot say rightly.

7524. Did it exist two years ?—No.

7525. Did it exist one ?—Perhaps it might do.

7526. Do you know what they did there ?—No. I never was there.

7527. You never went into the investigating committee ?—No.

7528. Were you ever in arrear to the club ?—Yes.

7529. Did not you go into the investigating committee when you were in arrear ?—I did not owe enough to go there.

7530. How much must you owe before you go there ?—Over 1*l.*

7531. You never owed enough ?—No.

7532. You were never sent before that tribunal ?—No.

7533. On this night in question, when the committee was sitting, was it sitting upstairs ?—What night ?

7534. On the night when this paper was written ?—Yes.

7535. Do you recollect Shaw being there ?—Yes ; that night.

7536. Did he go and ask for scale that night ?—Not that I heard him ; he did not ? not to my knowledge.

7537. You never heard Shaw ask for scale that night ?—No.

7538. Would he apply to you as one of the committee for scale if he wanted any ?—No.

7539. Whom would he apply to ?—He would apply to Broadhead for his scale.

7540. Did Broadhead say to the committee that he had applied to him for scale ?—I am sure I do not know.

7541. Do you mean to say that you attended the committee on the business of your union to which you belong, and you do not recollect whether Broadhead mentioned it to you ?—No ; I was not up at that time.

7542. Was it before you got up ?—I should perhaps be, but might have gone downstairs.

7543. What do you mean "perhaps" ?—When he were up perhaps I was down.

7544. What do you mean by "when he was up perhaps you were down" ?—I was not in in time.

7545. When did you come in ?—We sat at 6 o'clock.

7546. Did you see Shaw up there ?—Yes.

7547. Did you see him sent downstairs ?—No.

7548. Did you see him come up ?—I saw him when he was upstairs.

7549. Did you see him come up ?—No.

7550. He was in the room ?—Yes.

7551. Did he ever leave the room while you were there ?—Yes.

7552. What did he leave it for ?—He was ordered to go downstairs.

7553. Did he afterwards come up again ?—I am sure I do not know whether he did or not.

7554. Do you recollect Mr. Broadhead saying anything at all about him or about his case on this night when you were asked to sign this paper ?—I think I do not.

7555. Then this paper was never read to you ?—No.

7556. And you know nothing about what was in it ?—No ; I cannot read or write, except my own name.

7557. All that you were required to do was to sign your name ?—That was all.

7558. You do not know to this day what is in this paper ?—No.

7559. Do you know whether Shaw signed his name to it or not ?—I believe he did.

7560. Did you see him ?—I am sure I do not know whether I saw him or not ; I cannot say.

7561. Then you are as good a witness as you are a committee man ; it appears you do not know whether Shaw signed his name or not ?—No ; I do not know.

7562. Did you see who drew it up ; did you draw it up ?—No ; I cannot write.

7563. Who drew it up ?—I am sure I do not know, without Broadhead did.

7564. Do you know whether Broadhead did or not ?—No ; I do not know whether he did or not.

7565. It was not drawn up in the committee room ?—I am sure I do not know whether it was or was not.

7566. Might it have been drawn up in the committee room and you not know anything about it ?—It might have been drawn up while I was out.

7567. If it was drawn up in the committee room while you were there would you have known whether it was so or not ?—I should think so.

7568. As you think that, tell me, was it drawn up

EIGHTH DAY.

H. Garfit.

14 June 1867.

in your presence?—I do not know rightly whether it was or was not.

7569. You cannot tell me that, but if it were drawn up in your presence, you say, that you would know? if you do not know, would you say that it was not drawn up in your presence?—I cannot say rightly whether it was or not.

7570. If it was drawn up in your presence you would have seen it?—Yes; I should have seen it if it had been.

7571. You can tell me whether it was drawn up in your presence or not?—There was a deal of writing, I believe, but I do not know what was done.

7572. Was anything told you about it whilst it was being drawn up?—No.

7573. You never knew why it was drawn up, or anything about it?—No; I did not know nought about it.

7574. And Broadhead had never told you that it was drawn up for any purpose at all? He never told you what it was for, did he?—Not to my knowledge he did not.

7575. You say that you could not have seen Shaw sign it or you must have recollected it. You do not know whether it has Shaw's signature to it?—I do not know whether he signed it or not.

7576. Do you recollect Shaw being in the room? Yes; I recollect Shaw being in the room.

7577. Was he in the room while you signed that or not?—I do not know whether he was or not.

7578. Do you recollect whether he went downstairs after he signed it?—Yes; he went down the stairs. I do not know whether he signed it, or what he did.

7579. Do you recollect his coming upstairs after he signed it?—No; I do not recollect Shaw coming upstairs.

7580. You do not recollect his leaving the room and coming back again?—No; I do not.

7581. Are there many intelligent men like yourself on the committee?—I do not know I am sure.

7582. Are there many men equally clever with you on the committee?—I cannot tell you that.

7583. Can they all write?—I cannot answer for that.

7584. I see Broadhead is a marksman; he cannot write at all; here is his cross. Can you tell me whether Ellis can write or not?—I do not know whether he can or not.

7585. Can Matthew Frith write?—I do not know whether he can or not.

7586. And Coldwell; can he write?—I do not know.

7587. How long had these men been on the committee, Coldwell, Baxter, Frith, and Ellis, when this paper was signed?—I do not know at all.

7588. You do not know what this paper was for, why you signed it, or whether Shaw signed it, or anything about it?—No; I do not know anything about it.

7589. Then you signed it I suppose because Broadhead asked you to sign it?—I do not know whether Broadhead asked me to sign it, or who did.

7590. Somebody asked you to sign it?—Somebody asked me to put my name to it.

7591. You call that signing it?—Yes.

7592. It is the same thing?—Yes.

7593. Who asked you?—I do not know.

7594. Did Broadhead ask you to sign it?—I cannot say.

7595. Do you sign your name to papers whenever you are asked?—I do not know.

7596. Do you sign your name to a paper without knowing what is in it? What is the good of your signature if you do not know who signs, and if you do not know what is in it?—I can neither read nor write.

7597. But you can hear reading and writing and understand it; it is simple English?—I am sure I do not know.

7598. What is the good of your signature if you did not know what was in it, and did not know whether any person had signed it or not? What do you think your name appeared there for?—I should think as a witness.

7599. To what?—That paper.

7600. What paper?—That you showed me now.

7601. What were you to witness?—I do not know.

7602. Then it was never read over to you?—Not to my knowledge.

7603. And there was never any complaint made by Broadhead that Shaw had been doing anything at all?—Not that I know of.

7604. No complaint of any sort?—Not that I know of.

7605. No complaint against Shaw of misconduct?—There was not that night, as I know of.

7606. How long were you there that night?—Perhaps two hours.

7607. What time did you go?—Six o'clock.

7608. Were you there till eight?—Yes.

7609. During that time there was no complaint made by Broadhead against Shaw or anything of the kind?—I was downstairs a good deal that night.

7610. Was there at any time during that night a complaint by Broadhead against Shaw?—I am sure I forget now.

7611. Will you swear that there was not?—I am sure I do not know whether there was or was not.

7612. Do you recollect whether Shaw said anything that night as to whether he asked for scale?—No; I do not recollect anything about it.

7613. Have you had any conversation with Mr. Broadhead about this or not?—No.

7614. You had not?—No.

7615. Not at all?—No.

7616. Have you been in company with Dennis Clarke this morning?—Yes; we have been at the wheel together.

7617. Is Dennis Clarke in court? You say that you have been in company with Dennis Clarke?—Yes.

7618. Where have you been to?—At the Harvest Lane Works.

7619. Where is that?—We have been just up here at Lambert's.

7620. How long were you with him at Lambert's?—Perhaps 10 minutes.

7621. Where have you been with him besides?—Up above, the "Angel," t'other side of road.

7622. Where is that?—Opposite the "Brown Bear."

7623. How long were you there?—Ten minutes.

7624. Is that the same place as Lambert's?—No; t'other side of road.

7625. You were opposite the "Brown Bear" 10 minutes?—Yes.

7626. Where else?—Only where I work.

7627. Where is that?—Harvest Lane.

7628. Where is that?—At Taylor's works.

7629. Do you work together?—Yes.

7630. Have you talked to him about what you were going to say to-day?—No, sir.

7631. You know Clarke very well, do you?—Yes.

7632. Were you ever at Alvey's public house; the saw makers house?—Harvest Lane.

7633. Were you ever there with him?—Yes; many a time I have been there with him.

7634. Have you heard Clarke say that he would have Shaw and Old Smitem lagged?—Never.

7635. And have them run in?—Never.

7636. Did you not on one occasion, in Alvey's public house, hear him say that he would have Shaw lagged?—Never.

7637. You never heard him talk about Shaw?—No; nothing about it.

7638. What have you heard him say about Shaw?—Many different things.

7639. Have you heard him say that he could have him lagged?—No, never.

7640. Nothing of the kind?—No.

EIGHTH DAY.

H. Garfit.

14 June 1867.

7641. Nor ever say that he could have anything done to Broadhead ?—No, never.

7642. Do you know that Shaw was not on good terms with Broadhead ?—No, sir.

7643. You do not ?—No.

7644. (*Mr. Barstow.*) When you were with Mr. Wilson what work did you do ?—Hand saws, cross cuts, and pit saws.

7645. Was that all ?—Yes.

7646. What work did Helliwell do ?—He used to grind, and then he glazed. He ground when I was there. We had a trough apiece.

7647. That was a different sort of work to what you did ?—Grinding ?

7648. Yes ?—No ; just the same.

7649. You said you hung stones ?—I never hung a stone there but for myself.

7650. I asked you whether you hung stones, and you answered my question that you did. Did you do the same work that Helliwell did ?—Yes.

7651. Do you mean that all the time you were there you never used any bad language to him ?—None whatever, only the time I was quarrelling.

7652. How did you come to quarrel with him at that time ?—About work.

7653. How did you come to quarrel with him ?—He wanted more work than me, and I would not stand it.

7654. How do you mean, that he wanted more work than you ?—He wanted a bigger share.

7655. He took what Mr. Wilson gave him ?—No, it was not done in that way ; it was sent down in a cart and shared.

7656. Did you ever try to persuade Helliwell to join the Union ?—No, never.

7657. You never used any persuasion for that purpose ?—No.

7658. Did you ever hear Shaw do so ?—No.

7659. Or Clarke ?—No.

7660. You never heard any man try to persuade him to join the Union ?—No.

7661. After you had fought with him what happened ?—Nothing ; we worked as friendly as usual.

7662. Did you use any abusive language to him at the time ?—No.

7663. How did you come to fight if you used no abusive language ?—He shoved me and I shoved him, and then we let into one another. There was not a word spoken.

7664. Neither before or after ?—No ; we were friendly enough after.

7665. Did you tell him he was worth nothing as a workman ?—I do not know whether I did or not.

7666. As to this document, did you never hear it read ?—No.

7667. Do you mean that you put your hand to it without knowing what was in it ?—I put my name to it, and that was all I knowed.

7668. How came you to put your name to it ?—It was put down ; I put my name to it.

7669. Did you put your name to anything that they put down ?—I do not know about that.

7670. Who asked you to put your name to it ?—I do not know I am sure.

7671. On what day of the week is scale paid ?—Saturday.

7672. The scale is paid on Saturday ?—Yes.

7673. Who pays the scale ?—Broadhead.

7674. Does he pay it himself ?—No ; I think there is somebody else with him.

7675. From whose hands does the money pass ?—I do not know. I think there is a committee that pays it.

7676. I want to know from whose hands the money passes ? If you went for scale who would give you the money ?—Broadhead has given me the money when I went for my scale.

7677. Who was present at the time it was paid ?—I cannot tell you that.

7678. I do not mean what man, but what officers; what are they called ?—I do not know what they are called.

7679. I do not want to know their names. I want to know what officers of the Union were present ?—I cannot tell you what they call them.

7680. How many were present ?—I think there were two besides Broadhead.

The witness withdrew.

JOHN CLARKE sworn and examined.

J. Clarke.

7681. (*Chairman.*) You have been convicted of rattening ?—Yes.

7682. When was that ? at Leeds Assizes ?—Yes.

7683. How long ago ; nine months ago ?—Ten months ago. I have been out five weeks since I was punished.

7684. Whose goods did you ratten ?—Mr. Darwin's.

7685. You were caught with the things upon you ?—Yes.

7686. How did you happen to do this act of rattening ?—Mr. Darwin wanted to sacrifice me 10 per cent. ; he wanted to give me some work out the morning that I finished the last lot ; he said I should have to sacrifice 10 per cent. I said I should have to see Thompson the secretary of the trade about it.

7687. Did you see Thompson ?—Yes, the morning after. I told him that Mr. Darwin wanted me to sacrifice 10 per cent ; he told me I must do nothing of the sort ; he said I must take other means with him.

7688. Did he mention the means you were to take ? Yes.

7689. What did he say ?—He told me that I was to go and destroy some of Darwin's tools. I asked him how I was to enter into the shop. He says, "I will show thee very soon." He pulls down a piece of chalk and draws a pattern of tools that would enter into his shop.

7690. That would enable you to get in ?—Yes ; and I went and succeeded with those things the night after.

7691. He gave you the pattern of the tools ?—I went to my shop, and made them myself after he drew them out with chalk.

7692. Were they house breaking tools ?—They were shop breaking tools.

7693. What kind of tools were they ?—They was queer tools. I could not show you unless I had something to draw them out by.

7694. Are they like false keys ? or what are they like ?—Yes ; they are rum looking things of course.

7695. Do they look like keys, or what do they look like ? is it a jemmy ?—No ; I had a jemmy of course.

7696. Were they to operate on the locks ?—They were to operate upon the locks what he drew out.

7697. Besides that you had your jemmy ?—Yes.

7698. Had you had that jemmy long ?—I made it the same time as I made the other.

7699. He drew you this pattern of tools and you made them, and you then went in ?—I went in the night after, and I succeeded. I went into this place of Mr. Darwin.

7700. And when you got in what did you do ?—I destroyed all I could lay my hands on, and there were a pair of bellows that I cut.

7701. Who told you to do that ?—Thompson.

7702. Thompson told you to cut the bellows ; what did he tell you to do besides ?—He told me to do another place where I was apprehended. Of course he has stated what he knows of it before me ; he took the first chance.

EIGHTH DAY.

J. Clarke.

14 June 1867.

7703. Have you seen the account he has given of it ?—No ; I have had to suffer for it.

7704. You say that Thompson has told us all about it ?—Yes ; he has stated his case.

7705. Do you know what he has said ?—No ; I cannot read.

7706. Has nobody told you what he has said ?—I have never inquired much ; I know I have had to suffer for it.

7707. He told you to go to the place where you were apprehended ; where were you apprehended ?—In Cornish Place.

7708. Where ? at Mr. Dixon's ?—At the back of Butcher Bland's.

7709. What were you to go there for ?—For the same purpose that I had been to the other.

7710. Has Mr. Darwin a place there ?—No ; this was another place.

7711. He told you to go to this other place ?—Yes.

7712. Whose was it ?—It was some one akin to this Hague that was working at Darwin's ; it was a brother of his.

7713. It was where a man was working who was a brother of a man who was working for Darwin—Yes.

7714. Do you know what the name of the person was where you went according to his directions when you were apprehended ? what was the name of the wheel or place ?—It was a scissors shop.

7715. Whose scissors shop was it ?—Hague rents this shop.

7716. What did you do there ?—I did nothing. I was apprehended there.

7717. Did you get in ?—No.

7718. How were you apprehended ?—I was apprehended at the bottom of the yard.

7719. Were you going to his place ?—Yes, I was going.

7720. Had you the things you got from Darwin's upon you, or how did they apprehend you ?—They found me with a jemmy, and I was without shoes at the time they apprehended me there.

7721. And they took you up for that ?—Yes, they took me up for that, and I got to Leeds assizes over it.

7722. You were charged with Darwin's business ?—Yes ; they came the morning after and charged me with breaking into Mr. Darwin's shop.

7723. How did they find you out ?—In this way : they took this jemmy from me and it corresponded with the marks on the door where they said I had broken in, and where I did break in of course ; I did do it.

7724. So you got nine months ?—Yes.

7725. Had Thompson told you to go to this Hague's shop ?—Yes.

7726. What did he tell you to do there ?—He told me to destroy the machinery, the same as I had done at Darwin's.

7727. When was it that you destroyed it at Darwin's ? do you recollect the day of the week ?—Thursday night I destroyed it at Darwin's ; I was apprehended at the other place on the same night ; it was all in the same night.

7728. You first went to Darwin's ?—Yes, and then went to the other place.

7729. Where is that ?—In Snow Lane.

7730. You went to Darwin's in Snow Lane and then to Hague's ?—Yes.

7731. You took some bands away ?—No ; there are no bands there.

7732. Are there any small tools belonging to the men ?—Plenty.

7733. Had you taken any small tools away ?—No.

7734. Are you quite sure that Thompson told you you were not to take away the small tools but that you were to destroy the machinery ?—He told me I was to destroy the machinery and the other tools and all.

7735. And you did ?—Yes.

7736. Have you never taken any small tools away ?—I took two hammers away.

7737. What became of them ?—I put them away.

7738. Have you returned them, or have you got them still ?—No.

7739. Have you got them ?—No.

7740. Do you know where they are ?—I chucked them into the river.

7741. Did he give you any instructions about the mode in which you were to destroy the machinery ?—He drew out the way I was to get into the place ; and I was to destroy the bellows, and take the hammers.

7742. Are you quite sure that he told you to destroy the bellows ?—I am quite sure.

7743. Did he tell you how to destroy them ?—He told me I was to have my knife and cut them.

7744. Did he tell you to do so ?—Yes, he did.

7745. Did he tell you whether he would give you anything for doing it ?—Yes.

7746. What was he to give you ?—He said he would give me a sovereign for doing it ; of course I was doing it a little out of spite in consequence of Mr. Darwin wanting to sacrifice me 10 per cent.

7747. You did it partly for the sovereign and partly out of spite ?—Yes, I did it partly for spite.

7748. Did you propose doing the damage to Mr. Darwin or did he propose it ? Who proposed that you should destroy the bellows and take the hammers ?—When I stated the case to him he proposed it.

7749. He proposed the damaging, it was not your proposal ?—No, it was not my proposal at all.

7750. Did this occur ? did you ask him to give you permission to rip open Hague's bellows ?—No.

7751. And to take away all the tools that you could take away ?—No.

7752. Did be say in answer to that " If there is " one thing more than another I detest it is this " knife business "?—No ; he never said such a thing to me.

7753. Did he tell you not to cut the bellows ?—No.

7754. He did not tell you not to cut the bellows, but to take away the tools ?—No.

7755. Did he say that by destroying the bellows you would make enemies of the employers, but by taking away the small tools and hiding them you might return them when the men commenced paying ?—No.

7756. He never said anything of the kind ?—No.

7757. Are you quite clear, because I must caution you about this ; are you quite sure that it was not your suggestion to cut open the bellows ?—I am quite sure.

7758. Are you quite sure that it was Thompson who suggested it ?—Yes, quite sure.

7759. Are you quite sure about it ?—I am quite sure. Why should I have any other reasons ? When I went down he put the question to me at once.

7760. Why could not you have taken away the small tools and hidden them and returned them, why should you cut the bellows ? Was it your own business or was it suggested by Thompson ?—It was suggested by Thompson ; he never mentioned the small tools, that was done on my own account. I thought I might as well, to fill up my time, as not.

7761. Repeat what he directed you to do ?—He directed me to cut the bellows and take the tools.

7762. And you persist in that statement ?—Yes, and I did do it.

7763. I know you did it, but did Thompson tell you to do it ?—Yes, sir.

7764. You say that he told you to destroy the bellows and take the small tools ?—He told me to destroy the bellows and take the tools.

7765. Only a moment ago you told me that he never mentioned the small tools ?—He told me to destroy the bellows and take the tools of course ; I only took two hammers.

7766. I want to know whether he distinctly told you to cut the bellows ?—Of course he told me.

7767. It is not of course. I cannot tell that. Will you swear that he told you to do it ?—I will swear he told me to cut the bellows.

7768. Did you ever see him after you did this and were in custody?—No. I got apprehended that night.

7769. Did he come to you in prison?—No. I never saw him till I came home.

7770. Did you write to him?—No.

7771. Did you instruct your wife to write to him?—No, never.

7772. Do you know whether he has done anything for your wife?—Yes.

7773. What has he done for your wife?—He has done 6*s.* a week, that is all he has done.

7774. Is your wife here?—No.

7775. Where is she?—At home in Sheffield.

7776. 6*s.* a week?—6*s.* a week he allowed her while I was away.

7777. How long for?—Nine months.

7778. Did he give your wife 6*s.* a week for nine months?—Yes; he gave her 6*s.* a week for nine months.

7779. But you were in custody before the assizes and you got nine months after?—I was in custody a few days. I was apprehended on the Thursday, and the Leeds Assizes began on the Wednesday after.

7780. Did your wife get 6*s.* a week for nine months and those odd days; that odd week?—There were no odd days in it at all; he allowed her that since I got my time. I got nine months and he allowed her 6*s.* a week.

7781. Have you ever talked to Holmshaw at all?—No.

7782. Is Holmshaw in your union?—No.

7783. Thompson is your man?—Thompson is our Secretary.

7784. He was, but he is no longer?—No.

7785. Are you a member now?—No.

7786. You are a member of the Union now?—Yes.

7787. Were you present at a meeting where Thompson appeared and told the meeting, after he had been summoned here, that he had paid your wife 6*s.* a week?—Yes.

7788. You were present at that meeting?—Yes.

7789. And I believe you joined in passing a vote of thanks to him for paying your wife?—Not me.

7790. Did you join in it?—No.

7791. Did you see whether it was carried unanimously or not?—I see there were two or three parties that carried it whom he had bribed; they were only two or three that he had got there to sanction it, and there was only a few parties that did sanction it.

7792. It was not passed unanimously?—It was passed by some parties.

7793. Was there any opposition to it?—Yes; there was opposition to it; plenty.

7794. Was it expressed?—Yes.

7795. There was expressed opposition?—Yes.

7796. Who opposed it?—I do not know their names. I cannot mention names.

7797. Were you known as the person who had destroyed this machinery?—Yes; they all knew me; they knowed me when they heard my name mentioned; they had seen it.

7798. You are a member of your union notwithstanding your having been convicted?—Yes; I am still a member.

7799. Do you mean to say that they continue in their body persons who have been convicted of offences like this?—The trade have nothing at all to do with it; he did that entirely on his own bottom did Thompson; nobody mentioned such a thing to me but Thompson; never.

7800. Has he ever suggested to you to do anything of the kind before?—No; I never had such a thing put to me before.

7801. Did you ever do it before?—No, never.

7802. Nobody ever put it to you before?—No.

7803. You had heard of such things before?—I had heard tell of rattening before, but it was never put to me before, and I never did it before, and I am sorry that I have done it.

7804. You were caught?—I was caught, that is right enough.

7805. You never did it before?—No.

7806. If you had never done it before and he made this proposal to you why did not you turn round to him and say, what do you mean by asking me, a respectable man, to go and damage a man's tools?—I asked him which way I was to get in.

7807. That is all you wanted to know then? you only wanted to know which way you were to get in? Have you had any talk with Thompson about this since you came out?—I have been in his house several times.

7808. Since you came out?—Yes.

7809. He keeps a beer-house?—Yes.

7810. All the secretaries keep beer-houses?—Not to my recollection. I do not know anything about any other secretary.

7811. Do you know any other secretary who does not keep a beer-house?—I only know our own secretary.

7812. Is there any secretary who does not keep a beer-house?—They can suit themselves what they keep.

7813. On the several occasions that you have been in his house since you came back, has he ever complained to you that you did wrong in cutting the bellows?—No, never.

7814. How long do you say you have been at home?—Five weeks last Thursday.

7815. When were you at his house last?—I have not been since we have had this meeting.

7816. What meeting?—Since we have had this general meeting; I have never been since he was examined.

7817. How long before he was examined were you at his house?—I went just as I came out.

7818. When was the last time you were there?—Perhaps a fortnight last Saturday night since I was there.

7819. Did you see him?—Oh yes.

7820. You talked to him?—Yes.

7821. Quite in a friendly way?—Yes.

7822. Did he tell you that he was coming to give evidence before us?—No.

7823. He did not tell you that?—No.

7824. It took you by surprise when you heard he had been coming and telling us a story about you?—It made no difference to me; I have served my time for it and it did not matter to me.

7825. If he proposed this to you and rather urged you to do it and was the cause of it being done and you got into all this trouble through him, did not you blame him for it?—Yes of course, I had to blame him, there was no one else to blame but him and me.

7826. Did not you blame him when you came back and say, "If I had not listened to your bad advice I should not have got into this scrape"?—I did not blame him; I never mentioned such a thing.

7827. If he got you into this scrape why did not you blame him?—I did not wish to blame anybody.

7828. Is it true that he suggested it or that you suggested it?—It is true he suggested it.

7829. Did you take those tools on your own account or was it suggested by Thompson?—By Thompson.

7830. And you adhere to that?—Yes.

7831. Now I tell you distinctly he has told us that you wanted to destroy the bellows, and he told you that he detested that kind of thing?—He did no such thing.

7832. And that he hated the knife business, you might take the tools and keep them, and when the master came to terms with the Union you could restore them. He tells us that he warned you against cutting the bellows, is that true or not?—He never said such a thing, on my oath.

EIGHTH DAY.

J. Clarke.

14 June 1867.

7833. Notwithstanding I tell you that he has sworn that, do you still tell me that he authorized you to cut the bellows ?—Yes, he told me to get a knife and cut the bellows.

7834. Did anybody know besides your wife that he was paying money to her ; was it known that your wife was receiving money ?—No, I suppose not. He did it all on his own bottom. I do not believe our trade knew anything at all about it. Why should he want to keep this in darkness if the trade knew anything about it. He never allowed the trade to know anything about this affair.

7835. Are you at work now ?—No.

7836. Are you on the Union ?—I have nothing to do.

7837. What do they allow you at the Union ?—My scale, the same as they allow other men.

7838. What do they allow you ?—They allow me 8*s.* a week, the same as they allow other men ?

7839. How long have you had 8*s.* a week. Had you it all the time you were in prison ?—No, they did not allow it. Our trade has never allowed me a penny.

7840. When did they begin to allow it to you ?—Since I came out. I chucked myself on the box when I came out. I had nothing to do.

7841. They have supported you ever since ; they have given you 8*s.* a week ?—Yes ; I was straight with the trade, and I can force it the same as any man can when he is out of work. I get nothing but what is due to me. I have received nothing for doing this here.

7842. You got a sovereign ?—I have not received a sovereign. I got apprehended the night that I ought to have received something after.

7843. Have you applied for it ?—No, never.

7844. Why did not you go to Thompson if he did this all on his own account, and get your sovereign ?—No doubt I should have got the money after if things had come off all right.

7845. But you have never applied for it since you came out ?—I have never asked him to give it me ; if he had offered it to me I should have taken it, no doubt of that, but our trade seems all against it ; they will not do nothing.

7846. (*Mr. Chance.*) Have you any family ?—No.

7847. Does your wife earn any wages ?—No.

7848. Then during the time that you were in confinement she was not earning any wages ?—No.

7849. She was living upon what was allowed her by Thompson ?—She had only 6*s.* allowed her ; two relations lived at our house, and what we had coming in kept my wife.

7850. Was anything said to you from time to time whether Thompson was supporting her ?—Of course Thompson did support her.

7851. That was well known ?—It was well known between the two.

7852. Was not it well known to other people ?—No ; they tried to keep it from other people. Thompson would not allow any one to know anything about it because he kept it from the trade.

7853. How did you know that, if you were in prison all the time ?—I have known it since I came out by what he stated himself.

7854. Did not anyone in the trade ask you whether anything had been done for her by anybody ? Did not anybody ask your wife while you were in prison ?—I do not know what they asked my wife while I was in prison. I cannot answer what was said to her, or what was done while I was in prison.

7855. (*Chairman.*) Do you mean to say that your wife never wrote to you to say how she was living ?—She wrote three letters, and she told me that she was doing first rate.

7856. Did she tell you where she got her money from ?—She told me she had 6*s.* a week ; that was all she had. She got nothing from the trade. The trade turned their backs upon her.

7857. (*Mr. Chance.*) Do you suppose that the Union and your friends had no curiosity to know how she was supported ?—I knew before I went away she was all right.

7858. Was there not some curiosity among her friends to know how she was living while you were in prison ?—She had 6*s.* a week.

7859. How did the trade know how she was living ?—I do not know how they knew ; I do not know what they knew about it.

7860. They would have inquired from her how she was living while you were in prison ; do not you know that there was a report that the trade was supporting her ?—I knew nothing about what the trade was doing.

7861. Do not you know that there was a report about that the trade was supporting her ?—No, the trade did nothing for her at all. Thompson did it all on his own bottom, he states in his case that that has cost him a lot of money on his own account, he ought to suffer for it. I do not believe that the trade knows anything at all about his affairs. They all seemed to turn their backs both upon me and her. They have done nothing for her while I was away.

7862. (*Mr. Barstow.*) You are drawing scale now ?—Any man can force his scale that is straight with the trade. If he is straight with the trade he can force his scale when he has nothing to do ; but if they can find him any work he is forced to go to do it.

7863. (*Mr. Chance.*) While you were in prison your wife was earning nothing ?—No.

7864. She was supported by money from Thompson ?—She was supported by 6*s.* a week from Thompson, that was all she got from him.

The witness withdrew.

Adjourned to to-morrow at 11 o'clock.

NINTH DAY.

Council Hall, Sheffield, Saturday, 15th June 1867.

PRESENT :

WILLIAM OVEREND, Esq., Q.C.
THOMAS IRWIN BARSTOW, Esq.
GEORGE CHANCE, Esq.
J. E. BARKER, Esq. Secretary.

WILLIAM OVEREND, Esq., Q.C., IN THE CHAIR.

NINTH DAY.

D. Clarke.

15 June 1867.

DENNIS CLARKE sworn and examined.

7865. (*Chairman.*) You are a saw grinder I believe, are you not?—Yes.

7866. To whom were you apprenticed?—Linley.

7867. And then what became of you?—I was loosed.

7868. After you were loosed where did you go?—I worked for Wilson.

7869. Then afterwards what did you do?—I joined the union.

7870. Did you leave Wilson to join the union?—Yes.

7871. Who joined the union at the same time?—A good many of us.

7872. Can you mention any person?—Fearnehough joined, and Copley and Garfit.

7873. Did Shaw join?—I do not know whether Shaw joined or not.

7874. Who besides? was Myers a member?—I am sure I cannot remember.

7875. You and Shaw were apprentices together, were you not?—Yes.

7876. Have you known Shaw ever since?—Yes.

7877. Did Matthew Woollen join at the same time? I am sure I cannot tell you.

7878. Did Ibbotson join?—I think Ibbotson did.

7879. Did James Linley join at the same time?—Yes.

7880. And did Charles Baxter join?—I do not know.

7881. Christopher Frith?—Yes.

7882. And you have been intimate with Shaw ever since I believe?—We have gone together a bit sometimes.

7883. You are a member of the union I believe?—Yes.

7884. How long have you been a member of the union?—I do not know whether it is eight or nine years since.

7885. It is since 1859 I believe?—I do not know when it was.

7886. Have you been a member somewhere about eight years?—I dare say I have, I do not know how long it is since.

7887. Is it about eight years?—It is somewhere about eight or nine years.

7888. Have you ever been employed by the secretary to do any business for the union?—No.

7889. No business at all of any sort?—I have never done any business at all for the union.

7890. Has the secretary, Mr. Broadhead, ever employed you to do anything for the trade, for the union?—No.

7891. Nor anyone connected with the committee?—No, I have never done any.

7892. Do you know that persons are sometimes watched to see whether they do business in conformity with the rules of the society?—I know naught about it, I have never been watched that I know of.

7893. You do not know that people are ever watched to see whether they conform to the rules of the union?—I do not know, I have never been watched yet.

7894. I did not ask you that, I asked you if it was not the custom to watch people to see if they did or did not conform to the rules of the union?—I do not know.

7895. Is that your answer?—Yes.

7896. You are quite clear about that?—I know naught about it.

7897. You yourself were never set to watch?—Not that I know of.

7898. Were you ever set to watch and see whether persons conformed to the union rules?—Not that I know of.

7899. Will you swear that you never were set to watch?—Not that I know of.

7900. I do not ask you that; I shall send you to prison if you begin to trifle with me?—You do not want me to swear to a thing that I cannot think on.

7901. No I do not, but you know whether you have been employed to watch and see whether persons conformed to the union rules?—I cannot recollect it.

7902. Will you swear that you have not?—I cannot recollect it.

7903. Will you swear that you have not?—I cannot swear if I cannot think of it.

7904. You can remember it. Will you swear that you do not know?—I will not swear at all.

7905. Do you say that you will not swear?—I cannot swear if I do not know anything about it.

7906. I ask you if you have ever been employed by the union to watch and see whether people conformed to the union rules?—I cannot swear if I do not know.

7907. Have you or have you not?—I know naught about it.

7908. Have you or have you not?—Not that I know of.

7909. Will you swear that you do not know that you have?—How can I swear if I do not know anything about it.

7910. You must not ask me questions, but you must answer mine. Have you or have you not been set to watch?—Not that I know of.

7911. In the month of January 1860 were you set to watch a man?—Not that I know of.

7912. Mind what you are about; you must know it?—Not that I know of.

7913. Will you swear that you were not in the month of January 1860 set to watch whether a man was conforming to the rules of the society or not?—I tell you I cannot remember the time. I cannot remember it.

7914. Will you swear that you were, or that you were not?—I cannot swear what I do not know.

7915. I know you cannot, but will you swear that you were not employed in January 1860 for that purpose?—I cannot remember it.

7916. You must remember it if you were so employed?—I cannot remember it.

7917. Will you swear that you were not?—How can I swear when I cannot remember anything at all about it?

7918. Will you swear that you were not. I will send you to prison if you trifle with me much longer?—I cannot swear a thing that I cannot remember.

7919. I do not want you to do so, but you must remember this fact: whether you were employed by the union and whether you did watch?—I cannot remember.

7920. Did you not in the month of January 1860

NINTH DAY.

D. Clarke.

15 June 1867.

receive 2*s.* from the secretary for going out to watch ?—I cannot remember so long back as that.

7921. Yes, you can. On the 16th of January 1860 did not the secretary give you 2*s.* for going out to watch ?—It is so long since.

7922. Never mind; it is only 1860. Will you swear that he did not ?—I cannot swear when I cannot recollect it.

7923. Then you cannot recollect it; is that what you say ?—Yes.

7924. Were you not paid 2*s.* a day for some time by the union for watching ?—I tell you I cannot recollect it.

7925. Did you not complain to the society that 2*s.* a day was too little ?—I cannot recollect it.

7926. You can recollect it if it occurred. Will you swear that you do not recollect that ?—I cannot recollect it.

7927. Will you swear that it did not occur ? that you did not complain to the union that 2*s.* a day was too little for employing you to watch ?—I cannot recollect it.

7928. Will you swear that it did not occur ?—I cannot swear what I do not know.

7929. May it have occurred ?—It might have occurred for aught I know.

7930. Then you may have watched for them and forgotten it ?—I may have.

7931. Is that so ? may you have watched and forgotten it ?—I may have, but if I have I have forgotten it.

7932. Were you drinking last night with Joseph Copley ?—Yes, I went and had a pint of porter ; that was all I had.

7933. Did Joseph Copley boast to you last night that the Commissioners had got very little out of him ?—I was not in the same room with him all the time.

7934. Did Joseph Copley tell you last night that we had got very little out of him ?—I am sure I do not know; I had had a sup of beer and all.

7935. Did Joseph Copley tell you last night that we had got very little out of him ?—I do not remember ; I heard him talking some, but I do not know what it was.

7936. No doubt you heard him talking, but I ask you if you heard him talking that way ?—I had had some beer myself.

7937. There is no getting out of it ; did Joseph Copley talk to you and boast that we had got very little out of him ?—He did not say so to me.

7938. Did he say it in your presence ?—He said something, but I forget what it was.

7939. Did you hear him say so ?—About getting very little out of him ?

7940. Yes ?—I do not know what he said ; I know he said summat.

7941. I know he said something, but did he say that ? Will you swear one way or the other ?—I cannot think of everything that is said up and down the town.

7942. That is no answer. You have said that you cannot recollect what occurred in 1860 ; I now want to see whether it is a question of memory, or because you will not tell me, and I speak now of what occurred last night ?—I do not know what it was now ; I was fresh and all.

7943. Did he boast that we had got very little out of him ?—I cannot swear that.

7944. Will you swear that he did not ?—No.

7945. Will you swear that he did ?—No; he said something, but I do not know what it was.

7946. Did he say that ?—I do not know what he said.

7947. Did he say that or not ?—I do not know.

7948. You know whether he said that or not ?—He said something.

7949. Did he say that or not ?—I do not know what he said.

7950. You know whether he said that or not ?—I did not notice what was said at all.

7951. You knew very well you were going to be a witness yourself the next day. Do you mean to tell me that he boasted and said we had got very little out of him ; there were others there at the time, remember ?—Yes, I saw the others there. I saw Shaw there.

7952. In the presence of others did he not say openly and boast that we had got very little out of him ?—I do not know what it was that he said now.

7953. Will you swear that he did not say that ?—I cannot remember now what it was they were talking about. He was drunk and I was fresh and all.

7954. Will you swear you did not hear him say that ?—I do not know whether it was that or what it was.

7955. Do you think that anybody believes a word that you say about it ? Did he say that or not ?—If a fellow is drunk he does not recollect a deal the day after I should think.

7956. Did he say that or not ?—I cannot swear what he said.

7957. Did he say that or not ?—I heard him talking very hard.

7958. And when he was talking very hard, did he say we had got very little out of him ?—I cannot swear that. I do not know what he said. I was fresh and all.

7959. Do you recollect ever being at the "Blue Pig," and Helliwell coming in ?—No, I was never at the "Blue Pig" with Helliwell.

7960. Have you ever been at the "Blue Pig" ?—Yes, many a time.

7961. Do you recollect Mr. and Mrs. Helliwell coming there ?—No.

7962. Have you ever at the "Corner Pin" seen Mr. and Mrs. Helliwell ?—Never.

7963. And you swear you did not say to Mr. Helliwell in the presence of his wife, "I will do thee yet" ?—Yes, I will swear that.

7964. Did you ever say so to him ?—Never.

7965. Nor ever anything of the kind ?—No.

7966. And you never threatened Helliwell in your life ?—Never.

7967. Helliwell worked for Wilson did he not ?—Yes.

7968. Do you ever recollect being at the wheel when Garfit and he fought ?—Yes.

7969. Were you there as the friend of Garfit ?—Yes.

7970. Do you recollect Helliwell being blown up ?—Yes.

7971. How long was that before he was blown up ?—I do not know ; I remember his being blown up.

7972. How long before he was blown up was it that you were there with Garfit when he fought Helliwell ?—We were all working there.

7973. Are you sure about it ?—Yes.

7974. What were you doing ?—Grinding.

7975. What did they fight about ?—I think it was summat about work, they were drunk.

7976. What about the work ?—Garfit thought he did not get his share of the work or summat.

7977. Have you ever abused Helliwell and called him names ?—I called him names the same as he called me.

7978. What have you called him ?—"Topsey."

7979. Have you abused him for not joining the union ?—Never.

7980. Have you abused him for not working according to the rules of the union ?—Never.

7981. Have you abused him for anything ?—No ; he was a man that I knew very little about was Helliwell.

7982. Have you ever heard Garfit abuse him ?—No.

7983. Do you recollect ever being at the "Greyhound" inn ?—I have been there many a time.

7984. Do you recollect being there on one occasion when Shaw was there ?—Shaw has been there many a time, the same as me, for his scale.

7985. Who kept the "Greyhound" ?—Broadhead.

7986. Did you ever go to Shaw and ask him if he would do a job ?—Who ?

7987. Did you ever ask Shaw if he would do a job ?—No.

NINTH DAY.

D. Clarke.

15 June 1867.

7988. After you had been in the union about a fortnight did you ask him if he would do a job?—No.

7989. Did you at any time ask him if he would do a job?—Never.

7990. Did you ever ask Shaw if he would blow up "Old Topsey"?—No, never in my life. I will swear it.

7991. Did you ever tell him that you could have 3*l.* for doing it?—No.

7992. Will you swear that?—Yes.

7993. Or any sum of money for blowing up "Old Topsey"?—No.

7994. Have you seen Mr. Broadhead about this matter?—Yes.

7995. Have you seen Mr. Broadhead since Shaw gave his evidence?—No; I have never seen him since last Sunday.

7996. Have you received any message from him since that time?—No.

7997. So you never told Shaw that you could get 3*l.* for blowing Helliwell up?—No; I have sworn I never did.

7998. Did you not go up to Broadhead and receive from Broadhead some cans of powder?—No.

7999. Never in all your life?—No.

8000. You have never got any powder from him?—No.

8001. Have you ever had powder in your possession when you were in Broadhead's house?—No.

8002. Had you ever three cans of powder?—No, I never had money enough to buy three cans of powder.

8003. I do not ask you whether you had money enough; had you ever three cans of powder in your possession?—I had never two ounces of powder in my life.

8004. Never?—Never.

8005. Then what Shaw says is not true, that you went upstairs and brought down three cans of powder?—It is not true.

8006. That is not true?—It is not.

8007. Did you ever go with Shaw to Simmonite?—No.

8008. Did you ever see Simmonite when you were in company with Shaw?—No, I am almost sure I did not.

8009. You never did?—No.

8010. Are you sure you never saw Simmonite when you were in company with Shaw?—I am sure I did not.

8011. Did you ever go to Shaw's house?—Yes, I have been in Shaw's house many a time.

8012. Did you know where he slept?—No.

8013. Did you ever go into the room where his bed was?—No.

8014. Did Mrs. Shaw ever speak to you at all about any powder?—No, never.

8015. Or speak to her son in your presence?—No.

8016. Do you recollect ever going to the "Green Man" with Shaw shortly after you had joined the union?—I do not.

8017. Did you ever go to the "Green Man" in company with Shaw?—I might have been with him but I do not know when.

8018. But did you go in with him?—I can hardly swear that. We have been in a many places together.

8019. Have you been in the "Green Man" together?—We have not boen to the "Green Man" together.

8020. Did you ever go with him to the "Corner Pin" in the Wicker?—Many a time.

8021. Now did you not on one day shortly after you had joined the union go first to the "Green Man," and then afterwards to the "Corner Pin" and get drunk there?—I never was with Shaw at the "Green Man" to my knowledge.

8022. Did you ever go with him from the "Green Man" to the "Corner Pin," and get drunk with him?—I have been drunk at the "Corner Pin" many a time.

8023. Did you get drunk with Shaw at the "Corner Pin" a short time after you joined the union?—It is hard for me to say where I have been drunk at.

8024. I daresay it is, but you will recollect very well whether you went down to the "Corner Pin" shortly after you joined the union and got drunk there in company with Shaw, is that so?—I have been there many a time since.

8025. That is not an answer; did you shortly after joining the union go there with Shaw and get drunk?—I have been in the "Corner Pin" many a time.

8026. I do not ask you that; I ask you whether shortly after you joined the union you got drunk there once?—I daresay I may, but I do not know.

8027. What were you doing after you joined the union?—Hanging and holeing stones.

8028. Where were you hanging and holeing stones?—Anywhere where they wanted them done.

8029. Can you mention a place within the first fortnight after you had joined the union where you have hung a stone or holed it. You know you were loosed, and then you joined the union, and you surely can recollect what you were doing for the first fortnight. Tell me any person whose stones you hung or whose stones you holed during the first fortnight?—I holed some of the trade tools.

8030. Are they trade tools which the trade had bought of you or what are they?—No; they belong to themselves.

8031. And did they supply you with tools, or how was it that you holed some of the trade tools?—I got them ready for hanging; they wanted holeing.

8032. And you did this for the union?—Yes.

8033. Where did you hole any?—At the Tower.

8034. In the first fortnight?—Yes.

8035. How many did you hole?—I cannot recollect now how many I holed.

8036. Who paid you for doing it?—Broadhead.

8037. How much did he pay you?—A shilling apiece.

8038. How many did you do?—I do not know.

8039. How many will you swear that you did during the first fortnight?—I do not know.

8040. How many did you do in the first fortnight?—I do not know.

8041. Did you do two?—Yes, and more than two.

8042. Did you do three?—I do not know.

8043. Will you swear that you holed three stones during the first fortnight after you joined the union?—I do not know how many I holed; it is so long since.

8044. You can recollect about your one shilling apiece; will you swear that you holed three?—I cannot swear how many I holed during the first fortnight.

8045. Were you on the box during the first fortnight?—Yes.

8046. How much did you get?—I got so much a week.

8047. How much a week did you get?—I do not know how much it was now.

8048. How long were you on the box after you joined the union?—I would be on a good while.

8049. How long?—Before I had a situation?

8050. Yes.—Four or five years very likely.

8051. You were four or five years out of situation after you joined the union, is that what you say?—Yes.

8052. What were you doing during those four or five years?—Working at whatever I could get.

8053. For whom have you worked?—I have worked for my father the biggest part.

8054. What did you do for him?—Rubbing stone; labouring for him.

8055. What did you do for your father?—Laboured for him.

8056. But what kind of labour was it?—Any kind that wanted doing.

8057. But what kind of work did he give you to do?—He learned me to be a mason.

8058. Where did you work for him?—At Walkley.

NINTH DAY.

D. Clarke.

15 June 1867.

8059. Where at Walkley?—At the top of Break-back, I think. I do not know what they call the street.

8060. Was it in a quarry or what?—No, it was in some cottage houses.

8061. How long did you work at those houses?—A good while.

8062. How long?—I do not know rightly.

8063. Yes, you do?—No, I do not.

8064. How long did you work?—I do not know; I worked there a good while.

8065. That gives me no information; how long did you work?—I cannot tell you how long I worked.

8066. Did you work a month?—Yes, many a month.

8067. How many months did you work there?—A good many.

8068. Will you swear that you worked there three months?—Yes.

8069. Four months?—I cannot tell how many months.

8070. Will you swear that you worked four months at those cottage houses?—I worked above four months. I cannot tell to a month.

8071. Will you swear that you worked five months at those cottage houses?—I can swear that I worked above 12 months, but I cannot tell how much above.

8072. Did you work 18 months?—I do not know how long it was.

8073. Did you work 18 months?—I do not know how long it was. I cannot think of things so long back.

8074. Did you work 18 months?—I do not know how long I worked.

8075. Did you work 18 months?—I have worked and played all four years.

8076. You worked 18 months? do you say 18 months or not?—I said I had worked above 12 months.

8077. What did your father pay you?—He paid me 3*s.* a day when I started.

8078. And what afterwards?—He raised me to 4*s.*, and he kept me at 4*s.*

8079. Was your father a mason?—Yes.

8080. Where did he live?—At the top of Tom Cross Lane.

8081. Did he employ anybody besides you?—Yes.

8082. Whom?—My brother.

8083. For how long did he pay you 3*s.* a day? for six months?—I cannot tell you how long it was.

8084. Was it for six months?—I cannot tell you how long it was.

8085. You must tell me about how long it was?—I think it would be about six months.

8086. And 4*s.* for the remainder of the time?—Yes.

8087. Now will you swear that he paid you 3*s.* a day every day or not every day?—He paid me every day I worked.

8088. How many days did you work?—I do not know.

8089. Three days a week?—Yes, and sometimes four.

8090. Now then, you have accounted for 12 months; during the three other years what were you doing?—Working.

8091. For whom?—For anybody that would give me a job.

8092. Whom did you work for?—I have worked for many a one.

8093. Tell me for whom you worked?—I afterwards worked for Mr. Worth.

8094. How long did you work for him?—I do not know.

8095. About how long?—I cannot tell.

8096. Was it a week?—I cannot tell; I worked for him two or three weeks.

8097. For whom have you worked besides?—I worked for Hawley.

8098. How long did you work for him?—I cannot tell you.

8099. What number of weeks did you work for him?—I cannot tell; I never keep that in my head.

8100. What Hawley is that?—Joseph Hawley they call him.

8101. Where does he live?—He lives somewhere agen the "Fox and Duck."

8102. What is Mr. Hawley?—A mason.

8103. What is Worth?—A mason.

8104. How long did you work for Hawley?—I cannot tell you.

8105. I do not want to know to a day, or even to a week, but about how long have you worked for Hawley?—About two or three weeks.

8106. For whom have you worked besides?—I have worked for mysen.

8107. How have you worked for yourself?—I picked a bit of masoning up, and did it myself.

8108. What masonry have you done yourself?—I have done some for Dawson.

8109. Who is Dawson?—I do not know; they call him Josh Dawson; that is all I know about him.

8110. Where does he live?—He lives up against the "Fox and Duck."

8111. What did you do for him?—I did 11 or 12 houses; I do not know which.

8112. Did you build them altogether?—I did the stone work.

8113. How long ago was that?—I got it done two or three weeks since.

8114. How long were you employed at those houses?—I do not know how long we were agate on them.

8115. Yes you do?—No I do not.

8116. How long were you employed at those houses?—I do not know.

8117. Were you employed a year on them?—No.

8118. Were you six months there?—I cannot tell you.

8119. Yes you can?—I cannot tell you to two or three months.

8120. Were you three months?—I cannot tell you.

8121. Were you there six months?—I do not know.

8122. Was it more than six months?—I do not know; I could not tell you how long I was agate upon them; I do not keep an almanack in my head.

8123. Do not be impertinent to me, or I will send you to prison?—I cannot think of everything; you want me to swear things that I do not know.

8124. Were you employed there six months or not?—It might be six months or it might be under.

8125. What is your belief about it? do you believe that you were engaged there six months?—I should not be far off.

8126. Are those all the employments that you know of, which you have had since the year 1859?—What other bit I have done, I have done with my brother; I have a brother a mason and all.

8127. What do you mean by that?—I worked for him when I could get no other work.

8128. How long have you worked for him?—I cannot tell you; I should work for him when I could not get work anywhere else.

8129. Have you worked a month for him during the whole of those seven years?—Seven years?

8130. Yes; it is more than seven years, it is eight years; have you ever worked for him a month altogether in all those eight years?—I should think I worked for him many a month; I used to go to him when I could not go anywhere else.

8131. How long have you worked for him altogether?—I cannot tell that.

8132. Have you worked a month for him altogether?—I should think I have worked about a month.

8133. Are those all the employments that you have had that you can recollect?—That is all I can recollect, and I think it is plenty and all.

8134. I have taken down the account which you have given of the time during which you have been occupied since 1859, and I see that you have been engaged exactly 20 months in the eight years; what were you doing the other part of the time?—I do not know.

8135. Have you ever worked at the saw grinding?—Yes.

8136. For whom ?—Mr. Taylor.

8137. How long have you worked for him ?—I worked for him this time eight or nine weeks. I worked for him twice before.

8138. And how long did you work for him then ?—I do not know.

8139. Eight or nine weeks or how long ?—I do not know. I worked while he stopped me.

8140. How long had you worked for him on the previous occasion ?—I cannot tell you.

8141. Was it three or four weeks ?—It would be many a week ; I cannot tell.

8142. Was it two months ?—It was many a week I tell you.

8143. Was it two months ?—Above two months.

8144. Was it jobbing or a situation ?—One was a situation and the other was jobbing.

8145. How long is it since you had the situation ?—I cannot tell.

8146. Is it two, or three, or four years ago that you got the situation ?—I cannot tell whether it is two or three years since.

8147. With whom had you a situation ?—Taylor.

8148. How long is it since you had a situation with Taylor ?—I have one now.

8149. With Taylor ?—Yes.

8150. How long have you had the situation ?—I do not know how long it is since.

8151. How long did the situation last ?—I cannot tell you.

8152. Was it a month, or two months, or three months, or how long ?—I cannot tell you how long it was.

8153. Yes you can ?—I cannot.

8154. You can ?—You do not want me to tell you a lie about it.

8155. I do not want you to tell a lie, though I daresay you will do so ; how long did you hold that situation ?—Perhaps two or three months.

8156. Had you it more than two or three months ?—Yes, I daresay I had.

8157. Had you it for more than six months ?—I do not know.

8158. Do you believe that you had it for six months ?—I daresay that would be about the time.

8159. And when you afterwards worked on a job how long were you at that ?—As long as the men came.

8160. How long was that ?—A week or two.

8161. And how long have you been working in a situation now ?—Eight or nine weeks happens.

8162. You see that you have only given now what will make up a little over two years out of the eight years, therefore there are six years to account for ; how were you living during those six years ?—With my father.

8163. Are you a married man ?—I have been.

8164. When were you married ?—I do not know long it is since.

8165. How many years is it ago since you were married ?—I do not know, I should think it is nine or ten years.

8166. You were not married before you were of age were you ?—No, I should be about loosed.

8167. How long did your wife live ?—She lived while the flood.

8168. Till the bursting of the Dale Dyke reservoir ?—Yes.

8169. And was she lost in the flood ?—No, she was confined.

8170. Did she die afterwards ?—She got a cold and died the same week.

8171. Then were you and your wife both living with your father ?—No.

8172. Where was your wife living ?—We were both living in Harvest Lane.

8173. You told me you were living with your father ?—You asked me who kept me, and I said my father and my mother and all.

8174. Your father kept you in Harvest Lane ?—Yes, he kept all of us.

8175. Have you any children ?—Two.

8176. Are you a pretty good workman ?—I do not know ; master knows that best. I can do my share.

8177. Have you been on the box in the Saw Grinders union ?—Yes.

8178. How long ?—I do not know altogether. I cannot tell you how long I have been on altogether.

8179. Have you ever been off ?—Yes.

8180. When were you off ?—I was off that time when I was in a regular situation at Taylor's and I am off now.

8181. Were you ever off the box, except on those two occasions when you got a regular situation, and now when you have a situation ?—No, only when I was jobbing a bit.

8182. When were you off the box when you were jobbing ?—I cannot tell you when it was.

8183. Have you not been on the box with the exception of about 18 months during the whole of that time ?—I daresay I have.

8184. And what have you received from the scale ?—We receive now 9*s.* 6*d.* for me and two children.

8185. And you have been receiving this for years ?—Yes, I have been receiving it when I have been on the box.

8186. Have you always received 9*s.* 6*d.* a week ?—I received more when we had more scale.

8187. How much have you received a week ?—I do not know.

8188. What has been the highest you have got ?—I am sure I do not know now.

8189. You do know. A man who is not in employ at all, and who has his family to keep knows what he gets. How much did you get ?—I do not know. I think it was 7*s.* for a man, 2*s.* 6*d.* for his wife, and 2*s.* for each child.

8190. If that was so you would be receiving 13*s.* 6*d.* a week ?—I do not know what we received ; I buried two children. I have two living.

8191. Have you been paid for four children ?—Yes.

8192. How long were you paid for four children ?—While they lived.

8193. How long is it since they died ?—One of them died at the flood, and I do not know how long it is since the other died.

8194. Has the other died since ?—Yes, the other got scalded.

8195. That would make the 17*s.* 6*d.* a week for four years doing nothing, is that so ?—I do not know how much a week it was. It was not bad wage.

8196. Do you mean to say that during that time the union paid you all this sum of money and never asked you to do anything for them ?—Yes.

8197. And you rendered no services at all to the union ?—Never one.

8198. Was there plenty of work in the trade during those four years ?—If there had been plenty of work they would have made me have gone.

8199. Did you ever apply for work ?—No.

8200. Is there a list made out in your union of the persons who are out of employment and ready to be engaged by the masters ?—Yes, there is a list of unemployed.

8201. And nobody is at liberty to apply for work in your union unless his name is on the list, is he ?—No.

8202. Have you ever been sent by the trade to any master for the purpose of being engaged ?—No, I have never been sent to be engaged.

8203. So that all that you have done has been to go about as you pleased and present yourself on a Saturday night, and then you got your scale ?—Yes, I used to have my scale when I wanted it.

8204. And this has been going on since 1859. When you joined the union did you pay anything ?—5*l.*

8205. Have you paid anything to the union since ?—No.

8206. Do you mean to say you never paid any contributions at all ?—Yes. I paid my contribution, but I thought you meant besides the 5*l.*

NINTH DAY.

D. Clarke.

15 June 1867.

8207. When have you paid the contributions?—I have paid it when they came for it.

8208. Have you paid it when you have been in situations only or at other times?—When I have been in situations only.

8209. And how much did you pay a week when you were in a situation?—I pay 5*s.* a week now.

8210. But how much did you pay before?—A poundage. So much in the pound.

8211. How much was it on your wages formerly?—3*s.* 4*d.* in the pound.

8212. Now you say it is 5*s.*?—Yes.

8213. Then as you make it out you paid 5*l.*; you paid your poundage while you were in service for about 12 months?—I do not know how long I had a situation.

8214. You told us you were 12 months in a situation?—I never told you I was 12 months.

8215. How much could you earn a week when you were in that first situation with Mr. Taylor for about six months?—Sometimes 2*l.*

8216. But what was the average which you earned with Mr. Taylor?—I cannot tell.

8217. Did you earn as much as 30*s.* a week?—I do not know.

8218. Did you earn 30*s.* a week?—We used to have a tale as well.

8219. Did you make from 30*s.* to 2*l.*?—Yes, some weeks I did; some weeks less and some weeks more.

8220. Did you ever make 2*l.*?—Yes.

8221. Will you swear that?—Yes and above.

8222. How often have you made 2*l.*?—Many a week.

8223. But is 30*s.* an average?—I cannot tell what will be the average,

8224. But it was sometimes more than 2*l.* you say and sometimes less than 30*s.*?—Yes, sometimes less than 1*l.* and sometimes nought.

8225. If you earned nothing you had nothing to pay?—We could pay nothing.

8226. Then in point of fact whether you paid by poundage or by a fixed rate, it appears you would pay somewhere about 5*s.* a week?—I do not know what I paid.

8227. Your 5*l.* on your entrance and your other contributions is all that you have paid to the club?—I do not know what I have paid to the club. Broadhead would know quite well.

8228. And for this you have been on the box now between five and six years?—I cannot tell you to two or three months how long it was.

8229. Did you get scale while you were working as a mason?—Yes.

8230. Then it is eight years all but six months and six weeks that you have been getting scale, and you would not even swear that it was six months, and do you mean to tell us that the club have a member who only brought in 5*l.* and contributed 5*s.* a week during six months, and they have been paying you all this money for eight years?—They have been paying me while I was on the box.

8231. There surely are not many in the same position as you?—There are about 80.

8232. But if there are 80 men on the same system as you that would ruin any society?—If it were not upheld it would.

8233. Who upholds it?—Those that work.

8234. And those that play are to receive?—Yes.

8235. But why did you not work?—I did not seek for it.

8236. Why did not the secretary put your name on the list?—He did put it on the list.

8237. And how was it that you did not happen to be engaged?—I do not know.

8238. Have you ever seen the list with your name upon it?—No.

8239. Then how do you know that your name was on it?—I should expect he would put all box men on it.

8240. But you never saw it?—No.

8241. Did you know a man of the name of Martin?—Yes.

8242. He was a member of the union too, was he not?—Yes.

8243. Do you know his christian name?—Joe Martin.

8244. Was he a friend of yours?—Yes, we were all apprentices together.

8245. Did he often go to Broadhead's?—He went to Broadhead's when he was dry.

8246. Did you and he keep company together?—Not a deal.

8247. Was he at work or was he on the box?—We were both working and on the box and all.

8248. For whom have you ever known him work?—I do not know; I know he worked at Screw Mill?

8249. How long?—I do not know how long he worked there.

8250. How long have you known him to be on the box?—I cannot tell.

8251. Have you seen him going about doing nothing?—Yes many a time.

8252. I mean to say out of employment?—Yes.

8253. On those occasions have you seen him at Broadheads?—I have seen him go for his scale on Saturday nights sometimes.

8254. Where is he now?—He is in America I expect.

8255. When did he leave?—About eight weeks since.

8256. How came it that you joined the union?—Because all the others joined.

8257. Had any pressure been put upon you to join the union? had anybody been to you to ask you to join the union?—Nobody had asked me; I joined because the others did.

8258. There was nothing said to you to force you to join the union?—No.

8259. It was of your own free will and voluntary act that you went?—I volunteered to go so soon as the others went.

8260. It has not been a bad thing for you I think?—No, it has not.

8261. Where did you get your 5*l.* from?—I paid it at so much a week out of my scale.

8262. So you paid the 5*l.* out of the scale at so much a week did you?—Yes.

8263. Then in point of fact you have never paid anything, they have got their own money back again, that is all?—It would be their own money, but it would be mine before it was theirs.

8264. No, it was theirs before it was yours?—Then they got it back again.

8265. Supposing you are jobbing, have you to give an account of what you are doing by your jobbing?—No, you have to pay 5*s.* a week for your jobbing.

8266. But supposing that you do not earn 5*s.*, but only 4*s.*, what then?—You pay 5*s.* if you are there a week.

8267. Whatever you earn you pay 5*s.*?—Yes.

8268. Is that a new regulation?—Yes.

8269. How long has that regulation existed?—I do not know how long it is since.

8270. But formerly did you pay 5*s.*?—No, there was a poundage.

8271. But supposing that you were jobbing under the former system how did you pay then?—You paid according to what you earned.

8272. And they deducted that from your scale?—We had no scale at all then.

8273. You said that you only paid contribution when you were in a situation, did you pay anything when you were jobbing?—Yes, I should pay the same when we were jobbing as when we were in a situation.

8274. Did you pay the contribution except when you were in a situation?—Yes, jobbing is just the same as being in a situation. We have to grind.

8275. It is not the same. I have seen your rules. I ask you whether you pay the same when you are jobbing as you do when you are in a situation?—I say yes.

NINTH DAY.

D. Clarke.

15 June 1867.

8276. You have always done so ?—Yes.

8277. Is it not in this way ; that they deduct what you earn from the scale which they allow ?—If you earn 1*l.*, 3*s.* 4*d.* is paid you.

8278. Supposing you earn 10*s.* and are entitled to scale of 17*s.* 6*d.*, would they not deduct the 10*s.* and give you 7*s.* 6*d.* ?—No, they would give you 3*d.* in the shilling.

8279. What do you mean by that ?—Every shilling you earned under your scale they would give you 3*d.* on.

8280. Do you mean that you are not entitled to it all ?—They have 9*d.* and you have 3*d.*

8281. Supposing that you were to earn 10*s.*, you would not be entitled to have the whole 10*s.* yourself, but you would take 2*s.* 6*d.* out of it for yourself, and they would take the remainder ?—Yes, I should have the 3*d.* in the shilling.

8282. Then how much would they allow you ? would they make it up to 17*s.* 6*d.* ?—They would give me this 3*d.* in the shilling above my scale.

8283. Therefore if you are jobbing they give you 3*d.* above your scale, they do not deduct from your scale ?—You have all the threepences above your scale. If you had 17*s.* 6*d.* a week and earned 15*s.*, you would have 15 threepences to draw, to put on the top of the 17*s.* 6*d.*

8284. Therefore when you are in a situation you have to pay 5*s.* a week ?—Yes.

8285. When you are jobbing you still get your scale and you get 3*d.* in the shilling for every shilling that you earn besides ?—If you earn above your scale you have to pay.

8286. But if it is under your scale ?—Then you have your 3*d.*

8287. And that you add to your scale ?—Yes, if you do not earn above it.

8288. And you say that the 5*l.* you paid was to be taken out of your scale, was it in point of fact deducted out of your scale ?—Yes, it was regularly deducted out.

8289. It was regularly deducted all the time till it got paid off ?—Yes.

8290. You have been a very useful member ?—I have been a very good one.

8291. Mr. Chance tells me he has been calculating what you have received ; and he makes out that you have got from this union upwards of 200*l.* ?—Not very bad that.

8292. For that you have contributed nothing, and done nothing in the world. That is the use of which you have been to the union. That is not bad pay for a man doing nothing ?—It is not, but if there had been work I should have had it to do.

8293. Having told you that you have been this expense to the union and cost them 200*l.* while you have been a member, I ask you, if you have done no services to the trade during the time that you have been on scale ?—Not one.

8294. Have you ever been asked to do anything at all for Mr. Broadhead during that time ?—No.

8295. Has Mr. Broadhead ever sent you to any master offering you as a man ready to work ?—No, he has never sent me to any master.

8296. You have already said that you did not get any gunpowder from Mr. Broadhead. In the following week after Helliwell was blown up did you not go to the "Clock" public house and meet Shaw there ?—I don't know that I ever met him at the "Clock."

8297. I call your attention to the time. In the middle of the week following the one in which Helliwell was blown up you did not meet him then at the "Clock ?"—No, I never was in the "Clock" with Shaw in my life.

8298. Did Shaw within about a fortnight or some short time after Helliwell was blown up ask you if you had got it ? and did you say you had got three quid ? —No, I will swear that; I never had three quid of my own in my life.

8299. You never had three sovereigns of your own in your life ?—No, not at once.

8300. Did you give Shaw 30*s.* ?—I never gave him a halfpenny.

8301. Never in your life ?—No.

8302. On a Thursday, somewhere about eight weeks ago, do you recollect being in a public house in Spring Street, called the "King William" ?—Yes.

8303. Did you there say that you had blown up Helliwell ?—No.

8304. That you and Shaw had done it ?—No.

8305. Did you there boast that you and Shaw had done anything to Helliwell ?—No, I never did nought to him in my life.

8306. But did you boast that you had done it ?—No, I have never once.

8307. Do you recollect a person of the name of Jonathan Crapper ?—Yes.

8308. Was he there ?—Yes.

8309. Was John Woodhead there ?—Yes.

8310. Was James Hallam there ?—Yes.

8311. Now I ask you whether upon that occasion you did not say that if he would give the word you would "lag" "Old Smit'em ?"—I did not. How could I lag him when I knew nought about him ?

8312. You have heard Mr. Broadhead called "Smit'em," have you not ?—Yes.

8313. Do you know what "lagging" a man is ?—Giving him time, sending him to prison I expect it is.

8314. Not transporting him ? — Yes, transporting him if you have a mind to call it so.

8315. Does it mean transporting or not ?—I don't know what it means ; I should think it does.

8316. And you never said that if he would give the word, you would "lag" "Old Smit'em" ?—No.

8317. Did Shaw tell you you had better mind your own business ?—No, he was glad to get out.

8318. What was he glad to get out for ?—Because he wanted to fight.

8319. Whom did he want to fight ?—He wanted to fight Crapper—he said he would bust his old guts or summat—and Thompson.

8320. He wanted to fight Thompson also ?—Yes—and then I wanted to fight him, nobody else would fight him.

8321. Then was it for the love of the thing, or for what was it that you wanted to fight him for ?—I do not know. We had got some beer into us.

8322. But what was it that you were to fight about ? —Because he was agate calling everybody in the place names.

8323. And what did he call them ?—He called them "muck-tubs" or summat ; I do not know what he meant by it.

8324. Did you have any quarrel with Woodhead ? —No.

8325. Was Woodhead there ?—He was there.

8326. Was there any quarrel between you and him ?—No.

8327. Do you know a public house they call Alvey's ?—Yes, I know a many public houses.

8328. Do you know Alvey's public house ?—Yes, in Harvest Lane.

8329. Do you recollect a week last Thursday being at that public house ?—I was not there then.

8330. Do you recollect being there when Yellott and Lee were there ?—Yellott was not there ; I was there on Wednesday afternoon, but I was not there on the Thursday.

8331. Were Yellott and Lee there ?—Yellott was not there, but Lee was.

8332. Have you ever been there when Yellott and Lee were both there ?—No.

8333. You have never been there when Yellott and Lee have been both there ?—I cannot say I have been there when they were both there. They were not there on Thursday afternoon ; Yellott was not.

8334. Did you ever say that it was too hot for Shaw ?—No, I never did.

8335. Did you ever say you had got 20 crowns from the Commissioners to give evidence against

NINTH DAY.

D. Clarke.

5 June 1867.

Broadhead and Shaw?—No, I never said such a thing.

8336. Either Wednesday or Thursday, or any other day, have you ever said in the presence of Yellott and Lee, or either of them, that you had got 20 crowns from the Commissioners to give evidence against Broadhead and Shaw?—I have not.

8337. You never said it?—No.

8338. At any time?—No.

8339. And in no place?—No.

8340. Do you know a person called Gillott?—Yes.

8341. Who is he?—He is a file grinder.

8342. Did you ever say that Gillott had stopped you in the Wicker and squared you?—No, I said Gillott had stopped me as I was going down to our house in a light cart. He said I should have the Commissioners to face. He said Wilson or somebody, he said, he was in at the same time as Wilson was.

8343. Who was in?—This Gillott; I think he said Chambers; the same time as Wilson came in.

8344. Who can understand such nonsense as that; what do you mean?—I mean that.

8345. Do you mean that Wilson was at Mr. Chambers'? what do you say Gillott said?—Gillott said Wilson came there while he was in there.

8346. To Mr. Chambers?—Yes.

8347. What about that?—He said he would tell him something about me and that I should have the Commissioners to face.

8348. What did you say to that?—I said, "What is it for?" He said he did not know.

8349. And you never told either Yellott or Lee that Gillott had squared you?—How do you mean squared me?

8350. Do you not know what squaring means?—I do not know.

8351. Made it all right with you—made it better for you not to tell?—Gillott never told me he had squared me—he had nought to square me for.

8352. Did you ever say that you had been squared?—No.

8353. Do you recollect the night when Linley was shot?—Yes.

8354. Where were you that night?—Working.

8355. Where?—For Fearnehough at Blonkwheel.

8356. Did you work all night?—No, up to when the wheel stopped.

8357. Up to what time did you work?—Seven o'clock I think.

8358. Do you know at what hour of the night Linley was shot?—No.

8359. He was shot in Scotland Street, was he not?—No, in the Wicker.

8360. Do you happen to know what time of the day it was, whether it was in the night or the day?—I do not know.

8361. You never heard?—I never heard what time it was.

8362. You never heard whether it was in the night or the day?—It was in the daytime I expect, because I went to see him when I had done at night.

8363. He was shot at twice I am told; the first time was in the Wicker and the second time in Scotland Street; do you know whether when he was shot at in Scotland Street it was in the night or in the day?—I heard talk of it, it was in the night-time I think.

8364. That is the night to which I am calling your attention—where were you on that night?—What night?

8365. That night when he was shot?—I should be at home I should expect.

8366. Were you at home?—I do not know where I was that night.

8367. Were you not out from your home during the greater part of that night?—Not that I am aware of.

8368. Will you swear that you were not?—I cannot swear where I was that night.

8369. Were you out, not at your home nor at your work, but out the greater part of that night?—I do not know where I was; I should ten to one go out for an hour or two.

8370. Were you in Scotland Street that night?—No.

8371. On your oath, were you not in Scotland Street that night?—Upon my oath I was not.

8372. You were never near it?—No.

8373. Never near Scotland Street?—No.

8374. Where were you?—I do not know; but I know that I was not there.

8375. How do you know that?—I do.

8376. If you do not know where you were, how do you know that you were not in Scotland Street?—I know that I was not in Scotland Street.

8377. Do you know where Scotland Street is?—I know where Scotland Street is.

8378. Were you never near Scotland Street that night?—That night I was not.

8379. You swear that?—Yes; I have some recollections of reading it on some placards.

8380. Will you swear that you were not in Scotland Street that night?—I know that I was not in Scotland Street.

8381. Mind, we have a police in this town. Will you swear you were not in Scotland Street that night?—I was not in Scotland Street.

8382. How near were you to Scotland Street that night?—I do not know.

8383. Will you swear that you were not close to Scotland Street that night; if you were not in the street, were you in an adjoining street?—I cannot swear. I generally go on to West Bar, and that road.

8384. Were you in West Bar that night?—Yes; I should go over that road, but I do not know where I should go to.

8385. Were you in West Bar that night?—Yes; I should be in West Bar.

8386. Scotland Street does not go into West Bar, does it?—It is not so far off.

8387. Were you never nearer to Scotland Street that night than West Bar?—I was never nearer than at West Bar.

8388. Now do not make a mistake. On that night when Linley was shot I ask you on your oath whether you never were nearer to Scotland Street than West Bar?—I never was any nearer than West Bar.

8389. Do you know a man called Ogden?—Yes.

8390. Do you ever work all night at your work?—Not very often.

8391. Do you ever do so?—We have done.

8392. Where did Ogden work?—He would be at the Tower, I expect. He was a file grinder, and he worked somewhere about.

8393. At the time when Linley was shot at in Scotland Street, where were you working?—I do not know; at the Tower; I should think I should be working at the Tower; I do not know whether I was not working for him.

8394. Where was Shaw working then?—He would be working at the Tower.

8395. Were you jobbing or had you a situation?—We had a situation when we were there.

8396. Who was there with you?—I do not know whether I was in one.

8397. Do not you know as a fact that you were working for Linley at that time?—I do not.

8398. Do not you believe it?—I cannot tell you where I worked.

8399. Do not you believe when Linley was shot that you were at that time working for him?—I do not.

8400. Do you believe that you were?—I think I was.

8401. Was Ogden working for him?—No; Ogden is a file grinder.

8402. Did you work in the same wheel?—He worked at the same place.

8403. In the same hull?—No.

8404. Did the police ever come to you after Linley was shot, about his being shot?—No.

8405. They never came to you?—No.

NINTH DAY.

D. Clarke.

15 June 1867.

8406. Are you sure of that?—Yes.
8407. You never were inquired about by the police?—Not that I know of; they never said naught to me.
8408. Were you ever charged with being implicated in that murder?—No.
8409. Never?—No.
8410. With no one?—No.
8411. Did you tell Ogden not to tell the police about your being absent from your work that night?—No.
8412. Are you sure about that?—Yes.
8413. Did you give Ogden 15*s.* to keep it secret?—No.
8414. Did you give him any money?—No.
8415. Did Shaw or both of you together give him money?—No.
8416. Did you see Shaw give him money?—No.
8417. Did Shaw tell you that he gave him money?—No.
8418. Did you give him money?—No.
8419. Did you see money paid to him by anybody?—Not for a job of that sort; we gave him 10*s*.
8420. Why did you give him 10*s*.?—We had been grinding saws for Brown of Bailey Lane, and Ogden came and helped us to wheel them out, and we gave him the money to keep because we had no pockets to put it in.
8421. You gave Ogden 10*s*. because you had no pockets to put it in?—Yes.
8422. When was that?—When we had been grinding saws for Brown of Bailey Lane, that is all the money he has seen of mine.
8423. When was it you gave him that?—When we had done them.
8424. When was it that you worked for Brown?—A good while since; since I have been loose.
8425. Was it about the time that Linley was shot?—I cannot say; it was I should think before then.
8426. Will you swear that it was before?—Yes.
8427. Will you swear that you did not pay him 10*s*. after Linley was shot?—I think Linley was not shot then.
8428. Will you swear that he was not?—I will not swear he was not shot; it is so long since.
8429. Will you swear that it was not after he was shot?—I cannot remember whether it was before or after.
8430. Now I ask you upon your oath, when you paid this 10*s*., was not it upon the express understanding that he was not to say you were absent on the night Linley was shot?—No.
8431. There was no bargain of that kind?—No; I did not care who knowed whether I worked or played either.
8432. Did you ask him not to say where you were on that night when Linley was shot?—No.
8433. Did you ever tell him that you were afraid of the police?—No.
8434. Did you ever tell him that you thought that the police would inquire for you?—No.
8435. Was anything said about the police by you?—No.
8436. Did you ever say to him anything about Linley's death?—No.
8437. Or of anyone being suspected?—No, I do not know that anyone was suspected but Brown.
8438. You never told him that you were afraid of being brought up and implicated in it?—No, I never told him anything of the sort.
8439. Was Brown tried for it?—Yes, I expect so.
8440. And was acquitted?—He would be acquitted.
8441. Do you know how long Yellott was on the box?—He has been on longer than me.
8442. He has been on four years, has he not?—I do not know.
8443. Has Lee been on the box a long time?—No, only a week or two.
8444. Did Yellott join when you did?—No.
8445. Did Yellott join at the same time you did?—No.
8446. How long has he been in the union?—He has been in some years, he is an oldish man.
8447. During the time that you have been a member of this union have you ever gone into a dark room?—No, not yet.
8448. You have never gone into the dark room at Broadhead's?—No.
8449. Never?—I do not know that there is a dark room.
8450. Have you ever gone into the room when the light was excluded from it, at Broadhead's?—No, never.
8451. Has a bag or box ever been brought round?—I never saw one.
8452. You never saw a bag produced containing balls?—No.
8453. Or a hat?—No.
8454. Did you ever go in with other people to put your hand into anything in order to get a ball?—No, never.
8455. Never?—No, never.
8456. Did you ever see it done?—No.
8457. Are you sure of that?—I am sure, I will swear it.
8458. Have you ever been asked to do so?—No, never.
8459. Has any member of your union ever told you that he had done it?—No, nobody ever told me naught about who has done it, because nobody knows except those who have done it.
8460. Except those who had done what?—What you are talking about.
8461. What am I talking about?—Drawing balls out.
8462. Have you ever heard of it before?—I heard you mention it.
8463. Have you never heard of it except from me?—No, never.
8464. You have never on any occasion gone and drawn out a ball?—I have never drawn naught out.
8465. You have not?—No.
8466. Nor seen it done?—No, nor seen it done.
8467. And have you never heard of its being done?—No.
8468. Not on any ground, for any purpose?—No.
8469. Neither for a good nor a bad one?—No.
8470. It is never done at your union?—Not that I know of; I have never seen it done.
8471. And you have never heard of it being done for any purpose by any person, either by Broadhead, or his daughter, or a member of the club, or anybody?—I never heard of it being done afore you just mentioned it.
8472. Have you ever said in the presence of Hallam, that you had got the order to do Damms, and that you would do him. I mean at the "Blue Pig?"—I have not.
8473. Did you ever say in the presence of James Hallam that you had got the order to do Damms; and that you would do him?—No; I never told Hallam so.
8474. Do you know a person called Damms?—Yes.
8475. What is he?—A saw grinder.
8476. Was he an outlaw?—No.
8477. Did he pay to the club?—Yes.
8478. There was no complaint of him that you know of?—I never heard of any.
8479. Did you ever hear any complaint by the union of Damms?—No.
8480. Not from Mr. Broadhead nor anybody?—Mr. Broadhead never told me naught about it.
8481. And you never at the "Blue Pig" said in the presence of Hallam that you had got orders to do Damms, and that you would do him or do for him?—I never did say such a thing to Hallam.

The witness withdrew.

NINTH DAY.

Mrs. A. Clarke.

15 June 1867.

Mrs. Ann Clarke sworn and examined.

8482. (*Mr. Barstow.*) Are you the wife of John Clarke?—Yes.

8483. He was convicted of cutting bellows?—Yes.

8484. That was last year?—Yes.

8485. For how long was he sentenced?—Nine months.

8486. When he was away how were you supported? —By the secretary of the trade, Mr. Thompson.

8487. How were you supported?—He used to bring me 6*s*. a week.

8488. To your own house?—Yes.

8489. Did you make any application to him for this?—My husband sent for me when he was in prison.

8490. Whom did he send?—His brother-in-law saw them bring him up, and he said he wanted to see me. I went to Mr. Jackson, and I asked to see him, and I got to see him.

8491. Where was he in prison?—At the Town Hall in Sheffield; he told me to go to Mr. Thompson, and ask him if he would do anything for me while he was away, and he would still be a man.

8492. Did he say anything else to you at the time? —No; I went to Mr. Thompson.

8493. You had known Mr. Thompson before?—I had never talked to him before; I had seen him by his coming to see our master for his natty money.

8494. Your husband's natty money?—Yes.

8495. Then you went to Thompson?—Yes.

8496. Where did you go?—To the "Star" at the bottom of Cooper Street.

8497. What did you say to him?—I told him what my husband had repeated to me.

8498. What did he say to you?—I told him it was a very bad job, and I thought of going to his master and seeing if he would let me replace the things that he had destroyed, and he would not hear of it.

8499. Whom do you mean when you say "he" would not hear of it?—It was Mr. Thompson; he said, "You must not do anything of the kind."

8500. What did he say next?—He said, however, that he would see my husband righted; he would do whatever he could, but I was not to go near Mr. Darwin.

8501. What did he propose to do?—He went to Mr. Chambers with me—he paid Mr. Chambers I believe two guineas as far as I can remember.

8502. What did Thompson do for you during your husband's absence?—He brought me 6*s*. a week.

8503. When did he first promise to allow you that?—As soon as my husband was gone.

8504. Did he promise that to you at the interview which you had with him at the "Star"?—No, when I went to the "Star" inn with him, my husband had only been taken on the Thursday.

8505. You mean as soon as your husband had gone to Wakefield?—He was not gone away when I went to the "Star."

8506. (*Chairman.*) They sent him to Wakefield first did not they?—No, he was here a week in the Town Hall.

8507. Then he went to the assizes at once?—Yes.

8508. (*Mr. Barstow.*) When did Thompson promise you the 6*s*. a week?—He did not promise me till after my husband's trial. He said he would be a man to him and see him righted—he did not say what he would give me or anything of that kind.

8509. Do you remember the first time that he brought you this money?—I do not rightly remember the day he brought it to me.

8510. Did he bring it to your house?—Yes, I always had it. If he missed one week he paid me double the week after.

8511. What did he tell you that the money was for?—He said that it was to help to support me while my husband was away.

8512. Did he tell you where it came from?—No.

8513. Did you hear from any one where it came from?—No, only when he asked me to sign this paper, I said, "Well it was strange if the trade did "not know about this crime, and that if my husband "was suffering, that they should want me to sign my "hand to a paper." He said the trade knew nothing about it, he was allowing it to me himself.

8514. What was this paper?—I am not a scholar, but he read it to me. It was to say that I was not receiving any maintenance from the trade.

8515. When did he bring you that paper?—My husband had about three months to stop then; he might have 13 weeks to stay then.

8516. How long ago was that?—My husband has been out six weeks last Thursday.

8517. At that time he had about 13 weeks to stop?—Yes.

8518. That would be about 19 weeks ago?—Yes.

8519. Was that the first time that he had said anything to you about its not being from the trade?— When my husband was first sent, Thompson said that he would allow me this money. I said I wished to see the committee myself, and Thompson said he would see the committee.

8520. Did he say anything more?—Yes, he said they was a disagreeable lot of men, and he would call a meeting to gather me something; the trade seemed so disagreeable.

8521. Did you say anything upon that?—No, I could not say anything upon that. I knew nothing except what I heard him say.

8522. You assented to that?—I said I should not like a meeting called.

8523. Did he say anything upon that?—No, he did not say anything more.

8524. Then the conversation ended?—Yes.

8525. How soon after that did he bring you any money?—He had brought me money during this time.

8526. How was it that you wanted to see the committee, if you got that allowance?—Because he said they were going on so; he contradicted himself so.

8527. He kept telling you such contradictory stories?—Yes.

8528. What stories for instance did he tell you?— He kept saying that he had seen the committee, and then he said the trade had nothing to do with it, and I did not know which way he concluded to when he kept contradicting himself.

8529. That made you wish to see the committee yourself?—Yes, because he kept telling me one tale and then another.

8530. You wanted to ascertain from them whether it was the real truth or what they would do for you?— I wanted to know in what way they meant doing something for me. I wished to see them myself when he kept telling me such tales.

8531. What did you wish to see them for?—When he kept coming and saying that those parties had heard such a thing and such a thing.

8532. Did you want to see what they would do for you?—I thought they had a right to do something for me as long as my husband was suffering. We were both suffering too.

8533. (*Chairman.*) You wanted to see what the trade would do for you?—Yes.

8534. (*Mr. Barstow.*) What did he say to prevent your going?—He said he had seen the committee himself.

8535. Had you before this known anything of the trade?—No.

8536. Had your husband ever been receiving scale? —Yes; he did about two years since for about five weeks, and during the time he has been home he has received the scale.

8537. Do you know anything about how the scale is paid?—I know they go to the "Star" inn for their scale.

8538. Do you know about what sums were paid to particular classes of people?—Yes; we had 11*s*., 3*s*. for me and 8*s*. for him; that is what I got.

8539. How did Thompson come to bring you this

NINTH DAY.

Mrs. A. Clarke.

15 June 1867.

note to sign?—I do not know I am sure. For about a week I would not sign the note.

8540. How did he happen to come to you at first with it?—He came to our house in my husband's trouble to see me.

8541. You say that it was about 19 weeks ago that he brought the note?—Yes, but he had been before.

8542. But when he brought the note what did he say to you?—He said there had been a deal of bother amongst the trade, and that it had caused a great deal of bother amongst the trade, and if I would sign the note, saying that I did not receive anything, it would make it a deal pleasanter for him.

8543. Did you know at that time from whom the 6*s.* came?—No.

8544. You do not know whether it came from the trade or not?—It was his paying me the 6*s.* which made me sign the paper.

8545. Before he said anything about signing the paper you did not know whether the 6*s.* came from the trade or not?—No, I did not.

8546. You had nothing but Thompson's word for it?—No.

8547. You knew nothing of your own knowledge?—No.

8548. Until he showed you the note which you signed you had no idea that he was paying it?—Yes, I had an idea, because I was receiving it.

8549. You did not know that he was paying it for himself?—I did not know but what the trade was paying it.

8550. Did you think that the trade was paying it?—I did up to that time while he contradicted himself so.

8551. Why did you object to sign it?—I wanted to see a friend and to see what he wanted me to sign this note for.

8552. You wanted to see a friend?—Yes, before I signed the note.

8553. What was the objection in your own mind to signing the note at once?—I do not know. I thought it was very strange to bring a note for me to sign like that.

8554. I suppose it did not matter to your friend where you got the money so long as you got it?—I thought so long as my husband was suffering all this, Thompson had a right to keep and support me. I was suffering—it was not 6*s.* a week that was keeping me—I was a great deal better off and my husband too before the trade was together.

8555. The trade has been no good to you?—It has not been much good by getting me in trouble like that.

8556. Do you mean to say that you had more money for yourself before you joined the trade?—I mean to say we were a great deal more comfortable.

8557. Had you more money to spend before then?—I wished to live comfortable.

8558. What do you mean by "living more comfortable?"—I mean this, that my husband had more hours to work for the money, but he was a deal different and more comfortable.

8559. If he had more hours to work he earned more money?—I do not know that; he did not tell me what he earned; he did not give it to me; he would not let me reckon for him.

8560. Do you know what made your husband join the union?—No, I do not.

8561. Do you know who asked him to join?—No.

8562. The first time that Thompson asked you about signing the note you did not sign it?—No.

8563. Did you see this friend?—Yes.

8564. Who was your friend?—My friend was a neighbour; he had nothing to do with their trade.

8565. Did you show the note to your neighbour?—No, because Thompson did not leave it with me; I stated it to him——

8566. Did you tell your neighbour what the contents of the note were?—Yes.

8567. What did the neighbour say?—He said he should have nothing to do with the trade at all; of course I could not help my husband having had to do with it.

8568. Did your neighbour give you any advice?—He gave me the advice not to have anything to do with it.

8569. Then you did not sign this note in consequence of anything your neighbour said?—No.

8570. What made you sign it?—Thompson promised me that my husband should have plenty of work when he came out. I said my husband had lost a very good place by doing it.

8571. He had lost a very good place by doing it?—Yes, he had.

8572. Has he been at work since?—No.

8573. Do you know what his wages were then?—No.

8574. (*Chairman.*) After you had signed this paper, did you give it to him?—Yes.

8575. And he has got it now?—Yes.

8576. Can you tell us at all what was in it; as far as you recollect what was in the note?—"This is to "certify that the wife of John Clarke, Ann Clarke, "does not receive any maintenance from the trades "union."

8577. Had you heard any reports in the town that you were receiving relief from the union?—Yes, it was reported.

8578. Where had you heard it talked of?—In many places.

8579. Did not they say that it was a great shame that the union should support you while your husband was in prison, and that the union should support him there?—I never heard it.

8580. What was the talk about it?—People asked me if they allowed me anything; I did not tell everyone my business.

8581. Was it in consequence of what you said that this report got about that the trade was supporting you?—No.

8582. It was not in consequence of what you said?—No.

8583. How did the report get abroad?—I do not know how reports do get about.

8584. Reports did get about that the trade was supporting you?—Yes.

8585. Did Thompson say that the union men were very angry about it?—Yes, he said the union men were.

8586. And that it would make it easier for him, if they had the note to say that you were getting nothing from the trade?—That it would make it a great deal better for him if I signed the note to say that I was not receiving anything from the trade; he did not say from himself.

8587. It would make it a great deal better for him?—Yes.

8588. That was the reason you signed it, was it?—Yes. I did not receive it from the trade, I received it from Thompson himself, or else I should not have signed it.

8589. Therefore, you signed the paper because he asked you to do it, in order to make it right for him?—Yes. I knew I was receiving it from him; I did not receive it from anyone else.

8590. (*Mr. Chance.*) It was pretty well known in the town that you were receiving support from some one?—That report got up and down, but not from me. It was not 6*s.* a week that kept the old man.

8591. Were you ever asked by anybody from whom you were receiving support?—No, not in particular.

8592. Not particularly, but were you ever asked at all?—Perhaps my neighbours might mention it, but I do not make my neighbours as wise as myself. I keep my business to myself; I do not let my neighbours know my business.

8593. Still it was talked of at the time?—There were several reports in the neighbourhood; I did not take notice of what was talked of in the neighbourhood.

8594. But they would ask you about this matter?—Yes, but it was not my place to answer them, and I pleased myself whether I answered them or not; I

NINTH DAY.

Mrs. A. Clarke.

15 June 1867.

have spoken the truth and nothing else, and I did not interfere with my neighbours, or them with me.

8595. (*Mr. Barstow.*) I have these questions put into my hands to ask you: did you ever see any member of the trade except Thompson?—Not one. I have seen them, but not to talk to them.

8596. You are aware that your husband was examined yesterday?—Yes.

8597. Were you in court when he was examined?—No, I was at home.

8598. Have you read your husband's evidence?—No.

8599. Have you had it read to you?—No.

8600. Did he tell you what he said?—He might tell me a few words. Of course he did not tell me all. I have nothing to do with my husband's evidence. He was not here when I had to do with Thompson. I am speaking the truth for myself. I cannot answer what my husband and Thompson may have had to do, but I am answering for myself now.

8601. Since your husband gave his evidence yesterday here, have you had any conversation with him about the evidence?—No.

8602. Not about what he said?—No. I have had bother enough over it.

8603. Do you know that your husband stated yesterday that the trade had nothing to do with the matter for which your husband was convicted?—I do not know. I know no one but Thompson in the trade. Nobody came to me except him.

8604. Do you know that your husband stated yesterday that the trade had nothing to do with the matter for which he was convicted?—I cannot answer for that. I am answering as far as I know what I have had to do with Thompson.

8605. (*Chairman.*) Was Thompson at your house last night?—No; he came to our house the morning that he had to appear here, to see if my husband had a summons to appear the same day as he had. I have never seen him since.

8606. You have not seen your husband in company with Thompson yesterday?—No.

8607. Your husband and Thompson talked about these matters, did they?—Not that I am aware of.

8608. He saw your husband when he came to him?—The morning he was to appear here with a summons—not the morning that my husband was, but the morning that Thompson was summoned—he called and asked if he had received a summons, and he said "No;" that was all he said.

8609. (*Mr. Barstow.*) Are you aware that your husband received a considerable increase in his wages by reason of the union being established?—No, it did not make any difference to me.

8610. That is not quite an answer to the question. Are you aware whether your husband received a considerable increase?—He never told me his earnings.

8611. You do not know whether he did or not?—No, he never told me his earnings.

8612. Do you know at what time the union was established?—No.

8613. (*Chairman.*) How many years ago is it, do you think?—I am sure I do not recollect.

8614. Five or six years ago?—I do not know. I never took any notice.

8615. Do not you know how long it is since your husband joined?—I do not know when he joined. I was not with him. I was at home.

The witness withdrew.

T. Gillott.

THOMAS GILLOTT sworn and examined.

8616. (*Mr. Chance.*) What are you?—I am a scissor forger.

8617. Are you president of the Scissor Forgers Union?—Yes.

8618. How long have you been president of the union?—About five months.

8619. And how long have you been a member of the union?—About two and a half years.

8620. Do you remember Clarke being convicted for taking the tools and destroying the bellows belonging to Mr. Darwin?—Yes.

8621. At that time who was the secretary to your union?—Mr. Thompson.

8622. Have you got the books of the union here?—No, I have not.

8623. Could you let us have them?—I have not any books. Mr. Thompson had all the books, I believe. Our new secretary has the books now. Mr. Earnshaw has the books.

8624. What is Earnshaw's christian name?—John, I believe.

8625. Have you been attending here every day during the course of the examination?—No.

8626. How many times have you been here before?—Once.

8627. When was that?—Yesterday.

8628. Did you know yesterday that Clarke was to be examined?—Yes, I had heard he was to be examined here.

8629. Was that the reason why you came here?—No, I came here expecting to be examined the first witness yesterday morning. I met with Mr. Barker and made a statement to him, and he said that I must be here in the morning.

8630. Have you been summoned?—No.

8631. You came expecting to be examined?—Yes.

8632. Did not you bring your books in order that you might give information in your examination?—No; the evidence that I wished to give was nothing in respect of the books; it was with respect to the resolution which was reported to be passed at the general meeting of our trade last week.

8633. Was not that resolution entered on the books—No I believe not.

8634. Taking you back to the case of Clarke's conviction what were the circumstances of that case so far as you remember them?—As far as I remember I heard the report the following morning that Mr. Darwin had been rattened.

8635. You say that after Darwin had been rattened you heard the report?—Yes, and that Clarke had been arrested for it.

8636. After you heard the report of his being rattened what did you do? did you take any notice of it?—I did not take any notice except as far as this; we talked one among another in the places that we work at.

8637. Were you president of the union at that time?—No.

8638. How long before you became president did this happen?—Perhaps it would be six months.

8639. You say that you talked about it amongst yourselves?—Yes.

8640. Was any reason given that you remember why Darwin was rattened?—No.

8641. Do you mean to say that you never heard any reason given why Darwin was rattened?—None.

8642. Did not you inquire as to why it was?—No, I did not.

8643. Had you no belief as to what was the cause of his being rattened?—None.

8644. Do you mean to tell me that you did not make an inquiry as to the cause of his being rattened?—No.

8645. Was Clarke a member of the union at that time?—Yes, I believe he was.

8646. Had you any conversation with Thompson about it?—No, I never attended any of the meetings at that time.

8647. Not any of the union meetings?—No.

8648. You have been a member of the union about two years?—Yes.

8649. Do you mean to say that you did not attend any meetings during the whole of the two years?—No, except the quarterly meetings.

8650. After Clarke was convicted had you no conversation with Thompson about Clarke's conviction? —Not that I can remember.

8651. Surely you can remember whether you had a conversation with him or not as to that conviction?—I do not think that I mentioned the subject at all to Thompson.

8652. Did he mention the subject to you?—Not that I am aware of; I do not remember having any conversation with Thompson with respect to it at all.

8653. Surely if you were to have any conversation you could hardly forget it?—I should think I hardly could, but if I had any conversation it would be in a casual way, and supposing he came to my shop for contribution, which he always did, I might say I understood Clarke has done this or that, but I do not remember that I said anything to him.

8654. He came to you for the contribution?—Yes, and I might mention the circumstance of Clarke being arrested when he came there.

8655. Did not you mention it to him? cannot you remember that you mentioned it to him?—No, I cannot say positively whether I did or not.

8656. Take your recollection back; it is no great distance of time since the event occurred?—I cannot say positively that I mentioned it to Thompson.

8657. Did he mention it to you?—No, on the same grounds that I cannot say there was any conversation between us on the subject.

8658. It was well known that it was a trade affair?—I do not know that it was well known, it was well known it had been done.

8659. Had you any doubt in your own mind that it had been a trade affair?—I made the best of inquiries, and I could not get any information.

8660. Then you did make inquiries?—Yes.

8661. What inquiries did you make?—In reference to Mrs. Clarke receiving her weekly allowance.

8662. Then you were aware that Mrs. Clarke was in receipt of a weekly allowance?—I had heard a report.

8663. How long after Clarke had been convicted was it that you heard the report that Mrs. Clarke was in receipt of that weekly allowance?—It would be about December when I heard the report.

8664. When was Clarke sentenced?—I do not remember.

8665. It was in December 1866, that you heard the report?—Yes.

8666. It was just after he had been convicted?—I heard of it in December.

8667. You heard of this by report you say?—Yes.

8668. (*Chairman.*) How long was he in prison; four or nine months?—Nine months.

8669. You say that you heard it in December?—Yes.

8670. It was during the time that she was receiving the allowance?—So I believe.

8671. You say that you heard it reported?—Yes.

8672. (*Mr. Chance.*) Was the report to the effect that she was receiving a weekly allowance?—I heard of it only from one party, and I believe they had got the information in a direct manner, so I made it my business to inquire.

8673. Who was the party from whom you heard it?—The manager of our place.

8674. Did you hear the amount that she was receiving?—No.

8675. Upon hearing the report that she was receiving this allowance, what did you do?—I made up my mind to get to know for a positive fact what I possibly could, and I used my best endeavours to do so, and one of the endeavours was to be elected president, so that I should have power to get to know.

8676. But could not you get to know without becoming president?—I thought it would be the best way of getting to know. I inquired and nobody seemed to know anything about it.

8677. Whom did you inquire from?—From several parties, I cannot say distinctly whom.

8678. Did you inquire from several members of the union?—Yes.

8679. Did you inquire from the officers of the union?—No, I believe I did not mention it to any officer.

8680. Did not it strike you as a very strange thing that she should be receiving this allowance?—It did.

8681. Whom did you suppose she was receiving the allowance from?—I did not know whether she was receiving it or not, and I wished to ascertain the truth.

8682. Did you ever see Mrs. Clarke about it?—No.

8683. I believe you asked her about it?—No, I never knew her.

8684. Till you became president you attended no meetings except the quarterly meetings?—No, except the quarterly meetings. I believe I was once president three months, previous to that about two years ago.

8685. When you were so president, did any rattenings of this kind ever take place?—Not that I know of.

8686. Surely you must know if they did take place?—I cannot remember any such circumstances taking place during the time that I was president.

8687. Do you know of any taking place during the time that you were a member and not president?—Yes, I know there has been such things transpire during the time I have been a member.

8688. Have those been done at the instance of the union?—I do not know.

8689. You do not know whether they have?—I do not know.

8690. Do not you believe that they have been done at the instance of the trade?—I do not; it is my belief that the trade has nothing to do with it.

8691. At whose instigation would they have been done?—I am sure I do not know.

8692. Do you mean to say, with the experience which you have, that the rattenings which have taken place have been done for any other than trade purposes?—I cannot say the purposes that they have been done for; it is my belief that the trade has had nothing to do with them.

8693. Are you speaking of your own particular trade or the unions generally?—I speak of the scissor forgers trade at present.

8694. Are you well up in the course generally adopted in order to obtain the contributions of the members?—I am up to the course we adopt to obtain contributions.

8695. Supposing a man is in arrear, what course do you adopt for the purpose of getting his contribution? —We go to him and ask him if he will not pay.

8696. Then supposing that he will not pay?—We let him do as he thinks proper, that is as far as my knowledge of the business goes.

8697. Is that the only course that you adopt in the event of a man not paying his arrears?—It is the only course as far as I have had any experience in it. I believe there have been other courses adopted such as taking out the grinders and stopping them till those men have paid.

8698. Is it not a well recognised course of proceeding when a man does not pay his contributions to take out the grinders?—It has been in our trade; that was done on two occasions I believe.

8699. Has that been done because the men would not pay their contributions?—Yes.

8700. When a man does not pay his contributions do not you then wait upon the master?—I believe that our secretary has waited upon the master.

8701. Is it not the practice which is generally adopted?—Yes, generally speaking it is the practice adopted to wait upon the masters after they have waited upon the men and see whether the masters will not persuade the men to pay.

8702. Supposing that to fail, what is the course

NINTH DAY.

T. Gillott.

15 June 1867.

which is adopted then ?—The next course is I believe to take out the grinders.

8703. You say that in your experience you do not know that that has been done, but that is the system generally adopted ?—That is what has been done.

8704. You do not know that the grinders have been taken out, from your experience as president ?—Yes, it has been done in my experience.

8705. Now as to the resolution to which you referred, there was a resolution brought before your meeting in reference to the evidence given by Thompson here ?—A resolution was brought before the meeting in reference to his having embezzled the monies.

8706. When was that ?—Last Thursday week.

8707. Was that a meeting especially called or was it the ordinary committee meeting ?—It was a special general meeting of the whole trade which was called.

8708. And called for what purpose ?—For the purpose of calling upon Joseph Thompson to deliver up his books and the possession of all the property that he had belonging to us.

8709. At whose instance was that meeting called ?—At the committee's.

8710. There was some person deputed by the committee to call the meeting ?—I took it upon myself after hearing what had been said here to call the committee together.

8711. Do I understand that it was you who called the meeting ?—No, we called a committee meeting on the Wednesday evening, and we sent for Joseph Thompson from his house to come and tell us what he had to say, and it was agreed amongst us that we should call a general meeting for the night following.

8712. For the purpose of taking into consideration that case ?—Yes.

8713. Was Thompson present at this previous committee meeting ?—After we sent for him he came.

8714. Was this committee meeting called at the suggestion of Thompson ?—No, it was my own suggestion.

8715. Had he made any representation or suggestion of any kind to you previously ?—No.

8716. Was it entirely at your own suggestion that the meeting was called ?—Yes, the committee meeting.

8717. And at the committee meeting it was resolved to call a special meeting ?—Yes.

8718. When was the special meeting held ?—On the night following, Thursday week.

8719. What took place at the special meeting ?—When the meeting was opened we called upon Mr. Thompson to explain his conduct. Of course there were many remarks made at the meeting.

8720. How many people were present at this special meeting ?—Above 100—rather over 100.

8721. You called upon Thompson to explain his conduct ?—Yes.

8722. Did Thompson get up and explain his conduct ?—Yes.

8723. What was the substance of what he told you ?—He wished to show to the meeting, that the monies that he had taken (which was the principal object of the meeting), he had not embezzled, as he had not applied them to his own use.

8724. He wanted to show that the monies were not embezzled because they had not been applied to his own use ?—Yes; he did not approve of the term "embezzlement" as far as I could understand him. They heard what he had to say and then there was an uproar amongst them, and they made various remarks about his conduct, and talked about hanging him and throwing him out of the window, and such remarks as those.

8725. (*Chairman.*) They do not hang people and throw them out of the window in your trade, do they ?—They considered that he deserved it.

8726. (*Mr. Chance.*) There was a great deal of uproar, and they made various remarks upon him ?—Yes.

8727. What was the upshot of it ?—I do not know what the upshot was. We quieted them in course of time and proceeded to elect a new secretary.

8728. Before electing the new secretary, was anything said to Thompson about resigning his secretaryship ?—It was proposed that another person should be elected for the post of secretary.

8729. Thompson was the secretary then ?—Yes.

8730. Was there any proposition that he should resign ?—Yes; he tendered his resignation in the course of making his speech. There was a proposition that it should be accepted in a formal way. He said that after what had been said and done he could not think of having any more connexion with the business of the union, and he would tender his resignation. Of course it was accepted, and a new man elected in his place.

8731. Who was elected in his place ?—Mr. John Earnshaw.

8732. Was there any resolution passed in reference to Thompson's conduct ?—No; I believe not.

8733. Was there any resolution passed at the meeting ?—There was only the resolution that I have been speaking of; there was no resolution passed about his conduct. They seemed to be satisfied with talking among themselves about it.

8734. Just call it to mind. You say that there was no resolution passed except in reference to his secretaryship ?—There was a resolution passed that his resignation should be accepted.

8735. Was there not a resolution passed that the monies were not embezzled ?—Yes, that is the resolution that I wish to speak of. The meeting was called for 8 o'clock, and this uproar and the business and different things that transpired, took to near upon 11 o'clock, and then Mr. Thompson, when we were going to break up, put a paper into my hand and asked me whether I would read it to the meeting.

8736. Was this before the meeting had broken up ?—Yes, it was before the meeting had broken up. I read it to the meeting. There was a discussion on the resolution and then many went away.

8737. What was the resolution. Was it to the effect that the money had not been embezzled, but was taken to be applied to the purposes of the trade ?—I cannot think of the exact words, but something to that effect.

8738. (*Chairman.*) It appeared in the newspaper the next day ?—Yes.

8739. (*Mr. Chance.*) Was the resolution as it appeared in the newspaper, the resolution put to the meeting and carried ?—It was word for word the resolution that Mr. Thompson wrote; but when the resolution passed there was a discussion, and on that many went away. They said they would not stop any more at such proceedings as that. At the time the resolution was put to the meeting the meeting was in a fearful state of excitement, owing to the interruptions of a certain person in the room that would not let anyone talk but himself.

8740. Who was it ?—Charles Thomas; I had repeatedly to call him to order, to allow anybody to get a word in. The meeting was in a fearful state of excitement when that resolution was carried, and a great many of them went away. Everybody had got upon their feet and were standing round the door ready to go, and they kept saying "Put it! Put it!" There was 20 or 25 people in the room.

8741. Was the resolution put ?—Yes.

8742. How many people were remaining in the meeting when the resolution was put ?—Twenty-five as near as I can guess.

8743. Were you one of them ?—Yes.

8744. What number of those 25 voted in favour of the resolution ?—About 18 I should think.

8745. Then it was not carried unanimously ?—No, it was not carried unanimously by three-fourths of the trade as was stated in the newspaper.

8746. Do you know who sent the advertisement to the paper ?—Yes.

8747. Who sent it ?—Mr. Thompson. The reporter was downstairs waiting I believe until he had done.

8748. As we understand, Thompson wrote the resolution and proposed it at the meeting?—He gave it to me to propose to the meeting.

8749. And he sent the advertisement himself to the paper?—Yes; that is a strict account.

8750. Did you vote in favour of the resolution?—No.

8751. Did you vote against it?—No, I did not vote at all.

8752. You were president upon that occasion?—Yes.

8753. When the resolution was put were any hands held up against it?—No; as soon as the hands were put up for it they all rushed down the stairs.

8754. Then the contrary proposition was never put?—There was no time to put any proposition.

8755. Then it was not put?—No, there was not any.

8756. Then was it put to the meeting at all as to who were in favour of it and who were against it?—It was put to the meeting who were in favour. They were all standing round the doorway ready to go away, and they kept calling out "Put it! Put it!" and I said, "All that are in favour of it hold up their hands." Those that were in favour held up their hands and at that instant walked away; there was no time to ask who were against it; it was a quarter past 11 in the evening.

8757. You said just now that you called a meeting?—I called a committee meeting.

8758. And that committee decided upon calling a special meeting?—Yes.

8759. Then it is not true, as Thompson said, that he called a meeting?—Mr. Thompson was there at the time and wrote the advertisement to go to the newspaper to call the meeting.

8760. Was it he who suggested that a special meeting should be called?—I do not know that it was; I believe it was the unanimous decision amongst us all to call a meeting.

8761. Did he suggest calling a meeting for the purpose of tendering his resignation?—I believe he had said that he thought of calling a meeting.

8762. Did he say for what purpose the meeting was to be called?—No.

8763. At the committee meeting which was called did he then say anything about tendering his resignation?—No, he did not say anything about tendering his resignation. We had taken certain steps and he felt annoyed at it, and he said he thought of calling a general meeting.

8764. Then he tendered his resignation and it was accepted and Mr. Earnshaw was appointed in his place?—Yes.

8765. (*Chairman.*) You say that Mr. Thompson made a speech and proposed to resign?—Yes.

8766. When he proposed to resign was not he pressed very much to continue?—He was not pressed very much.

8767. Was he pressed at all?—Well, I believe he was not pressed.

8768. Did they ask him to stay?—There were some parties in the room that asked him, if he was proposed again, if he would stand.

8769. Was there any objection raised to that?—Yes.

8770. Who objected?—I cannot say the person's name.

8771. Was there more than one who objected?—Oh yes.

8772. Who besides you?—I do not know any names.

8773. You know your own members and you were the president, can you tell me the names of the persons objecting to his continuing any more? you say he was asked to continue?—I cannot tell any names for this reason, there was a general clamour raised in the meeting.

8774. You cannot tell me the names of any members who objected?—No.

8775. I asked you if there was any person who objected, did they stand up in their places and say "I object to that"?—No, they sat down and made complaints about it.

8776. Do you stand up when you speak at your meetings?—Yes.

8777. Was there any man who got up in his place and said "I object to that"?—No, I do not know that there was.

8778. How did the reporter happen to be present on that night?—I do not know.

8779. You know that he was there and that Thompson took him this resolution?—I knew when Thompson told me.

8780. You were aware that it was a question for your consideration, and a very important question, whether Mrs. Clarke had been kept by the union while her husband was in prison?—Yes, I knew it was a very important question for us.

8781. You knew it?—Yes.

8782. If his wife was kept at the expense of the trade ought the money that was paid to her to have appeared in your books?—I understand that the monies that are paid ought to appear in the books.

8783. You have books then?—Yes.

8784. Do not you think it would have been well if you were coming here as the president of that union to have brought your books with you?

(*Mr. Sugg.*) He is examined on the spur of the moment.

(*Chairman.*) He is not examined on the spur of the moment.

(*Mr. Barker.*) This gentleman was at my office the day before yesterday, and he was called in court to-day at his own request.

8785. (*Chairman to the witness.*) Two days ago you told the secretary that you wished to give evidence to clear the society?—I wished to give evidence to contradict the report of the resolution.

8786. If you are the president of this society your character is as much at stake as anybody's—do not you think that it would have been well to have brought your books to-day when you came to give your evidence in order to show what the books contained?—It did not occur to me to bring the books.

8787. Will you be good enough to produce the books on Monday morning?—Yes, I think I can venture to say that I will make it my business to see Mr. Earnshaw.

The Chairman inquired of Mr. Sugg, whether there would be any objection on the part of the trades unions, to produce their books to Mr. Chambers, in order to enable him to bring before the Commissioners any cases which he might deem worthy of their notice.

Mr. Sugg stated that there would be no objection to this course being pursued provided some one on behalf of the trades unions were present during the examination of the books.

8788. (*Mr. Barstow to the witness.*) You think it a very serious crime that this money was paid to Mrs. Clarke?—Yes, I do.

8789. And in conseqneuce of that and with the view of learning more about it you became president of the union?—Yes.

8790. Have you looked over the books of the union to see whether any money was paid to Mrs. Clarke?—No, not particularly more than casting my eye over them in doing our business.

8791. You have not made any particular search into the books of the union?—Yes.

8792. Have you asked Mrs. Clarke herself?—No.

8793. Have you ever asked the secretary himself?—Yes.

8794. When did you first ask him?—I believe it was the first night that I was in office.

8795. How long ago is that?—Five months ago.

8796. What did he tell you?—I told him I had heard a report that she was receiving a sum of money and I wished to know whether it was true or not.

NINTH DAY.

T. Gillott.

15 June 1867.

He said if we would leave it to him he would satisfy us in the course of a week.

8797. Do you know any reason why he should not have satisfied you then?—No.

8798. He had the books I suppose?—He had some of them I believe. I do not know whether he had all of them or not.

8799. Did he give you any reason for wishing the matter to stand over for a week?—It was suggested that a paper should be drawn up.

8800. Who suggested that a paper should be drawn up?—I cannot bring to mind who suggested it.

8801. Can you recollect whether it was Thompson?—No, I believe it was some of the committee.

8802. Who was it?—I cannot recollect who it was.

8803. We wish very much to know?—I cannot remember the person who suggested it.

8804. Who were the members on the committee?—I cannot recollect who were the members.

8805. Was it Earnshaw?—No, Mr. Thompson's book will show who were the members.

8806. Cannot you really tell us who it was?—No, I cannot tell who it was that suggested it.

8807. Are you prepared to swear that it was not Thompson himsalf?—I am prepared to swear it was not Thompson.

8808. You swear that it was not Thompson who suggested that the paper should be drawn up?—No, because he fell in with it, and he said he would satisfy us the next week or the week after, but I cannot remember everything.

8809. When did you see that paper?—I saw it the Monday after Mrs. Clarke had signed it.

8810. We have heard all about it from Mrs. Clarke?—I did not see it before she had signed it.

8811. You say that Thompson wrote out a resolution?—Yes.

8812. When was that?—I do not know when he wrote out the resolution; he brought it with him when he came.

8813. He brought the resolution, and he brought the reporter?—I do not know whether he brought the reporter or not, the reporter was there.

8814. Is it usual to have a reporter in the room when your meetings are held?—I never saw one before.

8815. Is it usual to have the resolutions passed at the trades meetings published in the newspaper the next day?—No.

8816. Have you ever seen it before?—No, I have never seen one.

8817. If Thompson says that that resolution was passed unanimously, I understand that that is false?—It was passed unanimously with the parties that was left; but not by three-fourths of the trade as is stated in the paper.

8818. What is the whole number of your trade?—I think about 160 or something of that sort; I cannot say to a few.

8819. How many were present when it was put?—25, or something of that sort, as near as I can guess.

8820. When he read it the first time 25 were present?—When he read it the first time there were considerably more.

8821. How many voted for it?—About 18 as near as I can guess; I will not say more.

8822. Is that number fairly represented by the word "unanimously"?—18?

8823. Yes?—It was unanimous with what was left in the room.

8824. I thought you told us that it was not?—With what was left in the room—about 25.

8825. That is not unanimous?—I call it the majority.

8826. When did you see the advertisement in the "Telegraph"?—The following morning.

8827. It was there described as a resolution passed unanimously?—Yes, it was.

8828. Did it strike you as being a true representation or an untrue representation?—As being an untrue representation.

8829. Did you do anything upon that?—Yes.

8830. What did you do?—I went to Mr. Thompson.

8831. What did you say to him?—I asked him how it was he got it put in the paper.

8832. Did you urge him to come forward and contradict it?—No.

8833. Why did not you do that?—I do not know. I told him he had been rather quick over it.

8834. The credit of your trade was at stake, it went forth to the world as a true account of what passed at the trade meeting and yet you took no steps to contradict it?—Only when I went to Mr. Barker to come here myself.

8835. You did not volunteer that statement to us, it was after Thompson had been examined. Of the 160 members how many are on the box?—They vary according to the men that are out of situations.

8836. At present, on this day, how many are there?—Perhaps a dozen.

8837. Not more than that?—I think not.

8838. Are any of the members in arrear?—Yes.

8839. From time to time, I suppose?—Yes.

8840. Is any list of the members in arrear read over?—No.

8841. None whatever?—No.

8842. Not on any occasion?—Not on any occasion.

8843. Have you a committee before whom the names of the members in arrear are submitted?—Yes.

8844. You call it the "investigating" committee?—We have a committee which we call the "arbitration" committee.

8845. What are their duties with respect to men in arrear?—When a man receives a note as to how much arrear he owes, he can elect to go before the investigating committee or the arbitration committee, and if he shows cause why he ought not to pay the whole they reduce it as they think proper.

8846. Supposing that he does not show cause?—He is obliged to pay it.

8847. Supposing he does not pay it?—There has not been a circumstance where they have not paid it.

8848. Thompson said there had been; do you mean to say that there are no arrears unpaid?—Yes, there are arrears unpaid.

8849. Do you mean to say that there is no case of a man going before the Arbitration Committee whose arrears are unpaid?—Yes, there are many of them yet.

8850. What do you do when they are unpaid?—I do not know that anything is done.

8851. Nothing whatever?—No.

8852. Is anything done?—Not that I am aware of.

8853. Have you heard of anything being done?—No, I have not heard of anything being done.

8854. Do you allow the men to go on remaining in debt, and take no steps to compel payment?—We have done, since the arbitration committee was established.

8855. You take no steps whatever to induce the men to pay?—No, only to persuade them to pay.

8856. What is the use of the arbitration committee if the men do not pay up?—I suppose when the men see they are dealt leniently with they will pay.

8857. Are no steps taken to compel the men to pay?—There are no compulsory steps taken to make the men pay.

8858. Do you swear that in your union a man's bands or property are not taken to compel him to pay?—Yes.

8859. That no such steps are taken in your union?—Yes, I swear that.

8860. I mean that a man being in arrear in your union is safe from any person taking his bands to coerce him to pay?—We have not any bands in our trade.

8861. From taking his tools then?—I never knew

NINTH DAY.

T. Gillott.

15 June 1867.

a circumstance of a man having his tools taken to make him pay.

8862. You never knew it ?—No.

8863. Nor his property injured ?—No.

8864. Have you never known any rattening taking place in your trade ?—No.

8865. (*Chairman.*) Was no scissor grinder ever rattened ?—I have not anything to do with scissor grinders but with scissor forgers.

8866. Have you never heard of a scissor forger being rattened ?—No, not to make him pay his contribution.

8867. (*Mr. Barstow.*) Have you never known a scissor forger rattened ?—Not to make him pay his contribution.

8868. For any purpose whatever ?—There have been scissor forgers rattened.

8869. What would it be for ?—I do not know.

8870. You really do not know ?—No, I do not.

8871. Do you know whether that rattening was connected with the trade rules ?—No.

8872. You do not know whether it was or not ?—No.

8873. What would it be for then ?—I do not know that they have been rattened in connexion with the trade at all.

8874. What use would it be for anyone not in the trade to ratten a man ?—I do not know.

8875. Would they have any earthly object in it ?—Not to my knowledge.

8876. Who else could do it but a man in the trade ?—I do not know.

8877. Is that all the explanation which you have to give of rattening in the scissor forgers trade ?—I never knew of any rattening except on two occasions in the scissor forgers trade. Mr. Gill's in Lambert Street was one.

8878. What was the other ?—Robert Winter's.

8879. Where is Robert Winter's place ?—In Cooper Street.

8880. We have heard that when men are in arrear in your trade it has been the practice to call out the grinders ?—Yes.

8881. That is to compel payment ?—Yes.

8882. Who supports the grinders when they are taken out ?—The forgers.

8883. In your union ?—Yes.

8884. That is a heavy expense to you, I suppose ?—I do not perfectly understand the expense ; it is according, I believe, to the merits of the men.

8885. If you have to pay a body of men, that is an expense to your box ?—Yes.

8886. It is larger, of course, in proportion to the number thrown out ?—Yes.

8887. Is not taking a man's tools or his scissors a much more effective way of enforcing payment ?—I never knew that course taken to enforce payment.

8888. You never knew it done ?—No.

8889. Do you know where that paper is which was signed by Mrs. Clarke ?—I do not.

8890. (*Chairman.*) You say that Gill's is one case ?—Yes ; I heard of Mr. Gill being rattened.

8891. That was in 1864 ?—I do not know the year.

8892. Do you know that before he was rattened he had had a threatening letter sent to him ?—I do not.

8893. Do you know that before he was rattened he had received a letter from the secretary of your union requesting him to attend the meetings ?—I do not.

8894. Do you know that before he was rattened Joseph Hague had refused to join the union ?—I do not. That was before I had much to do with it.

8895. Did you never hear that Joseph Hague had refused to join the union ?—No.

8896. Do you know that his bellows were cut ?—I know that some bellows were cut.

8897. Were you a member of the union at that time—on the 24th of February 1864 ?—I might be a member.

8898. Do not you know that at the time when Hague's bellows were cut he was a defaulter to your union ?—No, I do not.

8899. Did not you hear it said so in the union ?—No.

8900. You know that his bellows were cut ?—I remember a pair of bellows being cut. I did not know whether they were his or not.

8901. Was that at Gill's ?—Yes.

8902. Was he a member of the union ?—I do not know.

8903. Do not you know whether Hague was a member of the union or not ?—I do not know.

8904. Had he refused to become a member ?—I do not know.

8905. Do you know that besides Hague's there were another pair of bellows cut at the same time ?—No, I do not remember any more.

8906. Were you a member of the committee at that time ?—No.

8907. When a man comes and asks you about these kind of things, do you make entries in your minute books ?—I do not know whether the secretary does or not. I have never seen him make any.

8908. What does the president do. You seem to know nothing ?—He presides at the meetings, and puts the various resolutions that have to be brought before the meetings.

8909. That is all he does ?—Yes.

8909*a*. That is all he does ?—Yes.

8910. He knows everything that is brought before the meetings ?—Yes.

8911. (*Mr. Chance.*) I am asked to put a question for Mr. Sugg. You stated that it was suggested that a paper should be drawn up and signed by Mrs. Clarke ?—Yes.

8912. Do you remember whether Thompson had stated before that, that he had himself paid Mrs. Clarke independently of the trade ?—No, I do not remember him ever saying anything of the sort. He distinctly said that he had not, that he knew nothing about it.

8913. He stated that he knew nothing about it ?—Yes.

8914. And also that she would sign to that effect ?—Yes.

8915. Did he say that she would sign to the effect that he had paid Mrs. Clarke independently of the trade ?—He said that she would sign to the effect that she had not received any money from the trade.

8916. The question I put to you for Mr. Sugg is this, whether Thompson did not state that he had paid Mrs. Clarke independently of the trade, and that she would sign to that effect ?—I never heard him say so.

8917. Are you a beer-house keeper ?—No.

8918. (*Chairman.*) What is your name ?—Thomas Gillott.

8919. Where do you live ?—In India Terrace, King Street.

8920. Do you keep a light cart ?—No.

8921. Do you ever go in a light cart ?—No.

8922. Do you know Dennis Clarke ?—No.

8923. Are you not the Gillott whose name was mentioned in reference to Clarke ? Clarke was asked whether Gillott had squared him in the Wicker. Are you that Gillott ?—No.

8924. Do you know what "squaring" is ?—I know what the common meaning of "squaring" is.

8925. What is it ?—To quiet a man.

8926. Then you did not quiet Dennis Clarke ?—I never saw Dennis Clarke before to-day.

The witness withdrew.

Adjourned to Monday next at 11 o'clock.

TENTH DAY.

Council Hall, Sheffield, Monday, 17th June 1867.

PRESENT:

William Overend, Esq., Q.C.
Thomas Irwin Barstow, Esq.

George Chance, Esq.
J. E. Barker, Esq., Secretary.

WILLIAM OVEREND, Esq., Q.C., in the Chair.

TENTH DAY.

G. Shaw.

17 June 1867.

George Shaw recalled and further examined.

8927. (*Chairman.*) I am now going to put some questions to you which Mr. Broadhead requests me to put, and I hope you will be very careful in the manner in which you answer them. You have stated to us that you have heard Clarke say that he would "lag" you, or could "lag" you and Broadhead?—Yes.

8928. When was the first time that you heard him say so?—I have heard him say so several times.

8929. But when was the first time?—Just after we did the deed.

8930. What deed?—Just after we blew up Helliwell.

8931. Where was it that he told you that?—He told me in the "Corner Pin."

8932. Was any person present?—No, not to my recollection.

8933. When was the next time that he told you?—I can hardly recollect; he told me several times.

8934. But why did he tell you that he could "lag" you and Broadhead? if you both did it, of course he could do so, and you all knew it?—He knew that I did the deed, but he knew that he employed us.

8935. Did he tell any person besides you?—No.

8936. Then what was his object in telling you this? had you quarrelled, or was it a threat, or how was it?—Yes, we used to quarrel frequently.

8937. Was it at a time when you had been quarrelling?—Yes.

8938. Have you not said that the first time that you heard him say this was in Alvey's public house?—No.

8939. You have never said so?—Not the first time. I said I heard him say it several times before I was in Alvey's public house. I heard him say it several times before he said it at Alvey's public house.

8940. Mr. Broadhead wants to know what was your reason for telling him every three or four months about this threatening?—Because Clarke boasted about it, but it was not every three or four months. I told him at several intervals, when I heard Clarke talk about it, and when he talked to me about it.

8941. To whom did he talk?—He talked about it in the "King William," when I told Mr. Broadhead about it, about eight or nine weeks since, perhaps it would be a week before Easter when I told him. I have a very good criterion to go by, that I was at Mr. Broadhead's the same night.

8942. Can you tell me what time it was that he was at the "King William?"—It was in the middle of the afternoon some time.

8943. But in what week or in what month was it?—It was a fortnight from last Thursday when I sat here. It was the week but one before Whitsuntide.

8944. What did he do the week but one before Whitsuntide?—He was talking in the "King William" that he could "lag" old "Smite'em" and me.

8945. Where was he, then, the week before Whitsuntide?—He was talking in Alvey's public house.

8946. How do you know that it was the week but one before Easter that he talked at the "King William"?—Because I was there.

8947. But how do you happen to know that you were there the week but one before Easter?—Because we worked a bit extra at Easter, as we do at Whitsuntide.

8948. You worked double work?—Yes, we worked harder. Our wheel works night and day; but there are other reasons.

8949. So that you might have your holiday?—Yes.

8950. And what other reasons have you?—I will state them when you have asked Mr. Broadhead if I was at his house on the following Saturday.

8951. Were you at his house on the following Saturday?—Yes, and I can prove that I was there.

8952. How can you prove it?—By what is in his books, and by my wife that went with me.

8953. How can you prove it by his books?—Joseph Copley left his situation on that very Saturday night; he left Peace Brothers. He worked for them when Darwin's bands were taken from him.

8954. And you know that it was that night?—Yes. Copley paid for a pint of beer for me in the dramshop while my wife was waiting in the street for me, and he asked me if he could earn a few shillings with me. There was no scale for him because he was in arrear. You will see in the books if he was in arrear at the time.

8955. And what did you say?—I told him if there was anything to do he could earn a few shillings.

8956. What kind of work was it?—Grinding. I am a sawgrinder, the same as he.

8957. Were you on scale then?—No, I had nothing to do with the trade. I had no business there at all, only to communicate to Mr. Broadhead what I had heard said about him and me.

8958. Were you in the union then?—No.

8959. You went there simply to tell Mr. Broadhead this?—Yes.

8960. (*To Mr. Broadhead.*) Will you be kind enough to let me look at the book to see whether or not Copley got his scale that night?— (*Witness.*) He went off a fortnight before Easter.

8961. What do you call Easter—Good Friday or Easter Monday?—Easter Monday.

8962. Easter Monday was on the 22d of April?—Yes.

8963. When was it that you say that you went to him?—I went when Copley's notice was up. It might be the Saturday before Easter or the Saturday after, but I went to tell him the day that Copley's notice was up. Copley told me in the dramshop.

8964. The Saturday but one before Easter would be the 13th of April, and the Saturday before Easter would be the 20th of April; which of those days do you think it was?—I scarcely know to a few days. I am telling you to the best of my recollection.

8965. But you say that you know that it was at that time, because you say that you had been working hard in order to get your holiday at Easter?—Yes.

TENTH DAY.

G. Shaw.

17 June 1867.

8966. And the Saturday after you went down to Broadhead's?—Yes, when I was there on Saturday night.

8967. Was that after you had been working hard or not?—No, I had not been working hard then.

8968. You say you know that he told you?—When I went to communicate to Broadhead what I had heard, Copley was there. He said his notice was up, and he was in arrear. If you look at the notice book you will soon see, if they had one.

(*Mr. Broadhead.*) Here is Copley's name receiving no scale on the 16th.

8969. But on the 16th Copley receives nothing?—(*Witness.*) No, he said he was not allowed to receive scale because he was in arrear.

8970. (*To Mr. Broadhead.*) According to this Copley received nothing that day?—He received nothing.

8971. Have you any notice book?—No, we enter the notices as they come in the minute book.

(*Witness.*) His notice was up a short time after Damms' bands went.

8972. (*To witness.*) How do you know that on the occasion you talk about, about the week but one before Whitsuntide you went and told Broadhead in Alvey's?—I told Broadhead in Green Lane what I I had heard.

8973. And it was in Alvey's public house, you say, the week but one before Whitsuntide. How do you remember that?—It was this very last Whitsuntide.

8974. And you recollect it because it was such a short time ago?—Yes, I told Mr. Broadhead about it in the street, and we had a row about it. Copley had above one notice.

8975. I see in the notice book that Copley gives notice to the society on the 11th of May. Now the 11th of May was long after Easter?—Well, I can scarcely call to mind to a day or two or a week or two how long it was, but I was there the night Copley went on the box, and he asked me if he could earn a few shillings with me.

8976. It is the custom to give a month's notice they tell me?—Yes.

8977. Then he would leave his employment a month after the 11th of May?—Yes.

8978. That would bring him into June?—Why, he has been working for Mr. Taylor these seven or eight weeks, close beside our place. Copley has left his situation since I have been in mine, and I did not take to my situation while five weeks after Christmas.

8979. You are speaking of this year, are you not?—Yes.

8980. Not of 1866?—No, I am speaking of this year, 1867.

8981. There is a notice entered there, "Notice to the box on the 11th of May." The 11th of May is not above a month ago?—No.

8982. Are you sure he has not been in employment since that time?—He has been in employment at Mr. Taylor's two months; you can inquire at the Adelaide Works.

8983. How then is it that he should give notice on the 11th of May, that could not be right?—He did not give any notice. The master would not have him because he was always drunk and would not attend to his work. He had above one notice at the situation he was in.

8984. But are you quite sure that he was in work in the months of May and June?—I never took any notice when he was in work.

8985. I thought you said he was at work in the Adelaide Works?—He is at the Adelaide Works now.

8986. How long has he been there?—To my recollection about two months, he came with "Currant," that's Martin, to see me just before he went to America.

8987. Who came to see you?—Copley came with Martin to see me.

8988. Copley came with Martin to see you before Martin went to America?—Yes.

8989. Where did he work before he went to the Adelaide Works?—He worked for Mr. Peace; you will find if you inquire at the works of Messrs. Peace Brothers when he went to the Adelaide Works.

8990. Do you know whether he was dismissed from Messrs. Peace's without notice?—I do not. When I was not in the trade I did not bother my head with anything about the trade. I merely took his suggestion which he made to me.

8991. Did Martin tell you who was sending him to America?—No, he did not.

8992. Nor Copley?—No.

8993. Did he appear to know?—Martin had been very bad with the trade about some row or some business which I did not understand, and they stopped his scale, and then he had to face the general body of the meeting. They granted his scale, and in a few weeks after that he disappeared and went to America. I know no more of Martin or anybody else. I daresay you will find in the scale book how it was granted to Martin and everything else. I do not know how it was stopped.

8994. When you were examined here at first, you would not make a statement, and then you were afterwards recalled, and you made a statement, to whom had you made that statement before you came here?—I simply called at Broadhead's to ask him where the place was.

8995. What place?—This place. He said it was at the top of Norfolk Street. He read the paper to me; I said I knew nothing about the man who had brought me into this affair, and I left Woodhead with him having a "four" of brandy; I went home to change my clothes, and I had only half an hour before it was time to come here, and I never spoke a word about the affair to anybody.

8996. Mr. Broadhead wants to know to whom you told that he had given you money about blowing up Helliwell?—I never told that story.

8997. Not to Clarke?—No.

8998. Who was the man to whom you told that?—I told Mr. Peace at Little London that I did not do what I ought to have done. I told him that I blew him up with smithy-slake instead of powder. I give that in my statement.

8999. You say you told Mr. Peace; who is he?—Mr. George Peace, the man that I work with. I went to warn him before I left the meeting. The man that found me employment said Broadhead would not let 500 men grind saws that was wanted, and he asked me if I was willing to earn my living, and I said, I was willing to earn my living anywhere. He said he did not wish to go to any more of Broadhead's meetings because he had joined another trade.

9000. Was it then that you told him about blowing up Helliwell?—No, it was afterwards when I was talking to him.

9001. How long afterwards was it that you told Mr. Peace?—Perhaps it was a fortnight, and then I had to face the committee. It was betwixt a week and a fortnight, but I cannot tell to a day or two.

9002. Did you mention the name of Dennis Clarke?—Yes, I said me and "Tucker" had to do it.

9003. And what did you tell him besides?—I told him that we blew the man up with smithy-slake instead of powder.

9004. Did you tell him anything about Broadhead at that time?—No.

9005. Did you tell him who had given Clarke the can?—I told him I had got it at "Old Smite'em's."

9006. How along ago is that?—Perhaps six or seven weeks before I left the trade—six or seven or eight weeks before Christmas. I can scarcely tell—happens a week more or less, but that is the best of my recollections.

9007. Nobody else heard you besides Peace?—No. Well, Jonathan Crapper paid us a visit one day. He asked me what I was working at there. I told him I

TENTH DAY.

G. Shaw.

17 June 1867.

neither cared for the trade nor anyone else. I considered that I had a right to have a living. He was the one that wanted me to go to Mr. Jackson to tell him how badly I had been used by Martin; I went as far as Bank Street, and I left Martin, as I supposed, to go towards the Town Hall, and I went the other way.

9008. What had Martin done to you?—He had gouged me, and there are marks on my face that will never go off, and my throat and all. When I went to work with Fearnehough I was ordered not to labour at all by Mr. Broadhead.

9009. Have you been paid anything by the association of the masters in order to make this statement? —No, by no one living; I have merely defended myself.

9010. As to the statement which you have made here Mr. Broadhead requests you to be asked (and I should ask you if he did not do so) whether you have been paid anything by any association?—No, by no man or gentleman living.

9011. Have you been offered any advantages of any sort?—No, only that Hallam came to our house and said we should get 25*l.* if we spoke. I was not in the house. My aunt was in. Some seven or eight weeks since Hallam came to my aunt's with two or three men with him,—who was with him I do not know,—and he said supposing I should come I should get a reward or something of that sort, but I never took any notice of him. I thought I had better mind my own business.

9012. He came and saw your aunt, did he?—Yes, and he asked for me to come to the "King William" and see James Hallam.

9013. And you went to see James Hallam?—No, I never went near him.

9014. Hallam came to your house and saw your aunt, and left a message for you that if you would go and give evidence you would get a reward of 25*l.*?—He said that should be all right, and that if I came down and gave evidence I should get a reward.

9015. Was that the reason why you came here?—To tell you?

9015. Yes?—Because I knew he had been here and told before me.

9016. You were summoned here, were you not?—Yes.

9017. You never communicated at all to Mr. Chambers?—No. I received a summons to come here.

9018. And you have never told anybody until you came into this court?—No, only when I came here on Saturday. After I had been here on Saturday I told Mr. Barker.

9019. Was that after I had warned you that you had already committed perjury and put yourself in peril?—Yes, I went into that room (*pointing to the ante-room*) and told him.

9020. Did you tell him the same story that you have told us?—Thereabouts.

9021. Then afterwards you were called up again and another chance was granted to you, and then you told the story?—Yes, I told the whole truth and nothing else but the truth.

9022. What did you know about Hallam having been down here before you?—Hallam and several others stopped me in Fitzwilliam Street the very day that I gave the warning, and he said that Clarke had told him, that supposing I would speak what we knew we could do for "Smite'em." We were in a public-house in Fitzwilliam Street together. I told him that I did not wish to have anything at all to do with it, and then he made applications at my home for me where I live.

9023. Hallam did?—Yes, but I never interfered with him.

9024. Did you see him?—No. He left word that I was to see him at the "King William," and I should be rewarded.

9025. You say that the reason that you came was that you knew Hallam had been down before you. How long have you known that Hallam had made any disclosures?—I had heard by public-house talk that he had been to Mr. Jackson about it.

9026. Had it been talked about in public-houses that Hallam had been?—Yes, and I had another reason to believe it. I went to Crapper's house to show how I had been used, and he got me down from the bottom of Glossop Road to the end of Bank Street to tell Mr. Jackson. I said that I did not like to bother myself or bother anyone about it, and I left Crapper, and I suppose that he went to the Town Hall.

9027. When have you heard it talked about in a public-house that Hallam had spoken to Jackson?—He told me in Fitzwilliam Street that if I would come and tell the truth I should get well paid, and I told him I did not wish to interfere with it.

9028. Where have you heard it talked of in a public-house that Hallam had been with Jackson?—When I began to hear it talked of I used to go out; I was sick of hearing it talked about. Hallam told me when I was sitting in the "King William."

9029. That he had been to Mr. Jackson?—Yes, and he told me all about it.

9030. Told you all about what?—He said that he had made a disclosure of what he knew and that I ought to do the same, and I told him that I knew nothing.

9031. Then he did not tell you what he had said? —Yes, he said that he had got to know from Tucker what I had done, and he wished me to come and say the same.

9032. That is from Dennis Clarke?—Yes, I knew nothing any more about it. I never bothered about it.

9033. Then there has been no inducement at all except that which Hallam held out to you, to induce you to come here and tell this story?—No; no man has come and spoken to me about it.

9034. You saw Mr. Barker in the adjoining room? —Yes.

9035. Did you afterwards go to Mr. Chambers?—Yes.

9036. Why did you go to Mr. Chambers?—I went to ask Mr. Brammer to accompany me up to Simmonite, to ask him if he had bought the powder or not. I knew he had bought it, and I only wished him to speak the truth the same as I had done.

9037. You have said that you did not care a pin for the society, or anything for the society at the time you were in Little London working for Peace, but were you not at that very time receiving scale from the society?—Yes, but it was stopped when they thought I was picking up a few shillings by hanging stones and such as that.

9038. Did your scale continue during the whole time that you were working for Mr. Peace?—No, I could not live on 6*s.* a week.

9039. But was it stopped?—Yes, it stopped when they knew by Martin that I was going there; Martin ordered Broadhead to stop it.

9040. Martin was tracking you up and down to see whether you were working or not?—Yes, he was, and he said that my eyes looked dim, and he said I had been working at night, and I told him that he told a falsehood and a lie.

9041. Was Martin acting for himself or acting for the committee, or Broadhead, or whom?—He authorized my scale to be stopped; I suppose he was acting for Mr. Broadhead and the trades union.

9042. Were you receiving scale and doing work, and at the same time telling the society that you were doing no work?—I earned a few shillings.

9043. But did you give that in to the society? —No, I did not; I think I earned it with walking up there.

9044. Was not your scale stopped in consequence of their finding out that you were working, and had not reported your work to the society?—Yes.

TENTH DAY.

G. Shaw.

17 June 1867.

9045. Martin reported you ?—Yes, of course.

9046. You said that when you blew up Helliwell, Clarke stood beside you ?—He stood where he could see me as I did it.

9047. But you said that he stood beside you, what did you mean by that ?—There was of course only the wall that parted us.

9048. And afterwards you stated that he was in the adjoining hull ?—That was the wall that parted us.

9049. How far was he from you ?—I was about three yards from him.

9050. Then what you meant by standing beside you, was not that he stood by your side, but in the adjoining hull ?—Yes, he could see me do it (*describing the same*).

9051. It is not precisely accurate to say that he was close beside you if he was in the adjoining hull. I asked you (and in this you committed perjury) whether you had not seen Mr. Broadhead on the morning before you appeared here, and you said that you had not seen him ?—Well, I did not wish to be implicated with him at all.

9052. Was that the reason that you told us that ?—Yes, I had had enough of Mr. Broadhead.

9053. Had Mr. Broadhead told you to say that you had not seen him ?—No, he had not.

9054. Do you know Joseph Woollen ?—Yes.

9055. After you had committed the perjury which you committed here in saying that you had not seen Mr. Broadhead, did you see Joseph Woollen ?—Yes, he lives close by me.

9056. And did you tell him that you had got into a mess, and that you would leave the country if you could ?—I knew they had something to tell about me. I saw Mr. Broadhead here and I saw Mr. Sugg here with the compact in his hand that I had signed, and I told Woollen that I had been with him that morning. He had brought the document that I had signed, and I spoke the truth then when he did. I out with it at once, and made a clean breast of it, and Mr. Sugg can ask me anything he thinks proper, and Woollen can come forward in front of me and ask me what I told him.

9057. Woollen brings the books for Broadhead ?—Yes, he has told me this morning in the presence of another man, he told me he had to come and carry the books, and he left me to carry them, and there is a man in court that saw him.

9058. What was it that you said about Mr. Sugg ?—I said that I saw Mr. Sugg with the assignment I had signed in his hand, and that compelled me to speak the truth, and I have done it. I have never seen Mr. Broadhead only when I have seen him here.

9059. When you told Woollen that you were in a mess and so on, did you tell him that he must go to Broadhead and ask him to find you the money to leave the country, and that it would be well worth their while to do it ?—No, I did not. I merely simply said to Woollen that I did not like to be in the mess I was brought in, and I was compelled to speak the truth when I saw Mr. Sugg bring out that document on Saturday. That was it and nothing else.

9060. Where did you first see that paper, you say that the document was produced by Mr. Sugg ?—I saw it on that table (*pointing to the table*), Mr Sugg had it in his hand. He said he had something to say against "that man Shaw" on Saturday.

9061. (*Mr. Sugg.*) Do not blow me up.—I do not wish to blow anyone up. I dare say my life will be attempted to be taken after what has taken place here. I do not wish any insinuations to be thrown out by Mr. Sugg.

9062. (*Chairman.*) You must not speak to Mr. Sugg in that way. What ground have you for supposing that your life is in danger ?—There are a many men who have their lives in danger for less grounds than I have now to depend upon.

9063. How do you mean ?—Men have been shot at for less than I have done.

9064. How do you know ?—From paper reports. I am giving evidence against the great Mr. Broadhead. I went into a public-house last Wednesday night and I heard a murmur that they would like to cut me in two.

9065. What ground have you for saying that your life is in danger ?—Well, I have not a minute to call my own now.

9066. Since you have given your evidence has anything been done to you, or said to you ?—Clarke was in a public house where I called in and I heard him murmur that he would like to cut me in two, it was when me and Mr. Brammer were together. Mr. Brammer was at the door, and I told him what had been said.

9067. Where was that ?—That was at the place facing Taylor's. It was at Mr. Parr's where I went in and had a pint of ale.

9068. Was Mr. Brammer there ?—He was at the door, and I told him what had passed when I had been in, and I told him that I did not care for it.

9069. Was anybody there besides Mr. Brammer, Clarke and you ?—No, he and I came away together. There was Copley, and a whole host of them.

9070. Did Copley say anything to you ?—No.

9071. But they could hear what Dennis Clarke said ?—I do not know whether they heard it or not, they perhaps turned dumb-foundered and would hear nothing.

9072. Clarke made that statement after you had given your evidence ?—Yes.

9073. You had given it on the Thursday ?—Yes, and that was on Friday night between 7 and 8 o'clock.

9074. And he said that he should like to cut you in two ?—Yes.

9075. And you came out immediately and told Mr. Brammer what had happened ?—Yes.

9076. Has anybody else besides Clarke used either threatening language to you, or molested you since you gave your evidence ?—No.

9077. It is Clarke only ?—Yes, we have always been at variance ever since a few months after we joined the trade.

9078. Did he tell you at all why it was that he should like to cut you in two ?—No. There is another man in court, Woodhead, who said to a man, a saw grinder, that he should like me to be cut in two for the evidence I had given, because I had spoken the truth.

9079. Did Woodhead say this ?—Yes.

9080. For the evidence which you had given two days before ?—He said it to a man named Hague who is no relation to me, and who had been up here for having his tools destroyed or something.

9081. What relation is Hague to you ?—Nothing ; he worked with me at the Tower when I did, and I have not seen him since.

9082. Who told you that ?—Hague told me when I was in Bank Street on Saturday.

9083. Has there been any direct threat held out to you by anybody since this occurred ?—No, there has not.

9084. If there should be let us know ?—I will. I have merely spoken the truth, I do not care who knows it. It is trnth what I have said and nothing more.

9085. You have been examined on that side, and you have told us a good deal of matter ; do you think that you have told us everything that you know ?—Yes, which is within my knowledge. I have told you everything I know, and as for Mr. Wilson saying I was a man about five feet six inches or five feet eight inches, I am about five feet six and a half. I was not above eight stone when I joined the trade, and I was not above five feet four ; and no detective or policeman can come forward and say that black was my character ; and Mr. Wilson told a complete falsehood

TENTH DAY.

G. Shaw.

17 June 1867.

when he was here the other day. I never earned a shilling from Wilson in my life. When I was working I was fetched out of the wheel and Dennis Clarke, and who the other man was I do not know. When my master was shot in the ribs there were not two bullets in the ribs, but he was shot in the ribs. He bought me a suit of clothes the week before.

9086. Who was your master ?—James Linley. He was shot in the Nursery.

9087. You say that he was shot in the Nursery, and that he had given you a suit of clothes the week before ?—Yes, his brother-in-law had made it, where he was shot at. We were fetched by Mr. Jackson who delivers warrants, I and Tucker and the others.

9088. You said that you were sought out by the police ?—They fetched us out of the wheel where we were working, I and Dennis Clarke.

9089. When was that ?—The very night that he was shot when he was sitting on the table. There was three of us, but which of the apprentices I can scarcely tell, there was so many of us. That was the first time he was shot; he was shot twice.

9090. This was the first time ?—Yes.

9091. Was a person of the name of Ogden working there ?—He was working for Mr. Gillatt, file grinder.

9092. At the same wheel ?—Yes, there was above 100 grinders worked there.

9093. Then the police did come and take you up too ?—Yes, I and Clarke and another man, but who was working with us I can scarcely tell now. It was about 18 months or perhaps two years before we joined the union.

9094. On that occasion you say that Linley was shot in the side ?—Yes, I think it was in the side.

9095. Was it a pistol shot ?—I do not know. There were two lumps in his ribs one below the other. Whatever was shot at him did not enter him. It made two lumps; that is all I know of.

9096. Do you know at what time of the night he was shot ?—We were fetched perhaps between 7 and 8 o'clock. I and Clarke worked while the wheel stopped and the other.

9097. Were you ever present at a conversation when Clarke spoke to Ogden about the police being likely to come ?—No; Clarke and he used to keep pigeons together, but I do not know what they talked about. I was never with him.

9098. When you were taken up what became of you ?—We came back to our work, and we ceased it after.

9099. You were not troubled any more about it ?—No.

9100. Were you examined before the magistrate ?—No.

9101. Were you merely taken up by the police ?—No, merely brought to see our master in the state he was in.

9102. But for what reason were you brought ?—The police came and said, "Come and see your master, he has been shot."

9103. You were not charged with it ?—No.

9104. Neither of you ?—I do not know whether Clarke was; I was not. Jackson fetched us that delivers out warrants at this present time.

9105. Then you were merely brought down to look at your master ?—Yes, to see him.

9106. At that time had you any conversation with Clarke about it ?—No.

9107. Afterwards, Linley was shot again, was he not ?—He was shot twice, my master was.

9108. He was shot the first time in the Nursery ?—Yes.

9109. And the second time in Scotland Street ?—Yes.

9110. The second time, was it in the open street ?—He was sat on a table in his brother-in-law's house. I do not know whether it was his brother-in-law or his brother. They sell oatcakes in the same house.

9111. When he was shot the second time, were you at the Tower wheel ?—I believe so.

9112. Do you know in what month he was shot ?—I have no idea. He was a great fisher was our master. He went to see how he was to go about the fishing. That is all I ever heard about his being shot.

9113. He was shot in Scotland Street the second time ?—Yes.

9114. And was Clarke working for him then ?—I am not quite well aware whether he was working for him or Mr. Wilson.

9115. But you were working at that time ?—I was apprentice-boy at that time.

9116. And Clarke too ?—No, Clarke was older than me a deal. He worked for both Fearnehough and Wilson.

9117. Was he at work on the night when Linley was shot ?—No, we should have ceased work then; he was shot late at night.

9118. Were you working all night or not ?—We never worked all night. We gave over every night about 7 o'clock.

9119. Was Ogden at work there then ?—He worked at the wheel the same as we did.

9120. On the occasion of the last shooting ?—Yes, all the shootings.

9121. Do you recollect Clarke speaking to Ogden about the police coming to him ?—No, I was never in Clarke's company at all.

9122. You never heard him say anything to Ogden about the police coming ?—No.

9123. Did you work in the same hull with Clarke ?—Sometimes; I had various places.

9124. But did you occasionally work in the same hull with Clarke ?—Perhaps three months at once, and then I went and worked in another hull.

9125. In what hull were you working the last time when Linley was shot ?—I think it was at the back of Henry Garfit. I think I was glazing there.

9126. Where was Clarke working then ?—Clarke would be working for Mr. Wilson, I think, at that time, or Fearnehough; I do not know which.

9127. But was it the same hull ?—No.

9128. A different hull to yours ?—Yes.

9129. Did he work in the same hull with Ogden ?—The file grinders had a hull to themselves.

9130. Do you recollect a pistol being found after ?—No, I never heard about that.

9131. You never saw the pistol ?—No.

9132. Did you ever talk to Clarke about a pistol being found ?—No.

9133. Did you ever talk to Ogden about it ?—No; he and I scarcely ever speak to one another.

9134. He has never shown you a pistol ?—No, he has never shown me anything.

9135. Did you ever hear that a pistol had been found in the hull where Clarke worked ?—No.

The witness withdrew.

Mr. H. Holdsworth.

Mr. Harry Holdsworth sworn and examined.

9136. (*Mr. Chance.*) Were you in partnership with Mr. Ashburner ?—Yes.

9137. When did you first commence partnership with him ?—In September 1861.

9138. And what business did you carry on ?—Crinoline steel manufacturers, saw manufacturers, and tool manufacturers.

9139. Where were your works situate ?—In New George Street.

9140. Are you in business now ?—As a manager only.

9141. You are speaking now of September 1861, when you were in business ?—Yes.

9142. While you were in business had you anything to do with the union?—No, I never acknowledged the union in any shape or way.

9143. Did you employ union men?—Yes, I had union men and also non-union men; I did not object to them, because they were union men.

9144. While in business did you receive, at any time, any threatening letters?——Yes, I received several at different times.

9145. Have you any of those letters that you have received?—I have not.

9146. Have you destroyed them?—Yes, some I destroyed, and I believe some were given to Mr. Jackson.

9147. Were they given by you?—They were handed over by me and my clerks to Mr. Jackson.

9148. Do you remember when you received the first of those threatening letters?—I believe it was in October 1861.

9149. Can you remember at all what the nature of the letter was?—It was a demand to discharge a man of the name of Jonathan Crapper, who was then in my employ.

9150. Was there any threat in the event of your not discharging him?—In the event of my not discharging him, there were vague threats of personal injury, but I do not recollect the exact terms in which they were couched.

9151. You are clear that there were threats of personal injury?—Yes, in the first letter, but they were rather vague.

9152. What was Crapper?—A grinder.

9153. A saw grinder?—A saw grinder.

9154. Did you discharge Crapper upon that?—Oh, no.

9155. I believe you took no notice of the letter?—None at all.

9156. About the same time did you receive any other letter?—In about a fortnight after I received another letter.

9157. What was the nature of that?—It repeated the demands, and it was something to the effect that the nights were getting dark, and that I was to look out as I was going home. It was signed "Tantia Topee."

9158. Was the demand there, the same as the demand in the other letter?—Yes.

9159. What did you do upon that?—I did nothing. I burnt the letter, and took proper precautions to defend myself. That was all.

9160. Did you have any other letters upon the same subject?—Yes, I had other letters after, but there was an occurrence took place before that.

9161. Will you describe that occurrence to which you refer?—I had some long saws that were sent down to the Sheaf Island Works to grind; they were taken away from the grinding wheel.

9162. Do you know the reason why they were taken?—Personally I do not, but I am told they were taken on account of this man, Crapper. Crapper told me he believed they had been taken on his account.

9163. Did he tell you the reason why he thought they were taken upon his account?—He was under some dispute with the union, the nature of which I do not recollect. It was some dispute apart from my business. Those saws were restored in a day or two; they were found in the wheel again.

9164. How long was that after they were missing?—I believe in two days.

9165. Do you know at all how it was that they were restored?—I am sorry to say I do not recollect. We had taken precautions to have the place watched; but they were restored without the restorer being discovered.

9166. Did anything more take place with regard to those saws?—Nothing more took place with regard to those saws.

9167. Did you receive a threatening letter in reference to those saws?—Yes, I received a further threatening letter.

9168. (*Chairman.*) How long was that after they were restored?—I should think it might be about a week after to the best of my recollection.

9169. (*Mr. Chance.*) Do you remember what the nature of that letter was?—It did not contain I believe any allusion, except an allusion to the former letter, and a demand that I should comply with the former requests.

9170. Was there any threat held out if you did not comply with those requests?—Yes, a similar threat to the previous one.

9171. (*Chairman.*) As to the night's being dark?—It was signed: "One whose hand never flinches."

9172. (*Mr. Chance.*) Were they threats of personal violence?—Yes.

9173. And about the same time did you receive other letters?—Yes, I believe I received one more letter, which I handed to Mr. Jackson at the time.

9174. Was that upon the same subject?—Yes.

9175. And containing similar threats?—Yes, similar threats.

9176. Do you remember any occurrence taking place soon after you received the last of the threatening letters to which you have referred?—On the 2nd of December in the same year, 1861, on a Monday, on returning to business, I discovered there had been an explosion.

9177. Was that on Monday morning?—On Monday morning. I was shown the remains of a can or canister which had been discovered in a cellar underneath part of the warehouse.

9178. Who showed you the can?—My own manager.

9179. Who was he?—William Roberts.

9180. You say it was discovered in a cellar under the warehouse?—Yes, the buildings were damaged to the extent of about 100*l.* or upwards.

9181. Do you know any reason why the powder had been put there?—No personal reason, other than what I derived from those threatening letters.

9182. Had you any dispute at all with your workmen?—None at all.

9183. Or had you a dispute with anybody else that you know of?—None at all.

9184. Do you imagine it was done by one of your own men?—I do not.

9185. Have you any reason for supposing that it was not so done?—Yes, because the grate of the cellar had been soldered down, and it had been removed to insert this can of powder. There was another grate which was well known to our workmen, which was only chained down, and which could have been removed very much more easily.

9186. If one of your own workmen had done it he would have done it in a different way?—Yes.

9187. (*Chairman.*) In an easier way you say?—Yes.

9188. (*Mr. Chance.*) And would it produce a good deal of damage?—It might have been done at several places where it would have produced greater damage.

9189. After this explosion took place, was any remark made to you by any of your workmen?—Yes, I was advised, or I should scarcely say advised, but it was suggested to me whether it would not be better to ask Crapper to leave me.

9190. Did you ask Crapper to go?—Oh no, certainly not.

9191. Was there any suggestion that you should settle with the union?—It was suggested that I should advise Crapper to settle with them.

9192. Did you suggest that to Crapper?—No; I told him that I would stick to him as long as he would stick to me.

9193. Do you know whether shortly after that Crapper did, as a fact, settle with the union?—I was informed that he did.

9194. After your were so informed, did you receive

TENTH DAY.

Mr. H. Holdsworth.

17 June 1867.

any other injury of any kind, or any threatening letters?—None at all.

9195. Did there seem to be a feeling amongst your men that you would not be molested in any way again?—Yes, I was congratulated by some of the men upon having escaped a great danger.

9196. You told us just now that you believe the injury received was connected with some trade affair?—Yes.

9197. It was no personal feeling to yourself, or spite against yourself in any way?—No, I had no personal feeling; but I think it right to make one remark; and that is, that I had other men working for me who were not connected with the union, and I received no molestation about them in any shape or way.

9198. The union men and non-union men, then, went on well together?—Yes, and I received no communication about them.

9199. (*Chairman.*) Have you ever seen any person connected with the trade upon the subject of those letters?—No one.

9200. Have you been to the secretary about them at all?—No.

9201. You have been a bankrupt, I believe?—Yes, I have.

9202. Were you committed for twelve months as a fraudulent bankrupt?—Yes, I was.

9203. When was that?—In March 1863.

9204. You say you are now a manager?—Yes.

9205. For whom are you manager?—For Mr. Primrose, lead and glass merchant.

9206. Where does he live?—In Corporation Street, Sheffield, but I am managing a branch establishment which he has at Hull.

9207. How long have you done that?—Since February of the present year. May I be allowed to make a remark, as I have been asked this question?

9208. Certainly.—I wish to say that immediately after the bankruptcy I was proffered the sympathy of, and a situation if I required it by Messrs. Wilson, Hawksworth, Ellison, and Company, to whom I had served my apprenticeship.

9209. After you had been committed to prison?—After I had been committed. A great deal has been said about it. I actually held a situation with Mr. Henry Taylor, who had been previously a partner with Messrs. Wilson and Company.

The witness withdrew.

Isaac Taylor.

ISAAC TAYLOR sworn and examined.

9210. (*Mr. Barstow.*) You live at Sharrow Vale, do you not?—Yes.

9211. Are you a saw grinder?—Yes.

9212. For whom do you work?—I work for Mr. Naylor.

9213. For whom were you working in 1862?—For Mr. Naylor.

9214. Are you a member of the saw grinders union?—Yes.

9215. When did you first join it?—I joined it in 1849.

9216. Did you continue a member until 1862?—Yes, or the beginning of 1863.

9217. Do you remember one Monday morning in April 1862 going to your work with your apprentice?—Yes.

9218. On that occasion did you find your work ready for you?—No, we had not any work there.

9219. I believe that the regulation in your trade is that the master shall carry the work to the place where it is to be done?—Yes.

9220. What did you then do to get your work?—I asked my boy to go down to Mr. Naylor's.

9221. What to do?—To ask him if we were going to have anything to do on that day.

9222. Did he bring up the work?—Yes, he brought one dozen of saws.

9223. What is your boy's name?—Luke Frith.

9224. Next morning did you find a letter?—We found that the nuts were gone off the axles.

9225. Did you find any writing about your place?—Yes, we found a note on the horses.

9226. Is that the note (*handing a paper to the witness*)?—Yes, that is the note.

9227. "Do thy own work and let the carriage alone. Keep the lad for something better than master"?—That is it.

9228. What did you do?—I thought that they were not using me the same as they were other people, and I tried to go on working.

9229. You contrived to go on without your nuts?—Yes.

9230. How was that?—I wedged the pulleys on; I tried wedging.

9231. Did you make any inquiry about your nuts?—No, not until Mr. Broadhead came.

9232. And you went on working in that way until the end of the week?—Yes.

9233. Do you recollect anything occurring on the following Monday?—The Monday following, Mr. Broadhead came for the contribution as usual.

9234. What did he say to you?—He asked me what I had earned during that week, and I told him.

9235. Do you remember how much it was?—Well, I believe it was 4*l.* 6*s.* 0*d.*, me and a boy.

9236. What would you have to pay upon 4*l.* 6*s.* 0*d.*?—I believe we were paying 2*s.* 6*d.* in the pound at that time.

9237. That would be about 10*s.* 9*d.*, would it not?—Yes.

9238. What did he say then?—He asked me how much I was going to pay. He said I was 13*s.* 7*d.* in arrear. I told him that I would pay all off if he would bring me back my nuts.

9239. What did he say to that?—He said I should not have them back yet unless I paid something.

9240. What did he mean by "something"?—I suppose he meant that I must pay my contribution.

9241. Your 13*s.* 7*d.* was the contribution, but there was something besides?—Yes. The week before we had those nuts taken, I promised to pay this 13*s.* 7*d.* as soon as I did any work.

9242. But there was something more than the 13*s.* 7*d.*?—Only the weekly contribution.

9243. Broadhead told you that you should not have back your nuts unless you paid something?—Yes.

9244. What did he mean by that?—I understood that I was to pay the money; it was my duty to call at his house and tell him our nuts were gone, and he would have called a meeting; but I had not done so.

9245. Did he say so at the time?—Yes.

9246. What would have been the result of the meeting?—Very likely I should have been fined.

9247. You said that Broadhead said that yon should not have them back unless you paid something: is that which you have just told us what you meant?—I understood this, that I should have to pay the money.

9248. (*Chairman.*) What money?—The contribution and this 13*s.* 7*d.*

9249. (*Mr. Barstow.*) Then the 13*s.* 7*d.* was besides the contributions?—Yes, that 13*s.* 7*d.* was what was in arrear.

9250. What you call contributions I understand to be the payment for the current week?—Yes.

9251. And 13*s.* 7*d.* was arrears?—Yes.

9252. Would there be anything to pay besides those two sums?—No, I am not aware that there was.

9253. What did you tell him?—I told him that I should not pay him anything while he brought me back the nuts, so he went away.

9254. Then, in fact, you paid nothing at that time?—No.

9255. How did he go; did he go away pleasantly?—He went away pleasantly.

9256. He did not say anything uncivil, did he?—No, not that day.

9257. When did you see Broadhead next?—I worked that week following again, then he came again on Monday as usual.

9258. And I suppose he asked you what you had earned that week?—Yes.

9259. How much was it?—It was 6*l.* 0*s.* 8*d.*

9260. Was your contribution on that 2*s.* 6*d.* in the pound?—Yes.

9261. That would be something over 15*s.*?—Yes.

9262. Did he ask you anything?—He asked me what I was going to pay.

9263. What did you say?—I told him that I should not bring him anything till he brought back the nuts.

9264. What did he say to that?—He said that I was both a fool and a rogue; I told him I was not as big a rogue as he was.

9265. What then?—He was for fighting then.

9266. What did you do?—I ordered him away about his business; I told him to come again when I sent for him.

9267. What did you do?—I began to think that they would come and fetch the bands, and I began to roll them up that night and put them in a box and lock them up. On the Thursday morning following, when I got down to my work, I found somebody had broken the box open and taken the bands.

9268. Had you left the box locked on Wednesday night?—Yes.

9269. And your bands were gone?—Yes.

9270. What did you do when you missed your bands?—I got some more bands; we had two old bands that we had thrown off, and I put these old bands back and went on working again.

9271. Did you tell anybody what had happened?—Yes.

9272. Whom did you tell?—I sent a word down to Mr. Naylor.

9273. You were working for him then?—Yes.

9274. What did Mr. Naylor do?—He said he was very angry.

9275. Did anybody come to watch the wheel?—Yes, Mr. Naylor then went down to Mr. Jackson, I believe.

9276. I believe, in fact, some one came to watch the wheel?—Yes, I came to watch the wheel.

9277. Was not a constable set to watch the wheel?—Yes.

9278. (*Chairman.*) Were you and the constable together?—No, when the constable came on I went off.

9279. Now we will go to the Saturday night following; while you were watching that night did anything happen?—There were three men came.

9280. (*Mr. Barstow.*) What time was this?—It would be about 10 o'clock; and they got put off by me.

9281. (*Chairman.*) They saw you?—I think so; they ran away.

9282. (*Mr. Barstow.*) Did they leave anything behind them?—I found a spanner, with which I expect they were going to unscrew the stones.

9283. Was it a spanner with which they could unscrew the stones?—Yes, it just fitted the stone-end nuts.

9284. It would be a very large instrument?—Yes.

9285. (*Chairman.*) There was no work going on at this time?—No.

9286. Nobody had any business there at that time at night?—No, all were away; there was no one, I believe, there except Mr. Davenport.

9287. (*Mr. Barstow.*) What did you do with the spanner?—I took it away.

9288. Where is it?—I have it now.

9289. Did you give any information of this to any one?—I went down to our master and told him.

9290. That was Naylor?—Yes, I went on Monday.

9291. What did he say to you?—He said I had better go and settle it; he said we should be having tools broken up.

9292. Did you go and settle?—No, I told him I would not go an inch towards it.

9293. What occurred upon that?—He said he could go himself.

9294. Do you know whether he did go?—Yes, he asked me to call at his warehouse the morning after, and I did so.

9295. What happened there?—I saw him the morning after, and he told me that he had been to Broadhead's and seen Mr. Broadhead, and he said that I had 2*l.* to pay to get back the bands and nuts; I told him I should not pay 2*l.* at first.

9296. But did you in consequence of this conversation see Broadhead?—Yes, I considered in the course of an hour that I would go and settle it.

9297. Where did you go?—I went to Mr. Broadhead's.

9298. Is that the "Royal George" in Carver Street?—Yes.

9299. Did you see Broadhead?—Yes.

9300. Did you speak first or did he?—No, he spoke first.

9301. What did he say to you?—He said, "Now "then, my lad, hast thou come to settle it?"

9302. What did you say?—I said, "I do not know "yet, we will see about it."

9303. What did Broadhead say to that?—I said, "What shall I have to pay to get back the things?"

9304. What did he say?—He says, "Your master "has told you, has not he?"

9305. What did you say to that?—He said, "He "was here last night."

9306. Did you in fact pay the 2*l.* to Broadhead?—Yes.

9307. When you had paid it did you ask for the nuts?—Before I paid the 2*l.* I asked him if he would give me a receipt for 2*l.*; he said, "No, that was "quite out of reason," but he would guarantee that I should have the things back.

9308. What did you say; had you any more conversation with him?—I asked him if I were to pay him the 2*l.* whether I would be the same as I had been before; whether I should be used well in a meeting.

9309. Had you ever been ill-used at any meeting?—At one meeting after that.

9310. Was anything more said about your being well received at the meetings?—Yes, he told me that I was to come to the meetings as usual, it would be all settled and I should never hear anything more about it.

9311. Can you give us his exact words?—I think, as near as I can remember, that is what he said. I was to come to the meetings as I had been used to do, and there should be never anything more said about it.

9312. Next day did you receive a letter?—Yes, Mr. Davenport brought me a letter in.

9313. Is that the letter (*showing a paper to witness.*)?—That is as much of it as can be found.

9314. "You will find your nuts in the hen-roost, "where you settled your grievances. (Signed) Mary. "Mary thought you would not like to fetch them." What did you do upon receiving that note?—I set off to fetch them.

9315. Where did you go to fetch them?—To Broadhead's house.

9316. By yourself?—No.

9317. Did anybody go with you?—Yes.

9318. Who was that?—A man named Thomas Weaver.

9319. Did you see Broadhead?—When we got to

TENTH DAY.

Isaac Taylor.

17 June 1867.

the door, Thomas Weaver would not go in; he said he would wait outside, he did not like to go in.

9320. You went in, I suppose?—Yes.

9321. Did you see Broadhead?—Yes, he was getting his breakfast in the kitchen.

9322. Which of you spoke first?—Broadhead spoke first; he said, "Good morning," and I said "Good "morning." He says, "Hast thou got back thy "things yet?" I said "No." I said, "You have "got them in your hen-roost."

9323. Had anyone told you that they were in the hen-roost?—No one, only the letter.

9324. What did he say?—He says, "Come on then, we will go and look for them."

9325. Did you go with him?—Yes, I went with him, we went up to the top of the yard.

9326. Describe what happened to you?—He opened the door.

9327. The door of what?—It was a sort of standing for a horse, and there was a lot of straw all round. I says, "Where are they?" as soon as we got in; and he lifts up some straw, and brings some nuts out. He says, "Here are the nuts." I says, "Where are "the bands?" He says, "You must look round the "place for them." I began turning the straw over, and when I got up towards the top end, there were two hens sitting; he says, "Do not go there, they are not there."

9328. You found your bands, I believe?—He says, "Thou must go up on the top here."

9329. On the top of what?—It was a sort of chamber, but the boards had been pulled up, and there was nothing but the baulks to walk on over another stable.

9330. Before you went to this chamber had you seen some bands?—No, not before we went into this chamber.

9331. You say that the boards were up?—Yes.

9332. Did you go along the baulks?—Yes, to the far end.

9333. What did you see at the far end?—There was a sort of joiner's bench at the far end, there were some grinding bands on this bench.

9334. I suppose you looked for yours amongst them?—Yes; we had one band marked "Naylor," the other band was not marked at all.

9335. How many grinding bands were there on this bench?—Something like five or six bands.

9336. You wanted two?—Yes; he shouted out and asked me if I had found them.

9337. Broadhead was below stairs, was he?—Yes: I told him I had found some bands, and I told him I could not pick ours out of them. I asked him to lend me a light.

9338. Did he bring one?—No; he told me to come down and he would let me have the bands in the afternoon.

9339. Did you get your bands in the afternoon?—Yes; they flung them over out of Peace's wheel yard into Davenport's yard.

9340. Davenport's yard was where you were working?—Yes; it was not the same yard I was working at. Mr. Davenport had two wheels, one each side of the street.

9341. They were in Davenport's wheel, but not the wheel that you were working at?—Yes.

9342. They were the very bands that you missed?—Yes.

9343. Can you say how they happened to be found there?—There was a little boy comes to me about 4 o'clock in the afternoon; he says, "Have you "found your bands master?" I said "No." He says "There are two bands flung over into Daven- "port's yard, the other side, you are to go directly."

9344. Do you know the boy?—No, I cannot say that I do; it was some boy that had been sent in.

9345. Sent in from Davenport's?—Yes. I did not know the boy at that time.

9346. Sometime after that you went to a general meeting at Broadhead's?—Yes.

9347. Was it the next general meeting?—Yes; a fortnight after that.

9348. What took place there?—I went upstairs and as soon as they called my name over I went downstairs.

9349. Was the committee sitting downstairs, or how was it?—No, I went down to get a glass of beer.

9350. The meeting was upstairs, was it?—Yes.

9351. I understand that as soon as your name was called over you were released from attendance?—Yes; I sat downstairs till about half-past 4—about an hour and a half I was down. I was fetched upstairs by a man of the name of William Barker. He told me that my case was coming off.

9352. Did you know anything about the case that was coming off?—No; I did not know that I had a case. He says, "Come on with me upstairs," so I went up with him.

9353. Then you went upstairs, and whom did you see there?—When I went upstairs the room was quite full—the door was shut after me as soon as I got in.

9354. Were there men standing keeping the door? Yes, I believe there were.

9355. Were the meeting sitting or standing, or how was it?—I went up about the middle of the room, getting to where Mr. Broadhead was sitting at one side, at a desk. He asked me what I had got to say for myself. I got up to explain how it was about these two notes getting to John Wilson—it was these two notes that had got to John Wilson.

9356. The notes that we have read?—Yes, he had exposed them in the newspaper.

9357. (*Chairman.*) John Wilson?—John Wilson.

9358. Who was that—John Wilson, who works for Messrs. Joseph Rodgers and Sons?—Yes.

9359. Were these the two notes which had been put in the paper by John Wilson?—Yes.

9360. (*Mr. Barstow.*) That was your case, I suppose?—Yes; I got up to explain it, and they told me if I did not sit down they would knock me down.

9361. Then they asked you to explain and would not hear your explanation?—No, they would not.

9362. Who said so?—I turned round to a man of the name of William Barker that just stood behind me. I cannot say whether it was him or not, but it sounded like his voice. I spoke to him and told him he could do so as soon as he liked.

9363. Was it Barker who fetched you upstairs?—Yes.

9364. Can you tell me who was in the chair at the meeting?—John Skelton.

9365. What did Barker say?—Barker never said anything to me after I spoke to him. Broadhead got on his legs then, and he said that I was the biggest scamp that there was in the trade.

9366. What occurred next?—John Skelton declined being in the chair any longer, and the meeting got in an uproar.

9367. What made him decline being in the chair any longer?—He could not keep order.

9368. What was done then?—They got another chairman.

9369. Who was it—do you remember?—I cannot exactly say who it was. I got up then as soon as they silenced them, and I told him that I had paid the money they charged me to pay, and I expected all was settled.

9370. Did any one answer you?—They hooted me and shouted at me, and told me they could do without me. I said I should go out of the meeting and never come in any more.

9371. Did you leave the room?—Yes, I left the room and went home.

9372. That was not quite all, was it?—I left the room and went downstairs.

9373. What was the consequence of your leaving the room?—They fined me 5*s*.

9374. For what?—For leaving the room.

9375. Have you paid it?—No, I did not; they put me this on after.

9376. You have never paid it?—No.

9377. You went on paying for some time?—I went down next morning to Mr. Naylor and told him what took place at the meeting, and I told him I should not go near any more meetings; and I told him we had better go somewhere where we could be safe. He asked me where we were to go.

9378. And where did you go?—I told him we could go down to Butcher's.

9379. You went to Mr. Butcher's wheel?—Yes; he advised me to go and pay.

9380. Did you pay after you went to Mr. Butcher's wheel?—Yes.

9381. You had a man named Gleddow working for you?—Yes, after I went down to Mr. Butcher's wheel I had a man that came to work with me, named Stephen Gleddow.

9382. Did you see Broadhead?—Yes, he had been working with us for a week, and Broadhead came down on Monday for my contribution, which he did every week.

9383. What did he say to you?—He asked me what we had earned, and I told him, and we paid him.

9384. You paid him the contribution?—Yes.

9385. Then did he ask anything more of you?—Yes, he turned round and said he wanted 30*s*. more of me.

9386. What was that for?—I asked him what it was for, and he said for fines, for not attending the general meeting. I told him I should not pay it.

9387. What did he say to you then?—He said, "Won't thou"?—I said, "No I shall not." Then he says, "I shall stop this man of thine."

9388. Did he stop the man?—I said, "You can stop him as soon as you like."

9389. Did he stop him?—Yes. I said he could stop him as soon as he liked.

9390. (*Chairman.*) He took him away?—Yes, he took him away there and then.

9391. (*Mr. Barstow.*) Did he ever come back to you?—He never came back to work; he came back the week following; I had to begin to do his work myself.

9392. Gleddow came back the week after?—He came back the week after for a waistcoat and smock that he had left that he worked in.

9393. He went away with Broadhead on the spot? Yes.

9394. He came for his things? — Yes, and he asked me how it was I was doing his work. I told him I was forced to do it. He said it was not right that I should do his work. I said, "If you come back "you shall have your work back." He says, "I shall "not come back till you have paid this money to "Broadhead."

9395. Was that all that he said?—I says, "You "will not come back yet then?" and he says, "Yes, "you will go on until you get your head knocked off." I asked him if he could knock it off, and he said, "No," but he said there would be a party who would either knock it off or blow it off some night when I was going home.

9396. What did you do upon that?—I told him that he was to go out and not to come in any more. I said, "If anybody harms me, or anybody belonging "to me, I will blow Broadhead's brains out."

9397. Did you say anything more?—He said that I had better mind what I said, for he would go and tell him. I told him he could do as soon as he liked; and he went out.

9398. Did you show him anything?—Yes, I pulled a pistol out of my pocket at the time. I told him I was ready to defend myself.

9399. Had you really bought that pistol to defend yourself?—No, I had not bought it then, I had bought it some time; I always kept a double-barrelled gun loaded at home.

9400. Was that for protection?—Yes.

9401. Did you always carry a pistol about with you?—I did at that time, for I expected being shot at.

9402. What made you expect that you would be shot at?—Because they had used these threats.

9403. People use threats of that sort without carrying them into execution?—Yes, of course.

9404. Do you mean seriously to say that you were afraid of being shot at?—I only said it to this man; he told me that I should either have my head knocked off or blown off, and I was frightened; I felt very much frightened after I spoke it; I put my coat on after he went out of the hull and followed him at a distance to see whether he went to Broadhead's house. I saw he did go; I thought very likely Mr. Broadhead would have me up about it, but it did pass off and I never heard anything more about it.

9405. I ask you if after that time you carried a pistol about with you?—No, not after that time. I always kept a double-barrelled gun loaded at home at night.

9406. You ceased after that to contribute to the union?—Yes.

9407. You have not been a member ever since that?—No.

9408. You have not been molested since?—No.

9409. Have you ever been asked to go and join the union?—Yes.

9410. By whom was that?—I believe it was by a man named Thomas Green and Mr. Fearnehough. I cannot say so to be certain, but I think it was; one was Green.

9411. You have never joined it?—No.

9412. Just carry your mind back as early as 1862; do you remember somebody else coming to you with Mr. Broadhead?—Yes.

9413. Who was that?—A man named William Hides.

9414. Who is he?—Secretary to the saw makers.

9415. That was at Davenport's wheel?—Yes.

9416. What did they want with you?—They came in and asked me if I would go and have a sup of beer with them at the public house. I asked them what they wanted me for, and they said that they should not want me long.

9417. Did they say anything about anyone in your master's employment?—Yes.

9418. What did they say about that?—When we got to the public house they said my master had got a man that did not join the union.

9419. (*Chairman.*) Who was your master then?—Mr. Naylor. I asked them who he was, and they told me. I said, "Cannot you take him into the trade?" They said no, they would neither have him in the trade nor out.

9420. (*Mr. Barstow.*) Did they give any reason?—They said he did not belong to the trade; he was an Irishman.

9421. Did they wish you to do anything about him?—They asked me to go down and see Mr. Naylor there and then, and they told me they would call and see me in the morning to see how I had gone on.

9422. Did you see Mr. Naylor?—Yes, I saw Mr. Naylor.

9423. Did you report to him what they had said?—Yes, I told him what I had come about.

9424. What did he say?—He said he should not get "shut" of the man.

9425. Did they come to you the next morning?—Yes, they came to me the next morning, and asked me how I had gone on. I told them; so Broadhead said there would have to be something done, and Hides said before there was anything done they would see me again.

9426. Did they see you again?—I went down the Saturday after to Broadhead's house, and he asked me to sit down.

9427. You did not see Hides again after that, did

TENTH DAY.

Isaac Taylor.

17 June 1867.

you ?—No; and when the room was at liberty he asked me to close the door.

9428. You and Broadhead were at this time alone in the room, were you ?—Yes.

9429. Did you close the door ?—Yes. He asked me if I could do a little job for him.

9430. What was the job ?—I asked him what it was. He said he wanted me to roll our bands up.

9431. Whose bands ?—My bands.

9432. Your own bands ?—Yes ; and put them away where nobody could find them.

9433. (*Chairman.*) Did the bands belong to Mr. Naylor ?—Yes.

9434. (*Mr. Barstow.*) Did he say anything more at the time ?—He said he would pay me well for it.

9435. What did you say ?—I told him I would consider about it. "Well," he says, "the sooner the better." So between that and Monday morning I considered I would not have anything to do with it. So the Saturday following I goes again. He says, "Thou hast not done that little job yet." I said, "No, and I am not bound to do it." He says, "How is that ?" I says, "You must do it yourself."

9436. What did he say to that ?—He turned quite sour, and I turned out of the room and left him.

9437. Were the bands ever taken ?—No, a week after that I had a man that was working for me of the name of Alfred Broadhead ; he was uncle to Mr. Broadhead. He told me that some one had asked him to take our bands.

9438. What is the largest sum which you ever paid in weekly contributions ?—3*s.* 4*d.*, I believe.

9439. Is that the largest sum that you have ever paid ?—Yes.

9440. That is the largest poundage ?—Yes.

9441. How much is the largest sum that you have paid on a Saturday altogether ? What are your largest earnings ?—I cannot say. I have been looking for my natty book, but I could not find it.

9442. Can you give us a notion of the largest sum that you have ever paid ?—I have paid 10*s.*

9443. You must have paid as much as 15*s.* ?—Yes.

9444. Do you think that you ever paid as much as 1*l.* ?—I cannot say.

9445. Have you ever paid as much as between 15*s.* and 1*l.* ?—I might have done, but I cannot be sure.

9446. Can you tell us what you think your average payment has been ?—No, I could not. At my place of work sometimes we had little and sometimes more. Sometimes I had a good week and sometimes a bad week.

9447. You could not say what the average was ?—No.

9448. Have you ever been receiving scale ?—When I was working ?

9449. When you were not working ?—Yes, I had once seven weeks scale when I was out of a situation

9450. How much did they allow you a week ?—I had 16*s.* a week at that time—me and my wife and three children.

9451. Was that the only time ?—I believe I had been on once before.

9452. For how long was it ?—It is a long time since that.

9453. For how long were you on the box ?—I cannot say how long I was on.

9454. (*Chairman.*) About how long were you on the first time ?—I might be on 11 or 12 weeks that time—that is many years since.

9455. (*Mr. Barstow.*) What did you get then ?—We should have the same number then I believe.

9456. Were you married the first time when you received scale ?—Yes.

9457. (*Chairman.*) And you got about 16*s.* then ?—Yes.

9458. (*Mr. Barstow.*) Do you remember any other time ?—No, only in 1849, when the strike took place.

9459. What did you get then ?—Only 5*s.* a week.

9460. For how long was that ?—I was on for 13 or 14 weeks.

9461. Those are the only times that you have been on the box ?—Yes.

9462. Have you ever calculated how much you have paid altogether ?—No.

9463. How long have you contributed, from 1849 to 1862 ?—Yes.

9464. You have contributed 13 years ?—Yes.

Mr. Sugg submitted that the Commissioners had no power to go into the question of contributions which had been paid prior to the ten years over which this inquiry extended.

The Commissioners overruled the objection.

9465. (*Chairman to the witness.*) Can you tell us the average of your contributions for that time—how much on the average have you contributed ?—I cannot say.

9466. (*Mr. Barstow.*) There is a question which I omitted to ask you. In 1862, when Broadhead asked you to take your own bands, what reason did he give for taking them ?—He said I might as well have the job as anyone else.

9467. What reason did he give to you ?—It was on account of Mr. Naylor not turning this man away.

9468. Did he say so at the time ?—Yes.

9469. Do you recollect what he said ?—He said, "Your master has not turned this man away yet." I said "No."

9470. (*Chairman.*) And the bands belong to Mr. Naylor ?—Yes.

The witness withdrew.

Mr. G. Naylor.

Mr. George Naylor sworn and examined.

9471. (*Mr. Chance.*) Do you carry on a saw manufactory at Victoria Park, Clarkhouse Road ?—That is my residence.

9472. You carry on your business in Arundel Lane ?—Yes.

9473. Under the name of George Naylor and Company ?—Yes.

9474. How long have you carried on your business there ?—Since Christmas.

9475. Where were you carrying on your business in 1861 ?—In Porter Street.

9476. Was Isaac Taylor at that time in your employ ?—Yes.

9477. Had he been in your employ for some time ?—About nine years.

9478. Do you remember his nuts, and also his bands being taken in the year 1862 ?—Yes.

9479. Were the nuts and bands your property ?—Yes, they were my property.

9480. And he was working upon them ?—He was working upon them.

9481. Upon their being taken did you supply him with a fresh set of bands ?—Yes.

9482. Do you remember what he did with them every night ?—The second set of bands he brought down to our warehouse every night.

9483. For what purpose was that ?—For safety.

9484. To prevent them being taken ?—To prevent them being taken ; he had had the others taken.

9485. Did he tell you of an attempt that was made to take them again, or to do any injury to them ?—Yes, he told me.

9486. Of the attempt that had been made ?—Of the attempt that had been made.

9487. What was that attempt ?—One evening he had been watching the premises, and he told me that he had seen some one enter the premises.

9488. Nothing was done then ? that attempt was not carried out ?—The attempt was not carried out.

9489. Upon that attempt did you give him any advice ?—Yes.

9490. What did you tell him to do ?—I told him he

had better have the matter settled with the trade, and he objected to it.

9491. Did you tell him how he had better have the matter settled ?—I told him he had better have the matter settled with the trade by going to the secretary.

9492. Who was the secretary ?—Broadhead.

9493. Then he said something ?—He said he would not do it. We were busy at the time.

9494. Why did you tell him that ?—We were busy at the time, and afraid of being hindered in our work.

9495. When you say you were afraid of being hindered, in what way were you afraid ?—By some fresh attack upon us.

9496. Upon Taylor refusing to go to Broadhead, what did you do ?—I told him I would go, and I went. I saw Broadhead at his own house, the "Royal George."

9497. Did you go by yourself ?—Yes.

9498. Whad did you say to him ?—I told him I had come to ask why the nuts and bands had been taken ; he said he did not know. I said, "Well, of course "not, but at any rate you will, perhaps, tell me what "the cost will be to have them brought back." He appeared to consider a little, and said he did not know, but somewhere about 2*l.* he thought. I said "very "well," and left him.

9499. Did he appear to be ignorant of the transaction ?—Yes, he did appear to be ignorant of it.

9500. Then you left him ?—I left him.

9501. Upon going back again, did you advise Taylor to do anything ?—The following morning Taylor called upon me at the warehouse, and I told him he had better see Broadhead, and try to settle the matter.

9502. What did he say to that ?—After a little conversation he consented to see Broadhead.

9503. Do you know whether he went to Broadhead ? —I found he had been to Broadhead.

9504. After that, did he get back the nuts and the bands ?—He got back the nuts and the bands sometime after.

9505. After that did you have any other communication with Broadhead ?—Not to my knowledge.

9506. Did you afterwards remove from the premises where you then were to other premises ?—Yes.

9507. Where did you go to ?—To Mr. Butcher's wheel.

9508. What was the reason of your going there ?— It was more secure from attacks of a similar kind.

9509. Why could you be more secure there than where you were before ?—The premises were watched both day and night.

9510. (*Chairman.*) Had they closed doors besides ? —Yes.

9511. It is a covered archway ?—Yes.

9512. (*Mr Chance.*) Since you have been at these premises, have you been free from these attacks ?— We have had none since.

9513. What do you pay for the power which you rent at Mr. Butcher's wheel ?—About 84*l.* or 85*l.* for power.

9514. How much did you pay at Davenport's where you were before ?—I do not remember, but somewhere about 50*l.*

9515. (*Chairman.*) For the same amount of power ? —The same amount of power.

9516. (*Mr. Chance.*) Was the sole reason of your leaving Davenport's and going to Butcher's that you might be safe from damage ?—Yes.

9517. Was that the only reason ?—It was the only reason.

9518. Could you find premises of a much less rent than what you pay at Butcher's if it were not for that fear ?—Yes.

9519. (*Chairman.*) Even less than what you paid at Davenport's ?—Yes.

9520. In the country ?—Yes, in the country.

9521. (*Mr. Chance.*) At what rent would you be able to obtain power at some other place further in the country; were you able to remove there ?—A neighbour of mine is having the same amount of power for 35*l.* in the country.

9522. (*Chairman.*) The same amount of power for which you pay 85*l.* ?—Yes.

2523. (*Mr. Chance.*) Would not there be the expense of carriage to be considered in paying rent in the country ?—Yes, there would.

9524. Does the figure that you give us, the 35*l.*, include the expense of carriage ?—No ; I wish to say that the carriage is managed for about 8*l.* or 10*l.*

9525. Including the cost of carriage, it would be somewhere about 45*l.* that you would have to pay instead of the 85*l.* that you are paying at Butcher's ? —Yes.

9526. The only reason you do not go into the country is the fear of damage to your machinery ?— Yes.

9527. Do you remember having a workman, an Irishman ?—Yes.

9528. What was his name ?—Tom Weaver.

9529. Was any objection made to his working ?— There was some objection, but not a very strong objection, from the saw makers.

9530. (*Chairman.*) Not the saw grinders but the saw-makers ?—The saw makers.

9531. (*Mr. Chance.*) Who made the objection ?— We did not hear it from our own men, but from the secretary.

9532. The secretary of the saw makers ?—Yes.

9533. Who is that ?—William Hides.

9534. Did you hear it from the secretary himself ? —No.

9535. How was it communicated to you ?—He sent a slip of paper into our warehouse by one of our men.

9536. What was the name of your man ?—Robert Carlton, saw-handle maker.

9537. Was it delivered to you ?—It was delivered to me.

9538. Do you remember what the contents of that paper were ?—Not the exact contents.

9539. Then the substance of it ?—It requested that a deputation might see me respecting Tom Weaver.

9540. Was that signed by the secretary ?—I do not remember whom it was signed by.

9541. Have you the paper, or is it lost ?—I tore it in two and gave it the man back, and told him to take it back to the person who gave it him.

9542. You refused to accede to his requst ?—Yes.

9543. Did you ever suffer any inconvenience from the course you took ?—Not that I remember at present, excepting through the grinding. The saw makers did not take any further steps.

9544. Were any steps taken by the saw grinders or any other body ?—No, not to my knowledge, only what I heard from Isaac Taylor.

9545. (*Chairman.*) Did you hear from Taylor shortly after this ?—Yes.

9546. What did he tell you ?—It is a long while ago. I do not remember the exact time, but it was some time after the thing occurred, he told me that Broadhead had asked him to roll up his own bands.

9547. (*Mr. Chance.*) Did he tell you the reason why Broadhead had asked him to do so ?—Yes.

9548. What did he say was the reason ?—That Tom Weaver was objectionable to the union and he wished me to turn him away.

9549. Did he give you any further particulars ?— No ; he did not that I remember.

9550. You did not turn Weaver away ?—I did not turn him away. I said that he had worked for me something like six years, and worked to the trade a number of years before somewhere else, and I did not see that I should turn him away.

9551. He was not a member of the union, I believe ? —He was not, but he agreed to become a member of the union and pay what they required to pay if they would take him in.

TENTH DAY.

Mr. G. Naylor.

17 June 1867.

9552. And they refused?—They refused.

9553. Have you anything further to tell us?—Not of any great importance.

9554. Have you ever lost any bands or nuts on other occasions?—Yes; before the ten years.

9555. But since the ten years have you?—Not since the ten years.

The witness withdrew.

Isaac Taylor.

ISAAC TAYLOR re-called and further examined.

9556. (*Chairman.*) Do you know Mr. Broadhead's handwriting?—Yes.

9557. You say that you received two notes?—Yes.

9558. Have you seen Broadhead write?—Yes.

9559. Is it your belief that either of those notes is in Broadhead's handwriting?—Yes, the first note is.

9560. Do you mean the one commencing "Do thy "own work?"—Yes.

9561. That is the one that was found on the horsing?—Yes.

9562. You believe that that one, which was found on the horsing, was in Mr. Broadhead's handwriting?—Yes.

9563. How often have you seen him write?—I have seen him write very often.

9564. Just look at it again—are you quite sure about it—that is the document (*handing the same to the witness*)?—Yes.

9565. According to your belief, having seen him write, is that his writing?—According to my belief it is his writing.

9566. You do not know the writing of the other?—No; I cannot say about the other.

9567. Do you know whose writing the other is?—No, I do not; it might be Mr. Broadhead's. He can write in three or four different ways.

9568. Have you seen him write in three or four different ways?—I have seen different ways that he has wrote.

9569. Have you ever seen him write them? how did it occur that you have seen him write in different ways?—I have had notes from him before, that have been just the same as that first note.

9570. When?—At different times I have done work for him.

9571. Were those notes which you have received before anonymous notes, or notes with his signature to them?—They were such like notes as those.

9572. You have received similar notes to these?—Yes.

9573. How do you know that they were written by him?—He was the man that we always had to apply to, and then we could get back the things.

9574. Have you ever shewn him one of these notes?—Yes.

9575. And have you spoken to him about them?—Yes.

9576. What note have you shown to Mr. Broadhead?—When I had my bands back a long time since.

9577. And you got a note written like this?—Yes.

9578. And you then went to Mr. Broadhead with the note?—Yes; I went to Mr. Broadhead.

9579. What did you say to Broadhead about it?—I asked him what I should have to pay to get the bands back. I was working at the Castle wheel at that time.

9580. What did he say?—He told me that he would let me know bye-and-bye.

9581. Did you ever ask him if it was his handwriting or anything of that sort?—I never asked whether it was his handwriting.

9582. What reason have you for saying that he had written it?—I have seen him write similar to it.

9583. What kind of thing was he writing then?—On account of setting work down. I have done work for him.

9584. Is this his common ordinary hand, or a disguised hand?—I cannot say; he can write three or four different ways.

9585. Have you seen him do it?—I have, at different times.

9586. You say that on one occasion Mr. Broadhead offered to fight?—Yes.

9587. Was any person present when he offered to fight?—Yes; there was always plenty of people in the same hull that I worked in, and the boy I had apprenticed was with me.

9588. Was anybody else present at the time that he offered to fight you?—There would be more but I cannot recall them by name.

9589. Are you quite sure that your boy was present?—Yes; very likely he would deny it now, he is turned of age now.

9590. This boy is loose now, and you say that he would deny it now?—Yes.

9591. Why?—Because they have got him over t'other side.

9592. Am I right in this, that I heard you say that you had seen Mr. Broadhead write notes in this very hand, the same as in the first note?—I have seen him write similar to that.

9593. What was it that you saw him write?—Not notes for these jobs, but different work. I have done work for him.

9594. And it is for doing work—that is, bills of account?—Yes.

9595. You have seen him write in that style?—Yes.

9596. And you believe that that note is in his handwriting?—Yes, the first note.

9597. What do you mean by "bills of work done?"—I have done work for him that belonged to the trades tools on to our master's tools, and I have gone to him on Saturday night on one or two occasions and told him what I had done, and he has wrote it down, and given me a bill of it what it was, and then he has paid me the money, and then he has taken back the bill. He put it down on a bit of paper.

9598. It was charging you for the amount that you had to pay for the trades tools which you have used?—Yes; I had to pay to the master.

9599. On what occasion has he done that?—At two or three different times.

9600. Mr. Sugg wants to know this—you say that he has written in two or three different hands—there is one hand, the common ordinary hand, and the other hand you say is like this,—now there is a third hand, what is that like?—The contribution book will show the different hands; that is not the book I allude to (*referring to the book shown by Mr. Broadhead*); it is what we call the natty book, every member is supplied with one of these books in a tin case.

9601. Just look at that (*handing a book to the witness*), whose handwriting is that?—Very likely it might be Broadhead's.

9602. That is Broadhead's?—Very likely.

9603. Is that his ordinary hand, or a different hand; is that the common hand that he writes?—Yes, that would be one of them.

9604. There is one that is his ordinary handwriting?—Yes.

9650. He is a man who has an ordinary style?—Yes.

9606. Then you say that there is another style which you have seen him write when he has made out his account to you, which is the same as this first letter?—Yes.

9607. That is No. 2?—Yes.

9608. Then there is No. 3; how does No. 3 differ from Nos. 1 and 2?—I have seen him write a smaller hand even than that.

9609. Here is the book partly kept by Mr. Broadhead, can you point out the two different hands to which you allude (*handing the book to the witness*). It is partly kept by Mr. Broadhead and partly by a stranger, but a great deal of it is written by Mr. Broadhead; can you there find out the two or three different kinds of writing to which you allude?—It seems to me to be all one writing.

9610. You do not find any of the third hand that we have talked of?—No.

9611. You say that he has written this writing to which you refer when he has been entering up the amount which you had to pay for tools which belonged to the union?—Yes.

9612. And that after he has written it and showed it to you he has has taken it away from you; you never kept it?—No, he just scribbled it down the same as that is scribbled.

9613. (*Mr. Chance.*) In your opinion is that written in the same hand as this?—No, it is a different writing.

9614. In your opinion, is this written by the same man, Mr. Broadhead, who wrote this?—Yes, of course; I should say so.

9615. Look at this; is that the third hand which you have seen him write (*handing a book to the witness*)?—Yes, I have seen that writing.

9616. Have you ever seen Mr. Broadhead write like that?—Yes.

9617. And you believe that to be his handwriting?—It may be.

9618. It may be, of course, just look at it?—I have seen him write similar to that.

9619. (*Chairman.*) Can you tell us, from your knowledge of his handwriting, whether that which is written in that book is the handwriting of Mr. Broadhead or not?—I should not like to swear.

9620. What is your belief of it?—I should say it would be.

9621. Why should you say so, from your knowledge of his writing, or because it happens to be his book?—I have not joined the trade so long but what I have seen him write a long time. I have seen him write in different ways when he has come round gathering the contribution.

9622. What is your belief as to it, is it written by him or not?—I should say it is.

9623. Were those names written by Mr. Broadhead (*handing a book to the witness*)?—I should think so.

9624. Do you mean to say that both of those are in his handwriting?—Yes.

9625. They are perfectly different hands?—This would be Broadhead's writing.

9626. You were asked whether they were written by the same person; it is quite clear that they cannot be written by the same person?—It is very hard for me to say.

9627. Can you write yourself?—Yes, I am not a very good writer, but I can write. I could only write one hand.

9628. You have been pressed about this, and it is a very serious thing. Supposing this kind of anonymous letter were sent (which is a disgraceful thing to do), are you still of opinion that that letter is in the handwriting of Mr. Broadhead?—I always believed that the first letter, which was left on the horsing, was written by Mr. Broadhead.

9629. And you still adhere to that?—Yes, I always believed so. I cannot give any reasons but one.

9630. What is the one reason?—Because I have had notes before wrote the same way.

9631. You are quite sure of that?—Yes.

9632. It is not because he happens to be the secretary and was likely to have written it, but because you believe that it is his handwriting?—Yes, I have seen his handwriting.

9633. Have you any notes in a similar handwriting to that note which you have produced to day?—I have not by me. I had one delivered to me at the time I worked at the Castle wheel, and another when I worked at the Park wheel.

9634. Have you got those?—No; but it was similar writing.

9635. Have not the trades unions tools of their own?—Yes.

9636. The bands of the union are in the possession of the secretary?—I should say they would keep the bands at the wheel.

9637. It is suggested that being secretary, Mr. Broadhead would, no doubt, have bands belonging to the union?—Yes, he might have.

9638. That would explain why the bands were found up in the loft of the hen-roost—is that the place where the secretary would keep his bands?—I should say he would keep his bands at the wheel.

9639. You say "kept at the wheel;" the union have not got a wheel have they?—No, but they rent power.

9640. They rent troughs?—Yes.

9641. You would expect the bands to be kept in one of the troughs in the hulls which they have rented?—Yes.

9642. If they had more bands than they were using what would they do with them?—If they had more than what they were using they might keep them in a store place.

9643. When you went into this chamber and found on the bench a quantity of bands, did not you know as a fact that those bands were the bands belonging to the union?—No, not at all.

9644. Did any of them belong to the union?—I cannot say—some of them belonged to us, but I could not pick them out.

9645. How do you know they were yours if you could not pick them out?—Because Broadhead sent me up there and told me I should find them.

9646. But when you got there you could not find them?—No, it was dark at the far end of the room where the bands were on this bench. One of our bands was marked "Naylor," the other band was not marked, and I was looking for this band that was marked "Naylor." I asked him if he would lend me a light. He says, "No, come thee down, and I will "let thee have thy bands this afternoon."

9647. You told us that nobody had told you that they were in the hen-roost except by letter?—No. Mr. Davenport brought this letter to me in the morning; it came by post to Davenport's place. He brings this letter to me, and he says, "Here, I have "brought you this letter; I think you will make "something of it." He knew about these things going, and we found where they were gone to.

9648. The letter said, "You will find them in the hen-roost at the place where you have settled your grievance?—Yes.

9649. The place where you had settled your grievance was at Mr. Broadhead's?—Yes.

9650. So you went on to the same place where you had settled your grievance, which was the secretary's house?—Yes.

9651. And when you got up, he said, "Come up "to the hen-roost, and you will find them"?—Yes. Mr. Broadhead picked the nuts up himself, and gave them to me. He said, "Are these the nuts?" and I said "Yes."

9652. You say that you were charged 5*s.* for leaving the room; how do you know that?—I knew the quantity of meetings they had charged against me when he said I was 30*s.* in arrear by the fines after I got down to Mr. Butcher's works. I reckoned the meetings up, and they have reckoned that meeting; that was a 5*s.* meeting, and there was a 5*s.* meeting after that, and they have reckoned that in.

TENTH DAY.

Isaac Taylor.

17 June 1867

9653. That was not from any statement that had been made in the room ?—No.

9654. It was not any direct statement which was made that you would be fined for that non-attendance, but in calculating the amount you found that that must have been included ?—Yes. Mr. Broadhead had put me down and charged 5*s.* after I was gone. He called the names over a second time at the meeting when I was gone.

9655. You had a conversation with Gleddow ?—Yes.

9656. And you say that he said that you would have your head knocked off ?—Yes. He said I should go on working while I got my head knocked off.

9657. The question I was asked to put to you is, Was not it a fact that you threatened to knock Gleddow's head off ?—No, I never did so.

9658. Did you threaten to knock Broadhead's head off or blow his brains out ?—The first of it was that Gleddow said I should go on working when he came down to Butcher's works till I got my head knocked off. I asked him whether he could knock my head off. He said, "No," but he said, "You will get "your head knocked off or blown off some night when "you are going home." I said, "You must not come "in here any more."

9659. Did you say that you would knock old Smite'em's or Broadhead's or anybody's head off ?—I said, "If anybody will harm me or harm mine, I "will blow Mr. Broadhead's head off."

9660. Did you say that you would knock his brains out except in that way ?—No.

9661. Is there any pretence for saying that you at all threatened Broadhead ?—No, not besides that.

9662. You merely said that if you were attacked, or any of your family, you would go and blow his brains out ?—I used those expressions; it was in my own defence, I was threatened at the time.

9663. You used them in your own defence ?—Yes.

9664. You say that you were afraid that Mr. Broadhead would have you up; why should Broadhead have you up ?—I thought Gleddow would go and tell him what I had said to him and screen himself.

9665. All that you said was, if you or any of your family got damaged you would blow his brains out ?—Yes.

9666. What was Broadhead to do upon that ?—I was frightened at the time.

9667. What were you frightened that Broadhead would do ?—I was frightened of his fetching me up for saying I would blow his brains out.

9668. That fetching up means taking you before the magistrates ?—Yes.

9669. It seems a very curious thing; you carried a pistol about ?—Yes.

9670. And you were frightened that this man would go to Broadhead and tell him this ? if you were frightened of Broadhead before, surely what you said would make you twice as frightened as you were before? How was it, if you were frightened lest he should tell him, that you carried a pistol down to that time, and that you never carried a pistol after that time ?—I was put out of the books altogether; my name was never mentioned, and there was not anyone who ever spoke to me after this took place. My name was gone and it dropped all at once.

9671. How did you know that ?—It was done.

9672. How do you know ?—Because I never heard it mentioned.

9673. You did not go to the meetings ?—No.

9674. How did you know whether your name was mentioned or not ?—I had seen many saw grinders in the town, and there was none of them that would speak to me.

9675. That did not show a very friendly feeling if they would not speak to you; if you saw this unfriendly feeling how was it that you carried a pistol up to a certain time, and all at once put the pistol by and seemed perfectly secure ?—I only said so in defence, and I found out after that I had frightened some of them.

9676. Is that the only explanation you can give for giving up carrying the pistol ?—Yes.

9677. How long did you carry the pistol about with you ?—When I had to begin watching at Davenport's premises. I was not likely to stop there till half-past 10 at night without something. I had plenty of bottled porter. I had this pistol in my own defence. I got this pistol at that time.

9678. You got the pistol at the time you went to watch at Davenport's ?—Yes.

9679. How long did you watch at Davenport's ?—A fortnight.

9680. How long after you had been watching at Davenport's was this interview of which you have spoken ?—Six months after.

9681-2. Did you carry the pistol for six months from the time that you were watching at Davenport's up to the time of the interview ?—I kept it away from me till Broadhead came down to Butcher's wheel and took the men away, then I put it in my pocket occasionally to defend myself with when I went home of a night.

9683. (*Mr. Chance.*) Did the same charge remain in the pistol all the time you carried it ?—No.

9684. Was it never loaded ?—Sometimes I did load it, and sometimes I did not.

The witness withdrew.

Adjourned to to-morrow at 11 o'clock.

ELEVENTH DAY.

Tuesday, 18th June 1867.

PRESENT:

WILLIAM OVEREND, Esq., Q.C.	GEORGE CHANCE, Esq.
THOMAS IRWIN BARSTOW, Esq.	J. E. BARKER, Esq., Secretary.

WILLIAM OVEREND, Esq., Q.C., IN THE CHAIR.

ELEVENTH DAY.

18 June 1867.

Mr. Chambers stated, in reference to what had taken place on a former occasion between himself and Mr. Sugg, with regard to his having access to the books of the various Unions, that Mr. Sugg had informed him that the Unions refused to allow him (Mr. Chambers) to inspect the books, and that they would only be produced in open Court.

Mr. Sugg stated that he had made the arrangement with Mr. Chambers that the books should be produced in an adjoining room, but that he was instructed this morning that they would be produced in open Court.

The Chairman stated that in that case when the books were produced the Examiners would keep them.

Mr. Sugg stated that steps would be taken to see whether that could be done. He also stated that his clients were willing to produce the books to the Court, but that they were under the apprehension that the opposite party wished to see the state of the finances.

The Chairman pledged the word of the Examiners that no information so obtained should come to the knowledge of anybody except the Examiners themselves; and stated that if it would be a satisfaction to the Unions, the man who looked over the books should be publicly appointed and sworn to keep secret, except to the Examiners, anything that he might find in those books; but that if any impediment was thrown in their way the Examiners must exercise the powers which they possessed.

Mr. Sugg expressed his acquiescence in the course suggested being taken.

Mr. Chambers stated that it had not been his intention to inspect the books personally, but to employ a person to do it.

JOHN HAGUE sworn and examined.

J. Hague.

9685. (*Chairman.*) You live in Earle Street, do you not?—Yes.

9686. You have never been a member of a Union, I believe?—No.

9687. Was your father a shear grinder?—Yes.

9688. And were you brought up to the trade by him?—Yes.

9689. Is there a Shear Grinders Union?—Yes.

9690. What is a shear grinder? What do you grind?—Sheep shears and weaver shears.

9691. Have you been carrying on your business as a shear-grinder?—Sheep shears and edge tools; they are both in one trade.

9692. Is there a separate Union for edge tools?—No; they are both one now; they are joined together. They used to be separate.

9693. There is a Shear Grinding Union then and an Edge-tool Grinding Union then?—Yes.

9694. You say that you were with your father; were you what is called apprenticed to the trade?—No, I never was apprenticed; my father died when I was quite young.

9695. Have you never served an apprenticeship?—I never did. I worked for my mother.

9696. Since you have begun work on your own account have you been at all interfered with by the Union?—Yes.

9697. In what respect?—By different men calling me a "knobstick," and I have tried to join the trade.

9698. You mean men of the Union?—Yes.

9699. You say that you have tried to join the trade?—Yes.

9700. What have you done?—I have been five times to the committee.

9701. Whom have you seen?—I have seen Stacey.

9702. What is he?—He is the secretary, and he told me to come to the meeting, and I went to the meeting, and I waited downstairs till such time as I thought he would call me up to have inquiry into whether I belonged to the trade or not, which he did not do; and when all the men came downstairs they all stood laughing at me, and asked me what I was doing there.

9703. That was on one occasion?—That is one occasion. I have been five times in that way, and I have offered to pay 20*l.* to join that Union, 15*l.* down, and 5*l.* in three months. The last time I went to the meeting I saw Mr. Stacey, and he told me to come to the meeting again. This was the last time of the five.

9704. About how long ago was that?—It is about two years since, I should think. Two or three men came to my house and told me the time that the meeting was, and I was to go, and I went to the meeting again, and I saw those men. I thought I would wait while such time as they had done again. They never called me up again. This was the last time.

9705. How did they know that you were there?—The landlord of the public-house told them that I was there.

9706. You sent him up to tell them?—Yes, I sent him to tell them.

9707. Who was the landlord?—Well, I do not know the name of the man.

9708. Was he an officer of the Union or not?—He belonged to the Union. All the men came downstairs again, and I went upstairs myself. There were about 10 or 12 of the members left, and I went upstairs to Mr. Stacey, and I touched him over the shoulder (this was after the meeting was over), and I said, "You "have not called me upstairs"; and he said, "Oh! "I do not know anything at all about it," turning himself away from me; and I went downstairs then, and I have not been any more, and since that I have worked for a man called Greaves.

9709. Then up to that time, except being called a "knobstick," and so on, you had no interference?—I made a mistake; I worked for Greaves before that I worked for Greaves before I went to the meeting the last time. I engaged with him for six months, and when my six months were done I asked him if he would engage me again, and he said "No," and I asked what was the reason.

ELEVENTH DAY.

J. Hague.

18 June 1867.

9710. But were you at all molested before this last time ?—Not in my tools. They never did anything in any way except calling me a "knobstick."

9711. Have they in any way molested you ?—No.

9712. When you went the last time and Stacey said he had nothing to do with it, what happened to you ? You were engaged for six months ; what about that ?—When my six months was done I asked the man Greaves, that I was engaged for, to engage me again, and he said "No, I could not." I said, "How "is that ?" He said, "I have a reason for that." It was not Stacey, it was the other secretary ; but I do not know the other secretary's name over the sheepshear trade, but he told me.

9713. Was his name Reaney ?—Yes, it was Reaney. He went to my master and asked him for the work, either a week or two weeks after he had been there. I think it was about a week before my time had expired of those six months. I went to the wheel on Monday morning and my tools were all right, and I went on Tuesday morning, and as I was going in at the gate the man that tented the engine shouted to me and said, "Well, old ——, they have done thee at "last ;" and I said, "Well, what have they done" ?

9714. Did you go in and see what they had done ? —Yes, I will tell you. I said, "What have they "done?" and he said, "Come here, and I will shew "you," taking my axle-trees from underneath the boiler, and one by one throwing them down—"Here "they are," he says.

9715. How many axle-trees were there ?—There were 13 glazers.

9716. How many axle-trees ?—Thirteen.

9717. In what state were they when pulled out from under the boiler ?—The woodwork in the pulleys of the axle-trees was burnt, and the axle-trees to.

9718. Were they rendered unfit for use ?—Yes.

9719. Now what happened besides ?—There were 13 glazers.

9720. Where were they ?—They were burnt as well.

9721. What besides ?—Six wheel bands.

9722. What besides ?—Twelve pulleys and one shank stone was broken. Two horses were chopped up to kindle the fire-bed, I suppose. Part of the tools were burnt in the hull, and the other part underneath the boiler. They went up two flights of steps.

9723. Who did ?—The men that burnt them. I worked in the garret, and through another hull.

9724. How do you know all this ?—They are obliged to go through that hull to get to my wheel. They have to go up two flights of steps and through another hull to get to my door. My door was locked with two locks. One was a hang lock and the other was a regular house lock, and they broke both of them, and then started and knocked all the glazers from the axle-trees.

9725. The glazers were burnt, as I understood ?—Yes, but they had knocked them off the axle-trees. you know.

9726. We have had enough of the description of what has been done to you. Now, what was the damage that they did altogether to you ?—It turned out to be 15*l.* I had to stand still a month before I could start working again.

9727. Could you not get those things done at once ? —No.

9728. What did you do when you found those things done ?—I went to my master then.

9729. Who was your master ?—Mr. Greaves. I said, "Now, what is to be done now ?" and he said, "Well, what is the matter ?" I said, "I have got all "my tools burnt." "Well," he said, "I cannot help "that." "Well," I said, "Of course you cannot help "it, nor can I help it. Will you find me any money ?"

9730. Did you afterwards go to Mr. Stacey, the secretary ?—Yes, I did ; I went to the committee room.

9731. Where was it ?—At the bottom of Shambles.

9732. At the "Yellow Lion" ?—Yes, at the "Yel-"low Lion."

9733. Whom did you see there ?—I saw Mr. Stacey there, and a man of the name of Turner, I think.

9734. What did you tell them ?—I asked them if they would allow me to join their Trade.

9735. Did you tell them what had happened to you ? —Yes.

9736. What did they say to that ?—They said they did not know anything at all about it, and that they were very glad I had come ; and they said they would do all they could for me. I left them then, and I have not been to them since.

9737. But did they say whether they had any expectation of getting them or not ?—No, they said they did not know anything at all about it.

9738. Was anything said about your being in the Trade or serving your time, or anything of that kind ? —No. They said they would do what they could to get me in. They said it was not in their power to put me in, but that it was in the power of the general meeting.

9739. Did they say anything about your not getting your things for any reason or other ?—No, they did not. They said they did not know anything at all about it.

9740. Was anything said about their being destroyed at all ?—No. They said they were very sorry, but they did not know anything at all about it.

9741. What more passed then ?—About six or eight months since—

9742. Did you offer to pay any money to go into the Club ?—Yes.

9743. How much did you offer ?—20*l.*

9744. Did they say anything about whether they would let you in for that ?—They would never allow me to go upstairs. They never would give me a hearing.

9745. Is the 20*l.* that you now speak of the 20*l.* that you offered after the tools were burnt ?—Yes. I offered 10*l.* before that, and I offered 20*l.* afterwards ; but this 10*l.* I offered about twelve years' since.

9746. But when did you offer the 20*l.* that you now speak about ?—About two years since.

9747. Was that after your tools were destroyed ?—Yes.

9748. Did you give any information to the police at all ?—No.

9749. Why did you not do that ?—I thought the policeman did not know anything about it.

9750. You attributed it to the Trade ?—Yes.

9751. Since that how do you do your work ? Are you obliged to take your tools home ?—I will tell you how I have had to work. I have had to carry one glazer home at a time.

9752. Where to ?—Home. I have done it for weeks and months, carrying them as I wanted them, for fear they should destroy them.

9753. When you applied to Mr. Stacey did he say that he thought there was no possibility of bringing them back, because you did not belong to the Union ? —He never named them. About two years since I advertised them in the paper. I could not get a hearing of any one at all, but I paid 5*s.* to put them in the paper. The whole Trade—

9754. Did you get anything from them ?—No. That is the advertisement, that piece of paper hanging there (*pointing to the same*).

9755. "To the gentlemen of the Edge-tool and "Sheep-shear Grinding Trades. My father ground "weavers' shears. He died in the year 1830, leaving "five boys and one girl. I worked at the same trade "when a boy, but I had the misfortune in 1841 to be "transported for seven years. I returned in 1848. "I had no trade to fly to, but sheep shears and edge "tools. I have continued at the same up to the pre-"sent time. I am quite willing to join the trade and "pay to it. I think you are not behaving right to me "by you not allowing me a hearing. I have been five "times to the committee by their order, and they have "refused me a hearing. I have a wife and four "children depending on me for support, and one of "the four is capable to work, but is going to school "and does not work. I am willing to work for my "family while the Lord will allow me. I am also

ELEVENTH DAY.

J. Hague.

18 June 1867.

"willing to join you and pay to the trade. Yours "respectfully, JOHN HAGUE." You put this in the paper to show that you were disposed to do everything that you could, but they would not admit you?—No.

9756. Your goods were destroyed?—Yes.

9757. Have you ever been annoyed, or assaulted, or molested?—Well, at every public house I go to they call me "knobstick."

9758. Anything else besides that?—No, I do not know that I can say anything more.

9759. (*Mr. Chance.*) When you wished to become a member of the Union, and tried to become a member, was it because you wished to become a member, or was it from fear of injury?—It was from being afraid of having my tools burnt for one thing, and I would rather join the trade than be off it.

9760. (*Chairman.*) Why?—There was a deal of danger about working.

9761. And that was the reason why you wanted to join the Union?—Yes.

9562. (*Mr. Chance.*) Had you any wish otherwise to join the Union?—No; I wished to do just the same as another man.

9563. If you had been let alone should you have remained a non-Union man?—Yes, because they would not allow me to pay; if they would have allowed me to pay I should have paid, and I am willing to pay now.

9764. (*Chairman.*) There are certain advantages from the Union; if you are out of work you get scale do you not?—I think I never should be out of work.

9765. Then the Union does not offer you temptations in the way of money; it is only on the ground of the protection to your trade is it that you want to join?—Yes, that is all.

9766. Except at the time that your tools were destroyed and you could not work, have you been out of work?—No.

9767. You have always had work?—I have always had work.

9768. And are you a workman of such a character that you can always command work?—I can always get work.

9769. And of as good a paying kind as you would get if you joined the Union?—Every bit.

9770. Now you have nothing to pay to the Union, and you get nothing from it?—No.

9771. What are your earnings a week?—Well, I and my boy can earn from 3*l.* to 4*l.* a week; that is the wage that is down on that paper.

9772. (*Mr. Chance.*) Is the boy that you employ your own son or another boy?—It is my boy, my apprentice lad.

9773. Is he your son?—No, I have a son, but he does not work.

9774. (*Chairman.*) How old is the apprentice?—He is about 15 years old, and going on for 16, I think.

9775. And you have to keep him and find him clothes?—Yes.

9776. Do you give him money?—Yes.

9777. How much do you pay him?—Sometimes 1*s.*, sometimes 1*s.* 6*d.*, and sometimes nothing.

9778. You gave him so much a week?—Yes.

9779. With a gift now and then when the fair time comes?—Yes, 2*s.* 6*d.* or so, or 3*s.* There is another bit of a thing. About six or eight months since I and my wife were going out, and walking through the town and I lit upon a man, and he said, "Old lad, it "was a dammed shame to burn thy tools," and I said, "It was." He said, "I know who did it. Come "you here, and have a pint of ale." So according to that me and my wife went into this public house to have this pint of ale, and I said: "You had better "tell me who burnt them. I am sure I will not say "anything at all about it." He said: "If you and your "wife will come up to my house on Sunday to have "your tea I will tell you who burnt your tools." I said I would and begged of him to tell me then, but he would not tell me, but he said if I would go up on Sunday and have tea at his house he would tell me then. That was about six or eight months since.

9780. Have you got to know?—No, I have not, I did not go; my wife would not let me go.

9781. Why not?—I was getting over the tools, and I thought I would have no more bother about it.

9782. Who was the man who told you this?—They call him Dronfield; he is a pocket blade grinder who works at the same place where my tools were burnt at Ratcliff's wheel.

9783. Had you had any quarrel before your things were burnt with any man in that wheel?—No.

9784. And there is no person to whom you can attribute it as having done it out of spite or malice to you?—No.

9785. Had this Dronfield anything to do with the edge tools?—Not that I know of; he was a pocket blade grinder, and in another trade altogether.

9786. Where does Dronfield live?—He lives at Wadsley; somewhere near Wadsley; he is a grinder at Wadley; there is a grinding wheel there, and he lives at Wadsley.

9787. What is his name?—I do not know his name; he is a pocket blade grinder.

The witness withdrew.

JOHN TAYLOR sworn and examined.

J. Taylor.

9788. (*Mr. Barstow.*) Are you a saw grinder living at Dore?—Yes.

9789. Have you worked for the last ten years for Messrs. Newbold?—Yes.

9790. (*Chairman.*) Dore is about five miles from Sheffield, is it not?—Betwen four and five miles; $4\frac{1}{2}$ miles.

9791. (*Mr. Barstow.*) Were you a member of the Saw Grinders' Union from 1849 until February last?—Yes.

9792. Do you now belong to the jobbing grinders?—Yes.

9793. Do you remember in 1859 missing your bands?—Yes, from Bradwell wheel.

9794. Is that at Dore?—It is in Abbey Dale.

9795. Can you tell us what time of the year it was?—I believe it was in April.

9796. The next morning did you find anything there?—It was on the Monday morning when we went to work.

9797. Then you left them on the Saturday night?—We left them on the Saturday night, and on the Monday morning they were gone. I will not swear whether I was working there by myself or whether there was any one else working there at that time.

9798. (*Chairman.*) There was nobody there, I suppose, working on the Sunday?—No.

9799. (*Mr. Barstow.*) On the Monday morning did you return to your work?—Yes.

9800. Did you find anything?—I found a note.

9801. Where did no find it?—It was on my horsing, I believe (*producing a note*).

9802. Is that the note which you found on the horsing?—Yes.

9803. This is the note:—"When the blood is in "an impure state, brimstone and treacle is applied as "a mild purgative, &c. We have taken the bands as "a mild remedy. This is the brimstone and treacle; "but should the seat of disease be not reached we "shall administer something stronger; we shall take "away the treacle and shall add thereto a necessary "quantity of charcoal and saltpetre. (Signed) TANTIA "TOPEE." Were you at that time in any dispute with your Union?—Not that I can say, except through the saw makers.

9804. How could you be in dispute with the Saw

ELEVENTH DAY.

J. Taylor.

18 June 1867.

Grinders' Union owing to the saw makers ?—The saw makers had some dispute with the masters about one or two other men. I believe it was two, and an apprentice boy, I believe.

9805. Was that with the Messrs. Newbold ?—Yes.

9806. Why had they had a dispute about two men and a boy ?—I cannot swear what the dispute was, but they wanted us to give notice to leave when they did, and we would not.

9807. Who were those two men and the boy ?—I cannot mention their names.

9808. But what was the nature of the dispute which they said they had with them ?—It was something to the effect that they were not in the trade, or something; I cannot tell what it was about.

9809. You do not know ?—I do not know what the dispute was.

9810. Do you know whether they were members of the Saw Makers' Union ?—They were not members of the Saw Makers' Union.

9811. Are you aware that the Abbey Dale works belong to Messrs. Newbold ?—It does not belong to him; Mr. Newbold rents it; it belongs to Mr. Sanderson.

9812. (*Chairman.*) Newbold rents the wheel ?—Yes.

9813. What did you do when you missed your bands ?—When we missed the bands I went to Broadhead, and I believe there were several others; I believe there were eight or ten as well working for our firm at the same time.

9814. Were there others who lost their bands besides you ?—Yes, all the bands went the same night.

9815. How many went on that night ?—I believe there were eight or ten.

9816. (*Mr. Barstow.*) Can you tell us ther names or some of them ?—Yes, there was Samuel Dungworth, Henry Taylor, John Thorpe, George Parker, George Crooks, Joseph Daws, George Frith, and Elisha Parker, I cannot remember any more.

9817. (*Chairman.*) They all worked at this same wheel, did they all lose their bands ?—They worked at three separate wheels.

9818. Not at this wheel ?—Not all at this wheel; I believe there was but one more man who worked at the wheel where I did, but I cannot swear whether he was one of them at that time.

9819. (*Mr. Barstow.*) You say that those men worked at different wheels ?—Yes.

9820. They were all in Messrs. Newbold's employment, were they not ?—Yes.

9821. And they all lost their bands the same night ?—Yes.

9822. Where were those different wheels ?—There was one about 200 yards below where I was, which is called the Warp Mill.

9823. (*Chairman.*) Were there three wheels in Abbey Dale ?—I believe there were three or four, but they were not all grinding wheels.

9824. But still they were all in the same valley ?—Yes.

9825. And all belonging to Messrs. Newbold ?—No, they were not all belonging to Messrs. Newbold. He had only this wheel below, and partly this wheel above; they were only partly employed then, but now we have it all.

9826. (*Mr. Barstow.*) Do you remember the name of the other wheel? There was the one you worked at, there was the Broadway wheel, and the Warp mill, what was the other ?—There was the Broadway wheel and the Warp mill, and Vaughan's wheel, that was in Sheffield.

9827. You say that you all went to Broadhead ?—Yes.

9828. Where did you go to him ?—I will not swear whether he lived in Carver Street or on Shale's Moor at that time.

9829. Would it be at the "Greyhound"?—I will not swear which house he lived at.

9830. Did you see him ?—Yes.

9831. Were you altogether when you saw him ?—I believe we were not altogether that morning; I believe the biggest part of them went to his house that day.

9832. You and some others saw him ?—Yes.

9833. And I suppose that you told him that your bands were gone ?—Yes.

9834. Did you ask him the reason ?—I asked him the reason the bands were gone.

9835. What did he say ?—He said it was through the Saw Makers' accounts.

9836. Did you ask him how you were to get them back again ?—I asked him how we were to go on while we were standing, and he said we should be paid while we stood.

9837. And were you paid ?—Yes.

9838. How much were you paid ?—I got 1*l.* 19*s.* 0*d.* a week for me and an apprentice boy.

9839. How long did this dispute last ?—I believe it lasted five or six weeks, but I cannot tell to a week or two.

9840. And were you paid during the whole of that time ?—Yes, all the time while the bands came back.

9841. Could you tell me about how much a week you were earning at that time ?—I cannot say.

9842. About how much would it be ?—There were myself and a boy, and then it might be perhaps 3*l.* a week.

9843. At the end of those five weeks did you receive any information about your bands ?—No, I never received anything about the bands.

9844. Do you know whether any of the men received any information ?—I cannot say. We received nothing while there was one of our clerks came up to the place, and he brought a letter that they had bought us new bands.

9845. That letter was never in your possession, was it ?—Yes; he delivered all the grinders a note. This was the clerk of our factory. He delivered all of us a note, and said they had bought us new bands.

9846. Who had bought you new bands ?—He brought a note saying that Mr. Newbold had bought us new bands, and that if we did not commence working the day following we should be summoned before the magistrates.

9847. (*Mr. Barstow.*) What did you do upon that? —There was a meeting called the day after.

9848. A meeting of what ?—Of saw makers and grinders altogether.

9849. Did Mr. Newbold send the bands on to your place ?—No, he did not send them; they were sent to the factory. The bands were at the factory ready to start.

9850. There was a meeting ?—Yes; there was a meeting between the saw makers and the grinders.

9851. Did they come to any resolution ?—I believe there was a party picked out to go up to Mr. Newbold's to see if they could settle the matter.

9852. Were you present at the meeting ?—Yes.

9853. Do you remember what passed ? — I can remember some little, but not much.

9854. (*Chairman.*) There was a deputation sent ?—Yes; there were five or six sent, I believe.

9855. (*Mr. Barstow.*) And did they arrange the matter ?—Master told them that he should not be compelled to turn them away, but he said if they did come in he did not see why they should leave, but he would not say that he would be compelled to turn them away.

9856. (*Chairman.*) Did they come back and tell the meeting so ?—Yes.

9857. Did you hear them ?—Yes.

9858. They came back and said that Mr. Newbold said, what ?—He said that if they came back he would not say but what he should turn them away, but he would not be compelled to do so,

9859. (*Mr. Barstow.*) What followed upon that? did you go to work ?—Many of the grinders told the makers that they should start, but a few would not start.

9860. Then you did start, did you ?—I believe a note came the next morning to the wheel; one came to the Warp mill, I believe to tell where the bands

ELEVENTH DAY.

J. Taylor.

18 June 1867.

were; and I do not know where they found the note to the Sheffield grinders.

9861. But they were found ?—Yes.

9862. And they were found, I suppose, at the place mentioned in the note ?—No ; the bands were found in a wood near the wheel.

9863. You went and found them, did you ?—I was one amongst the party that went.

9864. Do you remember missing some bands in September of last year, 1866 ?—There was a cart book, a book that was taken out of a cart box, a book where our work was set down when it came from the warehouse, and then it was set down again when it came down again ; that was about two years since, last May. I believe it was last May but one.

9865. That was in May 1865 ?—I believe it was in May 1865.

9866. (*Chairman.*) What happened in May 1865 ?—A cart book was stolen.

9867. (*Mr. Barstow.*) What is a cart book ?—The foreman of the works set it down when the work comes up from the place before being ground, and then we checked it again in the same book on the contrary side when it was ground, when it went down from the wheel.

9868. Then that book would show the amount of your weekly earnings ?—Yes, it was to show what work we had done on the Saturday.

9869. At this time were you paying poundage ?—Yes.

9870. That is to say your contribution to the Union was paid by poundage ?—Yes ; we paid so much in the pound.

9871. (*Chairman.*) And therefore they wanted to know exactly how much you had done ?—They thought we were not delivering in the account right.

9872. And if they got hold of this book they would be able to ascertain whether you had sent in the right amount or not ?—Yes.

9873. And that was the interest that they had in that book ?—Yes.

9874. (*Mr. Barstow.*) Did you ever see that book again ?—Yes, I saw it again after it had been taken.

9875. Where did you see it ?—I believe it was the week after when I saw it.

9876. But where did you see it ?—At our warehouse, Mr. Newbold's warehouse.

9877. In the meantime had any use been made of the book ?—Yes, I believe there had.

9878. What use had been made of it ?—The man that brought the cart up, when he got to the wheel, said some one had broken the cart and broken the box open. This cart book was kept in a box in the cart.

9879. Was your contribution in any way altered on account of the information contained in that book ?—It was altered in this way, they said we had not delivered in what we ought to have done.

9880. Who was it said that you had not delivered in what you ought to have done ?—It was brought on before the meeting.

9881. What person said that you had not delivered in what you earned ?—It was read over at the meeting what we had delivered in, and then they had made an account of it in the book.

9882. (*Chairman.*) Was the book there ?—It was not at the meeting ; it was returned to this party that had taken it at first.

9883. (*Mr. Barstow.*) First of all, who said you had not delivered in your account accurately ?—It was brought on at the meeting. I will not positively say whether it was William Broadhead or not, but he said he had had the book brought to him.

9884. Was this meeting a committe meeting or a general meeting ?—It was a general meeting when it was brought on.

9885. Was Broadhead present at this meeting ?—Yes.

9886. Then at any rate it was some member of the meeting in Broadhead's presence who said that the account had been made out from the book ?—Yes.

9887. In consequence of that was the payment that you had to make raised ?—They put me 3*l.* or 4*l.* on, I cannot rightly say which.

9888. And the information on which they acted was contained in the book which was taken from the box in the cart ? Now the next case was in September last year, was it not ?—Yes ; but we found out the party who took that.

9889. Are you now speaking of last year, September 1866 ?—Yes.

9890. What did you miss in September 1866 ?—I should just like you to have this. I believe that Broadhead did not know anything about the book when it was taken ; it was the parties got it up unawares to him. I believe he never knew anything about it while it came to his house.

9891. (*Chairman.*) Here is the entry about it in the book : "John Taylor and Elisha Parker attend "and hear the charges against them delivering in false "accounts of earnings, as proved by the accounts copied "from their work book from January the 7th to April "the 8th and 15th, respecting Taylor down to April "the 15th, and Parker down to April the 8th. No "objections are raised as to the correctness of the "accounts, but they state they have a pull off for "broken saws, Taylor averaging about one dozen "per week ; and they assign as a reason for delivering in short that they knew that others were "doing the same, and they intended to bring a charge "to this effect against G. Parker, senior, before the "general meeting, which they would prove by his "work book, which they had in their possession. "They leave their own case in the hands of the committee and retire. After it being stated that Taylor's "deficiences delivered in are 15*l.* 14*s.* 6*d.*, and Parker's "deficiences are 7*l.* 5*s.* 3*d.*, after due deliberation "it is resolved that Parker and Taylor each pay "contribution upon the amounts proved to be "delivered in short, together with the amount of expenses incurred in obtaining the accounts ; the said "expenses to be paid between them, and any further "fines and penalties to be left for the consideration "and decision of the general meeting." That is the entry ?—Yes.

9892. (*Mr. Barstow.*) As a fact did you pay the expenses of obtaining that book ?—No, I believe that some arrears are in my book yet.

9893. You never paid that ?—No, because there was a lot set down false. There were some two or three weeks which they had put down more than I had earned.

9894. Have they ever been demanded of you ?—I cannot say ; I have paid perhaps now and then a few shillings towards it, but it was very little. I have my book.

9895. Has Broadhead ever asked you for any sum of money as expenses for obtaining that book ?—I believe they wanted 15*s.* each for the party that had taken it.

9896. Did he as a matter of fact ever ask you for 15*s.* ?—No, he never asked me, but I believe it was set down as something against us, and we found that it was one Henry Parker who had been doing all he could to get us in the same as himself, because he had not been delivering in his account right.

9897. But did you ever see that entry of 15*s.* for expenses to your name in Broadhead's book ?—I cannot say I ever saw expenses set down against me.

9898. You cannot say whether you ever saw that entry of 15*s.* for expenses against your name, or whether Broadhead ever asked you for the 15*s.* ?—No, I cannot.

9899. Do you remember your bands being missing in September 1866 ?—Yes.

9900. From where were they missing ?—Bradwell wheel.

9901. Were anyone else's bands missing at the same time as yours ?—Elisha Parkers and some others.

9902. Had you any dispute with the Union at that time ?—I do not know that I had any dispute, any further than I had some arrears ; but I have never been questioned about them for a long time.

9903. When you missed your bands what did you do ?—We went to Broadhead, I believe, on the Saturday. They were taken on the Friday night.

ELEVENTH DAY.

J. Taylor.

18 June 1867.

9904. That would be at the "Royal George"?—Yes.

9905. Did you see him there?—We saw him there on Saturday morning.

9906. What did you say to him?—When I got there I asked him the reason the bands were taken, and he said he expected they were taken for natty or arrears or something of that; he said arrears or natty, it was one of them.

9907. Did you ask what you had to pay?—Yes; he asked us how many bands were gone, and we told him there were four gone.

9908. Then what did he say?—He said it had been agreed by the committee that I should pay 19*s.*, and Parker 2*l.*, and 10*s.* each for "Mary Ann."

9909. Did you agree to do so?—No; we went away that day, and would not agree to it.

9910. What reason did you give for not paying?—I thought that I ought not to have my bands taken. I had paid 13*l.* 8*s.* 7*d.* in 36 weeks, except there is some little to deduct from a levy (I cannot rightly say what it was), which I reckon as extra money, because the box-men received extra scale on that account; but it is very little to deduct from it, I believe.

9911. Did you object to 10*s.* as being too large a sum to pay to "Mary Ann"?—I went on the Tuesday morning, I believe, and we went, I believe, determined to pay that morning, and when we got there he wanted 50*s.* for "Mary Ann."

9912. Did you ask him why he wanted so much?—We asked him the reason why he wanted so much, and he told us, through the difficulties, or something of that kind.

9913. (*Chairman.*) What difficulties were they?—I asked him what difficulties they were and he did not say; I told him to come up to our wheel; that he could get in either day or night, and that there were no difficulties at all.

9914. What did he say to that?—I cannot say that he said anything; we went away that day and I believe we went several times during the week.

9915. You went to Broadhead several times during the week?—We we went to Broadhead several times during the week and he said that he could not alter anything; that it was not in his power, but that it was in the committee's power.

9916. How much did you pay?—We went again on Saturday and he was still the same.

9917. That would be more than a week after?—Yes, the week following.

9918. Had you been out of work all this time?—Yes; we had not done anything. Our mistress called the same Saturday in the week following.

9919. Did you see anybody on the Saturday?—Our mistress called on the Saturday while I went to the warehouse, and she asked me the reason why he wanted to charge me so much for them; it was a kind of note. Parker had missed a nut some time before, and she said she did not want to pay for things belonging to other folk, and that Parker ought to have paid for his own, and Broadhead said if it had laid in his power I should not have had any bands taken at all.

9920. (*Chairman.*) Is your wife here?—No, my wife is not here.

9921. (*Mr. Barstow.*) Then what did you pay to get your bands back?—We went again on Monday morning.

9922. You did not get them on the Saturday?—No, I saw Broadhead on the Saturday, and our master told me that if I could get wheel room at Butcher's wheel I could go, but it had been taken up the same week by a man of the name of Fearnehough, and I could not go.

9923. There is more difficulty in getting into Butcher's wheel, is there not?—Yes, it is what they call the safe wheel. I was that angry with the trade that if I could have got a trough at Butcher's wheel I would have gone.

9924. But Fearnehough had taken all the places and you could not get room there?—Yes.

9925. On the Monday morning did you see anybody?—Yes, we went again on the Monday morning; he said he would agree to take 15*s.* a piece for the bands going.

9926. Who told you this?—William Broadhead; he said the committee had agreed to it, I believe.

2927. Did you pay your money?—Yes; Parker had begun rather hanging back, and I told him I would bring mine down. I had had running about enough, and I had plenty of it. I paid my 15*s.* for "Mary Ann" and 19*s.* for Natty; Parker only gave him 10*s.* and said it was all the money he had; 2*l.* for Natty and 10*s.*

9928. When you paid the money did you ask for the bands?—He took Parker's 10*s.*, but he said he would take it on that account; I told him I should expect my 5*s.* back to make it up.

9929. Never mind about that; did you get back your bands?—Yes.

9930. When?—It would be on the morning following.

9931. What did Broadhead say when you asked him for the bands?—After we had paid him the money we told him we should not want to be running about all day and the morning after.

9932. When you asked him for the bands, what did he say?—He said, "The bands will be all right if "you go home; you will not need to run about all "day; your bands will be all right in the morning;" and there was a note came by post in the morning.

9933. Did he say anything about a note when you asked for the bands?—I cannot say that he ever said anything about the note.

9934. But you got a note the next morning?—A note came through the post office the next morning.

9935. To whom as the note addressed?—To Elisha Parker.

9936. Have you that note with you?—I dare say Parker has the note. It contained where the bands were.

9937. You looked at that place and you found the bands I suppose?—Yes, we went and we found them.

9938. (*Chairman.*) You had been a member of the Union had you not?—I have been a member of it ever since 1849.

9939. What made you join the Union and keep in it?—At the first commencement when I joined the trade had been broken up for about six months.

9940. Did you join it for the purpose of securing assistance when you were out of work for the benefits it would give you as a member of the trade?—There were two ways; one was at that time that they had shut up the box for about six months, and some of the masters were taking such great advantage that the men were all willing to join. I believe there was but one man that was kept out and that was a man of the name of Sinley, and they thought he was not a man.

9941. All joined except Sinley?—Yes.

9942. Why did not Sinley join?—He was at that time a scissor grinder, and he had just started in the saw trade with a lot of common saws.

9943. And they would not let him join?—I do not think they ever asked him.

9944. But did he ever apply to go in?—I think not.

9945. That was, you say, the reason that the masters had taken advantage; what were the kind of advantages that the masters had taken at that time which induced you to join the Union?—At that time I worked for Moses Eadon, and Sons, and they took, I believe, 15 per cent. off at that time. It was either 10 per cent. or 15 per cent. at that time. I will not say which. They took off 10 or 15 per cent. discount.

9946. Discount off what?—Off the saws when we had done them.

9947. Off the price they had to pay?—Yes; off the week's wage.

9948. Supposing you had earned 3*l.* by saw grinding, what was it that Mr. Eadon would have done in that case?—If we had earned 3*l.*, 9*s.* would come off it, 15 per cent.

ELEVENTH DAY.

J. Taylor.

18 June 1867.

9949. Supposing you had earned 3*l.*, instead of paying you 3*l.* he would pay you only 2*l.* 11*s.*?—Yes.

9950. Why was that?—They did this and many others. There were some that took as much as 50 per cent. off the men.

9951. Was that a sudden reduction in the wages?—Yes. I have heard tell of plenty of parties that took as much as 50 per cent. off their men, and others 30, and others 20 per cent.

9952. That was a reduction of the price which they had paid?—Yes.

9953. Was that a sudden reduction?—After a man had earned wages of 3*l.*, if there was a reduction of 50 per cent., he would only get 30*s.* for it.

9954. Was there a list price in former times?—Yes, there had been a list, but the box had been closed for six months.

9955. Who had published the list price? Had the Union done it, or had the masters done it?—I cannot say, but there was a second list.

9956. Then you say the Union was broken up?—Yes; for about six months.

9957. When the Union was broken up then the masters diminished the price from the list price by this 50 per cent. and 15 per cent. as you mentioned?—Yes.

9958. Do you know who drew up that list?—Not the first, but the second list.

9959. But I am speaking of the first one. Do you know who it was that drew up the first list?—I do not.

9960. You do not know whether it was a list that was agreed to by the men and the masters, or whether it was a list laid down by the Union?—I cannot say; but the list had been in go for many years.

9961. How long was the Union broken up?—About six months I believe.

9962. When was that?—I believe it was in 1848 when the Union broke up; but I am not certain about it.

9963. And was it then that you joined?—That was the time I joined.

9964. When you joined did the Union make out a second list of higher prices?—After we got together we had to have a strike with many firms, and I believe we got the price at one place where I worked, at Moses Eadon and Sons, in about a month.

9965. You got your prices advanced, did you?—Yes, in about a month.

9966. As much as 15 per cent?—Yes.

9967. The full price according to the old list?—Yes; we got the old list.

9968. Then you had joined the Union?—Yes.

9969. And so you went on. Was there a second list published then?—There were several firms that stopped out for about twenty weeks.

9970. Then ultimately did you get a second list published?—They found out that there was a firm or two who had been standing out, and there were two or three that went in, and they thought the best way would be to realize the things, and there were some things that were deducted.

9971. The masters ultimately gave in, did they not?—Yes; except in some places; and then we realized the list, and took the things off it.

9972. Therefore as the masters did not come to terms, you made out a second list, in which you modified the first list?—Yes.

9973. A compromise?—Yes.

9974. And has that been the list upon which you have acted ever since?—Yes. I believe it was signed by Robert Jackson.

9975. Who is Robert Jackson?—Of the firm of Spear and Jackson. I believe it was signed by him, but I cannot say.

9976. This list was signed on behalf of the masters by Robert Jackson, of the firm of Spear and Jackson, was it?—Yes.

9977. Has that been the list upon which you have worked ever since?—Yes, I believe it has.

9978. The obtaining of this list from the masters secured to you certain advantages as you say. It secured to you a certain remuneration for your labour. In your judgment could you have got that without being in Union?—No.

9979. Have you continued in the Union for the purpose of keeping up prices, or for fear of having your property destroyed, or what has been the reason for your continuing a member of the Union?—Well, when I throwed out I was getting sick of many things. That was when I throwed out and went into the Jobbing Union. I had throwed out of the Old Union, and gone into the Jobbing Union.

9980. What did you do that for? what were you sick of?—I was continuing paying, and this man Parker that I worked with had given over, and I told Broadhead, if that was the way, I had as well give over myself; that it was no use my paying and then for them to come and take my bands. It made no difference.

9981. Elisha Parker did not pay then?—Since we have gotten our bands back I have paid better than 5*l.*, and I believe, from what Broadhead told me, he had paid somewhere about 10*s.* in the same time.

9982. You thought it was a shame that they should take your bands because Elisha Parker did not pay?—Yes.

9983. But was it for that reason that you left their Union and went to the Jobbers' Union?—When I told Parker of it he said he should not pay any more while Broadhead was the secretary, and he said that he would become a member of the jobbing trade. I said, "If thou can do it that way, and can get off with "paying 1*s.* 6*d.* a week, I will do it and all, and let "it go which way it will."

9984. And so you determined to join the jobbers?—I sent a note to the jobbers, and they agreed to take me in.

9985. For what reason did you join the jobbers? was it from any advantages which you were to gain in the way of prices or of getting scale when you were ill or out of work, or was it simply to protect your property?—They told me that if I was out of work I should get scale.

9986. But what was your reason for joining the jobbers?—I thought that I should be safer if I joined them than if I joined none.

9987. Can you at any time command work if you want it? are you at any time out of work?—In the jobbing trade?

9988. In your business?—According to the out rules, when a man is out he has to send a list of names.

9989. But supposing that you were not in the Union could you always get work?—I should have to run the risk of that.

9990. But is there any risk in it, or can you get work?—I cannot say; I have not been out lately.

9991. As I understand, you said that you thought you would be safer if you joined the Jobbers' Union than if you joined none. You joined the Jobbers' Union and left the Old Union. Did the members of the Old Union insult you, or did they do anything to you for this change in your course?—I have never been insulted at all.

9992. No steps have been taken against you because you changed from one Union to the other?—No.

9993. (*Mr. Chance.*) Supposing that you were left to yourself, and had no fear of consequences, would you be a member of a Trades Union or not?—I would be a member of Trades Unions when the prices get low if I could not do without, because I believe we could not.

9994. But as a general rule, taking all times and all circumstances without any fear of consequences, would you be a member of a Trades Union?—That depends on the masters principally, I believe. Our masters would not take an advantage, but others take an advantage, and then it must pull a good master down.

9995. And you make it depend upon the character of the master?—Yes.

ELEVENTH DAY.

J. Taylor.

18 June 1867.

9996. (*The Chairman.*) With a good master there is no advantage, and with a bad master the Union keeps him down ?—Yes.

9997. (*Mr. Chance.*) Which would you prefer, a good master with a chance of being rattened from time to time, or a bad master without the fear o being rattened ?—I am not very partial to being rattened, because it makes a good hole in your business.

9998. (*Mr. Barstow.*) When your bands were taken this last time on a Friday, and you did not get them back until the Tuesday, how much were you out of pocket by it ?—I should think, if I had been in full work, I should have been 3*l.* or 4*l.* out of pocket, I and my apprentice boy. I have a son who is as good a man as myself or better.

9999 Supposing that you had been in full work at that time, would you have made 3*l.* or 4*l.* ?—Yes.

10,000. (*The Chairman.*) When you and others joined the jobbing grinders were any of the men on the box of the old society taken into the new society ?—No.

10,001. Were the box men left to be supported by the old society ?—Yes.

10,002. (*Mr. Chance.*) Are you a brother of Isaac Taylor ?—Yes.

The witness withdrew.

J. Machin.

JOSEPH MACHIN sworn and examined.

10,003. (*The Chairman.*) Do you produce the books of your Union ?—Yes, I do (*producing the same*). Those are what I have, with the exception of receipts which are in the box ; they are found in a book here.

10,004. You have no other books than those ?—Not that I am aware of.

10,005. Are you the secretary ?—Yes.

10,006. Of what Union ?—Of the Scythe Grinders'.

10,007. How far do those books go back ?—I think they go back to about 1858 or 1859 perhaps.

10,008. Where are the books before that ?—They are destroyed. Those are all the books I know of.

10,009. Who destroyed them ?—I am sure I cannot tell you now.

10,010. How long have you been secretary ?—Something like eight or nine years. There are accounts in the books further back than I had been secretary.

10,011. When were they destroyed ?—I do not know. They were destroyed before I had the books.

10,012. They were destroyed more than eight or nine years ago ?—Yes.

10,013. You never saw them, did you ?—I think I have seen a scale book.

10,014. But have you seen any other books containing proceedings ?—Not more than these, that I am aware of, excepting a scale book.

10,015. Who was the secretary before you ?—John Thorpe.

10,016. Is he alive ?—He is alive.

10,017. Who destroyed the books ?—I cannot tell you.

10,018. Was it done by order of the committee ?—I dare say they were done in rotation, for they never kept any after they were filled at that time.

10,019. And when a book was full they destroyed it ?—When a book was full they destroyed it, and started with a fresh one the same as they did with the scale book in my time ; in the commencement ; the one that is in there (*pointing to the books*).

10,020. And you do not know who destroyed the books ?—No, I do not.

10,021. Nor what was the reason of it ?—I do not know any other reason than that, that they were filled and then destroyed.

10,022. And those are all the books ?—That I know of.

10,023. Not only that you have, but has anybody else any books ?—Not that I am aware of.

10,024. You believe that those are the only books belonging to the Union ?—Yes.

10,025. We wish to keep these books for a day or two to look at them; I believe you have no objection to our looking at them ?—I have no objection. I suppose they will remain there ; I have brought them here just as I take them backwards and forwards to the Union.

10,026. We are much obliged to you. Who was secretary before Thorpe ?—A young man named Benjamin Cochrane. He is dead some years since.

10,027. Do you know a person called Thompson ?—Yes, I do ; I believe he was secretary a little bit between these two.

10,028. What Thompson was that ?— Michael Thompson.

10,029. Where did he live ?— He lived at Millhouses, I think.

10,030. Is he alive now ?—Yes.

10,031. Where is he ?—He is working.

10,032. Where does he live ?—He lives at Sheffield now.

10,033. Where at ?—In Clarence Street.

10,034. He is a man well known is he not, if we should want him ?—He is well known.

10,035. Where does Thorpe live ?—He keeps Peter's Hotel in Lord Street, Park.

10,036. I dare say we shall get a gentleman to look through these books to save us trouble, but we shall swear him before he looks into them, that he will never divulge to anybody but ourselves whatever he finds there ?—I should have some objections to the public altogether looking at the accounts, but I have no objection whatever to you or the officials you appoint looking at them.

The witness withdrew.

J. Hague.

JOHN HAGUE recalled and further examined.

10,037. (*Mr. Barstow.*) By desire of Mr. Sugg I am going to ask you some questions ?—Any questions he thinks proper to give I will answer.

10,038. First I wish to ask you what was the Union of which you desired to become a member ?—My father belongs to that.

10,039. But what was the name of the Union to which you wished to be admitted ?—The Edge Tools and Sheep Shearers'.

10,040. In the first place are you not aware that if you are incapacitated from sickness or accident you would receive 5s. a week if you were a member ?—I do not know ; I have never joined a Union.

10,041. But have you never inquired what advantages you would receive as an equivalent for the payments which you would make to the Union ?—No, never.

At this point *Mr. Joseph James Shrubsole* was called in.

The Chairman informed Mr. Shrubsole that the Examiners appointed him as the person to go through the books of the various Unions, and to call the attention of the Examiners to anything which he might find therein which he considered should properly be brought under their notice; and further that he was not to divulge to any person whatever, except the Examiners themselves, anything that he might find in the books.

[*Mr. Shrubsole* was then sworn to secresy as to the contents of the books which he should examine.]

ELEVENTH DAY.

J. Hague.

18 June 1867.

10,042. (*Mr. Barstow to the witness.*) Have you never inquired what would be the advantage to yourself from joining this Union?—No.

10,043. Have you never heard it said?—I have never heard it said.

10,044. Has no one asked you to belong to it?—They have told me to go to try to get in.

10,045 Have they never given you any reason?—I say that I ought to be in the trade although I am out.

10,046. Has no one ever pointed out to you the advantages of the Union?—Never.

10,047. Are you aware that when you are out of work you would receive 8*s*. a week?—No; I was not aware of that, not exactly aware of it.

10,048. Were you aware that you would receive some payment when you were out of work?—My opinion and my own feeling was that I thought that I never should be out of work.

10,049. Answer the question. Were you aware that in the event of your joining the Union you would receive some sum of money when you were out of work?—No, I was not aware of that. Supposing I had nothing to do if I joined the trade, if they took me out of a place, I was aware I should have something to draw, some kind of scale.

10,050. But if you were thrown out of work by your master having no work, then were you not aware that you would receive so much a week?—I do not think I should ever have been out of work; I must speak the truth, I cannot say any more.

10,051. Accidents happen to everybody, you might have been thrown out of work if you were ill, or if you had broken your leg, or if the wheel was lame?—If the wheel was lame I should be out of work. If I broke my leg no doubt I should have pay from my trade.

10,052. Have you been to Mr. Greaves' and requested him to come before the Examiners to say that Stacey has been to him, Greaves, to request Greaves to discharge you?—Never; I have been to Mr. Greaves.

10,053. When were you with Mr. Greaves;—I think it is somewhere about a week since but I am certain I cannot tell exactly.

10,054. Had you any conversation with him about this enquiry?—Yes.

10,055. Did you ask your master, Mr. Greaves, to come here as a witness?—Yes.

10,056. Why was that?—The reason I went to him was because he was my master, and I went and asked him if he could give me a character, and he said, Yes he could.

10,057. Why should you ask him to come and give you a character?—The time just before my tools were burnt the secretary came to his place, as he told me himself, and asked for the work which I was doing. He had four lathes and I was doing all the work. There was no other man could take the work away unless Greaves had a mind.

10,058. Did you not ask him to come and say that Stacey had desired him to discharge you?—No.

10,059. That you swear to us?—I will swear that.

10,060. Is it true or untrue that Stacey ever went to Mr. Greaves and ever asked him to discharge you?—Not that I know of.

10,061. You do not know whether it is so or not?—I do not know that, not Mr. Stacey but the other Secretary, I do not know his name.

10,062. Reaney?—Reaney, he went there, Mr. Greaves told me that before. He did not discharge me.

10,063. I have no desire to ask questions about Reaney. Now, I have to ask you this question—Why were you transported?—Well I will tell you, me and another boy—

10,064. Say shortly for what it was?—For stealing a pair of trousers, me and another boy.

10,065. How long ago was that?—In 1841. I came back in 1848. I went to Van Dieman's Land.

10,067. Do you mean seriously to say that you and another boy were transported were stealing one pair of trousers?—No; the other boy got one month, and I got seven years.

10,067. Now just tell your story. You came back in 1848?—Yes.

10,068. Where were you tried?—At Rotherham.

10,069. How old were you?—I think I was about 17 or 18.

10,070. How came it to pass that the boy who was with you got a month and that you got seven years?—That I cannot tell, but this boy——

10,071. (*Chaiman.*) Was the boy much younger than you?—I think he was.

10,072. Then they thought that you had led him into the mischief?—Very likely; no doubt about that.

10,073. Was it your first offence?—Well, I think I had been a time or two.

10,074. You had been a time or two and had got a little boy into this trouble?—Yes; I shall tell nothing but the truth I can tell you.

10,075. (*Mr. Barstow.*) Have you been in any trouble since 1848?—Yes.

10,076. What was it?—I once had three months.

10,077. (*Chairman.*) When was that?—I am sure I cannot recollect. It is a few years back. I cannot read very well myself.

10,078. It is nothing to be proud of, you need not laugh?—No, it is not.

10,079. When was it?—I cannot tell, three or four years ago.

10,080. (*Mr. Barstow.*) What was that for?—It was for burning my own clothes.

10,081. I am not aware that that is a crime at all?—But it is a crime.

10,082. Will you explain what you mean?—I will explain it. I will show you how I burnt my own clothes. My wife died and I got in company with another girl.

10,083. Do not laugh about it, but speak the truth?—Of course I bought those clothes and the girl wore them. I bought everything she had on her back from her foot to her head, and the girl left me then, and I thonght I would be revenged upon her, and I thought I would buy two pennyworth of vitriol, and I thought I would sprinkle her with it just a bit.

10,084. (*The Chairman.*) You are a greater scoundrel than I thought you were?—Yes, no doubt.

(*Mr. Barstow.*) I need not ask you the questions which I intended to ask you, as to your admission into the Union.

The witness withdrew.

THOMAS HURST sworn and examined.

T. Hurst.

10,085. (*Mr. Chance.*) Are you a saw grinder?—Yes.

10,086. Do you work for Messrs. Beardshaw and Sons at Attercliffe?—Yes.

10,087. How long have you been working for them?—44 years.

10,088. You are a member of the Union?—Yes.

10,089. Which Union?—The Saw Grinders'.

10,090. How long have you been a member of the Saw Grinders' Union?—About 46 years.

10,091. Have you regularly paid up your contributions to the Union?—Yes.

10,092. Have you ever been in arrear?—No.

10,093. Do you remember in the year 1864 your tools being taken away from Messrs. Beardshaw's?—I remember in 1864, if I am right, on the second day of August, our bands were missing.

10,094. Was that the band that you were working with?—Yes.

ELEVENTH DAY.

T. Hurst.

18 June 1867.

10,095. Had you any quarrel or dispute at the time with any union ?—No.

10,096. Had you paid up your contribution money? —Yes.

10,097. Had you given any cause for their having been taken away?—I cannot give any cause. They were taken away; we were without them from Tuesday morning until Saturday morning.

10,098. Upon missing them what did you do?—On Friday morning Mr. Beardshaw asked me if I had heard anything of the bands or found them. I said "No." He said if the bands were not forthcoming he should buy new ones. I went to the wheel and told the remainder of the grinders what Mr. Beardshaw had said; with that we had a meeting in the wheel yard.

10,099. You and the other workmen?—Yes, I and the other workmen.

10,100. What did you do upon that, after you had a meeting to discuss the matter?—At that meeting it was advised that me and Edward Crookes should go to William Broadhead. We went to William Broadhead and told him what had occurred.

10,101. You say "we"; who besides yourself?—Me and Edward Crooks was the deputation that went to William Broadhead chosen out of that meeting.

10,102. Where did you go to; was it to the "Greyhound"?—No.

10,103. Where did you go?—It was in Carver Street, at the "Royal George" inn.

10,104. At Broadhead's house?—Yes, we saw William Broadhead; we told him that our bands had been missing from Tuesday a few days. We asked him if he could not lend us some bands belonging to the trade; he told us that he would see what there were, and he would lend us all the bands that they had so that we could begin work again. He asked us if we had seen a person of the name of William Hides, the secretary of the Saw Makers' Union.

10,105. What did you say to that?—We told him that we had not seen him. He advised us to see him. We asked him where we should see him, where would be a likely place to meet with him. He told us at the "Moseley Arms." We went to the "Moseley Arms," and saw William Hides, and we told him what had happened, that we had had a meeting in the wheel yard, and a deputation had waited upon William Broadhead, and William Broadhead had said he would render us all the assistance he could by way of lending us bands so that we could begin our work. Mr. Beardshaw wanted the work, and we wanted the the tools.

10,106. What did Hides say?—Hides said he knew nothing about the bands; he hoped that we should soon find them again. I went to the wheel on Saturday morning.

10,107. On what day did you go to Hides?—Friday.

10,108. The same day that you went to Broadhead's?—Yes.

10,109. You went to the wheel on Saturday morning? — I went to the wheel on Saturday morning; my band was on the horsing. Mr. Beardshaw had received a note that morning.

10,110. Did you see the note?—No; I do not know whether the note was not given to Mr. Jackson.

10,111. Did you see it when it was received?—No; it was received by master.

10,112. Did you see the note after it had been received?—No.

10,113. (*Chairman.*) Did Mr. Beardshaw tell you that he had got a note?—Mr. Beardshaw told me he had received a note.

10,114. (*Mr. Chance.*) Did he tell you what was in the note?—It was telling where the bands were.

10,115. Were the bands in the place where the note said that they would be?—The bands were found in the bottom hull and the top hull.

10,116. Was that what the note said?—I believe that was the case. Mr. Beardshaw went to the hull and found the bands underneath the horsing in the bottom hull.

10,117. Were you with him when he found them? —No.

10,118. You did not see the bands again till you found them on the horsing?—My bands were on the horsing, not the place where I left them on Monday night when I had done work. It was round the pulley.

10,119. Is that all that you have to tell us about the loss of the bands upon that occasion?—Yes. As soon as we found the bands we commenced working.

10,120. Have you lost bands at any other time?—No.

10,121. You have not told us whether there was any reason for supposing by whom your bands were taken away. Was there any cause that you could assign for their being taken away?—If there was any reason it was from the saw makers.

10,122. Why should the saw makers take them away?—I do not know.

10,123. Was there any quarrel of any kind?—No.

10,124. (*Chairman.*) Why should the saw makers take them?—I do not know.

10,125. Then why do you suspect them?—Mr. Beardshaw said that the saw makers were in arrear with their Union.

10,126. The saw makers were in arrear, and they had taken your bands?—Yes.

10,127. (*Mr. Chance.*) You mean that the saw makers at Beardshaw's were in arrear?—Yes.

10,128. You know of no other cause except that? —No.

10,129. (*Chairman.*) Do you know when the Union closed its box and broke up?—I think it was in 1849.

10,130. What was the effect to the members of their closing the box and breaking up the Union? Were they put in a bad situation, were they at all damaged by the Union having been broken up?—Do you mean Mr. Beardshaw?

10,131. No. The Union existed, and then it got broken up. What was the consequence of that to the men? Did the men suffer in consequence of the Union being broken up? Was it a bad thing for the men that there should be a Union or not?—The Union was a good thing for the men.

10,132. Did the prices come down?—The prices fell down after the Union broke up.

10,133. Is it customary for the Saw Grinders' Union to have spare bands?—I do not know whether it is customary for all the unions, but it so happened that the saw grinders had spare bands at that time; we were informed so; that was the reason we went to Broadhead to ask for the bands. That was a deputation that waited upon Broadhead, me and Edward Crookes.

The witness withdrew.

G. Glossop.

GEORGE GLOSSOP sworn and examined.

10,134. (*Mr. Chance.*) Are you a saw maker?—Yes.

10,135. In the year 1864 were you working for Messrs. Beardshaw at Attercliffe?—Yes.

10,136. How long had you been working for Messrs. Beardshaw?—At that time about 10 years.

10,137. Were you a member of the Saw Makers' Union?—I had been, but was not then contributing.

10,138. How long had you ceased to be a member then?—Perhas 12 months; not quite that.

10,139. Do you remember in the year 1864 receiving a note, or Messrs. Beardshaw receiving a note?—Messrs. Beardshaw received a note.

10,140. Did you see that note?—I did not see the note.

10,141. Was the note read over to you?—No.

10,142. Did you at any time hear the contents of that note ?—I heard from the manager that a note had been received stating that the saw makers were in arrear.

10,143. Was that from Hernshaw ?—Yes.

10,144. You heard that a note had been received from whom ?—I do not know who from.

10,145. It stated that the saw makers were in arrear ?—Yes.

10,146. Do you know as a fact that any saw grinders in Messrs. Beardshaw's employment were in arrear ?—Yes ; others besides myself ; I was considered to be in arrear.

10,147. You were considered as a member of the Union at the time ?—They asked me still to contribute, which I had not done.

10,148. Then the other saw makers at that time were in arrear ?—Yes.

10,149. Do you remember in what part of 1864 that was ?—In August.

10,150. Was anything stated in the note about your paying up ?—Something was said that the saw makers were in arrear, and if they did not pay up something would be done, but I do not know what it was.

10,151. Do you know how the note came ?—I do not know.

10,152. After receiving that note did anything take place ?—Yes, the bands were taken.

10,153. How many bands were taken ?—I do not know how many bands.

10,154. Were your bands taken ?—I had not any.

10,155. Did you receive any information from anybody with regard to the nonpayment of your arrears ?—There was a member of the committee worked at the place ; his name was Joseph May.

10,156. What did he say ?—We had a meeting when the bands were missing, and they advised that we should go to see the committee.

10,157. (*Chairman.*) The committee of the saw grinders or the saw makers ?—The saw makers' committee would sit on the Thursday evening.

10,158. What happened ?—A good many as could go went to see the committee.

10,159. Did you go ?—I did not go ; I could not, I was otherwise engaged.

10,160. (*Mr. Chance.*) You were going to say something that May said ; what did he say ?—May said as many as could go were to go before the committee.

10,161. Was that all that he said ?—All that I can remember his saying.

10,162. Did he say anything about your not paying up ?—There was something about paying up, but I cannot say what was said at the time ; it was said that it would have to be done.

10,163. Was anything said about paying up or taking the consequences ?—It was said afterwards.

10,164. When was that ?—There was a committee meeting, and the levy was put on that every man would have to pay a certain amount, which was decided, I suppose, by the committee. Joseph May told me on the Friday morning that I had *2l.* to pay by Friday noon, or take the consequences.

10,165. Did you pay the *2l.* ?—I gave Joseph May the *2l.*, and I of course heard no more about it till I got to the works the next morning, when I was told that the bands were found.

10,166. Where did you find them ?—I do not know ; they were found when I got to the works.

The witness withdrew.

William Hernshaw sworn and examined.

W. Hernshaw.

10,167. (*Mr. Chance.*) Are you a workman at Messrs. Beardshaw and Sons ?—Yes.

10,168. Have you been workman there for some years ?—Eighteen years.

10,169. Do you remember in 1864 some bands being taken away from Messrs. Beardshaw ?—Yes.

10,170. About that time did you receive any notice ?—No ; Beardshaw received one.

10,171. Did you see the note ?—Yes.

10,172. Look at that note and see if that is the one which he received (*handing the same to the witness*) ?—This is not the one that came to them.

10,173. Is that the note (*handing another letter to the witness*) ?—That is the one.

10,174. When was it received ?—On the Saturday morning after the bands were taken.

10,175. " Gentlemen, In the bottom hull, turn up " the horsing, and in the trough the bands of both " hulls will be found. Apologising for the little in- " terruption, it is satisfactory things are arranged " without damage, which will make things a little " more agreeable when the rough edge is worn off. " Trusting these nocturnal visits will be no longer " necessary, I remain (signed), The Shy Maiden. " P.S. It is depended that A. Latham will either " come up or be discharged at the end of the reported " notice." You saw that note at the time it was received ?—Yes.

10,176. The bands were found at the place spoken of in that letter ?—Yes.

10,177. Did you receive about that time any other letters ?—No.

10,178. Did Mr. Beardshaw ?—No.

10,179. Do you know anything of this letter (*handing the same to the witness*) ?—That came afterwards.

10,180. How long after this occasion was it that you received this letter ?—About 12 months after.

10,181. Was that received by Messrs. Beardshaw and shown to you ?—Yes.

10,182. This was sent to Messrs. Beardshaw :—" Gentlemen, I understand Latham is still not con- " tributing to his trade society." Who is Latham ?—The chief handle maker.

10,183. Was he working at Messrs. Beardshaw's ?—Yes.

10,184. " I understand Latham is still not contri- " buting to his trade society, and as this is one of the " principal causes of the bands to be missing on the " last occasion, I think it right you should be made " acquainted with the fact of the non-settlement of " of this business, and that G. Peck has not kept his " engagement." Who is G. Peck ?—Another handle maker.

10,185. Did anything take place after receiving this note ?—No.

10,186. Did you at any time lose any other bands or tools from Messssrs. Beardshaw's premises ?—No ; 18 years ago the bands were taken.

10,187. I mean since the year 1864 ?—No.

10,188. Have you ever had any communication with Mr. Broadhead about missing bands ?—No.

10,189. The occasion of which you first spoke is the only occasion of bands being missing from Messrs. Beardshaw's ?—Yes.

10,190. Have you had any other letters besides these two which I put into your hands ?—No.

The witness withdrew.

Elisha Parker sworn and examined.

E. Parker.

10,191. (*Mr. Barstow.*) You are a saw grinder, living at Dore ?—Yes.

10,192. Do you now belong to the Saw Grinders' Union ?—The Little Saw Grinders' Union.

ELEVENTH DAY.

E. Parker.

18 June 1867.

10,193. You did belong to the Saw Grinders' Union?—Yes, once.

10,194. When did you join it?—The beginning of this year.

10,195. When did you join the old Saw Grinders' Union?—As soon as I was loose.

10,196. How long is that ago?—I am 47 years of age.

10,197. Is that 26 years ago?—Yes.

10,198. Do you remember, in September 1866, your bands being taken?—Yes.

10,199. Were John Taylor's bands missing at the same time?—Yes, and many more than John Taylor's.

10,200. Did you go with him to Broadhead?—Yes.

10,201. Were you with him all the time that he was at Broadhead's?—Yes; there was many more than John Taylor went at the time. I think there were ten.

10,202. Did you hear him ask what had become of the bands?—Yes.

10,203. What did Broadhead say to him?—Broadhead told him it was owing to the saw grinders.

10,204. Did he ask how he should get them back again?—He said they would have "play wages" while they were out.

10,205. That was said both to you and Taylor and the others?—Yes.

10,206. Did you receive "play wages"?—I did not receive money for a long time after that.

10,207. Perhaps you were in arrear?—No.

10,208. What were your "play wages"?—They wanted to give me 24*s.* a week, and I was not satisfied with that.

10,209. What did you want?—I wanted more than that. I thought I ought to have as much as any other man.

10,210. What did you ask for?—I asked for something in reason.

10,211. I suppose you proposed some sum which you ought to receive?—I cannot say what I asked.

10,212. In point of fact what did you receive?—I suppose what Broadhead gave me after. There were brother and me were five or six weeks before we got the money.

10,213. You do not remember how much it was?—No.

10,214. Was it more than at the rate of 24*s.* a week?—I cannot say.

10,215. Did he tell you that there would be anything to pay for expenses?—No.

10,216. Did not he say that there would be anything for "Mary Ann"?—No.

10,217. When are you speaking of? I am asking you about 1866.—I speak of this letter here (*handing a letter to the Commissioners*).

10,218. This was in 1859 that you are speaking of now, a long time ago?—Yes, the saw makers.

10,219. Then you received this letter?—Yes.

10,220, The post mark is April 24th?—Yes.

10,221. "When the blood is in an impure state, "brimstone and treacle is given as a mild purgative," is that the same letter we have read before?—Yes. This is another letter that came by post too (*handing the same to the Commissioners*).

10,222. At the same time?—It might be a few days after, April the 7th, 1859.

10,223. Did these two come in the same envelope?—No.

10,224. They are in the same handwriting as the other, and signed exactly in the same way, "Tantia Topee"?—Yes.

10,225. You say that these letters came at different times?—They are not the same date; they came at two different times. You will find the date on the enveloep.

10,226. The letters are not dated?—No.

10,227. They came at different times?—The two you have in your hand came together at the same time, when we were out on strike.

10,228. "To Elisha Parker. Dear sir, I take the "liberty of addressing you on the subject of making "yourself such a busy tool in the hands of Messrs. "Newbold Brothers. Let me tell you that your con- "duct is closely watched, and if you refuse to act with "the men I would advise you not to act against them "by running about to find men to fill their places. "It is a filthy job, and I am sure if you act wisely "for your own interest's sake, you will keep out of it. "There is an abundannce of means of paying you back "with interest for all the mischief you are capable of "doing in this case. The truth of this your past expe- "rience ought to teach you. Messrs. Newbold cannot "compensate you for the consequences you are surely "bringing upon yourself. It is out of mortal power "to do so. Be advised ere it is too late. (Signed) "A GRINDER." "To Messrs. Newbold's saw grinders "working at Vaughan's wheel. Gentlemen, Since "you have refused to assist the saw makers in the "present strike after having been desired to do so, "let me advise you not to act against them, as some "of you may have cause to regret if persisted in, and "let me particularly advise Aaron to keep his trap "shut, as it has been heard of him bleating about it "being a great thing that the grinders must be called "upon to turn out for the makers, and so forth. He "ought to be ashamed of himself. He has refused "to turn out, and therefore he had better hold his "tongue about the affair, as it will only tend to vex "the already irritated minds of the members of your "own branch of the trade more still at your repre- "hensible conduct; but it was not he who was speak- "ing it, but the sentiments of some one else above "him. The poor fool has not sense for it; when "Balaam could not speak his ass spoke for him. "(Signed) A GRINDER." Do you remember losing you bands in September 1866, not quite a year ago?—Yes.

10,229. And John Taylor's were taken at the same time?—Yes.

10,230. Did you go to Broadhead's?—Yes.

10,231. Did you ask him why they had been taken?—Yes.

10,232. What did he say?—Owing to our arrears.

10,233. Did he say what you would have to pay?—2*l.* I had to pay, and "Mary Ann."

10,234. How much for "Mary Ann"?—It was 1*l.* for us both. It was on a Saturday.

10,235. 2*l.* for arrears and 2*l.* for "Mary Ann"?—2*l.* for arrears that he charged us, and "Mary Ann."

10,236. What was "Mary Ann"?—1*l.*

10,237. That was the amount between you?—Yes. That was on Saturday.

10,238. You went to him again?—Yes, we went to him again on Tuesday.

10,239. And then he told you that you would have something more to pay?—He said we should have 2*l.* to pay, and 50*s.* for "Mary Ann."

10,240. How much did you pay?—I paid 2*l.*, and 10*s.* for "Mary Ann," and Mr. Broadhead wished to lend me 5*s.*, and I said it should not ever be said that I had borrowed 5*s.* from a man like him to make the 15*s.* up.

10,241. Did he tell you how you were to get the bands back?—He said we must go home when we paid the money, and we should have the bands in the morning.

10,242. Did you receive a letter the next morning?—Yes, I received a letter the next morning. I keep the post office. It came to the house.

10,243. Have you kept the letter?—No; it was sent to my employer. I do not know what became of it.

10,244. Do you remember the contents of it?—Yes; it said where the bands were, and we went down to the place by the side of Mr. Robinson's, and found the bands where the letter stated.

The witness withdrew.

Mr. JAMES SMITH BECKETT sworn and examined.

10,245. (*Chairman.*) You are a saw manufacturer, and one of the firm of Alfred Beckett and Sons, in Green Lane?—Yes.

10,246. Your father was in business some 26 years?—Yes, about that time.

10,247. He died last September?—Yes.

10,248. In February 1859 had you a quantity of bands taken?—Yes.

10,249. Can you assign any reason why the bands had been taken away?—I believe it was because the saw makers were in arrears.

10,250. The saw makers?—Yes.

10,251. Did they afterwards pay the money?—Yes.

10,252. Did you get the bands back?—Yes; we lent them the money.

10,253. Do you know how they came back?—We got a note saying where they were to be found, and our grinders went but they could not find them, but the day after they were in the "George" public house at Owlerton.

10,254. Do you know what the note said?—Yes; I have the note here (*producing the same*).

10,255. "The bands is in the house of Tom Booth, "lying in the slack in the cellar, the nut in the top of "the wall in the corner on the ivy at the corner going "to Balmford Wood, near to Dearton's brewery. "(Signed) MARY" and addressed to Thomas Godley, who is Thomas Godley?—A grinder that works for us.

10,256. Did you search in Booth's cellar?—Yes.

10,257. Did you find them?—No.

10,258. What did you do?—A few days afterwards, or a day afterwards, our grinders were at the public house at Ollerton, when Hides, the saw makers' secretary, came in. They told him they could not find the bands.

10,259. Hides is alive then?—I believe he is dead.

10,260. What happened?—He said he would go and help to look for them, and he went and he could not find them.

10,261. What else?—So the day afterwards my father went down to Broadhead, when he kept the "Greyhound" in Gibraltar Street.

10,262. Were you with him?—Yes.

10,263. Then you both went?—Yes.

10,264. Did you see him?—Yes.

10,265. What did you say to him?—My father told him that now the affair was settled he wanted his bands back.

10,266. He paid the money?—Yes, the men had.

10,267. Your father said, "Now the affair is settled I want my bands back"?—Yes.

10,268. What did Broadhead say to that?—He said he knew nothing about them. My father then told him if they were not forthcoming the next day at 12 o'clock he should put the screw on to one of their great men, and he said he would send down at 10 o'clock in the morning for the answer. I went down the next morning, and I do not remember the words he said, but he led me to believe that either those bands or some others would be forthcoming at the appointed time, at 12 o'clock, and at 2 o'clock the same day this grinder of ours that is here, Godby, went to some leather dealer on the West Bar, and got new bands and took them on to our grinding wheel.

10,269. On your account?—No. I do not know who paid for them; we did not.

10,270. Godby went to the leather dealer and bought you some new bands?—Yes.

10,271. The same number as you lost exactly?—Yes; something to substitute for those that we had lost.

10,272. You never paid for them?—No.

10,273. Godby is here, is he not?—Yes.

10,274. What happened else? you set to work with your bands?—Yes; that is the whole of it.

10,275. That was in 1859?—Yes.

10,276. In the beginning of 1860 do you remember anything taking place?—Yes; we had some bands taken on the 9th of August 1860.

10,277. How many bands were taken?—I think about four.

10,278. Can you say what was the reason of that?—It was on account of the saw makers being in arrear, the same as before.

10,279. What was done then, did your father lend the money to pay?—Yes, he lent them the money.

10,280. How much did he lend them?—7*l.* 10*s.*

10,281. What became of that, had you a note or how?—I believe we had a note; I am not sure.

10,282. Were the bands returned?—Yes.

10,283. How were the bands returned?—I think the grinders got a note saying where they would be after the affair was settled, and they got them back.

10,284. Had you any communication with Broadhead about it at that time, in August 1860?—One day, before we got the bands back, my father went down to Peace's Wheel, Eagle Works, where Godby, this man of ours, was working; my father had found him some other tools and set him to work, so that we had one man working, and he used to go twice a day to see that he attended to it, and one day when he went down Broadhead was at the gateway.

10,285. What happened?—I do not know for what purpose he was there, but it rather exasperated my father, and he called him an idle skulking vagabond, or something very appropriate, and he got out the note.

10,286. He used bad language?—It was not bad language. Broadhead jumped up and struck him just under the eye.

10,287. And then they had a fight over it?—Yes.

10,288. Have you received other letters than those which you have shown?—Yes. I do not know anything about the dates, they are here.

10,289. You have got them?—Yes, they are here (*producing the same to the Examiners*).

10,290. One is dated Sheffield, 1860, to Mr. Beckett, signed by the committee. "We are informed that "you are determined to annoy us by setting parties "not belonging to our trade to do work which ought "be done by saw makers. Now, sir, we wish to be "on friendly terms with you, and it is in your power "to promote that good feeling which should exist "between yourself, your men, and the trade generally "by keeping parties in your employ at work which "belongs to them and not infringing on the rights of "others. We speak truly when we say we wish to "live at peace with all, consider then calmly if it "not be better to work in harmony with the saw "makers employed by you and the trade generally." The next is "December 14th, 1860. Mr. Beckett, "Sir, It appears your saw and handle makers are "a considerable sum in arrears again, and as the "wishes of Amalgamated Society of the Saw Trade "are well known to them it is deemed necessary to "draw your attention to the subject, knowing *that* "*you have suffered loss and inconvenience* through "*their* neglect *before*, and as you can apply a remedy "it is considered best to give you an *opportunity* of "so doing, Yours respectfully, WM. HIDES." And here is a list—"R. Wragg, 12*s.*, William Hawood, "4*s.* 8*d.*, William Ibbetson, 6*s.* 2*d.*, J. Mallender, "5*s.* 10*d.*, J. Walker, 1*s.*, J. Arnley, 9*s.* 2*d.*, H. "Fearnehough, 5*s.* 2*d.*, E. Taylor, 7*s.* 8*d.*, J. Tuppett, "6*s.* 8*d.*, 2*l.* 18*s.* 4*d.*" The next is "November 4, "if them handel makers of yores dosent send their "money i shall com an feth strings if the devil stands "it road." The next is "James Godby bands wil "be Found at the Dike Side under the bank in Steads "Fild opersite the club mil 2 at each side the edg. "MARY." The next is "Jonas Haywood, your bands "will come back when the saw makers pay to thare "money." "beckett And Slaks must pay their natty." "Mr. Beckett, If you dont see at thes maters "settled I shall com ageen an then yol now on it

ELEVENTH DAY.

J. S. Beckett.

18 June 1867.

" yore men's workin, but if hell stans it road you can " reckin on it and it will cos you summat next time. " Mally." Then there is a small one " Make saw " makers pay." Those are the ones ?—Yes.

The witness withdrew.

W. Broadhead.

Mr. William Broadhead recalled and further examined.

10,291. (*Chairman.*) Have you a book called the investigating committee book ?—No.

10,292. Have you never had a book containing entries of monies paid by the investigating committee ?—No, only the books which you have here.

10,293. Is there a book containing entries by the investigating committee ?—There is only the appointment of the investigating committee.

10,294. What is that ?—The minute book when the appointment takes place, it will be at the general meetings when they are changed from time to time.

10,295. I speak independently of that; beyond that have you any book kept by the investigating committee in which their proceedings are entered ?—No, the only entries that we ever had were the arrears selected out from the contribution book on a foolscap sheet of paper and placed in the investigating committee's hands.

10,296. Had you in the month of June of last year any book of that description ?—No.

12,297. And you have none now ?—I have none now.

10,298. You know Joseph Chapman, who has been examined ?—Yes.

10,299. You do recollect in the month of June of last year his coming to you about his arrears ?—I remember him coming at a certain time; I do not remember the exact time.

10,300. You do recollect his coming ?—Yes.

10,301. Did you show him a book about an inch or an inch and a half thick and five or six inches wide which was called the investigating committee book ? —No, I should show him a book if he came about his arrears.

10,302. What book would you show him ?—The contribution book for one; this would be the book (*showing a book to the Commissioners*), and I might show him my own pocket book, which showed the same account.

10,303. That is nothing like an inch and a half thick and five or six inches wide. Is your private collecting book more than half an inch thick and five inches wide ?—It would be an inch thick and more, and it would be four or five inches wide.

10,304. Have you got that book ?—It would be a book similar to this, but thicker than this.

10,305. (*Mr. Broadhead to Mr. Chapman.*) Was it anything like that in size (*pointing to a book on the table*) ?

(*Mr. Chapman.*) No.

10,306. (*Chairman.*) Was it as large as that ?

(*Mr. Chapman.*) It would be as wide as that, but longer.

10,307. (*Mr. Broadhead.*) What was the colour of the book ?

(*Mr. Chapman.*) Like that one.

(*Mr. Broadhead.*) You must be mistaken.

10,308. (*Chairman to Mr. Broadhead.*) Did not you show him a book like that described which was called the investigating committee book ?—I say no, because it would be impossible.

10,309. Did you show him a book in order to satisfy him that he was not worse off than his uncle ?—I could not do that.

10,310. Did you show him a book to prove that his uncle was not worse off than others ?—Do you ask me the question, did I show him a book.

10,311. Yes ?—Very likely I did.

10,312. What book could you show him to satisfy him that he was not worse off than others ?—It might be my pocket contribution book, or it might be a large red book.

10,313. Those are the only two books that you could show him ?—Those are the only two books that I could show him, except I might show him a foolscap sheet of paper of the investigating committee's.

10,314. Have you the foolscap sheet ?—No; we do not keep it by us.

10,315. You have got the ledger ?—Yes.

10,316. And your own private book you have kept back ?—I have it; it is not here, a man is doing my business to-day and he has got the collecting book with him.

10,317. When it is called for it will be produced ?— Yes.

10,318. Did not you show him a book and point out a thing to him to show that there was an instruction in it, that his contribution was to be got by force ?—If I showed him anything at all——

10,319. Did you show him that ?—Do you mean a book ?

10,320. Did you show him an entry in a book in which there was a statement that his contribution was to be got by force ?—No.

10,321. Did you show him an entry of that kind, not in a book, but in anything in anyway ? did you show him such as entry as that ?—It is very possible that I might.

10,322. In point of fact did you do it ?—I cannot remember it, but if he says so I am ready to believe him; but it would not be from a book.

10,323. What would it be from ?—From a foolscap sheet of paper.

10,324. You swear that you had no book containing an entry of that description ?—I swear that.

10,325. And you keep no investigating committee book ?—I keep no investigating committee book.

10,326. And you swear that you have produced us all the books that you possess ?—All the books that we possess. If you permit me, an idea has struck me how he might suppose that it is possible——

(*Chairman.*) I will ask you about your idea afterwards. We will hear what Chapman has got to say first.

The witness withdrew.

J. Chapman.

Joseph Chapman recalled and further examined.

10,327. (*Chairman.*) Do you recollect calling upon Broadhead some time in the month of June 1866 ?— Yes.

10,328. Did he produce a book to you ?—Yes.

10,359. What size was it ?—The first book that he opened was the regular ledger book, and while he was reckoning my arrears up we got in conversation. I told him I thought I was used worse than another member; I told him that I had a brother that was owing near on 10*l.* that I knew of, and they had not made any bother with him, and he got a book to convince me that I was not used worse than another member, and there was my name in it, and at the end of my name it was written that my arrears must be got by force.

10,330. You read that yourself in the book ?—Yes.

10,331. Did you read anything as to what the book was called, was it headed anything ?—I understood that it was the investigating committee book.

10,332. How did you understand it so ?—It is not often that they transact business as a committee without a book.

10,333. You know the investigating committee ?— Yes.

10,334. How many formed the investigating committee ?—Three.

ELEVENTH DAY.

J. Chapman.

18 June 1867.

10,335. Who are the investigating committee?—If I am right there was one William Barber, and the othere were Jonathan Renshaw and George Allen; I am not certain, but I believe so. I know two of them.

10,336. Have you ever been before them?—Yes, I have been before the investigating committee.

10,337. At the time you were before them had they a book or not on the table, when they were investigating their affairs?—I cannot say whether they had or not, they had every man's account before them, but I cannot say whether it was in a book or not.

10,338. It might have been on sheets?—Yes, it might have been on sheets.

10,339. They had every man's account before them, but you cannot say whether it was in a book?—No.

10,340. Can you say whether you had seen this book or not before Mr. Broadhead showed it to you that day?—No, I cannot.

10,341. You called it the investigating committee's book?—Yes.

10,342. Why did you say that it was the investigating committee's book?—They had their instructions from the investigating committee.

10,343. Why did you say that it was the investigating committee's book?—It was there besides for me to look at.

10,344. Did Broadhead say what the book was?—No, he did not.

10,345. Have you ever seen a book in the possession of Broadhead containing any account of acts of violence done or to be done?—No; not further than that.

10,346. Is that the only time that you have seen the book?—Yes.

10,347. Have you never seen a book containing an account of acts of violence done or to be done?—No, sir, I have not.

10,348. Never?—No; I never saw a book excepting that time.

10,349. What did you see in that book besides what you mentioned, that your arrears were to be got by force?—I saw some parties' names in it.

10,350. What was to be done to the other parties?—Their money was to be got by force, the same as mine.

10,351. Can you recollect the expression that was used?—Betwixt Broadhead and me?

10,352. What was written in the book about the other men?—I could not see anything except the names, there were names in that book that there was not anything against.

10,353. There were some names which had nothing written at the end?—Yes.

10,354. There were other names to which something was added?—They had written at the end of them the same as mine, that their money was to be got by force.

10,355. Was the kind of force mentioned by which the money was to be got?—There was not anything named excepting that.

10,356. Are you quite sure that the words "by force" were used?—Yes.

10,357. Was that book which you saw a bound book or loose sheets?—It was a bound book.

10,358. Amongst those books just point out the kind of book that you saw; look at that lot and select the book nearest in size (*alluding to a number of books on the table*)?—It was like this book (*selecting one from the bundle on the table*).

10,359. Was the one that you saw like that one?—There is very little difference between the two.

The witness withdrew.

WILLIAM BROADHEAD recalled and further examined.

W. Broadhead.

10,360. (*Chairman.*) Do you produce to me the book which contains the entry that these men's arrears are to be got by force?—No.

10,361. The other witness has sworn that he has seen a book in your possession a book in which there is an entry that his arrears are to be got by force. I ask you to produce that book?—We have not such a book, and never had.

10,362. You had a loose sheet in which it was written?—I do not dispute what he says, though I do not remember it. I want to show you how it might occur; these accounts, as I tell you, used to be taken on the sheets to submit to the investigating committee, and to keep them clean I frequently used to put them in a book of this kind. I have borrowed this sheet of paper of Mr. Sugg just to explain what I mean. It was no uncommon thing to place the sheet in the book, and it might be in the book on that occasion; it was a double sheet, one side had the names and the amount of arrears, the remaining part of the line would be for remarks to be entered upon it. I might open the book like that, and the sheet might be in it, and he might take this to be a part of the book.

10,363. You do not deny that there was in that book an entry that the arrears were to be got by force?—With regard to the word "force" I do not remember making such an entry, but I admit that we used to make such remarks as this "This case to be pressed by the best means it can," and such as that.

10,364. It is said that Chapman's arrears were to be got by force?—He is mistaken, I believe, I do not remember; I cannot tax my memory with that.

10,365. You swear that you have no such book?—I swear that we have no such book.

10,366 And never had?—And never had.

The witness withdrew.

JOSEPH CHAPMAN recalled and further examined.

J. Chapman.

10,367. (*Chairman.*) Mr. Broadhead has given his explanation; he says that you may be mistaken in supposing that it was a book, and that it was only a sheet of paper that was laid in the book; do you still adhere to your statement that it was a book, or do you accept that explanation and say that it possibly might be a sheet of paper?—It is quite possible it might be a sheet of paper in that book; I just looked at my name, I did not read more than three besides my own, I turned away and was paying him some money; it possibly might have been a sheet of paper.

10,368. You believed it to be a book, but since you have heard the explanation given by Mr. Broadhead you will not swear that it was not a sheet of paper?—I will not swear it was not a sheet of paper.

10,369. But until you heard the explanation you always believed that it was a book?—Yes, I always believed it was a book.

10,370. This is about the size of the book (*producing a book*)?—Yes.

(*Chairman.*) I do not know any sheet of paper that would be the size of this book.

The witness withdrew.

THOMAS FEARNEHOUGH sworn and examined.

T. Fearnehough.

10,371. (*Chairman.*) You are suffering, are you not?—Yes.

10,372. How old are you?—50.

10,373. Have you served your apprenticeship to the trade of saw grinders?—Yes, the jobbing grinders and saw grinders together.

ELEVENTH DAY.

T. Fearnehough.

18 June 1867.

10,374. How long ago did you join the Union ?—About eight years ago, as near as I can remember.

10,375. Did you leave them ?—Yes, I left them last year.

10,376. But you had left them before that, and joined them again ?—Yes.

10,377. When did you first leave them ?—A good bit since, I cannot say how long.

10,378. How long did you cease to be a member? were you absent from them for some time ?—Yes.

10,379. And then you joined them again ?—Yes.

10,380. Why did you leave them ?—I cannot exactly say why I left them at that time.

10,381. Why did you join them again ?—I joined them because they all went in and it would not do for me to stop out myself.

10,382. The remainder went in ?—Yes, and so did I along with the rest.

10,383. You thought that it would not do for you to stay out ?—No.

10,384. Why did you think that it would not do for you to stay out ?—I thought they might do me some bodily harm.

10,385. I believe it was in 1859 when you first joined ?—Yes, I think it was, I am not certain.

10,386. It was for your own protection, and not from any advantage that you expected from the Union that you joined ?—Yes.

10,387. I believe you left them on the 23d of October 1865 ?—Perhaps it might be that.

10,388. In 1865, that was two years ago ?—Yes, but I joined them again.

10,389. You left them altogether in October 1865 ?—Yes, I did.

10,390. And you have never belonged to them since ?—No.

10,391. When you were a member how much did you pay ?—When we were paying poundage I was paying about 6*s.* a week, and when we were paying 5*s.* a week it cost me 7*s.* 6*d.* a week, 5*s.* for myself and 2*s.* 6*d.* for my son.

10,392. Do you know how many members there are belonging to the Union ?—A little over 200.

10,393. Do you know how many there are on the box ?—No, I do not know at present.

10,394. Have you ever been yourself on the box ?—Yes, I had been on the box about three months when I joined them the last time.

10,395. Had you an accident ? How was it you were on the box ?—I was out of a place of work.

10,396. What did they allow you when you were on the box ?—I think I drew somewhere about 1*l.* a week when I was on the box for me and my family.

10,397. Were you on the box three months ?—Yes, about three months.

10,398. And with the exception of that 1*l.* a week for three months, which you received, have you ever received any other aid from the trade ?—No.

10,399. Did you ever have a house at Birkendale ?—Yes.

10,400. What became of it ?—I sold it; the reason for selling it was that I received a threatening letter.

10,401. When did you have a house at Birkendale ?—It is five or six years ago since I sold it.

10,402. Why did you sell it ? because you received a threatening letter ?—Yes, threatening to blow it up, and I thought they should not have the chance.

10,403. Have you got the letter ?—No, sir, I have not.

10,404. What was the value of your house ?—I think I sold it for 200*l.*

10,405. Did you work at Hague's at any time ?—Yes.

10,406. When was that ?—I began to work for them in 1864.

10,407. Was there any trouble between you and the Union at that time ?—Yes, I left the Union on purpose to work for them.

10,408. What was the consequence of your going to work for Hague's ?—I worked for them up to the 25th of September 1865; that was the time I left them.

10,409. Was anything done in consequence of your going to Hague's ?—Do you mean in reference to taking bands or anything of that kind ?

19,410. Yes; tell us anything that happened ?—Nine months after that I joined them again, for Broadhead came up for the contribution. It was the latter end of November or the beginning of December; and he says, "I want you to do a bit of a job "for me." I said, "What is it for ?" and he said, "The handle-makers are not paying to the trade." I said, "It required consideration." He said, "Well, "it will do next week"; and he came up the week following, and as soon as he saw me he put a note into my hands. He said, "When thou hast taken "the bands put that note on to the horsing."

10,411. What was in that note ?—I do not remember what was in the note.

10,412. Did you do what he asked you ?—No; I told him I should not do it, or let anybody else do it if I could help it. That is what I said to him. So I made it my duty to see Mr. Hague, and he advised me to take the bands from there myself and put them away, and so I did.

10,413. Did you follow his advice and take them away ?—Yes; that is all I have to say on that subject.

10,414. In January 1866, were you working on your own tools ?—I began working on my own tools in 1865.

10,415. Were you working upon them in January 1866, last year ?—Yes.

10,416. Do you know Mr. Green, the pork butcher, in Gibraltar-street ?—Yes.

10,417. Did you ask him to speak to Mr. Broadhead about your joining the Union ?—Yes, I did.

10,418. You asked him to see Mr. Broadhead upon the subject ?—Yes, I asked Mr. Green to see Mr. Broadhead, to see if he could arrange matters for me to come in again.

10,419. Had you had any bands taken away just about that time ?—They took two bands from Mr. Butcher's wheel on the 24th of November 1865.

10,420. Did you buy two other bands for them ?—Yes, I bought two other bands for them.

10,421. What did they cost you ?—5*l.* all but a shilling.

10,422. Did you leave them at the timekeeper's house ?—Yes.

10,423. I believe you fell in with his suggestion, and it was Green who advised you to try and make it up ?—Yes; I was down at that time with the liver complaint.

10,424. Is Green a saw grinder as well as a butcher ?—Yes.

10,425. I believe Green spoke to Broadhead, and Broadhead met you by arrangement at Green's house, did he not ?—Yes he did.

10,426. What did Broadhead say to you when he came ?—I will try to tell you as near as I can. I think he told me I should have nearly 16*l.* to pay to make me straight. I offered to pay a certain sum down.

10,427. How much did you offer to pay down ?—I think it was 3*l.* I am not certain how much it was just now. I think it was 3*l.*, or it might be more.

10,428. You offered to pay 3*l.* or something more ?—Yes.

10,429. What about the new bands which you had bought ?—I wanted him to stop the remainder out of my instalments. He said that it could not be done in that way; I must pay it all down, and then I should have my bands back again. I have rather overrun my story. I wanted them to take 5*l.* off what I had to pay, and they said I must pay the whole money down, and then I could have my bands back.

10,430. Was your son working with you at that time ?—Yes.

10,431. How old is your son ?—22 last Christmas.

10,432. Did you arrange with Broadhead or not ?—

No, I did not agree with Broadhead at all. I told him I should not pay the money ; I would go on as I was.

10,433. At that time were you working at Gray's, in New George Street ?—Yes.

10,434. Your son was working there at the same time ?—Yes.

10,435. In February 1866 did you begin to work at Gray's ?—Yes, I did.

10,436. You worked there till June ?—I worked there till the 25th of December.

10,437. After that did you engage with Slack, Sellars, and Co. ?—Yes, I did.

10,438. Did they want you to work for them entirely ?—Yes.

10,439. Did they belong to the Union ?—Not at that time.

10,440. And you did not ?—No.

10,441. And you agreed to work for them and continued to work for them till the 25th of September ?—Yes, and I am working for them now.

10,442. Have you worked for them ever since ?—Yes, at Mr. Butcher's wheel.

10,443. Has anything been said to you or done to you by the Saw Grinders' Union for working in this way, not being a Union man and not paying this sum of money ?—Yes, I got blown up for it.

10,444. You were blown up on the 8th of October ?—Yes.

10,445. Had you, between the time when you saw Broadhead, when he wanted you to pay the money, and the time you were blown up, suffered any annoyance from the Union ?—No.

10,446. Had they asked you to pay to the Union ?—No.

10,447. Had Broadhead been to you ?—No.

10,448. Nobody had been to you at all ?—No.

10,449. Did they know that you were working at Butcher's wheel for Slack, Sellars, and Co. ?—Yes.

10,450. And that you had not paid the money ?—Yes.

10,451. You say that on the 8th of October you were blown up ?—Yes.

10,452. Is that the outrage in Hereford Street ?—Yes.

10,453. There has been a reward of 1,100*l.* for it ?—Yes.

10,454. To whom do you attribute that blowing up ? have you any reason to suspect any person or any body of persons of being the cause of that blowing up ?—I have as much right to back my opinion as Broadhead to deny the truth,

10,455. What is your belief ?—I believe Broadhead knows all about it, and knows the man that did it, if it was not himself.

10,456. Is it of trade origin or private malice ?—It is a trade affair, I am certain, through me going to Slack, Sellars, and Co.

10,457. Are you aware of possessing any enemy at all who would be likely to do you such an injury ?—No.

10,458. Have you any enemy that you are aware of ?—Not that I am aware of, only that party.

10,459. Have you given offence in any way, except to the Union ?—No, not to the best of my knowledge.

10,460. Have you given offence to any private individual ?—No ; not to the best of my knowledge.

10,461. Have you ever had any threat of any sort from any private individual ?—No.

10,462. Was there any person you had quarrelled with before that time ?—No.

10,463. Are you a married man ?—Yes.

10,464. And with a family ?—Yes.

10,465. Have you any reason to suppose that any of your family had quarrelled with any person ?—No, they had not.

10,466. How old is your family ? One son is of age ; is he your eldest son ?—I have two sons of age.

10,467. Do they live with you ?—No.

10,468. Are there any younger ones ?—I have two boys and a girl living with me.

10,469. You have no suspicion of any person at all on the ground of private malice ?—No.

10,470. You say that you are entitled to an opinion, and you believe that Broadhead knows all about it ?—Yes.

10,471. What ground have you for saying that ?—On account of my going to Slack, Sellars, and Co. ; that is the reason.

10,472. What right have you to say that you believe Mr. Broadhead knows all about it ?—I have as much right to back my opinion as Broadhead has to deny the truth of it.

10,473. Though you have a right to back your opinion in a matter so serious as that affecting your own happiness, what right have you to say that Broadhead knows anything about it ?—I know he does ; I am certain he does ; he knows all about it ; he knows who has blown me up, and everything ; he knows how much money has been paid for the job being done, and everything.

10,474. This is a very serious charge against Mr. Broadhead ; what right have you to make such a charge against him ?—I told you I have as much right to back my opinion as Broadhead has to deny the truth of it ; that is my opinion.

10,475. Upon what is your opinion based ?—On account of my going to Slack, Sellars, and Co.

10,476. Has Broadhead ever used any threat to you at any time ?—Yes ; I had one about 11 years ago, and I had one either the second or third day after they blew me up.

10,477. From whom was the threat 11 years ago ?—I expect it came from Broadhead.

10,478. Why do you expect that it came from Broadhead ?—Because I was just going to engage to do some work for Ibbetson ; he said if I did not leave it alone they would blow this house up at Birkendale.

10,479. He told you this himself ?—No ; he said so in his threatening letter.

Mr. Sugg submitted that a transaction which had taken place 11 years ago was out of the scope of this inquiry.

The Chairman stated that a threat which had been made 11 years ago could be gone into as an important fact, showing that previous malice existed.

10,480. (*Chairman, to the Witness.*) You say that you had a threat some long time ago, when you were going to work for Ibbetson ?—I was going to do some work for him, and he told me if I did it——

10,481. Who told you ?—It was in the threatening letter.

10,482. How do you know that Broadhead sent the letter ?—It came to me.

10,483. How did it come to you ?—It came by the post.

10,484. Who wrote it ?—I cannot say who wrote it.

10,485. How do you know that it was Mr. Broadhead who wrote it ?—Because nobody had any business to send it but him.

10,486. Was Broadhead secretary at that time ?—Yes.

10,487. Then it comes to this, that you received a threatening note ?—Yes.

10,488. What did it say ?—It said if I did the work I should have the house blown up at Birkendale.

10,489. Was that the reason why you parted with the house ?—Not just then it was not.

10,490. You had a letter ?—I did not do the work, I left it alone, I daresn't meddle with it any further.

10,491. That note came by post you say ?—Yes.

10,492. Can you recollect the contents of it ?—No.

10,493. It told you that if you did that work your house would be blown up.—Yes.

10,494. And Broadhead was the secretary at that time to the Union ?—Yes.

10,495. Had you any quarrel with any person about that work except with the Union ?—No.

10,496. You were a member of the Union then ?—No, I was not.

ELEVENTH DAY.

T. Fearnehough.

18 June 1867.

10,497. What is your other ground? you say that two days before the blowing up, something occurred?—The day after the blowing up I received another letter, I gave that letter to Mr. Jackson; the threatening letter I got the day after the blowing up; I gave it to Mr. Jackson.

10,498. You say that you received a letter which you gave to Mr. Jackson?—Yes.

10,499. Do you know who it came from?—I guessed from Broadhead.

10,500. What reason have you for saying that that letter came from Broadhead?—Because I know he is a man of that description that does send such like letters.

10,501. It is not in his handwriting, is it?—It is wrote in red pencil I think.

10,502. Do you recollect what it was?—No, it mentioned something about a cat's foot, &c.

10,503. You gave that to Mr. Jackson did you?—Yes.

10,504. You say that you believe that the letter came from Broadhead because he is a man who sends such letters?—Yes.

10,505. How do you know that he sends such letters?—I know that he does.

10,506. How do you know it?—It is his business to do it I suppose.

10,507. What right have you to say that Mr. Broadhead is the man who sends anonymous letters about?—I say it is nobody else but him.

10,508. What right have you to say that? it is very easy to say that of a person? but what ground have you for saying that Broadhead is the man who sent you that anonymous note?—There is no one else that has any business to send them but him.

10,509. What right have you to say that it was he, any bad man can send such a letter as that? Why should you fix upon Mr. Broadhead?—I still back my opinion, and I do believe that it is him and nobody else.

10,510. You ought to have some reason for such an opinion; what are your reasons for coming to such a conclusion as that?—I cannot change my opinion from what I say.

10,511. Have you ever seen Broadhead write such a note?—I have seen him write letters many a time.

10,512. Have you ever seen him write anonymous letters? letters without signing his name to them?—No.

10,513. Have you ever seen him write a letter and sign it "Tantia Topee?"—It requires a little bit of study over that.

10,514. Think for a moment. Have you ever seen him write a letter which he signed "Tantia Topee"?—I believe I have heard him speak about that name many a time when I was there.

10,515. You have heard him speak of the name "Tantia Topee" when you have been there?—Yes.

10,516. Have you ever seen him write a letter and put that signature at the bottom of it?—I will not say whether I have or not.

10,517. Have you ever seen him write a letter of a threatening character to anybody?—No, sir, I have not; I am not a scholar myself.

10,518. You have never seen him write a letter of that description?—He has not let me see it.

10,519. What right have you to say that Broadhead is the man who sent you that letter? you cannot swear to his writing, and you never saw him write a threatening letter?—I know Broadhead can write three or four different hands.

10,520. How do you know that?—I have seen him do it.

10,521. You are no scholar, and you are sure that you have seen him write in three or four different hands. What has been his object in writing before you in two or three different hands; why did he do that?—So that nobody should know his writing.

10,522. On what occasions have you seen him write different from his ordinary hand?—I cannot say exactly; I know he can write three or four different hands.

10,523. How do you know that? this may be a groundless suspicion of yours?—I have seen him.

10,524. Sometimes better and sometimes worse, or a different character or what?—Some larger and some smaller.

10,525. Having seen him write so often as you say you have, can you tell us whether the letter that you received two mornings after you were blown up was in Mr. Broadhead's handwriting or not?—I cannot say that.

10,526. Have you ever heard Broadhead talk about threatening letters?—I cannot say positively just this moment whether I have or not.

10,527. Then you have no ground except the simple fact of his being the secretary, and the suspicion that this is a trade matter that this letter was written by Broadhead?—Yes, that is all.

10,528. There is nobody else to whom you can attribute it?—No.

10,529. At the time that you were blown up were your sons working as well as yourself for Slack, Sellars, and Company?—No.

10,530. It is against the law of the Union to work on your own tools?—Yes.

10,531. You owed the Union some money, and you were working against the Union on your own tools, and that was the ground of offence as far as you are concerned?—Yes.

10,532. Had you any fear of being blown up before you were blown up?—Yes, I was aware they would do me some bodily harm or blow me up.

10,533. Did you take any precaution to prevent it?—I fastened the cellar grate as well as I could.

10,534. What besides?—That was all I could do just then.

10,535. Had you a fanlight over the door?—Yes.

10,536. What did you do with that? did you let it remain as it was?—I believe I got a board that would fit the fanlight.

10,537. Did you, after this occurred, ever go to Broadhead and complain to him that he was at the bottom of it, or anything of that kind?—No.

10,538. If you thought he was why did not you?—I thought I had better stop away from him; I did not like the man at all.

10,539. Have you had any quarrel with Broadhead?—Yes.

10,540. Is this a charge made by you out of malice to Broadhead?—We have not had much of a quarrel, but we have had a few words.

10,541. When was that?—That was when I was working on the Trade's tools at Well's wheel.

10,542. How long ago is that?—That would be in 1864.

10,543. Did you fight?—No, I did not say anything to him myself; I never spoke to him.

10,544. What did he say to you?—He called me everything but a gentleman; I never spoke to him.

10,545. What things did he say to you?—We had no work to do on the Friday and Saturday, and we went to his house with a man who had paid for a sup of beer.

10,546. Did you go to Broadhead's house?—We went to Broadhead's house on Friday afternoon, and this man paid for a sup of beer, and when we were done we stopped there until we went home at night; we were there on Saturday morning, we did not work any more that week.

10,547. What did Broadhead say to you on that occasion?—We got to work on Monday morning and worked till Friday.

10,548. What did Broadhead say to you? he called you everything but a gentleman?—I went on Friday to put the work down, and then he started calling me everything.

10,549. Tell me what he said?—I cannot remember what he said.

10,550. What names did he call you, or what did he complain of?—That I was drunk, and everything

ELEVENTH DAY.

T. Fearnehough.

18 June 1867.

that was bad. He said we ought to be minding our work, but we had no work to do, and it was not his place to speak to me at all; it was his place to fetch me up before the committee if there was anything amiss; but he took it on himself, and that was my reason for giving a month's warning to leave.

10,551. It was in consequence of his speaking to you that you gave a month's warning to leave?—Yes.

10,552. You gave notice to leave the Union?—Yes.

10,553. You thought that he had no business to speak to you, and you gave a month's warning to leave?—Yes.

10,554. Is that the only occasion on which you have had any quarrel with Broadhead?—Yes.

10,555. Have you had any quarrel with him at all except on the ground of trade questions?—No.

10,556. Upon no private ground, but upon trade questions?—Yes.

10,557. Have you ever quarrelled with anybody else?—No; I have told you all the quarrels I have had with him.

10,558. Your bands were taken at Hague's and the glazers cut to pieces?—Yes; that was at the bottom of Arundel Street.

10,559. Before the bands were stolen do you recollect any person giving you warning?—Yes.

10,560. What did they tell you?—They said I had better look out, there was something amiss.

10,561. Before your bands were taken you were told to look out?—Yes.

10,562. Who told you to look out?—William Woodhead.

10,563. Were your bands taken shortly after Woodhead told you?—I took the grinding band and hid it myself, and I left two bands about, and they came either that night or the night after and took one away and left the other and cut the glazer.

10,564. You told us that Broadhead once offered you some money to take Hague's bands?—Yes.

10,565. Are you quite sure that you told that to Mr. Hague?—I told Mr. Hague, I went the same day and told him.

10,566. How did you happen to join the Union first, in 1859?—You mean the first time?

10,567. Yes?—Because they took all in.

10,568. Do you know the names of those that went in 1859?—They took all in at that time and I was one amongst those that went in.

10,569. Did Linley go in to?—No.

10,570. Linley went in afterwards?—Yes.

10,571. You remained in the Union some time at first?—Yes.

10,572. And you stayed some time and went out?—Yes.

10,573. What was the reason you went in the second time?—I went in the second time with Linley and a lot more, I do not know their names exactly now, but I went in with Linley and a lot more.

10,574. What time was that when you went in with Linley?—Perhaps seven or eight years ago.

10,575. Would not that be about 1859?—Perhaps so, I cannot say positively.

10,576. Linley died in February 1860?—It would be the year before.

10,577. You went in with Linley long before he died?—Yes.

10,578. How was it that you happened to go in then?—They took us all in.

10,579. The letter which you gave to Mr. Jackson is lost, do you know what was in that letter?—No; I cannot remember the whole of it, it talked a great deal about the "cat's foot."

10,580. What did it say about the "cat's foot"?—I do not know, I could not read it myself, but a person read it to me, I put it my pocket and gave it to Mr. Jackson.

10,581. Do you recollect no more about it than that?—No.

10,582. Did it say anything about blowing up or not?—No.

10,583. What about the "cat's foot"?—It meant that they would give me a right 'un next.

10,584. Did they say in the note that they would give you a "right 'un" the next time?—It mentioned nothing more, but I thought it went that length.

10,585. (*Mr. Chance.*) When you refused to roll the bands at Mr. Broadhead's request, did Mr. Broadhead express any annoyance at you not doing it?—No.

10,586. Did he ever express any annoyance at your working for Slack's? Did he express any anger, or remonstrate with you?—No; nor any one else.

10,587. Or because you worked upon your own tools?—It was partly for working upon my own tools, and partly for going to work for Slack, Sellars and Company.

10,588. What was?—Being blown up,

10,589. Did Broadhead ever say anything to you about working upon your own tools?—Yes, he did several times, but not then.

10,590. When did he say anything to you about it?—When Linley joined them. I sold them my tools. I sold my tools to the trade.

10,591. Did Broadhead, in the year 1866, ever say anything to you about your working upon your own tools?—I think he said it was not allowed. I am sure I cannot remember.

10,592. Do not say that you do not remember. I ask if he did?—I think he mentioned once it was not right for any one to work on his own tools.

10,593. When was that?—That was when I was working at Park, at Raynor's wheel.

10,594. How long before the blowing up in October did that take place?—It would be in 1865 when Broadhead said that to me.

10,595. (*Chairman.*) Were you a member of the Union at that time?—Yes, I was.

10,596. And it was against the rules for a man to work on his own tools, was it not?—Yes, it was.

10,597. (*Mr. Barstow.*) Before you joined in 1859 had you been threatened at all by any Union men?—No.

10,598. You say you joined with Linley and others?—Yes, but I threw myself out again after that.

10,599. But you can recollect your joining with Linley and others, can you not?—Yes.

10,600. Before that time had you been threatened by any Union men if you did not join?—No.

10,601. No one had done so?—No.

10,602. Then it was quite of your own goodwill that you went into the Union?—Yes; it was a good deal of it through my goodwill, and from the others going in at the same time.

10,603. You did not like to be left out?—No.

10,604. Did you break the Union rules in any other respect besides working on your own tools?—I like the Union very well so long as it is governed right.

10,605. You know the Union rules, I suppose?—Yes.

10,606. Did you break them in any other way besides working on your own tools?—Not that I can remember, except that I did not pay up sometimes.

10,607. Were you always straight in respect of apprentices?—I have had none but my own sons for the last ten years.

10,608. (*Chairman*). I am desired by Mr. Sugg to put this question to you. Have you been in the habit of absenting yourself from your work and your family for a week at a time, drinking?—I have done so; I ought to tell the truth, I have I believe.

10,609. Have you been in the habit of stopping out from your family and passing the night in debauchery?—I believe I have been out once or twice, but I have not been in a house of that description.

10,610. Has it been drinking then?—Yes.

10,611. Were you discharged from Hague and Barton's for bad conduct?—They did not turn me away at all; I gave them a month's warning and left them when the month was up.

10,612. You say that Broadhead asked you to ratten Mr. Hague?—Yes, he did.

10,613. Now instead of that did not you ask

ELEVENTH DAY.

T. Fearnehough.

18 June 1867.

Woodhead to take away the bands?—I never asked any one; I did not.

10,614. You never asked Woodhead?—I did not.

10,615. You never offered him money to do it?—No, I did not; I will take an oath of it.

10,616. You are quite sure about it?—Yes, I am.

10,617. You have charged Broadhead with having asked you to do it; did you ask Woodhead to do it?—No, I am confident of that; I did not know that I mentioned such a thing, except to Mr. Hague; I might mention such a thing to Woodhead.

10,618. But did you ask Woodhead to do it himself?—I did not.

10,619. You say that Broadhead said you were to pay 14*l.*; did Broadhead say what those 14*l.* were for; whether they were for arrears, or what they were for?—It was for arrears, and contributions, and fines, &c.

10,620. But did he mention what the 14*l.* were for?—I have forgotten whether he did mention it or not.

10,621. Were you aware that it was not simply for fines and contributions?—It was for contributions and fines.

10,622. And nothing for either "Mary Ann" or for taking away your bands or anything?—"Mary Ann" would be put to it.

10,623. Were you aware that the 14*l.* included any charge for "Mary Ann"?—I will not say that it was not in separately.

10,624. But was the 14*l.* composed of a fine for "Mary Ann" as well as for contributions and fines?—It was all put together.

10,625. Are you sure that it included a charge for "Mary Ann?"—I am not sure; it was all summed up together on a paper. I did not think that "Mary "Ann" was mentioned then.

10,626. Had you any means from your own knowledge of knowing what your contributions were, and what your fines were?—Yes.

10,627. How much would be owing for contributions at that time?—I think I was paying 7*s.* 6*d.* a week at that time.

10,628. But how much were you in arrear?—Perhaps four or five weeks, perhaps more. I cannot say.

10,629. That would be under 2*l.*?—Yes.

10,630. How much was due from you for fines?—I cannot exactly say how much I was behind in fines. It was for not attending meetings, I suppose.

10,631. But how much was due for fines?—I cannot say how many meetings I missed.

10,632. But you can tell us one way or the other whether that sum of 14*l.* included a charge for "Mary "Ann" or not?—No; I cannot answer you that question.

10,633. When were you blown up?—October 8th, 1866.

10,634. This is before that; this the 23rd January, 1866: "The secretary reports Thomas Fearnehough "having made known to Thomas Green that he, "Fearnehough, was desirous of coming to terms with "this society by giving up the present places he was "working for, and coming on the box, and thus taking "his chance for a situation according to the rules of "the society. At the request of Green, the secretary "had made out an account of arrears against Fearne-"hough up to June 13th, and that between 13*l.* and "14*l.*, without fines or penalties, since Fearnehough "left the society, which had been furnished to Fearne-"hough, Green being present, in this house, he, "Green, having just stated to the secretary, on "Fearnehough's behalf, that Fearnehough proposed "to pay the same, and the residue to be stopped by "2*s.* 6*d.* a week out of the scale, after an additional "5*l.* was deducted for arrears or missing bands. "After very brief consideration, it was resolved that "the following be the only terms on which Fearne-"hough ought to be accepted: That half the arrears "be paid down, and that for the residue the whole of "his scale be stopped until he is straight the same "as other members commence on the box who are in "arrear. As to the missing bands, the committee "have nothing to do with them, and refuses to enter-"tain this as any part of the case, beyond that should "arrangements be made the committee has no objec-"tion to use any influence it may possess to get them "restored, provided Fearnehough will pay any ex-"penses which may be incurred to obtain them." Is that a true story of what occurred?—Yes; it is true so far as it goes, except that they wanted me to stand on the box till I was straight.

10,635. They say that half the arrears are to be paid down, and that for the residue the whole of the scale is to be stopped until you are straight; did they tell you that you were to pay half, and that then the remainder should be stopped until you were straight?—Yes, I was not to have any scale at all until I was straight.

10,636. They say all members who came on the box do the same?—Yes.

10,637. Then you have no right to complain of any injustice as having been selected for a different course from others?—Yes, but what was I to live on until I got straight, and what was my family to live on?

10,638. You had stopped working?—Yes.

10,639. You were out of employment?—Yes.

13,640. And you would have no scale?—No.

10,641. And therefore you would be without a farthing if that proposition on the part of the Society were really in earnest?—Yes, and without any means.

10,642. Without any means of livelihood?—Yes.

10,643. *Chairman* (*To Mr. Broadhead.*) Is that so?—The proposition is that he should pay half the money down, and that the rest should be stopped out of his scale, 2*s.* 6*d.* a week.

10,644. This is your entry, "That half the arrears be paid down, and that for the residue the whole of the scale be stopped until he be straight"?—Bar 2*s.* 6*d.* a week.

10,645. Nothing of the kind; that was the proposition I think. He proposed to stop out of his scale 2*s.* 6*d.* a week, and to deduct the cost of the bands; but you said, "No, he should pay half down and then he shall not work, and he shall not get anything for his family until he is quite straight;" of course no man could accept such a proposition as that?—They refused to take him until all arrears were paid.

10,646. (*To the Witness.*) I dare say that they did not want you at all; you had been off and on with them?—Well, I did not want them very badly.

10,647. And I dare say they did not want you very badly. I am desired to ask you this question, and to press you upon it:—You say that you have seen Broadhead write three different hands?—Yes, I have; I have seen it when it has been written. I have seen his writing up at the desk in the place.

10,648. Have you seen him write?—Yes, I have.

10,649. Have you seen him write three different hands yourself?—I have seen him write different hands, but I cannot say how many.

10,650. But when you say different hands, is it one larger than the other, or what is it?—Different styles.

10,651. Did it occur to you that there was any reason for this?—I did not know why he was writing so many different hands. It did not matter anything to me, and I did not take much notice of it. I thought he was doing what he could do. As far as that goes a man has a right to learn what he can while he lives.

10,652. Can you tell us where you saw him write those different hands?—In his own house.

10,653. When have you seen him write those different hands?—When I worked on the Trade's tools; that would be in the year 1864.

10,654. Was it in the books which he was writing?—Not particularly in the books, on different occasions. (*A book was shown to the witness.*) I cannot read writing.

10,655. Broadhead knew quite well that you could not read writing?—No, I cannot read writing.

10,656. He knew that ?—Yes, he did.

10,657. Thereupon there was no occasion for him to write different hands before you ?—I can tell when a man is writing in one hand and when he is writing in another.

10,658. But what is the good of Broadhead writing in a different hand before you ?—I cannot shut my eyes.

10,659. No, but if you cannot read you might as well have them shut ?—No, but I can look at it.

10,660. But was he writing in books when he wrote these different hands ?—I believe he might be making notes out.

10,661. Was it on bits of paper or was it in books that he was writing ?—They were on paper, I believe.

10,662. What kind of paper ?—Writing paper.

10,663. Were they like notes or what were they like ?—Yes.

10,664. Like notes ?—Yes.

10,665. I suppose that whatever he was writing he would not be frightened of your seeing it. Where were you standing when he was writing those notes ?—I might be standing as close to him as this gentleman here (*pointing to the shorthand writer*).

10,666. As close as that ?—Yes.

10,667. And you were looking over it ?—Yes, I might be looking over it.

10,668. Was any one else present at the time ?—There might be another or two.

10,669. (*Mr. Chance.*) Were you sitting opposite to him when he wrote ?—Yes ; he was sitting just the same as I might be sitting now opposite this gentleman here (*pointing to the shorthand writer*).

10,670. I am desired to ask you this question. Why were you under alarm of being blown up if you had never been threatened except 11 years before ?—On account of my going to Slack, Sellars, and Co.

10,671. But why should you be frightened at being blown up particularly for going to them ? was there any quarrel between Slack, Sellars, and Co. and the trade ?—Because they had turned their grinders away and employed me. At least their grinders left them ; I believe they did not turn them away ; I believe they turned themselves away ; they left their employment of their own accord.

10,672. But I suppose that Sellars and Co, were in no worse a condition than other people in the trade. Any person else might have employed you ; why should it have been because it was Slack, Sellars, and Co. ?—It was because somebody had taken the nuts and burnt them on account of their handle maker, who was working for them, and they wanted them to turn this handle maker away, and they would not. They said he suited them, and they would keep him.

10,673. They would not turn away their handle maker ?—Yes ; they would not turn him away to please the handle makers, so they said they would keep him.

10,674. That was with the Saw Makers' Company ?—Yes.

10,675. You are not a saw maker ; you are a saw grinder ?—Yes, but this brings the truth out.

10,676. How is that ?—They came to me in June ; I believe it was in June last.

10,677. Who came to you ?—I think it was Mr. Wragg, but I am not positive. He asked me if I would do some work for them, and I said "Yes," and they sent me some work, and I did it ; and they sent me some more, and I did it. They came down themselves, but whether it was Wragg or Mr. Sellars I am not certain ; I think that it was Wragg who came down again, but I am not positive. They said that I did not do enough for them. "Well," I said, "I am "working for three or four parties, and I durst not "give up a certain thing for an uncertainty." I said, "If you like, I will give up the other work, and I "will work for you and nobody else." If I would do so, they said they would stick to me if I would stick to them, and I said, "I will ; I will stick to you" ; and so I have done up to the present moment, and that is the reason of my being blown up.

10,678. Have you not been complained of by the masters for going off work and for drinking ?—By Slack, Sellars, and Company ?

10,679. Have they complained ?—No.

10,680. Have no masters for whom you have worked complained of your going off drinking ?—Perhaps Messrs. Hague and Clegg might do so, but I cannot say.

10,681. Do you recollect having something to do for Thomas Shelton and Son ?—Yes, there were nine webs.

10,682. That was in April 1863, was it not ?—Yes, I believe it was.

10,683. Did they not complain to Mr. Broadhead of your neglecting their work ?—There was but nine, and I left my boy to do them.

10,684. Did not they complain to Mr. Broadhead of your neglecting their work ?—I think they did.

10,685. And did not you write this letter, "Sir, I "hereby give you notice that I shall quit your em-"ployment in one month from the date hereof. "(Signed) Thomas Fearnehough. I have taken this "step considering the language you used to me last "Friday much too strong for the offence I had com-"mitted, as you will find, on inquiry, that instead of "there being plenty of work in the wheel there were "only six band saws and three working out webs. I "should have thought that I was highly to blame "had I gone away and inconvenienced any party, but "that not being the case I must again repeat your "severe remarks were uncalled for." Was that what you wrote ?—I did not write it myself but I got it written.

10,686. Who wrote it for you ?—MacLachlan they called him.

10,687. At all events they had to complain of your neglecting your work ?—That is right, I will tell the truth.

10,688. Was that the time that Broadhead called you anything but a gentleman ?—Yes, it was over that—quite right.

10,689. You were in the service of the trade ?—Yes.

10,690. You say that the language used was sadly too strong for the offence which you had committed ; what do you mean by the offence which you had committed ?—I say he had no right to say anything to me. If he had anything to say it was his duty to bring it before the committee as a man, and not to blackguard me himself.

10,691. It was simply from your not having done the work as quickly as you ought to have done ?—Yes, that was it.

10,692. What was the damage done to your house when you were blown up ?—I think it cost 25*l.* 10*s.* repairing it up again, but I am not certain.

10,693. It was blown up by gunpowder, I believe ?—Yes.

10,694. A can of gunpowder was thrown into the cellar ?—Yes.

10,695. Was your family in the house at the time ?—Yes.

10,696. And they escaped ?—Yes.

10,697. Was there much destruction done to the house ?—Oh ! yes.

10,698. Is Hereford Street in the middle of the town ?—No, it is outside, by St. Mary's Church.

10,699. Is it a detached house, or in a row ?—In a row.

10,700. Is it the last house, or a middle house ?—About the middle.

The witness withdrew.

Adjourned to to-morrow at 11 o'clock.

TWELFTH DAY.

Council Hall, Sheffield, Wednesday, 19th June 1867.

PRESENT:

WILLIAM OVEREND, Esq., Q.C.	GEORGE CHANCE, Esq.
THOMAS IRWIN BARSTOW, Esq.	J. E. BARKER, Esq., Secretary.

WILLIAM OVEREND, ESQ., Q.C., IN THE CHAIR.

TWELFTH DAY.

J. Hallam.

19 June 1867.

JAMES HALLAM recalled and further examined.

10,701. (*Chairman.*) The last time you were here you refused to tell us who was the person who was with you when you rattened Taylor. You have come here to-day again. Are you now prepared to tell us who that person is?—Yes.

10,702. Who was that person?—Samuel Crooks.

10,703. After you had rattened him, did you see Mr. Broadhead?—No.

10,704. Did you go to Mr. Broadhead?—Yes.

10,705. You and Crooks together?—Yes.

10,706. How soon was that after you had done it?—The day but one after, I believe.

10,707. What happened; did either of you see him, or did both of you see him?—Crooks saw him.

10,708. Where were you then?—Downstairs.

10,709. Did he come down presently?—Yes.

10,710. Did you go with him anywhere?—We went to John Woollen's.

10,711. Crooks came down, you say, and you went with him to John Woollen's?—Yes.

10,712. When you got there did Crooks pay you anything?—He paid me 25*s.*

10,713. Have you ever rattened any person besides?—Only Charles Damms.

10,714. When was that?—I could not say when it was.

10,715. What was your reason for rattening him?—Clarke was going to do it.

10,716. Dennis Clarke?—Yes.

10,717. Did he tell you so?—Yes.

10,718. Why did he say that he was going to do it?—He said that he had got the order.

10,719. Did you see Damms that day?—He agreed to pay for 5*s.* worth of ale for us not to do it.

10,720. Not to be rattened?—Yes.

10,721. Did Clarke say anything upon that?—He said that if he paid for 10*s.* worth he should do it.

10,722. Did you go together and get some ale?—Yes.

10,723. Where?—At the "Blue Pig."

10,724. While the others were there did you go away?—Yes.

10,725. And what did you do?—I took the nuts.

10,726. You went to his place and took the nuts?—Yes.

10,727. Did you tell anybody after you had done it?—I told Copley.

10,728. After the drinking was over, did Clarke and you go anywhere together?—We went to the wheel, but of course I had done him.

10,729. But you had done it already. You had got the nuts, had you not?—Yes.

10,730. After that did you go back to the "Blue Pig"?—Yes.

10,731. Did you afterwards see Broadhead?—Yes.

10,732. How soon after?—About an hour.

10,733. Did you tell Broadhead what you had done?—Yes.

10,734. Did you show him the nut?—No.

10,735. What did you tell him?—I told him we had got Damms' nuts.

10,736. Whom do you mean by "we"?—Copley and me.

10,737. What did he say?—"All right."

10,738. Did he pay you anything?—No.

10,739. Afterwards, did you hear that the master, Mr. Peace, had paid the money which was in arrear?—Yes.

10,740. Did you send a note?—Yes.

10,741. Telling him where the nut would be found?—Yes.

10,742. On the day that you sent the note were Copley and you at Broadhead's?—Yes.

10,743. Did Copley go upstairs, or did you go upstairs?—Copley went upstairs.

10,744. And did he bring you down any money?—He came down, and we went away together.

10,745. Where did you go?—We went down to the "Blue Pig" again.

10,746. Did he give you any money?—He gave me 1*s.* 6*d.*

10,747. Did he tell you where he had got it?—No.

10,748. Was there any person besides who got any money?—Yes, he gave Joel Yellatt 1*s.* 6*d.*

10,749. What was there besides?—He spent the remainder.

10,750. What was the money given for? Did he owe you money, or what was it for?—No.

10,751. What was the money given for?—I suppose it was for the nut.

10,752. When you were here before I spoke to you about Wheatman's; were you ever at Wheatman's?—Yes.

10,753. How did you happen to go to Wheatman's? What was the reason that you went? Did any person speak to you about going before you went?—Yes; Crooks.

10,754. What did he say to you?—He said that we had a job to do there, to blow it up.

10,755. What did he say was to be done?—We were to blow it up.

10,756. After he had told you this, did you go to Broadhead's?—Yes.

10,757. Did you see him?—Yes.

10,758. Did both of you see him?—We both saw him, but Crooks went upstairs with him.

10,759. When you came down did Crooks say anything to you about this?—He told me he had got 2*l.*

10,760. Did he tell you what for?—As we were going away he did.

10,761. What did he say it was for?—To buy powder with.

10,762. Did he give you any part of that 2*l.*?—He gave me a sovereign.

10,763. And what did you do with the sovereign?—I went to Milner's and bought some powder.

10,764. Where does Milner live?—In Fargate.

10,765. How much did you buy?—I could not tell you exactly what was the amount we bought at that time.

10,766. Did you get any more elsewhere?—Yes.

10,767. Where?—I got some more at the bottom of Pinstone Lane.

10,768. Did you get any more powder besides at other places?—No, only at those two places.

10,769. As you got the powder what did you do with it? How much did you buy altogether?—About 24 lbs.

10,770. Were you alone, or was Crooks in company

with you at the time you bought the powder ?—He was in company with me when I bought it.

10,771. After you had bought the powder what did you do with it ?—I gave it to Crookes, and he put it by.

10,772. Do you know where he put it ?—He told me he put it in a quarry at Bole Hill.

10,773. Did you buy anything else ?—Yes.

10,774. What else did you buy ?—I bought a bottle to put the powder in.

10,775. Where did you buy it ?—At Milner's.

10,776. Close by here ?—In Fargate.

10,777. What kind of a bottle was it ?—It was a large one.

10,778. Was it made of glass, or what was it made of ?—No, it was a tin bottle.

10,779. Did you buy anything else ?—A fuze.

10,780. Where did you buy the fuze ?—On Snig Hill.

10,781. Anything else ?—I bought a lash line to lap the bottle up in.

10,782. Do you know where you got it at Snig Hill ? do you know the name of the shop ?—No.

10,783. Do you not know where it was in Snig Hill where you bought that ?—Nearly at the top.

10,784. Do you not know the name of the person ?—I did not at that time, but I believe it is Twibell.

10,785. And what did you do with the lash line ?—Wrapped it round the bottle.

10,786. Where did you get the lash line ?—In Division Street.

10,787. Do you know the place ?—I could not tell now. It has been altered.

10,788. Do you know how long ago this was ?—Six or seven years, perhaps.

10,789. After you had bought your powder, and your bottle, and your fuze, what did you do ?—We went on the Saturday night to Wheatman's.

10,790. When you got to Wheatman's, what did you do ?—They were working.

10,791. Had you the powder with you then ?—Yes.

10,792. What did you do with it ?—We put it by in a waste place.

10,793. They were working, you say ?—Yes.

10,794. And you did nothing ?—No.

10,795. Now, when did you go next ?—I went on the Sunday night.

10,796. Yourself alone ?—I cannot swear whether I was by myself or not that time.

10,797. Did you do anything that night ?—No, they were working again.

10,798. When did you go again ?—On the Monday night.

10,799. Were you alone, or was any person with you then ?—Crookes was with me.

10,800. When you got there on the Monday night, what did you do ?—We put the bottle in the sough, in the drain.

10,801. Did you attempt at all to do anything before you put it in the sough ?—Yes, we tried to get inside, but the men were working.

10,802. What were you going to do if you got inside ?—We should have put it in the chimney bottom.

10,803. What to do ?—To blow it down.

10,804. You say that they were working, and that therefore you could not put it in because the powder would have gone off at once, and you say that you put in the sough ; did you put it there to do anything with it ?—Yes.

10,805. In order to put it in the sough, how did you get there ?—We went across the river.

10,806. Did you both cross the river ?—Yes.

10,807. When you put it in the sough, what did you do with it ?—I lit the fuze.

10,808. And after you had lit the fuze, what did you do ?—We crossed the river again.

10,809. And where did you go to ?—We were on Rutland Bridge when it went off.

10,810. Did it make a great explosion ?—Yes.

10,811. After that what did you do ?—We parted directly.

TWELFTH DAY.

J. Hallam.

19 June 1867.

10,812. Where did you go ?—We went towards Crookes.

10,813. Did you see any handbills out the next day ?—Yes.

10,814. And did you find whether you had done a great deal or only a little damage ?—Very little.

10,815. Were there persons in the place at work when you let this off ?—Yes.

10,816. Did you see Broadhead after that ?—Yes.

10,817. How soon was that after you had blown up this place ?—The day but one after.

10,818. Where did you see him ?—In his own house.

10,819. Did you speak to him ?—Yes.

10,820. What did you say to him ?—I cannot say what I said to him.

10,821. Did you speak to him about this matter ?—Yes.

10,822. Did you tell him that you had done it ?—Yes.

10,823. Are you quite sure that you told him that you had done it ?—Yes.

10,824. What did he say upon that ?—He said it would do very well.

10,825. Did you ask him for payment ?—No, he told me he was not prepared to pay me that day.

10,826. And what did you do ?—He lent me 10*s*.

10,827. Did you see Crookes after that ?—Yes.

10,828. When ?—I believe it would be the same day.

10,829. Where was that ?—At the public house in Harvest Lane.

10,830. Do you know the sign of it ?—The "Mowbray," I believe.

10,831. Did you talk to him about this matter ?—There was another person with him, and we said very little about it, and we agreed to meet on Saturday.

10,832. Did you meet on Saturday ?—Yes.

10,833. Where ?—At John Woollen's.

10,834. And when you met at John Woollen's did you get anything ?—Yes.

10,835. What did you get ?—Instead of 7*l.* 10*s.* I got 4*l.*

10,836. Who paid it to you ?—Crookes.

10,837. Why do you say instead of 7*l.* 10*s.* ?—Because he told me we were to have 15*l.* for it.

10,838. Did he tell you when the remainder was to come, or anything of that kind ?—He told me that Broadhead had only given him half.

10,839. Did he say anything about when the remainder was to come ?—He told me that he would pay me the remainder on the Saturday after.

10,840. On the Saturday after did you see him ?—Yes.

10,841. Did he pay you the remainder ?—I saw him and he only gave me a sovereign.

10,842. What did he say about not paying the remainder ?—He said he had not got settled.

10,843. The week after this did you see Broadhead ?—Yes.

10,844. Did you ask him for anything ?—Yes, I asked him for some money.

10,845. What did you say to him ?—I told him he could stop it when he paid Sam the remainder.

10,846. What did he say to that ?—He said he had paid him on Saturday night.

10,847. He said he had paid him what ?—The money, he did not say how much.

10,848. He meant what was due to him ?—Yes.

10,849. He said he had paid him the money on Saturday night ?—Yes.

10,850. How many pounds of powder did you say you were to buy ?—We were to buy 28 lbs. or 30 lbs.

10,851. And you only bought 24 lbs. ?—No.

10,852. Who told you that you were to buy 28 lbs. or 30 lbs. ?—That was what Sam told me.

10,853. When did he tell you that ?—The first night as we were going.

TWELFTH DAY.

J. Hallam.

19 June 1867.

10,854. Do you know why Wheatman and Smith were blown up?—For putting a machine down.

10,855. Now do you recollect the time when Linley was shot?—Yes.

10,856. On the Saturday night before Linley was shot were you not seen in Wilson's "Snug," in West Bar with a pistol in your pocket? Say yes or no?—Yes.

10,857. Where did you get that pistol from?—I bought it.

10,858. For what purpose did you buy the pistol? (*The witness hesitated.*) You know if you tell the truth you have nothing to be afraid of. You will be entitled to your certificate if you tell the whole truth. I ask you for what purpose did you buy that pistol? Answer the question.—(*After some hesitation.*) I will tell the truth if I may have my certificate.

10,859. You shall have your certificate, and if the man whom you are going to implicate will come forward and ask for his indemnity, he shall have it, so that you need not fear for anyone, because you will be indemnified by having our certificate; and if the man, whoever he may be, whom you implicate, will come forward and make a clear statement, he shall have his indemnity. (*The witness fainted, and eventually had to be removed from the Hall; on his return*)—

10,860. (*Chairman to the witness.*) You say that you bought a pistol, for what purpose did you buy it?—To shoot Linley.

10,861. Was there anybody associated with you in shooting Linley?—Yes.

10,862. Who was it?—Crookes.

10,863. Who shot him? Did you or Crookes shoot him?—I compelled Crookes to shoot him.

10,864. With what did he shoot him?—An air gun.

10,865. Had anybody set you to do this?—Not to shoot him.

10,866. Had any person set you to do anything to him?—I asked Broadhead one day what he was doing with Linley, and he told me he would have conversation with me on the following day.

10,867. Did you see him the next day?—Yes.

10,868. What did he say to you?—He asked me if I remembered the conversation of the previous day. I told him I did.

10,869. What did he say?—He asked me what I could do with him.

10,870. What did you say?—I told him I would make him as he would not work any more.

10,871. What did he say to that?—He asked me what I should want for doing it.

10,872. What did you say?—I asked him if 20*l.* would be too much.

10,873. What did he say?—He said, No, he should think not.

10,874. Did you say that you would do it?—Yes.

10,875. Did you tell him how you would do it?—No.

10,876. How was it that Crookes came into the matter?—I saw him.

10,877. When?—I think it was the following day.

10,878. What did you say to him?—I told him I had got the job to do Linley.

10,879. What did he say?—He asked me who I had seen.

10,880. What did you tell him?—I told him I had seen Broadhead; I told him we were to have 20*l.*

10,881. What did he say to that?—He said he thought we should not get 20*l.* Then I saw him again.

10,882. When was that?—It would be the week following. We went to Broadhead's to see what we were to have.

10,883. Did you see him?—Yes, Crookes saw him alone; when he came down he said we were to have 15*l.* that was all he would give. Then I went up and he told me that he could not give above 15*l.* for it, and I agreed to do it and I got 3*l.* of him and I bought a revolver.

10,884. Did Crookes buy a revolver?—I do not know, he had one.

10,885. If you and Crookes arranged to do this matter, how did you do it?—We followed him from one place to another; we found there was no chance with a revolver, so Crookes got the air gun.

10,886. Do you know where he got the air gun?—No.

10,887. You were not with him when he got the air gun?—No.

10,888. What did you do with the air gun, did you try it, or what did you do?—That was what he shot him with.

10,889. Was Crookes a good shot?—He was pretty fair, to get where he did I think.

10,890. How do you mean "to get where he did"?—To hit Linley.

10,891. Had you ever used the air gun at all before you went to Linley to shoot him? had you ever seen him shoot with it at all?—Yes.

10,892. Where had you seen him shoot with it?—In Ecclesall Wood.

10,893. What was he doing shooting with it? shooting with it in Ecclesall Wood?—Rabbits.

10,894. Why did he go to shoot rabbits?—We both went.

10,895. Now you say you followed him, how long do you think you followed Linley about before he was shot; between the time of your talking to Mr. Broadhead and the time Linley was shot, how long an interval elapsed?—I could not tell exactly; five or six weeks, or perhaps more.

10,896. And how often did you go in those five or six weeks after him for the purpose of finding an opportunity of shooting him?—Nearly every night, but Sunday night.

10,897. How was it at last? where was he shot? in Scotland Street?—Yes.

10,898. Tell us how it took place, where was he?—He was in the back room.

10,899. Where were you and Crookes?—We followed him from the American stores.

10,900. You followed him from the American stores to Scotland Street, was it a public house?—Yes.

10,901. Do you know what they call it?—The "Crown Inn," I believe.

10,902. And you say that he was in a back room?—Yes.

10,903. Did you go into the public house?—No.

10,904. What did you do?—I went into the back yard to look.

10,905. Could you see from the back yard into the room where Linley was sitting?—Yes.

10,906. Where was he sitting?—He was sitting with his left hand to the window.

10,907. What time at night was it?—Perhaps about nine, but I cannot say to what hour it was. It was just dark.

10,908. Where was Crookes?—Crookes was in the street when I saw him.

10,909. What did you do after you had seen him there?—We did not know which room he had gone into while I saw him.

10,910. When you saw him what did you do?—I told Crooks that he was there.

10,911. Were there any other persons in the room?—Yes.

10,912. When you told Crookes that he was there what did Crookes do?—He came and looked at him. He refused to shoot then.

10,913. What did he do? Where was the gun? Had he a gun with him or not?—He had his air gun.

10,914. What did he do with the air gun?—(*The witness hesitated*).

10,915. What did he do?—He would not shoot because there was no way of exit.

10,916. Do you mean that there was no exit from the yard?—No.

10,917. What did you do?—I went through the yard and found a way out.

10,918. Did you come back and tell him that you

had found a way out?—Yes; he said there were too many people about.

10,919. What did you say?—I told him he was either to do it or I would do him.

10,920. When you had told him that what did he do?—He said there was no chance.

10,921. What did you say?—I said I would do it myself and risk it. He told me (*the witness hesitated*).

10,922. What did he tell you?—He said I must not attempt; I might miss him, and that he would risk it.

10,923. When he said that he would risk it what did he do?—(*The witness hesitated*).

10,924. What did he do when he said that he would risk it?—He shot him.

10,925. After he shot him what did you both do?—We run away.

10,926. Which way did you run?—Through the alley into Peacroft.

10,927. Did you meet anybody as you went out, or was the whole course clear?—There was a man and woman.

10,928. Where were they?—In the entry.

10,929. In order to get into Peacroft had you to pass by this man and woman?—Yes.

10,930. Did you go near them?—I stumbled against them.

10,931. And then what did you do? where did you go to after you got into Peacroft?—Then we ran.

10,932. In which direction did you run?—Towards St. George's Church.

10,933. Where did you separate, if you did separate?—At Crookes.

10,934. Where did Crookes go to?—I do not know.

10,935. Where did you go to?—To Joel Winterbottoms.

10,936. When did you next see Crookes?—On the following morning by agreement.

10,937. Where did you see him?—I saw him in Wylie's.

10,938. That is in the Haymarket, is it not?—Yes.

10,939. Had you any talk to him?—No.

10,940. Did you see him afterwards?—I got a sovereign of him there.

10,941. What did you do when you had got your sovereign?—I and Palfryman went to Tasker's.

10,942. Did you after that at all see Broadhead?—No.

10,943. Did you never see Broadhead after Linley was shot?—Yes.

10,944. When was it?—I do not know.

10,945. About how long afterwards was it?—Before the Saturday.

10,946. What did you say to him?—I said nothing.

10,947. What did he say to you?—He told me that I had better not go there too much.

10,948. Did he say anything else besides that?—No.

10,949. Did he say anything about your having shot Linley, whether it was right or whether it was wrong?—No.

10,950. Have you ever had any conversation with Broadhead about Linley being shot since then?—No.

10,951. Have you received any money from Broadhead since Linley was shot?—No.

10,952. What did you get for shooting Linley?—7*l.* 10*s.*

10,953. Who paid you the money?—Crookes gave me 4*l.* 10*s.*

10,954. And who gave you the 3*l.*?—Broadhead.

10,955. Did Broadhead give you the 3*l.* after Linley was shot, or before he was shot?—Before.

10,956. I believe that Linley lived a good while, several months after he was shot, did he not?—Yes.

10,957. Was he shot in the head?—Yes.

10,958. And ultimately he died, I believe?—Yes.

10,959. Was there a coroner's inquest?—Yes.

10,960. They found a verdict of murder against some person unknown, did they not?—I do not know.

10,961. But there was a verdict of murder found, was there not?—Yes.

10,962. Did you see Crookes after the verdict of the coroner's jury had been returned?—I saw him many times.

10,963. Have you talked to Crookes about their finding this verdict of murder?—It was unimportant.

10,964. What you talked to him about?—Yes.

10,965. Did he ever say anything to you about the verdict?—Merely a passing word.

10,966. Did you pledge yourselves to keep it secret, or anything of that kind?—Yes.

10,967. Did you bind yourselves by any oath, or anything of that kind?—No, at that time I did not think we should need it. He is true and I am false.

10,968. You have told us a very different story when you were here before about Crookes; you would not mention his name, and you said all that you had told about going to Wheatman's was false. What was the reason you said that what you had told Mr. Fretson about it was false?—It was to save Crookes and myself.

10,969. But how do you mean to save you both, because I told you that if you made a full disclosure, no civil proceedings or criminal proceedings would ever be instituted against you for whatever you have done; therefore there was no occasion for you to make a false statement; was that the only reason for your making that false statement?—It was a true statement that I made to Mr. Jackson and Mr. Fretson, only in the two cases when I said I had not received the money, and that Crookes was not with me at the firing of the fuze. I drew the money from Broadhead.

10,970. Why was it that you made that false statement to Mr. Fretson with respect to Crookes not being with you and that you drew the money?—In the first place I had reason to believe that it had not been kept secret as I had kept it about Wheatman's being blown up.

10,971. You say in the first place you had reason to believe that it had not ben kept secret about Wheatman's being blown up as you had kept it; what besides?—In the second place I thought I would take all the blame upon myself if it was possible.

10,972. Was there any other reason?—No. I wish to state one thing.

10,973. State it by all means?—Mr. Jackson supplied me with a paper yesterday, where Shaw had mentioned my name.

10,974. Was it a newspaper?—Yes. He told the Commissioners that I had told him that I had disclosed everything I knew. That statement was false. The first statement that ever I made to Mr. Jackson and Mr. Fretson was on Easter Monday, but he said it was seven or eight months since that I told him that.

10,975. And you say that what Shaw said about that is not true?—No, it is false. The only conversation that ever Shaw and I had it is true was in Fitzwilliam Street, but not in a public house. He called me back and asked me if I could set him on working, and I told him that I could not. He said, "What dost thou think about the old sod stopping my scale?"

10,976. Who is the "old sod"?—I said, "What, "Broadhead"? He said, "Aye. I could waken him "up if I were to speak out." I said "What dost "thou mean about Helliwell"? He said, "Aye." I said, "Well, please thyself." He said, "Thou knowest "all about it." I said, "Aye, but it makes no differ-"ence to me," and I left him.

10,977. Did you know all about it?—He told me the same week.

10,978. Shaw told you the same week, did he?—Yes.

10,979. That he had blown up Helliwell?—Yes, I will here take the liberty to mention that he said that I had got it from Clarke all about it in a public house conversation. I never heard Clarke mention that in my life, upon my oath. He told me the week

TWELFTH DAY.

J. Hallam.

19 June 1867.

that it occurred that Clarke had got the job, but he had not the pluck to do it, and he asked him. He told me that he only put half a pound of powder in and sold the other. In his evidence he said that I had first told him that he could get 25*l.* for it. I never said anything of the kind. The day after I saw him in Fitzwilliam Street I told Jonathan Crapper what he had said to me. Crapper asked me if I would go with him to their house.

10,980. To whose house?—To Shaw's. I said I would. We went but he was not in. Crapper told his aunt to inform him to come to the "King William" and meet me. I have never seen him since to have any conversation with him, only the time he is alluding to in the "King William" in his evidence, and Clarke never mentioned either lagging him or "Old Smit'em" at all.

10,981. Were you there all the time that Shaw and Clarke were there?—I was in all the time.

10,982. Could Clarke have said so, and you not have heard it?—No.

10,983. Did you never hear Clarke say, that he could "lag" him, or "Old Smit'em"?—Never in my life.

10,984. Have you heard Shaw say so?—No, only in Fitzwilliam Street.

10,985. You did hear him say it there?—Yes.

10,986. He said he could "lag" him?—No, he did not say he could lag him. He said what he could do for him. He did mention lagging of course.

10,987. What did he say?—I do not remember the exact words.

10,988. "I could waken him up"?—Yes.

10,989. You have told us this about yourself, is there anything else that you have done that you have not told us?—Yes. I wish to make that statement to refute him, that I had told him that he would get the reward. I have previously stated that the first time I ever made a statement was on Easter Monday in Mr. Jackson's presence.

10,990. You wish to make the statement now, that you had never made any statement before Easter Monday?—No.

10,991. I have taken that down. Had you any quarrel with Linley, or what was your reason for shooting Linley?—I did not know him at that time.

10,992. Had you ever spoken to him in your life?—No, I never did do so.

10,993. Had you any malice against him in any way?—Only for being obnoxious to the trade. I urged Mr. Broadhead to it.

10,994. How do you mean that you urged Mr. Broadhead to it?—By mentioning it to him first, and seeing him again about it afterwards. He had never previously mentioned anything of the kind to me.

10,995. I will go from this at present. Is there anything else that you have done that has been against the law that you have not mentioned to us?—Yes.

10,996. What have you done besides?—Old Sammy Sutcliffe.

10,997. What did you do to Sammy Sutcliffe?—I waylaid him.

10,998. Where did Sammy Sutcliffe live? — In Hoyle Street.

10,999. What was he? — A surgical instrument grinder.

11,000. Had you had any quarrel with him?—No.

11,001. When was this?—I cannot say to a year.

11,002. Is it two years ago?—It is about six years since. I cannot say to a year.

11,003. Why did you waylay him?—I was employed to do it.

11,004. Who employed you?—John Broomhead and another man.

11,005. Who was the other man?—I do not know; I do not know his name.

11,006. What was John Broomhead?—Secretary to the Pen and Pocket Blade Grinders.

11,007. What did he tell you that you were to waylay Sutcliffe for?—I was to make him so that he could not go to work for a week or two.

11,008. Why were you to do that?—Because of his not paying to the trade.

11,009. Who told you that he had not paid to the trade?—It was conversation between me and the other man and John Broomhead.

11,010. Do you know what the other man was?—He was in the same trade.

11,011. Do you not know his name at all?—I never heard his name mentioned.

11,012. About how old was he?—He might be about 50 years of age, or near that.

11,013. Was he tall, or thin, or broad?—He was a little old man; old looking.

11,014. He had not paid to the trade, you say?—No.

11,015. You waylaid him, you say; where did you waylay him?—At the "Entry" End.

11,016. What did you do to him?—I struck him with a life preserver several times.

11,017. Where did you strike him?—On his head.

11,018. What was the result of your striking him?—He was in bed a week or better.

11,019. You say that you were set on to do it by a person of the name of Broomhead?—Yes.

11,020. Did you get any pay for it?—I was to have 7*l.*

11,021. Who promised you that?—Broomhead.

11,022. Did you get paid?—Yes.

11,023. Who paid you?—John Braithwaite paid me a sovereign the day after.

11,024. Who is John Braithwaite?—He is one of the same trade.

11,025. Where did he pay you?—At Tetlow's in Eldon Street.

11,026. Was anybody present when he paid you?—No.

11,027. Did he tell you what it was for?—Yes.

11,028. For what did he say that it was?—It was for doing Sutcliffe. He asked me if that was sufficient then for that day.

11,029. What did you say?—I told him it was.

11,030. Did he say anything about your being paid anything else? Did he say when you were to be paid the remainder?—He told me that Broomhead would see me on the Saturday.

11,031. Did Broomhead see you on the Saturday?—Yes.

11,032. Where?—At the Washington Hotel. He paid me five sovereigns there, and told me that was all the committee would allow him to give me.

11,033. What did you say to that?—I told him he would have to pay me the other sovereign. He told me I must meet him on Tuesday.

11,034. Did you meet him on Tuesday?—Yes.

11,035. Where?—On Snig Hill.

11,036. Was it in a public house?—I beckoned him out of the public house.

11,037. Out of what public house?—The "Swan," I believe it was.

11,038. He came; and when did he pay you?—He and the man that had engaged me came out into the archway, and he refused to pay me the sovereign while I forced it from him.

11,039. How do you mean "forced it from him"?—I held him while the other man went and fetched it. The man came out with him that engaged me.

11,040. Whom did you hold, the other man or Broomhead?—Broomhead.

11,041. You held Broomhead till the other man fetched the money?—Yes.

11,042. Did he go and fetch the money?—Yes.

11,043. How much did he bring you? — A sovereign.

11,044. And that was all that you were entitled to receive?—Yes.

11,045. Who is Broomhead; is he alive?—No.

11,046. When did he die?—I do not know, but he is dead now.

11,047. Who is Braithwaite?—He is one in their trade.

11,048. Do you know whether he is alive or not?—Oh, yes, he is alive.

TWELFTH DAY.

J. Hallam.

19 June 1867.

11,049. Do you know where he lives?—The Hampton View, I believe.

11,050. What had you got a life preserver for?—To thrash him.

11,051. Did you buy it for that purpose?—I made it myself from gutta-percha.

11,052. How was it that Broomhead came to you; you were not in that trade, were you?—No.

11,053. How was it, then, that Broomhead applied to you?—It was hinted to me that he wanted to see me. I have forgotten how it was brought about.

11,054. Did some person tell you that he wanted to see you?—Yes.

11,055. You do not recollect who it was, do you?—No.

11,056. Is there anything else that you have done?—No.

11,057. That is all that you can recollect; you believe you have told us everything that you have done?—Yes, and it has not been a bad share.

11,058. That is true enough; but I want to give you, if I can, protection, and I must be satisfied that you have told me everything. Is there anything else?—Not the slightest; nothing in my recollection.

11,059. Are you quite sure that you have told us everything?—Yes.

11,060. Everything?—Yes.

11,061. Have you done nothing of any sort which you have not told us?—No.

11,062. Now, be satisfied about it, because you know your safety depends upon it?—Not in connexion with the trades unions or any trade.

11,063. You have told us everything in connexion with trades?—Yes.

11,064. Now, I will ask you another question. Do you know a person of the name of Fearnehough?—Yes.

11,065. Do you recollect his working at Hague and Clegg's?—Yes.

11,066. While he was working at Hague and Clegg's had you ever any conversation with Broadhead about blowing up Hague and Clegg's works?—Yes, once.

11,067. What did Broadhead say on that occasion?—I asked him (*the witness hesitated*).

11,068. What did you ask him?—I asked him if there was anything doing.

11,069. Anything doing about what?—If there was anything doing.

11,070. What did he say to that?—He said there was Fearnehough's place, but that had better be let alone while the Social Science Congress had passed.

11,071. Was there a Social Science Congress expected in Sheffield then?—Yes.

11,072. How soon after?—I cannot say.

11,073. About how soon after?—I have no idea; it might be weeks, or it might be months.

11,074. However, a Social Science Congress was then expected in Sheffield?—Yes.

11,075. And what did he say was the reason that he would rather have it put off till the Social Science Congress had passed?—It might spoil it.

11,076. How spoil it?—I do not know.

11,077. At the time that you talked to him about it?—He told me it would be easy to do.

11,078. You say that he told you that it would be very easy to do?—Yes.

11,079. Did he show you how it could be done?—He made a kind of sketch on his book.

11,080. How do you mean a sketch on his book?—Of the entrance to the places I suppose.

11,081. And what were you to do at the place?—He never mentioned that.

11,082. But what were you to do at the spot?—I told him I would blow it up, and he said that I had better let it be at present.

11,083. Do you know who blew up Fearnehough, ultimately?—No.

11,084. You do not know that?—No.

11,085. Have you never been told who blew up Fearnehough?—No.

11,086. Are you sure about it?—Yes.

11,087. You did not do it yourself?—No.

11,088. When you were there when he made you a sketch on his book, did he offer to find you anything for getting the nuts?—He told me if I had a spanner, a square spanner would do all that was required, and that he could find me one.

11,089. And what were you to do with the spanner?—That he did not say to me, nor me to him.

11,090. What would the spanner do?—The spanner would unscrew anything that I thought was necessary.

11,091. Do you know who blew up Tyzack's?—No.

11,092. Have you never been told?—No.

11,093. Has no one told you who shot at Tyzack?—No.

11,094. Are you quite sure that you do not know who shot at Tyzack?—No.

11,095. Now be careful; mind what you are about. Are you quite sure that you do not know who shot at Tyzack?—No.

11,096. Have you never heard?—No.

11,097. Has no one ever told you that he shot at him?—No.

11,098. Are you sure about that?—Upon my oath.

11,099. Do you know Needham, who was sent for three or four years into penal servitude?—Thomas?

11,100. Thomas Needham?—Not personally.

11,101. Have you ever had any conversation with Crooks about him?—Crooks told me that he was going to London for him.

11,102. What did he say he was going to London to Needham for when he came out of prison?—To fetch him home.

11,103. But why should he go to fetch him home?—I do not know.

11,104. Be cautious. Did he not tell you why he fetched him home?—He did not give me any reason, only that he was to get at him first.

11,105. But why should he get at him first? did he not tell you?—No, not those particulars.

11,106. You know something about it, I am sure. Now be cautious what you are stating. He said that he was going to fetch him home as soon as he got out, and that he wanted to get at him first. What was his object in wishing to get at him first?—There had been a difference betwixt his wife and the trade, so I believe.

11,107. What of that? After he got out did you see Crooks, and did he tell you anything about him that he had seen him?—No.

11,108. Did he never tell you that he had seen him?—Of course I knew that he had seen him.

11,109. Did he ever tell you that he had said anything to him when he came out?—No.

11,110. He never told you anything?—No.

11,111. Did he ever tell you that he told him, that if he ever told he would blow his brains out?—No.

11,112. And say, "Here is a 5*l.* note for you, but if you tell I will blow your brains out"?—Upon my oath, no.

11,113. He never told you that?—No.

11,114. You never heard it?—No.

11,115. And did you not know who did Tyzack's business?—No.

11,116. Do you know a person called Martin?—Yes.

11,117. Do you know where Needham is now?—No.

11,118. Have you been associated with Martin?—Well, more or less; I worked with him once.

11,119. Was he often in work?—I never knew him in work only once.

11,120. How long was he in work?—I cannot say.

11,121. About how long?—I have no idea.

11,122. How long have you known him?—I have known him since I was 20 years of age.

11,123. And only on one occasion have you known him in work?—No.

11,124. For how long a time do you think that

TWELFTH DAY.

J. Hallam.

19 June 1867.

he was in work? for a year?—I could not say I am sure.

11,125. For how many years have you known him off work?—I do not know that he worked these last eight years to my knowledge.

11,126. Was he often at Broadhead's?—I cannot say.

11,127. Do you know how he supported himself?—His mother kept a public house, and he had the box pay.

11,128. What became of that revolver which you bought, you never told us that?—You never asked me.

11,129. I want to know what became of it?—It was pawned to pay a part of the money that I should have had for Wheatman's without it.

11,130. Where did you pawn it?—I did not pawn it.

11,131. Who pawned it?—I gave it to Sam.

11,132. Do you know where he pawned it?—No.

11,133. Did he never tell you, you must recollect that?—He never told me.

11,134. He told you that he had pawned it, but did he never tell you where?—No.

11,135. Are you sure about that?—Yes.

11,136. Do you know where Sam got his air gun?—No.

11,137. Do you know what Sam did with the air gun?—No.

11,138. Has he it now?—I do not know.

11,139. Do you know whether he parted with it or not?—No.

11,140. Have you ever seen it since that night?—No, never.

11,141. How long before had you seen it; did he tell you whether he had bought it for the occasion or had had it a long time in his possession? what did he tell you about that air gun?—I had no conversation about it.

11,142. Remember, you must have had some conversation about it. If a man brings an air gun for an offence like this you must have talked to him as to how long he had had it, or where he had bought it, or something about it?—He told me it came from Birmingham, but when or how I do not know.

11,143. Although you have told us that you have never done anything else, do you know of any other offence against the law that has been connected with trade matters? do you know of any person who has done anything else?—No.

11,144. Are you quite sure about it?—Only Shaw.

11,145. What do you know that Shaw has done?—He told me himself about Helliwell.

11,146. Is that all you know against Shaw?—Yes.

11,147. Do you know nothing against Crookes besides what you have told us?—No.

11,148. Do you know anything against any other person?—No.

11,149. Do you know anything against Martin?—No, nothing in the least.

11,150. Do you know anything against Copley?—No, only that, where we were together in Damms'.

11,151. Is there any person that you know who has committed any offence connected with the trade, you are to make a complete disclosure of everything that you know?—No, not to my knowledge.

11,152. You are sure about that?—Yes.

11,153. I caution you; are you quite sure that you do not know of any person who has committed any other offence, about which you can give us any information?—No.

11,154. You know that if they had done so, and if they come forward and make a full disclosure they will be entitled to protection, and they will not be liable to be inculpated for their share in the transaction. Do you know of any other person who has committed any trade offence which is contrary to law?—No.

11,155. Will you swear you do not know any person?—Yes.

11,156. Are you sure you do not?—Not to my knowledge.

11,157. But if you had heard it, you must know it, because it is talked about?—No.

11,158. Are you sure about it?—I do not know, but there is one thing, I never was with anybody except Crookes.

11,159. Have you ever been asked to commit any other thing besides those that you have mentioned?—No.

11,160. By no one?—No.

11,161. Have you never been asked to it?—No.

11,162. Have you never been offered money to do it?—No.

11,163. By no one?—No.

11,164. I believe you are pretty general in work are you not?—Yes, I am in a very good situation, or was before I came here.

11,165. I do not know that you are worse off now, I believe you have removed a load from your breast that must have borne you down. However it is not for me to comment upon that. Are you quite sure you have told us everything?—I have told you everything in my knowledge and recollection up to this present time.

11,166. I suppose you prefer going back with Mr. Jackson, do you not?—Yes, I should like you to prove this statement of Shaw's false, because it is false every word, when he said I had told him I had made the disclosures. It was on Easter Monday that I made the disclosures to Mr. Jackson and Mr. Fretson.

11,167. And you wish Shaw to be examined about that?—Yes. Clarke never in his life mentioned anything about Helliwell at all, and it was Shaw that told me about it.

The witness withdrew.

Mr. Sugg stated that the evidence which had been given this morning had taken the Defence Committee completely by surprise; that that Committee was composed of the Trades, and that Mr. Broadhead was not a member of the Committee; and that he would consult with his clients and decide what course to adopt.

The *Chairman* stated that the witness could be recalled for cross-examination at a future time, and that the Examiners would give Mr. Sugg every advantage which they thought at all reasonable in dealing with so grave a charge as that which had been brought.

W. Overend.

WILLIAM OVEREND sworn and examined.

11,168. (*Mr. Barstow.*) You live at No. 3 Court, Pye Bank, Bridgehouses?—Yes.

11,169. And you are a razor grinder?—Yes.

11,170. How long have you been a razor grinder?—Near upon 40 years.

11,171. Were you ever a member of a union?—Yes.

11,172. When did you become a member of the union?—Perhaps four years since.

11,173. Are you a member now?—No.

11,174. Why did you cease to be a member of the union?—Because I did not like to pay to support the idle fellows that would not work.

11,175. Why did you join the union? you have been nearly 40 years in the trade and five years ago you joined the union?—Yes, because it has only been agait four or five years this time, this is the second time.

11,176. What made you join it?—Because the others did.

11,177. Is that the only reason; you had been 35 years in the trade and you are a man of great

TWELFTH DAY.

W. Overend.

19 June 1867.

experience ; was that the only reason that you joined because the others did ?—Yes.

11,178. You ceased to be a member ; why was that? —Because I did not like the to pay money to support a lot of idle fellows.

11,179. Is it your experience that the men on the box are generally idle and bad workmen ?—I can hardly speak to that.

11,180. What do you mean by saying that you did not like to support a lot of idle fellows ?—Because there was a party of them that would not work.

11,181. Were those the men you mean whom you would have to support ?—Yes.

11,182. What do the fellows do that will not work? —I cannot tell you that.

11,183. Is it in your experience a common thing for a good workman to be supported on the box ?—I do not know.

11,184. You do not know whether it is or not ; you have been nearly 40 years in the trade and cannot you tell me that ?—I never was on the box myself.

11,185. Have you ever known good workmen in your trade on the box ?—Very seldom.

11,186. Can a good workman generally get employment at razor grinding ?—Yes.

11,187. When a razor grinder is out of employment is it generally because he is an idle fellow or a bad workman ?—No. I do not know the reason of it.

11,188. You do not know the reason of it ?—No.

11,189. You have been in the employment of Mr. Gilbert of the Oxford Works have you not ?—Yes.

11,190. Are you in his employment now ?—Yes I have been so for some time.

11,191. Were you ever stopped working for him ? —No.

11,192. (*Chairman.*) Were you prevented ?—No, I have never been stopped working for him.

11,193. (*Mr. Barstow.*) Have you worked for Mr. Crooks ?—Yes.

11,194. Have you ever been stopped there ?—Yes.

11,195. What do you mean by "stopped" ?—Because I would not pay to the union.

11,196. How were you stopped, did you apply for work to Mr. Crooks ?—Yes.

11,197. To Mr. Crooks himself ?—No, to the manager.

11,198. That is Mr. Westby ?—Yes.

11,199. Did he give you work ?—Yes.

11,200. What do you mean by saying that you were stopped ?—They sent me work before I was stopped.

11,201. You say that you applied for work to Mr. Westby and that they stopped you, how did they stop you ?—If they employed me they were going to take the other men away.

11,202. When you applied to him for work on this occasion what did he say to you ?—He gave me some work and then when he stopped me he said he dare not employ me any more.

11,203. Are you aware whether your work was satisfactory ?—Yes.

11,204. What reason did he give for not daring to employ you ?—They were frightened of their taking the other men away from them.

11,205. Did he say anything more ?—No.

11,206. Did not he say anything about their having work for you ?—Yes, there would have been work for me supposing our trade had allowed me to go on for them.

11,207. Have you had as much employment since that as you had before ?—No.

11,208. You would be glad to have more work than you get at present ?—Yes, to get more money.

11,209. Do you know Mr. Nicholson near Sheffield Moor ?—Yes.

11,210. Have you applied to him for work ?—Yes.

11,211. Did he give you any ?—Yes.

11,212. About what time was that ?—The 15th of May last.

11,213. Were you disturbed at all in your work ?—Yes, they went and tried to stop me there.

11,214. Whom do you mean by "they" ?—Our secretary.

11,215. What is his name ?—Joseph Mallinson.

11,216. In what way did he try to stop you ?—He went to Mr. Nicholson and told Mr. Nicholson if he sent away the men that he had he could find him a lot fresh ones from the box, and Mr. Nicholson told him that he was satisfied with the men that he had.

11,217. Then he did not in fact stop you ?—No, the master would not stop us.

11,218. Are you working now for Mr. Nicholson ? —Yes, a little.

11,219. Have you ever gone back to Mr. Crooks ? —No, I have not been back since I was stopped.

11,220. You have never been since ?—No, not since I was stopped, the 17th of November.

11,221. Have you never applied to him for work since the 17th of November ?—I think only once.

11,222. Did you get any ?—No.

11,223. To what do you attribute your not getting the work ?—I do not know I am sure.

11,224. You do not know why ?—No.

11,225. Have you made any effort to join the union again ?—Yes.

11,226. When was that ?—In January this year.

11,227. What made you do that ?—We heard that they would take us in if we would go, a party of us.

11,228. What made you want to join the union ? —They tried to stop me, and I thought we should be better joined than not.

11,229. Would you have joined the union if you could have got work without ?—No, but I wanted to join them again if they would have taken me.

11,230. (*Chairman.*) Why did you want to join them ?—On account of getting my places of work back again at Mr. Crooks.

11,231. You wanted to join them to get Mr. Crooks work back again ?—Yes.

11,232. (*Mr. Barstow.*) Supposing that you could have got Mr. Crooks' work without joining the union would you then have wished to join them ?—No.

11,233. Did you go to see Mallinson ?—In January when we went to see him we offered to pay poundage to go into the trade again, five or six of us, and they would not take the poundage. They wanted to force us to pay the whole of the money down at once which we owed, mine was 8*l.* 11*s.* 6*d.*, and one owed as much as 16*l.*, and more than that, and they wanted us to pay it all and go on the box.

11,234. (*Chairman.*) Then when you had paid it all they wanted you immediately to go on the box ?—Yes.

11,235. (*Mr. Barstow.*) What would be the effect of going on the box ?—I do not know.

11,236. Would you have had to give up work or not ?—Yes, I should have had to give up work if I went on the box.

11,237. How would you live whilst you were out of work ?—I do not know how I should live.

11,238. Would they allow you anything ?—Yes, I do not know exactly what the scale was, but I think either 9*s.* or 10*s.* a week for a man and wife.

11,239. How much can you earn in a week when you have a good week ?—30*s.* up to 2*l.*, it depends on the work, and it depends on the job.

11,240. What was the decision of the committee ?—They said they could not do any more with us than bring the case before the general meeting.

11,241. Did they bring the case before the general meeting ?—No.

11,242. Did they tell you anything about working at Gilbert's ?—Yes, they said we could stop and work at Gilbert's, but we were not allowed to go to seek work anywhere else.

11,243. Are there any non-union men employed at Gilbert's ?—No.

11,244. When you left the union were you in arrear ?—Yes.

11,245. Did you give any notice to them ?—No.

11,246. You only stopped paying that is all ?—I stopped paying.

The witness withdrew.

TWELFTH DAY.

Mr. G. Gill.

19 June 1867.

Mr. GEORGE GILL sworn and examined.

11,247. (*Mr. Chance.*) Are you a scissors manufacturer?—Yes.

11,248. At Lambert Street?—Yes.

11,249. How long have you been a scissors manufacturer?—Eighteen years.

11,250. Do you work for yourself or for anybody else?—For any of the merchants in the town.

11,251. What do you call you yourself?—A scissors manufacturer.

11,252. Are you a member of any union?—No.

11,253. Have you ever been?—No, I have never been asked.

11,254. Have you never been asked?—No.

11,255. Do you remember in 1864 that there was an attempt to form a scissor forgers union?—Yes, I had a letter sent to me by Thompson, the secretary, soon after that time. I left it in Mr. Fretson's office in Bank Street a few weeks since.

11,256. When had you the letter?—Perhaps some two or three years ago. I cannot say to a few months.

11,257. What were the contents of that letter?—He said they had been trying to form a union of scissors forgers and my men had not contributed towards their funds, and he asked me to show them the letter to see if they would contribute towards their funds.

11,258. You as a manufacturer would not be eligible to join the union?—No.

11,259. Upon receiving that letter from Mr. Thompson, did you make the application to your men which he requested you to do?—Yes, I gave it to the men and they had it there for about a week, and then of course they returned it to me after that time.

11,260. Did any of the men join the union in consequence of that letter?—There are two or three of them that have contributed since, because they cut a pair of bellows of the men after.

11,261. When you received the letter you showed it to the men; after you gave it to the men did any of them contribute to the union?—Yes.

11,262. In consequence of that letter, did any of your men contribute to the union?—Yes.

11,263. They joined the union in consequence of this letter?—Yes.

11,264. Some of your men joined and some did not?—Yes.

11,265. Do you know how many joined?—There are four out of the six that belong to the union; two did not join. I employed six forgers.

11,266. Some of the men refused to join?—Yes.

11,267. Is there a man of the name of Joseph Hague who with others refused to join?—Yes.

11,268. Do you remember after his refusal to join being called upon by anyone?—Yes, there were three parties of them that called.

11,269. Who were they that called?—There was Richard Newbold, and Robert Lingard, and Joseph Thompson, the secretary.

11,270. They called at your manufactory to see your men?—Yes, they called to see Joseph Hague.

11,271. Do you know what they said to Joseph Hague?—No, I was not in the shop at the time.

11,272. Did he tell you what they said to him?—He said that he had had a deputation from the committee respecting their contributing to their union.

11,273. Did he say that any threats were uttered in the event of his not joining?—Yes, if he did not contribute to their union, they said they would do something for him.

11,274. After that deputation which you speak of, was anything done?—Yes, about three weeks afterwards a pair of bellows was cut; that was on the 22nd of February 1865.

11,275. Those bellows belonged to you?—Yes.

11,276. And Hague was working upon them?—Yes.

11,277. What did they cost repairing?—1*l.* 1*s.* I left the invoice at Mr. Fretson's office.

11,278. At the same time did there happen to be another pair of bellows belonging to a man who was a member of the union?—Yes, he had contributed sometimes; but he is a man who does not enjoy very good health, and they would not have him a member of the union.

11,279. Was there a pair of bellows there on which the union man was working?—Yes, he has contributed sometimes.

11,280. Were those bellows cut?—No.

11,281. After the cutting of the bellows, did you go to the committee?—Yes.

11,282. Was that immediately afterwards?—About four months afterwards.

11,283. Who was at the committee?—Thompson was the secretary, and of course there was a lot more men there.

11,284. Did you say anything to them about the bellows?—Yes, the men working for me at the time mentioned it to the committee, and they said they would make it right for me if I would wait, and that was the reason I waited.

11,285. The men told you before you went to the committee that they would make it all right?—Yes.

11,286. Was that the reason why you did not go to the committee?—Yes.

11,287. When you went to the committee, what was done?—I saw Thompson and a lot more of the committee men, and they said they did not know anything about it; they had only been fresh elected on the committee a fortnight, or something of that sort.

11,288. Was anything more said?—No; they did not do anything to reimburse me for the outlay.

11,289. They did not reimburse you, they did not do anything for you, and they denied all knowledge of it?—Yes.

11,290. Have you seen any of them since?—No; I do not know that I have mentioned the affair to any of the committee since.

The witness withdrew.

S. Crookes.

SAMUEL CROOKES sworn and examined.

11,291. (*Chairman.*) Do you know that this morning Hallam has been here as a witness?—I have heard so.

11,292. Have you heard that he has made a serious charge against you?—Yes.

11,293. I do not know, and we can none of us know at present, whether that is a true statement or not; but if it is a true statement, and you know it to be true, you are guilty of a very great crime indeed, and you are in very great peril in respect of that crime. If now you like to make a full and clear disclosure of that crime, if you committed it, and if you satisfy us that you have told us the whole truth, you will obtain a certificate, which will free you from the consequences of your act. If, on the other hand, you are guilty, and if you do not tell us the truth so as to entitle you to the certificate, you will hereafter be liable to be prosecuted for that offence, and you will have to be tried for your life. Now you may do as you please. I do not know whether you are guilty or not guilty, but now, at any rate, you have an opportunity if you like by making a full disclosure of having a certificate, which will protect you from the consequences of your crime if you have committed it. If you have not committed it, you have nothing to confess. Now take whatever course you like. I have warned you, and told you what you can do, what protection you can get; you alone know, and can know, what is the proper course to pursue, but I did not like you to give evidence after so serious a charge had been brought

TWELFTH DAY.

S. Crooks.

19 June 1867.

against you, without letting you know the peril in which you stand, and also letting you know the security which you may obtain if you make a full disclosure. You know James Hallam?—Yes.

11,294. Were you at all concerned in rattening a person of the name of Taylor?—Yes.

11,295. Was Hallam along with you?—Yes.

11,296. Before you rattened Taylor had you seen Broadhead?—William Broadhead?

11,297. Yes?—I cannot remember whether I had or not, it is so long since.

11,298. Be careful?—I am speaking the truth; I cannot do more.

11,299. Did Broadhead give you any money for rattening Taylor?—Yes; 50*s*., I believe.

11,300. Were you concerned at all in blowing up Wheatman's?—Yes.

11,301. Who was with you? was Hallam with you?—Yes, James Hallam.

11,302. Where did you get the money from to buy the powder?—I do not know; James Hallam got the money, if I recollect right.

11,303. Are you quite sure about that; did not you get the money?—I think not.

11,304. Hallam got the money, you think?—Yes.

11,305. Who gave it to him; do you not know?—I expect Broadhead gave it him; I do not know rightly, I am sure.

11,306. How much did you get, 2*l*.?—I am sure I cannot say.

11,307. Was it about that sum?—It might be about that sum; I cannot swear to it, it is so long since.

11,308. Did not you get 2*l*. yourself, and did not you give him a sovereign to buy powder?—I think not, but I cannot swear to it.

11,309. Was the powder bought?—Yes, I expect it was bought.

11,310. Do not you know that he bought some at Milner's, in Fargate?—I cannot say whether he bought it at Fargate or at Twibell's.

11,311. How much did you buy altogether?—I cannot say rightly, but there was not as much as he said there was.

11,312. There was not 24 lbs.?—No.

11,313. How do you know what he said?—I saw it in the paper what he said.

11,314. It was not as much as 24 lbs.?—I am sure it was not.

11,315. Did you take the powder and conceal it near Crookes at Bole Hill?—I am going to speak the truth; it never was in Bole Hill.

11,316. Where was it?—At our house.

11,317. You kept the powder at your house; after having kept the powder at your house, did you ultimately go down to Wheatman's on the Saturday night?—Yes.

11,318. What did you do with the powder?—We put the powder in a bottle.

11,319. And what became of it?—We hid the bottle; we could not do it that night.

11,320. When did you next go?—I cannot swear to the night exactly; but we went down another night and they were working, but I cannot swear what night it was.

11,321. Did you go again after that?—No, I think we did it that night.

11,322. How did you do it?—We put it up a hole that there was, and put it underneath the floor.

11,323. Who lighted the fuze?—I cannot say whether he lighted it or whether I did, I do not know.

11,324. Where did you stand when it went off?—We were on the bridge above while it blew up.

11,325. Did you, after that blow up, go to Broadhead's?—That night?

11,326. No, at any time afterwards?—Yes, I went to Broadhead's.

11,327. How soon after did you go to Broadhead's?—I cannot say.

11,328. About what time?—I am sure I cannot say. We went in the course of a few days.

11,329. When you went to Broadhead's, why did you go?—We went to fetch some money.

11,330. Did you see him?—Yes.

11,331. What money did he give you?—I think it was 15*l*., but I am not sure.

11,332. Was that the sum. I thought that you were to have 20*l*.?—I think it was only 15*l*. that he gave me, I could not swear to that, I think it was 15*l*.

11,333. I believe Wheatman and Smith had put up a new machine?—Yes, they were putting one up.

11,334. Did Broadhead tell you at all why you were to blow up this place of Wheatman's?—Did he tell us why we should do it?

11,335. Yes?—No, he did not say anything to me.

11,336. He merely told you to blow them up, and that he would give you 15*l*. for doing it?—Yes.

11,337. And after you had done it he gave you the 15*l*.?—Yes.

11,338. Did he tell you how you had done it, did he say that you had done it well or not?—He was satisfied I expect; he did not complain about it.

11,339. You did not do a great deal of mischief I believe?—No; it was not intended I believe to do a great deal of mischief.

11,340. Did not you want in the first place to blow up the chimney?—No, we did not; that was a falsehood altogether; we went direct to do it in the place we did do it.

11,341. When have you heard and where have you heard that Hallam has been making a statement against you. Was it from what you saw in the newspaper?—Yes, I saw it in the newspaper; he made many statements false in that paper.

11,342. Have you heard what he said to-day?—No, I have not heard what he said to-day, but I heard he implicated me in it.

11,343. Your name was not in the newspaper before, he would not tell your name?—There was "Sam" in it, he might as well have told it.

11,344. You knew quite well whom he meant?—Yes, of course I did.

11,345. I do not know what you have heard. I will tell you what he has said because I think that you ought to be made acquainted with it. He has said that you and he were employed by Broadhead to do an injury to Linley, and he says that you and he went together, and that you had an air gun and that he and you followed Linley about for a long time from place to place for nearly five or six weeks, having been promised 20*l*. by Broadhead to do this deed, and that you then, having followed him into a public-house in Scotland Street, with your air gun shot Linley in the head, and he says that he compelled you to do it, that you were unwilling to do it, but that he compelled you to do it and you did it. That is what he said against you, and that he was by you when you did it. Have you heard that statement?—No.

11,346. That is what he says and has sworn to this morning. Now it is about this that I want to caution you, if you are guilty of this, you are guilty of murder, if you are guilty of murder you will be tried for your life, if you make a clean breast of it and make a candid disclosure of that fact, we have power to grant you a certificate which will protect you even from the consequences of such a deed as that. That is the only protection that you can ever have in your life. Now then it is for you to say, did you do that deed or not?—Yes; I did it.

11,347. You did shoot Linley?—Yes.

11,348. Had you any quarrel with Linley?—No.

11,349. How came you to be disposed to shoot at him or to do him an injury?—I did not intend to kill him.

11,350. Who first suggested to you doing any harm to him, was it Broadhead?—Yes, I think it was. I do not know whether he suggested it or whether he suggested that Linley was doing us a great deal of injury. I cannot say whether we suggested it or whether Mr. Broadhead suggested it.

11,351. How was he doing you a deal of injury?—He was setting a whole lot of lads on, filling the trade

TWELFTH DAY.

S. Crooks.

19 June 1867.

with lads and spoiling the trade altogether; that was it. Doing all the harm he could.

11,352. He was spoiling the trade by filling it with lads and doing all the harm that he could?—Yes.

11,353. Had you talked to Broadhead about his doing this damage to the trade?—Yes.

11,354. What did Broadhead say to you?—I cannot say what he said exactly. I cannot remember, it is so long since.

11,355. But you are not likely to have forgotten a thing of that kind. Did he offer you money?—To do it?

11,356. Yes?—I cannot say whether we went to him or he told us.

11,357. Did he agree to give you money?—Yes.

11,358. How much did he agree to give you?—I think it was 20*l*.

11,359. What did you agree to do?—We agreed to do something to Linley. We did not want to kill him, but we could not help but hitting him where we did. There was a lot of people in the room. Hallam would have me to shoot. I did not want to shoot.

11,360. You did not want to shoot but he compelled you to shoot?—I did not want to hit him where I did. I wanted to hit him in the shoulder. I was compelled to hit him where I did.

11,361. You say that you wanted to hit him in the shoulder, but you were compelled to hit him as you did?—He was bending forward this way (*describing the same*) and I was shooting at his shoulder. I tried to get it just into the shoulder here, not into his head at all, and he had his head laid down talking. I did not want to hit him over the head.

11,362. After you had got these instructions did you get any money at all from Broadhead? Did he pay you anything on account? I mean when you agreed to do him this harm?—I cannot say whether he did or not.

11,363. Did he give you anything on account?—I daresay he might.

11,364. Do you recollect whether he did or not?—I cannot recollect it; he gave us it according to what we agreed to.

11,365. Did he give it you after you had done it, or did he give you a part before you had done it?—I do not know. I cannot swear that.

11,366. You do know whether he paid it before or after?—He paid us after it was done of course.

11,367. Did not he pay you beforehand?—No.

11,368. Do you recollect a revolver being bought?—No.

11,369. Do you recollect whether Hallam bought a revolver?—I recollect Hallam having one, but I do not recollect whether he bought it.

11,370. Do you recollect Broadhead giving Hallam some money?—I cannot say; he might give me some. I cannot swear to that.

11,371. Had you a revolver?—No, I had not a revolver. Hallam had a revolver.

11,372. Had you never a revolver—are you certain of that?—No, I never had one in my life.

11,373. You never had one in your life?—No, not of my own.

11,374. Did you borrow a revolver?—No.

11,375. Did you ever carry a revolver about at that time?—We bought a revolver, Hallam and me.

11,376. What did you give for it?—I do not know. I think it was 50s. It was in pawn. I bought it out of a pawnshop.

11,377. Where did you buy it?—We bought it out of "Pot" Square.

11,378. Paradise Square?—Yes.

11,379. Do you know the name of the pawnbroker?—I do not know his name exactly.

11,380. Whereabouts is it? Is it a corner house—the corner of Bank Street?—Yes.

11,381. The corner shop, I think it used to be a pawnbroker's shop?—Bowman, I think they call him. I do not know whether I am right or not.

11,382. Was that the only revolver that you had, either of you?—Yes, we had only one revolver.

11,383. What did you get the revolver for? did you intend shooting him with the revolver?—Hallam told me he would want a revolver, he would want something to defend himself with, and I bought him a revolver. James Hallam gave me the money to buy it with.

11,384. Did you know Linley yourself?—Yes, I knew him.

11,385. Did you know him to speak to?—No, I never spoke to him, but I knew him.

11,386. You had no quarrel with him—the only thing was that you were annoyed about the trade?—Yes, that was all.

11,387. When you had agreed to do this harm to him, did you always intend to shoot him?—No, I intended to shoot him, but not to kill him.

11,388. You always intended to shoot him?—I always intended to wound him to make him know he was doing wrong, but not to kill him.

11,389. But not to kill him?—No.

11,390. You intended to wound him I suppose with this pistol?—With this pistol?

11,391. Yes?—No.

11,392. How did you intend to wound him?—His pistol was never used at all.

11,393. Did you ever intend to use it?—He intended using it if anybody attacked him.

11,394. Did you ever intend to use that pistol against Linley?—No.

11,395. How did you intend to wound him? how were you to do it?—With an air gun.

11,396. You always intended that?—I intended to do it after I had set my mind to do it.

11,397. Where did you get your air gun?—I bought it at Snig Hill, at Naylor's. Naylor lived on Snig Hill at that time.

11,398. Did you buy it in order to do this deed?—Yes.

11,399. What did you give for it?—I cannot say now.

11,400. But you bought it at Naylor's?—Yes, when they lived on Snig Hill, not where they do now.

11,401. They then lived on Snig Hill, where do they live now?—They live on West Bar now.

11,402. Were you alone, or was Hallam with you when you bought it?—I was alone when I bought it, I believe. The first time I bought it was to go shooting with it to kill grouse with, but just as I had got it I got this Linley affair to do and I used it for that; but I did not buy it expressly to do him with, because I had had it a long time before I ever knew anything about Linley, a little bit before.

11,403. Having this for the purpose of killing grouse, you determined to use it for the purpose of shooting Linley?—Yes.

11,404. After you had agreed to shoot him and had made up you mind to shoot him, how long was it before you did shoot him?—A long time.

11,405. How long?—I cannot say, but it was a very long time.

11,406. Several weeks?—Yes, we were after him many weeks before we could get the chance.

11,407. Did you go after him up and down to try and get a chance?—Yes.

11,408. Where did you go?—We went up and down the town to light on him; we lit on him at one place and then another as it happened, we was a long time agait.

11,409. Did you go out almost every day to look after him except Sundays?—We went out very often at nights, not in the daytime.

11,410. Did you go to the public-houses to which he went?—Yes.

11,411. And you could not succeed? why did not you succeed before?—Because we never got a right chance.

11,412. On the day on which he was shot where did you first see him?—I cannot exactly say, but just before, I believe we saw him at the American stores; I cannot be certain.

11,413. After that what became of him?—He went

up to John Raike's, I believe it was, and he went into the back room.

11,414. That is in Scotland Street?—Yes, and we went up the entry; he went into the room where the window came into the yard; Hallam went first, and he saw him through the window and he came to me and told me he could see him through the window, and I told him it would not do. I followed him up, and looked through the window and saw him. I could only just see him. I said, "It will not do to do him now." I says, "We should hit somebody else," and he said, "If you do not do him, give hold of it, and I will do him if you will not do him." Well, I kept it myself because he was not fit to handle it; he would have shot somebody else; he did not understand it, and we went down.

11,415. He said he would do it if you would not?—Yes.

11,416. Did you do it afterwards?—Yes, I watched my opportunity for the first chance I could get of course, and I shot at him, and intended to hit him in the shoulder.

11,417. Did you know where you had hit him?—No, I did not know while I saw next day.

11,418. Directly you had shot him what did you do?—We ran down the back side; there was an entry went into some Croft; I do not know what Croft it is.

11,419. Is it Peacroft?—I cannot say; it comes out the back side of Raike's.

11,420. Had there been any question as to whethor you could get out that way at first?—Yes, Hallam went to look before we shot him.

11,421. Then you found that you could get out that way, and you ran out that way?—Yes.

11,422. As you ran out was there anyone in the passage?—Yes, there was a man and woman in the passage.

11,423. What did you do?—We ran away.

11,424. Did you run against them?—I do not know whether we ran against them; we ran close to them but they said something, I do not know what it was.

11,425. Which way did you run?—We went down. I cannot tell you, but we went down the hill and up towards Crookes.

11,426. Did you pass up by St. George's Church?—Yes, I daresay we did.

11,427. Did you separate there?—Yes.

11,428. When did you next see Hallam?—I cannot say, to say right.

11,429. Did not you see him the next day?—Very likely, but I could not say whether it would be the next day or the day after, but I daresay it would be the next day.

11,430. The next day, you believe, that you saw him? there was a great commotion in the town, was not there?—Yes.

11,431. Were you at Wylie's in the Haymarket?—I cannot say.

11,432. Where do you recollect meeting him?—I went to work myself the next day.

11,433. When do you recollect meeting with Hallam next?—I am sure I cannot say.

11,434. After having done a thing like this, and it being so much more serious than you wished, had you never any talk with him about what you had done?—Yes, we talked after; but I cannot say how long it was after.

11,435. Shortly after he had done this you met him and talked of it, did you?—Yes.

11,436. Did you go to Broadhead?—I do not rightly know.

11,437. We have had Hallam to tell his story, I will tell it to you. He said that you gave him at Wylie's the next day a sovereign; was there a man called Palfryman there?—I do not know.

11,438. Did you see Broadhead after this?—Yes.

11,439. How long after this did you see Broadhead?—I cannot say.

11,440. How many days do you think that it was before the Saturday?—I daresay it would be on the Saturday, but I will not swear to that.

11,441. What did Broadhead say to you, or you say to Broadhead about this matter?—I do not know, I am sure, exactly what he said.

11,442. You must have talked about it if he gave you money to shoot at him?—It was so long since.

11,443. You must recollect after you had done it what passed between you?—I am sure I cannot say.

11,444. Did he pay you for it?—I believe he did, but I will not swear whether he paid me or Hallam.

11,445. In your presence?—I only speak the truth, but I will not swear without I know it.

11,446. Did Broadhead after he knew that you had shot Linley pay you the money?—Broadhead?

11,447. Yes?—I believe he did, but I am not certain; I believe he did pay me, but I will not be sure.

11,448. You are not sure whether he paid you, but are you sure that he paid either you or Hallam?—Yes, he paid one of us.

11,449. Did you get your share of the money?—Yes. I have never made any complaints, so I expect I got it.

11,450. How much did you get for your share?—I think I got 10*l.*, I think so. I think it was 10*l.* but I will not swear, my memory slips me whether it was 15*l.* or 20*l.* that we had for that job.

11,451. Do not you think that you had some money before that; if you got only 15*l.* your share was only 7*l.* 10*s.*?—It might be so, it is so long since I cannot tell.

11,452. Where was it that Broadhead paid you?—I think he paid us at his house.

11,453. Did he ever say anything to you about your having shot him in the head, or that it was all right, or what?—No; he never said anything of that sort.

11,454. What did he say about the shooting?—He said that it was a very good job we had not killed him; he lived a good while after; we did not kill him then; he did not want us to kill him.

11,455. But you told Broadhead that you were going to shoot at him?—Yes.

11,456. Did he tell you when you told him that you were going to shoot Linley that you were not to kill him?—He said we were not to kill him, but just to wound him, so as to let him know that he was not doing right.

11,457. You were not to kill him if you could help it?—He did not say "if we could help it," he said we were "not to kill him but to wound him."

11.458. Did you see that there had been a coroner's inquest after he died?—Yes.

11,459. The verdict was murder against somebody whom they did not know?—Yes.

11,460. When this turned out to be murder in this way did you and Hallam have a talk together about keeping it secret?—Yes.

11,461. What did you say to each other?—We pledged ourselves to keep it still, and not to let nobody know about it.

11,462. Had you any talk to Broadhead about it?—No, I think not.

11,463. He knew the secret as well as you?—Of course we did not need to talk to him.

11,464. Did you bind him over to keep the secret because he knew it as well as you?—No, we did not bind him over; we expected that he would be able to do it himself, without us.

11,465. You could trust him?—Yes.

11,466. And you did not have any agreement with him?—No, I think not.

11,467. Are you quite sure of that?—I am quite sure I have not.

11,468. You do not know that Hallam had?—I do not know whether he had or not.

11,469. You have told us about this; you know that, in order to get a certificate from us you must not only tell us about this, but we must be satisfied that you have told us everything else that you have

TWELFTH DAY.

S. Crooks.

19 June 1867.

done which has been illegal or unlawful about trade matters. Can you tell me who shot at Linley the first time that he was shot at?—Yes.

11,470. Who shot at him then?—Me.

11,471. Where was it that he was shot at?—In Nursery Street.

11,472. How long was that before the second time when he was shot?—A long while.

11,473. How long before?—I could not say I am sure; it was a good time before. I cannot say how long.

11,474. Were you alone when you shot him in Nursery Street?—Yes.

11,475. With what did you shoot him?—I shot him with the air gun; just the same thing.

11,476. The same air gun?—Yes.

11,477. And there was nobody with you?—No, nobody was with me; I had it to myself.

11,478. Who asked you to do it?—I had a bit of talk with Broadhead, we did it between us.

11,479. Did Broadhead give you anything for doing that?—Yes.

11,480. How much did he give you?—I think I had 20*l*. I think so.

11,481. Did he pay it before or after you shot him the first time?—After.

11,482. He was then wounded in the side, was not he?—Yes.

11,483. Where was he when you shot him the first time?—He sat on the table with his back towards the window.

11,484. Were you outside in the street?—Yes.

11,485. What time of the night or day was it?—It was soonish on at night, it would be sometime in the night. I cannot say when.

11,486. Seven or eight o'clock?—Yes.

11,487. Was there a light inside the room where he was?—Yes.

11,488. Was there anybody with him when you shot him the first time?—No.

11,489. He was alone?—He went by himself into the house. There was somebody in the house with him. Nobody went into the house with him. They were in before he went in.

11,490. How long were you before you got to shoot him the first time after you had agreed with Broadhead? You say that you had a little talk with Broadhead and agreed with him; how long after you had agreed with Broadhead was it that you got your chance of shooting him the first time?—A good while.

11,491. During this time while you were trying to get your chance did you see Broadhead about it for him to know whether you were getting on or not?—Yes, I saw him oft enough, he knew I was not getting on or he would have heard of it.

11,492. Did he ask you how you were getting on or anything of that kind?—No.

11,493. Did you tell him that you had not had a chance?—I told him I had not had a chance.

11,494. How often did you tell him this?—Two or three times, every time I saw him.

11,495. Were you pursuing him up and down the streets from day to day wherever he went in order for you to get a chance?—I generally knew where to find him. He was generally to be found at such like places as the "American Stores," and such like places as them, these lowish houses, he was generally there. I generally went to look for him there. I do not watch for him. I generally found him at such like places.

11,496. You were looking after him all this time to get your opportunity?—Yes; but I did not want to do him a deal of harm that time. There were very little air in the gun—it never did enter him—it never was intended—there was not air enough. I had very little air in the gun on purpose just to warm him.

11,497. You are a good shot I believe?—I cannot say about that.

11,498. You can shoot rabbits with an air gun?—Yes.

11,499. Then you are not a bad shot?—No; I have shot many a one.

11,500. Have you shot grouse with an air gun?—Yes.

11,501. But you intended to hit him though not to hurt him very much?—Yes.

11,502. Where did you shoot at him?—I shot at him in the back. I knew that it could not hurt him a deal because I knew there was not a deal of air in the gun.

11,503. Whereabouts. Can you put your hand at the place which you shot at?—It was somewhere at the back here (*describing the same*). He was sitting on the table.

11,504. If your gun had been a little stronger and there had been a little more air than you intended in it, it would have been a serious business?—You could depend about that. I can always tell about it.

11,505. What distance were you from him when you shot at him the first time?—About four or five yards. I knew I should not be far off him or I should have had more. If I wanted to do him any injury it would have done injury enough, but I did not want to kill him.

11,506. You have told me that you have shot at Linley twice, and you have told me of two rattenings in which you have been engaged, are there any other offences of which you have been guilty in connexion with the trade?—I have never been guilty of anything only that time—only one that I intended to be at, but we never got at it. That was Helliwell.

11,507. You intended to be at Helliwell?—Yes, but we never did get at him.

11,508. When you say "we," whom do you mean?—Jem Hallam and me, at the time that Wheatman and Smith's job were agait.

11,509. How did you happen to be in for the Helliwell business, who asked you to do it?—We had that the same as we had the other, Hallam and me. I do not know whether Hallam undertook that, or whether I did.

11,510. Who proposed it to you?—We went to Broadhead and we got the job.

11,511. What were you to do?—I do not know rightly what we were to do to him.

11,512. Where was he working?—He was working at Firth's.

11,513. Are you quite clear that it was Firth's, or was it Hague and Clegg's?—I know nothing about Hague and Clegg's. It was at Firth's.

11,514. Were you to blow him up or destroy his bands, or what were you to do?—I do not know rightly now, it is so long since, whether we were watching to get to hammer him, or what it was. I cannot say what we had to do to him.

11,515. You were to do some harm to him?—Yes.

11,516. What were you to have for doing this—how much money?—I cannot remember. It was not a deal. I cannot remember what it was.

11,517. But you were to have some money for doing it?—Yes.

11,518. And you say that somehow or other it did not come off. How was it?—We did Wheatman's job, and we never got a chance at him. I never did naught to him at all.

11,519. Is there any other thing which has been done besides in reference to the trade. Have you done anything in reference to trade matters which is illegal or contrary to the law?—No, I do not know that I have ever done anything except what I told you.

11,520. You do not think so?—I believe I never have.

11,521. Are you quite sure that you never have?—I am quite sure I never have.

11,522. You have never done anything at all except what you have told me?—I never did anything since.

11,523. Since when?—Wheatman and Smith's I believe was the last job.

11,524. You have never had anything to do with anything since?—No.

TWELFTH DAY.

S. Crooks.

19 June 1867.

11,525. Do you know Needham?—What Needham?

11,526. The man who had four years penal servitude?—Tom Needham?

11,527. Yes, Tom Needham?—Yes, I know Tom Needham.

11,528. What did he do that caused him to be transported?—He did something at Dronfield.

11,529. He blew up a manufactory there?—Yes, he and his brother I believe.

11,530. Do you know what they made at the manufactory at Dronfield?—No.

11,531. Was it a scythe works?—I do not know I am sure.

11,532. I believe that Needham was tried at Derby and had four years penal servitude?—I know he was tried there for it; that made me know that he did it, but that is above 10 years back.

11,533. Were you concerned in that?—No I was not concerned in that.

11,534. You had nothing to do with it?—No.

11,535. Nothing at all?—No, I was blamed for it, but I never had anything to do with it.

11,536. Did you know Needham's wife?—Yes, they lived beside us.

11,537. You lived beside her?—Yes.

11,538. After Needham was sent to prison did not you go and pay his wife a sum of money from week to week?—No.

11,539. Now mind?—I will speak the truth, I never did.

11,540. You never paid her any money?—No.

11,541. She is here now?—I am prepared to meet her; I never paid her a penny.

11,542. I wish to caution you upon this matter?—I never paid her a penny, she washed for us.

11,543. You never paid her any money except for washing?—No.

11,544. I want you to make a full disclosure; you have disclosed a very serious crime and you are in very great peril if you do not get your certificate, and it becomes very important that you should tell the truth. Did not you send her money immediately after her husband went to prison, and after paying her for some time did not you then hand her over to Michael Thompson, the secretary of the union?—No, I never handed her over at all. I never knowed that she were.

11,545. Did you go to see Needham in prison?—No.

11,546. Are you sure about that?—I am certain.

11,547. Did you go with his wife?—No.

11,548. And did you tell her to pass you off as her brother?—No, I never went with her at all.

11,549. Is there any crime which has been committed connected with trade matters as to which you can tell me who did it although you did not do it?—No.

11,550. You cannot?—No, I have never known anybody doing anything.

11,551. Who blew up Fearnehough?—I cannot say.

11,552. On your oath do not you know?—On my oath I know nothing about it, and never had anything to do with Fearnehough in my life.

11,553. And you do not know who did it?—No, I do not.

11,554. Now again, did you go to see Needham after he came out of prison?—Yes.

11,555. To see him did you go to London?—Yes.

11,556. What did you go to London for?—I went to see him come out. I went to meet him come out.

11,557. Who was with you?—Nobody.

11,558. Was Hallam there?—No Hallam had nothing to do with it.

11,569. Did you tell him that he must keep secret the names of the persons who had been engaged in it or that you would blow his brains out?—No, never; we were always on good terms.

11,560. Why did you go to London?—I went to meet him.

11,561. Why did you meet him?—Because we were mates; before he went he lived beside me; I went for an out.

11,562. And you had nothing at all to do with that matter of his?—No, I had not.

11,563. Who sent you? did anybody send you to meet him?—No, I went on my own account.

11,564. Did anybody supply you with funds to enable you to go there?—No, I found my own, I wanted to go to London.

11,565. Do you know who kept his wife while he was in prison?—No, I do not.

11,566. Are you sure?—I am certain, I know nothing about it.

11,567. What became of Needham after he came back?—He went to America.

11,568. When?—A good while since; he has been in America I should think six or seven years.

11,569. How long did he remain in England after he came out of prison?—I do not know, it would be a good while.

11,570. How long?—I cannot say.

11,571. A year?—It was a good while.

11,572. Was it a year?—I will not swear to the time, because I cannot tell; it was a good while.

11,573. Might it be less than a year?—It might or it might not be, I cannot say.

11,574. Did you ever lend your air gun to anybody?—No. How do you mean, lend it to anybody?

11,575. Lend it for anything?—No.

11,576. Had you any other gun besides the air gun?—Yes; I take a licence out every year. I have had a gun many a year.

11,577. Did you ever lend your gun to anybody?—I have lent my gun to many a one, but I do not know anybody particular.

11,578. Do you recollect Elisha Parker being shot at?—Yes.

11,579. At the time when Elisha Parker was shot had you not then lent your gun?—Not that I am aware of.

11,580. Are you sure that you had not?—Not that I am aware of.

11,581. Think for a moment; you heard of his being shot at?—Yes, that was the reason that I know.

11,582. If you had lent your gun at the time when he was shot at you would recollect the fact—had you lent your gun to anybody at the time when he was shot at?—Not that I am aware of.

11,583. Will you swear that you had not?—I will swear I do not know that I had lent it at that time. I do not know that I lent my gun, I cannot tell.

11,584. Do not you believe that you lent it at that time?—No, I do not believe that I had. I do not know that I had.

11,585. Who borrowed it about that time from you?—I cannot tell you. I cannot tell I am sure. I never lent my gun a great deal.

11,586. To whom have you lent it?—I have lent it to several about home.

11,587. To whom have you lent it?—I have both lent my gun and borrowed guns.

11,588. To whom have you lent your guns?—I cannot say.

11,589. Mention the name of a person to whom you have lent your gun?—I cannot say particularly whom I have lent it to.

11,590. Mind, it is a very serious matter. You must satisfy us?—I will speak the truth.

11,591. To whom have you lent your gun?—I cannot tell, not particular.

11,592. Do you know a person called Elijah Smith?—Yes.

11,593. Have you lent your gun to him?—Never in my life. Elijah Smith never had my gun in his life, on my oath. I will take my dying oath he has not. He never asked me for it.

11,594. Do you know a person of the name of Bamford?—Yes.

11,595. Did you lend it to him?—No.

11,596. Did you ever lend it to him?—Never in my life.

11,597. Do you know who shot at Mr. Parker?—No, I will take my oath I do not, and never knew in my life.

11,598. You do not know at all?—No.

11,599. You have now told us all you know?—I have told you all I know that I have had aught to do with.

11,600. There is an Investigating Committee at Broadhead's?—No, not now.

11,601. Was there at the time when you shot at Linley?—I cannot say.

11,602. Had you any communication with any other person than Broadhead?—No, never anybody but him.

11,603. Had you any communication with anyone but Broadhead at the time when you did these rattenings?—No; I have never had anything to do with anybody but Broadhead.

11,604. Broadhead was the only person who employed you?—Yes.

11,605. And no other member of the union?—No. I have never had any talk to anybody else.

11,606. I want to know this, were you aware before you came into this room this afternoon of what Hallam had said about your shooting at Linley?—All that I was aware of was this, they came into the wheel just before the policeman came; there was a person who is working against our place doing somewhat who told another person that Hallam had been telling all about it.

11,607. All about what?—All about Jemmy Linley, and they said that it was some Crooks that he had told on; that was all I knew; that was all I got to hear before the policeman came.

11,608. Did you talk with the policeman when you came here?—No.

11,609. Did he tell you that Hallam had implicated you?—No.

11,610. Did anybody tell you how Hallam had said it was done or the details of it?—No, that is all that I heard.

11,611. All you heard was an observation in the wheel that Hallam had been up before us to-day and had told us all about Linley, and that one Crooks was in it?—Yes; some Crooks.

11,612. You never knew that he had said how you tracked Linley about from one place to the other, and that you had gone up to the public-house and looked in at the window and tried whether there was a back exit or anything of that kind. You did not know that he said that?—No.

11,613. You do not know that now?—I do not know that he said aught about it.

11,614. Did you give Mrs. Needham 10*s*. once?—No.

11,615. Do you recollect going with her to Derby and saying that you were her brother?—No, I never did.

11,616. Do you recollect her going a second time and your saying that you dared not go, but that you gave her 10*s*.?—No.

11,617. Did you send your wife with her?—No; my wife never was at Derby I should think.

11,618. Did you say that she might go to Michael Thompson, the secretary of the Scythe Grinders Union, and ask him if he would find her money to bury her child?—No.

11,619. Do you know whether Linley was blown up at Poole's in the Wicker?—I do not know anything about it.

11,620. You do not know who did it?—No.

The witness withdrew.

Mr. Sugg applied to have the witness recalled for cross-examination at the end of the week, and stated that the evidence given to-day had completely startled both himself and his clients. He stated that he thought that a line might be drawn between the defence of Mr. Broadhead and the defence of the Trades Unions.

The Chairman suggested that it would be desirable that Mr. Sugg should meet his clients to-night, if possible, and decide what course he would adopt.

Mr. Sugg stated that he feared it would be impossible for him to be prepared to-morrow to cross-examine the witnesses who had given evidence to-day on the statements which they had made, on account of the great amount of investigation and detail which it would involve.

The Chairman stated that the Examiners were not prepared to state at present what course they would take.

After some further discussion, it was arranged that to-day's witnesses should be recalled on Friday for cross-examination on behalf of the Trades Union Committee; but the Examiners intimated that they considered that Mr. Broadhead stood in no different position from that of Hallam or Crooks, and that he must hold himself in readiness to be examined to-morrow, or whenever the Examiners might deem it expedient to examine him.

Adjourned to to-morrow at 11 o'clock.

THIRTEENTH DAY.

Council Hall, Sheffield, Thursday, 20th June 1867.

PRESENT:

WILLIAM OVEREND, Esq. Q.C.	GEORGE CHANCE, Esq.
THOMAS IRWIN BARSTOW, Esq.	J. E. BARKER, Esq., Secretary.

THIRTEENTH DAY.

20 June 1867.

WILLIAM OVEREND, Esq., Q.C., IN THE CHAIR.

Mr. J. J. Shrubsole, the person appointed yesterday to examine the books of the unions, delivered in the books of the Scissor Forgers Union, together with his report thereon, under seal, to the Commissioners.

The Chairman inquired whether Mr. Broadhead was present.

Mr. Sugg stated that the Defence Committee had held a meeting last night, and that, having taken into consideration the disclosures made yesterday, they felt that they must from that time be dissevered from the saw trade, and they had therefore passed the following resolution : " Moved by Mr Austin, seconded by Mr. " Dronfield—That in consequence of the very serious charges now pending against the saw trade before the " Examiners, this committee hereby resolves to hold itself aloof from such trade, until the charges have been " further investigated, this committee being astounded at the revelations made during the inquiry, believing " at the time that the application was made by the trades for the Commission of Inquiry that such outrages " were not countenanced or connived at by the officers of any union."

The Chairman inquired whether there was any person present who had attended the meeting.

Mr. Sugg stated that Mr. Dronfield was present.

The *Court* ordered Mr. Dronfield to be sworn.

Mr. WILLIAM DRONFIELD sworn and examined.

Mr. W. Dronfield.

11,621. (*Chairman.*) Will you be kind enough to give me that resolution to which Mr. Sugg has referred ?—Yes (*handing in the same*).

11,622. Who was present at this meeting ?—Mr. Austin.

11,623. What is he ?—George Austin, secretary to the Railway Spring Makers Union.

11,624. Who was there besides ?—Mr. Thomas Smith.

11,625. Who is he ?—Secretary to the saw makers.

11,626. Who else ?—Mr. William Blenkiron, secretary to the amalgamated joiners, Sheffield; Mr. Charles Bagshaw, secretary to the fork grinders; I was there myself.

11,627. In what capacity were you there ?—I attended as honorary secretary to the Defence Committee.

11,628. Who was there besides ?—Mr. Sugg was there.

11,629. As solicitor to the Defence Committee ?—As solicitor to the Defence Committee.

11,630. Were those all the persons that were present ?—Mr. Broadhead was present during a portion of the time, but he was called in. He is not a member of that committee.

11,631. Who was there besides ?—I think that that is all. I have not a list with me. There was Mr. James, secretary to the table knife hafters.

11,632. Where did you meet ?—We met at Mr. Broadhead's.

11,633. You went to Mr. Broadhead's house yesterday ?—The meeting had been called there, and we had no other place to hold it in at that time. It was thought to meet in Mr. Sugg's office, but he had not convenience for the whole of the committee.

11,634. But you went on to Mr. Broadhead's ?—Yes.

11,635. For what purpose was Mr. Broadhead called in ?—He was called in to ask him with respect to statements which had been made against him yesterday.

11,636. What was said to him, and who said it ?—Mr. Sugg had a long conversation with him.

11,637. But what did he say about this ?—What did Mr. Sugg say ?

11,638. No, what did Mr. Broadhead say, and what did you say to him ?—I said scarcely anything.

11,639. What was said to him in your hearing ?—I am sure that I cannot tax my memory with what was said.

11,640. Yes you can. What was said to him about those charges ?—Mr. Sugg told him that the charges against him were of a very serious nature, and that he had been completely astounded at the revelations which had been made, and I think that the committee generally agreed with what Mr. Sugg stated, that they themselves had been taken by surprise at the revelations, and they hoped that those charges were not true, but that pending any further inquiry into them it was thought better that the saw trade should be kept distinct altogether.

11,641. What besides ?—Until the charges had been investigated.

11,642. How long ?—The committee at its formation not having any notion that such things existed, and not being formed for the purpose of defending such things. The committee I may say expressed their great abhorrence of such acts as had been perpetrated.

11,643. What did Mr. Broadhead say ?—Mr. Broadhead did not satisfy myself.

11,644. I did not ask you whether he satisfied you. We are not here to inquire into that. I am asking you what Mr. Broadhead said ?—Mr. Broadhead had a consultation with Mr. Sugg.

11,645. I did not ask you that. I asked you what Broadhead said at the meeting ?—Mr. Broadhead said that he did not recollect some of the circumstances that had been stated by some of the witnesses.

11,646. Anything more ?—He said that there might be some truth in some portions of the statement. I am not pledging myself to the words.

11,647. You need not state the words, but give us the substance ?—After hearing his statement the committee were not satisfied.

11,648. But what did the statement contain besides that ? did he say nothing as to his having been accessory before the fact to murder ?—No ; he did not say anything about it.

11,649. And the committee did not ask him about it ?—No.

11,650. Do you mean to say that nothing was said by the committee to him about this charge of murder ? —There was something said to him about its being true about Linley being shot, and his knowing about it, but he did not satisfy the committee whether it was so or not.

11,651. What did he say ?—I do not think that he said anything directly bearing upon it.

11,652. If he did not satisfy them, it was because he said something which was not satisfactory; what did he say ?—I have told you that I do not remember what he did say upon it, and I do not.

11,653. Do you mean to say that when a charge is brought against a man of so serious a nature as this, and you are acting as secretary to the Defence Com-

THIR-TEENTH DAY.

Mr. W. Dronfield.

20 June 1867.

mittee, you do not listen to every word and bear it in your memory ?—I heard all he said.

11,654. Then what did he say ?—I am giving it as nearly as I can. I do not intend to say anything but what I believe to be truthful. He stated, as I said before, that there might be some truth in some portion of the statement.

11,655. Of whom ?—Which Hallam had made, but that he was not prepared to give us any further explanation then. I am telling you as nearly as I can, but I do not want to pledge myself to the exact words. He said that he was not prepared then to tell us more about it.

11,656. When you say that he said there might be some truth in what Hallam had said, to what part of the evidence which Hallam had given was he referring ? —I understood that it had reference to the several charges which had been made.

11,657. Of course ; but which charge did he allude to ? the charge of shooting at Linley ?—I cannot swear whether it was or not.

11,658. Yes you can ?—I cannot indeed.

Mr. Sugg stated that that matter was not discussed at all.

(*Witness.*) I was going to tell you that after hearing his statement the committee wished him to retire and they then passed that resolution.

11,659. He entered into no defence of his conduct there ?—No.

11,660. And he was not asked to do so ?—No ; we thought that was Mr. Sugg's business and yours. I told you that we were not satisfied with what he said, and we passed that resolution and he then retired.

11,661. How long did the meeting take ? how long were you sitting together ?—It would be about 7 o'clock when I got there, and I think the committee broke up about 10, but there was other business besides that.

11,662. How long were you engaged on the business of Broadhead ?—I do not know. Mr. Broadhead was called in and then he was requested to retire, and he was called in to hear that resolution. That business might take probably an hour and a half. Of course we had a good deal of conversation on the general evidence that had been given.

11,663. Broadhead's business took about an hour and a half, did it ?—About that.

11,664. That was as to the charges brought against Broadhead ?—It was the conversation about the evidence that had been given and as to those charges. I think it was about an hour and a half. I cannot say. I know what time I went and what time the business was over. There was other business.

11,665. Was there no question put to Broadhead about the fact of his having paid any money ?—No, I did not hear any question put about any money. I may say that I was not in the room all the time. I was called out of the room several times by parties on other business, so that I really do not know all that was said, and of course I am only speaking of what I heard. I was called out by the reporters and others once or twice.

11,666. There was no question put to him about having paid money and there was no explanation given by him ; and then there was this resolution that it would be more prudent to be separated from him until the thing was ended ?—I do not know that it was more prudent, whether that is your interpretation or not.

11,667. "Pending the inquiry it was thought better "that the saw trade should be kept distinct." Was that the expression, or, "That it would be more prudent" ?—Not "more prudent."

11,668. What was the expression ?—I do not remember. You have the copy there. I may say that we do not want to be implicated in such charges, and that was the reason we passed that resolution and that we had no sympathy with the perpetrators of such acts.

11,669. Have you a notice for another meeting ?—No.

11,670. You have no other meetings, have you ?—It is to be left to be called, if necessary, but we are not going to hold any more meetings at Mr. Broadhead's. That was decided by the committee last night.

11,671. Have you notes made of the proceedings at that meeting ?—They are entered on a loose sheet. I have no book.

11,672. Have you got the sheet ?—I have not.

11,673. Will you be good enough to produce that sheet ?—I can produce it after dinner ; I can fetch it if you wish.

11,674. I should like you to fetch it now ?—I have given you a copy of the resolution itself.

11,675. I want the notes of what was passed at that meeting, and you say you can get it ?—I will bring you the sheet ; it is on a sheet something like that (*pointing to a paper*).

The witness withdrew.

Mr. Sugg objected to this course being taken, and advised Mr. Dronfield not to go for the paper. He stated that this proceeding was an expression of disbelief in what Mr. Dronfield had stated on oath.

The Chairman remarked that it was not so, and that the Examiners only took this course in discharge of their duty to the public.

The Examiners ordered William Broadhead to be called.

Mr. Sugg stated that Mr. Broadhead would not answer, and that he wished it to go forth to the public that he had yesterday applied to the Court that Mr. Broadhead might have to-day to prepare himself to be examined.

The Chairman stated that if Mr. Broadhead did not appear to-day the Examiners would take what steps they could to make him do so.

Mr. Sugg stated that he would undertake, as a professional man, that Mr. Broadhead should be here to-morrow morning, but that the number and extent of the charges brought against him were so considerable that it was necessary that he should have a little time.

The Chairman stated that if Mr. Broadhead said he was embarassed as a witness every lenience should be shown to him ; but that it might have been supposed that a man against whom such grave charges had been brought would be only too anxious to repel them.

The Court called for the officer who had served the summons on Broadhead.

J. Thorpe.

JOHN THORPE sworn and examined.

11,676. (*Chairman.*) Have you been this morning for the purpose of serving a summons upon William Broadhead ?—Yes.

11,677. Where did you go ?—I went to his house.

11,678. Whom did you see ?—I saw his wife.

11,679. Did you tell her for what purpose you had come ?—Yes.

11,680. What answer did she give ?—She made answer and said he had left at a quarter to 11.

11,681. To-day ?—Yes ; and she supposed that he was coming here.

11,682. And you have not been able to meet with him ?—No.

The witness withdrew.

THIR-TEENTH DAY.

20 June 1867.

The Chairman read the following letter, addressed by Sir William Erle, the Chairman of the Trades Union Commission, to Mr. Gathorne Hardy: "To the Right Honourable the Secretary of State for the Home "Department. Sir,—I have the honour of forwarding to you herewith a letter from Mr. Barker, secretary to "the Trades Union Commission at Sheffield, and of requesting you to give, in your official capacity, your "written sanction for inquiry (by the Examiners appointed under the 30th Victoria, chapter VIII.) into the "case described in Mr. Barker's letter, sent herewith.—I have the honour to be, sir, your obedient servant, "W. Erle, Chairman of the Trades Union Commission. 12, Princes Gardens, 17th June 1867. Allow me "to suggest that your sanction, written on the opposite page, and annexed to Mr. Barker's letter, would give "all legal authority if sent to Sheffield." He also read Mr. Gathorne Hardy's note, which was as follows:— "I sanction the inquiry into the case of Elisha Parker, mentioned in Mr. Barker's letter annexed. (Signed) "Gathorne Hardy. Home Office, June 17th, 1867;" and stated that this was an authority to enter into a case which took place more than 10 years ago.

Elisha Parker recalled and further examined.

E. Parker.

11,683. (*Chairman.*) You live at Dore, I believe, and are a saw grinder?—Yes.

11,684. And you have been a saw grinder, I believe, for 33 years?—Rather more than 33 years.

11,685. And you have been a member of the union from the commencement of your apprenticeship?—Yes.

11,686. And you continued a member, I believe, until 1853?—It might be the latter end of 1852 or 1853, I cannot say.

11,687. At that time were you working for Mr. Newbold at Bridgefield Works, Sheffield Moor?—Yes.

11,688. Did Mr. Newbold give the grinders a month's notice to leave because they refused to work at reduced wages?—Yes.

11,689. At the end of the month did you strike work?—At the end of the month we did.

11,690. How long were you on strike?—21 weeks as near as I can think.

11,691. How were you maintained during that time?—I received 8*s.* 6*d.* a week from the Saw Grinders Union.

11,692. Not the saw forgers?—No, the grinders.

11,693. At the end of the 21 weeks did Mr. Newbold offer you the full price if you would come in again?—Yes.

11,694. You began work again, I believe?—Yes.

11,695. And did Mr. Newbold engage two men who did not belong to the union?—Yes.

11,696. Was one a man of the name of Jackson?—I think that was his name, but I cannot be certain.

11,697. Do you know the name of the other man?—I do not. I think one of them was Jackson.

11,698. But he was a non-union man?—Yes.

11,699. Where did those men work?—They worked at a wheel near Sheffield Moor, but I cannot tell you exactly the place.

11,700. For Mr. Newbold?—Yes.

11,701. Where did you live at this time?—I lived at Dore.

11,702. About six miles from Sheffield?—Yes, I kept the post-office there.

11,703. A few days after you had commenced work did Broadhead and a man called Edwin Machin come to your house at Dore?—Yes.

11,704. Which Broadhead was that?—William Broadhead.

11,705. Had he anything to do with the union then?—He was the secretary.

11,706. At that time?—Yes.

11,707. What time was it that they came to your house?—At about 12 o'clock at night.

11,708. Did they call you up; were you in bed?—All the family were in bed.

11,709. What did they say to you?—They wished me to give over working, and they said that the trade had had a meeting, and they did not wish me to go on, on account of the two men that Mr. Newbold had set on. They came in a cab. I told them that I should not, and that I should go on working.

11,710. What did they say to that?—I told them that they could have my contribution as usual, but that I should go on working.

11,711. What did they say to that?—Broadhead gave me no answer to that.

11,712. What become of them?—We had a little more conversation, and they left me to tell my brother in the morning.

11,713. You were to tell your brother?—Yes.

11,714. Did your brother work for Mr. Newbold also?—Yes.

11,715. Did they want him to give up work as well?—Well, that is what they told me. They told me to tell my brother.

11,716. They went away then?—Yes.

11,717. How long did they stay with you?—Perhaps half an hour. There was a good deal of conversation, but that is the most that I can call to memory.

11,718. After they had gone away that night, did you go on working?—Yes.

11,719. Did you hear anything more about this?—A man they call Roebuck came in a few days to the wheel.

11,720. Is that Benjamin Roebuck?—Yes, and he wanted us to give up work and go away. I asked him where we were to go to, he said "Any where you like." He said the trade would find us money for us to go with.

11,721. What was this man Roebuck? was he a man connected with the union?—Yes, he was a saw grinder.

11,722. Had he any office, connected with the union?—I do not know, I am sure, whether he had any office or not. He said that he would leave us to consider of it for a day or two, and he came but I cannot say whether it was the next day or in a day or two. We told him that we were not going away.

11,723. You said that you would not go away?—Yes.

11,724. And you went on working?—Yes.

11,725. You say it was in the year 1853?—It was either in the year 1852 or 1853 that we turned out, but I cannot say which.

11,726. How long was it after you turned out that Broadhead came to you?—It was after we commenced working, after the 21 weeks.

11,727. Was that in 1852 or 1853?—I cannot say that.

11,728. In what month was it, do you think that he called upon you?—I could not say that because I am not certain in which year it was.

11,729. But you can tell me in what month it was, was it in summer or winter?—No, I could not.

11,730. Did you go on working?—Yes.

11,731. How long did you work without being interrupted and interfered with?—I was interrupted in 1853 (*referring to a paper*).

11,732. From what are you reading?—This is the 'Sheffield and Rotherham Journal' of July 23rd 1853.

11,733. Were those some proceedings before a magistrate?—No, it is an account which is given of my horse being hamstrung.

11,734. You had been working up to what time; what happened to you in July 1853?—I had this horse hamstrung in July 1853.

11,735. What horse? had you a horse?—Yes.

11,736. Where was he?—He was in the field.

11,737. Where was the field?—Near Dore Moor Inn.

11,738. How far from your house?—Half a mile.

11,739. Had you had the horse long?—I bought it

THIRTEENTH DAY.

E. Parker.

20 June 1867.

to ride backwards and forwards on when I commenced working.

11,740. Was the field yours ?—I took the eating of it.

11,741. You rode the horse backwards and forwards to your work ?—Yes.

11,742. What happened to it ?—It was hamstrung.

11,743. Did you go to the field ?—Yes, when I got to hear.

11,744. You heard something had happened to your horse, and you went to the field ?—Yes.

11,745. And when you got to the field what did you find ?—I found it hamstrung.

11,746. What do you mean by hamstrung ?—The hind leg was cut just above the hocks.

11,747. In what state was it ?—It was bleeding very badly.

11,748. In what state ?—It was cut to the bone.

11,749. And what did you do with it ?—I sent for a veterinary surgeon, Mr. Nelson, and he advised me to have it destroyed.

11,750. Was it destroyed ?—Yes.

11,751. What was its value ?—About 20*l*.

11,752. Had you paid to the union at all since Machin and Broadhead had been to your house ?—No.

11,753. Did you still continue to work for Newbold ?—Yes.

11,754. And did you work for him all the winter forward ?—Yes.

11,755. Did anything happen to you after this ?—Yes ; I had some gunpowder laid.

11,756. When was that ?—That was the date when I got the Reverend Mr. Aldred to write to Mr Tasker (*handing a paper to the Chairman*).

11,757. I find that is March the 9th, 1854 ; was that the date this happened ?—That was, I believe, the morning it happened.

11,758. Then it would be on the 8th of March that this occurred ?—Yes.

11,759. Tell us what happened ? — I had some powder laid at my door.

11,760. How do you mean, some powder laid at your door ?—It was a very wet night, that night, and I had got very wet through coming from Sheffield. I and my missus went to bed, and the rest of the family except her mother, and she was up drying some clothes. She smelt some powder. We had two doors out of the house ; one was into a kitchen, and knowing the outer door was bolted (there were three bolts to it and the kitchen door had only one) she went towards the kitchen door to open it, and when she opened it there was a man on the floor laying some more powder. She could smell the powder as she went.

11,761. Where was he laying it ?—Against the kitchen door, trying to thrust it under the door.

11,762. That is your mother ?—My mother-in-law, my wife's mother.

11,763. What happened next ?—She came upstairs, and waked me ; and I went down just as I was, out of bed, and did not stop to put anything on, and when I got out by the kitchen door, the powder that was laid against the house door exploded.

11,764. Were you hurt ?—No, I was not hurt ; I had not got to it.

11,765. Did it do any damage to your house ?—It shook the door a little.

11,766. Was it a great noise ?—Oh ! it was a good noise.

11,767. Was it loose powder, or in a can, or how was it ?—It seemed to be wrapped up in some kind of a parcel.

11,768. Did you find any fragments about ?—Only the fuse.

11,769. You found the fuse, did you ?—Yes.

11,770. Did you find anything else ?—Just at the time when I was going into the house I heard another explosion.

11,771. Did you go out of the house then ?—Yes, I went out.

11,772. And then you came back again ?—Yes.

11,773. How long were you out ?—Perhaps about a minute or two.

11,774. Just as you came into the house you say that you heard another explosion ?—Yes.

11,775. Where was the other explosion ?—It seemed to be a distance off, but I did hear the next morning it was a little higher, at a house they call Bishop's.

11,776. Who is Bishop ?—Thomas Bishop, scythe maker.

11,777. Was he at all concerned in trade matters ? I do not know.

11,778. But do you know whether he had given offence to that trade ?—He had put a son to the handle maker's trade, but I cannot say anything more.

11,779. Do you know whether in putting that son to the handle makers trade he had broken the rules of the handle makers union ?—I cannot tell you that.

11,780. But, however, you know that he had done that ?—Yes.

11,781. Of what kind of handle makers are you speaking ?—The saw handle makers.

11,782. Did anyone come the next day to look at it ?—Yes, Thomas Bamford.

11,783. Who is Thomas Bamford ?—He is a scythe grinder.

11,784. You are a saw grinder, are you not ?—Yes.

11,785. He has nothing to do with the saw grinders, has he ?—No.

11,786. He came to look at the damage ; I suppose everybody did so in the neighbourhood ?—I think he came as soon as any man.

11,787. How early did he come ?—I think he came about six o'clock or seven.

11,788. Where did he live ?—Just below.

11,789. He was close to you ?—Perhaps about 50 yards or 60 yards. I cannot say to a few yards.

11,790. Had you any quarrel with him at all ?—I had not.

11,791. Had any of your family ?—Not that I remember.

11,792. You had had no quarrel at all ?—I think not.

11,793. However he came to look at it, that was all ?—Yes.

11,794. Had you any reason to suspect anybody of having done this to you ?—The only suspicion I had was as to his shoes ; I saw the print of a shoe on the floor. I looked at his shoes when he was sitting in the house, because my mother thought it was him when she saw him on the floor, but she would not swear to that.

11,795. Where did you see a print ?—Just at the outside, and being a wet night, it left the print of his shoe.

11,796. What did you notice peculiar about the shoe ?—I looked at the nails, and they seemed to match what I saw.

11,797. Did he wear different shoes from the ordinary working men ?—He has not a big foot ; it was a little foot.

11,798. What about the shoes which you noticed ?—I looked at them, and I thought they nearly matched what I saw there.

11,799. But you never compared them ?—No.

11,800. You never charged him with it ?—No.

11,801. And you never told him that you thought he was the man ?—No.

11,802. But in your own mind at the time you thought that the print of his foot corresponded with the print that you had seen outside ?—Yes.

11,803. You say that your mother told you that it was he that she saw laying the powder ?—She thought that it was he.

11,804. But do you not think that that was the reason that you thought that his foot was like the print ?—That made me look at his foot certainly.

11,805. There was nothing particular about his shoe, was there, except that it was a small one ?—No.

11,806. Had Bamford ever threatened you at all, or

done anything to you ?—Not then ; he threatened my wife, but I think it was after that.

11,807. How did he happen to threaten your wife ?—I do not know how it started ; I was not there.

11,808. How did it happen ?—I do not know how it happened. I fetched him up before the magistrate.

11,809. When was that ? — I cannot speak for certain.

11,810. But was it after this ?—I think it was.

11,811. Did you borrow a gun to protect yourself ?—Yes.

11,812. From whom did you borrow the gun ?——From my master.

11,813. What master ?—Samuel Newbold.

11,814. Did you ever see any anonymous letter after that about a gun ?—Yes.

11,815. Who had it ?—Bennett Ward, I think, if I remember right.

11,816. Who is Bennett Ward ?—He is a farmer.

11,817. Had you ever borrowed a gun of Bennett Ward ?—Yes.

11,818. At the time when Bennett Ward received this anonymous letter, had you the gun which he had lent you in your possession ?—Yes.

11,819. And did Ward show you the letter ?—Yes.

11,820. What was in the letter ?—I cannot swear to it now.

11,821. But what did it say ?—I cannot say.

11,822. Was there any allusion to the gun ? —I could not answer to save my life.

11,823. Did you go before the magistrates. Look at that (*handing a paper to the witness*) ? — I went before the magistrates.

11,824. Just look at that statement, and after you have read it perhaps you may remember. Can you recollect what was in the letter ?—I cannot recollect, only I believe that is my statement that was in it, but I could not repeat it.

11,825. But you made a statement at the time ?—Yes.

11,826. Was it about getting back the gun ?—Yes.

11,827. Therefore, this letter addressed to Bennett Ward, who had lent you the gun, was a letter to him threatening him if he did not get back the gun ?—Yes, I remember it, but I could not tell you what was in it now.

11,828. How soon was it after you had had the gunpowder laid that this letter came ?—I could not swear to when it was, but it was a little time after.

11,829. Do you recollect afterwards one Whit Sunday night ?—Yes.

11,830. How long was that afterwards ?—That was in 1854 I think.

11,831. Your horse was ham-strung in July, was it not ?—Yes.

11,832. That was in 1853 ?—Yes.

11,833. Then in March in the following year gunpowder was placed against your house door ?—Yes.

11,834. Then on Whit Sunday of the same year did you hear anything in your house ?—Yes, I heard some stones thrown on the slates.

11,835. At what time ?—It had gone 12 ; between 12 and 1.

11,836. At night ?—Yes.

11,837. At that time had you got the gun ?—I had got Mr. Newbold's gun at that time.

11,838. When you heard the stones come upon the slates of the house what did you do ?—I unloosened a big dog that I had, and I took a double-barrelled gun and went out of doors.

11,839. You opened the door ?—Yes, I went out to the end of the house to see what was on the slates. As soon as I got there, there was a shot, a gun went off.

11,840. How far off from you was the gun discharged ?—By the flash I should say somewhere about 20 yards ; I could not tell to a yard or two.

11,841. Did you see anybody ?—No, it came from the planting ; I saw the flash. The planting was on the opposite side of the road from my house. As soon as that had gone off there was one went off on the low side.

11,842. How do you mean on the "low side" ?—On the low side of the planting below our house.

11,843. Could you tell how far that was off ?—That was perhaps 20 or 30 yards. I could not swear to a few yards.

11,844. But in your judgment it was about 20 or 30 yards ?—It might be a little more ; I cannot speak to that.

11,845. Was it on the opposite side of the road also ?—Yes.

11,846. Did you see any person firing ?—No ; I saw the flash.

11,847. But you did not see anybody ?—No.

11,848. How far must the person who fired off the second gun have been from the person who fired off the first gun ?—I should think they would be 20 or 30 yards apart or more than that perhaps. I cannot tell.

11,849. One above and the other below ?—Yes.

11,850. So that if you had gone out of your door you were ready to be caught on that side, and if you went the other way you were ready to be caught the other side ?—Yes. The second shot caught my right arm and covered me all over with pellets right up to my neck. It went as far as my chin. It went through my handkerchief.

11,851. Did you get any of the pellets out ?—They had to work out after.

11,852. What sized shot was it ?—I could not speak to that.

11,853. Are you not a sporting man at all ?—No.

11,854. Cannot you tell us whether it was dust shot or not ?—It was not dust shot, it was not the smallest shot.

11,855. What size shot was it ?—I could not tell you the number of it, I am not a shooter myself ; I got enough then without being a shooter.

11,856. It was not dust shot at all events ?—No.

11,857. Did any of it enter deeply into you ?—Yes.

11,858. How deeply ?—It went inside the flesh.

11,859. Not simply through the skin, but into the flesh ?—It went through the skin into the flesh.

11,860. How deep was it in ?—I do not know, they put poultices on to draw it out.

11,861. Are you quite sure that it was the second shot or was it the first shot which hit you ?—To the best of my recollection I think it was the second, but I could not be certain. They were as near together that you could hardly tell, only it was the low shot that caught my arm.

11,862. That is your impression now ?—Yes.

11,863. You are not quite certain which it was ?—I am not quite certain which it was. The top side I know missed me, but I cannot say which went off the first.

11,864. When you were shot in this way did you cross the road ?—Yes.

11,865. Had you crossed the road before you were shot ?—No.

11,866. You crossed the road after you were shot ?—Yes.

11,867. And after you had got across the road, what did you do ?—Well ; I went to cross the road, I had gone a few yards when a man's head appeared and another gun. That was fair opposite me, when I saw him I put the gun that I had in my hand to my shoulder, when I was levelling for his head, for I could see nothing else only his head and the gun as far as the shoulder, his gun caught my arm.

11,868. The same arm or the other one ?—The other one.

11,869. What did it do to you ?—Well, it knocked me down, and my gun went off and catched the coping-stone underneath the wall.

11,870. Was that shot or bullet, or what was it ?—It was shot.

11,871. What sized shot was it ?—I could not speak to the number of it.

11,872. Was it the same size as the other ?—Something similar.

THIRTEENTH DAY.

E. Parker.

20 June 1867.

11,873. Did that enter into you or not?—If you would allow me I will show you and you can judge for yourselves. (*The witness bared his arm and showed it to the Examiners.*)

11,874. You are disabled to the present day then?—Yes, I can only straighten my arm now to a small extent. I have been disabled ever since.

11,875. Did you lose a good deal of blood?—Yes.

11,876. You were sent to the infirmary I believe and remained there 11 weeks?—Yes, but before that I just wish to mention one little affair; I was carried into the house by my neighbour and my wife and the Reverend Mr. Aldred was sent for, and he came, and the doctor was sent for, and he wanted me to go to the infirmary. When I got there I had some doctors to look at it and they wanted to take my arm off; I would not agree to that, and I laid there 11 weeks.

11,877. How long was it before you were able to do any work at all?—About twelve months I think.

11,878. You never saw anybody, you saw a man's head, but whose head it was you do not know?—No, of course it was only by a flash of a gun, and I would not swear to any man by the flash of a gun.

11,879. And you never saw any person at all to whom you can swear?—No.

11,880. Had there been any bad blood between you and the other people at all?—I do not know that there was anything, only my missus had had Thomas Bamford up.

11,881. Was Thomas Bamford a man who went shooting?—Yes.

11,882. You say that he lived 50 yards from you, do you recollect whether before you were shot in this way Bamford was in the habit of shooting?—He was in the habit of shooting in the middle of the night.

11,883. For how long had he been in the habit of shooting in the middle of the night?—For five or six weeks.

11,884. At what did he shoot?—I cannot tell that, he used to come out of doors and let his guns off.

11,885. What sense was there in that?—I cannot tell that there was any sense in it at all, but of course we judged afterwards what it was for.

11,886. He let his gun off?—He used to fire two or three off, whether it was a double-barrelled gun or not I cannot tell you.

11,887. Two or three shots?—Two or three shots.

11,888. Was there game there, or what was there?—No. He used to stand at the door and shoot through the window.

11,889. You have seen him do that have you?—I have seen him do that.

11,890. There are grouse at Dore are there not?—Yes, but there would not be grouse on a man's doorstone.

11,891. But are you sure that you have seen him shoot from his doorstone?—Yes.

11,892. At night?—Yes. My family hardly ever went to bed, we were always up.

11,893. Why?—Because the house was tried several times, but it could not be got to.

11,894. Besides these times?—Yes.

11,895. But how did they try?—They used to come about the place, but my dog always warned me of it, and always put them off.

11,896. Did you ever see anybody?—My nephew once shot at a man who was in the stack yard, the missus's nephew, not mine.

11,897. And you were in this state you say, and somebody always sat up?—Yes.

11,898. To keep guard?—Yes.

11,899. How long?—It was after I had the powder laid.

11,900. For how long did that continue?—Until I was shot.

11,901. But at the time when you were shot nobody was up, because you say that you got up?—Yes, the missus and me were up at the time.

11,902. When they threw it on the slates?—Yes.

11,903. You were not in bed?—I was not in bed, nor the missus neither.

11,904. Had you taken precautions as to the shutters and doors to make secure?—I have to this day.

11,905. How do you do it?—I have shutters both inside and outside.

11,906. Against whom do you protect yourself then?—Against the trades union.

11,907. It is from no fear of robbers?—No.

11,908. Do you remember a person called John Hill being taken up or going before a magistrate? I believe that he went before my brother as a magistrate, did he not?—Yes, he did.

11,909. After you had come out of the infirmary did you go and see Broadhead?—No.

11,910. Did Broadhead see you?—Yes.

11,911. What did Broadhead say to you?—He had been to my brother before he came to me.

11,912. But what did he say to you?—Well, he wanted the thing settling, and of course my brother persuaded me to begin to pay to the union.

11,913. Do you recollect whether when you left the infirmary the Sawgrinder's Union made any present to the infirmary?—Yes.

11,914. What did they give?—I cannot say, I think I heard that it was 20*l.*, but I cannot say what it was particularly.

11,915. Was there any other saw grinder in the infirmary besides yourself at that time?—No.

11,916. Had you ever any communication with the union about your horse? did you ever complain to them that it was done by the trade?—I complained this way, they wanted me to pay to the trade, and I said I would not unless my horse was paid for.

11,917. What did they say?—They gave me no answer to it.

11,918. Did you have any communication with them about those blowings up?—No.

11,919. Did you complain to Broadhead about those blowings up?—No, I never saw him, it was my brother who went to him and told him to meet me at Mr. Jackson's wheel, and when we met he said; "Well, "Parker, let us see if we cannot settle it, let the bye-"gones be gonebyes."

11,920. What did you say to that?—I told him it was very hard work when a man had got lamed to let those things go by.

11,921. What did he say to that?—He did not say anything to it. I did not begin paying them. I was not able to work. I did not begin paying for myself, but I paid for a boy from that day until I began to work, and then I paid for myself afterwards.

11,922. Did they allow you anything from the union at that time or not?—No.

11,923. I believe that the Duke of Rutland is the proprietor of the land in that district?—No, the Duke of Devonshire. The Duke of Rutland I believe owns the moor, but to the Duke of Devonshire belong most of the farms.

11,924. But the Duke of Devonshire is the proprietor of most of the land about your house, is he not?—Yes.

11,925. The Duke of Rutland owns the moors?—Yes.

11,926. How far are you from the moor at your house?—Perhaps a mile.

11,927. And the moors were then strictly preserved, were they not?—Yes.

11,928. Did grouse at that time come down to near your house?—Not that I am aware of. I never saw one in my life near our house.

11,929. Did any other sort of game come near your house?—Not that I am aware of.

11,930. Did any come near the house of Bamford?—I never saw any in my life down there.

11,931. Had you had any dispute with any poacher at Dore?—No.

18,932. Did you give information against any person for poaching on your land?—No.

11,933. Had you had any quarrel with any person so that you might believe that he would have some private malice against you?—No man had ever had an angry word with me at Dore.

THIRTEENTH DAY.

E. Parker.

20 June 1867.

11,934. Who owned the plantation? Whose plantation was it ?—I cannot speak to whom it belonged to at that time, but I could tell to whom it belongs now, whether it belonged to Offley Shore I do not know ; formerly it did, I know, but I do not know whether it was sold or not at that time; I cannot say. I will not swear to his name. It was sold when the estate was sold.

11,935. To Mr. Shore of Norton ?—No, it was not him.

11,936. Of Meersbrook. Mr. Offley Shore the banker ?—I do not know the gentleman to whom it belonged. I cannot speak to the name; I will not swear to the name.

11,937. Do you know whether he preserved game or not ?—Not that I am aware of.

11,938. Have you ever seen any game in that plantation ?—No.

11,939. Have you ever known of any case of poaching at Dore ?—Not that I am aware of.

11,940. Have you never heard of any poaching at Dore ?—There might have been some, but I never heard of any.

11,941. Do not the moors go down as low as Dore ? —The Dore Moor does, but that is a long way from our house, it is a mile.

11,942. When did your wife first quarrel with Bamford ?—I think it was soon after the powder was laid. He quarrelled with her not she with him.

11,943. Do you know what the quarrel was about ? —He went drunk to the house and insulted her.

11,944. How do you mean insulted her ?—He called her everything but a lady I suppose. I was not there and so I cannot speak to the words.

11,945. But was there any particular thing that he went about ? was there any quarrel that he had before? —No, there was nothing before that.

11,946. Was there anything that he was annoyed about ?—No, nothing.

11,947. He simply went drunk and used abusive language ?—Yes.

11,948. Had she ever quarrelled with him before ? —No, he could not. He had borrowed many a dozen pounds of mine before to carry on his shop.

11,949. You had been a friend to him ?—Yes, at the same time that the powder was laid, he had 2*l.* of mine.

11,950. You say he is a scythe grinder ?—Yes.

11,951. Is he at all connected with the saw grinders? I cannot tell you that.

11,952. Is there any relation of his who is a saw grinder ?—I cannot speak to his relations.

11,953. How much was the reduction which Messrs. Newbold insisted upon your working at ?—They asked us for 10 per cent.

11,954. They reduced you 10 per cent ?—They did not reduce us anything.

11,955. But they asked you to work at 10 per cent. reduction ?—Yes.

11,956. You struck and you got your price, the old price ?—Yes.

11,957. It is suggested that you may have been alarmed without any kind of cause at all; you say persons tried to get into your house, might not the persons who got there have come there for the purpose inquiring about letters, because you keep a post office ?—Not in the middle of the night.

11,958. But it is suggested that somebody might be inquiring for you on business, and that they merely wanted to speak to you, and that you were afraid that they came to do mischief ?—What, at the backside of the buildings among the stacks ?

11,959. But what did they do there ?—I do not know, they had no business there.

11,960. What did they do? you say they had tried the house, what do you mean by that ?—They came on the premises, but they were always put off.

11,961. Did they do anything ?—They had never the chance.

11,962. Did they do anything at all when they were on the premises ?—They were always seen before they could get to do anything.

11,963. How many times were they seen ?—Many times, I could not speak to that.

11,964. And at what time ?—Generally after 12 o'clock.

11,965. Twelve o'clock at night ?—Yes.

11,966. In the middle of the night ?—Yes.

11,967. When they were seen what did they do ?—They always ran away.

11,968. It was not very much like inquiring for letters certainly ?—No.

11,969. As postmaster you had to deliver the letters. Did you ever quarrel with anybody about the mode in which you carried on your business as a postmaster ? —I do not know that I ever had a complaint in 16 years.

11,970. There was no cause of complaint for that? —No.

11,971. (*Mr. Chance.*) Do you remember Mr. Broadhead once calling upon you when you had a bad elbow ?—Yes.

11,972. Was that elbow bad in consequence of being shot ?—I had fallen down at that time and caught the elbow.

11,973. What did he come for ?—He came to me because I could not work, and we had a sick society in our union, and I set a man on to work for me.

11,974. What did he come to you for ?—He came, do you see, for my contribution, and I told him I wanted sick pay for this, because I had been sick some weeks. He refused to give it me, and I would not pay while I had it.

11,975. Did he come for arrears then ?—No, I had been off six weeks, and I said, "I have set a man to work that is off your box, and I have saved you 8*l.*"

11,976. Did you ask for anything ?—I asked him for the 15*s.* that I considered belonged to me, according to the rules.

11,977. Did he pay that ? — He would not pay then.

11,978. What was done upon that ?—It was brought before the meeting ; Broadhead brought it forward himself, and they ordered him to pay me my money.

11,979. Did he pay you ?—Yes, I got it the week after.

11,980. (*Mr. Barstow*). Were you in arrear at the time they shot at you ?—I had not paid anything; they would not take my money after I commenced working.

11,981. (*Chairman.*) Mr. Sugg desires me to ask you whether ham-stringing a horse has anything to do with a trade, and whether it is not more probably the result of agricultural malice than the malice of a person connected with trade. What is your judgment about that ?—I never knew a farmer who had a horse hamstrung ; not through farming, I do not know that I have.

11,982. You had only taken, as I understand, the eatage of the field ?—I had taken it of the man whom it belonged to.

11,983. Who would know you had taken it ? How long had you had it ?—I had had it a few months.

11,984. How was it known that you had taken the eatage of this field ?—I do not know, but the man would know that I had paid the money to, no doubt ; and plenty of parties would see my horse in it, no doubt.

11,985. Was your horse well known ?—Certainly, it was well known.

11,986. What kind of horse was it ?—It was a brown horse.

11,987. Had it any particular mark upon it ?—No, it was a nag horse I rode on.

11,988. And you had ridden it day by day from Dore to Sheffield for some months ?—Yes.

11,989. So that it was well known ?—Yes.

11,990. Is Bennett Ward alive ?—Yes.

11,991. Does he live at Dore ?—Yes.

The witness withdrew.

THIRTEENTH DAY.

Rev. J. Aldred.

20 June 1867.

The Reverend JOHN ALDRED sworn and examined.

11,992. (*Chairman.*) You are vicar of Dore, I think?—I am the incumbent.

11,993. And did you know this man Bamford?—Yes.

11,994. Do you recollect, just a short time before this man Elisha Parker was shot, noticing whether Bamford was in the habit of firing off his gun?—I do not recollect that he shot the guns off, but guns were frequently shot at night about that time. It was the talk of the village.

11,995. Have you heard them yourself?—I have occasionally.

11,996. At what time of night have you heard them?—That I cannot recollect.

11,997. But can you give us a notion, was it at 7 o'clock in the evening or in the middle of the night?—No, 8 or 9 o'clock.

11,998. And it was the talk of the village, you say?—Yes.

11,999. How long were those shootings-off at night before the talk of the village, Parker was shot?—A few weeks.

12,000. And how long did the shootings continue?—Up to the time.

12,001. Do you know whether there was shooting afterwards?—That I do not recollect.

The witness withdrew.

E. Parker.

ELISHA PARKER recalled and further examined.

12,002. (*Chairman.*) You say you had heard shootings at night frequently near your house, and at Bamford's before you were shot; did you hear any more of those shootings at night after you were shot?—I could not; I was in the infirmary 11 weeks.

The witness withdrew.

Mr. W. Dronfield.

Mr. WILLIAM DRONFIELD recalled and further examined.

12,003. (*Chairman.*) Have you those minutes?—Yes (*handing the same to the Commissioners*).

12,004. Those are all the minutes that were taken, are they?—Yes.

12,005. Nothing more took place?—No.

12,006. Do you not make more ample notes than these, as a rule?—No, I am very often absent from the committee on account of my other occupation.

The witness withdrew.

W. Broadhead.

WILLIAM BROADHEAD recalled and further examined.

12,007. (*Chairman.*) You are the secretary, I believe, of the Sawgrinders Union?—Yes.

12,008. And you have been so since 1847, I think?—Not quite so long as that. I think it would be 1848 or 1849, but I was secretary some five or six years previously, on one occasion.

12,009. You were secretary some time previously?—Yes, some four or five years at the least I had been secretary on a former occasion.

12,010. What is the number of the union? how many members are there?—The number of the old union at the present time would be somewhere about 190 members.

12,011. Does that include apprentices?—No.

12,012. It includes simply the persons who contribute?—The members themselves. There would, perhaps, be from 50 to 60 apprentices.

12,013. Who are eligible to become members of your union?—All who have served an apprenticeship to society members.

12,014. And no one else?—No one else, unless they are taken in by the society by a special arrangement.

12,015. Then occasionally you take in persons who have not been brought up as apprentices to the trade?—The trade has taken them in large numbers at various times.

12,016. There must be a special case to induce them to do it?—Yes, they could not claim a right to it.

12,017. The rule is that they must be apprentices?—Yes.

12,018. If they have not been apprentices there must be a special application under special circumstances, and they are admitted?—Yes.

12,019. Have you any reference to character at all, as to whether a man is a person of respectable character or not?—No, that is not a question of consideration so much as his qualities as a workman. It would be a consideration, no doubt, but it would be a secondary one.

12,020. The real question is his being a good workman?—That is it.

12,021. As a matter of fact, is your society composed, amongst others, of ticket-of-leave men?—I am not aware that we have one.

12,022. Have you your books here?—No, but I can send for them if you require them.

12,023. We shall feel obliged to you if you will do so?—(*Turning to the people in Court.*) Are there any saw grinders in Court who will be kind enough to go to our house and bring the whole of the books that are labelled? (*To the Court.*) There are two books which have been in the possession of the Examiners which have not a label upon them, the minute books.

12,024. Was there a person called Henry Bradshaw?—There I am wrong. Yes.

12,025. He was a ticket-of-leave man, was he not? Yes; I did not think of him.

12,026. Do you know why he was sent to prison?—No, I do not.

12,027. Do you recollect that he entered into the society and was allowed money during the time that he was in prison?—No.

12,028. I had better refresh your memory when I get those books?—Very good.

12,029. Was a person of the name of Needham sentenced to four years' penal servitude?—I do not know such a person.

12,030. Do you not know Needham?—No.

12,031. Did you never hear of such a man?—To my knowledge I never heard of such a man.

12,032. You never heard of such a man?—Not to my knowledge.

12,033. Did you know a person of the name of Joseph Myers?—Yes.

12,034. He was hanged, I believe?—Yes.

12,035. For murder?—Yes.

12,036. You say that character is a secondary thing altogether?—Yes, we generally look to their qualities as workmen; we think they are amenable to the law for character and so forth.

12,037. It is merely a question of trade?—Yes.

12,038. And the question of a man being a drunkard, if he is a good workman, is one at which you do not look?—The first question is whether he is capable of earning a living at his trade and filling a situation.

12,039. What are the officers of the union; have you a chairman?—There is a chairman elected at every general meeting and every committee meeting. There is no permanent chairman.

12,040. He acts for the day?—For the day

12,041. And the chairman who is elected there is only chairman for the day ?—That is all.

12,042. Are there any other officers ?—There are committee men.

12,043. How many committee men are there ?—Seven, the regular committee.

12,044. You have been in court and have heard those very serious charges which have been brought against you ?—I have.

12,045. They are so serious as to amount to this that if they are true, you are liable to be put on your trial for murder, because you, certainly if they were true, were an accessory before the fact to murder. An accessory before the fact is treated in the same way as a principal, and therefore you are liable to be tried for that. You are liable to be tried also for having attempted to blow up Helliwell. You are liable to be tried for various breaches of the law; for rattening and taking away property. That is as far as we have got yet. I do not know that anyone of those charges is true at all, but they are charged against you, and you are liable to be tried for them. If you are guilty you are aware that by this Act of Parliament you may make a confession and say that you are guilty. If you are not guilty of course you know best, and you can take what course you like. If you make a full disclosure not only of the facts which have been charged against you, but of all the facts within your knowledge (because you must satisfy us not only on these matters but upon every subject), you are then entitled to a certificate which will protect you from the consequences both criminal and civil. With this warning which I give to you under the circumstances, because I feel it my duty to do so, I ask you to make a full disclosure of everything connected with the unions, in relation to these matters, or connected with other matters to which I shall call your attention. You say that there are seven regular committee men ?—Yes.

12,046. What are their duties ?—Their duties are to attend once a week, every Tuesday, except on some special occasions, when they may have occasion to be specially called together; and I ought to say that on the week of the general meeting which takes place on a Tuesday the committee meeting that week is held on a Monday, in order that we should not have the general meeting's business and the committee meeting's business running into one.

12,047. Therefore in that week you meet on two days; one the Monday, and the other the Tuesday ?—Monday is the committee meeting, and Tuesday the general meeting.

12,048. You say that their duty is to attend. What are they to attend to ?—To attend to any business which may be brought before them appertaining to the society.

12,049. Is it their business to have the control and general management of all matters connected with the society ?—In the absence of the general meeting.

12,050. What do you mean by saying, "In the absence of the general meeting" ?—Business appertaining to the society. The society only meeting once in every two months it would be too long for members to wait to get their matters attended to. It is once in two months at the present time.

12,051. Then the committee have power to deal with all the affairs of the trade, subject to its being reviewed by the general meeting ?—Yes. If it be any case of special importance they may refer it to the general meeting for approval.

12,052. But if it is not of special importance, have they power to deal with it themselves ?—In ordinary cases.

12,053. And do all questions connected with the trade come before the committee ?—Not all questions have come before the committee.

12,054. What questions have not come before the committee ?—Such questions as those that engaged the attention of the Court yesterday.

12,055. Have such questions as those which engaged the attention of the Court yesterday taken place? —In the committee, do you mean ?

12,056. Anywhere ?—Yes.

12,057. To what questions do you allude ?—To those that engaged the attention of the Court yesterday.

12,058. What do you mean? Be specific, if you please ?—The outrages.

12,059. What outrages ?—The Linley outrage.

12,060. Before whom did the Linley outrage come ? —Before myself and the parties who named them.

12,061. Hallam and Crooks ?—I am prepared to endorse in substance the whole of their statements. Some of the details, I think, they are mistaken in, but the substance is correct. There is some slight deviation in the details, but they are immaterial.

12,062. Am I to understand from you then, that you did hire Crooks to shoot at Linley in the first instance ?—I regret to say that I did.

12,063. And did your pay him 20*l.* for it ?—That I cannot say. My impression is that it was 15*l.*, but I will not be certain about it.

12,064. You paid him then either 20*l.* or 15*l.* ?—Yes. My impression is that it was 15*l.*

12,065. Did you hire Crooks and Hallam to shoot a second time at Linley ?—Yes.

12,066. Did you pay to Crooks and Hallam the sum of 20*l.* for the second shooting ?—My impression is that it was 15*l.* on both occasions, but I will not be certain. They might be right, but that is my impression.

12,067. Had you any personal quarrel with Linley ? —No. I have no personal quarrel with any man.

12,068. What induced you to hire Crooks to shoot at Linley on the first occasion ?—Well, I have no wish to extenuate anything in my own conduct, but I have a wish and a desire to state here the whole truth. They came to me separately.

12,069. But the first time they did not come separately ?—I am not aware that ever I had a joint interview with them.

12,070. But Crooks you say is right in what he says, that he was employed by you to shoot, on the first occasion, at Linley. I ask you what induced you, if you had no personal quarrel with Linley, to hire Crooks to shoot at him ?—He came to me and made the offer, and what induced me was, that Linley was doing a great amount of harm to the society. Having recently left his own trade, in consequence of the poor remuneration of labour and want of union, he entered into the saw grinding trade because it was better paid and was supported by the union. Having recently left his own trade, in consequence of the poor remuneration caused by the want of union, he was desirous to enter into a trade which was better paid, which had been obtained by its union.

12,071. Are you speaking of your own impression, or did he tell you so ?—My impression, and what had been told to me, as his remarks, by other people.

12,072. Have you ever heard him say so himself ?—I cannot say that I ever heard him state it himself.

12,073. Then you were induced to do this, he having done a great amount of harm to the society, and having left his own trade and come into yours ? —It was not so much in coming into the society as it was setting all the rules of the society at defiance and taking in a large number of apprentices.

12,074. Was that your ground ?—That was my ground.

12,075. His injury to the trade ?—I considered that he was ruining it. I thought he was bringing ruin upon us all.

12,076. What induced you on the second occasion to engage with Crooks and Hallam to shoot him ?—Well, I had begun to dismiss the thing from my mind; but being one day down at the Eagle Works, I think it was (in fact I am certain it was) collecting my contributions, and being about to leave the wheel Hallam came up to me and he said something to this effect: "What about Linley? He can be done for 15*l.*" I think that was the money named. I paused. It came upon me as an unpleasant subject. Something was said about the mischief and injury he was doing.

THIR-TEENTH DAY.

W. Broadhead.

20 June 1867.

After consideration for a time, I said, "I will consider about it." I left him. The subject, as I have before stated, was a painful one; but I felt that, for the salvation of the society, it was necessary that something must be done. But it crossed my mind that Hallam was not a man to be trusted, and I reflected upon it several days, until Crooks came to me upstairs and mentioned the subject to me again.

12,077. He had not mentioned it before?—Not Crooks. I do not remember that he had ever mentioned it, or, at all events if he had it was a considerable time previous. He said he had come to see me about that matter that I and Hallam had talked over. I felt myself more at liberty to be free with him. I asked him what he proposed to do. He detailed it to me in the manner that he gave his evidence yesterday.

12,078. Did he tell you that he proposed to shoot him?—Yes, but not to kill him.

12,079. But to shoot him?—Yes, but not to kill him.

12,080. You say not to kill him?—Yes, that was the understanding between us.

12,081. He said he should shoot him; was anything said as to where he was to be shot?—No, that was to find.

12,082. But was anything said as to what part of the body he was to be shot in?—Oh, not in a vital part. I cannot say now whether any particular part was pointed out, only I can speak distinctly to this, that the understanding was that he was to wound him and not to kill him. I had confidence to believe in both his nerve and in him as a marksman. With this understanding, with very great pain, I assented. Nothing further took place at the interview.

12,083. But if you had so much pain, how was it that you assented to it?—Because I felt the necessity for it, or otherwise the union would be destroyed, knowing that there was no legal protection for the unions, and viewing it (wrongly if you will) as an absolute necessity.

12,084. So you said before. I believe he had taken five apprentices, had he not?—I cannot tell you how many it was, he had a wheel full.

12,085. Do you know how many apprentices he had taken against your rules?—No, I do not. I think he had had some become loose; I think so, but they were apprentices that he had had in the scissors trade, and that he brought out of the scissors trade along with him. I am not quite certain, but I think so.

12,086. Were they all admitted at the same time?—Into the union?

12,087. Yes?—I think they were.

12,088. Had he one called Joseph Myers? Were they admitted on September the 26th, 1859?—Myers was not an apprentice of his; he was apprenticed to a man of the name of Woodhead.

12,089. Was there a man called Woollen who was his apprentice?—I think one of the Woollen's was apprenticed to him.

12,090. Was it Matthew Woollen?—I cannot say.

12,091. Joseph Ibbotson?—I cannot say whether Ibbotson was apprenticed to him or Fearnehough, but it was to one of the two, I think.

12,092. Joseph Copley?—Copley was apprenticed to him.

12,093. Baxter?—No, he was not apprenticed to him.

12,094. Dennis Clarke?—Yes.

12,095. Christopher Frith?—Yes.

12,096. Henry Garfit?—Yes.

12,097. Then there were about six apprentices?—I should say so.

12,098. Was that all the offence you had against him?—That was all.

12,099. This taking six apprentices into the trade against your rules was all the ground you had for shooting that poor man?—I considered that he was ruining the whole body.

12,100. Although he was violating the rule, how was he ruining the whole body?—By bringing in this large number of apprentices, for if it was permitted to him, a person coming out of another trade, forcing himself into ours, to bring a wheelful of apprentices, while our own members were bound and tied down, the example, if followed by others, would soon bring such an increased number to support on the box that it would be utterly impossible for it to exist, and that has had its effect upon the society. In five years time the society has paid something like 9,000*l.* to sick and unemployed.

12,101. Then it was entirely upon trade considerations that you came to this horrible conclusion?—It was a very painful thing to me.

12,102. Were you aware that Hallam and Crooks were dodging about from public house to public house, during a course of five or six weeks, in order to take away this man's life?—Yes, from remarks made to me at various times; at several times.

12,103. As one of them described it, "in order to get a chance at him," is that what they described to you?—Before he was shot at?

12,104. Yes?—No, I have no recollection of it.

12,105. But did they not come and tell from time to time that they had not done it?—Yes.

12,106. You had engaged them to do it, and did not they say that they had not had "a chance at him" yet?—Yes, they mentioned it on several occasions, when they had met him. Within my heart I wish they never had met him, and I did then.

12,107. No doubt. When did you first hear that they had met him, and that one of them had shot him? was it the same night?—I think not; it could not be the same night from one circumstance; I had not seen them for a considerable time previous, and I began to think that they had given it up and I was not sorry; but getting hold of the newspaper on the morning following the shooting I read from one of the daily papers the account of the man being shot in Scotland Street.

12,108. The next morning then? — The next morning.

12,109. When did you next see either of them?—I think not that day, but I daresay it would be the day following; but I cannot speak positively as to the time.

12,110. Did you then give them money or not? you had paid them part to buy powder had you not?—I daresay I should give them something; but I cannot remember at what time I gave it to them.

12,111. But you paid it both before and after?—I see Hallam says I did; but my impression was that I did not; that was one of the matters——

12,112. What was your impression?—My impression was that I had not paid anything before. My impression was that I paid it aferwards and that the whole of it was paid to Crooks; but I wish you to understand that I will not be certain, but the money was paid.

12,113. Now then I will ask you the next question. Did you engage Shaw and Clarke to put gunpowder in the trough of Helliwell?—No.

12,114. I caution you?—I am prepared to say that.

12,115. You are prepared to say that you did not? I am prepared to take any oath upon it that you may deem necessary to administer.

12,116. You never gave any money, or asked them to put gunpowder in his trough?—No.

12,117. Neither of them?—No.

12,118. Neither the one nor the other?—No.

12,119. Did you ever give money to anyone for the purpose of getting powder to blow up Helliwell?—No.

12,120. Did you ever employ or agree with any other person or persons to blow up Helliwell?—No.

12,121. No one in the world?—No one in the world.

12,122. And when Helliwell says he was blown up, and Shaw says he blew him up, and blew him up by your direction and received 3*l.* for doing it, it is false?—False.

12,123. Did anyone ever apply to you for money after Helliwell was blown up?—No, it is a thing I could not forget; understand me, not for that purpose.

THIR-TEENTH DAY.

W. Broadhead.

20 June 1867.

12,124. If you want to qualify it in any way, qualify it ?—That is the only qualification.

12,125. No one ever applied to you for money in respect of having blown up Helliwell ?—No.

12,126. Were you aware that Helliwell was about to be blown up ?—No.

12,127. Do you know who put powder into his trough when he was blown up ?—No.

12,128. Did you employ Hallam and Crooks to blow up Wheatman's ?—Yes.

12,129. Why did you employ them to blow up Wheatman's ?—Because they had introduced a machine for grinding the straight saws ; I mean not circular saws.

12,130. And you thought that would interfere with the wages that would be earned by hand labour by the people in the trade ?—At that time.

12,131. You thought so then ?—Yes, but my opinion has now changed and has been for some time past.

12,132. Your opinion has since changed ?—Yes, quite so.

12,133. Then what orders did you give for them, or what agreement did you come to with them, when you wanted them to blow up Wheatman's ?—Well, I think the orders were that the job might be done, and they were to have a certain sum of money, I think it was 15*l.*, but, as I said before, I cannot be certain as to the amounts.

12,134. Were they to blow down the chimney if they could ?—Well, it was an arrangement of their own making.

12,135. Did they tell you that that was their intention ?—There was something of that kind named to me at some of the interviews, but I never saw them jointly that I remember.

12,136. But there was something of the kind, that they should blow the chimney down mentioned to you before they went ?—Yes, I have some recollection of it at the time, but afterwards it was stated at another interview that it was impracticable. This I believe was Crooks, for I never felt very much at liberty to talk to Hallam on this.

12,137. But you afterwards ascertained that they had blown it up by means of putting gunpowder in the sough ?—Yes.

12,138. And you paid them their 15*l.* ?—Yes, by instalments.

12,139. By how many instalments have you paid them ?—I cannot say by how many instalments.

12,140. They say that you paid them all at once ? —My impression is that I paid them in instalments.

12,141. Are you quite sure that you did not pay it all at once ?—No, I cannot be sure.

12,142. You gave 2*l.* in the first instance to get powder, was that right ?—It might be, but as I observed my impression was that I paid it all to Crooks ; I will not be certain.

12,143. You might have given them 2*l.* to buy powder and have paid them the remainder altogether ? —My impression is that I did not. I had, in fact, an objection to do with Hallam.

12,144. That was no reason why you should not pay him all the money ?—I did not want to have anything to do with him.

12,145. The sooner paid the sooner discharged. The longer you are in paying the longer you would have to do with him ?—I should have preferred paying it to Crook's, because I should think the secret more likely to be better kept.

12,146. Can you swear confidently one way or the other, you paid 2*l.* to buy powder, can you say confidently whether the remainder was paid at one time or at more times than one ?—No, I cannot.

12,147. It has been stated by a great many witnesses that you have employed them to do rattening ?—Yes.

12,148. Is that true ?—It is true, and if you permit me to state this ——

12,149. On those occasions did you send notes to the parties, if they came to your terms, stating where the bands were to be found ?—Occasionally I may have written them, but the parties who took them wrote the notes.

12,150. Was the system of rattening adopted by you to compel payment of contributions, and also as a sort of punishment for any person who violated the laws of the union ?—As a rule they did not need employing, they took it upon themselves.

12,151. I ask you whether you did employ them for the purpose of compelling persons to pay their subscriptions ?—Yes.

12,152. Did you also employ them to ratten people if they had broken any rules of your society, for instance, by having too many apprentices ?—They got rattened very often.

12,153. Did you employ them is the question which I put ?—I may have done so.

12,154. On their introducing new machinery, have you employed them to ratten them for that ?—In the case named, I never knew any machinery introduced except that in the circular saw trade.

12,155. Except for having many apprentices, and not paying subscriptions, upon what other ground have you employed persons to ratten them ?—Members have been rattened for various infringements upon the rules.

12,156. What kind of infringements ?—Infringements of any rule which was in existence.

12,157. What kind of infringements ?—I cannot say, such as taking a situation without being selected from the list. There are 150 different ways in which it might occur.

12,158. And when they complied with the rules of the society, a note was sent to them and generally their bands were returned ?—Yes.

12,159. If they did not comply with the rules of the society, they did not get them back ?—On some occasions they did not ; there have been occasions where the society have bought new ones.

12,160. In the course of your secretaryship, can you tell me at all how many times you have employed persons to ratten others ?—No, I cannot.

12,161. 100 ?—Oh, yes!

12,162. As many as 500 ?—That is very many, but in 20 years time ——

12,163. Within the last 10 years have you rattened people more than 100 time ?—It would be difficult to get at.

12,164. Would it be an extravagant thing to say 100 times ?—I could not dispute it.

12,165. Would you dispute 200 ?—I should not like to be certain about it, though I do not think it is so, but there have been very few occasions on which I have sent them myself.

12,166. Who have been the persons whom you have employed to ratten ?—It would be difficult to make selections, because I could not fix the particular cases.

12,167. When you have employed persons to ratten for you, have they told you that they have rattened, and have you seen them about it ?—Yes.

12,168. Now tell me the names of the men whom you have employed ?—Some of Moses Eadon and Sons.

12,169. Whom did you employ for that ?—They got rattened, but they were not employed by me.

12,170. Whom have you employed to ratten ?— When the note was found in the fender——.

12,171. Whom did you employ to ratten ?—I did not employ anyone.

12,172. Did a man come to you ?—Yes.

12,173. Who was that man who rattened them ?— Abraham Green.

12,174. Is Abraham Green dead ?—Yes.

12,175. He was one of Eadon's workmen ?—Yes.

12,176. Tell me the name of any other person whom you have employed ?—I could not give you the name of anyone whom I have employed, but there have been some. I have no desire to fence with the question. Rattening is a matter I am quite prepared to make a clean breast of. I do not look upon it as a matter of any interest at all. I would tell you if I could fix upon a case.

12,177. You know quite well whom you have employed ?—I have given you the best answer I can.

12,178. No, you have not mentioned a single name

THIRTEENTH DAY.

W. Broadhead.

20 June 1867.

of the persons whom you have employed, and you will not?—That is not correct, pardon me.

12,179. You must know. A man who has employed persons as you say to ratten others must know whom he has employed; now mention their names?—I have mentioned such as I can remember.

12,180. You have not mentioned one?—Yes, I have.

12,181. You mentioned a dead man, Green?—I cannot remember the others.

12,182. I caution you. You know what peril you are in. You have acknowledged yourself to be a participator in a murder, and your only chance of not being prosecuted for that is telling the truth in every particular. If you do not satisfy us that you have told the plain truth as to everything, I tell you that nothing will induce us to grant you a certificate?—I must do another thing besides that; I must have the satisfaction myself that I am telling the truth.

12,183. Whom have you employed?—I cannot give their names.

12,184. Cannot you give me the name of one man who is alive whom you have employed to ratten?—There are many living who have rattened a score of times, but I cannot select a particular case where they have rattened.

12,185. Tell me the name of a man who has rattened?—I would do it directly if I could fix upon a specific case.

12,186. Never mind a case, tell me a man who has rattened?—I cannot give you a case of a man rattening a certain place.

12,187. I do not ask that; tell me a man who has been sent upon an act of rattening?—I cannot.

12,188. Do persons ratten and then come and tell you?—Yes.

12,189. You say that the persons who have done rattening have come to you and have told you that they have done it?—There have been parties come.

12,190. Who are they?—I cannot give their names; I really cannot remember. I speak the truth.

12,191. It is very difficult to believe that?—If I cannot I am sure you would not have me tell an untruth.

12,192. It is very difficult to believe that; it looks very much to my mind as if you were attempting to screen others. If you tell only that which you are obliged to tell you can get no certificate?—I quite understand my position and must stand the consequences.

12,193. You say that persons who have rattened have come to you and told you that they have done so; who has done that?—I cannot give you a specific name; I cannot remember to fix any specified party. Yes, I can, now I come to recollect; you are putting these questions and I am trying to recollect. There was a case named yesterday of Hallam and Crooks rattening Hallam's father, and Matthew Broadhead, and I remember that case. Had I not heard it in court and have asked the question as you are now asking it, I could not have remembered it; but I thought it over as it was named and I remember that circumstance, but had I been asked about it, and had it not been named I could not have remembered it.

12,194. You mention the facts spoken of by Hallam, but you will not mention the name of any person?—I cannot.

12,195. And you want us to believe that you who have been engaged in rattening either by hiring people to do it, or they having done it and having come and told you that they had done it, and then having got the price for it, do not know a single man who has done it?—I cannot fix it upon them.

12,196. I do not ask you to fix it upon them. I ask you to tell of a person who has done an act of rattening?—I cannot give any name.

12,197. I shall go through all the evidence with which your name has been mentioned particularly presently, but I am doing it now generally, you shall have an opportunity of saying whether you remember them or not; you say that all the rattening was always done for the benefit of the trade, and that it was not done to gratify any malice of yours?—No.

12,198. It was for the benefit of the trade?—Parties took it upon themselves to do it as a general rule.

12,199. But you employed them sometimes?—I cannot dispute that.

12,200. And it was done, as you say, for the benefit of the trade?—It was either done for that or presumed to be done for it; it was not always done for the benefit of the trade.

12,201. But where you have done it?—When I have done it it has been for the benefit of the trade.

12,202. In no case have you done it where you have had any private malice or anything of that kind?—Never in my life.

12,203. It has always been for the benefit of the union?—Yes, and in no other light, and I wish to God for it to be abandoned and the protection of the law given in its stead.

12,204. Do I understand you that you used it for the purpose of getting the rules of the society obeyed because the law did not give you power to enforce them?—So far as I was concerned it was so.

12,205. Do you know whether that system is adopted by other unions besides your own?—I believe it is.

12,206. Can you mention the name of any union who adopt the system of rattening besides your own? There have been cases occur in the sawmaker's trade.

12,207. Where besides?—The saw-handle makers, but the grinders bands have gone on various occasions.

12,208. In what trades besides? have you known whether the scissor grinders have been so?—I have had no connection with them.

12,209. Who else besides the saw handle makers, the saw makers, and the saw grinders?—Every grinding branch in Sheffield, either in union or out of union, do so.

12,210. I do not quite understand you when you say "either in or out of union;" if they are out of union, I do not know what they would have to ratten about, there would be no rules?—No; there is an old adage "two of a trade seldom agree," and there are private quarrels, one man imagining he is suffering an injury from another would be induced to ratten him.

12,211. That is private malice?—It would not always occur in the case of private malice, it would be in the case where one man might consider another man was taking his work, or reducing the price.

12,212. Have you ever known a case of a non-union man rattening another?—I cannot bring one to mind.

12,213. I believe that the practice is in the town of Sheffield, among all the grinding branches, for unions to ratten when their members do not obey the rules?—Yes, and in every other branch where the trades have bands.

12,214. Or nuts?—Yes, if it is tailors, they will take the sleeve-boards; it is the same thing.

12,215. Did I understand you to say that this system of rattening was a matter not only done by you, but one which was done by the union?—It is an old custom of the town that was in existence long before I was born, or anyone in this room.

12,216. Is it a custom which was adopted by the union, as a body, or adopted by you alone?—It was adopted by the members of the union, and I cannot plead innocence any more than any other members.

12,217. But they all do it?—They all do it; it is most frequently done by their fellow-wheelmates, one fellow wheelmate will ratten another.

12,218. Supposing the union wanted a man to be rattened, what was the course which they pursued, if it did not employ the man?—I will tell you how the thing most generally comes about in our own branch of the trade. Our books are open for the inspection of every member in the trade at any time he chooses to come without me as an officer having the right to question them why they want to look into the books, if I was present.

12,219. It is done without any question from anyone?—Yes; each man's account is always to be seen in the book, and they will make their own selections.

12,220. That is an ordinary case, you say?—Yes.

12,221. If a man is in arrear with his money, is his

THIR-TEENTH DAY.

W. Broadhead.

20 June 1867.

name called over ?—It was at one time, but it is given up now ; it is not so now.

12,222. Formerly his name was called over?—Yes, before the body.

12,223. What is done with it now ?—There is an investigating committee, or rather there was an investigating committee, who used to meet for the purpose of examining accounts of arrears. I used to prepare a list of them selecting them from the ledger writing down the names with the arrears at the commencement of the month.

12,224. And you then handed it over to the investigating committee ?—Yes, and the arrears at the close of the month, showing the increase.

12,225. You wrote them down on a slip of paper and handed them over to the committee ?—I presented them to the committee.

12,226. Formerly the names were read over ; when was the investigating committee first established ?—I cannot say here but the minutes will show.

12,227. What book is that which you hold in your hand ?—It is a memorandum ; I made some selections from the contribution book ; I was going to see if I could find it.

12,228. I find this as regards the investigating committee in 1861. I find that in October 22nd, 1861, when Joel Yellatt was in the chair : "8 case. J. Coldwell, J. Turner, T. Parkin, E. Machin," formed the investigating committee ?—I daresay that is so.

12,229. Can you say whether that investigating committee was established before 1861 ?—I think that was the time it was established.

12,230. You think that the investigating committee was established in 1861 ?—Yes ; I think it was about that time.

12,231. Before 1861, was it your practice to have a meeting of the body to call over the names of the persons whose conduct was disapproved of ?—There would be occasions when it was done, but it became more constantly the practice after the investigating committee was established.

12,232. The reading them over ?—Yes ; but you must understand——

12,233. I speak of the general meeting ; at the general meeting if men were in arrear or had violated any law of the union before the investigating committee was established, was not it your practice in full meeting to read over the names of the defaulters ?—On certain occasions it would occur.

12,234. Was that at a full meeting ?—Yes, when it was intended to be read.

12,235. I find that in 1860 at a general meeting there is an entry in your books ; just refer to it : "July 30th," there is an entry of " George Bradshaw, Henry Bollington, Francis Crooks, George Crooks, senior, highly disapproved of ?—That was read out.

12,236. Was that the way in which you dealt with a man at the public meeting ?—Yes, it was ; but you must understand that first if the investigating committee had been established——

12,237. You say that it was established in 1861 ?—I said I thought so.

12,238. Go on, I do not want to be harsh with you? —When the investigating committee was established they met on the same day that the general meeting met, but they met a couple of hours before the general meeting to go through the accounts of arrears, and the parties who were in arrears on the list were to be summoned to attend the investigating committee, and make arrangements with them that would shorten the business of the general meeting, but there would be cases occur where the parties might not attend, or the committee would refuse to entertain their case at all, and in either of such cases they would send the case before the general meeting.

12,239. And, therefore, if they had not made a special arrangement with the investigating committee, there names would be called over, and they would have a statement put against them in their book as being highly disapproved of ?—Yes, there would be similar remarks to those made.

12,240. I see that on September the 3rd this entry : " Crooks, Cutler, J. Hallam, J. Gee, G. Peace, C. Stainforth highly disapproved of," at the general meeting ?—I have no doubt that is so.

12,241. "Conduct stripes 30 ?"—That would be the remark made in the general meeting by some member.

12,242. What did it mean ?—It meant that he would deserve to pay a heavy amount of arrears.

12,243. What would 30 stripes mean ?—It would mean the same as a party who might be punished in the army for misconduct.

12,244. It means that highly disapproved of conduct merits 30 stripes, does it not ?—I cannot define it in any other way, it would be a mere joke.

12,245. I find again an entry, " Henry Bollington, Baxter, Crooks, disapproved of," and another " A. Godby, A. Green, and H. Edwin, highly disapproved of," all read at the meeting. Then the next is John Lea, three crosses, recommended, what does that mean ?—I cannot tell you.

12,246. What does this mean—" John Lee called over, and it was passed that John should have 30 for censure " ?—I cannot account for that at all ; it would be the fancy of the man who wrote it down, or some remark made at the meeting.

12,247. Are you in the habit of entering jokes in your books which have been uttered in the meetings ? —That is not my entering.

12,248. I ask you to explain the book ?—I am not in the habit of entering it.

12,249. Can you explain what the 30 meant ?—No, I cannot.

12,250. Who entered about the 30 stripes ? do you know his handwriting ?—Is there a signature to it ?

12,251. September the 3rd, 1861, is the date, whose writing is that ?—I really cannot tell you.

12,252. You know better than that ?—I cannot, I really cannot tell you.

12,253. You were the secretary ?—Yes, but this is not my writing.

12,254. I do not say it is, but surely the secretary knows whose writing it is ; who made the entries ?—A person selected from the body of the meeting for the occasion.

12,255. Do you mean to say that he acted for you ? —On those occasions for me, as secretary. I had the business to introduce. In fact, I had a great deal of the chairman's duties to do.

12,256. But the first volume is all in that handwriting ; the entries of the general meeting are all in the same handwriting ?—This is not mine.

12,257. Whose is it ?—I cannot tell you.

12,258. You know better than that, you know whose it is—whose handwriting is that ?—I do not know.

12,259. You cannot tell me whose writing that is ? —I could not tell you if the certificate was to be withheld from me for it.

12,260. I have mentioned certain names—there is " Bradshaw, Broadhead, Hawksley, Parker, Roebuck, Shaw, and Bollington, highly disapproved of " ?—Yes, and you will find those names at every meeting generally.

12,261. Can you tell me whether this is the same Crooks who gave evidence ?—I cannot tell. There are many Crooks in the Society.

12,262. Do you know a person of the name of Cutler ?—Yes, several.

12,263. And James Hallam ?—Yes.

12,264. And J. Lee, who is he ?—He is the person who last worked at Taylor Brothers.

12,265. Do you know G. Peace ?—There are two.

12,266. And Charles Stainforth ?—Yes.

12,267. And Henry Bollington ?—Yes.

12,268. And Baxter ?—There are several Baxters.

12,269. And Crooks ?—There are several Crooks.

12,270. And Abraham Godby ?—Yes.

12,271. Abraham Green ?—Yes.

12,272. Henry Edwin ?—Yes.

12,273. John Lee ?—You read that.

12,274. Have any of those men ever been rattened ? —I believe, sir, they have.

THIRTEENTH DAY.

W. Broadhead.

20 June 1867.

12,275. Were not they rattened after their names had been read over in that meeting?—Very likely.

12,276. Were not their names read over for the purpose of getting them rattened?—No.

12,277. Was not that the object of reading them over?—The object was to expose them before the body. We were quite aware that they exposed themselves to the chances of it, and it had a very salutary effect upon many of them; in fact, the members who were straight in the book required that they should know how others were paying who were not straight.

12,278. All these names, Bollington, Baxter, Crooks, Godby, Green, Edwin, and others, were men who had been rattened?—Yes, I should say so; and a good many others.

12,279. That was for not paying their contributions?—Yes.

12,280. On some occasions I find there is a case like this—"W. Ashforth censured"?—Yes.

12,281. Why was that?—That would be probably on account of his arrears.

12,282. Censured openly before the meeting?—It was by resolution. It might be done in the committee, and it may have occurred in both.

12,283. It may have occurred both in the committee and in the general meeting?—Yes.

12,284. There is another case, "Case 9, William Crook's case passed over in despair"?—Yes.

12,285. What was that?—Simply that he was hopeless of improving, he had so repeatedly been in arrears, which had accumulated from time to time. The remark of some of them was, "We will give him his time out."

12,286. Was he rattened?—He has been rattened.

12,287. Often?—More than once; I cannot tell you how often, and I cannot fix the particular time.

12,288. There is another entry that I find here, about which I should like to know. Were these entries of what had passed at one meeting read over at the next meeting?—No, I think they would not be read at the next unless they had not fulfilled their engagement the last time. In certain cases it would occur.

12,289. In certain cases the proceedings of the previous meeting would be read over at the subsequent meeting?—No, the list that was prepared for that meeting would be the only list.

12,290. The list furnished by the investigating committee?—Yes.

12,291. I find here something of this kind, "C. Bradshaw, G. Bradshaw, and W. Crooks transferred to our black books." What is that; that is July 29th, 1862. What did you mean by transferring the men to the black books?—I cannot say what the man might mean who set that down. It is just according to the fancy of the individual who might write it down. I cannot tell.

12,292. It is case 9: "This man to be transferred into our black books, Charles Bradshaw; Charles Damms passed over; William Crooks a black book gentleman of the first order, A 1, copper-bottomed"? —I think you will see it was a mere joke on the part of the parties who wrote it.

12,293. What do you mean by transferring to the black book?—We had no black book. All the books are here.

12,294. Are there any books in which you enter persons names who are defaulters?—No, that list was the only thing.

12,295. You have a list made out, I know?—Yes, of such entries as those in that book.

12,296. You had no book, then, which you called the black book?—No.

12,297. Although there is an entry there saying that he is to be transferred?—No.

12,298. Who wrote that entry (*showing the same to the witness*)?—It would be John Oaks.

12,299. That is the man who wrote it?—Yes.

12,300. Who is John Oaks?—A man who used to work for Slack, Sellars, and Company.

12,301. Is he alive?—For anything that I know, he is in America.

12,302. I find here one in 1863, "Ashworth disapproved of; Bradshaw disapproved of; Green, Hattersley and Sharp, and Bollington disapproved of. "May 5th, general meeting. Baxter, Bollington, "Godby, Stainforth, Yellatt, and Myers to be handled "by the committee"—what does that mean?—That might be the regular committee, but I should think it would be the investigating committee. Those would be the minutes taken at the general meeting. That entry which is signed John Oaks looks very much like the names which were called over to me, namely, "Henry Bollington, and the others which were to be "handled over by the committee." That would be left in the hands of the investigating committee.

12,303. Had you a case of Crook's on May 12th, 1864. I see there is an entry there, "Crook's case and others all to come under the law;" what is your law?—I do not know what rule that refers to; it would be there—12th of January 1864.

12,304. We will not go into any further explanations about this?—I think I could shorten your labours if you would permit me. Those accounts which you have been reading to me would be the list that had gone from the investigating committee from this sheet that is made out of the arrears and which were considered bad cases to go before the general meeting. Those would be remarks made at the general meeting as the cases came before the general meeting by the party who was appointed to take the minutes.

12,305. What is the meaning of the entry "7th "case arrears; reading over William Crook's case "and others whose names are read over, all to come "under the law; Joseph Crapper's case to stand over "another month, and Abraham Green highly cen"sured?"—The meaning of that would be an arrangement that had been made for the payment of arrears. It was a custom; in fact we might call it a rule that parties being in arrear should discharge those arrears by so much per week in addition to contributions according to the amount of those arrears—say 1*s*. or 2*s*. in addition to their contribution, that would be the meaning of it.

12,306. That is your explanation of coming under the law?—Yes, that would be the meaning of it.

12,307. What were the duties of the investigating committee?—The duties of the investigating committee were to inquire into these arrears and get the payments the best way that they could.

12,308. Then the management of the question of arrears was left to the investigating committee?—It was left to the investigating committee, except the bad cases, and the bad cases were then sent before the body.

12,309. You say that these were appointed; had they nothing else to do but to manage these cases?—That was what they called the investigating committee.

12,310. Is that all that they had to do?—That is all they had to do.

12,311. Nothing else?—I do not remember anything else.

12,312. Are you quite sure that the investigating committee had nothing else to do but to ascertain what people were in arrear?—Yes; I think I could say that.

12,313. They had nothing else to do?—I do not know that they had.

13,314. Will you swear that they had not?—I think I could.

12,315. You will swear that?—I do not know that they had anything else to do.

12,316. Tell me the names of the investigating committee?—Indeed I cannot; you will find them in the book as they were appointed.

12,317. They are all there?—Yes.

12,318. You say that they have no other duties besides those of investigating accounts brought before them?—At the time the entries were made that you are now reading.

12,319. At any time had the investigating committee any duties except the duty of investigating the accounts?—There was an alteration in the rule; it may be a year or 18 months ago.

THIRTEENTH DAY.

W. Broadhead.

20 June 1867.

12,320. What was the alteration?—The alteration was that the question of arrears should be left entirely in the hands of the investigating committee. You will find a minute upon it, and rather a strong one it is.

12,321. Was the rule carried out that all the cases should be left entirely in the hands of the committee?—As far as they could be.

12,322. Were you on the committee?—Yes.

12,323. Were you permanently on?—Yes.

12,324. Whenever there was an investigating committee you were one of its members?—Yes, previous to the alteration I was with the investigating committee.

12,325. That was a thing which was done on the 20th of June 1865; I mean that minute that you are talking of, of the change in the system?—I cannot say when it was done.

12,326. It is in these words—will you correct me if I am wrong: "That an investigating committee "be elected every monthly meeting as usual, but instead of its duties being only to sit to hear parties "excuses for nonpayment, and accept such propositions which may be made, which are frequently not "fulfilled, or send such cases before the general "meeting, the investigating committee's duties shall be "in future to meet every fourth Wednesday previous "to the books being audited, and oftener if necessary, "and to examine the arrears of all defaulting members, and other matters"?—Yes, I remember that being passed.

12,327. "And this committee shall be furnished "with full powers from this society to take any and "whatever steps this committee may deem necessary "to compel payment of arrears, &c., and to enforce "observance of all rules and regulations of all this "society's members; and any expenses incurred "in carrying out these objects, this committee shall "not be bound to make such expenses public to the "body, but such expenses shall be met as the committee may see best; nor shall any member have "the right to question any expenses of this kind "that may become known, but members serving on "this committee, for the time being, when such expenses are incurred—that members who have failed "to give an account of earnings and pay contributions, &c., since May 9, 1864, when dividends were "declared. Such cases shall be left in the hands of "the investigating committee to arrange with such "parties; if the parties are so disposed, or if failing "to effect an arrangement with such parties, this "business shall be left in the hands of the investigating committee to take whatever steps it may see "necessary under the rule before provided"?—I believe that is a correct copy.

12,328. (*Mr. Chance.*) That is in your own handwriting, is it not?—That is my own handwriting.

12,329. (*Chairman.*) According to that rule not only was the investigating committee furnished with powers to investigate the arrears of defaulting members, but they said that other matters were to be referred to them; what other matters were to be referred to them?—Any course that they might deem to be necessary to be taken.

12,330. "Any course"?—"Any course," but that is not meant to imply outrages and things of that sort.

12,331. But any course which they liked to employ they might employ?—Yes.

12,332. And they were to have any money which they liked for it?—Yes, without giving an account.

12,333. Without giving any account?—Not without giving any account.

12,334. "And any expenses in carrying out these "objects this committee shall not be bound to make "such expenses public to the body"?—Yes, just so, but they had to keep an account without making it public.

12,335. Amongst themselves?—Yes, and any members could come and look at the entry in the book.

12,336. What do you mean by that, you have told me already that that regulation was carried out?—As far as it could be.

12,337. By this regulation they are at liberty to incur any expenses they please, and no member of the body has any right to inquire what the expenses are?—But they are bound to make an entry of the expenses without a regulation.

12,338. Then what is the use of such a rule as that?—Simply that they should not have to state what it was for; it would be entered in this form, "investigating committee's expenses," without stating what it was for.

12,339. But they had the power of getting money and using it in any way they pleased, and were not bound to account to anybody for it?—Yes, but it was in the balance sheet notwithstanding.

12,340. And it was only entered in your books as expenses by the investigating committee?—Yes.

12,341. If the object was a lawful one, and if they intended to do that which was right with that money, what was the object of that rule?—The objects would be these: they would be various, I will give you a case in point, by way of illustration. If a person who was paying poundage at one time delivered in a false account we should have to find it out, and the only means of finding it out would be to find some one, if we could, to take an account of his work, just as was named in the case of Parker, and we should give instructions to some one to adopt such means as he could, to get to know this. We should get to know in some cases, and in some cases we should not get the information we desired; but it would not do for the society to read over how those expenses were incurred in obtaining information about it.

12,342. Why not?—Because we should be telling the party what we had been after, and that would put him on his guard for a future time.

12,343. Did not the people know very well that you were employing men? you had many men whom you employed to watch the trade?—No.

12,344. How many had you?—Occasionally they would be employed to get the information.

12,345. Had you many men employed?—No.

12,346. How many had you?—I cannot tell.

12,347. Whom did you employ?—The last that was employed was Joseph Martin.

12,348. How long had you employed Joseph Martin?—Not a very long time; he got 10*s.* for doing it.

12,349. How long had you employed Joseph Martin?—We employed him to ascertain whether Shaw was working with George Peace.

12,350. How long had you employed Martin?—I cannot say.

12,351. Had he done any work for the last eight years?—He had only come from America three or four months.

12,352. How long was he in America?—I think six years.

12,353. Was he as long as that?—Yes, somewhere about that.

12,354. Then, except for these expenses incurred by employing men to go and cut the bands of others who were not rendering a full account of their work, can you give any reason why a rule so singular as this, giving them such powers as those, and placing such large means in their hands, they giving no account of it, should have been passed?—Another reason would be an unlawful means of using it.

12,355. What was that?—That would be in case it was necessary that a person's bands should be taken, and that there were no means of making the individual pay the money, to give power to the committee, in such cases as they might have, to pay for it; and they would have to enter it in the way I have described, "expenses incurred by the investigating committee."

12,356. Then you might as well have told us at first, that it was to cover payment made for illegal purposes?—I wish to explain it to you as explicitly as I can; I have described a case.

12,357. Supposing money had been given to a man to blow up a mill, or to blow up a man, that would come equally within that rule?—Yes, and it would be entered as expenses of the investigating committee.

THIRTEENTH DAY.

W. Broadhead.

20 June 1867.

12,358. It would be entered as expenses of the investigating committee ?—Yes.

12,359. When you got the 15*l.* to pay for Wheatman's blowing up, where did you get it from ?—I got it out of the contribution book as I collected the contributions, taking a little out at a time.

12,360. Is there an entry in the investigating committee's expenses of the 15*l.* ?—No, it was before those accounts were kept in that form.

12,361. In Linley's time, where did you get your 15*l.* ?—I got it in the same way in which I have described that it was got for Wheatman and Smith's.

12,362. Had you any authority to apply that money, or did you embezzle it out of the funds of the union ?—Call it "embezzled" if you will, I had no authority.

12,363. Then you took the money without authority, and applied it in your own way ?—I did.

12,364. You did exactly as Thompson, the secretary of the Scissor Forgers, has done ?—Just so.

12,365. When you paid for rattening where did you get the money ?—The men had to pay for it themselves except in cases where you will find entries made. I do not know what you will find.

12,366. But under this rule supposing you wished to put an entry for blowing up a man or giving a reward for shooting a person, it could easily be covered by getting it entered "expenses of the investigating committee" and there would be an end of it ?—Yes.

12,367. Where did the investigating committee get its money from ?—The investigating committee got its money from the funds.

12,368. What funds ?—From the general funds of the society.

12,369. Who keeps the money ? have you any banking account ?—No.

12,370. Who keeps the money ?—The treasurer paid all monies that I brought an account of before the investigating committee, and if it were ordered to be paid it would be so paid and entered.

12,371. Was the treasurer a member of the investigating committee ?—No.

12,372. Did your money go from you to the investigating committee or from you to the treasurer ?—It went from me to the treasurer.

12,373. If the money went from you to the treasurer how did the investigating committee get it ?—The investigating committee passed a resolution. It could never go into the investigating committee's hands.

12,374. "And any expenses incurred in carrying out these objects this committee shall not be bound to make such expenses public to the body." Where did they get their money from ?—They did not get it at all; the case went before them and they passed a resolution upon it as to whether it should be paid or not, and upon those instructions I paid the money. I drew it from the treasurer when the finance committee sat.

12,375. They passed their resolution and gave you authority and you drew the money from the treasurer; that was the course of proceeding ?—Yes.

12,376. Do you mean to say that you went to the treasurer without any order in writing from the committee ?—I went with the account entered as passed by the investigating committee.

12,377. Did they never keep any book containing their resolutions ?—No.

12,378. Who was the treasurer ?—We have had two or three.

12,379. Were you treasurer and secretary as well, because we heard Staniforth complain that he would be no longer a member of the union because you were both ?—Of course you have had that explanation of it.

12,380. Were you treasurer and secretary or not ? —At one time I was, but it was not my wish.

12,381. Then you drew on yourself ?—They forced it upon me ; the society did.

12,382. Was that after this rule was passed ?—I cannot tell how long it is since that was instituted ; it would commence at the time that I commenced collecting the contributions.

12,383. This was a power that the committee had ? —Yes.

12,384. They kept no books ; why did not they keep books ?—Simply because it was all entered on a sheet ; they had nothing to do with the accounts ; they had to say whether anything should be paid for or not, and all they had paid for I am prepared to explain.

12,385. They kept no books did they ? — Only sheets.

12,386. What has become of them ?—The sheets got destroyed.

12,387. Therefore there is no memorandum existing of anything passed at those meetings?—No, not to my knowledge.

12,388. Had you an auditor ?—Yes.

12,389. Was it your duty to lay your accounts before the auditor ?—Yes ; there were two.

12,390. Now Mr. Broadhead, you say that you paid as much as 20*l.* for one transaction, and you will not deny that you paid 60*l.* for only three transactions ; but taking the 20*l.* for Wheatman's affair and the two attacks upon Linley that makes 60*l.*, what were the contributions which you had to levy ?—I cannot say what the amount of the contributions would be at that time, but our contributions during the time that we were paying poundage would range from a penny in the shilling to three-halfpence in the shilling.

12,391. How much in a week did you levy for the union at the time that you ordered Wheatman to be blown up ? how much were you getting altogether ? —Contributions ?

12,392.—Yes ?—I cannot say how much ; I daresay it would average 40*l.* a week, without speaking correctly.

12,393. In what period of time did you abstract this money from the 40*l.* a week ?—I cannot tell you that.

12,394. Tell me the name of a person whose name you put down improperly ?—I cannot.

12,395. You cannot ?—No.

12,396. You say that you made false entries in that book ; those are not the payments ?—No.

12,397. Then how was it ?—It was done simply in the way I described.

12,398. You did not put his name down ?—His name was down ; he would pay to me a certain amount of contributions, it might be 12*s.*, or 10*s.*, or what not.

12,399. You put it down ?—No, instead of doing so, I should enter him 7*s.* or 8*s.* ; but I should not take too much at one time, and so with others, and at that time we had not check books for each member, as we have now.

12,400. Tell me name of anyone whose money you have put down improperly, as having paid you 10*s.* when in fact he had paid you 12*s.*, or 14*s.*, or 16*s.* ?— I cannot tell you a name.

12,401. Upon your oath, is not that altogether a lie ? is it not money drawn from the society ?—No, upon my oath it is the truth.

12,402. Upon your oath, did not the investigating committee know all about it ?—They did not.

12,403. If it were not for matters of this kind, what is the good of this rule ?—It was never intended. I quite expected I was going to be severely cross-examined on that rule ; but it was never wrote out for such a purpose as I am now suffering this examination upon. It was intended in such cases as these rattenings, where it was deemed fit to pay a little additional money to give them power to do so ; but in all cases it is entered "expenses of investigating committee," or some such entry.

12,404. There is another expression in your book, not only "expenses of investigating committee," but I find that there is an entry which is peculiar, "services rendered to trade ;" what does that mean ?—There are sums varying here from 1*s.* and 1*s.* 6*d.* a-piece. Out of 13,000*l.* I have various items, and among them is 1*s.*, 6*d.*, and as much as 2*s.* and 2*s.* 6*d.* here occurring. Out of 13,000*l.* there is 9*l.* 11*s.* 7½*d.* that is entered without thorough explanation ; that passes over a period of five years.

12,405. I see one entry of 10*s.* to a man called Jessop, a wheelwright, for services rendered to the trade ?—I recollect that man worked at the Tower wheel; it would be somewhere about the time when Linley came into the society, and he had used his good offices to get us the room. We rented a room there, and he used his good offices to get us a room, and it was brought before either the committee or a general meeting, I forget which, and he got a grant of 10*s.* for his services.

12,406. After Linley was shot, and was recovering, did you write a number of letters to his employers, warning them not to let wheel room to Linley, as he had more than once drawn upon himself the vengeance of the whole trade?—I do not remember ever doing so.

12,407. Did not you?—I do not remember.

12,408. Did you write any anonymous letters after Linley was shot?—I have given you my answer; I do not remember.

12,409. Will you swear that you did not?—I do not remember.

12,410. Will you swear that you did not?—I have given you my answer.

12,411. Did you after Linley was shot the second time?—Am I obliged to swear to a thing that I cannot answer? I cannot swear to that.

12,412. You must swear to it one way or the other? —With all due deference to this Court I want to answer the questions that I can, and you will not want me to answer questions that I cannot.

12,413. Did you say that it had brought upon him the vengeance of the whole trade?—I do not remember ever writing.

12,414. Will you swear that you did not?—I do not remember ever writing anything of the kind.

12,415. Will you swear that you did not? you cannot get out of it in that way, may you have done so?—I really cannot undertake to say that.

12,416. Will you undertake to say that you did not?—I will rather undertake to say I never did than that I did; it strikes me from the remark you made that I have seen it somewhere, but it has not emanated from me.

12,417. Will you swear that you did not write it? —I have no recollection.

12,418. Will you swear that you did not write it? —Do you wish me to swear a thing that I cannot remember.

12,419. I do wish you to swear that you did or did not?—If you wish me to swear one way or the other I would rather swear ——.

12,420. You cannot forget whether you wrote that letter immediately after you had caused a man to be murdered; you must recollect whether you wrote a letter to the merchants asking them not let him wheel room, because he had drawn upon himself the vengeance of the whole trade?—I have no recollection.

12,421. Do you mean that the man who is engaged in a sanguinary business like that cannot recollect whether he wrote such a letter as that?—No, I cannot recollect.

12,422. You cannot recollect?—No, I cannot; I would sooner say that I never did than that I did.

12,423. You say that in order to get the money to pay for Linley's shooting you took it out in small sums from the contributions?—Yes.

12,424. Were those contributions examined from week to week?—No, they were gone through from month to month, and the amount was reckoned up from week to week by the committee, but they had not check books.

12,425. The accounts were gone through week by week by the committee, and reckoned up and passed every month by the general committee; is that so?—By the auditor, but allow me to be correct; what I mean by being passed through the committee is that all the accounts there are taken and reckoned up after me. They would not stop to examine every account, and check it as against every member, and that was the way the money was got.

12,426. You knew they would not examine every account, and that was the reason that enabled you to take out the money?—Yes.

12,427. Then if they had found you out you would have been liable to be treated as an embezzler of their money?—I should have been liable to that.

12,428. Do you mean to tell me that, having no grudge against the men and having nothing to gain, but only acting for the benefit of the trade, you put yourself in such a situation with the committee, not having their authority for it?—I do, positively.

12,429. All you had at heart was the good of the trade, and so had they?—I cannot tell you what theirs was, it was mine.

12,430. So you risked being found out embezzling people's money for no good to yourself only to benefit the trade? —Yes, that is true.

12,431. Who examined your contributions from week to week?—Various parties who were on the committee.

12,432. Tell me their names at Linley's time; just refer to the book?—We have not the book.

12,433. What has become of the books of the time when Linley was shot?—They are destroyed.

12,434. Who destroyed the books?—I destroyed them.

12,435. If they had appeared would they have shown that you had taken part in injuring Linley?—They would have shown all that I have now been telling you.

12,436. What would they have shown?—They would have shown where there had been figures altered, the contributions scratched out, and others put in their places.

12,437. Did you, in fact, scratch out figures and put others in their places?—Occasionally; the money was got in various ways.

12,438. Then any auditor looking at those books would immediately see that there had been a scratching out?—They do not always see it.

12,439. How could they avoid it if the books were scrached out and defaced in the way you mention—how could they escape the sight of the auditor?—They could escape as they went through the accounts, not stopping to examine them. You must understand it was not scratched out in such large numbers that it would strike your eye—it would only be done at certain places and at certain times. I made the selections of them in such a way that they should not see them.

12,440. At this time were the books open to every member of the union?—Yes.

12,441. Then any member who came to look at them could have found them out?—They could have found them out, and I had that risk to run.

12,442. Were the contributions entered singly?—They were entered singly.

12,443. How many deductions must you have made in order to make up the 20*l.* for the first shooting of Linley—several hundreds?—Probably a good many.

12,444. And yet you would run the risk of being found out simply to benefit the trade—is that what you wish us to believe?—Yes, I did.

12,445. Then, according to your mode of dealing with the members you entered the amount of payment short?—Yes.

12,446. And the accounts were audited and open to the inspection of the whole body?—Yes.

12,447. How did the men ever get right?—I placed the amount of a man's earnings to equal his contributions—he did not get into arrears. I took so much off the amount he delivered in as earned, and that made his contribution less.

12,448. If you went to a man you said to him, "How much are you earning?" and if he said 6*l.*, then you had to take out of that your poundage—that would entitle you to 15*s.*, but instead of that you only put down that he earned 5*l.*?—Yes, for illustration.

12,449. Of course you would put down that you would be entitled to so much only?—Yes, making him so that he would not get into arrear.

12,450. You put down that he was earning less?—Yes.

12,451. Show me an instance where you have done that?—I cannot from that book, because it is not done in that book.

12,452. Is there any book in which you can show that—if you had not done so a man would get into arrear and never get right again; but if you did it in that way, show me a single case in which you have

THIRTEENTH DAY.

W. Broadhead.

20 June 1867.

put down a man's work at less than he was earning?—All the books we have now are correct; there are none of those alterations.

12,453. Then that was only done at the time of Linley's affair?—Yes.

12,454. When was Wheatman blown up?—I do not know when it was.

12,455. The books were all open to the trade?—Yes.

12,456. Was there ever a single case—there were hundreds of them you say?—I said hundreds; it was a guess.

12,457. Was there ever a case, although there were hundreds of persons whose contributions or earnings were falsely entered, of a man complaining to the society that you had falsely entered their earnings in the books?—They frequently complained of it, but in the cases they complained of there were was no truth in it. In those cases where I got the money from members I never took it from those in arrears, it was those who were straight on the books.

12,458. Is there one case amongst the lot in which you have acted improperly of a man having paid so much coming into the union and saying, "Mr. Broad-"head has put me down 5*l.* and I earned 6*l.*, and I have paid him on that scale"?—I do not know of a single one.

12,459. Did you ever order anybody to do anything by the authority of the investigating committee?—No, sir. There are cases that have occurred where appeals have been made to me for monies that I have brought before the investigating committee after those things have been done, and I have got the money from them; but I did not explain to the committee I think in all the cases what it was for. I think not, but there was one in particular, it was George Peace, and you will find 2*l.* 10*s.* entered November 29th, 1865. There is an entry made there of expenses of the investigating committee. This person at that time was coming month by month and claiming to have the scale made up, instead of paying contributions, on the ground of being short of employment; he produced his notes and so forth, but there was a report that he was not delivering in correctly. We consequently instructed a person to what we call clerk him, that would be to go to his wheel day by day and night by night and get the amount of his work.

12,460. Who was the man whom you employed to do that?—Thomas Broadhead.

12,461. You employed Broadhead to watch him, did you?—Yes.

12,462. Was the auditor who investigated these earnings a man in the trade?—He had been a member, but during the latter part of his investigating duties he was not a member.

12,463. But he would know what a man could fairly earn in his trade?—Yes.

12,464. It was this man's duty every week to go over the books and examine these entries?—But understand me, the party I allude to had never had any of the accounts to examine that were so falsely entered, it was before his time.

12,465. Who did them?—I cannot say; we did not keep the balance sheets at that time as we do now.

12,466. Was there no entry of earnings?—Not now, but there were then.

12,467. Who had to examine those earnings?—Nobody examined the earnings; they examined the accounts.

12,468. And they examined the earnings?—No, they did not examine the earnings.

12,469. It was their duty to have done it?—No, it was not.

12,470. Who did it?—Nobody but myself; I made the account out.

12,471. Therefore all these poor men who had contributed their money upon their earnings were entirely at your mercy, was no person to have a check upon you?—That was so.

12,472. Was the book that you destroyed as big as that book (*referring to a book*)?—No.

12,473. How large was it?—It was not half the size.

12,474. You say that the committee knew all about the rattening, and the trade knew all about the rattenings?—No, I did not say that it was made a committee question at all. I said these rattening cases would arise without their going before the committee in the way I have described.

12,475. Have you on any occasion dealt as a committee in restoring or ordering things to be restored?—There have been cases where the men who have been rattened have brought their cases occasionally before the committee and there have been certain resolutions passed upon them.

12,476. That they should be restored?—Something like that.

12,477. Do you recollect an instance where some men have had their things rattened which in your estimation you thought had been improperly rattened, they having committed no fault, where you as a member of the union wrote to the Saw Makers Union telling them that unless they prevented a thing of that kind occurring you would withdraw as a body from the amalgamated society?—Yes, there is a minute on the book to that effect.

12,478. Is that minute correct?—Yes.

12,479. Then you, as one body, wrote to another body treating them as the parties who ordered the rattening?—We thought so.

12,480. Did you believe that the union as a body had ordered the rattening?—It was doubtful.

12,481. Did you believe it?—I doubted it.

12,482. Why did you write to them?—Simply to make them acquainted with the fact that it had been done, and as it was through some circumstances (I forget what now) connected with themselves. I thought it was our duty to see that the property was restored.

12,483. And you told them that if they did not restore it you would no longer belong to the amalgamated union?—Yes.

12,484. That is a case which occurred on the 10th of November 1862?—Yes.

12,485. It was this: "Resolved that the nuts of "Messrs. Russell and Company, Messrs. Tooley, and "Messrs. Marsden, are removed without cause"?—I think you have not got it correct.

12,486. "That there must be an investigation of saw makers or saw handle makers; that a note be sent from this meeting to the secretary of the saw makers and saw-handle makers that if any case of a similar nature occurs we should at once withdraw from the union of the four branches"?—Yes, the latter part is correct.

12,487. Then you as a union sent that notice that if ever your men were rattened again, you would withdraw from the amalgamated union?—Yes, the four branches of the saw trade.

12,488. It is one union talking to another union?—Yes.

12,489. And one union giving them to understand that they consider the rattening to be done by the unions, and telling them that if the rattenings go on they will withdraw from all future connexion with them?—We thought it had been done to serve their society.

12,490. And it was done to serve their society?—I cannot say.

12,491. But you thought so?—Yes.

12,492. Did not you compel the saw handle makers to make it good?—They got restored without compelling.

12,493. You wrote this letter, and thereupon the things were restored?—They got restored, I believe.

12,494. You wrote to them, telling them what you would do if they were not restored, and they were restored?—Yes.

12,495. That was union to union?—Yes.

12,496. You cannot ratten the saw makers, can you?—No.

12,497. And if you wanted to have some kind of influence upon the saw makers, you are obliged to ratten some other branch of the trade?—That has been the case.

THIR-TEENTH DAY.

W. Broadhead.

20 June 1867.

12,498. You thought that was the kind of case which had been done then?—Yes.

12,499. Your men had done nothing—something had to be done in order to put the screw upon the other branch, and your men were the sufferers by it?—That was the opinion.

12,500. That was the opinion of your union?—Yes.

12,501. We have not had this thing explained. A nut is a thing which if it is taken away and a man goes to work upon his stone and he does not see that it is gone, the probability is that the stone will blow up into the air and kill him on the spot?—No, you labour under a misunderstanding. It would be impossible for him to draw the band on the stone without discovering the nut was gone. The stone would be loose, and he would discover at once that he could not work.

12,502. Does the nut often come off. I have heard of cases of stones flying up to the top of the ceiling and nearly killing the man that was working at the time?—That would not be taking away the nut.

12,503. Taking away the nut does not endanger life?—No, it would only stop him from working.

12,504. Have you ever authorized the cutting of bellows?—What have I to do with bellows?

12,505. I did not ask you that—have you authorized or sent any person to cut bellows?—No, never in my life.

12,506. You have never done that?—No.

12,507. All that you have done has been the simple thing rattening. Have you ever blown up a man or ordered a man to have gunpowder put in his trough?—Yes, this case of Linley's

12,508. You did not put gunpowder into his trough?—I never authorized any blowing up—you have got the cases.

12,509. I have a good many cases to talk to you of, we are only approaching the cases, there are a good many cases behind. Have you ever authorized or been a party in any way to putting gunpowder into a man's trough?—No.

12,510. Never?—No, never.

12,511. And you had nothing to do with Helliwell?—Nothing to do with Helliwell.

12,512. How many persons have you on the box as a rule?—I believe they range between 40 and 50, at the present time trade is very bad.

12,513. As a rule you have between 40 and 50 men on the box doing nothing?—At the present time.

12,514. Have you had as many as 80 on the box?—Yes.

12,515. There are 40 now. Have you had men on the box who have never done any work for years?—Yes, we have some.

12,516. How many?—I have not counted them up.

12,517. But about how many?—There would not be many who have been for years. Out of the 40 there might be such a thing as half a dozen. I am not speaking correctly.

12,518. There might be as many as half a dozen on the box who have never done any work for years?—Yes.

12,519. And the working men were keeping these men and their families in idleness?—Yes, they thought it well worth their while to buy their labour out of the market.

12,520. If they could have done work they would have been on the list which was sent to the employers?—Yes.

12,521. What good was it to the trade to keep the men out of it?—The good of it was this, and this is the vital part. It regulated the supply of labour in the market according to its demand. In case of any manufacturer requiring a man the society give him his choice of all out of employ, but the society do not permit members to go to seek for employment; that is, he must not present himself in the labour market before others have the same chance; just as lawyers or barristers go on a circuit they must all be there on a day. Consequently, while a list is furnished to the employer to take his choice from, to make what selection he chooses, any member being known to make any overtures for any place is liable to have his name struck from the list for so doing. The object obtained is this, that surplus labour is not seen in the market until it is required.

12,522. Go on?—I have nothing more to say upon that subject.

12,523. Tucker Clarke was about as consummate a scoundrel as there is in the town of Sheffield?—He might be a good deal better if he chose to be.

12,524. Martin is about as great a scoundrel as ever existed?—Martin had his faults.

12,525. I suppose Myers had a few faults as well?—Yes, and pretty large ones.

12,526. If they were not in the union no man would ever employ such men?—They did when they were out.

12,527. What advantage could it be to the poor industrious men to be keeping these men idle?—Simply this. If they did not keep them they would be obliged to live at some price. They could not live on air, and they would have to offer themselves to work at such prices as they could get. It would be an inducement to an employer to take them, and they got into situations by that means.

12,528. Amongst these six or seven men who were doing nothing for years, did you employ any to watch for you or employ them to do jobs for you?—They have rattened many a time, but the rattening would occur in the way that has been described.

12,529. They were all ratteners, in fact?—Begging your pardon, the bulk of the rattening was not done by that class; their fellow wheelmates were the larger class, men who worked at the same places.

12,530. Were those respectable gentlemen engaged in rattening a good deal?—I do not want to say anything about their character; you know it as well as I do.

12,531. Were they engaged in rattening? The price was 5*s*. for a band?—They looked after a job of that description.

12,532. Did they get 5*s*. for a band?—Yes, that was the custom.

12,533. How much for a nut?—It would be about the same. There would be occasions where they had a good deal of trouble, and there would be additional charges made.

12,534. And you used to give them to them?—Sometimes.

12,535. How often have you paid Martin?—I have not paid him very often, because we have not had him often. Since he returned he has never been paid for any unlawful purpose.

12,536. What did you pay him?—10*s*.

12,537. For what?—He received 10*s*., for it is on the minute book.

12,538. Why did he receive 10*s*.?—It is on the minute book for detecting Shaw; and speaking upon this I wish to correct myself. I said he had never received anything for any unlawful purpose. I think that there was a case, if my memory serves me rightly, that occurred to Elisha Parker recently, and I believe that he was the man that applied for the money.

12,539. What did they do to Elisha Parker?—I believe some bands or something were taken, as far as my memory serves me. Whoever it was, Martin was the man who applied for the money. You asked me if I could remember sometime back, but I could not remember.

12,540. Did he apply for any money for blowing up Fearnehough?—No.

12,541. Did not he?—No.

12,542. Did not you employ him to blow up Fearnehough?—If looking you in the face and telling you—

12,543. Did not you employ Martin to blow up Fearnehough?—No.

12,544. Martin went to America?—Yes.

12,545. According to the rules of your society a man has a certain sum advanced to him if he goes out to America?—Yes.

THIRTEENTH DAY.

W. Broadhead.

20 June 1867.

12,546. It is only to go out once?—It was so, and it is altered.

12,547. I know it is. I will call your attention to the alteration. Before Fearnehough was blown up what was Martin's scale?—I cannot say, it will tell you in the book, somewhere about 10*s*.

12,548. It was 6*s*.?—Then he did not receive for his wife, because she was not living with him.

12,549. Is it not true that before the blowing up he received 6*s*., and after the blowing up immediately his scale was increased to 10*s*.?—I cannot say whether it was before or after, but the fact is that at one time he received 6*s*. and then 10*s*. I do not know the particular time, the book will tell.

12,550. Up to Fearnehough's blowing up it was 6*s*., after Fearnehough's blowing up it was 10*s*.?—If you refer to the book it will tell you; the minute book will tell you when it is advanced.

12,551. No, it will not. I see Joseph Martin here 10*s*. 3*d*. The 8th of October 1866 was the date on which Fearnehough was blown up?—Yes.

12,552. (*Mr. Chance.*) Would the payments of Martin's scale appear in that little cash book?—It would appear in the scale book.

12,553. (*Chairman.*) Is this the one: "March "12th, 1867. Joseph Martin applies for 5*l*. and to "assist him in paying his passage to America. Martin "retires, when Martin having had a grant of money "for this same purpose on a former occasion and "he had returned, the rule passed April the 5th, 1864, "on such cases is referred to, and finding there is no "provision made for any second grant to emigrants "it is therefore resolved to leave this case in the hands "of the general meeting. Martin is called up and "made acquainted with this decision. Martin then "asks for scale to be allowed until the general meeting, "but having resigned the situation at the trades tools "after notice had been given him, scale is therefore "refused. He is told he can work his month out at "the trades tools if he refuses. This Martin declines "to do. The secretary also states Martin having "declined to work the month's notice out, he had "set on Thomas Cutler to job the month out, which "the committee approves of." Then I find on the 9th of April this resolution come to: "The various rewards "offered for the detection of the perpetrator of the "New Hereford Street outrage having failed, and the "reward of 1,100*l*. having been already withdrawn, "and a Parliamentary Commission having been ap- "pointed to inquire into the outrages that have oc- "curred within a period of 10 years back in Sheffield "and the neighbourhood, therefore the reward of 10*l*. "offered by the society for the same object be also "withdrawn, in conjunction with the rewards offered "by other trades, &c., so soon as arrangements can be "effected to do so." On the very same day that you got to know about the Commission Joseph Martin having decided to emigrate to America he applies for 5*l*. which he now is entitled to from the society as a member, you having passed a rule in the interval that he was not entitled to it because he had come back from America after having the allowance to go there; now on the very day on which you found out that there is to be an inquiry by us grant him the sum of 5*l*. to carry him out?—Yes, the body did it against the wish of the committee; that is what the committee did, and you see what the body did, so that he did not get more favour at the hands of the committee.

12,554. But it was done?—It was done at a general meeting.

12,555. At that time had it been currently reported that Martin was the man who blew up Fearnehough? —I never heard his name at that time mentioned as being connected with it up to that time.

12,556. You have since?—I have heard it talked of since.

12,557. Now I put it to you very solemnly again, did not you hire him to blow up that house?—No, sir.

12,558. Did not you give him the 5*l*. to get him out of the way to prevent him being examined upon this inquiry?—If I may never rise again, I did not.

12,559. Did the body do it for that purpose?—No, they did not.

12,560. Was it to screen him from a cross-examination upon that point that he was taken away?—No.

12,561. For what purpose was the 5*l*. advanced to him, to take him out of the way?—Because he wanted it, and the body considered that it would be an advantage to them to get as many members away as they could even if they had been away before, and it is now a general rule of which any other member can avail himself. It was not done for Martin; it was done as a general rule.

12,562. Has it ever been applied to any other person than Martin?—No, the committee before would not pay it, but the body ——.

12,563. Who has said that Martin did it?—I cannot tell you. I have heard it reported.

12,564. How soon after you had passed this resolution; where did you first hear it?—I cannot tell you.

12,565. Had you heard it before this resolution was passed?—I think not.

12,566. Will you swear that?—No, I will not swear it.

12,567. I put it to you, if you will not swear that you had heard it before this resolution was passed; and if it was not public talk that he had done it, on what ground do you say that the committee had sent him out of the country?—On the grounds that he applied for the money to go with and we could spare him.

12,568. And none other?—None other.

12,569. Did you bring it before the committee or a meeting, and say, "It is a very foolish thing for you to "give this man money to go out of the country, why "we are going to have an inquiry, and if, according "to public opinion, Martin is the man, you must not "send him out"?—I never do remember saying such a thing.

12,570. Do not you think that it would have been a very prudent thing to have told them that they must not advance any money because he was suspected, and that the Commission was coming down?—I did not know that he was suspected at that time. Now you name it, I feel convinced that it was after that time that I heard the report.

12,571. Do you know where he is in America?—No, we would not pay him the money until we had a guarantee that he went.

12,572. And did you get a gurrantee that he was gone?—Yes, and a man paid the money for him and we would not pay the man until we were sure he was gone.

12,573. Until you were perfectly sure that he had left the country?—Yes; if you apply to Mr. Priest he will tell you, he carries on business; he found the money and he had a particular reason for finding it.

12,574. You would not pay the money until you got a guarantee that this man was out of the country?—Yes, that is correct.

12,575. But if it was an advantage to you for him to go out of the country why was there a necessity for all this caution and guarantee and the rest of it?—Because it was considered to be just possible that he would not go out of the country if he got it, that he would spend it, and that we should have him again; that was it.

12,576. Then he was a very great ruffian?—You will see our opinion of him in the book.

12,577. Was he frequently at your house?—He came pretty frequently, but I had not much conversation with him.

12,578. I have a great deal more to inquire about? —I shall be very happy to be at your service any time.

The witness withdrew.

Adjourned to to-morrow at 11 o'clock.

FOURTEENTH DAY.

Council Hall, Sheffield, Friday, 21st June 1867.

PRESENT :

William Overend, Esq., Q.C.
Thomas Irwin Barstow, Esq.
George Chance, Esq.
J. E. Barker, Esq., Secretary.

WILLIAM OVEREND, Esq., Q.C., in the Chair.

FOURTEENTH DAY.

W. Broadhead.

21 June 1867

William Broadhead recalled and further examined.

12,579. (*Chairman.*) I think it my duty in the interest both of yourself and of public justice, and in the interest of those whom you might implicate to give you another warning. I dare say you may have a false sense of honour that you will not implicate others; but I have looked over my notes and I find that you have not told us the name of a single person whom you have caused to do rattening. You have never disclosed a single fact which has not been proved by two witnesses. You have never admitted anything which could not have been proved without your evidence. Remember, that to obtain a certificate you will have to tell us all that you know, and we must be satisfied that you tell us all that you know. It is not merely telling about those things which have been mentioned, but if it should turn out in the result that there are other things with which you are proved to be associated, and you have not told us about them, unquestionably your certificate will be withheld. Again, it is not in the interests of any men who may have been associated with you that you should screen their names, because if they, believing that you screen their names and their guilt, should not appear, and they do not come forward, you may be the cause of their actually being brought to punishment. If they knew now that you told all that you knew about them, they most likely would come forward themselves and state that which they have done. If they did so they would be entitled, if they spoke truly, to their certificate. By concealing their names, if you know them, you are not only putting yourself in peril, but you are putting them in peril; and, therefore, I caution you again with reference to other transactions of which you have not spoken, to be explicit, clear, and candid in your disclosures?—Pardon me. Will you permit me to ask you one question?

12,580. Yes.—Can I rely upon it that the same mercy will be extended to those men that will be extended to myself, provided that I will own to the truth?

12,581. Undoubtedly?—Then I will give you a true statement.

(*Mr. Chance.*) It is your only chance; you must do it.

12,582. (*Chairman.*) Is there any statement which you would like to make before I put questions to you? —Yes; to begin with, the statement which I made to you yesterday relative to the Helliwell affair was untrue; I hired Dennis Clark.

12,583. To blow up Helliwell?—Yes.

12,584. What did you give him?—Well, my memory will not serve me what the amount was.

12,585. Was it 3*l.*?—I believe it would be either 3*l.* or 5*l.*

12,586. Do you know that Clark did blow him up? —That Shaw blew him up.

12,587. You say that you hired Dennis Clark to blow him up; that Dennis Clark did not blow him up, but that Shaw did?—So I was told.

12,588. Who told you so?—Clark, I think.

12,589. Did you pay the money to Shaw or to Clark?—I think I paid the money to Clark.

12,590. Then for what purpose am I to understand that that paper which you drew up was drawn up?—That paper was drawn up because I had heard of Shaw circulating reports of that kind, and when I learned of him drawing scale, and at the same time working, it became my duty, let the consequences be what they might, to detect him if I could in drawing scale which he had no right to. He was detected doing so?

12,591. By whom?—By Martin, and I was obliged to bring it before the committee; feeling that if I did so, to be revenged upon me he probably might put into practice what I had heard he had talked about. I consequently drew up that document and said nothing to anyone for the purpose, when the case was brought before the committee; in the first place questioning him as to the reports which he had put in circulation, which I believed he would deny, and in the next place to ask him before the committee in their presence.

12,592. Is that the investigating committee?—No, the regular committee—to ask him in their presence if I ever did employ him to do such a thing, which I believed also he would deny, thinking that he would get his scale stopped if he did not; and then to call upon the committee in his presence to witness that document and to hold that document as a protection against any statement he afterwards might make. When the committee met I carried into effect.

12,593. Are your books here this morning?—Yes.

12,594. Have you the paper which you yourself drew up?—I think I have it. When the committee met I carried my plan into effect and as the minute states, asked permission to ask Shaw a few questions, which they granted. I then put the questions to him as given in the statement, and as anticipated, he answered them. The committee afterwards signed them. Feeling myself somewhat secure against any course which he might take, I then went into the business, and that terminated as expressed in the minute; that is all I think.

12,595. Now, will you be kind enough to let me see your paper?—(*The witness searched for the paper.*) I do not appear to have it; I may have left it at home upon the desk; I shall find it no doubt.

12,596. I wanted to have asked you a question upon it, and I am very sorry that it is not here?—It is here (*handing the paper to the Commissioners*).

12,597. You require it no longer now?—No.

12,598. Then I will put in my book "George Shaw " being present, William Broadhead states he had " heard a report that George Shaw had been circula- " ting to the effect that he, Broadhead, had several " years ago"———— I call your attention to this? —I am listening.

12,599. " Employed and paid Shaw to force his " way through the cog wheel race at the Castle Mills

FOURTEENTH DAY.

W. Broadhead.

21 June 1867.

"Blonk Street, to commit an outrage with gun-"powder upon a person named Joseph Helliwell; "Broadhead in the presence of the committee "interrogates him upon it, upon which Shaw declares "he never had been employed for any such purpose, "and therefore willingly signs the following state-"ment, 'I hereby declare that I never at any time "'was either employed or paid by William Broadhead "'to commit any such outrage as is above described, "'nor did Broadhead ever make such an offer to me.'" You see that this document confines itself very much, entirely in fact, to Helliwell's case?—It does.

12,600. Now, I will read you the whole, and you will see what a story you have made: "George Shaw "attends in consequence of his scale having been "stopped on Saturday last week; but William "Broadhead, the secretary, previous to the business "being gone into requests to ask Shaw a few ques-"tions on another subject, to which assent has been "given. Broadhead says he had heard a report that "he, Shaw, had been circulating that he, Broadhead, "had several years ago employed and paid Shaw to "commit an outrage with gunpowder upon a person "at the Castle Grinding Mills, Blonk Street. Shaw "denied having put such a report in circulation. "When Broadhead further puts the question to him, "was he ever employed or paid by Broadhead to com-"mit such an outrage as is here spoken of, to which "Shaw replies, he never was." Therefore, you see your document here, of which you have an entry in your books goes further than this; it goes to say that he was never employed at any time for any outrage, whereas the document which you gave him to sign is merely confined to the blowing up of Helliwell.

12,601. How is it that you have made the entry in your book much larger than the document which he gave; was it for your own protection?—Yes; but understand me; it was only to make it sufficiently large, that is the only affair that ever he was connected with me in, to my knowledge. There may have been rattening cases, but I do not remember them.

12,602. And you had confined your questions before the committee, I suppose to Helliwell's case only?—Yes. Now, is it true as Hallam says, that you asked Hallam and Crooks to do the job for you?—The evidence which I gave to you respecting that matter yesterday is all truthful to the best of my knowledge.

12,603. Were Hallam and Crooks intended in the first instance to be at Helliwell's?—No.

12,604. Never?—Never.

12,605. Was Hallam intended to be in Helliwell's case?—No.

12,606. Then this is the true story, is it?—Yes.

12,607. Where was Helliwell working? he was working at Hague and Cleg's was he not?—No; Helliwell was working at Castle Mills, otherwise Tower Wheel.

12,608. Before I go forward, have you anything more to say?—Nothing further about Helliwell.

12,609. Is there anything else with regard to which you wish to make any statement?—Not on that case.

12,610. On any case that you have been engaged in?—Yes; you had a case on yesterday of Elisha Parker. He had a horse destroyed; that was done I believe by Elijah Smith, John Taylor, and Phineas Dean.

12,611. And Joseph Bradshaw?—I do not know about Bradshaw. He might, but I do not know. I am here to speak the truth; all that I know.

12,612. I believe you are disposed to speak the truth, but I have a good deal of private information on this subject, and therefore I ask you before you talk about Elisha Parker, was not Bradshaw one of the parties?—I do not know; I do not indeed. Those were the only parties that I am aware of.

12,613. Has Bradshaw ever spoken to you of Parker's horse being destroyed?—I do not think that he has.

12,614. Will you swear that he has not?—No, I will not.

12,615. Do you believe he has?—I believe he has not.

12,616. Where is John Taylor?—He is dead—they are all three dead.

12,617. I thought so?—I tell you the truth.

12,618. You tell me the names, and all three are dead. Now I will ask you is Bradshaw alive?—Yes.

12,619. But you know those other three are dead?—Yes.

12,620. Did you hire them to do it?—Well they came to me after it was done; I believe I am correct in that.

12,621. Did you hire them to do it; you know you were there at 12 o'clock at night with Machin some time before. Did you hire them to do that?—I have no recollection of that, but I paid the money.

12,622. How much?—I cannot say what was the amount now, but it was not a large amount.

12,623. Will you swear you did not pay them before they went?—I have no recollection that I did.

12,624. Will you swear you did not?—No, I will not.

12,625. Will you say that you did not promise them something before they did it?—I have no recollection of having any conversation with them until afterwards. The impression upon my mind is that they came to me afterwards and that I paid them money, and that is the only impression on my mind.

12,626. But you will not swear that you did not speak to them before?—I cannot speak positively to that.

12,627. You will not swear you did not?—I should not like to do it, because it is possible.

12,628. Did you not speak to Bradshaw about this being done before it was done?—I have no recollection of it.

12,629. Will you swear that you did not?—I tell you sincerely I have no recollection of it.

12,630. But will you swear that you did not?—I can say no more.

12,631. I tell you that I have evidence behind?—I am speaking now to the best of my knowledge.

12,632. I want you to have your certificate if I can give it to you?—Well, I wish to speak the truth in everything.

12,633. Have you ever spoken to Bradshaw about it?—I have no recollection of ever having conversation with Bradshaw on the subject at all.

12,634. Was Bradshaw present when the money was paid?—I have no recollection when the money was paid, nor whom I paid it to.

12,635. Will you swear that Bradshaw was not present when you paid it?—I have no recollection of it.

12,636. You must know?—I can say no more.

12,637. You know who the person was?—I might get rid of this question by saying who it was, but I should be saying that which I really do not know.

12,638. What is your belief?—My belief is that he was not present, but I have no recollection.

12,639. Do you know a man who was spoken of yesterday who lived near who was a "shooter," Bamford?—Yes.

12,640. Do you know his house?—No; he lives at Dore, or did live there.

12,641. Was he one of the parties who damaged that horse?—Not to my knowledge.

12,642. You must know?—No; I will give you the names of those that I have a knowledge of.

12,643. They are all dead men, you know?—They are not all dead.

12,644. Taylor is alive, you say?—No; that is the question of the destroying of the horse.

12,645. Smith, Taylor, and Dean are all dead?—Yes.

12,646. That is as to the horse?—Yes.

12,647. Now perhaps you can tell us something about the shooting at Mr. Parker himself?—Yes; a person named George Peace, senior, was hired by me to do something to stop him from working.

FOURTEENTH DAY.

W. Broadhead.

21 June 1867.

12,648. How long was that after the horse was destroyed?—Well, I cannot say; but it could not be a very long time. He had seen me several times; he had come to see me several times.

12,649. Was he a member of the Union?—Yes.

12,650. Is he alive?—He is alive. He had come to see me several times on the subject, but I think nothing up to this time had been decided upon so far as my memory will give it me. I am now speaking to the best of my recollection. It is a long time since now, but to the best of my recollection I think that I went up to his house one Sunday.

12,651. Where did he live?—At Dore.

12,652. Is it George Peace's house of which you are speaking?—George Peace's house. I saw him on the subject. We left his house together and went down into some fields. I think it was in the summer time. I remember the day I am speaking of was a very beautiful day, and there, as far as my memory carries me, we had conversation and agreed upon something to be done, but whether he defined what that something was to be or not I really cannot say.

12,653. Did you suggest that he should blow up Parker's house with gunpowder?—Of that affair I know nothing.

12,654. You do not know anything about putting gunpowder under the door?—I know nothing of that affair at all.

12.655. Something was to be done, you say, but what it was you do not know?—I have forgotten whether it was defined what was to be done or not; but there, so far as my memory serves me, it was finally settled that something should be done; that is, so far as my memory will carry me.

12,656. Will you swear that you did not agree that he should shoot him?—No, I cannot swear it because I will not say that I did not say so.

12,657. Did you agree that he was to call Parker up at night by throwing stones at his house?—The mode in which they were to go about the business I knew nothing of until afterwards.

12,658. You say "they," who were "they?"—The parties who had it to do.

12,659. Who were the parties?—He told me that he had a servant man of his own who would do it.

12,660. Did he mention his name?—I believe he did, but I have forgotten the name. He told me that this man would see to the affair being done, that he had employed him. The affair got done and the amount that he was to receive, I cannot say what it was, but it was a large amount.

12,661. How much was it, was it 20*l.*?—It was more, I believe.

12,662. Was it 50*l.*?—I do not think it was. I cannot say what the amount was, but it would be, I have no doubt, between 20*l.* and 30*l.*, or perhaps it might be even more than 30*l.* I really cannot say what the amount was. He was a long time before he got the whole of the money, but he ultimately did get it.

12,663. Did he tell you who did it?—Yes, he gave me the man's name, but I have forgotten his name; I have seen the man.

12,664. Do you know him?—No, I have never had conversation with him. He came to my house.

12,665. Was it Bamford?—No.

12,666. Was it Elijah Smith?—No, Elijah Smith was a member of their own trade. I knew Elijah well enough.

12,667. Was Elijah Smith one of them?—Not that I am aware of. Let me see; I think I gave three names for the horse. I am not quite clear whether Elijah was not one also, since you have named it.

12,668. For the shooting?—No.

12,669. You have given the name of Elijah for the horse, but I am talking now about the shooting?—I have no knowledge of his having anything whatever to do with it. I have every belief that he had nothing whatever to do with it.

12,670. Are you aware that Elijah Smith before his death made a confession, and confessed that he was one of the men?—I am not.

13,671. Then I will tell you that he did, and it was stated to a person, and that we have his confession?—I did not know it.

12,672. Do you know that fact, that Elijah Smith before his death confessed to a man whom we have and can produce that he was one of the men?—I was not aware of that.

12,673. Having told you that, I ask you again was Elijah Smith one of the men?—I do not know that he was.

12,674. Mind, I have evidence here, you see; was Elijah Smith one of the men?—If you repeat that question to me till this time tomorrow I can say no more.

12,675. Is there any other person besides that man to whom you have alluded and Peace, who you know was there?—The only person that I am acquainted with as having been connected with it is the party that I have given.

12,676. Again, I will put a name to you, and I caution you to remember that we have many secret sources of information. Was Sam Crooks there?—No.

12,677. That you swear?—So far as my knowledge goes I believe he was not. He has always told me so whenever we have met.

12,678. Have you ever asked him if he was?—Yes.

12,679. Did he ever tell you that he had lent his gun for the purpose of its being done?—No. I have seen him this morning, and asked him that question, and he tells me he did not.

12,680. So you have had a conversation with Sam Crooks this morning, have you?—This morning.

12,681. What was your object in talking to Crooks this morning?—My object in talking to Crooks this morning was to arrange what we should do in the situation in which we are placed.

12,682. Was not your object in talking to Crooks this morning to decide between yourselves how much you should confess, and how much you should withhold?—Yes.

12,683. What did you agree to withhold?—We agreed to withhold the Hereford Street outrage.

12,684. Then you were a party to that?—Yes; at last. Do you allude to the ——?

12,685. To the Hereford Street outrage?—Oh! to the outrage itself?

12,686. Yes?—Yes.

12,687. Who committed it?—Samuel Crooks.

12,688. Was Martin there? — No. Martin is entirely innocent, and the minutes in that book are genuine.

12,689. Now we will go forward; we will talk about that presently. I ask you again, was Sam Crooks present at the time when Elisha Parker was shot, to your knowledge?—To my knowledge he was not, and I believe he was not.

12,690. Sam Crooks, you say, was not there?—To my knowledge, and I believe, he was not there.

12,691. Whenever you have had any shooting business to do, has not Crooks been the man to whom you have always entrusted it?—Yes.

12,692. How often have you employed him to shoot for you?—Well, I do not know of any cases but those which have been named.

12,693. You do not know any others?—No.

12,694. It is impossible that you can make us believe that if you employed this man to shoot Parker, and if Parker was shot, and you paid him money for shooting him, you cannot know who shot him. You must know who shot him, and you have heard the account I daresay, (or read it in the paper if you were not present) that he was shot at from at least two places. One man was placed above his house, another man was placed below his house, and, at all events, two were concerned in that matter.—I have always understood that there were two.

12,695. Now who is the other?—I do not know.

FOURTEENTH DAY.

W. Broadhead.

21 June 1867.

There has been a report in circulation that Thomas Bamford was the other, but I do not know it.

12,696. Had Thomas Bamford anything to do with you or the trade?—Not with our trade.

12,697. Was he connected in any way with trade?—He was a scythe grinder, and he belongs to the Scythe Grinders' Union.

12,698. And you say that there has been a report that he was so? You know that Peace did it?—Yes.

12,699. Have you ever talked to Peace on the subject, and asked him whether Bamford was there or not?—I think we have had conversation about it. At least that is the impression I have.

12,700. Was he there or not? Did Peace say that he was there or not?—I think I have heard Peace say so, but I want to be correct, and I really cannot say. I cannot be certain.

12,701. Was Peace in your Union?—Yes.

12,702. Were the three other men whom you have mentioned, who are dead, all members of the Union?—Yes.

12,703. Now had you had any personal quarrel with Parker?—Not a personal quarrel. We had disagreed frequently when we had met together on matters connected with the trade.

12,704. And were these things done, both the maiming of the horse and the shooting of Parker himself, in consequence of his disobeying the rules of the trade?—I believe it was.

12,705. And only for that reason?—As far as I am concerned.

12,706. And was not the only thing which he had done working at Mr. Newbold's, Mr. Newbold being unwilling to turn out his non-union men?—I think it arose out of something of that kind. I think that was it. I believe it was.

12,707. What is the next thing about which you have to tell us? Have you employed Crooks in anything else of any kind, and at any time, to your knowledge?—I think that he was once employed, but I am not certain. I really am not certain. My impression is that he was once employed to blow up the boilers at Firth and Sons, but I cannot be certain. Somebody was. That is a good many years ago.

12,708. How many years ago is that?—I really cannot say.

12,709. Was there any attempt made to blow them up before?—I do not recollect.

12,710. I think it is not so simple a matter but that you must recollect whether an attempt was made to blow up Messrs. Firth's boilers?—I recollect that an attempt was made to blow them up.

12,711. How far did that attempt succeed?—It did not do much damage.

12,712. Did the gunpowder go off? Was gunpowder used?—I think it went off.

12,713. Was it one of their boilers situated down beyond the Wicker?—Yes.

12,714. Did you employ the man, whoever he was, to do it?—Yes, I believe I did.

12,715. Who was that man?—I can give you no more information upon it than I have given.

12,716. Whom is it your belief that you employed?—My belief is that it was Crooks.

12,717. Was any person else besides Crooks engaged in that blowing up?—I do not recollect that there was.

12,718. Can you swear that no one else was engaged in it?—No, I cannot do that. If there was, my impression is that they would be employed by himself if there was anyone besides.

12,719. How much did you give him for that?—I do not know.

12,720. But about how much; was it a large sum?—No.

12,721. It was a dangerous thing to do?—Yes, but it would not be a large sum.

12,722. How much was it; was it 10*l.*?—I do not think it would be that.

12,723. How much?—It might be 5*l.*, but I do not know what it would be. I do not want to be making a lot of statements about a man that have never occurred.

13,724. Did Helliwell work for Firth?—There were two Helliwells, and they were brothers.

12,725. Did one of the Helliwells work at Firth's?—They both worked at Firth's at one time. I think so.

12,726. Have you ever employed Crooks to watch at Firth's in order to shoot Helliwell?—I think he was employed, but I do not remember that it was defined what it was to be. He was to do something to stop him.

12,727. Now, upon your oath, was it not to shoot him?—It is unnecessary to put the oath to me; I should speak the truth.

12,728. Very well, I will not put it to you in that form. Was it to shoot him?—I do not think it was.

12,729. Do you believe that it was or that it was not?—I believe it was not.

12,730. What do you believe that it was to do?—I believe it was to stop him from working.

12,731. How to stop him from working?—By maiming a limb or something of that kind.

12,732. Did Crooks tell you that he was there watching for many nights?—I believe he did.

12,733. And did he tell you that on one occasion he got on to the Midland railway in order to shoot at him?—I do not remember that.

12,734. Did he tell you that he went on the Midland railway every night to shoot at him?—I do not remember his telling me that.

12,735. Firth's is close to the Midland railway, is it not?—Yes.

12,736. Did he never tell you that he went on the Midland line every night to shoot him?—Stop a bit. On one occasion (now that you remind me) he told me something about getting on the Midland railway. That might be the occasion. I think it was.

12,737. Did he not tell you that he got his gun up to shoot at him, but that Woodhead's head came between him and Helliwell's, and he did not shoot?—I do not remember that. He told me that he had watched him, and now you remind me, he told me something about having a gun for the purpose, but I do not remember that.

12,738. Did he tell you that he had got his gun and was standing on the railway about to shoot when he came from work, but that Woodhead's head was between him and Helliwell, and he did not shoot?—Well, I do not remember that.

12,739. Did he ever mention Woodhead's being there and interfering with his shooting?—I have no recollection of it.

12,740. Now, did he shoot him or not?—I think not.

12,741. Did he tell you the reason why?—I think he said that he could not get a chance or something.

12,742. How long was he trying to get a chance to shoot him?—I do not know.

12,743. Is that your handwriting (*handing a paper to the witness*)? *The witness hesitated.* You need not read it?—No.

12,744. You know your own handwriting; is that your writing or not?—I really cannot say.

12,745. Do you mean to tell me you do not know your own handwriting?—It is, very likely it is.

12,746. Do you not believe it is?—I am disposed to think so, but I cannot be certain.

12,747. I see it is not in your usual hand. Do you write in different hands occasionally?—I have done so.

12,748. It is addressed, I see, to "Mr. John "Helliwell, saw grinder, at Messrs. Firth and Sons, "Saw Manufacturers, Saville Street, Sheffield," and it bears the post mark of August the 24th, but the year does not appear. I cannot make out the year. "To Messrs. Firth and Sons, saw grinders,— "Gentlemen,—The game works merrily, and we "brush away all obstacles before us. If we appear "to be rather long about it you see we are none the "less sure. It is your turn next, and the man that "hangs back will be the first to get it; and if I but "move my finger you are sent to eternity as sure as "faith. Be advised, and take the hint in time." Do you think you wrote that letter?—I think I did.

12,749. Was any person concerned in the attempt to shoot Helliwell besides Crooks?—I do not know.

12,750. Yes you do know quite well?—I do not.

12,751. You do know?—I do not.

12,752. Was any person concerned in the attempt to shoot Helliwell besides Crooks?—I do not know.

12,753. Will you swear that no other person was employed by you to watch Helliwell?—I do not remember.

12,754. Will you swear there was no one else employed?—I know of no one but Crooks.

12,755. I warn you again. You may be attempting to screen other people. It is very easy to implicate Crooks, who has already implicated himself; you may be attempting now to screen another. I ask you whether there is any other person besides Crooks?—I do not know of any other person.

12,756. Was there no other person besides Crooks employed to watch him?—Not by me.

12,757. By anybody that you know of?—I think I have heard Crooks say that he got somebody.

12,758. Who was the man that he got?—I do not know who the man was.

12,759. I tell you distinctly that it does not satisfy my mind (I do not know whether it satisfies the minds of my colleagues) that you do not know who that other man was?—I do not.

12,760. You persist in that?—I persist in that. I think I have heard them call him by the name of "Nunk."

12,761. What does "Nunk" mean?—I do not know.

12,762. Do you know a man who goes by the name of "Nunk"?—No.

12,763. But you say that Crooks told you that he had got with him a man who went by the name of "Nunk"?—That is the impression that I had.

12,764. Did you never ask him who it was?—No, I never wanted to know.

12,765. You have been talking with him this morning; it will not do to screen anybody; tell me who this man "Nunk" was?—I can tell you no more.

12,766. Why was Helliwell to be shot at; had you had a quarrel with Helliwell?—No.

12,767. Helliwell and his wife had come to your house, and he had offered 10*l*. to be admitted into the Union, had he not?—But you are in error there. It was the brother that was attempted to be shot at.

12,768. Quite right. Was this Helliwell that was to be shot a member of your Union?—At one time he was but not then.

12,769. What was the name of the Helliwell that was to be shot?—John.

12,770. What was the thing which caused offence to the trade with regard to Helliwell?—He left the society. There had been a dispute at Newbold's respecting price. He was one of the men that left Newbold's, but I don't know how far that affair had connexion with this; but this is a circumstance that occurred; he left Newbold's.

12,771. But what was it that caused him particularly to be selected by you as a proper person to be maimed in his limbs?—On account of his leaving the society and going to Firth's and working at discount, and I think he had an apprentice boy or two. I think that was it.

12,772. Had his matters frequently been brought before the Union?—You see you are pressing me very closely upon questions, and I want to be very careful. I am here, let the consequences be what they may. I know they are serious to me, but of course I must bear them. I want to be truthful upon it, and I do not want to exceed the truth.

12,773. Had Helliwell's case been frequently brought before the Union?—Those outrages and those matters were never transacted to my knowledge by the trade.

12,774. I did not ask you that. I asked you whether Helliwell's case had frequently been brought before the committee of the Union?—It had frequently been talked about.

12,775. Had his name been called over at the general meeting?—I do not remember, but there is no doubt it has.

12,776. Had any entry been made in the books saying that he was open to censure?—I do not remember such an entry. Whatever you find in those books is truthfully recorded. If it is there, it is a fact.

12,777. Do you recollect whether the Union were very angry with Helliwell for the course that he had pursued?—There was a very strong feeling among the members.

12,778. Was he ever rattened?—I think he was.

12,779. How long before this was he rattened?—I think that would be at the Tower Wheel. I cannot say whether it would be before or after; but I think he was rattened.

12,780. Are you not quite aware that he had been rattened before, and that it had not succeeded?—My impression is that he had been rattened before, and that it had succeeded.

12,781. But if he had been rattened before and it had succeeded, he had still violated your laws afterwards, had he not, by going to Firth's?—Just so

12,782. Therefore the rattening did not do any good?—No.

12,783. Was it in consequence of the rattening not being successful that you then adopted the resolution of maiming him in his limbs?—Very likely it would be so.

12,784. Do you know how many times he was rattened before this happened?—No, I do not.

12,785. He was not shot?—I think not.

12,786. What was done? Was his case brought again before committee?—Those affairs we are talking of, those outrages were no part of the trade's at all. I did it in the interest of the trade, but not by their authority, or with their knowledge.

12,787. Do you recollect that 12 days before Firth's boiler was blown up a canister of powder was put down the chimney of Samuel Baxter, a saw grinder, at Loxley?—I remember that circumstance. I do not know what length of time it was.

12,788. But a short time before. It was on the 24th of May 1854?—I remember the circumstance.

12,789. Do you know who put that there?—I think it was Crooks.

12,790. Was anybody else engaged in doing it?—I am not aware.

12,791. Now it is not a likely thing that you should not know it.—Well, I am not aware.

12,792. I caution you again. Will you swear that nobody but Crooks put that can down that chimney?—I am speaking to the best of my knowledge.

12,793. Will you swear that nobody but Crooks put that can of gunpowder down that chimney?—I can swear to nothing beyond this, that it was done with my knowledge.

12,794. Did you pay Crooks for doing it?—I believe I did.

12,795. How much did you pay him?—I do not know. I cannot remember.

12,796. What is your belief as to the amount? Was it 10*l*., or 5*l*., or 3*l*., or what was it?—It would not be less than 5*l*.

12,797. Are you aware that Samuel Baxter's chimney had a can of gunpowder put into it on the 24th of May?—Yes.

12,798. That Firth's was blown up on June the 5th, and that Elisha Parker was shot on the same day?—I am aware that those circumstances took place, but I am not aware——

12,799. Do you mean to say that the man who blew up Firth's was engaged also in Elisha Parker's business on the same day?—No.

12,800. You say that Peace shot Parker?—I said

FOURTEENTH DAY.

W. Broadhead.

21 June 1867.

Peace engaged to do it. My understanding was that Peace was only a man between the actual party and myself.

12,801. He hired the man?—Yes, and he was a servant of his own.

12,802. Is there any other matter to which you can call our attention?—Yes, there is the Hereford Street outrage.

12,803. But before we go to that I would call your attention to another incident. You recollect Linley being shot. He was shot at your instigation was he not?—Yes.

12,804. He was shot at first on November the 12th 1857. He was ultimately shot on August the 1st 1859, and he died I believe in the February following. Is not that so?—He died in six or eight months afterwards.

12,805. Did you know a person of the name of Poole, who lived in a house in the Wicker?—No.

12,806. Do you not know that Linley had a brother-in-law of the name of Poole?—I know he had a brother-in-law a butcher, but I do not know his name.

12,807. He is a butcher in the Wicker is he not?—Yes.

12,808. Are you not aware that on the 11th of January, 1859, six months before Linley was shot, a can of gunpowder was thrown into this man's house in the Wicker?—I remember the circumstance.

12,809. By whose authority was that done?—By mine.

12,810. Whom did you employ to do it?—Crooks.

12,811. What did you give him for that?—I do not remember.

12,812. But what would it be worth for a man to risk his life; because if he were detected in throwing gunpowder into a place where persons were living he would be liable to be hanged, what would you pay him for that?—I do not remember what it was, but it would be 5*l.* or 10*l.*

12,813. Now you see you had not mentioned that until I reminded you of it?—No.

12,814. Is there anything else now? you are not very candid; is there any other occasion on which you have employed him?—I do not remember any.

12,815. Do you know that on November 4th 1859 Joseph Wilson's house was attempted to be blown up?—Yes.

12,816. Did you cause that to be done?—Yes.

12,817. Whom did you employ to do that?—Crooks.

12,818. Did you employ anyone else?—No.

12,819. You swear that?—Yes.

12,820. How much did you give him for doing that?—I cannot remember.

12,821. Yes you can?—I have told you the truth; I shall tell you all I know now.

12,822. How much did you give him for that?—I cannot tell you that.

12,823. But did you give him 20*l.* for blowing up a man and his family?—I do not think it was anything like that.

12,824. How much do you think it would be?—I think somewhere about the same amount as was named before.

12,825. Would it be 10*l.*?—Somewhere about that probably; I do not know exactly.

12,826. I did not ask you before as I ought to have done, what was the offence which that man at Loxley had committed?—He was one of Firth's men.

12,827. Was that his only fault?—He was keeping aloof from the trade and he had received a great deal of money out of the society and I thought he ought to contribute.

12,828. Do you know whether he was a man with a family, and that his family was living with him in the house at the time that this can of gunpowder was put down his chimney?—He had a family but I think they were all grown up.

12,829. Were they living with him?—I think not.

12,830. Was his wife with him?—Yes; I do not know whether his family were living with him.

12,831. You had had no quarrel with him except on trade matters?—No.

12,832. Had you had any quarrel with Wilson?—No, only difference upon affairs of the trade.

12,833. What was your object in throwing a can of gunpowder into Poole's house, the butcher in the Wicker?—The object was to bring Linley to.

12,834. Were you to hurt Linley by it?—It was to alarm him and to cause him to come into the trade. We hazarded the consequence.

12,835. Did Linley lodge at his brother-in-law's?—Yes, I think he did.

12,836. This poor butcher then had nothing to do with you?—No.

12,837. Was this butcher a married man? had he a family who lived with him?—I do not know He was married of course, he married Linley's sister.

12,838. But was his wife alive?—The butcher's wife?

12,839. Yes?—Yes.

12,840. Now what had Wilson done?—Well, he had set the society at defiance, and determined to have no one connected with the Union.

12,841. Do you know a person of the name of Harry Holdsworth?—Yes.

12,842. Did you do anything to him?—Yes.

12,843. I believe that was on the 1st December 1861?—Yes.

12,844. What did you do to Holdsworth?—The place was blown up.

12,845. You put, or caused to be put, I believe, (I do not say that you did it), a quantity of powder in the cellar of his manufactory?—Yes, I think that was it.

12,846. Whom did you employ to do that?—Crooks.

12,847. No one else?—No.

12,848. Was anybody else engaged in it besides Crooks?—I do not know; I think not.

12,849. What did you give him for that?—I think it was somewhere about 6*l.*

12,850. Do you recollect that in 1863 on June the 7th there was an attempt made to blow up Reaney's engine house in Bernard Street?—Yes.

12,851. Who did that?—Crooks.

12,852. Any one else?—I do not know.

12,853. Mind what you say?—I had nothing to do with anybody else.

12,854. Did Crooks ever tell you of any person who helped him in any of those jobs?—The jobs named?

12,855. Yes? — There is this "Nunk" that I spoke of.

12,856. How often did he mention "Nunk"?—I cannot say.

12,857. How many times do you believe that he told you that "Nunk" helped him?—I cannot tell how many times, not in all the cases.

12,858. In all but which cases?—I cannot select them.

12,859. Tell me in which cases he said that "Nunk" helped him?—Well, a many of them, but I cannot select the cases. Of course there was Hallam in the cases that are named.

12,860. We know that, but did he never mention anybody besides Hallam and Nunk?—Not in the cases named that I know of.

12,861. Did he ever mention anybody else in any other cases (not in the cases named), besides Hallam and Nunk?—Yes.

12,862. Whom did he mention?—Copley.

12,863. In what case did he say that Copley helped him?—The Hereford Street outrage.

12,864. Now, what had Reaney done?—Fearnehough had gone there to work.

12,865. How much did you give him for doing that?—I cannot remember.

12,866. I did not ask you what Holdsworth had done to have his place blown up?—He was employing men not belonging to the society.

12,867. Then you had had no private quarrel with

him and that was the only ground?—That was the only ground.

12,868. You say you do not recollect what you paid for Reaney's house, but how much do you believe it was?—I could only fix about the same amount as the others.

12,869. Was it 10*l.*?—I should scarcely think it was as much.

12,870. Not to blow up a man's house?—Reaney's was a wheel I think.

12,871. Do you think that it would be 6*l.*? had you a regular settled price for blowing up a place?—There is no fixed price, but it would not vary a great deal.

12,872. But what was the general price? — It might be 5*l.*, or 6*l.*, or a little more according to the difficulties.

12,873. Mr. Chance tells me that you have not told us how much you gave Crooks for watching Helliwell with a view of shooting him?—I think I told you that I could not recollect.

12,874. What is your belief? about how much was it?—I can but fix it at that amount which has been named before.

12,875. What is that?—Varying from 5*l.* to 10*l.*

12,876. Is there any other matter in which you have employed him?—I do not recollect.

12,877. You called my attention to the Hereford Street outrage?—Yes.

12,878. On October the 8th 1866 Thomas Fearnehough's house in Hereford Street was blown up?—Yes.

12,879. Who caused that to be done?—Me.

12,880. Whom did you employ?—Crooks.

12,881. Who did that?—Crooks.

12,882. You said just now that Copley did it?—Copley was with him. He told me so; I do not know that he was, but I have no doubt that it is correct.

12,883. Copley is a member of the Union I believe as well as Crooks?—Yes.

12,884. Have you ever seen Copley on the subject?—No; Copley and I never exhanged a word on the subject at all, at any time.

12,885. How much did you give Crooks for doing that?—I think it was 15*l.*

12,886. You had no quarrel with Fearnehough either, it was only a trade matter I believe?—That was all.

12,887. Did you introduce Hallam to Broomhead?—I do not recollect.

12,888. May you have done so; did Broomhead ever apply to you for a fit man to do a job for him?—(*The witness hesitated.*)

12,889. Did Broomhead ever apply to you for a fit man to do a job for him?—I am trying to think on it.

12,890. Do so by all means, do not be hurried.—(*After a pause*) I do not remember.

12,891. You would not say that he did not?—No; but I do not remember.

12,892. Did you not tell Broomhead that he was the man who would what was wanted in Sutcliffe's case?—I have no recollection of it.

12,893. Will you swear that you did not tell Broomhead that Hallam was a fit man to do his business in Sutcliffe's case?—I do not remember.

12,894. Will you swear that you did not?—No.

12,895. Did you know of Sutcliffe's case?—I never knew of it until my attention was drawn to it in the court.

12,896. Did you never hear of it at the time?—Not to notice it.

12,897. Then you may have told Broomhead that Hallam was a fit man to do a job for him?—I may have done so but I do not remember.

12,898. You will not swear that you did not?—No.

12,899. Has he ever applied to you for a fit man to do a job of that kind?—Well I think that he has at some time said something of that kind.

12,900. He has said something to you?—I think he has.

12,901. You know whether a man has said such a thing to you or not?—No.

12,902. Oh! Yes you know that. I have tried you with all leniency, but to tell me that you do not know whether a man has asked you to find a fit man to do such a job as this for him is simply trifling with one's understanding.—And if I were to say that I did, it would be simply hazarding a statement which I could not be sure had taken place.

12,903. You will not swear whether Broomhead applied to you or not?—No.

12,904. What is your belief?—I believe he never did make such an application, he may have mentioned such a thing when we casually met together and I think I remember hearing some conversation, but I have no recollection.

12,905. What was the substance of the conversation which you think you remember?—Talking about some one that would be likely; but I cannot remember where, nor do I think that I pointed any one out.

12,906. You knew that Broomhead was the secretary of the Pen and Pocket Grinders Blade Union?—Yes; I knew him.

12,907. And what you meant by a man that was likely, was a man who was likely to do some act of violence on trade matters?—With Broomhead I think we had once some conversation.

12,908. About a man who would do some act of violence in a trade matter?—Yes; but I do not recollect ever naming one.

12,909. You talked to Broomhead? have you ever talked to any other secretary of any other Union as to a fit person to do an act of violence in a trade matter?—I do not remember.

12,910. Mind; have you ever talked to the secretary of any other Union as to finding or knowing a fit man to do an act of violence in a trade matter?—I do not remember.

12,911. Will you swear you have not?—No; because if I could do that I could engage to say what conversation I had had with people; I do not remember.

12,912. Have you had conversations with secretaries of other Unions about their defaulters?—Oh! frequently about defaulters; nothing was more common; pardon me, I think I catch what you are wanting to get at.

12,913. I daresay you do. What do you catch?—The branches of the saw trade.

12,914. What occurs to your mind on the discovery of that fact?—The officers of the branches of the saw trade and I have frequently arranged ourselves for rattenings to be done.

12,915. What officers have you arranged with? mention them.—William Hague, Henry Skidmore, and the secretaries of the Handle Makers and the Jobbing Grinders too.

12,916. Who were they?—I am speaking of that, I remember Holdsworth's case was a joint affair between them and me.

12,917. What do mean by saying it was a joint affair between them and you?—To be at the expense of it.

12,918. Were you the treasurer of the Amalgamated Society?—Yes; of the saw trade.

12,919. Are you the treasurer also of the National Association?—I was until last night, when I resigned.

12,920. What is the National Association?—It is an association composed of various trades throughout the kingdom.

12,921. What office did you hold in it?—I was treasurer.

12,922. When where you treasurer?—Up to last evening.

12,923. For how long a time had you been treasurer?—Since its creation.

12,924. Which are the trades that are in the National Association?—Indeed I cannot tell you that; there are so many.

12,925. Are all the Sheffield trades in it?—Not all, many out of Sheffield.

12,926. Does it involve the carpenters and the

FOURTEENTH DAY.

W. Broadhead.

21 June 1867.

joiners, and the masons and tailors?—Yes, it involves———

12,927. (*To Dronfield*); I believe you are the Secretary, are you not?—Yes.

12,928. Can you furnish me with a list of the various trades?—I have not them, but I can get them.

12,929. I wish you would if you please, I should very much like to see what they are?—I have not them now.

12,930. Not now, to-morrow morning will do?—I will get them.

12,931. (*To the witness*:) How long has the National Association been created?—Since last Christmas.

12,932. Do you know what are its objects?—Its objects are to resist lock-outs.

12,933. Lock-outs by masters?—Yes.

12,934. Are there subscriptions to this National Association?—Yes.

12,935. What is paid by the members?—According to the requirements.

12,936. What has been paid to this association? do you know how many members there are in Sheffield?—I could not say; 6,000 or 8,000, or something of that sort. Mr. Dronfield is better acquainted with the numbers than I am.

12,937. And how many do you think it extends to in the kingdom?—Well, I think it would extend to something like about 60,000.

12,938. Is this the head place of them?—Yes.

12,939. And you are its principal officer?—No, Mr. Austin is the principal officer; Mr. Dronfield is the secretary, ; and I have been treasurer up to last evening. Mr. Austin is president.

12,940. What is Mr. Austin?—He is a railway spring maker, and secretary to the Railway Spring Makers' Union.

12,941. Who is the secretary?—Mr. Dronfield.

12,942. And you are the treasurer?—I was up to last evening.

12,943. Do you know what money has been collected during the time that you have been treasurer? —No; I cannot tell that, Mr. Dronfield has the account, the books will show.

12,944. But what was the subscription that parties paid to resist this lock-out?—They paid by levies; there are two levies of $\frac{1}{2}$d. per head I think, levied every year for working expenses. It has power to levy further sums per head according to the requirements.

12,945. Who is to judge of that?—The Judicial Council.

12,946. Where do they sit?—They have sat hitherto I think at Sheffield.

12,947. Were you a member of that Judicial Council?—No, not beyond that as treasurer, I am one of the executive, or was one.

12,948. Do you know what money has been raised in Sheffield?—I cannot tell here; the books would show.

12,949. But could you give us a sort of general notion; have you raised thousands of pounds?—There have been some thousands, I should think.

12,950. How many thousands of pounds according to your recollection have been raised?—Not many thousands.

12,951. 10,000*l.*?—No.

12,952. 5,000*l.*?—Not 2,000*l.* I think.

Mr. Sugg stated that he was instructed that the National Association had had nothing whatever to do with these matters in any way.

Witness.—Permit me to say that there is no connection in any degree whatever between associations of that description, and such cases as are now being examined into by the Commission; and I am anxious that that should be most clearly understood.

12,953. Let me put that down. I am glad to have it, and it is fair that it should be clearly understood. That society has no connection with any trade outrage whatever?—No.

12,954. Then there is another society besides this National Society, of which you are treasurer, and that it is called the Amalgamated Society?—Yes, of the organised trades of Sheffield, and I wish to say the same thing of that association.

12,955. So I understand. Are you still treasurer of that Association?—Yes, but I intend to resign.

Mr. Sugg stated that he was instructed by Mr. Dronfield, the secretary of the National Association to say that that association had nothing whatever to do with any local trades in any way, or with the Defence Committee in this matter, and that they had not subscribed a single farthing in any way connected with it; and he requested the Court to examine Mr. Broadhead as to the position and functions of the Judicial Council.

12,956. (*Chairman to the witness.*) Would you prefer to retire for a short time or to go on with your examination till it is finished?—I should like to get it over as soon as I can.

12,957. I do not go into the question of the National Association; I understand it has nothing all to do with this, but it is merely to resist lock outs generally?—That is all.

12,958. And is composed of most of the trades in England?—Yes.

12,959. And they have had the misfortune to have you for their treasurer?—Yes.

12,960. What are the amalgamated trades of Sheffield?—The amalgamated trades of Sheffield is formed for the purpose of aiding and assisting each other, as far as each trade may see necessary, or be in a position to do, the funds being in the hands of each individual society, given according to the circumstances or otherwise. There are three levies each year of one penny per head for the working of the society, such as printing, indorsing, appeals for aid and assistance to other trades, issuing reports and so forth.

12,961. That is the object of the society?—Yes.

12,962. To assist one another in case of strikes?—Yes, or lock outs.

12,963. Now I will go back to Linley's affair. After Linley was shot at, and also after he was killed, did not you write a series of letters to the papers, pronouncing your great abhorrence of the perpetrators of that deed?—I did, and for this I know that I shall be held up to the execration of the whole world.

12,964. After Wheatman's place was blown up, did you not put a letter in the paper suggesting that Messrs. Wheatman had blown up the place themselves?—I never said so, but I conveyed this inference: while they were charging the trades with it, there were causes to suppose that it was just as likely to emanate from the manufacturers as from the trades; and the arguments which I adduced were based upon facts that had taken place; I never thought——

12,965. Now, I beg you not to go on like this—I want to speak truthfully.

12,966. I have here private information; this is a letter of yours that appeared in the *Independent* of the 4th of January, 1862. Did you not in that letter say,—"I have better evidence than any that has been "advanced, of suspicion pointing quite in another "quarter, and that is to their own order"?—Yes, that is correct, but if you will read forward to the end you will find that I qualified it.

12,967. Did you say,—"On the very day or the "night on which the outrage was committed a saw "manufacturer expressed his regret and disappoint-"ment strongly in my presence at the small amount "of damage done"?—Yes, and that is the truth; but I at the same time stated that I did not believe that that gentleman did entertain opinions of that kind, and he expressed regret afterwards that he had said as much, I merely mentioned it as an argument to show that it might arise from a cause of that kind, I at the same time was fully convinced that that gentleman had nothing to do with it. In fact, knowing as I did that it was my own act, he could not be guilty of it.

12,968. But you wished the public to believe that it was done by a manufacturer, and not by the trades?

—No, I wished them to understand this, that while they imputed this to the trade from motives of difference there were motives on the other side.

12,969. And therefore you wished it to be imputed that the other side had done it ?—Yes, as far as motives went; that motives might be taken into account.

12,970. That the act might be the act of the masters ?—Yes, that was used to shield the wrong that I had done, and if you will permit me to make the observation, I took this view (wrongly, as I expressed yesterday if you will), that there being no law for the trades I conceived the notion that I had a right to take those courses in the absence of the law, and that the end would justify the means. They were acts that in the whole course of my lifetime in my own private capacity, and the character I have maintained is as spotless as any man's ——

12,971. You have really maintained a spotless character, have you ?—Yes, but I lent myself to those things, and I lent myself to them for their interest and benefit, and brought myself to this shame and disgrace, so that I sincerely hope and trust you will permit me —— but as far as my private transactions went, do not let me be misunderstood ——.

12,972. I think you had better go on; I do not wish you to be misunderstood. Did you in that letter which you wrote, describe this as a hellish deed, blowing up Wheatman ?—I think I did.

12,973. You blew up Mr. Wilson, too ?—Yes.

12,974. When Mr. Wilson came forward to explain how he had been blown up, and his family put in peril, was it you who suggested that he had been summoned before the magistrates for cruelty to his apprentices? —I believed I named it. At that time I had no intention of making this confession.

12,975. I suppose not. Do you recollect that when a person stated that you had directed him to your hen-roost ?—Yes, and I want to state something relative to that.

12,976. And that you had pointed out to him to go on to an adjoining house, and to look on to a bench, where he would find a quantity of bands; you came up to me and said that you should satisfy me beyond all doubt that these were superfluous bands ?—Yes, and those bands that he spoke of, if any were there, belonged to the society.

12,977. You still stick to that ?—I stick to that most firmly; but I believe there were no bands there at all.

12,978. Then why did you send him there ?—He suggested it; he said he wanted his bands, and he said something about their being in the chamber, and then I said: " Then go and look for them thyself," but I had stumbled upon the nuts though I knew nothing about their being there, and I thought that as they had placed the nuts there as he had suggested they might have placed the bands there, and that therefore he might look for them there; but why did he not bring them down there himself? they were not there; that is the truth.

12,979. After Fearnehough was blown up did you not address a letter to the newspapers, in which you described the conduct of the perpetrators as of the most infamous description ?—Yes, I did.

12,980. Did you at the same time say that Fearnehough's conduct was as bad as it could be, and almost merited what he met with ?—Yes, and I really thought it did.

12,981. Do you still continue of that opinion ?—No.

12,982. Did you offer a reward out of your own pocket for the discovery of the perpetrators of that offence ?—Yes I thought it would never be called for.

12,983. You offered a reward of 5*l.* did you not ?—Yes.

12,984. Did your Union offer a sum of money for the discovery of the perpetrators ?—Yes, and they were induced to do it by me.

12,985. Then but for you they never would have done it ?—I cannot say that.

12,986. I thought you said they were induced to offer a reward by you ?—So they were; I mean they were induced to offer the reward.

12,987. And but for you there would have been no reward offered by them ?—It is very likely not.

12,988. Now were you very much censured for the letter which you had written in the paper after Fearnehough's blowing up ?—Yes.

12,989. There was a meeting of your body, and you offered your resignation, I believe ?—Yes.

12,990. You protested your innocence before them did you not ?—Yes.

12,991. Was there a meeting of your body and did they then pass a resolution saying that they had the most perfect confidence in you ?—Yes.

12,992. A vote of confidence was passed in your favour and you were pressed to become secretary again ?—Yes.

12,993. I believe a gentleman of the name of Mr. Verity came down to Sheffield did he not ?—Yes.

12,994. Was that after the Hereford Street outrage ?—No.

12,995. How long was it before it ? was it shortly after the Acorn Street murder ?—I think it was.

12,996. Mr. Verity I believe, was a gentleman who delivered lectures in favour of Trades' Unions was he not ?—Yes.

12,997. And your conduct was then the subject of considerable reproach was it not by many people at that time ?—For what ?

12,998. Why they even said that you had to do with that murder in Acorn Street did they not ?—Oh ! yes they did.

12,999. Did you not hear Mr. Verity describe you as a man possessed of a calm Christian spirit ?—I heard Mr. Verity speak complimentarily of me.

13,000. Did he not speak of your " calm Christian " spirit " ?—I could not quote his exact words.

13,001. You had enjoyed a good character up to that time and so had imposed upon the world ?—Yes.

13,002. While we are upon that subject I will ask you a question; where you engaged in the Acorn Street murder ?—Not at all, I am as innocent as the child that is unborn of anything of that, and I wish I was as innocent of all the rest.

13,003. Do you know who was concerned in it ?—No; I know nothing of it.

13,004. Is there any murder or any blowing up (not in your own union only) of which you have knowledge beside those which you have mentioned this morning ?—Within what period ?

13,005. Within ten years ?—No.

13,006. Do you know anything about Tyzack's case ?—No.

13,007. Do you not know that Crooks shot at Tyzack? —No; I know nothing whatever about it; nothing.

13,008. Are you sure about that ?—I am quite sure. Permit me the phrase, you are quite off the scent about that so far as I am concerned.

13,009. I am off the scent am I ?—As far as I am concerned.

13,010. Which way does the scent run ? — Not towards me. Therefore——

13,011. What do you know about Tyzack's case ?—I know nothing.

13,012. Then why do you say that I am off the scent ? — Because you directed yourself to me. Therefore you are off the scent.

13,013. Do you know who shot Tyzack ?—No; I know nothing whatever of it; I neither was connected with it nor have I the slightest knowledge of who was connected with it. That is what I mean.

13,014. I understand you. Before I go further did you once offer a boy 5*l.* to steal some bands ?—I offered him a sum of money.

13,015. It was the case of Dawson at Butcher's works was it not ?—It was at Butcher's works but not Dawson, it was Frith.

13,016. Was it not a sum of 5*l.* ?—I have forgotten what the amount was.

13,017. Was it not 5*l.* ?—It might be.

FOURTEENTH DAY.

W. Broadhead.

21 June 1867.

13,018. To steal some bands ?—Not to steal them.

13,019. To take them ?—Yes.

13,020. From Butcher's ?—From Butcher's wheel.

13,021. Was that matter investigated, and was it brought to the knowledge of Mr. Dronfield, that you had offered a boy 5*l*. to take those bands from Butcher's wheel ?—Mr Dronfield never knew anything of it.

13,022. Was there not a letter in the newspaper by a person of the name of James Dodworth ?—Yes.

13,023. Did he not state in that letter that you had offered that money and that the matter had been brought before Mr. Dronfield, the secretary of the organised society, and that you had not denied that you had done so ?—And that I had not denied ?

13,024. Yes ?—I had denied.

13,025. No ; you never denied that you had done so.—I had denied that I had done this when I had done it.

13,026. Mr. Dodworth says : "When I got this " information I told Mr. Dawson I should use it and " suggested we should relate it to Mr. Dronfield as " a member of the organised trades (and as one who " we thought wished right things) with a view to its " being inquired into, and the same information was " repeated to him by Mr. Dawson in my presence. " He said it should be inquired into. I afterwards " went to Mr. Broadhead and related it to him. I " asked him 'Is it true or false ?' He said it was " false that the brother had threatened him, but he " could not then remember the whole of the circum- " stances to give an answer as to whether the boy's " statement was true, but he said, although I had not " mentioned any names to him, he well knew who the " parties were that I had referred to ?"—Yes, but Mr. Dodworth made a wrong statement about that, I called Mr. Dodworth's attention to it. The statement that I made to Mr. Dodworth at the time he came to me was this : I listened to his statement, and after I had listened to the end of his statement, I commenced by telling him that when he commenced his statement I was at a loss to understand who it was he alluded to, but when he came to mention the boy's brother as having come to me, I remembered the circumstance of a person of the name of Frith coming and charging me with offering to pay his brother 5*l*., which I told him was not the case; and from that circumstance I told Mr. Dodworth I remembered then the circumstances that he had alluded to, but of course denying that such was the case ; but it was the case.

13,027. Did you deny it to Mr. Dodworth ?—I denied it to Mr. Dodworth.

13,028. Did you deny that you had ever given 5*l*. to the boy to steal some bands ?—Not given—offered.

13,029. You denied that ? — I denied to Mr. Dodworth that I had ever offered it.

13,030. Did you deny it to Mr. Dronfield ?—I denied to Mr. Dronfield that I had ever offered it.

13,031. Then it was never known that you had offered it to anybody ?—It was never known that I had offered it to anybody. I said that I had never known that it was ever offered to anybody. That is as you put the question to me.

13,032. Now you have mentioned one or two names, and only one or two names. I call your attention to the fact that in all those outrages, blowing up houses, shooting at people, and so on, Crooks and "Nunk" are the only persons whose names you mention ?—Are they the only persons ?

13,033. And Copley and Peace ?—Yes.

13,034. This is a practice which has been going on for 10 years ?—It extends further.

13,035. Do you think that we believe you when you state that those are the only parties whose names you can mention ?—I cannot tell what you believe, but I have the consciousness within me that I have spoken the truth.

13,036. Is there no other man whom you can mention who has been mixed up with these outrages ?—None that I can mention.

13,037. You swear that ?—I swear that—to my knowledge.

13,038. That there is no other man of whom you know who has been mixed up with these transactions ?—Not to my knowledge.

13,039. Has Clarke been mixed up with these matters ?—Only in the way I have named.

13,040 In what way ?—In Helliwell's affair.

13,041. Has he to your knowledge been mixed up with any other affairs ?—He has been at rattenings at various times, but I could not select any.

13,042. Has he been constantly employed by you to ratten other people ?—Rattenings got done in the way described.

13,043. And have you employed him for that purpose ?—I may have done so as I stated yesterday, but I could not select one. As a general rule they were taken in the way I described to you.

13,044. Had he a general retainer from you to ratten ?—He would get paid by me when the money was obtained from the parties whom he had rattened.

13,045. Then he had authority from you to ratten on his own behalf, with the understanding that you would pay him whenever he did it ?—It was an authority of this description ; that any person being in arrear was subject to this sort of thing, and it could be ascertained without appealing to me, from the books as I have described.

13,046. Did you authorise any one person besides Clarke to ratten on behalf of the society ?—No doubt there has been.

13,047. Whom have you authorized besides Clarke ?—I cannot call them to memory.

13,048. Yes you can. Mind, you are in great peril if you do not do so. What do you say to Garfit ?—Garfit has been in a rattening.

13,049. Has Garfit been employed by you to ratten ?—He has been at them, I think, but do not let me put men into things that I know nothing about. I can say no more than I have done.

13,050. Yes you can. You know whether you have employed Garfit or not ?—I can say no more.

13,051. I am not inquiring into a particular fact ; I want to know as a fact whether you have employed Garfit to do rattening for you ?—I do not remember.

13,052. Will you swear that you have not employed Garfit to do rattening for you ?—I cannot call to recollection any particular act.

13,053. Will you swear that you have not employed Garfit to do rattening for you ?—I can give you no more information than I have done.

13,054. Will you swear that you have not employed Garfit to do rattening for you ?—I will neither swear that I have nor that I have not.

13,055. Do you mean to say that you do not know whether you have employed men to do rattening ?—I mean to say that I cannot speak to Garfit.

13,056. Has Garfit done rattening ?—I believe he has.

13,057. Have you paid him money for doing it ?—I cannot say; I do not remember paying him money.

13,058. Will you swear that you have not paid him money ?—I cannot in a number of cases ; it is only in a case of this description I must bear the infliction.

13,059. You have done those deeds and you must know. Is Garfit one of them ?—I intend you to know, as far as I can give you the information.

13,060. I am not complaining. I will see how you go on ?—I can give you no further information than I have given.

13,061. Do you believe Garfit to have been at them ?—I believe Garfit to have been in the rattening, but I can give you no more information.

13,062. Has Garfit been in at the blowings up ?—No; I do not think he has been in at any, none to my knowledge.

13,063. Copley has been at one blowing up ?—I only know of one name, and I do not know that from him ; we never had a word of conversation.

13,064. Has he been in at rattenings for you ?—Yes;

FOURTEENTH DAY.

W. Broadhead.

21 June 1867.

I think he has; in fact I think he was named the other day as one.

13,065. Has he been employed by you often to ratten?—Often.

13,066. How often?—Well I cannot say how often it might be. I have told you that there have been many cases of rattening.

13,067. Can you tell me the names of persons whom you have paid for rattening? You will protect them best by telling their names, because if they do not come forward and we find them out they will be punished.—I am trying to get out that but I cannot.

13,068. It is an opportunity which no country has ever before afforded to criminals, I believe?—I am doing all that I can.

13,069. And if criminals like to come forward and state what they have done they have the means of escaping from punishment. It is the only opportunity that has ever occurred that I am aware of, and now your best mode of serving your friends as you may call them is by coming forward and telling their names, if you know anything about them.

13,070. (*Mr. Chance*). And of serving your turn too.—I want to do what I can. I remember one occasion but I cannot give them all in detail; I remember on one occasion Mr. Armitage being rattened and that was done by some of his own men working at the place.

13,071. Tell me the names of the men who did it?—I cannot give you the names, Hallam was I think connected as one. He worked for him at that time I believe. I am going at a venture from your pressing me upon it, but as far as my knowledge goes I am speaking correctly.

13,072. You believe that Hallam was one?—I think he was one.

13,073. Who were the others?—I think young George Peace was another, but it is from your pressing me and I wish to qualify it, pardon me, but you may press a witness beyond the truth.

13,074. I do not think that I am using any pressure upon you at all, I am only asking you the question.—Well I am doing what I can and I can do no more.

13,075. You go every week collecting this natty money?—I do.

13,076. You go to every master's wheel and know what men are in arrears and all that?—Yes.

13,077. And you must know who has done it when a man comes and tells you he has done a thing and tells you where the things are and knows all about it?—Yes; if particular cases were pointed out it might come to my recollection, but I cannot give you any more than I have.

13,078. It is not worth my while to go into it but before this inquiry is over I may have to send for you two or three times again?—What would be the use of my keeping back these trivial affairs when there are those great affairs that I have spoken of?

13,079. Only that you do not disclose any other persons' names. Now I will take you back to Linley's case. In Linley's case you say that all the books are destroyed?—Yes.

13,080. You have no books?—No.

13,081. You paid that large sum of money and you got it you say by making false entries in the books and by putting the earnings down at less than they were?—Yes.

13,082. After Linley was shot, was there any meeting of the trade at all expressing their abhorrence of the thing?—I do not remember; there were meetings of the trade to take the men into the society who came in after, and he was one that was taken in.

13,083. I ask you again; after Linley was shot, did not you write a letter telling the masters not to allow him to have hull room?—That is the letter you were alluding to the other day, but I do not remember it.

13,084. Will you swear that you did not write it?—I remember having read a letter of that description somewhere.

13,085. Did not you write it?—No, I do not remember writing that letter myself; upon my word I do not.

13,086. Do you believe that you wrote it?—I will not swear that it was not written by me; I do not remember writing it.

13,087. Did you help to compose it?—I have no recollection of that either.

13,088. Will you swear that you did not?—No.

13,089. Who had any interest in preventing the masters letting him have hull room, except the trade, and you as their organ?—I do not know, I am sure.

13,090. Who was likely to have written it, if you did not?—I confess there is nobody seems so likely as me, but I do not remember.

13,091. Now I ask you whether you were suspected in being concerned in shooting Linley, after Linley was shot?—Yes.

13,092. Was there any meeting of the trade to investigate that matter, to see whether you were guilty or not?—I do not remember one.

13,093. Do you mean to say that the trade had an officer in it who was suspected of being a party to the murder of a poor man, and still continued him as their officer without question or inquiry?—Yes; and I do not believe the society believed it, you must understand.

13,094. These matters, rattenings, blowings up, cans of gunpowder thrown into houses, gunpowder thrown in through the windows, people shot at, and men murdered, went on from time to time with the knowledge of the Union; is that so?—Not with the knowledge of the Union.

13,095. Was it known to them that they occurred?—It was known to them that they occurred.

13,096. Was it known to them that in many instances you were believed to be a participator in them yourself?—I have no doubt it was.

13,097. Was there ever any meeting called except after the Hereford street outrage, to inquire into your conduct, to see whether you had been a participator in them or not?—Public meeting, do you mean?

13,098. Any meeting you like of your trade?—I do not remember one.

13,099. After the Hereford Street outrage, your name having been pointed out prominently, were any steps taken by your trade, except to receive your own statement, that you were innocent, in order to pass a vote of disapprobation upon your conduct?—Any investigation made, do you mean?

13,100. Was there any investigation of the matter to see who had done it?—By my own trade?

13,101. Yes, or did they take your own word for it?—They took my word, I believe.

13,102. Was it not well known to your society that all these outrages were the result of trades differences?—I believe such was believed to be so.

13,103. Such was the belief?—Yes.

13,104. Still they took no steps to investigate how they were done or to stop it; is that so?—Not beyond what has been spoken to.

13,105. Beyond what, do you mean?—The rewards, and so forth.

13,106. That is all they did; there was no calling up of members?—There had been property made good occasionally.

13,107. Property has been made good for rattenings?—Yes, occasionally.

13,108. Has property ever been made good when houses have been blown up?—I am not aware.

13,109. Has compensation been given when persons have been injured?—I do not know of any.

13,110. Do not you know that in the case where that man Parker was shot at, that the trade itself actually gave him a sum of money to compensate him for the injury he received?—If it did I have forgotten it.

13,111. Did the trade pay him a sum of money?—What interest would it be to me to deny a thing of that sort.

FOURTEENTH DAY.

W. Broadhead.

1 June 1867.

13,112. I do not care about your interest; tell me?—I do not remember.

13,113. Will you swear that the trade did not pay a sum of money as compensation for his injury?—I will not swear that.

13,114. Do you believe they did not?—That is as far as my knowledge goes.

13,115. Do you know of any case in which the trade have paid a sum of money to compensate a man for an injury received in this way?—I do not.

13,116. Will you swear that it did not?—No, I will not, to the best of my knowledge.

13,117. Will you swear that the fact of a man being injured in his person or property has not been brought before one of your meetings and money ordered to be given to him as compensation?—It may be so if a case can be cited.

13,118. Do not you believe it has?—I do not remember one; if a case was cited to me I would say at once.

13,119. Did not you yourself say that the 10*l.* which was given to the infirmary was to compensate them for the injury the funds of the infirmary had sustained by reason of a man being injured for a trade difference?—I have no recollection of having made the remark.

13,120. It was paid by you?—The infirmary was paid two or three instalments.

13,121. Was not that in consequence of Parker being laid up there at a great cost to the infirmary, that you were induced to pay that sum of money?—It was in consequence, I believe, of a number of cases of saw grinders having been taken in, members who had broken bones, and so forth.

13,122. It was not in consequence of Parker?—I have no recollection of its being in consequence of Parker.

13,123. Will you swear that it was not?—No.

13,124. Will you swear that Parker's case was not distinctly brought before the meeting, and they were told that this was a trade outrage, and in consequence of that the funds of the infirmary ought not to suffer, and they voted 10*l.* to recoup them for what they had lost?—I do not think that that could occur without my knowing it; I do not know that.

13,125. You swear that nothing of the kind ever occurred at any of your meetings?—I have no recollection.

13,126. Will you swear that that did not occur?—I will repeat what I said before.

13,127. Will you swear that nothing of that kind came before a meeting of your society?—I have no recollection of it. I can say no more.

13,128. Yes, you must recollect it. Has your society on any occasion ever discussed the question of these trade outrages?—The society?

13,129. Yes.—In its general meetings?

13,130. Either in its general meetings or in its other meetings?—I cannot tell whether members may have talked about, but the society in its corporate capacity never discussed subjects of that kind to my recollection.

13,131. Although they were perfectly cognisant of all these rattenings and outrages they never discussed the subject?—Not to my recollection, only when the subject might be raised they would express their disapprobation of it.

13,132. Have you any entry in any of your books of such disapprobation?—I do not know whether there are any entries in those books or not. They are all at your service.

13,133. After the Hereford Street affair there is a strong declaration of your abhorrence of the crime written by yourself?—Yes.

Mr. Sugg stated that he was instructed that Mr. Dodworth called upon Mr, Dronfield about the order to the boy, and that Mr. Dodworth had asked Mr. Broadhead about it, but that he had denied it; and he requested that the witness might be asked whether the other trades did not send a deputation to the Home Secretary to get this special Commission issued.

13,134. *Chairman.* Do I understand you to say that your society did not join in the application to the Home Secretary for a Commission to inquire into trade outrages?—Yes. Our society being a part of the Amalgamated Society did join in it.

13,135. It was not confined to other Unions, but you were a party to it as well as the other Unions?—Yes, the Unions were combined. Permit me to observe I am not aware that the saw grinders ever did recommend it; they simply did not oppose it since it appeared that there was a disposition for the inquiry to take place.

13,136. You tell me that in the case of Linley you have explained how you got your money?—Yes.

13,137. You have now been speaking of the outrages and supplies of money to Crooks which altogether amount, according to your rough approximation, to the sum of from 130*l.* to 150*l.*?—Yes.

13,138. Where did you get those monies from?—It was got in the way already described.

13,139. Those books are in existence?—No, they are not.

13,140. Where did you get the money for the Hereford Street outrage?—For the Hereford Street outrage, I got 15*l.* from the other branches.

13,141. How much did you give for the Hereford Street outrage, 30*l.*?—I think it was somewhere about 21*l.* or 22*l.* for the Hereford Street outrage. I think so.

13,142. Where did you get that money from?—I got 15*l.* from Mr. Skidmore.

13,143. Who is Mr. Skidmore?—He is treasurer to the Saw Makers' Society.

13,144. What did you tell him you wanted it for?—It was not paid until after.

13,145. What did you tell him you wanted the 15*l.* for?—I did not tell him what I wanted it for, but the manner in which it was done was, there was a dispute with Fearnehough and Slack Sellars and Grayson. Fearnehough was out of the trade. It was their dispute together, and it was done for the whole of them.

13,146. And you told them that it was on Fearnehough's business that you wanted the 15*l.*?—Yes; but it was left in my hands.

13,147. Did you tell Skidmore that it was on Fearnehough's business you wanted the 15*l.*?—He understood that.

13,148. Did you tell him that it was on Fearnehough's business you wanted the 15*l.*?—I do not remember telling him that, but it was understood.

13,149. Will you swear that you did not tell him?—I will not swear that I did or did not, but it was understood.

13,150. It was perfectly understood?—Yes.

13,151. Where did you get the money paid?—At my house.

13,152. When?—I cannot give you the day.

13,153. How long after Fearnehough's house was blown up?—It would not be a long time. A few days.

13,154. And Skidmore knew that it was paid for blowing up Fearnehough's house?—Yes, he knew it was paid for that affair, though you must permit me to say that when the arrangement was made there were no explanations of what was to be done beyond this, that there was to be something done that would be likely to bring about a settlement. I did not state to them what would be done, but it was understood that it was to be something that would be likely to bring about a settlement.

13,155. So that this conversation was a conversation which you had with Skidmore and some other people about bringing Fearnehough to terms?—Skidmore, Joseph Barker, and myself.

13,156. So you three talked about the misconduct of Fearnehough, and how he had been going against the rules of your Union, and they agreed to advance you a sum of money to bring him to terms?—But it was also connected with Slack, Sellars, and Grayson, whom Fearnehough was working for.

13,157. And they agreed to give you a sum of money to do his business in fact?—Yes.

13,158. Who is Joseph Barker?—The secretary to the saw handle makers.

13,159. They said that if you would do something to Fearnehough to do his business and to settle with him they would find you 15*l.*?—I think the amount was not named.

13,160. But they would give you what money was necessary?—Yes.

13,161. After you had blown up Fearnehough did you tell them what money you wanted?—Yes.

13,162. Did they thereupon pay you the 15*l.* for the expenses that you had been put to?—Mr. Skidmore paid it me.

13,163. Was Barker present?—No.

13,164. Was anything said about the course of proceeding which had been adopted with regard to Fearnehough?—Not beyond this, that it appeared to give satisfaction; but I ought to state this, that they have expressed regret since that it ever occurred. Since you ask the question of one part of it I have the right to give an answer to it.

13,165. I have no doubt that you are sorry for it now?—Yes.

13,166. When did they express their regret? since this inquiry began?—Mr. Barker has since this inquiry began; but it was before this inquiry began that I refer to.

13,167. It was before the inquiry began that Mr. Skidmore mentioned that they were sorry that this had been done?—Both did.

13,168. That was after the 1000*l.* reward was offered?—I cannot say how long it was since.

13,169. You have explained where you got the 15*l.* Now there are other monies. There is "Peace's 30*l.*" Where did you get that from; that is Elisha Parker's affair?—I believe in the same way that I have described, from the contributions.

13,170. That was in a book which you have destroyed?—Yes.

13,171. You say that the books were all open to inspection, and that they were regularly audited?—Yes.

13,172. Has there been a single person in the world who has ever complained of the books being wrong?—Not about those things, because when I took those items out I took them out of places where I thought they were least likely to be detected.

13,173. Helliwell's case was not long ago; where did you get that 10*l.* from for shooting Helliwell?—In the same way.

13,174. Then you have the books for them?—No, sir.

13,175. Yes you have?—No.

13,176. Yes you have?—If you look at them you will see that I have not.

13,177. Up to what date do your books go back containing the amount of contributions?—The contribution book is from 1862.

13,178. They have all been destroyed before 1862?—Yes.

13,179. When did you destroy them?—When this Commission talked about coming I thought there was a possibility that it might come, and I consequently began to destroy them. I let no one see me. I did not destroy them all at one time.

13,180. Are you aware whether the books of other Unions have been destroyed in the same way?—No, I am not.

13,181. Have you had any communication with any secretary of any other Union at to the advisability of their destroying their books before we commenced this inquiry?—I do not remember. I should imagine they thought the same as me, that it would be a thing they could do without consulting anyone, and they would consequently do it. I consulted no one.

13,182. And you did it?—Yes.

13,183. And you believe that they have done the same thing?—I should think those who had them.

13,184. Do you know any one case in which the secretary or any one connected with any Union has destroyed their books?—I do not.

13,185. Can you suggest any reason why the books should be destroyed except for the concealment of the facts which would be contained in them?—Only this, that some of the other books were not all destroyed for that reason. Some of our books were destroyed just in the manner stated, that they were used up for waste paper.

13,186. Up to what date do you keep them?—We keep them three or four years, or something of that sort, some of them less.

13,187. Then can you give me any explanation of the 130*l.* except as to 15*l.* of it?—I can only give you that in the way I mentioned to you.

13,188. Do you mean that you have been abstracting such large sums of money as that, falsifying the books and passing them before the auditor from week to week, and have never been detected?—Yes.

13,189. And you wish us to believe that that is a true story?—I wish you to believe that it is true. I cannot make you believe it, but I know that it is true.

13,190. Have you never received from any other Union, except on the occasion that you alluded to in the Hereford Street case, any sum of money for assistance?—Yes, there have been other cases of rattenings and what not.

13,191. You have received money from Unions in other cases of rattening?—Yes.

13,192. What Union has paid you for rattening?—Branches of the saw trade.

13,193. Have all the branches of the Saw Trade paid you for rattening?—Hides has paid me on several occasions.

13,194. Who besides? has Bagshaw paid you?—Never a penny. If you permit me an observation, I believe that man's character is as stainless from anything of this description as any man's in Sheffield.

13,195. I know nothing against him. I do not insinuate anything against Mr. Bagshaw; it is my duty to enumerate each case to you?—Yes, and I am glad you have put it.

13,196. Is there any other person except the persons in the same trade who has paid you money for rattening?—I have no recollection.

13,197. Not the Scythe Grinders' Union?—They have paid us for some bands which had gone on some occasions which you will find in the books.

13,198. Has the secretary of the Scythe Grinders' Union ever paid you money for rattenings?—Only what you can see entered upon those books.

13,199. Tell me what it was.—I cannot tell you what it was. I think it was something respecting some bands at Mr. Horne's, I cannot say what it was, I looked the books over and saw the entry but I cannot remember the particulars of it.

13,200. Looking at that entry are you not aware that the Scythe Grinders have paid you money for rattening persons in the scythe trade?—No.

13,201. What was it then?—It is something relative to some bands. I cannot say whether it was paid by our society to them or by them to us.

13,202. Either their society paid it to you or you paid it to them?—Yes.

13,203. You recollect your society paying it do you then?—No; I do not recollect it; I saw the entry there.

13,204. I find an entry on the 4th July, 1861 of your having paid Joseph Machin for the Scythe Grinders' committee a sum of 1*l.* 4s. 10d. for the third part of the cost of the missing bands?—Yes.

13,205. What was that? why did you pay a third part?—It had been a band that had been missing and it would be one third that we had agreed to pay for it, but I do not recollect what band it was.

FOURTEENTH DAY.

W. Broadhead.

21 June 1867.

13,206. Who would be the other parties that would have to pay the other two thirds ?—I do not know, that is the item I alluded to, but if my memory serves me right I can recollect as far as this, I think it was a band that would be missing from Mr. Horne's wheel.

13,207. Who had to get it ?—I think the Scythe Grinders would get the band, I think that would be the way they would get the band and it would be that part that we should agree to pay for.

13,208. Who would agree with the Union besides yourselves ?—The Scythe Grinders Union. It would be an agreement between them.

13,209. That is two, the Scythe Grinders and you ?—I do not know who the other party would be, I give the best information I can.

13,210. I see there is this man Myers, who was hanged, he has been constantly employed by you in performing services for trade ; what has he done ?—What is the amount ?

13,211. 4*s.* and 2*s.* and so on.—That would be some trifling service, it would be nothing of a nature that would be unlawful.

13,212. What would it be ?—Perhaps running errands and other matters, general items.

13,213. Have you employed Myers to do anything for you in this unlawful way ?—No.

13,214. You know Smith the secretary of the Saw Smiths ?—Yes.

13,215. Did he know of the 15*l.* being paid to you by Skidmore and the other man ?—I do not know, he has known since that there has been something paid to me but whether he knew the amount or not, I cannot say.

13,216. He knew that the Hereford street outrage had been done by their connivance or instigation ?—I should think he did.

13,217. His name is Thomas Smith I believe ?—Thomas Smith.

13,218. How do know that he has known of it ? has he ever spoken to you about it ?—We have had conversations at various times about things ; I never let them know who had done it.

13,219. But that it had been paid for by you ?—We have had conversations.

13,220. Have you in your conversations told him that it had been paid for by the Unions ?—I never told him anything about who it had been paid by; when I got the money I paid for it and we have had no conversation about paying or what not since.

13,221. It had been arranged before hand, you must all of you have been alert about this Hereford Street affair; there had been this great reward offered when you talked to Smith, and you said that he knew you had been concerned in it; what did you say to him ?—I never made any admission to him about it at all.

13,222. How did he know it ?—He would judge.

13,223. How would he judge ?—I cannot tell you how he would judge; I never told him.

13,224. Did he ever tell you that he knew ?—No.

13,225. Did he give you to understand that he knew ?—I understood it without anything further.

13,226. Were you from certain knowledge which you possessed aware that he knew all about it ?—There was nothing to be gathered from conversation or remarks.

13,227. By any other means were you aware that he knew about it ?—I believe that he was aware of it.

13,228. Is there any person besides Crooks, Copley, Skidmore, Barker and Smith, and yourself who know of this Hereford Street business ?—No.

13,229. It has been in the keeping of all these people all this time notwithstanding the reward ?—Yes.

13,230. Do you believe that it was pretty well known to the secretaries of the other Unions as to who had done it ?—No; I do not think it was.

13,231. Do you think they made a good guess ?—No; I do not think they did.

13,232. Do you think that any one in his senses could think that it was otherwise than a trade matter ? Would not all the town believe that it was a trade matter ? and that it was in fact believed to be a trade matter ?—I think it is a very curious investigation to search into a man's thoughts.

13,233. I think you are right, I think that that is a question that I ought not to put ; was it not the general opinion of the town ?—It was the general talk, the trades were mixed up a great deal in the conversation about it.

13,234. Is there a trade in the town in which rattening has not been known to its members to exist in connection with the Union ?—My impression is that rattening has existed in every trade before any of this assembly here were born.

13,235. And it has been continued ever since ?—Yes.

13,236. And every Union has known that that practice has been resorted to ?—That has been the belief.

13,237. And knowledge ?—It has been the established custom in existence.

13,238. And known to all the members of the Unions ? — Oh ! Yes, it has been known in the grinding trade.

13,239. According to your opinion and judgment and knowledge all the trades in Sheffield have adopted, it and it has been known that they have adopted the ancient custom of rattening ; is that your evidence ?—The way that it has been adopted has been the way it is described, not by rule or regulation of the society, but members, as a matter of course, when others have been in arrear have taken upon themselves to roll up their bands until the payments were made, and there have been payments made to them for the expense of it ; and as a rule the parties rattened have had to pay those expenses. The society themselves as a rule have not given orders but it has simply been an understanding.

13,240. You are rather qualifying what you said yesterday, you said that it was not confined to Sheffield but that it was in all trades, and you said that tailors would even take away the goose and the sleeve boards ?—Yes.

13,241. Is it your opinion that in all trades whether at Sheffield or otherwise they will, from not having means of enforcing the payment of contributions or the means of enforcing their rules, resort to rattening of some sort or other ?—Yes sir, and I believe this, that if the law would give them some power, if there was a law created to give them some power to recover contributions without having recourse to such measures there would be no more heard of them.

13,242. I daresay there is something in that, and it is for that reason I want it clearly shown to the legislature that they may have the means of legislating properly upon the subject if it ought to be legislated upon ?—It is for that reason I make the statement.

13,243. I understand you to state without equivocation or anything of that sort, that in your judgment as a man connected with trades for a great number of years, that in every trade of Sheffield rattening prevails ?—Yes ; and my character must suffer for this afterwards ; as a man of experience, judging by nothing but my experience, I now wish to say for the benefit of my fellow working men and the country at large that if a legislative measure was adopted to meet these things it would destroy these acts that have taken place and which have placed me in this painful position.

13,244. As a man of experience in trade matters have you found throughout the trades that where rattening would not succeed stronger measures have been resorted to ? have you any knowledge of it ?—They have occurred.

13,245. In all trades ?—No, not in all trades.

13,246. In which of the trades have they been resorted to ?—I can speak of none but my own, and the disgrace lies at my own door.

13,247. Do you know of no other trade but your own in which it has been done ?—I should be very

FOUR-TEENTH DAY

W. Broadhead.

21 June 1867.

sorry to impute these things to any other trades if I do not know.

13,258. Do you know of any other ?—No other in which such things as I have named have taken place.

13,249. As a man of experience do not you believe that if rattening is obliged to be resorted to and unlawful measures resorted to the natural result is that from one error you go to another and that other outrages are necessary in consequence ?—I am sorry to say that it has been the case with me.

13,250. In your judgment is not that the inevitable consequence of commencing by unlawful proceedings like those ?—Others are subject to the same temptations as I have been, that is all I can say, I am now very glad that there are no others that have done this thing to the extent that I have done.

13,251. You have to a certain extent taken the whole blame of this matter upon yourself ?—I have done so truthfully.

13,252. You had an investigating committee ?—Yes.

13,253. And you have told us somewhat what the duties of the investigating committee were ?—Yes.

13,254. You were challenged by a man who said that he had seen a book which was the investigating committee's book, in which he had seen his own name where it was stated that the money was to be obtained by force ?—He was mistaken.

13,255. When you were asked the question whether such an entry as that might have occurred in the book you said that it was possible "If he said so I "will not contradict him" was your expression to me ?—I do not remember making use of that remark but I speak now of what I believe to be correct.

13,256. I am calling your attention to what you have said already in this inquiry. A man came forward and said "I saw a book in which there was an "entry of my own name and my deficiency" and there was beyond that a remark "To be obtained by "force" or something equivalent to that. You said "If the man says so I will not deny it" ?—I think I can undertake to take my oath that such an entry as that was not made—"by force."

13,257. You did not say that at the time Chapman was examined. You said "The expression might be "used but the man is mistaken in supposing that it "was a book, because we never kept a book, it was "simply on a sheet of paper" ? — I was not paying particular attention to the word "force." It would be what was entered that I paid attention to.

13,258. I can quite understand that you have an object to shield your committee, but, I cannot allow you to say that your attention was not called to the word "force," because it was with that object alone that you were recalled and your attention drawn to it ?—If I said that it was in a book I should be saying that which is not true.

13,259. (*Mr. Chance.*) You said this "I did not "show a book in which it was stated that his con- "tribution was to be got by force" ?—I did not show him a book.

13,260. It is very possible I might have shown an entry of this kind, if he says so I believe I did so ; I should have shown him such an entry on a foolscap sheet of paper.

(*Mr. Barstow.*) Chapman says—"I am quite sure "the words 'by force' were used." He speaks particularly to the words "by force."

13,261. (*Chairman.*) Therefore you cannot tell me that your attention was not called to that fact ; your attention was directed to the words "by force" in the investigating committee's book on sheets ; I ask you now how it is that you go away from that statement ?—I come to that because I believe what I am now stating to be the truth.

13,262. Bearing in mind what you have once said, and the effect that it has produced upon our minds, I ask you again, knowing what you said, will you say upon your oath that there was not the entry in your book "to be obtained by force ?"—I do not believe that ever the word "force" was used.

13,263. Will you swear that in that sheet or book the word "force" was not used ?—I could no more swear to that than I could swear to a volume of writing that might be placed before me.

13,264. Is it possible that the word "force" might be used in that book ?—I should hardly think it could ; I have never made an entry of that description ; the word "press" was frequently used.

13,265. I am not asking about the word "press," I ask about the words "by force." You were asked and you said that it was true that it was there. Now I ask you whether you stick to that ?—It is a very trivial affair, and would not be worth my while to deny it.

13,266. So far from a trivial affair it is a most important affair ?—I do not see it.

13,267. It is one of the essences of this inquiry, whether there existed in the accounts of the investigating committee an entry of that description ; if it were true it would be followed by enormous results ? —Then if it is I am all the more called upon to persist in the statement that I have made as far as my knowledge goes.

13,268. Then you have altered your statement now from what you said before ?—I do not remember making a remark to apply to the word "force."

13,269. Do not think that it is a question of book, I am speaking of a sheet of foolscap paper ?—Yes.

13,270. Will you now swear that "by force" was not on that sheet of foolscap paper ?—I will not swear that it was ; I will swear to the best of my recollection it never was, and I have confidence to believe it.

13,271. Will you swear that it was not there ?—I cannot do that, but I do not believe it was. I believe I am telling the truth when I say that.

13,272. If you believe now that you are telling me the truth, why, when Chapman came here and swore that he saw it, did you not deny it then ?—I was paying attention to the entry.

13,273. (*Mr. Barstow.*) You used the expression "by force" three times. He first said that you showed him a book in which the arrears were to be got by force ; then he says "he knows the inves- "tigating committee ;" and then he says he had seen the entry appended to other names that their arrears were to be got by force the same as his. Then he says he is sure that the word "force" was used ?— I am aware that Chapman made use of the word "force," but my answer to it and the interpretation of its being so confirm what he stated has been misunderstood. I never could have made such a statement, because it was the first time I ever heard the term "force" used in reference to those sheets, and I do not believe it ever was.

13,274. (*Chairman.*) We know what you said, and we know under what circumstances you said it. We know how this man was called expressly forward to show that the investigating committee had made an entry, and that they were conscious that force was used. We called your attention to it and you did not deny it. Now, if you change your evidence we shall have reason to believe that you have some reason for changing your evidence ?—I shall have confidence that I have spoken the truth, and I should have very great hesitation indeed in saying that the word "force" was used there, because I do not believe it ever was.

13,275. Now, taking the statement of this man who has already said that he saw the word "force" used in those sheets, I ask you to explain how it was necessary (except in that trumpery way which you explained yesterday, of not wanting anyone to find out what you were doing) for you to have minute made by which the affairs of the investigating committee were to be kept secret ?—Nearly all our books of regulations have taken their commencement from a course of that description at the first, and the investigating committee when it was created did not con-

FOURTEENTH DAY.

W. Broadhead.

21 June 1867.

sider it necessary to keep a book. It was only to take accounts from the books which were selected to the investigating committee. It was not to carry them forward or anything of that description, it was only to make the accounts out and lay them before the committee. The money got by contributions and so forth went into the book; they were kept for a month or so until they were no longer wanted.

13,276. You would never keep any entry of an outrage?—No.

13,277. Nor of a rattening?—No.

13,278. Nor of a blowing up?—No.

13,279. And if they were parties to that it would be essential to you to have a minute of that description?—If they were parties to it.

13,280. If they were parties to it it would be essential to have a minute of that description?—If they were parties to it there might be one, or there might not be one; but they never were parties to it, and I transacted the business as you are already made acquainted with.

13,281. Then do you mean to tell me that for no personal gain whatever, from time to time you put your own life in jeopardy, and your person and freedom in jeopardy, simply for the benefit of the trade without any co-operation of the other members of the trade?—It may appear incredible, but I did.

13,282. Since this inquiry has been instituted or since it was known that it was about to take place, have you had any communication with the members of the investigating committee as to the course of evidence you should give?—No.

13,283. Have you talked it over?—No.

13,284. With no one?—No.

13,285. With no member of the Union?—No; they are totally unacquainted with it.

13,286. Have you talked to them at all about what evidence was to be given at this inquiry?—No; when the report of this day's proceedings comes to be known they will be as much surprised as any one.

13,287. They knew of the outrages?—They knew of the outrages; everybody new of them.

13,288. They knew that they were trade matters for the benefit of the saw grinders?—It occurred in the trade.

13,289. And they knew that the outrages as well as the rattenings were for the benefit of the saw grinders?—Very likely.

13,290. If it could be no good to you, and only for the benefit of the trade for which it had been done, and they knew it?—I left them to form their own judgment.

13,291. Had you any doubt that they knew it quite well?—I cannot say; I do not know.

13,292. Did not the Union, as a body, know it?—As a body they did not know it.

13,293. Did not they know that these outrages were done for their benefit?—I am not aware.

13,294. Did you ever have them discussed?—In general subjects they have been discussed.

13,295. Have you ever at any of your meetings had any person stand up and protest against such conduct on the part of the trade?—Oh, yes.

13,296. When?—I cannot tell.

13,297. Tell me an instance of a man standing up and protesting against such outrages on the part of the trade. I believe that you have done it yourself?—Yes, I have.

13,298. After the Hereford Street outrages we know that everybody did; but before the Hereford Street outrage can you tell me of any occasion where a person came forward and protested against outrages being committed, such as blowing up houses, and so on?—There have been members both in a general and private meeting.

13,299. Tell me any one man who in a general meeting protested against it?—The very man who went with me to see Parker, Machin.

13,300. Machin has protested against it at general meetings?—Both in general meetings and in private conversation.

13,301. At those general meetings, for I speak of general meetings, private conversation I cannot deal with, has Machin come forward in the presence of the meeting and declared that these outrages were a disgrace to the trade?—Yes, he has, and he has sincerely felt that they were.

13,302. Has he declared that they were done by the trade?—No.

13,303. Has he called upon the trade to reject them and repudiate them in every way?—They have done so.

13,304. Have they not been defended at your meetings?—No.

13,305. Never?—It has been protested against.

13,306. Who protested against it?—I mean the meetings have protested against the outrages.

13,307. Where have you any entry in your books of such a protest?—I do not know whether there are any or not.

13,308. How many have protested?—I cannot tell that; it would be a very singular thing if I could.

13,309. I should think it would not; I should think that if you were carrying on these outrages yourself without any authority, and the meeting were all against you, you would never have dared to go on with such lawless proceedings?—I was not very likely to make a note of every one who protested.

13,310. I should have thought you were?—But I did not do so, at all events.

13,311. Have not the protests been by one or two isolated individuals, not by the body of the meeting?—I simply selected Machin as one who has done so. There are others, but I cannot go on enumerating others.

13,312 There is no entry of any resolution in the books of any protest on behalf of the meeting?—I cannot say, but I believe not.

13,313. There is one thing which I have omitted to ask you. There was Helliwell who was watched, and was to have been shot at, and there was a Helliwell to be blown up; I never knew what was the cause of the offence of the Helliwell who was to be blown up?—He had simply come into the trade. I believe he was a labouring man or something of that kind; his brother had brought him in and gave him wages; I thought there was quite sufficient in the trade; it would only end by bringing him on the box and making him a burden to it.

13,314. So for coming into the trade, having been a labouring man, you thought it consistent with your duty to hire a man to put gunpowder into his trough and blow him up with a chance of killing him on the spot?—That induced me to do it.

13,315. You had no personal malice against him?—Not a bit against any one of them; I am aware that the world will not credit what I say.

13,316. He offered 10*l*. for being taken in?—Yes.

13,317. You would not have it, and went and blew him up?—The society would not have it; it went before the society, but they would not have it.

13,318. You knew it?—I knew that the society would not have it.

13,319. You knew that this poor man had offered his 10*l*. to come in, and had offered to conform to the rules of the society; you knew that the society would not have him, and then you went and hired a ruffian to blow him up?—Put it just in what light you please.

13,320. Now, Mr. Broadhead, I think that I have asked you all the questions that occur to my mind at present; but this is a very long and serious inquiry, and there are many points raised to-day of the truth of which I know nothing at present. It will be our duty to inquire fully into all that you have said, and you must be in attendance, if you please, so as to come back and give us further information, if that information should be required?—Will it be necessary for me to attend every day?

FOURTEENTH DAY.

W. Broadhead.

21 June 1867.

13,321. No, certainly not. I cannot think that it will be pleasant for you after this to attend in a Court of this kind. I do not ask you to do so, but you must be in a place where you can be found if necessary ?—I am ruined, but I cannot complain, I must bear it.

13,322. There is no reason for you to remain here any longer; you may go home when you like, but you must not leave the town, and you must be here when called upon if we should require any further information, and you shall not be sent for until it is necessary for the ends of justice ?—There is one matter I should like to explain before I leave. I stated that I had received 15*l.* for the Hereford Street affair, that is true, and I was told by the parties that I must pay myself something. Part of that money I gave to this man, and I took something of it myself, it being in another trade, and not in my own.

13,323. Part of the 15*l.* you paid to the man, and part of the 15*l.* you have appropriated to yourself, it not being in the trade ?—Yes.

13,324. You speak of the Hereford Street outrage ?—Yes. There is another part that was to have been paid to make up the 15*l.* to the man; that would have had to have come after the Commission had done sitting, and it was agreed that instead of receiving it in money he should have a certain amount of his arrears taken off which stood against him. All the arrears would not have been likely to have been examined, and he would have stood so much less in arrears. I wish to explain this because I do not wish to have the pain of again having to come here to explain it at a future time.

13,325. Who was the certain person whose money was to have been paid in that way ?—I was to have been paid something myself, as it was done in the interest of the other two branches.

15,326. What did you take yourself ?—Perhaps 5*l.*

15,327. And 10*l.* you gave to the man ?—I do not speak positively to the amount,

13,328. Skidmore gave you the 15*l.*, and there was this other person and Barker, and you say that there was another man mixed up in it, who is he ?—Smith. I am not aware of that except in conversation; it was brought into our private conversations, and it seems in our private conversations I gathered it from nothing but this, that he had been cognizant of this having taken place.

13,329. But what about this man, and the arrears being let off, who is he ?—Crooks was to be let off. I name that because I do not want the pain of explaining these things again.

13,330. There is one question I forgot to ask you; there have been a good many threatening letters sent ?—Yes.

13,331. Were those written by you ?—Most of them I did write, but not all of them.

13,332. Most of them were written by you ?—Yes.

13,333. Who wrote the others ?—I do not know.

13,334. Most of the threatening letters were written by you ?—Yes, numbers were written by me.

13,335. Were those signed "Tantia Topee" written by you ?—I believe they were.

13,336. In which you told persons that they might expect to be shot, and all that kind of thing ?—Yes.

The witness withdrew.

J. Chapman.

JOSEPH CHAPMAN recalled and further examined.

13,337. (*Mr. Barstow.*) What age are you ?—32.

13,338. When you were about 18 years old, did you live with an uncle of yours at the "Stag" Inn, Wadsley Bottom ?—Yes.

13,339. Do you remember one night being awakened by a loud knocking at the door ?—Yes.

13,340. Did you hear talking ?—Yes.

13,341. Did you know the voices ?—Yes, I thought that I did.

13,342. Was this about three o'clock in the morning ?—Yes, about that time, I cannot exactly say.

13,343. You knew the voices ?—Yes.

13,344. Whose voices were those ?—Phineas Dean was one.

13,345. Who else ?—The other was, I believe, John Taylor; he went under the name of "Noisey."

13,346. Who besides ?—Elijah Smith and Joseph Bradshaw.

13,347. Had you known these men before ?—Yes, I had known them very well, that was the reason why I knew the voices.

13,348. Did you see them that night ?—No.

13,349. Did they come in ?—They knocked at the door. I was not allowed to let any one in, and my uncle had to come out of his room across mine to the window in the bedroom where I slept, and he opened the window. He shouted out and wanted to know who it was. I cannot exactly say how they answered him, but he did answer them, and he asked them what they were after.

13,350. Did any of them mention any of their names ?—No, I did not hear any name mentioned.

13,351. He did not say any such thing, as "who are you" ?—I cannot exactly say, it is a long while ago.

13,352. You cannot say whether any names were mentioned ?—No.

13,353. Did he ask what they were doing about at that hour, or anything of that sort ?—He asked them where they had been, and if I heard right, Phineas Dean said they had been up in the low country.

13,354. What did you understand by "the low "country" ?—Well, I do not know.

13,355. Do you know it now ?—Yes, I knowed it the day following.

13,356. I want to know what is meant by "the "low country"; does it mean any place about here ?—No, there is a place called "the low country," Lincolnshire and there.

13,357. But not about here ?—No.

13,358. Is that any "cant" talk ? is it "slang" at all ? does it mean doing mischief, or anything of that sort ?—No, not that I am aware of.

13,359. Did they say what they had been doing ?—No, I did not hear that they said anything. My uncle went down to them and let them in.

13,360. You did not see them ?—No, I never saw them.

13,361. Did you hear anything the next morning ?—Yes; when I was going to my work I heard that a horse had got his hamstrings cut.

13,362. Whose horse was it ?—Elisha Parker's.

13,363. Have you seen Joseph Bradshaw lately ?—Yes, I saw him yesterday.

13,364. Where does he live ?—I cannot say where he lives; I do not know. I know the neighbourhood.

13,365. Where did he live at this time, do you know ?—I do not, but I believe he lived in Dun Street.

13,366. Do you know where Phineas Dean, Taylor, and Smith lived ?—I think Smith lived on Shales Moor, but I am not certain. I do not know where any of them lived particularly.

13,367. (*The Chairman.*) Were they Sheffield men or Dore men ?—Smith was a Sheffield man, as far as I know anything about him.

13,368. Do you remember some time after this meeting Elijah Smith on Shales Moor ?—Yes, it would be a very long time after that.

13,369. But how long ago ?—I cannot say exactly, I am sure, not to be certain.

13,370. Was it five or six years ago ?—Perhaps six or seven years ago; I cannot exactly say; but I should think it would be about that time.

13,371. Did he want you to buy a pawn ticket of him ?—Yes.

FOURTEENTH DAY.

J. Chapman.

21 June 1867.

13,372. What was the pawn ticket?—A pawn ticket of a six-barrelled revolver he told me.

13,373. Did you make any remark about it?—Yes.

13,374. What did you say?—I told him at first I did not want to buy such a thing; it was of no use to me. I said to him, "I expect that is what you have "played your games with."

13,375. Did you mention where?—No, I did not mention where particularly, not just at that moment.

13,376. What did you say then?—I says to him, "I guess you would had that with you when you "went to Dore," or something to that effect. I cannot say exactly the words.

13,377. What did he say to that?—He said "Yes," he had it in the house.

13,378. Was anything more said about the pistol?—He said he had it in use that night when Parker was shot.

13,379. Do you remember when the Globe Works were blown up?—No, I do not think that I do; perhaps I can just recollect something about it.

13,380. How long ago do you think it was? was it more than ten years?—Yes.

The witness withdrew.

H. Chapman.

HENRY CHAPMAN sworn and examined.

13,381. (*Mr. Barstow.*) In 1852 or 1853 did you keep the "Stag" at Wadsley Bottom?—Yes.

13,382. Do you remember at three o'clock in the morning some people coming to your house?—Yes.

13,383. Did you let them in?—Yes.

13,384. Who were they?—Phineas Dean, Elijah Smith, John Taylor, and Joseph Bradshaw.

13,385. When you let them in had you any conversation with them?—Yes.

13,386. What did you say?—I asked them what games they had been on this morning, and they said they had been on rattening business for the trade.

13,387. Did you ask them what the business was?—Yes I did, and they said I should hear more about it.

13,388. That is all they said at the time, was it?—They said they had come by a cross country road to get out of the way; that is all they said to me.

13,389. Did they say anything more?—No, not about rattening business that I am aware of.

13,390. Did you hear what that business was the next day?—Yes, I heard that Elisha Parker's horse was hamstrung.

The witness withdrew.

J. Bradshaw.

JOSEPH BRADSHAW sworn and examined.

(*Chairman.*) I caution you that if you have been engaged in any unlawful proceedings, if you like to make a clear disclosure of everything within your knowledge you will obtain a certificate to protect you against the consequences of your misconduct. If you do not you are liable to be prosecuted.

13,391. (*Mr. Barstow.*) Are you a saw grinder?—Yes.

13,392. Do you remember in 1852 or 1853 going with Elijah Smith, John Taylor, and Phineas Dean to Dore?—No.

13,393. Did you go with them to Wadsley?—I have let on them several times. I came from Wadsley.

13,394. Were you at Chapman's public house?—Yes, I have been there all hours.

13,395. Do you remember being there with them at three o'clock one morning?—We have been there several times.

13,396. With John Taylor, Elijah Smith, and Phineas Dean?—No, I cannot remember being with them all three together.

13,397. Were you never there with them all three together?—No, not to my knowledge.

13,398. You must remember; at three o'clock in the morning?—I have been there all hours; I have lived at the "Stag."

13,399. Do you remember the last witness coming and letting you and three men into the house at three o'clock one morning?—I cannot remember to my knowledge. I have been there all hours.

13,400. You do not remember whether he did or not?—No.

13,401. Will you swear that you were not there with these three men at three o'clock one morning?—I cannot swear that. I have been there with Dean many a time.

13,402. Did you hear what the last witness, Henry Chapman, said?—I was up there, but I could not get to hear right.

13,403. He said that you and Elijah Smith and John Taylor and Phineas Dean came to his house at three o'clock one morning at Wadsley, and that he let you in, and that when you came in he asked you what games you had been up to, and that you said that you had been on a rattening business for the trade; do you remember that?—Not to my knowledge. I never heard anything of that sort mentioned in my life witn either Phineas Dean or Smith.

13,404. Is it true, or not true?—I cannot say, it is so many years ago since, I cannot tell.

13,405. Were you ever on a rattening expedition?—Yes; I have been once and served my time for it.

13,406. Were was that?—At Moses Eadon's.

13,407. Who was with you?—No one.

13,408. You were taken, were you not?—Yes.

13,409. And sentenced?—Yes.

13,410. Have you ever been on any other rattening expedition?—No.

13,411. Never?—No.

13,412. How long were you in prison for that?—Six months.

13,413. Do you swear that that was the only time you have been rattening?—Yes.

12,414. Can you say that on your oath?—Yes.

13,415. Then if Henry Chapman and Joseph Chapman say that you were at Dore that is not true?—I did not know where Dore was at that time.

13,416. (*Chairman*). Perhaps you do not know now?—Yes; I have been at it several times.

13,417. (*Mr. Barstow*). Do you mean to swear that you were never in company with the three men whom I have named at Henry Chapman's house?—Not all three together to my knowledge. I have been to Chapman's, his sister kept the public house before him. I once trained to run there, I have been there in all shapes, and in all forms and at all hours.

13,418. Have you ever been there with Elijah Smith, Phineas Dean, and John Taylor at three o'clock in the morning?—I cannot say so.

13,419. Will you swear that you have not?—I will swear, not to my knowledge.

13,420. Will you swear that you have not been there at that time, at three o'clock in the morning?—Unless it has been at feast time, I cannot remember any other time.

13,421. You remember quite well?—No; I do not.

13,422. You must remember whether you were there or not?—No; I cannot I am certain.

13,423. Do you mean to say you were never there?—I have been there scores of times.

13,424. You have been there with the three men?—No.

13,425. Will you swear that you were not there with the three men, all together?—No; not to my knowledge I was not.

13,426. Why do you answer not to your knowledge? you must remember whether you were there at three

FOUR-TEENTH DAY.

J. Bradshaw.

21 June 1867.

o'clock in the morning with those three men, you remember it well enough ?—No, I do not.

13,427. Were you ever out in the morning about that time ?—Yes; I have been getting mushrooms at one and two o'clock in the morning.

13,428. Have you known these two Chapmans ?—Yes.

13,429. You know them well ?—Yes; as well I know my own brother.

13,430. If they were to see you could they be mistaken in you ?—No ; I should think they would not be mistaken in me, I have been brought up amongst them all my life.

13,431. Are you aware whether the Chapmans are acquainted with Elijah Smith ?—Elijah Smith and me, we have hung stones for Henry Chapman often time, and we have gone to the "Stag" to have the money, we had the money all in drink.

13,432. Are you acquainted with the Chapmans ? do you know Phineas Dean ?—Yes; Phineas Dean worked for them, I believe.

13,433. Do you know whether they were acquainted with John Taylor ?—Not to my knowledge; I know nothing about John Taylor.

13,434. You were not acquainted with John Taylor ?—Very little; I knowed him in our line, we almost know every man that is in the branch.

13,435. You know every man in the branch ?—Yes ; very nearly, we do in our trade.

13,436. Were you ever with these three men at Dore or near Dore ?—Yes ; not with those three men, I have been with Smith and Taylor at Dore.

13,437. What did you do there ?—We went to see a person of the name of Broadhead that lived at Abbey Dale. From Abbey Dale we went to Henry Yellatt of the "Hare and Hounds" at Dore.

13,438. Is that Joel Yellatt ?—No; Henry Yellatt the mason. He is uncle to this Taylor, I believe.

13,439. What did you do there ?—We got some ale there, we all four got drunk, and there was a man named George Peace who lived there; he says "you "can find these four chaps beds, they will not return "to Sheffield to night," and we had beds and left at seven o'clock the next morning.

13,440. When was this ?—I cannot say to a year or two, it might be seven years since.

13,441. It might be a little more ?—It might be more, I cannot say.

13,442. Did you all sleep there that night ?—Yes.

13,443. Did you do nothing more ?—No, except drink some ale.

13,444. You did nothing but drink some ale and then go to bed ?—Yes ? that was all.

13,445. Do you know Elisha Parker ?—Yes, very well; I know him.

13,446. Did you go to Elisha Parker's that night ?—No ; I have worked for Elisha Parker since several times.

13,447. Did you go with these men into any field there ?—No.

13,448. Did you see them do any thing to a horse, any of them ?—No.

13,449. Did they say anything to you about doing anything to a horse ?—No.

13,450. Did you do anything to a horse ?—No.

13,451. Do you remember hearing of Elisha Parker's horse being hamstrung ?—Yes.

13,452. What time was that ?—I am sure I cannot tell. I am no scholar. I cannot remember anything about it.

13,453. Was that about the time that you were speaking of ?—I am certain I cannot say what time it was. I think, to my own knowledge, since we were at Dore, it is six or seven years since.

13,454. Was it about the same time you were at Dore that you heard of Elijah Parker's horse being hamstrung ?—At the time I heard of his horse, there was a man working at the same wheel as I was ; and I was told the next morning, but I cannot say when it was, it was the next morning or the morning after.

13,455. If you were told the next morning after the horse was hamstrung, you must know whether you were at Chapman's the night before ?—I do not know about Chapman's, I have been there many times.

13,456. You know now when Elisha Parker's horse was hamstrung, because you were told the next morning ; on the night before that were you at Chapman's ?—I do not know that I was at Chapman's that morning to my knowledge.

13,457. (*Chairman.*) Will you swear that you were not ?—That morning that Henry Taylor told me about Elisha Parker's horse I had not been from home above ten minutes.

13,458. (*Mr. Barstow.*) Will you swear that you were not at Wadsley that same night on which Elisha Parker's horse was hamstrung ?—I cannot say to that.

13,459. Will you swear that you were not there ?—I cannot say. I do not remember any time or anything of it ; but I was told that he had got cut, or something ; I did not know what hamstringing meant.

13,460. Were you present that night at a conversation between Phineas Dean, and Elijah Smith, and John Jaylor ?—No, I never was there with John Taylor to my knowledge.

13,461. Were you there the night that Elisha Parker's horse was hamstrung, with Phineas Dean, Elijah Smith, and John Taylor ?—I might be ; I have been there at all hours in the morning and stayed there all night.

13,462. Did you hear any talk between Henry Chapman, and Phineas Dean, and Elijah Smith ?—No.

13,463. You heard no talk between them ?—No.

13,464. Do you mean to say that at this time you did not know where Dore was ?—Not at that time.

13,465. Do you swear that the day before Parker's horse was hamstrung you did not call at Parker's wheel with a man named Henry Taylor ?—No, I never went anywhere the day after.

13,466. The day before his horse was hamstrung, I asked about ?—The day before ?

13,467. Yes ?—No, not to my knowledge ; I have been at Parker's wheel many a score times and I have worked for Parker.

13,468. You know quite well the day upon which Parker's horse was hamstrung ; were you at his wheel the day before his horse was hamstrung ?—No ; I did not know where Elisha Parker worked at that time.

13,469. Were you at his wheel wherever he worked ?—Yes.

13,470. The day before his horse was hamstrung ?—Not to my knowledge ; I was not there the day before the horse was hamstrung.

13,471. (*Chairman.*) Now mind what you are about ; you know if you do not tell us the truth you will not get a certificate, and if you have been guilty of this great offence you will be punished ?—I have not been guilty.

13,472. Now answer this ; here are these two men, the Chapmans one is the nephew, and the other is the uncle ; one said that he heard you on the morning that this horse was hamstrung, and the other says that he saw you. There are two witnesses now, mind that, who swear that on that very night they saw you in their house. Do you swear that you were not there ?—I might be there.

13,473. Will you swear that you were or not ?—I cannot.

13,474. Will you swear you were not ?—I have been there many a time.

13,475. Will you swear that you were not there on that night. They swear that you were ?—I cannot say to my knowledge that I was.

13,476. Will you swear that you were not ?—I was never there so early in the morning.

13,477. Were you there that night at that public house when the horse was hamstrung ?—I cannot swear that I was.

13,478. Will you swear that you were not ?—I cannot take a solemn oath on it.

13,479. Then you will not swear that you were not there ; will you swear that you were not there in company with those three men that night ?—I was never

FOURTEENTH DAY.

J. Bradshaw.

21 June 1867.

there in company with three of them. I have been there in company with Phineas Dean all hours of the night.

13,480. Were you there that night with those three or any of them? They both swear that you were in company with all three. Will you swear that you were not?—I will swear I was not there. I have been there many times.

13,481. Were you there that night with them, you shall answer that?—I have been there with two.

13,482. Were you there that night with them?—Not to my knowledge.

13,483. Will you swear that you were not?—I cannot swear.

13,484. You cannot swear that you were there. Two people swear that you were there. Will you swear that on that night one of those men in your presence did not say that they had been out rattening?—I never heard anything of it.

13,485. Will you swear that they did not?—Yes, I will swear it.

13,486. Will you swear that they did not say so in your hearing?—I never heard such a word mentioned in my life at Henry Chapman's.

13,487. Did they say in your hearing that they would hear more of it the next day?—Not to my knowledge.

13,488. Will you swear that they did not? There are two witnesses who swear it.—I am not bound to swear a falsehood.

13,489. Will you swear that one of them did not in your presence say that they had been out rattening, and that you would hear more of it the next day?—I never heard such a thing mentioned.

13,490. Will you swear that that did not happen?—Never in my life at the "Stag."

13,491. Were you at Mr. Parker's wheel the day before his horse was hamstrung?—No, not to my knowledge.

13,492. Will you swear that you were not at his wheel the day before his horse was cut. You shall swear one way or the other. If you were there and it is proved against you——?—I was not there to my knowledge. Never in my life.

13,493. You knew of it the day after the horse was hamstrung?—The day what horse was cut?

13,494. You must know that you were at Parker's wheel the day before his horse was hamstrung?—I was not there.

13,495. You swear that you were not there?—Yes, I will swear I was not at Parker's wheel.

13,496. Were you at Dore?—I have been at Dore.

13,497. Were you at Dore the same night that the horse was cut?—No, never at night.

13,498. How near were you to Dore that night?—I never was nearer to Dore that night than Wadsley Bottom or Owlerton.

13,499. You swear that you never were nearer to the place than that?—Yes, I swear that.

13,500. Will you swear that you were not there the day before?—At Parker's wheel?

13,501. Yes.—I will swear that.

13,502. But you will not swear that you were not at the "Stag" at three o'clock the next morning?—I have been there all times and all hours.

13,503. Did you ever tell Chapman that you had been out rattening, and kept out of the way in the bye-lanes?—No.

13,504. Nor has anybody told him in your presence?—No, I never heard anything mentioned I think.

13,505. Will you swear that you were not keeping in the bye-roads with Phineas Dean and Smith to avoid the public?—No.

13,506. You have never done such a thing?—No.

13,507. On no occasion?—No.

13,508. You say all this at your peril; if this all turns out to be false you are liable to be prosecuted?—I have spoken the truth as far as my knowledge goes.

The witness withdrew.

Adjourned to to-morrow at 11 o'clock.

FIFTEENTH DAY.

Council Hall, Sheffield, Saturday, 22nd June 1867.

PRESENT:

WILLIAM OVEREND, Esq., Q.C.	GEORGE CHANCE, Esq.
THOMAS IRWIN BARSTOW, Esq.	J. E. BARKER, Esq., Secretary.

FIFTEENTH DAY.

S. Crooks.

22 June 1867.

WILLIAM OVEREND, Esq., Q.C., IN THE CHAIR.

SAMUEL CROOKS recalled and further examined.

13,509. (*Chairman.*) We promised Mr. Broadhead yesterday that as regards any person whom he should criminate, if they came forward and offered their evidence we would hear what they had to say, and that in the event of their telling us the truth, and making to us a full disclosure of all matters within their knowledge, we would, if we were satisfied of that, grant them a certificate of protection. Your evidence is of no consequence to us at all, we do not want it, the only reason why we allow you to give evidence now is that you may have an opportunity of getting your certificate, and that we may fulfil the pledge which we gave to Mr. Broadhead. You have already told us that which is false, and which we knew to be false, and you are liable to be prosecuted for all the offences which can be proved against you. You are now in that situation, and but for the pledge which we gave Mr. Broadhead we should not allow you to appear again; but, as we gave that pledge, we shall keep our word to Mr. Broadhead; and, although some of these persons who have been examined, as we believe, have not spoken the truth, yet even to them, if they come forward and give their evidence in a manner which satisfies us, we shall extend our protection. Our business here is not to detect parties, our business is to see, after having ascertained whether offences have been committed, whether these offences are in any way associated with Trades Unions. So far as your offences are concerned they are proved beyond any question at all. Therefore, it is only for the purpose of enabling you to obtain a certificate that we allow you to be examined again before us; and let me give you this caution: standing as you do in the greatest possible peril, your life being in great jeopardy at this moment, if you do not state everything which is within your knowledge, not only concerning the matters which have been spoken to by Mr. Broadhead, but concerning everything which may be within your knowledge, we shall certainly withdraw our protection from you?—I just want to ask

FIFTEENTH DAY.

S. Crooks.

22 June 1867.

you this : supposing I make a clean breast of all that I know, will you look over all that I said on the previous occasion which was wrong ; for I did say what was wrong ?

13,509. Quite so. If you only tell us now truly and sincerely what has occurred, we shall look over that falsehood in your previous statement. With respect to Linley's case you have already stated that you were the person who shot him ?—Yes.

13,510. Now you have stated that you shot him in the shoulder ?—No, I shot at his shoulder.

13,511. Now I ask you if you have not stated that you intended to shoot him in the ear ?—In the ear.

13,512. Yes ?—No.

13,513. Have you not told Hallam so ?—No.

13,514. Did you not tell him that your instructions were to shoot him in the ear ?—No, I did not.

13,515. Where did you shoot him ?—I hit him here (*describing the same*). I will show how it was done.

13,516. In what part of his head did you shoot him ?—It was somewhere about his temples, I believe.

13,517. And you swear that you were not instructed by Mr. Broadhead to shoot him in the ear ?—No, I was not ; I will swear that.

13,518. Was anything said about shooting him in the ear ?—No, not to my knowledge. He said we were not to shoot him to try to kill him.

13,519. Did you say to Hallam that you were instructed to shoot him in the ear ?—No.

13,520. Will you swear that ?—Yes, I will swear that.

13,521. After the event did not Hallam tell you that he thought you were a man of great nerve, and a very good shot, and that he was astonished that having aimed at his ear you should have hit him in the temple ?—No, I never recollect that he ever said anything of the kind.

13,522. Was there any conversation about your having missed your mark ?—No, no more than when I saw it in the papers that he was hit in the forehead ; he was leaning forward in this way, he was sat in this predicament, and leaning forwards in this way (*describing Linley's position*), and with my shooting at the shoulder and the party being in the room it accidentally hit him in the temples. I never intended hitting him in the head at all. My intention was the shoulder.

13,523. Is there anything in reference to Linley's case which you stated in your last examination which was not true ?—I have only one thing to say respecting Linley : everything that I said respecting Linley to the best of my knowledge is correctly true, except one thing that I omitted to tell you respecting the first time of Linley's shooting. At the first time I did it myself, and I left a pistol in the street to make it appear that it had been done by a pistol. That was the only thing that I did not tell you the last time. I omitted to tell you that. That is everything correctly true as far as I can say.

13,524. Then that is all that you have to alter of your statement about Linley ?—Yes, as regards the shooting of Linley, it is all I have to say respecting it.

13,525. Have you anything to say in any other respect about Linley ?—I have nothing to say except that I blew him up at Poole's ; I have nothing more to say respecting Linley. I never had anything else to do with him.

13,526. How did you do that ?—I put it in the cellar grate.

13,527. Was it at night ?—It was in the morning.

13,528. Early in the morning ?—Early in the morning. I put it into the cellar grate, and all that I can say is that I put it in and it went off.

13,529. You lighted the fuse and it went off ?—Yes.

13,530. Do you know who was living in the house at the time ?—There was a butcher living at the house at the time; it was a butcher's shop.

13,531. Was Linley lodging with him ?—Well, I expect he was; he lived there. I had watched him in and out a time or two ; I knew that was his house ; I expected he was lodging with him ; I do not know which of them held the house.

13,532. Did you know that other people lived there as well, that Mr. Poole lived there ?—Yes. I knew that a butcher lived there ; I did not know his name.

13,533. Was he a married man with a family ?—I did not know that.

13,534. You put it under the cellar grate ; under the shop or under the house ?—It was a round grate very near the middle of the causeway. It is a very broad causeway there. The grate did not go against the shop, and it did not open against the wall ; I put it in there and I flung it in as far as I could get it by throwing it in.

13,535. You knew nothing about Linley and had no enmity against him ?—No.

13,536. Did any person engage you to do this ?—Yes, Mr. Broadhead.

13,537. What did he pay you for the job ?—I think it would be 15*l.*, but I cannot pledge myself to remember everything; I have had so many cases that I cannot pledge myself to remember things. The general thing I think was about 15*l.*, but it was sometimes less.

13,538. As to the second time that you shot at him, have you anything to alter in your statement about that ?—No, I am not aware that I have made an untruthful statement in that ; I am not aware that I have.

13,539. Now about blowing up Wheatman and Smith's, have you anything to say ?—No, I do not know that I have any additions to make to that. I believe it is as right as I can possibly remember it ; I cannot alter it to the best of my knowledge.

13,540. Do you know Samuel Baxter, at Loxley ?—Yes.

13,541. Did you blow him up ?—Yes.

13,542. By putting a quantity of gunpowder down the chimney ?—Yes.

13,543. Who was with you ?—Thomas Needham.

13,544. Who employed you to do that ?—Broadhead.

13,545. How much did he pay you ?—Well, I cannot say. I think it would be 15*l.* ; that was about the regular sum, I think, generally. I might have had less on different occasions, but I think at that time it would be 15*l.*, but I cannot positively swear to that.

13,546. Had you any animosity at all against Baxter personally ?—No.

13,547. Did you know him ?—I knew him.

13,548. Have you drunk with him and known him ?—I have drunk with him, but I never had much to do with him.

13,549. Why did you do it ?—Because I was told to do it; I did it because Broadhead employed me to do it. When I got those jobs, I did them ; I did not ask any questions ; I did not ask the reason always.

13,550. Were Needham and Broadhead at all intimate ?—No. I do not know that ever Needham had anything to do with Broadhead ; not of my own knowledge ; never had to my knowledge. I employed Needham in that job ; he assisted me in that job.

13,551. Do you know Joseph Wilson, in Hereford Street ?—Yes.

13,552. Did you blow him up ?—Yes.

13,553. Who employed you to do that ? or did you do it on your own account ?—Broadhead.

13,554. Did you know him too ?—No, I did not know him.

13,555. What did he give you for that ?—I think it was about 15*l.*, the same as usual I think.

13,556. Now Reaney's wheel is in the Park ?—Yes.

13,557. Did you blow that up ?—Yes, I attempted it, but I did not do a deal at it.

13,558. Who employed you to do that ?—Broadhead.

13,559. Who was with you there ?—No one.

13,560. What did you get for that ?—15*l.*

FIFTEENTH DAY.

S. Crooks.

22 June 1867.

13,561. Had you any animosity or any personal feeling against Reaney, or was it merely because Broadhead employed you that you did it ?—It was merely because Broadhead employed me. I believe Fearnehough was working there at the time, I believe he was; I am not certain but I almost feel certain that it was so.

13,562. Did you do anything to Joseph Helliwell at Blonk wheel ?—I had nothing to do with him.

13,563. Did you do anything to Messrs. Firth's boiler ?—That I never knew anything about. I have had a bit of talk this morning with Mr. Broadhead respecting that: I never did do that, and I have never had anything to do with the boiler.

13,564. He has said you did ?—He says that he believes that he has said so. I saw it in the paper and I have been asking him respecting it. He says that he believes it is——. I will explain the matter afterwards.

13,565. You had better explain it now, I think ?—Very good. I did go to Firth's to put some powder down the chimney once, and I could not get it down the chimney. I went by myself—I carried a ladder. That will be remembered, I took a ladder from some place just below where they were building some houses. I took this ladder and when I got it to Firth's place I was so weak that I could not raise it up to the chimney, and I laid the ladder out of the gate of the trains (it was on the railway line) and I heard someone walking about and I resolved to push it through the window into the wheel, but there was some bars and I could not get it through, and I believe I laid it on the window sill or fastened it in some way to the bars so that it hung and went off and it blew the panes out and I believe that was all that it did. That was it that Broadhead thinks was the boiler. That was the job that I did. I had never anything to do with the boiler.

13,566. Has Broadhead told you who the man was that did it ?—No, he has not; he cannot recollect anything about the boiler. I do not know anything about the boiler myself, nor that they had done anything respecting the boiler. At any rate I never did anything respecting the boiler.

13,567. Did you watch at Firth's to try to shoot John Helliwell ?—Yes.

13,568. On that first occasion were you paid by Broadhead ?—I have always been paid by Broadhead.

13,569. Do you know how much he paid you to put the gunpowder down the chimney ?—Well I believe I got 15*l.* I told him a statement at that time. He did not want to give me the full amount at that time because I had not done anything. He said I did not do any damage at all. He said it was not deserving of the money, but I told him that I must have the full amount of money because I told him I had another with me; but that was false; I had not, I had done it myself. He said "Who hadst thou with thee ?" I said, "A chap called 'My Nunk.'" He said, "Thou hadst better have done it thysen." I said, "I shall have him to pay whether you give me the full amount or not, and I expect the full amount." (15*l.* I believe it was.) "Well" he says, "I will "give it thee, but thou hast not done it as thou ought "to have done;" and I got the 15*l.* I do not think that I should have got the 15*l.* if I had not told him that I had another man to pay out of it.

13,570. So that you recollect quite well that he paid you 15*l.* ?—Yes.

13.571. You have mentioned the name of a person called "My Nunk" ?—Yes.

13,572. Who is that ?—That is the man who I told you I had with me.

13,573. Who is he ?—I merely called him "My Nunk" on several occasions to Broadhead. I would not tell him who the man was, but I made him believe that I had another man with me.

13,574. Mind what you are about ?—Yes. I am come to speak the truth this time. I am going to divulge it all this time, I should have done so before.

13,575. Let me caution you, you know your peril. You mentioned a man called "My Nunk" ?—Yes.

13,576. Who is that man ?—I never knew him. I merely used the man's name. I merely wanted to make him believe that I had a man with me, but I never had a man with me.

13,577. Then there is no person that you know or have known that went by the name of "My Nunk"?—No.

13,578. What does "My Nunk" mean ?—I did it to suit my purposes.

13,579. But it is a very funny name, what does "My Nunk" mean ?—It was a nickname.

13,580. Have you ever heard that nickname applied to anybody ?—No.

13,581. Then was it an invention of your own ?—It was an invention of my own to get the money.

13,582. But what does "My Nunk" mean ?—I do not know.

13,583. Have you an uncle ?—I have many a one.

13,584. Have you heard an uncle sometimes called "Nunky" ?—No, I have never called an uncle that I had "Nunky."

13,585. Is it not a common thing in the town of Sheffield to call an uncle "Nunk" or "Nunky" ?—Yes, I dare say it is.

13,586. Now upon your oath was not one of your uncles employed with you to do this deed ?—Upon my oath I never had an uncle implicated at all. I generally did those things myself. I am bound to divulge all that I know.

13,587. But I want to keep you to "My Nunk"?—Very good.

13,588. Had you no uncle that has ever been engaged with you in any of these matters ?—Never in my life.

13,589. You say this was an invention of your own, and there is no such person as "My Nunk" ?—There is no such person that I have ever had to do with. This was merely an instrument, if I may say so, to get the money when he did not want to pay me. I put it on thinking that if I told him I had another man with me he would not be able to get out of paying all the money.

13,590. How many times have you told him that you had "My Nunk" with you ?—I do not know. I might have told him many a time, I cannot say, I do not call to mind the cases.

13,591. You say that on that occasion he did not want to pay you the full price, because you had not done as much mischief as he expected, and there might be a good reason why you should say that you had another man with you then to get the pay; but if you had done all that he expected of you there was no occasion to put in the name of another man, because your bargain was your bargain whatever it was ?—Yes, but the thing is here: a bargain is a bargain, that is right enough; but in many cases if the thing had not done anything there was a shuffle. There was not the money always very freely. There was a shuffle; and in those cases I had to shuffle anent that to get the money, and I told him that I could not do it for any less and that I must have it, because I had another man to pay out of it. This was false but it suited my end; and that is the reason that I said that I had another man with me. He has often asked me what this t'other man was when I told him so, but I never told him aught but "Nunk." I told him I did not know him by anything but the name of "Nunk." He wanted to know who I had with me on several occasions, but I could not pretend to implicate any man that was innocent, and I gave him this name to satisfy him that I had somebody with me on purpose to get the money. I believe that that case which I have mentioned just now was the case where there was not a deal done, and he complained that he did not ought to have to pay the whole amount.

13,592. Did you on one occasion attempt to shoot John Helliwell at Firth's ?—Yes.

13,593. Were you alone then, had you company?—I had James Hallam with me.

FIFTEENTH DAY.

S. Crooks.

22 June 1867.

13,594. Did you go several times on to the Midland Railway and watch through the window or whatever it was to see him at work ?—Yes.

13,595. What were your instructions with respect to shooting at Helliwell,were you to kill him ?—No, my instructions were these, that I was to do him ; that I was to shoot at him to do him harm ; not to kill him. I was never instructed to kill anyone. I was never told to do that.

13,596. Who instructed you to shoot Helliwell ?—Broadhead.

13,597. Did you attempt to shoot him with a gun ?—I took the air-gun to shoot him with.

13,598. On one occasion do you recollect pointing your gun at him, and a man called Woodhead getting up and his head coming between Helliwell's head and your aim ?—No, I will tell you what it was.

13,599. What was it ?—We went down, Hallam and me, and they were gassing. It was just before Christmas, I believe, and there was Woodhead and Joe Woollen working. Helliwell, I believe, did not work in that hull at all ; he had a little hull, as far as we ascertained after, at the back somewhere. He did not work in that wheel, I believe, where Woodhead did, or if he did, he was not working in it that night. I never saw him, to the best of my knowledge. I did not see Helliwell. I saw Woodhead and Joe Woollen. I never saw Helliwell at all. I never attempted to shoot at any one, but I should have done if I had had the chance at Helliwell, but I believe I never saw him that night.

13,600. Did you ever get up your gun to shoot and find that it was Woodhead instead of Helliwell ?—When we first got to the window we thought that Woodhead was Helliwell.

13,601. I thought so. Did you get up your gun to shoot at him ?—I cannot say whether I did or not, but I found out that it was not him. I cannot say ; I might get the gun ready.

13,602. How was it that you never did pick up Helliwell ?—How was it I never got at him ?

13,603. Yes ?—I never had a chance. At the time that we had Helliwell agate Wheatman and Smith's case turned up, and Broadhead said that we had better attend to Wheatman's, because it was wanted to be done more than Helliwell, and that we had better let Helliwell alone a bit, and we did do so, and we never went after that. To the best of my knowledge Helliwell's case was never taken up after it was given up.

13,604. What did you get for shooting at Helliwell ?—We never got anything. I am not aware that we got anything for Helliwell. We did not get money that easy.

13,605. Then you never were paid till you had done the job ?—We might get trifles to buy things with sometimes. but we never got paid while it was done.

13,606. With respect to Elisha Parker at Dore, have you anything to say ?—I never had anything to do with Elisha Parker. That is not my case. I will not take to that. I shall have plenty to answer for before I have done. I will not answer to that.

13,607. Do you know Elisha Parker ?—I know him, and I know he got shot ; but I never knew anything about that.

13,608. Do you know who shot him ?—No, I never knew anything about that.

13,609. Do you know who shot him ?—No, I never did any harm to Elisha Parker in my life, and I never did know any one who did any harm to him in my life.

13,610. Do you know a person of the name of Needham ?—Yes.

13,611. Did you ever go to Derby to see him ?—Yes. I made a false oath last time respecting that.

13,612. Then you did go to Derby ?—Yes.

13,613. How often ?—Only once.

13,614. Did you go with Needham's wife ?—Yes.

13,615. Who found you the money to go there ?—Michael Thompson, I believe.

13,616. He was the secretary of the Scythe Grinders' Union, was he not ?—Yes.

13,617. Did you go to see Needham when he came out of prison in London ?—Yes, I went to meet him, and saw him come out of prison.

13,618. Why did you go and meet him—who sent you ?—Well, I got the money from Michael Thompson to go to meet him.

13,619. Why were you to meet him ?—I went to meet him, he had been away, and I went to see him, of course to explain matters. There had been a deal of talk respecting his wife and his brother.

13,620. But why did Thompson give you the money to go to meet him ?—He gave me money to pay my expenses with, because I expect he was implicated with Needham. It was not my case then. It was Needham and Thompson. I did not engage in that case. It was Needham that engaged me to assist him that time.

13,621. In what were you to assist him ?—I assisted him in doing the act.

13,622. What was it ?—Putting some powder down a chimney at Dronfield.

13,623 Was it Ward and Camm's ?—Yes, I believe it was.

13,624. And you say that you were engaged by Needham, but it was Thompson's business ?—Yes, Needham told me that he had a job from Michael Thompson, and he said if I had a mind I could join him in it, and me and him and his wife's brother (they called him Henry Bradley) went to Dronfield, and put the powder and can down the chimney.

13,625. What did you get for that ?—I never got anything ; I never got a penny.

13,626. But you say that you got money from Michael Thompson to go to London. Did he tell you what you were to go and see Needham for ? Were you to tell him to keep the secret or anything of that sort ?—Before I went to London I had been in the habit of fetching money from Thompson for Needham's wife. They did not pay very regularly ; they were very irregular with it. I went many a time and did not get anything, and I daresay she thought that I had got it and did not give it her, but that was false. I gave her always what I got ; for my own sake I gave it her, every penny, and many a shilling out of my own pocket to keep the thing quiet. I did not want to be exposed in it.

13,627. And why did you go to London ? I do not quite understand.—I went up to London to fetch him to make it all right I expect. I do not know what I went up for. I went to meet him and keep him all right that he would not tell when he came out ; that was it.

13,628. Did you not know that Mr. Tyzack was hunting about for Needham ?—No, I did not know anything about it.

13,629. Did you not know that Tyzack was hunting about to get hold of Needham, when he came out of prison, and that it was in consequence of his trying to get hold of Needham that he was shot at ?—I never heard of that.

13,630. You never heard that it was in consequence of his trying to get hold of Needham that he was shot at ?—No, I never heard that he had been shot at. I never heard anything about Tyzack's case, never to my knowledge. I never heard that he had been shot at. I never knew anything about Tyzack. I never had anything to do with that.

13,631. Then you never heard that it was in consequence of his trying to get hold of the persons concerned in this affair, after they got out of prison, that he was shot at ?—No, I never heard of that business at all, as regards shooting at Tyzack. I never knew anything about it, and I never heard tell of it.

13,632. Was Needham at large for some time ?—Yes.

13,633. How long did he live in the country ?—Well, I could not say how long, but we were not very friendly for a while after that, Needham and me, because when his wife and he got together, she told

FIFTEENTH DAY.

S. Crooks.

22 June 1867.

him a lot of tales and we were rather at outs. We did not fall out but we kept aloof from one another. I did not see him very oft after that.

13,634. He is dead now, is he not?—No, I believe not.

13,635. Is he in America?—He is in America I believe.

13,636. Do you know who paid for his going there? —No, I do not know anything about that.

13,637. Now the next thing about which I will ask you is the Hereford Street outrage. Did you blow up Fearnehough?—Yes, I am sorry to say that I did.

13,638. Who employed you to do that?—Broadhead.

13,639. Had you any quarrel at all with Fearnehough?—No.

13,640. Was it merely because you were set on by Broadhead that you blew him up?—Yes.

13,641. How much did he pay you for that?—Well, I think it was 15*l.*

13,642. Did you see anybody but Broadhead about that?—I saw Joseph Copley.

13,643. Who was with you?—Joseph Copley was with me when I blew up Fearnehough, but I did not see anybody but Broadhead.

13,644. And you say that Broadhead paid you?—Yes.

13,645. How low long was it after the explosion that you were paid?—Well, I cannot say, but I believe it was getting on; it was during that week I believe, but I cannot swear to that exactly.

13,646. Were you paid in one sum or in different sums?—Well, I believe I was paid all at once, only I got the stuff to buy the powder beforehand I daresay. I believe I did.

13,647. Did he give you the money to buy the powder?—Yes, I believe he did, I believe so.

13,648. Did he tell you why he wanted Fearnehough blown up?—Yes, he was doing us a deal of injury. He did not say particularly; I understood that he was doing wrong in some way according to the rules, you know, of the trade. I did not ask him any very great particulars about it I think.

13,649. Did he tell you whether it was a joint business of the saw smiths and the saw handle makers and the saw grinders, or whether it was his own private matter?—I could not say that, I never asked him that.

13,650. Did he tell you whether there was any combination of unions who were determined to get rid of Fearnehough?—No, he did not say anything to me. I never asked him.

13,651. Did you ever see any of the secretaries connected with the saw smiths' union about that?—No, not particular that I know of.

13,652. Do you know Skidmore?—I know Skidmore. I have seen him at Broadheads, but I have never seen him in conversation or anything of that kind.

13,653. Did you talk to him about the Hereford street business?—No, I never spoke to anybody about it.

13,654. Had you any talk to Skidmore before it was done or after it was done about it?—No, not respecting that job.

13,655. Had you any about any other job?—No. I have never had anything to do with Skidmore, not as regards his engaging me or anything of that kind. I never had anything more to do with Skidmore than talking in regular private conversation at a public-house.

13,656. Regular private conversation?—Regular pnblic conversation, not private.

13,657. What have you talked to him about, was it about the persons whom you had blown up?—No.

13,658. Did you ever speak to him about the persons whom you had blown up or shot at?—No.

13,659. Did he ever speak to you about the persons whom you had blown up or shot at?—No. I have never had any talk to him of that sort.

13,660. Do you know a person named Thomas Smith?—The secretary to the saw makers? Yes, I know him.

13,661. Had you ever had any talk with him?—No.

13,662. Have you ever received any money from him?—No.

13,663. Do you know a person named Barker?—Yes.

13,664. What is he?—He is the secretary to the handle-makers, I believe.

13,665. Had you any talk to him about the Hereford Street business?—No.

13,666. Nor has he paid you any money?—Never.

13,667. You have had no communication with him either before or since about that affair?—No.

13,668. Do you know anything about Holdsworth? —Yes.

13,669. What did you do to Holdsworth?—I put some powder in the cellar.

13,670. Did it blow his works up?—Yes.

13,671. Who hired you to do that?—Broadhead.

13,672. You had no quarrel with him I suppose?—No.

13,673. Did he tell you what Holdsworth had done? —He said there were some outlaws working there or summat.

13,614. How much did he pay you for that?—It would be about 15*l.* I think. I think I generally had 15*l.* at that time. It might be less, but it would not be any more.

13,675. Did you generally receive the whole amount at a time?—No, not always. I had it deducted off my arrears sometimes.

13,676. But as a rule was it paid down in sums of 10*l.* or 15*l.*?—Well on a many occasions when I did owe anything at times he used to take so much towards it, but still I reckoned to receive 15*l.*

13,677. Were you generally in work?—Yes.

13,678. Then I suppose you generally paid your contributions, you were not much in arrear, were you?—Yes, I generally kept a little in arrear.

13,679. What amount then did you receive in money as a rule?—Oh, I cannot say that. I cannot answer that with truthfulness because I cannot say. That was just as it depended.

13,680. Were you engaged in Sutcliffe's business also?—Yes. I wish to say a little bit about that. Hallam has not implicated me in that business I believe, but I was with him.

13,681. Who struck him?—Both of us.

13,682. With what did you strike him?—We had two gutta-percha life preservers, one a-piece.

13,683. Who hired you to do that?—I do not know. I believe it was Broomhead, not Broadhead.

13,684. Did he hire you or did he hire Hallam to do that?—Hallam had that, and he engaged me to do that.

13,685. Did you get part of the money?—Yes.

13,686. What did you get?—I believe I got 3*l.* 10*s.* if my memory carries me right.

13,687. How much did you get altogether for that business?—Well, I understood him it was to be 7*l.* if I can recollect the thing right. I believe it was 7*l.*

13,688. And you got 3*l.* 10*s.* of it?—I got half of it let it be what it would, but I believe it was 7*l.*

13,689. You saw Broomhead, did you not, about it? —I did not see Broomhead. I went with Jem Hallam to fetch the last sovereign, and I strayed down Snig Hill while Jem went into that passage archway up Snig Hill, and when he came back he said he had to hold him up, he would not let him go while t'other chap fetched the sovereign or summat. I did not see Broomhead myself.

13,690. Now is there any other outrage of that description of which you have been guilty?—Yes, there is Crook's and Roberts's.

13,691. What did you do to them?—I and Needham put some powder in underneath the packing warehouse, I believe. It was through a cellar grate.

13,692. Did it blow them up?—Yes, it blew them up.

13,623. Who are Crooks and Roberts?—They are saw manufacturers.

FIFTEENTH DAY.

S. Crooks.

22 June 1867.

13,694. Whereabouts are their works ?—In Shoreham Street, I think they call it, down Doctors' Field.

13,695. What did you do that for ?—There was some variance or other ; Broadhead told us to do it, you know ; I do not know what there was or whether it went off.

13,696. How much did you get for that ?—I expect it would be 15*l*., but it is so long since that I cannot remember exactly.

13,697. How long ago is that ?—Oh, it is a many years back.

13,698. Is it more than ten years back ?—Yes.

13,699. Then we need not inquire into it. Was it before Needham was convicted of felony ?—Yes. I shall have to come out with all these things that I have been guilty of, whether it was ten or twenty years since.

13,700. We are not at liberty to examine you upon matters which occurred more than 10 years since, without the consent of the Home Secretary, unless they throw light upon something that has occurred within the last 10 years. If that which occurred more than 10 years ago was in connexion with something which occurred after 10 years ago, we are at liberty to go into it, but if it was an independent transaction of more than 10 years ago, we are not at liberty to go into it ?—But I am here to make a clean breast of everything.

13,701. Have you told us all the matters which you have done within 10 years ?—Would you just read them over to me. There might be something which I had forgotten.

13,702. There is Linley twice ; Wheatman and Smith, Baxter, Joseph Wilson, Reaney's wheel in the Park, John Helliwell at Firth's, Joseph Helliwell at Blonk wheel ?—I never did do anything to John Helliwell at Firth's.

13,703. You did not succeed. There was Elisha Parker that you say you had nothing to do with ?—No.

13,704. And then the Hereford Street outrage ?—Yes.

13,705. Are there any other cases which you know of within the last 10 years ?—I think not.

13,706. Have you ever sent any threatening letters ?—I am not aware that I have. I do not know that I have ever sent any.

13,707. Have you ever thrown letters into a house or put them into the post-office for Broadhead ?—Yes, for Matthew Broadhead. James Hallam and me when we took Matthew Broadhead's nuts.

13,708. What did you do ?—I will not be certain whether it was a note which Hallam flung into Matthew Broadhead's or whether it was the nut. I cannot swear to that.

13,709. Who wrote the letter ?—I believe it was Hallam. I do not know that I ever wrote any letters. Not to my knowledge.

13,710. I am speaking not of notes telling people where they could find their bands, but I mean notes telling a person that if he did not do so and so and so and so he might expect to have some serious injury done to him ?—I do not know that I ever sent any of them.

13,711. You cannot write perhaps ? Yes, I can write, but I certainly took the caution not to send notes ; that was my main aim. I never did a deal of that business ; the note business. I used to leave that job to Broadhead to do. The note system I had nothing to do with.

13,712. Did Broadhead tell you that he sent notes occasionally ?—Yes.

13,713. Have you ever posted them for him ?—Not that I am aware of. I generally used to keep out of that business.

13,714. I suppose that you have rattened a good many people in your time ?—No, I have not done a deal of the rattenings. I have done very little of that business.

13,715. Then your business was the blowing up and the shooting at people ?—Yes, it has generally been that I am sorry to say. They were not worth bothering with, those other cases, and I did not much with them.

13,716. Have you done any business for any secretary of any union except for Michael Thompson and Broadhead ?—And Broomhead ; that case that I was in with Hallam.

13,717. Have you done any for any other secretary ?—Those are the only cases which I ever had. I have never had to do with any secretary or anyone to the best of my knowledge.

13,718. Have you been employed by any person connected with any trade in Sheffield to do any outrage or anything against the law, except by the persons whom you have mentioned ?—No.

13,719. Will you swear that ?—I do not know that I ever have in my life.

13,720. Do you know of any person who has done any outrage besides those whom you have mentioned ?—No ; I do not know anybody that has ever done any.

13,721. You do not know ?—I do not know anybody who has ever done them. I have heard tell of things being done, but I do not know who did them.

13,722. Do you know who did the Acorn Street murder ?—No. I had nothing to do with it ; I never knew anything about that.

13,723. Are you sure about that ?—I am quite certain ; I am innocent of that.

13,724. You do not know who did it ?—No.

13,725. Thompson was tried for it you know, and got off ?—Yes, I know that, but I know nothing connected with that affair.

13,726. And you do not know ?—I do not know. It was rumoured at the time that "Slipper Jack" had done it, but I did not know "Slipper Jack." I did not know anything about it.

13,727. How was it rumoured, was it rumoured among men of your class ?—I do not know how it was rumoured. I do not know whether he was fetched up or not, but it was the talk at that time.

13,728. Who talked about it, was it Hallam ?—No.

13,729. Did anybody ever tell you that "Slipper Jack" had done it ?—I do not recollect any personally.

13,730. Do you never recollect anybody telling you that "Slipper Jack" had done it ?—No.

13,731. Who is "Slipper Jack ?"—I cannot answer that ; I do not know him.

13,732. Amongst whom was the rumour ?—It was almost anywhere you went at that time ; at almost any public house there would be somebody talking about it at that time. There was a great talk about it.

13,733. Did they say "Slipper Jack" had done it, or what did they say ?—They said it was "Slipper Jack ;" I did not hear aught about Thompson.

13,734. Was "Slipper Jack" a man known in the town ?—He had a great name, but I did not know him.

13,735. What had he a great name for ?—They always called him "Slipper Jack."

13,736. But what had he a great name for ? if you had been known to have done all these things, you would have had a great name ?—But there was not a many that did know.

13,737. What had he a great name for ?—I cannot say.

13,738. But what do you mean by his having a great name ?—He was a deal talked about.

13,739. Have you ever heard him talked about in connexion with anything else ?—No.

13,740. Have you ever heard that he had done anything else besides that Acorn Street murder ?—No.

13,741. What do you mean by his having a great name ?—I cannot answer any more.

13,742. Yes you can. What had he a great name for ?—Well, I have got a great name you know.

13,743. Yes, but what was he ?—I never knew this man, and I cannot say anything about it. I cannot say anything to implicate a man that I know nothing about.

FIFTEENTH DAY.

S. Crooks.

22 June 1867.

13,744. Has anybody told you that he knew that "Slipper Jack" had done it?—No; nobody that I can recollect. I never heard anybody say so, only at the time it was rumoured that "Slipper Jack" was suspected of it.

13,745. But you know a rumour cannot exist without it being talked about. Who told you that "Slipper Jack" had done it?—I cannot say, I heard it; I cannot say that anybody has told me particularly.

13,746. Where did you hear it?—I cannot say; I heard it in many a place where I went.

13,747. Tell me then a place where you heard it said that "Slipper Jack" had done it?—I cannot pledge myself to name one.

13,748. Everybody was talking about this murder; it was a very atrocious murder, and you must recollect where it took place if anybody talked about "Slipper Jack" having done it?—I cannot say particularly; I went to a many public houses. I heard it at every public house; it was town's talk.

13,749. But who was it that told you that it was "Slipper Jack" who had done it?—I cannot say.

13,750. Was it one of your own companions?—No.

13,751. Was it Hallam?—I do not know that I ever heard Hallam say anything about it.

13,752. Was it Needham, or any of those men that you have mentioned?—No; none of them knew him that I know of. It was after Needham's time.

13,753. Is there anything else that you know, that you think it is your duty to tell us which has occurred within 10 years?—I have told you all that I have done to the best of my knowledge, that I can think of. I do not know that I have omitted anything.

13,754. You know best; we cannot tell, of course?—I believe I have not omitted anything: I believe I have told you everything.

13,755. It is your only chance of safety to do so?—I believe I have told you everything, to the best of my knowledge. I take my oath that I have.

13,756. It is not only what you have done, but what you know?—I do not know anything about anybody. I never took the business of inquiry; I always took care to look after my own, and did not look after anybody elses, and to keep my own as private as possible.

13,757. Now you have come here to make this statement, and it is for the purpose of getting your certificate. We cannot tell at all at present whether or not we shall grant your certificate, because this inquiry is far from being finished, and things may turn up which may show that your story is not a true one. If it should turn out that it is not a true one, then you will not get your certificate, and you will be liable to be punished for these misdeeds?—Very well; it is this way. I have told the truth; there can be nought come up against me unless somebody swears false. I have told the truth now. I pledged myself not to divulge, and I never should have done, but Broadhead has done it. We agreed not to do it. Yesterday morning we agreed not to do it about this Hereford Street affair. It was such a disgraceful affair that I was alarmed at it, and I was so disgusted with myself that I told him I would not admit it. Now then he comes and admits it, and now I have come to tell you the truth and nothing but the truth, and I have told it you, and I cannot alter my statement. Whether I get a certificate or not I have told you the whole truth to the best of my knowledge.

13,758. If you have told the truth, you will get a certificate?—Well, I hope I shall, but my character is gone, I am sorry to say———

13,759. Never mind; we have nothing to do with that. We cannot talk about the character of a man who has committed crimes like yours: you may go?—It is a bad one, and I am ashamed of it.

The witness withdrew.

J. Copley.

JOSEPH COPLEY recalled and further examined.

13,760. (*Chairman.*) I understand that you wish to make a statement to us. When you were here on the last occasion you made a statement. According to the terms of the Act of Parliament, any person summoned before us, if he makes a true statement in our judgment, is entitled to a certificate to protect him; but if he makes a false statement in our judgment, he is not entitled to one. You have made a statement which may be, and which we think is false; and if so you will be prosecuted for what you have done; but, however, we gave a pledge to Mr. Broadhead yesterday that if he compromised any person we would give that person another chance, and allow him to come before us and make a statement. Do you wish to make a further statement?—Yes.

13,761. Now mind, it is no benefit to us; we have got the facts; it is only for your protection that this is done, and your only chance of protection is in telling the whole truth, not only as to the matters in which you are implicated, but as to everything you know about the matters connected with trades unions and outrages. If you know anything you are bound to tell it, whoever you may compromise, no matter what the consequences may be; and if you do not tell it, and we find that you have not told it, you will not get your certificate. When you were last before us, did you make a false or true statement?—A true statement to what I knew of, as to what you asked me.

13,762. I will read you what you said: "I "am a saw grinder, and I work at Mr. Taylor's in "Mowbray Street. I have worked for him about "four years, off and on. I am a member of the "union and I have been so for about seven or eight "years. I knew 'Putty' Shaw and Joseph Helli-"well. I never worked with him. I was never in "the wheel when he was there. I know a person "called Henry Garfit. He is my brother-in-law. I "might have been in the wheel with Helliwell when "he worked at the Tower wheel. I have seen him "there. I believe I have seen Henry Garfit fighting "with him. Garfit is rather older than I am. I "think I shall be 31 next birthday. Garfit is per-"haps six months older than I am, or something of "that sort. He is a low crooked leg man, middling "strong built. I do not know how old Helliwell is. "I should think he would be older than I was. He "was rather bigger than Garfit, but he was straight "legged. It was a toss up which won the fight. I "think Garfit had the best of him." Is that true?—Yes.

13,763. What statement do you want to make?—Concerning this outrage?

13,764. What outrage?—Hereford Street.

13,765. Did you do it?—No.

13,766. Were you there when it was done?—I was there.

13,767. Who did it?—Sam Crooks.

13,768. We know how it was done; by throwing in some gunpowder?—Yes.

13,769. Do you know how he happened to do it?—He engaged me himself.

13,770. Did he tell you who had employed him?—Broadhead.

13,771. What did you get for doing it?—A sovereign.

13,772. Did you see Broadhead about it?—No.

13,773. Broadhead never spoke to you?—No.

13,774. Had you any quarrel with Fearnehough?—No.

13,775. What did you do it for? simply because Crooks asked you to do it?—Yes.

13,776. Had you ever done anything of the kind before?—No, never in my life.

13,777. Had you done any rattening?—I was once in with James Hallam doing Damms.

FIFTEENTH DAY.

J. Copley.

22 June 1867.

13,778. I believe Hallam went out, did he not, and did it ?—Yes.

13,779. And told you he had done it, and then you shared the money ?—Yes.

13,780. Did you see "Tucker" Clarke that night ?—He was with us when it was done, I was talking to him while Hallam went and did it.

13,781. Did he know about it ?—He had got the job.

13,782. Did he say so ?—Yes.

13,783. Now you say you have never done anything but the Hereford Street outrage ; that is to say, blown a person up : have you ever shot at a man ?—No.

13,784. Have you ever been with any other man that did ?—No, never in my life.

13,785. Have you been asked to shoot a man ?—No.

13,786. Have you ever shot at a man ?—No.

13,787. Have you thrown any combustibles at a man, or anything of that kind ?—No, never in my life.

13,788. Have you ever thrown any powder into a house ?—No.

13,789. Have you done any outrage of any kind ?—No, only this one.

13,790. How old are you ?—I shall be 31 next birthday.

13,791. Are you married ?—Yes.

13,792. And yet for a paltry sovereign you engaged in blowing up a whole household of people ; is that so ?—Yes.

13,793. Had you any quarrel with Fearnehough ?—No.

13,794. You are a saw grinder, I think ?—Yes.

13,795. Is that all you wish to tell us ?—It is all I know.

13,796. Do you know any person who has committed an outrage, if you have not done one yourself ?—No, never.

13,797. Do you know any person who has done one ?—Only Crooks.

13,798. Do you know anybody who has done anything for any other union besides the saw grinders ?—No.

13,799. Do you know nobody who has been engaged in any of those matters ?—Not to my knowledge.

13,800. You have told us falsely once ; do not tell us anything about your knowledge ; I know what that means. Do not be frightened about compromising your friends ; if they come forward and make a full statement, and we find it to be true, we will grant them a certificate which will free them from the consequences of their acts. Is there anybody that you know at all who has ever been engaged in any outrage that you are aware of ?—No.

13,801. Not in any ?—No, I never knew about any but this here.

13,802. Do you know who committed the Acorn Street murder ?—No.

13,803. Have you ever heard anybody say that he knew who had done it ?—No, never in my life.

13,804. Did you ever hear the name of the man called "Slipper Jack" ?—I have heard tell of his name.

13,805. Who is he ?—I do not know I am sure.

13,806. Where does he live ?—I do not know.

13,807. What is he ?—I do not know.

13,808. Did anybody ever tell you that he knew that he was engaged in the Acorn Street matter ?—No, never in my life.

13,809. Never ?—No.

13,810. Is there any other outrage at all, committed by anybody, of which you have been told by any of your friends that they knew who had done it ?—No, never in my life. I know nothing about aught but this here.

13,811. You say that you got a sovereign ?—Yes.

13,812. Did you see Broadhead about it ?—No.

13,813. Did you talk to Broadhead about it ?—No.

13,814. Did you talk to any member of any other union about it ?—No, I had nought to do with anybody but only Crooks.

13,815. You may be thankful that you have been permitted to come forward and to say this. If you had not come forward you would have been in great peril, and it is only because we gave an undertaking to Broadhead that any man whom he implicated should be allowed to come forward that we have allowed you to come forward. You had once had your chance and you had gone away and not told us the truth ?—I am very sorry for it.

13,816. It is not only because you do not tell that which is true that you are in peril, but because you keep back that which you know ; and I told you distinctly, as I have told all the witnesses, that it is their duty to tell us all they know with reference to any outrage which has been committed. You knew about the Hereford Street outrage, and you never told us, and if you had not been allowed to come back and it had been found out that you had kept that back, you would never have got your certificate, and you would have been punished for this Hereford Street business. We have given no undertaking to anybody but Broadhead, but if any witness who comes forward keeps back a matter, and it is proved that he has kept it back, he will get no certificate from us ?—I have told the truth, what I know.

The witness withdrew.

GEORGE PEACE sworn and examined.

G. Peace.

13,817. (*Chairman.*) What are you ?—A saw grinder.

13,818. Where do you live ?—At No. 11, Washington Road.

13,819. Mr. Broadhead said yesterday that you engaged to find a man to do something to stop Elisha Parker from working. Is that true ?—Partly. Not particularly to stop him from working, but there was to be something done to him—not to do him any bodily harm.

13,820. What were they to do ?—That was not named. They were to frighten him principally, that was the thing to do.

13,821. Did you find a man ?—Yes.

13,822. Who was the man ?—They called him John Hall.

13,823. What was he ?—Well, he was brought up, I believe, in a scythe forge, but he was a labouring man at the time.

13,824. Had you had a talk with Broadhead before you engaged this man ?—He came up to my house.

13,825. Had you had any quarrel with Parker ?—No particular quarrel.

13,826. Why was it that you found a man to do something to him ?—Well, Broadhead came up to my house about six months previous almost to the time of this taking place about my finding one, and I objected at the time to find anybody or to have anything at all to do with it.

13,827. Was that three months before it happened ?—More than that. I should say it would be four or five months.

13,828. Broadhead came to you and said he wanted you to find a man, but you say you objected ?—Yes.

13,829. Why did you object ?—Because I did not want to have anything to do with him. I saw him pretty nearly every fortnight. I had to go to Sheffield and used to call and pay him my money as contributions, and so on, and he was continually at me to find him some one to do this business.

13,830. At this time you lived at Dore, and so did Parker ?—Yes.

13,831. How near did you live to Parker ?—Perhaps 200 to 300 yards distant.

FIFTEENTH DAY.

G. Peace.

22 June 1867.

13,832. At that time were you a married man?—Yes.

13,833. A housekeeper?—Yes, and a farmer as well.

13,834. Was this man Hall employed by you on the farm?—I have employed him occasionally at times.

13,835. Broadhead asked you frequently to find him a man to do this job?—Yes.

13,836. At last you consented?—I consented. The reason of his asking me that was, I asked him if there was nobody in Sheffield he could send, and let me be out of it altogether. He said he had sent parties from Sheffield, but they had not accomplished the purpose.

13,837. What did he tell you they had done. Did he tell you that they had hamstrung his horse in the night?—I heard of it.

13,838. You knew that they had hamstrung his horse?—Yes.

13,839. And he told you that they had been sent by him?—He said he had sent them to Parker several times, and they had not done it.

13,840. Did he tell you that he had told them to hamstring the horse, and that they had cut the horse's legs?—It was known throughout the country.

13,841. You knew therefore that Broadhead had sent them?—He never mentioned any case except what I had a hand in.

13,842. Did you know at the time when you were talking about this that Broadhead had sent some men to hamstring his horse?—I knew the horse was hamstrung. I did not know who had sent them.

13,843. Did not you know that Broadhead had caused the horse to be hamstrung?—I had no doubt that he had, but I did not hear him say so.

13,844. Did you yourself employ this man?—Yes.

13,845. How much were you to give him?—There was no stated price. It was in this way. He was not to do him any serious bodily harm, or anything of that sort.

13,846. What was he to do to him?—He was to frighten him. There was a train of powder laid to frighten him outside the house, and I suppose that it made some kind of blow up, but not anything particular.

13,847. Now mind, we know what the train of powder was, and if you tell us that it was merely a train of powder to frighten him, when there was such a quantity as to blow open the door, you will not get a certificate?—I do not know anything of that. I have nothing to do with that.

13,848. There was a train of powder laid at his house door to frighten him?—Yes.

13,849. Did you tell him that he was to lay this train of powder?—No.

13,850. Did you know that he had laid a train of powder?—I knowed the thing was done after.

13,851. Did your servant tell you so?—No, he did not tell me.

13,852. How did you know?—It was the country talk.

13,853. After that what did you do?—He was engaged to do something. There was nothing specified, only he was not to do him any bodily harm.

13,854. Did you engage him the second time?—No, one time only I engaged him.

13,855. I will read you what he says?—It was one agreement altogether.

13,856. Before I tell you what Broadhead said, I will ask you was it not suggested that the man should shoot him?—No.

13,857. Or blow him up?—No; there was neither blowing him up nor shooting at him mentioned.

13,858. Nor shooting at him?—No.

13,859. He was neither to shoot him nor shoot at him?—No, nor blow him up.

13,860. Nor blow up his house?—No.

13,861. What was to be done?—It was left to their discretion what they did as far as it went.

13,862. Did you give instructions to the man as to what he was to do?—No, I did not.

13,863. Did you tell Hall what he was to do?—No, I did not.

13,864. What did you say to Hall when you engaged him?—I told him what Broadhead had said to me.

13,865. Tell me what you said to him?—I told him Broadhead's words, what he said to me.

13,866. Tell me what you said to Hall, because we shall call Hall and see whether you are entitled to your certificate?—I said to Hall that he wanted something doing; that Elisha Parker was in default according to Broadhead's statement, and that Broadhead had been to me to get somebody to do the job. I wished him first to have gone to Broadhead, but Broadhead would not have it for fear it should be found out by his going to his house to receive the money. He wanted it passed through my hands; there was no arrangement what was to be done.

13,867. What did you tell him to do?—I did not order him to do anything.

13,868. What did you say Broadhead wanted doing? to say that he wanted a job doing is to tell him nothing; what did you say was the job that Broadhead wanted him to do?—As far as rattenings goes it was his business.

13,869. You know that it was not rattening. Did you tell him what kind of a job Broadhead wanted him to do?—He was not to do him any serious bodily harm; he was to keep from that in every shape and form.

13,870. You have told us what he was not to do, but you have not told us what he was to do?—Then he had to do what he thought proper after.

13,871. He was to do anything that he thought proper?—Yes, but not to do him any serious bodily harm.

13,872. Was he to do something to his person?—It was not stated what he was to do.

13,873. He was to do the job, but he was not to do him any serious bodily harm?—Yes.

13,874. Was he to do something to him?—It went as far as that, not to go to shoot or injure him in any way.

13,875. But he was to do something to him?—Yes.

13,876. You knew that?—Yes.

13,877. And you did not limit it in any way except that he was not to do him any serious bodily harm?—Yes.

13,878. Had your man a gun?—Had the man a gun when I engaged him?

13,879. Yes?—No.

13,880. Did you supply him with one?—No.

13,881. Had he powder?—No.

13,882. Did you supply him with powder?—No.

13,883. Did you hear afterwards that he had blown him up or shot at him?—I heard that he had shot at him.

13,884. You heard that he had shot at him?—I did not hear that Hall had, but I heard that he was shot at.

13,885. Did not you know that Hall was one of the men who shot at him?—I did not know personally, but he engaged to do the job. I did not see him do it. I know no more about it.

13,886. He was engaged in it when he was shot you say?—Yes.

13,887. How do you know that he was engaged in it?—Engaged in what?

13,888. In shooting at Parker?—I do not know that he was engaged in it.

13,889. Why did you say that he had the job?—He had the job, but I do not know that he shot the man.

13,890. I do not say that he shot him, but was he in the job when he was shot?—I do not know; he never told me that clearly.

13,891. What did he tell you?—Of course it was suspected that he had done it. That was as near as we could come to, but he never said the particulars. He said he had done the job or something to that effect.

FIFTEENTH DAY.

G. Peace.

22 June 1867.

13,892. He told you that he had done the job ?—Yes.

13,893. Did you pay him the money ?—It was put in my stackyard under a stone.

13,894. Who put it there ?—I put it there myself.

13,895. How much did you put there ?—I believe the first money was 6*l.*

13,896. What was the second money ?—He was a man out of work, and after this job was done he was hanging on me, and I paid him money—lots of money.

13,897. How much ?—Altogether I cannot swear, but at least 13*l.* to send him to America ; perhaps from 9*l.* to 11*l.* altogether I daresay he had.

13,898. And you paid him ?—I put it under that stone.

13,899. Did you always put it under the stone ?—Yes.

13,900. Did you never pay him anything into his hands ?—No.

13,901. Did you tell him that it was under the stone ?—Yes, I told him where it would be when I went down to get it from Broadhead.

13,902. Did you go and fetch it after Parker had been shot ?—Not directly after, but I kept going different times, and Broadhead paid me by trifling amounts. He did not pay me it altogether.

13,903. You know that Parker had been shot seriously, and was lying in the infirmary ?—Yes, and very sorry I was.

13,904. And you put this money that you got for shooting him under the stone to pay the man that you had engaged ?—Yes.

13,905. You say that you engaged him simply to frighten him ?—Yes.

13,906. That is what you say ?—Yes.

13,907. Does it occur to your mind that 6*l.* is a large sum to pay to one man simply to frighten another ?—Yes, but he had done this other deed when this came forward. He had done the deed when he got the money.

13,908. He knew what he was to have for it ?—No, there was no agreement about the price whatever.

13,909. What induced the man to shoot him if you had hired him to frighten him ?—From my statement to him from Broadhead that there was no tie about the money.

13,910. How did he come to shoot him ?—I believe, according to his statement, that Elisha Parker was holding up his hands, pointing his gun at him, and he said he was going to shoot him, and to save himself he shot first.

13,911. You told me that you never heard from him that he had shot him ; you told me only a minute ago that you never heard from him that he had shot him, but only that he was in that job ?—I told you he had done it.

13,912. You did not tell me that he said he had shot him. Now did he tell you that he had shot him ?—He said he had done the job, as I told you.

13,913. You told me also that he never told you any particulars, and a minute after you say that he told you all the particulars by saying that Parker held up his arm, and he thought he was going to shoot him and then he shot ?—He said he did not want to harm him, but the position he was in made him do it.

13,914. At first you said that he had told you no particulars, and now it turns out that he told you the full particulars of how he shot him ?—The reason he told me that was I found great fault with him for doing it, and he said he could not help it.

13,915. He is in America now ?—Yes.

13,916. Who found the funds for him to go to America ?—Broadhead.

13,917. Did the money go through your hands ?—Yes, I went to Liverpool with him.

13,918. Why did you go to Liverpool with him ? were you frightened that he would implicate you ?—I quite expected it would come out, and the man was hanging on me altogether ; he was always hanging on me for money.

13,919. Of course he would hang on you, if you induced him to do it ; you had induced him to shoot him. Now make a clean breast of it ?—No, not to shoot him.

13,920. To shoot at him ?—Not to do any bodily harm.

13,921. To shoot at him ?—There was nothing specified about it.

13,922. Did you know that he was going to shoot him ?—No, not previously.

13,923. Did you know that he was going out with a gun ?—I did not know he had any gun at all, he had no gun of his own.

13,924. Whose gun was it ?—I do not know.

13,925. Did he tell you whose gun it was ?—No.

13,926. Did he tell you it was Crooks' gun ?—No.

13,927. Did not he tell you that Crooks' was there ?—No, he never named such a man.

13,928. Did he say that it was Crooks' gun ?—No.

13,929. Did not you ask him ?—No.

13,930. When you did not know that he had a gun, and when he used a gun without your instructions, did not you ask him where he got the gun from ?—No.

13,931. Nothing was said ?—No, in no shape or form whatever whether it was a gun or a pistol. I do not know whatever it might be.

13,932. We have heard from Parker that there two shots, one above and the other below the house ?—Yes.

13,933. Who was the other man ?—I do not know.

13,934. You had heard the whole story, that it was the country's talk when the poor man was sent to the hospital ?—Yes.

13,935. You know that it was known quite well that he was shot, there were three shots ?—That I do not know.

13,936. Did he never tell you who was with him ?—No.

13,937. Do not you know ?—No.

13,938. Do you know a man called Bamford ?—Yes.

13,939. Did you ever hear him shooting his gun shortly before that night when Parker was shot ?—I do not remember hearing it, he might do it.

13,940. Do you mean to say that you did not hear him ?—I do not remember.

13,941. Did not you hear him ? You would know if a man was shooting off his gun at 8 or 9 o'clock at night ?—He might be.

13,942. The clergyman of your district has been here and said that he heard him ; do not you know that is so ?—I might not be at home when it was done.

13,943. You might not, but were you ?—I cannot say.

13,944. Will you swear that you were not ?—I cannot say whether I was at home or not.

13,945. Did you hear Bamford shoot off his gun at night ?—What night ?

13,946. Several nights before this occurred ?—I heard shots go off, but I did not know whose they were.

13,947. You heard them late at night ?—I heard shots go off ; I did not know whose they were.

13,948. You had heard shots late at night ?—Yes.

13,949. Upon your oath, do not you know that Bamford was one of the men who was out that night when Hall shot at Parker ?—No, I did not.

13,950. Will you swear that Bamford was not one of the men ?—I swear I do not know anything about him.

13,951. Did Hall tell you so ?—No.

13,952. Has Bamford told you ?—No, he never has.

13,953. You talk of the money that you put under a stone ; you say that you put 11*l.* or 12*l.* there ?—Not as much as that.

13,954. Say 11*l.* ?—Yes.

13,955. Broadhead has sworn that he paid you 30*l.* ?—Yes, but it is wrong ; there was 13*l.* at least sending the man to America, and he paid me from 20*l.* to 30*l.* altogether.

13,956. Broadhead paid you from 20*l.* to 30*l* altogether, but not a great deal over 20*l.* ?—No.

FIFTEENTH DAY.

G. Peace.

22 June 1867.

13,957. How much did the man get? Did you pay more than one?—No.

13,958. Will you swear that you did not?—Yes.

13,959. Do you swear that you do not know that more than one man was engaged in it?—No, I do not.

13,960. There were three shots, it was well known all over the country; do you mean to tell me that when you found that your man had shot him and described all about it, you did not ask the particulars as to who was there besides?—No, I did not, it was not my business. I could not be seen with him. I was as little with him as possible.

13,961. Did not you say to him, "You have employed other men?" Did not you put that to him? No, I had nothing to do with that. He employed who he liked, it was nothing to me.

13,962. Have you talked to Bamford about it?—No, not particular.

13,963. Was Bamford a neighbour of yours?—Do you mean to say did I talk to him at the time it was done about it?

13,964. Yes?—It was rumoured that it was Bamford. I think he was fetched up for it.

13,965. Did you speak to Bamford about it?—About what.

13,966. About shooting Parker?—Of course if we got into discourse we should talk about it.

13,967. Of course you would. Now in your discourse with Bamford did not you hear from him that he was one of the party out that night?—I had heard it said many a time over.

13,968. Did not he tell you so?—Do you mean Bamford?

13,969. Yes?—No, he did not.

13,970. Did not Hall tell you so?—No.

13,971. Did not you know that he was out that night?—No, I did not.

13,972. Do not you believe it?—I cannot say anything about it. I will not say whether he was in or out. I do not know.

13,973. Did he get any of your money?—Bamford.

13,974. Yes?—Not to my knowledge.

13,975. What are you?—I am a saw grinder.

13,976. Are you a master?—Not particularly so.

13,977. Do you employ hands?—Yes, I employ hands.

13,978. What number of hands do you employ?—Merely my own son and an apprentice who is nearly at age, and another man I set on occasionally as my work runs.

13,979. Do you hire a hull or a trough?—My son has a wheel.

13,980. Is it your son's own property?—It belongs to Offley Shore.

13,981. But your son rents it?—Yes.

13,982. What rent do you pay for your house?—10*l.* a year.

13,983. Were you in the same position of life then as you are now?—No.

13,984. You have gone down in the world?—Yes.

13,985. What were you formerly?—I was formerly a grinder and a colliery master, and I don't know what.

13,986. Did you employ several hands at that time?—A many.

13,987. Then you, in your station of life, being an owner of a colliery, a farmer, and so on, hired one of your men to go and do a deed of this kind; and after he had done it, you paid him money for shooting at a neighbour whom you had no quarrel with, is that the state of things at Dore?—Yes, he was not much of a man of mine, he worked for me occasionally, but very seldom, it was six months before I would have anything to do with it.

The witness withdrew.

Adjourned to Monday next at 11 o'clock.

SIXTEENTH DAY.

Monday, 24th June 1867.

PRESENT:

William Overend, Esq., Q.C.
Thomas Irwin Barstow, Esq.
George Chance, Esq.
J. E. Barker, Esq., Secretary.

WILLIAM OVEREND, Esq., Q.C., in the Chair.

SIXTEENTH DAY.

D. Clarke.

24 June 1867.

Dennis Clarke recalled and further examined.

13,988. (*Mr. Barstow.*) You are sworn in this inquiry, not that that makes much matter to you. We are going to give you another chance to clear yourself; you have confessed that you have committed perjury, and that the story which you told us before was untrue. You have one more chance, and this is your last one. Do you remember Helliwell being blown up?—Yes.

13,989. Some time before that did you receive some powder from Broadhead?—Yes.

13,990. How much did you receive?—I cannot tell you how much it was; there was a good deal.

13,991. Did Broadhead give you any directions when he gave you the powder?—He told me to go and blow Helliwell up with it.

13,992. Did you go?—Yes, me and Shaw went.

13,993. What were you given for blowing him up?—3*l.*

13,994. What did you do with the powder?—I gave Shaw some of it, and some of it I had myself.

13,995. Did you sell any of it?—Yes.

13,996. To whom did you sell it?—To Simmointe.

13,997. What did you do with what remained?—What remained I used.

13,998. How did you use it?—Shaw used it to put in Helliwell's trough.

13,999. Were you present?—Yes, I was in the other hull. I could see what he was doing.

14,000. You saw Shaw put it in?—Yes.

14,001. Have you ever done any other job for the trade?—Yes.

14,002. What was that?—Rattening.

14,003. Whom did you ratten?—They call him Thomas Broadhead.

14,004. When was that?—That is a good while since; I cannot tell how long it was since.

14,005. Where did he work?—At Lovell wheel on Ran Moor.

14,006. How did you ratten him?—I took his bands.

14,007. What was that for?—Because he had not paid his contribution, I expect. It was either that or grinding some saws that he had no business to grind. I do not know which it was.

SIXTEENTH DAY.

D. Clarke.

24 June 1867.

14,008. Did you get anything for that?—Yes, we got summat, but I cannot tell to a halfpenny who got it.

14,009. Who was in it?—I can but think of one, and that is George Peace.

14,010. Who is he?—He is a saw grinder.

14,011. Does he live at Dore?—No, he lives somewhere near the infirmary.

14,012. (*Chairman.*) Is he the man who gave evidence on Saturday?—I think not.

14,013. Are there two George Peaces?—Yes, young George and old George.

14,014. (*Mr. Barstow.*) Was this young George or old George?—Young George.

14,015. What is he by trade?—A saw grinder.

14,016. Who set you to do this?—Well, Thompson gave me the ticket.

14,017. (*Chairman.*) What Thompson? — They call him Bill Thompson.

14,018. (*Mr. Barstow.*) Who is Bill Thompson?—He is a saw grinder, and works at the Eagle.

14,019. How did he give you the ticket?—He said he had got a ticket to go and do this Broadhead, and he would not do it, and he gave it to me.

14,020. What sort of a thing is this ticket?—It is to fetch t' bands.

14,021. Was it a piece of paper?—Yes.

14,022. Can you read?—A little.

14,023. What was written on that piece of paper?—I am sure I cannot tell you; it was to fetch t' bands.

14,024. Was there anything said about what you were to have for it?—No.

14,025. Who paid you for fetching the bands?—Broadhead paid some of it, but I do not know which of us he paid now.

14,026. Is George Peace the son of the man who used to live at Dore?—He is the son of David Peace.

14,027. Have you ever done any other job?—No, I had a ticket out for one.

14,028. That was Charley Damms, was it?—Yes.

14,029. You had a ticket—what sort of a ticket was it?—It was a bit of a paper.

14,030. What was written on it?—I am sure I cannot tell you.

14,031. You had two?—Yes, but I cannot tell you what was written on it.

14,032. There must have been directions of some sort on it, what were they?—I cannot tell you. I think it was a ticket to fetch t' bands.

14,033. Is that all that you can tell us?—Yes.

14,034. Was the name of the man whose bands you were to fetch written on the ticket?—I am sure I cannot tell you, they give you a ticket telling you where you were to go to.

14,035. That is all you have done is it?—Yes, for the union.

14,036. We have nothing to do with what you have done on your own account. Those are all the trade things with which you have been concerned are they?—Yes, I have not been so bad as folks think.

14,037. (*Chairman.*) Do you know of any other person who has done any other trade outrage or mischief at all?—I do not know. I have never been with anybody.

14,038. Do you know of any person who has done anything?—I have never been with them.

14,039. But have you known of any person doing anything of the kind?—I have heard talk of Copley doing rattening.

14,040. What do you know about Copley?—That he has done a good deal of rattening.

14,041. Have you talked with Copley on the subject?—No.

14,042. Where have you heard talk about it?—At the club-house.

14,043. What club-house?—The saw grinders club-house.

14,044. Then do you talk about what rattening is done at the club-house at Broadhead's when you are there?—Yes, I heard talk about a deal of rattening.

14,045. Amongst the members?—Yes.

14,046. And was it a well known fact to them there that Copley was engaged in rattening—did they all know it?—I expect so.

14,047. Did they know that you had rattened also? No, I do not know that anybody knew besides Peace and me. I have only rattened one. I have had a ticket for two.

14,048. But was it known amongst the members of the union that rattening was going on?—Yes, I should expect so.

14,049. Do you know of any person who has done anything like a blowing up?—Not besides myself and Shaw.

14,050. Was it known who had done that amongst the union people?—No, it was known to nobody but Shaw and me and Broadhead.

14,051. But was it talked over at the Union club-house that it had been done for the benefit of the trade?—I do not know.

14,052. But what was said in the public-house after you had done it?—Nobody knew who had done it.

14,053. But what was said about it?—I cannot tell I am sure.

14,054. But did they say that it was done for the trade or not?—They did not mention what it was done for to my knowledge.

14,055. Did you ever hear of that Hereford Street business?—I never heard of it while I heard it here.

14,056. Did you hear it talked of at your club?—No.

14,057. You never did?—No.

14,058. You never heard of blowing up chimneys talked of at your club?—No.

14,059. You never heard of blowing up houses and things of that so?—No.

14,060. Do you mean to say that you never heard it talked of at the club-house?—No.

14,061. But rattening is common enough?—That is common enough.

14,062. (*Mr. Barstow.*) I do not think I asked you what Broadhead was to give you for that job?—3*l.*

14,063. (*Mr. Chance.*) I suppose you had no quarrel with Helliwell had you?—No, he took my work.

14,064. And was it because he took your work that you helped to blow him up?—Yes.

14,065. Did you ever hear of a man called "Slipper Jack"?—I have heard him mentioned many a time when I was a boy.

14,066. What is he?—He used to be a fighting man, that is what I have heard of him.

14,067. What is his name?—"Slipper Jack."

14,068. But what is his real name?—I could not tell you his other name.

14,069. Have you ever seen him fight?—No.

14,070. But you have heard of his fighting?—Yes.

14,071. Then you have heard him spoken of by some other name?—I never heard of his name to my knowledge.

14,072. But you know the man?—No.

14,073. Have you seen him?—No, I might have seen him, but I could not pick him out.

14,074. And have you seen him and heard of him as "Slipper Jack"?—I have heard him spoken of as "Slipper Jack."

14,075. But you said you had seen him?—No, not to my knowledge.

14,076. You know him by sight, do you not?—No.

The witness withdrew.

HENRY SKIDMORE sworn and examined.

H. Skidmore.

14,077. (*Chairman.*) Do you wish to give evidence before us?—Yes, I do. I was summoned to appear here this morning.

14,078. What are you?—A saw maker.

14,079. Do you belong to any union?—The saw makers society.

SIXTEENTH DAY.

H. Skidmore.

24 June 1867.

14,080. Do you hold any offices?—I am president of the saw makers society.

14,081. Who is your secretary?—Thomas Smith.

14,082. What other officers have you?—There is no more besides the committee; there are only two officials of the trade.

14,083. Have you no treasurer?—No, there is no treasurer, the secretary is treasurer.

14,084. Have you brought your books with you?—I have not any; the secretary has brought his books.

14,085. Does the secretary keep the books?—Yes.

14,086. And he has brought them has he?—He has brought them.

14,087. What communication do you wish to make to us?—Regarding our trade.

14,088. You offer yourself as a witness, and I want to know what communication you wish to make to us?—I thought that Broadhead had stated things about which I had to appear here this morning.

14,089. What have you to say about them? I had better put it to you?—I think it would be better.

14,090. Is it true that you paid a sum of money to Broadhead, in order to get the blowing up done in New Hereford Street?—No, after it was done a sum of money was paid to him. I paid the money.

14,091. How much was it?—It was 15*l.*; it was lapped up in a piece of paper when I gave it to him.

14,092. You gave him 15*l.*, did you?—He said it was 15*l.*, but I do not know what sum it was, because I never counted it.

14,093. You know it was money?—I know it was money.

14,094. And you know that it was for doing that job in New Hereford Street?—Yes.

14,095. Had you known that that Hereford Street offence was to be committed before it was committed?—No, or else it never would have been.

14,096. Who told you that it had been done?—Mr. Broadhead.

14,097. When did he tell you?—I am sure I cannot remember the day.

14,098. How soon after the outrage was it?—I think it was Wednesday or Thursday night.

14,099. What day of the week was the outrage?—I think it was Wednesday when he told us.

14,100. When was the outrage, on a Monday, or Tuesday, or Wednesday?—I think it was a Monday, but I hardly know; I never took any particular notice of the day of the week. It was on the Wednesday night that we had an interview with him.

14,101. Where did he tell you?—In the room upstairs.

14,102. In his own house?—Yes.

14,103. Who was present?—Joseph Barker.

14,104. Who besides?—Nobody else, besides Mr. Broadhead.

14,105. And yourself?—Yes, and Joseph Barker.

14,106. You and Joseph Barker and Broadhead were together?—Yes.

14,107. Were you on the saw grinders investigating committee?—No.

14,108. Were you ever on it?—Not the saw grinders, on the saw makers I was.

14,109. Why did you go there that Wednesday night?—Well, the reason why we went there was respecting this Hereford Street affair; we were surprised how it occurred, and we wanted an understanding, so long as we had never given orders for it.

14,110. What did you say to him?—Should I tell you the first interview we had with Broadhead, or only this one?

14,111. If you please, we should like to have it all?—The first interview with him——

14,112. When was that; was it on the Wednesday?—No, it was previous to that.

14,113. When was the first interview?—I should think it was two or three months previous; two months perhaps before this occurred; I never took particular notice of the dates.

14,114. What took place then?—There was I and Joseph Barker went to him, and this Fearnehough was doing some of Slack's work; he was working for Slack, Sellar's and Company, and the saw grinders were out. We went to him and asked him if anything could be done respecting Fearnehough. He was grinding saws for Slack, and their grinders, and the saw makers, and the handle makers were out of employ, and this Fearnehough was grinding the work. We asked Broadhead if something could be done to stop him respecting rattening him and taking his nuts; and he said he would see if something could be done. That was the first interview, but we were not aware that there was going to be a blow up or else we should have put a stop to it. It would never have occurred, I am certain.

14,115. Have you, as a member of the union and as representing your union, been in the habit of rattening?—No.

14,116. Then this was a special case, was it?—Yes.

14,117. Do you mean to say you had never ordered any rattening before?—No; I do not say that, because I have ordered rattening.

14,118. Has your union ordered rattening before? Yes; there was rattening in our union before I was born.

14,119. I daresay there was. Have you ordered the taking away of nuts as well as bands?—I do not know; I have ordered the taking away of bands.

14,120. Have you ordered the taking away of nuts?—Well, I cannot say. Yes, I daresay nuts and bands too. I do not know whether they took away nuts at the same time, but I will say nuts and bands.

14,121. That was for enforcing the payment of contributions, was it?—Contributions and other things.

14,122. Had you done anything else before this in the way of enforcing your rules besides taking away bands and nuts?—No.

14,123. Had you never in your life been a party to anything being done to a man besides his bands and nuts being taken away before this?—No, and I never sided with it.

14,124. Has any person in your union been blown up?—No, not in the saw makers department.

14,125. No person in the saw makers department has ever been blown up?—No, nor ever been injured in any way.

14,126. Has anything been done to him personally?—No.

14,127. Not in your saw makers union at all? Remember I have a long list here. I do not want you to make a mistake?—I will tell you what I know respecting the union since I joined it, and that is enough.

14,128. How long have you joined the union?—I was put an apprentice in 1826; I think about 31 or 32 years almost. I have joined ever since 1826, when I was put an apprentice.

14,129. During that time that you have been a member of the union, has no saw maker been injured at all?—All that I can remember is, that one person had his garden destroyed about 20 years since.

14,130. But within the last 10 years?—No; that is 20 years since.

14,131. Confining yourself to the last 10 years, has no saw maker been personally injured?—No, not one.

14,132. You believe that is a fact?—Yes; I cannot recollect anyone that has ever been injured in any way whatever.

14,133. No saw maker?—No.

14,134. Has any saw maker lost anything besides bands and nuts within 10 years?—A saw maker never lost bands and nuts.

14,135. But you have rattened?—Yes; the grinders you mean?

14,136. But has any saw maker lost any of his property?—No.

SIXTEENTH DAY.

T. Smith.

24 June 1867.

THOMAS SMITH sworn and examined.

14,328. (*Mr. Chance.*) What are you ?—I am the secretary belonging to the Saw Makers Society, and I am a saw maker or a saw smith by trade, whichever you have a mind to term it.

14,329. How long have you been secretary to the Saw Makers Society ?—I took office on the 1st April 1866. You will find it recorded in the minute book. I have been in office about 15 months I think.

14,330. Had you held any office in that society previously to that ?—I have been on the committee several times, but it is sometime since.

14,331. How long have you been a member of that society ?—I have been between 20 and 30 years a member of that society.

14,332. Do you remember the Hereford Street outrage ?—I do very well to my great grief.

14,333. Had you known anything of that previously to its taking place ?—I had not ; it was done without my knowledge.

14,334. Did you know Fearnehough ?—No, not before I saw him in the Court the other day—I mean speaking the truth.

14,335. (*Chairman.*) If you say that so often we shall begin to doubt you. There is no necessity for your making statements of that kind.

14,336. (*Mr. Chance.*) Have you ever heard of him ?—Yes.

14,337. You know his name ?—I know his name.

14,338. Did you know that he was a saw grinder ?—Yes.

14,339. After the outrage took place did you see Broadhead ?—No.

14,340. Did you ever see anything of Broadhead after that ?—I have seen him several times, but we had no conversation on the Hereford Street outrage at all.

14,341. How long after the outrage had taken place had you any communication with anyone upon it ?—A few days. Our president came to me.

14,342. (*Chairman.*) What is his name ?—Skidmore.

14,343. (*Mr. Chance.*) Which day was it ?—It was either Wednesday or Thursday. I should not like to be positive on that matter, but it was either Wednesday or Thursday.

14,344. Did he come by himself or with anybody else ?—He came by himself.

14,345. When he came what did he say to you ?—He said that he had seen Mr. Broadhead, and he came and wanted the money from me. I ought to remark that before this he came to me and named about the Hereford Street outrage and about the blow up, and he wanted some money from me.

14,346. (*Chairman.*) At this interview or before it ?—It was after the Hereford Street outrage.

14,347. What was the interview you are talking about ?—The only interview.

14,348. What did he say ?—He said he wanted some money.

14,349. What else did he say to you ?—He came to me and he said " We are in a mess," and I asked him what was the nature of the mess.

The witness withdrew.

J. Reaney.

JAMES REANEY sworn and examined.

14,350. (*Chairman.*) You are I believe the secretary of the Edge Tool Makers Union ?—Yes.

14,351. And I understand that you have brought, first, a cash book, commencing 10th October 1866 ; secondly, a roll book, commencing January 1865 and ending December 17th, 1866; thirdly, a roll book, commencing January 1867; and, fourthly, a ledger commencing in 1846, but which is so incomplete that there there must be another ledger, and from which it is impossible, we are informed, to make any account. Have you a cash book ?—I have given it to Mr. Barker. I never brought any books except three.

14,352. Is there a cash book ?—No.

14,353. Have you a cash book ?—I have, and entered all the monies in.

14,354. Have you a cash book ?—No.

14,355. Have you ever had one ?—No.

14,356. Have you any book showing your cash transactions for the last 10 years, or during any portion of that time ?—Yes, that book will do it (*producing a book and explaining it to Mr. Shrubsole*).

14,357. Then that begins in 1861 ?—Yes.

14,358. Have you no book earlier than 1861 ?—Only what I call my ledger.

14,359. What has become of a similar book to that antecedent to 1861 ?—I think for seven or eight years since we have kept nothing but the contribution book. We have destroyed nothing that I know of.

14,359*a*. You do not produce any such books ?—No.

14,360. Have you a minute book of your proceedings ?—Yes.

14,361. That begins in 1864 ?—We never had a minute book before that.

14,362. Had you never a minute book before 1864 ?—No.

14,363. Had you any ledger besides that which you have there ? we are told that that there ought to be another and that that is not a complete ledger ?—You see the contribution book contains all that we receive. Then this book shows you what we have paid out of that, and all the accounts are entered in this ledger.

14,364. I am told that the cash book commences in 1864 ?—That is not brought.

14,365. But we want all your books for the last 10 years ?—I was not aware of that, we shall have to fetch that ; do you want it now ?

14,366. Yes, every book which you have. On your oath, have you never kept a minute book besides this ?—Only this one.

14,367. Nothing else ?—Nothing else.

14,368. Have you no entries of your proceedings ?—We have made entries of all monies paid, and of all monies paid out, and what they are for.

14,369. Do you make an entry of resolutions passed ?—Not at all times.

14,370. Have you any book recording proceedings at your meetings ?—Recording resolutions, I cannot speak to that. If I may be allowed to go I will fetch all that I have.

14,371. What you have brought are not enough for our purpose, and you must produce all the books which you have had for 10 years past, and bring us a copy of your rules ?—I have sent those to London, but I dare say I can get you a copy. The secretary holds that copy of the rules.

14,372. Very well. You ought to be very glad to come here and lay these books before us for the sake of the union itself ?—I am very proud to come here to answer your questions.

14,373. Do not let all that is bad go against the unions in Sheffield, surely there must be something to their credit, do let us have it ?—I will bring them. I will get back as soon as I can.

The witness withdrew.

T. Smith.

THOMAS SMITH recalled and further examined.

14,374. (*Mr. Chance.*) The last thing you said was that you asked Skidmore the nature of the mess ?—Yes; he stated to me with reference to Fearnehough's blowing up.

14,375. What did he say ?—He said it was a bad job.

14,376. (*Chairman.*) He could not say it was a bad job, that is not the way people talk about such

it. We were never parties to it, and we abhor the " whole thing ?"—Well, I must admit that I committed myself in that error, and I do regret it sincerely from the bottom of my heart, although I was not a partaker in it.

14,548. Can you tell me the date when you paid this money ?—I never paid it.

14,549. You gave an order for it to be paid out of your money. Do not quibble in that way ?—Mr.

there were such indignation meetings, ... a person who was perfectly innocent should have had it just confided to him. Did you know nothing about it ?—Mr. Skidmore came to me and told me about it.

14,571. It is a very odd thing that he should come and tell you, why should he tell you ?—I did not know that it belonged to the saw trade at all.

14,572. Then why should he tell you, when he was not sure that you would not the next minute go

—Yes ; when I thought we were going to have a Commission of Inquiry down here I thought I would make my book right.

14,658. So when you thought that there was going to be an inquiry you thought that it would better your case to destroy the leaves of one of your books ?—I thought so at the time ; I do not now ; I regret it very much.

14,659. Is Kenworthy alive ?—No ; he died in January 1862.

14,660. He died in January 1862 ?—Yes.

14,661. Did not it occur to you that if you wanted

14,689. Is it only known now for the first time to anybody but yourself that you have mutilated one of the books and made a false entry in the other ?—I have named it to several of our members.

14,690. When have you mentioned it ?—Two or three weeks ago the first time.

14,691. To whom ?—I mentioned it to James Gorbidge.

14,692. Who is he ?—He works with me.

14,693. What is he ?—A fender grinder.

14,694. Where do you work ?—At Mr. Robertson's Chancery works.

SIXTEENTH DAY.

T. Smith.

24 June 1867.

14,480. Do you mean to say that your auditors passed your accounts in that way? If you said that they were expenses paid by Mr. Barker, did they not ask you what they were paid for, and did you not tell them?—I did not.

14,481. Do you mean to say that they passed those expenses?—Yes, just the same as they had passed these other accounts.

14,482. Do you mean to say that the unions had no

14,504. And you say that there are eight or nine months entries torn out?—Yes, there are.

14,505. Who tore those out?—I tore them out, and that one entry went with the rest.

14,506. Why did you tear out the eight or nine months entries?—I do not know; just for this very same reason.

14,507. Did the other pages extending over eight or nine months contain entries of similar expenses?

SIXTEENTH DAY.

T. Smith.

24 June 1867.

and tell of him; why did he tell you?—Because he had been and seen Broadhead about it.

14,573. I know that, but why did he tell you?—Well, I do not know hardly what to say to you with reference to that. I did not know about it before he was blown up.

14,574. But why did he tell you?—We were in conversation.

14,575. But persons do not tell people about such a thing in conversation if they had not to do with it before. They do not say, "I have been concerned and I have been asked by a man to pay him money" for an outrage like this for which a reward of upwards

14,581. Was that the reason?—That was the reason, and because I did not want to leave old England and I did not want to get the reward; I had done nothing amiss myself, and that was the reason and the only reason.

14,582. You knew Fearnehough was obnoxious to the trade?—Yes, I had heard about it.

14,583. Do you know him yourself?—No, I never saw him in my life or spoke to him before I saw him in this chair the other day.

14,584. Did you know that Barker and Skidmore had had this interview with Broadhead?—Yes, I

SIXTEENTH DAY.

J. Robertson.

24 June 1867.

14,695. How did you happen to mention it to him; is it since this inquiry began?—Yes.

14,696. Is it since I made the announcement that we should require the books of the various unions?—It was before you gentlemen came down here to sit.

14,697. Did you tell him that you supposed that the persons who were sent down would have to see your books?—No, I did not.

14,698. How did you happen to talk to him about it?—I told him this, that I received from Mr. Kenworthy 24*l.* 15*s.* 3*d.*, whereas I ought to have received 30*l.* 15*s.* 3*d.* I told him that I got a new book and had entered all afresh, and put it down received 30*l.* 15*s.* 3*d.*, whereas I only received 24*l.* 15*s.* 3*d.*, and he asked me my reasons for doing so, and I told him this, that I remembered well the first or second night in November 1861, when I officiated for our secretary, that he gave me 6*l.* to give to William Bayles, and I paid him, and that this 6*l.* would make it correct.

14,699. You say that you said to him that you had received 30*l.* from Mr. Kenworthy, whereas you had only received 24*l.*?—Yes.

14,700. If you received only 24*l.* how would his paying you 6*l* to give to Bayles make it right?—(*No answer.*)

14,701. If Mrs. Kennedy paid you 30*l.* you ought to have put down 30*l.*?—Yes.

14,702. But instead of putting down 30*l.* you put down 24*l.*?—That was what I received from him.

14,703. You received from her 30*l.*?—I put down 30*l.*

14,704. You received 30*l.*, did you put down 30*l.*?—No, 24*l.*

14,705. You said that you had received 30*l.* from her?—If I said so I said wrong.

14,706. You only received 24*l.* from her?—24*l.* 15*s.* 3*d.*

14,707. You put down 24*l.* as you received it?—Yes.

14,708. Then the accounts did not balance by 6*l.*? No.

14,709. Then you say that you believe that the way the accounts would be made to balance would be by Kenworthy paying you the sum of 6*l.* that you paid to Bayles?—Yes.

14,710. What happened?—The Acorn Street outrage happened immediately after this.

14,711. The Acorn Street outrage was a murder?—Yes.

14,712. Then do not call it by its wrong name. When was it that you paid the money to Bayles? it happened just after what?—I should think the money that I paid to Bayles would be the first night I officiated for our secretary. I believe it was on the 12th of November, if I recollect right. Our secretary did not tell me what the 6*l.* was for.

14,713. What about the Acorn Street murder?—I do not know.

14,714. When did it take place?—It took place some time the latter end of November.

14,715. Let me refresh your memory. Did not the Acorn Street murder take place on November the 23rd?—I am sure I could not say.

14,716. It is the fact; there is no doubt about it. You paid the money on the 12th of November?—I believe so.

14,717. On the 12th of November 1861 you paid this money, and on the 23rd of November the Acorn Street murder took place?—(*No answer.*)

14,718. You say that the secretary did not tell you what the money was for?—No; he requested me to give it to William Bayles; there was nothing more than that.

14,719. Was it because you believed that the 6*l.* was paid to William Bayles to do this murder that you altered the books?—No.

14,720. Do you believe that it made you alter them?—No.

14,721. Did you think that we should think so?—I cannot say that.

14,722. Was the reason that you destroyed the books because you thought that we should think so?—No.

14,723. What was your reason?—Because I wanted the book to correspond.

14,724. What was the inference that you thought we should draw from the books being wrong?—I did not know that I had anything to fear from the old book—the old book would have proved that I was correct.

14,725. You had nothing to fear?—No.

14,726. You thought it was a very singular thing that the 6*l.* should be unaccounted for in your books?—Not in my books.

14,727. In Kenworthy's books, the books of your secretary?—Yes.

14,728. And that you had been asked by him to pay the sum of 6*l.* to a man called Bayles; you did not know what for?—No, sir, I did not.

14,729. What was Bayles?—He was a grinder; one of our members.

14,730. Do you know whether Bayles had ever been employed to do any act of outrage?—No, I never did.

14,731. Did you know there was a man called Sybray?—Yes, I have heard talk of Sybray.

14,732. Did you ever hear that he was attacked?—I do not remember that I ever did.

14,733. Did you never hear that Bayles was said to have attacked him?—I do not recollect anything of the kind.

14,734. Do you recollect in the Acorn Street murder inquiry whether it was not distinctly proved?—No, I do not recollect.

14,735. You do not recollect anything of that kind occurring?—No, I do not.

14,736. Did you never hear it from one of your union men?—(*No answer.*)

14,737. Was Sybray one of Mr. Hoole's men?—Yes, I believe he was.

14,738. Do you mean to say that at the time the investigation of the Acorn Street murder went on you never heard of a man called Sybray having been severely beaten and attacked?—I do not recollect it, I might have, I would not say that I have not heard it.

14,739. Did not you know at that time that Bayles was charged with taking part in the attack upon Sybray?—No, I never knew it.

14,740. You never heard of it?—I could not say whether I have or not, I do not recollect it, it is so long since now.

14,741. Will you swear that you never heard of it?—No, I will not swear it.

14,742. You will not swear that you have not heard that Bayles was engaged in making the attack upon Sybray?—No, I never heard it.

14,743. What have you heard that you will not swear?—I will not swear that I have not heard that Sybray was attacked, but I never heard by whom.

14,744. Not by Bayles?—No, I never heard that.

14,745. You swear that?—Yes.

14,746. Did you read the newspaper report of the trial of Thompson for the Acorn Street murder?—Yes, I did.

14,747. We will refresh your memory. Having called your attention to that, did not you see in the report of his trial an account that Bayles had been engaged in making the attack upon Sybray?—I do not recollect seeing anything of that kind.

14,748. You swear that you do not recollect it?—Yes.

14,749. Did you never hear that Bayles had been engaged in any outrage of that sort?—I never recollect any outrage of that kind.

14,750. Of any kind?—I never heard of Bayles being engaged in any case of that kind.

14,751. Of any kind?—Of attacking Sybray.

14,752. Or as being engaged in any outrage of that kind?—No, I never heard anything of that kind—I never remember it.

SIXTEENTH DAY.

T. Smith.

24 June 1867.

THOMAS SMITH sworn and examined.

14,328. (*Mr. Chance.*) What are you ?—I am the secretary belonging to the Saw Makers Society, and I am a saw maker or a saw smith by trade, whichever you have a mind to term it.

14,329. How long have you been secretary to the Saw Makers Society ?—I took office on the 1st April 1866. You will find it recorded in the minute book. I have been in office about 15 months I think.

14,330. Had you held any office in that society previously to that ?—I have been on the committee several times, but it is sometime since.

14,331. How long have you been a member of that society ?—I have been between 20 and 30 years a member of that society.

14,332. Do you remember the Hereford Street outrage ?—I do very well to my great grief.

14,333. Had you known anything of that previously to its taking place ?—I had not ; it was done without my knowledge.

14,334. Did you know Fearnehough ?—No, not before I saw him in the Court the other day—I mean speaking the truth.

14.335. (*Chairman.*) If you say that so often we shall begin to doubt you. There is no necessity for your making statements of that kind.

14,336. (*Mr. Chance.*) Have you ever heard of him ?—Yes.

14,337. You know his name ?—I know his name.

14,338. Did you know that he was a saw grinder ?—Yes.

14,339. After the outrage took place did you see Broadhead ?—No.

14,340. Did you ever see anything of Broadhead after that ?—I have seen him several times, but we had no conversation on the Hereford Street outrage at all.

14,341. How long after the outrage had taken place had you any communication with anyone upon it ?—A few days. Our president came to me.

14,342. (*Chairman.*) What is his name ?—Skidmore.

14,343. (*Mr. Chance.*) Which day was it ?—It was either Wednesday or Thursday. I should not like to be positive on that matter, but it was either Wednesday or Thursday.

14,344. Did he come by himself or with anybody else ?—He came by himself.

14,345. When he came what did he say to you ?—He said that he had seen Mr. Broadhead, and he came and wanted the money from me. I ought to remark that before this he came to me and named about the Hereford Street outrage and about the blow up, and he wanted some money from me.

14,346. (*Chairman.*) At this interview or before it ?—It was after the Hereford Street outrage.

14,347. What was the interview you are talking about ?—The only interview.

14,348. What did he say ?—He said he wanted some money.

14,349. What else did he say to you ?—He came to me and he said "We are in a mess," and I asked him what was the nature of the mess.

The witness withdrew.

J. Reaney.

JAMES REANEY sworn and examined.

14,350. (*Chairman.*) You are I believe the secretary of the Edge Tool Makers Union ?—Yes.

14,351. And I understand that you have brought, first, a cash book, commencing 10th October 1866 ; secondly, a roll book, commencing January 1865 and ending December 17th, 1866; thirdly, a roll book, commencing January 1867; and, fourthly, a ledger commencing in 1846, but which is so incomplete that there there must be another ledger, and from which it is impossible, we are informed, to make any account. Have you a cash book ?—I have given it to Mr. Barker. I never brought any books except three.

14,352. Is there a cash book ?—No.

14,353. Have you a cash book ?—I have, and entered all the monies in.

14,354. Have you a cash book ?—No.

14,355. Have you ever had one ?—No.

14,356. Have you any book showing your cash transactions for the last 10 years, or during any portion of that time ?—Yes, that book will do it (*producing a book and explaining it to Mr. Shrubsole*).

14,357. Then that begins in 1861 ?—Yes.

14,358. Have you no book earlier than 1861 ?—Only what I call my ledger.

14,359. What has become of a similar book to that antecedent to 1861 ?—I think for seven or eight years since we have kept nothing but the contribution book. We have destroyed nothing that I know of.

14,359*a*. You do not produce any such books ?—No.

14,360. Have you a minute book of your proceedings ?—Yes.

14,361. That begins in 1864 ?—We never had a minute book before that.

14,362. Had you never a minute book before 1864 ?—No.

14,363. Had you any ledger besides that which you have there ? we are told that that there ought to be another and that that is not a complete ledger ?—You see the contribution book contains all that we receive. Then this book shows you what we have paid out of that, and all the accounts are entered in this ledger.

14,364. I am told that the cash book commences in 1864 ?—That is not brought.

14,365. But we want all your books for the last 10 years ?—I was not aware of that, we shall have to fetch that ; do you want it now ?

14,366. Yes, every book which you have. On your oath, have you never kept a minute book besides this ?—Only this one.

14,367. Nothing else ?—Nothing else.

14,368. Have you no entries of your proceedings ?—We have made entries of all monies paid, and of all monies paid out, and what they are for.

14,369. Do you make an entry of resolutions passed ?—Not at all times.

14,370. Have you any book recording proceedings at your meetings ?—Recording resolutions, I cannot speak to that. If I may be allowed to go I will fetch all that I have.

14,371. What you have brought are not enough for our purpose, and you must produce all the books which you have had for 10 years past, and bring us a copy of your rules ?—I have sent those to London, but I dare say I can get you a copy. The secretary holds that copy of the rules.

14,372. Very well. You ought to be very glad to come here and lay these books before us for the sake of the union itself ?—I am very proud to come here to answer your questions.

14,373. Do not let all that is bad go against the unions in Sheffield, surely there must be something to their credit, do let us have it ?—I will bring them. I will get back as soon as I can.

The witness withdrew.

T. Smith.

THOMAS SMITH recalled and further examined.

14,374. (*Mr. Chance.*) The last thing you said was that you asked Skidmore the nature of the mess ?—Yes; he stated to me with reference to Fearnehough's blowing up.

14,375. What did he say ?—He said it was a bad job.

14,376. (*Chairman.*) He could not say it was a bad job, that is not the way people talk about such

SIXTEENTH DAY.

T. Smith.

24 June 1867.

things?—He mentioned Fearnebough's blow up to me.

14,377. What did he say?—He said he wanted money.

14,378. What did he say?—I cannot remember the very words.

14,379. Yes, you can?—Begging your pardon I cannot—I cannot remember every word. I am going to tell you all I know and I hope that you will give me credit for it.

14,380. What did he say afterwards?—He said that he wanted some money to pay for it and he asked me for some money and I told him I would not find him any. He said, "Why?" I said, "You have got "yourself into the mess, I have nothing to do with "it, and I will not find you a penny." That is the whole truth.

14,381. (*Mr. Chance.*) What took place upon that, was anything more said?—I told him that he must go to Joseph Barker if he wanted any money for I had not had anything to do with it and I was not going to find any monies. Joseph Barker found him the money.

14,382. What made you say that he was to go to Joseph Barker?—I thought Joseph Barker and he were the likeliest parties to find the money, because they had been implicated in some way in this affair.

14,383. Had anything been said about Joseph Barker before this?—I believe Mr. Skidmore named him. I do not know whether Mr. Skidmore had seen Joseph Barker previously.

14,384. You say you thought that Joseph Barker was the likeliest person. Why did you say that?—Because he told me that he and Joseph Barker and Mr. Skidmore had seen Broadhead.

14,385. You say "he," Joseph Barker, and Skidmore, whom do you mean by "he"?—I mean Joseph Barker and Skidmore.

14,386. Was that the reason why you thought he was most likely to pay the money?—They informed me of this.

14,387. (*Chairman.*) Why do you say that you thought they were the likeliest parties to find the money because they had been implicated?—For this reason, they went to Mr. Broadhead.

14,388. You shall not get out of it in that way?—That was the reason.

14,389. No. Why did you say they were the likeliest parties to find the money because they had been implicated?—Well, I thought Joseph Barker and Mr. Skidmore had been to Broadhead.

14,390. Why did you think so?—I did think so.

14,391. You must have known it—you did not think it. Why did you say that—they must have either told you so or not?—Mr. Skidmore told me that they had been to Broadhead's and they wanted the money. I beg your pardon that is the reason.

14,392. And so they told you they had been to Broadhead and that they were implicated, how did they get implicated? going to Broadhead did not implicate them?—They went to Broadhead for this reason, to tell Broadhead to roll up Fearnehough's bands. That was what they told me and that was the reason I stated that. I thought they had been implicated with going to Broadhead; but they told me that they had not implicated themselves at all, only rolling up the bands. That was the reason that I thought they had been implicated, but they cleared themselves to me.

14,393. You thought they were not implicated, because you thought they were?—I thought they were not implicated in the blowing-up affair, that was what I thought.

14,394. (*Mr. Chance.*) Then you say you had told him to go to Barker?—Yes.

14,395. Did he tell you the amount of money he wanted?—7*l.* 10*s.*

14,396. Did he go to Barker?—I expect he did. I did not see him any more; I expect he went directly to Barker when he had had an interview with me.

14,397. Did you see Barker yourself?—No, not after I had had an interview with Skidmore before the money was paid.

14,398. After the interview with Skidmore, had you an interview with Barker?—I had not.

14,399. Just think?—I had not respecting the money payment.

14,400. Did you not say to Barker that there was an account against him upon the saw makers account?—I told Mr. Skidmore that Barker was the likeliest man to find the money as I had had nothing at all to do with it, and as there was an account against them they could please themselves whether they took it or not. Mr. Skidmore said he could charge the saw makers and Mr. Barker would have an account of that, on the 13th of October, 7*l.* 10*s.*

14,401. Did you give any authority to Barker to pay this money?—I did not. I did not see Barker to ask him to pay the money.

14,402. Did you not see him after that?—I saw him after Mr. Skidmore had given an order to pay the money.

14,403. Did you give any order to Skidmore upon Barker?—I said this to Mr. Skidmore, "You have "got yourself in a mess, and you must get the money "from Mr. Barker."

14,404. (*Chairman.*) Why was he to get it from it Barker?—Because Barker owed the saw makers something like 17*l.* or 18*l.*, I believe it was.

14,405. Owed you?—Owed the saw makers society.

14,406. Therefore you would have been entitled to be paid this 17*l.* or 18*l.* out of that money that was due to you; he was to debit you with the amount?—Yes.

14,407. Therefore in point of fact you ordered him to get of your money the sum of 7*l.* 10*s.*?—I did not order him; I told Mr. Skidmore that Barker was to find the money, I had not found any.

14,408. But he was to deduct the money that he was to pay you?—Just one word of explanation.

14,409. Answer the question; he was to deduct the money that he was to pay to you?—I did not tell Mr. Barker so.

14,410. But they owed you 17*l.* or 18*l.*, and instead of paying you the money he was to pay 7*l.* 10*s.* of it over to Skidmore?—Yes, but just allow me one word.

14,411. (*Mr. Chance.*) Did you after that get any account from Barker?—Yes.

14,412. What was the account which you got from Mr. Barker?—I did not get any monies from him; he charged our trade with the amount of 7*l.* 10*s.* Just allow me one word.

14,413. (*Chairman.*) Did he render you an account?—Yes, I had an account.

14,414. Let us look at it?—I have not it here, but the account was put in the book, the same as I have here with the handle makers. But allow me to make one remark.

14,415. No, make no remarks. Show us your books?—This is a small account that we had with the handle makers, but I have not that account I am sorry to say.

14,416. You were summoned to bring your books; why have you not brought that account?—I have not it.

14,417. Why have you not it?—I expect the account has been destroyed.

14,418. Have you destroyed it?—I do not know; I might have; I daresay I have.

14,419. You daresay you have?—Yes, I think I have.

14,420. You know you have?—Yes; the accounts had been audited.

14,421. Stop a minute; have you destroyed it?—Yes, I have; I cannot find it anywhere, and I must have destroyed it.

14,422. (*Mr. Chance.*) Is there an auditor of your society?—Yes.

14,423. Who is he?—John Wood and John Blenkiron.

14,424. Did that amount of 7*l*. 10*s*. pass into the accounts?—Yes, it was put to the accounts.

14,425. (*Chairman.*) It passed the audit, did it?—Yes, I showed them the account in the books; it was put down in this memorandum book.

14,426. Show me where it is put down in the memorandum book?—I have not it. I am sorry it is missing; for my credit I am sorry it is missing.

14,427. You have brought the book without the entry; is it torn out?—Well, it must be torn out or something.

14,428. You said it was a memorandum?—It is a memorandum.

14,429. Was it a loose memorandum, or was it a memorandum in the book?—It was a memorandum in that book.

14,430. You tore it out, did you?—Yes.

14,431. Where was the place you tore it out from?—It was somewhere about there (*showing the book to the Chairman*).

14,432. But where was it exactly?—I will find it if I can, so far as my judgment will allow. I believe it was there (*handing the book to the Examiners*). I have kept the account you see from January, and there has not been anything destroyed there.

14,433. Nothing has been destroyed since January, you are quite right; the money was paid and the memorandum was entered, when, in October, the man was blown up?—It was entered after he was blown up.

14,434. How long after?—Well, perhaps it might be a week or two after.

14,435. When does your audit take place?—Sometimes once a month, and two months, and three months.

14,436. On this occasion when did the October audit take place?—The books would tell; I do not remember; it would be in December.

14,437. Then your account in which this money was paid was entered before December?—It was entered before December.

14,438. You say the entry was between October and December?—Yes.

14,439. And the audit took place in December, and you say that the entry which you have torn out was an entry which took place before December?—I have no doubt but what it was.

14,440. Are you certain it was?—I am certain that it was.

14,441. You will swear it was?—Yes; it is an error if I have done it.

14,442. I first asked you if that was so, and you said, "Yes." Then I asked whether you had any doubt about it, and then you said, "No," and then you say that you must look at the book. That is the entry before the place where you had taken it out. The entry refers to January 1867; now explain that if you can?—This was the balance of January 1867, and therefore the leaves would be torn out there.

14,443. Do you mean to tell me that there are entries of transactions of October and December coming in after January, February, and March of the following year?—Yes; I will tell you how it has been done (*going up to the Examiners*).

14,444. Take the book, then, and sit down; I do not want you here?—The book has been done in this way; I have kept a debtor and creditor account, and that is the reason that it is put in one opposite the other: "Debtor and Creditor account of the Saw-handle Makers and the Saw Makers Society."

14,445. But look at these items and read me one that takes place in the year 1866, in the page that is before the one that you tore out; you tore out a page you say after that, and the page which comes in after that is a page relating to matters which took place in January 1866?—It was the balance that took place in 1866. This was the balance that took place, "Balance to the Saw Makers Society."

14,446. But how could an entry upon matters in 1866 come in a page after 1867?—I was in the habit of going to Mr. Barker, and we generally balanced up about once a week, and after we had balanced up I took the balance forward a fortnight; and that was the balance due at that time.

14,447. But how does the page of 1866 come in after 1867?—This was January 1867. "Saw Makers "in account with the Saw-handle Makers Society, "January 21 to balance 2*l*. 18*s*. 9*d*." That was due to us on that day.

14,448. In 1867?—In 1867; not in 1866.

14,449. Was that the proper place?—I put it in there; I might be in error.

14,450. But how could that page refer to that matter of 1866, the year before?—It was the balance after we had balanced the accounts; the balance was due.

14,451. It is enough for our purpose that you tore out the page?—Yes, and I am sorry that it is done.

14,452. Did you tear out the page for the purpose of screening your own transaction?—Not at all.

14,453. What did you do it for?—It was very foolish of me———

14,454. Answer my question, what did you do it for?—I had no sinister purpose.

14,455. For what purpose did you do it?—I do not know that I had any purpose.

14,456. A man does nothing without a purpose?—I do not know that I had any purpose.

14,457. Why did you tear it out?—It was an act of my own.

14,458. Why did you tear it out?—Well, it was my own act; I do not know any other reason.

14,459. When did you do it?—In December perhaps; I cannot say when I tore it out.

14,460. On your oath, did you not tear it out after you knew that this Commission was coming down?—No, I did not; I will swear it on oath.

14,461. Has any person audited your books?—Yes, they did audit them.

14,462. Was the Commission talked of in December?—Yes, it was.

14,463. Was it not in consequence of that that you tore it out?—No, it was not.

14,464. Then for what purpose was it?—Well, it was a foolish act of my own; I had no business to tear it out. That is the only reason I can give, and I give it truthfully.

14,465. What did you charge the entry of 7*l*. 10*s*. for?—It was one that Mr. Barker harged our trade with.

14,466. But what was the charge for?—Expenses for the Hereford Street outrage.

14,467. You entered that, did you?—I put it in this book.

14,468. Did you put it in, "Expenses of Hereford Street outrage"?—No, I did not; I was not going to be so foolish as that.

14,469. How did you enter it then?—I entered it, "Expenses paid by Mr. Barker on the saw makers "account."

14,470. Now mind what you are about; are you sure that you entered it into the book as "Expenses paid by Mr. Barker"?—Yes.

14,471. That was the language you used, was it?—Yes.

14,472. Are you sure that that is the expression which you used?—Yes.

14,473. There is no mistake about that?—There is no mistake about it.

14,474. When the auditor came to examine your books, did he not say, "What are those expenses"?—I said———

14,475. Answer the question. When the auditor came to examine your books, did he not say, "What are those expenses"?—Yes.

14,476. Who was he?—It was John Wood and John Blenkiron.

14,477. What did you say to that?—I said they were expenses paid by Mr. Barker.

14,478. But for what?—I did not name the reason.

14,479. Do you mean to say that you gave no voucher, or anything of the kind?—No.

SIXTEENTH DAY.

T. Smith.

24 June 1867.

14,480. Do you mean to say that your auditors passed your accounts in that way? If you said that they were expenses paid by Mr. Barker, did they not ask you what they were paid for, and did you not tell them?—I did not.

14,481. Do you mean to say that they passed those expenses?—Yes, just the same as they had passed these other accounts.

14,482. Do you mean to say that the unions had no further security than your statement that they were expenses paid without vouchers of any kind? do you mean to say that the auditors would pass a thing merely upon your representation that they were expenses?—They did so; undoubtedly they did. They believed me.

14,483. Would that be a common thing? do you mean to say that you have entries there which are merely entries, expenses paid, without any voucher at all, and that the auditors were satisfied?—They were satisfied with me.

14,484. They were satisfied with you on account of your good conduct, I suppose?—Yes; and honesty. I never robbed anybody of anything in my life.

14,485. Your unions must be in a nice condition if they are represented in that way. Do you mean to say that the poor men who pay in their contributions to you in this way have no securtiy from their auditors, but a representation from their secretary that expenses have been paid?—Our union did not know anything about it.

14,486. Because you put "expenses paid" without telling them what they are?—Yes.

14,487. And the auditors passed it in that way?—Yes.

14,488. You say that you have torn out the entry?—Yes.

14,489. But they were expenses paid. Is Mr. Wood here? he saw these entries before you tore them out, I suppose?—Yes; I have no doubt they were in the book for him to look at, just the same as I get the balance in those other items.

14,490. And you say, of course, that it was for no sinister purpose that you tore them out?—No.

14,491. It was accidental, perhaps?—Well, you can just have it which way you think proper.

14,492. Do you think that that is an answer which will be satisfactory to the public? If you produce a mutilated book, and I ask you whether it was done intentionally or accidentally, and you tell me I can have it which way I like?—It was not done intentionally; it was done through my foolishness.

14,493. Do you call it accidental?—You may call it carelessness.

14,494. You are the honest man on whom the auditors rely, are you?—Yes.

14,495. Did you tear it out accidentally or intentionally?—I did not tear it out for any purpose, strictly speaking.

14,496. Did you tear it out at all?—Yes.

14,497. Then why did you tear it out?—I tore it out because I thought it was done with, that was my reason for tearing it out.

14,498. Then why did you not tear out the other leaves which were done with?—Because for instance——

14,499. Answer the question. Why did you not tear out the other leaves which were done with?—I do not know. I have kept them since.

14,500. And you had kept them before?—Yes, I had.

14,501. Then why did you tear that one out?—I cannot give you any other answer I am sure; and I have given you an honest answer to the best of my ability and to the best of my judgment.

14,502. You had torn out one leaf which contained the entry of the payment to Mr. Broadhead and you have left all the remainder, and I ask you why you have done it?—There are many entries which have been torn out. There are eight or nine months entries which have been torn out, not that one alone but others.

14,503. Where are those?—They are torn out with the others. One of those pages contain about twelve weeks account.

14,504. And you say that there are eight or nine months entries torn out?—Yes, there are.

14,505. Who tore those out?—I tore them out, and that one entry went with the rest.

14,506. Why did you tear out the eight or nine months entries?—I do not know; just for this very same reason.

14,507. Did the other pages extending over eight or nine months contain entries of similar expenses?—One, and only one.

14,508. But besides this one?—Yes, besides this one, only one more.

14,509. What was that?—2*l.* 10*s.* was in.

14,510. What was that for?—It was paying Mr. Peace at Little London. Damms had been rattened.

14,511. Did you pay him?—No, I did not pay him; Mr. Barker settled the affair.

14,512. And you paid it out of the funds of the society did you?—No, Mr. Barker charged that to our trade.

14,513. It was allowed in your accounts?—Yes, it passed in our accounts in this memorandum book of mine. I am very glad that I have this memorandum book, and I wished it had had the whole of the facts in it.

14,514. Then you did not want it to be known that the money had been used for paying the charges of Mr. Peace, was it for that reason that you tore it out?—It was known to several individuals.

14,515. Then why did you tear it out if it was known to several individuals for eight or nine months?—I give the same reason as I have given for tearing the other out.

14,516. Was it in point of fact to conceal it?—No, it was not at all.

14,517. What was it for?—It was paying Peace in compensation.

14,518. But why did you tear it out?—I do not know, for the same reason as I did the other.

14,519. But you gave no reason for that; you said it was foolish; we all agree in that. but your folly is no reason, was it to conceal the entry?—No, not at all.

14,520. Then why was it?—I do not know, it was not anything of the sort. I was called in here to speak the truth and I shall do it.

14,521. You have not spoken the truth in this respect because you have not told us the reason. Those entries are both of them improper entries to be made; do you mean to tell us that your tearing them out was not for the purpose of concealing them?—No, it was not on my part, I do not think.

14,522. On whose part do you think that it was?—No one but mine, not to the best of my knowledge; no one knew anything about it but me after the auditors had passed them.

14,523. Will you swear that you did not tear it out in order that nobody else should know anything about it?—I will not swear it—there.

14,524. What do you mean by "there"?—That I did not tear it out that no other parties might know anything about it.

14,525. Why did you tear it out?—Well, it was a foolish purpose, if I may use the term.

14,526. What was the foolish purpose?—It was foolish on my part to tear the leaves out.

14,527. But what did you do it for? if you wanted to light a pipe with it that might be a reason?—I might throw it into our waste paper cupboard to light the fire. I have no doubt it did go in there.

14,528. Did you tear it out for that purpose?—I reckoned it as waste paper when the auditor had passed it.

14,529. Did you tear it out for that purpose?—I tore it out and threw it into the cupboard when the auditor had passed it.

14,530. Had you no other reason?—No, I had no other reason. If I had one I would give it you honestly and truthfully.

14,531. Recollect that we must be satisfied that you are telling the truth, you have a certificate to get?—I have no doubt that Mr. Barker will satisfy you on these matters.

14,532. How ?—Mr. Barker kept a distinct account of what each of us paid during the week.

14,533. I told Broadhead that we should give you a certificate upon your telling the whole truth, but we did not tell Broadhead that we should give you a certificate if you did not tell the whole truth, and if we believe that you are not telling us the truth with respect to this leaf we shall not be justified in granting your certificate ?—It is true what I have told you.

14,534. I give you an ample caution, and if you do not tell us why you tore that out in a manner which will satisfy us that you are telling the truth you must take the consequences upon yourself; and recollect that you have identified yourself with the Hereford Street outrage and may be tried for it. Now bearing in mind that, no matter how foolish you have been up to this time, why did you tear out that leaf ?—I had no reasons. I really cannot give you any other reasons.

14,535. I give you ample caution ?—I am aware of it.

14,536. You have ample caution, and you have to satisfy us three; and when we come, at the end of this inquiry, to look over the names of the various witnesses who have appeared before us your name will appear amongst them, and we shall have to see whether you have told the truth; and, amongst other things, we shall have to consider the questions which have been put to you about that leaf, and if we are satisfied that you have not told the truth we shall not be justified in giving you a certificate. Now, what was the reason that you tore out that leaf ?—I had no reason at all.

14,537. Was it for concealment ?—No, there was no concealment at all. I had nothing to conceal at all, and I shall speak the truth whether I get a certificate or not.

14,538. You had seen Broadhead, you say, and Skidmore told you that he had been up to Broadhead about rolling up Fearnehough's bands; they told you that they had not implicated themselves except in rolling up the bands, and you said that you did not think that they were implicated in the blowing up. At that time they knew that they were implicated in the blowing up ?—Yes, at that time when Skidmore came to me for the money.

14,539. You knew that it was money to be paid for blowing this man up ?—Mr. Skidmore told me so. I should not say for blowing up. I do not know that it was for that exactly.

14,540. Having been told by Skidmore that it was money for blowing this man up, and you having nothing to do with it before, how was it that you gave an order and implicated yourself to pay for that which you had not ordered ?—I told Mr. Skidmore.

14,541. How was it, if you had never ordered it, that you came to implicate yourself in this matter, which was against your principles and wishes ?—Well, it was so.

14,542. Then why did you give an order for the payment ?—I told him to go to Barker.

14,543. Why ?—I told him to go to Barker.

14,544. Why did you tell him to go to Barker ?—I had nothing to do with it.

14,545. Then why, if you had nothing to do with it, and if your principles were all against it, and if you knew that it was for blowing him up, did you give him an order for money for doing a thing with which you had nothing to do ?—Allow me to explain.

14,546. Why did you do it ?—Mr. Skidmore came to me, and he said that Barker must find the money, and if he found the money it would come out of our trade.

14,547. Why did you not say, "We never ordered "it. We were never parties to it, and we abhor the "whole thing ?"—Well, I must admit that I committed myself in that error, and I do regret it sincerely from the bottom of my heart, although I was not a partaker in it.

14,548. Can you tell me the date when you paid this money ?—I never paid it.

14,549. You gave an order for it to be paid out of your money. Do not quibble in that way ?—Mr. Skidmore went to Mr. Barker, and they made arrangements about the money; I had nothing to do with it.

14,550. Barker was your debtor, and you told him to go there ?—I told him Barker and he might find the money. I would not find the money.

14,551. You told us that you ordered Barker to be paid out of your funds ?—I do not know that I did.

14,552. You told us so ?—I told Skidmore.

14,553. Do not go on chattering like that. It is a serious thing for you. Although you had given an order to Barker to be paid for blowing this man up, did you not afterwards enter an indignation minute in your books about it ?—I did. It was passed by the general meeting.

14,554. You proposed it, I believe ?—No, I did not. I had nothing to do with it. I do not propose resolutions nor second them. I enter them down as they pass.

14,555. You entered that indignation minute, you at that time sitting there, and knowing that you had paid for doing the very job ?—I did know, and I dared not tell.

14,556. Why ? You had nothing to fear; you had nothing to do with it ?—I should have brought several other parties in, and I did not know who had done it at that time. I kept it secret for the sake of my own life. I might have been molested.

14,557. Who would have molested you ?—Look at the shooting that there has been of late in Sheffield, and the blowings up, &c.; and those villains might have come and pounced upon me if I had divulged anything.

14,558. But you say you did not know anything ?—I knew that this money had been paid. I did know that.

14,559. There was a reward offered, and the whole town was indignant at the kind of disgrace which had come upon it. Why did you not come forward and say, "I know who has done it. I know the man who "has asked for payment for doing it, and I will pro- "claim it" ?—I dared not, because I should have brought Mr. Skidmore in and Mr. Barker.

14,560. That is just what you ought to have done ?—They were innocent of the blowing up, and that was the sole reason why I did not divulge it, because I should have brought Mr. Barker and Mr. Skidmore in.

14,561. You were all in together ?—Yes, we were. We knew about it, no doubt.

14,562. How long before it took place did you know about it ?—I did not know anything about it before it took place.

14,563. I thought you said that you did. How soon did you know of it—the day after ?—I knew the same day, Monday.

14,564. Did you know who did it ?—I did not.

14,565. Did you go to Broadhead's ?—No.

14,566. Never ?—Never.

14,567. To whom did you go ?—I did not go to anyone.

14,568. Did it never occur to you that this blowing up might be the consequence of that little order which was given ?—I did not know; I did not know any particulars about it or how it originated while our president came and told me about it.

14,569. Had you any doubt how it had been done ?—I had no doubt about it; at this time I had had no knowledge how it had been done, or the instigators of it.

14,570. It is a very curious thing if you knew nothing at all about it, and were perfectly ignorant, while the whole town were protesting against it, and there were such indignation meetings, and so on, that a person who was perfectly innocent should have had it just confided to him. Did you know nothing about it ?—Mr. Skidmore came to me and told me about it.

14,571. It is a very odd thing that he should come and tell you, why should he tell you ?—I did not know that it belonged to the saw trade at all.

14,572. Then why should he tell you, when he was not sure that you would not the next minute go

SIXTEENTH DAY.

T. Smith.

24 June 1867.

and tell of him; why did he tell you?—Because he had been and seen Broadhead about it.

14,573. I know that, but why did he tell you?—Well, I do not know hardly what to say to you with reference to that. I did not know about it before he was blown up.

14,574. But why did he tell you?—We were in conversation.

14,575. But persons do not tell people about such a thing in conversation if they had not to do with it before. They do not say, "I have been concerned and I have been asked by a man to pay him money" for an outrage like this for which a reward of upwards of 1,000*l.* had been offered. You were a stranger to the affair and knew nothing about it, and were quite innocent?—I did not at that time; I did not know that it was a trade affair at all before they came to me.

14,576. But why should they tell you?—I did not know it was a trade affair at all, I thought it might have been private malice; I did not know who was the cause of it, or the instigators, or anything; I was quite as green as this book.

14,577. Then why did you not turn round and say, "Why do you tell me, I shall proclaim you"?—I dared not.

14,578. Why not?—I have given you the reason why I dared not. My life would have been at stake.

14,579. At stake by whom?—If I had divulged the facts, I should have been shot.

14,580. Who would have shot you?—These bad people who were going about; do you not think that Broadhead or some of those parties implicated might have employed some one to shoot me; some of those that had done the job.

14,581. Was that the reason?—That was the reason, and because I did not want to leave old England and I did not want to get the reward; I had done nothing amiss myself, and that was the reason and the only reason.

14,582. You knew Fearnehough was obnoxious to the trade?—Yes, I had heard about it.

14,583. Do you know him yourself?—No, I never saw him in my life or spoke to him before I saw him in this chair the other day.

14,584. Did you know that Barker and Skidmore had had this interview with Broadhead?—Yes, I knew about their going; I admit that.

14,585. Did you doubt for a moment when you heard of this that it was all done in consequence of the interview with Broadhead? you knew Broadhead had a reputation for these matters?—Not until the other day; I hear many things said about men that they are not guilty of; I did not think the man had been so vile as what he is; I harboured a better opinion of him.

14,586. You have been a friend of his?—As far as going to the house several times on business. I know no more of him than that, being the secretary of the saw grinders union.

14,587. Was the other 7*l.* 10*s.* paid by the saw-handle makers, do you know?—Barker paid 7*l.* 10*s.* for them and 7*l.* 10*s.* for the saw makers, and I had to put it down in the book, and I deeply regret that I ever entered it at all. I deeply regret it. That is where I have missed my way. I was no participator in the affair at all.

The witness withdrew.

J. Robertson.

JAMES ROBERTSON sworn and examined.

14,588. (*Chairman.*) Are you the secretary of the Fender Grinders' Union?—Yes.

14,589. We have asked you to produce your books?—Yes.

14,590. Have you produced all the books in your possession?—Yes, every one.

14,591. How far do they go back?—I am sure I cannot say exactly, but they go back beyond 10 years, I believe.

14,592. Have you got the minute book of your proceedings?—There is a resolution book there.

14,593. Do you mind our keeping them for a short time in order that we may look over them?—No.

14,594. Have you produced all the books connected with the union?—Yes.

14,595. Are you aware of any being destroyed?—Yes.

14,596. Which have been destroyed?—A portion of the cash book has been destroyed; a portion of that is here.

14,597. Which portion has been destroyed? this is the cash book (*pointing out the same*)?—Yes, that has been the cash book.

14,598. With all the entries torn out?—Yes.

14,599. That must be half the book, or nearly so?—Yes.

14,600. Do you know who tore them out?—Yes, I did myself.

14,601. When did you tear them out?—About January or February this year.

14,602. How far did the entries go back?—To January 1862.

14,603. Are there any other books that are mutilated?—No, sir, none whatever.

14,604. This is the only book from which you have torn out the entries?—Yes.

14,605. Is there any book that has been destroyed?—No, sir, not one.

14,606. Is there any book with any false entries that you are aware of?—Yes, sir.

14,607. Which is that?—It is one of mine.

14,608. This contains false entries?—Yes, one.

14,609. What do you call this book?—The cash book.

14,610. Will you be good enough to point out to me the false entry?—Yes, this is it (*pointing out the same*).

14,611. On January the 14th, 1862, there is a false entry?—Yes. "Received of Mrs. Kenworthy 30*l.* 15*s.* 3*d.*"

14,612. In what respect is that a false entry?—It was 24*l.* 15*s.* 3*d.*

14,613. Then there is a difference of 6*l.*?—Yes.

14,614. Did you make that entry yourself?—Yes.

14,615. And where did you do it at the time?—About February this year, when I took the leaves out of the other cash book. That is an exact copy of the other cash book, with that one exception.

14,616. Do I understand that these leaves were torn out?—Yes.

14,617. And you copied the leaves in there?—Yes.

14,618. And this was done in January?—January or February, I will not be certain which.

14,619. Then you copied the leaves into this book, and all this has been written since January?—Yes, it is an exact copy of the other book, with that exception.

14,620. It is a copy of the old cash book which you have mutilated?—Yes.

14,621. It is a correct copy except the Kenworthy item?—Yes.

14,622. Will you be good enough to tell me your reason for tearing out the leaves?—Yes.

14,623. What was the reason?—I entered in that book 24*l.* 15*s.* 3*d.* which I received from Mrs. Kenworthy; the exact amount.

14,624. You entered on the leaves 24*l.* 15*s.* 3*d.*?—Yes; the reason I did it was that it did not correspond with Mrs. Kennedy's books. There was 6*l.* deficient.

14,625. Have you Mrs. Kennedy's book here?—Yes.

14,626. Show it to me?—(*The witness produced the book.*)

14,627. What book is this?—It is Mr. Kenworthy's book.

14,628. What is Mr. Kenworthy?—He was our secretary.

14,629. Show me the item which you say did not

correspond with his book; where is the item?—Here (*pointing out the same*).

14,630. Is this side for receipts, and that for payments (*referring to the cash book*)?—Yes.

14,631. You ought to have received from Kenworthy the secretary 30*l.* 15*s.* 3*d.*?—Yes.

14,632. And he only paid you 24*l.* 15*s.* 3*d.*?—I believe he only paid me 24*l.* 15*s.* 3*d.*

14,633. When was it? on what settlement?—I believe it is dated at the bottom in his son's handwriting; it is the 21st of January 1862.

14,634. The castings are wrong, are they?—Yes.

14,635. You say that you tore this out because it represented that you had received only 24*l.* 15*s.* 3*d.*?—Yes.

14,636. Did you receive 30*l.*?—No.

14,637. You say you believe that he paid you 24*l.* 15*s.* 3*d.*?—There was 6*l.* which was not accounted for in that book, and it was not accounted for in that which you have in your hand either.

14,638. The 6*l.* was not accounted for in the leaves nor in Kenworthy's book?—No; and I account for it in that last book of mine.

14,639. But this a transaction of 1862?—Yes.

14,640. You have only done this lately?—Yes.

14,641. You have copied upwards of 100 pages of book in order to make this little mistake right?—Yes.

14,642. Why did you do this? what was your object in correcting this mistake?—I wanted to make it correspond with the old book.

14,643. Why were you so anxious to do it?—Because I knew that that 6*l.* was not wanting.

14,644. How do you mean that that was not wanting?—I knew that 6*l.* had been paid.

14,645. But paid by whom and to whom?—By our other secretary to me.

14,646. By Kenworthy to you?—Yes; he gave it to me to give to one of our members William Bayles.

14,647. When did you give it him?—I cannot say exactly, but I can tell you to a week I daresay; it was in November 1861.

14,648. What did you give it to Bayles for?—Our secretary was ill, and he asked whether I would go and officiate for him, and I did go, and he gave me 6*l.* to give to William Bayles, but he did not say what the 6*l.* was for, nor did Bayles; but I knew that the 6*l.* did come.

14,649. Does that 6*l.* appear in your books anywhere as payment to Bayles?—No, it is not accounted for in Kenworthy's books.

14,650. Kenworthy was the secretary then?—Yes.

14,651. If it was his duty to pay those 6*l.* to Bayles and also to enter them in the book, why were you at the trouble to tear out all the leaves of this book, and make a fresh book, and write out nearly 100 pages in order to correct so trifling an error as that? I thought I would get my books to correspond with his.

14,652. That was all?—Yes.

14,653. Is William Bayles alive?—No; he got killed.

14,654. Did anyone see you pay William Bayles? Yes, I paid it at our meeting.

14,655. Then if you paid it at your meeting there is no doubt that you have an entry of it somewhere?—I was not secretary at the time.

14,656. Is there no entry of it anywhere?—No; I never could find one.

14,657. It occurred to you in February this year?—Yes; when I thought we were going to have a Commission of Inquiry down here I thought I would make my book right.

14,658. So when you thought that there was going to be an inquiry you thought that it would better your case to destroy the leaves of one of your books?—I thought so at the time; I do not now; I regret it very much.

14,659. Is Kenworthy alive?—No; he died in January 1862.

14,660. He died in January 1862?—Yes.

14,661. Did not it occur to you that if you wanted your book to look right and correspond, at all events it would be quite as well to have kept the old leaves so that they might have been seen?—It would have been better.

14,662. Have you done so?—No.

14,663. What did you do with the leaves which you tore out?—I burnt them.

14,664. Then you were afraid of us seeing the original book?—Yes; because I thought that if I entered that 6*l.* received from Mr. Kenworthy you would not know about it; that was the reason.

14,665. What inference should we draw from that?—I made up my mind to tell you respecting it as long as I had not the old book.

14,666. What inference did you suppose that we should draw from the fact of there being a wrong entry in that book?—Well, I do not know.

14,667. I mean at that time?—My intention was to make my book correspond with the other.

14,668. Did you think if it did not correspond that we should come to some conclusion about it?—Yes.

14,669. What conclusion?—You would see that there was 6*l.* short.

14,670. Therefore we may conclude that that 6*l.* was paid in a way of which there was no explanation?—Yes.

14,671. So that you thought we should think that 6*l.* was paid in a way of which there was no explanation?—Yes.

14,672. You thought that it was a thing that might be taken against yourself?—Yes.

14,673. And accordingly you altered the books?—Yes; I got a new book and entered all a fresh.

14,674. You got a new book, and put the whole thing right?—Yes, during my secretaryship.

14,675. Is Mrs. Kenworthy alive?—Yes, for anything I know of.

14,676. Is there anybody whom you can bring forward to show that the payment had been made in accordance with the entries in your books besides yourself?—I can bring witnesses to prove that I have paid them weekly scale.

14,677. That will not do. Here is an entry by which you appear to have received 30*l.*, and so it was entered in the old book?—30*l.* 15*s.* 3*d.*

14,678. And you had entered it so?—Yes.

14,679. It ought to be 24*l.*?—Yes.

14,680. How do you account for the 6*l.* except by giving it to this man. If you wanted to make it right why did not you put it into the book as being 6*l.* paid to Bayles, because that would have made it all right?—It was not in my account, it was in the other secretary's account.

14,681. You mean Kenworthy?—Yes.

14,682. Is Kenworthy's book here?—That is it that I have given to you since.

14,683. It does not appear in that?—No.

14,684. The 6*l.* does not appear in Kenworthy's book?—No.

14,685. One was a manufactured book and the other is a mutilated book?—Yes.

14,686. It is to your credit that you have kept the book, mutilated as it is; before you did this did you take the advice of any man as to the propriety of what you should do?—No.

14,687. You never consulted anybody?—No; it is my own act.

14,688. Did you tell anybody that you were doing it?—No.

14,689. Is it only known now for the first time to anybody but yourself that you have mutilated one of the books and made a false entry in the other?—I have named it to several of our members.

14,690. When have you mentioned it?—Two or three weeks ago the first time.

14,691. To whom?—I mentioned it to James Gorbidge.

14,692. Who is he?—He works with me.

14,693. What is he?—A fender grinder.

14,694. Where do you work?—At Mr. Robertson's Chancery works.

SIXTEENTH DAY.

J. Robertson.

24 June 1867.

14,695. How did you happen to mention it to him; is it since this inquiry began?—Yes.

14,696. Is it since I made the announcement that we should require the books of the various unions?—It was before you gentlemen came down here to sit.

14,697. Did you tell him that you supposed that the persons who were sent down would have to see your books?—No, I did not.

14,698. How did you happen to talk to him about it?—I told him this, that I received from Mr. Kenworthy 24*l.* 15*s.* 3*d.*, whereas I ought to have received 30*l.* 15*s.* 3*d.* I told him that I got a new book and had entered all afresh, and put it down received 30*l.* 15*s.* 3*d.*, whereas I only received 24*l.* 15*s.* 3*d.*, and he asked me my reasons for doing so, and I told him this, that I remembered well the first or second night in November 1861, when I officiated for our secretary, that he gave me 6*l.* to give to William Bayles, and I paid him, and that this 6*l.* would make it correct.

14,699. You say that you said to him that you had received 30*l.* from Mr. Kenworthy, whereas you had only received 24*l.*?—Yes.

14,700. If you received only 24*l.* how would his paying you 6*l* to give to Bayles make it right?—(*No answer.*)

14,701. If Mrs. Kennedy paid you 30*l.* you ought to have put down 30*l.*?—Yes.

14,702. But instead of putting down 30*l.* you put down 24*l.*?—That was what I received from him.

14,703. You received from her 30*l.*?—I put down 30*l.*

14,704. You received 30*l.*, did you put down 30*l.*?—No, 24*l.*

14,705. You said that you had received 30*l.* from her?—If I said so I said wrong.

14,706. You only received 24*l.* from her?—24*l.* 15*s.* 3*d.*

14,707. You put down 24*l.* as you received it?—Yes.

14,708. Then the accounts did not balance by 6*l.*? No.

14,709. Then you say that you believe that the way the accounts would be made to balance would be by Kenworthy paying you the sum of 6*l.* that you paid to Bayles?—Yes.

14,710. What happened?—The Acorn Street outrage happened immediately after this.

14,711. The Acorn Street outrage was a murder?—Yes.

14,712. Then do not call it by its wrong name. When was it that you paid the money to Bayles? it happened just after what?—I should think the money that I paid to Bayles would be the first night I officiated for our secretary. I believe it was on the 12th of November, if I recollect right. Our secretary did not tell me what the 6*l.* was for.

14,713. What about the Acorn Street murder?—I do not know.

14,714. When did it take place?—It took place some time the latter end of November.

14,715. Let me refresh your memory. Did not the Acorn Street murder take place on November the 23rd?—I am sure I could not say.

14,716. It is the fact; there is no doubt about it. You paid the money on the 12th of November?—I believe so.

14,717. On the 12th of November 1861 you paid this money, and on the 23rd of November the Acorn Street murder took place?—(*No answer.*)

14,718. You say that the secretary did not tell you what the money was for?—No; he requested me to give it to William Bayles; there was nothing more than that.

14,719. Was it because you believed that the 6*l.* was paid to William Bayles to do this murder that you altered the books?—No.

14,720. Do you believe that it made you alter them?—No.

14,721. Did you think that we should think so?—I cannot say that.

14,722. Was the reason that you destroyed the books because you thought that we should think so?—No.

14,723. What was your reason?—Because I wanted the book to correspond.

14,724. What was the inference that you thought we should draw from the books being wrong?—I did not know that I had anything to fear from the old book—the old book would have proved that I was correct.

14,725. You had nothing to fear?—No.

14,726. You thought it was a very singular thing that the 6*l.* should be unaccounted for in your books?—Not in my books.

14,727. In Kenworthy's books, the books of your secretary?—Yes.

14,728. And that you had been asked by him to pay the sum of 6*l.* to a man called Bayles; you did not know what for?—No, sir, I did not.

14,729. What was Bayles?—He was a grinder; one of our members.

14,730. Do you know whether Bayles had ever been employed to do any act of outrage?—No, I never did.

14,731. Did you know there was a man called Sybray?—Yes, I have heard talk of Sybray.

14,732. Did you ever hear that he was attacked?—I do not remember that I ever did.

14,733. Did you never hear that Bayles was said to have attacked him?—I do not recollect anything of the kind.

14,734. Do you recollect in the Acorn Street murder inquiry whether it was not distinctly proved?—No, I do not recollect.

14,735. You do not recollect anything of that kind occurring?—No, I do not.

14,736. Did you never hear it from one of your union men?—(*No answer.*)

14,737. Was Sybray one of Mr. Hoole's men?—Yes, I believe he was.

14,738. Do you mean to say that at the time the investigation of the Acorn Street murder went on you never heard of a man called Sybray having been severely beaten and attacked?—I do not recollect it, I might have, I would not say that I have not heard it.

14,739. Did not you know at that time that Bayles was charged with taking part in the attack upon Sybray?—No, I never knew it.

14,740. You never heard of it?—I could not say whether I have or not, I do not recollect it, it is so long since now.

14,741. Will you swear that you never heard of it?—No, I will not swear it.

14,742. You will not swear that you have not heard that Bayles was engaged in making the attack upon Sybray?—No, I never heard it.

14,743. What have you heard that you will not swear?—I will not swear that I have not heard that Sybray was attacked, but I never heard by whom.

14,744. Not by Bayles?—No, I never heard that.

14,745. You swear that?—Yes.

14,746. Did you read the newspaper report of the trial of Thompson for the Acorn Street murder?—Yes, I did.

14,747. We will refresh your memory. Having called your attention to that, did not you see in the report of his trial an account that Bayles had been engaged in making the attack upon Sybray?—I do not recollect seeing anything of that kind.

14,748. You swear that you do not recollect it?—Yes.

14,749. Did you never hear that Bayles had been engaged in any outrage of that sort?—I never recollect any outrage of that kind.

14,750. Of any kind?—I never heard of Bayles being engaged in any case of that kind.

14,751. Of any kind?—Of attacking Sybray.

14,752. Or as being engaged in any outrage of that kind?—No, I never heard anything of that kind—I never remember it.

SIXTEENTH DAY.

J. Robertson.

24 June 1867.

14,753. Are you secretary now?—Yes.

14,754. Did you ever bring the fact of your having mutilated one book and fabricated another before your committee?—No, I think not to my knowledge.

14,755. And why did not you do that?—It was a matter affecting our whole trade.

14,756. Why did not you tell them of this mistake in the books, and that you had corrected it and had mutilated the books? these are not your books, they are the books of the trade?—Yes, they are.

14,757. Why did not you tell the committee?—I did not tell them.

14,758. Why?—I did not wish it. I was very loath to say anything about it till I came here.

14,759. Why should you wish to keep it secret till you came here?—I do not know that I had any motive for doing so. I thought I had better let it come out here.

14,760. How do you mean "come out." What do you mean by coming out?—So that they would know all about it here.

14,761. Perhaps we might not have found it out?—Yes, I should have explained it to you.

14,762. However, you did not want to explain it yourself to the committee?—No, I would rather explain it to you gentlemen.

14,763. This Acorn Street murder occurred on the 23rd of November; what is this book (*referring to a book*)?—That is the cash book.

14,764. In this book what ought to appear, simply payments or receipts?—Both.

14,765. Receipts and payments?—Yes.

14,766. Have you cut out that leaf (*referring to a leaf which was cut out of the book*)?—No, I never cut out a leaf in that book in my life.

14,767. Two leaves are out there?—I never cut any leaves out.

14,768. Look at it; there are two leaves cut out there?—Yes, there would seem to be two leaves out here.

14,769. Who cut them out?—I do not know.

14,770. It is quite clear that two leaves are cut out?—Yes, I never noticed it before.

14,771. You never noticed this before?—No.

14,772. Do you mean to tell me that your attention being called to these books up to the casting, you found that the casting was not correct, and in consequence of the casting not being correct you went and copied this book and never looked at that book of exactly the same date?—Never; I never knew that it was out.

14,773. I find that the first entry here is November. Whose writing is that?—Not mine.

14,774. That is November the 12th?—Yes.

14,775. Here we come to November the 5th. Whose writing is that?—John Kenworthy's.

14,776. That is John Kenworthy's too, is not it?—Yes.

14,777. Which is yours?—This (*referring to the same*).

14,778. You begin only in January?—Yes.

14,779. Your writing appears for the first time on January the 18th, 1862?—That is the first time I had these books.

14,780. Then all the writing that appears before that time is writing in the hand of Kenworthy?—Yes.

14,781. But there is in his account, in the month of November, at the very time when this Acorn Street murder took place, two leaves which are cut out?—Just so.

14,782. At that very moment?—Yes.

14,783. Who cut them out?—I do not know.

14,784. Who has had this book ever since?—Myself.

14,785. It has been in your charge and care?—Yes.

14,786. When were these entries made (*referring to some pencil entries*)?—I do not know; they are not mine.

14,787. When were these made (*referring to some more pencil entries*)?—They are not mine.

14,788. Do you mean to say that you made these entries here on this page when you had the book in your hand for the first time, and you did not notice that?—Yes, I did not notice it.

14,789. You never saw it?—Never; not till you showed it to me.

14,790. Can you at all explain how it was?—No, sir, I cannot, I am certain of that.

14,791. Kenworthy is dead?—Yes.

14,792. You have had the book in your own custody ever since?—Yes.

14,793. Is there any book at all corresponding with this, any ledger or book in which the entries in this book appear again?—No.

14,794. There is no check upon this in any way?—No.

14,795. Have you vouchers at all for payments? No.

14,796. Have you no contribution book?—Yes, we have a contribution book.

14,797. Let me look at the contribution book of November the 19th, 1861?—(*The witness produced and explained the contribution book to the Examiners.*)

14,798. I see a letter to Birmingham, what have you to do with Birmingham?—We have one member working there, and he has been so for a number of years; 20 years I should think.

14,799. Do you know a man named "Slipper Jack"?—Yes, I do.

14,800. What is his name?—I do not know his name.

14,801. Where does he live?—I do not know.

14,802. Do you know a person called John Aldam?—No, not to my knowledge.

14,803. Do not you know that "Slipper Jack's" name is John Aldam?—No.

14,804. Have you any member of the name of John Aldam in your union?—No.

14,805. How do you happen to know "Slipper Jack"?—I know him by going to a public house in Green Lane. I have seen him there.

14,806. What is the name of the public house?—The Napoleon inn.

14,807. Did you ever see him in company with Wastnidge?—No.

14,808. You do not know Wastnidge?—No.

14,809. Have you ever seen him in company with a man who was tried, Thompson?—Yes, I have seen them at that public house together.

14,810. Have you ever seen him in company with Bayles?—No.

14,811. Neither of them?—No.

14,812. This is a matter which is quite new to us. I daresay we shall have to ask you further about the matter, when we have investigated it; but you swear that you have produced all the books now in your possession?—Yes.

14,813. And you swear that the leaves that are cut out of this book are destroyed?—Yes, they are.

14,814. You swear that?—Yes; I am very sorry for it.

14,815. At the time when you destroyed this book, had you any intention of explaining to us that you had destroyed it?—No, sir, not at the time I destroyed it.

14,816. At the time that you destroyed it, you did not intend telling us about destroying it?—No.

14,817. What did you intend to tell us?—I thought the other book would pass; that you would take it as the old one.

14,818. When did you change your determination which induced you to produce these books?—In April, as near as I can guess it.

14,819. And who advised you to do it?—No one.

14,820. No one advised you?—No.

14,821. Then at all events you have been wise?—It is true what I have told you.

14,822. And you swear that it is not done by reason of some person suggesting it to you?—Yes.

14,823. It is your own suggestion; you destroyed

SIXTEENTH DAY.

J. Robertson.

24 June 1867.

that leaf and determined to repair it as far as you could by making this statement?—That is true.

14,824. I am bound to put this question. From the entries which appeared in the book, did not you come to the conclusion that Kenworthy had so conducted himself that had we seen the books we should draw an inference hostile to the trade?—No.

14,825. Did not you believe that we might have suspected Kenworthy?—Yes; I did not understand you before.

14,826. Did not you believe that if we had seen the books we should have thought that Kenworthy had paid something for the commission of this murder. Was not it your belief that that would be the inference which we should draw from it?—Yes.

14,827. And it was to prevent us coming to that conclusion that you destroyed the books?—No, I cannot say that it was, not to speak honestly.

14,828. You said you thought that if we saw the books we should come to the conclusion that he had paid money for that purpose, and you destroyed them to prevent us coming to that conclusion?—Yes, I did not understand the question.

14,829. I do not see any reason to doubt your statement at all, but in the interests of the public themselves, I want to know, as you have gone through the books, whether you can give us any clue whatever to the discovery of that Acorn Street murder?—I really cannot.

14,830. Have you any reason to suppose that any person whom you could point at did it?—No, I do not know.

14,831. Have you any ground of suspicion against any man?—No.

14,832. Not merely a vague suspicion, but nothing upon which you could found a suspicion?—No, I have not.

14,833. Have you found no entry in your books that you have mutilated or otherwise, which if they were produced would give us any information on the subject?—No, none whatever.

14,834. No entry of a name?—No, none whatever, I am certain of that.

14,835. Have you any ground of suspicion against "Slipper Jack"?—No.

14,836. He was suspected?—No, not to my knowledge, not before I saw it in the paper this morning; never before did I hear such a thing named.

14,837. 6*l.* we have been talking of. I do not see 6*l.* entered as payment for anything; what would 6*l.* be paid for. It is a larger sum than is usually paid is it not?—Yes, it is.

14,838. Supposing it were an improper payment to make for this purpose, it seems a very curious thing Kenworthy should have paid you the money to hand over to the man; I should have thought if he wanted to employ him he would have paid him himself? however, it is a large payment?—Yes.

14,839. And you never asked him what it was for?—No; I do not know that a word passed between us.

14,840. When you took to the books and you were responsible for keeping the accounts, did not it occur to you to see whether that amount was entered, it being a large amount?—Yes; I did look at the book to see if I could find it.

14,841. If you looked through it to see if you could find it when you took to the books, explain why you did not call Kenworthy's attention to it?—He was dead before I took to the books.

14,842. Did you know that Wastnidge was obnoxious to the fender grinders' trade?—Yes.

14,843. Had Kenworthy ever spoken of him disrespectfully, or spoken of him in an angry manner as a man violating the rules?—No; I never heard him speak of him in an angry manner.

14,844. Have you ever heard him speak of him as having broken your rules?—No.

14,845. Was he a contributor?—No.

14,846. In respect of what was it that the union was angry with Wastnidge. I forget what he had done?—It was for a little bit of unpleasantness that took place between Mr. Hoole and his grinders.

14,847. He would work for Mr. Hoole when they wanted him to strike?—Our men struck against him.

14,848. Did Wastnidge work for him?—Yes.

14,849. Your men had struck and you did not want anybody to work for Hoole, and instead of doing as you wanted Wastnidge worked for Hoole; that was it was not it?—Our men struck of their own accord; they did not come for the consent of the trade society.

14,850. But they struck?—They struck, and they had a meeting on the night of the day they struck and represented to the trade society why they had struck, and the society wanted them to go back and offer their services the next morning. They turned round and did do so, and Mr. Hoole refused their services.

14,851. What did Wastnidge do to make you angry with him?—I do not know that he did anything particular more than the rest of them. I am not aware that he did; he was a man I was not acquainted with at all.

14,852. Was not he a man who came from Masborough?—Yes.

14,853. And he came from Masborough to work against the trade at Sheffield?—Yes.

14,854. That was the offence?—Yes.

14,855. When did you discover this error of the 6*l.*?—Last Christmas I should think or before.

14,856. You had not seen the error when you first took to the books?—No.

14,857. You did not know that the payment to Bayles was not in?—No, I did not know that the payment to Bayles was in at all.

14,858. Did you know that it was not in?—I knew it was not in.

14,859. Did not it occur to you that it was an odd thing that it was not in?—No.

14,860. When did you find that it was not in the books?—When I found it out first, it would be the first year that I had the books.

14,861. But having found it out the first year that you had the books, did not it occur to you that there was 6*l.* unexplained, and that you did not know how it was?—Yes; I knew that the money that I received from Mrs. Kennedy and the 6*l.* I had to give Bayles was perfectly right.

14,862. Did not it occur to you that the payment of 6*l.* to Bayles was probably a payment for doing some mischief to Wastnidge?—No.

14,863. Did it not occur to your mind?—No; I did not know that money was paid for the Acorn Street affair.

14,864. It was just nine days before the Acorn Street outrage, and you found that it was not entered in the books, still it did not occur to your mind that it might have been paid in some way in connexion with that outrage?—No, it did not occur to me.

14,865. What could 6*l.* be due to Bayles for?—I do not know.

14,866. And you do not know now?—No, I do not know now.

14,867. It is an unexplained amount that you paid to a man and you did not know who to?—I did not.

14,868. Could it have been a lawful amount?—I do not know. I was not aware of the amounts at the time, because I was not the secretary.

14,869. We must have it looked into. I am bound to say that as far as you have gone your evidence is satisfactory.

Mr. Sugg suggested that the witness should be called another time.

The Chairman stated that he did not intend to ask the witness any questions to-day were it not for the strange appearance of the books.

14,870. (*Mr. Barstow to the witness.*) I see that Bayles was not in arrear of his contribution?—No.

14,871. He was not receiving scale?—He was not receiving scale at that time.

14,872. (*Chairman.*) He was not receiving scale, and he was paying his contributions regularly?—Yes.

14,873. Did not it appear to you that if he was

SIXTEENTH DAY.

J. Robertson.

24 June 1867.

not receiving scale and was paying his contributions regularly 6*l.* was a large payment to be made to him? did not it astonish you then?—I certainly could not understand it.

14,874. As you could not understand it and thought it was a large sum of money, and the man was paying contributions and was not on scale when you heard of this outrage at Acorn Street, did not you connect the things together and say "Here is 6*l.* gone. I wonder whether it was paid to damage him"?—I did wonder at that time whether the 6*l.* was not for that affair.

14,875. Did not you believe that it was?—No, I could not come to that conclusion.

14,876. But you wondered whether it might not have been?—Yes.

14,877. The trade was accused of having done it, and Kenworthy was the secretary of the union?—Yes, the trade was accused of having done it.

14,878. Did you mention your state of wonder and curiosity to anybody at that time?—No, sir, I never did.

14,879. Did not you?—No, I did not.

14,880. Do not you think that it would have been a good deal the wiser course if you had said, "Upon "my word with reference to the charge against the "trade generally, we ought to have our books square "at all events"?—I do think so now, but I did not mention it to anybody.

14,881. But it did pass your mind did it not, and you wondered at the time?—Yes.

14,882. Had you ever known Kenworthy engaged in any matter of this kind?—None whatever.

14,883. Was he a man who spoke violently and used strong language at people who violated your rules?—No.

14,884. Was he a very strong union man?—He was a very good union man; he was a very good man altogether I believe.

14,885. As far as you know?—Yes.

14,886. Do you ratten in your trade?—No, there has been no one charge of rattening since I knew the trade.

14,887. Not a charge against fender grinders?—Not to my knowledge. I never knew of one.

14,888. I suppose your people sometimes do not pay their subscriptions regularly?—Not very.

14,889. Supposing that they do not, what course do you pursue? you have no legal remedy?—We allow them to pursue their own course which our books will show.

14,890. You allow the people to pursue their own course?—Those that do not pay regularly.

14,891. How do you deal with them?—They pay when they think proper.

14,892. Supposing they do not pay?—We never interfere with them further than asking them.

14,893. Is yours a benefit society as well?—We have a funeral fund.

14,894. Do you mean to say that in your society there are some who pay and some who do not, and that they are all entitled to benefits?—No, they are not all entitled to benefits if they run beyond eight weeks they run financial and are not entitled to any benefits.

14,895. If they are eight weeks in arrear and do not make it up, they cease to be members?—No, they do not cease to be members, they are not entitled to benefits.

14,896. They still remain on the books, but they are not entitled to benefits?—Yes.

14,897. Do the men amongst one another ever ratten?—I never heard tell of such a thing.

14,898. Have you ever heard, except of that Acorn Street murder, of any person in your trade, in consequence of any violation of any of the rules of your trade, having been injured?—I never heard tell of it.

14,899. Except the Acorn Street outrage?—Excepting that; not to my recollection; I do not remember anything of the kind.

14,900. Mr. Barstow tells me that the contributions seem very well paid, and the balances are very small indeed, and the balance of 6*l.* is a thing quite unusual?—Yes.

14,901. That makes it very much more surprising to me that you, having had to pay over such a large sum as that, not knowing for what, a few days before the Acorn Street murder took place, had taken no steps to investigate whether the 6*l.* did not go in some way towards that matter; it is a very foolish thing not to have done so?—It is true. I did not take any steps in it at all.

The witness withdrew.

JOSEPH BARKER sworn and examined.

J. Barker.

14,902. (*Chairman.*) You are secretary of what society?—The Saw-handle Makers Society.

14,903. You have heard what Mr. Broadhead has said?—Yes, through the papers.

14,904. Were you present when he gave his evidence?—I was present the first hour that he was examined at the bottom end of the court, but I could not hear all that he said.

14,905. Do you know anything at all about this Hereford Street outrage?—Yes.

14,906. When did you first hear of it?—The same day that it took place.

14,907. Were you aware that anything was to be done to Fearnehough before this outrage took place?—Yes.

14,908. When did you first hear of it?—Hear of what was to be done to him?

14,909. No, that something was to be done?—Perhaps about two months before that time I and Skidmore went to Broadhead, I cannot state exactly, I think it is about two months or a little more. We told him, and we believed he was quite aware of the fact, that Fearnehough was doing work for Messrs. Slack, Sellars, and Grayson, and by so doing was injuring our trade. We asked him if nothing could be done to stop him. He said he did not know. We said then that he was doing us a very serious injury, and if by any means his nuts and bands could be taken we should not mind about the expense. Broadhead said that their trade was also interested in him, as he was an obstacle, and that they would pay their share of the expenses along with us.

14,910. I suppose you ratten in your union?—We ratten through the saw grinders; the saw grinders ratten for us. I have come here to tell you all I know.

14,911. I believe that there are certain unions which ratten and some that do not; if we can have it clearly stated it is best; you ratten through them?—Yes.

14,912. They have frequently done it?—Yes. Well, I think that was all that took place at that time.

14,913. Are you quite sure that on that occasion anything was said about bands or nuts?—Yes, I am sure both bands and nuts were mentioned, and I never had any other idea of anything else. Perhaps two or three weeks elapsed and I heard nothing. I daily expected to hear of Fearnehough's nuts and bands being gone; but not hearing of anything we went and asked Broadhead again whether he had taken any steps to get his nuts and bands taken. He said that the thing was in progress, but he was very awkward to get to.

14,914. Did he not tell you that at the time he was working for Butcher?—No.

14,915. At Butcher's wheel?—No, I am not aware.

14,916. Mind; did not he tell you that at that time he was working at Butcher's wheel?—No, he did not.

14,917. When did you first hear that he was

IXTEENTH DAY.

J. Barker.

24 June 1867.

working at Butcher's wheel?—I cannot say; but if he was working at Butcher's wheel at that time I should have been aware of it.

14,918. In point of fact he was working at Butcher's wheel at the time when he was blown up, you know that?—No, I think he would not; I cannot say now for certain.

14,919. We know it quite well, because he has been here, and he told us that he had been working there some time; they could not have his nuts and bands taken. Slack, Sellars, and Company took a trough at Butcher's wheel, and Butcher's were so protected that no person could get into the wheel; therefore his bands and nuts could not be taken there. Now how do you answer that?—I believe——

14,920. How do you answer that?—I tell you why I thought they could take his bands and nuts there, because I heard that his bands had been taken some time previously.

14,921. Not there?—Yes, I heard so.

14,922. That is not so, they never were?—I am not able to answer the fact whether they were or not.

14,923. Do not you know in point of fact that that was a building where the entrance was covered over so that you could not get in, and that there was a man who watched the place, and that they could not get about on account of the watchman?—I know there was a watchman.

14,924. Whether there was a watchmon or not the entrance was a covered one; did not you know that the expense of taking a man's nuts and bands was a mere nothing?—I knew what the expense was.

14,925. 5*s.* is the price for a nut and 5*s.* for a band?—Yes.

14,926. Why were the three unions to join in simply taking away a man's nuts?—If it had cost only 15*s.* we should have to pay 5*s.* each.

14,927. Do you mean to say that there was a necessity for these serious cogitations and these meetings about a question of 5*s.* a-piece?—The serious meetings were this: Fearnehough was hard to get to, to ratten him, and I thought this that if any man could ratten Fearnehough, Broadhead was the man to do it.

14,928. So you knew that he was hard to do?—Yes.

14,929. So hard probably that you could not ratten him?—I knew if Broadhead could not get him rattened, no one else could.

14,930. Was it commonly talked of how he could be got at?—No, but I can explain how my ideas were that he could be got at.

14,931. I should like to know what your ideas were?—I will take a case where a rattening took place and I will just give you my ideas. I will just tell the way in which he could have been done at Butcher's.

14,932. You think that it could have been done? you could have rattened the man yourself?—If I had known all the grinders at work at Butcher's wheel, I think I could have got him rattened.

14,933. You had a talk about him, and you went frequently to ask him, and he said that it was in progress?—Yes, the second time.

14,934. What happened next?—The next thing that happened was that on the Monday I went out in the street and saw a placard announcing the Hereford Street outrage. It immediately flashed across my mind that Broadhead must have had something to do with it.

14,935. Why?—Because I knew that Broadhead wanted Fearnehough stopped in some manner or other.

14,936. And you did too?—Yes, and so did we.

14,937. And so knowing that you all wanted him to be stopped, you concluded that he had been stopped?—Yes, I did.

14,938. Had you any doubt in the least that Broadhead had stopped him in consequence of your conversation?—I thought it was in consequence of our conversation.

14,939. What did you do upon that?—I felt in such a way I scarcely knew what to do. I thought I should then be getting into trouble if Broadhead said anything about it to anyone.

14,940. You thought you would be getting into trouble if Broadhead said anything about it to any one?—Yes.

14,941. So what did you do?—I did nothing that day.

14,942. Did not you go to Broadhead?—No.

14,943. Did not you go to stop his mouth?—No.

14,944. What did you do?—I did not go till the following night.

14,945. Did you see anybody about it before then?—I saw Skidmore the day following.

14,946. What did you say to Skidmore?—I said to Skidmore that I believed Broadhead was at the bottom of this, and we had better go and see him.

14,947. If you had had nothing at all to do with it and had only done rattening I should have thought the less you had to say to Broadhead the better?—Yes, and I think so now.

14,948. However you thought then that the best thing you could do was to go to Broadhead?—Yes.

14,949. And you went?—Yes.

14,950. What was said to Broadhead?—We inquired for him, and went into his house. He was up-stairs. We went up-stairs to him. He sat at his desk by himself, and I cannot exactly remember the words that were said at the time, only I do remember this that I protested ——

14,951. What did you say when you first went in?—I cannot really remember the exact words that I should say to him.

14,952. Did you say, "Well, I say Broadhead, you did him at last?—No.

14,953. What did you say?—I said something of this sort, "Well this is a rum affair."

14,954. And he would say, "It is a rum affair too?—He smiled.

14,955. It was rather a joke than otherwise with you?—It was no joke for me.

14,956. You thought this was a rum affair and he smiled, what else?—I said, "We never engaged for anything of this sort you know."

14,957. You said that; what did Broadhead say?—He said nothing.

14,958. He said nothing; then what did you say?—We did not know what to say, we were so confused and so frightened at what took place that we scarcely knew what we did, but I remember him telling us that we had 7*l.* 10*s.* each to pay.

14,959. And you paid it too?—Yes.

14,960. You paid it?—Yes, I found the money.

14,961. You paid 15*l.* did not you—5*l.* a-piece?—7*l.* 10*s.* each.

14,962. Was Broadhead to have anything for doing it?—Well we made an arrangement with Broadhead about the rattening.

14,963. Was Broadhead to have anything for doing it?—We never asked him any questions concerning that.

14,964. Did you agree when you asked him to do rattening to give him 15*l.*?—No, the sum was never mentioned at the time.

14,965. But you said something about money?—When do you refer to?

14,966. I refer to that first conversation, what did you say about the payment?—We told him it would not matter about the expense if he would get him rattened, and knowing he would be at considerable trouble to do this we told him he could pay himself or charge his own expenses.

14,967. What did you tell him besides?—That was all we told him on that occasion.

14,968. Does not it occur to you as a curious kind of thing (because if it is a mere question for rattening you say that you can get any common workman working in the same place with him to do it) that you should bargain with Broadhead to pay him a sum of money for expenses?—We had done it before.

14,969. You had paid him a sum of money before for expenses?—Yes.

SIXTEENTH DAY.

J. Barker.

24 June 1867.

14,970. In rattening ?—Yes.

14,971. What was that ?—I could begin and go through them all.

14,972. But you have paid this ?—Yes.

14,973. For himself ?—No.

14,974. I speak of the case where you paid him himself ?—It is always understood that he charges something for his own trouble.

14,975. But you paid him this 15*l.* ?—Yes.

14,976. Let me look at your books ; where is the entry in your books ? You paid Broadhead on the 11th November, what does this mean that the place where you call my attention to has been all cut out ?—The writing is erased.

14,977. Who erased the writing ?—I did.

14,978. When did you do it ?—About a few months ago.

14,979. How did you happen to do it ?—When I knew this inquiry was going to take place I expected to be closely questioned concerning the payment of that 7*l.* 10*s.* I had paid it to Mr. Skidmore, understanding that he had the authority of their secretary through me to pay it on their account, and I thought I will scratch this out and put the other paid to the saw makers society—you will see there " Sy." (for secretary) " for scale due."

14,980. What had you scratched out ?—For scale due is scratched out.

14,981. But you have got it in ?—Yes, I thought I could not put anything better in.

14,982. You first scratched it out and then having scratched it out you put in at the top the same thing that you had scratched out because you thought that you could put nothing better in ?—Yes.

14,983. When did you originally put in " for scale due " ?—The first time, when I entered that entry.

14,984. That is the 13th of October ?—Yes.

14,985. Then that was a false entry ?—No, it was due to them for scale.

14,986. Do you call it scale due 7*l.* 10*s.* if you pay a man money for blowing a house up ?—I will explain how that scale was due to their society.

14,987. But you paid it for blowing up Fearnebough's house ?—I paid it to their society.

14,988. It was paying to the society ; but it was paying to the society for blowing up Fearnehough's house ?—Yes certainly, in one way it was.

14,989. And you called it for scale whereas there was no scale ?—Yes, I rubbed 7*l.* 10*s.* off that we owed for scale ; when we took Slack, Sellars, and Company's saw makers out we agreed to pay an equal portion of the expenses of these men.

14,990. Therefore 7*l.* 10*s.* was for that, but you paid 15*l.*—Yes.

14,991. Where is the other 7*l.* 10*s.* accounted for ?—It is not accounted for in the book at all.

14,992. How did you make your book balance ?—I will tell you, I drew, I think, it was 4*l.* 10*s.* monies on account of saw handles that I had sold, the other 3*l.* I paid at that time out of my own pocket.

14,993. That would not enter into the accounts ?—No, the 3*l.* I simply charged at the time as expenses by small instalments.

14,994. Where are those ?—Here (*showing the same to the Examiners*). I charged the 3*l.* amongst weekly expenses by small instalments.

14,995. All these were false entries ?—No, I did it by way of incidental expenses.

14,996. And you put down more than you had paid in order to recoup yourself the 3*l.* ?—Yes.

14,997. Those were false entries ?—Yes.

14,998. And these accounts were passed by your auditor ?—Yes.

14,999. You say that you entered your solemn protest against this proceeding ?—I did.

15,000. But notwithstanding your protest and abhorence, you paid the money out of your own pocket ?—Yes, I thought it was the best thing that I could do then.

15,001. I daresay you had an indignation meeting ?—Yes.

15,002. And you protested yourself ?—Yes.

15,003. Did you move the resolution ?—No.

15,004. Did you call it a horrid, or fiendish, or devilish act ?—I felt it was both horrid, fiendish, and devilish.

15,005. It was so passed at your meeting ?—Yes.

15,006. Did you speak on the question yourself ?—Yes.

15,007. Before the meeting ?—Yes.

15,008. And you paid for it all the while ?—Yes.

15,009. How long have you been secretary ?—Three years and four months.

15,010. Who was secretary before you ?—George Hinchcliffe.

15,011. You say that rattening is a very common thing with you ?—Yes.

15,012. Have you ever had the misfortune to pay for any other outrage which was committed against your will ?—No.

15,013. Never ?—No, never.

15,014. Have you ever paid for any outrage committed with your sanction ?—No.

15,015. Have you ever been concerned in any other outrage ?—No.

15,016. Have you ever been concerned in any other outrage or breach of the law in connexion with the trade, except the Hereford Street outrage ?—No.

15,017. Do you know any other persons who have ?—No, except rattening.

15,018. Do you know any person who has been engaged in any outrage at all ?—No.

15,019. Will you leave your books with us ?—Yes.

15,020. Have you produced all your books ?—Yes, all but one.

15,021. Which is that ?—The one I have destroyed.

15,022. What was the book which you destroyed ?—A cash book.

15,023. When did you destroy it ?—I think it was about last June.

15,024. A year ago ?—Yes.

15,025. What did you destroy it in June for ?—Our society was broken up in a way that I disapproved of, and many of the effects were divided. I considered that my father had been wrong in his affairs, and I was only curious to see the books of the society for a time back when that occurred. When I took to the secretaryship there could not be any books found save an old contribution book, and the books then in use. Hinchliffe told me that he had given me all the books he had. I then inquired of William Birkinshaw who had been the secretary previous to him. Birkinshaw said he had not any books, and he referred us to Charles Birkinshaw who told me the same ; he had been secretary before him. We removed our premises last June or somewhere about that time. I burned a deal of waste paper and this book among the rest. I said, " I cannot see anybody else's books, they shall not see mine." That was the reason I destroyed it.

15,026. They said that they had not any books, and therefore you thought that because they had not produced the books to you, you would destroy your own ?—Yes.

15,027. What period of time did your books go over ?—From the time I took to the secretaryship till I began to use that cash book, a year and a half ago.

15,028. When does that begin ? You have been secretary three or four years ?—Three years and five months.

15,029. That would be January 1864 ?—It was February 1864, when I was elected secretary.

15,030. That book extended from January 1864, to February 1866 ?—Yes ; two years.

15,031. Do you mean to tell us that for so foolish a reason as that you destroyed that book ?—Yes.

15,032. And none other ?—No ; I had no other reason for destroying it at that time ; but since then we have got all the old books back ; the persons have all given them up.

15,033. You have produced everybody's book but that one ?—Yes.

SIXTEENTH DAY.

J. Barker.

24 June 1867.

15,034. You have produced everybody's book but your own?—For 10 years.

15,035. Everybody's book but your own is produced, save the book from January 1864 to February 1866, which you have destroyed?—Yes, all those.

15,036. Have you delivered all the other books up?—They are all here.

15,037. Even this book looks very much as if it were written a good deal at the same time?—It has been written week by week.

15,038. That you swear?—I swear that; there may have been a time or two when I have written two week's accounts down running; that is not a got up book.

15,039. You pledge your word that you have not been engaged in anything except rattening, and that you have been concerned in rattening in a great number of cases?—Yes, to some extent.

15,040. I do not think that it is needful for us to go into the question of rattening. We only want to know the fact. Was it known in your trade that there was rattening done?—Yes.

15,041. It was known generally in the trade that rattening was going on?—Yes.

15,042. Can you tell us whether rattening was known to exist in other trades beside your own?—I think that it has existed in the grinding trades.

15,043. The grinders are liable to be rattened?—I think so.

15,044. And all the grinders unions know it?—Yes.

15,045. Are there several trades in Sheffield that are not concerned in rattening at all?—It is quite possible.

15,046. As far as the grinders unions are concerned they all ratten? — Yes; to some extent I think they do.

15,047. Did you ever know of any bellows being cut at all?—No; we have nothing to do with bellows in our trade.

15,048. Do you know whether or not that has been done by members in other trades?—I never heard anything about bellows cutting till I came here.

15,049. Do you know any union at all which has sanctioned in any way the beating of men?—No.

15,050. Or frightening men?—No.

15,051. Did you ever write any threatening letters? No.

15,052. Never?—No.

15,053. Have you been aware of any threatening letters being sent in respect of your society?—No.

15,054. Never?—No, never; but I heard of a letter being sent to Messrs. Slack, Sellars, and Grayson, and I can explain to you what that letter was if it is true that it was sent.

15,055. What is that?—The man we had in dispute was named Henry Martin, and I have been informed by a person I could name that he wrote that letter.

15,056. You never wrote one yourself?—No.

The witness withdrew.

J. Hoyle.

JOSEPH HOYLE sworn and examined.

15,057. (*Mr. Barstow.*) Are you secretary to the jobbing grinders?—Yes.

15,058. How long have you been secretary?—It is about 10 years since the first time; but I have been off; there has been another person in.

15,059. You have been secretary off and on ever since?—Yes.

15,060. Your union have tools and bands?—Yes; generally we find our own tools.

15,061. Has rattening been pretty common in your union?—No; not much rattening.

15,062. Has it existed?—Yes.

15,063. Do you remember an attempt being made to blow up Mr. Holdsworth's factory?—Yes, I remember something about that.

15,064. That was on the 2nd of December 1861?—Yes, I saw an account of it in the newspaper.

15,065. Were you at that time secretary of your union?—Yes.

15,066. Had you anything to do with that? did you induce anyone to blow up Mr. Holdsworth's factory?—No, I will tell you how it was.

15,067. You had not anything to do with it?—No; I had not anything to do with blowing up in any form. We had some jobbing grinders that went down to Holdsworth's, and they did not belong to the union, and did not pay to the union. Mr. Broadhead came down to the wheel to me and said they had a case there, that they were going to make their men pay to the union.

15,068. He said that he intended to make his grinders pay?—Yes; so he asked whether we had any grievance at that place, and I said, "Not particular, but that there was some men working at our trade." So he said, "Do you wish to make them join?" I said, "Well, we should like them." He said, "Have "you any objections in going shares with us in the "expenses? we are going to make them pay." I said, "What are you going to do?" So he said, "We are going to ratten them." I said, "What do you mean?"——

15,069. (*Chairman.*) Do you mean to say that you, a Sheffield man, did not know what rattening meant?—Sometimes we rattened the bands and sometimes the nuts.

15,070. (*Mr. Barstow.*) The effect of rattening is really to stop the men going on grinding?—Sometimes the nuts go, and it stops them without taking a lot of stuff from the place.

15,071. Was that what you meant when you asked him what he was going to do?—Yes; and he said that he was going to take the bands and nuts. He went away and left me, and I heard no more of him till I heard tell of the place being blown up.

15,072. Till you heard of Holdsworth's place being blown up?—I did not hear any more.

15,073. Was any claim ever made upon you for the expenses?—Yes; he came down to the wheel to me and told me about it. I said, "Broadhead, you ought "not to have done it. I did not bargain for any "blowing up." He said, "Never mind, it will work "well for us."

15,074. Did he desire you to pay a share of the expenses?—Yes; he told me that our share of the expenses would be 6*l.* I thought it would be about 16*s.* when we started in it; when I got my money from the society I paid the 6*l.*

15,075. How did you get the money from the society?—The committee, which was sitting, gave me the money.

15,076. The committee gave you the money?—Yes.

15,077. How many sat on the committee?—I think that night there were two on.

15,078. Who were they?—There was one called John Thompson and Jonathan Hazlewood.

15,079. When they went into the committee room you asked them for the money?—I told them what had happened, and they did not want to pay me the money; so I told them they would have to pay it to keep the matter quiet and still.

15,080. I suppose, in short, they did pay?—Yes, they paid.

15,081. You keep books, I suppose?—Yes, we have some books.

15,082. Is that payment which you made entered in your books?—I do not know whether it was.

15,083. You are secretary and you ought to know whether it was so or not?—Yes.

15,084. Where were the books?—I do not know

whether it was entered in the book at that time, or whether it was deferred.

15,085. Does it appear in your books at all?—I think it does.

15,086. (*Chairman.*) Where are the books?—I took them to Mr. Fretson.

15,087. (*Mr. Barstow.*) Can you tell us how it appears?—No.

15,088. It is 6*l.* is it?—Yes.

15,089. (*Chairman.*) You did not pay it for blowing up Holdsworth?—No, we did not pay it for blowing up; but it was there and after I tried to get out from Mr. Broadhead the best way we could, and we withdrew from the amalgamated society altogether.

15,090. (*Mr. Barstow.*) This was on the 2nd December 1861, that it was blown up; were you at that time amalgamated with the saw grinders union?—Yes.

15,091. What were the other unions?—The handle makers and saw smiths.

15,092. You tell us that after you paid this money you withdrew from the union?—Yes, as soon as it was convenient for us to withdraw from the society we did.

15,093. When did you withdraw from the society?—Two or three years after, perhaps three years.

15,094. Did you ever hear what was the whole sum which was paid for Holdsworth's job?—No, I did not know that anybody else had anything to do with it until I saw an account in the newspaper of Broadhead's evidence, where I saw that the saw smiths and handle makers had something to do with it. I fancy I heard it from the newspaper.

15,095. Yow saw it from Broadhead's evidence?—Yes.

15,096. Do you mean to tell us that the payment to Broadhead was the reason why you withdrew from the union with the other three unions?—Yes.

15,097. It took place three years after?—Yes, but we could not get out of it till we saw a chance.

15,098. How was it that you could not get out?—We could not get out comfortable so as to be agreeable.

15,099. How so?—We were so mixed up with one another.

15,100. Could not you have said, "We want nothing to do with such outrages as these"?—I could not exactly.

15,101. In point of fact you did not think that this was a sufficient ground for withdrawing yourselves from union with the other branches?—It was the main one.

15,102. You thought that you could not give that as a reason for withdrawing?—No.

15,103. Why could not you give it as a reason for withdrawing?—I do not know, we were so mixed up with one another that we could not get out there and then.

15,104. Do you mean that your trade would not consider it a sufficient reason for withdrawing yourselves from union with the other three branches?—No, the trade wanted to join all along with Broadhead, but I did not want to join in with him. I wanted to be left to ourselves.

15,105. Then you feared that the payment of that money for that outrage would not be regarded by your trade as a sufficient reason for withdrawing?—We never mentioned it to the trade.

15,106. You feared that the trade would not regard it as a sufficient reason for withdrawing at once?—No.

15,107. Perhaps you mean that you could not then tell the trade that you dare not tell them, and that if you had told them the thing would have been out that you had been engaged in this outrage?—I do not know about dare not, but I did not tell.

15,108. (*Chairman.*) Then you would have dared to tell them?—Yes, I dare have told them.

15,109. If you had told them that you had blown up Holdsworth what would the trade have said to you for that?—It would have been all over the town.

15,110. Then you dared not tell them, in point of fact it would have been all over the town, and you would have been taken up?—Yes, we had to keep it secret.

15,111. That is the only outrage you know of?—It is the only blowing-up case I have ever had anything to do with, and I should not have had that if Broadhead had explained what he was going to do. I did not know anything about the other branches being in at all.

15,112. This is the only outrage you ever had anything to do with?—Yes, we have had rattening cases.

15,113. Have you ever known anyone beaten for not complying with the rules of the union?—Only from what I have seen in the newspaper.

15,114. Has it never happened in your trade?—No.

15,115. Nor has there been any personal annoyance to a man who chose to keep out of the union?—We have had a few rattening cases with men.

15,116. But you have not insulted them in any way?—No.

15,117. (*Mr. Chance.*) The jobbing grinders grind several kinds of tools?—Yes.

15,118. Have you been in the habit of grinding machine knives?—Yes, I have been grinding 36 years.

15,119. Do you grind machine knives?—Yes.

15,120. Do the jobbing grinders generally speaking grind machine knives?—Yes, we have a statement of articles.

15,121. Has that caused any dissatisfaction on the part of the scythe makers?—I think it has, and in the scythe trade and the saw trade as well.

15,122. Do you know whether the scythe grinders at any time have sent any threatening letters in consequence of you grinding machine knives?—No, I do not.

15,123. Do you know whether any threatening letters have been sent to Mr. Hazlewood?—No, I do not know, except what I have seen in the papers.

15,124. You do not know of any that have been sent of your own knowledge?—I know Hazlewood once had his bands taken for taking an apprentice boy on.

15,125. Hazlewood once worked at Tysack and Sons?—Yes.

15,126. While he was working at Tysack's did not he receive a threatening letter from the scythe makers?—Yes, I have seen it in the newspaper.

15,127. Do you know of your own knowledge that he did?—No.

15,128. You do not know whether Hazlewood gave up working for Tysack's in consequence of threatening letters from the scythe grinders?—No, he did not give over, his son works for them now.

15,129. He did not give over?—No.

15,130. Do I understand that you cannot speak from your own knowledge of any threatening letters from the scythe grinders?—No, I do not know anything about them.

15,131. That is so is it?—Yes.

15,132. (*Mr. Barstow.*) Do you produce all the books in your possession?—We have another old book or two.

15,133. Are they more than 10 years old?—No, we have only been organized about 10 years.

15,134. Have you produced to us all the books which have been in use in the union for 10 years?—No, we had one book short eight or nine years since.

15,135. What book is that?—It is a scale book.

15,136. Have you destroyed any books?—No, I have not destroyed any books.

15,137. Have you mutilated any?—Well——

15,138. Then you have altered them?—We have had bits of scratching out when we have made mistakes.

15,139. Have you altered any with reference to this inquiry?—I do not know that I have.

15,140. What do you mean by altering the books?—When we have made mistakes in the figures.

15,141. You have not intentionally falsified your books?—No.

SIXTEENTH DAY.

J. Hoyle.

24 June 1867.

15,142. You are sure of that?—Yes.

15,143. Those are all the books kept by you for trade purposes?—Yes, except the book that we have short.

15,144. You can produce that book cannot you?—No, it is gone, I cannot produce it.

15,145. Do you know whether there was any trade outrage by your union about that time?—There was not any outrage at all in our society at that time.

15,146. You have told us of the only outrage which you knew of in the last 10 years, the Holdsworth affair?—Yes, that is the only outrage I know of in our society.

15,147. You say that you never originated any yourselves?—No.

15,148. (*Chairman.*) Can you give us any explanation why that book is missing?—No, I do not know where it is, it was lost.

15,149. When was it discovered to be lost?—We had a lot of contribution books burnt.

15,150. When did you discover that that book was lost?—I did not discover it till some few weeks back when I was looking for it.

15,151. It was simply your account of the scale?—Yes.

15,152. You are quite sure that you did not destroy it?—Yes.

15,153. Do you know any person who has destroyed it?—No, we had a lot of books taken away when Jonathan Hazlewood was secretary; a lot of contribution books and statements. The box was not big enough. He took them out, and laid them on a form, and locked the box up, and there was another meeting the same night in the room, and somebody took them.

15,154. Are you quite sure that it has not been abstracted, and kept away from us that we might not see it?—No, sir, I am sure that it has not.

15,155. (*Mr. Barstow.*) Do you know in what book this entry would appear?—I do not think it is all in one sum.

15,156. How was it entered?—I do not know, it is so long since. I did not know that I should be called upon till Broadhead mentioned it.

15,157. It was six years since, and it was entered in small sums?—I cannot say how it was entered.

16,158. (*Chairman.*) A false entry was made?—Yes, I suppose it was.

15,159. And you made an entry to disguise it?—No, I did not. I made the entry with a lot of other things. I do not know how it was made.

The witness withdrew.

Adjourned to to-morrow at 11 o'clock.

SEVENTEENTH DAY.

Tuesday, 25th June 1867.

PRESENT:

WILLIAM OVEREND, Esq., Q.C.	GEORGE CHANCE, Esq.
THOMAS IRWIN BARSTOW, Esq.	J. E. BARKER, Esq., Secretary.

WILLIAM OVEREND, Esq., Q.C., in the Chair.

SEVENTEENTH DAY.

J. Wood.

25 June 1867.

JOHN WOOD sworn and examined.

15,160. (*Mr. Barstow.*) What are you?—A saw maker.

15,161. I understand that you were auditor to the saw makers union?—Yes.

15,162. Are you so now?—Yes.

15,163. How long have you been auditor?—Since last April but one.

15,164. I believe you wish to make a statement with reference to what was said by Thomas Smith, your secretary, yesterday on the matter of the accounts?—Yes.

15,165. Will you have the goodness to make it?—I say that I never saw an item as I have seen in the report in the papers about expenses paid to Mr. Barker.

15,166. If I remember right, he said that he entered in the account 4*l.* of the 7*l.* 10*s.* which he paid altogether, and that he paid the other in advance out of his own pocket, and that he then repaid himself by small items?—I do not know anything about that.

15,167. Was not this Smith's statement, "We "had charged our trade with 7*l.* 10*l.*; I have de- "stroyed that account. There are two auditors to "our trade, John Wood and John Blenkiron; they "passed the audit."

15,168. (*Chairman.*) This is Smith's evidence yesterday, "When the auditor came to examine your "your books did he not say, 'What are these "expenses'?—*A.* Yes. *Q.* Who was he?—*A.* It "was John Wood and John Blenkiron. *Q.* What "did you say to that?—*A.* I said that they were ex- "penses paid by Mr. Barker. *Q.* But for what?— "*A.* I did not name the reason. *Q.* Do you mean to "say that you gave no vouchers or anything of the "kind?—*A.* No. *Q.* Do you mean to say that your "auditor, passed the accounts in that way? If "you said that they were expenses paid by Mr. "Barker, did they not ask you what they were paid "for, and did not you tell them?—*A.* I did not. *Q.* "Do you mean to say that they passed those ex- "penses?—*A.* Yes, just the same as they had passed "these other accounts. *Q.* Do you mean to say that "the unions have no further security than your "statement, that they were expenses paid without "vouchers of any kind? do you mean to say that the "auditors would pass a thing merely upon your "representation that they were expenses?—*A.* They "did so; undoubtedly they did; they believed me. "*Q.* Would that be a common thing? do you mean "to say that you have entries there which are "merely entries of expenses paid without any "vouchers at all, and that the auditors were satis- "fied?—*A.* They were satisfied with me. *Q.* They "were satisfied with you on account of your good "conduct, I suppose?—*A.* Yes, and honesty; I never "robbed anybody of anything in my life."

15,169. (*Mr. Barstow.*) You have heard what Mr. Overend has read?—Yes.

15,170. Is that correct? first of all, did you pass the account of 7*l.* 10*s.*?—No, we did not.

15,171. Do you remember seeing such an item?—We never saw such an item.

15,172. Were you aware that Barker was in debt to your union between 17*l.* and 18*l.*?—Yes, I think it was in last September or October.

15,173. Are you aware whether that sum was ever repaid?—No, I am not.

SEVENTEENTH DAY.

J. Wood.

25 June 1867.

15,174. So far as you know there is no entry of the repayment of that sum in the books of your society?—I will explain to you the way in which Smith has told you; he has stated that the grinders belonging to Slack, Sellars, and Grayson (where there was some dispute) were paid by the trade jointly, the saw makers and the saw-handle makers; that at the commencement the saw makers were paid considerably more than the saw-handle makers, and that was the the way this got on. We kept asking him to bring us the account of the handle makers; he never did so, but the handle makers were paying the grinders instead of us, and that was the way it was getting reduced.

15,174*a*. Did he say you were in debt to the grinders?—No.

15,175. I understand the saw-handle makers were in debt to you?—Yes.

15,176. Well, then how did the fact of the saw-handle makers paying the grinders make any difference to you, if the grinders were not in your debt?—Allow me to explain: the saw grinders were out of employment by a dispute, and the saw makers and the saw-handle makers paid them their scale, and the saw makers paid more than what the saw-handle makers did towards that, and that was the way that that originated.

15,177. (*Chairman.*) You say the saw makers paid more than the saw-handle makers, how much more did they pay?—I cannot tell; 17*l.* or 18*l.*

15,178. (*Mr. Barstow.*) Was this Smith's assertion to you, or do you know it of your own knowledge?—Only his assertion; we have no proofs.

15,179. Then I understand you pressed him for an account?—For a balance.

15,180. And he never rendered one?—No.

15,181. (*Chairman.*) He said he destroyed the book, but are you sure there was not an item of 7*l.* 10*s.* paid to Barker in the book?—I never saw the book.

15,182. Although you say you never saw it, are you prepared to swear that there was no such item in the book?—I will swear I never saw it. I believe I just stated that I did not see a book; I did see a book last Monday night but one. I should have said that I never saw the entry, but I did see a book last Monday night but one.

15,183. And there was no entry in Smith's book that you saw?—No, not that I saw.

15,184. There would not be an entry in Smith's book, I presume. Whom did Smith represent; he was secretary of what union?—The saw makers.

15,185. It was the saw-handle makers that had to pay, was it not?—Yes.

15,186. Then if they paid any money there would be an entry in their books, but there would be nothing at all about it in the saw makers book; there ought to be credit given in his book for 7*l.* 10*s.*?—Yes.

15,187. And you say you never saw such a credit?—No, never.

15,188. You might have balanced his books right if that money had been paid?—Yes.

15,189. (*Mr. Chance.*) But there ought to have been a balance of 17*l.* or 18*l.* to the credit of the saw makers in the saw makers book?—Yes.

15,190. Was there such an item; was there an item giving credit to the saw makers, or rather debiting the saw-handle makers to the extent of 17*l.* or 18*l.*?—You mean separately?

15,191. Yes?—No, there was not.

15,192. You say the saw-handle makers owed the saw makers some 17*l.* or 18*l.*, inasmuch as the saw makers had paid more than their share to the saw grinders?—Yes.

15,193. Therefore, there ought to have been an item in the saw makers book debiting the saw-handle makers?—Yes, if there was it would be in the cash book with the scale paid.

15,194. Was it so?—Yes, I believe it would be that way.

15,195. Did you see the entry?—No, I cannot say that I did. In the cash book would be the scale paid. It would be in that way.

15,196. Then if there is no entry of 7*l.* 10*s.* credited from the saw-handle makers there still must be an item of 17*l.* or 18*l.* as due from the saw-handle makers to the saw makers?—There is no item of 7*l.* 10*s.* that I have seen.

15,196*a*. Therefore, ought not the books to show that there is still 17*l.* or 18*l.* due from the saw-handle makers to the saw makers?—No; as I stated before, he told us there was something paid back again on the scale account over and above what had been due, and that reduced it.

15,197. How much was it?—I cannot tell.

15,198. (*Mr. Barstow.*) As I understand, Mr. Chance is asking you about the original sum of 17*l.* or 18*l.*; unless that was entered to the debit of the saw-handle makers in your accounts, how could you balance your books?—They have never been properly balanced.

15,199. (*Chairman.*) Then you have been a very bad auditor?—Well, I must allow that.

15,200. (*Mr. Chance.*) Any item might have been put in, and you would take no notice of them?—Yes.

15,201. (*Chairman.*) I do not think that you have benefitted yourself much by coming with this explanation; you have only shown that you have not audited their accounts properly, and that there may have been an item, but you did not see it if there was one.

The witness withdrew.

JOHN BLENKIRON sworn and examined.

J. Blenkiron.

15,202. (*Mr. Chance.*) Are you one of the auditors of the Saw Makers Union?—Yes.

15,203. With the last witness, John Wood?—Yes.

15,204. How long have you been an auditor?—Eighteen months.

15,205. You come here wishing to make a statement, do you not?—Yes.

15,206. What have you to say?—The statement which I wish to make is that there never was such an entry as "Cash paid to Mr. Barker, 7*l.* 10*s.* 0*d.*" in any account.

15,207. But nobody has ever said that there was such an entry?—According to the newspapers this morning it states so.

15,208. An entry paid to Mr. Barker?—Yes, that there was an item "Cash paid to Mr. Barker, 7*l.* 10*s.* 0*d.*"

15,209. It was stated that there was charged an item of 7*l.* 10*s.*, you say that that is not down?—I think it was stated that we saw an item of 7*l.* 10*s.* cash paid to Mr. Barker.

15,210. Was there any item of 7*l.* 10*s.* as having been paid by Mr. Barker to the saw makers union? No, not to my knowledge.

15,211. Was there any item by which Mr. Barker was credited to the extent of 7*l.* 10*s.*?—Not to my knowledge.

15,212. Is it a fact that the saw-handle makers were debtors to the saw makers society to the extent of about 17*l.* or 18*l.*?—I will try to explain to you the circumstance——

15,213. Can you answer that question first?—We had that report verbally from Mr. Smith, and since that audit to the present time I have applied to him for a proper account, but have never been satisfied with that account, and to see how that money has been rubbed off, but he has never furnished us with it.

15,214. Then he has told you that there was a debt of 17*l.* or 18*l.* from the saw-handle makers?—Yes, we had that account, and from that time we do not know how it has been rubbed out.

15,215. And you say that you have from time to time applied to Mr. Smith for an account of that?—Yes.

15,216. Then no entry of that has appeared in the book?—He has shuffled it off in a manner that did not

SEVENTEENTH DAY.

J. Blenkiron.

25 June 1867.

give us satisfaction, and we told him that that was not a proper account. He referred the small book to us the last Monday but one, but it only gave an account of how the saw-handle makers had reduced their debt since January.

15,217. And how was that?—By paying more scale to the saw grinders.

15,218. To what extent?—That was only to a few pounds since then.

15,219. Would those few pounds and the other sums, entered in a book, go to the extent of 17*l.* or 18*l.* which he said were due to you?—That was all we saw, and I repeatedly asked him myself for a proper account, and he has passed it off that we should have it at the next audit.

15,220. Have you ever complained to any of the committee that Smith would not render his account?—No.

15,221. But if he refused to render any account, why did you not complain to the committee?—I have not seen the committee since, but I took his word that we should have it.

15,222. But it is the duty of an auditor to see the books balanced?—Certainly.

15,223. But they did not balance?—His books balanced.

15,224. Not if there was a debt due which was not accounted for?—The regular trade book balanced, but we had this account against him.

15,225. You say that you from time to time applied to him, and he refused to render you the account?—Yes.

15,226. And you never complained to the committee of his refusal?—No, I have made no complaint to the committee, expecting to get it.

15,227. How long is it since you first asked him?—Last October.

15,228. And you have allowed it to go on from last October to the present time?—Yes.

15,229. And you have never complained to the committee?—No; they were only audited, I think, once in three months; there has not been above two audits since. I may have asked him twice for it.

15,230. (*Mr. Barstow.*) Does this sum of 17*l.* or 18*l.* appear in your books as given to the saw-handle makers?—Only week by week; it is an excess of scale; it is represented in our books as an excess of scale.

15,231. But have you such an entry in your books?—No, not in one sum. I repeat that we only got it verbally from Smith.

15,232. Do you know when this debt of 17*l.* or 18*l.* was incurred?—It would be at the time Slack and Sellars' grinders were out.

15,232*a*. (*Chairman.*) That is all. You have been a very bad auditor.

The witness withdrew.

Mr. W. Dronfield.

Mr. William Dronfield recalled and further examined.

15,233. (*Chairman.*) You are the honorary secretary of the Sheffield Trades Defence Committee, I believe?—I am.

15,234. Have you any office besides that?—Yes, I am secretary of the United Kingdom Alliance of Organized Trades.

15,235. Do you hold any other office?—I am secretary to the Organized Trades of Sheffield, that is the local society.

15,236. Have you any other office?—By trade I am a printer, and am secretary to the Printers Society of Sheffield.

15,237. Have you any other offices?—No.

15,238. Those are your offices?—Yes.

15,239. Did you not some time ago issue a circular on behalf of the United Kingdom Alliance Organized Trades Society?—I have issued a number of circulars, but nothing in connexion with this business.

15,240. Will you allow me to see the circular?—(*The witness handed a paper to the Chairman.*)

15,241. As secretary of the defence committee to whom did you issue the circular?—To the secretaries of the trades societies of Sheffield and its neighbourhood.

15,242. When was that?—I think the date is February 26th, 1867.

15,243. Was that in reference to this inquiry?—It had reference both to this and the general Commission now sitting in London.

15,244. Will you give me a copy of that?—That is one of the series (*handing a paper to the Chairman*).

15,245. How many answers did you get to the questions in this paper?—I think 39 or 40.

15,246. What answers did you get as to outrages?—Well, I believe that with the exception of the saw trade there were no outrages admitted.

15,247. Would you allow me to see what the saw trade said?—I will (*handing a paper to the Chairman*).

15,248. Does Broadhead answer this?—Yes.

15,249. "Have there been any outrages committed "in your trade during the last 10 years? If so, state "what particulars you are able, and also the probable "cause." Broadhead writes this to you, "James "Linley was once blown up and twice shot at. He "died seven months after the last time, but whether "those outrages on Linley were done by union men "or others has never been ascertained. Henry Jackson "and Joseph Helliwell were burnt by an explosion of "powder at two separate times at Tower wheel. Mr. "Joseph Wilson's house was also blown up, and there "was also the outrage at Russell works, and the "threatening letters to Messrs. Smith and Wheatman. "There is also the Hereford Street outrage, which I "was nearly forgetting (if it is to be attributed to "our trade). *Q.* Are you or any of your members "prepared to give evidence on oath upon the above "charges should you be called upon to do so?—*A.* We "are prepared to give evidence upon what we know, "but that is very little. *Q.* What method have "you of collecting your contributions?—*A.* The "finance committee sits every Saturday to pay scale "and receive contributions, and examine and balance "all other accounts, but the secretary collects the "bulk of the contributions during the week, which "are handed over to the finance committee on the "Saturday following. If they cannot be prevailed "upon to observe the rules and regulations they often "get rattened, but as a general rule the bands are "restored when the difference gets settled." Therefore the saw grinders admitted rattening?—Yes.

15,250. Perhaps you will allow us to see the others?—Oh, yes, certainly, but I thought you wanted the saw trade.

15,251. Which is the next that you have?—There is the saw trade (*handing a paper to the Chairman*).

15,252. There is no answer given, I see, by Thomas Smith as to the outrages?—I am not aware. I do not remember the answer, but you have it there.

15,253. With respect to the mode of enforcing their claims, he says, "The rule is to call upon the "men, and moral persuasion is used; and if this does "not succeed, the masters are seen." That is all the information Thomas Smith gave you?—Yes.

15,254. Joseph Barker, secretary to the saw-handle makers made you a report also?—Yes.

15,255. It is not signed?—He had not room on his schedule.

15,256. March 12th, 1867, "Have there been any "outrages committed in your trade during the last 10 "years?" He says, "Not to our knowledge." *Q.* "What method have you of collecting your contribu- "tions?—*A.* We do not collect it, but each member "sends or brings it voluntarily to the committee on "Saturday night. *Q.* What method have you of "enforcing your claims upon refractory members?—

SEVENTEENTH DAY.

Mr. W. Dronfield.

25 June 1867.

"*A.* None." That is all; that is the saw-handle makers. What is the next?—I think the jobbing grinders did not return theirs. I have been looking them over this morning, and I cannot find it. Mr. Sugg has had them for some time.

15,257. Are the saw makers all together connected with the saw trade?—Quite so.

15,258. What is the next?—I think you have next the file smiths union, which is the largest trades union in Sheffield (*handing a paper to the Chairman*).

15,259. The secretary says that they know of no outrages in the file trade, and he says, "The mode "of enforcing claims is that we decline working with "them, thereby giving our employers the choice of "unionists or non-unionists. In all cases of dispute we "see the employers, if they will allow us, before any "action takes place." There is no admission there of either rattening or of outrage?—No, I think not.

15,260. Are there any others?—Yes, the stove grate and fender grinders (*handing in a paper*).

15,261. As to outrages, the secretary says, "There "has been the Acorn Street outrage, as to which you "are no doubt in a position to get information by "referring to the papers of that date. The man "Thompson that was put on his trial for the said "outrage made a statement damaging to our society, "for which they expelled him from the society; for our "trade has no knowledge of that outrage. *Q.* What "method have you of enforcing your claims on "refractory members?—*A.* We have had only one "case of enforcing our claims, and that was with the "man Thompson alluded to above. We wished him to "pay his arrears, and he would not. We waited upon "Mr. Hoole, and he told us to pump upon Thompson; "but the same day he paid his arrears." There is no admission of rattening?—No. (*The witness handed in a paper.*)

15,262. The next is the carpenters and joiners, and their secretary states, "At Mr. Fewsdale's (now Cra- "ven, Brothers), W. Champion, a non-society man, shot "H. Grayson, the then secretary of the local society, "and attempted to shoot others in the shop, for which "he was tried at York assizes, and sentenced to a term "of imprisonment. *Q.* What method have you of "collecting your contributions?—*A.* Fortnightly, at "the branch meeting house." That is no answer at all; what does that mean?—They are paid fortnightly at the meeting house.

15,263. As to the method of enforcing their claims, the secretary says, "When owing 10*s.*, suspension "from benefit, and after 26 weeks, exclusion from the "society." They do not admit rattening?—They do not practice rattening.

15,264. (*Mr. Chance.*) Who is the secretary of the carpenters?—William Blenkiron.

15,265. Then we have the razor-blade grinders, and their secretary says, "There have been no out- "rages since our union was established. *Q.* What "method have you of enforcing your claims?—*A.* Exclusion from benefits." Then there is something crossed out; do you know what that is?—I do not know; I have not crossed anything out (*after examining the papers*). It is not my doing. I do not know who did it.

15,266. In the case of the file grinders there is no allusion to outrages. They enforce their claims "only by referring them to the district meetings"?—Is there not something about No. 9?

15,267. There is no admission at all. Who is the secretary to the razor-blade grinders?—His name is Joseph Mallinson. Those are the scythe grinders (*handing a paper to the Examiners*).

15,268. The secretary is Joseph Machin?—Yes, the secretary is Joseph Machin.

15,269. He says that there have been no outrages. "We first remonstrate with the refractory members; "that failing, we then see the employers, if they are "agreeable. If that does not do, if there are any more "men at the place they cease work. If there be no "more men at the place the bands generally disappear. "If that fails, we generally expel him from the union. "The bands are generally returned when the thing "is settled." He admits rattening in that case?—Yes. Then there are the common scythe makers, whose secretary is William Linacre.

15,270. In reply to the question, "Have there been "any outrages committed in your trade during the "last 10 years?" the answer is, "The destruction "of property; tools have been removed. *Q.* What is the "mode of collecting contributions? *A.* The finance "committee sit every alternate week on Saturday to "receive them, and members come or send at that "time." There is no answer to the question "What "method have you of enforcing your claims?" What is the next?—The sickle and hook forgers (*handing in a paper*).

15,271. No outrages are alluded to in this, "What "is the method of enforcing claims?"—*A.* If a member "be out of employment (or under notice to leave his "employ), and is more than six weeks in arrear of con- "tributions, he can only pay those arrears by paying "what we call double contributions to bring him finan- "cial. Some have paid for months before they could "come on the funds. In some cases tools have been "removed." That is rattening. William Webster is the secretary. What is the next?—The fork makers.

15,272. George Bulloss is the secretary, and he says there are no outrages, and that the only mode of enforcing payment is "by persuasion, or by any other legal means in our power." What are the next?—The bone, haft, and scale cutters society.

15,273. John Pickin, the secretary, says that there are no outrages, and there is no answer as to the mode of enforcing claims upon refractory members. What is the next?—The table blade forgers.

15,274. Their secretary, Joshua Walker, says there are no outrages; the answer is, "None." As to the mode of enforcing their claims, he says there is none?—Yes, the secretary of that is Joshua Walker.

15,275. What is the next?—The table knife hafters.

15,276. The secretary says there are no outrages, and the mode of enforcing claims is "persuasion." James James is the secretary. What is the next?—The pen and pocket blade forgers.

15,277. There is no trade outrage, and they use "moral suasion" for enforcing their claims upon refractory members. The secretary is W. J. Holden. Was "moral suasion" applied to Sutcliffe, because he had his head broken; they say that they enforce payments by "moral suasion"?—No, that was the grinders.

15,278. The next are the Britannia metal smiths, No. 1 Society, of which the secretary is William Mounsey. There is no outrage of any kind, and their mode of enforcing contributions is that, "If a mem- "ber becomes refractory, and will not comply with "the rules of the trade, we call a meeting in the "manufactory of the members, and if they do not "settle we give a legal month's notice." What is the next?—The Britannia metal smiths, No. 2 (*handing in a paper*).

15,279. The secretary says there is no outrage, and no answer is given as to the mode of enforcing claims?—I thought there was a remark as to that.

15,280. Who is the secretary of that?—His name is Jenkinson; but I do not know his actual name, he has not signed his name (*handing in a paper*).

15,281. What is the next?—The next is the railway spring makers, of which George Austin is the secretary (*handing in a paper*).

15,282. They say there have been no outrages; and as to enforcing their claims their method is, "Suspending them from the benefits of the society." What is the next?—The edge tool forgers, of which James Reaney is the secretary (*handing in a paper*).

15,283. He says there have been no outrages, "Not "one from any cause whatever;" and that they have no method of enforcing claims. "We do all we pos- "sibly can by persuading; but in some cases we have "to use stronger measures, namely, stopping them

SEVENTEENTH DAY.

Mr. W. Dronfield.

25 June 1867.

" from working until the matter is settled." That is very vague; we do not know whether that is rattening or not. What is the next?—The cabinet-case makers, Walter Nield, secretary (*handing in a paper*).

15,284. He says there have been no outrages, and that there is no method of enforcing claims, " but loss " of benefits unfinancial." What is the next?—The razor scale pressers, Joshua Vickers, secretary (*handing in a paper*).

15,285. No answer is given as to outrages, and then with respect to the mode of enforcing payments, he says, " We have been very fortunate with persua- " sion. On one or two occasions we have had to " write to our employers to state that if such a man " did not pay we should stop the others." What is the next?—The British plate, spoon, and fork filers (*handing in a paper*).

15,286. They answer, "No," as to the outrage, and as to the mode of enforcing claims, they say their " moral suasion only " is resorted to.

15,287. (*Mr. Barstow.*) Who is the secretary to that society?—Henry John Woodward.

15,288. (*Chairman.*) What is the next? — The Rotherham and Masbro' stove grate fitters (*handing in a paper*).

15,289. That is hardly within our limits ; it is scarcely in the neighbourhood. The secretary says, as to outrages, " None whatever to my knowledge ;" and as to the mode of enforcing payment he says, " None ; but each member who allows his contri- " bution to exceed eight weeks is not entitled to the " benefit of the society." The secretary signs his name as Joseph Norburn. What is the next?—The fork grinders (*handing in a paper*).

15,290. No answer is given as to the outrages, and the mode of enforcing claims, he says, is " persuasion ; " and in an extreme case society men leaves off work." Charles Bagshaw is the secretary. What is the next? —The cork cutter's society (*handing in a paper.*)

15,291. (*Mr. Chance.*) Are those the cutters of cork, or are they the makers of tools for cutting cork? —The cutters of cork.

15,292. (*Chairman.*) The secretary says there have been no outrages, and that the mode of enforcing claims is expulsion from the society. Who is the secretary?—George Wood.

15,293. What is the next?—The steam hammer drivers (*handing in a paper.*)

15,294. The secretary says, " We are not aware of any outrages ;" and that the mode of enforcing claims is " by fines and expulsion from our society." Who is the secretary?—William Matthewman.

15,295. What is the next?—The patent scythe and hook makers (*handing in a paper*).

15,296. There is no answer given to the outrage inquiry, and it is stated that the method of enforcing claims is by the " society men leaving off work." Who is the secretary?—Charles Bagshaw.

15,297. Is he the same Bagshaw as the other?— Yes.

15,298. What is the next?—The engineers tool and hammer makers' society (*handing in a paper*).

15,299. It is stated that there have been no outrages, and in answer to the question as to the mode of enforcing claims they say " None." Who is the secretary?—Joseph Rowland Hill.

15,300. What is the next? — The edge tools grinders society, Samuel Stacey, secretary (*handing in a paper*).

15,301. They say, " We are not aware that there have been any outrages whatsoever," and that they have no method of enforcing their claims except " by " annoying them, or ceasing to work in their com- " pany." In answer to the question, " What is the " mode in which you collect your contributions?" They say, " Monthly ; it is brought to us in committee " on the last Saturday in every month ; if on the " first Saturday in the following month 6*d.* forfeit ; if " not paid then. 5*s.* forfeit; if not paid then some " kind of annoyance is often practised." That is not Samuel Stacey, is it?—Yes.

15,302. What is the next? — The file hardeners society, secretary, Edward Memmott (*handing in a paper*).

15,303. As to outrages, the secretary says, " None to my knowledge ; " and as to enforcing claims, " We try persuasive means." What is the next? —The workboard hands, scissor trade, William Simpson, secretary (*handing in a paper*).

15,304. As to outrages he says, " Not to my " knowledge," and he gives no answer as to the method of enforcing claims. What is the next?— The wire drawers society, Henry Bond, secretary (*handing in a paper.*)

15,305. As to the outrages he says, "Not any," as to the method of enforcing claims, " There is no compulsion ; it is optional." What is the next?—The letterpress printers, William Dronfield, secretary (*handing in a paper*).

15,306. It is stated that there have been no outrages whatever, and that the method of enforcing claims is " expulsion from the society, and if needs " be remonstrance with the employers ; this failing, " sending in a month's notice to leave." What is the next?—The spring knife cutlers, Francis Brownes, secretary (*handing in a paper*).

15,307. He says as to the outrages that there have been " None more than individual grievances arising " from one shopmate paying to the union, and others " not, they receiving equal benefits in the prices by " allowances to those who regularly pay their contri- " butions." As to the method of enforcing claims he says there are " none but moral suasion ; we greatly " require some power by Act of Parliament for " enforcing such claims." What is the next?—The wool shear forgers, secretary, George Fox (*handing in a paper*).

15,308. As to outrages, they say there have been " no outrages within 10 years. We have answered, " No, to the above questions inasmuch as the cases we " found occurred nearly 20 years ago." As to the mode of enforcing contributions they say " Moral suasion." What is the next?—The rollers and roll turners (*handing in a paper*).

15,309. As to outrages, the secretary says, " None " that I know of ; " and as to the method of enforcing claims, " Persuasion and fines ;" and then Thomas Crook, the secretary, says that, " We earnestly hope " that trades unions will become legal institutions, " and the protection of the law granted to us, and if " it were so we have not the least doubt that our " society would speedily be in a flourishing state." Are those all that you have?—I think those are all that I have.

15,310. Are they all that you have received?—I believe that they are all there, but without I had gone through them myself I could not swear to that. There was a list of them kept, which I think Mr. Sugg has.

Mr. Sugg stated that he should like to have a synopsis made of those unions, showing the number of members of unions, and those not members of unions.

The Chairman remarked that there were only two cases where there had been any rattening admitted.

15,311. (*Chairman.*) Can you tell us of your own knowledge what is the number of saw grinders—those who have admitted rattening?—Somewhere about 200.

15,312. And of the scythe grinders, how many are there?—They return 60 in our association.

15,313. And those are the only two, are they?— The sickle and hook forgers.

15,314. How many are there of those?—I believe it is 190. The numbers are all on those schedules.

15,315. You are very well acquainted with the trades of the town, are you not?—Yes. Allow me to me to ask whether you have the edge tool grinders? I think they admitted rattening.

(*Mr. Chance.*) They admit annoyance, but not rattening, I think.

15,316. (*Chairman.*) You say that there are several unions which have not answered your questions?—

SEVENTEENTH DAY.

Mr. W. Dronfield.

25 June 1867.

Yes. I sent out about 60 of those schedules, I think.

15,317. And you got 40 answers ?—Yes.

15,318. How many unions are there in Sheffield? —Sixty is about the number. I sent to all that I could get to, whether they were large or small.

15,319. Do you know what is the number of the other unions, that do not admit rattening ?—There are two trades of about 4,000 members which do not admit it. I cannot give you the numbers of any trade except that in the Organized Trades Association, who have 6,000 members.

15,320. How long have you been connected with trades unions ?—I was on the executive of the Provincial Typographic Association for 15 years. That was an amalgamated society of the printers of the country.

15,321. I believe amongst the printers it was never suggested that there was any rattening at all ?—I never heard of any.

15,322. So far as your knowledge goes, although those were the returns ; what is your opinions as to rattening prevailing. Broadhead said that it prevailed extensively ?—Well, I cannot speak to it of my own knowledge, and I was unprepared for the statement which Mr. Broadhead made, and not only that but for many more of the statements that he made of course, and I do not believe that it does exist to the extent which he stated.

15,323. To what extent do you believe that it exists ?—I believe that it is confined, if not exclusively almost exclusively, to the grinding branches.

15,324. Do you believe that all the grinders ratten? —I believe so, but I have no personal knowledge of it.

15,325. It has been the system of enforcing their rules, as we hear, for almost time out of mind ?—Yes, for want of legal protection.

15,326. And you say that according to your judgment, as being acquainted with the trade, the grinders universally ratten?—That is my belief from my connexion with the organized trades. I have been secretary since its formation in 1859.

15,327. Are there in your judgment any other trades besides the grinders which ratten ?—I do not think there are. I do not know of any. I have never been told of any, and I have never heard the thing talked of in our meetings.

15,328. There are persons who are not grinders who are rattened, are there not ?—I believe there is some kind of annoyance practised towards them, but I cannot speak to what it is.

15,329. For instance, the scissors forgers ?—I never heard of that case before I heard of it in Court.

15,330. Have you never heard of any other persons besides grinders who have been rattened ?—No.

15,331. Nobody but grinders ?—No, unless I have read as much in the papers ; but I have heard so much during this inquiry that I cannot say whether it was before or since this inquiry commenced, but I believe that it is since this inquiry has been going on that I have heard of those cases.

15,332. Speaking to you as a respectable man, and as being trusted amongst the unions, I want you to give us information ?—Yes, and I am most anxious to do so.

15,333. I believe you are. In your judgment, are there various trades who for the purpose of enforcing their rules upon the master and also upon the other branches, ask the grinders, and the grinders ratten them ?—Well, there are grinders rattening. I believe, as a rule, they have some kind of amalgamation the same as they have in the saw trade, and one branch assists the other in that way ; that is to say, if there are forgers in other branches and there are grinders in connexion with them, I believe that the other branches complain to the grinders and the grinders are rattened ; and in that way it may extend to the other branches in which grinding is done.

15,334. Therefore, any man who is engaged in any trade in Sheffield where grinding is done, is liable to be rattened ?—I believe so.

15,335. It extends to all persons engaged in a trade in which grinding is a process ?—That is my belief.

15,336. Do you know how many trades there are in which grinding is used ?—I do not.

15,337. How many unions are there in which grinding is used. I suppose almost every trade in Sheffield has more or less grinding connected with it ? —I could give you a list of the grinding trades.

15,338. But I want to know where grinding comes in, because everybody who is connected with grinding is liable if he does a thing which is not pleasant to the unions to be interfered with by the grinders ?—Would you allow me to run through this list ?

15,339. By all means ?—(*After referring to a paper.*) Out of 34 trades which we have in our association, there appear to be about 18 in which, to my knowledge, grinding is done. It appears to be so from this schedule.

15,340. Therefore all those 18 would be subject to be rattened ?—I believe so.

15,341. Is it necessary that they should be amalgamated with the grinders in order to cause them to ratten for them or not ?—So far as I know of those amalgamations (and I am speaking now of the trades being amalgamated amongst themselves, and not of the general amalgamation), the saw trade, the scythe, sickle, and hook trade, the scissors grinders, and forgers, and I believe the sickle grinders and scythe forgers are in amalgamation among themselves.

15,342. And if anything happens to one branch they call upon the others to assist them in enforcing their rules ?—That is what I understand to be the case.

15,343. Are the file cutters in that position ?—Yes, I beg your pardon.

15,344. That had escaped you ?—Yes, it had.

15,345. I do not know whether the file cutters have sent in a return ?—They have.

15,346. Do they admit rattening ?—I think not.

15,347. Do you not know that it is notorious in Sheffield, as a fact, that rattening prevails extensively amongst file cutters ?—Among file grinders.

15,348. You believe that it is only amongst the file grinders ?—I believe so. I have heard of cases in the union, but the smiths and the cutlers deny them.

15,349. But the file grinders you believe, like the others, do enforce their rules by rattening ?—I believe so.

15,350. Do you know of your own knowledge, as being secretary of this society, and so on, whether resort is had to destroying bellows or destroying property in any way ?—I cannot of my own knowledge speak to it. I may say that what I have heard has been from the newspapers, or since this Commission commenced.

15,351. You know of no union at all in which when they cannot enforce their rules they compel the men not to work ?—That is common in all the trades. They will give notice or something of that kind.

15,352. Do you know whether in any of the trades any recourse is had to injuring property ? —I never heard of it, nor heard it named at any of the meetings.

15,353. Not as being done by the authority of the society ?—No ; there may have been cases, but they may arise from private malice in some of the trades.

15,354. Or a bad secretary, if they happened to have one, might do it ?—Yes, he might. We have cases where secretaries themselves have been rattened, and had their bands taken ; more than once that has happened.

15,355. Were they grinders ?—Yes ; only last November there was a reward offered for a similar purpose ; a secretary had had his bands taken.

15,356. I believe that in the majority of cases, after the money is paid, or the rule which has been broken has been complied with, as the case may be, the bands are returned, are they not ?—I understand so.

15,357. You cannot speak to that ?—I cannot, indeed.

SEVENTEENTH DAY.

Mr. W. Dronfield.

25 June 1867.

15,358. But in many cases they are not restored, they throw the nuts into the river, do they not, sometimes ?—I understand so, sometimes. You will understand that what I am giving is from the report.

15,359. Have you known a case where persons instead of taking the nuts have taken them off and then put them on again, or wedged them in such a way that when the person was going to work, and the wheel going round with velocity, the stone would be liable to fly and so hurt the man who was working at it ?—I never heard of such a case as that, and I do not remember reading of it either.

15,360. But that would be the effect, would it not ?—That would be the effect, doubtless, if such a thing had been done.

15,361. Slightly wedging the nut so that the man would suspect nothing, and directly he got the stone in motion up it would fly and knock his head off ?—That may be so.

15,362. You have heard cases of men being nearly killed from the stone going up in that way ?—Not in that way ; I have heard of their being injured from the breaking of the stone, or from the stone being cracked ; but not in the way you mention.

15,363. Do you suppose that if we were to send for the secretaries of all the grinders they would come and admit this rattening, because that would shorten our labours very much ?—I believe that they would, I hope they would. However, that would be the wish of the committee ; we had a conversation about it, and that is our recommendation to them, but of course, we cannot enforce it either one way or the other ; we would advise them to do that.

15,364. It would shorten our labours very much if the secretaries would come forward and say that it has been unfortunately their position that they have had to resort to rattening, but that it has been done. If they would come and tell us that it would shorten our labours very much ; then I think, that for the satisfaction of the town, we ought to have those secretaries to pledge their words, or their oaths rather, that so far as their knowledge goes no rattening is done in their unions. I think for the satisfaction of the town and of the country we ought to know where the evil is, and how it has been carried on. It would be for the clearing the character of the town if those people who have not been engaged in it would come forward and say so ?—Yes, I think this announcement will have the effect of calling their attention to it, and I hope that it will bring them forward.

15,365. If the gentlemen who are secretaries of those various unions who are prepared to admit that rattening has been carried on in their unions would give a list to Mr. Barker, we would take them shortly and just ask each of them the question, "Has rattening "prevailed in your union to your knowledge ?" If he says, "Yes, it has," we shall have done with it, and we shall go no further into questions of rattening. It is not important to us to discover who has done the rattening ; our inquiry is as to what extent it has prevailed amongst the unions. We could get through all the rattening question in a morning, and then the only question left for us would be the question of inquiring into outrages ; those are few I think, and then we should go into them, and then our inquiry would very soon terminate.—I hope for the credit of my native town that the outrages are pretty nearly gone through now. I assure you that we have been deceived to a very great extent.

15,366. I have asked you for this information that it should be talked of amongst the unions themselves, and that they should see how we stand, and what we want to do. If the secretaries will come forward and say, "We are prepared to admit it," or "We are prepared to deny it," very few questions would dispose of the thing, and then we should have done with the rattening. We have been talking it over together, and we have decided that that is the proper course that we should pursue. We are much obliged to you for your evidence ?—Will you allow me to put in these rules (*handing in a paper*). I should like to call your attention to the third annual report, and if you would read those, I should be obliged as an act of justice to the trades.

15,367. We wish to do whatever is right and proper. This (*referring to a paper*) was an address to Lord Palmerston ?—This was an address to Lord Palmerston on the occasion of his visit to Sheffield in 1863.

15,368. It was not signed by Mr. Broadhead, I suppose ?—No.

15,369. This is a respectable thing, "The question, too, of more fully legislating for trades unions so "as to give powers for compelling payment in the "county courts by defaulting members, is one to "which they attach much importance, and would "respectfully recommend the same to your lordship's "most serious attention. Your lordship will see "from the accompanying documents the steps the "executive have taken in reference to those most "disgraceful and abominable outrages attributed to "trades unions, and their utter abhorrence of all "such acts of violence, and they beg to assure your "lordship that they should be only too glad to co-"operate in any movement for their suppression, "being fully convinced that such acts are not only a "disgrace on those who commit them, but also an "injury on the town and trade of Sheffield, in the "prosperity of which none are more deeply interested "than the working community of this large and "populous borough. The fact that their secretary "is also honorary secretary to a committee appointed "at a public meeting to take steps for the suppression "of these outrages, and is now in communication "with the mayor thereon, will, it is hoped, convince "your lordship of their sincerity on this matter" ?—Yes, I was the secretary to that committee. We had some correspondence with Mr. Brown, who was then mayor ; that was immediately after the Acorn Street outrage ; but I am sorry to say that the commitee fell through for the want of co-operation, chiefly on the part of the manufacturers. They thought that it could not get at the perpetration of this outrage, and the committee after some few months dissolved and paid their own expenses.

15,370. If every society had so respectable a secretary as you, I do not doubt that they would be very much better off than they are.

15,371. (*Mr. Chance.*) To what do you attribute the fact of rattening existing among the grinders and not among other trades ?—I believe that it is chiefly owing to the great facility which exists for its being done. For instance, formerly the wheels were on the outside of the town, and a very great number of them are there even yet ; they are ready of access, and the bands are very easy to get at, and the nuts are quite as convenient and more portable to carry away. The men, not having the legal protection which they think that they should have, use those means of enforcing their claims upon refractory members.

15,372. And you attribute this rattening to the necessity which they feel for enforcing their claims by taking the bands ?—Yes.

15,372*a*. Supposing that legal means were given of enforcing the payments of contributions, would that in your opinion do away with rattening ?—I believe it would.

15,373. But supposing you had legal means to enforce the payments of contributions, would there not still be a danger of rattening for an infringement of the other rules of the unions ?—I think not, because I believe that the protection which the law would give them in that way would dispense with the necessity of it to a very great extent, if not do away with it altogether.

15,374. I only wanted to know your opinion in reference to the tendency to rattening ; you think that if you had a legal means of enforcing the contributions rattening for other infringements of the rules would not occur ?—That is my belief.

15,375. Supposing that a man has more apprentices

SEVENTEENTH DAY.

Mr. W. Dronfield.

25 June 1867.

than he ought to have according to the rules of the union, would he not be likely to be rattened for that?—In that case the men would leave his employment.

15,376. (*Chairman.*) But supposing the man was refractory and would not leave, a remedy in a court of justice would not meet the case?—Probably not, but I think that it would be a great step towards it.

15,377. (*Mr. Chance.*) Then again, supposing that there are certain members of the union and certain non-members, would not rattening be resorted to as it has been for the purpose of preventing the non-union men from working?—I think that in that case the men would be withdrawn, and the parties who were not eligible to the benefits of the society would see that it would be for their interest to join the union and pay to one common fund for the general benefit of all.

15,378. Do I understand you to say that a legal mode of enforcing contributions would do away with those other temptations to rattening for the infringement of other rules?—I think so to a very considerable extent, if it would not altogether do away with them.

15,379. Do you think that the enforcement of the payment of contributions by Act of Parliament would be so great a benefit that the temptation to rattening would be done away with?—Yes; and I think also it would be the means of bringing about a better understanding between the employers and the employed, which is not only very desirable in Sheffield but elsewhere; but you will find in the evidence given that those offences were first commenced when attempted reductions were about to be made.

15,380. (*Chairman.*) The pressure is often upon the masters as much as upon the men, is it not?—The pressure is an attempt to reduce the wages.

15,381. But it is a pressure upon the masters almost as much as upon the men?—Yes.

15,382. (*Mr. Chance.*) Do not the trades unions in this town still intend to enforce the non-employment of all beyond a certain number of apprentices?—They have rules about that, I believe.

15,383. Is that likely to continue a rule of the unions?—I should think so. There are two cases which have been called to my knowledge in which when the trade has been out of the union prices have gone down as much as 50 per cent.

15,384. That is another question. We are only inquiring as to those cases which are likely to produce rattening, and you say that if you had legal power to enforce contributions rattening would be done away with. Do you propose to do away with the rule restricting the number of apprentices, or is that still to be the law of the union?—That is a law at present in Sheffield, but it is not a law throughout all the trades, and the Sheffield trades only form a unit in the number of trades societies; but I do not think it would be intended to give up the apprentice question.

15,385. Then I gather that your opinion is that the apprentice question would still remain a law of the unions?—I think so.

15,386. Then supposing that you had legal power to enforce your contributions from the members of the union, and then supposing that a man had more apprentices than he ought to have according to the rules of the union, what protection will the power given to you to enforce your contributions be against rattening for too many apprentices?—It will not give the protection. I cannot see that it will give the protection.

15,387. Then how will that legal power do away with the rattening for the infringement of that rule?—I do not think it will; but I do think that the light which has been thrown upon the working of trades in this inquiry will be, with the legal protection which we hope to get, the means of stopping all those illegal practices.

15,388. (*Chairman.*) Do you know whether rattening prevails in other towns?—I cannot speak of it to my own knowledge. I have heard of things being done.

15,389. Grinding exists in other towns, does it not?—Yes, on a very small scale.

15,390. Originally the grinding wheels were moved by water power, were they not?—That is so.

15,391. And the wheels were on those little streams in the neighbourhood of the town?—Yes.

15,392. And they were in exposed situations?—Yes.

15,393. There were no neighbours round them, and they were often by themselves and very easy of access, and a person could easily get in and destroy property there?—Yes.

15,394. In your judgment was the origin of rattening the facility with which they could be got at?—Yes, that in my judgment was the origin of rattening.

15,395. Latterly, people dared not have their wheels outside the town?—But there are a great number of wheels outside the town, at Loxley and on the Rivelin and on the Don.

15,396. But has not the tendency rather been, in consequence of this rattening, to desert those old wheels and to come into the town, to places such as the Tower wheel, and so on?—I do not know that it has been in consequence of rattening, but it has been chiefly, I think, on account of the facility of getting steam power, and of getting a large wheel, so that they can have a greater number of hulls and have grinding going on at the same time, and by that means they economize the labour; and it is a protection to a certain extent against rattenings, because—take this case of Fearnehough's at Butcher's wheel—it was stated by a witness yesterday that if Broadhead could not ratten him he did not know who could, and he was working I understand at Butcher's wheel.

15,397. Then it was hardly possible to ratten him, and one would almost say, that of necessity, if anybody was employed to ratten him there must be something else done?—I cannot speak to that, but of course there must be great difficulty in getting at him from what I have heard since.

15,398. (*Mr. Chance.*) Do you know anything of the town of Birmingham?—No, I have been in it several times.

15,399. I suppose that it is one of the largest manufacturing towns in the kingdom?—Yes, but there is no grinding there.

15,400. Do you know Wolverhampton?—There is no grinding there, I think; the iron trade is the chief thing in Wolverhampton and in the neighbourhood.

15,401. Did you ever hear of any case of rattening either in Birmingham or Wolverhampton?—No, I never did.

15,402. (*Chairman.*) Then it is almost entirely confined to Sheffield?—So far as I know it is; I have an explanation to make, if you will allow me, before I leave the chair. When Mr. Broadhead was under examination on Thursday or Friday (I am not sure which) you asked him a question with respect to his connexion with the United Kingdom Alliance of Organized Trades, and he stated that he was treasurer up to the night previous. I think in justice to that society, of which I am secretary and in which of course I am deeply interested, as it has gone forth that his connexion was with it in the way it was, you should allow me to put in this document to show the way in which our business is done, so as to show his connexion with it as treasurer could not by any means have any connexion with outrages or with the misappropriated money towards the payment for those outrages (*handing in a paper*).

15,403. He is a very bad man, and he has imposed upon the public and upon you, no doubt, with the rest?—He has, indeed.

The witness withdrew.

SEVENTEENTH DAY.

J. Wilson.

25 June 1867.

JOHN WILSON sworn and examined.

15,404. (*Chairman.*) What are you?—A pen and pocket blade grinder.

15,405. Have you been a member of a union?—Not since it was last formed.

15,406. Up to that time were you a member?—I was a member from being of age till I was about three and twenty.

15,407. For about two years?—Yes, it might be three; I cannot say exactly.

15,408. And then you ceased to be a member, and the union was broken up?—Not then. I left the union because I would not be mixed up with things that I was ashamed of. If you would allow me to make a statement that would skip over the intervening period to come to the present union I should be glad. I saw a man come for his money for blowing up a boiler at Dronfield wheel. It is beyond the date, and I simply state the fact. It has been imputed by the secretary of my own trade that I paid that money and that I was treasurer. I did not pay the money. I withdrew shortly after. I could not withdraw just then. I would have brought the man to justice if I had had it in my power. I did not know the man or who had employed him, but I take some little credit to myself for ferretting out that he was employed by the other committee. You will understand what that means by the investigations which have taken place. I daresay you will remember prosecuting some razor-grinders who were transported for inciting to destroy machinery. That broke up many of the unions.

15,409. How long ago is that?—That was in 1847, and our trade was out of union from 1847 or 1848 up to about 1859 or 1858. I was waited upon by a deputation and asked to join. I refused, stating my reasons to the deputation that I had not confidence in the men at the head of it. That was Broomhead. I had lost confidence in Broadhead long before that period. Broomhead asked me the reason why I had not confidence. I told him that he had not managed his affairs with that degree of prudence which would induce me to trust men to his management. Besides, I said, there were practices connived at by the unions which I utterly abhorred, and he answered me then that the union should be a purely voluntary association. "Well," I said, "I would wait a little before I volunteered." While they had no power they were tolerant, but as soon as they got power they became intolerant.

15,410. How do you mean "got power"?—When they had got a great many men in the union they began to put the screw upon the few that remained out as far as they could. A deputation came to me and waited upon me at my own place of work along with my own fellow-workmen ——

15,411. You were working at Rodgers', were you not?—Yes. They alleged that I was the obstacle which caused some others to stand aloof from the union and they were going to try and make me pay.

15,412. They told you so?—Yes.

15,413. Who were the parties?—John Broomhead was one. I could not be certain to all the deputation, because I have had so many at various times, so that I could not swear to any other parties; but Broomhead has always been there. Once or twice he has been accompanied by a man of the name of William Thorpe who, I believe, has been treasurer of the trade and may be so now for anything I know.

15,414. The committee said that they would make you pay?—I do not know that it was they who used the threats, but that was the purpose of the deputation. I said, I understood that their union was a voluntary thing; "So it is" they said. I said, "Surely you do not wish to make a man a volunteer." They said I should have to pay. I said, "Then I shall wait while you make me."

15,415. When was this?—That was in 1859. About that time I was coming down to work and I saw the capture of some ratteners in the newspapers. I thought it very probable that they were connected with our trade, because they had had a general meeting the afternoon before and had begun then to restrict the apprentices. I went down to the town-hall to see the men tried and my suspicions were verified. They were two of my own trade. The case was brought before Mr. H. E. Hoole, who was then mayor, and I saw them committed to York for the assizes; but when I went down along with another fellow-workman, I saw a man who has taken an active part since then in the district where I work, a person of the name of Cushworth. I said, "Henry, why do you not pay your money and not have this"? "It is not about the money" he said. I said, "What is it about?" He said, "John Critch will not take his lad off." He was the person who worked at Mr. Worrall's wheel in Bernard Lane. There was one suspicious thing about it; there was one witness whose evidence had been taken the day before; the deposition had been taken by Mr. Alfred Smith's clerk, and that was not forthcoming, and it was stated that the trade had got him out of the way. This was most indignantly repudiated by the trade, but before I got back to my work that day I heard that the affair was compromised, and that it would come to nothing. At the trial at York the most direct perjury was committed. The counsel for the defence alleged that the indictment was bad, because Critch was placed along with Mr. Worrall as prosecutor and Critch was not the prosecutor and did not wish to prosecute, and he raised a story of this kind; he had had some gambling transactions with one of the ratteners and he had lost on a handicap foot race. He had failed to pay his bet, but he told him that if he did not pay him by a certain time he was to fetch his bands. He went, I believe, about half-past 10 at night, broke the iron stanchions from the grinding-wheel window, and got in, but one of the night watchmen happened to catch him.

15,416. And so he said that was the result of a bet?—Yes, that was the result of a bet.

15,417. That was altogether false, you say?—Yes.

15,418. How do you know that it was false?—I will come to that directly, but I will finish the trial. I think Baron Martin tried the case. I will not be certain, because I know that he has tried several rattening cases. He called Mr. Worrall (they had taken the bands of Mr. Worrall in mistake) and asked him if he had any dispute with the union of the trade. "Oh, no," he said, "he had no dispute with the trade; they had never interfered with him." His lordship said that if he had thought it was a trade case he would have made a severe example of him. His lordship said that he did not understand the case. Mr. Worrall was a hackle-pin manufacturer, to whom some rooms had been sub-let by the grinders, and they had rattened him by mistake. Now the week after Mr. Hoole committed him to prison, the first dinner of the organized trades took place. Mr. Hoole presided, and announced at that meeting amidst great applause that he was very happy to assure them that the case of the man whom he committed for rattening a week before was not in any way connected with the trade. "Of course," he said, "it would have been "improper for me to have made that statement on the "bench; but I have great pleasure in making it now." A particular friend of mine, who was present with me and saw the trial, said that Mr. Broomhead was especially rapturous at that announcement. The very Monday following that meeting, the collector came round in the room where I worked to collect natty. He had another person with him with a book. Not personally knowing me, he came to ask me what I would give. I said, "What for?" "Oh," he said, "you have heard of those two men being sent to "York." "Yes," I said, "I did hear of two men, but "what of them?" They were collecting to defend those men. Being aware at that time that they were making it a case of stealing, I said, "What! do you want me to subscribe money to defend two thieves?" I said, "You know the grinders would not defend thieves." Many of my fellow-workmen were foolish enough to contribute. I dismissed them with the assurance that I would have been very glad to have contributed to buy a rope to hang them.

15,419. They were collecting money for the trade?—For the defence of these men.

15,420. Were they officers of the union?—Yes, he came with the officer of the union.

15,421. Do you know in your position as a pocket-blade grinder, and one of the most experienced grinders in Sheffield, that rattening is extensively practised?—Certainly; I could bring men to swear before you that they have never seen a farthing paid in their lives for rattening, and they could tell you directly afterwards that they had seen scores of pounds paid. They are men who are not in the trade now.

15,422. Do you know that rattening has been carried on?—Certainly.

15,423. In what trade?—My own very extensively in the last union; but as Broomhead has been named, I would come to a more recent case connected with Sutcliffe; Hallam was wrong when he stated that Sutcliffe was in arrear of contribution. They do not take such violent measures to recover the contribution. There was a strike at Messrs. Mappin's; Braithwaite, who was one of the witnesses, who had paid Hallam a sovereign, I think, was one of the men that turned out. All the men went out, but for some cause or other they came in again, and then went out again, which very much annoyed Mr. Mappin, and he set on two persons who worked on the Beeswax wheel, Sutcliffe and a man of the name of Brammer. One winter fair afternoon, which is a holiday in Sheffield, Brammer's tools were destroyed at the Beeswax wheel. The paper stated that no motive could be assigned for the act. I put a short letter in the "Independent" on the Saturday following, simply inquiring if any reason could be assigned for that outrage. I daresay it was suspected who the Enquirer was—I signed the letter "Enquirer"—but my object was to direct the attention of the more moral part of the trade to repudiate those things as a method of stopping them. I have that letter in my pocket.

15,424. We shall be very glad to have any information you can give us, but our inquiry must be directed to this: do you know whether rattening has prevailed, and whether it has prevailed in connexion with any trades union?—Oh, yes, with many of them. There is not a grinder's secretary who would come and tell me in private conversation that it had not; neither Mr. Wragg, the secretary of the table blade grinders, or Mr. Rolley, or anyone.

15,425. You believe it has been very extensively practised?—Yes.

15,426. Do you believe that it has been practised by any but the grinders?—I have known of bellows cutting even more than those that have come out in the present inquiry, but more beyond the period of 10 years.

15,427. But within 10 years have you known of bellows cuttings?—Not except from newspaper reports; I was aware of the cases that have occurred from seeing the cases as a general reader of newspapers.

15,428. Have you any knowledge at all from your acquaintance with workmen, or otherwise, that this bellows cutting has been the result of trade quarrels?—I never knew one that was not, or where there was not every reason to suppose it was. I knew a man who was once engaged by a trade secretary to cut one.

15,429. Who was that?—That is beyond the period; but he is a respectable man working at our place now.

15,430. Do you know of any other method of enforcing contributions, or of enforcing compliance with the rules besides that?—Yes; if rattening will not do, as a general thing, they will try to bring force to bear either on the workman or on his employer.

15,431. How?—By threatening to withdraw the other men, or sometimes by going to the manager and asking the manager to use his good offices. I believe they have been to our manager many a time about me to ask him to use his good offices. I know what it means; it means putting the screw on.

15,432. Do you know of any case where any outrage has been practised by the authority of the union where other means have failed?—Not within 10 years; of course I have not been connected with them.

15,433. In your judgment do people join the union voluntarily, or from what reason?—I could only illustrate it by what a person told me a few weeks ago; a young man came to grind a few blades with me, he was an apprentice at our place but is now working out; the wheel where he worked was standing for repairs. The person took a lad and he was summoned before the committee. I believe about the 1st of April he had to turn that lad off.

15,434. But you did not answer my question. In your judgment is it a voluntary thing for persons to go into the union, or do they join because they fear that if they do not join something will happen to them?—I believe the majority voluntarily go in, because they believe unions to be decidedly beneficial. I believe others go in because they are frightened not to go it; and there are others that stand aloof and leave the consequences.

15,435. Do you know the proportion of union men to non-union men in Sheffield?—I do not; they are very few.

15,436. Who are very few?—There are very few non-union men who are non-union men from principle.

15,437. Then do you believe that most of the workmen in Sheffield are in union?—Yes.

15,438. And generally they go in from a belief that unions are good things for them and keep up the price of labour?—I believe that is so, but I may think it is a mistaken opinion.

15,439. But, however, that is their opinion?—Yes.

15,440. And you say that there are some who go in from fear; what proportion do you suppose they bear to the others?—I should think a much larger proportion go in from fear than those who stand out from fear of their tools being destroyed, in fact it has been stated in the newspapers on more than one occasion that if I did not work in a well protected place my tools would be destroyed.

15,441. You work in a place where they cannot get at you?—Yes.

15,442. (*Mr. Barstow.*) You seem to be a stiff non-unionist; you are what they call a "knobstick," I suppose?—Yes.

15,443. Is your union the same as that of which Broomhead is secretary?—Yes.

15,444. Have they ever served you as they served "Old Sammy Sutcliffe"?—No.

15,445. Have they ever molested you?—No; they came to try and make me turn a lad off; not personally.

15,446. Have you suffered any personal violence?—No; I perhaps never committed the same crimes as Sutcliffe did; I have set them at defiance.

15,447. You have set them at defiance, and they have not molested you?—Yes; I may say I have been annoyed, and persons have told me; in fact a person last week, when I was going home, told me that he should like to hang me, but I despise all those things.

15,448. (*Mr. Chance.*) Have you ever received any threatening letters?—Yes; I received one shortly after the Hereford Street outrage, but whether it was to try to frighten me or to have a joke at my expense I do not know.

15,449. What did it say?—It was to assure me I should not come to harm. I had written some letters about the Hereford street outrages in the "Telegraph," and this was sent to me; I daresay I have the letter in my pocket.

15,450. Never mind about it. Was it written ironically?—It said that it was written to warn me, but there was this thing about it. It named two or three of the persons that had written, and I was to hasten to them to assure them of these things, and to say the same to them. I have no means of knowing who the writer was. He said in his letter I had received a number of threatening letters which had

SEVENTEENTH DAY.

J. Wilson. 25 June 1867.

caused me to have a number of sleepless nights. I had not received anything of the kind; that was the only letter I received. If you would allow me I would say that I heard a statement of Mr. Dronfield's that was not strictly correct. I believe he intended speaking what was strictly correct. He was one of the committee for the suppression of outrages. I was on that committee too. I was voted on. I had never any opinion of its being effectual; it would have been if the committee had had the manliness to carry out a proposition which I submitted to them, but which did not meet with a seconder. We tried to get rewards. I was sure we could never raise the rewards that had been offered. 1,000*l.* had been offered 25 years ago, and we had offered large rewards in other cases, but I did suggest as not being in connexion with the organized trades, that the organized trades should pass a resolution refusing all association whatever with any trade in which these outrages occurred, because I believe that would be far more effectual than offering rewards. You have seen what rewards have done, and how men will offer rewards. I believe I was the only dissentient in that. He was quite correct in saying that we paid our own expenses and settled the thing.

15,451. (*Mr. Chance.*) Will you answer this shortly; in your opinion as a practical man, supposing there were a power given by law to enforce contributions to trades unions, would that have the effect of doing away with rattening?—Certainly not.

The witness withdrew.

H. Cutts.

HENRY CUTTS sworn and examined.

15,452. (*Mr. Barstow.*) You are the secretary of the file trade, are you not?—No, of the file smiths union.

15,453. What is that union?—It consists of the file cutters and forgers.

15,454. Then you are not in connexion with the file grinders, are you?—We are in alliance with them and the hardeners too; the grinders, hardeners, forgers, and cutters.

15,455. What do you mean by being in alliance with them?—We assist each other mutually to carry out the rules and regulations of the trade.

15,456. You know what our inquiry is about; do you give one another that peculiar assistance about which we have been sent down here to inquire?—In what respect?

15,457. Rattening?—No.

15,458. Do I understand you to say that you have never been a party to rattening?—Never.

15,459. Do you know of any instances of rattening connected with the trade of which you are secretary?—I know of some instances of rattening, but not in connexion with the trade.

15,460. Do you mean that there are people in your trade who have been rattened?—Yes, there are, but they are very few to my knowledge.

15,461. (*Chairman.*) But not in consequence of trade matters?—The trade have not participated in them.

15,462. (*Mr. Barstow.*) I do not understand that; do you know of any person connected with your trade who has been rattened?—Yes.

15,463. Would you give us the instances to which you refer?—One was John Wilkinson. He lived somewhere about Malin Bridge, I think.

15,464. When was this?—During our lock-out.

15,465. When was that?—In 1866.

15,466. Do you know how he came to be rattened?—No, I do not.

15,467. Was he working for anyone?—Yes. Will you allow me to explain? You will soon get at it. He had been on our funds during the lock-out, eight weeks. Then Mr. Joel, a file manufacturer, required men and he agreed to give the price until the thing was decided. Wilkinson was sent to work for him; he took a note of recommendation from us to Mr. Joel and he had only worked for him a short time before his shop was broken into and his chisels, lead, and files taken away, and as he tells me since, thrown into the river. Mr. Joel at that time was collecting "natty-brass" for us (of course you know what "natty-brass" is), and gave us a check on his bankers for the money as often as we required it.

15,468. That was during a strike, was it?—During a lock-out.

15,469. A lock-out is when the masters lock-out the men?—Yes.

15,470. And Joel, I suppose, was a sort of master "knobstick," was he?—No.

15,471. (*Chairman.*) What had Wilkinson done? Nothing whatever to the trade. He was in strict compliance with the rules. He had been on our box eight weeks. We sent him to this work and the master was in compliance with the trade rules too.

15,472. (*Mr. Barstow.*) Then this is an instance where a man lost his tools though he had not broken any rule of the union?—Yes.

15,473. In your own mind to what do you attribute this?—Well, in my own mind I think there was some private malice connected with it. There was certainly no trade grievance.

15,474. Were you ever told what that private malice was?—No; I forgot it until he was summoned here, and then he came to me and told me.

15,475. Did you ever hear it at the time?—No.

15,476. Did Wilkinson ever tell you?—He came during the lock-out, but I entirely forgot it until he told me after he had got his summons.

15,477. Did he tell you any reason why he thought that his tools had been taken?—No; I referred him to my colleague, Mr. Rolley, up-stairs.

15,478. Did he come to you to get them back?—Yes; he thought we were in some way connected with it.

15,479. Do you know of any other instance?—Yes, there was a case at Turton Brothers.

15,480. How long ago was that?—It was during the lock-out.

15,481. But I do not know when the lock-out was you know?—In 1866.

15,482. What was the name of the person rattened?—He generally goes by the name of Kit Machin. I cannot remember his other name.

15,483. What happened to him?—His shop was broken into.

15,484. And were his tools taken?—Yes; and others as well.

15,485. Was he in any dispute with the trade?—No, he was receiving box pay.

15,486. At that time he was receiving box pay, was he?—At the very time.

15,487. Did he come to you?—No; one of the men in the shop came and told me.

15,488. Did he say then that he thought that it was a trade outrage?—He did.

15,489. And he asked you to explain it?—Yes; he wanted his tools back he said.

15,490. Did he get his tools back?—I never knew.

15,491. You did not get them back?—No, we had no grievance against him.

15,492. Do you know Mr. William Torr?—Yes.

15,493. Do you remember in 1864 his men being turned out?—Either late in 1864 or the beginning of 1865. I cannot speak to it just now.

15,494. This would be the beginning of 1864, if I am rightly informed; in February 1864?—Probably so.

15,495. What was that for?—He was not paying them the statement price. I might say that his men were out three times, so that you will probably be right.

15,496. Did you call upon him?—I do not know that either I myself or anyone connected with the trade did. His men came to us.

SEVENTEENTH DAY.

H. Cutts.

25 June 1867.

15,497. Did you write to him?—No.

15,498. Are you sure that you did not write to him?—If I ever wrote anything to him my name is attached to it. I never wrote but one letter in my life without my name to it.

15,499. Did you make a demand upon him that he should allow his men to collect natty money at the gates?—We should request it.

15,500. But did you do so?—We should request it then.

15,501. But had you demanded it?—I am not aware; but that is our way of business, we request it.

15,502. (*Chairman.*) Did you, in this case, ask Mr. Torr to allow you to collect the natty money?—I never had an interview with him on the subject.

15,503. Did you write to him on the subject?—No.

15,504. Who would write to him if you did not?—Nobody; I do the correspondence, unless when it has happened unfortunately that I have been ill.

15,505. Do you swear that you did not write to him? did you, or did you not?—I never wrote to him; I do all the correspondence in the trade.

15,506. And you never wrote to him?—Never.

15,507. Who could have written to him?—I do not know; my colleague is in Court, there is a probability that he might write to him unknown to me.

15,508. Then why do you say that you do all the correspondence in the trade?—That is my duty.

15,509. You do not know then whether he was written to or not?—I know that I did not write to him. Perhaps, for your information, I might say that we have two secretaries, Mr. Rolley and myself, so that it might seem strange the way I answer this question to you unless I were to explain it.

15,510. (*Mr. Barstow.*) Do you remember, in 1864, Mr. Torr's hardening cistern being pierced?—I heard of it.

15,511. How did you hear of it?—Through rumour.

15,512. Had you any communication with Mr. Torr on the subject?—No; his manager always came to us when there was business to do with the trade.

15,513. Had you a communication with his manager then?—Well, he came to us.

15,514. Do you know how much water was in the cistern?—I do not.

15,515. You never heard?—No, I never saw the cistern, so that I cannot give an estimate.

15,516. What would be the value per gallon of this hardening water?—I am not aware.

15,517. It is used in your trade, I suppose, is it not?—Yes.

15,518. Do you answer that you really do not know what is the value of it per gallon?—I do not.

15,519. Have you ever worked at that trade?—All my life, I served an apprenticeship to it.

15,520. Have you ever used this water?—No; I do not think it is very valuable.

15,521. I am told it is worth as much as 3*s.* 6*d.* a gallon?—Oh! that is perfect nonsense; I should think not three-farthings a gallon.

15,522. What did his manager say to you when he came to you?—He came respecting the men being out.

15,523. Did he mention the cistern being bored?—No.

15,524. Was nothing said to you about it at all?—Not anything. I will explain what was said in that respect; he came because the men were out, and he wanted to know on what condition the men were to return to the work; I said, "He has only to pay "the price, and the men will go back to the work." A good many manufacturers at that time were taking a discount off the men, and he among the rest.

15,525. Do you remember in November 1864, Mr. Torr's warehouse being broken into?—I remember, about the latter end of 1864, or the beginning of 1865; I am not sure about the date.

15,526. Had you any correspondence with him about that?—No.

15,527. Were you never spoken to about it?—Not by him. It has occurred to him because papers were put up offering a reward.

15,528. By his manager?—No.

15,529. Do you really mean to say that no one ever spoke to you on Mr. Torr's behalf, about his books being taken?—No, no one in the world.

15,530. Where were you on the night that those books were taken?—Can you tell me the night it occurred?

15,531. The 5th of November 1864.—What day would it be?

15,532. That I cannot tell you.—I cannot tell you where I should be. I warrant every Saturday night and Sunday night I should be at liberty; every other night in the week I should be in my office, up to 9, 10, 11, 12, or even 2 o'clock in the morning.

15,533. Do you know nothing about his warehouse being broken into?—No further than rumour.

15,534. At this time he was in dispute with the trade, was he not?—Yes, and his factory picketed day by day.

15,535. Why did you picket his factory?—So that when men applied for work, not knowing that there was a dispute, they should inform them of it. We do so in all cases of dispute.

15,536. Had you no knowledge that this warehouse was about to be broken into?—No.

15,537. Had you ever given or offered any reward in respect of the warehouse being broken into?—For the discovery?

15,538. Not for the discovery, but for the person who did it?—No.

15,539. (*Chairman.*) You never employed anybody?—No.

15,540. (*Mr. Barstow.*) Did you ever at any time know where Mr. Torr's books were after they were taken from the warehouse?—No, I was never in the place but once.

15,541. That has nothing to do with it; did you know where the books were?—No.

15,542. Nor what became of them after they had been taken?—No.

15,543. Then you say that you had nothing whatever to do with it?—Nothing whatever.

15,544. To what do you attribute this warehouse being broken into?—I cannot think at all.

15,545. You have not a notion?—No, I can only look at it in this way. I do not think he has had a man in his employ who has left him who has not left him with the bitterest hatred towards him.

15,546. Was not Mr. Torr very obnoxious to your trade?—No further than other manufacturers.

15,547. I suppose that those men who left him with such bitter feelings were members of the trade?—Not at that time; they consisted generally of the lowest class of our trade.

15,548. Do you mean that Mr. Torr's men were not members of your union?—No they were not; he had not a union man.

15,549. Have they never become so?—Yes.

15,550. At the time that they had left him had they became members of your trade?—Since then they have.

15,551. But how soon since?—Oh, immediately.

15,552. Then those men who left him with the bitterest feelings of hatred became members of your trade?—Some of them.

15,553. Do you tell us that Mr. Torr was not particularly obnoxious to your trade?—No further than not paying the price, and taking a discount off the men.

15,554. Do you mean to say that all men leave their masters with feelings of the bitterest hatred?—No, he had a way of dealing with the men that I cannot explain. The men might explain it themselves better than I can.

15,555. Why cannot you explain it?—I do not

SEVENTEENTH DAY.

H. Cutts.

25 June 1867.

see how I can. I cannot explain men's feelings, but I know that great feeling against him did exist.

15,556. How did you know their feelings ?—From what they had expressed.

15,557. Had you any negotiations with Mr. Torr about becoming a member of the trade ?—I had not. In fact I might sum it up in this way. I got so disgusted with him after a while, that I determined that I would wash my hands of him entirely.

15,558. About what time was this ?—I cannot give you the date. We had a very many cases at the town hall, and he made himself very obnoxious there. He threatened Mr. Albert Smith that he would have him removed, and so on, and I have no doubt they got disgusted too.

15,559. And Mr. Torr summoned some of your men, did he not ?—Yes.

15,560. They were convicted ?—Yes, and I should like to explain that.

15,561. They were fined were they not ?—Yes, they suffered in prison.

15,562. Who paid their expenses ?—They had to suffer in prison. I should like to explain that—because I know it is necessary, or at least I think it is necessary—if you will allow me.

15,563. What did Mr. Torr summon those men for ?—I suppose it would be for notice generally.

15,564. (*Chairman.*) But what were they summoned for ?—For leaving their employment without giving notice, but in these cases, if you will allow me to explain, those men were picketed, and we always warn the men when they are picketed not to commit any violence or break the laws in any shape or way. We always tell them if they do that they must stand the consequences; and these men got drunk, they picked a quarrel with one of Torr's men, they fought, and they were brought up for it.

15,565. (*Chairman.*) For fighting as well ?—Yes, they fought I believe.

15,566. They were brought up not for leaving without giving notice ?—Not in this case.

15,567. What were they brought up before the magistrates for ?—These particular men were fetched up for assault.

15,568. (*Mr. Barstow.*) Were they convicted ?—Yes.

15,569. What were they sentenced to ?—I cannot speak to that now. I think it was two months or the option of a fine.

15,570. Were they defended ?—I am not aware; we did not defend them.

15,571. Did you not pay the costs ?—We did not.

15,572. Do not you know that the costs were paid by the trade ?—No.

15,573. Do not you know that Holland paid the costs ?—They were imprisoned.

15,574. They were defended before the magistrates ?—I am not aware.

15,575. I do not mean who paid the fines, but who paid the costs of defending them ?—I am not aware that they were defended. I cannot answer that question. If they were defended it will appear in our cash book, but I think to the best of my knowledge they were not defended by the trade.

15,576. Do you mean to say that you do not know that Holland, the secretary of the trade, paid the expenses of their defence ?—I do.

15,577. You do not know that he did ?—I do not know that he did.

15,578. You say that you have never seen any entry of the sum of 6*l.* 18*s.* paid for defending these men in your books ?—I should have to make that entry.

15,579. And you never made that entry ?—Not to my knowledge. I can nearly swear that.

15,580. Can you swear it ?—I could when I have seen my books.

15,581. (*Chairman.*) Are your books here ?—No, sir. I arranged with Mr. Barker respecting the books yesterday; we have a large trade, and they are a large quantity, and really we could not carry them here, but everything is there for some 40 or 50 years back to the present time.

15,582. I believe at the end Mr. Torr made terms with you ?—He did.

15,583. Do you remember what conditions were imposed upon him ?—Yes; as his men came out the third time he sent his manager up to us to see on what conditions he could settle the matter, and he would pay the price in full in future, which he had promised three times before and did not fulfil; and we looked at the list that we paid the men on, and found that it was somewhere between 8*l.* and 9*l.* I think it was 8*l.* 15*s.* I wish to correct the statement; I see that I am mistaken. His manager came to me, and I told him the cost of these men, and what they had received from us; he wished to know so that he could pay and have his men back and settle the matter, and I wrote him the names and what they had received. He afterwards published it in the local papers, so that I had written to him, and yet I would not be writing to him in a manner of speaking on that occasion; that is the only time I have written to him.

15,584. You say that you had written to him, and that you had not written to him ?—I did not call that addressing a letter to him. When Mr. Barstow asked the question I expected he referred to sending a letter to him.

15,585. You made out a list ?—I made out a list of the men we had paid, and the amount we had paid them.

15,586. (*Mr. Barstow.*) You made a sort of bill out against him ?—Yes, it would be what you might call a bill.

15,587. And he paid it, did he ?—Yes, but not for a long time after that.

15,588. Did he say anything to you then about his books ?—I had nothing to do with the transaction.

15,589. Answer my question; did he say anything to you then about the books ?—Not to me; my friend Holland had an interview with him.

15,590. Was that on the subject of his books ?—No; it was with regard to having books.

15,591. Did he at that time say anything to you about his books ?—Not to me.

15,592. In your presence did he say anything ?—No, I never would see him.

15,593. Did you ever hear from Holland or any other person that he had demanded to have his books back from you ?—He had an interview with Holland, and it might be two of our members, and what passed at that interview I cannot tell.

15,594. Can you or not tell me whether he demanded from you or from Holland to have the books back ?—I cannot.

15,595. You do not know that he did ?—I do not know it.

15,596. Did you promise him that whatever might be the damage it should be made up ?—No.

15,597. Do you know whether he has had his books back ?—I do not.

15,598. Has he ever since that time applied to you for the books ?—No.

15,599. Never at all ?—Never to me.

15,600. Has he ever applied to Holland ?—Mr. Holland must answer that question.

15,601. You do not know whether he has or not ?—No.

15,602. Did you ever hear of a man named George Gillott ?—Yes, I know him.

15,603. Did you ever hear of anything happening to him ?—Yes, I have heard some years back that he was blown up.

15,604. Were you then secretary of that union ?—No.

15,605. (*Chairman.*) What trade was Gillott ?—A file grinder.

15,606. Do you know when it was ?—No, I do not know the time, it was previous to my becoming secretary.

15,607. (*Mr. Barstow.*) Do you know whether Gillott was all straight with the trade ?—I do not

SEVENTEENTH DAY.

H. Cutts.

25 June 1867.

know anything about him; we had no connection with the grinders at that time.

15,608. (*Chairman.*) I do not at all understand what you say about Wilkinson; now let us understand about the state of the trade. There was a lock-out in 1866?—Yes.

15,609. How long did that last?—16 weeks.

15,610. What was the lock-out for?—The grinders asked for an advance of prices; they gave notice for that with us being in alliance with them. The manufacturers would not believe but that we had something to do with their movements, but we had not.

15,611. And did the masters refuse to employ the men for this reason?—They gave us notice because the grinders had given us notice for the advance.

15,612. What was the lock out for?—They had no cause to lock us out.

15,613. Why did they not let them work?—Because the grinders had given them notice for an advance.

15,614. The grinders said that they would not work for them unless they gave them an advance on their then wages?—That is so.

15,615. And the masters said "No, if you do not work for the old prices we will not employ you"?—No, they were a separate branch from us.

15,616. You are a file smith?—Yes.

15,617. What is a file smith?—Both forgers and cutters are called file smiths generally.

15,618. Then yours is the first process?—Yes, forging is the first, grinding the second, after that cutting, then hardening.

15,619. The cause of the lock out was that the grinders wanted an advance?—Yes.

15,620. And the masters said "No, unless you work at these prices we will not employ you"?—Yes, then they gave us notice.

15,621. What to do?—To turn us away without work.

15,622. They turned you off?—Yes, in fact we were at that time considering the advisability of asking for a rise on our list.

15,623. They gave you notice and turned you off?—Yes.

15,624. Then you were out for 16 weeks?—Yes.

15,625. And during the time that you were out John Wilkinson, of Malin Bridge, had his shop broken into, and Dick Machin?—Yes.

15,626. And who besides?—I do not know of any other.

15,627. You told me "and others;" you said there was Machin and others had their houses broken into, what other men were they?—The men that work in the shop; in a file cutter's shop we will perhaps have eight or 10 cutting stocks or blocks, and the man lets them for 6*d.* a week for other men to work on.

15,628. In this place there were not only Machin's taken, but several other people's?—Yes.

15,629. How many do you think?—I do not know.

15,630. Wilkinson's is at Malin Bridge, three miles from Sheffield?—Yes.

15,631. Machin's was taken out of Turton Brothers?—It is in some yard adjoining Turton Brothers works in Cross Smithfield.

15,632. Were Turtons one of the masters who had locked out?—Yes.

15,633. Whom did Wilkinson work for?—Hugh Joel, manufacturer, in the Jericho works.

15,634. Do you know whether at the time when Wilkinson's was broken into Wilkinson was working for Joel at the advanced prices, or the prices of the masters?—I know that Joel came——

15,635. Answer the question; was he working at the high price or the low price, you must answer me yes or no?—I must qualify that; I believe it was at the advanced price which was demanded.

15,636. You say that you must qualify it, now qualify the last statement; do not you know that he was working at the low prices?—I do not.

15,637. Do not you believe it?—I do not.

15,638. Will you swear that you think he was working at the high prices?—I believe that he was working at the high prices, because Mr. Joel agreed to pay it until the thing was settled; if there was any abatement, if they did work, there were several besides him. There was an understanding with the men that it should be returned when the price was settled.

15,639. At the time did not rattening take place, or whatever it was, at Machin's, at Turton Brothers? Was Machin working for Turtons?—He was receiving scale from our box.

15,640. I did not ask you that; was Machin working for Turtons at that time?—I do not know that he was.

15,641. Will you swear that he was not?—I cannot.

15,642. Do not you know that he was?—I do not, and I believe not.

15,643. His tools were taken away you say?—I believe so.

15,644. What were his tools doing at Turton's shop if he was not working for him?—That would not be Turton's shop; he was one of Turton Brothers' men; it was his own shop that he rented.

15,645. It was his own shop in Cross Smithfield which he rented?—Yes.

15,646. How many persons tools were taken at the same place at the same time?—I do not know.

15,647. About how many?—I do not know.

15,648. You are in the trade, and therefore you do know?—I do not know.

15,649. You do know; you told us that Dick Machin and others were in the shop?—I do not know; I was not in the shop.

15,650. How many were there?—I do not know.

15,651. Did you hear that there were several besides Machin and Hall?—No.

15,652. Will you swear that you have not heard of others besides Machin and Hall at that shop?—No.

15,653. Did you hear that there were others besides Machin and Hall?—I understood that everything was gone belonging to everybody. I was not there; it was Hall that told me.

15,654. Were you not aware at that time that these men were working at under prices?—No; I believe they were not working at all; they were receiving scale from us.

15,655. They were not working at all, and had not been working?—Not to my knowledge.

15,656. You say that they were receiving scale?—Yes.

15,657. They had no business to receive scale and work?—No.

15,658. Was Wilkinson receiving scale?—No.

15,659. Was Machin, the other man; were they all receiving scale?—Yes.

15,660. Did you know at that time that they were working or not?—I did not.

15,661. Was it said in the trade that they were?—I never heard of it.

15,662. You never heard it suggested?—I never heard such a thing intimated.

15,663. What was the value of the things which they destroyed or took away, were they valuable?—They were taken away.

15,664. All of them?—So Hall told me.

15,665. They were all taken away?—Yes.

15,666. What was the kind of things taken?—Chisels, and lead, and very likely hammers.

15,667. You said it puzzled you; you could understand private malice against Wilkinson, but how can you understand private malice against a whole shop full of people?—They might quarrel amongst themselves.

15,668. It is like the Kilkenny cats, they fight till they destroy each other; was it a quarrel so fierce that every one destroyed his neighbour?—They are that sort of people.

15,669. There would be one left who surely would not destroy his own tools?—No.

SEVENTEENTH DAY.

H. Cutts.

25 June 1867.

15,670. They are all taken, however?—Yes.

15,671. Do not trifle with us; it is either a robbery of the whole of the things by a thief, or it must be private malice. There is no pretence for saying that this is private malice against the whole shop full of people; to what do you attribute it?—I cannot attribute it to anything. I am confident the trade had nothing to do with it in any way or shape.

15,672. But supposing they had violated the laws of the trade, that would have been a mode punishing them for doing it?—No, we do not do that; we strike them off the box.

15,673. You never have known in your trade of a case of rattening?—Never in my experience.

15,674. In your experience have you known of any person in your trade being rattened?—Only with those exceptions that have been named in my examination.

15,675. Namely, Wilkinson's and Machin's cases? —Yes.

15,676. I want to know whether you know of any persons being rattened besides those two instances? No, not besides those that you have named.

15,677. Torr, Wilkinson, and Machin?—Yes.

15,678. Was there a third?—Yes.

15,679. None else?—I do not know of anyone else.

15,680. Will you swear that no one else in your trade has been rattened besides those three persons?—None else have ever come to my knowledge; ours is a large trade.

15,681. You are the secretary, and so you know all about it, and we shall get to know if, there have been others, and then we shall see how far you are correct. You think yourself that there have been no more than those three?—I do not recollect an instance.

15,682. Now about Torr; Torr's warehouse was broken open, and he was very obnoxious to the trade? —So far as regards paying price but no more than others.

15,683. You were so disgusted with him that you determined to wash your hands of him?—Yes.

15,684. You had a strong feeling against him?—I was disgusted with him.

15,685. Were there many besides you who were disgusted with him?—I cannot say any farther than I know that the men expressed great hatred against him.

15,686. You were disgusted with him; had you ever talked his conduct over at your meetings; had his conduct been mentioned at your meetings?—It had been named, and I daresay in respect to him not paying the price; we always had to appeal to the meeting before any action was taken in regard to the men because the men not being payers, we had to have the sanction of the meeting before we could pay them the money.

15,687. Then his conduct had been brought before a public meeting?—I believe it had.

15,688. You know it?—I believe it.

15,689. You recollect it?—I know this, that every place when they did not pay the price we should name at the meeting.

15,690. Do not you recollect bringing his conduct before a meeting yourself?—I do not recollect the proceedings, but I should say, so far as I remember, that I would do.

15,691. And did do?—No doubt.

15,692. You did bring his matter before a public meeting; how many times did you do so?—Every time, I should think, that he failed in carrying out his promise I should do so.

15,693. How many times do you think that you had done this before he was rattened?—I cannot speak to dates.

15,694. We will not call it rattening. How many times had his conduct been brought before the union before his cistern was bored?—I cannot answer to that.

15,695. Do you know that it had several times been brought before the union?—I should report it every time that he did not carry out his promise.

15,696. Had you not done so several times before that?—I cannot tell about the date; we had so many factories of the same kind on hand.

15,697. If you had bored his cistern you would take away all his water for hardening?—Yes, if they bored it in the bottom.

15,698. It takes months before you can get water right for hardening?—I believe that aged water is considered the best.

15,699. It requires months before you can get water in a proper state for hardening?—Yes, unless you are acquainted with what is required.

15,700. If you deprive a man of the water for hardening his files you stop his trade for months?—I have known instances——

15,701. Answer me that; if you take away a man's water for hardening his files you stop his work for months?—No.

15,702. For how long?—While the cistern is being filled again.

15,703. Of course; but it is only good when it is old?—I have known instances where a manager has gone fresh to a place and has dispensed with the water, and has filled the cisterns afresh to his own liking.

15,704. Does not it require some time before the water is fit for use?—It is generally stated so.

15,705. Was not it three times that he had his water tapped?—I am not aware.

15,706. A man must have had a very bad feeling against him if he tapped his cistern three times?—There is no doubt of that.

15,707. And the tools were taken away?—I never heard of that.

15,708. You did not hear of it?—No.

15,709. Did you hear of his books being taken away? —Yes.

15,710. What kind of books were they; they were not library books—they were the books of his trade, showing what people owed him?—Yes.

15,711. It would stop the means of getting in his debts or anything?—Yes.

15,712. If the man was not connected with the trade he must have had a very bad feeling against him?—It really has that appearance.

15,713. Do not you believe that it was done by some person in consequence of his connexion with the trade?—Not in connexion with the trade.

15,714. Was it in connexion with the society?—No.

15,715. You never ordered it?—No.

15,716. But who could do it if it were not for the trade purpose?—I cannot tell.

15,717. You cannot imagine?—No. I only know, as I told you before, that he had one of the lowest lot of men in the trade; we had some few who turned out good men, and were glad to get away from him.

15,718. Did not you pay a man 50*l.* for about 12 months in order to induce him to leave?—No.

15,719. Did not you pay a man of the name of Joseph Wolstenholm 50*l.* in order to leave him?—No.

15,720. Did you pay him anything?—He turned out the same as the rest of the men.

15,721. How much did you pay him?—My books will tell.

15,722. Have you not paid him 50*l.* for leaving him?—No.

15,723. 1*l.* a week?—Yes, he had 1*l.* a week scale.

15,724. Did not his money that he did receive in consequence of his leaving work amount to 50*l.*?—I do not think it would be.

15,725. Will you swear that it would not?—I will swear to my books.

15,726. Will you swear that it was not 50*l.*?—No, because I do not know the amount.

15,727. Will you swear that it was not 50*l.*?—No.

15,728. Something near that; he was nearly a year without work?—Yes, and he would have been longer if we would have kept him.

15,729. Did you spend 50*l.* to keep him out?—That was the way we rattened them.

SEVENTEENTH DAY.
H. Cutts.
25 June 1867.

15,730. He did not want to come out?—Then why did he come out?

15,731. Did he want to come out, or how did he come out?—We had no compulsion, it was a voluntary act.

15,732. Did you send him a threatening letter?—No.

15,733. Did you tell him that if he did not come out something would happen to him?—No.

15,734. Was he told by your authority?—No, we did not give such authority; we did not do it.

15,735. Do you remember a person of the name of Marshall coming to the committee with Torr?—Edward Marshall, a file manufacturer?

15,736. Yes.—He came by himself.

15,737. Did he talk to you about Mr. Torr?—Marshall came to me, and now you name it I do not know whether he did not have an interview with my colleague, Holland, and others, but Marshall came to me about those things being settled. I said it could be settled in a minute if he would pay the expenses.

15,738. What expenses?—8*l.* odd that we paid the men, and the third time he paid the price.

15,739. He was to pay 8*l.* 10*s.*?—I think it was 8*l.* 15*s.*

15,740. You said if he would pay 8*l.* 15*s.* you would settle the matter?—Yes.

15,741. What matter were you to settle?—The men would all go back to work.

15,742. Do you call that a settlement?—Yes.

15,743. And you call that fair?—Yes.

15,744. After a man has all his water taken out of the cistern three times, and his books taken out of his place, do you call that a settlement?—If we had called it a settlement we should have asked the value of his things and paid for them.

15,745. You never offered to pay him?—No.

15,746. You never did?—No.

15,747. And he has never got paid?—No, we have not paid him. I do not believe we ever shall do so.

15,748. Perhaps, presently, you will be induced to pay him?—I cannot tell.

15,749. Do you recollect Torr sending some work on to Ecclesfield?—No.

15,750. Did you follow his work wherever it went?—The pickets would look to that. If he sent any steel out of his place the men would follow the steel to see where it went to.

15,751. Did Wilkinson work for Torr?—Not to my knowledge.

15,752. Will you swear that he did not?—I will swear that I do not know that he did.

15,753. Did Wilkinson work for Torr?—I never knew him work for him.

15,754. Whom did Wilkinson work for?—He worked at the Globe Works for Messrs. Ibbetson.

15,755. Were they lock-outs?—Yes.

15,756. At the time, I think, he was locked out from Ibbetson Brothers?—Yes.

15,757. Had any work been sent out by any manufacturer to Wilkinson before he was rattened?—I do not know, except from Joel.

15,758. Had Joel sent him work?—He was his man.

15,759. Was Joel a lock-out?—No.

15,760. He was right in the trade?—Yes.

15,761. You swear that you have no entry at all in the books of any payment for the defence of these men who were taken up for the assault?—I do not believe they were defended. I am speaking to the best of my belief.

15,762. We can see whether they were defended?—We had a good many things before the magistrates and the County Court about that time.

15,763. Who had?—The men.

15,764. What do you mean by "the men"?—The men belonging to the different factories.

15,765. What do you mean by "we had?"—The trade.

15,766. The trade had several cases before the magistrates?—Yes, a good many.

15,767. What were they for?—In the general way it would be for notice before leaving, and in some cases it would be in the County Court for wages instead of work as compensation.

15,768. Had you many cases of assaults and injury to persons and intimidation or anything of that kind?—No, only the three I have named for intimidation or assault.

15,769. Only these three?—Yes.

15,770. And you swear that the trade did not pay for the defence of those?—I do not believe it paid for it, but my friend Holland will be better able to say.

15,771. Who is your lawyer?—Sometimes Mr. Broadbent and sometimes Mr. Chambers, and Mr. Fretson and Mr. Branson.

15,772. That was for County Court business?—Anything that turned up.

15,773. Did the trade pay Mr. Branson or Mr. Fretson?—Yes, when a man is trying to compel a manufacturer to pay him wages when he has been turned away without any notice, we are compelled to take that case up.

15,774. Then you go to law for him?—Yes, the same if it is a case of notice that we are disputing. It is their way of fighting the manufacturers that we shall find the men legal assistance.

15,775. But you do not take up cases of assault; if a man knocks another down you have nothing to say to it?—If he does that he may get out of it the best way he can; our men would not stand paying money for that.

15,776. Did you hear that Torr sent out some files to a person called Tyatt?—Yes.

15,777. You did hear of that?—Yes, it slipped my memory.

15,778. Was that when there was a lock-out?—No, it was during the time that Torr's men were out.

15,779. Then Torr not having any men and wanting his work done sent it out to a person of the name of Tyatt, who lives out in the country?—I do not know where he lives.

15,780. At Crookes?—I do not know where he lives.

15,781. Do not you know that when the work got down to Tyatt's place his shop was immediately broken into and the things taken away?—I know it was done, I do not know whether it was immediately.

15,782. But it was done?—Yes, it was reported to us so.

15,783. Do not you know that it had not been broken open at all, but that the things had been taken without breaking into it?—No.

15,784. You know that the property was taken away?—I know what the man explained to me—he became a member after that.

15,785. Can you explain it? does it look like a trade business?—It certainly does.

15,786. Have you any doubt that it was a trade business?—Yes, I have a doubt, because I do not know.

15,787. Have you a doubt about everything that you do not know?—No, there are things that I have not much doubt about, but being connected with the trade as I am I should have an idea.

15,788. All these things which we have mentioned you say look very much like trade business?—I do not say all of them.

15,789. Which do you say is not a trade business?—That looks like one.

15,790. And the others look like it?—The premises being broken into looks like one.

15,791. The things thrown into a goit at Mr. Wilkinson's looks like one?—No, it does not.

15,792. Wilkinson's does not look so much like one?—No, nor the others.

15,793. We shall see your books?—Yes.

15,794. (*Mr. Chance.*) Do you send out men to look after the men to see that they are working?—No,

SEVENTEENTH DAY.

H. Cutts.

25 June 1867.

we do not do that, when a factory is taken out the men watch it.

15,795. Do you employ those men to watch it?—We allow them something more than the scale to do it.

15,796. You employ men to watch?—Yes, we give them two pints of ale a day, 6*d.* each, and they take it in turns.

15,797. Supposing the men go to work are the pickets to report to you?—They would go and tell the parties that apply for work that there is a dispute in the factory.

15,798. Are they instructed to use any intimidation to people?—They are warned against it.

15,799. (*Chairman.*) You say "Do not duck him in the horse pond"?—We caution them against it, and we tell them not to commit themselves; if they do they will have to stand to it.

15,800. (*Mr. Chance.*) You say that Torr's conduct was brought before the committee from time to time?—Yes.

15,801. Does not that have a great tendency to cause men to do people some injury?—We cannot help what personal annoyance there might be. We have one purpose in view—that is, to enforce the price.

15,802. (*Chairman.*) To enforce the price at any cost; you mean by fair means? You do not mean that you do it by any means?—I know it costs us a good deal sometimes.

15,803. When you hear of these rattenings taking place do you discourage them, and tell the men not to do them?—We tell them to keep their hands clear of it.

15,804. You know that these things do take place, even in your trade?—In these few instances; and they are few, considering the size of our trade.

15,805. You know rattening to prevail everywhere in Sheffield?—It is generally understood.

15,806. And very well understood?—Too well, I am sorry to say.

15,807. Is it confined to certain trades?—We seldom hear of it except in the grinders.

15,808. You believe that it does extend to the grinders almost universally?—I believe so, nearly. There may be grinders who do not practise it.

15,809. But you believe it prevails almost universally?—Yes, we believe it.

15,810. In what other trades besides grinders?—I do not know that I have ever heard of a case of rattening except what has been reported since this inquiry commenced.

15,811. You have not?—No.

15,812. Have you heard of bellows cutting?—A great many years since. Mr. Butcher's bellows were cut.

15,813. Is that all that you know of?—It is all I can call to my mind.

15,814. We have a few which we are going into presently.—If you name anything I will give an answer.

15,815. Did not Torr himself have his bellows cut?—Yes, so I believe.

15,816. That looks rather like a trade affair?—It does indeed.

15,817. His trade books are gone, his bellows cut, his things for carrying on his business are abstracted, his water is taken; what can that be but the trade?—One thing brings on another. As to trade matters (*handing a letter to the Chairman*)——

15,818. Here is a pistol and a coffin with an inscription in memory of Cutts. Below the coffin are the words—"Death is sure and time is short;" and it is addressed to Cutts, file manufacturer, Sheffield Lane, Sheffield, Yorkshire. That is in March 1864?—Yes, it was the eventful year when we had so many factories out.

15,819. Then you must have done something to render yourself obnoxious?—Very obnoxious to the class of men that had been made such bad use of.

15,820. You think that it came from them?—Yes, I believe I have traced it the men.

15,821. To what men?—To some non-unionists. I reported it to Mr. Jackson and the late officer Brayshaw and Wynn, and they satisfied themselves of the man that had sent it, and so did I; but we could not get a direct proof. I have had others that have been committed to hard labour for intimidation to myself.

15,822. For intimidation to yourself?—Yes.

15,823. How had they intimidated you?—Meeting one of the committee as he came to his work, and knocking him down, and coming to me with their pockets full of rubble to smash my windows. I have one particular place that I sit to my breakfast.

15,824. Who smashed your windows?—I do not know, but a brick came through in a line with where I always sit, and nearly went through the panel on the other side of the room.

15,825. What year was that?—The same year, 1864.

15,826. This you attribute to some men who were non-unionists?—Yes.

15,827. Have your pickets called out at the time, and hooted them as they went to their work?—No.

15,828. I have known instances where men have been called knobsticks and hooted at as they go to their work; is that done?—We discountenance it entirely.

15,829. And it is not done by you?—Never.

15,830. None of your pickets do it?—We warned them not to do it.

15,831. You do not know that they do it?—I do not know that they do, and if they did they would be brought up for it.

15,832. Do you know that they do it?—I do not know that they do it. I believe they do not.

15,833. You received this threatening letter, and you say you think you know who sent it?—I am not particular about telling you.

15,834. Who was it?—I suppose anything that I say here cannot be used against me for libel?

15,835. No, certainly not.—I traced it to a man of the name of Benjamin Taylor. He was at that time a knobstick.

15,836–7. Had you ever any interviews with him?—No.

15,838. Have you ever seen him?—No.

15,839. Whom was he working for?—For Jackson, at the Sheaf ironworks.

15,840. You think you traced it to him?—I put Brayshaw on him, and he went to the place; and from the manner in which he received him and all this, he said he was confident I was on the right man. One man carried a knife and a knobstick, weighted with lead, and another man carried a double-barrelled pistol, waiting for me.

15,841. How did they carry them?—They carried them about for me.

15,842. You were so obnoxious as well as the masters?—Yes, to these men; they knew we must win the battle; they of course felt they would have a little bit of revenge against me beforehand.

15,843. (*Mr. Barstow.*) No one ever assaulted you?—No; at that time it was not every man that would tackle me.

14,844. As a matter of fact no one ever did?—No, I have not been struck.

15,845. Did this man who carried the pistol to shoot you show it to you?—No.

15,846. The biggest man may be shot with a pistol however big he is. Did you ever receive any injury from this man?—No.

15,847. Did you say that you had a man committed for assaulting you?—No; he knocked a committeeman down as he came along the street, and he had his pocket full of stones to come to me.

15,848. He knocked down a committeeman?—Yes, and he got stopped before he got to my house. He got stopped at the entry.

SEVENTEENTH DAY.

H. Cutts.

25 June 1867.

15,849. He knocked down a committeeman in the street?—Yes.

15,850. What was done to him?—I think he had to find security to keep the peace, and failing to do so he was committed.

15,851. You never saw that letter before you received it by post, did you?—No; certainly not.

15,852. You are quite sure of that?—Yes.

15,853. Mr. Sugg desires me to put a question to you; you mentioned to us the cases of Torr and Wilkinson?—Yes.

15,854. And Machin and the other man?—Yes.

15,855. And Tyatt?—Yes.

15,856. Have those cases ever been brought before the society?—No.

15,857. You swear that none of them have ever been brought before the society at any time?—Never.

15,858. They were never publicly mentioned at any of the meetings?—Not at any meetings.

15,859. Either general or committee meetings?—No; I do not know that it has been named.

15,860. You have no memorandums beyond these books?—Only what has been presented to you, but no books.

15,861. (*Chairman.*) If they looked so like trade matters, did not you say that you hoped none of your members had been doing this?—We always caution them.

15,862. As it was done, did not you mention it to them?—No.

15,863. (*Mr. Barstow.*) Mr. Sugg asked, have they ever been treated by the society as trade matters?—No.

15,864. How many members are there in your union?—We have about 3,500 on the books.

15,865. Of your union?—Yes.

15,866. (*Chairman.*) What are their contributions?—It varies according to the requirements. At the present time it is 1*s.* 6*d.* per week.

15,867. (*Mr. Barstow.*) Are there 3,500 file smiths?—Yes, good payers and bad.

15,868. Do you mean of all the four unions?—Of the file smiths union. I mean the cutters and forgers.

15,869. That is exclusive of the grinders and hardeners?—Yes; we have branches in other towns.

15,870. I mean in Sheffield?—In Sheffield we have over 3,000.

15,871. How nany non-union men are there in Sheffield?—Probably there may be 100.

15,872. Not more?—I do not think there are much more.

15,873. (*Chairman.*) They are all in the union except 100?—Yes; good and bad payers which compose the rest.

15,874. Are Turton's men out now?—Yes.

15,875. What are they out now for?—They are out against an individual called Jeffcock, a grinder.

15,876. What has he done?—I believe he has seven apprentices.

15,877. Jeffcock has seven apprentices?—Yes; and that is contrary to the rule.

15,878. How many apprentices do you allow?—He belongs to the grinders and we do not interfere with each other's rules, further than asking each other mutually to carry them out.

15,879. How many apprentices do you allow in your union?—A man is allowed to have one apprentice, and no matter how many sons he has he can have them all.

15,880. May he have one apprentice, not being his son?—Yes, other people's sons; for instance hardeners' sons and strikers' sons.

15,881. He must be some person in the trade?—Yes; a journeyman.

15,882. Supposing I were in your trade, could I take from the joiners an apprentice?—If you were a manufacturer you could.

15,883. If I were a man and not a master?—We will not take non-freemen's sons.

15,884. All that are taken must be the sons of persons in the trade?—Yes.

15,885. All apprentices must be their sons?—Yes, and there are instances where they are not. In 1854 we admitted 200 to meet the requirements of the manufacturers.

15,886. The rule is that no person must have an apprentice who is not the son of a man in the trade?—Yes, except under special circumstances.

15,887. Jeffcock has got seven apprentices you say?—Yes.

15,888. I am informed that he has only four?—I can produce 50 or 60 men who know he was present at one of our meetings this month and he acknowledged seven.

15,889. Why are Turton's men out?—To assist the grinders to enforce their rules; that is an alliance.

15,890. The grinders say, "You shall not have apprentices," and this man has taken apprentices contrary to the rule?—Yes.

15,891. Why do Turton's men go out?—Because we have agreed together to mutually assist each other, and Turton is a file manufacturer.

15,892. So you compel his men to come out?—We did not compel them.

15,893. They do come out?—We call a meeting and lay the case before them, and they can come to what decision they like; if the men think it is a case in which they are called upon to compel the rules to be complied with they give a month's notice and then leave.

15,894. This is done because Turton employs Jeffcock?—Yes.

15,895. They leave Turton unless Jeffcock is turned away?—It is not so; they wish him to reduce the number of apprentices according to the rule, and they do not want him to be turned away. If the grinders had persisted in that course our men would not have taken it up. The manufacturers on the other hand have issued a black list of their men to prevent other manufacturers employing them.

15,896. (*Mr. Chance.*) If Turton were to turn Jeffcock away the men would go back again?—Yes, of course, the rule would be enforced.

15,897. You wish Jeffcock to reduce his number of apprentices, or what will happen?—Or the men will not work where he is.

15,898. You would be satisfied with Turton sending the man away?—Yes; there would be an end of the case as far as he is concerned.

The witness withdrew.

C. Rotherham

Mr. Christopher Rotherham sworn and examined.

15,899. (*Mr. Chance.*) Are you a sickle manufacturer?—Yes, and have been for nearly 60 years on my own bottom.

15,900. Are you a member of the union?—No, I am quite against the union. I have not belonged to them for 40 years.

15,901. Have you ever been a member of a union?—No, I have been a member against them.

15,902. During the last 10 years have you had any disputes with the unions?—Yes, I have been at it above 50 years; they cut all our bands.

15,903. Do you remember in the year 1860 anything happening to you about a boiler?—We had a boiler blown up; there was a cask of powder put under it; they found some fragments of wood by which they could tell.

15,904. Was that where you were working?—That was where we were working and are working now.

15,905. Do you know why the boiler was blown up?—Because our men would not pay to the union, we supposed; at least they sent me threatening letters to that effect.

15,906. Did you receive the threatening letters before the boiler was blown up?—Before and since.

SEVENTEENTH DAY.

Mr. C. Rotherham.

25 June 1867.

I have had a dozen threatening letters, enough to scare you out of your wits, but I never took any notice of them.

15,907. Were those letters to ask your men to pay to the union?—It was intended for me to force them. I would not force the men. I said, "If you like to join the union, join it, if not I will not force you." They said it was no use their going into the union.

15,908. Did any of those letters say that you would be blown up if they would not join?—Worse than that. I was to be blown to pieces.

15,909. What did the letter say?—Mr. Hutton of Ridgway has one of the letters by him.

15,910. Can you tell us more particularly what the letter said?—I cannot, I never kept them by me at all. I saw what they meant; it was nought but destruction.

15,911. Did they say what you would be blown to pieces for?—I do not know that they expressed what for.

15,912. What did they tell you that they wanted you to do?—To make the men pay to the union; that was the meaning of it.

15,913. After your boiler was blown up did you offer any reward?—I offered 100*l.* out of my own pocket; the police went to work.

15,914. Did you ever find the man who did blow the boiler up?—No, we did not.

15,915. Was there a man of the name of Coggin arrested?—Yes, there was, but they could not bring it against him.

15,916. He was discharged?—Yes.

15,917. Have you ever had any bands or tools taken?—The bands and tools were cut to pieces, and nine pair of bellows and 12 bands at the same time.

15,918. (*Chairman.*) What besides?—They threw the anvils into the dams to stop them from working.

15,919. When was that?—I forget.

15,920. (*Mr. Chance.*) Have those been at different times, or were they all done at the same time?—They did it twice.

15,921. How long ago was this?—I think it is above 10 years.

15,922. Have you had any bellows cut or bands taken within 10 years?—We have had plenty of rattening and bellows taken; we have been blown up twice, and they have tried to do so since.

15,923. You have told us about the first time the blowing up took place, tell us when the next occurred?—They blew the boiler up, and I offered this reward, and it did not answer, and we could make nothing of it. I have three nephews, grinders, and they lived at Troway; somebody threw a cannister of gunpowder into one of these nephew's windows, the one that grinds for me; two lived in the house by themselves, and one was married. They threw it into the house where the single ones lived, just as they had gone to bed.

15,924. Your two nephews lived together?—Yes, and one lived in a house a bit off.

15,925. How long ago was this?—That happened some eight years ago.

15,926. Do you know what was the reason of that? They blew the boiler up to make these grinders pay to the union. I took no notice of it, and then they followed them to Troway with this gunpowder, they tried to blow the house up.

15,927. Were your nephews members of the union?—No, they were not.

15,928. Were your two nephews sickle grinders?—Yes; there were three of them.

15,929. Was much damage done to the house?—It was my own house; it took the roof off and blew the windows out; I had it all to repair.

15,930. Did you live in the house?—No.

15,931. It belonged to you, and your two nephews lived there?—Yes, it belonged to me; it was two or three miles off where I live.

15,932. Was anybody injured?—No; they were all upstairs in bed; they threw the gunpowder into the lower window; it blew the floor up and the windows out, it damaged the walls and blew the roof to pieces.

15,933. Both your nephews were in the house at the time?—Yes, and were not injured, they were in bed.

15,934. Into which window was the gunpowder thrown?—Into the window on the floor at the back.

15,935. Your nephews were sleeping upstairs?—There were two of them sleeping upstairs, at least the whole family were.

15,936. Had you received any threatening letters before this took place?—Yes, plenty; I took no notice of them.

15,937. What did they say?—I forget; they were very bad threatening language.

15,938. What did they tell you that you must do?—I forget, but I know that one said they thought I was enjoying myself over my pipe at night, and it said something about gunpowder, and something else; I took no notice of it.

15,939. Did they say you must make your men pay to the union?—They said so before.

15,940. Was there anything else which they told you you had to do?—Yes, but I forget now. I knew what they wanted; they wanted me to make the men to pay to the union.

15,941. That is the second blow up. Now, do you remember a year and a half ago?—Yes; about two years ago.

15,942. What took place then?—We did not know but that all was right, and we got up in the morning and opened the warehouse door, and there was a two-gallon bottle of gunpowder, and a very long fuse from the door led to it, and it had burnt within this much (*describing the same*) of the bottle; it had to go round like this, and somehow it had gone out before it got to the bottle.

15,943. At what time did you discover this?—In the morning.

15,944. (*Chairman.*) The bottle was inside the warehouse?—Yes, a two-gallon bottle, and I gave it to the police.

15,945. (*Mr. Chance.*) Was the bottle filled with powder?—Yes, it was filled up to the top they tell me, I did not examine it.

15,946. Whereabout in the warehouse was it?—Inside the warehouse, they would all have been killed together.

15,947. Whereabouts in the warehouse was the powder placed?—At the far end of the warehouse.

15,948. Was the door shut or open in the morning?—Of course it was broken open.

15,949. Then was the fuse inside the warehouse or partly outside the warehouse?—The fuse was altogether inside the warehouse; it had burnt within a little of the powder.

15,950. Was anyone in the warehouse at the time?—No, it was at night.

15,951. There was nobody there?—No.

15,952. Had you received any threatening letters before that?—I think we had not; but I got threatening enough then, for I forced all the men to join the union. I could not stand it any longer, it was like death.

15,953. You say that you made your men join the union, when was that?—They had done me then. I persuaded my men to join the union. When they had put the powder there I forced the men to join the union. There were four young men, all the family, the mother and children, in the house. It would have killed all. I persuaded the men, I did not force them, to join the union. I said, "Now how are things going on?" They said they had demanded a sovereign a-piece for the first payment, and in a month they were to pay another sovereign, and they were to be so long before they could have anything from the funds."

15,954. (*Chairman.*) They did pay the sovereign?—Yes.

15,955. And then afterwards they paid another sovereign?—I understood them so; and then they were to be so long before they could get any relief.

SEVENTEENTH DAY.

Mr. C. Rotherham.

25 June 1867.

15,956. Have you ever paid any money to the union?—No, I think not, I would sooner rob it if I could.

15,957. I mean since your men joined the union?—We have been as quiet as bees since, we are not afraid of anything now.

15,958. Is there anything else that you have to tell us?—No. I could tell you plenty of former days, it is too far back.

15,959. We do not want anything further back than 10 years?—There is nothing I can further say. I do not want to say anything more than I know.

15,960. (*Mr. Barstow.*) This last bottle with the fuse attached to it was in the warehouse?—Yes, in the warehouse.

15,961. How near is that to where any people sleep?—The rooms join the warehouse.

15,962. Were those rooms inhabited?—Yes, by my nephews and nieces, the mother, niece; and three fine sons, grown up, would have been all destroyed.

15,963. How many people were inhabiting the rooms adjoining the warehouse?—Five; the mother, three sons, and her daughter.

15,964. If the gunpowder had gone off they would all have been destroyed?—Nothing could have saved them.

15,965. You told my friend the size of the bottle in which the powder was?—It was a two-gallon bottle. I gave it to the police and they came and took charge of it.

15,966. Was the two-gallon bottle full of powder?—It was top full of powder. I did not examine it, the police did.

15,967. (*Chairman.*) What reason have you for supposing that your place was blown up on account of a trade matter?—Certainly it was a trade matter.

15,968. Why do you say so?—Because the men told me they had some threatening before then.

15,969. Who had had threatening before then?—Our workmen.

15,970. And who had threatened them?—Letters which they expected came from the union.

15,971. What right have you to say that they came from the union?—They would have great knowledge of it when they had to be about paying their natty money.

15,972. That is your reason for believing that it was done by the trade?—The men would not join their union at all, that was it.

15,973. Why do you say so? had you any person that you had quarrelled with at all?—I had not.

15,974. What did you mean by saying that you had been at war with the union for 40 years?—I am sure I have.

15,975. How have you been at war with them?—In the first place they wanted to put men on me that I did not like. A man had been to prison and he had gone to America and left his family in distress, and he came back in distress and asked me if I could find him employment and the parish would set him at liberty, and as soon as I found what he was, I told this man that I did not like him.

15,976. Mr. Sugg wants to know whether it is not because you have had this war with the union for 40 years that you have come to the conclusion that they had done it, and not because the men had any threats and fears?—I have had threats, and they came from the union, no doubt.

15,977. Have you ever had any secretaries calling upon you?—Yes, I have.

15,978. Who has called upon you?—I do not know, and they have called upon our men; they do not like me, and I cannot bear the sight of them.

15,979. Therefore they call upon the men, and not upon you?—Yes, upon the men, and what they have said I do not know and I do not want to know.

15,980. Can you at all recollect what they said in those letters, just think for a moment?—I am sure I cannot recollect it; but I think Mr. Hutton, of Ridgway, copied one of my letters.

15,981. And he kept it?—Yes.

15,982. Cannot you recollect what was said in any one of the letters?—It was very threatening and bad language.

15,983. What did they say that it was for, did they mention it in the letter?—It was because I would not make the men pay to the union.

15,984. Did it say so in the letter?—Not exactly. I have had it before and since.

15,985. Did you at any time after the blowing up go to the secretary of the union and complain that they had been the cause of it?—No, I was not going to them. I would sooner blow them up.

15,986. (*Mr. Chance.*) Had you any private quarrel with anybody?—No, never in my life. I never had any malice against any man in my life. I have no malice in me, not against my biggest enemies, not against those who have done me the mischief. I could not like them, but I should not like hurting them.

The witness withdrew.

THOMAS HOLLAND sworn and examined.

T. Holland.

15,987. (*Chairman.*) Of what are you the secretary?—Of the file smiths union.

15,988. Are you joint secretary with Mr. Cutts?—Yes.

15,989. Do you know of any rattening done in your trade except those instances mentioned by Mr. Cutts?—No.

15,990. Did Wilkinson's affair look to you very much like a trade matter?—I do not know anything about it, and did not till very recently.

15,991. It only took place in 1866?—I know that.

15,992. You have heard of the circumstances, does it not strike your mind as looking very much like a trade matter?—I cannot answer that question.

15,993. Does not it strike your mind as being a trade matter?—I do not believe that it was.

15,994. You do not believe it?—I do not believe it.

15,995. What do you think it is?—I cannot tell, it is not for me to say what it is.

15,996. You do not think that it is a trade matter? I do not think it is.

15,997. Do you think that Machin's was a trade matter?—No.

15,998. Do you not believe it was?—No.

15,999. You do not believe that taking away all this man's tools was a trade matter?—I did not know that they had done it.

16,000. Now do you believe that it is a trade matter?—No.

16,001. You mean to say that your union has not authorized it, that is what you mean by trade matters?—Yes.

16,002. You mean that your trade has not authorized it?—No.

16,003. Had you in 1866, at the time when Machin's tools were taken, mentioned at any of your meetings that Machin had done anything wrong?—No.

16,004. His case had never been brought before the society?—No.

16,005. Nor Wilkinson's?—No.

16,006. There was no fault found with them in any way?—None whatever.

16,007. What is Wilkinson?—He is a file cutter, I believe.

16,008. You are file smith, is that a file cutter?—Yes.

16,009. Is that the same trade?—Yes.

16,010. If he had offended the grinders, the grinders would have done it?—I cannot answer for that.

16,011. All that you say is that it was not a trade case so far as your society is concerned?—Yes.

16,012. Whether it was a trade case as done by the grinders or not you do not know?—I was

SEVENTEENTH DAY.

T Holland.

25 June 1867.

strengthened therein from what he confessed to me last Saturday but one, he told me he believed himself it was not.

16,013. Who was that, Wilkinson ?—Yes.

16,014. Do you know Mr. Torr ?—Yes.

16,015. Have you been to his place ?—Yes.

16,016. Was not he in dispute with you ?—We very seldom have any conversation with Mr. Torr. I believe it was always with his manager.

16,017. You have been to his manager ?—Yes.

16,018. You have been to his manager and asked him whether he would not come into your terms ?—Yes.

15,019. How often have you been to the managers ?—Perhaps two or three times.

16,020. Have you told his manager if he did not come into your terms of any course which would be pursued by your society ?—No, of course the men were taken out.

16,021. You did not tell him ?—No.

16,022. You did not tell him when you were going to take the men out ?—No.

16,023. Do you avoid doing that for fear it should be considered a threat ?—Certainly.

16,024. Although you dare do it you dare not threaten to do it ?—Yes.

16,025. You avoid making use of a threat although you take the men out ?—Yes, afterwards, if it is not complied with.

16,026. So you say nothing at the time of what you are going to do ?—No.

16,027. You say, "Are you going to pay or are you going to get your men to pay" ?—That is the conversation we generally have with the manager.

16,028. What do you see his manager for ?—To ask him whether he will do anything to assist us in making the men comply with our wishes.

16,029. If he says that he will not, what do you do ?—We order the men to come away.

16,030. Did you ever hear of his losing his tempering water ?—Yes, I have heard of it.

16,031. Does that look like the trade ?—Decidedly it looks like the trade, there is no question about that.

16,032. Did you hear of his bellows being cut ?—No.

16,033. You never heard of that ?—No.

16,034. Supposing it had been so, can you suppose anything else but that it was a trade business ?—I do not suppose that it would be a trade matter.

16,035. Supposing his bellows were cut, do you think that would be anything but a trade matter ?—I cannot say.

16,036. But could you suppose anybody would do that except in connexion with the trade ?—I cannot say.

16,037. It looks like a trade matter, does not it ?—It certainly looks like it.

16,038. Did not the manager complain to you of having his water taken away and being stopped in his business ?—No, never.

16,039. He never complained at all ?—No, never.

16,040. You thought that Mr. Torr was not an ill-used man at all ?—I have nothing to do with Mr. Torr being an ill-used man. I do not think anything about it.

16,041. Do you know how often he has been damaged ?—No.

16,042. Is he now one of the men whom you are out against ?—No.

16,043. Do you allow your men to work for him now ?—Yes.

16,044. Did not you hear that his books were taken away ?—Yes, I have heard of it.

16,045. Did not you see 8*l.* 15*s.* paid by him or his manager ?—Yes, I received it.

16,046. And on that occasion did not you propose that his books should be restored ?—No, sir.

16,047. Now mind, did you propose that his books should be restored upon the payment of that money ?—No.

16,048. Was any allusion made to his books ?—None whatever.

16,049. He never said anything about his books being gone ?—Not when the money was paid.

16,050. Did you at any time ?—Yes.

16.051. What was said ?—On the Saturday morning when the money was paid he asked about the books; I said I had nothing to do with the books, I knew nothing about them; and if the books were in the case I would receive no money at his hands. At that time there were two or three persons present, and they could be produced as witnesses.

16,052. You repudiated altogether your connexion with the books ?—Yes.

16,053. And never promised to get them, or do your best to get them, or anything ?—Never.

16,054. You are perfectly sure of that ?—Perfectly sure of it.

16,055. Taking a man's books must be, of course, the trade ?—I do not know what benefit it could be to the trade.

16,056. It would be no benefit to the trade, but it would be a great injury to him if he lost them ?—I cannot say.

16,057. You and I could not have any benefit by taking a man's books—no robber could benefit by it—they do not steal waste paper ?—No.

16,058. We can only conceive that it must be for the purpose of stopping the man's business; does not it look like it ?—Of course, it looks like it.

16,059. There were some men taken before the magistrates for an assault, did you defend them ?—No.

16,060. I ask you now, did not you pay 6*l.* 18*s.* for defending these very men ?—No.

16.061. Have you ever paid 6*l.* 18*s.* ?—I do not recollect ever paying 6*l.* 18*s.*; I am not prepared to say I have not, but not for that case.

16,062. Which case was it ?—It was a case in reference to Torr, where he summoned his man for notices, and we as a trade defended the man before the magistrates, but not in that case was a single fraction ever paid or recognized in any shape for that assault.

16,063. I speak of the assault cases ?—Yes.

16,064. You are quite sure that that amount of 6*l.* 18*s.* was not paid by you; that it never was paid in respect of defending those men for an assault ?—I am.

16,065. Did you defend those men for an assault ? No.

16,066. Did you instruct anybody to appear for them ?—No.

16,067. Did you see them tried ?—I was at the Town Hall at the time.

16,068. Had they any counsel or attorney ?—Not to my knowledge.

16,069. What did you go to the Town Hall for ?—To wait till the trial was over; to see the men get through.

16,070. If you had not employed them to commit the assault, what had you to do with it ?—I had no interest in it, except in seeing what the matter would come to, having heard that the men had committed an assault; we did not countenance it or have anything to do with it.

16,071. You went down to see how the thing came off ?—Yes.

16,072. Can you tell me who appeared for them ?—No one appeared for them.

16,073. They had no attorney ?—They had not.

The witness withdrew.

SEVENTEENTH DAY.

J. Rolley.

25 June 1867.

JOSEPH ROLLEY sworn and examined.

16,074. (*Mr. Barstow.*) You are secretary to the file grinders ?—Yes.

16,075. We have heard to-day that rattening prevails in all unions connected with the grinders ; is that your belief ?—Yes, I believe that it is so ; I believe it is in our branch ; I cannot speak to others.

16,076. Do you know of any case of outrage that has occurred in your branch within the last 10 years ?—I believe there was one of the name of Gillott, but I was not aware at the time they sent that paper in that it was within 10 years.

16,077. Gillott's case occurred on the 25th of April 1857 ?—Yes.

16,078. (*Chairman.*) The Act was passed on the 5th of April 1867.

16,079. (*Mr. Barstow.*) Have you heard any particulars of that case ?—No, only the report at the time.

16,080. How long have you been secretary ?—Better than 13 years.

16,081. Do you admit that that was a trade outrage ?—I do not admit that it was a trade outrage upon our part ; not as far as I know.

16,082. Was that outrage brought before your notice at all as secretary of the grinders union ?—No.

16,083. It never was ?—No.

16,084. Do you mean that it was never mentioned at any meeting of your union ?—I have heard it talked about.

16,085. (*Chairman.*) Was it brought before the body as a matter of business ?—No.

16,086. (*Mr. Barstow.*) Have you ever paid any money for the defence of any one ?—No.

16,087. Did you yourself instigate anyone to commit that outrage ?—No.

16,088. Are you aware from your own knowledge of any member of your taade who did so ?—No.

16,089. Or anyone ?—No.

16,090. Who was Gillott ?—A file grinder.

16,091. Was he at this time a member of your union ?—I believe hs was not subscribing at the time.

16,092. Did he subscribe at the time that he was blown up ?—Yes.

16,093. Had he been subscribing previous to that time ?—I cannot be certain, I am sure, unless I refer to the books.

16,094. (*Chairman.*) Have you got the books here ?—Yes ; they are here.

16,095. Look at the 25th of April 1857 ?—He was not subscribing then ; I have him here in January.

16,096. (*Mr. Barstow.*) He was a subscriber in January 1857 ?—No, he was not subscribing then.

16,097. I ask when was the last time that he was subscribing before then ?—I see him in three or four different places ; I do not see his name there.

16,098. Was he a subscriber in the course of that year ?—No ; I have him here, August 4th, 1856, and as far as August 1857, and we have nothing from him after that time at all.

16,099. What course do you take in your union with men who are in arrear ? what course did you take at that time ?—I believe it was the same then as it is now ; we had district meetings once in every month in most of the districts ; some of them had them once a fortnight. At that time I should not have George Gillott in our district books, because he was not subscribing ; we call over the names in the district.

16,100. Would Gillott's name be called over ?—No.

16,101. He had entirely ceased to be a member of the trade ?—Yes, he was not a member of us at all then.

16,102. He was what you call a "knobstick"?—Yes.

16,103. Do you interfere with men not in the trade at all ?—I do not myself, I do not know whether anybody else does.

16,104. Does your society ?—No, I cannot say that they do.

16,105. You are not aware that any mention was made in your union of Gillott's name about this time ?—Not to my knowledge. I do not know that it was.

16,106. I think I understand you to say that he was not a member at all ?—He had not been subscribing for above a year.

16,107. (*Chairman.*) His name is in the book, but he did not pay his subscriptions ?—Yes, he was a file grinder, but we could not say he had joined the union.

16,108. He had been a member before ?—Yes.

16,109. And you had already before that seen his name as subscribing ?—I do not find it for a year before that time ; he might have been subscribing.

16,110. For a year ?—Yes, I have only looked for a year before that time.

16,111. He had not subscribed for a year ?—No, he had not subscribed in 1856 or 1857.

16,112. What rule have you as to non-subscribing members terminating their connexion with the union?—They have no benefit from the union if they cease paying.

16,113. (*Mr. Barstow.*) How long in arrear must a man be before he ceases to be a member of the union ?—We never turn them out, if they like to pay again they can ; if George Gillott had told me to call for his subscription I should have called, and he would have been a member just the same as any other man. If any of them like to become members again, and tell me of it, I should call at their wheel and receive their money.

16,114. And receive the arrears ?—Yes.

16,115. If they commenced paying ?—Yes, and if a man wanted his case gone into, so as to be made a financial member, he would have to go to the general meeting of the trade, and I should bring the matter before the meeting, and the meeting would settle his business.

16,116. Do you know a man named Royston ?—Yes.

16,117. Was he taken into custody ?—Yes.

16,118. Did you do anything to defend him ?—I believe I gave 2*s.* 6*d.* ; there was a subscription made.

16,119. Was anything contributed from the funds of the union ?—No.

16,120. Was there a subscription amongst the members of the union ?—From anybody that would give anything.

16,121. Was it made in the meeting room ?—No.

16,122. Was it gathered in the club room ?—No.

16,123. (*Chairman.*) Where was it gathered ?—In different factories.

16,124. Did you go round to collect ?—No.

16,125. Who did ?—Different parties, but I did not.

16,126. Who was it ?—I do not recollect whom I gave my 2*s.* 6*d.* to. I subscribed my 2*s.* 6*d.* on the list.

16,127. (*Mr. Barstow.*) Do you know of any other outrage ?—No, not one any further than bands being taken.

16,128. That you have admitted ?—Yes.

16,129. How many members have you ?—About 300 now.

16,130. What is your subscription ?—We are paying 2*s.* 6*d.* a man, and 1*s.* 3*d.* a boy ; we have paid less than that, and sometimes more.

16,131. I believe you produce your books to-day ?—They are all here.

16,132. (*Chairman.*) You have never heard of any outrage besides Gillots ?—No.

16,133. The outrage was committed upon Gillott upon the 25th of April, 1857 ?—Yes.

SEVENTEENTH DAY.

J. Rolley.

25 June 1867.

16,134. Two days before that did not you have a general meeting in reference to the men who were in arrear ?—Yes.

16,135. What happened to Gillott; he had his house blown up by a can of gunpowder being thrown in, did he not ?—That is the report.

16,136. His house was blown up by a can of gunpowder being thrown into it on the 25th of April. He did not subscribe to your union for nearly a year; now look and see if you did not have a general meeting of your union on the 23rd of April in reference to these men who would not pay their arrears; it was two days before the blowing up, is not that so ?—I see it is so.

16,137. "April 23rd, 1857, resolved, that all the " men that are in arrear be applied to, and that money " be lent to them for the purpose of having them " straight with the trade, and that means be taken " for the purpose of obtaining the statement price for " those who have not it, and that the following six " men be appointed to wait upon them and carry out " the law," (*reading the names*). Therefore there had been actually a committee appointed in reference to these men who were in arrear just two days before Gillott was blown up ?—I will explain that.

16,138. It does appear in your books that though there is no order to blow up there is a committee appointed to investigate the cases of men not paying ?—Yes, I will tell you how that is; there were a number in arrear, and by their being in arrear they could not have any relief from our trade, and it was agreed that they should be waited upon ; and there was a number of them that had not the price for their work, and it was agreed that the trade should lend the money if they were willing to make themselves right with the trade, and that they should sign a promissory note for that amount.

16,139. If men were willing to join and had not the money, you would lend it to them ?—Yes, to make them straight with the society.

16,140. If the master did not give them the full price they could go on the box; your rule is not to take a man on the box without he is straight with his contribution ?—We could not get them on the box if they were not straight, and they could not get the price by themselves unless we assisted.

16,141. Were you having at that time any quarrel with the masters ?—No, not particularly.

16,142. You say that you could not put them on the box. The resolution says " That means be taken for " obtaining the statement price for those that have not " it " ?—Yes, it would be by taking them on the box.

16,143. Was there at that time any quarrel with the masters ?—No.

16,144. Was there a quarrel with the men ?—No, it would be some few masters, such as Gillott would be working for ; there were a number besides Gillott who were not paying, and it was on account of their not paying that they had not the price, and they could not pay. That was passed at the meeting in order to make them right, so that they could be taken on the box and get the statement price.

16,145. At all events the case of men who were not getting the price as you thought was brought prominently before a meeting, and a committee was appointed two days before the blowing up ?—There would be a committee appointed to go with them if they applied to that committee.

16,146. You have in your society taken the matter up of men who were either not getting the price, or were not paying their subscriptions; the thing was brought prominently forward at the meeting ?—Yes, apparently by that.

16,147. Do you recollect the fact of it ?—No ; but I have no doubt of it, because it is my writing.

16,148. This was a resolution adopted at the general meeting ?—Yes, that would be so.

16,149. At the general meetings would the names of the persons who were in arrears, or men who were not doing right, be mentioned ?—I do not think they would. If anybody asked for them they would be. I do not recollect that anything of the kind was done.

16,150. Will you pledge your word that their names were not mentioned at the meeting ?—I will say that I believe they were not.

16,151. Is your knowledge such as to enable you to swear that they were not ?—I should not like to do that ; but if I were to swear any way I would swear that they were not.

16,152. If anybody asked for their names they might have them ?—Yes.

16,153. At that time was Gillott at all obnoxious to the trade ?—I do not know that he was more obnoxious than others in similar situations.

16,154. Was any complaint made to him of his not having paid ?—I do not think so.

16,155. I want to know whether you had ever complained of his not paying his subscription, or doing anything to the trade ?—I do not recollect that I ever did.

16,156. Had anything been done to him, will you pledge your word to that ?—I do not recollect.

16,157. You had had a meeting at an important time, two days before he was blown up, and I ask you now if you did not shortly before that time go to him and want him to comply with your rules ?—I might have done that, I cannot say.

16,158. You might have been to him; how long before this had you gone to him to ask him to comply with your rules ?—I have no idea, I do not recollect ; but it would be my business to go to him, because I had to go round every week to every member, and when rules of that sort were passed it would be my business to see him when I went to his wheel, and I might ask him.

16,159. Would there be any other persons besides whose business it would be ?—No.

16,160. Have you ever rattened him ?—No ; I never knew him to be rattened.

16,161. Where did he work ?—At Castle wheel, I believe.

16,162. The Tower wheel you mean ?—Yes; it is the same place.

16,163. There would be no difficulty in rattening him ?—I should think there would be.

16,164. Why ?—Because it was considered a secure place.

16,165. Then you could not ratten him ?—I should think not.

16,166. Then if the trade wanted you to put pressure upon him, they could not ratten him ; there was nothing for it except doing something to him personally or his property ?—I should not like anything of the sort to be done.

16,167. That is the only way of doing it ?—I cannot say that it would be.

16,168. But there was nothing else for it ?—I cannot say.

16,169. Whom did you generally employ to ratten at this time ?—We have very little rattening now.

16,170. I talk about 1857 ; who was your rattener in those days ?—We had not anyone particularly.

16,171. Did not you employ the men ?—No, we did not employ them at all ; they employed themselves. If you would allow me to show you the district book, I could show you how it would be, but we do not take that course now.

16,172. You do not do it any more ?—Though it has been my business to get the men to work as well as possible, I do not like it.

16,173. I should like to have the names of the men that you employed about this time ?—If you tell me a person who was rattened, I will give you the name if I can.

16,174. I do not know one ?—And I do not know.

16,175. You are the secretary, and went about getting it done ?—No ; it is not my business to get it done ; it is my business to get the money of the members. No, I will not say it is my business to get it done.

SEVENTEENTH DAY.

J. Rolley.

25 June 1867.

16,176. Whose business is it ?—It is the district's business.

16,177. What do you call the district ?—Our trade is divided into 10 districts, and they hold meetings once a month. This morning before I received my summons to come here I had been preparing the books at four district meetings to-day. I should have gone to one at one o'clock.

16,178. Each district takes the thing in its own hand ;—Yes ; we have to call over the accounts of every district every month, stating what every man has paid and what he owes.

16,179. That is called over ?—Yes.

16,180. And then this book is the general meeting's book (*referring to a book*) ?—Yes.

16,181. Besides this there is a meeting of the district ?—There is a district meeting every month.

16,182. The districts will have their own ratteners ? —If they think proper they have.

16,183. You do not know who was the rattener at that time ?—No.

16,184. What district was Gillott in ?—That would be Castle mills, but I think that wheel did not join the district at all.

16,185. Where did Gillott live ?—At Tomcross Lane, it was stated in the paper. I do not know where he did live.

16,186. Bramber Street, Tomcross Lane ?—Yes.

16,187. Whose district would that be in ?—The district would be where he worked, not where he lived, but I do not think the Castle wheel was joining the district ; it was a secure place, and very few were working there except those who went there for security.

16,188. They went in there for security. Was the wheel built for the purpose of giving security to people against ratteners ?—I do not know that, but it was considered a secure place when they commenced working there, though we had some men paying that worked there.

16,189. (*Mr. Barstow.*) You say that a resolution was passed that anyone might by a loan put himself straight ?—Yes.

16,190. Did Gillott make any application to the union ?—No.

16,191. He took no steps to put himself straight at all ?—No.

16,192. He kept himself quite aloof from them ?—Yes.

16,193. You do not know whether he was getting the price or not ?—No, I do not.

16,194. He was one of the men who were lowering the price ?—We should think so, because if those persons were not straight with the trade, and the masters wanted them to allow a discount, unless they were well to do themselves, they would be obliged to give way to the manufacturers.

The witness withdrew.

G. Gillott.

GEORGE GILLOTT sworn and examined.

16,195. (*Mr. Chance.*) You are a saw grinder ?—Yes.

16,196. Living in Rockingham Street ?—Yes.

16,197. In the year 1857 did you reside in Bramber Street ?—Yes.

16,198. Tomcross Lane, Sheffield ?—Yes.

16,198*a*. Do you remember in April 1857 anything happening to you ?—Yes.

16,199. Just describe to us what happened to you ? —Some one broke the cellar grate and put a canister containing gunpowder in the cellar ; there was part of a canister found afterwards.

16,200. When did you first find the can of gunpowder ?—The canister was found in a few hours after, but you mean when was it put in.

16,201. Do you know about what time it was put in ?—Yes, it was about half-past 12 ; I was quiet in bed at the time.

16,202. How many of your family were in the house ?—My wife and son and daughter, and two apprentice boys ; I had two pointer dogs in the kitchen, and they barked gently ; they did not bark right out, they gave a gentle bark each, and directly I heard a crash, and I knowed at once that I was done. I waked my wife and she says, " Whatever is the matter," I said " Lie still, you will hear it enow ;" in about a minute or a minute and a half the powder exploded.

16,203. Did the crash take place before the powder exploded ?—Yes, it was the same as a hammer striking.

16,204. Was the crash the exploding of the powder ? —The crash was the cellar grate ; in about a minute or a minute and a half the powder went off.

16,205. Did you go downstairs ?—Yes.

16,206. What did you find when you got downstairs ?—The place blown all to atoms in all directions.

16,207. What damage was done ?—It blowed the front windows out, the door, the two kitchen windows, and the chamber windows.

16,208. Anything else ?—It knocked the cellar door out, the kitchen door out, and there was a partition wall went up the side and it knocked that down altogether in a great heap ; it was only held up by one wall. If it had not been for that wall it would have blown the house down altogether.

16,209. Did you find the can of powder afterwards ? —I did not go in the cellar ; the policeman went in the cellar and found the remains of a can containing the powder, and there was a rope and a piece of brown cloth that had, I believe, been wrapped round the powder.

16,210. What did you do upon that, after you went down ?—I began to look about, and the first man I saw was a man called Sam Brammer.

16,211. Where did you see him ?—He was where the kitchen used to be ; he came to look, and I says to Sammy, " What are you doing here this time of the morning." It was about 20 minutes to one.

16,212. Does Brammer live near to you ?—He lives a little way off.

16,213. What is he ?—A file cutter ; it is not far, perhaps 300 or 400 yards, perhaps half a mile ; he lived in the neighbourhood.

16,214. What did you say to him ?—He said that he had been to the Casino, that was all that passed between Brammer and me ; and soon there were plenty of people about ; the watchman and the neighbours came. We got the family out ; then a watchman asked me whether I had any suspicion of anybody. I said, Yes, I thought they had run into a house across the road. He asked me what was the reason of my thinking that. I said after I had heard the crash I heard somebody run across that appeared to be either in their stocking feet or a pair of slippers, and all at once the sound ceased, and I said it appears to me as if they had run into this house of Royston.

16,215. Who was Royston ?—He was a file grinder.

16,216. Royston was taken up on suspicion, was he not ?—Yes.

16,217. And afterwards discharged ?—No, the bill was ignored.

16,218. Were you a member of the file grinders union at that time ?—No.

16,219. Had you been a member ?—Yes.

16,220. For how long had you ceased to be a member ?—I believe the last time I paid anything was just before a man called Watts was attempted to be blown up ; he had been attempted to be blown up. A can of powder was flung up at the window, but it did not go in ; that was at Allen Street yonder ; that would be perhaps a year or a year and a half before I was blown up.

16,221. Was that the time that you ceased to be a

SEVENTEENTH DAY.

G. Gillott.

25 June 1867.

member ?—Yes, Rolley came to me for my contribution, but I said, "I shall pay no more, George."

16,222. Is that the last witness ?—Yes; I said it is no use my paying any more towards being at the expense of blowing myself up. I have been blown up once, I said, and you shall have no more money towards blowing me up again.

16,223. You had not been blown up then ?—I have been blown up twice.

16,224. When was it that you were first blown up? 21 years since.

16,225. Then you were referring to that blowing up when you spoke to Rolley ?—Yes. I said, "I shall not pay any more money to blow myself up again," and I considered I had paid my money and I had no thanks for paying it, and I knew they would do me all the injury they could.

16,226. That was the reason why you refused to pay any more contributions ?—Yes.

16,227. After that did you cease altogether to pay contributions to the union ?—Yes, I never paid it after Watts was attempted to be blown up on the Thursday or Friday night; Rolley came to me on Monday morning, and I never paid again.

16,228. Did Rolley apply to you often for the contributions ?—I do not think that he did.

16,229. Did any other member of the union apply to you for the contributions ?—No.

16,230. After you told Rolley that you would not be any longer a member of the union, did anyone call upon you to ask you for your contributions ?—Not often; they might come to me and ask me whether I would join, but I always refused.

16,231. Was there any threat ever used to you if you did not join the union ?—No, no threats.

16,232. Did Royston ever use any threat to you ?—He once threatened me, but that was above a year before this happened.

16,233. What did he say to you upon that occasion ? —We came together at night, and we were going home together, and we were talking about me not joining the union. I said I would not join. He said they would make me join. I said I should not. He said "Thou " hast been blown up once, and thou wilt be blown up " again, if thou doesn't." I said, "It doesn't matter " for that, I will never join it again till I am forced."

16,234. Was he quite sober when he said that ?—In a moderate way; we had a glass or two together.

16,235. You were sober; you must not tell us any drunken conversation ?—Yes, I was sober.

16,236. Did you have a quarrel upon that; he said said that he would blow you up again ?—Yes; we went on talking. I said, "I shall not join, if " they shoot me. I will suffer death first. I will " never be forced to join the union again." He says, "We will make thee." I says, "Who will make me ?" He says, "Thou wilt be blown up again, and I will do thee myself." I says, "Thou hadst not better let me catch thee, or thou wilt blow no more up if I do." He says, "Well, I think not, what couldst thou do ?" I said, "I am only half a man." You see, sir, I have had a water cancer in my wrist (*showing his arm to the Examiners*). He thought he could do as he liked. I said to him, "If thou think'st thou can'st do " ought, I don't mind having a couple of friendly " rounds with thee, and we will not fall out about it."

16,237. Had you two friendly rounds ?—Yes; I tied up this hand first and had two or three hits at him, but when I found I could not hit him hard enough with my left hand, I took the other out of the sling, and let slip at him with it.

16,238. Did you join the union in consequence of what he said to you ?—No; this was August or September. I was so lame I could not lift the arm up.

16,239. Do you know what was the reason of your being blown up ?—Yes.

16,240. What was the cause of it ?—My opinion was, that it was because I did not join the union.

16,241. (*Chairman.*) Between this time that you had a quarrel with this man and the blowing up, had there been any application to you to join the union ?—I cannot say.

16,242. How long before you were last blown up had you any application to join the union ?—I should think it would be a year and a half.

16,243. (*Mr. Chance.*) This was about a year before it took place ?—I think something about that, because I vowed vengeance against them, and they did not come near me.

16,244. Had you any private quarrel with anyone ? —No, never in my life.

16,245. Have you ever received any injury or had anything done to you since that ?—I have lost two grinding bands two or three times. I lost one four years last December—the latter end of December. I lost one grinding band about two years ago, just before Christmas or just after; it is in the Town Hall report. I offered 2*l.* reward.

16,246. At the time you lost the bands were you a member of the union ?—Yes, I joined them then.

16,247. When did you become a member of the union ?—Rolley and Griffen came down to me and said that the makers, cutters, hardeners, and grinders, had all joined in together; that was three years since last March or April.

16,248. They said that they were all going to join ? —Yes, he said they had been to several, and they had all agreed to join, and there were two more to go, that was Jeffcock and Hudson; they had all agreed except these two. I said if they had all joined but me I would join. I thought I had been fighting them long enough. I said if I was the only one left, then I would join.

16,249. Did you join ?—Yes, but I was forced to do it.

16,250. Was it since you joined the union that your bands were taken ?—Yes.

16,251. The first time and the second time ?—Yes, I believe I joined both times. I did not regularly join when I first went. I paid occasionally. Rolley came down to me and said that there were many men upon the box, and asked me to contribute a little towards them. I said I would pay 3*s.* a week for the man and myself on condition that they would not interfere with either me or the man, and I was paying on those conditions at the time this first band was stolen.

16,252. What was the reason the first band was taken ?—I do not know whether it was the trade, or who it was that stole it; it was a very good band three inches broad.

16,253. Were you in arrears of the contributions which you had promised ?—When my bands were taken I was paying 3*s.* sometimes, and sometimes 6*s.*

16,254. At that time were you in arrear of what you ought to have paid ?—I might be or I might not, I paid when I saw him. I was not a regular member.

16,255. The second time the bands were taken were you in arrear ?—No.

16,256. Can you give any reason why your band was taken ?—I think the band was regularly thieved.

16,257. When you say "thieved," do you mean that it was not taken on the trade account ?—I do not know anything about that; when I liked I paid.

16,258. After the bands had been taken did you make any application to anybody about them ?—I went to the Town Hall the last time and offered 2*l.* reward.

16,259. Did you go to Rolley or the other secretary of the union about them ?—I told the other secretary; I do not remember telling Rolley.

16,260. Did you ask them if they could do anything for you in getting the bands back ?—The other secretary said they would be a couple of pounds or 5*l.* towards it if they could find it out. I forget what amount they said they would be, but they said they would be something towards it besides my reward.

16,261. That they would offer a reward ?—Yes.

16,262. Did they deny all knowledge of it ?—I did not ask them whether the bands were taken. I bought two bands, and set to work again directly.

16,263. You believed that they were stolen, and that it was not a trade affair?—I think they were stolen. Of course they had nothing to do it for then.

16,264. (*Mr. Barstow.*) At the time you were blown up was there any rule in the trade about apprentices?—Yes.

16,265. Had you more than the number allowed by the trade?—Yes.

16,266. Had anything been said to you about that? —Yes; frequently people used to meet me and tell me about it.

16,267. Members of the same trade used to tell you about it?—Yes.

16,268. Were you applied to to discharge any of them?—Not particularly.

16,269. Do you think that that may have been the cause of ill-will on the part of the trade towards you? —Yes, it was not for working under price. The place I worked for I have worked for since I was a boy, and when trade was down they never took the discount at all—they always paid full price; they never took a penny of discount; and as for Rolley saying that Gillott and suchlike were working under price for this master, I can only say that I worked for the most respectable masters in the town.

16,270. I do not think Rolley said that you worked under price?—He made the remark that Gillott and suchlike (and he pointed back to me) were working for this master under price. I can prove that my master paid me full statement when the trade was broken up.

16,271. Where were you working at this time?—At the Tower wheel.

16,272. Would it have been an easy matter to have rattened you there?—No, they could not have got there; there were two or three watchmen there.

16,273. (*Chairman.*) And the doors are closed?—Yes, and the watchmen lived on the premises inside.

16,274. Have you ever had any threat from anyone?—No.

16,275. Never?—No.

16,276. When you had the friendly round with Royston where had you been to?—We had called up at the "Hen and Chicken," in Castle Green, and had a drain, and from there on our road home we called at the "Corner Pin," and had a glass of whisky together.

16,277. Were you sober?—I was as sober as I am this minute.

16,278. Are you sober now?—I think so.

16,279. You were quite sober?—I had enough to make me sober when I was going to be blown up.

16,280. What time of night was it that you had this friendly turn with your friend?—Half-past 12 or one in the morning.

16,281. In the night?—Yes.

16,282. Where was it that you had a friendly turn? —Up Spittal Hill.

16,283. Had you any persons to look at you?—Royston and me and another person that was with me, "Old Tommy Sykes."

16,284. So you had this friendly turn at the top of Spittal Hill?—Yes.

The witness withdrew.

Adjourned to to-morrow at 11 o'clock.

EIGHTEENTH DAY.

Council Hall, Sheffield, Wednesday, 26th June 1867.

PRESENT:

WILLIAM OVEREND, Esq., Q.C.	GEORGE CHANCE, Esq.
THOMAS IRWIN BARSTOW, Esq.	J. E. BARKER, Esq., Secretary.

WILLIAM OVEREND, Esq., Q.C., IN THE CHAIR.

GEORGE CASTLES sworn and examined.

16,285. (*Chairman.*) You are the secretary of one of the unions; which is it?—The sickle and reaping-hook grinders.

16,286. How long have you been secretary?—It will be four years next August, I believe.

16,287. Do you produce the books of your union? —Yes.

16,288. How far back do they go?—There is one which only goes back to September last.

16,289. Have you complete books up to any period? —I do not know how far the books do go back except the one book which I refer to; I have not looked.

16,290. What is that book?—It goes back to the 5th of last September.

16,291. What book is that?—It is the book where the general accounts are entered.

16,292. Will you allow me to look at those books? —Yes (*handing the books to the Chairman*).

16,293. Are those all the books which you have? —Those are all which I have.

16,294. How long have they been in your possession?—I took them till this morning.

16,295. Who has had the custody of them?—There are three of us.

16,296. Who are they?—George Barker, James Haslam, and I keep the keys of the box in which the books are deposited.

16,297. To the best of your belief are those the only books which the club possesses?—With the exception of the bank books.

16,298. Where is the bank book?—It is in the box.

16,299. Why did you not bring it?—I did not know that the bank book would be required.

16,300. Do you keep a banking account, then?—Yes.

16,301. With whom?—With the savings bank, I suppose; it is a little above. That is the only banking account we have.

16,302. I have not seen the books, and we have had it from one secretary who has come before us that he had torn out some leaves and made some alterations; have there been any leaves torn out of any of your books?—Not that I am aware of.

16,303. Have any alterations been made?—No; the books are just as they were.

16,304. And do they contain an account of all your proceedings?—Yes.

16,305. Have you a minute book containing entries of your proceedings at your meetings?—Yes, there is a book in which we enter minutes.

16,306. Have you any books applicable to the year 1860?—No, except that book there (*pointing to a book*) goes back to there. I have never looked how far it went back.

EIGHTEENTH DAY.

G. Castles.

26 June 1867.

16,307. Have you any book in reference to the year 1860?—No; not that I am aware of.

16,308. What book is this (*holding up a book*)?—It is what we had for a minute book before I got that new one.

16,309. This is not a minute book; this is something else. Just come and look at this, will you (*the witness walked towards the Chairman*). "Resolution passed at a general meeting held August 26th, 1861." This then would apply to an earlier period?—Yes, that was before I had anything to do with the books.

16,310. The first entry and date of the resolutions is the 26th August 1861; then in all human probability this would not refer to 1860?—It is just as I found it.

16,311. Never mind; would this apply to proceedings in the year before?—It would apply to proceedings in that year.

16,312. There is "October 7th," but there is no year. October 7th is the first entry in the book, and I want to know what year that was?—Well, it is not my writing; I cannot tell you.

16,313. I only want you to explain the book; the first entry of the resolutions in the year is 1861; before that there are various entries, all of the month of October, but which October does not appear; it was before this was written, therefore it must be 1860, or 1859, or any year before?—It may be October 1860.

16,314. Can you tell me who has torn out those leaves?—No, I cannot.

16,315. The period which we want to investigate is the month of August 1860, and I find just before October a great number of leaves were cut out?—Yes.

16,316. Do you know who did that?—No.

16,317. When did you notice that those leaves were cut out?—I noticed it first when I became secretary.

16,318. Then that would be four years ago?—About four years ago.

16,319. Do you swear that you saw them out four years ago?—Yes.

16,320. Do you know for what reason they were torn out?—I do not.

16,321. Will you swear that you do not know the reason at all?—I will.

16,322. From whom did you get your books?—I got them at the meeting place.

16,323. Who was your predecessor?—John Morton.

16,324. Is John Morton alive?—Yes.

16,325. How long was he secretary?—I think he was in office 12 months.

16,326. Who was his predecessor?—Well, I believe it was William Widdison, I think so.

16,327. Is he alive?—Yes.

16,328. How long was he secretary?—Either one or two years, I could not say which.

16,329. Did you never when you got those books in this mutilated condition inquire of anybody the reason why they were so mutilated?—No, I never took any notice.

16,330. You have a book here beginning with "Resolution at general meeting held," so and so, "William Widdison, chairman: First, that the 11th "rule remain in its present form; third, that an "apprentice be allowed to be set on during the current "year," and so on with various resolutions. They go on all right enough but on April 6th, 1863, there are a lot of resolutions, and on the 4th August 1863 there are further resolutions. In November 1863 there are further resolution, and in 1864, and then there is a page out. This goes down to 1864, and I find that this book contains entries of the year 1843. Then there is a blank, and then there are a lot of pages cut out again; then there is half a leaf cut out. Where is the resolution book previous to 1861?—I never saw one. Those are the only books which I have seen with the exception of one, those are the only books with that exception that I ever saw.

16,331. Do you know who was secretary in August 1860?—No, I do not.

16,332. Have you no book, think for a moment, who was secretary for 1860?—I think it would be George Widdison or William Widdison, but which of the two I cannot swear.

16,333. Are they both alive?—Yes.

16,334. You were secretary for four years, that brings it to 1863?—Yes.

16,335. Then John Morton was your predecessor for 12 months, that would make it 1862; then was William Widdison before him one or two years?—I could not say.

16,336. That would make it 1861 or 1860?—No.

16,337. But at all events George was before William?—I think he was.

16,338. Then it would be either in George's time or William's time?—I think so.

16,339. Have you ever had any conversation with any person at all about the state of this book?—No, not with anyone.

16,340. Will you swear that this book was torn in this way when you got it?—Yes.

16,341. Four years ago?—Four years since next August.

16,342. Have you any knowledge why it was torn in that way?—I have not the least.

16,343. Would your book go back to the year 1860?—No.

16,344. Had you any banking account in the year 1860?—I do not know that we had.

16,345. Do you know one way or the other?—The bank book does not go back to that time.

16,346. But had you a banking account?—Not that I am aware of.

16,347. Where does William Widdison live?—At Eckington.

16,348. Where does George Widdison live?—At Handsworth Woodhouse.

16,349. Now mind, you swear distinctly that that book was in that state when you got it?—I do.

16,350. Has it never been defaced or altered in any way?—Not to my knowledge.

16,351. Will you swear that you have never defaced or altered it in any way since you got it?—I will swear that it is as near as possible like what it was when I got it as a book can be.

16,352. Have you any knowledge at all of why those leaves were torn out?—I have not.

16,353. You have had no conversation with any member of the union about it?—Not a word about any of the leaves being taken out.

16,354. You know it is particularly unfortunate for your union. We find in the year 1860 there is a charge made against your union for having been engaged in blowing up a gentleman of the name of Rotherham, and it is suggested that money was paid for doing it. We want to see your accounts for that very year 1860, and to see if we could by any means find out whether any payment of that description was made, and when we come to look at the books we find that for that very year the leaves are torn out. It is a little difficult to say so, but the edges of those leaves are very clean if you look at them (*handing the book to the witness*), and they look very much like recent removal?—This is the book just as I got it.

16,355. But look at the edges; what do you say to them; they are clean?—They are.

16,356. Are you sure that you noticed the leaves out, or did you not notice them?—I have noticed the leaves being out of the book, and that was part of the reason why I got the new book.

16,357. Is this the new book (*showing a book to the witness*)?—Yes, that is the new book.

16,358. But it was in 1864 that you got this new book?—When I got the book I found it in such a mutilated condition——

16,359. You found it in such a mutilated condition that you then got the new book in which all the proceedings have been entered since?—Yes.

16,360. Has that book been in any use at all since you have had it?—Only for the entries that I have made in it. It has been locked up in the box ever since.

16,361. If it has not been used that may account for its being clean ?—It has been locked up in the box ever since.

16,362. You had to pay for this book, had you not ?—Yes.

16,363. Out of the funds of the society ?—Yes.

16,364. When you did that some person would know that you bought it; was anything said about the condition of the other book at the time this was bought ?—No, only that——

16,365. To whom did you mention that the other book was in such a dilapidated condition that you must buy a new one ?—To the committee then sitting.

16,366. Who were the committee to whom you then mentioned it ?—The 1864 committee ; there are the names in the book, I believe.

16,367. John Atkin Chappell ?—No, I believe the names are here (*showing the book to the Commissioners*).

16,368. In 1863 and 1864 were James Renshaw, Thomas Staniforth, Joseph Staniforth, George Statham, George Cartridge, George Fox, and William Renshaw, your committee ?—Yes, at that time.

16,369. And they say the key holders are James Renshaw, George Statham, and George Fox ?—Yes, at that time.

16,370. Some person ought to be able to give us some information about this. Do you suppose that Widdison could give us some information about this book being torn ?—Well, he is the likeliest person that I know of to give any information about it.

16,371. You are quite sure (I am obliged to put the question) that those leaves have not been torn out for the purpose of preventing our having an opportunity of seeing them ?—I am quite sure they have not.

16,372. Or for any such purpose ?—For no such purpose, not since I have been in possession of the books.

16,373. And that they have not been torn out within the last four years ?—They have not.

16,374. You say when a new book is required it is mentioned to the committee ?—Yes, I mentioned that.

16,375. Then any one of those persons who are on the committee would be able to tell us that you called the attention of the committee to the condition of this book ?—Well, I should think they would.

16,376. You know the book was not by any means full ?—No.

16,377. There were plenty of leaves to fill. You swear that those entries are all made in this book at the date under which they appear ?—They are.

16,378. They have not been made since ?—No.

16,379. And they are all in your own handwriting ?—I believe they are in that book.

16,380. We will look over the book, if you will leave it with us, but I want to ask you a question. For the purpose for which we wanted it, it is of no use, because the entries are gone; there are no entries, but for other purposes we may find it useful. You are a grinder of sickles and reaping hooks, are you not ?—Yes.

16,381. In your union do you ratten ?—Yes, there is some little rattening done.

16,382. When you ratten do you pay men for doing it ?—Never since I have been in office.

16,383. You have never paid any men ?—No.

16,384. Has the man got payment from the person to whom the bands were restored ?—If he has got any at all it has been got in that way.

16,385. But you have never paid anything out of the funds of the union ?—I never did.

16,386. But you have instructed a man to ratten for not complying with rules ?—No.

16,387. You never have ?—No.

16,388. You have never known of its being done ?—I have known that parties bands were gone when parties have come and told me.

16,389. And they have been done for the trade ?—Yes, I have reason to believe that they have.

16,390. Have you districts ? I see there are various districts alluded to in this book. There is Hallam, Hackenthorpe, Pudding Mill, Birley Moor, and other places ?—Yes.

16,391. And are those places which are mentioned as districts under the management of district committees ?—There is a committeeman for each place.

16,392. And that committee meets once a month or something of that sort ?—Yes, and once a fortnight.

16,393. They come from all the districts around ?—Yes.

16,394. Where do you meet ?—At Hackenthorpe.

16,395. In cases where rattening has been done, has it been done by the district or by a separate committeeman ?—I do not know who has done it.

16,396. But you know it has been done for the trade ?—Yes, I have reason to believe that it has.

16,397. But would the orders be given by the committees of the different districts ?—No, there have never been any orders given since I was in office.

16,398. Then how is it done ? Have you pointed out that a man has been a defaulter, and then have his bands been taken or something of that kind ?—The books will tell.

16,399. Show me an entry about rattening in your book ?—(*The witness explained the book to the Examiners.*) This book shows every man's arrears.

16,400. Have you a meeting for the purpose of calling over the names of the persons in arrear ?—Yes, they are called over at a general meeting.

16,401. And at a general meeting the names of the persons who are in arrear are called over ?—Yes.

16,402. Can you tell me whether when the rattenings have occurred, they have been shortly after those names have been called over ?—No, I do not know that they have.

16,403. How many rattenings have you known in your time ?—In my time of office ?

16,404. Yes ?—Only some three or four.

16,405. In the four years ?—Yes.

16,406. Do you mean to say that in the four years that you have been in office there have not been more than three or four rattenings ?—There have not been above half-a-dozen.

16,407. In those cases have bands or nuts been taken ?—Bands.

16,408. Have they been destroyed or have they been restored ?—They have been restored.

16,409. In all cases ?—Yes.

16,410. Have you a price for taking bands ?—No.

16,411. Is it 5*s.* ?—No, I have never heard of it.

16,412. You have heard of 5*s.* being the regular price for bands being taken, have you heard of any regular payment for Mary Ann or anything of that sort ?—I have heard something respecting it. When I was a boy, I have heard my father say that he had to pay 5*s.* for his band.

16,413. How long ago is that ?—I should think it is 20 years since.

16,414. Then in your trade rattening has been going on, and Mary Ann has existed for upwards of 20 years ?—Yes.

16,415. Do you know of any other trade in which there has been rattening besides the grinders ?—No, I do not.

16,416. You have never known of any person being rattened ?—Yes, I have heard speak of some of the sickle smiths being rattened, but not to my knowledge.

16,417. Have you a union of sickle smiths and sickle grinders ?—Yes.

16,418. Are you amalgamated ?—Yes.

16,419. How many branches are there ? there are sickle smiths, and what besides ?—Sickle grinders.

16,420. And what besides ?—Scythe grinders.

16,421. You are in connexion with the scythe grinders ?—Yes, there are five branches, I believe.

16,422. What are those ?—Sickle smiths, sickle

EIGHTEENTH DAY.

G. Castles.

26 June 1867.

grinders, scythe smiths, scythe grinders, and patent scythe and hook makers, that is all.

16,423. And you help one another; if one wants rattening you do a little business for them, and they do for you as you want them?—I do not know of anything of that kind.

16,424. Then what is the benefit of your amalgamation? how do you help one another?—We assist one another by any legal means, such as giving advice or anything of that kind.

16,425. Contributing from your funds?—Yes, we contribute funds.

16,426. From one society to the other?—Yes.

16,427. In fact you help one another to the best of your power?—Yes.

16,428. When a rule of the society is broken, and a man is at work, do you draw your men off and tell them they must come away off the work?—I have never known a case of that kind. I have never been in connexion with it on the committee in any way.

16,429. Have you ever known a case of that kind in your trade?—Yes, I believe there has been one. but I cannot say that it was through the committee, because I have never had anything to do with it.

16,430. But you have known that it was so?—I believe it was so.

16,431. How long have you been in the union?—I have been in the union ever since 1848. I was loosed in 1848.

16,432. Do you know Mr Rotherham?—No.

16,433. Did you know nothing of him?—No.

16,434. You know there is such a man, do you not?—I have heard speak of him.

16,435. There is no great kindness between him and your union, is there? I believe you do not like him in your union?—I do not know but what we like him as well as any other man; I had never any ill feeling against the man. I never saw him to my knowledge.

16,436. He lives at Dronfield, does he not?—Yes.

16,437. Did you hear that he was blown up?—I believe I did, some many years since.

16,438. But I am speaking of 1860; that is seven years ago?—Yes, I believe I heard of it at the time.

16,439. Had you any talk to your committee about it?—No.

16,440. Have you had any talk to any of your union about it?—No.

16,441. On your oath do you know at all who it was that committed that outrage upon Mr. Rotherham?—No.

16,442. Are you aware whether any money was paid by any member of your union for that?—I am not.

16,443. Have you ever seen any entry in any of your books in reference to that?—Never.

16,444. Have you ever been present at any meeting of the union when that outrage was spoken of?—No.

16,445. Never?—Never.

16,446. And no member of the union has ever told you that it was done on behalf of the trade?—No.

16,447. I suppose that when a man has his bellows cut, twelve bands cut to pieces, anvils thrown into the dam, his house blown up, and a two-gallon jar of gunpowder put into his warehouse, he being a man that had no quarrel with his neighbours that he knew of, that looks like a trade affair, does it not?—I was very much surprised to see it in the paper this morning, for I never heard of the occurrence while I saw it in the paper this morning.

16,448. And you never heard about that two-gallon jar?—I never heard of it to my knowledge while this morning I saw it in the paper.

16,449. And that was only two years ago?—No.

16,450. Have you never heard of it?—To the best of my knowledge——

16,451. You must go further than that. Will you swear you never heard of it?—I will swear I never knew such a thing or heard it named while I saw it in the "Independent" this morning.

16,452. Do you recollect any pressure being put upon the young Rotherhams to make them join your union?—No.

16,453. Did you ever go to them and speak to them, and ask them to join?—No. I never saw them in my life to the best of my knowledge.

16,454. Who went round to collect the natty money from Dronfield?—The committeemen from each district.

16,455. Who would be the committeeman from Dronfield?—We have not had one from Dronfield.

16,456. But whose business would it be to go round at Dronfield and try and get members for your union?—No one since I have been in office; no one has ever been sent to try and get anyone to join the union at Dronfield since I have been there.

16,457. Has anybody ever been sent to Dronfield to get people to join the union?—No; I was sent there once myself.

16,458. When was that?—Last year.

16,459. What was that for?—It was to go to Mr. Harrison's at Dronfield to try and get some work.

16,460. What district is the nearest to Dronfield?—There is a young man of the name of Fox, who lives at Trowey. His district was Skelper or thereabouts.

16,461. How near is that to Dronfield?—I never was that way to Dronfield, but I should think it might be two or three miles off.

16,462. Was it his business to collect the natty?—Yes, at his own wheel and in his own district.

16,463. Is Dronfield out of your district?—We have no committeeman for it.

16,464. Have you any union men in Dronfield?—We could scarcely call them union men.

16,465. Did they pay to your funds?—They paid occasionally.

16,466. What is the name of those men?—John Rotherham, I believe, Christopher Rotherham, and I think George Rotherham.

16,467. Those are the nephews of old Rotherham, are they?—I believe so.

16,468. Now to whom did they pay their natty?—To Mark Fox; in fact he brought it to the committee.

16,469. They have only done so lately have they?—Some two or three years I think.

16,470. Do you not know that they had been applied to frequently on behalf of the union to join the union before they would consent to do so?—Not since I have been in office.

16,471. Not to your knowledge?—Not since I have been in office to my knowledge.

16,472. Has anybody told you that he has gone?—Fox has told me that he has seen them respecting it.

16,473. Did he tell you that he told them that they must join or else that it would be the worse for them?—No.

16,474. What has he told you?—He told me that he had seen the Rotherhams, and they had said that they would send money and so and so. That is the chief of what he said to me.

16,475. Have you ever caused it to be said to persons that if they did not join your union it would be worse for them?—No.

16,476. Have you ever known of its being done?—No.

16,477. Have you ever known a case of bellows being cut?—No, not of my own knowledge.

16,478. Have you heard of it?—I have heard of it through the papers, but that is all.

16,479. At the time?—Yes.

16,480. Were the persons in connexion with your trade?—No.

16,481. How many times have you heard of bellows being cut?—Only once.

16,482. When was that?—At Dronfield.

16,483. Did you hear of that?—Yes.

16,484. What interest could anybody have in cutting a person's bellows except for the purposes of the trade?—I do not know.

EIGHTEENTH DAY.

G. Castles.

26 June 1867.

16,485. Not being able to assign any reason, does it occur to your mind that it is a trade matter ?—No, I did not connect it with the trade at all, because I knew we were clear from it as far as our committee was concerned at the time, and I thought it might be a trade matter or might not.

16,486. If it might be a trade matter or it might not, and if you disapproved of proceedings like that, why did you not bring it before your committee and make enquiries about it ?—Well, I never thought that our committee had anything to do with it.

16,487. You never did bring it before the committee ?—No ; it was talked of in the committee that so and so had had their bellows cut, that was all.

16,488. What did you say about it ?—Well, our committee did not approve of it, and never have done. Since I have been on we have always set our faces against anything of the kind.

16,489. But did you not think it worth while to make inquiry about it ?—I did not think it was connected with our society at all.

16,490. But you thought that it was a trade matter ?—I thought that it might be.

16,491. The character of your own union was involved in that; why did you not call a meeting, and investigate it amongst your members ?—Because I did not think that it affected us at all; I knew that we had nothing to do with it. We had no dispute with the man, and we had no ill feeling against them.

16,492. Why, old Rotherham had refused to join you, and had defied you all his life ?—I do not know that he was ever asked; he was not a grinder to my knowledge.

16,493. But he was a master who employed grinders ?—The masters never do join us.

16,494. But he had employed men who did not belong to your union, had he not ?—Yes.

16,495. And you swear that you do not know anything at all about Rotherham's business ?—I do.

16,496. And you do not know who did it ?—No, I do not.

16,497. Do you know where the cash book previous to last September is ?—Yes; I know where I saw it last.

16,498. Where is that ?—I saw it on the fire last.

16,499. Who placed it there ?—Well, it was either Elias Havenhand, or Oliver Turner, or Mark Fox.

16,500. Where did they place it on the fire ?—In the committee room.

16,501. When ?—In September last.

16,502. Why did they do that ?—Well, I will tell you how it was, if you will allow me to explain. The book was full, and I had got a new one. There were some of the leaves which were not quite filled up, and they were cutttng the blank leaves off; the bottom of the leaf that was not completely filled up they were cutting off to make bills to put the work down on to send in to the masters. I noticed them doing that ; I was writing at the time, and they were turning it over and cutting them off; and one of the party took it at last and threw it into the fire, but which of the three I cannot say.

16,503. You know who threw it into the fire ?—I did not see it while it was on the fire.

16,504. And you swear that you do not know who threw it on the fire ?—I will swear that I do not know which of the parties I have named did it, but I have reason to believe that it was one of them.

16,505. Were they all there at the time ?—They were all there at the time.

16,506. You see we have two dates as to which we want to inquire. We have the year 1860, and we have two years ago. We find the first leaves out of one book, and the other book thrown into the fire ; now this is a very suspicious circumstance ?—It is.

16,507. You acknowledge that it is a very suspicious circumstance ?—I do.

16,508. Was no remark ever made about throwing it into the fire ?—Not any; only they seemed to be not exactly falling out, but trying which could get the most out of those blank leaves that were not filled up at the bottom, and one of them took it and threw it into the fire.

16,509. But that is not the way to get leaves out ; nobody got any leaves if they threw it into the fire ; you do not give us a sufficient reason for their throwing it into the fire ?—That is all I know ; I was busy writing ; I have come to tell you the truth and nothing but the truth, and that is all that I know.

16,510. I do not say that you are not telling the truth, but I must inquire about this you know ?—Yes.

16,511. Was anything said about it ?—No.

16,512. It was a record of your proceedings until September last, and you might be called up by any of your members who might say that your accounts were not properly kept ?—Yes.

16,513. When does the new book begin ?—On the 5th of September.

16,514. And when was the book destroyed ?—Sometime during the month ; whether it was that night or the night after I could not swear.

16,515. Now look at what a situation you have placed yourself in. You get a new book the same night you burn the old one ; was it the same night as this was bought ?—I do not know whether it was that night or the night after.

16,516. The same night or the night after you got a new book ; you actually destroyed the records of all your proceedings, and if any member challenged you with misconduct in your office you had not any document at all to show. Do you mean to say that you have done such a thing as that ?—I mean to say it was done.

16,517. That book came up till the very time ; the very week before; and if a man had said that he had paid his contributions or anything of that sort what would you have done ?—The contributions would not be in that book.

16,518. What was in it ?—It was a general account similar to that book which you see there.

16,519. (*Mr. Chance.*) With a credit side and a debit side ?—Yes.

16,520. (*Chairman.*) If you had paid a man 10*l.* for putting a can of gunpowder under a man's place, that 10*l.* ought to have been in that book ?—Yes.

16,521. And you have no better reason to give for destroying that book than this ?—That is the only reason that we had for destroying it that I am aware of.

16,522. You were no party to the destruction according to your statement ?—No.

16,523. Did you not say, " What business have you to throw it into the fire " ?—Yes ; and if I could have got it off again I would have done so.

16,524. What kind of a book was it ?—It would be a square book somewhat similar to that which you have before you, only rather thicker.

16,525. What kind of a back had it ?—It had a stronger back than that one.

16,526. And you tell me that when you saw it done if you could have got it off the fire you would have saved it. Do you mean to tell me that if a man throws this book into the fire it gets so much ignited at once that you could not save it ?—I mean to say that when I saw that book on the fire it was all in flames.

16,527. You say that you saw them throw it into the fire ?—No, I beg your pardon.

16,528. You saw it on the fire ?—Yes.

16,529. And in flames ?—Yes.

16,530. A book like this would not burn in that way. Why did you not get hold of it with the tongs ?—There were not any.

16,531. Why did not you remove it with the poker ? you might soon have slipped it off from the top of the fire ?—It was all in flames when I saw it.

16,532. That is all your explanation ?—That is all I have to say.

16,533. And you mean to say that you saw the book of your society (you being the secretary) burning on the fire, and did not try to save it ?—I did not. Of course if I had had any idea of this taking place I should have done so.

EIGHTEENTH DAY.

G. Castles.

26 June 1867.

16,534. What business had you to allow your members to cut away your book?—Why, they do just as they think proper. They say that it is just as much their book as mine, and they use it.

16,535. You are responsible as secretary. You have the charge of it, it is your book, and they are your entries, and if that book had to be investigated by any of your own men, by the very fact of part of it being cut out, they would have said, "You have falsified the books, and cut out entries." What business had they to cut it out?—Well, I do not know. They did not cut any writing out.

16,536. That is what you tell us, but how could you explain it to your own union, how would they know that there was not writing cut out?—Because one page would correspond with another. The balance would go over each leaf, and they could see very plainly that there had been nothing cut out.

16,537. But surely, if you saw this book thrown on the fire, you must have said, "What business have you to throw it on the fire?" To whom did you speak?—I did not see it thrown on.

16,538. But when you saw it on the fire did you not say, "Who did it"?—I believe I did, but——

16,539. Who answered?—I do not know that there was any answer who it was. They were laughing and talking among themselves, all in confusion at the moment.

16,540. At that time had there been a rumour of a commission or investigation?—No.

16,541. Did you contribute at all towards the expense of defending the man Thompson for murder?—Not that I am aware of.

16,542. Did you contribute at all towards the expenses of defending Thompson for murder?—There has never been one penny gone out of our box for anything of the kind since I have been secretary.

16,543. Did you yourself personally contribute?—No.

16,544. How many members are there in your union?—I think there are somewhere about 60.

16,545. Has any person complained about the book being destroyed?—No.

16,546. Has it ever been mentioned at all?—Yes.

16,547. Where?—In the works where I work.

16,548. Where?—At Hackenthorpe.

16,549. To whom have you mentioned it?—To most of the grinders.

16,550. Name the man to whom you told it?—I told it before most of them when we were on the hearth. There might be five or six.

16,551. Tell me the name of the men to whom you told it?—I do not know who really. I believe there would be a man of the name of Reaney.

16,552. What is his name?—Mark.

16,553. And to put down that, you told Mark Reaney?—I believe he would be one of the parties.

16,554. Will you swear that you told Mark Reaney?—I will swear that to the best of my knowledge he was there.

16,555. Will you swear that you told Mark Reaney?—I would not like to swear that I told him, but to the best of my knowledge——

16,556. Was there any man there to whom you can swear you named it?—I believe Reaney is a man that heard me say that the book was destroyed.

16,557. When will you swear that you mentioned it to Reaney?—Oh! months back, just at the time of the occurrence, just afterwards.

16,558. You know that this was in September last?—Yes.

16,559. How soon after September last did you mention to Reaney that you had burnt the book?—Just after. I could not say to a week or so, but it was just directly after the occurrence.

16,560. Who was present besides Reaney?—I could not say; there might be James Renshaw and Samuel Morton, but I should not like to swear that they were there. I could not do it.

16,561. Did Reaney say anything when you told him that it had been burnt?—Not particularly.

16,562. Did he say that it was a right thing to do or a wrong thing to do?—He said that it didn't ought to have been done.

16,563. In September last you knew about this Commission of Inquiry did you not?—No.

16,564. Are you sure that the 5th of September was the date?—Yes, the date of the commencement of that book.

16,565. You are sure that the 5th of September was the date when you destroyed that book?—No, I am not sure of that. I say it was either on the 5th of September or the committee night after the 5th.

16,566. In the month of September?—Yes.

16,567. And not later?—No.

16,568. You will swear that it was in the month of September?—Yes.

16,569. And that this book was immediately made and kept in the usual course from that time forward?—Yes.

16,570. Will you swear that those earlier entries in this book are not entries copied from another book?—I will.

16,571. Were they made at the the time when they bear date?—Yes.

16,572. They were not made all at once?—No.

16,573. Now look at this page (*the witness looked at the book.*) Will you swear that that page was not all written at the same time?—I will.

16,574. Was it written week by week?—Fortnight by fortnight.

16,575. And this was not written all at the same time?—No.

16,576. And it is not a transcript from another book?—No; those accounts never were in any other book besides that.

16,577. And you swear that the old book has not been destroyed lately, and that you have not put these in from the old book?—I will.

16,578. You fixed the date when that book was destroyed as September the 5th?—Yes, I will swear that.

16,579. What time of the day do you meet?—We meet at 7 o'clock at night.

16,580. Do you meet at a public house?—Yes.

16,581. At whose house?—At George Staniforth's the New Inn, Hackenthorpe.

16,582. Did he see it destroyed?—No.

16,583. Was anybody but those men, Havenhand, Turner, and Fox there?—Yes, several of us were in the room.

16,584. They saw it destroyed?—Yes, they saw it on the fire.

16,585. September was a cold month I believe, but is not September rather an early time to have fires?—I do not know; we had a fire.

16,586. You are sure about it?—Yes.

16,587. You did not take it into the kitchen to destroy it?—No, it was burnt in the room.

16,588. Now look at this again. (*The witness looked to the book.*) Those two entries are very much alike?—Yes, it is all in my handwriting.

16,589. But when we come further on, this is your writing too is it not?—Yes.

16,590. It is very different to the other?—It is mine.

16,591. But one is not at all like the other. This looks very much like a copy?—There is a difference in the ink.

16,592. It is not a difference in the ink. This looks very much like a copy all through January, and when we get to February it is a perfectly different hand, and it is dirty while the other is as clean as possible. It is not as if it were written from day to day, but as if it were all transcribed from something else, and then when you come to February it is going regularly on. Will you explain that if you please?—I cannot; it is different ink and it is cleaner, if you will allow me to explain.

16,593. This is a very suspicious thing indeed, I want you to explain this; if this was done in the regular course of business, and each entry made at

EIGHTEENTH DAY.

G. Castles.

26 June 1867.

the end of a fortnight, one would expect it to be dirty as having been used, but instead of that, it is as clean as possible all the way through until we get to the month of February, and then there is a different style of writing altogether, and then I find that the book is dirty and it looks like a book in use (*showing the book to the witness*) ?—Yes, it is not so clean I admit that.

16,594. You admit that it is not so clean; you admit that the handwriting is perfectly different?—It is my handwriting.

16,595. I know that it is your handwriting, but compare that handwriting with the entries in February; it is quite different?—It is the pen.

16,596. That is carelessly written and the other is very carefully written?—If you look at this I think you will find——

16,597. Give me an instance where, in the course of your regular business, you have made entries in the same careful manner as those first entries are made in. It strikes me very much that it is a copy of another book?—I think you will see there that this is written in very much the same way as that, if you will examine it.

The Chairman inquired of Mr. Dronfield when the deputation to London took place.

Mr. Dronfield replied that it was on the 17th of November.

16,598. (*Mr. Barstow to the witness.*) Where did you make the entries in this book?—In the committee room.

16,599. (*Chairman.*) You say that the book was mutilated and so on, but I think you said that it was not full?—The book which was burnt was full.

16,600. Where did you buy this book?—At Messrs. Pawson and Brailsford's, Church Gates.

16,601. When did you buy it?—At the latter end of last August or the first week in September. I could not swear which.

16,602. If you bought it you would have an entry of payment for it, would you not?—Yes.

16,603. Would it be in this book or in the other?—I should think it would be in that book, but I do not know. If I bought it in the first week in September it would.

16,604. If it were August it would be in the other book, because this book begins at the 5th of September?—Yes, if I bought it the latter end of August.

16,605. Are you sure that you bought it in August?—I am not sure whether it was the latter end of August or the first week in September.

16,606. Had you a bill of it?—No.

16,607. Did you buy it over the counter?—Yes.

16,608. Was it before or after the general meeting?—It was after the general meeting.

16,609. When was your general meeting?—It was in August.

16,610. But it was after the general meeting?—When I bought that book?

16,611. Yes?—Yes.

16,612. I find that your general meeting was on the 29th of August?—Well, I could not say whether it was or not.

16,613. Look at that book (*handing a book to the witness*) and tell me when it was?—(*After referring to the book*) It would be so by this.

16,614. Then it must be after the 29th of August that you bought it?—Yes, I should say so.

16,615. Ought it to appear in that book (*handing the book again to the witness*) if you bought it after that?—Yes, it ought to appear here.

16,616. There is no entry then on the 5th of September you see?—No.

16,617. Do you know whether when you made your last entry in the old one it would be a fortnight before the 5th of September?—It would be on the 29th of August, I think, or sometime about then.

16,618. If the 29th of August was the last entry in that book, and you bought this book after the general meeting on the 29th of August, it ought to appear here, and there is no entry of it. How do you explain that?—I do not know. I cannot explain it without it has been forgotten to be put down.

16,619. How could you balance your books?—I should have been out of pocket for it if I did not charge for it.

16,620. What did it cost?—I am sure I do not know. It was either half-a-crown or a shilling, or something; I believe it was half-a-crown.

16,621. Was anybody with you when you bought it?—No.

16,622. Of whom did you buy it?—I bought it in the shop.

16,623. Was it from a young lady or from a man that you bought it?—I think it was a boy.

16,624. What time of day was it?—I am sure I do not know; very likely it would be in the afternoon.

16,625. For what did you tell him that you wanted it?—I did not tell him that I wanted it for anything, only I wanted an account book.

16,626. For what did you ask?—I said that I wanted an account book.

16,627. Were you dressed as you are now?—Well, I believe I should be.

16,628. Were there any persons in the shop at the time when you bought it besides this boy?—Yes, I think there would be one or two. I think there were customers going in and out at the time.

16,629. You do not know any of the persons?—I do not know any of the persons.

16,630. Did you see either Mr. Pawson or Mr. Brailsford?—I do not know them personally.

The witness withdrew.

S. Stacey.

SAMUEL STACEY sworn and examined.

16,631. (*Mr. Barstow.*) You are the secretary of the edge tool grinders union are you not?—Yes.

16,632. How long have you been secretary?—About five years and a half.

16,633. Do you admit the practice of rattening in your union?—Yes, and consider it no sin.

(*Chairman.*) I believe that is the fact; there is no doubt about it.

16,634. (*Mr. Barstow.*) Are you aware that any violence has been committed upon anybody by your union?—Not that I am aware of.

16,635. I mean has any violence been committed on any one in your trade?—Certainly not.

16,636. Not within the last ten years?—Not within the last ten years.

16,637. I believe that is the case; how many members are there in your union?—Upon our books there would be something like 226 or 228, I think.

16,638. Do you produce your books?—Yes.

16,639. Have any threatening letters been sent?—Not to my knowledge.

16,640. In the rattening you have spoken of do you destroy property?—We merely remove them; we hide them.

16,641. And when the man settles you restore them to him, is that so?—Certainly.

16,642. But if he does not settle what then?—Perhaps they are never found again then; perhaps they get them back again as a matter of course.

16,643. (*Chairman.*) If they settle they get them back, but if they do not settle they do not get them back?—Oh yes, that is quite right. If you will allow me I will name an instance or two where they have rattened. I do not wish to close, but just to illustrate the thing; if you will allow me I will relate a case or two since Christmas. A person named George Steer was in arrear 10*s.* to us, and his band was taken and that made 15*s.*

EIGHTEENTH DAY.

S. Stacey.

26 June 1867.

16,644. What, 5*s*. for the expenses?—Certainly: It is a very good job is the rattening business you know. The person that took the band told me that he had taken it, and Steer came to me and said, "Why were not two others done?" (namely William Swallow and Henry Fawcett). I said, "I do not know." He said, "Should I be justified in taking theirs?" I said, "Perhaps there would be nobody more pleased to hear it than I should be. Do as thee will George, but nobody would be more pleased to hear it than I." The next day he came to me along with a witness, who is in court now, and he said, "How much have I to pay," and I said "15*s*." And that night he came to me and said, "Didn't you "say that I should be justified in taking the others?" I said, "No, I said I should not be sorry about it." He said, "I have 15*s*. to pay you haven't I?" I said, "Yes;" he said, "Here is 5*s*. then, and I have done the other two."

16,645. He owed 10*s*. and was rattened for it, and that made it with the expenses 15*s*., and then he went and rattened two other men, so that he only had to pay 5*s*.?—Yes, but he had the trouble.

16,646. You ratten not only for arrears of contributions, but also if a man breaks your rules in any way, do you not?—Well, not particularly. If he wishes to leave us we allow him to leave us.

16,647. (*Mr. Barstow.*) But supposing a master employs a man who is not a member of your trade, what do you do?—We leave him.

16,648. Is that the only thing you do?—Yes.

16,649. You never do anything else?—Not in our society.

16,650. (*Chairman.*) Do you remember Addis being employed?—Yes.

16,651. (*Mr. Barstow.*) Do you recollect calling upon Mr. Ward about Addis?—Yes.

16,652. James Reaney was with you, was he not? —Yes.

16,653. Did you not tell Mr. Ward that if he discharged Addis he would get his things back again?—No.

16,654. Or that the men would go back again to work?—No, never in my life.

16,655. You never said such a thing?—I never said such a thing. That belonged to the edge tool forgers, not us.

16,656. Did you not demand some money from Mr. Ward?—No, I was one of the deputation.

16,657. (*Mr. Chance.*) Did you go to Mr. Ward? —Yes, along with the others.

16,658. You went to Mr. Ward with James Reaney?—Certainly; yes.

16,659. Did you not ask him if the matter could be brought to a conclusion?—Certainly; that is comfortable. I think that it should be.

16,660. (*Mr. Barstow.*) But how was the matter to be brought to a conclusion?—By the men working again.

16,661. Were you not aware that Mr. Ward's nuts had been taken?—Yes.

16,662. Did you not offer to make an arrangement with him?—Not personally. I was there when the arrangement was made.

16,663. Reaney did it in your presence, did he?—Certainly.

16,664. What was the nature of the arrangement that you proposed?—I did not propose anything.

16,665. What was the nature of the arrangement which Reaney proposed in your presence?—That he should turn away Addis and pay the expenses.

16,666. (*Chairman.*) What do you mean by "expenses"?—The men's wages that were walking about.

16,667. Was anything said about his things being restored?—We certainly hinted that things would be made comfortable if he would oblige us.

16,668. Did you mean that you would restore his nuts?—Yes.

16,669. (*Mr. Barstow.*) What did you mean by wishing Addis to be turned away?—We did not wish it.

16,670. I thought you said just now that part of the arrangement was that Addis should be turned away?—We did not suggest that. I heard it suggested.

16,671. You were part of the deputation?—Certainly, but there was a deputation previous to that.

16,672. (*Chairman.*) You had better answer the questions which are put to you?—Certainly.

16,673. (*Mr. Barstow.*) Were you aware that Addis was assaulted?—Yes, by reading of it.

16,674. You never knew of it before?—Never before. By reading of it at the time, I mean.

16,675. But did you hear at the time when he was assaulted that he had been assaulted?—Yes, when the case came before the magistrates, I then heard it.

16,676. Who were the men who assaulted him?—They did not belong to my trade.

16,677. (*Chairman.*) That is not an answer to the question. Who were the men who assaulted him?—Well, I do not know.

16,678. You have answered about the rattening. Did you ever authorize a man's bellows to be cut?—The bellows do not belong to us; most decidedly not.

16,679. Did you ever do anything else in that way, except authorizing a man's bands or nuts to be taken? —Certainly, we would take his sofa if we could.

16,680. You would steal anything if you could, under those circumstances?—We would be bailiffs if we could.

16,681. The law does not give you the power to act as a sheriff's officer or anything of that kind?—No, we have to shut our eyes to the facts.

16,682. And seize upon other people's property?—Yes, and we ask them to shut their eyes and not to look at us.

16,683. But if a man's eyes happen to be open, you are aware that you would be liable to be taken up for stealing?—Yes, and we should have to have whatever they had a mind to give us.

16,684. And you would suffer it?—Yes, we should suffer it.

16,685. You would risk it?—Yes, we should risk it.

16,686. You take upon yourself the duty of a bailiff?—Yes, I belong to two unions; I belong to the Poor Law union myself, and if I do not pay my contributions they will ratten me for them.

16,687. What are you?—I am secretary of the edge tool and wool shear grinders.

16,688. But are you working now at the trade?—No.

16,689. What are you?—I am secretary.

16,690. But how do you make your living?—I am paid.

16,691. But what is your business?—Secretary.

16,692. (*Mr. Barstow.*) Are you nothing but secretary?—Nothing.

16,693. (*Chairman.*) Have you a public house?—No; I am a public house customer sometimes.

16,694. Have you a minute book?—Yes, I believe we have.

16.695. Have you it with you?—No.

16,696. Why have you not brought it?—Our minute keeper keeps it.

16,697. Who is your minute keeper?—Charles Styring.

16,698. (*Mr. Chance.*) If there were legal powers given to you to enforce the payment of contributions do you think that that would do away with rattening? —Most decidedly, yes. It would make my job a lot easier.

The witness withdrew.

EIGHTEENTH DAY.

J. Cann.

26 June 1867.

JAMES CANN sworn and examined.

16,699. (*Chairman.*) What are you ?—I am secretary to the united joiners tool makers.

16,700. How many branches are there in your society ?—Four branches.

16,701. What are they ?—Joiners tool makers, brace-bit forgers, filers, and grinders.

16,702. How long have you been secretary ?—About three and a half years.

16,703. How long have you been a member of the union ?—Ever since there was a union. There have been various unions ever since I was 21—I suppose for 20 years.

16,704. Has there been any rattening in your society ?—Yes.

16,705. Has it been a usual practice ?—Well, it has been a practice. It has occurred about three or four times during the three and a half years that I have been secretary of that society.

16,706. And I suppose a great many times before that ?—Well, it has occurred, but not often in any cases.

16,707. What do you ratten for ?—For arrears of contribution principally, and generally if the rules are broken, but principally for arrears of contribution.

16,708. But you do ratten for the breaking of the rules of the society ?—Yes, we have no other way of doing it.

16,709. During the time that you have been secretary have there been any outrages in any of the branches of your society ?—No, not the slightest.

16,710. (*Chairman.*) You are not quite correct. Do you know Messrs. Craven ?—I have heard the name, but it is not connected with our trade in the least.

16,711. Do you remember whether on the 19th of May 1862 Messrs. Craven were not rattened ?—It is not in our business. We are the joiner's tool makers and not the joiners.

16,712. (*Mr. Chance.*) Is the joiners society a different society from the joiners tools society ?—Entirely.

16,713. I understand you to say that during your time you know of no outrages having been committed by your society ?—There have not been any.

16,714. (*Chairman.*) They have never been reported to you ?—They have never been imputed to us. There have not been any.

16,715. (*Mr. Chance.*) Supposing that you were to obtain a mode of enforcing your contributions by a legal process, do you think that it would do away with rattening ?—I think that if we had this, that if a man once entered himself a member, we should have power to claim contribution in the county court, or in some other summary mode until he should give a month's notice ; that would do away with rattening altogether. So far as we are concerned I am sure that it would.

16,716. But supposing that you had power to enforce payments of your contributions would that do away with rattening for other infringements of your rules ?—I never knew a man scarcely that infringed the rule if he was straight upon the books.

16,717. But do you limit your number of apprentices ?—Not the number.

16,718. But do you limit the sources from which they are taken ?—Members sons.

16,719. But may not a member infringe a rule with regard to apprentices and yet be straight upon your books ?—Well, very rarely ; I have never known a case of that sort.

16,720. What is the connexion between the two ?—Well, he might of course infringe the rule in that respect, and still be a clear member upon our books.

16,721. I should have thought so. Supposing that you had that legal power to enforce your contributions ; if a man takes apprentices from other people except those which are allowed by your society, would that legal power to enforce contributions prevent rattening on the ground of taking apprentices from other sources ?—I cannot state what course would be taken.

16,722. But supposing that you had legal power to enforce your contributions, if a man takes apprentices from other people except those which are allowed by your society, would that legal power prevent rattening on the ground of taking apprentices from other people ?—I should not think that it would, but I think that the principal part of the rattening arises from nonpayment of contributions.

16,723. And doing away with rattening in the one case you think would have a tendency to do away with it in the other ?—Yes.

16,724. (*Chairman.*) You have a rule against taking apprentices have you not ?—Yes, for the present, except members sons. Our trade is over-handed at present. If we were under-handed we should extend it and take in other than members sons, but at present we are over-handed.

16,725. (*Mr. Barstow.*) How many members have you ?—About 160.

16,725*a*. How many men have you on the box ?—At the present time we have about a dozen as near as I can state.

16,726. Do you call that overhanded ?—There are more branches than one, and some of the branches are over-handed. The joiners tool branch to which I belong is decidedly over-handed.

16,727. How much can a man earn a week at your trade in your branch ?—A good man on an average might earn 27*s*. a week or something like that (decidedly not more) at the present prices. That would not be the average of the trade by any means.

16,728. Which of those four is the most highly paid branch ?—That is a very much disputed point. If I had to decide it I should think the grinders were the best paid branch.

16,729. And what would a grinder make a week ?—Well, 2*l*. perhaps ; but not being a grinder I cannot speak exactly. Then he has heavier expenses than other men.

16,730. (*Mr. Chance.*) Do you consider that the rule with regard to restricting the number of apprentices in the way that you have mentioned is a fair rule to be adopted in trades ?—Well, I consider it an expedient rule in the present state of our society. I speak of nothing beyond that.

16,731. But supposing that all trades adopted the same rule, what then ?—Well, I think that the trades unions are things altogether of expediency, and not a matter of positive right.

16,732. But supposing that as a matter of expediency all trades adopted the same principle, what would happen ?—Well, I would rather speak about our own trade and not go into general matters.

16,733. (*Mr. Barstow.*) I am told just now that you claim the sole right to grind skates ?—Yes ; in connexion with our union skates and brace bits.

16,734. (*Chairman.*) You would not allow anybody else to do it ?—I do not know about allowing ; there are men that grind skates who do not contribute to us.

16,735. (*Mr. Barstow.*) Have you ever endeavoured to prohibit a man who was not in your union from grinding skates ?—We have endeavoured to prevent it.

16,736. (*Chairman.*) And have you rattened him if he did it ?—No ; we have never rattened a man for grinding skates.

16,737. (*Mr. Barstow.*) How have you endeavoured to prevent a man from grinding skates ?—I do not remember that we have had any specific case of the kind.

16,738. Perhaps I may be able to remind you ; how have you endeavoured to prevent a man from grinding skates ?—I cannot remember any special case, but I was speaking merely of what we should do.

16,739. Did you ever hear of a man named Widdison ?—Yes.

16,740. Do you remember whether he was so prohibited ?—Now you name it, he was.

16,741. For whom was he working ?—He was

EIGHTEENTH DAY.

J. Cann.

26 June 1867.

working at Messrs. Ibbetson's wheel, but he was working for Mr. Cann.

16,742. What is Mr. Cann ?—A skate maker.

16,743. I suppose that Widdison ground skates for him ?—Yes ; he was a surgical instrument grinder himself, and secretary of the surgical instrument grinders trade.

16,744. How long ago is this ?—It may be about 18 months or two years ; it will be within two years.

16,745. I am informed that you prohibited him from grinding skates ?—Well, we had a meeting upon the subject to which we invited him, and he came and he laid down his case why he thought he should grind them. We passed a resolution upon it that as he had a good trade of his own and good places in it, we requested him to let our trade alone and stick to his own. There was no more prohibition than that.

16,746. (*Chairman.*) He was told not to grind skates ?—We requested him not to do it ; there was nothing further done.

16,747. (*Mr. Barstow.*) Did he comply ?—He did comply. I believe there was nothing further done than that.

16,748. What would you have done to him if he had not complied ?—Well, I am sure I cannot tell you. We should not have committed an outrage upon him, most certainly.

16,749. (*Mr. Chance.*) Do you ever use any mode of intimidation for the purpose of obtaining your object ?—Not the slightest.

16,750. You never have done so ?—We never have done, nor has anybody belonging to us.

16,751. (*Chairman.*) Are you aware of any threatening letters having been sent ?—I have not sent any, and I do not know of any.

16,752. You do not know of any in your union ?—I do not.

16,753. Is it your belief that none have been sent ?—It is. We have carried on very peaceably.

16,754. Have you heard of any violence being practised towards the person of any man, or of any man being beaten or molested in any way ?—Not that I have heard of.

16,755. All that you have done is to ratten ?—That is the worst we have done, and not a great deal of that. It has been the last resource.

The witness withdrew.

H. Cutts.

HENRY CUTTS recalled and further examined.

16,756. (*Chairman.*) I think you said yesterday you had no rattening in your trade ?—Not connected with the trade.

16,757.—But do you recognize rattening in your trade ?—No, we do not; we have a more expensive method, that of withdrawing men.

16,758. I did not ask you about that ; I ask you about rattening. Do you ratten in your trade or not ?—We do not.

16,759. You said so before, I know. Have you ever in any case caused the goods that have been rattened—bands or otherwise—to be restored ?—No, we have had no connexion with it.

16,760. You have never done so ?—Never.

16,761. Have you ever given a note to a man, telling him where his tools would be found ?—Never.

16,762. Do you know Jonathan Woolhouse, who lives near the Grange at Butterthwaite Wheel in the parish of Ecclesfield ?—I do not know such a man.

16,763. You do not recollect his being rattened ?—I do not. I do not even know what trade he belongs to.

16,764. Where do you live ?—At 92, Arundel Street, on the trade premises.

16,765. Is it a public house where you meet ?—We have premises of our own where we meet.

16,766. Where do you meet ?—The general meeting meets at the Temperance Hall, but for the monthly meetings we meet at the bottom room of the Temperance Hall. All the other business is done at the society's private office.

16,767. You are not aware of any case of a person applying for his bands ?—We were formerly, up to last September, in Cambridge Street.

16,768. Do you know the "Moseley Arms ?"—Yes, very well.

16,769. Is that where the file grinders meet ?—Yes.

16,770. Have you anything to do with them ?—No. We are in alliance with them.

16,771. Do you know any case where an application has been made to the file grinders, and bands have been restored ?—No, I do not know any single instance.

16,772. Dut do you know that they ratten ?—They admit it.

16,773. Do you know a person of the name of Benjamin Morton ?—I know three at least.

16,774. Then you know one ?—Oh, yes.

16,775. He works at Hill and Sons, I believe ?—Yes.

16,776. You know that man ?—Yes.

16,777. Did he come to you a day or two ago ?—Yes.

16,778. Yesterday ?—Yes, he was here yesterday.

16,779. I thought so. What did he come to you about ?—He had a summons to attend here.

16,780. I know that; what did he come to you about ? To see if we knew anything about it.

16,781. About what ?—About what he had got summoned for.

16,782. Did he ask you if it was about Torr's case ?—It was in this way: he said he had got a summons, and I said what about, and he said it was something about Torr's case.

16,783. Did he tell you how he happened to know that it was about Torr's case ? for the summons was simply to attend here ?—No, he did not.

16,784. He must have been very cunning then to know that it was about Torr's case ?—Well, that is not for me to say.

16,785. How did he know ?—I do not know.

16,786. Did he ask you about Torr's case ?—No.

16,787. Did he not ask you if it were a trade business ?—No.

16,788. Mind ; did he not ask you if it were a trade business ?—No.

16,789. Are you certain about it ?—I am.

16,790. Did he not ask you if it were a trade busi ness ?—He did not.

16,791. Did he tell you who had done it ?—No.

16,792. Do you know a person of the name of Sam Owen ?—Yes, he is on strike.

16,793. Now I ask you, having called your attention to his name, whether you know who did it ?—I do not.

16,794. Did you ever hear that Sam Owen did it ?—No.

16,795. Do you know a person of the name of Dicky Dyott ?—I know Dicky Dyott.

16,796. Do you know whether he did it or not ?—I do not.

16,797. Did not Morton tell you that he knew about it ?—No, he told me that he himself and a man working at the same place, called Thomas Rawson, had been having a spree and had been jawing about this thing, and I said "Very well, in this case——"

16,798. Did he not tell you that Rawson had told him that he had taken his box, cut his bellows, and tapped his cistern ?—No, he did not tell me that.

16,799. Did he not tell you that Dicky Dyott was with him and that Dicky Dyott lay upon the privy while the watchman went away ?—He did not.

16,800. Will you swear he did not ?—I will swear he did not.

16,801. Nothing of the kind ?—Nothing of the kind.

EIGHTEENTH DAY.

H. Cutts.

26 June 1867.

16,802. And you did not know when you gave your evidence that Rawson was the man that cut Mr. Torr's bellows?—No.

16,803. Have you never heard of that?—No; I said, "If you have had any drunken spree or anything "of that kind amongst you you must do your own "business."

16,804. Have you an executive committee?—Yes.

16,805. Have you produced their books?—No; the minutes?

16,806. Yes?—Yes.

16,807. Have we seen them?—No.

16,808. Where are they?—They are at the office. I have arranged with Mr. Barker that whenever you like to order a person to go you can have them.

16,809. I should like it to he arranged that we can have the books of the executive committee?—Very well, you can have them. I have arranged that you can have them, but being a large trade they are heavy and we could not lug them backwards and forwards.

16,810. You have minutes of the executive committee have you not?—Yes, we have a minute book of the delegate meetings, which are held monthly, of the general meetings which are held quarterly, and of the executive committee meetings which are held monthly.

16,811. How many books are there?—There are two books which go back a great many years, I cannot say how many.

16,812. But does it contain the minutes of the executive committee?—Yes, of every case that comes before it.

16,813. A proper entry of every case that comes before it?—Yes, as proper as we can make it.

16,814. You say you do know Sam Owen?—Yes.

16,815. Do you recollect when Mr. Torr's bellows were cut?—I remember the time.

16,816. Do not you recollect that immediately after his bellows were cut you sent Sam Owen up to Newcastle?—Sam Owen went to work at Newburn, but I do not know the time.

16,817. Did he go to work at Newburn at the expense of the trade? did you find him the money?—If he was on the box (I am not sure whether he was or not) we should pay his fare; we always do.

16,818. Nothing more?—No.

16,819. You gave him nothing for his fare up to Newburn?—He would get 15*s*. His fare is 10*s*. 10*d*. and the other is a start for him in any little matter that he may want.

16,820. Do you recollect his going?—I recollect his going.

16,821. You recollect the sum paid?—I recollect the sum paid; it is always that sum either to Sunderland or Newburn. We have a district in each of those places.

16,822. Did he not go to Newburn almost immediately after Torr's bellows were cut?—I cannot speak to that.

16,823. Do you not believe that?—No, I think not.

16,824. Did he not go to get out of the way because he was suspected?—Certainly not.

16,825. And the trade did not find him the means of getting out of the way because he was suspected?—Certainly not.

16,826. Nothing of the kind?—Nothing of the kind, it was his own freewill. We generally at the roll call say, "We want a man for so and so," and whoever volunteers in that line goes.

16,827. You know I asked you about Torr's case yesterday, and I asked you if you knew anything about it, and you said No. Why did you not tell me that this man Morton had been calling upon you to inquire about that business?—We never got to that, I should have concealed nothing.

16,828. That is what I complain of. Why did you not tell us that?—I never saw any reason for it.

15,829. We are here you know to inquire into all the outrages committed?—Yes, I am here to answer all the questions you put to me.

16,830. If you knew about Morton calling upon you, and you knew that it was about Torr's business, why did you not mention it?—He told me he expected it would be that, and he seemed to me to be perplexed in his mind about it; and I said to him, "Well, if you have anything on your mind about it it is amongst you and you must do it as you like," and besides I then knew he was aiming here.

16,831. And that was your reason for keeping it back?—I should think that would be my sole reason. I knew he was waiting in the court. He sent for me and said, "I am the wrong man." I said, "In that "case they must have intended to have summoned "Benjamin Morton that managed for Torr," the party that came to see me respecting the dispute. There are three Benjamin Mortons, his son, and the manager for him, and I think there is another besides them.

The witness withdrew.

CHARLES BAGSHAW sworn and examined.

C. Bagshaw.

16,832. (*Chairman.*) What are you?—I am a razor smith by trade, but I am a clerk.

16,833. Are you secretary of a union?—I am secretary of the fork grinders and secretary of the patent scythe makers.

16,834. How long have you been secretary?—About six years of the patent scythe trade, and better than two years to the fork grinders.

16,835. In your trade do you ratten?—Well, I have never paid anything for rattening, but still they do ratten, and I do not know of anything that has ever been paid in either branch for rattening.

16,836. But rattening is done?—Yes; it is done in both, but there have been very few cases indeed.

16,837. Do you know how many cases of rattening have occurred during the last two years?—Well, I only know of them by report. Perhaps there have been some half-dozen. I think so; that is all I know of.

16,838. Is it for failure of payment of contributions?—I think it is.

16,839. But I suppose that if there were any violation of any other rule that would be the way in which you would enforce it?—No; that would not be the way. If there is a violation of any rule we have an amalgamation of three branches, and we should withdraw, but there would be no rattening.

16,840. It would be only for payment of contributions?—Well, that is not sanctioned by the trade.

16,841. But it is done, you say?—It is done, but in what way I do not know.

16,842. And I suppose that if a man came to you and said, "I have rattened another, and have got his bands here," and asked for the money, you would get the five shillings for him, would you not?—No; I never charged a penny in my life, and would not. I would not be a party to it.

16,843. Then what do you mean by saying that it is done, although you do not know of it?—I mean that parties do it, but I do not know of any given case. I know only of one belonging to the patent scythe trade, where Joseph Hopkinson came to me and said he had taken the screws off at the Globe Works, and he said he wanted paying for it. I said, "Thou must go to them that set thee on; I shall not pay thee aught for it." He said I was a very shabby fellow. I said I should not pay. He came to the committee. I told the committee that I came to be secretary for them with a distinct understanding that there was to be no rattening, and that I should not be secretary if there was any rattening. He only said last week that I was a very shabby fellow, and put some very bad language to it because I had not paid him.

16,844. Did the committee pay it?—The committee

EIGHTEENTH DAY.

C. Bagshaw.

26 June 1867.

have not paid it in any way to my knowledge. If they have paid it, they have paid it from private subscription and not from the funds.

16,845. You say that it is paid from private subscription?—No, I cannot say that; but if they have paid it they have paid it from private subscription. I cannot say that they have paid it at all.

16,846. But nobody rattens for nothing, you know? —They do not, but I have an impression that the reason why there have been so few cases is because the society does not pay them.

16,847. There have been very few lately?—There have been few, but when I went to them as secretary I went with a distinct understanding that there should be no rattening.

16,848. But before your time there was a good deal of rattening, was there?—Yes.

16,849. Since you have taken this office I suppose that you have not taken the view which Mr. Stacey has taken, that you do not consider it a sin to ratten? —I do consider it a sin.

16,850. Therefore you differ from Mr. Stacey on that point?—I do so far as my own individual opinion is concerned.

16,851. And you say that you have discountenanced it, and that you believe that in consequence it is less done?—I do.

16,852. And any secretary might easily discountenance it?—Yes, but then he would have to take this firm action to prevent it.

16,853. And if rattening prevailed you would, I suppose, at once come to the conclusion that the secretary was a little lax?—I should at once come to the conclusion that the secretary must have some knowledge of it, unless he was to take the stand which I took.

16,854. And if he took the stand which you have taken then the rattening would be finished?—Yes.

16,855. And if the rattening continued you would say "It is quite clear that we must not go on in that way"?—I should.

16,856. Have you had any outrages at all?—None that I know of.

16,857. I think that I can refresh your memory a little about the fork grinders. Did you ever hear of a person called William Mason?—Yes, I have heard of him.

16,858. Have you ever heard of Samuel Gunson? —Yes, I have heard of Samuel Gunson.

16,859. Have you heard of a man of the name of Roebuck?—Yes.

16,860. Have you heard that outrages were committed upon all those three men on the very same day? —Yes, but not while I was secretary.

16,861. That was I think on February 17th, 1859? —I cannot tell anything about that; only I know that I made inquiry about it and that the general conversation when I went to be secretary was that it was done, but they did not state when. In the meeting two or three voices at once called out, saying that I was quite right in making the statement that I would not be secretary if those things were done.

16,862. I understand from that that your impression was when you made that statement to the meeting, that they had been done by the trade, and that you would have nothing to do with them if they were so continued?—I had that impression but I could not prove it.

16,863. Do you know what was done to Mason?— I do not, except so far as this. They said some gunpowder was put in the trough; that is all I know. I cannot say it positively.

16,864. But that was the story?—Yes.

16,865. And was he blown up?—Well, I do not know I am sure.

16,866. You recollect what was said. I only want to have a notion of what was said?—I cannot say that anything was said beyond what I have said now.

16,867. And what about Gunson, what was done to him?—Well, I understood that they were all three similar.

16,868. All three alike?—Yes.

16,869. All three blown up?—Well, they were blown up by powder being put in the troughs.

16,870. Do you know what they were?—Fork grinders.

16,871. Were they "at outs" with the union?— I do not know. I do not know anything about that.

16,872. You do not know whether at that time there was any dispute between them and the union? —I do not.

16,873. Then why did you think that it was a trade matter?—I never inquired, only I took general outside observation; I might say this: "How could this be done if the trade was not mixed up with it?" but I never began to inquire.

16,874. You said that at the general meeting did you?—I said that to the committee, and I made a public statement that I would not be secretary if there was any rattening or anything done contrary to the law of the country, and that they would have to deal with refractory members in a different way.

16,875. What did the society say to that?—Three or four voices called out "Quite right."

16,876. What did the committee say?—The committee said I was perfectly right.

16,877. Well, but did they say nothing more than that?—They said nothing more, only they said this, that I was right in taking the stand that I took, and that they would not be on the committee if there was anything of the sort done.

16,878. Was that all that was said?—That was all that was said.

16,879. That was all that passed?—Yes.

16,880. Then there was no person to come forward and say that it was not connected with the trade?— Yes, there was one person.

16,881. You told me that that was all that passed. Now you see I have refreshed your memory; was there anybody who said that it was not connected with trade?—There was one person who said it was not connected with trade.

16,882. Who said that?—I do not know he was, but one member of the committee said it was not in connexion with trade.

16,883. Do you know who he was?—I do not know now.

16,884. What did you say to that?—"That seems "strange to me;" and there was no other remark made.

16,885. It was strange and it is hard to conceive, is it not, how three separate men all in the same trade could have been blown up unless it was a trade business?—I think so.

16,886. And you believe that it was a trade business?—I do.

16,887. Who was secretary then?—I do not know. I know who was secretary when I took to the affair, but I do not know who was secretary then.

16,888. Have you the books of that time?—No, I have no books, only one book that they did business with; I brought the books of both trades though I was not summoned to do so.

16,889. That was quite right. Have you brought all the books which you have?—I have brought all the books I have.

16,890. You have been secretary of the fork grinders for two years have you not?—Yes, better than two years.

16,891. Have you all the fork grinders' books?—I have got all that they said they had (*producing the same*).

16,892. What books have you?—They are all there.

16,893. What are they?—There is a cash book, a scale book, a contribution book, and a minute book.

16,894. There are three minute books, are there?— Two; one of them was given into my hands when I became secretary.

16,895. Are those all the books which you are aware that they possess?—Yes, I looked in the box and I saw no other.

16,896. How far back do your minute books go?—The cash book goes back to November 1865.

16,897. An outrage like this, blowing up three men, could not be done by the trade without money being paid for it?—Well, I think not.

16,898. I should like to see the cash book of that period to see whether in point of fact any money was paid?—When I asked the committee about the books, they said that their society had been broken up.

16,899. The fork grinders'?—Yes.

16,900. When was that?—When I took to the secretaryship. They said that the society had been broken up and that they had not any more books, only that one that is there (*pointing to a book*).

16,901. They said that they had no other book but the minute book?—Yes, there is contribution and everything in one book.

16,902. (*Mr. Chance.*) Is this the minute book of 1863?—I think so, it is the only book they gave me without they gave me this (*referring to a book*). I would not be certain about this, but I think that it is the only book.

16,903. (*Chairman.*) When was the trade broken up?—They waited upon me about two years and a half since, I think——

16,904. When was the trade broken up?—I do not know; they had been broken up some time then, and they wanted me to——

16,905. When was the trade broken up?—I cannot say positively; they had been broken up perhaps seven or eight months when they came to me to try and reorganize them.

16,906. That is two years ago?—Better than two years ago.

16,907. Then they would be in union in 1857, at the time when those men, Mason, Gunson, and Roebuck were blown up?—I believe they were.

16,908. They would be in union for four or five years after that, would they not?—Yes, I think they would, but I cannot speak to it because I knew very little of them. They have been in union and out of union many times.

16,909. They were in union when those men were blown up, and then for four or five years after they were out of union, and then you started them and re-organized them?—Yes.

16,910. Where are the books? what account did they give you about the books?—The account they gave me was that that was all the books they had; that is either one or two.

16,911. The earliest book, according to this, begins in 1863; there is nothing before 1863; where are those other books applicable to 1857?—I do not know; they said they had not them; they said they had been broken up; the secretary had them, and they knew nothing about them.

16,912. You do not know who was the secretary in 1859?—No; I know who was the secretary at the time I went.

16,913. Who was he?—Joseph Sanderson.

16,914. You succeeded Joseph Sanderson?—Yes.

16,915. How long was he secretary?—I do not know.

16,916. Is he alive?—Yes.

16,917. Where does he live?—He lives in Healy, but he works at Sanderson's, in Carver Street; he is some relative, I do not know what.

16,918. Was he secretary for a number of years?—I think not, but I am not certain.

16,919. Do you know of any other person being secretary?—No.

16,920. In 1863 I understand there was a man named, not Sanderson, but Rowan?—They tell me that those parties were trying to get the trade together, and that they were only temporary secretaries of the committee; but they did not succeed.

16,921. (*Mr. Chance.*) Thomas Rowan would be secretary in 1863?—Yes, I should think he would.

16,922. (*Chairman.*) Is Rowan alive?—Yes.

16,923. Where does he live?—I cannot tell you where he lives; I know where he works.

16,924. Where?—At Drabble's, in Orchard Lane.

16,925. Was it a proper proceeding to destroy the books?—No.

16,926. Did you make some complaint about it?—Yes, I said it was a strange way of doing business, and I could not do business that way.

16,927. Whom did you say that to?—The committee.

16,928. Whom did you say that to?—To the committee at the time.

16,929. Can you tell me who they were when you entered three years ago?—No.

16,930. You told them that there were these books missing, and that you thought that it was a very improper mode of proceeding?—Yes. They said I was to get the books that I thought were requisite.

16,931. You had books to go on with? I speak of the past record of what they had been doing; had they a record of your proceedings in 1859? did you complain that they were missing?—Yes.

16,932. What did they say to that?—They said the society had been broken up, and they knew nothing at all about them.

16,933. Are you quite sure that you have never had any books since you have been there containing entries of payments during the year 1859?—I am quite sure I have never had any books but what are there.

16,934. Are you quite sure of that?—Yes.

16,935. And you have never seen any?—I have never seen any.

16,936. And you do not know what has become of them?—I do not know what has become of them.

16,937. And you do not know who has got them?—I do not know who has got them.

16,938. Do you know whether they are in existence?—I do not; I do not believe they are.

16,939. For what purpose should they have been destroyed?—If they are destroyed they would be destroyed for the purpose of hiding things; but I cannot say they are destroyed for all that.

16,940. Will you pledge your word that they have not been destroyed since there was any question about this inquiry?—I will; I am certain of that, because I had the books all in my possession, there have been no books destroyed.

16,941. Do you know whether the practices of the union had been otherwise wrong? there have been these outrages; have you known of any other things that they have done besides the rattenings?—There has been a good deal of rattening. I know by newspaper reports, and I come to the conclusion that the other things have taken place in the same way.

16,942. Have you heard of any other things which they have done?—Only by reading in the paper.

16,943. Have you seen in the papers that other things were attributable to them which in your judgment were trade matters?—No, I cannot say I have.

16,944. If they have done a good deal of rattening and other things, and have paid for it, there would be a reason why the books have been destroyed?—Yes.

16,945. Did you ever hear from any committeeman or members of your union that they were destroyed for that purpose?—No.

16,946. Or that there was anything in them that they would not like to be seen?—No.

16,947. Have you seen any entry in any book which would at all show that money had been paid for a purpose of this description?—No, I have not.

16,948. Have you auditors?—Yes, we have a committee. I have nothing to do with receiving the money or paying it over; we have a collector that goes round and collects the money called the financial secretary, and then the committee both receives and pays all the monies over, and the committee is changed from time to time, as you see by that book.

16,949. It is a very unfortunate thing if it is done for no dishonest purpose that they are not here. Did you write this first entry—it is strange language,—in 1863?—No, that was before my time.

16,950. I see, "General meeting, January 20th, "1863. Thomas Roebuck in the chair: Resolved,

EIGHTEENTH DAY.

C. Bagshaw.

26 June 1867.

"that it is the opinion of this meeting that the "great amount of competition of rival producers "produces the great amount of poverty, misery, "crime, and degradation that prevails over the whole "trade, and unless some stringent measures be adopted "to retard the progress of the two monster evils, the "whole trade will become recipient of parish relief, "and ultimately be hurried off to an untimely pauper's "grave." What were the two monster evils ?—I will show you a work of Dr. Holland.

16,951. Never mind Dr. Holland. What are the two monster evils ?—I do not know. I know nothing about it; only when men are reduced to something like from 75 to 200 per cent., and by being in the union they get advanced from 75 to 200 per cent., and when men work at 10*d.* a gross out of the trade, and at 2*s.* 6*d.* a gross when in the trade, and less than that, they might use that strange language on account of that, I cannot say,—not being there and not knowing anything about it; but when men are reduced from 2*l.* a week to 10*s.* a week, it might make them use strong language, and do many things that they might not otherwise do.

16,952. You can throw no more light upon it ?—No, I cannot; if I could I would.

16,953. What is the number of your fork grinders ?—About 130 in the union, and 30 out, taking it at an average.

16,954. How many are on the box ?—We have had on the average from 30 to 40 per week I should think for the last eight months.

16,955. There has been nothing in the patent scythe grinders ?—I do not belong to the patent scythe grinders trade.

16,956. You are the secretary ?—I am secretary to the patent scythe makers, not the grinders.

16,957. Has there been any rattening among the patent scythe makers ?—Only in the case of Marshall, that is the only one that I can recollect belonging to them.

16,958. Have there been no outrages connected with them ?—No, not that I know of.

16,959. How many are they in number ?—They number about 60; the books are here.

16,960. How many non-members are there in the trade ?—I think there would be about a dozen, but I cannot say positively.

16,961. How many are there at the box ?—Not many now.

16,962. How many on the box on an average ?—There are three now.

16,963. What are the wages of the fork grinders ?—When working they will get about 2*l.* a week, that is the report given to me, and those that are out, 10*s.*; the fact is that that is a statement made publicly to me.

16,964. Do you suppose that the 30 members who are out only get 10*s.* a week ?—No, I think they get nearly the same price as those that are in, but the union men are keeping the price up for them.

16,965. The men who are out are getting the same price, and not contributing to the union; what is the contribution to the union ?—4*s.* a week.

16,966. Therefore the men out of the union would save that ?—Yes, they would save that; but they might happen to lose 4*s.* or 5*s.* in other ways.

16,967. Why ?—In little reductions. They get nearly the same price, but there would be some little reductions to get work in some cases.

16,968. If they had a good master there would not be ?—The fork trade is the most unfortunate trade in Sheffield, they are master journeymen, nearly all of them; they are masters that take their wallets on their backs. They get the fork from the maker, and they go to the table knife manufacturers and sell them, and I daresay that the reduction will come down upon them as much as 30*s.* a week.

16,969. Who reduces it ?—It is from competition among themselves when out of the union; they are little masters; working masters.

16,970. They do it for less price ?—Yes, they compete one against the other.

16,971. The union is to avoid competition ?—Yes.

16,972. What do the patent scythe makers earn ?—According to the best information that I have received they get somewhere about 30*s.* a week, but I could not be quite sure about that. I have questioned some of them, and that has been their general answer. Some of them might get more than that even.

16,973. How many days does a fork grinder work to earn 2*l.* a week ?—Five days at present; sometimes they have to limit themselves to four days, and sometimes three days, and sometimes two days.

16,974. Have they got as much as 2*l.* in two days ?—No. They would have to submit to earning 18*s.* or 1*l.* if they worked two days.

16,975. (*Mr. Chance.*) Do you attribute it to the fact of having a number of small masters that there is a necessity for the union ?—No, not exactly, but I believe there is a greater necessity on account of all of them being working masters as it were.

16,976. Supposing that the trade were in the hands of the larger manufacturers, would there be the same danger of the prices being lowered ?—No, I wish it was in their hands. I believe the manufacturers as a class would not reduce them in that way.

16,977. Would there be so great a necessity for trades unions if the business was in the hands of the larger manufacturers ?—There would be a necessity for trades unions even if there were larger manufacturers, but not so great a necessity as there is now. Human nature is human nature with masters and men, and there are even masters who think of nothing but getting money, and there are many masters who think about their workmen, and some do not care about them if they may be rich, and therefore the honest master is compelled to reduce his workmen many times in consequence of the dishonest masters reducing them, and going into the market and cutting him out.

The witness withdrew.

G. Bulloss.

George Bulloss sworn and examined.

16,978. (*Mr. Barstow.*) You are the secretary of the Fork Grinders Union ?—Yes.

16,979. How long have you been secretary ?—Better than two years—nearly three years.

16,980. Have you any rattening in your union ?—We do not recognise it at present. It was done.

16,981. Does it exist ?—No, not at present.

16,982. What was the last case of rattening that you heard of in your union ?—Nearly three years since, when we first formed. We have only been formed about three years.

16,983. You are the first secretary ?—No, there was one before me three or four months.

16,984. I suppose we may take it, according to your evidence, that your union is quite free from it now ?—Yes.

16,985. Are you aware of any cases of personal violence that have been used to any member of your union ?—No.

16,986. Or to any non-union men working in your trade ?—No.

16,987. What course do you adopt to enforce the payment of contributions ?—At present we are amalgamated with the grinders and casters, and we take their men out, of course.

16,988. That is the only mode employed ?—Yes.

16,989. Do you ever ratten the grinders ?—No.

16,990. Or get them to ratten one another ?—No.

16,991. (*Chairman.*) Or to ratten for you ?—No.

16,992. Now you are amalgamated ?—Yes.

16,993. And the grinders ratten ?—Of course I do not say they do now.

16,994. They say they do?—All grinders do more or less, I daresay.

16,995. Do they ever ratten for you?—No.

16,996. If they stop the trade it is much the same as if you do it yourselves?—We never asked them such a question as that, and I do not suppose we shall do.

16,997. (*Mr. Barstow.*) What is the number in your union?—134 union men.

16,998. How many non-union men are there?—About 40.

16,999. How many men have you at present on the box?—About 17.

17,000. I am told that you have a good many small masters who are contributing members of your union?—Yes.

17,001. (*Chairman.*) You never heard of any rattening?—No.

17,002. If a man does not submit to your rules, or pay his contribution, how do you enforce it?—We let them run themselves clean out.

17,003. How "run clean out"?—We do not meddle with them unless we can meddle with them by taking their grinders away from them and paying them the wages for standing still.

17,004. That is the only course you have?—That is the only course we have.

17,005. Do you never adopt any measures of violence?—No.

17,006. Or intimidation?—No.

17,007. Do you hoot them or picket them?—No, we never do anything of that kind.

17,008. (*Mr. Chance.*) Do you use any forcible measure to make men join your union if they are not members?—No.

17,009. You try to persuade them?—Yes, all we can.

17,010. (*Mr. Barstow.*) What is your contribution?—2*s.* for a man and 1*s.* for a boy.

17,011. What wages can a fair average workman earn?—4*s.* 6*d.* a day, working eight hours. We work hours according to the demand; we are working seven hours a day at present.

17,012. Does that contribution include the apprentice too?—It is 3*s.* for a man and a boy.

17,013. Does the wage include a man and a boy?—One man's wages, not a man and a boy.

17,014. How much do a man and boy get, 6*s.*?—They will get more than that; 7*s.* 6*d.* perhaps for a man and boy.

17,015. (*Mr. Chance.*) Do the union men and non-union men work friendly together?—Yes; I believe they would speak to one another as though they were brothers in the streets. I do not think they have any malice at all whatever.

17,016. (*Chairman.*) Not in the shop?—I never heard tell or saw any in the shops either.

The witness withdrew.

GEORGE AUSTIN sworn and examined.

G. Austin.

17,017. (*Mr. Chance.*) What are you?—I am secretary to the railway spring makers, and I am also secretary to the scythe makers.

17,018. How long have you been secretary to the railway spring makers?—About nine and half years.

17,019. And the scythe makers?—About six years.

17,020. Are the two branches amalgamated?—No, they have no connexion whatever. I have been a member of the union since the union commenced, that is since September 1857, 10 years; that is the railway spring makers union.

17,021. You are not a member of the other, you are simply secretary?—Yes.

17,022. Has there been any rattening in your trade?—Such a thing was never known.

17,023. Are you speaking of either of those unions?—I speak of the railway spring makers.

17,024. Has there been any rattening amongst the scythe makers that you know of?—Yes, I can recollect four cases during the last six and a half years that I have been in connexion with them.

17,025. Have those cases of rattening been cases of rattening on account of the trade?—I believe they have, though they have kept them back from me.

17,026. Has not any notice of them been given to you while you were secretary?—None whatever.

17,027. (*Chairman.*) Who has done it?—I really cannot tell, I never knew.

17,028. (*Mr. Chance.*) No one who has rattened has come to you to ask for money?—Never.

17,029. Have you never paid any money?—No, I never knew anything of the kind.

17,030. Have any rattening cases ever been brought before the committee?—Yes.

17,031. Do you know what the committee have done upon those cases?—The committee never paid a farthing in my presence.

17,032. They know that rattening has been done?—Yes.

17,033. Have you ever found them discourage it or deny it?—They have denied it.

17,034. But not discouraged it?—No, they have not discouraged it, only it is purely on my account and I believe from my influence that it is discouraged altogether now. I do not think that another case will ever happen in connexion with it.

17,035. As far as your belief is concerned were those cases, although denied, encouraged by the trade before your time?—The trade had encouraged them, and had done for a number of years, they did it with impunity thinking they were doing right.

17,036. As far as you are concerned you have no personal knowledge of rattening?—No.

17,037. (*Chairman.*) You have set your face against it?—Yes, as every man will testify.

17,038. (*Mr. Chance.*) Since you have set your face against it has rattening ceased?—Yes, I have not heard of a single case for 18 months.

17,039. Have you ever heard of any outrages in connexion with the railway spring makers?—Never.

17,040. Have you with regard to the scythe makers?—A case came under my notice, I believe, in January 1866; a man waited upon me, an utter stranger to me, and informed me that a pair of bellows had been cut at some place that I did not know, near Bole Hill I think they called it. We had some conversation upon the matter, and I told the man, "If you can prove to "me that it has been done by our trade I will not only "resign my office but I will do all I can to bring the "parties to justice."

17,041. What trade was he in?—This man was a scythe grinder that came to me, and he was an utter stranger to me.

17,042. He was not in your union?—No; I asked him his name; before I had any conversation with him he gave me his name; his name was Cartledge. He could not satisfy me that it was connected with the trade, but in order to bring the matter right I called the committee together immediately to investigate the affair. I called a committee together the day or day but one following; that was a committee of scythe makers; they are quite exempt from the railway spring makers.

17,043. (*Chairman.*) This may have been done by the scythe grinders?—The secretary of the scythe grinders was with him when he came to me. They could not trace it to their trade, and so they came to me.

17,044. Then you brought it before the committee?—Yes, and I asked this man to attend; I called the committee for Friday night; I investigated the affair and asked the committee. They all denied it, but this man failed to attend. I brought it before the members at the next general meeting, and there I fully inquired into it and I could make nothing of it, and

EIGHTEENTH DAY.

G. Austin.

26 June 1867.

heard nothing more of it, and I have heard nothing of it from that day to this.

17,045. (*Mr. Chance.*) Are the scythe makers amalgamated with any other union?—They are amalgamated with the Association of Organised Trades of Sheffield.

17,046. They are not amalgamated with the scythe grinders?—Yes, I believe they are.

17,047. That will explain the reason why he came to you as the secretary of the scythe makers?—Yes.

17,048. You heard nothing more about it?—No, that was the last case I heard of.

17,049. (*Chairman.*) The secretary of one union came to the secretary of another union to inquire how it was that the bellows had been cut?—The secretary accompanied this man that came to me.

17,050. It is a funny thing that the secretary of one union should come to the secretary of another union to ask how it was that the bellows were cut; it is rather significant of what he thought?—However strange it may appear it was so.

17,051. (*Mr. Chance.*) That would be consistent with the fact of rattenings and things of that kind having been done previously?—Yes.

17,052. Do you know of any act of intimidation or of any threatening letters in either of those unions?—I never heard of it in either of them.

17,053. How many members are there in the railway spring makers union?—360; we vary sometimes; they are all the same class.

17,054. How many are there not in the union?—About five or six, and they are dissolute characters which we do not recognise.

17,055. (*Chairman.*) In your union do you consider the question of character?—It is the first question we consider.

17,056. We have unfortunately heard that in the saw grinders' union they do not consider character at all; they take in ticket-of-leave men and all sorts of men?—The first thing we inquire into is the character for the men.

17,057. (*Mr. Chance.*) In the saw grinders' union the only question was whether a man was a good workman?—That is hardly a question with us, because a man, according to his capabilities, is able to earn his wages.

17,058. What wages do they earn?—There are two branches. One is the forehand, and the other is the underhand; the underhand will earn from 25*s.* to 30*s.* a week; the overhand will earn from 2*l.* to 2*l.* 10*s.*, and rather more.

17,059. What is the contribution?—1*s.* 6*d.* the overhand, and 1*s.* 3*d.* the underhand.

17,060. How many men have you on the box on the average?—64*l.* 13*s.* we paid last week. They are not regular box men. We have a rule in our union stating that if a man is off a second clear week from his employment from no fault of his own he shall be entitled to 4*l.* out of the funds. Trade is now very bad, and we are paying from 50*l.* to 60*l.* or 70*l.* a week. Sometimes we have a week when the men are all employed, and at the present time all the men are in situations with the exception of six; the manufacturers do not turn them away, but they share the work alike, and I am happy to say that we have a very good feeling with the manufacturers. I never met with a discourteous word from any manufacturer in Sheffield, and no manufacturer can come forward and say that I have a bad character or ever did them a dishonest act. The scale we pay is 8*s.* for a single man, 2*s.* for his wife, and 1*s.* each child under 14 years of age.

17,061. How many members have you in the scythe makers union?—48.

17,062. How many out?—I cannot tell you, they are scattered about the country, five miles out this way and five miles that way.

17,063. Are there many out of the union?—No.

17,064. They are scattered about, so that you cannot say how many there are?—Yes.

17,065. Would there be as many as there are in the union?—No, only about a dozen.

17,066. What do the scythe makers earn?—2*l.* a week, I should think. I may say I only meet them once a fortnight; they come out of the country to meet me. I know very little about them.

The witness withdrew.

J. Mallinson.

JOSEPH MALLINSON sworn and examined.

17,067. (*Chairman.*) Are you secretary to the Razor Grinders' Union?—Yes.

17,068. Are you ratteners?—No.

17,069. Rattening does not exist in your union?—No, it does not.

17,070. Then, although it has been said that all the grinders ratten, it is not true with respect to your union?—No, it is not true with respect to our union.

17,071. Have they never rattened?—Yes.

17,072. Up to what time?—This union was established in February 1862, when I was made secretary, and there has never been any rattening since that time.

17,073. Before that there was?—Yes, our trade suffered very much in consequence of the rattening previous to that.

17,074. Are you able to get in your contributions?—Yes.

17,075. Are the contributions pretty well paid?—Yes.

17,076. Do persons observe your rules pretty well in your trade?—Yes.

17,077. Then it is not correct to state that rattening is a necessity; you can do without it?—Yes.

17,078. And in your judgment if there were a secretary and a committee who set their faces against rattening, would there be rattening in that trade?—No.

17,079. And where rattening occurs, from your knowledge of the trade, in your judgment is it attributable always or almost always to trade matters? I mean taking away the bands?—I should think in almost every case it is so.

17,080. How many members have you in your union?—About 290 I think.

17,081. How many out?—Somewhere about 30 perhaps.

17,082. What are your contributions?—2*s.* per week a man and 1*s.* per week a boy.

17,083. What can a man and a boy earn per week?—There are various branches, as we may term them, and different work given out, and according to the work given out men will earn more and men will earn less.

17,084. What is a fair average statement of what the razor grinders of your trade will make?—A man and a boy working at what we term common work at the present rate of wages would get about 36*s.* to 2*l.* a week, but there has been an advance in prices.

17,085. Do you mean common razors?—Common razors.

17,086. If they were to do the finer kind of razors how much would a man and a boy get?—A good workman would get from 3*l.* to 3*l.* 10*s.* doing a certain class of work.

17,087. In getting into your union, do you respect characters or not?—When our union was first formed we were anxious to get all into the union that we possibly could, irrespective of character.

17,088. But what do you do now? is there any difference in your rule?—No, they are still in the trade.

17,089. You do not inquire into character?—We cannot refuse them into the union if they have served their apprenticeship to the trade.

17,090. You have rules in your trade?—Yes.

EIGHTEENTH DAY.

J. Mallinson.

26 June 1867.

17,091. You find that you can always secure the observance of the rules of your trade as well without rattening as with rattening?—Yes.

17,092. Have there been any outrages since you joined?—There was a man of the name of John Green had some damage done to his tools in 1862, a few weeks after our union was first formed.

17,093. He had his tools damaged?—Yes.

17,094. What kind of tools were they?—Grinding tools.

17,095. What kind of grinding tools?—His glazer.

17,096. His glazer was cut?—Yes.

17,097. Was that a trade business?—No.

17,098. What was it?—I saw a report the day following in the paper that he had been to the Town Hall attributing it to private malevolence.

17,099. Do you believe that that was true?—Yes.

17,100. It is not reported to us as a trade case, therefore I daresay that you are right. Are you aware of any case of outrage attributable to the trade in your union?—No.

17,101. You have never been charged with it have you?—Damage done to tools?

17,102. Yes, any outrage of any sort?—If I remember right, just now, there was another case of a person of the name of George Fisher, he had what we term caps knocked off the axle, and the wood and the lead taken away which the axles were kept up with, that is what I know of that affair.

17,103. Do you attribute that to the trade?—No.

17,104. Do you believe that it was a theft?—Yes.

17,105. Simply for the purpose of gain to the man who took them?—Yes.

17,106. Had this man any dispute with the union?—No.

17,107. Although you do know of persons having their tools damaged, you are not aware of any trade outrage that has ever been charged against your union?—I am not aware of any.

17,108. That is a very creditable account. That is all that I have to ask you; I wish everybody had followed your example?—I wish they had.

17,109. (*Mr. Chance.*) You ratten in no case?—In no case.

17,110. Do you generally do what you can to make men join your union?—We have an understanding among our men that if there are any connected with any firm that do not contribute to the trade or conform to the rules of the trade, they should cease work until such persons conform to the rules.

17,111. That is as regards the union men. My question was rather directed to men who are not members of the union?—That is in regard to the union men.

17,112. You are telling me about union men. I want to know, supposing that there are men who will not join your union, do you take any measures to induce them to do so?—Yes.

17,113. What measures do you adopt to induce members to join your union?—If such an individual is working for a certain firm or manufacturer in the town, where he employs other hands, we go to the manufacturer and ask him to use his influence with the person working for him in that capacity, and in some cases we have been enabled to make terms and in some cases such a man has been refused work any more at that place.

17,114. Supposing he does not join the union, do you adopt any other measure?—No.

17,115. If all your efforts in that direction fail, do not you draw off the men?—We have only had one instance where that has failed, and the men ceased working until those parties conformed to the rules of the trade.

17,116. (*Chairman.*) You did draw them off?—Yes.

17,117. (*Mr. Chance.*) You speak of the union men conforming to the rules of the trade. I speak of the non-union men; do you know Samuel Sharp?—Yes.

17,118. He was not a member of your union?—He contributed to the union.

17,119. Did not he at one time refuse to join the union?—Yes.

17,120. At his last refusal to join the union did not you call upon him?—I wait upon every man for his subscription.

17,121. I speak now of the time before he became a member before he became a member of your union did you call upon him?—Yes.

17,122. What did you call upon him for?—To ask him to contribute to the union.

17,123. Did he refuse to contribute to the union?—For a certain time.

17,124. Did you upon his refusing to contribute to the union take any measures to compel him?—Not in the first instance.

17,125. Have you at any time, whether the first time or the second time, adopted any measures to compel him to come into the union?—As he had refused to contribute to the union we adopted measures to compel him.

17,126. What did you do? did you take the men out with whom he was working?—Yes.

17,127. You took the men out with whom he was working in order to compel him to join the union?—Yes.

17,128. Is that the system adopted by you for the purpose of making the men join the union?—That is the system we have among the men and the best system under existing circumstances.

17,129. Is that the system adopted by you?—Yes.

17,130. If a man will not join the union you draw off the men with whom he is working, in order to compel him to do so?—Yes.

The witness withdrew.

GEORGE CASTLES recalled and further examined.

G. Castles.

17,131. (*Chairman.*) I have asked Mr. Brailsford whether he can tell when the book was sold to you, and he says he cannot tell, therefore the thing is left entirely upon your statement?—Very well, sir.

The witness withdrew.

WILLIAM SIMPSON sworn and examined.

W. Simpson.

17,132. (*Mr. Barstow.*) You are secretary of the work board hands of the scissors trade?—Yes.

17,133. How long have you been secretary?—About 15 months, since February last year.

17,134. Is that trade amalgamated with the other branches of the scissors trade?—Yes.

17,135. In your branch of the trade do you ratten?—No, we have no rattening cases in our society at all in any way.

17,136. Do not you cause a scissor grinder to ratten?—No.

17,137. You have never done so since you have been secretary?—No; we do not recognize rattening in any shape.

17,138. You do not recognize it?—No, it is not done in our trade.

17,139. Do you know of any cases of rattening occurring in your trade?—No, not any.

17,140. Not at any time?—No, not at at any time.

17,141. You are aware, I suppose, that they occur in some of the branches with whom you are amalgamated?—I have read of them, but I cannot speak any further of them than reading the accounts in the papers.

EIGHTEENTH DAY.

W. Simpson.

26 June 1867.

17,142. You mean at the time they occurred?—I cannot tell you the time they occurred.

17,143. Then you never heard of Mr. Darwin's bellows being cut?—Yes, I heard of it.

17,144. That was in the trade?—In the forgers trade.

17,145. The forgers trade is the one you are amalgamated with?—Yes; we are amalgamated to give each other assistance when we require it.

17,146. Do you know of rattening occurring in the associated trade in consequence of quarrels you have with your masters?—We have had none.

17,147. Do you speak of when you were secretary or before?—Since 1864, when this society started.

17,148. If you do not ratten, you do not know of any case of personal violence to any of your members? No, I am not aware of any of the kind.

17,149. Or any violence offered to non-union men in your branch of the trade?—No.

17,150. Do you know anything of the committee of the file smiths' union?—No.

17,151. Have you never attended that committee? —No.

17,152. Have you never personally attended the committee of the file smiths' union?—In what shape do you put the question to me? Do you mean a committee entirely in connexion with the file trade, or the committee of organized trades?

17,153. I understand that there is a file smiths' union?—Yes.

17,154. Have you attended the committee of the file smiths' union?—No.

17,155. Have you ever said that you were going to attend the committee of the file smiths' union?—No.

17,156. It is quite a mistake.—Yes, I thought so.

17,157. What is the number of the members of your union?—Somewhere about 190 in the union.

17,158. Can you tell me at all how many non-union men there are in your branch of the trade?—I should think somewhere about 40.

17,159. What is the rate of your contribution?—6*d*. a week for a man and 3*d*. a week for a boy.

17,160. How many men have you on the box?—We have had five or six. I think this week we shall have a dozen, or rather better. The masters are turning the men away because they will not work for less money.

17,161. What do you think the average number of men on the box is?—The average on the box has been four or five per week.

17,162. Can you tell us what wages a fairly good workman can earn in your branch of the trade?—I might say from about 24*s*. to 27*s*. per week on the average. A good workman to do his work in a workmanlike style would not get more than 27*s*. a week.

17,163. How much could a man and a boy make?—I cannot tell you that.

17,164. Cannot you possibly tell us?—I never made an inquiry of anyone who has a boy what they can earn.

17,165. It is a common thing for a man to work with a boy?—No, it is not a common thing, and very many do not have boys, they are more in the way than anything else.

17,166. You cannot answer how much a man and a boy would earn?—I cannot; there are three branches. I am not aware of the average of a man and a boy.

The witness withdrew.

J. Reaney.

JAMES REANEY recalled and further examined.

17,167. (*Chairman.*) What are you?—I am secretary to the edge tool forgers.

17,168. You ratten I believe?—In extreme cases we do, we cannot get any further without we ratten.

17,169. How often have you rattened?—I cannot answer that, not many times.

17,170. One hundred?—No.

17,171. How often have you rattened?—Never in my life.

17,172. How often have your trade rattened within the 10 years?—Not more than a dozen times.

17,173. Not more than one a year?—Not more than one a year. I do not think it will be.

17,174. In olden times you used to ratten more than you do now?—Yes, formerly. I call rattening rolling up bands, we have an understanding that we will take the bands, we do not destroy anything.

17,175. You merely take the things?—Yes.

17,176. And if they agree to your terms they get their things back again?—Yes.

17,177. They pay 5*s*. to "Mary Ann" for the bands?—Yes.

17,178. 5*s*. for a nut?—No.

17,179. How much is the price for a nut?—They take nuts generally speaking.

17,180. How much have they to pay for a nut, if it is 5*s*. for a band?—If they take both band and nut it would be the same thing, that reckons for one trough, if there were six troughs that would be six 5*s*.

18,181. For every trough you stop, you charge 5*s*.? —Yes.

17,182. So if they do not come into you terms they never get their bands?—We never had a case of that sort, they are generally too proud to come in and glad when they get in.

17,183. Not too proud to come in, they are too glad to come in?—They are too glad to come in.

17,184. They are satisfied when they get in?—Yes.

17,185. And you ratten them I suppose when they do not pay their money for the contributions?—Yes.

17 186. And if they take an apprentice when they ought not you ratten them then?—We can do that generally without that. There is not much extravagance about taking apprentices.

17,187. Supposing a man employs a workman who is not in the union, do you ratten the master?—We should lay down work and leave him to himself.

17,188. And you would ratten him some time?—Yes.

17,189. Do you recollect Addis coming?—Yes.

17,190. He was a good workman?—Yes.

17,191. And he came from London?—Yes.

17,192. And you did not like it?—We did not.

17,193. He went to work for David Ward?—I believe so.

17,194. You were determined that he should not work for him?—No; we were not determined he should not; we wanted him out of the yard. We were not willing to work with that man; we wanted to remove him from that place, not to stop him working for David Ward.

17,195. And you rattened him?—Yes.

17,196. When you say "remove him from that place" you mean remove him out of the town?—It cannot be so; the thing is settled now. He is working out of the town, and away from the men he was insulting.

17,197. He insulted the men by getting his head broken?—He was invited into a public house to assist one of the men.

17,198. And he got his head broken?—He did, I believe.

17,199. Four men set upon him?—That was the report; I was not there.

17,200. They were charged and convicted for it?—Yes.

17,201. You say that it was to get him out of the yard from the other men?—Yes.

17,202. He never worked with the other men; he worked with a master?—He came and insulted the men. He would come into our yard to get steel.

17,203. At first you say that he was not to work with the men; and when I asked you if he never did

EIGHTEENTH DAY.

J. Reaney.

26 June 1867.

work with the men, you say that it was because he came into your yard to get steel ?—Yes.

17,204. That you call working with the men ?—He was in the yard every day fetching steel.

17,205. He had a place to himself and was working by himself, and you would not allow him to come and get steel out of the same yard ?—We were frightened of his insulting the men.

17,206. That was your reason ?—Yes.

17,207. He got his head broken; four men were convicted of having assaulted him; and furthermore did not you say that they took the man away from Mr. Ward's ?—No.

17,208. Were not they compelled to go away ?—They were fetched down to the Town Hall by a special summons.

17,209. Did you withdraw your men from his employment ?—No.

17,210. Mr. Ward was very anxious to have this man ?—Yes.

17,211. Did not you go and see him about it?—Yes.

17,212. Did not he say that it was a hard case that his hands should be taken away to stop his work in that way, and did not he plead very hard with you to retain that man?—Yes, he did.

17,213. Did not you tell him that that was the way you did it to compel the manufacturers to comply with your demands ?—Those were not the words; the meaning would be somewhat of that sort.

17,214. And then Stacey, Fox, Higginbottom, and Machin went and made that statement to him ?—I think Higginbottom was not there; the other four were.

17,215. Did you tell him that he had no alternative but to consent to discharge the man ?—I told him the thing could not be settled unless he removed him from the place and sent him away. He said he would send him to Birmingham.

17,216. He did send him to Rockingham Street ?—Yes.

17,217. Did you send him to Jerico ?—No.

17,218. You sent him to Coventry ?—If you call it Coventry, he has gone I suppose.

17,219. Did not you tell Mr. Ward that he would have 30*l.* to pay ?—Yes, I believe I did; I was fetched away from my work to do the job.

17,220. You had taken this man's goods away and rattened him ? did not you make him pay 30*l.* before you would allow him to be square ?—Yes.

17,221. And you actually sent him a receipt for the money ?—Yes; it is most natural that I should do so.

17,222. Did not Addis offer to become a member of your union ?—He called upon me and offered to become a member.

17,223. And offered to pay you something ?—He offered 5*l.*

17,224. You told him that you would not have him at any price ?—We did; it would have been very bad policy on our part to have had him.

17,225. What do you say about him ? you are thinking of yourself, but not about him ?—He wanted to come in and pay 5*l.*, but there is not a manufacturer in the town that can employ a man like that in trade; he had four boys with him, and he would have learnt the four boys the trade, and when he had learnt them we should have had these boys to keep when they came upon the box if we had taken Addis into the trade.

17,226. He had not four boys ?—He says he has only one now, but he has three now.

17,227. You never said a word about boys in your interview with Ward; you never complained of the boys then ?—We saw what he was doing.

17,228. He was a better workman than you were at the trade, that is it ?—No. Will you allow me to explain the matter; this was tried to be made a trade matter.

17,229. You have got your books have you not ?—Yes.

17,230. Have any leaves in your books been torn out ?—There have not.

17,231. None ?—Not that I am aware of.

17,232. Do not you recollect that your books were asked for, and you said that your children had been playing with the books and had torn a good many leaves out ?—That is 15 years ago, my books for 10 years are here.

17,233. They are none of them torn ?—No.

17,234. They are all complete for 10 years, without any tearing out at all ?—They are, every one; I do not care who sees them.

17,235. You say that you do admit rattening ?—Yes.

17,236. You have admitted all the other things fairly enough; I think you did very foolishly, but you have admitted it; how many are there in your union ?—370 I should think ——.

17,237. How many out ?—About 30. I cannot exactly tell; there are two or three houses which we call slop places which we do not recognize.

17,238. What are the contributions ?—1*s.* for a man and 6*d.* for a boy under 18.

17,239. How many are there on the box ?—Eight at present I should think.

17,240. What can they earn a day in your trade ?—We are double-handed, two men would average about 2*l.* 15*s.* a week, from that to 3*l.*

17,241. 3*l.* a week the two ?—Yes.

17,242. Would they divide it ?—The foreman takes three-fifths; if they earn 50*s.* the foreman takes 30*s.* and the stoker 20*s.*; it is rather more than three-fifths in some branches.

17,243. (*Mr. Chance.*) Is eight the average number on the box at the present time ?—We have eight old men that cannot work at all, some of them have been on 20 years. They are men past work.

17,244. Are the eight workmen that you speak of the number on the box now ?—Yes.

17,245. (*Chairman.*) You have plenty of work, have you not ?—Not quite sufficient work for all of us.

17,246. If you had none on the box when Addis came, you must have been very jealous that you would not let him have a bit of work ?—We did not care about him.

17,247. He has set up as a master, he is not a workman any longer ?—Yes, he said he could do better as a little master.

17,248. He has set up as a master ?—Yes.

17,249. (*Mr. Barstow.*) He says that he and his boy sometimes earn 10*l.* a week ?—I heard him say that in this hall.

17,250. There is a great difference between him and his boy earning it and a man earning 50*s.* ?—Yes, but he is a wonderful man, and I thought so when he was making use of that expression.

17,251. He seems to be thought a wonderful man ?—Yes.

17,252. (*Chairman.*) He is the only man that gets prizes at the exhibition ?—I should not like to explain what I know about that; that gentleman would not like to tell you what I know about his affairs.

17,253. Amongst the edge tool forgers, except the case of outrage against the man Addis, are you aware of any charge of outrage for the last 10 years ?—Never.

17,254. Not against you personally, but against the trade ?—None.

17,255. There is no charge of cutting a man's bellows, or injury to property in any way ?—Not at all.

17,256. Or intimidation ?—No.

17,257. (*Mr. Barstow.*) We do not know as a fact that Jephson and the other man were workmen of your trade ?—They were Mr. Ward's men.

17,258. Were they members of your union ?—Yes.

The witness withdrew.

EIGHTEENTH DAY.

R. Winter, jun.

26 June 1867.

ROBERT WINTER, jun., sworn and examined.

17,259. (*Mr. Chance.*) Are you a scissor forger? —Yes.

17,260. From Copper Street?—Yes.

17,261. Are you a member of any union?—No.

17,262. Have you ever been?—No.

17,263. Do you remember some years back, when the union commenced, being called upon by Mr. Mills the treasurer?—I met him accidentally in the street.

17,264. How long ago was that? do you remember? —I cannot tell.

17,265. Two, three, four, or five years?—Two and a half years ago.

17,266. You met Mr. Mills the treasurer in the street?—Yes.

17,267. Did he say anything to you?—He asked me if I was not going to join the trade, he said I had better join it. I told him that I should not, and he told me that if I did not "Nathan" would come.

17,268. What did you say to that?—I did not say anything to it that I am aware of, unless it was that I said I did not care whether he came or not. I said I should not join the trade whether he came or not.

17,269. Did anything happen to you after that?— Yes.

17,270. What was it?—I found the dog dead in the house.

17,271. How long after was that?—I cannot say exactly what time it was when I met with him, but it was on the 10th of August when we found the dog dead.

17,272. Was it after your conversation with him in the street?—Yes.

17,273. Did anything happen to you besides? did you have any tools taken?—Not belonging to me.

17,274. To anyone working with you?—The men that were working with my father; the men on the premises had their bosses taken.

17,275. You say that they were working with your father?—Yes.

17,276. Are you all working together for your father?—Yes.

17,277. How long was it after the conversation that you had in the street?—I cannot tell you how long it was, because I do not know the exact time when I met with Mills.

17,278. Do you know the reason why the bosses were taken?—It was on account of the men not paying to the trade, we thought.

17,279. Did you know that they were in arrear to the trade?—Yes.

17,280. Have they told you so?—I have heard them speak of it frequently.

17,281. Do you remember in 1865 seeing Joseph Thompson?—Yes.

17,282. Is he secretary to the scissor forgers union? —Yes.

17,283. Did he say anything to you about joining the union?—He asked me whether I was going to join the union, and I said I should not join it at all. He said, "All masters and masters sons that work at the trade will have to join."

17,284. You refused to join?—Yes.

17,285. Was this interview that you had with Thompson before the bosses went or after?—Before; it was the Sunday before.

17,286. On what day did the bosses go?—We found it out on Thursday morning, the 10th of August.

17,287. Was anything done to a pair of bellows that your father had?—Two pairs were cut, and the leather completely destroyed.

17,288. Who were using the bellows that were cut? —The two men that had the bosses taken, Henry Pressley and James Hallas.

17,289. Were they union men or non-union men? —They had belonged to the trade, but they had withdrawn. They had paid into the trade; I do not know how much, but they were a good deal in arrear, in fact they had given it up altogether.

17,290. They had not paid their contributions, but they were union men?—Not for some time.

17,291. Did they cut your bellows too?—No.

17,292. How was that?—We had a large dog on the premises, and they could not get into the shop where I worked unless they made some noise.

17,293. Did you ever after that make any application to Joseph Thompson about your bellows?— No.

17,294. Or about the bosses?—No.

17,295. Or to the treasurer, Mills?—No.

17,296. Did you never take any measure whatever about them?—We went down to Mr. Jackson, the chief constable.

17,297. Did you ever hear who had done it or was suspected of doing it?—We suspected a person of doing it.

17,298. Who was that?—William Fernley.

17,299. Why did you suspect him?—He came up to me a day or two after, and said he thought it was a bad job the bellows being cut, and I said it was a bad job; anyone knows that. We were making new shutters for the shop windows, and putting iron on them, and it commenced raining. On Friday afternoon we went up into the shop chamber to nail the iron on, and he said we had only gone up there to hinder him, but he did not care, the trade would pay him for his lost time.

17,300. Was Fernley a member of the scissor forgers union?—Yes.

17,301. Did he say anything else upon the matter? —No, he did not say anything else, but the morning that it was found out he was the first to come, and the man that kept the key called out and told him they had been, and he asked, "Who had been," and he said, "The ratteners."

17,302. Did you hear him say that?—No.

17,303. Is that what was told you by somebody else?—Yes.

17,304. Have you any other reason besides that which you have told us for suspecting that he was the man that did it?—No, I am not aware that I have.

17,305. Had you ever had any quarrel with him? —No, I had not.

17,306. If he or anybody else did it, do you believe that it was a trade affair?—Yes, I believe it was a trade affair.

17,307. Had you had any quarrel with any other person?—No, I do not know that I have ever had a quarrel with anyone in the trade.

17,308. Has your father had a quarrel with anybody in the trade?—No, I believe not.

17,309. Do you think that poisoning the dog was a trade affair?—I took it to a chemist, and he said his stomach would have to be had out, and he would send it up to London, and it would cost me two guineas. I did not like to go to the cost.

17,310. You do not know what the cause of death was?—No.

17,311. Where was the dog?—He was in the house the day before; he was healthy the day before, and we found him dead in the morning.

17,312. If the dog was in the house was it possible for anybody to get at him?—He was running about the yard all day.

17,313. The dog was dead the day after?—Yes, in the house.

17,314. It had been down the yard the night previous?—Yes.

17,315. Was it the same dog that kept guard over your bellows?—No; it was quite a little dog that we found dead.

17,316. Would there have been any difficulty in getting at the other dog that guarded the bellows?— No.

17,317. Would it have been as easy to have poisoned one dog as the other?—Anybody coming down the yard might give anything to them to eat.

EIGHTEENTH DAY.

R. Winter, jun.

26 June 1867.

17,318. Was the dog that guarded the bellows at large?—No; he was chained up.

17,319. The other was running about?—Yes.

17,320. (*Chairman.*) Would he have barked if anybody came?—In the night time I believe he would have barked at anybody.

17,321. Would he have barked at Fernley?—At night I believe he would. Fernley used to bring bits of bread to him.

17,322. He said that the trade would pay him for his lost time; what did he mean by that?—Whilst we were upstairs hammering and driving the nails he chucked dust down through the boards on to us. He said he could not work, but he did not care; the trade would pay him for his lost time—for whatever time we caused him to lose.

17,323. (*Mr. Chance.*) If a man is in work and he loses time will the trade pay for it?—I do not know; that is what he said.

17,324. (*Chairman.*) Mr. Sugg wants to know how you connect the trade with this matter. You have had no quarrel with anybody?—No.

17,325. You had two men in your employment whom you knew to be in arrear?—Yes.

17,326. What right have you to say that the persons, whoever they were, that cut your bellows, did it for trade purposes?—We think they did.

17,327. Can you assign any motive to any person for cutting them except it was to compel the men to pay their arrears?—That is all we can assign it to.

17,328. Before that had Mr. Thompson told you that he would make you join the union?—Yes, he told me before.

17,329. Before that he told you that he would make you join the union?—Yes, the Sunday before.

17,330. (*Mr. Chance.*) You say that Mr. Mills, the treasurer, had already told you that "Nathan" would come if you did not join the union?—Yes; the dog that was poisoned belonged to me, and they knew it.

The witness withdrew.

HENRY PRESSLEY sworn and examined.

H. Pressley.

17,331. (*Mr. Barstow.*) You were formerly a member of the scissor forgers union?—Yes.

17,332. And I believe in January 1865 you ceased to contribute to the union?—Yes.

17,333. After that time did you frequently see Thompson, the secretary of the union?—Yes.

17,334. What did he say to you?—He wanted me to pay.

17,335. And you refused?—Yes; he stopped me in the street.

17,336. Did he say anything to you by way of inducing you to join?—Not anything, particular, only he said it would be better for me.

17,337. How many men were there in the shop in which you worked?—Five of us.

17,338. I believe some of them were union men?—Yes.

17,339. How many were union men?—Three of them.

17,340. And you and Hallas were non-union men?—Yes.

17,341. Do you remember something happening one night in August 1865?—Yes.

17,342. What was it?—They cut my bellows and took 14 of my tools.

17,343. Were any bellows besides yours cut?—Yes, Hallas's.

17,344. The two non-union men's bellows were cut?—Yes.

17,345. Were any of the union men's bellows cut?—No.

17,346. You had some bosses taken at the same time?—Yes.

17,347. Did Hallas lose his bosses at the same time?—Yes.

17,348. Did the union men lose any of their bosses?—No.

17,349. How were the bosses left?—On the side upon a shelf.

17,350. Were they left altogether?—Mine were, and he kept his to himself. I had some belonging to our master and they left them; I had five all on the shelf together, and they left his and took mine.

17,351. Would they know which was which?—I think those that took them would know, but a stranger would not know.

17,352. Was there any mark on the bellows to distinguish them from any of the others?—No.

17,353. Strangers would not have known yours from any of the others?—No.

17,354. In this interval of time between January and August 1865, had you ever been threatened by anyone?—Yes.

17,355. By whom?—John Smith and a man named Fernley, and they said it would be better if I would pay, and if not they would make me.

17,356. How often was that?—Several times in the shop.

17,357. But you never would pay?—No.

17,358. Was Fernley a man who worked in the shop?—Yes.

17,359. Have you since that belonged to the union?—No.

17,360.—To whom did you first tell this statement?—To Mr. Fretson.

17,361. When was that?—Last month.

17,362. Do you recollect what day last month?—No, I do not; he sent for us down to his office.

17,363. Mr. Fretson sent for you?—Yes.

17,364. I suppose your case was commonly known?—Yes.

17,365. Did you make any complaint about it?—No, not to anybody in particular.

17,366. You had not gone to Mr. Jackson about it?—No, our master sent down to the Town Hall, and one or two detectives came.

17,367. Then it would be known to the police?—Yes, that was the morning we found it out.

The witness withdrew.

JAMES HALLAS sworn and examined.

J. Hallas.

17,368. (*Mr. Barstow.*) You are a fellow-workman of the last witness?—Yes.

17,369. And you have been here and heard his evidence?—Yes.

17,370. Is it true?—Yes.

17,371. And the same things occurred to you at the same time that it occurred to him?—Yes.

17,372. These are bosses (*showing the same to the witness*)?—Yes.

17,373. Where are they used?—In the stithy.

17,374. In your trade do these things belong to the workmen or the master?—Those were on the top of mine, and they shifted those and took mine.

The witness withdrew.

WILLIAM FERNLEY sworn and examined.

W. Fernley.

17,375. (*Chairman.*) I am going to ask you a few questions. I suppose you are aware that if you have committed this act of which you are charged you are liable to be punished for having done malicious mischief, and it is a very serious offence; if you tell the whole truth about this matter we have the power

EIGHTEENTH DAY.

W. Fernley.

26 June 1867.

of granting you a certificate which will exonerate you from the consequences of your misconduct; and therefore you have the chance of escaping from the result of your misconduct. If you are not guilty you have nothing to confess; but if it is found out that you have done this and do not confess to it, you will be liable to be tried for it and be punished. Now then, were you working at Winter's at the time when Hallas and Pressley's bellows were cut?—Yes.

17,376. Who kept the key of the place?—John Barlow.

17,377. Who was the last in the shop on the night before the bellows were cut?—Smith.

17,378. Mind, will you swear that you were not the last man in the shop that night?—Yes, Smith was the last; he took Barlow the key.

17,379. I have private information about this, will you swear that you were not the last man in the shop that night?—Yes.

17,380. What was the name of the man who was in the shop last?—John Smith.

17,381. Was he a fellow-workman?—Yes, and not a very good payer; he did not pay his money right.

17,382. How do you mean pay his money right?—He did not pay his natty money right.

17,383. Then he did not always pay to the union?—He did not pay as he ought to do; he did pay, but not as he ought to do.

17,384. How do you know that John Smith was there the last man?—Because I left him working.

17,385. What time did you leave?—I believe between 8 and 9, and he followed me down the yard.

17,386. You left between 8 and 9?—Yes, he followed me just after down the yard, he and a man named Jubb came down the yard together and went away together.

17,387. And were they last?—Yes.

17,388. Who gave the key that night to John Barlow?—Smith, I expect.

17,389. On your oath did not you give it yourself?—No, on my oath I did not.

17,390. Now mind?—I do mind. I am bound to speak the truth.

17,391. Will you swear that that night you did not with your own hand deliver to John Barlow the key of that shop?—Yes.

17,392. You swear this?—Yes.

17,393. Were you with Smith when he delivered it?—No, Smith followed me out, and also locked the shop up himself.

17,394. You saw him lock the shop?—No.

17,395. Then how do you say that he did?—I say right, they followed me down the yard.

17,396. They were just after you?—He went out of the shop just after me.

17,397. There was not a minute's time between the two going out?—No.

17,398. Then as I understand you, in point of fact you all left together?—No, I went just after them.

17,399. There was not a minute's time between you?—I do not think there was.

17,400. And he followed you down the passage?—Yes, he followed after me down the yard, he and Jubb came together.

17,401. What did you mean by saying just now that you left him working?—It would not take him a minute to lock the shop up and come down the yard.

17,402. You told me just now that you left him working?—(*No answer.*)

17,403. You said just now that you did not leave more than a minute before him, he followed you down the passage?—Yes.

17,404. Who was there first next morning?—I was.

17,405. Did you open the door?—Yes.

17,406. Who was present at the time?—When I opened the shop door? Nobody.

17,407. You were alone?—Yes.

17,408. Did you see Hallas and Pressley?—I saw them when they came to the shop in the morning.

17,409. How soon after you came there did they come?—Hallas came not long after, he generally comes about 9 or 10.

17,410. What time did you get there?—About 7.

17,411. What time did Hallas come?—I tell you about 10 I think.

17,412. What time did Pressley come?—He was just after me, he was not much after.

17,413. What did you say to Pressley when he came?—I asked him if he had missed aught.

17,414. What did you say that to him for?—Because I knew it was done.

17,415. You knew it was done and you asked him if he had missed aught?—Yes.

17,416. Is that the way you tell a man when you know that his property is destroyed?—Yes, I am speaking truth.

17,417. You said, "Have you missed aught"?—Yes.

17,418. You knew that his bellows had been cut?—Yes, I cut them myself the night before, while Smith was working.

17,419. You cut them?—Yes.

17,420. Was Smith working with you at the time?—Yes.

17,421. And he saw you do it?—I dare say he did.

17,422. Had Smith helped you to do it?—No, I did it myself. I have the knife in my pocket yet, it is here (*producing the same.*)

17,423. You cut the bellows yourself, and that is the knife you cut them with?—Yes.

17,424. Did you cut them because Pressley and Hallas had not paid to the union?—Partly; and I cut them because master persuaded people not to pay, he said he would have a lot of nail makers out of the low country and Pressley would learn them to make scissors, that is what I cut them for and nought else.

17,425. Where is the low country?—I do not know, it is somewhere where the nail makers work.

17,426. That is what you call the low country?—Yes.

17,427. Who put it into your head to do this?—I put it in myself.

17,428. Who is the secretary of your union?—Thompson.

17,429. Have you ever talked to Thompson about Pressley not paying and about Hallas?—I knew they were not paying; he used to come every week.

17,430. Of course you used to have a talk with him, and he said that it was a great shame?—No, he did not. I saw him go out of the shop.

17,431. Did you ever talk to him about Pressley and Hallas not paying?—No, I never talked to Thompson much myself.

17,432. Did Smith?—He was a regular rum old dodger, Smith; they knew that Smith used to say many a lot of things he did not mean.

17,433. What kind of things did he say?—I have heard Smith say many a time that if Hallas came on his side he would knock his brains out with the hammer.

17,434. If he would not join the union?—No.

17,435. Why should he knock his brains out?—Pressley used to try to get his rag out, and he would say it in a bit of a passion.

17,436. This was a pleasant kind of conversation. He tried to make himself agreeable with him by saying he would knock his brains out?—It used to happen very often.

17,437. You have heard him say this?—Yes.

17,438. Have you heard him say unless he joined the union he would knock his brains out with a hammer?—Never.

17,439. Have you ever talked to Pressley about joining the union?—Yes, I persuaded him many times to join the union and he would be better off.

17,440. And would be worse off if he did not?—I did not say so to him, I am too little for him.

17,441. You are not too little to cut his bellows?—No.

EIGHTEENTH DAY.

W. Fernley.

26 June 1867.

17,442. There are many ways of damaging a man; you need not fight him, you can cut his bellows?—He has damaged me. He owes me some money and he has not paid it; he has not the principle to pay 2*d*.

17,443. Are you sure that the secretary has never told you to do this?—I am certain he has not.

17,444. He has never said a word to you about it?—No; I did it entirely on my own bottom from what master said and from them not paying.

17,445. Have you ever been present at the club when they have said that it was a great shame that Pressley and Hallas did not pay?—I have heard them say he was not paying at the general meeting.

17,446. After you had done this did you go and tell the secretary that you had done it?—No.

17,447. Will you swear that you did not?—Yes.

17,448. What did you get for doing it?—Not a farthing. I did it entirely on my own bottom.

17,449. Have you never been paid by the union?—Never a farthing. I have had my scale. One day they went upstairs and started working, knocking nails into the shutters, and the muck came down my chimney, so I went to Thompson and told him, and so it happened the next day, and I went to the shop on the next day. After that I did not go there any more that week. I went to the trade, and they gave me 6*s*. to make my scale up, 14*s*. altogether.

17,450. How long did you get 6*s*.?—Only that week; I worked the week after at Winter's.

17,451. Had you anything the week before?—No.

17,452. The week that you cut the bellows you got 6*s*. from the union?—Yes.

17,453. You never had anything before or after?—Never after, only my scale. I never had a farthing.

17,454. You went on the box when you were at Winter's?—Yes.

17,455. You were not on the box after. Notwithstanding that you were not on the box, the very week this was done you got 6*s*. from the secretary of the union?—Yes, to make my scale up.

17,456. Have you not in your union to give notice before you receive scale?—No, I can go any time. I work for a widow, and they let me go on when she has no work.

17,457. Is this the only case when you have cut a man's bellows?—Yes, it is the first time and I hope it will be the last time. I have had it on my mind ever since.

17,458. Have you done anything else?—Yes, I took the bosses and I chucked them in the Green Lane Dyke.

17,459. Have you talked to Thompson at all about this matter since the inquiry began?—I have never talked to him, and have never seen him, except when he was at the meeting at night. I did not talk to him, but they were passing a resolution, and I asked whether he would stand secretary again, and I believe he would have been re-elected if he would.

17,460. That was the time when he told you he had been embezzling all your money?—Yes, that was the only time.

17,461. Did not you talk to him about this little bit of business, about the bosses?—No, never at all.

17,462. You have never seen him since?—Yes, I saw him on Saturday afternoon. I was on the box, and he paid my scale.

17,463. Has he been paying money since the time when he ceased to be secretary?—He did not pay it to me.

17,464. I thought you said he did?—He put it down in the book.

17,465. He has been acting as secretary though he has resigned?—He was acting as secretary that night I expect, because he put it down in the book.

17,466. And he gave you the money?—No, Abbigan gave me the money, he is the treasurer.

17,467. I believe you were asked about this a day or two ago?—Never.

17,468. You were never asked about it?—No. There was not a living man in Sheffield knowed it until I told it here, not one.

17,469. Did you vote at that time for Thompson being re-elected?—No, I did not vote for him, it was not any use when he would not stand.

17,470. You held up your hand?—No, it was such a hobble cobble of a meeting I did not vote at all, and I went away before it was over.

17,471. (*Mr. Chance.*) You would have voted for him?—I do not know exactly whether I would or not. I might have done. I never saw nought amiss with him before, he is a nice young chap.

17,472. You do not believe that he embezzled the monies?—I do not know that he had money to pay the woman with, or he would have paid it without taking it out of the trade money. I do not think he had the money.

17,473. You think that he must have taken it out of the trade money?—He took it out of the trade money.

17,474. And on account of the trade?—I do not know for that.

17,475. What do you think he did it for?—I believe he was asked several times about Mrs. Clarke, whether he was giving her 6*s*. or not, and he said that he was not.

17,476. You think that he did it for the trade when he paid Mrs. Clarke?—I know he did take it from the trade, because he put me down 14*s*., and I had not had it. I believe he put it down 15*s*.

The witness withdrew.

Adjourned to to-morrow at 11 o'clock.

NINETEENTH DAY.

Council Hall, Sheffield, Thursday, 27th June 1867.

PRESENT:

WILLIAM OVEREND, Esq., Q.C.
THOMAS IRWIN BARSTOW, Esq.
GEORGE CHANCE, Esq.
J. E. BARKER, Esq., Secretary.

WILLIAM OVEREND, Esq., Q.C., IN THE CHAIR.

NINETEENTH DAY.

W. Stanley.

27 June 1867.

WILLIAM STANLEY sworn and examined.

17,477. (*Chairman.*) What are you?—I am a brickmaker and an employer of labour.

17,478. Are you secretary of any union?—Yes, I am the secretary of the brickmakers society at present.

17,479. How long have you been secretary?—I took to it on the 13th May 1867.

17,480. Who was secretary before you?—William Henry Owen was the last.

17,481. How long was he secretary?—Somewhere

NINETEENTH DAY.

W. Stanley.

27 June 1867.

between two and three years; two years I think, I do not exactly know, but I think it was two years.

17,482. Who was secretary before him?—Mr. Palmer, or I think it is Pawmer.

17,483. How long was he secretary?—To the best of my remembrance I think he was secretary some 15 or 18 months.

17,484. In 1860 and 1861 do you know who were secretaries; just look at your books and tell me?—We have not a minute book at all.

17,485. Do you produce all the books of your society?—Yes, all that I know of, all that I have seen.

17,486. How long have you been a member of the union?—Somewhere about 13 or 14 years I believe, to the best of my remembrance.

17,487. You say that you have produced all the books which you have ever seen since you have been a member of that society?—All the books that I have seen since my secretaryship I have brought into your presence.

17,488. That is not an answer; have you produced all the books you have ever seen since you have been a member of that union?—For anything I know; I do not know that there are any more books.

17,489. I did not ask you that either. Have you produced all the books which you have ever seen since you have been a member of that union?—There might have been books before I was in office, I cannot answer for that.

17,490. I know that; but have you produced all the books which you have ever seen since you have been in office?—I have to the best of my knowledge.

17,491. Be a little more distinct than that if you please. Will you swear that you have produced all the books which you have ever seen since you have been in office?—Well, I cannot swear that which I do not know to be correct; but I will swear that I have produced all the books that I have had the handling of.

17,492. That will not quite answer the question. Have you had any books at all in your society during the time that you have been in office which you have not produced?—No, I think not.

17,493. Will you swear that you have not?—Well, I cannot swear it; I do not want to take a false oath.

17,494. But as secretary you know what books you have?—All the books which I have brought are all the books which I have seen since my secretaryship.

17,495. That is a clear answer; there are all the books that you have seen since you have been in office?—Yes.

17,496. Are you sure about that?—I am sure about it.

17,497. Do you produce all the books which you have seen during the time that you have been a member of the union?—I am in office.

17,498. But I am speaking of the time before you were in office; do you produce all the books that you have seen since you have been a member of the union?—For many years.

17,499. Do answer my question; do you or do you not produce all the books which you have ever seen belonging to the union since you have been a member of the union?—I might have seen other books, but I have not taken that notice of them; but I do not think that I have seen others.

17,500. Do you produce all the books that you have seen?—I produce all the books that I have knowingly seen since I have been a member of that union.

17,501. I will put it in another way; are there any books which you ever saw belonging to the union which you have not produced?—No, I do not know that there are.

17,502. Will you swear that there are not any other books which you do not produce?—Yes, I could swear that.

17,503. Well, do so if you can, and I will put it down. Do you swear that there have never been any books during the time that you have been a member which you do not produce?—Well, there might be some new books perhaps, at the time when I was first a member, and perhaps those books might have been full, I cannot be answerable for that.

17,504. I do not say you are answerable or responsible in that sense, I only want to know the facts; do you know of any books which have been in existence during the time that you have been a member, which are not produced to-day. This looks very much as though there were some hanging back.

17,505. They are all the books which I have seen since I have been a member.

17,506. Will you swear that they are all you ever saw?—Yes, I will swear that they are the only books I have ever seen knowingly since I have been a member of our society.

17,507. That is a complete answer. Are you aware whether any false entries have been made in your books?—No I am not aware of it.

17,508. Have you made any false entries yourself in your books?—No, I have not.

17,509. Are you aware of anybody else who has done so?—No. I am not.

17,509*a*. We are obliged to put these questions, though it is rather an unpleasant duty, because we have found false entries made in other books. Are you aware whether any of your books have been mutilated or leaves torn out, or anything of that kind?—There have been leaves torn out previous to my secretaryship, I believe, as you will see by the books.

17,510. Do you know who tore them out?—No, I do not.

17,511. This book begins November the 24th, 1866. What do you call this book (*showing a book to the witness*). There are only four pages in it, although it is a thickish book?—I could tell you what book it is if I were to see the back of it. (*The witness looked at the book*). It is cash book receipts.

17,512. Then the cash book receipts begin at November the 24th, 1866. Where are the cash book receipts before November the 24th, 1866?—I am sure I do not know.

17,513. Do you enter receipts in this book from week to week?—Every fortnight in the winter; for 26 weeks in the winter season.

17,514. When did you begin to be secretary?—On the 13th of May 1867 I went into office.

17,515. There is a book with a loose sheet dated 8th of May 1867; whether it belongs to this book or not I do not know?—I think it belongs to that book.

17,516. Are there regular entries corresponding with those in the other book of expenditure, beginning November the 24th?—That is the expenditure book that you have now.

17,517. But I find the regular entries in the book begin exactly at the same date that the income begins at?—Somewhere about it, I believe.

17,518. They correspond to a day; and they begin at Novemver the 24th?—I know it is somewhere about the same date, but I could not swear to a day.

17,519. There is a sheet here of May the 8th, 1867?—It would go farther on a leaf or two, I think. If you turn over you will see that it corresponds.

17,520. Those leaves you know are all cut out; all the leaves, of which there must be upwards of 100 in both books, are cut out; that is so, is it not?—Yes, they have been cut out by the appearance of it.

17,521. Is this the contribution book (*showing a book to the witness*)?—It is the contribution book, I believe.

17,522. The contribution book begins November the 12th, 1866. Will you be good enough to look at that book and tell me whether all the leaves in that book at one end have not been cut out, and a sheet pasted over, and then whether you have not begun your entries here in the other end (*handing the book to the witness*)?—It looks as if some had been cut out, but I could not swear that there had. It was not while I have been in office.

17,523. Have you any books of contributions before November the 12th, 1866?—No, only what you see.

17,524. Have you any books of receipts or of payments before November the 24th, 1866?—No, not that I know of.

17,525. Have you any minute book?—No, we have not.

17,526. Have you never had any?—I cannot say that there ever was, and I cannot say that there was not, but there never was a minute——

17,527. Have you never seen a minute book since you have been a member of that society?—Not to my knowledge.

17,528. You must know whether you have seen one or not. Have you ever seen a minute book since you have been member of that society?—No, I have not.

17,529. You swear that deliberately?—Yes, I do.

17,530. That you have never seen a minute book?—Yes.

17,531. Have you no book in which you enter resolutions at which you arrive at your meeting?—They generally put it on a note of paper.

17,532. Do you mean to swear that resolutions come to by your body are not put in a book and recorded?—No, they are not, they are always put on a slip of paper.

17,533. What is the good of putting them on a piece of paper?—I cannot say. I have only been secretary six or seven weeks.

17,534. We know how long you have been secretary, but I ask you have you not a book into which you put those resolutions transferred from those slips of paper?—No.

17,535. You swear that?—Yes.

17,536. Are you aware there has never been such a thing in your book, because if it should be proved afterwards that anything of that kind occurred, it would be a very serious thing for you since you are liable to be indicted for perjury if it should turn out that it has been done and that you have seen it?—I do not know that I have seen one.

17,537. Will you swear that there has not been one?—I will swear I have not seen one.

17,538. You must go further than that. Will you swear that you never had a minute book?—I will swear I never saw one.

17,539. Will you swear there never has been one?—Well, I do not want to swear that which I do not know, or never took any notice of.

17,540. You never saw a minute book?—I never saw one to my knowledge.

17,541. In the hands of nobody?—In the hands of nobody to my knowledge.

17,542. Now who cut out those leaves?—Did you say who cut them out?

17,543. You heard me quite well; who cut out those leaves?—Well, I could not say who cut them out.

17,544. Did you cut them out?—No, I did not.

17,545. Has anybody ever told you that he had cut them out?—No, no one.

17,546. Has anybody ever told you that he knew who had cut them out?—No, nobody; not one.

17,547. Be kind enough to come here. (*The witness walked towards the Commissioners.*) You have sworn deliberately that there was no minute book containing resolutions. Look at that book (*handing a book to the witness*) and tell me what it is?—Well, I will take my oath that I have never knowingly seen that book.

17,548. After having sworn what you have is that a minute book containing resolutions?—I believe it is.

17,549. Although you have sworn that you had never had a minute book, it turns out that amongst your own books there is actually a minute book going back as far as Januury the 30th, 1865, but there are only entries of resolutions in 1865. I see "That it is "desirable to form a union of bricklayers and brick-"makers to aid and assist each other in contests "where their separate efforts fail to accomplish the "object in view," and so on. It then talks about mutual aid, settling by arbitration, and then about the rules; and then it says at an ordinary meeting "that "a deputation shall wait upon Mr. Anthony Hardy "with a view to settling the difference between them "and the bricklayers. Confirmed." Then there are minutes of a special meeting on the 3rd of March, "any member of the executive committee divulging "privately the transaction of any meeting shall be "fined 20*s*."?—That is a book which exists between the bricklayers and the brickmakers, I believe.

15,550. "That the committee wait upon Mr. "Joseph Marsden, the secretary to the master builders "association for the purpose of settling all disputes "by arbitration. Any member of the executive "committee absenting himself from business without "the consent of the president to be fined," and then he is to be expelled if he is intoxicated in the meeting. What do you say this book is?—It is between the bricklayers and the brickmakers now I come to look at it.

17,551. What officers have you?—We have a secretary, a treasurer, and a committee of six.

17,552. Do you call that the executive committee?—Well it manages all business.

17,553. Are those the officers?—Those are the officers.

17,554. Are this committee of six what you call the executive committee in those resolutions?—No, there is a committee of both branches.

17,555. The executive committee is a committee of both branches, is it?—The committee to which that book belongs is a committee of both branches, both of the bricklayers and the brickmakers.

17,556. Does your committee of six never make an entry of its proceedings?—No.

17,557. You have sworn that you do not know who has mutilated these three books?—Yes.

17,558. When you entered into your office did you notice that they were mutilated?—I looked at them.

17,559. Then you knew it?—I knew they were torn out.

17,560. Then?—Yes, then when I took to them.

17,561. On the 30th of May of the present year, 1867, do you swear that they were torn out?—Yes.

17,562. When you look to them and found that the last secretary had delivered up to you a set of books that were mutilated in this way, did you not ask him how it came to be that the books were so mutilated?—I told him that I should not sit except he continued forward with me to explain matters that might come up.

17,563. Did you ask him how it was that those books were mutilated? that was the question that I put to you?—No, I did not ask him any questions.

17,564. You knew at the time that you would have to produce your books did you not?—Well, I did not know whether we should or not.

17,565. You knew there was going to be the inquiry?—Yes, I expected there would be the inquiry.

17,566. Did it not occur to your mind that when the inquiry took place they would have to look at the books?—Well I did not know whether they would or not exactly, but I expected they would.

17,567. And if you knew or expected that we should want to look at these books, I ask you upon your oath whether you did not ask the secretary how it was that the books happened to be mutilated?—No, I did not.

17,568. You swear that?—I swear that.

17,569. It never was explained to you?—I never asked him, nor did he explain it to me.

17,570. Did anybody?—They did not, and I never asked anyone.

17,571. Has it ever been the subject of conversation in your committee?—Not that I know of.

17,572. You must know; it is a very important thing, you know. Do you mean to say that you have never talked about it?—It might have been talked about, but not to my hearing.

17,573. I did not ask you about what might have been. Have you never heard it talked about in your

NINETEENTH DAY.

W. Stanley.

27 June 1867.

union that those books were mutilated?—It has been talked about without a doubt.

17,574. Then why did you hesitate about it? who talked about it?—Well, I am sure I do not know who talked about it. The committee changes every three months.

17,575. When have you heard them talk about it, who talked?—I do not know who talked; I could not distinguish them personally.

17,576. When was it talked about?—That I do not know.

17,577. How long ago did you first hear it talked about?—It might be two or three weeks since, or I cannot say exactly how long it is since.

17,578. When is it your belief that you ever heard it first talked about?—(*The witness hesitated.*)

17,579. When will you swear was the first time you ever heard it talked about?—I could not swear to the time.

17,580. Within what time will you swear that you first heard it talked about?—Well, I could not swear that.

17,581. Did you ever hear it talked about before you became secretary?—Well, I never took that notice; I am sure I do not know.

17,582. Will you swear that you heard it talked about before you became secretary?—It might be talked about in the committee room.

17,583. I do not wish you to answer like that. Was it talked about before you became secretary?—It might be talked about in the committee room, without a doubt.

17,584. Was it talked about in the committee room without a doubt?—It might have been mentioned in the committee room.

17,585. Before you became secretary?—It might have been mentioned then, but the committee changes every three months.

17,586. Will you swear that it was mentioned before you became secretary that the books were mutilated?—It might have been mentioned in my hearing or out of my hearing.

17,587. It is of no use your talking of what might be. Was it mentioned in your hearing before you became secretary that those books were mutilated?—They said——

17,588. "Yes" or "no"; before you became secretary was it mentioned that the books were mutilated?—I was not on the committee before I became secretary.

17,589. Answer me, "yes" or "no"; you have been only two months secretary?—I have not been two months, only six or seven weeks.

17,590. I know that, that is why you can recollect. Was it mentioned before you became secretary?—No, not before.

17,591. Then it has never been mentioned since you became secretary?—Not in my presence.

17,592. Had you any office at all before you were secretary? were you a committeeman?—Well, I have been one on one or two occasions.

17,593. When were you last on a committee?—Last winter, I think, I was on a committee.

17,594. Fix the time; you must know when it was; do not trifle with us?—I was on the committee, I think, from last August up to February.

17,595. During that time you know whether it was ever mentioned or not in your committee about those books being mutilated?—They said when they heard that the Commissioners were coming down that it was a pity but what they had been kept, because every quarter's account is torn out.

17,596. Who said that?—I am sure I could not say who said so.

17,597. Yes, you can?—On my oath I could not.

17,598. When was it said?—It was sometime during that time, but I could not say what time.

17,599. At what period?—It might be the beginning of the six months or it might be the latter end of the six months.

17,600. But which was it?—I could not swear which it was.

17,601. When do you believe that it was? do you believe that it was said in the month of November?—I think it was in the beginning, but I do not know; I could not swear when it was.

17,602. You never heard about the Commission in the beginning, because the Commission was never talked about until after the Hereford Street outrage, and that was in October?—It might be at the middle of the time, I cannot say exactly, it might be at any time during the six months.

17603. I caution you; I do not want to threaten you, but you are not answering me at all satisfactorily, and I tell you so. At what time was it?—If it was at the beginning of the six months and I was to swear that it was the latter end of the six months——

17,604. Now see how foolishly you are talking. You say that it was when they heard that the Commission was coming down. There was no talk about the Commission coming until after October?—Then it must have been either at the centre or towards the back end of the time.

17,605. Do you mean to tell me that when they said that, nothing was said as to how it came to pass that those leaves were cut out?—No.

17,606. You had a conversation about it. Did they not say who had done it, and why they had done it?—No, I did not ask any particular questions.

17,607. Who said so?—I could not say.

17,608. You shall?—I could not.

17,609. You shall, or you will stand in peril. You can remember who said it?—No, they were not directing their discourse to me.

17,610. I know that; but you were present at the committee when that was discussed. Who said it?—I could not say who said it.

17,611. I caution you again. I give you fair warning?—Well, on my oath I could not say who said so.

17,612. Who was present at the committee meeting?—(*The witness hesitated.*) I am trying to think of it if I can.

17,613. Who was present at the committee meeting?—I think Francis Butt was one of the committee at the time, but I could not swear. Sometimes there were one or two of them away.

17,614. I am asking you not who were away but who was there besides Francis Butt?—Well, I could not swear who was there.

17,615. Mind what you are about!—I think a man of the name of Poole was on the committee, if I remember right.

17,616. What is his christian name?—Thomas Poole.

17,617. Who besides?—I am sure I could not say which of the members were there.

17,618. Yes you can. Who was there besides? Have you any book containing the names of your committee men?—No.

17,619. Who was on your committee at that time in November last? We may perhaps get it in that way.—(*The witness hesitated.*)

17,620. I will not give you much more time?—Well, I am trying to think of it as well as I can.

17,621. I will furnish myself with a document which will perhaps quicken your memory, if you do not go on.—I think Emmanuel Elms was one of the first three months out of the six.

17,622. I am speaking of November, when you heard of the inquiry. Was Emmanuel Elms on then?—He was on the first three months of the six.

17,623. I ask you whether he was on in November?—Yes, he would be.

17,624. Was he at that meeting when you talked about this matter?—Well, I could not swear that he was.

17,625. What is your belief?—He might be——

17,626. What is your belief?—Some meetings——

17,627. What is your belief—was he there or not?—I believe he was, but still he might not be any the more for that.

17,628 Do you believe that there were only three

NINETEENTH DAY.

W. Stanley.

27 June 1867.

there, or more than three ?—There might be three, or there might be four, or there might be all six of them there.

17,629. Do you believe that there were three, or more than three ?—There perhaps might be more than three.

17,630. Do you believe that there were three or more than three ?—Yes, I believe they were all there. They might be all five there. I could not swear to the number.

17,631. Who were the others who you believe were there ?—Alfred Ellesmere was on the committee, I believe, but I could not swear that he was there that night.

17,632. We have now Butt, Poole, Elms, and Ellesmere. Who were the others ?—Well, I am sure I could not swear who the others were.

17,633. Do you mean to say that you do not recollect who were on the committee in November last ?—No, I do not, on my oath.

17,634. But you know that Butt, and Poole, and Elms, and Ellesmere were there ?—Yes, I could almost swear they were on the first three months of the six.

17,635. I am speaking of November ; that was the time when you heard about the inquiry you know ?—I did not go on till August.

17,636. I want to know whether they were on in November ?—Of course I could not swear who were the others.

17,637. Do you believe that those persons were there in November ?—Yes, I believe those parties were on the committee in November.

17,638. Now you had heard that there was going to be an inquiry ; you thought it was a very important thing that those leaves had been cut out, and you discussed the matter in committee. What did you say about it ?—It was not discussed to my knowledge.

17,639. It was spoken about, was it not ?—It is a customary thing——

17,640. It was spoken about ; what was said about it ?—It was a customary thing——

17,641. Do not talk to me about "customary things ;" what was said about this book ?—It was said——

17,642. Who said it ?—I could not say.

17,643. Yes you can. You must know ?—On my oath ——

17,644. You must know ?—They were not directing their discourse to me.

17,645. That does not matter, you are not directing your discourse to those persons in the body of the the hall, but they hear what you are saying. Who said it ?—I cannot say.

17,646. You shall not get out of it in that way. Who said it ?—On my oath I cannot say who said it.

17,647. I will leave it there. When it was said by someone that it was a pity those leaves had been cut out, what observation was made ?—Well, I cannot say exactly what observation was made, because I cannot take account and keep things in my head so long.

17,648. Did they say why it was done ?—No, they did not to my knowledge.

17,649. Did they say who had done it ?—No.

17,650. Do you mean to say that they did not say why it was done ?—No, not to my knowledge.

17,651. Can you swear that it was not said why it was done ?—No, it was not; not to my knowledge.

17,652. Your knowledge will not protect you at all, because if you were there and it was said in your hearing, your qualifying it by saying that it was not said to your knowledge will not be any protection to you, because you must know ?—I do not want to swear what I do not know, and I could not swear that.

17,653. I do not want you to swear what you do not know. You heard it said that it was a pity that the books had been destroyed, because there was going to be a Commission, and I ask you what was said upon that ?—Well, I do not know particularly what was said.

17,654. Never mind about your not knowing particularly what was said ? (*The witness hesitated.*)

17,655. Do you refuse to tell me ?—I could not tell you——

17,656. Do you refuse to tell me ? (*The witness hesitated.*)

17,657. Do you refuse to tell me what was said when a member of the committee said it was a pity that the leaves had been cut out ?—Someone perhaps might have made a remark and said, "Is there nothing " to fear from their being cut out or from their stay- " ing in ? " but I could not swear.

17,658. Who said it ? it is no use telling us what might have been said ; what was said, I ask, upon that being mentioned ?—Well, I could not say upon my oath what was the reply nor yet who said it.

17,659. Will you swear that they did not say that they had cut them out to avoid your seeing what was in them ?—I do not think they were cut out with that intention.

17,660. Will you swear that it was not so said ?—I will, so far as my knowledge goes.

17,661. Will you swear that it was not so said ?—I will swear that it was not said in my hearing.

17,662. Will you swear that it was not so said ?—I could not swear that it was not said, but I will swear it was not said in my hearing.

17,663. Do you not know that they were cut out for that purpose ?—Not that I know of.

17,664. Do you not believe it ?—No, I do not beleive they were.

17,665. For what purpose do you believe they were cut out ?—It is a most customary thing for them to be cut out about every six months or so.

17,666. For what ? Have you ever known them cut out before ?—Yes, I have, I believe.

17,667. Who cut them out when you knew it ?—Well, I do not know who cut them out.

17,668. But who dare cut leaves out of a book of your public body ?—Well, I do not know——

17,669. When have you known them cut out before this last time ?—I have not been at the head of the office——

17,670. When have you known them cut out before this last time ?—I am sure I could not say.

17,671. You have said that you have known them cut before, and that it was customary. Now I will test you ; I ask you when you have known them cut out before ?—(*The witness hesitated*) They were cut out at intervals.

17,672. What I ask you is, when have you known them cut cut before, and you shall answer that question ?—Well, I could not swear at what time they were cut out.

17,673. Were they cut out six months before the last time that they were cut out ?—I could not swear that.

17,674. Were they cut out a year before ?—It might have been a year or it might have been 18 months or two years ; I could not swear.

17,675. Will you swear that they were cut out the year before ?—I will swear that it is a practical thing for them to be cut out, but I could not swear that they were cut out.

17,676. Will you swear that they were ever cut out before the last occasion when they were cut out ? —Well, I was not secretary at that time.

17,677. Will you swear that they were cut out before the last occasion when they were cut out; you shall answer the question ?—I could not swear it upon my oath.

17,678. Then how dare you say that it was the practice in your place to cut them out every six months if you never knew of their being cut out before (*the witness hesitated*).

17,679. Have you ever known them cut out before ? —I believe it is the practice ——.

17,680. I ask you if you have ever known them cut out before, and you shall fix the time ?—(*The witness hesitated*).

17,681. I should be very sorry to have to request

NINETEENTH DAY.

W. Stanley.

27 June 1867.

you to be prosecuted, but it will be my duty if you go on in this way; do you mean to say that all those leaves were not cut out at the same time?—Well, I could not swear that they were.

17,682. Can you swear that they were not?—It is a practical thing generally to cut——

17,683. You have told me about its being a "practical" thing, and you cannot bring an instance of its having been done before. Every one of the edges is quite fresh; will you swear that all those leaves were not cut out at the same time? (*The witness hesitated*)—I could not swear that they were.

17,684. I did dot ask you that; will you swear that they were not?—(*The witness hesitated*).

17,685. You had better not get yourself into trouble by giving answers of this kind. We have not gone into the affairs of your union, but I can assure you that your conduct puts your union in a very suspicious light indeed; can you give me no further information?—No, I cannot give you any further information.

17,686. Stand down and just think over this matter, and I will call you up again; do not leave the court.

H. Owen.

HENRY OWEN sworn and examined.

17,687. (*Chairman.*) You are a brickmaker, I believe?—Yes.

17,688. And you are secretary of the society, are you not?—Yes, I have been for two years up to May the 12th or 13th, I think.

17,689. Did you deliver over those books to Stanley?—I did.

17,690. Are you aware whether there is any minute book besides this?—There never was one to my knowledge.

17,691. What did you do with your resolutions?—They were mostly booked on a little paper and afterwards looked over, and then committed to the flames.

17,692. Then do you mean to say that you have no resolutions kept?—None, whatever, not belonging to the brickmakers society alone; there is one book which you have got there, which I brought this morning with me. No man has ever seen it only those who have been on the committee of the bricklayers and brickmakers; there are some minutes entered into that book of transactions which have taken place at those meetings jointly of the bricklayers and brickmakers. It was at the suggestion of the bricklayers that we should have a minute book; I told them that it was because——

17,693. I do not want you to tell me what it was; I want to know whether the brickmakers have a minute book of their own?—The brickmakers have not and never had.

17,694. Had the bricklayers?—Yes, I think they keep all theirs in a business-like manner; there are plenty of scholars amongst them; I believe they do.

17,695. These are not their books?—No, these are mine. That book which I brought here this morning to bring with these is in my keeping; I am the secretary of the two societies.

17,696. I wish you would answer questions and not make a speech?—Very well.

17,697. Do the bricklayers keep a book?—Yes, of their own.

17,698. You are a brickmaker?—Yes.

17,699. You have seen those books which have been handed in to us by Stanley?—I have.

17,700. In what state were they when you delivered them to Stanley?—They were mutilated.

17,701. When were they mutilated?—To the best of my recollection I mutilated them myself somewhere in the beginning of November.

17,702. At that time you had heard of this inquiry?—Yes, I had some idea that there was going to be one.

17,703. Did you do it of your own accord or by instructions from your committee?—Of my own accord.

17,704. Did you mention to the committee the fact that you had done it?—After it was done.

17,705. When did you tell the committee?—Somewhere about the date that they dated from. The lodge night, I think, began on the 12th of November, and I told them that I had mutilated the books.

17,706. You told the committee immediately after you had done it?—Yes, I told the committee then present on the 12th of November.

17,707. Was Stanley present?—I think he was.

17,708. Was Butt there?—Yes.

17,709. And Poole?—Yes.

17,710. And Ellesmere?—No. I think if you will look at the book when it was audited up it will tell you who was there that quarter, but neither Elms nor Ellesmere was there at that time.

17,711. But Butt and Poole were there?—Butt and Poole were there and myself and John White the treasurer. If you will just allow me to look at the book I shall be able to tell you.

17,712. By all means. You are giving us fair evidence, and we can deal with evidence like this?—(*After referring to the book.*) There would be myself, Francis Butt, George Sharp, John White, William Stanley, Thomas Poole, and I think a person of the name of Samuel Roberts, but I am almost sure, indeed I think I could swear to it. There are six who constitute the committee and two off it.

17,713. And you were all present at the meeting?—I think so, but we have no record of it.

17,714. And at the meeting you mentioned to the committee that you had mutilated the books?—I did after it was done.

17,715. Now why did you mutilate those books?—Well, I adopted it on my own authority, from what the practice of my predecessors had been.

17,716. You followed the practice of your predecessors?—Yes.

17,717. Who was the predecessor whose practice you followed?—Well, to the best of my recollection, Mr. Palmer was 15 months or 18 months——

17,718. I am speaking of the practice?—It was done when he was secretary.

17,719. How long before your time did he mutilate them?—About 15 months.

17,720. When you received the books on your becoming secretary were they mutilated or not?—They were mutilated.

17,721. And they were mutilated afterwards by you?—By me and by myself alone.

17,722. How many leaves do you think that you cut out? Did you cut out the whole of the proceedings for two years?—Our society's business occupies about from four to six leaves in 12 months, or a little more perhaps; the expenditure occupies rather more but the income less.

17,723. Therefore you would take out from eight to 12 leaves?—More than that.

17,724. How many did you cut out?—I might say up to 20. I cannot say precisely to one.

17,725. How many leaves had been cut out before you began with it?—I am sure I could not tell.

17,726. But about how many?—Well, the books were mutilated before Mr. Palmer took them, by his own record.

17,727. Is Mr. Palmer alive?—Yes.

17,728. Are there any books which you mutilated besides?—Only those present.

17,729. Only these three books?—Only these three books.

17,730. Are there any other books in your society which have been mutilated?—None which ever were in my possession.

17,731. I see that there is one book where there a good many leaves cut out at the end and turned down to the front?—There are. If you will show me I can point out the reasons, very likely. (*The book was handed to the witness.*) This is the contribution book; well I know this is my handywork, I cut them out.

NINETEENTH DAY.

H. Owen.

27 June 1867.

17,732. Was that mutilated also?—Yes.

17,733. And you pasted that leaf over?—I did.

17,734. What was your object in pasting that leaf over?—Well, I thought it would look rather better workmanship, pasting it over.

17,735. And it might conceal the fact of its having been mutilated?—That was the idea.

17,736. Now open that book at the first page of entry, when does that begin?—November the 12th. The arrears are carried over.

17,737. Supposing a man had paid his contributions for the previous year any time during the year, and you claimed arrears from him, and there had been a mistake, what means of proof would there be, if that book was destroyed, that his contributions had been paid?—None whatever, only we carry them over very often, which you will see if you look back.

17,738. Therefore, for a quarter past that man who paid the contribution would have no proof whatever that he had paid his contributions?—He carries receipts with him. They have check books against this themselves.

17,739. Therefore, he would have had simply his own check book?—He would have a receipt in his own book.

17,740. What was your object in mutilating the contribution book? What is the good which can accrue to anybody from cutting out leaves, showing what men have paid to your union?—I did it with a view of having the books corresponding one with the other.

17,741. But they corresponded before?—Yes, so they did.

17,742. Then that is not an answer. What was your reason?—I cannot give any other reason, only that I wanted the dates to correspond with each other.

17,743. But they had been mutilated to correspond before?—Yes, I mutilated them to correspond again.

17,744. But they did correspond all the way through; what was the good to anybody of cutting those leaves out?—I have given you a reason.

17,745. You have given us a reason, but it is a very insufficient one. Now, was it not to prevent us from having an opportunity of seeing what were the entries in those books?—I have stated that before, I think.

17,746. It was so?—Yes.

17,747. You have not stated it, but it is very candid to state so. What entry was it that you were afraid of our seeing?—None whatever that I know of.

17,748. There must have been an entry which you are afraid of our seeing, or else you would not have cut them out?—There are little expenses incurred on committees for refreshments which might look rather extravagant, and that sort of thing we had cut out.

17,749. Was that your sole reason?—That was the sole reason.

17,750. Were there entries in the book besides expenses of committees which might appear extravagant?—No, none whatever.

17,751. To what extent did the entry go, to how large a sum did you ever go?—I think eight of us consumed 2*l.* 2*s.* in a sitting in an afternoon for wages and refreshments.

17,752. Was there no larger sum than 2*l.* 2*s.* put in?—None.

17,753. On your oath, were there not payments in that book (I do not care under what name they come) which you did not wish us to see?—Will you please to put that question again?

17,754. I do not care under what names they were entered in your books, but I ask you whether there were not payments in those books which you did not wish us to see?—Not any but what I have stated.

17,755. Were there any omissions of entries so that the books would not correspond?—None whatever.

17,756. Were there any entries, so that if you checked one against the other you would see that there were monies which were not accounted for?—Just please to put the question again, so that I may properly understand before I answer it.

17,757. You are quite right. Were there any entries of which you know, which, if they had been examined, would show that there was a certain sum of money which had come into your hands as secretary, or to the treasurer, which had not been accounted for in the books?—None, whatever, with the exception of the committee's expenses.

17,758. Will you swear that the monies which you put down under the head of "committee's expenses" were monies expended by committees in drink and refreshment?—And in wages for losing their half day; I will swear that.

17,759. And in wages for their losing their half day in managing the affairs of the union?—Yes.

17,760. And there was no further entry under the name of the expenses of the committee whereas in point of fact they were expenses of a perfectly different character?—None whatever.

17,761. And you will swear that?—I will swear it.

17,762. We are obliged to stand by your statement, not having the books. When you mentioned this fact to your committee that you had mutilated the books, and that there was going to be an inquiry, what observation was made by your committee?—They said that I had not done a right action.

17,763. Did they not complain very much of your conduct?—Yes, they said I ought to get a new set, and I told them I thought they were quite good enough for the purpose.

17,764. And what did they say to that?—They gave me a calling, a little lecture, that I had done a very wrong thing at a very important time, and I told them that I felt quite satisfied with what I had done.

17,765. How long did this "calling" last?—About a minute.

17,766. Then after all they were not so sorry?—They did not appear to be.

17,767. What did you do with the leaves?—I put them in the fire.

17,768. Did anybody see you?—My own family. I take the books home regularly to audit them up.

17,769. What members of your family saw you put them in the fire?—Well, there are eight of us. There are plenty of them; they might be all there.

17,770. But we cannot know how many of them there were?—It is hard to count when there are so many round the hearth. There might be half of them.

17,771. But which of them?—My wife and two of my eldest sons, and I think two or three of the younger ones.

17,772. And they saw them consigned to the flames?—Yes.

17,773. It was done at your own home?—Yes.

17,774. And was not done at the committee room?—No.

17,775. Did you not talk about the matter, and say that you thought that we should make a great point and handle of this against the union directly we found that those things had been mutilated?—The committee made that remark to me that the Commissioners would make a great handle of it.

17,776. I thought they would. What did you say to that?—I do not know that I gave them any reply.

17,777. And I suppose you do not care so long as the leaves are gone?—Not I.

17,778. Did you say that it was "no matter"?—"No matter," I said, "they cannot speak."

17,779. Were you giving up office then?—I did not give up, nor have I positively given up office yet.

17,780. But you are not secretary, are you?—I have been officiating until this examination is over, at the request of Mr. Stanley, on account of those books being mutilated.

17,781. It was in consequence of the mutilation of those books was it that Stanley insisted on your remaining?—Yes, to give an answer.

17,782. You are kept on as the witness?—I do not know what I am kept on for.

17,783. You are kept on to satisfy him?—I am kept on to satisfy a wish of his.

17,784. Then it became a very serious thing for Stanley. He did not like the looks of things?—No,

NINETEENTH DAY.

H. Owen.

27 June 1867.

because he has worked himself into a respectable position, and he is with respectable employers, and he thought it would be a disgrace to him to have to show cause as to his books being in that mutilated state.

17,785. Then Mr. Stanley has been trifling with us altogether, when he said that he did not recollect all this conversation?—Well, he must recollect it, because it took place in Carlisle Street. He made some demur about taking to the books.

17,786. Then in all this pretence that he did not know anything about this mutilation, and that it was not mentioned in committee, Mr. Stanley has been trifling with us?—I think he has some knowledge about it. I may say that he has; he has not given you the candid answer that he ought to have done.

17,787. Have there been any charges at all against your union for damaging bricks?—Yes, I believe there have been some charges made, and there have been charges made without foundation.

17,788. But when were the charges made?—Well, to the best of my recollection there was a charge made of bands being taken away belonging to Mrs. Birch, which was supposed to be a society affair, and the society made the band good and bought a new band for about 7*l.* or 8*l.*

17,789. When was that?—I think that would be about the beginning of this last winter. Mrs. Birch is better known by the name of Mycock. She is Mr. Alderman Mycock's widow. We paid for a new band.

17,790. But in your trade you do not have rattening?—They straighten bricks sometimes when they are not straight enough. I might say they put their foot on them.

17,791. You employ persons then to put their feet upon bricks?—We never pay them.

17,792. But you get them?—Yes; they do one another. Unionists do non-unionists, and they retaliate again.

17,793. You get men to walk on the bricks and spoil them, in fact?—We do not get them, they employ themselves.

17,794. But they do go?—They do go.

17,795. They spoil the bricks?—Yes.

17,796. That is to say, they spoil the bricks of the non-unionists?—Yes.

17,797. When they do not comply with your rules? That is it.

17,798. Do they ever put pins and needles in the bricks?—I believe it is attributed to them that they do it.

17,799. Have there been many accusations against your union for having done so within the last 10 years?—No.

17,800. How often has it been charged?—That I do not know; I have only been secretary two years.

17,801. But during those two years?—There has been but one charge as to Mrs. Mycock's band. I saw it in the paper, but the charge was not made openly against us.

17,802. What was it?—The subject you named of pins and needles.

17,803. What other charge has been made against your union that you are aware of?—There has not been any charge made against the union or its officers for any bricks spoiling.

17,804. Has there been any charges of bricks having been spoiled belonging to parties who are obnoxious to the trade?—They have laid them, but they have never been brought against the officials.

17,805. They have not brought it home?—No.

17,806. They never brought it home to the union?—I did not ought to say no, because it is acknowledging that they have done it if I say no. The non-unionists have never brought it home to the officials.

17,807. But you mean to say that you know it was done in the interests of your trade?—I perfectly believe that it was done to enforce the rules.

17,808. A man can spoil a good many bricks in a night in that way, can he not?—Well, I never practised it.

17,809. If you tell me, I shall know how many I can do, you know, without practising it myself; you are a practical man?—Well; I am not a practical man at that.

17,810. But a man who was so disposed could do a considerable amount of damage in a night, could he not?—Yes; a considerable deal.

17,811. What amount of damage could a man do easily in a night. Could he do 100*l.* worth of damage?—No; nor 10*l.* worth.

17,812. But 10*l.* worth would be the amount of damage that he could do, would it?—Not easily, considering the space of ground that he would have to run over.

17,813. Have you ever heard of a case where 17,000 bricks were spoiled in one night?—Not to my knowledge.

17,814. But it might be done?—It is possible.

17,815. Is that the only remedy to be had by members of the union (not the officials)?—I suppose so.

17,816. I should like to know what that pins and needles case was?—Well, I read it in the "Telegraph" that at the Bradway tunnel the unionists had been putting pins and needles into the clay of Mr. Thompson. I believe he is the contractor.

17,817. Do you know how many they spoiled for him?—I do not.

17,818. But was a large number stated to have been spoiled?—It said a quantity of clay in preparation for brick making.

17,819. Did you hear whether it was a large quantity?—It did not give the quantity. It said, "A "large quantity of clay in preparation for brick "making."

17,820. Do you know when this was?—To the best of my recollection it would be about 18 months ago I think.

17,821. What would be the effect of putting pins and needles into the bricks?—It certainly would destroy the men's hands that had to work the clay in the making of the bricks.

17,822. That is 18 months ago, you say?—To the best of my knowledge it is.

17,823. Before that time, you having been in the trade, were there any charges of this kind besides this Bradway tunnel affair?—Not to my knowledge.

17,824. Have you never heard any other charge of pins and needles being put in the clay?—I never heard of any other charge.

17,825. I do not mean amongst your union, but as having been done?—No, I have not heard of it.

17,826. Have you heard in the last ten years of cases of the destruction of bricks by walking on them, or damaging them by putting stones on them, or anything of that kind?—Only the cases I have mentioned, and those only through the papers.

17,827. Do you mean to say that in the last ten years you have never heard of any other cases than those?—They have never been brought to my knowledge.

17,828. You are not aware of any?—I am not aware of any.

17,829. Have you ever heard it alleged against your union that parties have been shot at for disobeying your rules?—I have heard it and read of it in the papers.

17,830. Can you tell me a case where that has been charged? do you know a person of the name of Moorhouse?—I believe I do know a man of the name of Moorhouse.

17,831. Was there a charge of his being shot at?—Never.

17,832. What was done to him?—Nothing whatever that I know of.

17,833. You have never heard of anything being done to Moorhouse?—No, I have not.

17,834. Do you know a person of the name of Cotton?—Yes, I do, he is a member of the society.

17,835. Did you ever hear that he was shot at?—No.

17,836. Come, you do not know as much as I do

about it, though you are in the trade and I am not. You know Cotton you say?—I know Cotton well, we are very intimate.

17,837. Has he never told you that he has been shot at?—Never.

17,838. In drying, is gunpowder ever mixed with the bricks?—I never knew of any powder being put into the bricks.

17,839. Or into the stack?—No.

17,840. Have you ever heard of a man called Barnley?—I have heard of him, he is a member of the society.

17,841. Have you ever heard of his being threatened?—Yes.

17,842. Do you know a person of the name of Gascoigne Hickson?—No.

17,843. Do you know a person of the name of Glaives?—Yes, we have several persons of that name on the books of the society.

17,844. Have you ever heard of such a thing as Glaives being attacked?—No.

17,845. You never heard of such a thing?—I never heard of such a thing.

17,846. Do you know a person of the name of Peate?—Yes, he is a member of the society.

17,847. Has he ever been done anything to?—I am not acquainted with the matter, except what he once informed me himself.

17,848. What was that?—He was always a good workman, he said, and he had been only rattened once during the time, and that was when he worked for Mr. Chadwick, and the society paid him, he said, all the claims that he charged them.

17,849. Do you know a person of the name of Bridges?—Yes, he is a member of the society.

17,850. Was he ever done anything to?—I am sure I do not know.

17,851. Nor Robinson?—I know Robinson well.

17,852. Has he ever been done anything to?—I hear he has by report.

17,853. Do you mean by the report of a pistol?—I have heard it, but I do not know it.

17,854. What he suffered from?—He told me he had suffered from depredations.

17,855. What depredations?—From their trying to blow him up, and destroying his bricks.

17,856. How did they try to blow him up?—Putting a little gunpowder under his house, and under the window.

17,857. Did he tell you this?—Yes, he told me and my wife about it. We were on very intimate terms.

17,858. When was that?—To the best of my knowledge it would be seven or eight years ago.

17,859. At that time was there any quarrel between them and the society?—I believe at that time his men were not paying to the society.

17,860. And did they throw a can of gunpowder into his room?—So I heard from his own lips.

17,861. Is he alive?—He is, or he was the other day.

17,862. And he is now a member of your union, is he?—No, he is not.

17,863. Did he charge the union with having been at the bottom of this outrage?—He charged the union as instigators and perpetrators of it to me.

17,864. If you had paid anything at all for doing a job of this kind against Mr. Robinson, it ought to have appeared in these books, you know?—Yes.

17,865. And if you have cut out the leaves, we cannot see whether you have paid anything or not?—No, the entry would be cut out at the same time.

17,866. No doubt; that is quite clear. Have you any tariff or regular price, as they have among the grinders, for destroying a man's bands?—The society, since it came under my management, have never recognized nor paid any monies for either rattenings or outrages.

17,867. You have never paid any money for such purposes?—Never.

17,868. If a man has rattened another man does he ever come and tell you that he has done it?—Never.

17,869. Never in your time?—Never in my time.

17,870. Have you ever got bands restored?—The bands are only used in places where they have machinery to grind the clay.

17,871. But where they are used have they been taken?—There has never been but one instance and that is Mrs. Birch.

17,872. And there you restored it?—We replaced.

17,873. Why did you do that?—Because Mr. Birch was employing our labour, and her men were paying to our society, and we thought it our duty to reinstate it.

17,874. But why should you do it any more than I should do it?—If you had a copy of our rules you would see that our rules bind us to do it. If any employer employs our members, and his men pay to our society, if they should suffer any damage to any amount, we pay them the full compensation claimed.

17,875. Why should you have such a rule as that?—Because we find it to our benefit.

17,876. Why do you find it to your benefit?—The majority of the masters pay to our union, and by giving them compensation they pay with a better grace than they would if we did not grant them protection.

17,877. Then you not only insure your own property but you insure everybody's property for whom you work?—Who pays to the union. If they have property destroyed, and they are on our books, either their workmen or themselves, they get the value of the damages which are done to them.

17,878. Then you are insurers, in fact?—Well, it amounts to that.

17,879. Are you aware, before your time, though it may be better now, since you have come in, of any instance in which money has been paid by your trade for any outrage done to any person?—I have never known it.

17,880. It is not likely that you would know it?—If I knew it I should feel in duty bound to admit it, because I set my face against all such transactions.

17,881. I think that you have given your evidence very fairly. Have you ever heard of its being done by other people?—No, I have not.

17,882. By no secretary?—By no secretary.

17,883. Nothing of the kind?—Nothing of the kind for outrages or rattening by the society.

17,884. You are more lenient with your members for embezzlement than we are as lawyers, I find?—Are we? Then there is a little bit of grace about us in some things.

17,885. When persons are guilty of embezzlement they are punished for embezzlement; but I find that according to your rules you do not do anything of the kind. You say, "Should any member of the society "be detected in embezzling the funds belonging to the "society he shall be suspended until the money be "paid and the claim satisfied?"—There is no punishment except in that way.

17,886. Then there is no punishment in your society for any officer embezzling the funds of the society?—Only suspending his gifts.

17,887. Then I should be very glad to be a member of your society, because it would be easy enough to get 500*l*. of your money and go off with it, and nothing would happen?—We should be very glad to accept you, sir.

17,888. Then all you say is, "Go along and take the money along with you." It is a very pleasant way of getting the money, and they do not expel the man: they suspend him; it is not suspension by the neck, I suppose?—No; it is not lawful to hang a man in the brick trade.

17,889. It is quite clear what all this cutting out of leaves is for; it is quite evident that you did not want us to see those books?—Yes, that is the sum of it, that is the total.

17,890. We cannot tell what it is?—No.

17,891. And you are very glad that it is done?—I am not displeased.

NINETEENTH DAY.

H. Owen.

27 June 1867.

17,892. Well, I would much rather have a man who would come and speak out like you than one like the last witness?—Well, the fact is, there was a little impediment in his speech.

17,893. You are quite right, there was a very great impediment in his speech. I think you have been successful as to your books, because we can get nothing out of them?—And I am glad of it.

The witness withdrew.

W. Stanley.

William Stanley recalled and further examined.

78,894. (*Chairman.*) You have behaved in a most disingenuous way, and I cannot help thinking that you came here determined to commit perjury, which is a very serious offence?—No, I did not.

78,975. I do not know that we are right in not requesting that you should be prosecuted for perjury; because, of course, if the evidence of Mr. Owen is at all to be believed, you must have committed perjury, and you came here to deceive us. You knew quite well that the sole ground of your having retained Mr. Owen as secretary along with yourself was that the secretary would have to answer to us for the mutilation of the books; and you wished him to explain it. You knew, too, that it had been discussed in the committee, and that it had been considered a very serious question in the committee, and you evaded the various questions which we put to you on the subject. If we had not obtained the information which we have obtained from Mr. Owen, we should have had to con-consider whether we ought not to order you to be prosecuted forthwith for perjury; as it is, I do not think that there is a failure of justice, and we do not want to be too severe, or to do more than carry out this inquiry with due firmness; and, therefore, although you have conducted yourself in a manner which does you infinite discredit, and although you have disgraced yourself very much in the eyes of the town, yet we hardly feel called upon, under the circumstances, to prosecute you; still you may consider that you have been very lucky to escape that prosecution. You have been a very ill-conducted witness, and you may now go away with your books disgraced as you are.

The witness withdrew.

H. Cutts.

Henry Cutts recalled and further examined.

17,896. (*Chairman.*) We have not looked at many of your books, but we have looked at one of them. That is your one of your books (*handing a book to the witness*), is it not?—It is the executive committee book.

17,897. Will you turn to the entries in that book previous to April 23, 1867?—Yes (*referring to the book*).

17,898. Have you looked at them?—Yes.

17,899. Will you look at them though from the beginning to the end?—I have seen them.

17,900. You know what they are?—I know they are the transactions of the executive committee.

17,901. When did they begin?—Which do you mean?

17,902. I mean from the first to the last?—This book begins November 19th 1861, and ends the last Tuesday but one in last month.

17,903. There was a case of Samuel Owen, was there not?—Yes.

17,904. It was about Torr's case, was it not?—Yes.

17,905. Do you know when that was?—Do you mean in this book?

17,906. No; do you know when the occurrence happened at all?—At the latter end of 1864 or the beginning of 1865.

17,907. When did Torr's men turn out?—They turned out the first time, I think, early in 1864.

17,908. And the second time?—I do not know; they were out a fourth time.

17,909. But all transactions with Torr occurred in 1864 and 1865?—Yes.

17,910. Then they would be included in that book which begins November 19th 1861; if anything was done with regard to Torr it would appear in that book?—With reference to any of Torr's men, but I might explain——

17,911. Answer my question; you shall explain presently. If there were any committee resolution with reference to Torr it ought to appear in that book? Yes, any executive committee's resolution.

17,912. Now I call your attention to the entries before April 23rd, 1867; that would cover 1864 and 1865. Were those entries made at the time?—In April?

17,913. No; from April 23rd backwards; were those entries in that book made at the time when the occurrence to which they refer happened. (*The witness referred to the book.*) You know what I mean; you are too clever for that?—I am going to give you the full truth.

17,914. I know you are?—Then just allow me, if you please, to look at it.

17,915. Were your entries written down in the book at the time when the occurrences took place?—I will tell you when I have looked, but I will not until I have looked. I quite understand what you mean, March 19th, April 19th, and April 23rd, were all written on one day.

17,916. That is not an answer to my question at all. I want to know if all the entries before April 1867 were written at the dates at which they purport to be written in that book?—No; I can tell you every one.

17,917. I know you can. At how many different times were the entries made between November 19th, 1861 and April 23rd, 1867?—I will tell you as near as I can. In February 1865 I was taken ill of rheumatic fever. I was under Dr. Thompson and three other doctors——

17,918. Never mind that; you were very ill?—Yes, I was not expected to recover. About June I should resume business again, and I should make all the entries from that date to June together.

17,919. Then all the entries between February 1865 and June 1865 we entered at one time?—I believe so; it might be only up to May, but I think it was June.

17,920. Having been ill, you entered all the occurrences which took place then at one time in the month of June?—Yes; that would be about it as near as my memory will take me; I will admit that, because I believe it to be the fact.

17,921. Are there any other rules which were made in a similar way?—Yes.

17,922. Let us have those?—On the 30th January of this year I was seized with the same complaint, and was unable to get out of bed for six weeks; I should resume business at about two months' end.

17,923. Would that be in March?—Yes, I think that February and March and April would all be entered at one date; I believe so.

17,924. Were there any other entries which were all entered at one date except those?—There is not one but what was entered at the same time that the transactions are stated to occur.

17,925. Will you give me the book?—(*The witness handed the book to the chairman.*) I might say that if you referred to the cash-book you will find another person's writing at the dates I am telling you about.

17,926. Now you know we have a little experience in these kind of matters?—In cooking books? No doubt.

17,927. I do not mean in cooking books, I do not suggest it?—But I understand it, I understand what you mean.

17,928. Upon your oath is not every entry before the 21st April 1867 (and we have looked at them) a transcript from another book, and written out as a copy?—Certainly not.

17,929. You swear that?—Yes, I do.

NINETEENTH DAY.

H. Cutts.

27 June 1867.

17,930. Perhaps it was not a true copy; I daresay you are quite right?—They are as they have occurred, with the exception of those dates that I have named. I am not sure that there was not one during our lock out when I was away at London, and in that case the party that I had left to officiate for me would take it down, as in the other instances, on a slip of paper, and I might copy it; but with that exception every one of those was written at the time that they were dated to have occurred. I know there is a great similarity in the ink; we use one kind of ink continually, and that is where you may be led astray.

17,931. What kind of ink do you use?—We can get you a sample from our office; it is different from any I can find here.

17,932. Mr. Shrubsole, who has been very good about it, informs us that on every one of these pages you can take a letterpress impression?—I have no doubt of it; I think if you examine all our books, which we have used for four or five years back, you can have an impression from it; we have two quart bottles of the ink at our office now.

17,933. It is very good ink then; I understand that every page of this has a gloss upon it as if it were newly written, and every page is regularly written in the same hand, and every page admits of taking an impression from it as if it were newly written?—I daresay.

17,934. And it is new to me —— ?—Indeed.

17,935. That you can get hold of a book which has been written five or six years and take an impression from it?—That may be the case but such is the fact.

17,936. Having called your attention to these facts, I ask you now whether you swear that this book has not been copied from something else, or made up rather from some other book?—It has not; it is a continuation from the other.

17,937. Where is the other?—Mr. Shrubsole has it; it is there (*pointing out the same*).

17,938. But it is very odd; if you had all this ink, and it is the same sort of ink, why is not the ink of the latter part of the same character as the former? —There may be different bottles, and it may be blotted off.

17,939. But it is altogether of a different character; the last pages from the 23rd of April forward are in a perfectly different style?—How a different style?

17,940. It looks as if it had been written off carefully from some other book, and it does not at all look like a book which has been made up from time to time?—No doubt; if you will look at my books you will find that they correspond.

17,941. No doubt you are a very clean man?—I am not nasty in my work.

17,942. There is not a particle of dirt in this book? —Possibly not there because it has never been in regular use; you must bear in mind that it is put away from month's end to month's end.

17,943. That may be so, but from the date of November 19th 1861 to 1867 is six years, and for six whole years every month it has been a book to which you have had to refer as evidence of your proceedings in committee; during the whole of that time this book has been in use, and there is hardly a mark of soil or dirt upon it?—And I daresay it will remain so forward.

16,944. Have you any others which are as clean as this?—Yes, if no one else has interfered with them.

17,945. Let us see one of them?—You may get to any other.

17,946. (*Mr. Chance.*) Have you any other books written six or seven years ago with the same ink?—Yes, that one (*handing a book to the Commissioners*) is written six or seven years ago. For a short time after I took office we had a different kind of ink, but you will find that we made that change, and we have kept to the change ever since.

17,947. (*Chairman.*) I am bound to say that this is remarkably clean for a person in your condition in life; you are not a workman are you?—I am though; I do not work now, but I used to do.

17,948. I must say that this is remarkably clean? —I hope that that is not a fault.

7,949. No, but you know that we are bound to look with eyes of suspicion upon everything and everybody. We must see if anything is wrong; we are come down for that purpose?—Just so.

17,950. It certainly did strike us about this ink, and it did make a strong impression upon our minds? —Will you kindly examine the ink in that cash-book too, in both of them?

17,951. By all means; it is quite fair that we should do so. (*After having examined the books.*) It is quite fair to you to say that there is an entry here, and I daresay there is no reason why this should not be done in 1864, and there is great gloss upon that too? —There is upon the whole of it, if it is not blotted off, and even then it remains to a certain extent. I have not seen any ink like it in my whole life; it is a pity the man is not known of, because if he was in better circumstances I believe he might do well with it.

17,952. With what?—With his ink.

17,953. You say you sent Owen to Newburn?—Yes; he went from his own choice, you understand. We have a roll-call of the unemployed. He was not strictly belonging to us at that time, he was one of these men that were out. When we want a man we go to the roll-call and say, "We want so-and-so." He volunteered and we sent him.

17,954. Of course there would be an entry of the payment of 15*s.* to him?—It would be included in the item "unemployed."

17,955. Just find me the item?—If I could find you the date I would.

17,956. What is suggested is that you sent him out of the way?—Yes, but that is not the fact.

17,957. And if you did send him out of the way you would not be likely to put any items containing his name, and although you admit that you gave 15*s.* for sending him away, I want to see the item where that amount appears?—I should think it would be in the scale-book. We used to pay those that did not belong to us in a memorandum book or on a slip of paper.

17,958. Can you find a memorandum of 15*s.* paid to Samuel Owen?—I am not sure, otherwise it would be in the scale book. Mr. Shrubsole has been at it, I suppose.

17,959. He has been at it, as you say, but he has looked in vain for any payment of 15*s.* to Owen to enable him to go to Newburn?—He has not had it.

17,960. He has failed to find any payment of 15*s.* to Owen to go to Newburn?—Then it would be in the scale book perhaps, he has not had that I think.

17,961. You will let us see that, will you?—I will endeavour to do so. We do not enter a man that does not belong in the scale book on all occasions. We entered it sometimes on a slip of paper and filed it till the month's end.

17,962. Where is your cash-book?—That is it (*handing a book to the Commissioners*). Owen stayed but a short time at Newburn.

17,963. Did you pay for his coming back?—Oh, no.

17,964. Not at all?—No. If a man leaves his situation voluntarily it is his own affair.

17,965. Did you pay for his coming back?—No.

17,966. What is said against you is that Owen being employed by you to this business for Mr. Torr you sent him out of the country, and paid his expenses there, and paid them back again when the thing was hushed up, did you do so?—No. He came back of his own accord, and we sent another man in his place.

17,967. Are these your disbursements (*pointing to the book*)?—Yes.

17,968. Is not that the payment (*pointing to the book*), that sum of 1*l.* 0*s.* 4*d.*?—It will be cash that I have sent up there to make up their payments.

17,969. What payment?—Their unemployed, or something that they might be short of. They send all their cash down to Sheffield. You will find, "cash from Newburn" and "cash to Newburn," and the same from other out-districts in many instances.

17,970. "Cash to Manchester"?—Yes.

NINETEENTH DAY.

H. Cutts.

27 June 1867.

17,971. However, that "Cash to Newburn" was not cash sent to Owen to bring him back again?—No.

17,972. You are sure about it?—I am confident about it.

17,973. It looks very like a sovereign; 3*d.* for the post-office order and 1*d.* for postage makes up the 1*l.* 0*s.* 4*d.*?—Yes, it would be a post-office order. I see what you mean, but it is not so. I think you will find payments on several occasions if you will give me the date.

17,974. This is just the very time; it is 1864?—Is there no other cash besides that?

17,975. No. It is very much like a sum of 1*l.* to him, with the 3*d.* for the order and 1*d.* the postage?—Will you allow me to look at that book? (*The book was handed to the witness.*) What date is that?

17,976. That is in February 1864?—(*The witness referred to the book.*) You will find that it was connected with funeral money, Brian Bagnell, of Newburn

17,977. Here is "Brian Bagnell of Newburn." You paid 9*l.* to him?—He was entitled to 9*l.* funeral money, but there was that money short. If you look at the opposite side you will, perhaps, see that I have credited them with having paid 8*l.*

17,978. I cannot find that; where do you find that?—Probably, if there is not a balance sheet down from them, we should credit them with having sent the money.

17,979. That would be the same page, you know?—Yes. (*The witness referred to the book.*) It would be accounted for in the balance sheet that they sent to us.

17,980. But you have no account of it there?—No; it is not there seemingly.

17,981. There is not any entry then in your books of that 1*l.* which was sent over apparently to Newburn at that time?—I do not see it.

17,982. And it is suggested that you sent it to pay for Owen's coming back?—Yes, but it is not true, I will take my oath if I were going before my Maker this minute.

17,983. But you cannot prove it?—I will tell you how it can be proved; by writing to Newburn, they will tell you how much money they received at that date.

17,984. Will you look at your cash-book of January the 9th, 1864?—Yes. (*The witness referred to the book.*)

17,985. If you will cast up your account there you will find your debit is wrong by upwards of 10*s.*?—Oh! I daresay.

17,986. How do you account for that?—There would be a mistake somewhere.

17,987. But who got the money?—It would be carried forward somewhere.

17,988. There is no carrying forward?—I have not run it up; do the two run up alike?

17,989. They do not run up alike, and there is a certain sum of money either put in pocket or not accounted for; this is about January, 1864, and that is the time that is all important to us?—Yes, of course. (*The witness examined the book.*) It is a wonderful thing if the auditors have not discovered it; here is an error marked 4*s.*

17,990. That will not explain it; the auditors do not seem to be of much good amongst you, as far as I have seen?—We are looked after, I can tell you, in my trade.

17,991. Look at the 22nd of February; (*the witness referred to the book*) the debits are not added there, are they?—We received from them——

17,992. Are the debits added to that?—Yes.

17,993. Let me look at it? (*The witness handed the book to the Examiners.*)—We had sent the money on that occasion to pay for a funeral.

17,994. You have disbursements on one side and nothing on the other?—(*After referring to the book.*) I merely put the things down as they occur from day to day; I make up this book once a month.

17,995. At the very time when it is all important to us we find the debits not added up in this book?—I only use that to refresh my memory, and at the month's end I make it up.

17,996. On February 22nd, 1864, there is "paid with district monies;" paid whom? There is no account to whom you paid it?—It is the aged men.

17,997. It is very well to say so; "2*l.* 4*s.* paid with district monies," what does that mean?—You will find that in nearly every month's account.

17,998. Paid out of district fund, interlined, 1*l.* 2*s.*; paid in district cash, 1*l.* 2*s.*, interlineation again, not in the regular form; there is no occasion to interline?—Yes, it is my way of doing it.

17,999. You interline "district"?—Yes, you will find that in every month's accounts.

18,000. "Paid by district 19*s.*"?—That is the money of the aged men.

18,001. If you did pay 2*l.* 4*s.* of your district monies in a manner which you did not want to explain, is that the kind of entry you would make?—I protest against that.

18,002. Supposing a fraudulent man wanted to put into the accounts that he had paid some money and he did not want to account for it, what different entry could he make than this, "paid with district money, 2*l.* 4*s.*"?—Mr. Holland will go down and fetch the tickets that we received from Ecclesfield, that would prove what that money was spent for.

18,003. You paid Jackson's men one sum, and telegraphs another, and expenses of meeting another; but if you say that you paid district monies, without saying to whom, or on what account, or why it was paid, that looks very suspicious?—Yes.

18,004. That is the very time when Torr's case took place?—Yes.

18,005. There is an interlineation without any explanation at all?—It is paid to us. (*The witness further explains the accounts to the Examiners.*)

18,006. I should like to know this. There is an entry here of August the 2nd, 164, the union paid Mr. Broadbent, solicitor, a sum of money in respect of Torr's case, therefore it is quite clear that you had been employing a solicitor in Torr's matter?—In five or six cases.

18,007. You had him up before the County Court?—Yes, and when the men were summoned before the town hall we defended them.

18,008, It was not upon that case when his bellows were cut?—No, nor the assault case, the men were not defended at all. I asked my friend Holland who was at the Town Hall, and he says they were not defended at all.

18,009. If they were defended that would appear in the cash-book?—Yes.

18,010. There is an entry paying Broadbent 1*l.* 11*s.* 6*d.* for Torr's case?—Yes.

18,011. You said you did not pay for them being defended; if they were defended it would appear in the cash-book?—Yes.

18,012. The case is the 2d of August—you paid Mr. Broadbent on the 2d of August, then it was for services rendered before?—Yes.

18,013. Where is that entry in your book about Owen, that 1*l.* 0*s.* 4*d.* that occurred about nine months ago?—I do not know the date.

18,014. Just look at that date?—(*The witness referred to a book.*)

18,015. You say that you explain that by Richard Hedley having 7*l.*?—Yes, that is the man.

18,016. That is on the 7th of December?—No, there are others besides him.

18,017. Do you keep your letters?—Yes.

18,018. I am very curious about the Newburn business?—I will fetch all the letters from Newburn. I think I have them since 1864. I have no doubt in the Newburn letters you will see where they write for a striker, and we sent him and very shortly after another.

The witness withdrew.

THOMAS ROBERTS sworn and examined.

18,019. (*Mr. Barstow.*) What are you?—Secretary to the table blade grinders.

18,020. How long have you been secretary?—10 years off and on.

18,021. Do you admit that rattening has been common in your union?—I admit that rattening has been done in our union, but not common; we admit that rattening has been resorted to in extreme cases, and in a few cases only.

18,022. Are you aware of any act of outrage committed by your society?—No.

18,023. And no personal violence committed upon any member in your trade?—No.

18,024. Nor upon any non-union men working at your trade?—No.

18,025. Nor upon any master employing non-union men?—No, we have had nothing of that sort.

18,026. (*Chairman.*) And you have had nothing attributed to you?—No.

18,027. (*Mr. Barstow.*) How many members are there in your union?—About 450.

18,028. And how many are there out of the union? About 150.

18,029. How many men have you on the box?—I can hardly say to a few, say 50 in round numbers.

18,030. Is that the present number, or is it the average?—At present.

18,031. (*Chairman.*) What is the average?—Last year and the year before we had not more than 10 or a dozen, when trade was extremely good; it depends entirely upon the state of the trade.

18,032. (*Mr. Barstow.*) Can you say what has been the average number of men on the box for the last five years?—It would average 50 for five years.

18,033. You would have generally on the box 50 during the five years?—Yes, including good trade and bad, sometimes more and sometimes less; sometimes we have 100 men on the box.

18,034. Is trade good or bad at the present time?—It is very bad just now.

18,035. What could a fair average workman earn per week?—When we have our full list price and full work, in six cases out of every nine we reckon to average 2*l.* a man.

18,036. (*Chairman.*) For a man alone, or for a man and a boy?—A man.

18,037. How much could he make with a boy?—That depends upon the quality of the boy; a man and a boy will earn 3*l.* if he is pretty well up in his job.

18,038. (*Mr. Barstow.*) That would be for an average workman?—Yes, but you must understand we have a great reduction out of the 2*l.*

18,039. What is that for?—Wheel power, tools, bands, emery, bee's wax, &c., which cost us not less than 9*s.* a week. Then there is a contribution to pay to the trade of 2*s.* a week for himself and 1*s.* for the boy, but you must be aware that when our union is not in existence, in six cases out of nine the 2*l.* worth of work is to be done for 1*l.*, and the expenses out of it, which leaves a man 10*s.* or 11*s.* a week to take home to his family. The discount ranges as a rule 50 per cent., not for the whole of the trade because we have a portion of the workmen called country house grinders. They grind for the whole trade, and they are not reduced so low; the foreign trade as a rule reduces 50 per cent., and I have known it to be below that.

18,040. And the charges for expenses are the same?—Yes, the charges for the expenses are the same entirely.

18,041. How long has your union existed?—This union has been in existence about five years; there have been unions in the trade for 60 years at various times.

18,042. Are the masters in your trade generally large or small employers?—Most of them are small employers.

18,043. (*Mr. Chance.*) Do you remember what the wages were before this union was formed?—Yes, 10*s.* or 11*s.* a week when a man had paid his expenses and worked hard all the week, and when we were not in union invariably men with the heaviest family would be thrown upon the parish, while a man with small expenses would get the work.

18,044. Do you think the rise in wages is attributable to the union?—Yes.

18,045. Has not any alteration in the trade caused any alteration in the prices?—No, only when we have had unions at the back of them.

18,046. Do not the prices follow the price of provisions and other matters generally?—No.

18,047. Do you attribute the formation of the unions to your having been ground down?—Yes, I would not have unions if I could live without them.

18,048. Would you expect the prices to be reduced to some extent if the work was in the hands of larger manufacturers with capital?—Yes, the prices would be reduced; we have some of our larger manufacturers who have reduced the prices the lowest.

18,049. (*Chairman.*) Are there any cases of joint stock associations of masters and men, taking a percentage upon the profits?—No, we have no joint stock associations of masters and men. I tried to get it, but I could not.

18,050. You have not succeeded in that?—No, I wanted to get it.

10,051. (*Mr. Chance.*) Supposing you had legal means of enforcing your contributions, do you think that would do away with rattening?—Yes, as far as the trade is concerned.

18,052. Would not rattening still exist for the purpose of protecting you against other infringements of the rules?—No, the rattening would cease entirely if we had some method of enforcing payment.

18,053. Have you any rules in your unions as to the number of apprentices a man may keep?—Yes, we allow a man to have two.

18,054. You limit the number?—Yes.

18,055. You also limit the class of people from whom the apprentices are to be taken?—Yes, as far as we can.

18,056. If a man takes more than two apprentices he infringes your rules?—Yes, if he takes three he does.

18,057. What means do you adopt to prevent it?—We adopt none except by reasoning with the men.

18,058. (*Chairman.*) It is equally a violation of your rules to take more apprentices as not to pay contributions?—We should reason with the man.

18,059. Why should you use rattening in one case and not in the other?—Perhaps it has been used in that case as well.

18,060. (*Mr. Chance.*) Supposing you had the power to enforce contributions, as rattening exists in one case, why should it not exist in the other?—We should be able to keep up an uniform price, and that would enable a man to live with his two apprentices without taking more.

18,061. You do not understand me. You say that if you had power to enforce contributions you think rattening would cease?—Yes.

18,062. You say you know that you have had other infringements of your rules?—I do not know a case.

18,063. It is done?—It is done.

18,064. Why would legal power to enforce contributions do away with rattening?—Perhaps it would not in that instance.

18,065. Do you adopt any measure for persuading or compelling men to join your union who will not join?—No, we persuade them. When we had no unions the men were only too ready to join; they are anxious to have one formed; but it is when we have the union that the men become refractory, that is, they cease to pay or they take more apprentices than they ought.

18,066. Does not that look as if when they have the experience of them they do not like them?—They like the unions, but they do not like to pay for them.

18,067. (*Mr. Barstow.*) They like the advantage

NINETEENTH DAY.

T. Roberts.

27 June 1867.

of the advanced prices, but they do not like to pay towards keeping them up?—Yes.

18,068. (*Mr. Chance.*) What is your experience of the whole thing, taking the payment and the supposed advantage, would the men prefer belonging to the union or not?—The good men would; the bad men like the unions kept up at some one else's expense.

18,069. When a man pays to the union he likes it, but when he cannot, he does not?—Yes; when he cannot pay we do not compel him.

The witness withdrew.

E. Sykes.

EDWIN SYKES sworn and examined.

18,070. (*Mr. Chance.*) Are you a scissors manufacturer living in Wentworth Street?—Yes.

18,071. How long have you been a manufacturer? —Now about 40 years.

18,072. Have you been a member of a union at all?—Yes, sometimes.

18,073. Are you a member at the present time?—No.

18,074. Can you be a member of the union as a manufacturer?—I am a grinder and manufacturer; what they call a master grinder.

18,075. As a master grinder you were a member? —Yes.

18,076. Do you know Holmshaw, the secretary of that union?—Very well.

18,077. In December 1865 had you a boy named Leadbetter working for you?—Yes.

18,078. Was he working for you as an apprentice? —No. His master had gone out of town to Manchester, and his father brought him to me to ask me whether I would give him a week or two's work till his master came back again.

18,079. Would it have been contrary to the rules of the union for you to employ him?—In that case he was an apprentice to another man, but he had gone away, consequently his father could not keep him, and I said, "When his master comes back come and tell "me, and take the boy to the master."

18,080. And you took him to work for you during the time the other man was away?—Yes.

18,081. If you had taken him as an apprentice regularly would it have been contrary to the rules of the union?—I never asked them whether I was to do it or not.

18,082. Did Holmshaw come to you about that time?—Yes.

18,083. What did he come to you for?—He came on a Monday the last time when I paid; he came and got the 2*s*.

18,084. When was that?—December 11th, 1865.

18,085. Did he come to collect the money?—Yes.

18,086. Was that money due from you?—Yes.

18,087. Did he say anything about the boy?—No, he came again a day or two after. He says, "Come, you must get home;" and he pulled the lad off the horsing; and he said, "If you do not I will get a policeman to you;" and he went off, and I never saw him after.

18,088. Had the boy misbehaved himself?—No, Holmshaw had nothing to do with him.

18,089. What did you do? were you present at the time?—When he came and fetched the boy off the horsing I was down on the bottom. We had a little misfortune in the shop. The men said, "There is Holmshaw fetching the boy away." I said, "If you do not get off I will fetch a strap to you." I would have strapped him if I had got him, but he went off.

18,090. Did you see Holmshaw again some time after?—Yes.

18,091. Where did you see him?—In Pelham Street.

18,092. How long after?—About six months after; and he says, "You do not pay to the trade now." I said, "No, I never shall do." He said he would serve me out, and I told him if he would go out in the street I would dare take it out in his bones.

18,093. Did he say anything else at that time?—No, he was walking one way and I the other.

18,094. Did you do anything upon that?—No, I did not go to Mr. Jackson then; I told him after. He said he ought to have come at the same time that he threatened me.

18,095. Some time after that did you lose anything? —Yes.

18,096. How long after that time was it?—On December the 10th, 1866, I lost a set of bands; they took them all away.

18,097. Where were you working at that time?—At Gibson's wheel.

18,098. Previous to working at Gibson's wheel, where did you work?—We had a wheel of our own in my own yard. I gave it up; it stands there now.

18,099. Why did you stop it; it was not from fear of the union?—No.

18,100. Had you lost anything at the time when you were working at your own wheel?—We had several things taken out.

18,101. I speak of the time between 1865 and 1866, after you saw Holmshaw?—Yes, they broke into my place at Gibson's wheel.

18,102. Before you went to Gibson's wheel had you lost anything from your own wheel?—No, not bands.

18,103. Was there a difficulty in getting the bands from your wheel?—Yes.

18,104. Upon losing the bands, did you take any measures to ascertain what had become of them?—I went and told Jackson they were gone.

18,105. Did you make any application to Holmshaw?—No; I knew I should get nothing from him satisfactory.

18,106. What was the reason that your bands were taken?—They took them because I would not comply with the rules of the trade, and I would not have anything to do with them.

18,107. Do you consider that it was a trade matter? —Yes.

18,108. Not any private quarrel with anybody?—No, not any.

18,109. Do you remember on another occasion your shop being broken into?—Yes.

18,110. Where was that?—It was at the wheel where we were working; it was on the 26th of December, after they took the bands. I got new bands.

18,111. Did they take anything from you?—They broke many tools to the value of 24*l*. or 25*l*.

18,112. And put the remainder in the dam?—They put them into the well, and we found them on Easter Monday.

18,113. Do you know at all by whom it was done? —No, I did not see them do it.

18,114. Do you know why it was done?—It was done by the grinders, no doubt. Holmshaw told me he would serve me out.

18,115. Had you any grinders with you on your premises?—Yes.

18,116. How many men were working in the grinding hull?—Three.

18,117. (*Chairman.*) Did they pay to the union? —I do not know, I never asked them.

18,118. (*Mr. Chance.*) You do not know whether there were any arrears due from them?—No.

18,119. Have you taken any steps in the matter? —I went to Mr. Jackson; there were 17 large glazers taken out of the dam with a rope, they were not broken and were put in just as they were.

18,120. Do you attribute that case to the trade? —Certainly.

18,121. Was it because you would not join the union?—Yes.

18,122. That is the reason as you suppose why it was done?—I had a young man named Pryor.

18,123. What about him?—It was on account of him I was told.

NINETEENTH DAY.

E. Sykes.

27 June 1867.

18,124. How long had Pryor been working for you?—He is a grinder; he had been working for me four or five months, he was a grinder's son.

18,125. Was he a member of the union?—No.

18,126. Had he refused to be a member of the union?—He was not exactly of age, and his mother went to the committee in the committee room, where Holmshaw was; and they told her that they would not allow him to work in the trade at all.

18,127. You say that you would not turn Pryor away?—No.

18,128. Had anyone applied to you to turn him away?—No.

18,129. Who said that you must not have Pryor?—Many of them.

18,130. Who?—Holmshaw said so.

18,131. Did Holmshaw tell you that Pryor must not work for you?—Yes.

18,132. When?—It was when I met him in the wheel.

18,133. You say that you were rattened on the 26th of December?—Yes.

18,134. And Holmshaw spoke to you in January?—Yes.

18,135. That was after?—He spoke to me before that.

18,136. Therefore you cannot have been rattened in consequence of that?—Yes, I lay it to nothing else.

18,137. Had you no men who were in arrear to the union at the time?—Not that I know of; I do not know whether they were paying or not, I never asked them.

18,138. Did Holmshaw give any reason why Pryor should not work for you?—No.

18,139. Do you know any reason why Pryor was not allowed to work for you?—No, except what I was told, that they would not have him; his mother had been to the committee room and they told her that he should not work in the trade, he is a scissor grinder's son.

18,140. Do you know any reason why he should not be allowed to work?—No.

18,141. Was any reason given you by any member of the committee?—No.

18,142. You say that he was not of age to join the union?—No.

18,143. Had he done anything to offend the union?—He was 18 or 19 years of age.

18,144. (*Chairman.*) What are the rules about a man being of age? why did you say he was not of age?—He was not of age and had not been bound.

18,145. He had not been bound to anyone, and therefore he was working contrary to their rule?—Yes.

18,146. (*Mr. Chance.*) That is breaking the rules of the union?—Yes.

18,147. He had infringed the rules of the union by coming to you?—His father had died; he was not bound to his father, and they said they would not have him in the trade.

18,148. In your opinion is that the reason why you were rattened?—Yes.

18,149. Do you remember Holmshaw giving a man 5*l.* to go to America?—Yes; if that fellow had stopped here I could have got something out of him.

18,150. Who was the man?—Charles Young.

18,151. You say that Holmshaw gave Charles Young 5*l.* to go to America?—Yes.

18,152. How do you know that?—Young is my wife's brother, and he has sent a letter home; he is starving to death in America.

18,153. Young is your wife's brother?—Yes.

18,154. Why should Holmshaw give him 5*l.* to go to America?—He did it to get shut of him out of the way.

18,155. What had Young done that he should go to America?—He had done nothing; he had a good place and work.

18,156. Could he say anything or tell anything?—I do not know; he is in America now starving.

18,157. Do you know any reason why Holmshaw should give him 5*l.* to go to America?—He did not tell me the reason, but if he had stopped at home he would have told my wife something.

18,158. Sometimes members of the union do go to America?—Yes, he sent two or three there the same time.

18,159. Do you know any reason why they should not go to America?—No.

18,160. Do not you know that it is one of the rules of the union that when a man does go to America and out of your trade they give him 5*l.*?—They gave him 5*l.*; he was on the committee, and they were not aware he was my wife's brother until they found it out at last.

18,161. I do not understand why he should have 5*l.* to go to America?—I cannot tell you. That is what Holmshaw gave him to go.

18,162. You make no complaint of his having received 5*l.* to go to America?—No.

18,163. Do you know when he went to America?—Five months since or something like that. He wants to come home again.

18,164. Do you suppose that he had anything to do with the rattenings?—I do not know.

18,165. Is it only the fact of his going to America and receiving 5*l.* from Holmshaw that you speak to?—Yes, he went when they sent him to get him off there.

18,166. He knew nothing about rattening that you know of?—No, I do not know what he did.

18,167. (*Chairman.*) Mr. Sugg wants me to ask this: was not the reason of your wheel stopping because you used the water company's water?—No, I deny it, it is all humbug, it is all nothing of the kind.

18,168. Have you yourself rattened at the Union wheel?—Yes, if you call it rattening; I have fetched my own bands.

18,169. You say that what you rattened were your own bands?—Yes, they were my own bands.

18,170. Where did you take them from?—From Pryor's wheel, the same wheel as I worked at.

18,171. When was this?—It was 29 years since.

18,172. How did you happen to take these bands of your own from Pryor's wheel?—They took them from me; I had not a band left, and they were all committee men in that wheel, and I told them the night before "now you have made me play two days and "have laughed at me, you shall not get to work to-"morrow," and two men went and got them, and I with them.

18,173. Were you taken up?—That was the end of it.

18,174. Were you taken up?—Yes, and set at liberty again.

18,175. In point of fact 29 years ago after having been rattened yourself you said you would be revenged upon them, and went and got their bands?—Yes.

18,176. You said that you would be revenged upon them?—Yes.

18,177. And you went and took their goods?—Yes, and laughed at them the next day.

18,178. You say that a great many tools were destroyed, that there were 24 glazers thrown into the dam, and all that sort of thing; at that time had you any quarrel with your nephew?—No.

18,179. You had no quarrel at all?—No.

18,180. Had you any ground for supposing that this was done by your newhew in consequence of any animosity?—No, nothing of the kind.

18,181. You had had no quarrel?—No.

18,182. It is all nonsense suggesting that?—No, only I had been robbed by my nephew of a few thousand pounds, and I turned him out.

18,183. Your nephew has robbed you to the extent of a few thousand pounds?—Yes.

18,184. When was he found out?—At the time he was taken.

18,185. When did you find out that he had robbed you to the extent of several thousand pounds?—I had found it out several times that I had been robbed by him. I will tell you one instance; when my wife was

NINETEENTH DAY.

E. Sykes.

27 June 1867.

dying in bed he took her gold watch out of the drawers.

18,186. That did not make you very pleased with him?—No.

18,187. You quarrelled with him for that?—No, I told him I would not have him about the house.

18,188. Had he a father and mother?—Yes.

18,189. Was he a married man?—Yes.

18,190. Had he any claim upon you?—Not any.

18,191. Had you used violent language to him so that you might have reason to suppose that these things were done by your nephew?—Not a word.

18,192. How long is it since you found out that he robbed you?—Many times I found it out and forgave him. I was the uncle by my wife's side, and forgave him.

18,193. Then you overlooked his faults, and were indulgent to him?—Yes, and overlooked them many times.

18,194. Has there been any other quarrel between you?—No, not any; not a word.

18,195. He has robbed you, but you have been a benefactor to him?—Yes, I have.

18,196. What number of apprentices have you had at the same time?—One; he was not apprenticed to me.

18,197. You had an apprentice besides Pryor?—Yes.

18,198. That was according to the rules of the union?—I always took as many as I liked. I never asked the union what I should take.

18,199. At that time you had only one?—Yes, only one. I paid the money merely for quietness, when I did pay.

The witness withdrew.

Mr. J. Tyzack.

Mr. Joshua Tyzack sworn and examined.

18,200. (*Mr. Barstow.*) You are a member of the firm of William Tyzack and Sons?—I am.

18,201. What is your business?—Manufacturers of saws, scythes, and files, and of steel.

18,202. Are you in a large way of business?—There are a great many larger.

18,203. How many hands do you employ?—From 200 to 300; about 250 perhaps.

18,204. Are you what would be called a large master?—It may be said so.

18,205. I believe, in the course of your experience, you have been involved in a great many different disputes with the unions?—I am sorry to say, too many.

18,206. I understand that that is principally owing to the different unions claiming the sole making of different kinds of goods?—Not exactly that; it is from different causes.

18,207. Is that the principal cause?—It is a very important one.

18,208. That is a cause of quarrel over which you have no control yourself? — We have no control unless we submit to all their peculiar wishes.

18,209. (*Chairman.*) You must either comply or retire from the trade?—Just so.

18,210. (*Mr. Barstow.*) In January 1856 were you employing some men who were obnoxious to the trade?—I believe it was so reported.

18,211. Is that the fact, or not; I only ask you the fact?—I can say "yes" from the effects which followed after; I did not know then.

18,212. You know now, whether you knew then or not, that they were obnoxious to the trade?—Yes.

18,213. Was the place at which they were working blown up?—One of the places was.

18,214. Was a man named Needham convicted of blowing up that place?—Yes.

18,215. I believe he had four years penal servitude?—Yes.

18,216. Had you an interview with Needham in prison?—Yes.

18,217. In consequence of what you learned at that interview, were you afterwards anxious to see him when he came out of prison?—Not immediately after he came out.

18,218. Were you looking for Needham in the latter end of 1862?—Yes.

18,219. Have you reason to believe that it was known that you were looking for him? — Great reason.

18,220. Where did you hear Needham was at this time?—I may say from the result of the inquiry or discourse I had with him in prison that I traced him to Millbank.

18,221. That was after he was out of prison?—Yes; and from the manner in which I laid the case before our bench here, when I returned from the prison, I found that I could not handle the evidence I had got——

18,222. A great deal of this we cannot meddle with. Where did you hear he was in 1862?—I had overheard some of our men say that he had come out of confinement.

18,223. (*Chairman.*) Where had you heard he was?—In Sheffield.

18,224. (*Mr. Barstow.*) Had you heard whereabouts in Sheffield?—No.

18,225. Can you recollect a circumstance happening to you in 1862 on your way home?—I was shot at five times.

18,226. Whereabouts were you? what time of the evening was it?—Half-past 8.

18,227. What time of the year was it?—It was the first week in November.

18,228. You were going from Sheffield to your home?—Yes.

18,229. How do you generally go home?—I formerly used to ride on horseback, afterwards I took a gig, and since then I have gone in the phaeton.

18,230. (*Chairman.*) Was it known that you travelled on a certain way?—Yes.

18,231. Was it known that you travelled from Sheffield to your own home in a gig?—Very well indeed.

18,232. (*Mr. Barstow.*) What time did you usually return?—About half-past 8.

18,233. Was it your common practice? — Very regular, from that to a quarter to 9.

18,234. I suppose anyone who liked might see you returning in the night?—Yes; I heard the man at the gate say, "I must be ready for Mr. Tyzack at the gate."

18,235. You passed the turnpike at the same hour every night?—Yes.

18,236. What occurred when you were shot at? how far had you got from Sheffield?—About three-quarters of a mile.

18,237. That was just beyond Broadfield Bar, in a small plantation?

18,238. (*Chairman.*) You were not in the plantation, you were on the road?—Yes.

18,239. What happened?—I heard a shot fired.

18,240. Where did the shot come from?—I do not know.

18,241. (*Mr. Barstow.*) What followed?—Another shot immediately followed.

18,242. Then, I believe, you looked round?—I looked in the direction from where they sent them; the moment I turned my head in this position (*describing the same*) I saw a flash of a third shot.

18,243. Where did it come from?—In a diagonal position from the direction in which I was driving.

18,244. Was it from a man in the road or in the field?—From under a wall or broken down fence near Mr. Cockayne's residence.

18,245. How far off do you think it was from you?—From 12 to 15 yards.

18,246. Did the last seem to come from the same place that the other shots came from?—Distinctly so.

18,247. And from the same side of the road?—Yes.

18,248. You saw a flash, I believe?—Yes.

18,249. Did anything follow that?—Immediately I saw the flash a bullet went past my ear; it went through the brim of my hat and knocked a piece out of the size of half-a-crown.

18,250. What happened then to yourself?—I was thoroughly unconscious at the moment.

18,251. Did you continue standing as you were?—No, I dropped down from the excitement of the passing of the shot through the hair and hat; I both felt it and heard it.

18,252. (*Chairman.*) Were you knocked down?—No, it was excitement, momentary excitement; I dropped down into the bottom of the gig.

18,253. Could you tell from the report what the shot was fired from?—I should think it was a revolver, not a gun.

18,254. Is that from the fact of there being several shots, or from the fact of the noise of the report?—From the number of shots that were sent.

18,255. (*Mr. Barstow.*) Could you tell from the report whether it was loud enough for a gun?—It was not loud enough for an ordinary fowling piece.

18,256. Did anyone approach you?—No.

18,257. No one came near you?—No.

18,258. Do you know how long you were at the bottom of the gig?—It would be difficult to say; perhaps 30 or 40 seconds.

18,259. Just a short time?—Yes.

18,260. Half a minute?—I will say a moment.

18,261. Then you recovered yourself?—My impulse dictated that I should go.

18,262. What did you do?—I struck the horse.

18,263. You got up to sit again?—Yes, I struck the horse a violent blow.

18,264. And he went on; and what else happened?—There were two other shots as quickly upon each other as possible as soon as the horse got in action.

18,265. (*Chairman.*) Had you stopped the horse?—The horse had stopped by the act of my falling down; he was a very tractable horse; the horse in the gig was perfectly motionless for, perhaps, a quarter of a minute.

18,266. Directly you were gone there were two more shots?—Yes.

18,267. (*Mr. Barstow.*) Was the gig struck?—No.

18,268. (*Chairman.*) Neither you, nor your horse, nor gig were shot?—I could not trace any except the third, which came through my hair and hat.

18,269. (*Mr. Barstow.*) I suppose you drove on?—Yes.

18,270. (*Chairman.*) What kind of a night was it?—A fine night; I could clearly see the walk on the footpath from where I stood.

18,271. Was it moonlight?—It was moonlight.

18,272. Had you any quarrel with anyone?—Not that I am aware of.

18,273. To what do you attribute the attack upon you?—I was not aware at the time that there was anything further than that I had been very anxious to inquire for Needham.

18,274. Had you been busy in the neighbourhood making inquiries for him?—I had made frequent enquiries, and I had employed a young man to do the same for me.

18,275. (*Mr. Barstow.*) I believe you never saw Needham after this?—I never saw Needham after I left him in prison.

18,276. Do you know where he is?—He is in America.

18,277. Do you know when he went?—Since this Commission was talked about.

18,278. You told us that you were very anxious to see Needham, why was that?—Because I found that when I left him in prison and came back to Sheffield I was desirous of taking law proceedings against a person implicated in the blowing up.

18,279. What blowing up?—The blowing up at Dronfield, for which Needham was convicted.

18,280. Had Needham made any communication to you with regard to that person? did he give you his name?—Yes.

18,281. Who was it?—Michael Thompson.

18,282. What did he say of him?—He said that Michael Thompson had paid him several sums of money to blow me up.

18,283. Who was Michael Thompson?—The secretary of the scythe grinders union.

18,284. He had given Needham money to blow up the place at Dronfield, for which he has been convicted?—Yes.

18,285. What sum did he say that Thompson had given him?—The first amount was 3*l.*

18,286. We do not want to go into detail, tell us altogether what he gave him?—After he gave him the 3*l.* he blew up the shop.

18,287. Altogether how much did he say he had given him?—10*l.*

18,288. (*Chairman.*) You wanted to bring an action against Thompson, did you?—Yes.

18,289. Did you want to bring an action against him or prosecute him?—I wanted to prosecute Thompson.

18,290. And you wanted this man's evidence to convict him?—Yes.

18,291. (*Mr. Barstow.*) Do you attribute this attack upon you to the inquiries which you made for Needham?—I have no other cause to attribute it to.

18,292. (*Chairman.*) You had no quarrel with anybody at that time?—Not that I am aware of.

18,293. You had not made yourself obnoxious to the trade in any way?—Not in the least.

18,294. Had you violated any rules?—We are not aware of having done so at any time.

18,295. Did you employ their men?—Yes, all of them.

18,296. They were union men?—Yes all of them.

18,297. And you had violated none of their rules that you are aware of?—Not that we are aware of.

18,298. You were on good terms with them at the time?—Yes; save and except that the grinders in four different branches of the trade connected with this union claimed the same kind of work, and it appeared to be a quarrel between the two bodies of grinders.

18,299. That would not explain why you should be shot at; if two people quarrelled between themselves, that is no reason why a third man should be shot at five times?—No.

18,300. Is there any ground upon which you think any person should come under a wall and shoot at you five times?—None other than that case which I allude to.

18,301. Had you reason to believe that Thompson had any knowledge that you were making inquiries about Needham?—I am fully convinced of that.

18,302. How do you know that it had come to the ears of Thompson that you were inquiring after Needham?—He could not help knowing because he had had some letters from the prisoner Needham.

18,303. How do you know that?—Because they had passed through the hands of parties that had to deal with it.

18,304. That does not give us information; had you seen the letters? how did you know that Thompson knew that you were inquiring after Needham?—I have no reason to be certain that he did know it; but that was my suspicion.

18,305. Do you know now that at that time Thompson was aware that you were seeking for Needham?—No.

18,306. (*Mr. Barstow.*) During the last 10 years have you received any threatening letters?—Several.

18,307. Have you preserved any of them?—I believe there is only one.

18,308. What did you do with the others?—They were put in the hands of Mr. Rayner, the chief constable.

18,309. Have you made any search for them?—I have frequently asked that they should be restored.

18,310. (*Chairman.*) Without success?—Without success.

18,311. (*Mr. Barstow.*) Can you give us generally

NINETEENTH DAY.

Mr. J. Tyzack.

27 June 1867.

the contents of any of those letters ?—I believe this is out of the bounds of 10 years.

18,312. We must not go into any one beyond 10 years ?—I received one within the last 10 months. That is the envelope (*producing the same*). My attorney has got the letter; it is dated the 14th of February 1867.

18,313. Do you remember generally what the nature of these letters was which you received within the last 10 years ?—Threatening that if we sent any machine knives to grind to others than the scythe grinders we might expect something. Then they would sketch at the bottom of the letter something like a barrel of gunpowder.

18,314. It stated that you might expect to be blown up ?—Just so.

18,315. Was that the general tenour of the letters ?—Yes.

18,316. Now I am going into the question of rattening; in 1857 you were rattened ?—Yes.

18,317. Just say as shortly as you can what happened ?—The saw-grinders bands were taken.

18,318. How many bands were taken ?—Two or three upon that occasion.

18,319. From where ?—From Abbey Dale works.

18,320. To what do you attribute that ?—That was on account of work of the value of 3*d.* being done by a person who had not the professed claim upon that kind of work.

18,321. What was that man's name ?—His name was Hazlewood.

18,322. As a matter of fact, I believe, it was not in Hazlewood's province properly to do it ?—We admit that it was not so; but had he not done it we should have had to send three or four miles to have it done.

18,323. You thought in such a trumpery matter as that you might just as well have it done at home ?—Yes, that was our reason for doing it; it was a very small matter.

18,324. This was re-glazing the things that had been glazed by proper persons before ?—Yes; and we paid proper persons for it.

18,325. Have you any more to say upon that subject ?—I can only say that Mr. William Broadhead, the secretary of the saw grinders, on one occasion of his calling at our place, came to ask after some business. A messenger had to be sent into the works to communicate with some men that he inquired for, and while the messenger was away I said: "Broadhead, what was the reason that you sent for our bands for such a paltry affair as that ?" He said, "Well, my information was wrong, there was a great "exaggeration of the amount of work that had been "done; if I had known there had been such a small "quantity they probably would not have gone."

18,326. In 1858 were you rattened again ?—Three pairs of bellows were destroyed.

18,327. Where was that ?—At the Abbey Dale works.

18,328. What was the cause of that ?—Nonpayment of the natty money.

18,329. By whom ?—By the men who are called the scythe finishers.

18,330. By your workmen ? you had not to pay natty money ?—No.

18,331. That was for nonpayment of natty money by your workmen ?—Yes by the workmen.

18,332. Who is the secretary of that union ?—Mr. George Austin I believe.

18,333. Again in 1859 did something happen to you ?—There were 14 or 15 scythe grinders called from their situations and engagements contrary to the proper hiring.

18,334. (*Chairman.*) They took them away from you contrary to your hiring ?—Contrary to their hiring, without notice.

18,335. What was that for ?—In order to compel us to agree to terms in reference to giving the machine knives entirely to the scythe grinders.

18,336. Did you take summonses out against these men ?—No, they were sent out of the country altogether.

18,337. How do you know that they were sent out of the country ? how do you know that they did not go themselves ?—We made frequent inquiries at their homes and we could not hear of them in the district; any inquiry that we made the answer was from their own body or the persons associated with them that they were sailing on the high seas.

18,338. (*Mr. Barstow.*) Have you seen them since ?—They returned four or five weeks after.

18,339. I want to know how it was shown that they did not leave your business of their own motion without being sent out by the trade; what right have you to say that the trade sent them away ?—From the correspondence that took place afterwards.

18,340. Just tell us how you conect them with the trade ?—We wrote to the secretary of the trade to know the cause of the men being taken away; we addressed it to secretary Machin.

18,341. Is that the present secretary ?—Yes; we asked the reason why the men were taken away. I believe the words were couched in this way: Had there been anything wrong; and if so, had they spoken to us about it, the things might have been remedied without the men being taken away; they summoned us to attend a meeting at the public house, to show reasons why they should have done so, that was at the "Waggon and Horses" Mill houses. My brother and I drove there expecting to meet the secretary or one or two of our own men to negociate the matter. Instead of that there were about 30 people there, most of them strangers to us. We afterwards were informed that they were an amalgamated company of a number of unions together. After a good deal of discourse without much business being effected, they brought out a list of claims, which they wished us to submit to before these men could be brought back.

18,342. Did they do it in a respectable and quiet manner ?—In their style, I have no doubt they would call it so. The first demand was that we were to discontinue giving machine knives to grind to any other except the scythe grinders; secondly, that we immediately and without notice were to discharge Eccles and others from our service who were working at Ward's wheel at Dronfield that was blown up; thirdly, that we took no more apprentices; fourthly, that we changed our mode of managemant in the manufacture of scythes; fifthly, that we made a promise to retake all the men back to their old situations without taking any law proceedings against them for breaking their engagements by the union having withdrawn them from their situations and sent 10 or 12 of them out of the country for several weeks; we were to take them back without holding out any threat over them, and to take them back quietly; sixthly, that we should allow the union men from other rival mannfacturers to come in to inspect our works and mode of working when they thought fit; and, seventhly, that we should pay the expenses of those men while they were away from their work in their homes.

18,343. Those were the terms upon which they would allow these men to come back ?—Yes.

18,344. Did you submit to all those conditions ?—Most of them were compromised. I may say first that the meeting had to be adjourned till we could get the appetite to take the medicine.

18,345. Was it at this meeting that the question was put to you as to whether you had any scythes being made out for you by anyone ?—During the time the men were away we had a large foreign order.

18,346. Did anything occur upon that subject at this meeting ?—Yes.

18,347. Tell us what it was ?—We were very closely interrogated upon the subject of having employed a neighbouring manufacturer to assist us in getting an order away.

18,348. Who was the manufacturer ?—Mr. Horne, general manufacturer, in Sheffield.

18,349. I believe that some one in the meeting asked you if that was so ?—Yes.

18,350. Did you say "Yes" ?—We admitted the fact of that case, as it was known, and we made nothing strange in it.

NINETEENTH DAY.

Mr. J. Tyzack.

27 June 1867.

18,351. Upon your admitting it, what took place?—There appeared to be a secret discourse taking place for a few minutes with a few of the leading men.

18,352. Were you in the room all this time?—Yes.

18,353. Did you observe anything further?—We observed a number of men leave the room before the meeting was over.

18,354. Do you know who the men were?—I did not notice them at all, not knowing anything of their object.

18,355. You saw some of them leave the room?—Yes, three or four.

18,356. You cannot give us the names of any of them?—No, I did not know the name of the 20th part of the men that were there.

18,357. Did you hear something on the following morning?—I heard that Mr. Horne's establishment had been broken open and a quantity of tools destroyed.

18,358. Did you pay the expenses of the damage done at Mr. Horne's factory?—We paid a portion of them.

18,359. What was the amount of the damage done?—I do not know; I think that the amount we paid was from 5*l.* to 6*l.*

18,360. We have been talking now of the 18th of January?—Yes.

18,361. Now in July 1859 what happened to you?—13 scythe grinders bands were taken.

18,362. Where were they taken from?—From the Abbey Dale works.

18,363. What was that for?—Because we engaged a man without their consent, and the man commenced working some few days before the ordinary time.

18,364. What do you mean by "commenced working before the ordinary time"?—They have a peculiar time for the hiring of the men; we hire men at a certain time in the scythe trade for the season, which lasts a year, and we re-engage them every year.

18,365. When does the season begin?—On the 6th of July.

18,366. And he began before the 6th of July?—I believe so. Will you permit me to state how the bands were recovered?

18,367. Yes, as shortly as you can?—The man Kay was fined 10*l.*, and our place was stopped for a considerable time at the most important part of the year, when our goods were wanted for the harvest.

18,368. Do you mean to say that the whole of your works were stopped?—If one branch of our works stop, it stops the lot in a short time.

18,369. (*Chairman.*) Do I understand that the 13 bands being taken would stop your whole trade?—A great portion of that trade, almost entirely for that season.

18,370. (*Mr. Barstow.*) You lost almost the whole season?—No; the season was nearly over. The hay harvest was on then, and it prevented us sending a great many scythes out and sending a great many goods away.

18,371. For how long a time did you say they stopped you?—About ten days, I think it was.

18,372. (*Chairman.*) How did you get your bands back?—A note was stuck on to one of the workmen's doors, saying the bands were in a field of corn.

18,373. The bands were restored?—Yes. The note was signed "Tidd Pratt."

18,374. (*Mr. Barstow.*) In 1863 what happened?—Several shops were broken open in 1863, and tools taken away.

18,375. What was that for?—Nonpayment of natty money by the workmen.

18,376. In what trade was that?—The scythe finishers, the same as the other one. In 1865 two shops were broken open, and the tools thrown into the dams.

18,377. Because they would not join?—Yes, the same class of men.

18,378. For the same reason?—Yes.

18,379. You said that two shops were broken open; what was done at that time?—The tools were taken away; sometimes we found them and sometimes we did not.

18,380. Upon that occasion did you find them?—The excavators upon the Midland line had found them in some plantation where the line is coming through.

18,381. You did not find them at the time?—No.

18,382. They are of no use to you now?—We have replaced them, but they may come in some time or other.

18,383. In 1866 what happened?—A large quantity of grinders bands were taken.

18,384. Do you know what the reason of that was?—To compel the patent scythe makers to join the union.

18,385. That is, the patent scythe makers whom you employed?—Yes.

18,386. Did you get those bands back again?—After a similar code of concessions to those I repeated before.

18,387. They made terms at the same time?—Yes.

18,388. Was that a still further encroachment?—It was in a different branch of the trade, but a similar code of terms had to be conceded.

18,389. (*Chairman.*) I do not understand you. The men had not paid, and so they had not conformed to the rules of the union; they were the patent scythe makers?—The men had originally been members of the union, but they declined paying any longer. They said that we were paying more than most manufacturers and the union was of no use to them, and they did not want to join.

18,390. And this was done for the misconduct of your workmen?—Yes.

18,391. Did they say that they would not allow you to have these men, or what did they do?—The men made conditions and an agreement with Mr. Bagshaw, the secretary of the patent scythe makers union.

18,392. (*Mr. Barstow.*) Early in this year, I believe, you received a threatening letter?—Yes, the threatening letter is of a recent date; it is in connexion with the union, and occurred immediately after the men were united to the union to advance the prices.

18,393. (*Chairman.*) I understand you that after this large quantity of grinders bands were taken they made conditions and then the men joined again?—Yes.

18,394. (*Mr. Barstow.*) The date of the threatening letter is so dirty that I cannot read it; what was the date?—The 14th of February.

18,395. Is that the letter (*handing a letter to the witness*)?—Yes.

18,396. This is the letter "Sir, You say you will "not pay the price asked for, but you will have to "pay and glad you can. Mr. Charles Bagshaw says "we can make you pay any price we have a mind to "ask for. Mr. Bagshaw says you are robbing your "men of their rites for not letting them ave there own "apprentices; he says you are ruining the Trade for "aving so many lads in your firm insted of your men "having them, and men also working at the trade that "don't work in harmony with us for thay don't pay "to the trade. But Mr. Bagshaw says we must stop "it and very quick, he as sugested a plan which i "think will suckceed very well, that is to fire your "place at Abbydale insted of Blowing up the place "with gunpowder so as it cannot be detected as a "trade outrage. He says every man out to have two "pounds ten shillings that as a union if not it is there "own fault. He says yow out to give your men a price "that will earn that amount and live in smaller "mansions than you do, the Bargain is made to fire "your place if you don't give the price and get shut "of the Boys and men that Bore and lap up; i tell "you the money is paid and the job will be done by "the same man that took your bands and threw them "in the dam. Mr. Bagshaw says he got the fork "grinders their price which they are now having and "he says he can get us ours if we will stick to him, "and do as he tells us; we are sure to win the victory; "i think Mr. Bagshaw is worthy of great prase for "what he has done in Sheffield for the working men "that belong to a union; i hope this will be sufficient "warning to you to comply with the trade and save "your place from being burnt down." There is no

NINETEENTH DAY.

Mr. J. Tyzack.

27 June 1867.

signature but the writer seems to have been a connoisseur in Dresden china as there is something resembling a good pattern of ornamentation. Upon receiving that letter what did you do?—I put it into the hands of Mr. Jackson, the chief constable.

18,397. Besides that what did you do?—I called upon Mr. Albert Smith, the magistrate's clerk, and he said they would send for Mr. Bagshaw to the Town Hall.

18,398. Did you in fact see Mr. Bagshaw?—I did not see Mr. Bagshaw.

18,399. But, however, had you any negotiation in consequence of it?—I had not.

18,400. You had none?—No, none.

18,401. (*Chairman.*) I thought you got terms before you received that letter; you said that you had to make concessions, and you say next that the men made conditions with Bagshaw; when were the concessions made, and when were the conditions made? —The concessions and conditions of settlement which were made in connexion with this threatening letter occurred after the turn out with the men in reference to the prices, which was in February.

18,402. Was it after you had received that letter? —Yes.

18,403. (*Mr. Barstow.*) With whom did you make conditions, and to whom did you grant concessions?—With Mr. Bagshaw himself.

18,404. What were the terms proposed by Bagshaw?—There was a revision of the list of workmen's prices; the strike was a general one.

18,405. Did you give higher prices?—At a meeting of the manufacturers the matter was compromised.

18,406. Did you give higher prices?—We gave lower in some cases.

18,407. But generally were the prices advanced?—Very little indeed in our case.

18,408. Were they at all?—Yes.

18,409. Were the terms at all those proposed in that letter?—All the leading articles in that letter were endeavoured to be strictly enforced by Mr. Bagshaw when he came.

18,410. Have you ever had any difficulty with any unions connected with your trade except the grinding branch?—Principally with the scythe grinders; there is one instance with the saw grinders, but it is very paltry.

18,411. You have not had any difficulty except with the grinding branches connected with your trade?—I think I may say none, I mean in the scythe trade, that is in the making and grinding of scythes.

18,412. I understand that Mr. Dyson had a manufactory somewhere in Abbeydale?—I believe we succeeded to the works formerly occupied by him.

18,413. His wheel was blown up?—Yes.

18,414. That is more than 10 years ago, is it not? —It is more than 10 years ago.

18,415. Do you take any precautions? do you go about armed, or anything of that sort?—After I was shot at I provided myself with a revolver.

18,416. For how long did you carry it?—The whole of that winter through.

18,417. Do you generally carry one about in the winter now?—I do not since that time.

18,418. Do you ever sleep with fire-arms loaded?—Always.

18,419. (*Chairman.*) Your road home is rather a solitary road? there are not many houses along Abbeydale?—No.

18,420. How far down Abbeydale is your house? Three miles and a half.

18,421. Beyond the "Waggon and Horses"?—Three quarters of a mile bebond there.

18,422. (*Mr. Barstow.*) Have you commonly communicated with the police when these things were done to you?—I never made a case known. I kept them as quiet as possible.

18,423. What did you speak of?—I spoke about the shooting.

18,424. In cases of rattening on your property do you generally communicate with the police?—The only two occasions in which we have communicated with them were in connexion with the threatening letter and in connexion with the blow up at Dronfield, and the one that I gave you; those are the only two cases.

18,425. Why was that?—Because we thought it was of very little use; we never could get redress at all in these cases.

18,426. But you never tried?—We may have tried; other people have tried and been unsuccessful, and we took care to save ourselves the trouble.

18,427. Are you aware of any case of attempt to murder which has not been communicated to the police?—There was one of my own that I did not communicate.

18,428. You never communicated it to the police although you had been shot at five times?—No, I had a good reason for it.

18,429. Why? — The threatening letter in connexion with the affair with which Thompson was connected and Needham. It so happened that I had only very recently got married, and my wife was a stranger in this part of the country, and she was so unsettled that it caused a great amount of unhappiness.

18,430. So you wished to keep it concealed from her?—Yes.

18,431. Did she know that you were shot at?—Not till about a month after, when I gradually broke the matter to her.

18,432. That seems a very poor reason for not communicating it to the police; did not you think it your duty to come forward and try to find out the offender? —I do not see what advantage that could give anyone. I called upon Mr. Cockayne and communicated it to him; it was close to his residence where I was shot.

18,433. Do you think that you behaved in a manner consistent with your duty in not prosecuting the affair? —I saw no chance of redress.

18,434. You took no means to find it out?—I thought any further investigation would have been fatal to me.

18,435. Did you think that a manly course to be deterred by fear from doing what you were bound to do?—That was the course I took, and a straightforward course too.

18,436. It was a straightforward course one way but it was a straightforward course backwards. When the men had left without notice, had you taken out a summons against them?—No, because we are thoroughly cowed by the operation that is practised towards us. I did not for the same reasons that I spoke about in the shooting case.

18,437. Does not it strike you that if the perpetrators of these outrages had known that you would prosecute them vigorously, they might have been thoroughly cowed?—I believe that out of the number of cases occurring in Sheffield in reference to trade disputes there is not 1 in 50 that goes to our bench, for they are perfectly powerless in the matter.

18,438. Are you a magistrate?—I am.

18,439. (*Chairman.*) You believe that is the fact, that in trade cases not one in 50 goes before a magistrate?—I believe so. I never took one there out of the number which I have recited.

18,440. What do you suppose is the reason of that? —Because they are powerless.

18,441. Why are they powerless?—I may say that the revelations of this court would show you that there is a sort of compromise taking place between certain parties, and the magistrates cannot lend their ears to it. The magistrates can render no advantage and we as manufacturers have learned not to go near the bench with them.

18,442. If you had come before the magistrates and said, "Last night a man came into my wheel and took my bands away from me," do you mean to say that the magistrates would not set the police in motion, and send them about to inquire who were the persons who did it, and to prosecute and bring the men to justice?—I believe they did formerly, but it has been so unsuccessful that it has been dicontinued.

18,443. But you yourself must know of convictions following prosecutions for things of this kind?—Yes,

NINETEENTH DAY.

Mr. J. Tyzack.

27 June 1867.

but they are very rare; it is when they have been caught in the fact that they have been convicted in 19 cases out of 20.

18,444. Do you say that you did not go before the magistrates, not because the magistrates would not entertain the cases, but because you could not get evidence against the parties that the men who had done it are men connected with the trade? they would not give up the offenders?—I do not wish to slight the magistrates, but the cases are so frequent, and we as manufacturers find it is so little use to go to the bench, that we have given over going there or applying.

18,445. That is to say, you cannot get evidence up?—Yes.

18,446. (*Mr. Barstow.*) But in these cases, with the exception of two, you have never tried at all to get evidence, and never gone to the police?—Yes.

18,447. Do you think that that course is consistent with your duty?—I think the other manufacturers do the same thing.

18,448. Do you think that that course is consistent with your duty?—Perhaps not.

18,449. Do not you think that it is a very spiritless course to take?—It is one of the things which unfortunately has to be done at the present time.

18,450. Supposing people all through the country acted as you do, crimes would not be brought to justice at all, is not that so?—Very likely. If you would allow me to explain each rattening case in our establishment, you would see how powerless we are in the matter.

18,451. Do I gather from your evidence that the Sheffield manufacturers are such spiritless creatures that they allow these things to be committed upon them like a flock of sheep?—We are powerless to prevent it.

18,452. (*Mr. Chance.*) I suppose the fact is that the magistrates could not do that, which by paying and conceding terms, you are able to do?—Yes.

18,453. Is that the reason that you feel that there is no use in applying to the magistrates?—No, we have to submit to their tyrannical dictation. We would do anything if we could get relief otherwise.

18,454. You find that it is no use going to the magistrates because they cannot give you relief?—Yes.

18,455. It is only by consenting to the terms imposed upon you you are able to get relief?—Yes.

18,456. (*Mr. Barstow.*) Was that threatening letter which you received mentioned to Mr. Bagshaw at the interview which you had with him?—No.

18,457. (*Chairman.*) It looks as if you were throwing a reproach upon Mr. Bagshaw by having this letter read; you wished it to be read and you say that you settled upon the basis of the terms which were contained in the letter, and when Mr. Bagshaw called upon me and said that he was going to settle your case, you did not say to him, "But were you any party to this letter?"—The letter was in the hands of the chief constable.

18,458. Why did not you say, "There has been an " anonymous letter sent to me, Mr. Bagshaw, and I " think you were a party to it." If you said, "Mr. " Bagshaw, I have got a letter that can be got from " Mr. Jackson in which your name is mentioned, and " now I find that you are asking me to come to the " terms mentioned in it. I hope you were no party " to that letter," you would have given Mr. Bagshaw an opportunity of saying, "I never knew of it"?—The letter might have emanated from a different person. I thought it might have been written by one of our workmen.

18,459. Why did not you ask Bagshaw if he had written the letter?—He had denied all knowledge of it to Mr. Jackson.

18,460. The letter was brought to Mr. Bagshaw's knowledge and he had denied it?—He had denied all knowledge of it whatever.

18,461. (*Mr. Barstow.*) You say that in 1859 you wrote to the secretary of the scythe trade; do you mean the secretary of the scythe grinders?—Yes.

18,462. You say that Mr. Aston was the secretary of the patent scythe makers then?—That was the scythe finishers union.

18,463. Was he the secretary at the time that your bellows were cut?—Yes.

18,464. How do you know that?—Because I remember that on that occasion after the shops were broken open I went down to the works and the men that had been working were straying about. I said, "How is it you are not at work?" and they said that Aston had sent for my tools.

18,465. Did you see Mr. Aston on the subject?—I did not communicate with him.

18,466. How do you know that he was the secretary at that time?—I do not know.

18,467. He himself says that he was not the secretary. What reason have you for saying that the shooting at you was connected with the union?—Because there could be no other motive that I know of, nor any other party that I could attribute it to.

18,468. Did you see anyone connected with the union about it afterwards?—No.

18,469. Can you give any reason for saying that you were not attacked by robbers?—My reason for saying that it was more particularly on account of the union was that if robbers had attacked me, as soon as they saw I had fallen down in the gig they would have come up and rifled my pockets. I never saw the men.

18,470. Have you any other reason than that?—I do not know that I can give any other reason than that; it is the most powerful reason that I can give. If a robber had fired at anybody he would have pounced upon him after the shot taking effect. It was not the shot that knocked me down, it was the immediate palpitation and loss of nerve. It was a moonlight night.

18,471. (*Mr. Chance.*) How many unions have you connected with your particular trade?—11 or 12 in all.

18,472. (*Mr. Barstow.*) Have you any complaint against the file trade?—None whatever.

18,473. (*Chairman.*) You say that you were shot at?—Yes.

18,474. And you believe, as I understand you to suggest, that Mr. Thompson had something to do with it?—I can only attribute it to that.

18,475. To Mr. Thompson?—To Michael Thompson.

18,476. That is what you believe?—I firmly believe that Michael Thompson had something to do with it.

18.477. How long before you were shot at had this man, Needham, been out of prison?—I believe it was nearly two years, or about two years.

18,478. How long before you were shot at did you make those inquiries which you say were the cause of your having been shot at?—Only a very few days, perhaps a week.

18,479. It was only a few days before you were shot at? why did you postpone your inquiries till that time?—Because I had given up the idea of ever getting the address of Needham, and it had gone out of my mind till I heard some of our workmen say that Needham was seen in the district.

18,480. Had you mentioned that Needham had made any confession to you at all?—Yes, as soon as I found that could not handle Thompson by means of the law.

18,481. When was that?—Immediately on my return from the prison I spoke to eight or nine of his relations.

19,482. Whose relations?—Thompson's relations. I will mention them by name. There was John Fisher, the uncle, Thomas Fisher, the uncle, Francis Fisher, another uncle, and George Fisher.

12,483. These are the uncles of Thompson?—Yes. I told them the whole story of the confession of Needham, as to who paid the money to Needham to blow up these works, and to blow up my house.

18,484. And you told them that you had heard it from Needham?—Yes.

18,485. Therefore Thompson must have been perfectly cognisant that you had such a confession as

NINETEENTH DAY.

Mr. J. Tyzack.

27 June 1867.

that?—He was convinced of it, and I repeatedly asked the uncles if they had communicated the fact. They said they may have done so indirectly, but finding that it was only a probability I sent a messenger direct, not strictly direct, but I told him to tell him that if Needham has done it I would fetch Needham up for making the charge. I told the person to tell Thompson that I should prove that he had given 4*l.* to blow my house up.

18,486. Who was the man by whom you sent that message?—A person of the name of Hawk who assisted in the secretaryship at the club-house.

18,487. When was that?—During the four years servitude.

18,488. You sent that message to him?—Yes.

18,489. Did you get a message back from Thompson?—I said "You can tell the man so."

18,490. Have you any reason to believe that he did tell him?—I have every reason to believe it.

18,491. Has he told you that he did?—It has come repeatedly to my ears indirectly that he is aware of it.

18,492. Have you ever seen Thompson?—He lived in the same road, and I met him frequently.

18,493. Did you ever allude to it to him?—I never spoke to the man more than once in my life.

18,494. Have you ever alluded to it to him?—No; I beg pardon, on one occasion I happened to see him at an inn in the district, and I think my words were "Have you been to Dronfield lately?" or something to that effect; there was no reply, but I think he went away immediately after.

18,495. That was while Needham was in prison?—Yes.

18,496. The man had four years?—Yes.

18,497. The man came out of prison?—Yes.

18,498. How soon after he was sent to prison did you get the confession?—Between the time he was sentenced and the time he went away.

18,499. How long had he been in prison?—Two or three days after his conviction.

18,500. Therefore, it would be six years after the conviction that this shooting took place?—Yes.

18,501. And six years after the man had told you about it?—It was in 1862 that I was shot at.

18,502. A few weeks before you had been told that this man was in the neighbourhood?—Yes.

18,503. And you asked your men to make inquiries about him?—I never spoke to our men.

18,504. To whom did you speak?—To none of our men. I made personal inquiries about the district.

18,505. Where did you go?—In the neighbourhood of his house.

18,506. Whose house?—Thompson's house.

18,507. Thompson lives in the country?—Yes.

18,508. Did you go to some cottage houses?—Yes. The inquiries were promiscuous when I could not find anybody in connexion with Needham's family.

18,509. To whom did you go?—There was one man that I employed.

18,510. Tell me his name?—George Watson.

18,511. Who besides?—I cannot just now remember.

18,512. How many people did you go to?—There were two or three.

18,513. On the same day, or on different days?—On different days, just as the matter would come to my mind.

18,514. I wish you would be accurate about this. You went to two or three places; how many days before you were shot at did you make these inquiries?—It might be two or three weeks from days to weeks.

18,515. What ground have you for supposing that those persons would ever make any statement to Thompson?—I have no grounds for any idea of that sort. I may say I attribute the shooting itself to no other cause, because I had no personal quarrel.

18,516. You had taken steps a week or so before? you had inquired after Needham?—Yes.

18,517. What had you said?—I inquired if he had been seen in the country since he came back.

18,518. How near to Thompson's house were those men of whom you made these inquiries?—I think one was about a mile or a mile and a half, but he was acquainted with Thompson; that was the reason I inquired.

18,519. Was he on intimate terms with Thompson?—I do not know that. They lived in the district all together, and I casually inquired first of one and then of the other who were living in the district at the time the matter occurred. I am sure I could not recall the names of more than one.

18,520. A week after you made these inquiries this shooting took place?—Yes.

18,521. After you were shot at you did not go to him and charge him with it?—No.

18,522. You have told us that you never went to the police?—No.

18,523. Did you see Needham at all?—I never saw him.

18,524. Did you give any notice that you wanted to see him?—No.

18,525. You never were shot at again?—No.

18,526. When were you shot at in 1862?—In November 1862.

18,527. Do you know whether Needham remained in the country after that?—I believe he went to America directly.

18,528. How soon after?—I have traced these steps within the last few days. Immediately I was shot at I learned that he had been in Sheffield for a considerable period holding two situations.

18,529. Where?—One was at a person's of the name of Law, and the other at a man's of the name of Wolstenholme.

18,530. He was there just about the time that you were shot at?—Yes, and he immediately went to America; I believe so.

18,531. Had you ascertained at all by what means he went to America?—Not the first time.

18,532. Has he been twice?—He came back during the autumn of last year.

18,533. How soon after November 1862, after you were shot at, did he go to America?—That I cannot tell.

18,534. Do you know whether he went away directly after you were shot at?—Recent proofs say so.

18,535. Do you know that he went then? have you been told?—Yes.

18,536. Who told you?—A man of the name of Oates with whom he lodged.

18,537. Did he tell you when Needham went to America?—I think it was about the end of 1862.

18,538. You were shot at in November 1862, and at the end of the same year he went away?—Yes.

18,539. You had heard that he lodged at Oates's?—Yes.

18,540. Had you seen him?—I had seen him.

18,541. Had you ascertained whether Thompson was in communication with him at all?—No.

18,542. Have you tried to ascertain that?—No.

18,543. Have you asked the question whether he was with him or not?—No.

18,544. You are suggesting that a man has shot you or was a party to it, and that he got Needham out of the country?—He had two journeys to America.

18,545. He went to America, but he came back again?—Yes.

18,546. When?—The latter part of last year; I think about August last year; and after staying here for a very short period, report says that a little before Christmas, he was lodging with this Mr. Oates, and he showed Oates that he had had a large sum of money. Two people gave evidence as to that. He showed the money in the house to two men, and one estimated the amount at 150 sovereigns, another thought it was not quite so much.

The witness withdrew.

Adjourned to to-morrow at 11 o'clock.

TWENTIETH DAY.

Council Hall, Sheffield, Friday, 28th June 1867.

PRESENT:

WILLIAM OVEREND, Esq., Q.C.	GEORGE CHANCE, Esq.
THOMAS IRWIN BARSTOW, Esq.	J. E. BARKER, Esq., Secretary.

WILLIAM OVEREND, ESQ., Q.C., IN THE CHAIR.

Mr. JOSHUA TYZACK recalled and further examined.

TWENTIETH DAY.

Mr. J. Tyzack.

28 June 1867.

18,547. (*Chairman.*) On the night when you were shot at in Abbey Dale did any woman come to you and ask you if you would take her up in your gig?—No.

18,548. Did you say to anyone that you were loaded, and that you did not take anyone up at that time of night?—Nothing of the kind.

18,549. On which side of the road was the person who fired off the revolver at you?—On the right-hand side.

18,550. Going from Abbey Dale to Sheffield, on the footpath side?—On the footpath side.

18,551. Was that near the plantation?—It was in the plantation, at the very corner of it, adjoining Mr. Cockayne's premises. Would you allow me to state one little matter that occurred to me after I got on the road. The first person I met after I had proceeded a short distance after the report of the fifth shot was a man near Mr. Sam Young's lodge.

18,552. Coming towards Sheffield?—Yes, coming towards Sheffield. I stopped the horse again; I said, "My man, will you take hold of my horse while I run back." I ran back for about 15 or 20 yards and I stopped. I thought if the man had another barrel loaded and I was unarmed he would give it me, and I went back and reseated myself in the gig and went home. I do not know who the man was.

18,553. Did you tell him you had been shot at?—No.

18,554. When did you get the revolver first?—We had been in the habit of having one for a long time.

18,555. Had you had it for some years?—Yes, ever since it was invented.

18,556. How many years?—Perhaps 20 years.

18,557. You had had the revolver 20 years?—Yes, I may add that I have spent dozens of nights parading our premises from one time to another with this revolver for fear of these depredations; that was the reason we got the revolver in the first instance.

18,558. Were you ever shot at except upon that occasion?—No sir.

18,559. Did you ever yourself fire off a revolver when you were going home in your gig?—Never in my life.

18,560. Did you ever fire off a revolver at any time when you were going home?—Never at any time.

18,561. Did you ever tell Mr. Hall of the firm of Martin Hall and Company that you carried a revolver?—Yes, it was generally known throughout the district, for I wore a satchel in front of me, and carried it up to my bed-room at night, and down the next morning. I brought it into court yesterday.

18,562. You paraded it to let people know that you did carry one?—It was known unfortunately on one occasion amongst our men, because the string broke and it fell into a water-hole, when we were inspecting some works.

18,563. When was it known to your men that you carried a revolver?—I believe it was at the time of the accident I speak of; it fell out of the pouch into the water-hole. I got one of the men to fetch it out, and it was known ever after that.

18,564. Was it before you were shot at or after?—It was after. I did not carry one before that.

18,565. Were you carrying one at the time you were shot at?—No, I regret I had not got one. I would have faced him there.

18,566. Did you carry one in 1858?—I think not, we should occasionally take them up; we have had them at both places on account of being in the habit of watching sometimes.

18,567. Did you carry a revolver about your person in the year 1858?—We had occasionally done so, but not as a rule.

18,568. When you say "we" do you mean yourself and brother?—Yes. I will not say whether my brother really carried it, he has left the court; we had one revolver at one place and one at another, but they were not regularly carried. I carried them the whole of the winter after I was shot.

18,569. Why did you get them in respect of your premises?—At a period before the ten years that we are now speaking of, immediately after our entering our place, we had 10 pairs of bellows destroyed, and a number of rattening cases. I watched scores of nights the whole night through; I dressed myself up in a lantern and watchman's attire, with a revolver, and passed out, my brother being on one side of the place and I on the other. I have watched scores of nights and even more than that. I have spent the whole night through watching if these depredations should be committed.

18,570. Were you afraid of any attack in 1858?—I cannot remember that.

18,571. Had you your grinders out in 1858?—No, sir.

18,572. Were they out in 1859?—On January the 18th 1859 they left the works.

18,573. About that time had you mentioned to Mr. Hall that you carried a pistol to protect yourself against the grinders?—I cannot remember any discourse with Mr. Hall; he is my near neighbour and we often talk; it may have been mentioned in promiscuous conversation; I cannot swear to that.

18,574. Were you carrying a revolver in 1859 when the men were turned out?—No, I did not fear anything on that occasion at all.

18,575. What year do you say you were shot at?—In 1862.

18,576. Are you quite sure it was not in 1859 that you were shot at?—I am quite sure of that.

18,577. Did any woman ever mention to you about any shots?—No.

18,578. Did Mr. Hall ever tell you that any woman had mentioned to him about any shots?—No

The witness withdrew.

GEORGE FOX sworn and examined.

G. Fox.

18,579. (*Chairman.*) What are you?—I am a wool-shear forger.

18,580. What do you want to say?—I wish to call your attention to two questions that you put to Mr. Reaney when he was examined on Wednesday.

18,581. "*Q.* The witness went on to say that he went

TWENTIETH DAY.

G. Fox.

28 June 1867.

" to see Mr. Ward about employing Addis, and Mr. " Ward said, it was a hard case that his goods should " be taken and his work stopped." The question is, " Did you not tell him that was the way you did to " compel manufacturers to comply with your de- " mands?—*A.* That was not the word, but the " meaning was something of that sort. *Q.* You and " Stanley and Fox, and Higginbottom and Mitchell " all went and made that statement to him?—*A.* I " think Higginbottom was not there, but the other " four were." Is it in answer to that that you wish to say anything?—Yes. I wish to say that I was simply present there by Mr. Ward's request. I had no part either in the rattening or of exacting the 30*l.* for the expenses that they demanded from Mr. Ward.

18,582. It is quite correct that they did demand 30*l.* for the rattening that had been done?—Yes.

18,583. You appeared there as Mr. Ward's friend? —I appeared there at his request.

18,584. You think an impression has erroneously gone forth, and the public think that you were a party to exacting that sum of money?—I hope the public will not think I was a party to it.

18,585. You had nothing to do with the matter?— No.

18,586. (*Mr. Barstow.*) Were you in Mr. Ward's employment when Addis was working for him?— Yes; I was the foreman in the woolshear department at the time.

18,587. Had you anything to do with Addis?—No, I had not.

18,588. Used he to come into the warehouse for steel?—He might come, but I do not remember seeing him come; very likely he would.

18,589. You do not know whether he insulted or misconducted himself towards the other men?—I never saw him misbehave himself.

18,590. Did you ever hear them complain of him? —I never did.

18,591. There was something else that you wished to say?—I wished to call attention to that schedule which was read over by Mr. Dronfield. In that schedule it says, "woolshear forgers outrages, only one, nearly 20 years ago." It would appear from that that the public would believe that outrage had occurred in connexion with the wool shear forgers.

18,592. We cannot go into anything of that kind which occurred 20 years ago.

The witness withdrew.

M. A. Needham.

MARY ANN NEEDHAM sworn and examined.

18,593. (*Mr. Chance.*) Are you the wife of Thomas Needham?—Yes.

18,594. Was your husband an engine tenter at Messrs. Moss and Crooks?—Yes.

18,595. Was your husband convicted for the outrage committed in the year 1856?—Yes.

18,596. And sentenced to penal servitude?—Yes.

18,597. Where was the outrage committed?—I do not know.

18,598. Was it the outrage committed at Dronfield? —Yes.

18,599. Was he tried and convicted at Derby?— Yes.

18,600. After his conviction did you go to Derby to see him?—Yes.

18,601. Whom did you go with?—Sam Crooks.

18,602. Did Crooks ask you to go or did you ask him to go?—He asked me to go.

18,603. Who paid your railway fare?—Crooks.

18,604. Did he give you a new dress to go in?— That was the time when we went again.

18,605. How long did you remain at Derby?— Only a day.

18,606. Did you see your husband in prison?— Yes.

18,607. Did Crooks go with you to the prison?— Yes.

18,608. Did he go in his own name or pass himself off as somebody else?—He went in his own name.

18,609. Did he pass himself off as anybody else when he was there?—He said if they asked me I was to say he was my brother.

18,610. Did your husband say anything to Crooks about your being provided for while he was in prison?—No, he did not say so.

18,611. Did you ask Crooks for any money?—Yes.

18,612. Did he give you any?—Sometimes.

18,613. When did he first give you some money? —In the Town Hall in Sheffield.

18,614. How much?—8*s.*

18,615. How long after your visit to Derby was that?—It was before we visited Derby.

18,616. Did he give you any other money before you went to Derby?—No.

18,617. When you came back from Derby did he give you any money?—It was a long time before he did.

18,618. How long was it before he gave you any other money?—It might be a few months, I cannot say particularly.

18,619. How much did he give you then?—10*s.* I got again.

18,620. Did he give you any money after that?— Yes, a long time after that.

18,621. How long was it before he gave you any more money?—It might be four or five months.

18,622. How much did he give you then?—10*s.* again.

18,623. When next did he give you money?—It would be a long time again and then I got 10*s.* again.

18,624. How long, would it be many months?— Yes, but not many.

18,625. Did he give you any other money?—It came to 3*l.* what he gave me.

18,626. Did you make another visit to Derby to see your husband?—I made another visit a few months after the first visit before he was sent away.

18,627. Did you go of your own accord or did Crooks ask you to go?—Crooks asked me to go.

18,628. Who went with you?—His wife.

18,629. Did anybody else go?—My sister-in-law.

18,630. Anybody else?—My brother-in-law; he is dead now.

18,631. Was that John Needham?—Yes.

18,632. Who paid the railway fare to Derby?— Crooks.

18,633. Did he pay the fare of all of you?—I do not know whether he did for the others, he did for me.

18,634. And while you were there your expenses were paid?—I do not know who paid them.

18,635. Did you pay them?—No, I did not pay anything.

18,636. Did Crooks at any time make you a present of a new dress?—Yes; when we went the second time to Derby.

18,637. What did he give you the second time?— A new dress and a new bonnet.

18,638. Was that the only visit that you paid to Derby?—Yes.

18,639. How did you come to reside in Sheffield? —I left Crooks, and went to live in Garden Street, Sheffield.

18,640. Did you apply to Crooks after that for any more money?—Yes, many times.

18,641. Did you ever receive any?—Not after the 3*l.*

18,642. Why did you apply to Crooks for the money?—My brother told me I should have to ask him; he is dead.

18,643. Is Bradley a relation of yours?—He was my brother.

18,644. Who said that you were to go to Crooks to get the money?—My brother, Bradley.

TWENTIETH DAY.

M. A. Needham.

28 June 1867.

18,645. Did you lose a child some time ago?—Yes.

18,646. On the death of the child did you apply to Crooks for money to bury it?—Yes.

18,647. How long ago would that be?—It was a fortnight old when my husband was taken out, and lived for a year and three months.

18,648. When you asked Crooks for money to bury your child what did he say?—He said a very nasty word.

18,649. Did he tell you to go to anybody else?—I went to Michael Thompson.

18,650. Did he tell you to go to Michael Thompson?—No; Bradley told me to go to Mike Thompson.

18,651. Did you go to Michael Thompson?—Yes, I did.

18,652. What did you say to Thompson?—I told him my baby was dead; and he said he could not help it, he did not know me. I said, "I will make you know me."

18,653. What did he say to that?—I sat down in the house while he washed himself.

18,654. When he was washed what did you do?—I followed him as he went out; he said he could not do anything with me; I was to look to Crooks.

18,655. What did you mean by saying, "I will make you know me"?—I thought I had a right when my brother sent me there.

18,656. Why because your brother sent you there?—I do not know.

18,657. Why should that be any reason for saying "I will make you know me"?—I thought perhaps by my brother sending me that Thompson knew something.

18,658. About what?—About the affair for which my husband was suffering.

18,659. Had you ever heard from anybody that Thompson had had anything to do with it?—Only from my brother.

18,660. (*Chairman.*) What had he told you about it?—Not anything, only about going up when the baby died.

Mr. Sugg stated that the whole of this evidence related to what had taken place in 1856.

The *Chairman* stated that the object of the evidence was to show that Thompson was engaged in a trade outrage 10 years ago, which was an inducement to him to shoot Mr. Tyzack after Needham came out of prison, it having been proved that Mr. Tyzack had been inquiring after him.

18,661. (*Mr. Chance.*) Did Bradley say anything about Thompson?—No, only for me to go up there.

18,662. He only told you to go to him?—Yes.

18,663. Are you quite sure of that?—Yes.

18,664. You said just now that you followed Thompson out of the house, and that he told you to go to Crooks?—Yes.

18,665. Did you apply again to Crooks after that for money?—Yes.

18,666. And you got no more money from Crooks?—No.

18,667. Do you remember seeing your husband after he had served his time?—Yes.

18,668. That was four years afterwards?—Yes.

18,669. Did he ask you anything?—He asked me if I had had any money.

18,670. Did he say from whom?—From Crooks.

18,671. What did you say to him?—I told him I had, but my brother was living then, my brother told him.

18,672. What did you tell him?—I said I had had some, but he did not ask me anything more then.

18,673. You said that you had had some?—Yes.

18,674. Did you tell him how much?—Yes.

18,675. Did he ask you whether the trade had done anything for you?—No, he did not mention the trade.

18,676. Do you know whether your husband went to Crooks' afterwards?—Yes, he did.

18,677. Why did he go to Crooks?—He went to see why he did not give me the money.

18,678. Had your husband complained to you that Crooks had not given you as much money as he ought to have given you?—Yes.

18,679. Did he say anything when he came back from seeing Crooks?—He said that Crooks could have a bird box or anything there was.

18,680. What do you mean by that? was it a box of stuffed birds?—Yes.

18,681. Was it a box belonging to Crooks?—Yes.

18,682. Did your husband get anything more from Crooks?—I do not know.

18,683. You have told us of all the money you have received from him?—Yes, I have.

18,684. Did Crooks tell you at the time your husband was convicted that he would take care of you while your husband was in prison?—No; he did not say he would take care of me.

18,685. Did he say he would do anything for you while your husband was in prison?—Yes.

18,686. What did he say he would do?—He said he would do something for me while he was in prison.

18,687. Do you know when your husband came out of prison whether Crooks went to see him?—Yes.

18,688. Did Crooks tell you that he was going to see your husband?—No, I had not spoken to him for a long time then.

18,689. How do you know that he went to see your husband?—My little son told me he had.

18,690. How could your little son know?—He was not living with me, but he was living with his uncle at this date, he went there first.

18,691. Who is the uncle?—John Needham.

18,692. How did your little son know that Crooks had been to see your husband?—I cannot say that, but I know he did; my husband told me that Crooks did come to meet him.

18,693. Did you ever hear Crooks say afterwards that he had been to see your husband?—No.

18,694. How you knew it was through your little son, and your husband told you also?—Yes.

18,695. You knew nothing at all from Crooks?—No.

18,696. (*Chairman.*) Did he say why he went to meet your husband?—No.

18,697. (*Mr. Chance.*) Did your husband tell you why he went to meet him?—No.

18,698. Your husband is now in America?—Yes.

18,699. He has been to America twice?—I believe he has, I am not sure. I have not seen him five years come Christmas.

18,700. Did not you see him before he went to America the last time?—No.

18,701. (*Chairman.*) How long did he live with you before he went to America?—Three years, it might be a little better.

18,702. (*Mr. Chance.*) When did he go to America the first time, how long after his return from prison?—It would be between three and four years.

18,703. Between three and four years after he came out of prison?—Yes.

18,704. Now let us be clear about the dates; your husband was convicted in 1856?—I will not be sure.

18,705. You saw him when he came out of prison four years after his conviction?—Yes.

18,706. How long after he came out of prison was it that he went to America?—Between three and four years.

18,707. Between three and four years after?—Yes.

18,708. (*Chairman.*) Did he serve his whole time?—He served his four years.

18,709. (*Mr. Chance.*) How long after he came out of prison was it before he went to America?—Between three and four years.

18,710. Do you know why your husband went to America?—Yes.

18,711. Why did he go to America?—He said he could not look people in the face after he had been to prison.

18,712. How long before he went to America was it that he first talked about going to America?—A

TWENTIETH DAY.

M. A. Needham.

28 June 1867.

long while; he did not want to come home, he wanted to go to America then, but I would not go.

18,713. Between the time of coming out of prison and his going to America where did he live?—He lived in Sheffield.

18,714. Were you living with him?—Yes.

18,715. Did you ever see anything of Michael Thompson during that time?—No.

18,716. You never saw him come to see your husband?—No.

18,717. Did Crooks come to see your husband?—No.

18,718. (*Chairman.*) Your husband and Crooks had quarrelled had not they?—Yes, I fancy they had.

18,719. Had you heard before he went to America that Mr. Tyzack was inquiring for him?—No.

18,720. Did you hear after he went to America that Mr. Tyzack, was making inquiries about him?—No, sir.

18,721. (*Mr. Chance.*) How long did he remain in America?—I do not know how long; he will have been for five years in America come Christmas.

18,722. But he came home and then went back again?—I have not seen him.

18,723. Had you heard that he was in England?—I do not know; I cannot say.

18,724. How long did he stay in England?—I do not know.

18,725. How long did you hear he was in England?—I think he came to England and remained a few weeks.

18,726. (*Mr. Chance.*) Did you hear that he was going to America again?—No.

18,727. Do you know what time during the five years he was in England?—Lately—this last summer.

18,728. How long ago?—I cannot tell you.

18,729. Within a few months?—Perhaps it might be five or six months.

18,730. He was in England five or six months since?—Yes.

18,731. (*Chairman.*) Do you know whether he came to Sheffield or not?—He came to Sheffield but I had not seen him.

18,732. (*Mr. Chance.*) From whom did you hear that?—I heard from many people that he was in Sheffield, but I never saw him.

18,733. Up to what time did you hear that he was in Sheffield?—I heard he was in Sheffield I think on Friday.

18,734. (*Chairman.*) What time did you hear that he was in Sheffield?—I think about five or six months since.

18,735. Can you say whether it was this year?—I think it was this year.

18,736. (*Mr. Chance.*) How long after Christmas was it that you heard he was in Sheffield?—I cannot say, I took no notice.

18,737. Did you hear at the time that he was in Sheffield?—Yes.

18,738. You were told that he was in Sheffield?—Yes.

18,739. (*Chairman.*) Who told you?—Several people told my children and they came and told me.

18,740. (*Mr. Chance.*) That was five or six months ago?—Yes, as near as I can tell.

18,741. Did you hear of his going to America after that?—No; I heard he was gone, but I did not hear that he was going.

18,742. (*Chairman.*) What was your husband by trade?—An engine tenter.

18,743. He had nothing to do with the scythe grinders union?—No, not that I know of.

18,744. Did he belong to any union?—No, sir.

18,745. Do you know who found him the means of going out to America the first time?—We saved it amongst us.

18,746. You do not know Mr. Tyzack do you?—Yes I do.

18,747. Did you ever hear of Mr. Tyzack being shot at?—I once heard my brother talking of it, but it is a long time since; that is a brother that is dead now. He did not say Mr. Tyzack, he said a man.

18,748. Where was he shot at, did he say?—He did not say.

18,749. Did you hear of a man being shot at in Abbey Dale Road?—No.

18,750. You heard of a man being shot at?—No, not in Abbey Dale Road I did not.

18,751. Did you hear of Mr. Tyzack being shot?—No.

18,752. Who was it you heard of being shot at?—I do not know who it was.

18,753. How long after your husband came from prison was it?—I think it was while he was there.

18,754. Have you heard of any man being shot at after your husband came back from prison?—No.

18,755. And never did?—No.

18,756. Did you ever hear of anybody making inquiries where your husband was at this time?—No.

18,757. Did anybody come to you?—No.

18,758. Your husband lived with you?—Yes.

18,759. You never heard that anybody was asking for him?—There was a gentleman, after he was taken to prison, asked for him.

18,760. But after he came out of prison some three or four years, do you recollect anybody inquiring for him, to know where he was?—No.

18,761. You never heard of such a thing?—No.

18,762. Was his resolution to go to America a sudden thing, or how was it that he went?—It was always his motive to go.

18,763. But at last when he did go, did he go off in a hurry, or how did he go?—No, he did not go off in a hurry.

18,764. He did not go off in a hurry?—No.

18,765. You are quite sure about that?—Yes, I am sure he did not, because he did not go for three weeks after he left Mr. Wolstenholme.

18,766. He was out of work for three weeks?—Yes.

18,767. Who kept him?—I do not know where he lived, he did not live with me.

18,768. How long before he went to America did he leave you?—Three weeks.

18,769. What was he doing for those three weeks? had you quarrelled?—No, we had no quarrel.

18,770. It was a very funny thing if a man was living with his wife up to the time, and working with Wolstenholme, that all of a sudden he should go away?—That was owing to the bailiffs coming.

18,771. The bailiffs distrained upon you?—Yes, they did not take my goods.

18,772. Was your husband concealing himself from the bailiffs?—Yes.

18,773. How did he get money to go?—We saved the money for him to go to America.

18,774. What did you save, how much?—I do not know how much he had.

18,775. Who gave him any?—He used to job about the place.

18,776. What does it cost to go to America?—I am sure I cannot tell you.

18,777. Then he could have paid what he owed to his landlord if he got money to go to America?—It was not the landlord.

18,778. What were the bailiffs put in for?—A Scotchman.

18,779. You had bought goods of a Scotchman had you?—Yes.

18,780. And he did not pay the Scotchman?—No.

18,781. At first when I asked you, you said you had heard of Tyzack being shot?—I did not hear about it, I heard them talking about a man.

18,782. I said "Did you hear of Mr. Tyzack being shot at," and you said, "Yes" you had. Is that true, had you heard of Mr. Tyzack being shot at?—No.

18,783. Never?—No, never.

18,784. During the time your husband was living with you, the three or four years before he went to America, was he going about his work like an ordi-

TWENTIETH DAY.

M. A. Needham.

28 June 1867.

nary workman in the town ?—He was working with Mr. Wolstenholme.

18,785. And anybody who wished to find him out could have found him out ?—Yes.

18,786. Was he in regular employment at that time ?—Not regular, not when he came home from prison he was not.

18,787. He was sometimes in work and sometimes out of work ?—Yes.

18,788. He was in debt ?—Yes.

18,789. And suddenly he left you for three weeks, and the next thing you heard of him was that he had gone to America, and you have never seen him since ?—No.

18,790. Within this present year he has been in Sheffield for a few weeks, and has gone back again ?—Yes.

18,791. Was there any reason why your husband should not come to you ?—No, only he picked up another woman on the vessel.

18,792. Was that when he went out to America the first time ?—Yes.

18,793. Is she living with him ?—Yes.

18,794. Did he bring her to England when he came ?—Yes.

18,795. You heard all that ?—Yes.

The witness withdrew.

William Oates sworn and examined.

W. Oates.

18,796. (*Chairman.*) You live at Beauchief ?—No.

18,797. Have you ever lived there ?—No, never.

18,798. Did you live in Abbey Dale ?—Never.

18,799. Where did you live ?—I used to live at Crooks.

18,800. What are you ?—I am a blade forger.

18,801. Did a person of the name of Needham ever lodge with you ?—Yes.

18,802. When was that ?—Two weeks before last Christmas.

18,803. Was he the husband of the last witness ?—Yes.

18,804. How long was he with you ?—A month within a day.

18,805. Did he come alone or had he a woman with him ?—He came by himself first.

18,806. And afterwards a woman came, who lived with him as his wife ?—Yes.

18,807. And he went away you say in a month ?—Yes, from our house.

18,808. Where did he go to ?—He was in the town a day or two after he left our house, then he went to Dublin. He sent me a letter when he was in Dublin telling me he could sell some goods for me if he knew the prices, and I have never heard from him since.

18,809. Did he send for the goods ?—He sent for some goods.

18,810. Did you send them ?—His brother came for them, and I let his brother have them.

18,811. And you have never heard from him since ?—No.

18,812. Has he paid for the goods ?—No, I made him a present of them.

18,813. Did he tell you why he came over from America ?—Yes. The first time he said, "Bill, I have come for thee."

18,814. You had been a friend of his before ?—Yes. "Bill, I have come for thee and nine or ten other men."

18,815. That was all ?—Yes.

18,816. What did you say ?—I said it depends upon circumstances. I said I was doing very well, and I should not like to go.

18,817. He told you from the first that he intended to go back ?—He said he should go back to America.

18,818. Did he tell you at all who was to find him the means of going back ?—He had plenty of money.

18,819. He said that he had plenty of money ?—He showed it to me.

18,820. When did he show you the money ?—The day after he came.

18,821. How much did he show you ?—As near as my calculation goes, about 150*l*.

18,822. Did he tell you where he had got it from ?—He said he had earned it in America.

18,823. Had he ever lodged with you before ?—No.

18,824. Had you ever known him before he went to America the first time ?—Yes.

18,825. Did he tell you why he went to America the first time ?—For debt.

18,826. Did you hear of Mr. Tyzack being shot at ?—No.

18,827. You know him ?—He came to our house last week, or last week but one. This gentleman at the back of me (*pointing to Mr. Joshua Tyzack*).

18,828. Had you been intimate with Needham before he went to America the first time ?—Yes, but it is some years since.

18,829. You were intimate with him ?—A little bit. We went out together a bit, but not much.

18,830. Did he tell you that he wanted to get out of the way ?—No.

18,831. Did he tell you before he started that he was going to America ?—Yes.

18,832. How long before ?—Eight or nine months. He wanted me to go with him.

18,833. Before he went to America the first time ?—Yes.

18,834. Did he tell you how he would find the money ?—Hesaid he would pay my fare if I would go.

18,835. What was he, a scythe grinder ?—No, he was a spring-knife cutler.

18,836. He was originally an engine tenter ?—He was a spring-knife cutler ; I know nought about that ; he could tent engines.

18,837. He was a spring-knife cutler when he worked for Wolstenholme ?—No, he tented Wolstenholme's engines, but he is a spring-knife cutler by trade.

18,838. Do you know Michael Thompson ?—No.

18,839. You never saw him ?—I do not know him.

18,840. Did Needham ever talk to you about Michael Thompson ?—No.

18,841. Did he ever talk to you about the blowing up he did at Dronfield ?—Yes, we once went out seeking work and he showed me the place that he blew up.

18,842. He did ?—Yes.

18,843. Did he tell you who had sent him to do it ?—No.

18,844. He did not tell you that ?—No.

18,845. Do you know Bradley ?—No.

18,846. If Needham was in debt how did he happen to say that he would pay your fare if you went to America ? Did not you wonder where he got the money from ?—No, I knew how he got it.

18,847. How did he get it ?—He got into all the debt that laid in his power before he did go.

18,848. You knew that ?—Yes.

18,849. He was a very nice friend to be acquainted with ?—I had nothing at all to do with that ; if a man hangs himself I have nothing to do with it.

18,850. And if a man hung another you would have no objection to associate with him ?—I had nothing to do with it ; he said he would pay my fare if I would go.

18,851. Do you mean to say that you allowed a man to talk to you in that way when you knew he was cheating his creditors ?—No, I did not know it. What caused him to go as soon as he did, was he had quarrelled with Gregory, the bailiff, and he came to me at the shop and he said, "Bill, I shall get into trouble ; I have been insulting Gregory."

18,852. How long was that before he went ?—The very day that he was going when he came to me.

TWENTIETH DAY.

W. Oates.

28 June 1867.

18,853. He said, "I have been insulting Gregory" and he should get into trouble?—Yes, he said he should get into trouble and he said he was going.

18,854. Where was the money to come from?—I do not know no further.

18,855. Who was Gregory?—The County Court bailiff.

18,856. Do you know whom he got into debt with?—He got some things of a man named Neil.

18,857. He was a Scotchman?—Yes, that is the only man I know of, and that was the man he had the bother with.

18,858. What was that for?—Drapery.

18,859. Getting into debt with the man for drapery would not enable him to go to America and pay your fare. Where was the money to come from?—I do not know; that is what he said to me.

18,860. Where had he been lodging before he went to America?—He left his wife and went away from her.

18,861. He was three weeks in the town after that?—Not that I know of, I never saw him after.

18,862. Did he ever talk to you about Crooks?—Sam Crooks?

18,863. Yes?—Yes.

18,864. What did he say about Sam Crooks?—He said he believed Sam Crooks had robbed his wife out of some money.

18,865. Did he tell you who was to give Crooks the money?—No.

18,866. How had Crooks robbed his wife of some money?—I do not know.

18,867. But he did tell you that?—Yes.

18,868. What did you say to that?—I said I had nothing at all to do with that.

18,869. Did not you say "How is that, how did he happen to rob your wife"?—I had nothing to do with it.

18,870. When did he say, "Sam Crooks robbed my wife;" was it when he was in prison?—Yes; he ought to have allowed her so much a week.

18,871. How was that—why should Sam Crooks allow Needham's wife so much a week?—I do not know.

18,872. Did not you ask him?—I did not ask him anything at all about it.

18,873. Why not?—It was not my business.

18,874. He had shown you the place which he blew up and you were his intimate friend, and he did not mind telling you about the things, and you did not mind hearing of them; did not you say "How comes it that Sam Crooks was to have allowed your wife this"?—He said he was to have so much money for doing this job, but he did not say whether he received it or not.

18,875. And Crooks was to have allowed a certain part of it to his wife?—I do not know that he said Crooks robbed his wife out of so much money.

18,876. He did not mind telling you about doing it?—We were close by the place.

18,877. Did he tell you anything about Mr. Tyzack?—No.

18,878. Did he never mention his name?—Never.

18,879. Did you ever hear of a man being shot in Abbey Dale Road?—No.

18,880. Never?—No.

18,881. Not being shot at?—No.

18,882. Did he ever say whether Crooks employed him or whether he employed Crooks, or anything of that sort?—No, he was a man very close minded.

18,883. Do not tell me that?—His wife told me about this as well as about Crooks robbing her.

18,884. Needham told you so too?—Yes, and his wife as well.

The witness withdrew.

H. A. Morton.

HARRIETT ANN MORTON sworn and examined.

18,885. (*Mr. Barstow.*) What are you?—A sempstress.

18,886. Used you formerly to live at Bradway Bank, Abbey Dale?—Yes.

18,887. How long ago is that?—Seven years ago.

18,888. You left there seven years ago?—Yes.

18,889. Where do you live now?—West Street Lane.

18,890. Is that the "Angel Hotel"?—I lodge in West Street Lane. I am employed at the "Angel Hotel."

18,891. Do you do sewing work at the "Angel Hotel"?—Yes.

18,892. Do you remember one evening about 9 o'clock some one passing you in a gig?—Yes.

18,893. How long ago is that?—It is about nine years ago.

18,894. (*Chairman.*) Did you know that it was Mr. Tyzack?—Yes.

18,895. And you heard him fire off a gun?—I could not swear it was a gun, but I heard one fired off after I had spoken to him.

18,896. Was it Mr. Tyzack?—It was Mr. Tyzack, he was in a gig, and the revolver was fired after he had passed me about 100 yards further on the road.

18,897. You heard some one fire at him nine years ago?—Yes.

18,898. (*Mr. Barstow.*) What time in the evening was this?—Nine o'clock.

18,899. Where was it?—On Abbey Dale Road, near the nursery.

18,900. Where were you?—I was going from Sheffield home.

18,901. That is I suppose to Bradway Bank?—Yes.

18,902. Did the man overtake you in a gig—Yes.

18,903. Whereabouts was that?—Against the Norton Hammer nursery.

18,904. What time was it?—About 9 o'clock in the evening.

18,905. In what month?—I cannot say what month, I think it was about January.

18,906. What sort of a night was it?—It was a very dark night.

18,907. How far is Norton Hammer nursery from Sheffield?—About three miles I think.

18,908. How far is it from Bradway Bank?—Two and a half miles I think.

18,909. Is it near Mr. Cockayne's garden?—No, it is not very near Mr. Cockayne's.

18,910. How far is it from there?—Perhaps half a mile.

18,911. How far is it from Mr. Younge's lodge?—I do not know exactly, about five minutes walk I think.

18,912. Did you say anything to the man in the gig?—Yes, I asked him if he was going to Totley and if he would take me up.

18,913. Is Totley in the direction of Bradway Bank?—Yes, it is a mile further.

18,914. Did he pull up his horse?—Yes, he stopped and told me he could not take me up; he was loaded, and he did not take people up at that time of night.

18,915. Could you see him very well?—No, I could not see him very distinctly, because it was a very dark night.

18,916. You did not see him?—Yes, I saw him as I stood by the gig side.

18,917. Could you see him so as to see his features and tell who he was?—I could tell who he was when he spoke, because I knew his voice.

18,918. And could you see his features?—Yes, I could see his face.

18,919. And you knew who he was from seeing him?—Yes.

18,920. Can you tell us now who he was?—Mr. Tyzack.

18,921. Which Mr. Tyzack?—Mr. Joshua Tyzack.

18,922. Do you know him from any other reason?—No, I do not know him.

TWENTIETH DAY.

H. A. Morton.

28 June 1867.

18,923. You know him from seeing him?—Yes, I know him very well by sight.

18,924. That is the way that you knew it was Mr. Tyzack, because you saw him in the gig and knew that he was Mr. Tyzack?—Yes, I lived there many years and knew him from seeing him at the works.

18,925. (*Chairman.*) Had you heard him speak?—Yes.

18,926. You knew his voice?—Yes.

18,927. (*Mr. Barstow.*) You knew his voice?—No, I am not aware that I ever spoke to him, but I have heard him speak.

18,928. Then I suppose he drove on?—Yes, he drove on very fast after he had spoken to me.

18,929. What happened next? you walked on?—No, I did not walk on. I stood still waiting for company.

18,930. What happened next?—I heard a revolver go off.

18,931. How do you know it was a revolver?—Because I heard a report four or five times. I knew it was not a gun.

18,932. Had you ever heard a revolver go off before?—Yes, many a time.

18,933. You heard four or five reports?—Yes.

18,934. How long was it after the man in the gig left you, that you heard these reports?—Not more than a minute; he went very quick after I spoke to him.

18,935. Did you see the flash?—Yes, I saw a flash of fire every time there was a report.

18,936. How far were you from it?—I could not exactly tell, it was not very far.

18,937. How far do you suppose?—Perhaps 100 yards or so.

18,938. What did you do?—I went on a little further and Mr. Hall overtook me and I related the circumstance to him.

18,939. Where did you meet Mr. Hall?—By Mill Houses.

18,940. Which Mr. Hall is it?—Mr. Ebenezer Hall.

18,941. Of the firm of Martin Hall and Company?—Yes.

18,942. Did you tell him?—Yes, I related the circumstance to him.

18,943. Did you mention anyone's name?—I told him Mr. Tyzack had just passed me, and I asked him if he would take me up, and I told him about hearing the revolver go off.

18,944. What did Mr. Hall say to that?—He said very likely Mr. Tyzack would fire the revolver himself; there was some disturbance with his workmen, they had turned out the week before.

18,945. Did you tell anyone else this?—I mentioned it to several parties at the time.

18,946. I suppose you got home that night?—Yes, I went with Mr. Hall as far as he went, and I had not far to go after I left him.

18,947. Whom did you tell of it besides Mr. Hall?—I do not know, I am sure. I cannot mention any one now personally, but of course I told it to different parties that I had been very much terrified.

18,948. You were very much terrified were you?—Yes.

18,949. You never spoke to Mr. Tyzack?—No, I never spoke to him myself.

18,950. Would you think of asking a man whom you had never spoken to, to give you a lift in his gig?—I have very often done that when I have been out at night on a lonely road.

18,951. How long after Mr. Tyzack had passed you did you hear these reports?—It was not more than a minute after.

18,952. And you think that Mr. Tyzack must have heard it?—I do not know I am sure; I do not know who it was fired it off.

18,953. (*Chairman.*) If Mr. Tyzack had only gone a minute, and you heard the reports, he must have heard the reports?—He could not help but hear it.

18,954. He must have heard it, you think?—Yes.

18,955. (*Mr. Barstow.*) You are quite sure that he could not help hearing it?—No, he was going close past where the revolver was going off.

18,956. Mr. Tyzack was going past where the revolver was going off?—Yes.

18,957. Do you think that Mr. Hall could have heard the revolver?—No, Mr. Hall did not come up till some time after.

18,958. Was there anybody else on the road?—No, I did not see anybody else.

18,959. Is it a very lonely part of the road?—Yes, it is very lonely.

18,960. You walked a long way with Mr. Hall?—Yes, I walked home.

18,961. That would be about two miles?—Yes.

18,962. Did you walk with him all the way?—Yes.

18,963. You were talking about this most of the time?—Mostly; I told him as soon as he overtook me that I had been very much terrified.

18,964. You told us that he said Mr. Tyzack had very likely let off the pistol himself because some of the men were out?—He said very likely Mr. Tyzack was afraid and thought it was some one in disguise.

18,965. Did Mr. Hall explain why Mr. Tyzack should fire a gun off?—He said there was some disturbance, and his grinders had turned out the week before.

18,966. (*Chairman.*) He suggested that Mr. Tyzack took you for a person in disguise and took you for one of the trade?—Yes.

18,967. If he took you for a person in disguise that is a very good reason why he should have shot you, but why should he shoot when he was a long way on the road after leaving you?—I do not know.

18,968. Did Mr. Hall suggest any reason why, if he took you for a person in disguise, he should shoot when he had got so far away from you?—He said he might have shot to let people know he was prepared.

18,969. (*Mr. Barstow.*) How far was this from his own house?—About a mile and a half I think.

18,970. Did you pass Mr. Tyzack's house on the way home?—Yes.

18,971. Did you call to inquire whether he was hurt?—No.

18,972. Did Mr. Hall call?—No.

18,973. Mr. Hall is a friend of Mr. Tyzack's is he not?—I do not know.

18,974. (*Chairman.*) Was it your impression that some person had fired at him or that he had fired the pistol himself? could you see whether it came from the gig or from a person on the road?—It came from towards the gig.

18,975. Were the flashes towards the gig or not?—They were from the gig.

18,976. (*Mr. Barstow.*) Was the gig in sight? did you see the gig when you saw the flashes?—I could not see it if it had been daylight, because there was a turn in the road.

18,977. Did you hear the wheels of the gig?—Yes.

18,978. If you could not see the gig because there was a turn in the road, how did you manage to see the flashes that came from the gig?—I could see them so very plain.

18,979. How could they come from the gig if the gig could not be seen?—Because there is a turn in the road, the light came in the field by the roadside.

18,980. (*Mr. Chance.*) Was it on the right-hand side of the road or on the left-hand side of the road that you saw the light?—The left-hand side.

18,981. (*Mr. Barstow.*) When did you first tell this story with reference to your coming here?—I told it to Mr. Machin.

18,982. Who is Mr. Machin?—He is a scythe grinder. I think he is on the committee.

18,983. Do you know whether he is the secretary of the scythe grinders?—I do not know; I do not know much about him.

TWENTIETH DAY.

H. A. Morton.

28 June 1867.

18,984. How did you happen to see Mr. Machin? —He came to me this morning.

18,985. Did you tell him this?—Yes, I told him.

18,986. You told it to him this morning?—Yes.

18,987. Why should Mr. Machin come to see you, if you do not know much about him?—Because he had heard of the circumstances before.

18,988. Did he tell you so?—Yes.

18,989. What did he say to you?—He asked me if I would come and relate what I had seen.

18,990. A great many scythe grinders live up where you used to live do not they?—Yes.

18,991. Are you related to any of them?—My father was a scythe grinder when he was alive.

18,992. (*Chairman.*) Have you any brothers?—Yes, I have one brother.

18,993. What is he?—He is a painter.

18,994. Are you in any way related to Mr. Machin? —No.

18,995. Do you know Mr. Thompson?—Yes.

18,996. How long have you known him?—I have known him many years by sight, but I do not know that I ever spoke to him.

18,997. Do you know any of his family?—No.

18,998. How did you happen to know Mr. Thompson?—He used to live at Mill Houses, and I frequently met him going to his work.

18,999. Did he talk to you?—No.

19,000. Did he know your father?—Yes.

19,001. Do you know any of his family?—No.

19,002. To whom did Mr. Machin tell you that he had heard that you had told this story?—He did not mention anyone's name. He said he had heard that I had met with Mr. Tyzack some years back on the road, and all the particulars I have given you.

19,003. Did he tell you the particulars?—Yes.

19,004. Did he tell you he had heard that you had seen him riding in a gig and that you stopped him?—Yes.

19,005. And that you had asked him to take you up?—Yes.

19,006. And that after he had gone off you had seen five flashes of the pistol? he asked you if it was not so?—Yes.

19,007. And he asked if you would come here?—Yes.

19,008. So he told you all that?—Yes.

19,009. Then he knew it apparently as well as you did?—Yes, he must have heard something of it.

19,010. Have you got any relations at all connected with Thompson?—No.

19,011. No relations at all?—No.

19,012. You are in no way connected with him by marriage or otherwise?—No.

19,013. There has been no inducement offered you to come here to-day?—Not the slightest.

19,014. Were not you rather astonished that he knew these particulars so well?—Yes, I was.

19,015. Did you know what Mr. Tyzack had said yesterday?—No.

19,016. Did he tell you?—No.

19,017. Did not he tell you what Mr. Tyzack had said yesterday?—No, I do not know that he did.

19,018. Then what were you to come here for?—To give my evidence of what I saw.

19,019. Of what consequence would your evidence be about five shots being fired from a revolver nine years ago? what is to be the consequence of your evidence—why were you to come?—I do not know.

19,020. Did not he tell you?—No.

19,021. You are quite surprised to find that you are called?—He told me Mr. Tyzack had said he had been shot at some years back, and that he had heard the circumstance of my meeting him on the road, and he wished me to come to Mr. Sugg's office with him before I came here.

19,022. What do they call this place where you sew?—The "Angel" Hotel.

19,023. Have they any union meetings at that hotel?—No.

19,024. Are there none?—No, not that I am aware of.

19,025. You are not married I suppose?—No.

19,026. Having been in conversation with Mr. Hall along the road he must recollect it?—Yes, I should think he would.

19,027. There is no doubt about that?—He would be sure to recollect it I should think.

19,028. You are quite sure that it was Mr. Tyzack that you saw?—Yes.

19,029. There is no mistake about it?—No.

19,030. And you told him that it was Mr. Tyzack? —Yes.

19,031. (*Mr. Chance.*) Did the reports follow one after the other very quickly?—Yes.

19,032. Was there any interval?—They went successively one after the other.

19,033. Quickly? there was no stoppage?—Yes.

19,034. There is a turning in the road?—Yes.

19,035. Is the turning after you go up the road on the right-hand or the left-hand side?—It turns to the right; it goes round just where I was standing.

The witness withdrew.

Mr. J. Tyzack.

Mr. Joshua Tyzack recalled and further examined.

19,036. (*Chairman.*) You have heard what this young woman has said. Is there any truth in that story or not?—I am not aware that there is a single word of truth about it.

19,037. Is her story true or false?—There is not the slightest amount of truth in it.

19,038. You believe that it is thoroughly false?—Yes; I never saw her in my life.

19,039. Has there been any occasion when you have been asked to take up a young woman on the road?—Sometimes I may have been asked by drunken people, but I never stopped to listen to them.

19,040. Was there any report of a pistol after you had passed, at any time in the way she described?—Not in any circumstance to my knowledge; I never fired a pistol on the road.

19,041. Was any pistol ever fired after you except on the occasion which you have mentioned?—I never heard anything of the kind.

19,042. I must press you; she says that you must have heard it; if you did hear it, you can hardly forget it. I ask you, are you prepared to say on your oath that it never occurred?—It never occurred, on my solemn oath.

19,043. I will ask you another question, so far as the shooting is concerned it is a confirmation of your story, but the years are not the same; but supposing she is mistaken in the year, it is a confirmation of the story that there were shots on that road from a revolver five times in succession, but I want to know, on your oath, before you were shot at that night which you speak of, did any woman ask you to take her up into your gig?—Most positively not.

The witness withdrew.

Mr. E. Hall.

Mr. Ebenezer Hall sworn and examined.

19,044. (*Chairman.*) You are a partner in the firm of Martin Hall, and Company?—Yes.

19,045. Did you some nine years ago live on the Abbey Dale Road?—Yes.

19,046. Do you recollect on one night about nine years ago coming along that road and meeting with that young woman, Harriett Ann Morton?—I never saw her in my life to my knowledge. Mind, I may have seen her, but if I have seen her I did not know her.

19,047. Do you recollect about nine years ago when you were walking home at night meeting a woman in the road, who said to you that Mr. Tyzack had just gone on, and that she had heard the reports of four or five barrels from a revolver shot off?—No.

19,048. Never?—No.

19,049. Did she tell you that it was Mr. Tyzack?—No.

19,050. Did she tell you that she had asked him to take her into his gig, and he had declined, and that immediately he had gone on a revolver was fired?—Nothing of the sort could ever have been told to me; if so, I should remember it.

19,051. Did you say that it was possible that he was afraid of her, and thought she was some one in disguise, and that he had fired the revolver off himself?—I never said anything of the sort; I am quite sure that no such conversation ever took place between me and either that young woman or any other young woman.

19,052. Is this the first time that you have ever heard of the occurrence of any young woman ever being present when Mr. Tyzack was shot at?—Yes.

19,053. Have you heard that Mr. Tyzack was shot at?—I did not know that he was shot at till he told me or I saw it in the newspaper.

19,054. Till Tyzack told you a few days ago, were you aware that he had ever been shot at, or that there had been a revolver shot off when you passed along the road?—I may have heard that Mr. Tyzack had been shot at, but it would be in some incidental way. I cannot account for it now; but as to hearing that Mr. Tyzack had fired a revolver on the road, I have no recollection of anything of the kind.

19,055. Or anybody else?—Or anybody else, with regard to firing a revolver on the road. I do it frequently; I carry one in the winter nights, not to protect myself against the trade, but as a precaution against being molested.

19,056. You yourself have fired off a revolver?—Yes.

19,057. You never fired it at the time when Mr. Tyzack has been passing?—No, not to my knowledge; I do not know but he might pass.

19,058. You are a friend of his?—I know him very well.

19,059. You know his gig?—Yes.

19,060. He could hardly pass by without your knowing it?—Unless it was very dark he would not.

19,061. Did any conversation ever take place between you and any young woman about a revolver having been shot off?—No; I can say that very decidedly.

19,062. About nine years ago in January, in the winter, would you usually walk home or ride home?—Very likely ride home. I do not think I walk home once in three years in the winter evenings or once in six years.

19,063. You never walk home?—I will not say that I never walk home, but it is a very exceptional case; it is five miles from our works to my house.

19,064. She said that she walked with you after having told you what she had heard; that she told you that it was Mr. Tyzack, and that you made some observation about it, and that you walked along for two miles in her company?—I can only say that if such a thing had happened I should remember it. I have not the slightest recollection of it, and therefore I do not think that any such thing occurred.

19,065. Are you prepared to swear that it is untrue?—It is a very serious thing to take an oath upon a matter of that sort, but if you wish me to do so I will.

19,066. Will you do so?—I will.

19,067. You say that it is not true?—I say it is not true.

19,068. Were you aware that Mr. Tyzack carried a pistol?—No, not until I read it in the newspaper this morning.

19,069. Do you recollect Mr. Tyzack's men being out on strike in January 1859?—I cannot say that I remember anything about Mr. Tyzack's men being out on strike either nine years ago or any other time. I may have heard it. I am not prepared to give evidence whether I heard it or not. I do not know that I heard it; if they were out on strike I have no doubt I should hear of it.

19,070. Without going into the question of hearing the pistol, or the woman giving you an account of it, are you prepared to say that Mr. Tyzack may have shot off his pistol for the purpose of showing his men that he was prepared for them? Did you ever tell a young woman so on the road?—No.

19,071. How did you hear that Mr. Tyzack had been shot at?—I do not know how I heard about it. Mr. Tyzack named it to me the other day; he said he had a bullet through his hat. I may have incidentally heard of it before, but I have no recollection about it.

19,072. Have you any kind of impression on your mind that you have heard of it before?—Not the slightest.

19,073. You had never heard of it till Mr. Tyzack mentioned it?—I may have heard it; if I heard it it never made any impression upon me. I may hear it as I hear of many rattenings, outrages, and strikes.

19,074. You are a married man are you not?—No, I am not.

19,075. Did you ever go along and talk to young women on the road?—Very possibly.

19,076. Before you came into this court were you aware of what that young woman had said?—Yes.

19,077. Who had told you?—Mr. Chambers.

19,078. Mr. Chambers told you when he fetched you just now?—Yes; he said the young woman had stated she had walked along the road with me, and I understood Mr. Chambers to say that this young woman had been saying that I overtook her and she asked me if I would allow her to walk with me, and that Mr. Tyzack had been firing a revolver two or three times, that is all Mr. Chambers told me. He asked me if I recollected anything of the sort. I said, I did not remember anything of the sort. It is hardly likely I should come here without knowing what I was coming for.

19,079. Are you a member of any masters association?—No.

The witness withdrew.

HARRIETT ANN MORTON recalled and further examined.

H. A. Morton.

19,080. (*Chairman.*) Now, young woman, you have heard what Mr. Tyzack has said, and you have heard what Mr. Hall has said, the gentleman whom you vouched and said would support the truth of your story; if you have come here to tell us that which is untrue it will be our duty to cause you to be prosecuted for perjury?—I have not; it would not be any interest for me to come here.

19,081. If you have committed perjury we shall order you to be prosecuted. Now, I do not wish you to be prosecuted; you have time to withdraw what you have said; and if you have been induced by any person to come and tell a false story to us, you have now the opportunity of saving yourself by retracting it. Is the story which you have told us false or not?—It is not false.

19,082. You stand by it and take all the consequences?—Yes.

19,083. Again I caution you. You do not know how serious the consequences may be. You are a young woman; now think before you take upon yourself the responsibility of this. I have a right to caution you, having heard two witnesses who are contradicting you in the most emphatic manner on their oath. Would you like to have time to reflect?—No,

TWENTIETH DAY.

H. A. Morton.

28 June 1867.

it does not matter. I can say again what I have said before. Every word that I have said is correct.

19,084. Is that the Mr. Hall that you saw?—Yes, that is Mr. Ebenezer Hall.

19,085. And is that the man to whom you told that story?—Yes.

19,086. You stand by it?—Yes; he overtook me at Mill Houses and I walked with him to his own gates the same evening.

19,087. It is a very painful situation in which we are placed. Now no person has induced you to come and tell this story?—No.

19,088. You are quite sure of that?—No, I came of my own free will when I was asked this morning; and I said I would go and relate what I had seen and heard, and I have done so.

19,089. I should like to get at the bottom of this if I could. To whom did you mention this fact nine years ago besides to Mr. Hall?—I mentioned it to a good many.

19,090. Then it is more easy for you to tell me to whom you mentioned it. To whom did you mention it? Mention any one person to whom you told it nine years ago or later?—I have often related it later than that in the course of conversation.

19,091. Tell me one person to whom you have ever told it?—I told it to Mrs. Godbeer, the next door neighbour, the next morning.

19,092. Who is Mrs. Godbeer?—She was a scythe-grinder's wife, but she is dead now. Her husband perhaps might know the circumstance, because she would tell it to him as well.

19,093. Where is her husband?—He lives at Ridgway.

19,094. Where is that?—Near Ecclesall.

19,095. Is there any other person you can name to whom you told it—you say that you told several?—I cannot call anyone else to mind just now.

19,096. Where does the husband of Mrs. Godbeer work?—I do not know where he is employed just now.

19,097. What is his name?—George Godbeer.

19,098. Is there anybody else. I want to save you from being prosecuted if I can?—I told it to Thomas Bamford, a scythe grinder.

19,099. Where does he live?—Norton Wood Seats.

19,100. When did you tell him?—I told him about the time that it occurred.

19,101. You mentioned Mr. Tyzack's name?—Yes, I told him all the circumstances.

19,102. You told him immediately the occurrence happened?—I cannot say whether it was then or when, but in course of conversation on the day when I saw him.

19,103. Have you seen him this morning?—No.

19,104. From whom did Mr. Machin tell you that he had got his information?—He did not tell me where he had got it from.

19,105. Did not you ask him?—No, I did not ask any questions. They came and fetched me from my work this morning and I did not know anything about it till they asked me whether I would go to Mr. Sugg's office.

19,106. You cannot fix the time when you named it to Bamford. Can you tell us what time it was or how soon after it occurred?—No, I cannot tell the exact time.

The witness withdrew.

J. Machin.

JOSEPH MACHIN recalled and further examined.

19,107. (*Chairman.*) When you were here before you said that you were secretary to the scythe makers union?—Yes.

19,108. You produced the books from 1858?—Yes, I daresay they go so far back as that.

19,109. The other books had been destroyed eight or nine years ago?—I have only seen one destroyed; it was the scale book that was destroyed at the time the other commenced.

19,110. That will be nearly eight or nine years ago?—I daresay it will.

19,111. I am not going into the question of books, but I will go on the question which we have been discussing this morning. You went to that young woman Harriett Ann Morton this morning?—Yes.

19,112. What induced you to go to her this morning?—Because I had been to her mother last night. I had heard from one of our workers called William Thorpe on Saturday night——

19,113. What had you heard from William Thorpe?—I heard the circumstances she has related.

19,114. What did you hear?—I heard that Mrs. Morton was going from Sheffield on the Abbey Dale Road, and Mr. Joseph Tyzack was coming in a gig by himself, and she stepped off the causeway to ask him to give her a ride up the road, and instead of giving her a ride he struck the horse with the whip, and when he had gone on a few yards there was a pistol fired.

19,115. You heard that it was Mrs. Morton, her mother?—I heard it from William Thorpe on Saturday night. I asked him who had told him, and he told me that it was James Biggin had told him, and I says to him, "Well, now, just see that it is true."

19,116. When did he say that James Biggin had told him?—I did not ask him that. I am sure I told him to be sure and see whether it is true or not, and to let me know. He had not done so last night, and I took it upon myself to go to see Mrs. Morton at Bradway Bank.

19,117. You went to Mrs. Morton last night?—Yes.

19,118. Where does she live?—At Bradway Bank, that is the way I understand it; and I told her last night what I had heard. She says, "It is correct; but it is not me, it is my daughter." I asked her where to find her daughter, and she told me she was lodging with her aunt in Carver Lane, but very likely she might be at the "Angel Inn," and that she had to go there. I went to Miss Morton's aunt this morning, and the young woman was down at the "Angel Inn," and I went down to her.

19,119. What did you say to her?—I went in and asked whether I could see her, and they said I could, and they sent her out to the passage, and I related the story I heard.

19,120. What did you say to her?—I said, "Is it correct?" I think those were the words; I will not swear that those were the words. I said, "Is it "correct that you on a certain day were going from "Sheffield, where you had been down to see your "mother, who was then waiting on her uncle, Mr. "Stone, who owns the 'Crown Inn,' Little Sheffield." He was ill, then I understood he died. I said, "As "you were going home did you see Mr. Tyzack "and ask him to let you ride?" and she said, "Yes." I said, "Did you see anything else; was there any pistols fired?" That is about all that I said.

19,121. What did she say to that?—I said, "Would "you be willing to go to Mr. Sugg's office to give "your evidence, and to go before the Commissioners "to give that statement, or any other that is true, and "none but what is true?" She said, "Yes." She put on her things and went to Mr. Sugg's office and told everything there to Mr. Sugg. I might say that there was another man with me who went to her mother's, and who was with me this morning.

19,122. What is his name?—John Thorpe.

19,123. What relation is John Thorpe to William Thorpe?—John Thorpe is uncle to him.

19,124. That is all?—Yes, that is all I have to say.

19,125. You told her what you heard and asked her if it was so, and she said "Yes" to all you told her?—Yes.

19,126. Do not you think that it would have been a much more prudent course if you had asked her to

TWENTIETH DAY.

J. Machin.

28 June 1867.

tell her story instead of your telling her what you did?—Perhaps so. I told her the story and asked her if it was true.

19,127. That is as bad a mode of getting up evidence as you can have. If you wish a person to go and tell a story, according to your view the proper way is to tell them the story first and then to bring them up and ask them to tell their story?—I am not accustomed to getting up evidence; I do it in the best way I can; I have only the object of getting at the truth; if it was not so I did not want her to say so.

19,128. Had you known the girl before?—No, never known her before.

19,129. Had you known her mother?—Yes.

19,130. Is she any relation of yours?—No.

19,131. How long have you known her mother?—Some 20 years since I lived up at Abbey Dale, and I knew her then merely as a neighbour in going past sometimes when I was working in the neighbourhood. That is about all the correspondence I have had with her.

19,132. That was 20 years ago, and you have never seen her since?—I cannot say that I have not seen her since, because some 12 years since I had a nephew of hers apprenticed with me; it may be a little more than 12 years. I cannot be certain of that.

19,133. When was it that he was apprenticed with you?—I cannot swear exactly to the time. It will be 12 years or more, I daresay.

19,134. Twelve years ago?—Yes.

19,135. When was he out of his time?—He did not serve his time out with me. He was only with me about 2½ years; his indentures were cancelled.

19,136. What for?—He was unable to learn his trade.

19,137. Was he a bad boy?—He was incapable of working, he was incapacitated to learn. Another man tried him afterwards, but he could not learn him.

19,138. Had you any quarrel with him?—Not further than that.

19,139. Had you known anything at all about the relations of this girl Morton before?—No.

19,140. You had known nothing of her?—I have never seen one of them since the boy's indentures were cancelled.

19,141. And Thorpe told you this on Saturday?—Yes, it is the first time I heard of it.

19,142. How did Thorpe happen to tell you on Saturday?—He was passing by our house.

19,143. Thorpe is one of your unionists?—Yes, one of our trade.

19,144 He was passing your house, was he?—Yes, and called on his way home.

19,145. Where does he live?—He lives at Little Common.

19,146. Where is Little Common?—Above Ecclesshall, going on towards Dore.

19,147. He called on the Saturday night?—Yes, to have conversation as to the rumour that had come out of Mr. Joshua Tyzack being shot at.

19,148. What did he say about this rumour about Mr. Joshua Tyzack being shot at?—He says, "I "think it is a fabrication, because I have lived in the "neighbourhood all my life, and I have never heard "tell of it till now this Commission has been going "on." And my answer was, "Nor I either." I wished him to see if the statement was true, and let me know, and he promised me he would, which he did not. I do not know that I have anything more to say, only I took upon myself last night to go and see whether there was any truth in it, along with Thorpe.

19,149. That is your story?—That is my story.

19,150. Do not let me make any mistake about this. I will read what you have said, and ask you whether it is correct. "On Saturday Thorpe, who "is one of our trade, was passing our house, and he "called in respect of the rumour that Mr. Joshua "Tyzack had been shot at. He said, 'I think it is a "'fabrication. I have lived in the neighbourhood "'all my life, and I have never heard tell of it till "'now.' I said, 'Nor I either.' I asked him to see "if the statement was true, and let me know. He "promised me he would, but he did not. I took "upon myself to go and inquire about it." Is that the truth?—That is true.

19,151. Is it quite accurate?—Quite right, I think.

19,152. There is no mistake about it?—I think not. I do not remember that there is.

19,153. Now, how comes it then, if that was all he said to you, you knew about this story?—What story?

19,154. Why, you have told us that you went and told her the whole of this statement?—Yes. I told you at the first that he related the story to me first.

19,155. Mind what you are about. I asked you cautiously before I put that last question, if this was all which passed between you?—I think I told you that before, that he told me when he came what it was.

19,156. You told me that that was all he said?—He told me the story.

19,157. But you did not say so?—I understood that I had said so.

19,158. You did not, and I will show you that you could not have said it?—He did tell me, or else I should not have known it.

19,159. You said that was all that he told you?—I expected I told you that.

19,160. Then that was a mistake? — It was a mistake.

19,161. Then how was it that you told me that that was all he said, and then, if that were all he said, how was it that you came to know all about this occurrence, he never having mentioned it, according to your statement?—He told it to me at the first.

19,162. That is what you say now?—I do, and I expected I had said it before.

19,163. If he told you that at the first, how came it that you have said that you had never heard it in all your life of Mr. Tyzack's ever having been shot at?—From the conversation that he told me.

19,164. Why according to the conversation he had told you that Mr. Tyzack had been shot at?—He had heard so; he had told me this story.

19,165. Then how is it that you say that you thought this was a fabrication, and you had lived in the neighbourhood all your life?—He had lived in the neighbourhood all his life.

19,166. How do you explain that consistently with saying that he told you the story?—I do not understand you.

19,167. You said that you had never heard a word about it?—I had not about the shooting, till this Commission.

19,168. But if he had told you all about what Mrs. Morton had said you heard that Mr. Tyzack had been shot at?—When he told me on Saturday night, not before.

19,169. If he told you about that, how could he say, "I think it is a fabrication, I have lived in the neigh-"bourhood all my life, and never heard of it until "now," how should you say, "Nor I either?—To be sure I had not; not till that time we were talking then—I am giving my evidence to what we were talking about then.

19,170. Then he did tell you that?—He told me at the commencement.

19,171. And you thought it was a fabrication?—I did.

19,172. For what reason did you think that Mr. Tyzack had fabricated it?—I do not know.

19,173. But what purpose do you think that Mr. Tyzack had in fabricating it?—Perhaps to damage the character of the men belonging to the union.

19,174. You know that Mr. Tyzack did not give his evidence until yesterday?—No, I know nothing about it; I was not here yesterday.

19,175. Where had you heard this rumour about his having been shot at at all?—I saw it in the paper myself.

19,176. What—that Mr. Tyzack was shot at?—Yes.

TWENTIETH DAY.

J. Machin.

28 June 1867.

19,177. When ?—On the Saturday night, after this man had been talking to me; I saw it in the paper in the examination of Crooks.

19,178. What did you see about it in the examination of Crooks ?—Questions whether Crooks had shot at him ; I believe that was it ; I think so.

19,179. Then that is what you call rumour ?—That is what I call rumour ; I did not ask him where he had got his rumour any further than this; he said Biggin told him, and I do not know any more than that.

19,180. Biggin told him about Mrs. Morton ?—Yes, Biggin told him about Mrs. Morton. I asked him who told him and he said Biggin.

19,181. And Biggin is one of your trade is he ?—He is one of Mr. Tyzack's workmen.

19,182. Have you talked to Biggin about this matter ?—No, I have not seen him for some months.

19,183. What we are talking about is something which occurred in 1862 when Mr. Tyzack was shot at ?—Yes, I saw the statement yesterday in the paper that it was 1862, but the girl says it was 1859 I think.

19,184. Yes, you have got it, 1859 ?—I have not got it.

19,185. Who was secretary in 1862 ?—I should be ; I think I was elected at Midsummer 1859.

19,186. Do you know who shot at Mr. Tyzack ?—No, I know nothing about it.

19,187. Do you know who shot at Mr. Tyzack ?—No.

19,188. Was Mr. Tyzack very obnoxious to the trade ?—In one or two particular instances, at times.

19,189. Have you rattened him ?—He has been rattened, I believe.

19,190. By you ?—Not by me.

19,191. Not by you personally, but by your authority ?—No.

19,192. You have never authorized it ?—No.

19,193. Has he ever been rattened to your knowledge ?—Not until it was done.

19,194. But immediately it was done did you know it ?—Yes, very soon after.

19,195. Did you know who did it ?—No.

19,196, Did you get paid money for it ?—No.

19,197. Did you assist in restoring the bands ?—No.

19,198. How did you happen to know it ?—Because the committee called me in ; I was not on the committee when he was rattened the first time.

19,199. What did they call you in for ?—They called me in to try to settle it.

19,200. Then you knew he was rattened on behalf of the trade ?—Yes, I did. What I am speaking to now will be in the spring of 1859, soon after his men went away. I do not know exactly the date ; it might be in Midsummer ; I do not know the exact date.

19,201. Were you one of the persons that summoned him to attend a meeting at the "Wagon and Horses" ?—I was one that was there.

19,202. Did you know that Horne's property was destroyed at the same time ?—I heard of it, but I did not know anything about it.

19,203. He was rattened the same night, was he not ?—I am not aware what night it was.

19,204. You know as a fact that it was the same night, do you not ?—I do not know that it was the same night.

19,205. We do know it ?—I do not know it.

19,206. Was it done on behalf of the trade ?—I should say it was, but I do not know now ; I should say it was.

19,207. Do you recollect in July 13 scythe grinders' bands being taken ?—July 1859 ?

19,208. Yes ?—Yes, I do.

19,209. Was that on behalf of the trade ?—It was.

19.210. Was a man called Kay fined 10*l.* ?—He was.

19,211. And was a note sent in after the fine was paid, saying where the bands could be found ?—No, not after the fine was paid.

19,212. Before ?—Before ; but there was something done before that.

19,213. What was done ?—The arrangement was made with Mr. Tyzack before the note was sent in. I think he had a note sent him to say what the grievances were previous to that.

19,214. Is that the note (*handing a paper to the witness* ?)—I am sure I cannot say, I know nothing about that.

19,215. Was Bagshaw a party ?—That is not this time that I am talking about now, we will come to that afterwards if you please. I suppose you want me to make a clean breast of it ?

19,216. We do want you to make a clean breast of it ?—Very well, I will if I can. I will just go on and tell you all I can tell you. There was a note sent where the bands were taken to tell what the grievances were. That was in 1859 ; I believe I was sent for the next afternoon to go to Mr. Tyzack's office in Hockham Street to talk about that matter, and I went and he conceded to the agreement that was sent in the note, and he wrote me out the concessions and gave it to me and I took it.

19,217. When did you ratten him next ?—Perhaps you have not done with that yet ?

19,218. Yes, I have ?—But I have not done with it if you want to know it all.

19,219. I do not want to know any private arrangements. You offered him terms which he has accepted and the fine was paid and he got back his bands ?—A note went next morning to tell him where his bands were and they were restored.

19,220. We have that ?—Very well, I want you to have it all. A note was sent next morning to tell him where his bands were and they were restored.

19,221. When was the next time you rattened him ?—I do not know that he has been rattened by us since.

19,222. Have you anything more to say ?—I do know something about the rattening about a year or a year and a half ago respecting the patent scythe makers.

19,223. Do you know of anything before 1862, after 1859 ?—I know nothing about 1862 that I am aware of.

19,224. Was anything done before 1862 after 1859 ?—No, I think not, I do not think anything. If you can call it to my memory, I will take to it.

19,225. Was anything done to him in 1862 by you ?—Not to my knowledge.

19,226. Will you swear nothing was done to him in 1862 by you ?—I will swear that there was not anything done to my knowledge in 1862.

19,227. Did you ratten anybody in 1862 ?—No, not that I know of. I am not aware of it. It has slipped my memory if I did.

19,228. Did you commit any outrage upon anybody in the year 1862 ?—No.

19,229. Look at that book (*handing a book to the witness*), what book is it ?—It is the cash-book, and the incidental book, I believe.

19,230. In whose handwriting is that page which I brought before your notice ?—This page is in mine?

19,231. Does that indicate money taken out or what ?—This is money coming in; this is cash received.

19,232. Now let me look at it. (*The witness returned the book to the Examiners.*) Then you had in hand in November 1862 124*l.* 17*s.* ?—I believe it was so ; no doubt it was so.

19,233. What does "Cash from bank" mean ?—That is money.

19,234. Put into your hands ?—Not into my hands.

19,235. But at anyrate you had withdrawn from the bank the various sums mentioned ?—Yes, the cash from the bank is withdrawn on that side.

19,236. I find 10*l.* on the first of November ; 10*l.* on the 15th of November, and 10*l.* on the 1st of December ?—Very well, that will be right if it is there.

19,237. Besides that you have contributions, 22*l.* 7*s.*, then on the 15th of December you have

TWENTIETH DAY.

J. Machin.

28 June 1867.

29*l.* 16*s.*; on January the 12th, 21*l.* 7*s.*, and then you go on to November the 11th, 21*l.* 7*s.*, and you have cast it up rightly or wrongly, 124*l.* 17*s.*?—That is right.

19,238. That is right, you believe?—I think so.

19,239. I want to know how that money was spent? —The other books would show.

19,240. Bring me the book to show it. Bring me the scale book. (*The witness referred to the scale book.*) I want November the 3rd, 1862?—(*After referring to the book.*) I have it.

19,241. Are those payments to them?—They are payments to them. Those are fortnightly payments.

19,242. Will you just give me that book. (*The witness handed the book to the Examiners, and it was given to Mr. Shrubsole.*) Who tore out this leaf? —I do not know; not I. It was torn out when I took to it.

19,243. That cannot be so. There is "money received." You had got into your hands 125*l.* 17*s.* opposite that page which ought to have contained the payments?—Of what?

19,244. Of this?—No, this is the expense side (*explaining the book to the Examiners*).

19,245. Then on this side there ought to be the payments to explain the receipts on the other side?—That and this (*pointing out the leaves in the book*) will explain the payments.

19,246. But where is the sheet?—I know nothing about that sheet; I have never torn one out, and never saw one.

19,247. Did you never notice it before?—No.

19,248. About this time it is suggested that a sum of money was paid by your union, you know that?— I do not know it.

19,249. It is so suggested that it was done in order to get a man out of the country, and at the very time when this payment was made the leaf is torn out of the book?—There has been no money paid.

19,250. Never mind, there is the leaf torn out?— There is the account at the same time just the same. There have been no leaves torn out there by me or anyone else that I have seen.

19,251. But it is torn out?—It is torn out.

19,252. And you cannot explain it?—Now then, this transaction is November the 3rd, and here is November the 3rd, "Incomings and outgoings." (*The witness explained the accounts to the Examiners.*)

19,253. Now there is a leaf out; you cannot explain that?—No, and I know nothing about it.

19,254. Now look at June 1862 of the same year? —*The witness again referred to the books.*

19,255. I see you have contributions on that date to the amount of 77*l.* 8*s.* 6*d.* in your own hand?— That would be so if it is there.

19,256. In the contribution book dated June the 30th, 1862, we find there is a receipt by you of 33*l.* 4*s.*, and you have cast it up as only having received 30*l.* 14*s.* There is also another entry on the same date of 41*l.* 2*s.*, whereas it ought to have been added up 43*l.* You had therefore at that very time, on June the 30th alone, an error of upwards of 8*l.* How do you explain that?—I cannot explain it anything more than what there is in those books, and the money I have not received. If the items are wrongly cast up it is not my fault. I am not satisfied that those items are not added up right as I cast them up.

19,257. If you received money, you know——? —I do not receive it.

19,258. Who gets the money then?—The committee get the money. They sit and take the money, and I put it down; I never get any money except what members give me at the meeting.

19,259. You cast it up?—I cast it up.

19,260. Still the castings are false?—They should have tallied when we were there, otherwise we should have stayed while we got them right, if it was even till now.

19,261. You are so exact, are you, that if the accounts had not tallied you would have stayed even till now to make them right?—We at that time made the accounts up yearly, and we never went away without having it settled, and we generally have a big night. To the best of my knowledge we are generally satisfied; we have been at any rate.

19,262. In this case somehow or other either you or the committee have got into your books 8*l.* more as contributions received, and when you have entered it in this as a sort of general book instead of entering the full amount you have entered it short by 8*l.*?—I am not aware of it.

19,263. But it is so?—If you have cast it up right; it is not to my knowledge.

19,264. How do you explain it?—I cannot explain it.

19,265. If that 8*l.* had been improperly applied, would it explain it?—No, there has been none improperly applied.

19,266. That is what you say; but supposing there had been an entry which you did not want to appear in your books, would not that be a mode in which it might be accomplished?—It might have been accomplished, but it has not been.

19,267. But however, you cannot explain that deficiency of 8*l.*?—No; I do not believe it is a deficiency. If Mr. Sugg finds it right I will admit it. I have gone over it many a time since.

19,268. You see this is a matter of great importance?—Quite right. I wish you to know everything; you shall know everything that I know.

19,269. Had you any auditors then?—I think we had auditors then; the minute-book will tell whether we had auditors or not.

19,270. Just look at the minute book and see whether you had auditors then?—(*The witness referred to the minute book and explained it to the Examiners.*)

19,271. Are those the actual payments by the men and the amounts?—Yes.

19,272. Were all those sums of money received on June the 30th?—Yes they were.

19,273. I would not on any account have it thought that I am not dealing fairly with you. I am told that there are one or two entries in which you have charged yourself with having received more than you did receive?—I am not aware of it.

19,274. The difficulty with us is, that on this day, the one particular time to which we call attention in November, when it is suggested that Mr. Tyzack was shot, and when it is also suggested that a payment of money was made for a person to do it, there is a leaf torn out, and some months before there is an entry in your books as if it was a cooked account, in which there is 8*l.* unexplained at all, either by you or by the committee; it is 69*l.* 10*s.* 6*d.*?—What you have been talking about.

19,275. What I have been talking about, and therefore there are those two very strong facts of suspicion?—For anything I know that adding up is right to the best of my knowledge, and I declare upon my oath——

19,276. I only call your attention to the things which we discover. For the moment let us assume that our figures are correct and that you are wrong. Let us assume that your figures which you have put down are not the proper castings. Can you give us any explanation of the mode in which that 8*l.* went away in June?—No, I cannot.

19,277. You say you have auditors?—Yes, we have auditors.

19,278. Is it the duty of the auditors as well as of yourself to cast up those accounts?—Yes, it is their duty, and I am not quite sure whether the auditors are not down in that book. I generally put them down in the contribution book.

19,279. Of course if he is good for anything as an auditor he would cast up the amount of contributions to see if those contributions are correct?—He should do so.

19,280. Therefore he must have made a mistake as well as yourself if there is one?—Yes, he must.

TWENTIETH DAY.

J. Machin.

28 June 1867.

19,281. Does anybody else but the auditor and yourself cast up that contribution column?—Not that I am aware of.

19,282. Does the committee?—No.

19,283. Does the committee examine it?—No, not personally. There are some of them there when the auditors are auditing.

19,284. When was the audit of that year?—I cannot say.

19,285. Was it in December?—I cannot say without I looked at the book.

19,286. How soon after that November account was the audit made up?—The audit is the fortnight after the making-up night generally.

19,287. You say on the opposite side to the account for receipts there are disbursements?—Yes.

19,288. When do you enter those disbursements?—When we sit at the committee.

19,289. Every week?—No, once a fortnight.

19,290. And supposing an entry should have been made of a matter which, on consideration, you thought ought not to have appeared there, nothing would have been more easy than to have torn out the leaf to have copied what was written before, and to have gone on?—Off that leaf you mean.

19,291. Yes?—Perhaps so, but I will swear I have not done it and I have not seen anybody else, and the books are generally in my possession, for I have been in the habit of carrying them home with me for sometime, for people come to our house to know what they owe.

19,292. Then nobody could do it but you?—I think not.

19,293. And have you never seen that before to-day?—No, I have never noticed it. I brought them just as they were. I knew there were some leaves out at the farther end when I took to them.

19,294. But in 1862 you had been elected a couple of years?—Yes, I think it would be 1859, but the minutes will tell, because we had not any then; I think it was Midsummer, 1859.

19,295. You have had them three years then?—Yes.

19,296. And you cannot give us any explanation why a leaf should be torn out at that particular place?—No, I cannot. I have not done it and I do not know who has, and I will swear it has not been done for any sinister purpose if it has been done.

19,297. Have you a bank book?—Yes, we have.

19,298. Where is your bank book?—It is in the box; I cannot get it now.

19,299. You have not brought all your books then?—I did not know you wanted the bank book. They do not allow that to come into my possession.

19,300. We do not want to know what your financial position is?—You will find it in that book.

19,301. I am very glad to hear the error is not to the extent that was stated. We take it for granted that an experienced accountant will not make mistakes, but Mr. Shrubsole finds that he has mistaken one of your figures or something of that kind, and that it is 3*l.* 10*s.* instead of 8*l.* I should be very sorry indeed that from any mistake at all any erroneous impression should get abroad. We will deal fairly with you, you may depend upon it?—I want no more.

19,302. This book (*showing a book to the witness*) is kept by you is it not?—Yes.

19,303. Have you torn any leaves out of this?—No, there has never been one out. I will swear there has never been one out of that since I bought it, and it is in my opinion as it was bound.

The witness withdrew.

T. Bamford.

THOMAS BAMFORD sworn and examined.

19,304. (*Chairman.*) Have you been told at all why you were sent for here?—No, not particularly. I do not know that I have been told what for. I have been told I have been sent for.

19,305. Who went for you?—Mr. Chambers.

19,306. Mr. Chambers did not come for you, did he?—He served me with the summons.

19,307. That was some days ago?—That was the gentleman that fetched me to-day (*pointing him out*).

19,308. Is that gentleman whom you point out the person who fetched you just now?—Yes.

19,309. Has he told you what he wanted you for?—No.

19,310. And you do not know why you are come here to-day?—No.

19,311. Do you know Joseph Machin?—Yes.

19,312. Have you had any conversation with him lately?—Oh yes.

19,313. When did you see him last?—On Monday morning.

19,314. What did you see him about?—I saw him.

19,315. What did he talk to you about on Monday morning?—He went with me to Mr. Dronfield.

19,316. What did you go to Mr. Dronfield for?—I went to Mr. Dronfield to see him regarding this defence committee or outrage committee. (I do not know which the name is) regarding some information that I had received respecting myself.

19,317. What was that?—Regarding some information that I had received respecting myself.

19,318. What was that?—It was regarding Elisha Parker, some evidence that I had to give about it. That was all that we talked about.

19,319. Nothing else?—No.

19,320. Mind, we are very particular here. Did you talk to Machin about anything else?—Not that I am aware of. I do not know that we did.

19,321. Have you seen him since that?—No.

19,322. You have never seen Machin since then?—No.

19,323. Do you know a person of the name of Thorpe?—Yes.

19,324. Have you seen him?—No.

19,325. Have you had any conversation with him lately?—I saw him on Sunday.

19,326. What is his name?—John Thorpe I saw.

19,327. Do you know William Thorpe?—Yes.

19,328. When did you see him last?—William?

19,329. Yes?—I saw him on Sunday morning, but I did not speak to him.

19,330. With whom was he?—He was in a spring cart with his wife.

19,331. But he was not in company with any friend of yours?—No, he was going on the road.

19,332. Did he speak to you?—We just moved "Good morning," I believe that was what we did, there was nothing more.

19,333. Then you have neither seen Machin nor Thorpe. Do you know a person of the name of James Biggin?—Yes.

19,334. When did you see him?—I saw him on Tuesday morning.

19,335. Where?—In the "Bay Horse" public house on Sheffield moor.

19,336. Had you any conversation with him?—No, I do not know that I had any conversation with him.

19,337. On no subject?—If it was it would be on what was going on in the public room.

19,338. Do you know what you talked about with him?—I am sure I cannot say, nothing particular worth noting in any shape or other.

19,339. You have heard something about Parker, have you not?—Yes.

19,340. And is it true that you went out shooting at nights?—No.

19,341. You never went out shooting at nights?—I never went out shooting at nights in my life, and there is not a man living that can come and prove that I did.

19,342. But did you stand and shoot at your own door-stone?—I may have let my gun off at my own door sometimes, but very seldom; but it has not been on Parker's account, and I did not know anything about him. When I was shooting I was in the habit of taking out a certificate, and shooting in the shooting season.

19,343. You are a good shot, are you not?—Well, I can kill things sometimes; I have killed a good deal of game sometimes, and sometimes when my gun wanted cleaning out I have blown the powder out to clean the barrels out.

19,344. Did it get dirty towards night sometimes?—That depended upon the quantity of use that I had had for it. It did sometimes happen that it wanted cleaning.

19,345. Did it get dirty towards night sometimes?—Well, sometimes. It might be that I cleaned it out once in three months.

19,346. Did it not get dirty in the evening very often?—No.

19,347. Did you never find out that it was dirty, and fire it off at 9 o'clock at night?—Never.

19,348. Will you swear that?—Never.

19,349. I daresay you never shot at Tyzack either?—No, I did not.

19,350. And you never heard about it?—No, I never heard about it till I saw it in this inquiry. I never did.

19,351. You say that you never shot at Parker?—I do.

19,352. And you say that you never shot at Tyzack?—I do.

19,353. And you never heard perhaps that Parker was shot at?—Oh, yes.

19,354. Then you do know that he was shot at?—Yes.

19,355. You never heard that Tyzack was shot at?—I never did.

19,356. You never heard that Tyzack was shot at until this very day?—I never heard of it until I saw it in those reports.

19,357. When was it that you saw about Tyzack being shot at?—I think sometime in this inquiry in the paper.

19,358. When?—Well, last week. I did not note it down, but I saw an account of it in the "Telegraph" or the "Independent," the daily paper, about Tyzack being shot at.

19,359. Who had said that he had been shot at?—The account in the paper said that he had been shot at.

19,360. Who said it?—It was in the regular daily papers.

19,361. It took you very much by surprise to hear that, did it not?—I do not know that it surprised me much.

19,362. Did you not think that he was a likely man to be shot at?—Well, I did not take much notice of it.

19,363. Is it a very unlikely thing in Sheffield for a man to be shot at?—I do not know anything about it, and I do not think that I felt in any way particularly surprised about it.

19,364. You were not surprised at it?—I do not know whether I was or not. I saw it in the paper, and that is all I can say about it.

19,365. Then nobody had ever told you before that that he had been shot at?—No.

19,366. I will be bound that you have never heard until now that he has been shot at several times?—The most particulars I have heard about it are what I have read in this morning's paper. I read Mr. Tyzack's evidence yesterday in this morning's paper.

19,367. Well, did not that take you very much by surprise?—After I had read an account of his being shot at before; I do not know that I was affected in any way with it; not a bit.

19,368. But it came to you as news, I suppose?—I do not know that it would be any more news, when I had read about it last week.

19,369. You had heard about it last week. Did you hear last week that he had been shot at five times?—I only, as I have told you, read an account of it in the paper.

19,370. You had never heard of it before?—I had not.

19,371. You had never heard of it before you heard of it last week, and now you have read in this morning's paper that he had been shot at five times?—There is the account in the paper; that is all I know about it.

19,372. Then no person has ever told you before that he has been shot at five times?—No.

19,373. Will you swear that?—I will.

19,374. Upon your oath?—I will swear I never was told by one man or another that he had been shot, only I saw it in the paper.

19,375. (*To the witness Morton.*) Stand forward young woman.

Harriett Ann Morton stood forward.

19,376. (*To the witness Bamford.*) Now, on your oath, did not that young woman tell you that he had been shot at?—No, never.

19,377. Did she ever tell you anything about pistol firing connected with the case of Mr. Tyzack?—No, never.

19,378. Did she ever tell you that Mr. Tyzack ever fired a pistol?—No, she never told me anything, for I never had any talk with her about it, neither in one shape nor another, I am certain.

19,379. Did she ever tell you that nine years ago she met Mr. Tyzack or any man on the Abbey Dale Road; that she asked him to take her up, and that he refused, and that then he having gone on a little way past her, five shots were fired at him from a revolver?—No, never such a word.

19,380. Are you quite sure she never told you that at all?—I am, I have never had a word of conversation with her about it in my life.

19,381. Have you ever heard such a report as that until to-day?—Never until I saw this morning's paper.

19,382. Have you lived in that neighbourhood?—I lived at Dore.

19,383. How far was that from where she lived?—Well, she was living in Sheffield I understood.

19,384. But where does her mother live?—She lives in Abbey Dale.

19,385. How far from you?—About a mile.

19,386. Up to this morning had you ever heard it mentioned?—No.

19,387. Never?—Never.

19,388. Mind, it is nine years ago; may you have heard it and forgotten it?—I never heard it named that I am aware of in one shape or another.

19,389. Now I will give her the full benefit of this and mind what you are about?—I am speaking the truth.

19,390. Do you know that young woman (*pointing to the witness Morton*)?—Yes.

19,391. Has she ever told you that she ever was in the Abbey Dale Road and that she asked any one (not mentioning Mr. Tyzack's name) to take her up, but that he declined, and that after he had declined four or five shots were fired at him?—Never such a word has she told to me.

19,392. Or that the person in the gig fired shots himself?—She has never told me any such a word.

19,493. Either concerning Mr. Tyzack or anybody else?—I do not know that Mr. Tyzack's name has been spoken betwixt us.

19,394. But has she ever mentioned this occurrence to you either in reference to Mr. Tyzack or anybody else?—No, never.

The witness withdrew.

TWENTIETH DAY.

28 June 1867.

The *Chairman* informed Mr. Sugg that he was at liberty to put any questions which he might think proper to the witness Harriett Ann Morton.

Mr. Sugg applied for five minutes to consult with the witness.

The *Court* granted the request, and Mr. Sugg left the Court with the young woman, and after a short interval returned with her.

H. A. Morton.

HARRIETT ANN MORTON recalled and further examined.

19,395. (*Chairman.*) You see that now we have done all we could for you. You first of all said that Mr. Tyzack was the person to whom you had spoken, and he denies it. Then you said that you had told the fact to Mr. Hall, and that you walked along the road with him for two miles which you cannot have forgotten, and which he cannot have forgotten, and he denies it. We asked you to name a person to whom you had ever told it, and you mentioned a person and we sent for him, and he denies it. Now what have you to say in answer to that?—I told you that I had told him all about what I had mentioned, and I have told the truth.

19,396. And you still persist in it?—Yes. I have spoken truth all the time, and I will speak truth still whatever may be the consequences. It will do me no good to come and tell a falsehood. I do not know that I have any interest in it.

19,397. You say you have spoken the truth all the time, and still you persist in it that it is the truth?—Yes, I do; I told Thomas Bamford about it. He called one night on my mother; she keeps a small shop and sells tobacco, and he was partly intoxicated. He called for half an ounce of tobacco, and I told him of it.

19,398. You never said a word about his being partly intoxicated?—No; I knew of it, but of course I could not think of everything. I could not call to mind a many things that he might have said. I told James Biggin, the man whose name has been mentioned before about the first part that I did tell.

19,399. I think we cannot go more into this matter. If it should be thought that you have been committing perjury I do not know what course will be pursued; it is not for me to say; but you will be open to be indicted for perjury. Now bethink yourself; you have still a chance of escape if you have committed perjury. I will give you a chance more, and if you have been advised by any one to tell this story make a clean breast of it at once and tell us?—No; I have not been bribed in any way to come here and tell this story.

19,400. But have you been asked to tell it, knowing it to be untrue?—I have not.

19,401. And you persist in it that it is the truth?—Mr. Machin went to my mother's house last night and I had not seen her for a length of time and not spoken to her, and she told him the tale then.

The witness withdrew.

Mr. Sugg remarked that the statement which the witness had made to him in his office was precisely the same as she had made here.

The *Chairman* stated that there was no imputation upon Mr. Sugg.

Mr. Sugg applied to be allowed to bring further evidence on this point.

The *Chairman* said that it had gone far enough, but that if it should come to a question of prosecution further evidence might be given there. He inquired whether Mr. Sugg wished to put any questions through the Court to the witness Bamford?

Mr. Sugg replied that he should be glad to do so.

T. Bamford.

THOMAS BAMFORD recalled and further examined.

19,402. (*Chairman.*) Do you ever recollect being intoxicated, you often get drunk I suppose?—Well, sometimes I get a sup of beer you know.

19,403. This girl has said that she has told you all this?—No, never such a word. She stands here a perjured woman. She has never uttered such a word to me as sure as I sit in this chair.

19,404. She says that she is sure that she mentioned it to you and that you were slightly intoxicated, therefore you might have forgotten it?—No; she never said such a thing to me in one shape or another. As I stand before the Almighty at this moment I deny it.

The witness withdrew.

J. Machin.

JOSEPH MACHIN recalled and further examined.

19,405. (*Chairman.*) Will you look at the book and explain it to me (*handing a book to the witness*)?—Yes.

19,406. On December 29th, 1862, there are arrears paid?—Yes.

19,407. You received those arrears?—Not on that day.

19,408. When did you receive them?—(*The witness explained the accounts to the Court.*) It is arrears due and not paid.

19,409. What is the meaning of this column "arrears paid"?—It was paid previously to this at various times.

19,410. But when were they paid?—At those times.

19,411. But where is the entry of those sums—in what book?—This is 1862.

19,412. Will you explain it to Mr. Shrubsole, and then if there is any difficulty about it I will ask you questions upon it. You shall have a full opportunity of explaining that your books are all right if they are so?

The witness withdrew.

M. Thompson.

MICHAEL THOMPSON sworn and examined.

19,413. (*Chairman.*) Were you formerly secretary of the scythe-grinder's union?—Yes.

19,414. Were you secretary before Machin?—Yes.

19,415. Were you in office while Machin was secretary?—No.

19,416. Do you recollect a man called Needham being convicted for blowing up a place at Dronfield?—Yes, I remember something about it.

19,417. That was for putting some gunpowder in a chimney, I believe?—Yes, something of that sort.

19,418. Do you know who was concerned in that besides Needham?—Needham, myself, and Samuel Crooks, I believe.

Mr. Sugg submitted that as this offence had occurred more than ten years since, any certificate which the Court had power to grant would not cover it, and that if the witness answered these questions he would be criminating himself.

The Chairman stated that if it should be needful he would undertake that the witness should be indem-

TWENTIETH DAY.

M. Thompson.

28 June 1867.

nified from any consequences which might follow from his evidence.

19,419. *Chairman* (*to the witness*). Did you, after Needham was in prison, support his wife?—Yes, I believe there was some money paid towards supporting her.

19,420. Where did the money come from?—It came out of the trade box, I believe.

19,421. And you supplied Crooks from time to time with money I believe, did you not?—Yes.

19,422. I believe that you bought Mrs. Needham a bonnet, did you not?—No, never.

19,423. It was Crooks did that. But, however, you supplied Crooks with money?—I supplied Crooks with money.

19,424. Do you know that he went over to see Needham when he was in prison?—No, I do not know that he went over.

19,425. He did not tell you?—No, he did not.

19,426. And he did not ask you for money?—No, he did not.

19,427. Did you supply him with the means of going up to London to see Needham when he came out of prison?—No, I did not.

19,428. Were you aware that Crooks went up to see him?—No, I was not.

19,429. But you were aware that Needham knew that both you and Crooks were in it?—Yes.

19,430. Do you mean to say that you never supplied Crooks with money to go to Derby?—Yes, I mean to say that I never supplied Crooks with money to go to Derby.

19,431. Do you know that he went?—No, I did not know until afterwards that he had been.

19,432. Had you given him money before to give to Mrs. Needham?—Yes, before he went to Derby.

19,433. Therefore, instead of giving it to Mrs. Needham, he perhaps took it and went to Derby himself?—That I cannot say.

19,434. Now, when Needham came out of prison, were you aware that he had made a statement whilst in prison?—I heard such a report, but I did not know anything about it.

19,435. Do you know that in that statement he had declared that he had been engaged by you to do that job at Dronfield?—Yes, I heard so.

19,436. Now you say you sent Crooks up to meet him when he came out of prison?—No, I did not.

19,437. You gave him the money to go?—No, I did not.

19,438. Did you know that he went?—I did not know while afterwards.

19,439. You knew afterwards that he had been?—Yes, I knew it afterwards.

19,440. And you gave him money on behalf of Mrs. Needham?—On behalf of Mrs. Needham.

19,441. Therefore I presume, that what you suppose is, that instead of giving the money to her he kept it for himself?—That I do not know.

19,442. How much altogether did you give him?—I am sure I do not know.

19,443. How much do you believe that it was?—I cannot say.

19,444. Was it 30*l.*?—I cannot say.

19,445. Did you give it him 18*s.* at a time or 1*l.* at a time, or how much?—We arranged it in that way; we arranged it as it happened.

19,446. Have you paid him as much as 5*l.* at a time?—No.

19,447. How much?—Well sometimes 1*l.* and sometimes 15*s.*

19,448. How much altogether have you paid to him?—I cannot speak to that.

19,449. May you have paid him from first to last with regard to this thing, 20*l.*?—I cannot say.

19,450. May it have been as much as that?—I should think not as much as that.

19,451. May it have been 15*l.*?—I will not swear to it; I cannot say.

19,452. What is your belief about it?—I cannot positively say what it was.

19,453. Do you believe that you have paid him as much as 15*l.* in reference to this matter?—I cannot answer that question because I do not remember.

19,454. It might have been as much?—It is three miles out.

19,455. You got it out of the box you say?—Yes.

19,456. Did you make any entry of it in the books?—No, we made no entry in respect of the money.

19,457. Then how did you manage to get it?—I had possession of the key of the box at that time.

19,458. How long ago is it since you last paid anything—how long was it after he came out that you last paid?—I never gave him anything after he came out.

19,459. Were you continuing to pay up to the time that he came out?—No.

19,460. Up to how long before he came out?—I think it would not be continued above six months.

19,461. Are you sure that you never paid Crooks anything in respect of Needham's wife during the latter part of the time that Needham was in prison?—I am sure that I never did.

19,462. Why not?—Because I had not it.

19,463. Why not?—Because I had given up the situation as secretary and I did not apply to the trade afterwards.

19,464. Then it was only during the time that you were secretary that you paid him?—Yes.

19,465. When did Mr. Machin become secretary?—In 1859.

19,466. Then did you pay all the time that you were secretary? From the time of Needham being taken to the time of your ceasing to be secretary did you continue to pay money?—Yes.

19,467. That is clear enough. Was it not in 1859 that you ceased to be secretary?—Before that time.

19,468. How long before?—It would be about Midsummer 1856.

19,469. Then we cannot go into it. After Needham came out of prison did you see him?—No.

19,470. Were you in Sheffield?—No, I live at Mill Houses.

19,471. That is close to Sheffield, is it not?—It is three miles out.

19,472. Did you never see Needham after he came out?—No, I never saw him after he came out of prison.

19,473. Why not?—I do not know the reason why.

19,474. You and he had been concerned in a business like this, and you had got off, or at least you had never been convicted of it while he was imprisoned for it, and yet you say you never saw him afterwards?—No.

19,475. Did you send him any message?—Never.

19,476. I suppose you were offended at his making a statement about you?—No, I was not offended at all.

19,477. Why not?—Because I had no occasion to be offended with such a man.

19,478. But you had acted with him you know?—No, he acted while I stood in the background.

19,479. He did the thing and you stood in the background?—Yes.

19,480. Did you hear that he had said that you had set him on to do it?—I heard that he had said that I had set him on to do it.

19,481. Did you hear that he had told that to Mr. Tyzack?—Well, I heard a rumour of that sort.

19,482. You heard that he had told Mr. Tyzack this?—I did not say positively that I heard that he had told Mr. Tyzack that.

19,483. Then what do you say that you had heard that he told Mr. Tyzack?—There was a rumour of this going about.

19,484. When was that?—It would be after he was in prison.

19,485. How long after?—Well, perhaps it might be six months; I cannot speak positively.

19,486. Did you not think it worth your while to

TWENTIETH DAY.

M. Thompson.

28 June 1867.

get his mouth closed when he came back out of prison? —No, I did not.

19,487. Were you not afraid of Mr. Tyzack prosecuting you for this?—No, I was not.

19,488. Why not?—Because I did not believe what he stated.

19,489. You did not believe what he stated; how do you mean? you know that it was true?—No, there was not much truth in what Needham had stated.

19,490. There was all the truth, because you say that you were engaged in it, and therefore there was perfect truth in it?—Yes, but I say that I did not engage him myself.

19,491. How so?—I let Crooks engage him.

19,492. Then you engaged Crooks and Crooks engaged him?—No, I did not engage Crooks at all, that concerned Mr. Tyzack and his own men.

19,493. But you had to do with the Dronfield business?—Yes.

19,494. And it was with respect to Mr. Tyzack that you had engaged Crooks?—I had nothing to do with Mr. Tyzack's affair at all.

19,494. Were you alarmed at all about this man's disclosing what you had to do with this affair when he came out of prison?—No, I did not feel particularly uneasy about it.

19,495. Why not? if he had suffered his penalty he could have come forward and have said, "I will "tell you the party who set me on to do it. It was "Crooks, and he was set on by Thompson." Nothing would have been easier than for him to have said that. Were you not alarmed that he might have come some fine day and said it?—No.

19,496. And you never looked after that?—No, I did not.

19,497. And although you had heard that he had said so and that he had told Mr. Tyzack so——? It was rumoured so.

19,498. Were you quite contented about it?—I did not feel any way sorry about it.

19,499. You thought that it was a little pleasurable excitement perhaps?—No, I made no jest of it.

19,501. But you were not anxious about it?—No, I was not.

19,502. Did you ever see Mr. Tyzack himself?—In respect of that matter?

19,503. In respect of any matter?—No, never.

19,504. Do you recollect Mr. Tyzack once asking you if you were going to Dronfield?—Never.

19,505. Are you sure of that?—I am sure of that.

19,506. Are you sure that Mr. Tyzack never said to you, "When are you going to Dronfield again"?—No, I can swear to that.

19,507. Did he ever allude to Dronfield when he met you?—No, never.

19,508. Never?—Never.

19,509. Did you hear that he was inquiring about that?—I cannot say that ever I did.

19,510. Did you ever hear that he was inquiring for Needham?—No; I never heard that he was inquiring for him.

19,511. Never?—Never.

19,512. Do you know a person of the name of George Watson?—I cannot call to mind just now; I may know a person of the name.

19,513. Of course you may or you may not. Do you know a person of that name?—Yes, I believe I do.

19,514. What is he?—I think that he is a file cutter.

19,515. Do you know him very well?—No, I do not know anything particular about him.

19,516. Were you friendly with him?—No.

19,517. Did he ever tell you that Mr. Tyzack had been asking him where Needham was?—No, never.

19,518. Have you got any uncles?—Yes, I believe I have.

19,519. What are their names?—Well, there is John, and Thomas, and George.

19,520. Did they ever tell you that they heard that Mr. Tyzack was inquiring for Needham?—No, never.

19,521. Then in 1862 had you anything to do with the books?—No.

19,522. You say that you did not shoot at Mr. Tyzack?—That I am certain of; I am certain I never did that.

19,523. You never did that?—No.

19,524. Do you know who did?—No, I am sure I do not.

19,525. You are sure that you do not know who shot at him?—I am sure I do not know who shot at him, for I never knew he had been shot at, while I saw it in the paper the other day.

19,526. Do you know why it was that Needham went to America?—No, I do not.

19,527. Did you find him any money to go to America?—No.

19,528. You swear that?—I swear that.

19,529. Did the funds of your society find him any money to go to America?—Not that I am aware of.

19,530. Did you ever see him in possession of money which came from you or from the funds of the society?—No, never.

19,531. Did you ever hear it talked of in the society why he was gone to America?—No.

19,532. Do you know whether he was provided with money for going to America by the society?—No, I do not.

19,533. Are you still a member?—Yes.

19,534. And you do not know why he went?—No, I do not.

19,535. On your oath you have never shot at Mr. Tyzack?—On my oath I never shot at Mr. Tyzack.

19,536. And you never engaged any man to shoot at him?—I never engaged any man to shoot at him.

19,537. Nor do you know who did shoot at him?—No, I do not.

19,538. On your oath you do not know who shot at him?—On my oath I do not know.

19,539. Have you a revolver?—No.

19,540. Have you never had one?—I have never had one.

19,541. Never in your life?—Never in my life.

19,542. Have you ever had a double-barrelled pistol?—No; nor a gun neither.

19,543. Did anybody ever lend you a revolver?—No.

19,544. Did you ever buy powder?—No.

19,545. Were you ever seen in possession of a revolver?—No.

19,546. You never had one?—I never had one.

19,547. You never had one in any way, and never had one lent you by anybody?—No.

19,548. Did you ever shoot with one?—No.

19,549. Is your road home on Abbey Dale?—It was when I lived at Mill Houses.

19,550. Up to what time did you live at Mill Houses?—Till three and half years ago.

19,551. Did you know that girl Morton?—Yes, I think I do; she has been here to-day as a witness.

19,552. When did you talk to her last?—I had not seen her for nearly three years before I saw her to-day.

19,553. Have you sent to her to-day to come here? No.

19,554. Has she come here at your request?—No, she has not.

19,555. Have you communicated with any of her friends?—No.

19,556. Did you know that she was coming to swear to the story which she has told to-day?—No, I did not.

19,557. You swear that?—I swear it.

19,558. And you have never talked to her about that story?—No.

19,559. And you never heard until to-day that Mr. Tyzack was shot at?—It would be last week some time; I saw it in the paper.

19,560. Who did they say had shot at him?—I did not hear anybody had.

19,561. And did you hear how many times he was shot at?—No, not till this morning. I saw it in the paper this morning.

19,562. Do you know old Mrs. Morton?—I did know her, but I do not know whether she is living or what she is now. I cannot tell.

19,563. You have not seen her for some time?—No, not for several years.

19,564. It is a very hard case to have an imputation of this kind upon you, but if you go and mix yourself up in matters like blowing up chimneys, it is the consequence of your own misconduct to have inquiries of this sort put to you?—Just so.

The witness withdrew.

JOSEPH CROSSLAND sworn and examined.

J. Crossland.

19,565. (*Mr. Barstow.*) Are you secretary of the pen and pocket-blade grinders?—Yes, I have been so since the last first of April.

19,566. Who had been secretary before you?—John Broomhead.

19,567. Did you immediately succeed Broomhead?—No, there was a person called William Crapper, and a person called William Thorpe who acted while I was elected. That would be nearly a month I daresay.

19,568. Was Broomhead secretary at the time of his death?—Yes; he died very suddenly.

19,569. When did he die?—It would be about three weeks or a month before I took the office, I think.

19,570. (*Chairman.*) In what year?—In this year about three weeks or a month before I took office.

19,571. (*Mr. Barstow.*) Do you know at about what time, and at about what date he died?—Well, I could not name that. I think it would be about three or four weeks before I was elected.

19,572. That would be in the beginning of March?—Yes, about that. I believe there is the last writing in the book when he was at the committee.

19,573. (*Chairman.*) Crapper and Thorpe succeeded him?—Yes.

19,574. And they lasted for a month, and then you came on?—Yes.

19,575. (*Mr. Barstow.*) I believe you produce your books?—Yes, what I have got.

19,576. What books are they?—This is one with the committee's names in, and I have used it for a minute book since I have got it (*handing in the same*). Then we have a cash-book which I had given to me at Christmas.

19,577. Does any book which you produce go back beyond the first of January of last year?—Here are two old collecting books (*producing the same*).

19,578. (*Chairman.*) Except two old collecting books, do you produce a single book which goes back beyond the first of January of this year?—This has been used for the secretary's contribution book since November 5th apparently.

19,579. (*Mr. Barstow.*) When do the cash-book and minute book begin?—The cash-book begins at Christmas. The first entry apparently is on the 31st December 1866.

19,580. What is the first entry in the minute book?—This is the minute book (*producing a book*). April 2nd, 1867.

19,581. Have you any contribution book?—Yes, those are old collecting books here which were turned over to me.

19,582. (*Chairman.*) Do they bring the contribution from any time down to the present time or not?—This commences in November last year.

19,583. The contribution book begins in November 1866?—Yes, November 5th, 1866.

19,584. The 5th November was Gunpowder day you know?—Ay.

19,585. I daresay perhaps you had a little burning that day; did you have a gunpowder plot that day?—No, not at all.

19,586. (*Mr. Barstow.*) When you took to the books did you inquire for the old ones?—Yes.

19,587. Did you get any account of them?—No, they said they could not be found, or that they were destroyed, or something of that sort.

19,588. From whom did you inquire?—I inquired from the persons in office at the time. I inquired from the committee whose names are in that book.

19,589. What are the names of the members of the committee?—They are down in the book. There is one they call William Thorpe, he was one of the originals.

19,590. (*Chairman.*) Do you know how it happened that they were destroyed?—No, I do not.

19,591. (*Mr. Barstow.*) You do not know anything about it?—Not at all.

19,592. (*Chairman.*) All that they told you was that they had been destroyed?—Yes, that is all. Some said that they have buried the books with Broomhead, but I do not know whether that is true or not. It has been an umbrage all through the trade a long time, at least ever since it was known. You will see the last committee entered; that would be mine (*pointing to the entry*). I think that that committee book goes back as far as 1864.

19,593. (*Mr. Chance.*) That is a recent entry.

19,594. (*Mr. Barstow.*) On April 10th, 1867, I find this resolution: "Resolved, that after a great " deal of investigation, we are of opinion that the 70*l.* " was drawn out of the bank for trade purposes, but " at the same time we deprecate the manner in which " it has been drawn out, and hope in future the com- " mittee will be very particular in the mode of doing " their business." To what does that refer?—At the last general meeting we had before Broomhead's death (it did not say the date, but it is mentioned perhaps in this book here (*referring to the book*). No, it did not mention the date), a person complained of the 70*l.* being drawn out of the bank without his knowledge.

19,595. What was his name?—George Law they call him. He was on the check and had not been noticed about it. I think he was in the saving's bank—I am not certain, and he was one of the parties that took it to the bank, and it was drawn out without his knowledge. That was the reason he made his complaint, and they appointed a committee of investigation to see into it.

19,596. Was he an office bearer of the society?—Not at that time; he had been before. At the time the money was put into the bank.

19,596*a*. At the time it was drawn out ought he to have known of it?—Yes; that is the arrangement with the banker I understand. Here is a bank account. Here I have entered it since I have seen the notes (*handing a book to the Examiners*).

19,597. What was Law's office at this time?—He would be a committee man at the time.

19,598. What was done upon his complaint?—There was an investigation committee.

19,599. (*Chairman.*) Did not Thorpe tell Law before the whole meeting that he had paid part of it for rattening?—I believe he did not go so far as that. I believe he was very bold upon it, but I cannot answer for the very words.

19,600. Did not Thorpe, who was a beer-house keeper, tell Law that the money had been used for rattening?—I cannot say that he used those words; he said that it had been used for trade purposes.

19,601. What do you call a trade purpose?—Why anything that came before them at that time. I expect they said it was for a trade purpose. That was the investigation. Of course he was at the investigation committee and we could not get much more out of him than that.

19,602. (*Mr. Barstow.*) Did he explain for what

TWENTIETH DAY.

J. Crossland.

28 June 1867.

purposes it was ?—I believe no particular purpose was named. There was about five or six years ago, I understand, a strike in the trade, and it cost a great deal of money, but I did not take any active part.

19,603. That did not of course refer to the 70*l.* ?—I fancy it did ; I fancy it was somewhere about that time that it was drawn out.

19,604. Did Thorpe at the time he made this statement explain for what purpose that money had been spent?—No; not clearly.

19,605. (*Chairman.*) But it was an irregular payment of some sort, was it not?—Yes, very likely it was. They could not get it in any other way and so they came to that resolution, any further than its being for trade purposes.

19,606. (*Mr. Barstow.*) And the meeting understood that it was an irregular payment?—Of course that resolution was read over to them before they passed it.

19,607. And then they passed this resolution?—Yes.

19,608. I have not had time to look over this book, but are you aware of any other irregularity in your accounts than that which you have mentioned?—Of the money do you mean?

19,609. Yes?—I do not consider they have been regular or else we should have had the old books, and they would have been kept in a systematical manner of course. I think if you will examine mine, you will find they are correct.

19,610. Do you doubt that the books have been destroyed or withheld in order to prevent their being brought before this inquiry?—Yes ; I am afraid of that myself.

19,611. You have admitted that you ratten in your trade, have you not?—The trade have rattened a long time, ever since I was a lad, and longer than that a deal.

19,612. I hope you have come to the conclusion not to do it again?—Yes we have, and the committee that we have now are very staunch about it I assure you.

19,613. Are you aware of any acts of violence committed on any members of your trade?—Only from the report that I saw in the paper about Sutcliffe. I knew Sutcliffe very well.

19,614. You knew no other case beside Sutcliffe's ?—No I did not.

19,615. Do you know any non-union man working in your trade who has been assaulted in any way?—No.

19,616. Do you know of any acts of outrage towards masters?—No I cannot call to mind any ; I was not an active member.

19,617. Are you aware whether Sutcliffe was waylaid because he did not pay his contribution?—I cannot say. I understood there was some dispute on account of the master that he worked for ; it was either as to wages or because he had gone in when other men were out; I fancy that was the cause.

19,618. (*Chairman.*) 70*l.* were deposited in the savings bank, were they not?—I think it was in the savings bank, I will not be certain, but I think it was.

19,619. Was it not deposited in the name of Bell and Jowett and Law?—Yes, so far as I have heard.

19,620. And was it not suggested that somebody's name had been forged to get the money out?—Yes, at the meeting. It was in these terms as I understood ; that three out of the four could draw it.

19,621. And when they came they found it had been drawn, and did not Law say his name had been forged?—He said his name must have been forged to have got it.

19,621*a*. He denied having ever given his name?—Yes, he said he had not given it himself.

19,622. Was it imputed to anybody?—No.

19,623. To Broomhead?—No, it was not imputed to Broomhead at all ; he was at the meeting.

19,624. I understand Broomhead was a man of very good character?—He generally bore a very good character.

19,625. He was a local preacher, was he not?—Formerly I understand.

19,626. Was he the man that paid the money to beat Sutcliffe?—I believe he was ; I was not aware till I saw it in the paper, but I was surprised at it I can tell you.

19,627. Do you not know that Joe Brammer's tools were destroyed in the Beeswax Wheel?—No, I cannot call it to mind ; I should think it is not very lately if there has been anything of that sort.

19,628. Do you know whether a person called Gawthorne had nine of his bands cut entirely to pieces?—Yes, I have seen part of his bands.

19,629. How long is that ago?—As far as I can recollect from what I have heard it must be two or three years ago.

19,630. Do you recollect a person of the name of Bradshaw and Furniss being committed for nine months to prison for doing that little business?—No.

19,631. You must have heard of that in your trade?—No.

19,632. You must have heard of it in your trade?—No, I was not aware of it ; I have not heard of it in any shape.

19,633. For rattening and destroying machinery?—No ; I have heard tell of some one being sent, but I did not know the name.

19,634. But you did know that some of your trade had been sent?—Yes.

19,635. Well, you have destroyed your books you cannot do much more?—Nay, I have not destroyed them.

19,636. Not you personally?—Nor any of the committee so far as I am aware.

19,637. But it was to prevent our seeing them, and seeing how the money had been spent, I suppose?—I should almost think it was if I were to speak the truth.

19,638. Have you ever seen the books?—I have seen one book, a cash-book.

19,639. Have you seen any entries that you would not have liked us to have a peep at?—No, not myself.

19,640. Have they told you that they had some?—There were some entries that I made remark upon myself; I asked the reason that Mr. John Samuel Spooner was mentioned so often in that book ; that was when I audited the books at Christmas, I and William Eeles.

19,641. Who was Mr. Samuel Spooner?—He worked at the Beeswax Wheel.

19,642. Did he do any work for the trade?—I am not aware; I said it was very wrong to have a man's name mentioned so often, and the secretary Broomhead said he had been a very useful man. He had been on many deputations and they had made him a many presents. What I mean by presents was for losing his time, I do not mean presents for doing anything.

19,643. No, of course not. But you thought it was very wrong for his name to appear so often?—Yes, but it is a custom when a man goes out for a day anywhere and loses his time to pay him for it.

19,644. But why did you object?—I objected to his name appearing so often.

19,645. But was it because his name appeared when he did not go?—No, I do not know that.

19,646. Then why did you object? was it because you would have gone if he had not?—I was not one of the deputation, or else I should have gone very likely.

19,647. Have you heard whether Spooner was paid from the box? was he president?—Yes, he was president I believe.

19,648. Did he pay himself?—I am not aware that he received anything at all from that office.

19,649. But being president he had access to that money, had he not?—Along with the rest. I named it to him myself once, and I said, "How is it that your name appears so often in the books?" and he said, "When the key-holders have not been there, "I have frequently lent the committee money and "I have been paid back the next night;" and then he said, "I put down 'Spooner' so much," but he ought certainly to have put it down to the credit side. However, that is the explanation I got.

19,650. But that is a very bad way of keeping books, if a man puts down the repayment and does not put down the loan. If that was an improper payment that is just how it would be done?—I cannot answer to that, I cannot say whether it was an improper payment.

19,651. (*Mr. Barstow.*) How many members are there in your union?—Well, we calculate about 650 or 660 but there is not a quarter of them paying hardly I am sorry to say; or if I say half, I dare say I shall be nearer the mark.

19,652. How many non-union men are there working at your trade?—Well, there are none, or at least very few that say they will not be in the union. There are a few of that sort I understand. Of course the person that was examined this week, John Wilson, said he would not join, though he said that if he saw the trade carried on properly he would not mind giving his mite towards it.

19,653. (*Chairman.*) He is a respectable man no doubt, and would not have anything to do with those wrong doings?—No.

19,654. (*Mr. Barstow.*) How many men have you on the box at present?—None at present. The contribution is very small; they only pay 6*d.* a man and 3*d.* a boy if they all pay.

19,655. Then do you make no allowance to men when they are sick?—We have a funeral fund connected with it.

19,656. (*Chairman.*) Do you call a funeral fund a sick fund?—No, we have not anything to do with the sick, but we have a funeral fund connected with it. We allow 2*l.* for a woman and 3*l.* for a man if they are straight.

19,657. (*Mr. Barstow.*) Is the funeral money raised by levy?—No, it goes out of the contribution, if they are what are called "financial." We are in a very poor state. Our trade it is not half employed now.

19,658. (*Chairman*). What can a man earn in your trade?—I see that Broomhead gave it in 30*s.* a week, but if he did he exaggerated a good deal. He included the working expenses; that would be about 5*s.* a week.

19,659. How much can a man and a boy earn?—He might get 2*l.* 10*s.*, but he would have his wheel room and expenses to pay out, and that would reduce it to very little over 2*l.*

19,660. What does it cost for a man and a boy?—Well, we reckon 5*s.* 6*d.* a week for wheel room for a man and a boy now, but I think it is dearer now because the stones are dearer.

19,661. (*Mr. Chance.*) You say you have very few men on the box now?—We have none on the box.

19,662. But is not that rather singular if trade is so bad now?—We should have plenty, but we cannot afford it; there are many that tell me that they are not averaging more than 5*s.* or 6*s.* a week to take home after expenses are paid; if they have 12*s.* or 14*s.* they have a good week they say.

19,663. (*Mr. Barstow.*) To what do you attribute having so large a number of non-paying workmen?—They say they cannot afford to pay; they have nothing to pay with, because prices are so very low and trade is so very bad.

19,664. (*Chairman.*) We are much obliged to you for your evidence; I hope your influence will extend to your union?—It is my desire.

19,665. No doubt of it, a respectable man has very great influence upon his trade. You have given your evidence in a very candid manner?—I have testimonials to my character in my pocket.

(*Chairman.*) We do not need them, the manner in which you have given your evidence is quite sufficient.

The witness withdrew.

Adjourned to Monday next at 11 o'clock.

TWENTY-FIRST DAY.

Council Hall, Sheffield, Monday, 1st July 1867.

PRESENT:

Thomas Irwin Barstow, Esq.
George Chance, Esq.

J. E. Barker, Esq., Secretary.

THOMAS IRWIN BARSTOW, Esq., in the Chair.

Mr. Barker requested all witnesses who had been summoned to be in attendance at the Court to-day to be there to-morrow morning.

The *Chairman* stated that the learned Chief Examiner had met with a very serious accident, and that his medical attendant had pronounced it to be quite impossible for him to sit to-day, and that therefore the proceedings of the Court would be adjourned until to-morrow.

Adjourned to to-morrow at 11 o'clock.

TWENTY-SECOND DAY.

Council Hall, Sheffield, Tuesday, 2nd July 1867.

PRESENT:

William Overend, Esq., Q.C.
Thomas Irwin Barstow, Esq.
George Chance, Esq.
J. E. Barker, Esq., Secretary.

WILLIAM OVEREND, Esq., Q.C., in the Chair.

TWENTY-SECOND DAY.

Mr. J. G. Robson.

2 July 1867.

Mr. John George Robson sworn and examined.

19,666. (*Mr. Barstow.*) Are you in partnership with Mr. Hoole?—No, I am manager of the works.

19,667. How long have you been manager?—A great many years. I have been there 30 years altogether; part of the time as partner with Mr. Hoole, and recently as manager there.

19,668. You were manager, at all events, in 1862? —Yes.

12,669. And in 1861?—Yes.

19,670. Are you aware whether Mr. Hoole is in Sheffield?—He is not in Sheffield.

19,671. Do you know where he is?—He is in Paris.

19,672. Do you know when he went there?—He went on Saturday morning from London, not from Sheffield.

19,673. When did he leave Sheffield?—A week previously.

19,674. He left Sheffield on Monday week?—Yes.

19,675. I believe Mr. Hoole is a stove grate and ender manufacturer?—He is a stove grate and fender manufacturer.

19,676. Do you remember in the year 1861 there being some difficulty with the grinders at your place? —I do.

19,677. Those grinders who were members of the union left your employment, did they not?—They did.

19,678. Do you remember what the cause of their leaving was?—The introduction of other men into their places who were not in the union.

19,679. The taking of other men into Mr. Hoole's employment in their places cannot have been the reason for their leaving?—It was the reason for their leaving. They left because they would not work with men who were not in the union.

19,680. Had you a workman named Woolhouse then?—Yes, we had. He was not a regular hand.

19,681. Did they not allege as the cause of their leaving that you refused to employ Woolhouse?—Will you allow me to state the matter in my own way?

19,682. Certainly, if you please?—We had two sets of grinders, one in the heavy wheels, and the other in the light wheels. The grinders in the heavy wheels had been neglecting the work and drinking for a considerable time, for more than a week certainly. At that time we had a foreman named Mr. Sibray.

19,683. Was Sibray a member of the union?—I do not know. He was certainly not a member of the union. Mr. Hoole said to Sibray, "Can't you get me other men in the place of these drunken fellows?" and he said, "Yes." They brought a man from Rotherham named Charles Taylor, whom we set to work. When those men came to their work again they brought with them this Woolhouse. He had been many years in our employ previously, but had not been so for some months before this, and under the plea of going heavily to work to make up for lost ground they brought this additional man with them, who was a union man.

19,684. Not having at that time been discharged they went off drinking, I suppose, and then came back again?—They were not discharged.

19,685. The other men had not been discharged?—No; when they came to work on the Monday morning, bringing this Woolhouse with them, they found this Taylor at work in the lower wheel. They refused to work with this man and went up to the light grinder's wheel and said, "You must come with us;" and they agreed to go out altogether.

19,686. Then I suppose they all left work?—They all left work except this Charles Taylor.

19,687. All the union men left work?—Yes.

19,688. What was the date of that?—I cannot give you the date; I did not receive the summons till ten minutes ago, and I am not prepared to give it.

19,689. That was on the 3rd of June, I believe?—It was in June, but I do not remember the date.

19,690. On the following day did you receive an anonymous letter?—There was an anonymous letter received by Mr. Hoole, but I do not know on what day.

19,691. Have you that letter?—No.

19,692. Do you know what has become of it?—No; I expect that Mr. Hoole has it.

19,693. Do you remember what its contents were? —I do not.

19,694. Do you remember its general character?—I do not at present.

19,695. Was it what you would call a threatening letter?—It was what we understand by a threatening letter.

19,696. Do you remember what the threat contained in it was?—No; I cannot recollect. I dare say I could refer and see. I think we have some copies of it, but I do not know.

19,697. If you have it we should like to see it?—Very well.

19,698. What occurred after that?—The men came back to us; but previously I may say that Mr. Sibray was requested to engage men in the places of those who had left. He then engaged several men from Masbro'.

19,699. (*Chairman.*) Amongst whom was George Wastnidge?—George Wastnidge and others.

19,700. They came from Masbro', where there were no trades unions, I believe?—Yes; there were Richard White, George White, William Hulse, and Ripley.

19,701. (*Mr. Barstow.*) I believe that there are no unions at Masbro', where those men came from?—I do not know whether they had any unions in Masbro'; union men were not generally employed in Masbro'.

19,702. Were those men union men?—No; they were not union men.

19,703. None of them?—No.

19,704. Are you aware whether they were allowed to work quietly in your employment?—For a time they were. Those men who had left of their own accord came, I think, on the following day, when they found we were employing those other men, and they wished to make some arrangement, as they called it, to come to work again.

19,705. Are you aware whether those men whom you engaged were threatened?—I do not know much about that.

19,706. Had you any interview with anybody in respect of those men?—Yes; Broadhead and Charles Bagshaw called.

19,707. Do you remember when?—It was a day or two, or perhaps three days afterwards.

TWENTY-SECOND DAY.

J. G. Robson.

2 July 1867.

19,708. Two or three days after those Masbro' men had begun to work ?—Yes, a few days ; I do not know whether it was two or three or four days.

19,709. What did they want ?—They wished to know if they could not come to some arrangement to allow the union men to come and work again.

19,710. Did you see Broadhead and Bagshaw ?—Yes.

19,711. Did they propose any terms ?—No ; we would not hear of any terms being proposed. We said, "You may see the men, if you like, whom we employ now."

19,712. They may have proposed terms, although you would not listen to them ?—Just so.

19,713. Did they propose any terms ?—They said, "Had you not better keep to your own men whom have "been so many years in the trade instead of having "new ones ?" and so on. They argued in that way, but there was no other inducement.

19,714. Are you aware whether they saw those Masbro' men, the non-union men ?—Yes, I believe they did.

19,715. Was that in your presence ?—It was in my presence that he saw them, but I did not hear what he said.

19,716. I believe at some period or another between June and November, intimidation was used towards those non-union men ?—May I say that those men told me what terms they offered them ?

19,717. Yes ?—They were first offered 5*l.* each to leave.

19,718. (*Chairman.*) By whom ?—By Bagshaw and Broadhead. The men then came to ask what they were to do under the circumstance, what Mr. Hoole would advise them to do, and he said, "Do as you like." They refused the 5*l.* They then offered them 7*l.* or 7*l.* 10*s.*, (I forget which,) but they said they would not go for less than 20*l.*

19,719. 20*l.* each ?—20*l.* each.

19,720. Did you hear Bagshaw and Broadhead make those proposals ?—No, the men told me afterwards that they had done so. They afterwards offered them 10*l.* and they refused to go any further, and the men remained in our employ.

19,721. How many men had you from Masbro' ?—About half a dozen.

19,722. That would be 60*l.* then, at 10*l.* a piece ?—Yes, I do not know whether they offered the light grinders that amount ; some of them were light and some were heavy. I think so, but Sibray will be able to tell you more about that than I can.

19,723. (*Mr. Barstow.*) Are you aware that any intimidation was used towards these men, between June and November ?—I believe there were acts, but I really cannot tell you what they were. My memory does not serve me at this time ; I know Sibray was very much ill-used by them.

19,724. And I believe some of the other men were ill-used too ?—Yes, I do recollect that two of the Whites were struck at going home, between the works and their own house.

19,725. But before that did they ever complain to you of being threatened by the union men ?—I do not recollect that they did, but I recollect them falling upon this man White and ill-using and nearly killing him on his road home.

19,726. And anyone besides ?—I do not recollect.

19,727. You do not recollect whether anyone was ill-used besides White, do you ?—I know that Sibray was.

19,728. (*Chairman.*) Do you not recollect that on that occasion at Portmahon William White and George White and Richard Hulse were all attacked ?—Yes.

19,729. Why did you not say so ?—I did not recollect.

19,730. (*Mr. Barstow.*) What was done to them ?—They were beaten and bruised and one of them was left for dead, I think.

19,731. (*Chairman.*) Which of them was that ?—One of the Whites.

19,732. (*Mr. Barstow.*) Were Wastnidge and Cooper attacked ?—I do not recollect that they were.

19,733. Then you say Sibray was attacked ?—Yes.

19,734. What was done to him ?—He was suddenly surrounded by some six or eight men with something which he fancied at the time, was a bag with stones in it or some hard substance. They swung it round and struck him on the face and dislodged several of his teeth, and hurt him very much.

19,735. Are you aware of any other assaults committed on your men ?—I do not recollect.

19,736. Was any complaint made to the police about those assaults on the Whites, Hulse, and Sibray ?—Oh yes.

19,737. Was anyone brought to justice ?—No, the police for some weeks guarded those men to their homes from the works.

19,738. But was anyone brought to justice ?—I think not.

19,739. Was a reward offered ?—I think not.

19,740. (*Chairman.*) Do you recollect the case of George Wastnidge being blown up ?—I do.

19,741. That was on the 23rd of November, was it not ?—It was in November.

19,742. (*Mr. Barstow.*) Are you aware whether Mr. Hoole had desired Broadhead and Bagshaw to call upon him ?—I think he did.

19,743. Then you had better have told us so ?—I did not think of it.

19,744. Were not four members of the fender grinders union present with Broadhead and Bagshaw ?—They were some of them present.

19,745. Do you know who they were ?—I do not.

19,746. Had you ever seen any of those four members before ?—I do not know that I had.

19,747. Would you know their names if they were mentioned to you ?—Perhaps I might, I do not know.

19,748. Was Hellewell one ?—Hellewell was with us at the time ; I think he might be there.

19,749. But do you remember whether he was or was not ?—No, I do not.

19,750. Was Samuel Cutler there ?—I do not recollect ; he was not our man.

19,751. Was a man named Platts one ?—I cannot tell—I do not know these men.

19,752. Can you remember how long it was after this interview that these assaults upon the two Whites and Hulse took place ?—I do not recollect how long it was after.

19,753. Can you not recollect how long it was after ?—I do not know. I could find very readily on referring. I wish you to bear in mind that I am quite unprepared for this examination ; I only got the summons a quarter of an hour before I left, or otherwise I would have been prepared for it.

19,754. But the assaulting of one of your workmen and his being left for dead was a very remarkable circumstance ?—Yes, I dare say it would be two or three or five weeks afterwards.

19,755. Was it not at Mr. Hoole's request that those offers were made to the non-union men to buy them out ?—No, I believe not. I never heard of any such thing.

19,756. Do you know whether it was so or not ?—I believe not ; I do not know whether it was or not. I never heard of such an offer on the part of Mr. Hoole, nor do I believe there was any such offer made.

19,757. Are you aware whether Mr. Hoole desired Bagshaw and Broadhead to make the offer to pay money to the non-union men ?—I am not aware that he did so, and I cannot imagine what reason he could have for doing so.

19,758. (*Chairman.*) You say it is a week ago since Mr. Hoole went to London ?—Yes.

19,759. Was Mr. Hoole one of the persons who applied to Government to have an inquiry into these trades union matters ?—I do not know.

19,760. Mr. Hoole knew that this inquiry was going on, did he not ?—He knew that you were sitting.

19,761. He knew, as a matter of course, that this

TWENTY-SECOND DAY.

J. G. Robson.

2 July 1867.

Acorn Street investigation would come on?—Yes, and he said to me before leaving, "If I am applied "for, let me know directly, and I will come down."

19,762. Of course he must have known that he would be applied for. We could not conduct this case without Mr. Hoole. Now, in his absence, things are stated respecting him which, if he were here, he might contradict; and I think if he has an interest in the town, he has not shown it by going away when this inquiry is going on?—When he left here he was going on his London journey, and his instructions were that he should be brought here at once, but it appears that on the Saturday morning he went with Alderman Carter and his body of aldermen to Paris, and he has not sent me his address, and therefore I could not send this paper.

19,763. Well, we cannot get him, and that is a misfortune. I think that if he wished to have served the town, and to have these things investigated, he might have given us notice or been here?—I believe his opinion was that the case would not come on yet.

19,764. He could not know what our intentions were; nobody could know except ourselves what our proceedings would be. Do you not know Mr. Hoole's present address?—I do not know. I know his present address is Poste Restante.

19,765. It is very unsatisfactory that Mr. Hoole is not here?—I am very sorry, and I am sure he will be very sorry when he hears it.

19,766. (*Mr. Barstow.*) Do you know when Mr. Hoole will return?—On Saturday.

The witness withdrew.

Mr. JOHN SIBRAY sworn and examined.

J. Sibray.

19,767. (*Chairman.*) What are you?—A stove grate manufacturer.

19,768. In the year 1861 were you in Mr. Hoole's employment?—Yes.

19,769. How long had you been in his employment?—I went in April 1861, and left in November 1861.

19,770. In what capacity were you there?—As manager in the stove grate department.

19,771. How many men did Mr. Hoole employ at that time?—Perhaps from 80 to 100, I should say, or perhaps more; I cannot speak exactly.

19,772. When you went there were those men union men?—Yes.

19,773. All of them?—I believe they were.

19,774. In 1861 did Mr. Hoole ask you to get other men in place of some of those who were working for him?—Yes.

19,775. Why was that?—Because one of the men was very unsteady, and neglected his work a deal, and I was to get a man and put in his place.

19,776. One of the men or some of the men?—One of the men.

19,777. Were you to get one man or more?—One man then.

19,778. Did you get a man?—Yes.

19,779. Whom?—Charles Taylor.

19,780. Where did he come from?—From Masbro'.

19,781. Was he a union man or not?—He was not a union man.

19,782. Do you know whether there are any union men at Masbro' or not?—There were some years ago, but I do not think there are now in the grinding trade.

19,783. Were there any in 1861?—I think not. Those men wanted to join the union.

19,784. When Charles Taylor came to work for Mr. Hoole did anything take place?—All the grinders struck work directly he went into the wheel.

19,785. What was done upon that?—They left their work, and we had to get other men in their places.

19,786. Did Mr. Hoole request you to get other men?—Yes, and men applied.

19,787. And did you get other men?—Yes.

19,788. Whom did you get?—Taylor, Wastnidge, Ripley, Cooper, Townend, and the two Whites. I think that was all.

19,789. Where did you get those men from?—They came from Masbro' principally.

19,790. When they came to work, what did the other men do then?—They were not at the place, they had gone; the other men had left.

19,791. Did you go on peaceably?—Yes, for some time.

19,792. When was this?—It would be about the latter end of June, 1861 or it might be the beginning of July. I cannot speak to a day or two.

19,793. How long did they go on peaceably?—While November, I think, or somewhere about that.

19,794. But something took place before November, did it not?—Threatening letters came.

19,795. Have you ever seen any of them?—I believe I have. I believe Mr. Hoole read them over to me, but I am sure I forget now. They were referring to him and me.

19,796. You cannot remember what was in them?—I cannot remember what was in them now.

19,797. Did they use any threat?—I cannot speak to that, it was not very pleasant, but I cannot think of what was in them. Mr. Hoole has the letters, I daresay.

19,798. (*Chairman.*) Do you know by whom they purported to be signed?—I am sure I forget that.

19,799. (*Mr. Chance.*) Were they signed by anybody?—I am sure I do not know; I cannot tell you.

19,800. (*Chairman.*) Do you know whether one of them was signed, "One of your men," or "One of your workmen?"—I cannot speak to that, I am sure.

19,801. (*Mr. Chance.*) After receiving those threatening letters were there any disturbances with the union men?—Deputations were coming down, but I never had any interviews with them; they came to Mr. Hoole.

19,802. Did you ever see any of the deputations to Mr. Hoole?—Yes, I saw Broadhead and Bagshaw.

19,803. How often did they come down there?—I think three or four times.

19,804. Did they come by themselves or with others?—They came by themselves sometimes; three or four times; and to the best of my recollection they came with a body of unionists.

19,805. Do you know what Broadhead is?—He is a saw grinder.

19,806. What is Bagshaw?—I do not know.

19,807. Had they anything to do with the fender grinders?—They came as a deputation on behalf of the fender grinders to make some arrangement, as I suppose.

19,808. As I understand, Broadhead and Bagshaw are not in your trade, are they?—No.

19,809. Then what business had they there?—I am sure I do not know.

19,810. (*Mr. Chance.*) Have you any idea of what they said?—No.

19,811. You were not present while they spoke?—No.

19,812. Did you see them in communication with any of the men?—They came to the office, but they had communication with some of the men, by what the men told me.

19,813. You do not know that?—No, only by what the men told men.

19,814. When did this deputation take place?—About July, I think.

19,815. After that were there any quarrels between your men and the union men?—No, I had nothing further to do with them, except that one night they met me and ill-used me.

19,816. Was that the first time that anything had been done to you by them?—Yes.

19,817. What night was that?—It was on the 5th of November 1861.

19,818. Where was it that you were met and ill

TWENTY-SECOND DAY.

J. Sibray.

2 July 1867.

used?—Opposite the Union wheel, in Sheffield here. I was at the old workhouse as well.

19,819. What part of the day was that?—From six till half past in the evening.

19,820. (*Chairman.*) It would be dark then?—It was a very dark thick foggy night.

19,821. (*Mr. Chance.*) How many men were there? —Two.

19,822. Who were they?—I do not know.

19,823. Have you heard since who they were?—I think this Baylis, or Bayles, is one. I forget who told me that.

19,824. Who was the other?—I do not know I am sure.

19,825. What did they do to you?—When they got up to me they parted, and one gave me a stroke with his right hand, and I staggered a little, and as I was walking up to the other he ran away. The other man had gone on up by the side of the workhouse.

19,826. With what did they strike you?—I do not know what they had in their hands.

19,827. On what part of your body did they strike you?—On the lip and mouth.

19,828. Was it with a bag full of stones?—I never saw a bag full of stones.

19,829. Did it knock you down?—No; it staggered me a good deal.

19,830. Did it draw blood?—Yes. I went to a doctor the same night. It did not knock a tooth out, but it knocked it parallel with my mouth, and then it went back again.

19,831. Did both men hit you, or one only?—One only.

19,832. After the two men had left you what did you do?—I went to the police office, and Mr. Jackson was not in, so that there was nobody to attend to it, and I went home to Rotherham.

19,833. Did you go again to the police?—No; I believe Mr. Hoole made it known to the police after that.

19,834. Were no further steps taken by you to find out who had attacked you?—No; I think Mr. Hoole took it up then.

19,835. You say you went to a surgeon?—Yes, the same evening.

19,836. Were any other assaults made upon you? —No.

19,837. Were any other threats used towards you by union men?—No, they never came near me after that time.

19,838. What do you believe to have been the cause of the attack which was made upon you?—Because on account of this man being unsteady I got those other men to come, and then they all struck, and we had to get other men, and I got other men.

19,839. Was that the only reason?—That was the only reason; it was no price question at all.

19,840. And you had no private quarrel with any person?—No, I had not.

19,841. And there was no attempt to rob you?—No.

19,842. It was merely an attempt to beat you?—That was all.

19,843. Is that the only cause which you could assign for the attack which was made upon you on that night?—That is all; I do not know of anything else.

19,844. (*Mr. Barstow.*) You were the manager of the stove trade department at Mr. Hoole's you say?—Yes.

19,845. Did Mr. Hoole offer any reward for the detection of those men?—I think not, I am not aware of it.

19,846. Are you in Mr. Hoole's service now?—No.

19,847. How long did you remain in it after this attack was made upon you?—I left the Saturday after; that was on the Tuesday, and I left on the Saturday, I was on notice then.

19,848. Had Mr. Hoole given you notice?—No, I gave him notice.

19,849. What made you give Mr. Hoole notice?—Why we got threatening letters you know, and I thought it was not very pleasant to stop in Sheffield.

19,850. (*Chairman.*) Where had you come from? —From Rotherham.

19,851. (*Mr. Barstow.*) You were intimidated into giving him notice?—Well, I thought when these threatening letters came it was not safe to remain in Sheffield.

19,852. (*Mr. Chance.*) Were you one of the men who were guarded by the police afterwards?—No, because I only stopped four days after that. My time was up.

19,853. (*Mr. Barstow.*) Have you yourself ever received any threatening letters?—No.

The witness withdrew.

GEORGE WASTNIDGE sworn and examined.

G. Wastnidge.

19,854. (*Chairman.*) I believe you were working at Masbro', were you not, in the month of June in the year 1862?—No, I was not working there.

19,855. But you were at Masbro'?—Yes.

19,856. Were you suffering a good deal at that time from a strike which had occurred?—Yes.

19,857. In consequence of an application which was made to you by Mr. Sibray, did you come over to Sheffield to work for Mr. Hoole?—Yes.

19,858. Together with several others?—No, I came by myself; they were working when I came.

19,859. At what time of the year was it when you went there; was it about June?—It was about June.

19,860. Were Richard White and George White and William Hulse, and a man called Cooper all working there?—Yes, there was Richard White, and Joe White, and Hulse, and a man of the name of George Rodway, and one of the name of Henry Ripley.

19,861. Were they all non-union men?—Yes, I believe they were.

19,862. And so you worked for Mr. Hoole?—Yes.

19,863. While you were at work there, did you see anything of the union men? did the union men come to you at all asking you either to leave or do anything? —Mr. Broadhead came and Mr. Bagshaw and all.

19,864. Did they speak to you?—Yes.

19,865. And what did they say to you?—They took us to a public-house and treated us with some beer, and wanted to know what money or what recompense we would take to leave the place. I said I did not want any money or any recompense at all, and that if they would take me into their union I was willing to join.

19,866. What did they say to that?—They said that they could not do anything of the kind.

19,867. Did they make any proposal to you or name any sum of money?—Yes.

19,868. What did they offer you?—Well, I am sure I forget now what it was.

19,869. About how much was it?—I am sure, to tell the truth, I cannot say; perhaps some few pounds they offered us to leave the works.

19,870. And what did he say to that?—I said, Well, I was willing to take anything or leave without anything, provided they would find me another situation and let me join their union. What they wanted me to pay I was willing to pay.

19,871. What did they say to that?—They said, "No, they should not."

19,872. What happened next?—When we had had a sup of beer they left us, and we went and got on with the work again.

19,873. Did they come again?—Yes.

19,874. What did they say when they came again? —They were talking about the same thing; they wanted us to leave and offered us some money.

TWENTY-SECOND DAY.

G. Wastnidge.

2 July 1867.

19,875. You would not?—I did not see any money, but that was the proposal.

19,876. But they offered you money, and you said that you would not; is that so?—Yes.

19,877. How often did Broadhead and Bagshaw come to you offering you money to leave Mr. Hoole's employment?—Two or three times they came.

19,878. You did not leave?—No, not then.

19,879. At any of those interviews did they tell you that Mr. Hoole had sent them to you?—Yes, I believe they did.

19,880. What did they say?—They said that Mr. Hoole was agreeable for us to leave and take this recompense.

19,881. Did you ever speak to Mr. Hoole about it? —Yes.

19,882. What did Mr. Hoole say to you?—Well, he said that he knew nothing about it.

19,883. Did you tell Mr. Broadhead and Mr. Bagshaw that you had told Mr. Hoole what they had told you, namely, that Mr. Hole had said that you might take recompense, and that he had said he knew nothing about it?—I do not think I did.

19,884. However, you did not agree to leave?—No.

19,885. And you continued working then?—Yes.

19,886. Did you ever go to Broadhead's house at all?—Yes.

19,887. How did you happen to go there?—From the invitation of Mr. Bagshaw and Mr. Broadhead and all.

19,888. When was it?—I cannot tell you that.

19,889. How long was it after you had been to Mr. Hoole's?—I am sure I do not know; I cannot tell you I am sure.

19,890. Had you been there for a week or two?—Yes, a month or two.

19,891. Did you see Broadhead and Bagshaw at Broadhead's?—No; I saw Broadhead; I did not see Bagshaw.

19,892. And had you some kind of talk about receiving remuneration for leaving?—No.

19,893. What was done?—They had some business upstairs. We were downstairs, and all we had was plenty of beer.

19,894. Who paid for it?—I expect Bagshaw and Broadhead paid for it. We never paid for any.

19,895. How many of you went to Broadhead's on that occasion—all the men who were working?—No, not all. There was me and Rodway, and Cooper and Ripley. I think that was all.

19,896. Was any proposal made to you that night? —No.

19,897. And you did nothing?—No.

19,898. You merely drank beer and came away?—That was all.

19,899. During the time that you were at work at Mr. Hoole's, was anything said to you by those non-union men?—No.

19,900. Were you watched or not?—I believe we were.

19,901. Were you picketed?—Yes, middling.

19,902. Did you feel yourself safe to go home or were you obliged to have policemen to guard you home?—I felt safe enough; nobody said anything to me.

19,903. But do you know that policemen were employed to guard the men backwards and forwards to the works?—I believe they were.

19,904. For how long a time were they employed? —A few weeks.

19,905. The time when you went was in June?—Yes.

19,906. I believe nothing occurred to any of you until the month of November?—No.

19,907. In the meantime had you heard anything about any threatening letters?—No.

19,908. Had anything been said about the dark nights?—No, not to me.

19,909. Had that been said to anybody?—Not that I am aware of.

19,910. Did you get hurt at all in November?—Yes.

19,911. Who was with you when you were hurt?—Well, I was in the house.

19,912. Were you not attacked in the street?—No.

19,913. Never?—No.

19,914. Were you not once attacked with Cooper and did you not run into your house?—Well, yes, I believe we were. That was in Dun Street.

19,915. You had forgotton it I suppose?—Yes.

19,916. How many persons attacked you and Cooper then?—Well, there was one at first, and then a lot more came out of a publichouse.

19,917. Do you happen to know who they were?—No; I could tell one of them if I saw him.

19,918. But you did not know him before?—No.

19,919. Did you know the men who had left the employment of Mr. Hoole before you went there?—Yes.

19,920. Was it one of those men?—No.

19,921. Had you any quarrel with anybody in Sheffield except upon this union business?—Yes, I had once a quarrel.

19,922. With whom?—With a man; I forget what they call him now, but we had some few words, and there were two women started.

19,923. But was it the man with whom you had quarrelled, who attacked you on that occasion, when Cooper was with you?—No.

19,924. But you were attacked when you were with Cooper. Had you had any quarrel with anybody?—No.

19,925. After you had been attacked, were you in your house in the month of November?—Yes.

19,926. On the 23rd of November?—Yes.

19,927. Who lived in your house; there was you and your wife and your child, and Mrs. O'Rourke I believe?—Yes.

19,928. What time did you go to bed?—About eight or nine o'clock.

19,929. Did you leave Mrs. O'Rourke up at the time you went to bed?—Yes, I believe I did.

19,930. Where did you sleep?—In the garret.

19,931. Where did Mrs. O'Rourke sleep?—In the chamber.

19,932. Below you?—Below us.

19,933. And underneath that there was the parlour, was there not?—That was the house-place.

19,934. Did your child sleep in the same room with you and your wife?—Yes.

19,935. I believe that about midnight you were disturbed by a noise, were you not?—Yes.

19,936. What was the noise?—Something coming through the chamber window.

19,937. Had not your wife heard some people's feet before that?—I believe she had.

19,938. But then she heard something come through the window?—Yes.

19,939. What window was it? Was it the window of your room or the window of the room below?—The window of the room below.

19,940. That was the room where Mrs. O'Rourke slept?—Yes.

19,941. When she heard the noise of something coming through the window into Mrs. O'Rourke's chamber, what did you do? Did you get out of bed? —She said, "Oh dear! what is that."

19,942. Did she get out of bed?—She got out of bed.

19,943. What did she do?—She went downstairs.

19,944. Did she look through the window first?—Yes, she looked through the garret window first.

19,945. And then, after looking through the window, she went down stairs?—She said, "Am I to go and see what it is?" and I said "Yes," and she went and I followed her.

19,946. When you got into the room below, did you find Mrs. O'Rourke with something in her hands? —I did not get into the room before it exploded.

19,947. But did she get into the room?—Yes, my wife did.

19,948. She had got something in her hands?—Yes.

TWENTY-SECOND DAY.

G. Wastnidge.

2 July 1867.

19,949. And I believe sparks were coming from it?—Yes.

19,950. Did your wife take it from her?—She said she did. I did not see.

19,951. And while it was in her hands I believe it blew up?—Yes,

19,952. And that turned out to be, as you found out afterwards, a can of gunpowder, did it not?—Yes.

19,953. What was the result of that to your wife? It set her chemise on fire, did it not?—Oh, yes.

19,954. And what became of her?—She ran upstairs into the garret again, and I pulled the burning things off her; and my little lad had got out of bed, I was afraid of his being stifled and I picked him up—he had got under the bed—and before I could get to the window my wife was out.

19,955. She jumped through the window in her fear?—Yes.

19,956. Out of the garret window?—Yes.

19,957. She had nothing on her at all, had she?—No.

19,958. Was she perfectly naked?—Yes.

19,959. And what became of her?—When I got out of the window I found her in a house across the road.

19,960. Had she fallen on the footpath?—Yes; I expect she would have to do that.

19,961. What became of you?—I got out of the garret window too.

19,962. Did they bring you a ladder?—Yes, but the ladder was too short.

19,963. What became of your boy?—I took him out with me.

19,964. Did you drop him to the people below?—Yes.

19,965. And they caught him?—Yes.

19,966. And then you went down?—Then I went.

19,967. After that did you go into the house again to seek for Mrs. O'Rourke?—Yes.

19,968. Where did you find her?—She was in the cellar.

19,969. In what state was she?—She was dreadfully burned.

19,970. Your wife was taken insensible I believe to the infirmary?—Yes.

19,971. I believe Mrs. O'Rourke had all her night-dress and everything burnt off and she was very much burnt?—Oh, yes.

19,972. And she was removed to the infirmary?—Yes.

19,973. And, I believe in about a fortnight afterwards she died of her injuries?—Yes.

19,974. I believe you had jumped out of the window yourself had you not, and you lit on the ladder and that broke your fall?—Yes.

19,975. What had happened to the house, was it filled with smoke and sulphur?—Oh, yes.

19,976. Was it much damaged?—Yes, but not so much as one would expect.

19,977. How was the garret floor?—It hit the ceiling and it split a baulk, and it opened the ceiling, and that was where I got burnt; underneath the garret window the flames were all blazing up, while I was holding up the little boy to get some fresh air for him and for myself and all.

19,978. Then the house was on fire?—Yes.

19,979. After this took place I believe Mrs. O'Rourke died?—Yes.

19,980. How long was it before your wife recovered?—About a month or five weeks I daresay, or something like that.

19,981. She was in the infirmary four or five weeks?—Yes.

19,982. What were you doing?—I was in the infirmary with her a fortnight.

19,983. What had happened to you? were you burnt too?—Yes, I was burnt very badly; I was burnt in my legs holding my little boy at the window.

19,984. What became of you after the fortnight and when you came out?—I went to work.

19,985. For whom did you work?—Mr. Hoole.

19,986. He took you back into his employment?—Yes.

19,987. Who maintained you during the time that you were in the infirmary? I suppose you were maintained at the expense of the infirmary?—Yes; the infirmary maintained my wife; I maintained myself while I was there.

19,988. I believe you were sent to Wakefield were you not?—Yes.

19,989. For what?—For an assault.

19,990. When was that?—I think it was in April.

19,991. Before this took place?—No, after.

19,992. Had you worked from the month of November up to April for Mr. Hoole?—Yes.

19,993. And then you committed this assault and were sent to Wakefield, were you not?—Yes.

19,994. For how long?—For a month I stopped.

19,995. At the time when this happened to you had you any ground of quarrel with anybody?—No.

19,996. None at all?—Not a bit.

19,997. To what do you attribute the fact of this gunpowder being thrown into your house?—I suppose it was because I was working at Green Lane works.

19,998. Is there any other reason that you know of why a person should throw this combustible matter into your bedroom window except that?—No.

19,999. Was Mrs. O'Rourke on good terms with other people?—Yes.

20,000. And neither you nor your wife nor Mrs. O'Rourke had quarrelled with anybody?—No.

20,001. When you were not able to go to work did Mr. Hoole keep you?—I borrowed some money of him and I paid him back.

20,002. When did you borrow money of him?—I do not know when it was. Sometime in December.

20,003. How do you mean you borrowed some money of Mr. Hoole?—He advanced me some. I asked him for some and he let me have some.

20,004. When was that?—Sometime in December.

20,005. How did you happen to want money of Mr. Hoole? were you not at work?—Yes, I was in work, but then I was not so that I could do a deal of work.

20,006. Was that in consequence of being burnt?—Yes.

20,007. In consequence of being burnt you could not do a deal of work, and you had to borrow money of Mr. Hoole?—Yes.

20,008. And he advanced it to you?—Yes.

20,009. Had you to pay it back or not?—Yes, I paid it.

20,010. How did you pay it?—I believe I paid him 5*s*. a week.

20,011. He deducted it out of your wages?—Yes.

20,012. And you had sustained this injury in going and working for him?—Yes.

20,013. How soon did you pay off the money that you borrowed?—I paid him 5*s*. a week while it was paid.

20,014. How much did you borrow?—A few pounds—not a deal; a couple of pounds.

20,015. When you had paid your money, what became of you?—I left soon after.

20,016. How did you happen to leave?—Because I had had enough of the place, and of him and all.

20,017. Did you give notice, or did he give notice?—I believe I left without notice. I think I did.

20,018. Did you leave because you were afraid to stay in the place?—No, I was not at all frightened. It was because I was not satisfied with Mr. Hoole, because he had not behaved the gentleman that he ought to have done.

20,019. How was that, you borrowed money of him, and paid it him back?—Yes.

20,020. Then what were you dissatisfied with?—I should have thought I ought to have some recompense from a man like that, having had a job of this sort all through him.

20,021. You thought that you ought to have had a recompense for a job like that all through him, instead of borrowing money from him and repaying it

TWENTY-SECOND DAY.

G. Wastnidge.

2 July 1867.

by weekly instalments of 5*s*. from your wages?—Yes, all my furniture was burnt and things spoiled and lost.

20,022. Your furniture and things were damaged and lost?—Yes.

20,023. And did he make no recompense to you for that?—No, not at all. On the Saturday morning Mr. Hoole came to my house and put a sovereign into my hand, and sent for it back in the afternoon.

20,024. (*Mr. Barstow.*) Was that the morning after the blow up?—Yes.

20,025. (*Chairman.*) And therefore you sustained all the loss of this however it was?—Yes.

20,026. (*Mr. Chance.*) Was your dissatisfaction with Mr. Hoole the only reason why you left him?—Yes.

20,027. Had your differences with the union men no effect in inducing you to leave?—No, I had never had words with any of the men.

20,028. But you just now said, that you believe that you were blown up in consequence of it?—Certainly.

20,029. Had you no fear of the union men after the explosion had taken place?—No, not at all. I had no fear about it.

20,030. Then it was from no fear of the union men that you left Mr. Hoole's afterwards?—No, I had nothing against them, and I do not think they had anything against me.

The witness withdrew.

H. Wastnidge.

Mrs. Harriett Wastnidge sworn and examined.

20,031. (*Mr. Barstow.*) Are you the wife of George Wastnidge?—Yes.

20,032. You lived in November 1861 at No. 24 Acorn Street, did you not?—Yes.

20,033. With your husband and child and Mrs. O'Rourke?—Yes.

20,034. On the 23rd of November 1861 when you were in bed did you hear some men tramping about the street?—No.

20,035. Did you hear any men in the street?—I do not know that I did.

20,036. Were you awakened by anything?—Yes.

20,037. What waked you?—The smash through the window.

20,038. Through the chamber window?—Yes.

20,039. That was Mrs. O'Rourke's room, was it not?—Yes.

20,040. You went downstairs into the chamber?—Yes; I looked through the garret window first.

20,041. Never mind that; I will not ask you about that. I will just ask you what you saw in the chamber?—I went down into the chamber.

20,042. When you looked out of the window, did you see any men?—Yes.

20,043. What did you see?—I saw a lot running down the street; three or four.

20,044. (*Chairman.*) Are you quite sure that it was three or four, or only two?—I do not know, but they made a great clatter as they ran.

20,045. Were there more than one?—Yes, there were more than one.

20,046. (*Mr. Barstow.*) Were there more than two?—Well, I will not say.

20,047. When you went into the chamber, what did you see?—I saw this Mrs. O'Rourke standing in a corner against her bed; I told her to throw it out of the window.

20,048. To throw what out of the window?—Why, the parcel that was blazing.

20,049. Then she had a parcel that was blazing, had she?—Yes.

20,050. When you say that it was blazing, what do you mean?—Sparks were flying out. I said, "Throw it out of the window." She refused, and I snatched hold of it to throw it out myself, and it went off in my hand.

20,051. Did she say that she would or that she would not do it?—No, she said, "Take it!"

20,052. And it exploded in your hand?—Yes.

20,053. When it exploded in your hand, what happened to you?—I do not know.

20,054. You were very much burnt, were you not?—I do not know how I got into the garret again, but I did.

20,055. Did you immediately become insensible?—Yes, I went off.

20,056. (*Chairman.*) You do not recollect anything afterwards until you found yourself in the infirmary?—No, I do not.

20,057. (*Mr. Barstow.*) Were you very much burnt?—Yes.

20,058. Were you blinded at the time?—Yes.

20,059. Do you feel any injury from that now?—Yes, I do.

20,060. What is that?—My right knee fails me very badly, and I have no use in my right hand.

20,061. Is that from a burn?—Yes.

20,062. And is the knee also from the burn?—Yes.

20,063. How long were you blind?—I daresay about a fortnight.

20,064. You have the marks of the powder in one of your eyes now, I believe?—Yes.

20,065. Were you blackened all over with the powder?—Yes.

20,066. Do any of those marks continue about you now?—Oh, yes, fearful.

20,067. Had you any quarrel with anybody at that time?—No.

20,068. Do you know whether your master had?—Not that I am aware of. There was a neighbour lived next door but one to us, and she sent for me. I was a stranger in Sheffield; I had never been there before, and she asked me if we had our cellar grate fastened, and I said, "No, what for"? She said she heard tell there was a party lived in the next street that would blow us up if it was not fastened, and I told him and he fastened it. That would be about a fortnight before it happened, and the night it did happen I went into this woman's and asked her to allow me to sleep there, and she said "No."

20,069. All your furniture was destroyed?—Yes.

20,070. Shortly after that, we have heard from Wastnidge that he was sent to Wakefield?—Yes.

20,071. At that time you were in great destitution?—Yes, we were.

20,072. Did you apply to anyone for assistance?—Yes; I went to apply, but I had just got in when a policeman came to tell me that Mr. Jackson wanted me, and I did not see the overseer.

20,073. But did you apply to Mr. Hoole?—Yes.

The witness withdrew.

R. Renshaw.

Robert Renshaw sworn and examined.

20,074. (*Chairman.*) I am going to ask you some questions?—I will answer them then.

20,075. And I think it right to tell you beforehand that the inquiry which we are now upon, is an inquiry into the death of Mrs. O'Rourke which was a case of murder?—It is right enough.

20,076. And I am going to ask you whether you knew anything about that murder?—I do.

20,077. If you tell the truth and make a candid and clear confession of everything you know about the matter, if you know anything——?—I will tell you nought else.

20,078. We have the opportunity and the privilege of granting you a certificate which will not only free you from all the consequences of your own act, both criminal and civil, but also if you implicate any other person we shall do the same thing by him if he comes forward and makes a statement of the facts within his knowledge. But you must not only tell us what you did yourself but all that you know about; and having told you that you have an opportunity of getting a certificate if you tell the truth, I must also tell you that if you do not tell the truth that certificate will not be granted to you, and the consequences would be very serious to you if you are guilty?—I should never have told if somebody else had not; you might be sure about that.

20,079. Do you know a person of the name of Cutler?—Yes, I do.

20,080. What is he?—He is a stove-grate grinder; I am sorry I know him.

20,081. What are you yourself?—I am a file grinder.

20,082. Do you recollect seeing Cutler some time before Wastnidge was blown up at the time there was a disturbance amongst Hoole's men?—Yes, many a time.

20,083. What was Bayles?—He was a stove-grate grinder, and as good a lad as ever walked upon two legs, and Cutler is not fit to be in the same room with him.

20,084. Do you recollect Cutler asking you to meet him at the house of a person called Green?—Old Joe? Ay, I do.

20,085. How long was that before Wastnidge's house was blown up?—Happen two or three weeks; I cannot say.

20,086. Did you go on to Green's public house and meet him there?—Yes.

20,087. Who was there?—There were the "old swell" and Bill Bayles.

20,088. That was Cutler and Bayles?—Yes.

20,089. On that occasion did Cutler ask you to do anything?—Yes.

20,090. What did he ask you to do?—He asked me to go and knock a man on the head for 10*s*., and I would not do it.

20,091. Who was the man that he asked you to knock on the head for 10*s*. and you would not do it?—This man that you had up here just now; I do not know his name.

20,092. Wastnidge?—Yes; I have never seen him before to-day. I have seen him, but I did not know him.

20,093. And you said you would not do it?—Yes.

20,094. And when you said that what did Bayles say to you?—Well, I will tell you what he said; but I will tell you what I said before this. I said, "It would be deal better to do him at home than to do him in the street," and that was agreed upon.

20,095. How did you agree to "do him" at home?—Well, Sam gave me 10*s*. to buy powder with, and told me to put 3lbs. in; and instead of putting 3lbs. in I only put one.

20,096. Which is Sam, Cutler, or Bayles?—Cutler, that is him.

20,097. What were you to have for doing this?—Nay, I never got it yet.

20,098. But what were you to have?—I was to have 6*l*. at the first.

20,099. Who promised you that?—Cutler.

20,100. Who was present at the time?—Cutler and Bayles were present at Joe Green's at the time when this was made up to be done.

20,101. Did he give you any money to buy the powder?—He gave half-a-sovereign—gold you know.

20,102. And you bought the powder, did you?—I did.

20,103. When you had bought the powder what did you do with it?—I put it in a canister and a piece of fuse to it.

20,104. After you had bought the powder and put it into the canister and put a fuse to it, what did you do with it?—I will tell you what I did with it. I took it home, and I came to the theatre here, and I went to the theatre after it closed and threw it into the window, and now you know all about it.

20,105. Whose window?—I do not know the man; it was the same man; it was in Acorn Street, you know.

20,106. How did you throw it in? did you throw it from the street with your hand?—Of course; how could I throw it in without my hand?

20,107. After you had thrown it into the window what did you do?—I went into the Ebenezer chapel, and laid me down.

20,108. Into the chapel or the yard?—How could I get into the chapel if the door was locked?

20,109. But you said the chapel; you mean the yard?—Yes, I laid me down, and I laid till a crowd came, and two or three policemen, (they always come up when it is too late) and other folk besides, and I went to see how it had gone on.

20,110. When you came back what did you find?—I could see the old lady coming out of the window, and all that you know. I forgot this; they promised if I made a good job of it to give me 5*l*. more, and I never got it; that is 6*l*. I want out of that job.

20,111. Did you see Mrs. O'Rourke brought out?—Yes, I did; I helped to get her out.

20,112. Did you see Mrs. Wastnidge brought out?—No, she jumped out if you remember, and she was caught half way down.

20,113. But you helped to bring out Mrs. O'Rourke?—Yes, and I was grieved when I saw her come out.

20,114. Did you ever get any money for this?—I will tell you what I got.

20,115. What did you get?—I got 3*l*., and that was all I got for four or five weeks I should think.

20,116. Who paid you that?—Bill Bayles; he is dead. It is no use putting it on dead folk, but Sam Cutler is the man that drew the money and paid Bill, understand that.

20,117. Was it Bayles that paid you?—It was Bayles that paid me, 3*l*. and he paid me 2*l*.

20,118. When was it that he paid you the 3*l*.?—I will not be sure, you know, but it will be the day after, or two days; it will not be above two days I am sure.

20,119. After the blowing up?—Yes.

20,120. Then you say you got 2*l*. more?—Yes.

20,121. When was it that you got 2*l*. more?—Well, I will tell you about that and all. I goes to Sam Cutler's and I says, "Now, Sam, I want the 3*l*. you owe me." He says, "Bob, I have paid it to Bill." I goes to Bill and he had not got it, and I goes to Sam again. If you will ask me another question I will answer the truth.

20,122. When you saw Sam again, what did you say to him?—I told him I would serve him the same as I served t'other if he did not give me the 2*l*.

20,123. What did he say to that?—He said he had paid it to Bill.

20,124. Did you ever get it?—Aye, before I was up in the morning, he had come to our house.

20,125. Who did?—Bill Bayles brought it to me; I do not like to put nought on to dead folks mind you. Those innocent customers you see you don't know, you don't understand; they want to bring themselves clear off, and they are the guilty party.

20,126. This is the history that you have to give; you say that is the story of the way in which it happened?—Yes.

20,127. That is the whole truth?—Yes.

20,128. Where did you buy your powder?—I cannot say whether I bought it at Shepherd's or whether I bought it at Snig Hill, because it is such a long while since, but I bought it at one of those places.

20,129. Do you know Twibell's?—Yes, I do.

20,130. Have you ever bought powder at Twibell's?—Many a time.

20,131. Can you tell me whether you bought it

TWENTY-SECOND DAY.

R. Renshaw.

2 July 1867.

there that night?—I tell you I cannot say whether I did or not.

20,132. Do you know where you bought the fuse?—At the old Quaker's, just across here.

20,133. At Milner's?—Aye, that is him.

20,134. You say that Bayles asked you, and Cutler asked you; both of them?—Cutler is the scoundrel. He sent for me many a time.

20,135. What was the reason that you were to do this to this man Wastnidge?—For the money, that was all.

20,136. But what had the man done that he should be blown up more than anybody else?—I don't know, I never saw him in my life till to-day to know him.

20,137. Did they tell why you were to do this mischief in Acorn Street?—I was asked to come to do it.

20,138. What for?—They gave me the money to do it.

20,139. But what was the reason for which you were to do it?—Of course because he was wrong with the trade.

20,140. Did they say so?—Of course they did; they wanted him doing, you know.

20,141. Had Bayles any thing to do with the trade?—He was in the same line, the same as Cutler's; they are all a lot.

20,142. Is Cutler in the same line?—Yes, of course he is.

20,143. Do you know whether Cutler was at work for Hoole's?—It does not matter whether he worked for Hoole's or not? they all join together to do these things, and they get poor b——s like me to do these things, do you see.

20,144. What are you?—A file grinder.

20,145. You say you bought the powder, and put it in a can; do you know where you bought the can?—I do.

20,146. Where?—There was a tin shop at the bottom of the street, and I bought there; it is shut up now.

20,147. Did you buy the can, and the powder, and the fuze the same day that you blew them up, or when did you buy them?—No, I had it in my pocket a day or two before it was done.

20,148. Had anybody ever talked to you besides Cutler at all about blowing him up?—Never.

20,149. Did you know Broadhead?—Do I know Broadhead, poor old lad. I know him well enough, but I never had nought to do with him. I am bad enough and he is and all, but I never had nothing to do with him in my life.

20,150. Did Bagshaw ever talk to you about this matter?—What, Bob Bagshaw?

20,151. No, Charles Bagshaw. Do you see that man who stands up there (*pointing to Bagshaw*)?—Never in my life. I never saw him before.

20,152. Did anybody talk to you at all about doing this, or ask you to do it besides Cutler and Bayles?—I am telling you the truth.

20,153. But I want to know whether anybody ever talked to you about doing this, or asked you to do it besides Cutler and Bayles?—Never.

20,154. Do you know a man called Hellewell?—Aye, he is dead you know.

20,155. Did he ever talk to you about it?—No.

20,156. Did you ever know a man callled Platts?—I have heard speak of him, not to know him.

20,157. You have heard of a man called Thompson being together with those men?—I never saw him to know him.

20,158. Had you ever any talk with him about this matter?—Never.

20,159. Are you quite sure about that?—I am certain.

20,160. Whoever it was that put that can into the window——?—It was me and nobody else. Do not blame anybody but me.

20,161. Listen to what I am going to tell you. Mrs. Wastnidge says she got out of bed and looked out of the window, and saw the persons who had thrown it into the window running away?—She tells a lie then.

20,162. She says there were two at least?—Will you believe me when I am telling the truth? She is telling a lie and I won't.

20,163. Who were the other men?—There was never anybody else, there was me and nobody else, and there was never anybody knowed.

20,164. Mind you have confessed to a murder?—I do not care if I have confessed 10,000 murders; there was nobody but me did that job.

20,165. You have done more, you have confessed to attempting the lives of three persons?—She was soft you know; if she had walked downstairs that would never have been done.

20,166. You are liable now to be tried for those offences, and it is only in the event of our being satisfied that you have told the whole truth about it that you will have your certificate. Having cautioned you in that respect, and having told you what Mrs. Wastnidge said, I ask you again who was with you when you threw that can into the window?—Never a soul. I am telling you all now straight. She has told a lie.

20,167. You need not say that of the poor woman; you have abused her enough?—Look here, if you will believe me, there was never a soul saw that there besides myself, and there was never a soul did it but myself, and she told nought but lies when it went to be tried at York or wherever it went to be tried. You may take that for certain.

20,168. You still persist in that that nobody was with you?—I swear —— Well, if I was to swear it, you would not believe me I think, but there was never a soul besides myself.

20,169. And you never knew Thompson?—I never knew Thompson to know him to be Thompson in all my life. I might be in a public-house with him, but not to know it was Thompson.

20,170. Did you say Cutler had anything to do with it or was with you?—He only had the finding of the money; that is all Cutler had to do with it; that is all I can tell you.

20,171. How did you know that Wastnidge lived at that house?—Because Cutler went with me and showed me the house or else I should not have known. I did not know any more than you did, but he showed me.

20,172. When was it that Cutler showed you?—It might be a week or nine days before.

20,173. How did you happen to be dressed at the time when you did this?—What?

20,174. Did you wear a cap or a hat?—Well, I am sure I cannot tell you, but it is very seldom I wear a hat.

20,174*a*. You very seldom wear a hat?—Generally something like this (*producing his hat*).

20,175. Have you worn a beard always?—Yes.

20,176. As much beard as you wear now?—Yes.

20,177. Always?—Well, for as long a time as I can remember like. It might be that sometimes I would shave it off.

20,178. But at that time when Wastnidge was blown up were you wearing a beard?—I am sure; I am certain.

20,179. Do you happen to recollect what kind of a coat you had on at the time when you did this?—Yes, I can recollect it well.

20,180. What was it?—I was cleaned up a regular swell; I can remember that.

20,181. When you had done it you ran away, you say, to Ebenezer Chapel yard and hid yourself?—Yes.

20,182. As you ran away do you recollect whether your coat came in contact——?—I know what it is before you tell me. That is the biggest lie that ever was told in Sheffield.

20,183. You say that you never came in contact with the cotter of a shutter?—Nought of the sort. When I read that trial, and I read this paper, I knew it was the biggest lie that ever woman told in this world and I am likely to know.

20,184. Did you read that Mrs. Wastnidge said that

the man ran away, and that as he ran away he caught himself by the coat on the cotter of the shutter?—Yes; that was a lie.

20,185. She also said that two persons ran away?—She is telling you lies; there was never any cotter, and there was never two persons, and is not that good enough for anybody?

20,186. You may have a very good reason for telling about yourself, but you know we have private information?—You cannot have private information about this. I am telling you the truth.

20,187. But you may have a reason for concealing?—I am telling you the truth, and I cannot tell you more. There was nobody with me.

20,188. Were you ever in company with Thompson drinking before this happened?—I might be but I do not know Thompson.

20,189. Is Thompson in Court?—I do not know Thompson more than Adam.

20,190. Do you know that man (*pointing to a man*)?—I have seen him before.

20,191. Have you drunk with him?—Yes.

20,192. Did you see him at the time of that outrage with Hoole's men?—I have seen that chap many a time, but I did not know that he was Thompson.

20,193. Now then, were you ever in company with him a short time before this house was blown up?—I cannot say so.

20,194. You cannot?—No.

20,195. Will you swear one way or the other?—I cannot say that ever I was.

20,196. Who did you think that that man was?—There is two to one.

20,197. Who did you think that man was?—I knowed the man when I saw him, but I did not know his name.

20,198. Have you ever been in a public house with him?—Yes.

20,199. Where?—Well, I cannot exactly say where I was with him.

20,200. Have you been at Grew's public house with him?—I cannot say that I have.

20,201. Have you been in company with him and Cutler?—Yes.

20,202. And Cutler and he and you have been together?—Yes.

20,203. How long were you and Cutler and he in company together before Wastnidge was blown up?—I will tell you one thing. I cannot say that, because I do not know.

20,204. About how long?—I will not say.

20,205. Did that man ever talk to you about Hoole's men?—I never had aught to do with Hoole's men.

20,206. Yes you had. Wastnidge was one of Hoole's men?—Well, I never had anything to do with t'others.

20,207. Did he ever ask you to do any mischief to Wastnidge or to beat him?—Never in this world.

20,208. Did he ever offer to go and do the business with you?—No, I never had anybody with me to do that business. I always did that business myself; and if Sam Cutler had been the same as me he ought to have known nought.

20,209. Is this the only "business" you have done in these last ten years?—Yes, the first time in my life.

20,210. But you said just now that you always did them alone?—I said I should do them alone.

20,211. Had you never done anything of the kind before?—Never in my life.

20,212. Then how was it that you did this, never having done anything of the kind before?—Because Sam Cutler came begging and praying, and kept giving me half-crowns and paying for drink and all that, and now you know.

20,213. Was anybody present when you had interviews with Cutler?—No; they got me to come up at the latter end of the week when there was nobody in only Bill Bayles and me and Cutler.

20,214. Where did you meet?—At Joe Green's.

20,215. Always at Joe Green's?—No, not always.

20,216. Where else?—At Blackrock and at several other places; I could tell you a lot more.

20,217. Tell us one?—At the "Clock" at the top of Steelhouse Lane.

20,218. You were in company with Cutler and Bayles?—Yes.

20,219. On those occasions was not Thompson in your company?—He was never in my company to my knowledge.

20,220. He was not?—No; I will give you a straight tip if you will hear me. They have brought those chaps to square Cutler, you understand. I am telling you truth and nought else, and you may ask me any questions you like and I will answer you: I will, I am certain.

20,221. Have you had any quarrel with Cutler?—Yes, I have.

20,222. What has been your quarrel with Cutler?—Why, you know.

20,223. I do not?—Do you not?

20,224. No?—Then I will tell you. You know Cutler never sent me 3*l.* that I ought to have had for the job.

20,225. Then your quarrel has been with Cutler because you have never had the money for doing the job?—Yes.

20,226. And you have had no other quarrel with him?—Never in my life.

20,227. Have you ever demanded the money of him?—Yes.

20,228. Where?—In their entry.

20,229. Have you ever demanded the money of him before people?—Never; never to my knowledge or mind.

20,230. Have you ever told anybody that you had done this before to-day?—I never told a soul, nor never should have done.

20,231. Why did you tell it to-day?—Well, I will tell you the reason for that. I came yesterday, and you were not sitting, and I saw Jacob Twelves and his witnesses, you know, and I could see they were going to do me, you understand, and I thought I would go and say what I know.

20,232. Who is Jacob Twelves? — Why, Sam Cutler.

20,233. Cutler goes by the name of Jacob Twelves, does he?—Yes, he does. A scoundrel like him that will go and beg and pray folks to do things, and then half pay them, and then turn round first on them. That is the reason.

20,234. Then the reason you came here to-day is because you saw Cutler here, and you thought that he was going to tell against you?—I should not have come without.

20,235. Have you had any talk with Cutler about it?—No, I would not speak to him.

20,236. This took place you know in 1862, and here we are in 1867; that is five years ago. Have you never had any quarrel with him at all about the nonpayment of the money up to this time?—I do not doubt that when I have seen him in a public house I would say to him, just as I would say to anybody, "I "want a quid o' thee (that is a sovereign). Thou "hast paid me a pound short." I might say those things.

20,237. Have you said so?—I don't doubt it.

20,238. Do you remember any occasion on which you said so?—I cannot tell you a time; it is often. I will tell you another thing. I once went to their wheel, and he was working, and he came out and he says, "Bob, for God's sake, do not say anything "about this or we shall all be ruined together." He takes me into the "Bridge Inn," and pays for a pint of beer, and gives me half-a-crown, but he would not give me the pound that I wanted; he would not part with it; that was too big, too heavy.

20,239. When was that?—Happens it would be six or nine months after the job.

20,240. But if he was in your power altogether, and you knew all about this, and he knew it, he ought to have paid the money?—He ought to have done.

TWENTY-SECOND DAY.

R. Renshaw.

2 July 1867.

20,241. He was frightened of you, you know?—He was frightened of me, that is true, and he came to me and said, "Here is these Commissioners coming "down, let us be true to one another;" and you would never have known.

20,242. Do you mean if he had paid the sovereign we should never have known?—Well, if he had come and made it all right with me, you know, you would never have known.

20,243. Do you know a person called Scholey, who is a fender grinder?—I might know him, but I do not know him by his name.

20,244. Do you recollect going to Stringer's public house, in Green Lane?—Now, this is all gammon, let me tell you; I will back him to walk Sheffield streets as an honest man.

20,245. Did you ever say at that public house that Bayles and Hellewell and Cutler and Platts had employed you to do the job, and had not paid you?—I will swear on a bag of bibles that I never said such a thing.

20,246. You have said that Bayles and Cutler employed you; did Hellewell employ you?—I never said a word to Hellewell in all my life. It is no good talking about those dead folk. They are on to the dead ones, you understand.

20,247. Do you know Platts?—I do not know Platts. I do not know whether he is dead. I have never seen him in my life.

The *Chairman* inquired whether Edward Platts was in court?

Edward Platts answered, and was ordered to stand up.

20,248 (*To the witness.*) Do you know that man (*pointing to Platts*)?—I have never seen him before.

20,249. Was he one of the men who employed you to do the job?—No, he never was.

20,250. Are you quite sure about it?—I am certain of it.

20,251. Have you ever said that he was?—Never in my life.

20,252. And do you still persist in the story that there was nobody with you at the time when you did this job?—I have told you, haven't I.

20,253. You have, but do you persist in it?—I do.

20,254. And you say that Mrs. Wastnidge is not telling the truth?—I am sure she is not. I am certain of it.

20,255. On which side of the road did you run away, on the same side as the house or on the opposite side?—I can tell you; I banged it through the window, and went away. I got over the opposite railings. That is a lie, you know, of hers.

20,256. Where were you at the time when you threw it through the window?—There is a brewery just a bit above, and there is an entry, and I lit it in the entry; I lit the fuse and threw it through the window, and I walked away.

20,257. On which side of the road did you walk?—Well, now, I cannot tell you that, but I can tell you one thing, that nobody ever want to get their coat lap in, because they cannot do those things so. It is all nonsense.

20,258. When you went and bought the powder did you take a can with you?—No.

20,259. Are you quite sure about that?—Yes; certain.

20,260. Did you never put a can on the counter and say, "Put me two pounds of powder in this can and I will call again shortly"?—No, never in my life, because I bought the powder and put it in my pocket, and I went and bought a can at the bottom of the street here.

20,261. Did you buy it in paper or in what did you buy the powder?—I bought it in paper the same as you would do if you went to buy a pound of the best gunpowder if you were going shooting. You would go and buy the powder, and I did the same.

20,262. Was it shooting powder or blasting powder?—The best powder. Diamond powder.

20,263. Do you know what you gave for it?—I cannot exactly tell you that, but I bought it and I paid for it.

20,264. Have you seen Thompson lately?—Well, I do not know him.

20,265. Yes, you do know him you say?—I do not know him as regards meeting him or nought else. What I mean is, that he could go up the street without my knowing him or thinking he was Thompson.

20,266. Have you seen him at all since he came out of prison?—I cannot say that I have.

20,267. Have you ever spoken to him since he came out of prison?—I cannot say that I have without it is to-day, and I do not know whether it is him or not.

20,268. Do you know Mr. Powell of High Street, a gunsmith?—I know him well enough.

20,269. Did you go to Mr. Powell's to buy a fuse?—Never.

20,270. On the Friday night before Wastnidge was blown up did you go there and ask them if they sold fuses?—No, never in my life.

20,271. Do you know a person of the name of Wilson, a hairdresser, in Snig Hill?—I do not, to my knowledge, you know.

20,272. But do you recollect sometime before this place was blown up going to Mr. Wilson, a hairdresser, in Snig Hill, and asking him if he sold fuses?—I knew better.

20,273. You did not do so?—No.

20,274. Had you ever bought fuses before?—Well, you know I used to be sinking wells at one time when I had nought to do, and that was how I bought fuses, and blew fish up and all.

20,275. How do you mean "blew fish up"?—Why they throw it into the river and blow them up.

20,276. And you are sure that you never said that Hellewell engaged you as well as Bayles?—Hellewell never had nought to do with me. It is all very fine putting it on to dead folks. Don't you have it now. Let me tell you; don't you have it. It is all very well for a person like Sam Cutler.

20,277. Did you ever know a person named Henry Warburton?—I cannot say that I knowed him.

20,278. He lived in George Street, Philadelphia?—I cannot say I never knowed him.

The *Chairman* ordered Warburton to stand forward.

20,279. (*To the witness.*) Do you know that young man? I ask you if you have seen that young man at Mr. Stringer's at the "Ball" Inn in Green Lane?—That is one of Cutler's pals; he has brought him on purpose. I have seen him many a time.

20,280. Did you say to him that you had been engaged by Bayles, and Hellewell, and Cutler?—Never in my life.

20,281. To blow up Wastnidge's place in Acorn Street, and that they had not given you the amount of money they had agreed to give you, and that you would hide Cutler the first time you met him?—I would have done that and worse than that.

20,282. What would you have done?—I would have served him the same as I served the other for agreeing to give me 6*l.* and only giving me 5*l.*

20,283. Then would you have served him the same as you served the other?—Yes, as I served Wastnidge.

20,284. The same as you served an innocent woman?—No, that is all Dick. You agree with me to do a job for you; I get 5*l.* instead of 6*l.* and have something to do to get 5*l.*, and he does not give it me. Now what do you call a man like that?

20,285. I say he does not fulfil his agreement, no doubt; but do you mean to say that if a man did not pay you 1*l.* out of 6*l.* you would have gone and blown his house up and probably killed his lodger, or his wife, or his child?—Look here, I should never have got the 2*l.* but for that.

20,286. But for what?—For what I said to him.

20,287. You merely meant to threaten him then?—It depended you know.

20,288. Do you mean to say you would have blown his house up?—I will not say that.

20,289. But you threatened him with it?—Yes, I did.

20,290. But, however, the reason why you come forward to-day and tell us this story, is because you have seen Cutler here and you thought he was going to tell the story against you?—Yes, that is it and nought else.

20,291. We shall hear what others say; we have heard a good deal about you before you came here?—I know that.

20,292. Therefore, before you leave that chair I tell you this; we shall have to consider whether or not we are satisfied that you have told the truth and the whole truth about this. If we are satisfied we shall give you a certificate, if we are not satisfied we shall not give you a certificate?—What good will a certificate do me when I get it? In the street they all stare at me; they say here is the b—— wretch that has killed a woman.

20,293. A certificate will do you this good; it will prevent your being tried for your life?—We know all about it; we know all that as well can be.

20,294. You do not know perhaps that you are liable to be tried for your life?—I do not care if you try me to-morrow. I would rather put my head into any place than Sheffield.

20,295. You are liable to be tried for murder, and you are liable to be tried for throwing a can of gunpowder into a house with intent to murder George Wastnidge, Mrs. Wastnidge, and also their child. For all those different offences you are liable to be tried; and if we are not satisfied that you are telling the whole truth, we shall not give you a certificate. It is not enough for you to tell us that you did it, if we believe that two persons were concerned in it, and that you know it?—If you will not believe me, and I believe you, how can I help myself.

20,296. You still persist in saying that nobody was with you?—I do, and I tell you now what I told you before.

20,297. You will have no other chance?—I do not want any chance. I have told you truth; if you don't believe me I don't care.

20,298. We cannot do otherwise than endeavour to arrive at the whole truth?—Then what makes you keep boring me, and wanting me to tell you something else, and to tell you a lie?

20,299. In this painful inquiry we have had persons who have come up in the same way that you have come up, and they have only told us half the truth. They have then thought about it, and have come forward and told us the whole truth. At first they came forward and only told half the truth, in order to screen some friend as they thought?—There is no difference with me.

20,300. Do not believe that you do any good to yourself or to others by attempting to screen them, because if you implicate another man, and he comes forward, he has the same chance as you have of being protected by a certificate if he tells the truth?—I have nobody to implicate. I tell you the truth, and if I had I would not; it is straight.

20,301. That is what I am afraid of and that is the reason I have some difficulty, and I daresay my colleagues will have the same, with regard to giving you a certificate. If we think you are not telling the whole truth, we shall not be justified in giving you a certificate?—I have told you the whole truth, and what do you want more.

20,302. Think again?—It is no use thinking.

20,303. If there was another man——?—There never was. Sam Cutler, and me, and Bill Bayles was together, and Sam Cutler is the man that funked the job, and brought the money and paid it.

20,304. Have you been drinking at all this morning?—I have had a glass or two.

20,305. Are you sober?—Yes, I am. I had not a penny in the world, only Mr. Jackson gave me 6*d.* to get a glass with, or else I should not have had one.

The Court directed the witness to be detained for the present.

The witness withdrew.

Samuel Cutler sworn and examined.

S. Cutler.

20,306. (*Chairman.*) What are you?—A fender and stove grinder.

20,307. Have you ever worked at all for Mr. Hoole?—No.

20,308. Are you a member of the union?—Yes.

20,309. Do you know a man of the name of Bayles?—Yes.

20,310. What was he?—A fender grinder.

20,311. Had he anything to do with the union?—Yes.

20,312. What was he?—He was a member of the union.

20,313. Was he a secretary at that time?—No.

20,314. Do you know who was the secretary?—Kenworthy.

20,315. Did you hear of Hoole's men being out on strike?—Yes.

20,316. Did you watch the men whom they had got from Masbro' to work at his place?—No.

20,317. Do you know Thompson?—Yes.

20,318. Did Thompson watch the men?—Not that I am aware of.

20,319. Was Thompson a union man?—Yes.

20,320. Were you very angry with those men who had come from Masbro'?—No, I never spoke to them.

20,321. But were you angry at their breaking the rule and coming and working against the union?—Of course union men do not like it, certainly.

20,322. Did you hear of Mr. Sibray being attacked?—Yes.

20,323. Do you know who did it?—I know what Bayles told me. He did it, he and another.

20,324. Who was the other?—He would not say. I could not get him to tell me.

20,325. But Bayles told you that he and another man beat Sibray?—Yes.

20,326. Then you do not know who attacked Sibray?—Well, I know what Bayles said.

20,327. What did he say?—He said that he and another man did it.

20,328. You say that you know Thompson?—Yes.

20,329. Had you ever any meeting with Thompson with reference to whether you were to attack Sibray or not?—Yes.

20,330. Did Thompson ever ask you to attack Sibray?—No.

20,331. Was anything ever said to you about Sibray?—Yes.

20,332. What was said?—Bayles came to our house to ask me to show him where he lived, and he asked me if I knew where he lived, and I said I did not. He said to me, "Who does?" I said "I do not "know, unless Thompson knows." He said, "Will "you go with me and see?" It was on a Sunday, and so I went. I thought it would be a walk. I went and had a pint of ale, and Thompson came in and he told me where he lived. It was the Spital Hill Road. He went with me. He said if I would stop there while he cleaned himself he would go with me.

20,333. Did Thompson show you the house?—Yes.

20,334. Now I am going to ask you some questions which are very serious indeed. You know I daresay that if you give a true statement of all you know concerning any offence which you may have committed, and if you tell the truth and the whole truth, and everything you know about it, we have the power, if we are satisfied that you are telling the truth, to grant you a certificate, which will protect you from all proceedings either criminal or civil. Therefore if you

TWENTY-SECOND DAY.

S. Cutler.

2 July 1867.

like to tell us all you know about any offence of which you have been guilty, you will get the certificate, if we are satisfied that you have told the truth. But if you do not satisfy us the certificate will be withheld, and if you have no certificate and it is proved that you have committed any of these offences, you will be liable to be tried for them now. Be on your guard and tell the truth. Now you say you asked Thompson to point out Sibray's house and he pointed it out?—Yes.

20,335. Did you say who was to do the job?—No, I think not.

20,336. Did you say who was to do the job?—No, he said "He is just the man I want doing, him and "old Hoole." That is, Thompson told me, that Sibray and Hoole were just the men that he wanted doing.

20,337. Did you say that you knew a party who would kill all the lot for 5*l.* or so?—Well, I am not aware that I did. I was fresh when we were talking about it.

20,338. I am speaking of Sibray. Did you ever say that you knew a person who would "do" them all for 5*l.*?—Not that I am aware of.

20,339. Will you swear that you did not?—Not that I am aware of.

20,340. Will you swear that you did not?—When do you mean?

20,341. Before Sibray was attacked and you had the house pointed out to you, did you on that occasion when he said that he wanted Sibray and Hoole "doing," say that you knew a man who for 5*l.* would "do" them all?—No.

20,342. Did you say anything about doing Sibray on that occasion?—He got agate talking about Hoole first, and he said, "There is Hoole; I have watched "Hoole. He is watched home by a policeman. He "is turned over from one to the other, but he is to "be got at." "How is that?" I said, and he said, "Knock a brick out of his greenhouse and upset it."

20,343. That was as to Mr. Hoole?—Yes.

20,344. Did you offer to beat Sibray?—No.

20,345. And you did not beat him?—No.

20,346. And you do not know who did, unless it was Bayles?—I know Bayles told me that. That is all I know about it.

20,347. After Sibray was beaten, do you recollect some persons of the name of Hulse and others being beaten at Portmahon?—I have heard talk about it.

20,348. Where have you heard talk about it?—I have heard Bayles say so.

20,349. Have you heard anybody else say so?—I cannot pretend to say now.

20,350. Did he tell you who had done it?—No.

20,351. Did you know who had done it?—No.

20,352. Did you never inquire who had done it?—No, I did not want to know.

20,353. You were taking a strong part in the matter at that time were you not?—I did not want to know who had done it.

20,354. Why not?—Because I wanted to be out of that.

20,355. You knew that those men were going to be attacked, did you know what it was for?—For going out knobsticking.

20,356. After you had heard of those men being attacked, did it ever occur to you to do anything at all to Wastnidge?—No farther than I got that 6*l.*

20,357. Who gave you that 6*l.*?—Robinson, that is Bayles gave it me.

20,358. Who is Robinson?—He is secretary now.

20,359. Robinson, you said, first gave you 6*l.*?—No, it is a mistake.

20,360. Will you swear that Robinson did not give you 6*l.*?—Yes.

20,361. Who gave you the 6*l.*?—Bayles.

20,362. Did Bayles at the time when he gave you the 6*l.* tell you what it was for?—Yes.

20,363. What did he say that it was for?—To welt those fellows with. I asked him what it was for. He said "To welt those fellows with."

20,364. But you must have had some talk beforehand as to what was to be done?—I never heard a word about it.

20,365. When was it that he gave you the 6*l.*?—Coming out of the "King William."

20,366. Tell us what happened?—I saw Robinson give Bayles some money, but I do not know what it was. When we got outside he said, "Here take care of this. Thou art more capable of taking care of it than I am." I said "What is it for?" He said "It is to welt those fellows with."

20,367. What did you say to that?—Well I kept it. I am not sure whether it was a week or a fortnight.

20,368. What became of it last? did you go to any club meetings of the trade?—Yes.

20,369. Where did you go?—The "King William."

20,370. Who was the secretary at that time?—Robinson; Kenworthy was secretary, but Robinson was acting for him at that time.

20,371. Did you tell Robinson that you had got the money?—No.

20,372. Had you any talk to Robinson about it?—Never.

20,373. Did he give you any instruction?—Never.

20,374. And you went to the "King William," and there you went to a club meeting, did you meet Bayles again there?—Yes, he was there, and when we came away he said to me, "Hast heard about yon Redman?" I says "What is that?" He says, "He "has been in the public house bragging that he "would break the union up. I should like to give "him one or two."

20,375. Whom did they mean by "Redman"?—They call him "Redman" for a nickname. Wastnidge has red hair. I said I would have nothing to do with it. He said, "Well, then go with me to Joe "Green's. I think I can find one there that will "do it, if we can see him," and I said I did not care and I went with him. When we got there he was sitting there. There were two other men in the room.

20,376. Who were they?—There was an old man and a middle aged man.

20,377. What were their names?—One was Renshaw.

20,378. And who besides?—I am sure I cannot tell you the name of the old man.

20,379. Not Thompson?—No; we sat a bit, and then he called for a pint of ale and then Bayles went out and beckoned this Renshaw out, and they were out the best part of five minutes I should think, and then they beckoned me out and we went into the kitchen. There was nobody there and then Bayles got agate talking about this here thumping of those fellows; and he said that he reckoned nought of thumping of them—that it took no effect upon them. He did not say that. He talked more vulgar than that. He said we had better give them a bit of powder. I told him I would have nothing to do with it. He said, "Thou art up to nothing."

20,380. Was anything said about money?—Yes, he said he would do it for 10*l.*

20,381. Who said that?—Renshaw, and 5*l.* if it missed. I did not know what "missing" meant then, that is if he did not go in I suppose. I do not know.

20,382. He wanted 10*l.* and 5*l.* if it missed, that is to say if the thing did not blow up?—Yes.

20,383. If it was a failure he was to have 5*l.*, and if it was a success he was to have 10*l.*?—Yes.

20,384. What was said to that?—I told him that we would give this to give him a good thrashing or another 5*l.*

20,385. Where were you to get your money from?—I would get it from Bayles.

20,386. What did he say to that?—He hummed and ha'ed, and then a woman came in and we all three went away, Bayles and all, and he went right away; and when we were going away Bayles said to me, "I will see thee again to-morrow," and he never came.

20,387. How long was that before Wastnidge was blown up?—This was on the Tuesday night.

20,388. When was he blown up?—On the Saturday morning or Friday night.

20,389. What happened next?—He came to me about 4 o'clock the same day, Saturday.

20,390. Who did that?—Bayles.

20,391. What did he say to you?—He said, "I reckon thou hast heard of it."

20,392. Was that after the blowing up?—Yes.

20,393. What did you say?—I said I had heard of it of course. I said, "What have you done it for?" He said, "We could not get to him without, so we thought we would give him a bit of powder."

20,394. Was anything more said?—I told him he had done wrong.

20,395. Did he tell you who was there at the time when they had done this?—No.

20,396. Did he say that he and Renshaw were together when it was done?—He did not quite say it out. He talked in that way as if he were with him.

20,397. What kind of a man was Bayles?—He was a tall thinnish fellow.

20,398. Was he a taller man than Renshaw?—Yes.

20,399. Is he at all like Thompson?—He is as tall as I am very near. I should say he is about five feet eight or nine.

20,400. And he talked as if they had both done it?—Yes, he did.

20,401. Did you never have any talk to Bayles afterwards and ask him how they had done it?—He said they ran down the street, and he said they never saw a watchman while they got down the Wicker, and he said it was a good job they did not.

20,402. Then Bayles told you he was there too?—As good.

20,403. He told you that he was there?—Yes.

20,404. He said that they ran away together?—That was what he said.

20,405. Did he say that either of them went into the Ebenezer chapel yard?—No; he never said a word about it. He said he had some pistols with him and he would have blown the first man's brains out that they had seen if anybody had tackled to him.

20,406. It was Bayles that said that, was it?—He said Renshaw would.

20,407. But who had the pistols?—I suppose Renshaw had them by that.

20,408. But did he say whether he had them or Renshaw had them?—He did not say.

20,409. But one of them had pistols?—Yes.

20,410. Just repeat what he said?—He said they never met a watchman while they got down the Wicker, and that it was a good job, for if any watchman had tackled him he would have blown his brains out.

20,411. He did not say which would have done it?—He did not.

20,412. Are you quite sure that he said that Renshaw was there at the time that that was done?—Yes.

20,413. Did you ever speak to Renshaw about it afterwards?—I never saw him while the day after or the day but one. I would not be certain which it was, when he came for the money.

20,414. Bayles and he?—Yes.

20,415. Did you pay them?—Yes; I paid Bayles.

20,416. How much did you pay them?—I gave them 6*l.*

20,417. Was anything said about more being paid?—Yes; he said he should want another pound. He said he had agreed to do it for 7*l.*

20,418. Who said that?—Bayles. He said that he had agreed to do it with Renshaw for 7*l.*, and he said he wanted the other pound.

20,419. What did you say then?—I said I would have nothing to do with it. I said I did not engage him to do it. I said what I engaged him for was to do a thumping, and that I would have nothing to do with it. He said he would make that right.

20,420. Who said that?—Bayles.

20,421. Had you ever told Thompson, when speaking about Wastnidge, that you knew a person who would kill all the lot for 5*l.* or so?—Well, if I did, that was while we were at Wylie's, there when we were fresh. I will not swear whether I did or no. Thompson was talking that there ought to be something done.

20,422. And did you say that you knew a party who would kill all the lot for 5*l.* or so?—I said we had offered them 5*l.* to come out and they wanted 20*l.*

20,423. But did you at Wylie's shop say that you knew a party who would kill all the lot for 5*l.* or so?—I am not aware of it.

20,424. Will you swear that you did not say so?—No, I will not swear it. We were all getting fresh, so I will not swear it.

20,425. Did Thompson say that he knew a party who did not care about killing a chap and did he name him to Platts?—I did not hear him.

20,426. Did you and Platts say that Thompson was to see him?—Not that I am aware of.

20,427. Do you know a person called John Aldam?—Well, I did not know him while this week. I did not know him by name, but I had seen him.

20,428. Did you know him as "Slipper Jack"?—No, I did not.

20,429. Was his name mentioned to you?—Never; not in my hearing. If it was at Wylie's, it was not a very fitting place to name such things as this.

20,430. I think so too. Did Thompson ask you to send a man?—No.

20,431. Did you do anything in concert with Thompson?—No.

20,432. Did Thompson know anything about this matter being done to Wastnidge?—Not that I am aware of.

20,433. Will you swear that he did not?—Not that I am aware of.

20,434. Do you mean to say that you allowed Thompson to be tried for his life and that you knew that Bayles and this man had done it, and that you never came forward to give evidence to protect that man from the consequences of that verdict?—Well, we did the best we could for him as far as getting him a counsellor.

20,435. What did you do?—We got him a counsellor.

20,436-7. Who got him a counsellor?—I believe it was amongst us.

20,438. Which of you?—We all paid a pound a apiece, and then it was paid out of the box.

20,439. How much money did you raise?—I am certain I cannot tell you.

20,440. But about how much?—I have no idea.

20,441. How much did you raise for defending Thompson?—I could not swear how much it was.

20,442. But about how much was it?—It might be 60*l.* or 70*l.*

20,443. And who subscribed 1*l.* a piece out of the box, the trade—did it come out of the union?—Yes.

20,444. And you got him a counsellor?—Yes.

20,445. Do you mean to say that the trade defended Thompson?—Yes.

20,446. What business was it of Thompson's, or of the trade's, if Thompson had nothing to do with it?—They thought he was innocent.

20,447. Why did they think so?—I do not know,

20,448. Did you tell them you had done it?—No.

20,449. Then how did they know?—I do not know.

20,450. How did they happen to subscribe?—I do not know. We did it together, and at one meeting we agreed to gather 1*l.* a-piece and pay it out of the box.

20,451. Who did it?—We were all alike.

20,452. And you all agreed to pay him 1*l.* a-piece out of your pockets?—Yes.

20,453. And was the remainder to come out of the funds of the union?—Yes.

20,454. And who was the attorney whom you employed? what lawyer had you? was it Mr. Broadbent?—Yes, I think it was Mr. Broadbent.

20,455. Do you know who saw Mr. Broadbent?—Hellewell.

TWENTY-SECOND DAY.

S. Cutler.

2 July 1867.

20,456. Then did you tell Hellewell that this man was innocent?—No.

20,457. Did you not tell him that you knew that Thompson had nothing, to do with it?—I cannot recollect it.

20,458. Mind what you are about. Do you mean to say that you, knowing that you had engaged these men simply to beat Wastnidge, and not to do more, and they having done something which you had not instructed them to do, you did not go and tell Hellewell that this man Thompson was innocent?—No.

20,459. You never told him?—No.

20,460. Did Hellewell know it?—I do not know.

20,461. Have you talked to Hellewell about it?—No, I never have.

20,462. Was Hellewell at all mixed up in these matters with you?—Never.

20,463. Did Hellewell know that you had received money from Bayles?—I do not know whether he knew that or not.

20,464. Will you swear he did not know that you had received money from Bayles?—I cannot say whether he was in the room or not.

20,465. Was it at the "King William"?—Yes.

20,466. Was Hellewell there a short time before?—Not that I recollect.

20,467. Will you swear he was not there?—I I cannot swear it.

20,468. Be cautious. Was Hellewell there at the time when Bayles paid you the money?—I cannot swear it.

20,469. You make yourself now by your own confession liable for having engaged men to do mischief to another man. They may have exceeded your instructions, but you have rendered yourself liable to that. Now I ask you whether Hellewell was there when Bayles paid you that money?—I will not swear it.

20,470. Do you believe that he was there?—I cannot say. There was a room full, and I did not take notice of them.

20,471. Do you not know that Hellewell saw the money paid?—No, I do not.

20,472. Do you not believe it?—I do not know.

20,473. Do you not believe that Hellewell saw the money paid?—No, because I do not know.

20,474. Did you not tell Hellewell that they had exceeded your instructions, and that you had only engaged them to give him a beating?—No.

20,475. Did you say nothing of the kind to him?—I do not know that I ever spoke a word to him about it.

20,476. And you say that you only instructed them to give Wastnidge a beating?—That is all.

20,477. What did you point out the house to them for?—It was Bayles that pointed out the house.

20,478. Did you not point out the house?—No.

20,479. How do you know that Bayles pointed out the house?—What house?

20,480. Wastnidge's house?—I never knew where Wastnidge lived.

20,481. Are you quite sure that you never went and pointed out the house where Wastnidge lived?—I never knew where he did live.

20,482. Nor yet the house where he was blown up?—No.

20,483. You never pointed it out?—No, never.

20,484. Renshaw says that you pointed out the house?—Never in this world.

20,485. Renshaw says that you told him to buy three pounds of powder, and that he only bought one pound, is that so?—I never saw him after he went out of Joe Green's while it was done.

20,486. But did you tell him to buy three pounds of powder?—No, I never told him anything of the kind.

20,487. Did you give him money to buy powder with?—No.

20,488. Did you give him 10*s.*?—No.

20,489. Was Bayles with you when you gave him 10*s.*?—No.

20,490. Will you swear that?—Yes.

20,491. Did you know that Renshaw was going to buy powder?—No.

20,492. Will you swear that?—Yes.

20,493. Have you ever heard Renshaw say that he had done it?—I have never seen him since; I saw him in Hill Street once.

20,494. Did he ever ask you for the 1*l.*?—Yes, he asked me yesterday.

20,495. Yesterday?—No, about six months after it was done.

20,496. Six months after it was done he asked you for the powder?—Yes; there was him and Bayles together.

20,497. What did you say to that?—I said I did not engage him, he must ask Bayles to pay him; Bayles said he would make it all right.

20,498. Had you had any quarrel with Renshaw about it?—I never saw him.

20,499. Did he speak to you yesterday?—Yes.

20,500. What did he say to you yesterday?—He said I ought to go to hell for snitching.

20,501. What is snitching?—Telling.

20,502. Yesterday he said that you ought to go to hell for snitching?—Yes.

20,503. What did you say to that?—I told him it was his own fault.

20,504. How was it his own fault?—I told him I had heard he had been up and down telling it in public-houses.

20,505. What did he say to that?—He said it were a b——y lie.

20,506. What did you say to that?—I said no more to him; I walked away.

20,507. Did he say what he would do to you yesterday?—No, he did not to me.

20,508. Did he ask you where you had heard it told in public-houses?—No, that was all that passed between us.

20,509. Where was that?—Just at the top of the steps here.

20,510. He said that you deserved going to hell for snitching?—Yes.

20,511. Did he at all allude to any person whom you had with you?—No, I was with myself. He might have said something more, but there were policemen just outside, and he did not say any more.

20,512. What was the reason that all this was done to this poor man Wastnidge?—I believe it was because he was a knobstick.

20,513. Have you had any conversation with Broadhead about his being a knobstick?—I have not.

20,514. Have you had any conversation with Mr. Bagshaw?—No.

20,515. You were in the fender trade?—Yes.

20,516. What had Broadhead and Bagshaw to do with going down to Hoole's?—I believe they were chosen out.

20,517. Whom by?—I believe by two or three of our trade.

20,518. Wastnidge had had nothing to do with either Bagshaw or Broadhead, he was a fender man. What had they to do with it?—A deputation went to them.

20,519. A deputation went to whom?—To Broadhead.

20,520. What had Broadhead to do with it?—I do not know.

20,520*a*. Have you ever done anything for Broadhead?—No.

20,521. Have you ever done any job of this kind before?—Never in my life.

20,522. Have you paid any man to do a job of this kind?—No.

20,523. You have never paid any money for beating any man?—No.

20,524. And you never hired others to beat?—Yes. No (*the witness hesitated*).

20,525. What do you mean by that? Have you ever hired any person to beat another?—No, sir.

20,526. Had you anything to do with the beating of Sibray?—No.

20,527. Had you anything to do with Wastnidge being beaten?—No.

20,528. Nor Cooper, nor Hooles, nor Bailey ?—No.

20,529. You had nothing to do with any of these men ?—No, never.

20,530. Was any man beaten at the time of the strike with Hoole's men, that you are aware of ?—Yes, Sibray was beaten.

20,531. Had you anything to say to that ?—(*Hesitating*) No.

20,532. Did you know anything of that ?—Bayles sent me to Thompson to see where he lived, and Thompson went and showed me.

20,533. Do you know any person who joined in beating him at all ?—No.

20,534. Do you know anything else that was done by anybody connected with these trades unions ?—No.

20,535. You know of nothing else that has been done ?—No.

20,536. Do you know who wrote those letters ?—No.

20,537. Have you seen them ?—I am no scholar myself.

20,538. Has anybody told you that he had read letters that were sent to Hoole or his men, saying that it would be worse for them if they did not give up work ?—No.

20,539. Were you one of the pickets who were employed to stand and watch ?—No.

20,540. Then how was it that you received money from Bayles to hire Renshaw ?—I did not hire him, only to be thumped.

20,541. Did he never say that thumping would be no use ?—Yes.

20,542. He did say that ?—Renshaw said it would take no effect upon him ; better give him a bit of powder.

20,543. He told you that ?—Yes.

20,544. What did you say to that ?—I said it was no good. He said he would do it for a sovereign. I said it would be no good. I said, we will give you five sovereigns for giving him a thumping and another pound.

20,545. You never told Renshaw not to blow him up ?—No.

20,546. He told you that powder was the thing. He said that thumping him would do him no good, and you said that you would have nothing to say to that. Did you tell him not to blow him up ?—Who do you mean ?

20,547. Renshaw ?—Yes, I said I would have nothing to do with it.

20,548. Did you say that you would give him no money if he blew him up ?—No, I did not say anything to him.

20,549. And when you knew that he had blown him up you still gave him the money ?—I gave Bayles what I had.

20,550. What business had you to do that ?—I wanted to be shut of it.

20,551. You got shut of it by making yourself responsible for the act ?—I gave him the money.

20,552. But still you paid him for it ?—I gave him the money.

20,553. Was Platts present at any of these meetings about paying and engaging to blow Wastnidge up ?—Never a soul but us three. There was an old man.

20,554. Who was the old man ?—I do not know who the old man was.

20,555. You swear that ?—Yes.

20,556. And Robinson was never present at your meetings ?—Never.

20,557. Was not Platts present at the conversation at Wylie's ?—Yes.

20,558. Do you ever recollect Aldam passing by and Platts saying to you that he would not be a bad chap for the job ?—No.

20,559. Nothing of that kind ever occurred ?—No.

20,560. And you swear that ?—Yes.

20,561. Thompson had nothing to do with it. ?—I think not.

20,562. Will you swear that he had not anything to do with it ?—I had nothing to do with engaging him.

20,563. Had he anything to do with blowing up Wastnidge's house ?—I cannot say ; he might be with Renshaw.

20,564. How could he be with Renshaw when Bayles was with Renshaw ?—I do not know.

20,565. Do you believe that there were three ?—I do not know anything about it.

20,566. Have you ever heard Bayles say that there were three ?—No.

20,567. Have you ever heard anybody say that Thompson was there ?—No, never.

20,568. Do you believe that he was there ?—No, I do not. I believe it was Bayles and him.

20,569. You believe that it was Bayles and Renshaw ?—I do. I believe these were the two.

20,570. You say that the trade subscribed. Did all the members, 60 of you, subscribe to pay the 60*l.*—There were not 60 of us.

20,571. How many subscribed ? have you got a list ?—No.

20,572. Who was the man who kept the list ?—Robinson will have the list.

20,573. The list of the money which they subscribed ?—Yes.

20,574. How much was subscribed ?—I am sure I cannot tell you ; perhaps 30*l.*

20,575. 30*l.* was subscribed, and how much more was paid by the union ?—I cannot say.

20,576. This was a trade matter. Did you talk at all about it ?—We said we wanted to help him out.

20,577. Why should you help Thompson ?—They thought he was innocent.

20,578. But what has that to do with the trade ?—We try to help one another.

20,579. If a man goes and blows up another's house, or steals a man's watch, or commits a highway robbery, you do not defend him ; it is only when he does something connected with the trade ; is not that so ?—That is right.

20,580. Then why should you defend Thompson ?—Because they thought he had nothing to do with it.

20,581. Did you think that he had done something for the trade ?—It did not do for me to think. I thought he had not anything to do with it.

20,582. You thought that he had not anything to do with it ?—Yes.

20,583. But did you think that it was a trade matter ?—No.

20,584. You knew that it was ?—No, I did not.

20,585. Yes, you did ?—No ; it was not intended to be a blowing up.

20,586. It was a trade matter, though they exceeded your instructions ?—It would be a trade matter ; that is right enough.

20,587. It was a trade matter, but they exceeded your instructions ; your instructions were to thump him ?—Yes.

20,588. And instead of thumping they put in a can of powder ?—Yes.

20,589. And the man whom you told to thump, told you that that would be of no use, but that a can of powder would be necessary, and you paid him afterwards ?—Yes, I paid him what money I had on me ; he wanted 7*l.*, but I would not give it him.

20,590. On your oath did not you know quite well that he was going to blow that man up ?—No, I did not.

20,591. Mind, if we do not believe you you will not get a certificate ?—I am speaking the truth.

20,592. On your oath did not you believe that that man was going to be blown up ?—No, not while it was done.

20,593. On your oath had not you resolved amongst yourselves to blow him up ?—No, I never heard it named.

20,594. Yes you had heard it named, because he had said, "Better do him at home and give him a little powder." On your oath had not you deliberated about the mode in which it should be done ?—No.

TWENTY-SECOND DAY.

S. Cutler.

2 July 1867.

20,595. Nothing of the kind ?—No ; unless it was done after I left him, and they did not engage to do that when I was there. Both of them wanted to do it.

20,596. Both Bayles and Renshaw wanted to blow him up ?—Yes.

20,597. They both urged it upon you as the right thing to do ?—Yes, they wanted to urge it on me, and I would not hear of it.

20,598. And they were very anxious to do it ?—Yes, the pair of them.

20,599. Both of them ?—Yes.

20,600. They said that it was of no use thumping him ; that that was the only way to do the business ?—Renshaw said thumping took no effect upon him.

20,601. You never said that if they did anything like blowing up his house you would not pay them ?—No, I did not say that.

20,602. Did not you believe when they went away that they were going to blow his house up ?—No ; he said that he would see me on the Monday, and he never came.

20,603. Had you talked at all to Thompson about beating him ?—I cannot remember stating about it.

20,604. Will you swear that you have not talked to him about it ?—Unless it was at Wylie's.

20,605. Will you swear that you never called at Wylie's to ask Thompson to beat him ?—No ; I was fresh. I will not swear that at all.

20,606. Will you swear that you did not ask Thompson to beat Wastnidge ?—Yes, I did.

20,607. You did ask him ?—No, I say I will swear that.

20,608. You will swear that you did not ask him to beat Wastnidge ?—No, nothing of the kind ; he said that there ought to be something done.

20,609. Thompson said that ?—Thompson said that the whole night through.

20,610. Was Thompson anxious that he should be blown up ?—He never named blowing up.

20,611. What did he want ?—He wanted him to be thumped.

20,612. Did Platts ever say that something must be done to prevent him working ?—Not that I recollect.

20,613. Will you swear that he did not ?—No, I will not.

20,614. Was Platts also for having something done to him ?—No.

20,615. I caution you about this ; did Platts ever say anything about something being done to him ?—No.

20,616. He never said that something must be done ?—No, I never heard him.

20,617. You had known all along that it was Renshaw who did it ?—I had known what Bayles said when I paid him that money.

20,618. You never told your people ?—No.

20,619. You never mentioned it at your committee ?—No.

20,620. You never told the club that Thompson was innocent and that you knew it ?—No.

20,621. Would you have allowed him to be hanged if he had been found guilty, for he was very near it ?—I passed my word and he would have had to take his chance.

20,622. You had passed your word and he would have had to take his chance ?—Yes, I passed my word to Bayles and Renshaw.

20,623. You passed your word to Bayles and Renshaw that you would never divulge it ?—Yes.

20,624. And if Thompson had been hanged you would never have come forward to help him ?—I might have come forward, it might have made a difference.

20,625. You believe that he would have had to take his chance ?—I hoped it would not be so.

20,626. Supposing that he had been found guilty, what would you have done ?—I should not have felt very comfortable, still it was not my fault.

20,627. You as an innocent man could have come forward and said that Thompson was perfectly innocent, and that you knew the men who did it, and you could have come and said who the men were. I believe that the majority of people believe that Thompson did it to this moment—he has changed his name, has he not, in consequence ?—Not that I am aware of.

20,628. Will you swear that only two men were in it, and that those two men were Bayles and Renshaw ?—Yes.

20,629. You do not believe that Thompson was there ?—I do not.

20,630. Do you believe that any more money was paid besides the money that you paid ?—I do not believe there was.

20,631. Did you see Kenworthy about it ?—I never saw Kenworthy at all—he was badly a long while.

20,632. Did you see Robinson about it ?—About what ?

20,633. About this business ?—About it being done ?

20,634. Yes ?—No.

20,635. Did Robinson subscribe ?—Yes.

20,636. Was Robinson the man who managed the funds and who employed the attorney ?—He was acting while Kenworthy was bad.

20,637. Was he the man who got the money ?—Yes.

20,638. Have you ever had any conversation with Robinson about it since ?—No, never. I never heard it named.

20,639. (*Mr. Barstow.*) Where is the club meeting held ?—At the "King William."

20,640. Who were on your committee at this time ?—I do not know.

20,641. Were you on the committee at this time ?—Not that I am aware of.

20,642. You were on the committee were you not ?—He had been badly a long while; I do not think there was a committee at that time.

20,643. Were you not on the committee at that time ?—No, I cannot swear that.

20,644. Will you swear that you were not on the committee ?—No, I will not, because I do not know.

20,645. Have you ever been on the committee ?—I do not know.

20,646. You do not know whether you have been on the committee or not ?—I have been on the committee that is certain, but I will not swear whether I was on the committee then or not.

20,647. Do you know who was on the committee then ?—No, I do not.

20,648. Who generally takes the chair at your meetings ?—There is a fresh chairman every week.

20,649. Who most commonly took the chair at this time ?—I cannot swear to speak the truth.

20,650. Do you remember being in company with Thompson the Sunday before Sibray was beaten ?—I was never with him but one Sunday, that was when I went down to ask where Bayles was living.

20,651. Was that the Sunday before Sibray was beaten ?—I cannot say, I do not think it was.

20,652. Do you know whether it was before he was beaten or after he was beaten that you were in company with Thompson ?—I went down to tell him to do it, that would be before.

20,653. Did you ask Thompson if he knew where Sibray lived ?—Yes.

20,654. Did Thompson go with you and show you the house ?—Yes.

20,655. What did you want to know where he lived for ?—Bayles came to the house and asked me.

20,656. What did he want to know for ?—Bayles's wanting to know.

20,657. Bayles wanted to know is one thing, but why did you want to know ?—He asked me whether I knew where he lived.

20,658. That is no answer to my question, why did he want to know where he lived ?—He wanted to give him a thumping.

20,659. Did you want to know Sibray's house in order to tell Bayles where it was ?—Yes.

TWENTY-SECOND DAY.

S. Cutler.

2 July 1867.

20,660. And you knew at that time that Bayles wanted to give him a thumping ?—Yes.

20,661. Where were these conversations in the "King William" held ?—Whose ?

20,662. These conversations that you had in the "King William" with Bayles and Renshaw ?—I never told them at the "King William."

20,663. (*Chairman.*) Where were your conversations ? in what public house were they ?—At Joe Green's.

20,664. (*Mr. Barstow.*) Have you ever talked on the subject at the "King William" ?—No, never.

20,665. Have you ever heard it said in the "King William" that something was to be done ?—No, never.

20,666. You say you knew all this time that Thompson was innocent ?—I said I thought so.

20,667. Were you aware whether Thompson was expelled from the fender grinders' union ?—Yes, I believe he was.

20,668. Were you present at the meeting when he was expelled ?—No.

20,669. What was he expelled for ?—Because he had been saying falsehoods.

20,670. What year was he expelled ?—I cannot tell you.

20,671. (*Chairman.*) It was for a statement that he had made to Mr. Jackson ?—Yes.

20,672. (*Mr. Barstow.*) Do not you know when he was expelled ?—No.

20,673. Was it after he came back from York ?—Yes.

20,674. Do you know what was said at the meeting when he was expelled ?—I was not there.

20,675. Do you know what was said ?—No, I do not.

20,676. Do you know the grounds on which he was expelled ?—No, I do not.

20,677. Do you know how long it was after he came back from York ?—I have no idea.

20,678. Do not you know that it was the spring after he came back from York that he was expelled ?—I cannot say, but I know he was working at navvying before he came back again.

20,679. Was not it owing to the scandal created in the town from the blowing up in Acorn Street that he was expelled from the fender grinders' union ?—I am not aware of it.

20,680. What was the ground on which you heard he was expelled ?—It was because he had been making a false statement to Jackson.

20,681. (*Chairman.*) What was the falsehood that he had been stating to Jackson ?—I cannot say.

20,682. Who made a complaint of the falsehood ?—I believe it was Platts.

20,683. (*Mr. Barstow.*) Was Thompson at the meeting when he was expelled ?—I never saw Thompson there. I was not there myself.

20,684. Were not you all warned to attend the meeting ?—For two or three weeks, I never went after that.

20,685. What was the reason of that ?—Because I did not like to face it.

20,686. You thought that you knew too much ?—Yes.

20,687. What was it in Thompson's statement that gave offence to the union ?—Something had been said about Platts ; to tell the truth I hardly know what was said.

20,688. You know nothing about it ?—No.

20,689. You only know that he was expelled ?—I only know that he was expelled.

20,690. (*Mr. Chance.*) You said just now that you, Platts, and Thompson were at Wylie's ?—Yes.

20,691. Did not Platts, when you were at Wylie's together, say that something must be done ?—No ; Thompson kept saying that.

20,692. Was Platts listening and joining in the conversation at that time ?—There was a room full of company ; the room was right full—it was in the dram shop.

20,693. Were you, Platts, and Thompson together ?—Yes.

20,694. Were you talking together ?—Yes.

20,695. If Thompson said that, did Platts agree with what he said ?—I never heard that.

20,696. Did he disagree or not ?—I do not know that he said anything ; he said it many a time to me about there ought to be something done when we got a little fresh.

20,697. You say that you knew a man of the name of Aldam by the name of "Slipper Jack" ?—I never saw him ; I saw him when I came in here.

20,698. Did not you see him before ?—No.

20,699. Did you not know him as "Slipper Jack" ?—I heard talk of him.

20,700. When you, Thompson, and Platts were together at Wylie's, do you not remember a man passing by ?—No.

20,701. Did you see a man passing by there then or any time after, and was your attention called to him ?—No.

20,702. Did you hear Thompson speak about Aldam ?—I cannot say that I did.

20,703. Or "Slipper Jack"—I never heard his name while within a fortnight or so. I know nothing about him.

20,704. Do you remember a man being pointed out and Platts saying that he would not be a bad man for the job ?—I never heard him say so.

20,705. And then that Thompson said he would choose him if he must choose anybody ?—I never heard such a thing said.

20,706. Are you sure that you did not ?—I am certain.

20,707. Are you sure that Platts did not say that in your presence ?—No.

20,708. Did you hear Thompson say anything about Aldam at the meeting at Wylie's or any meeting after ?—No, never ; he had all the talking to himself. It was all his talk that there was something to be done.

20,709. Did Platts say nothing was to be done ?—I did not hear him.

20,710. Did he seem to agree with Thompson that something must be done ?—He said very little to him.

20,711. (*Chairman.*) Do you know anything about a man called Ripley ?—No.

20,712. Was he a man who worked for Hoole ?—I do not know.

20,713. You do not know anything about it ?—No.

20,714. Were you ever asked to blow anybody else up ?—No.

20,715. Were you ever asked anything about any person's house except Wastnidge's ?—No.

20,716. Do you know Ripley's house ?—No.

20,717. You never were asked about Ripley's house ?—No.

20,718. Did you ever attend a club meeting at the "King William" before Sibray was hurt ?—Many a one.

20,719. And do you recollect it being agreed by several persons that something must be done to Sibray at that meeting ?—No, I never heard such a thing named.

20,720. Did you hear it mentioned at any meeting that you had there that a boy called "James Dolphin's boy" had been engaged. Not there, I did not.

20,721. Where did you hear it ?—Thompson came down to the wheel and called me out of the wheel and told me of it.

20,722. Thompson called you out of your wheel and told you that Dolphin's boy had been engaged ?—Yes, he said, "We have been at Platt's and we must "meet him this afternoon, and he wanted to know "whether I would go with him." I said, "I would," that was in the forenoon. I had not come back, and he sent over between 3 and 4 o'clock. I got there at 4 o'clock, and we agreed to meet at Platt's. We

TWENTY-SECOND DAY.

S. Cutler.

2 July 1867.

met there, and we went down to Dolphin's till he came down the lane, and when he came, we asked him what he was going to do about the boy. He said that it was his wife's fault. Platts said something to him, that he knew he was doing wrong by letting him go; he said that it was his wife's fault, and it would be stopped altogether when he got home, and he would see what his wife said.

20,723. That was all that passed?—We were to see him again that night but I never went.

20,724. Did not Thompson say that something must be done; what was to be done?—He wanted to know what would be done about the boy.

20,725. If he did not send him away what were you to do?—I do not know that anything was to be done.

20,726. Did Dolphin satisfy you?—Yes.

20,727. How?—He said he should cut away; he should not go any more.

20,728. That was his own son?—Yes.

20,729. And he got him away?—Yes; he said it was his own wife's fault.

20,730. Did you threaten him, if he did not get him away?—Not the least bit in the world.

20,731. Did you tell him that something must be done if he did not get him away?—No.

20,732. What did you say?—We asked him whether he would take him away.

20,733. And if he did not?—He said it was his wife's fault, and he would see when he got home; he thought the thing could be stopped without any more bother.

20,734. Do you know a person called Charles Bagshaw?—Yes.

20,735. Had he anything to do with the defence?—I believe he was one that was chosen to go and see Mr. Hoole.

20,736. Had he anything to do with defending Thompson?—Not that I am aware of.

20,737. Are you not aware that he had?—No.

20,738. You do not know that Bagshaw actually retained Mr. Broadbent, and paid him a large sum of money. Do you know that?—No.

20,739. Did you see anything paid to Mr. Bagshaw?—Never.

20,740. What had Mr. Bagshaw to do with your society?—I do not know. I believe Hellewell paid him.

20,741. Paid whom?—Broadbent.

20,742. Did Broadbent get any money?—Yes.

20,743. You know Mr. Broadbent the solicitor?—Yes.

20,744. And you believe that Hellewell paid him?—Yes.

20,745. Are you sure that it was not Mr. Bagshaw?—No; I believe it was Hellewell that paid the money. I have heard it.

20,746. Why should you think so?—I have heard it said at the meeting.

20,747. It was discussed at the meeting who was to pay for Thompson's defence?—I heard the secretary say it. I heard Robinson say that Hellewell paid it.

20,748. Where did Hellewell get the money?—I daresay it was his own. I believe he paid it out of his own pocket.

20,749. What had Hellewell to do with defending Thompson?—I cannot say.

20,750. Do you mean to say that Hellewell, a man in no way connected with Thompson, found the money out of his own pocket?—I believe he laid it down.

20,751. For what?—To make this money up.

20,752. He laid it down for whom? He would not advance the money out of his own pocket for a man with whom he had nothing to do?—I believe Hellewell did.

20,753. Who asked him?—I do not know.

20,754. Who is Hellewell?—John Hellewell, who kept a public-house.

20,755. Fender grinder?—He was a fender grinder, keeping a public-house, and he advanced the money for Thompson's defence?—Yes.

20,756. You subscribed?—Yes.

20,757. It was made up?—We subscribed a sovereign apiece all of us.

20,758. How many were there of you?—I cannot say.

20,759. About——?—There might be 30.

20,760. I am requested to ask you this question. Had you any authority from the union or any of its officers to agree with Renshaw or Bayles to thrash or blow up any one?—No.

20,761. And you thought simply of your own notion that you wanted him to be thrashed?—Yes, I did.

20,762. And you had no authority at all?—Not the least.

20,763. And that 6*l.* was given by Bayles?—Bayles gave it to me.

20,764. Where did he get it from?—He got it from Robinson.

20,765. What had Robinson to do with it?—I do not know.

20,766. What business had you to pay the money that Robinson had given, unless it was given on the union account?—He sent it to me to take care of it.

20,767. You took care of it, by paying the money to blow a man up?—I did not agree to do it.

20,768. Robinson gave it to Bayles, and Bayles gave it to you. Robinson was acting as secretary, and you were to take care of it only. What business had you to part with it?—It was to flog him with.

20,769. Then it was paid by Robinson to flog him with?—I will not say that Bayles told me so.

20,770. How dared you tell me only this moment that you had never any authority from the union to pay a sum of money?—I had it from Bayles. I did not get it from the union.

20,771. (*Mr. Chance.*) You knew that the 6*l.* came from the union?—I saw him give him something, but I did not know what it was while I got out of doors.

20,772. You knew that the money which Bayles gave to you had come from the union?—I saw him give him something, but I did not know what it was. I heard him say it was from the regular meeting.

The witness withdrew.

J. Thompson.

JOSEPH THOMPSON sworn and examined.

20,773. (*Chairman.*) You have been tried for the murder of Bridget O'Rourke and you were acquitted, and you are not in any peril in respect of that murder. You never can be tried again for it, and our certificate has no effect upon you with reference to that charge. You are clear from it for all time; no person can charge you with that murder again; but I am bound to tell you this, that whoever it was that threw that can of powder, which resulted in the death of Bridget O'Rourke, into the house of Wastnidge, is liable to be tried now for throwing the can of gunpowder into the house where persons were living, with an intent to commit murder, and is liable to be tried at any time when evidence can be brought against him to establish his guilt. You are liable also for the same offence in respect of his wife, and also for the same offence in respect of the child, for there were three persons living in the house when the can of powder was thrown into it. Therefore, I tell you, that you must be on your guard, because although you are not liable to be tried for murder you are liable to be tried for any one of those three offences. You are also liable if you were an accessory to it in conjunction with any other person, and you knew of its being done; or if you bought the gunpowder for it or did anything to aid others in doing it, you are liable to be tried for that; or if you knew of it after and became an accessory after the fact, you are liable for that. Therefore, do not suppose that you are not liable to be tried; and having told you that you are liable to be tried, I tell you at the same time that if you have been guilty in respect of any of those offences and you like to come forward now and make a clear and full disclosure of all you know, and satisfy us that that which you tell us is the truth and the whole truth, we shall grant you a certificate which will protect you against all consequences criminal and civil. And I tell you also, that if in this statement which you are about to make, if you do make one, you implicate any other person, do not fear that; because if there is any other person whom you may implicate, he will have an opportunity of coming forward just as you have, and if he comes and tells the truth and satisfies us that he does tell the truth, he will get a certificate as well as you. That being so, having cautioned you, if you are innocent in respect of anything do not make yourself a criminal, but if you are a criminal you have now the means of making yourself free from any kind of prosecution hereafter by making a statement of all the facts within your knowledge. Now, I ask you in the first place, did you throw that can of gunpowder, which exploded in Wastnidge's house, in at the windows?—I did not.

20,774. Do you know who did?—I do not.

20,775. Did you ever enter into any kind of arrangements for Wastnidge's house being blown up?—No; never.

20,776. Did any person ever ask you to blow him up?—No; never.

20,777. Did any person ever ask you to beat him or otherwise illuse him?—No.

20,778. And you swear that you never threw that can of powder into the window?—I swear it.

20,779. And you swear that you do not know who did it?—I will swear I do not know who did it; no further than what I learn from the men examined here this morning.

20,780. And you never knew till this day who did it?—No; never.

20,781. Your name is Thompson?—Yes.

20,782. What were you by trade?—A stove grate and fender grinder.

20,783. Have you worked for Hoole?—Yes.

20,784. Were you one of the men that turned out in June?—Yes.

20,785. And you knew that Wastnidge had come over from Masbro' to work against your rules?—Yes.

20,786. And did you watch him?—Never.

20,787. Mind. Were you one of the persons employed to watch Wastnidge?—No.

20,788. Did you watch the workmen who did work for Hoole?—Never but once.

20,789. Who was that?—Sibray, but never with any intent of putting a finger on to him.

20,790. But you did watch him?—Yes.

20,791. What for?—To see where he went.

20,792. What object had you in that?—With respect to his not doing the thing that was right towards us in the trade.

20,793. Were you to watch him that another person should beat him?—I was to watch him to give information to another member where he lived.

20,794. What party?—Cutler.

20,795. What information was it that you gave?—Where he lived.

20,796. Why?—Because they should have the party in view that was going to drop on him.

20,797. What was the object of knowing where he lived, was it to blow him up?—No, I never heard anything of that sort named.

20,798. Why did they want to know where his house was?—On that account. I was lead by the nose by them.

20,799. By whom?—By the persons who were brought here this morning.

20,800. Who were they?—Platts, Cutler, Bayles, and Hellewell.

20,801. Did they all speak to you?—At different times.

20,802. What did they ask you to do?—They asked me to do nothing more than that.

20,803. To watch Sibray?—To watch Sibray, and to see where he lived and let them know.

20,804. Did you do so?—Yes.

20,805. Whom did you let know?—Cutler, he came to me on the Sunday following to ask whether I had traced him. I said I had.

20,806. When you were taken up who kept your family?—The trade.

20,807. When you were taken up who provided the means for your defence?—The trade, with the exception of a few pounds subscribed by my friends in a few public-houses.

20,808. When you were in custody did you make a statement to Mr. Jackson?—Yes.

20,809. Was that true?— I am sure I could not bear in mind everything that I said to him; I was in such a state of mind at the time.

20,810. Stop me when I come to anything you do not agree to. Did you say, "I suppose it is the club " that is finding the money to employ an attorney " and keep my family, our folks have nothing?"—I said something to that effect.

20,811. Did he say that he did not know, but he thought it was very likely. Did you say then on the Thursday in the week that the explosion took place, "John Hellewell came to my wife and said he wanted " to see me at his house?"—Yes.

20,812. That is true?—Yes.

20,813. That you went down between 7 and 8 o'clock?—Yes, he laid stress on my wife to tell me this; he went away and came back again and told her not to forget.

20,814. And you saw Hellewell and called for a glass of beer, and when you had nearly drunk it he called you to the kitchen door and said, which room did you sleep in when you lived in the house where Ripley lives, is that correct?—Yes.

20,815. Did you say it was in the front room?—Yes.

20,816. Did he say, "Whereabouts is it?"—Yes.

20,817. Did you say over the front door?—Yes.

20,818. Did you say "why"?—Yes.

20,819. Did he say, "They are going to blow old Ripley up this week?"—Yes.

20,820. Hellewell told you that?—Yes.

20,821. On going out did you say to Hellewell, "I shall perhaps come down to-morrow night?"—I will not swear that I said, I would come down the night after, or during the week.

20,822. Did he say you made haste home for fear something should happen whilst you were in the neighbourhood?—Yes.

20,823. What made you think something would happen while you were in the neighbourhood?—I had no idea further than what he said to me.

20,824. Then did you also say that on the Tuesday or the Thursday, but on or before the 5th of November when the attack was made on Sibray that you had a meeting at the "King William?"—Yes.

20,825. Did you say it was a club meeting in connexion with your union, and that it was said by several of you that something must be done?—Yes.

20,826. Did you say that it was stated that they had engaged James Dolphin's boy to go to work at Hoole's, and that they said something must be done to prevent his going, as his father was not in the trade?—Yes.

20,827. And that you and Platts and Cutler met at John Platts's at the Wentworth House on the Saturday?—Me and Platts did. I will not be certain whether Cutler was there or not.

20,828. But you and Platts were?—Yes.

20,829. At 4 o'clock did you go near Portmahon Chapel, and come down to Dolphins's on the same Saturday?—Yes.

20,830. Did you call him to you?—Yes.

20,831. And did Platts ask him if he knew that he was going against the rules of the trade?—Yes.

20,832. Did he ask him if he meant letting his lad go?—Yes.

TWENTY-SECOND DAY.

J. Thompson.

2 July 1867.

20,833. Did he say that it was his wife's doing, and that he would not let the lad go?—Yes, I believe he did.

20,834. Did you say that you were satisfied?—Yes.

20,835. Did you also say that you afterwards went to Wylie's and had something to drink, and that it was said amongst you that something must be done? —Yes.

20,836. And did Cutler say that he knew a party that would kill all the lot for 5*l.* or so?—Yes.

20,837. Did Cutler say that?—Yes; Cutler said he knew a party that would not mind killing the lot for 5*l.* or so.

20,838. Did Cutler say that?—Yes.

20,839. Who was present when that was said?—Platts.

20,840. Did he name him?—No, he never mentioned any names.

20,841. Did you ask who it was?—No.

20,842. Did you also say that Cutler said you were to see him, and that you had made it in your way to see him in a few days?—See who?

20,843. Cutler?—I am sure I cannot say.

20,844. Did you not say that the man was John Aldam, and that he lives in Hoyle Street?—I do not know that John Aldam was named at the time.

20,845. Did not you tell Mr. Jackson that Cutler said he was to see you and that you made it in your way to see him in a few days, and that the party in view was John Aldam, and that he lived in Hoyle Street, and that you asked him to drop on some of the men, and he said he could not, that he was working, or he would be glad of the job?—I do not remember.

20,846. Did you ever see Aldam?—Yes.

20,847. Did you ever ask him to drop on some of the men?—Yes, from Hellewell's request.

20,848. You did?—Yes.

20,849. And Hellewell requested you to see Aldam? —Yes.

20,850. And you asked Aldam if he would drop on some of the men?—Yes.

20,851. And he said that he could not as he was working, or he would be glad of the job; was that true?—Yes.

20,852. Did he say that he could tell the party, and that he would send him to you or bring him?—Yes.

20,853. Did he do so?—No.

20,854. Did you say that on the Tuesday night following Platts, Cutler, and yourself met together again?—I will not say; I cannot recollect.

20,855. On the Tuesday night when Sibray was attacked did a man named Bayles come in and say, "Well, they have done Sibray?"—No, I was going out and he followed me out and told me at the door that they had done Sibray, but he never came in and told me.

20,856. Did you say, "Where?"—Yes.

20,857. Did he say, "To-night?" did you say, "Where?" and did he say, "Just by the side of the union wheel?"—Yes, and Cutler came through at the time he was telling me.

20,858. Did he say they would have given him more, but that somebody was going by at the time?—Yes.

20,859. Did you say to him, "Who told you?"—I might do so.

20,860. Did he say, "Well, I have seen the party who did it?"—Something to that effect.

20,861. Did you tell Mr. Jackson that you supposed the club paid for doing Sibray's job?—Yes, I believe I did; I only supposed. I did not know it as a fact.

20,862. But you told him so?—Yes.

20,863. Did you tell him that you were confident that Bayles was on the committee that got Sibray's job done?—I will not say that; I said I was confident; I believe I did say he was on.

20,864. Did you think so at the time?—Yes.

20,865. Did you say that you once watched Sibray along the White Rails?—Yes.

20,866. Did Cutler come to you once and ask you if you knew where Sibray lived?—Yes.

20,867. And did you go with him and show him where the house was?—Yes.

20,868. Did Cutler leave you and say that he should go to see Bayles and arrange for it?—Yes.

20,869. Did he tell you that they were going to see the party who was going to do the job?—Yes.

20,870. And did he say that they meant doing it that week if they had the chance out of doors, and if not that they would fetch him out of the house?—Yes.

20,871. Did you ever see Platts about Dolphin's boy?—Yes.

20,872. Did he say that something must be done to prevent his working?—Yes.

20,873. Did you say that something ought to be done?—Yes.

20,874. And at that time while you were talking together did John Aldam pass by?—I believe he did; I will not swear that.

20,875. I am asking you whether you told Mr. Jackson these things. Did you tell him that Platts said John would not be a bad chap for the job?—Something to that effect.

20,876. And did you say that you would choose him if you must choose anybody?—Yes, I believe I did.

20,877. Did you say you were confident that Hellewell, Cutler, Platts, and Bayles were the persons who got it done?—Yes, I believe I did; the persons that were on the committee for the job to arrange about the affair as to blowing up, I never heard a sentence about it.

20,878. As to the beating of Sibray the committee were Hellewell, Cutler, Platts, and Bayles?—Yes, we are not alluding to any blowing up.

20,879. I am alluding to the beating of Sibray, were they on the committee for that?—I believe they were, if any one was not on it that would be Platts; but if he was not connected with that committee he was as thick as the other were.

20,880. Were you on the committee?—No.

20,881. Were you at the room at the union?—I was at several meetings.

20,882. How do you know that they were on the committee?—It was said to me that they would be the three likeliest men to be on the committee for the job, to arrange for attacks being made.

20,883. Who said that?—Platts said it. It was Cutler, Bayles, and Hellewell. I took it from that, that I believed they were the men who had the management of it.

20,884. When you said that they were the persons who got it done, did not Mr. Jackson ask you what you meant by it, and did not you reply, "Wastnidge's job?" What you said to Mr. Jackson was this, "I "am confident that Hellewell, Cutler, Platts, and "Bayles are the persons that got it done," and Mr. Jackson said "What do you mean by that?" and did not you reply, "Wastnidge's job?"—I have no doubt that I did.

20,885. Was it your belief that they were the persons who got Wastnidge's job done?—Yes.

20,886. Did you say that Edward Platts was generally the chairman of your union meetings?—Yes.

20,887. Did you say that Mr. Bagshaw came to your meeting on one occasion?—Yes, on two or three occasions.

20,888. And that he had seen the men working at Mr. Hoole's, and that if you would give them 20*l.* a man they would leave?—I will not say to the amount.

20,889. Was that what you said to Mr. Jackson? —Perhaps I might.

20,890. Did you then say that it was too much, and that you would agree to give them 5*l.*?—I will not swear to the amount.

20,891. And that they refused to take the amount, and that Mr. Bagshaw had offered them 7*l.* and they had refused it?—I do not remember it, all I remember I will tell you, there is no fear about that.

20,892. Did you tell Mr. Jackson that Hellewell sent for you ?—Yes.

20,893. Did you go to him and did he say, "I am glad you have come," and that he expected a party coming that night to know about Ripley's business that they intended blowing him up that week ?—It was all one night, the night or night but one before the job. That would be on Tuesday night in the same week.

20,894. Were you at the public-house after Wastnidge was blown up when the paper was read, and did you say, "Why, according to what the papers "state, there was sufficient time to have thrown it "out before it exploded," and did Hellewell make an answer, "Why, if they had thrown it out I would have thrown it back again ?"—Yes.

20,895. Who said that they would throw it back again ?—Hellewell said that they said so, or that one of the men said so.

20,896. Did you tell him that you never knew anything about the blowing up till Hellewell came to your house ?—I did.

20,897. Did you say, "If Aldam denies having anything to do with it, I will bring him into a bigger mess ?"—I do not remember saying that, but I might have let something slip when I was in such a state of mind, but as to knowing anything worse about him, is it possible to know anything worse about him?

20,898. I am going to ask you about that presently. Do you recollect saying that Mr. Kenworthy the secretary to your club had been ill, and that you recollected that the man who acted for him had told you that the party who assaulted Mr. Hoole's grinders in Water Lane, had been paid 6*l.* for his job ?—Something of that sort.

20,899. And they wanted 10*l.* and the union could not raise it without notice, did you say that ?—I will not be sure of that.

20,900. Did you say something of that kind ?—Something to that effect I believe.

20,901. Is what you have told Mr. Jackson true or false ?—I believe all that I have told him was true.

20,902. Who was the person who wanted to blow up Ripley ?—That is a mystery.

20,903. Who was to blow up Ripley ?—I do not know.

20,904. Hellewell inquired where he slept ?—He inquired where I slept.

20,905. Did you sleep in the same house where Ripley had lived ?—Yes.

20,906. Was Ripley ever blown up ?—No.

20,907. Was Ripley a man who had worked for Hoole ?—Yes.

20,908. Was he a "knobstick" ?—Yes, what is commonly called a "knobstick."

20,909. He had come from Masbro' with the others ?—Yes.

20,910. Where did he live ?—In the same house that I had been accustomed to live in, the second large house in Green Lane, Park Gate.

20,911. Had he a family ?—I believe he had two children.

20,912. Had he a wife ?—Yes.

20,913. Was the place which you pointed out as the place where you slept, over the front door ?—Yes, where I told them.

20,914. Was that the place where the family slept ?—Yes.

20,915. Where you slept with your wife ?—Yes.

20,916. You had been taking a great part in this strike ?—I cannot say that I had. I should never have struck at all or taken a foot out of the place unless I had been led by the nose by them.

20,917. Who led you by the nose ?—Several of them.

20,918. Tell me their names ?—Platts was one ; he said, "I never thought that you would have stood out "till now ; you have deceived me."

20,919. Where is Platts ?—There (*pointing to a man who was standing up*), and a very old particular enemy of mine.

20,920. Platts wanted you to turn out ?—No, he was glad I had stood ; and I was the only man he thought would not have stood out, after we had been out a certain time.

20,921. You said that you were at Wylie's, and that Platts was there ?—Yes.

20,922. And what did Platts say ?—The same as you asked me before.

20,923. That he knew a man who would kill the whole lot ?—No, Platts did not say that ; Cutler said that.

20,924. Was Platts there at the time ?—Yes.

20,925. What did Platts say to that ?—I do not recollect his making any answer. I do not say that he did not.

20,926. Could Platts hear it ?—I cannot say.

20,927. Do you believe that he heard it ?—I do not know whether he did or not.

20,928. Was Platts on that committee ?—I do not know.

20,929. You say that Hellewell was there ?—I believe he was.

20,930. What took place at your meetings with reference to that committee ? there were some persons on the committee for doing these jobs ?—I did not say for doing these jobs ; I said to arrange for them.

20,931. What was said at your meetings about it ?—I never was at one meeting of that kind.

20,932. What reason have you to say that they were the men who were appointed ?—From what Platts told me ; he said those were the most fittest men for it.

20,933. Did he say that they had been appointed ?—He said nothing more than what I have told you.

20,934. Did he say that they were the committee appointed to arrange ?—I do not think he did.

20,935. Will you swear that he did not tell you that they were appointed to arrange what was to be done to these men ?—He told me that they were the likeliest three men, Hellewell, Cutler, and Bayles.

20,936. Platts told you that ?—Yes, that led me to think they were the men to do it.

20,937. Did not he tell you that they were the men who were fixed upon to carry it out ?—I will not swear that.

20,938. Why do you use the word "committee ?"—They were chosen to meet at Hellewell's at different times to arrange those things.

20,939. You say that they were chosen to meet at Hellewell's ?—Yes.

20,940. How do you know that ?—He said they were the likeliest three to meet, and they were the men to do the affair.

20,941. Who was to choose them ?—I do not know.

20,942. You cannot have a man chosen unless he is chosen by somebody ; who were the parties to choose them ?—I do not know.

20,943. Who did he tell you had chosen them ?—It was his own suggestion.

20,944. Who could choose them ? he could not choose them himself ; was it the trade who chose them ?—Not that I am aware of.

20,945. Who did choose them if it was not the trade ?—I do not know.

20,946. What do you mean by choosing ?—It was only his own suggestion.

20,947. I want to know this ; you have made a statement to Mr. Jackson which you say is true ; did not you say that they were the persons chosen to arrange the matter ?—It was in my head from what he said to me.

20,948. And by whom had they been chosen ?—I do not know ; I told the truth to the nearest of my recollection.

20,949. By whom did Platts say that they were chosen ?—I did not hear him say anything of that kind.

20,950. By whom did you mean that they were chosen ?—It was from his suggestion that they had been chosen.

TWENTY-SECOND DAY.

J. Thompson.

2 July 1867.

20,951. By whom did you mean that they were chosen; you must have meant by somebody?—I do not know.

20,952. They must have been chosen by somebody, by whom did you mean that they were chosen?—I cannot say I am sure.

20,953. Mind you are in peril, by whom did you mean that they were chosen?—I cannot say.

20,954. Whom did you think?—My mind was in such a state at the time that I cannot recollect; there ought to be a little allowance.

20,955. If you still say they were the persons chosen, by whom were they chosen? they could not have been chosen except by somebody?—I am sure I do not know.

20,956. You answered just now that you thought they were chosen?—Yes, I did.

20,957. Chosen by whom?—By Platts, I suppose, for anything I know.

20,958. Platts could not choose them?—He could have made it known to them; he did tell Hellewell that they would be the likeliest chaps.

20,959. He told Hellewell that they would be the likeliest for what?—For the jobs in hand.

20,960. What jobs?—Respecting the attacks; as to the blowings up. I know nothing about it.

20,961. Was there a committee appointed by the trade to arrange about these attacks?—I will not swear that.

20,962. Do you believe it?—I believe it from what he told me.

20,963. You say that Hellewell asked you to get a man?—He asked me to go and see "Slipper Jack."

20,964. Is Hellewell alive?—No.

20,965. He is dead?—Yes.

20,966. What public-house did Hellewell keep?—The "Napoleon Inn," Green Lane.

20,967. Did you get any money at all? were you paid anything for any of these things?—No.

20,968. You were a member of the union?—I was after that time.

20,969. You say that you were asked to go and see "Slipper Jack?"—Yes.

20,970. And you said that if Aldam denied having anything to do with it, you would bring him into a bigger mess?—I might say something of that sort.

20,971. I know you did say so. What bigger mess do you know about "Slipper Jack" in connexion with trades unions?—None.

20,972. What mess connected with trades unions do you know relating to "Slipper Jack?"—I cannot say that I know of anything connected with trades unions of "Slipper Jack," not within 10 years.

20,973. The something that you alluded to was more than 10 years ago?—Yes.

20,974. You were a member of the union and when you were in prison the trade supported you and your family?—Yes.

20,975. Who paid for your defence?—The trade, within a few pounds.

20,976. How much did they subscribe?—I cannot exactly say, but between 40*l.* and 50*l.*

20,977. Was not it more?—I do not think it was.

20,978. Do you know who paid the money?—Hellewell paid one lot.

20,979. Did Bagshaw pay another?—Not that I am aware of; and my wife paid two lots.

20,980. Where did your wife get it from?—From the trade; she did not go to the trade committee for it.

20,981. Where did she get it?—One lot at Hellewell's, and the other at John Platt's.

20,982. How much did she get at Platts?—She did not know, the same as me—she was in such a state of mind.

20,983. When you were acquitted of the charge you came out of prison?—Yes.

20,984. Did you come back to the union?—Yes, I went.

20,985. The union kept your family all the time that you were in prison?—Yes.

20,986. Do you know how much they allowed you?—Pretty near.

20,987. How much?—There was 24*s.* when I was sent in custody and she remained having 24*s.* for some weeks after and they reduced it to 16*s.* or 18*s.*

20,988. She received the 16*s.* or 18*s.* up to the time that you were acquitted?—Yes.

20,989. When you came out what did they allow you?—I received one week's pay after and then they stopped it.

20,990. Why did they stop it?—I did not know. I went to the trade myself to see, the week after they had stopped it, and I asked the reason why they had stopped it, and they told me the reason that they had stopped my scale was that I was not financial at the time when we turned out from work at Green Lane.

20,991. Was that the fact?—No.

20,992. I think you are wrong, we have looked at the books and find that you were not financial, you were in arrear?—It was wrong as far as saying that they stopped my scale on that account—I was not financial, I had not been financial for some time—not one quarter of the time that I had been in the trade.

20,993. We have looked at it and we see that you were not financial?—That was not the reason they refused to give me my scale.

20,994. What was the reason that they refused to give you your scale?—Platts got the parties together and he said to them "Thompson has come respecting his scale being stopped and wants to know the reason why it is stopped." Well, he made answer and said he believed it was on account of my not being financial at the time when we turned out—who it was I cannot say, but he said it was on account of my not being financial at the time we struck. I got up and said "Providing I had been financial at the time we "turned out on that strike, would you have allowed "me scale to have kept me away from your fellows or "have refused me scale and let me work amongst "them?" One of them got up and said, "Decidedly, "we should have allowed you scale to keep you from "working amongst the men who were there at the "time." It was a man in the room who had a little feeling I suppose.

20,995. Did you continue in the union after that?—No.

20,996. When did you cease to be a member of the union?—As soon as I was discharged.

20,997. You were a member of the union up to the time of your coming out of prison?—Yes.

20,998. And you received scale the week after?—Once after.

20,999. Were you a member of the union after that?—No.

21,000. How did you happen to cease being a member of the union?—I have overrun my story. When I asked them if they would allow me to have scale they kept me out or refused me scale, and let me go to work amongst these fellows; they said they would have allowed me scale. Then Bayles went at me with a ginger-beer bottle, and would have taken my life if somebody had not come behind him; he took a spring at me with a ginger-beer bottle, and some one came behind him.

21,001. Why was it?—From what I stated to Mr. Jackson; I can see no other reason for it. It was Bayles that did it.

21,002. Did Bayles remain a member of the union after that?—For anything I know he did.

21,003. Were you turned out?—Yes.

21,004. Was Platts a member of the union then?—Yes.

21,005. Was Hellewell a member of the union?—Yes.

21,006. Did they continue so?—I believe they did.

21,007. After you were acquitted they had the bill to pay for your lawyer?—Yes.

21,008. That you say was done?—Yes.

21,009. In consequence of being tried for this dreadful crime did you change your name?—Never. That is the amount of one lot that was paid (*producing a paper*).

21,010. It is "Memorandum that I have received "of Mrs. Thompson, the sum of 23*l*. on account of "defence;" that is January 3rd, 1862, and is signed by Mr. Broadbent. Was that the second payment or the first?—I cannot say, and my wife cannot say.

21,011. She got the money from Hellewell?—She got one lot from Hellewell.

21,012. This amount mentioned in this paper?—I cannot say; she did not understand the paper.

21,013. Had you been engaged in anything connected with trades matters besides Mr. Sibray's affair?—Never.

21,014. You knew that there was a mischief intended to be done to Wastnidge?—I did on Thursday night, either to Wastnidge or Ripley, from what Hellewell said to me, but he did not name Wastnidge; but I suppose from Ripley not catching it they found the other place the most convenient.

21,015. That is from what Hellewell told you?—Yes; I suppose when they did not go to Ripley that they considered the other the most convenient place. But as to knowing any more about it while these men came down on Thursday night I do not. I never had any connexion with it. I was frightened out of my wits when I went from there.

21,016. Do you know who did this at Wastnidge's?—No.

21,017. You do not?—No.

21,018. You have heard what Renshaw said this morning?—Partly.

21,019. You have heard what Cutler has said?—No.

21,020. Do you know whether there were two men in it or only one?—I do not know.

21,021. Are you sure?—I am sure.

21,022. Did you ever hear any talk about it after it was done?—No.

21,023. Did you never hear that any person was suspected of it?—No.

21,024. Did you ever buy any powder?—Never.

21,025. For the purpose of pigeon shooting?—No.

21,026. Did you hear Twibell talk about your buying powder?—I heard him.

21,027. Was that true?—What he said was not true.

21,028. Did you buy any powder at Twibell's?—Never, that I am aware of.

21,029. Do you remember going into Powell's?—No, never.

21,030. You recollect what was said. You heard him say that?—Yes.

20,031. Do you recollect what was said about the fuse?—I recollect something being brought up about it.

20,032. Did you buy a fuse?—No, never.

20,033. Or inquired of the barber whether he knew where fuses were sold in Snig Hill?—I do not know what a fuse is to this moment.

21,034. Were you in the habit of wearing a velvet cap?—Yes, I never wore anything else for years.

21,035. Do you recollect having a coat?—Yes, I took two or three coats.

21,036. Do you recollect having a coat that was torn?—Yes, in about one place.

21,037. Do you recollect their pointing it out to you, and telling you that you had caught it on a shutter?—They did not need. I knew it was torn.

21,038. Did you not hear Mrs. Wastnidge say she saw you running away at night?—Yes, it was not worth my while listening to her.

21,039. I recollect her being examined.—If you had listened to her character you would have heard a nice one.

21,040. She swore she saw you that night running away; on your oath were not you there?—Never.

21,041. On your oath did not you run down that street that night?—Never.

21,042. On your oath did not your coat catch a cotter of a shutter, and get torn?—No, I was in a warmer place than in the street that night.

21,043. Where were you?—In bed.

21,044. Where were you in bed?—At my house.

21,045. Sleeping with your wife?—Yes.

21,046. She could not be called, and, therefore, you could not have the advantage of her evidence?—No.

21,047. You swear that you were not in that street at all?—Yes, I swear I was not.

21,048. You swear that you never bought any powder?—I swear I never bought any powder.

21,049. Nor a fuse?—Nor a fuse.

21,050. And had nothing at all to do with it?—Nothing.

21,051. I can give you a certificate.—I am aware of that.

21,052. You still persist in saying you had nothing to do with it?—I swear I had nothing to do with it. I will swear it if you ask me forty times over.

21,053. You do not know who did it, or whether there was more than one in it?—I do not. I have come here to speak the truth, and the truth I will speak, what I do not know I cannot say.

21,054. Where did you live at the time that this occurred?—In a lane called Wollen's Lane; I do not know whether it has not a fresh name; it is against Kelvin Grove near the old barracks.

21,055. Was there anybody living in your house with you at the time?—I believe my wife's father.

21,056. Why did not you call him at the trial?—He had lived from there.

21,057. I asked you if any person was living in the house with you that night?—My wife's father had gone a little before.

21,058. Was anybody living with you at the time—I believe not; I am sure not.

21,059. How was your coat torn?—The same as many other coats are torn, accidentally.

21,060. It was shown at the trial to be a recent tear; how did that coat get torn?—I do not know; it was constantly torn. I kept tearing it every now and then.

21,061. Can you explain how it got torn?—I will give you as good an explanation as I can. I was labouring with Mr. Chambers at his brewery. I had a deal of lifting amongst wood and stones and bricks, and one thing and another, and it is possible it might be torn that way. It was what I had to put on in such like weather as it is now.

21,062. You do not know how it was torn.

21,063. You swear that it was not torn at the cotter?—I swear it was not torn at that cotter or any other cotter.

21,064. (*Mr. Chance.*) What kind of a looking man was Bayles?—He stood 5 feet 9 inches.

21,065. You say that Bayles was a tall man?—Yes.

21,066. How much taller would that be than you?—About 5 inches.

21,067. Did he wear a moustache?—No, I do not know that he did.

21,068. Was he anything like you in appearance?—No, I could not see it myself.

21,069. Was Bayles at all like you?—I do not know that he was.

21,070. Did you wear a moustache at that time?—I do not know.

21,071. Did Bayles?—I do not know that he did.

21,072. Do you remember being present with four other men, and Twibell being asked to pick you out?—There were several parties besides Twibell that did.

21,073. You say that other parties did the same?—Yes.

21,074. Did he pick you out from amongst a number of other men?—Yes, but I was the only one amongst a lot who had a velvet cap on.

21,075. At the time you were picked out, did the man state that he picked you out because you had a velvet cap on?—I cannot say he picked me out for that.

21,076. Did you wear a velvet cap at the time you were with the other men?—Yes.

21,077. Did the other men have caps on?—Some

TWENTY-SECOND DAY.

J. Thompson.

2 July 1867.

had short hats and caps on; I do not think there was one in the lot with a velvet cap on besides myself.

21,078. How many men came to pick you out?—I cannot say.

21,079. (*Chairman.*) You were picked out three or four different times, and three or four different people swore that you were the man who went to Powell's, to Twibell's, and to Wilson's. They all said that you were the man?—Not to my face.

21,080. They did all swear that at the trial?—I do not remember it; I remember what Wilson said in the town hall when I was examined, when the question was put to him as to whether he did not think he was mistaken, he said, "That is not an every day "face; I am not so much mistaken."

21,081. Although you were so picked out you still persist that you did not do any of those things?—I did not.

21,082. Whereabouts was your coat torn? I believe at the side pocket was not it?—It was in several places.

21,083. There was one tear alluded to at the trial?—That was on the right side.

21,084. Near the pocket?—Near the pocket.

21,085. It was a rent which they said would have occurred if it was done by catching on a cotter?—They said so certainly.

21,086. Was not it said at your trial that the cotter was five feet from the ground?—I do not know.

21,087. Were you aware whether Mr. Hoole sent for Mr. Bagshaw and Mr. Broadhead or not?—I do not know.

21,088. Do you know why Bagshaw and Broadhead went at all and interfered in your strike?—No, not particularly; they went to see whether they could make any arrangements with Mr. Hoole to get the men away.

21,089. (*Mr. Chance.*) Did Aldam have anything to do with it?—Not that I am aware of.

21,090. What did you mean by telling Mr. Jackson that if Aldam denied having anything to do with it you would bring him into a bigger mess?—It is not possible to bring him into a worse mess.

21,091. If he denied it why should you try to bring him into a bigger mess if he had nothing to do with it?—I said if he had anything to do with it, that was my meaning.

21,092. Why should you, if he had anything to do with it, bring him into a bigger mess?—I cannot say that I could.

21,093. You said, "If Aldam denies having any-"thing to do with it, I will bring him into a bigger "mess"?—Is it not right that a little allowance should be made for me?

21,094. (*Chairman.*) The expression that you made use of was "I declare I never knew anything about "the blowing up affair; Hellewell came to my house; "if Aldam denies having anything to do with it, I "will bring him into a bigger mess"?—I did say so; I will not dispute it if Mr. Jackson says I said so.

21,095. (*Mr. Chance.*) Why should you bring him into a bigger mess if he denied having anything to do with it, if he never had anything to do with it?—I might say that I would bring him into another mess, but as to a worse mess, it is not possible to bring him into a worse mess.

21,096. (*Chairman.*) Did you say to Mr. Broadbent after your trial that the statement you had made to Mr. Jackson was false?—Not that I recollect.

21,097. Do you recollect whether you told him that or not? did you tell Mr. Broadbent after your trial that the statement which you made to Mr. Jackson was false?—No.

21,098. Did you say at the club afterwards when you were expelled that the statement you had made to Mr. Jackson was false?—I do not remember saying such a thing.

21,099. You were turned out on account of this statement which you made to Mr. Jackson? did you at that time tell them that the statement which you had made was false?—If I did say so I should not mean it.

21,100. Did you tell them so I ask you?—I will not say.

21,101. Will you swear one way or the other?—I cannot say.

21,102. Do you believe that you said so?—I do not remember.

21,103. Will you swear that you did not say so?—No.

21,104. Do not you know that you said so?—I do not know.

21,105. Do not you know whether you said it was false or not?—I cannot swear.

21,106. They brought up against you, before they expelled you from the society, your own statement to Mr. Jackson?—Yes.

21,107. I ask whether they brought that statement up against you, and whether you did not, before the union, tell them that the statement which you made to Mr. Jackson was false?—I might do so, but if I did so it was on my own account.

21,108. Why on your own account?—As regards being a little bit safer.

21,109. Why safer?—For fear of being attacked.

21,110. You say if you did say so it was because you were frightened and you dared not tell the truth?—Yes.

21,111. Was the statement which you made to Mr. Jackson true?—I believe the majority of it is.

21,112. Is any part of it false?—I cannot say

21,113. Is there any part that you would like to qualify in any way?—No.

21,114. Is it all true?—I cannot say all.

21,115. Which part is not true?—It may be all true; but I cannot give any answer about it. I do not remember.

21,116. As far as you remember is what you have said to Mr. Jackson true?—Yes, I believe it is.

21,117. (*Mr. Barstow.*) Have you been able to work at your trade since you left the union?—Yes.

21,118. You have?—Yes.

21,119. As a fender grinder?—Yes.

21,120. (*Chairman.*) Did you find work afterwards?—Yes.

21,121. Have you not been in difficulties?—I have not been in the union since then.

21,122. Have you never been at Ecclesall union?—Yes.

21,123. Have you ever made any statement there as to whether it was false or not?—Not that I am aware of.

21,124. Never?—Not that I am aware of.

21,125. Have you ever said to anyone at the union that you were guilty?—Never.

21,126. To any member of the union?—No, I never have said that I was guilty.

21,127. (*Mr. Barstow.*) What are you working at now?—As a fender grinder.

21,128. You have never been molested while working as a fender grinder?—No, not at my work, but I have been told by a party since that I must thank him I am existing.

21,129. Where do you work now?—For Mr. Hoole.

21,130. You still work for Mr. Hoole?—Yes, I have had it thrown in my face more than once. I think there should be some protection for it.

21,131. You may be thankful that this inquiry has taken place?—I am thankful.

21,132. Who has told you that you ought to thank him for your existence?—Mr. Platts.

21,133. Mr. Platts has told you what?—That I must thank him that I was existing, and that he tried his best to get my job done one night.

21,134. How do you mean?—He called a lot of fellows up, and there were two out of three of us very intimate together, because they did not agree with him he turned round upon us; there were three men coming up, and I believe they were going to kill all the lot of us.

21,135. Men do not generally tell people they are

going to kill them beforehand, do they ; that is not a likely thing ?—What I say is true.

21,136. It is quite clear that you have a strong feeling against Mr. Platts ?—Yes, and he has a strong feeling against me, but he has a different way of showing it.

The witness withdrew.

EDWARD PLATTS sworn and examined.

21,137. (*Chairman.*) Are you a fender grinder ?—Yes.

21,138. Have you been in the union ?—Yes.

21,139. Did you hold any office in the union ?—I have been on the committee.

21,140. Were you on the committee with Hellewell ?—I was not. I believe I have never sat on the committee in my life till this investigation took place. I will not swear it, but I believe not.

21,141. You have heard what has been said by Thompson about what Cutler said, that he knew a party who would kill all the lot of them for 5*l.*, and that it was told to you ?—They have both been in error. Joseph Thompson came to me and said that Dolphin's boy had gone, but I never heard of that matter all my life in our trade. Thompson told me me that Dolphin's boy had gone. Dolphin and me were fellow apprentices, and I said that if we could get somebody else to go and see Dolphin I had no doubt that Dolphin would take his boy away, it being a trade matter.

21,142. You are very far away from the point. The point is whether it was said to you that they knew a man who would do the job for 5*l.*, and kill the whole lot ?—I never heard that.

21,143. You swear that ?—I swear it.

21,144. Did you ever hear it mentioned that a man was to be found to do anybody's job ?—No.

21,145. You never heard it talked of ?—Never in my life.

21,146. Did you ever hear it talked about that any person was to be beaten ?—Never.

21,147. Did you suggest that any person should be beaten ?—Never.

21,148. Were you on the committee which had the management of beating people ? — I never had a moment's conversation with either Cutler, or Hellewell, or Bayles, in my life on the subject.

21,149. Do you know who found the money for this man being beaten ?—I do not.

21,150. Was it found by your club ?—I do not know.

21,151. Were you an associate of Bayle's ?—Never in my life.

21,152. Were you an associate of Hellewell's ?—Never in my life.

21,153. Did not you go to public-houses ?—I never was with Bayles in a public-house. I called sometimes coming from work.

21,154. Do you know Cutler ?—Yes.

21,155. Have you been an associate of his ?—No, never in my life.

21,156. Have you known Thompson ?—Yes. I do not know that Thompson has ever had a pint of ale with me in my life.

21,157. Never in your life ?—He has been speaking the truth about this. On the night when I was fresh I said he must thank me for being living, and I went down to the house the next morning and tendered an apology, and we shook hands, and there was no more about it.

21,158. You did one night, when you were fresh, say that he owed you his life ?—Yes, I got severely hurt for him, and my watch and guard were taken from me. I had no one with me. I had not an associate with me that night at all.

21,159. Did you know who blew up Wastnidge ?—No.

21,160. Had you ever known till to-day ?—I knew previous to to-day.

21,161. When ?—Yesterday it was told me.

21,162. Who told you ?—Cutler told me he should make a clean breast of it.

21,163. Cutler said so yesterday ?—Yes.

21,164. Before I examined him ?—Yes.

21,165. He told you that ?—Yes ; he said, " I shall speak the truth."

21,166. Have you known Renshaw ?—I take my solemn oath I never saw the man in my life.

21,167. Were you aware that any steps were taken by your trade to blow up any persons or to do a job ? —I am not aware of anything of the kind.

21,168. You swear that ?—I swear it upon my oath.

21,169. Were you aware that any money was paid to parties ?—I am not aware of anything of the kind.

21,170. When Thompson told you that he knew a party who would not care about killing a chap, did he name him to you ?—I do not know that Thompson ever said such a thing to me in this world.

21,171. Did you ever tell him that he was to see him ?—Never.

21,172. And there was no conversation about seeing a man who would kill a person ?—The afternoon we were to see James Dolphin we talked the matter over and we went into Wollen's public-house and vaults, and from there we went to Wylie's, and there was some conversation, but I am sure I cannot say what the conversation was about ; it was about trade matters a bit, but I took little interest in it in a place of that description, and Cutler was very fresh and I was getting fresh myself, and I do not know whether Thompson was or not.

21,173. Did you on that night talk about getting a person who was to kill any other ?—No.

21,174. Or at any other time ?—No.

21,175. Did you ask him to see the man who would do it ?—No.

21,176. You swear that you did not ?—No.

21,177. Did Thompson offer to see the man ?—No; not to my knowledge.

21,178. Did Thompson name the man to you who would not mind killing some people ?—I never heard Thompson say anything of the kind.

21,179. Did you watch the men who were out ?—I never watched a man in my life.

21,180. Did you ever beat a man ?—No.

21,181. Did you ever cast a canister into a man's house ?—No.

21,182. Were you aware who did it till yesterday ? —No.

21,183. Were you aware that any man had been paid by your union for doing it ?—No.

21,184. Did you know Robinson ?—Yes.

21,185. Did you know that he had given Bayles 6*l.*? I saw him give Bayles 6*l.*

21,186. Where did he give it to him ?—In the trades meeting.

21,187. Did not you inquire what he gave Bayles 6*l.* for ?—I did not.

21,188. Was not it your duty to inquire ?—It was partly my duty, but I was not dreaming anything wrong. I never heard the 6*l.* mentioned till this inquiry came on.

21,189. Did you subscribe ?—Yes.

21,190. How much did you subscribe ?—I do not know ; I subscribed my one 1*l.* in the first place.

21,191. How much did the union subscribe ?—I do not know ; I believe between 20*l.* and 30*l.*

21,192. Have you seen the books ?—No.

21,193. Had you anything to do with keeping the books ?—No.

21,194. Are you aware that there have been false entries made in them ?—No.

21,195. I believe you passed a vote of thanks to Mr. Bagshaw for the services which he had rendered to your society ?—Yes. We passed a vote of thanks to Mr. Bagshaw and Mr. Broadhead for their services.

TWENTY-SECOND DAY.

E. Platts.

2 July 1867.

21,196. What had they done ?—They had an interview with Mr. Hoole.

21,197. What had they done ?—Mr. Hoole called Mr. Bagshaw in to intercede in the matter.

21,198. What had Mr. Bagshaw to do with the fender trade ?—I will try to explain. Mr. Hoole had been a man that had a great deal to do with the organized trades. When their men went out he saw Mr. Bagshaw passing by, and Mr. Bagshaw came to us and said that Mr. Hoole desired to see some of the men. I was one of the men myself. He said, if we could arrange with the men he should be very happy for them to go out if he could by any means induce them to do so.

21,199. Did he want you to arrange with the men to go out ?—Yes ; Mr. Hoole did.

21,200. These men were men that Mr. Hoole had got from Masbro' ?—There were a few; there were not many at that time.

21,201. There were six of them ?—Yes.

21,202. Why were you to pay them out ?—Mr. Hoole said he would rather have his old men back again. He did not like to be seen in it and he came to us and said he would rather have the men back.

21,203. He could have arranged to have his own men, he had nothing to do but to send the men away ?—Mr. Hoole is a man who would not like to be seen in it—he wanted Bagshaw and Broadhead to do it.

21,204. You were to find the money?—Yes, the trade was to find the money—I would have given them 20*l.* a piece myself if they had been worth it.

21,205. Mr. Hoole had been chairman of the organized trades ?—I believe he had.

21,206. What are the organized trades ? — The delegates of all the men in Sheffield who contribute to the union.

21,207. Mr. Hoole is a master not a workman ?—Mr. Hoole used to mix a deal with working men.

21,208. Was he the chairman of the working men's union ?—I believe he was chairman to the association of delegates, and he asked Mr. Bagshaw to use his influence in the matter. I recollect Mr. Bagshaw stating that to us. He is here and he can say whether I am speaking truthfully or not.

21,209. I am requested to ask you whether Broadhead and Bagshaw did not retire from the matter before Sibray was beaten or whether they continued after that ?—I believe they had retired before.

21,210. Did they retire when they found that Sibray was beaten ?—I believe they had retired before, I believe so ; I will not swear that.

21,211. Are you quite sure that they had retired before ?—I am not quite sure, but I believe they had.

21,212. Had you not had frequent meetings at Broadhead's house ?—No.

21,213. You had meetings at his house ?—I do not know that I had meetings at his house at that time.

21,214. What is the date of the vote of thanks to Broadhead ?—I do not know.

21,215. Was it after Sibray was beaten or after Wastnidge's house was blown up ?—I believe it was before.

21,216. Was not it after ?—No.

21,217. Was not it three or four months after Wastnidge's house was blown up that you passed a vote of thanks to Broadhead and Bagshaw for their assistance to the trade ?—I cannot say, but I believe that it was before.

21,218. Upon your oath was not it the following June ?—I cannot say.

21,219. That took place in November; the man was tried in March, and was not it in the June following that the vote of thanks was passed ?—I cannot say, but my impression is that it was previous. Mr. Broadhead never gave us an item of ill advice in any way.

21,220. (*Mr. Chance.*) What do you mean by saying that Thompson owed his life to you ?—It is in this way. I was in my brother's one Saturday night and Thompson's wife came in ; it was at the time the attorney's expenses only had been paid by John Hellewell. Then came the matter for his defence—the raising of sums for his defence, and his wife came to me and she said that they were in very humble circumstances and they could not get him a counsel, they could not get him help, and from that night she enlisted my sympathy and I got our secretary Thomas Robinson and we did our best to raise funds for counsel for him, and when I have been having drink I very likely should lose my reason ; I do not deny saying that. When I awoke in the morning I knew that I had been saying something wrong and therefore I went across and told them.

21,221. (*Chairman.*) You meant by saving his life that you had got money for a counsel for him ?—Yes.

21,222. When you saw Robinson give Bayles 6*l.* what position did Bayles hold ?—I do not know that he ought to receive any money at all.

21,223. Did you know the amount that he received ?—No.

21,224. You did not know whether it was 6*l.* or any other sum ?—No.

21,225. You said just now that you saw Robinson give Bayles 6*l.* ?—Yes, I saw it.

21,226. You did not know the amount ?—I did not know the amount at that time, but since this inquiry came of course I have heard of it.

21,227. Is that the first time you ever heard of that amount being given to Bayles ?—Yes.

21,228. Did you subscribe more than once to defend Thompson ?—Yes, we had a deal of trouble to raise the counsel money.

21,229. Why did you subscribe to it ?—It was in this way. I went with his wife to his father and mother and they said that they were in the very greatest state of mind.

21,230. Did you go amongst the trade generally ?—Yes.

21,231. Was not the subscription confined to the members of your own union ?—The pound subscription was ; there was nothing wanting about it. We had a general meeting called.

21,232. Was not that subscription a trade matter ?—No.

21,233. Did not you subscribe the money because you believed that he was connected with the trade and had done something in connexion with the trade ?—I subscribed my money because he was connected with the trade.

21,234. Did not you subscribe the money because you believed he had done something connected with the trade ?—No.

21,235. Did you ever hear anybody say that Thompson had done it or not ?—I have heard something said here about " Slipper Jack " having done it.

21,236. Did you hear it said at the time he was in prison ?—No, after he came out. I never heard such a name as " Slipper Jack ; " I never spoke to such a man in my life.

21,237. Is it true that you said, pointing to " Slipper Jack," that he would not be a bad man for the job ?—To the best of my knowledge I never did say so.

21,238. You must know one way or the other ?—If it was at Wylies I could not say so.

21,239. Do you remember on any other occasion Thompson pointing to the man Aldam, or " Slipper Jack," or any one else, and your saying he would not be a bad chap for the job ?—I do not recollect anything of the kind.

21,240. Did you say so ? You cannot forget ?—I cannot remember anything of the kind ; if I did I would freely confess it.

21,241. Do you remember Thompson pointing out a man to you ?—No, I do not remember Thompson pointing any man out to me or hearing Thompson say anything about killing a man.

The witness withdrew.

TWENTY-SECOND DAY.

J. Mountain.

2 July 1867.

Mr. James Mountain sworn and examined.

21,242. (*Mr. Barstow.*) In 1862 were you a clerk to the late Mr. Broadbent, solicitor?—Yes.

21,243. Did he defend Joseph Thompson at the York Spring Assizes in 1862?—Yes, he did.

21,244. Do you know who retained him for defending?—Mr. Bagshaw and another gentleman.

21,245. Do you know who that other gentleman was?—I do not.

21,246. Did you make out a bill of costs?—No; the bill of costs was not made out.

21,247. What did you substitute for the bill of costs?—It was in a round sum.

21,248. How was the money paid?—My impression was, before this morning, that it was paid in a lump.

21,249. Do you remember what the amount was?—It was about 100*l.*

21,250. What is your impression now?—My impression now is that the money was paid in two or three instalments.

21,251. Do you know what instalments they were?—Only the one instalment that it was said Thompson had paid.

21,252. Is that Mr. Broadbent's signature (*handing paper to the witness*)?—Yes, that is Mr. Broadbent's signature.

21,253. Who paid the last instalment?—Mr. Bagshaw and another gentleman came and paid the money.

21,254. Was that the same gentleman who had come with Mr. Bagshaw to retain Mr. Broadbent?—I cannot say.

21,255. What was the amount of the last instalment?—I am sure I cannot say; my impression before to-day was that it was all paid in one sum.

21,256. Was it 100*l.* that he paid?—No.

21,257. You do not remember what it was?—No, I should not like to swear what it was. I have tried to make an inquiry, but I have been informed that the cash-books have been destroyed.

21,258. Do you know what the amount of the first instalment was?—I am sure I cannot tell you.

21,259. Do you know about what it was?—I think it was about 50*l.* if my memory serves me rightly.

21,260. (*Mr. Chance.*) When Mr. Bagshaw called upon you to defend Thompson, did you hear what was said by Bagshaw?—No, he took great interest in the defence; he was continually at the office.

21,261. Were you present when he called upon Mr. Broadbent?—I was present several times.

21,262. You said just now that he took great interest, what did he say?—He took interest in getting the evidence after instructing Mr. Broadbent about the defence.

21,263. Did he come to you more than once?—Yes, several times.

21,264. Did he suggest to you who should be called for the defence?—It was suggested by Mr. Broadbent and Mr. Bagshaw that there should be witnesses called to prove an *alibi.*

21,265. Mr. Bagshaw proposed that as well as Mr. Broadbent?—Yes.

21,266. Was the evidence put before Mr. Bagshaw at all?—I cannot say.

21,267. Were the facts brought before him as far they could be?—Yes, Mr. Bagshaw and Mr. Broadbent read the brief over when I was there.

21,268. And during the time the defence was being prepared, did Mr. Bagshaw call from time to time to see how it was being done?—Yes.

21,269. And took a great interest throughout the whole thing?—Yes, I thought so.

21,270. Were you present when Mr. Bagshaw retained him?—No, I was not present. I was present on several occasions, but I was not present at the time Bagshaw retained Mr. Broadbent. Mr. Broadbent told me to get the depositions as he had been retained by Mr. Bagshaw.

21,271. Were you present on any other occasion when Mr. Bagshaw was at the office consulting upon the case for the prisoner?—Yes, several times.

21,272. You were not present during the time he was retained, but afterwards when he came?—Yes.

The witness withdrew.

Mr. Sugg stated he would admit that the union had retained Mr. Broadbent for Thompson's defence.

J. Robertson.

James Robertson recalled and further examined.

21,273. (*Chairman.*) Take these books in your hand, one is a contribution book and the other is a cash-book?—Yes.

21,274. You have already shown us the book in which there were leaves cut out by you?—Yes.

21,275. And a false entry made by you to cover a payment of 6*l.*?—Yes.

21,276. That was a payment made by you to Bayles?—Yes.

21,277. In the committee room?—Yes, in our meeting room.

21,278. And you had been told as stated this morning, that some of the money was given for the purpose of beating Sibray?—I have heard it stated here to-day.

21,279. At the time that you paid over that money were you aware that it was for beating Sibray?—No; I had no knowledge what the money was for.

21,280. But it was paid by Kenworthy, your secretary, to give to Bayles?—Yes.

21,281. You kept the accounts afterwards?—Yes, from January 1862.

21,282. Did not you keep the accounts in October 1861?—No.

21,283. Look at those accounts in the contribution book, is that in your handwriting "October 1861"?—No.

21,284. Whose is it?—John Kenworthy's writing.

21,285. Who kept those on the 29th of October 1861?—John Kenworthy.

21,286. November the 5th?—John Kenworthy.

21,287. On October 22d, 1861, there is 3*l.* 14*s.* 6*d.*?—Yes.

21,288. Ought that to appear in the cash-book?—Yes.

21,289. Find me that entry in the cash-book?—(*The witness referred to the cash-book.*)

21,290. There is no such entry?—No.

21,291. Now look at October 29th, 2*l.* 6*s.* 6*d.* received?—(*The witness referred to the cash-book.*)

21,292. There is no such entry?—I do not see one.

21,293. Now look at November the 5th, just before the man was blown up 44*l.* 19*s.*?—(*The witness referred to the book.*)

21,294. Look in the cash-book and see if it is entered there?—I do not see it.

21,295. If that is so must not the 13*l.* 2*s.* 6*d.* have been embezzled?—I do not know.

21,296. It must have been either put into the man's own pocket or applied to purposes of which there has been no account rendered in your books?—I do not know that.

TWENTY-SECOND DAY.

J. Robertson.

2 July 1867.

21,297. Can you explain how that would be except in one of those two ways, either that the secretary had put the money into his pocket or that he applied the money in a way he did not like to acknowledge in the books?—No; I cannot say.

21,298. That is the only way to explain it, is it not?—I never had this book in my possession till the 21st of January.

21,299. I call your attention to the payment that had been made at the time just before this man's house was blown up, and where he ought to have entered the payment in his cash-book and it appears that that payment amounts to 13*l.* 2*s.* 6*d.*, of which there is no explanation in the cash-book?—I never noticed that book.

21,300. Can you give any explanation of it?—No, I cannot.

21,301. Now take warning never in the course of your life to go and cut out any leaves?—I will take notice of that. I will bear it in mind.

21,302. Now I come to another item. You paid for Thompson's defence?—Yes.

21,303. Give me the item in your book?—It is not in this book.

21,304. What book is it in?—It is in the other book of mine. You will see the defence expenses 30*l.* somewhere.

21,305. I understand that the expenses were 100*l.*?—No, sir. I will endeavour to explain that.

21,306. That is in the book which you have made up?—Yes.

21,307. It is not an account of things that happened at the time, that is what you call the transcript of another book?—Yes.

21,308. Defence expenses 30*l.*?—Yes.

21,309. We hear that his expenses were 100*l.*?—It was not so.

21,310. What was paid to Broadbent for the expenses of defending Thompson?—I cannot tell you. I did not engage Broadbent, but John Hellewell engaged Mr. Broadbent, and he engaged him without the knowledge of our society.

21,311. But your society paid 30*l.* towards it?—Yes.

21,312. Besides that did you each subscribe 1*l.*?—Yes, we had a voluntary subscription amongst ourselves; all did not pay, there was a portion paid.

21,313. There were 30*l.* out of the funds, and a portion besides, which was voluntary. Who paid the remainder?—Mrs. Thompson, the wife of Joseph Thompson, had some subscription cards printed and posted at different public-houses, and she got a few pounds that way, I could not say how many.

21,314. Did Mr. Bagshaw give anything?—No.

21,315. What had Bagshaw to do with this matter—I believe it was through Mr. Hoole's request, he requested Mr. Bagshaw to see some of the members of our society, to see whether they could come to some arrangement with respect to getting his old hands back again. I believe Mr. Bagshaw came to our meeting, though I do not remember it myself. I was not secretary, but I believe he came to our meeting and named it to our secretary, and Mr. Broadhead and Bagshaw were deputed to go and see Mr. Hoole with respect to terms of getting his grinders back again. They had an interview with my committee, and told our secretary respecting it. What took place at the interview I cannot say.

23,316. Mr. Bagshaw interfered on behalf of your society, was he paid any money by your society?—Yes.

23,317. Who paid him?—John Kenworthy.

23,318. How much?—I cannot say, but I saw John Kenworthy pay him.

23,319. He paid him for the trouble he had been to?—Yes.

23,320. Was Broadhead paid?—No, Broadhead would not have anything.

23,321. He was liberal towards you, but Mr. Bagshaw charged you?—Yes, he charged something, but I do not know what the amount was.

23,322. You began your time in January 1862, you say?—The 21st of January I believe.

23,323. How do you keep your accounts. Let us see whether your accounts are as just as other peoples?—The contribution book and the cash-book will tell.

23,324. Look at January 7th, 1862; there are some errors?—I do not say my accounts are exactly correct, there may be some trifling errors, but that I cannot help.

23,325. The great wrong which you have done is cutting out the leaves?—I am very sorry indeed for having done it. If I had the books they would prove that the amounts were correct.

The witness withdrew.

R. Renshaw.

ROBERT RENSHAW recalled and further examined.

21,326. (*Chairman.*) You have stated that you threw that can of gunpowder into the house of Wastnidge?—Yes.

21,327. And you have stated that you did it alone?—Yes.

21,328. Now we have information that in that respect you are not telling the truth?—I am certain I am.

21,329. We have information that not only you were there, but Bayles was there?—He never was.

21,330. And we have information that you and Bayles, after you had thrown it into the window, ran down all the way into the Wicker, and your story with respect to going into Ebenezer Chapel yard is not true?—Never.

21,331. Do you still stand to that, that you and you alone threw that can into the window?—Yes.

21,332. Was anybody in the street or watching you doing it?—No.

21,333. Was anyone keeping watch for you?—No.

21,334. Was Bayles out that night?—He was not with me.

21,335. Did you see him that night?—I cannot say that.

21,336. How long before that did you see him?—I saw him every day.

21,337. Did you see him after you had done it that night?—No.

21,338. Did he go out with you knowing you were going to do it?—He knowed it was going to be done.

21,339. Was he with you in the same street?—No.

21,340. Was anybody?—No.

21,341. And you swear that you did not go with him?—I will swear that.

21,342. You did it alone?—Yes.

21,343. Do you know where Bayles was that night?—I do not know where he was.

21,344. You are sure that he was not watching for you?—I am sure he was not.

21,345. He knew that you were going to do it?—Yes.

21,346. Did he know what time you were going to do it?—No.

21,347. Was he with you at the theatre?—No.

21,348. Was anybody with you at the theatre?—No.

21,349. Was it agreed that you were to go to the

TWENTY-SECOND DAY.

R. Renshaw.

2 July 1867.

theatre, and after coming from the theatre you were to do it ?—No.

21,350. Bayles did not know exactly the time that you would do it ?—No, nor Cutler either.

21,351. I have told you that we have information, Cutler has told us that Bayles told him that you and he did it together ?—It is very fine of Cutler talking about a dead man, is it not. I know.

21,352. He says that Bayles told him he himself did it ?—I would not believe Cutler if he was to go on his knees, because Bayles is not alive, and he never told him so. I would not believe him if he did tell him, but he did not, and I do not believe he did.

21,353. No one would tell him he was party to a murder unless he was ?—Cutler may hold out, and you will believe him ; you will not believe me, when I am speaking the truth.

21,354. Mrs. Wastnidge saw two men ?—She never did ; that was the biggest story ever told in a court.

21,355. Mrs. Thompson speaks to two, Cutler speaks to Bayles going, you were with another person. Do you still persist in that, that you were alone ?—I am certain ; Mrs. Thompson has told her at the top of the stairs that she never seed one.

21,356. Did you mention yesterday that you were going to tell this story ?—I must consider before I answer that question.

21,357. Did you mention yesterday that you were going to tell this story ?—I will not say that.

21,358. What did you say yesterday ?—I made up my mind yesterday when I saw the lot of people here to come straight to you with it, and I brought it.

Mrs. HARRIETT WASTNIDGE recalled and further examined.

Mrs. H. Wastnidge.

21,359. (*Chairman.*) When you looked out of the window how many men do you say you saw ?—I cannot say; there were some, but I cannot say how many.

21,360. Will you swear that there were more than one ?—Yes, I am sure there was.

21,361. Were they on both sides or on the same side of the street ?—No, they seemed to have parted.

21,362. Was the person you saw walking or running ?—He seemed to be running ; he looked as if he was stumbling.

21,363. Do you know whether that man (*pointing to Renshaw*) was one of the men ?—No, I am sure I do not.

21,364. (*Mr. Barstow.*) Did you hear where they ran to ?—The greatest run that I heard was the side the house was on ; I thought they stumbled against the window shutters in running towards the chapel ; that was the man I saw run away.

21,365. (*Chairman.*) You only saw one man ?—I saw him going on, but I am sure I did not know him.

21,366. You saw one man going towards the chapel ?—Yes.

21,367. You swear more particularly to one man than the other ?—Yes.

21,368. (*Mr. Barstow.*) Did you see the other men ?—No.

21,369. Or another man ?—No, I did not, they seemed to have divided.

21,370. What is your reason for saying that there was more than one man ?—I am positive that there was more than one man.

21,371. Why do you say so ?—I saw them as if they had parted, one on one side of the road and the other on the other side.

21,372. Did you see them part ?—No, I did not.

21,373. Did you see one man in the street ?—Yes, the other side of the road; this one man, who I thought was Thompson, was below our window, and when they got lower down they looked as if there two on the other side, and one on the side we lived on going towards the chapel.

21,374. (*Chairman to Renshaw.*) Did your coat catch the cotter of the shutter ?—No, nor nobody else's. I am telling you that is the biggest lie that ever could be imagined that this woman is telling. I am speaking candidly you know, and she knows that she is telling a lie.

21,375. (*Mr. Chance.*) Why should she tell a lie ?—Because she never see'd nobody.

21,376. (*Mr. Barstow to Mrs. Wastnidge.*) How far is the Ebenezer chapel from the house ?—Not many yards.

21,377. Could you hear the footsteps of the men that ran away ?—No.

21,378. Is your husband here ?—Yes.

The witness withdrew.

GEORGE WASTNIDGE recalled and further examined.

G. Wastnidge.

21,379. (*Chairman.*) Do you recollect Mrs. O'Rourke being brought out of the cellar of your house ?—Yes.

21,380. Do you remember whether that man was there (*pointing to Renshaw*) ?—No, I cannot recollect.

The witness withdrew.

21,381. (*Chairman to Renshaw.*) A man going to the Wicker would pass by the Ebenezer chapel ?—Yes, it would be a straight road to go.

The witness withdrew.

(*Chairman.*) Having got through the Acorn Street inquiry to-day much more rapidly than we expected, we have very few cases left to inquire into of outrage or matters connected with the trade of Sheffield. I therefore take this opportunity of inviting all persons, whoever they may be, to give us any information which they think will aid or assist us in the inquiry upon which we are engaged ; and if there are either masters who have to complain of outrages committed by the men, or men who have to complain of outrages committed by the masters, we shall be very glad to hear them and listen to any information which can be afforded us before we close this inquiry. We now give this invitation publicly and desire that whatever information is intended to be given should be given speedily.

Adjourned to to-morrow at 11 o'clock.

TWENTY-THIRD DAY.

3 July 1867.

TWENTY-THIRD DAY.

Council Hall, Sheffield, Wednesday, 3rd July 1867.

PRESENT:

WILLIAM OVEREND, Esq., Q.C.	GEORGE CHANCE, Esq.
THOMAS IRWIN BARSTOW, Esq.	J. E. BARKER, Esq. Secretary.

WILLIAM OVEREND, ESQ., Q.C., IN THE CHAIR.

Mr. Sugg, in reply to the remarks made by the Chairman at the close of yesterday's proceedings, stated that it was not the intention of the men to bring forward any charges against the masters.

The Chairman inquired whether the Examiners were to understand that the men did not bring any such charges, or that no such charges existed.

Mr. Sugg replied that the men did not bring forward any charges.

The Chairman stated that the business of the Commission was to inquire into any outrages or wrongs connected with the trades, and that if any such transaction came to their knowledge it would be their duty to inquire into it whether it was committed by masters or by men.

Mr. Chambers submitted that it would be fair on the part of Mr. Sugg to say whether or not any such accusations against the masters existed, and challenged Mr. Sugg, if they existed, to bring them forward that they might be investigated.

Mr. Sugg stated that whatever charges his clients made would be investigated in another place.

The Chairman again stated that the business of the Commission was to inquire into cases of outrage, and that if such cases came to their knowledge it would be their duty to inquire into them.

Mr. Sugg replied that he was instructed that there was no such case at present to bring before the Commissioners.

C. Baxter.

CHARLES BAXTER sworn and examined.

21,382. (*Chairman.*) What are you?—A saw grinder.

21,383. I believe you worked at Slack, Sellars, and Grayson's, in the next hull to Roebuck, Woolhouse, and Hague?—Yes.

21,384. And I believe they refused to come out on strike to help the saw-handle makers?—Yes.

21,385. I believe that Mr. Skidmore and Mr. Barker came to you on a Sunday and asked you to take the bands of those men?—Yes.

21,386. And did you take them?—Yes.

21,387. What became of them?—Well, I had them about six months.

21,388. What became of them?—I sold them. I went and asked Mr. Skidmore what I was to do with them. I did not like it.

21,389. And what did Skidmore give you?—30*s*.

21,390. And you have sold the bands?—I went to Mr. Skidmore and I told him I had these bands in my hands, and I wanted to be shut of them, and I asked him what I was to do with them. He said I was to do away with them the best way I could. There was a mark upon them and I thought I had better destroy them, and I sold them for 24*s*.

21,391. When was this?—I cannot tell you; it was six months after the bands were taken.

21,392. What is the date of the bands being taken?—It was somewhere about a twelvemonth since.

21,393. Then you stole the bands and put the money in your pocket?—Yes.

21,394. And Skidmore gave you 30*s*. for doing so?—Yes.

21,395. And all because those men would not join in the strike?—Well, I believe it was.

21,396. Was any person joined with you in that matter?—No.

21,397. Were you solicited in the first instance by Skidmore to do it?—I asked him who had sent him to me, and he said Mr. Broadhead had recommended him that so long as I worked at the wheel I should be the likeliest man to do it.

21,398. You were a grinder at the same wheel, were you?—No, in the next hull.

21,399. In the same wheel, but in the next hull?—Yes.

The witness withdrew.

W. Mason.

WILLIAM MASON sworn and examined.

21,400. (*Mr. Barstow.*) You are a fork maker, are you not?—I am a fork grinder.

21,401. And you were formerly a member of the fork grinders union?—Yes.

21,402. Do you remember that in 1859 it was resolved that no member of your union should work for any but one of 10 masters?—We chose 10 masters and we were not to work for any master in the town besides these 10.

21,403. You were then working for Mr. Thomas Jackson?—Yes.

21,404. And he was one of the 10?—Yes.

21,405. I believe he did not continue to find you work?—No; not for long.

21,406. To whom did you go then?—Mr. Samuel Burrowes.

21,407. He was not one of the 10 masters, was he?—No.

21,408. Do you remember the day on which you removed your tools to go to work for Mr. Burrowes?—I cannot say that I remember the day.

21,409. Where were you working for Burrowes?—At Furnace Hill wheel.

21,410. Where were you working for Jackson?—At Shiloh, at Mr. Chadburn's, in the Nursery.

21,411. Did you remove your tools from the Nursery to the Furnace Hill wheel?—No; first I removed them to Mr. Marsden's place.

21,412. Do you remember anything happening to you on that day when you removed your tools?—Yes.

21,413. What was it?—A party illused me the same night.

21,414. What time of the day was this?—I cannot say the exact time at night.

21,415. It was night time, was it?—Yes; it was night time.

21,416. And where was it?—The first time they met me in Corporation Street and took me as far as the iron bridge almost.

21,417. What happened?—Well, they knocked me down and kicked me.

TWENTY-THIRD DAY.

W. Mason.

3 July 1867.

21,418. Who were they?—There was John Smith.

21,419. And who else?—I cannot remember at present.

(*Chairman.*) Do not be in a hurry, think for a moment, who were the men.

21,420. (*Mr. Barstow.*) Tell us how many there were?—Five; I had five up, but I cannot think of their names at present; there were 30 in the party altogether, I should say, at least.

21,421. And you summoned five, did you?—Yes.

21,422. Were they union men?—Yes.

21,423. What was done with the men?—Two of them got fined.

21,424. Do you remember how much they were fined?—No.

21,425. What was done to the other three?—They were set at liberty.

21,426. Why were they set at liberty?—At the town hall.

21,427. But why were they set at liberty?—There was not witness enough.

21,428. (*Chairman.*) You could not identify them, I suppose?—No.

21,429. And you could not prove that they had done the thing, and so they were liberated?—Yes.

21,430. (*Mr. Barstow.*) After you had been a few weeks in Mr. Burrowe's service, do you remember anything happening to you?—Powder being put into the trough.

21,431. Do you know how long that was after you had been in his service?—About three weeks after I was in there; I had just commenced.

21,432. What happened to you?—It burnt my face.

21,433. Did it go off?—Yes, it went off and burnt my arms and face.

21,434. Did it burn you?—Yes; my arms right up here (*describing the same*), and my face.

21,435. I believe you had a pair of spectacles on?—Yes.

21,436. Do you think that that saved your eyes?—Yes, or else they would have been burnt out; I should not have seen any more.

21,437. Who was secretary at that time?—I cannot say whether it was Charles Sharpe or George Smith.

21,438. Did you give any information about this blowing up to the police?—No.

21,439. Why did you not give information about it?—To the police?

21,440. Yes?—They did not know anything about it.

21,441. You did so when you were assaulted?—Yes.

21,442. And two of the men were fined?—Yes.

21,443. Why did you not go to the police when you were blown up?—I could not tell who did it.

21,444. But it might have been found out, you know?—We did go to Mr. Jackson, but we could not find it.

21,445. (*Chairman.*) Did they try to find out who had done it?—Yes.

21,446. Did they send the police up to your place to see if they could find out who had done it?—Well, I expect so; I was fast abed. They came from the town hall in a cab to get me here.

21,447. (*Mr. Barstow.*) Had you any reason to suspect who did it?—No, I cannot believe who did it.

21,448. You had no guess who did it?—No.

41,449. Who do you think did it?—I cannot say?—I do not know.

41,450. Can you tell us why you think it was done?—Because I left off working for those 10 masters to go and work for Burrowes.

21,451. (*Chairman.*) Had any person any private grudge against you or quarrel with you?—No.

21,452. (*Mr. Barstow.*) Who was working in the next hull to you?—Well, there was some scissor grinders working at the same place; I do not know who the workmen were.

21,453. Do you know who they were?—No, I cannot tell you their names.

21,454. (*Chairman.*) You surely know the names of the scissor grinders who were working with you?—No, I do not.

The witness withdrew.

T. Roebuck.

THOMAS ROEBUCK sworn and examined.

21,455. (*Mr. Chance.*) Are you a fork grinder?—Yes.

21,456. Are you a member of any union?—No.

21,457. Have you ever been so?—Yes.

21,458. How long have you ceased to be so?—About two months.

21,459. How long were you a member of the union?—Well, I was a member of the union some four, or five, or weeks before then.

21,460. For how long?—For about six weeks.

21,461. (*Chairman.*) And you were only a member for six weeks?—No.

21,462. (*Mr. Chance.*) But have you been a member at other times besides those six weeks?—Yes.

21,463. How long is it since you first became a member at all?—Well, it is 10 or 11 years since.

21,464. Have you been a member at different times during those 10 or 11 years?—Yes.

21,465. Previous to the year 1859 did you work for Mr. Askham of Broad Lane?—Yes, I was a policeman for 12 months previously to that, but before that I worked for him.

21,466. When did you work for Mr. Askham?—I worked for him 10 or 11 years since.

21,467. After working for Mr. Askham did you enter the police force?—Yes.

21,468. Why was that?—Trade was very bad and prices very low, and I entered the police force to better my condition.

21,469. How long did you remain a policeman?—11 months.

21,470. And why did you leave the police force?—Mr. Askham sent for me back again.

21,471. Was that to work for him again as a fork grinder?—Yes.

21,472. Did you go back to him?—Yes.

21,473. When was that?—That was in 1859 in February.

21,474. Did you begin to work for him?—Yes.

21,475. After commencing work did you meet any of the committee of the fork grinders' union?—Well, I met several fork grinders, but I do not know whether they were on the committee. I never went down to the committee, and so I am not prepared to say whether they were on the committee or not.

21,476. Was that before or after commencing work with Mr. Askham?—Before.

21,477. Do you remember the names of those whom you met?—Yes, I met George Cooper for one.

21,478. Who besides?—A person named Sykes.

21,479. What was his Christian name?—Harry Sykes.

21,480. Who besides?—William Norton.

21,481. Who besides?—George Armitage.

21,482. Who besides?—Well, I did not notice anybody particularly.

21,483. Had you met them at different times?—Yes.

21,484. And did they say anything to you about commencing work?—Yes, George Cooper told me I had better not commence working, that I should be working in opposition to the rules of the trade. He said they had passed a resolution that nobody was to work for anybody that they did not approve of, and I was to work for the one that they appointed. I said I should work for Mr. Askham, that I had worked for him previous to being a policeman, and I thought I had a right to work for him, and that I should go back and work for him again. They said if I did I should get done. Those were the words that he made use of.

21,485. (*Chairman.*) Was that Cooper?—Yes.

TWENTY-THIRD DAY.

T. Roebuck.

3 July 1867.

21,486. (*Mr. Chance.*) Did he say anything more at that time?—No, I went away and left them. I thought it better to have nothing to do with them in any shape or form.

21,487. Did any other men have anything to say to you?—Well, Norton came to my house in our own yard and called me all kinds of names in my own house.

21,488. (*Chairman.*) What kind of names?—"Knobstick" and the like.

21,489. (*Mr. Chance.*) Was that before you went to Mr. Askham after?—It was before.

21,490. Did he say anything to you about working? —No, not particularly.

21,491. Did any of the others whom you mentioned just now say anything to you?—No, not particularly.

21,492. But did they call you bad names?—Well, nothing but bad names and swearing, and such like.

21,493. (*Chairman.*) But tell us what kind of language they used: whether it was simply abuse, or whether it was language connected with the union. What name did they call you?—They simply called me a "knobstick," and swore at me.

21,494. (*Mr. Chance.*) Did you go after that to work for Mr. Askham?—Yes, I was working there when he came to grind in the yard where I live.

21,495. When you were working for Mr. Askham did anything happen to you?—Yes, one morning when I went to work there was powder put in the grinding-trough.

21,496. Did you discover that yourself?—Yes, it so happened that that morning the sun shone in the trough and it glittered, and I took a handful of it out to see whether it was powder. I could not really think that it was, and I found that it was powder.

21,497. Do you know how much powder there would be in the trough?—Well, I should think there would be about a couple of pounds. It was laid all across the bottom of the trough; I should think I collected a pound and brought it down to Mr. Jackson. I had not it weighed; it might be more.

21,498. (*Chairman.*) Was it all powder, or mixed with smithy slack?—Well, I daresay it would be; I could see it among the dust in the bottom of the trough.

21,499. (*Mr. Chance.*) Supposing you had not discovered that and had set to work, would it have exploded?—As soon as ever I ground a fork it would have exploded.

21,500. What damage would it have done?—I do not know; it might have blown my head off. I should have been within two feet of it.

21,501. It probably would have done you most serious damage, would it not?—Yes.

21,502. It must have done so?—Yes.

21,503. Did you afterwards try to discover the person who had done it?—I told Mr. Jackson whom I suspected.

21,504. Whom did you suspect?—Well, I suspected a person of the name of Johnson.

21,505. What was his christian name?—Samuel.

21,506. Why did you suspect him?—Because he was the only person who was in the wheel when I went that same morning. As soon as I found the powder, I went and saw him in the room above. He was the only person about the wheel.

21,507. What was Johnson?—He was a fork grinder.

21,508. (*Chairman.*) Was he a union man?—Yes.

21,509. (*Mr. Chance.*) When you went to see him, did you say anything to him?—No; I simply went to see if anybody was in, and I saw him. I came down again.

21,510. Had you any other reason for supposing that it was Johnson who had done this?—Well, the door was not broken, and the lock the same as I left it the night previous, and so I could not think that anybody had done it during the night.

21,511. Was Johnson the only person who could have done it?—Well, he was the only man that I could suspect.

21,512. Was there any man who could have got to your trough besides Johnson?—Not without they had had a picklock and had picked the lock of the door.

21,513. Were no proceedings of any kind taken against Johnson?—No; I believe Mr. Jackson sent a detective to search his house, but they could not find any trace to lead to anything to convict him.

21,514. Had he ever made use of any threats against you?—No, no further than calling me a "knobstick."

21,515. He had called you a "knobstick"?—Yes. He frequently put his head in the door of my room, and called me names of that description when I was working.

21,516. (*Chairman.*) Is this man alive?—Yes.

21,517. Where does he work?—Well, I am sure I do not know. I think he works in Milton Street, but I will not be certain.

21,518. For whom does he work?—For Thomas Whiteley; he did do so sometime ago.

21,519. (*Mr. Chance.*) Had you ever had any quarrel with Johnson or any other person?—No, I had no quarrel with anyone.

21,520. And you believe that the putting of the powder in the trough was the result of some trade matter?—Yes, because there were several more who were blown up the same morning.

21,521. Give the names of those who were blown up?—A person of the name of William Mason was blown up the same morning, and Samuel Gunson, and James Gambles and Charles Royston; I think that was all.

21,522. Were they all working men?—Yes, they were all working; the powder exploded, and blew them up the same morning.

21,523. Were they all working at the same place? —No, at different parts of the town.

21,524. Were those men members of the union?—No, none of them.

21,525. Were they infringing the rule which you were said to be infringing?—Yes, it was the same.

21,526. Were they working for others than the 10 masters?—Yes.

21,527. (*Chairman.*) Do you know for whom James Gambles is working?—He is dead.

21,528. (*Mr. Chance.*) Do you know for whom Charles Royston is working?—He is working at the Bee Hive wheel in West Street; he is grinding hay-forks.

21,529. Is there a distinct union for the hay-fork grinders?—No; I think they have not unions amongst them.

21,530. Have you any notion or belief as to anyone who blew up any of these other men?—Well, there was one man who was apprehended and sent for six months to prison for blowing up Gambles; that was Sykes; he was sent to prison for 12 months, but before his time expired he was liberated and sent to America, and I have been told that it was the trade that sent him; he was liberated before the time was up out of the Wakefield House of Correction, and he went to America.

21,531. (*Chairman.*) How was that?—I do not know how it was; he was fined in the first onset, and he was sent to Wakefield for neglecting to pay the fine.

21,532. And then he paid the fine and went to America?—Yes, somebody paid the fine and he went to America.

21,533. (*Mr. Chance.*) Was Sykes one of the men that you met with about working for Mr. Askham? is that the same person?—That is the same person; he threatened Gambles, and it was proved against him, and he was fined for it.

21,534. He was fined for that, but was he convicted for putting powder into the trough; what was he sentenced to imprisonment for?—For neglecting to pay the fine.

21,535. Was he sent for 12 months?—Either six or 12 months, I cannot be certain which it was now; I was not there to hear the trial.

TWENTY-THIRD DAY.

T. Roebuck.

3 July 1867.

21,536. I thought you told us just now that he was convicted of blowing up Gambles?—No, it was not proved against him; he was convicted of threatening to blow him up and he was fined for it, and then sent to prison for refusing to pay the fine.

21,537. Do you know anything else about those other blowings up, or attempts to blow up? do you know any men who were suspected of them?—No, I do not know whether anybody was suspected.

21,538. (*Chairman.*) For whom were you working at the time when you had this powder put into your trough?—At Mr. Askham's.

21,539. Where are his works?—In Broad Lane.

21,540. How many persons worked in the place?—In the same room where I worked there was only one other man, and he was a pen-blade grinder.

21,541. What was his name?—Crofts.

21,542. What day of the week was it that you were blown up?—It was Tuesday I think.

21,543. Was the hull in which you worked a room that locked up?—Yes.

21,544. Who locked it up before you went away on the Monday night?—I locked it up.

21,545. What became of the key?—It was taken to the time-keeper, a person of the name of Sharpe.

21,546. What time of night was it when you locked it up?—Between 6 and 7 o'clock.

21,547. Is that place where you worked composed of various hulls?—There is not another hull on the same landing, there is one above, but not one on the same landing.

21,548. There is another hull you say up above?—Yes.

21,549. Who worked at that hull?—Several worked up there; this Johnson worked up there, and William Brown.

21,550. Who besides?—A person of the name of Eastwood.

21,551. Who besides?—There were two up there whose names I did not know.

21,552. What were those men who worked in the room above you?—They were all union men.

21,553. Were they all men in the same union whose rules you were violating?—Yes.

21,554. Was it a hull open to the street, or had they to pass through any gates?—They had to pass through the gates into the yard.

21,555. In order to pass through the gates would the gates have to be opened for them the first thing in the morning?—Yes.

21,556. Who would open the gates?—Sharpe; he lived at the gates.

21,557. Is Sharpe alive?—Yes.

21,558. What time did you go to the works on the Tuesday morning when you found the powder?—About a quarter to 8 o'clock.

21,559. Did you find the door locked as you had left it the night before?—Yes.

21,560. Could you tell whether any person had made an entry into the place?—No.

21,561. Not at all?—No, not at all.

21,562. You have been a policeman, have you not?—Yes.

21,563. Can you tell us whether any person had made his way by force into your room during the night?—Well, I should say not.

21,564. Then in order to have got into your room, if anybody had got in, in what way would he have got in?—He would have had to pick the lock.

21,565. Did you notice whether the windows were fastened?—There are not windows; at least there are not window shuts, there are windows, but they could not very well get into them.

21,566. Therefore the only mode by which a person could get into the hull would be by opening the door, and if the door was locked, by opening the lock?—Yes.

21,567. When you went in the morning did you find anything the matter with the lock?—No, it opened the same as usual.

21,568. You say you went into the place and you found the powder?—Yes, I found the powder.

21,569. You found your door fastened?—Yes.

21,570. And you opened it with your key in the regular way?—Yes.

21,571. And then when you found the powder you went upstairs; and whom did you find in the room up above?—This Johnson.

21,572. And he was the only man?—Yes.

21,573. Was there any other person in the wheel besides Johnson and yourself that morning when you went there?—No.

21,574. You were the only workmen of any sort?—There were some in the cutlers' shop, but not in the grinding-wheel.

21,575. Had you any quarrel with the cutlers?—No.

21,576. Not at all?—No, they had no interest in the matter.

21,577. Where were the cutlers' shops?—Down at the bottom; they did not go the same way; they go up another flight of steps altogether.

21,578. Do you know whether there was any person working upstairs at the time when you left on the Monday night?—No, I did not go up to see.

21,579. Supposing a man came in in the morning to get in and go upstairs and he passed your door, to get to the stairs above he would have first to apply at the outer door to be let in, would he not?—He would not go to my door, he would go to the outer door, to the time-keeper.

21,580. That you say was a man called Sharpe?—Yes.

21,581. Is Sharpe here?—He is living, I don't know whether he is here.

21,582. Did you inquire whether he had let anybody else in besides this man?—Yes, he had let a few cutlers in, but there was not a grinder besides them.

21,583. Did you ascertain whether any grinders had been left on the premises after you had left the night before?—I did not ascertain that.

21,584. You ought to have been sharp enough for that?—I was not aware that they were going to do it.

21,585. Then you went upstairs and you found him at work?—Yes.

21,586. You did not challenge him with it?—No.

21,587. And he had often threatened you?—Yes, he had called me names.

21,588. And you say the other man had done the same?—Yes, the names I have mentioned.

21,589. You say it was placed in your trough. In order to go to work, how would you sit in the trough with reference to the powder?—We sit in this position (*describing the same to the Examiners*).

21,590. With the powder under your legs?—Yes.

21,591. Therefore you would sit immediately above the powder?—Yes.

21,592. And if the powder blew up it would explode immediately underneath you?—Yes.

21,593. You say there were 2 lbs. of powder?—Yes, I should say 2 lbs. or 3 lbs.

21,594. And how far were you from it?—Betwixt two and three feet.

21,595. And you have never challenged this man with it at all?—No, I told Mr. Jackson and he made the necessary inquiry; but it could not be proved against him, and I thought it was better to let the thing stop as it was, if Mr. Jackson could not make anything of it.

21,596. You have been in the police force you say?—Yes.

21,597. Do you know whether the keys of the two rooms are of the same pattern, and whether your door-key would unlock the room above?—No it would not, I have tried it and it would not, and the outer door key would not. They were all separate keys and different locks.

21,598. Is yours a common key and lock?—Yes.

21,599. Having been in the police force you will

TWENTY-THIRD DAY.

T. Roebuck.

3 July 1867.

be able to tell me this—supposing a man were to use a picklock to unlock the door, would it be competent to him to lock it again ?—Yes, he might lock it again with a picklock.

21,600. What occurs to your mind as being the mode in which the room was entered ?—Well it is my opinion that it was entered while I went out. I unlocked the door and went down into the yard for perhaps three or four minutes, and it is my firm conviction that my room was entered and powder put in the trough while I was out.

21,601. When was that ?—Just after I had unlocked it. I went in to the wheel and took my coat off and then I went out.

21,602. I do not understand you ?—I unlocked it and took my coat off, at perhaps a few minutes to 8 o'clock; then I went down into the yard for three or four minutes, and I looked into the trough then, and I discovered the powder.

21,603. Your belief is that it was done during the time that you were absent from the hull going into the yard ? how long were you absent ?—About three or four minutes.

21,604. Could a man come down from above and go into your hull and do this, and go back again in three or four minutes ?—Yes, very easily.

21,605. In going into the yard could you see him come down ?—No ; there are two yards, and I was there perhaps three or four minutes.

21,606. Where had you gone to ? had you gone to the privy ?—Yes.

21,607. And you could not see any person who came down from above ?—No. I could not there because it was in another yard.

21,608. Did you inquire at all amongst the men below, the cutlers, who had done it ?—No.

21,609. Could the men below have easily got up into your room ?—If they felt disposed ; but there was nobody, only the blade makers, and they would have no difficulty in going up above.

21,610. Had you any quarrel with the blade makers ?—No, not at all.

21,611. Would this man above see you go downstairs ?—Oh yes.

21,612. He could see you going to the privy ?—He could not see the privy, because it was in the yard below, but he could see me go down and go across the yard.

21,613. What was he doing when you went upstairs and found him in his hull ?—He was putting some forks on the board.

21,614. Did you not speak to him ?—No, I saw him and came down, and I went right down to Mr. Sharpe and I took the powder down to Mr. Askham, and he said he would take me down to Mr. Jackson in half an hour or an hour; and I came down to see Mr. Jackson and brought the powder that I had collected out of the trough.

21,615. Supposing you had been blown up on your trough, how would that have affected the man in the room above ?—I do not suppose it would have blown the floor up ; there is a good strong floor.

21,616. (*Mr. Barstow.*) The window was open, was it not ?—Yes.

21,617. (*Chairman.*) When you went back did you leave the window open on anything of that kind ?—The windows are all open ; they are large windows with no glass in them.

21,618. Then in your judgment if the powder had blown up it would not have done damage to the man above ?—No, it would be very near to the windows, and it would have had free access out of the windows.

21,619. Because you know it is not a likely thing that a man would go and blow himself up ?—No, he would not.

21,620. In your judgment could you have been blown up without damage to the man above ?—I do not see how it could have done damage, because I was so near to the window that the pressure of the powder would have gone out of the window.

21,621. Did that man ever talk to you ? did you make it known that you had found the powder ?—Yes.

21,622. Did you ever say anything to him about it ?—I never talked to him about it.

21,623. Did you talk to others who had called you a "knobstick" ?—No, I did not say anything about it.

21,624. Did they say anything to you ?—No.

21,625. Did they know that you had been down to the police about it ?—Yes, they knew that.

21,626. Have you, since you took steps to have it investigated, had any powder put in your trough or had anything done to you ?—No.

21,627. The other men you say were working at other places ?—Yes.

21,628. We have had them before us already ; they are Mason and Gunson ?—Yes, there were several besides them.

21,629. Blown up ?—Yes, Gunson is in America.

21,630. Do you know whether Gunson was really working for men other than the prescribed ten ?—Yes, I was told that he was.

21,631. You were told at the time, were you ?—Yes.

21,632. And Mason too ?—Yes.

21,333. Do you know at what time of the day those men were blown up ?—It was all in the morning part; when they were beginning their work in the morning.

21,634. Do you happen to know whether any of the union men were working at the same wheel where Mason was ?—No, I think they were all working obnoxious to the trade where Mason was.

21,635. (*Mr. Chance*) What is Sharpe's christian name ?—I do not know.

21,636. Is he still there ?—No, he is not there now.

21,637. Where is he now ?—He is working in the saw trade as a saw smith.

21,638. Do you know where he is likely to be heard of ?—I am sure I do not know ; perhaps Mr. Askham might know ; Mr. Askham's first wife and he were relations, and so perhaps he might know where he was.

21,639. (*Chairman.*) Are you quite sure that there were no other persons connected with the grinding establishment but this man on the premises at the time ?—Oh yes, because I went up in the room to look, and I looked in at the door, and there was nobody in the room but this Johnson.

21,640. Were there any other grinders besides yourself and this man in that part of the building ?—No, not that way,

21,641. Did you apply at all to the union about it?—No.

21,642. This was in the month of February 1859, was it not ?—Yes, on the 17th of February.

21,643. Have you ever heard it stated who blew up these people, Mason and Gunson ?—Yes, I have heard say that it was Crooks since this inquiry commenced.

21,644. That is my impression ; but I have not my notes here, and I cannot refer to it. My own impression is that Crooks stated that he had blown them up.

21,645. (*Mr. Chance.*) Is Gunson dead ? — No, Gambles is dead.

21,646. (*Mr. Barstow.*) Do you know at all what the object of this rule is, limiting the men to work for only ten masters ?—It was to stop competition.

21,647. (*Chairman.*) What was to become of all the rest of the masters, who were not to have any men ?—They divided the trade and selected the men out.

21,648. But supposing there were 20 men in the trade, do you mean to say that the union appointed 10 masters who should have men to work for them, or else they should be driven out of the trade ?—They were compelled either to work for them, or else they would not be recognised at all.

21,649. But do you mean to say that the rule of

TWENTY-THIRD DAY.

T. Roebuck.

3 July 1867.

the union was that the men must only work for the 10 masters whom they had selected?—Yes.

21,650. How many fork grinders were there in Sheffield at that time?—Better than 100; about 120.

21,651. 120 masters?—120 grinders.

21,652. But there were 10 persons for whom you could work?—Yes.

21,653. How many masters were there in the same situation as those 10?—Several table-knife manufacturers were getting forks at that time, and they wanted to stop them altogether, and to force them to buy the forks of those 10.

21,654. It was to prevent the table-knife grinders from grinding forks, was it?—Yes, that was one object in it. The other object was to bring little masters out of the market.

21,655. Do you know whether the 10 masters made any arrangement at all, or did anything?—They were not allowed to work. The 10 that they appointed were not allowed to work at all. They were to manage the business and sell the forks and give them out to the men that ground them, and not work themselves at all.

21,656. That was the rule?—Yes, to bring their labour out of the market altogether.

21,657. They were not to work themselves, but to employ men appointed by the union?—Yes.

21,658. And all the other masters were not to be allowed to work at all, nor was any man to be allowed to work for them?—No. I had been in the habit of grinding forks and selling them. I was not allowed to do that. I was not appointed to be a master by the trade.

21,659. You were confined simply to your own part of the trade, and were not allowed to have anything to do with any other?—No, I was not allowed to work on my own account; but I was to go to people whom they had appointed.

21,660. And if you did not do that you were to give up work?—I might do as I liked, but they would not recognise me at all.

21,661. Does that rule exist now?—No, they must carry it out.

21,662. How long did it exist?—Towards two years; and it is carried out now to a certain extent, as far as they can carry it.

21,663. How far is that?—If they can keep grinders out of work and make them go to work for a master they select, it is all right.

21,664. Do you know where Gunson is now?—I have been told he is in America.

21,665. Do you know what was the reason why he went to America?—No.

21,666. Do you know whether he was sent out or not?—No.

21,667. Nor whether he went out by his own funds or how he went?—No, I never heard anything, only that he did go.

21,668. But he was driven out of the market?—Yes.

21,669. What wages can you earn as a fork grinder? Towards 2*l.* a week, a man that has full employment.

21,670. Have you boys under you?—Yes, we are allowed to have one boy.

21,671. How much can a mn and a boy earn?—Perhaps 2*l.* 10*s.* or 2*l.* 12*s.*

21,672. It was in order to keep up their prices that this rule was passed?—Yes.

21,673. If you had been allowed to work independently of the union, what would have been the price which you would have got for your work?—Well, the prices very often have gone down where there has not been a union.

21,674. How much?—They have gone down to half price.

21,675. If you were allowed to work as a master, what would you make?—It would all depend upon whether the union exists or not. If there was a union of course I could earn more.

21,676. When you worked as a master what did you make?—When the union was together I could make that and more. I could make as much as 3*l.* a week.

21,677. Therefore if a man was content with getting 30*s.* a week he was not allowed to do it?—No.

21,678. And they compelled him to work in such a way as to drive the other men out of the trade to such an extent that every man should be able to get 3*l.* or 2*l.* 10*s.* a week for himself and his boy; was that the object of the rule?—Yes.

21,679. The little master makes up the things, does he not?—Yes, we buy them in the rough state and sell them in the finished state.

21,680. Do you sell them to the merchants?—Yes, to both the merchants and the manufacturers.

21,681. Is there any rule in the union about a good workman and a bad workman by which a good workman only gets as much as a bad workman?—No, there is no particular rule about that.

21,682. Can one man get more than another?—Yes, a good workman can always get more than a bad workman.

21,683. According to the rules of the union, a good workman can always have his price?—He will have the best work.

21,684. Is there any fixed minimum price according to the rules of the union?—Yes.

21,685. What is the minimum price?—So much a gross.

21,686. According to that, how much wages can a man earn at the lowest?—At the lowest, where there has not been a union——

21,687. But when there was a union, according to the rules of the union, how much could a man make?—He could earn about 2*l.* a week; that is the lowest.

21,688. Do you recollect the time before unions existed, when there was no union?—No; there was a union when I was a boy.

21,689. There has been always a union, then?—The table-knife and steel fork grinders where all together, when I was a boy.

21,690. But have you never known the trade when there was no union?—Yes for years.

21,691. What was the effect of that?—Prices went down.

21,692. Was the reason of that because there were more men in the trade?—Because men had to do more work, and they overstocked the market; that is the reason that prices went down.

21,693. So the prices went down, and in order to get larger wages, they had to do more work?—Yes, they had to do four or five gross for the same wages as they now get for doing two or three gross.

21,694. (*Mr. Chance.*) I suppose that you are in favour of unions when they are properly conducted?—Well, I see the result of it; I see that the prices are down without the unions; I am in favour of them without blowing up, but I cannot do with blowing up.

21,695. (*Chairman.*) Have you ever thought what would be the effect upon the fork trade of Sheffield supposing you had a union and you only allowed the men to work for 10 masters? in that case Sheffield, as a fork making town would be very insignificant in competition with other towns, would it not?—Yes, but I am not in favour of the 10 masters system at all.

21,696. Of what are you in favour?—I think every man has a right, if he thinks proper, to buy tools and sell the articles which he makes.

21,697. That sounds very much like reason; but you say that you are in favour of the unions; of what are you in favour?—Paying a small contribution and having a certain fixed price, and if they cannot get the price they should go on scale.

21,698. You would have a small fixed contribution, that is to enable you to demand a certain price for your labour?—Yes.

21,699. And then those funds which you subscribe to the box would enable you in the case of a strike to be supported during the strike, so that you could compel the masters to come to your terms?—I do not think that we should need a strike at all. I believe a small contribution would do without a strike.

21,700. It would do it in this way; that the masters

TWENTY-THIRD DAY.

T. Roebuck.

3 July 1867.

would know that if they did not give the price that you insisted upon you would go on strike, and then you would have a fund to fall back upon during the time you were on strike?—Of course they would know that.

21,701. You say that you are in favour of that?—Yes.

21,702. But you are not in favour of interfering with a man's having an opportunity of buying his tools as he likes and working as he pleases at what price he chooses?—No.

21,703. (*Mr. Chance.*) Do you not think that that system has a tendency to encourage idle men?—Well, there are always idle men in any trade.

21,704. No doubt; but does not that system rather encourage them?—I believe that there are some men that it is better to keep by than to allow them to go into the market.

21,705. (*Chairman.*) Why?—Because they drink and booze, and waste their time, and then they want work, and they are determined to have work at what price they can get it, and then the masters get the advantage of them.

21,706. That is competition?—Yes.

21,707. Supposing that you are supplying goods to a man who is going to send forks, say to America or to Germany, he has to compete with all the persons who make forks at every place in the world?—Yes.

21,708. But if you are demanding those kind of wages and so on, you drive him out of the trade and you drive yourselves out too, and the other countries where they work at smaller wages must ultimately beat you?—Yes; but they do not make the same quantity of forks at the same price as we do; no other country in the world. I have been informed so.

21,709. We might discuss that to a considerable extent as to the benefit to the country or to the particular workman, but our business is simply with respect to outrages.

The witness withdrew.

Mr. JAMES ROBINSON sworn and examined.

J. Robinson.

21,710. (*Mr. Chance.*) Are you a brick manufacturer?—Yes.

21,711. Do you live at Park View, Intake Road?—Yes.

21,712. How long have you been a brick manufacturer?—I have worked at the business all my life nearly.

21,713. I suppose that is upwards of 40 years, is it not?—Yes; I have been in the trade 40 years, but I have not been a master so long.

21,714. Were you always a manufacturer?—No; I have been a journeyman perhaps half my time.

21,715. When you were a journeyman, were you a member of any union?—Yes; one portion of the time.

21,716. How long have you been a manufacturer?—I was along with my father for something like from five to seven years from the time when I was about 18 years of age when I joined with my father as a manufacturer.

21,717. Your father is a manufacturer, is he?—Yes.

21,718. Previously to 1859, had you any disputes with the brickmakers?—Yes.

21,719. What were those disputes about?—There was a brickyard which I took under Mrs. Addy, in Upperthorpe, and there I engaged a man to manage it with me. The man that I engaged had been off the trade for a number of years and had not worked at it. After he had been at work for some time he named it to me that the trade demanded 5*l.* of him, for him and his son. Of course he appealed to me whether he must pay or not, and I told him that he would be soft if he did, or something to that effect.

21,720. What was the name of the man?—Richard Lee.

21,721. What did you tell him?—I told him he would be soft if he paid the whole amount. I had no objection to his entering afresh. So the matter went on for a time until they spoilt me a quantity of bricks and rattened my tools as well.

21,722. But you are going rather too fast. Why was that a cause of quarrel with the union?—On account that he would not pay to the union.

21,723. You advised him not to pay to the union?—I advised him not to pay the 5*l.* Their ordinary entrance fee was 1*l.* 0*s.* 6*d.* or 1*l.* 1*s.* 6*d.*, I believe.

21,724. When was this?—It was in 1854 or 1855, I cannot tell which.

21,725. But I want to know whether just previous to 1859 you had any dispute with the union?—Things got straight then, and then we got on to 1857 or 1858; I hardly know the year. At that time they were charging non-union men for each shilling they had.

21,726. That was about 1859, was it?—1858 I think it was. Thus the trade being very good I had had several men to work for me for a number of years and there were four who had worked for me from three to six or seven years. They were very suitable men for me. Sometime in the back end of the year the committee sent four men to take these men's places.

21,727. (*Chairman.*) To you?—To me.

21,728. (*Mr. Chance.*) Those others you say were non-union men?—The four that they had been wishing me to turn away were so, but they had been paying to the trade.

21,729. Who were the committee who sent them on to you?—I could not say. I had nothing to do with the trade then.

21,730. What kind of communication did you get?—The men came from the committee, and we understand when they come in that way we have to turn the non-union men away.

21,731. Was that in the shape of a letter?—No; the men came that intended taking their places.

21,732. But did they bring any note or a written order of any kind?—No; I do not recollect that they brought any.

21,733. Did they simply tell you that they had come from the committee?—Yes; I objected to turn those four men off. Of course the men went away and I did not hear anything more for some time, until one morning on going into the yard after breakfast my men were all clubbed up together, all in a round ring, in a lump in the yard. One came from amongst them to me and wished me to go and have a few words with them. Of course I went amongst them. One of them spoke to me for the lot——

21,734. (*Chairman.*) Who was that?—I think he is dead now?—He draws my attention to whether I recollected when those four men came to me; I said I did. They said that on the regular meeting night following of the union, the committee or the trade wished them to leave me; the union, you must be aware, not the non-union men. Of course they objected to it; they would not leave me, nor yet did they say anything to me until that morning, and for that they put a fine upon them.

21,735. (*Mr. Chance.*) Why was that?—The committee put a fine on the union men, or at least they said so; I think it was 30*s.* on some and on some 2*l.* but something to that effect. They wished to know whether I had demanded them to pay the fine; I said that I had nothing in the affair and I would have nothing to do with it, but that they were soft if they did. I believe those were something like my words. They asked me if I would turn round upon them provided the committee came and made it up with me and turn them away. I said no, not so long as they suited me; any man if he did not do his work, or did not suit me, I should certainly turn him away, either in the society or out of it. With this they declined paying I suppose. However, we

TWENTY-THIRD DAY.

J. Robinson.

3 July 1867.

go on until the back end of the year; I think it was 1858, but I could not say whether it was 1858 or 1857, but it was somewhere about that time. I had a largish portion of bricks I daresay something like 16,000 or 15,000 bricks trampled upon.

21,736. Where were they?—In the Park.

21,737. On the brickfield?—On the brickfield.

21,738. Were they spread out drying?—Yes.

21,739. How long after this conversation which you speak of did that take place?—I think the summer passed between; I think it was the far end of the year when they fined the men, and it was the back end of the year when the bricks were spoilt but I did not make any minutes.

21,740. (*Chairman.*) How were they spoilt? by trampling on them?—Yes.

21,741. Were they so spoilt as to be of no use?—As it was a certain time of the year and I had three presses I managed to press a great quantity of them up again.

21,742. (*Mr. Chance.*) In what state were they when they were trodden upon?—They were partly dry, a third dry perhaps.

21,743. Just explain how the injury was done?—They ran upon them from row to row; there would be four or five men perhaps running on the bricks to spoil them; that was the way it was done.

21,744. (*Chairman.*) You say that they were not so entirely spoilt that you could not use some of them?—I took the advantage to press them up all as I could.

21,745. What was the loss to you?—They were not made for pressing, but of course I did not want to throw them away, and so I pressed what I could of them.

21,746. And what was the loss?—I could not say what was the loss; perhaps 5*l.* was the loss to me.

21,747. How many men do you suppose were engaged in doing that damage?—I do not doubt that there were five or six by the feet marks.

21,748. (*Mr. Chance.*) Have you endeavoured to ascertain who the men were who had done this?—I was at a deal of trouble; I was then a member of a protection society to commit felons and depredators. I went to Mr. Hallam at the needle factory, and laid information about the affair, expecting they would investigate it and they did offer a reward.

21,749. Was any discovery made of the people who did it?—No, I never could say positively that I was certain.

21,750. Had you any suspicion of anybody?—Yes, I had a suspicion.

21,751. Whom did you suspect; I could only suspect one or two.

21,752. Who were they?—Emanuel Elms was one, and Abraham Glaives was the other.

21,753. Where those the only two men that you had reason to suspect?—Yes, for what I could think.

21,754. (*Chairman.*) Why did you suspect them?—It would take me a little time to explain that, but the night previous to my finding them out, I was going up home, I think it was betwixt 10 and 11 o'clock at night, and as I was going past the yard I saw some boys playing about the fires. I could see the boys at the fires when I was in the dark. Of course that fixed my attention. I just watched them a moment, and whilst I was watching them two men came down the road past my gate; I went running into the yard after the boys then, and ran them right away out of the yard, and out of the yard I went home. I did not see that the bricks were spoilt then, but the next morning of course I learnt that they were spoilt. I go down and see them. I do not think of this Elms and Glaives then; I do not think it is them then, because my attention is taken by those boys; I think it is Mr. Bellamy and his men that are come down. After I had been to Mr. Hallam he questioned me. I said that I could not depose to anyone; I said I could not say, but I felt convinced directly after. During the day I happened to meet this Elms along with some more bricklayers, and then it struck me, and I was satisfied who it was.

21,755. Why?—Because I had seen them come down the road past my gate the night my attention was engaged by those boys.

21,756. (*Mr. Chance.*) You had seen them then?—Yes.

21,757. Whereabouts?—I saw them from my brickyard get down to the bottom of Hanson Street, then come down Duke Street, and the other came down the cross street; I do not know the name of the street.

21,758. Why should you suspect them? because they were there just then?—That was all the cause I had.

21,759. Was that the only reason that you had for suspecting them?—Yes, excepting that Elms had been past a time or two, but I do not know him; I had heard speak of his being about with different men. He was a stranger to me then.

21,760. Have you ever seen him on any other occasion near to your brickyard?—Not to know him. I have heard men say, "Yon is Elms," but I did not take any notice.

21,761. You have seen him, though you did not know him?—Yes, I have seen him but not to know him.

21,762. Is that the only reason you have for believing that it was he?—Something has transpired since which confirmed my suspicion.

21,763. What was that?—It is a customary thing for men of a trade to associate if all is right, but some time after this he went past the yard and I suspected something was not right, and after a time I got out of the yard and I got up to him as he had been past our house, and I said to him, "I would like you to mind "what you are doing; I shall not let you off next "time as I have done this last." His answer to this was (I suppose I must give it plain) "Why the hell do you not do right?"

21,764. What did you say to that?—I said it would be very well if they would do right; if they would keep themselves to themselves I would manage my my business. That is about all.

21,765. Is that the only occasion when you had any conversation with him about it?—Yes.

21,766. Have you any other reason for believing that Elms was engaged in it?—No, only as being a committee-man and having a great deal to do with the trade.

21,767. He was a committee-man, was he?—I think so. I did not go to the trade, but he has been in many instances.

21,768. Was Glaives also a member of the committee?—I am not aware.

21,769. How did you know about Elms? was it only by hearsay?—No, I was not a member of the union.

21,770. But you say he was a member of the union; how do you know that?—By my men repeatedly telling me.

21,771. After the bricks were destroyed in the way you have told us did you ever have any further disputes with the union?—I told the men that I should never encourage the union while they served me in that manner, and of course I encouraged them not to pay. So matters went on as we may say, and we were middling comfortable, only I kept hearing the men complain about being insulted, and that I did not take much notice of.

21,772. Did anything else happen to you after that?—In 1859 I had a cow graizing in a field opposite my house. When we got up in the morning she was stabbed between her bag and her forward bones so as to let all the entrails out.

21,773. Did you find her in this state?—My men found her the first thing. Of course I saw her.

21,774. How far is that from your brickyard?—It is all in one piece of land.

21,775. (*Chairman.*) Describe what happened to the cow?—There was the policeman; of course he was there at hand——

TWENTY-THIRD DAY.

J. Robinson.

3 July 1867.

21,776. Did the cow die?—It was in a dying state. This policeman said he was a butcher and he understood the affair. He advised me whatever I did to sell it.

21,777. Did the cow die in consequence of the wounds it received?—No, I sold it before it did die; it was in a dying state when I sold it.

21,778. But I suppose it was killed, was it not, to save the carcase?—Yes.

21,779. Do you know the reason of the injury that was done to the cow?—No, I have no evidence, only I have suspicion like—I have my own feeling; I have no grounds.

21,780. Do you know anyone that did it or that you suspected of having done it?—No, it would not do for me to say things that I hear in various ways.

21,781. Had you any quarrel with anyone?—No, only by the brick trade.

21,782. You believe it to have been in consequence of your disputes with the union?—Yes, I do.

21,783. Have you any reason for believing that, except that you had disputes with the union?—No; I do not know that I had disputes with any man.

21,784. Nothing took place with the union in consequence of that?—No. I am not aware that anything took place.

21,785. Did you ever speak to any member of the union about this?—A few friends I might speak to, such as are respectable in the trade.

21,786. But did you ever speak to any member of the committee about it?—No, I never went near the committee; not then.

21,787. And you do not know at all who did it?—No.

21,788. And you have no suspicion of who did it? —I have no suspicion, except that I heard that four men went up Park Hill about 1 or 2 o'clock in the morning. A woman said she saw them, but I took no further investigation about it. I did not bother about it.

21,789. You knew about them?—No.

21,790. After that, was an outrage committed against you at your house?—Yes.

21,791. When was that?—I think it was in October.

21,792. In what year?—1859. I might be wrong a year or two, because I did not make any minutes.

21,793. Will you describe what this was?—I was asleep and all my family was asleep in the house.

21,794. Of whom did your family consist?—Of my wife and son and four daughters. We were all asleep for anything I know. I was asleep. Sometime about 3 o'clock in the morning there was a tremendous crash. I was paralysed as you must be aware; I could not imagine what it was; only I jumped up in a moment and slipped on my slippers. I am not certain whether I heard three crashes to be satisfied that I heard them all three distinctly, but I heard them twice or three times.

21,795. (*Chairman.*) Did you hear two or three explosions?—No, crashes. After slipping my slippers on I found I was in the adjoining room to where we were sleeping.

21,796. In which room were you sleeping?—I was sleeping in the first front room.

21,797. On what floor?—On the second floor as you may call it; the chamber floor. I went into the room. The room door was partly open, a little bit open. It showed a reflection of light when I went there. The moment I went in I thought there was something a fire. I saw there was a burning fuse (though I did not know it was a burning fuse when I went in) near the length of my stick, or perhaps not quite so long. I put my foot on to it and kept trying to rub it out, and as I was doing that there were bits of powder like squibs (you know what squibs are) one igniting the other, I may say by scores, but they did not all go off at one time. Of course, I pressed on this to try to put it out until I got back and I found out my foot was on a bottle neck; then it struck me that there was something wrong. Of course I was alarmed then; my wife ran back.

21,798. (*Chairman.*) What did you do when you found the bottle neck?—I pushed my wife back and got to the door and said, "For God's sake "let us have the children out of bed, or else we shall "be blown up!" Of course she screams to the children, and they began dressing. I tried to slip my trousers on, and expected it to go off every moment, and it not going off I felt then——

21,799. Never mind what you felt; what did you do?—I thought it must have missed fire; I thought there was something wrong, and then after that I took up the rattle and rattled at the window for a moment or two, and then I ran downstairs with the rattle and rattled my men up. In time, of course, they got the police up, but they were a long time before they could get the police up.

21,800. What did you do then?—The police came to see what was the matter, and of course I took them upstairs. They could not get upstairs, they could not breathe, one of them.

21,801. Was that on account of the smoke?—Yes; I ran through to where they all were, and opened the window.

21,802. You opened the window and let out the smoke?—Yes.

21,803. And they came in?—Yes.

21,804. What did you find?—I examined upstairs first, and found this bottle in fragments, with the hobnails and glass——

21,805. Do not go on in that way; tell us what you saw?—We picked up the bottle neck.

21,806. What did you find in the bottle?—There was a deal of powder unexploded. There was nothing left scarcely in the bottle, only a cork and a part of the fuse, because the bottle had broken up towards the neck. There was a portion of the bottom left middling solid, and the neck was solid; the rest was broken in pieces. The police took charge of those, and in a short time they got Sills, Airey, and Brayshaw; those are detectives.

21,807. (*Mr. Chance.*) What was the result of the examination altogether?—They found three bottles altogether; two had fallen harmless outside the house.

21,808. (*Chairman.*) Where were the two bottles? —They had dropped down from the house on the grass plot.

21,809. How near to the house?—A yard or two; they had been intended to go through the house.

21,810. (*Mr. Chance.*) Had they exploded?—No, they had broken and fallen downwards.

21,811. Did you see what they contained?—Yes, the same as the others; powder and hobnails.

21,812. (*Chairman.*) Did they contain blasting powder and hobnails?—Yes.

21,813. Both of them?—Yes, for aught I can say; the detective took charge of them.

21,814. (*Mr. Chance.*) Were there fuses in them? —Yes.

21,815. Was there an appearance of any explosion in the room?—No, only as if you had spread powder about in trains, which we have done when we have been boys and lighted it, and it goes "swish."

21,816. Was there a mark on the wall where it appeared as if there had been an explosion?—Yes, there was a mark there for some time. The reporters and the police say so as well as me, and many others.

21,817. Was it the bottle which had burst and gone against the wall?—No, it would be the fuse and the powder that blackened it.

21,818. Was much damage done?—No.

21,819. Did you ascertain who had done this?—No.

21,820. (*Chairman.*) You said that you heard two cracks, did you not?—Yes, I am certain I heard two; my wife said she heard three.

21,821. You found only one bottle; would that be explained by the thing having been thrown into the room?—Yes.

21,822. How do you account for the other two crashes?—There was a mark against the wall; the powder left a black mark.

21,823. Where?—Within two or three inches of the window-casing on the stone wall. It caught, perhaps, within three or four inches of the casement or sash frame and fell harmless on the floor.

21,824. Was the mark above the place where those bottles were found ?—Yes.

21,825. As if men had thrown those two bottles against the window, and had failed in throwing them in ?—Yes, that is it.

21,826. (*Mr. Chance.*) One they succeeded in throwing in, and as to the other two they failed, leaving the marks on the wall ?—Yes.

21,827. You say that you do not know or suspect who did this ?—No, I do not know who did it ; I suspect the trade committee.

21,828. Did you make any inquiries about it afterwards ?—I did not go to the committee. To one who was in the union and was a respectable man, I said it was very strange that they should allow such work.

21,829. To whom did you say that ?—I said it to Mr. Webster and Mr. Hibberd, and I daresay to Mr. Jarrett.

21,830. There was nobody sleeping in the room into which it was thrown, was there ?—No, it was the best room ; it was what we call our spare room.

21,831. (*Chairman.*) But it was next to the room which was occupied by yourself and your wife and children ?—Yes.

21,832. What divided the one room from the other ? A $4\frac{1}{2}$-inch wall.

21,833. (*Mr. Chance.*) What was the size of the bottles ?—They would be common stone ginger-beer bottles.

21,834. Were they all the same ?—All the same.

21,835. Have you any notion how much powder they contained ?—I never calculated that.

21,836. You say you have spoken to Webster and another man ?—Yes, I named it to Mr. Webster and Mr. Hibberd ; they were each of them manufacturers but they were in the union.

21,837. What did you say to them ?—I said I thought it was very strange that they should be in a union that paid for such like work as that.

21,838. What did they say ?—That they were very sorry.

21,839. What did they say ?—It was at different times. I did not see them both together.

21,840. But the first time you saw Webster, what did he say ?—He was very sorry and he was ashamed that there had been anything of the sort, and he was sorry that he was almost forced to be in a society of that sort.

21,841. Did he say anything else ?—No ; we had very little conversation in that respect. We were generally friends.

21,842. Did you say anything to Hibberd about it ? —Yes, I named it to Mr. Hibberd, but I could not say now exactly what he said ; but he said to me in a similar way that he deprecated it, and that he was ashamed that they should do suchlike.

21,843. Do you know at all, or have you any suspicion, who did the act ?—I can only calculate on the committee being in the affair. I am satisfied as far as my own feeling goes.

21,844. Was there any reason why it should be done ?—I only attribute it to my men not paying to the union.

21,845. But you had done nothing yourself against the union ?—No. There was this : they called it a fault on my part by my setting a man on that was not in the union. They called that a fault.

21,846. But had they told you that it was a fault of yours at all ?—They never associated with me at all after the bricks were spoilt. For three or four years no committee ever came near me to my recollection.

21,847. Do you remember another attempt at injuring you taking place in 1860 ?—Yes.

21,848. Was that in November ?—I think it was.

21,849. What was that ?—I had a haystack that stood me in somewhere about 100*l.* or 150*l.*, and I had set it in a situation where I had taken a deal of clay out—I had been lowering my premises and I had been taking a deal of clay out—and consequently the end of the stack came up to a bank of four or five feet. One Sunday morning (I forget the date exactly) we laid a little longer than usual—my wife and I—and my daughter got up to milk ; and she noticed, as she thought, a quantity of linen put out to dry on this stack. She thought it rather strange when she went into the stable to milk, but she went on to milk. This would be between 7 and 8 o'clock in the morning. Before she had done milking, one of the men comes in to his horses, and I forget whether there was anything said about it then ; but when she came out she noticed that there was a strange smell, and she turned her head back and she thought it very strange that her mother was drying any clothes on Sunday morning. She went up to the stack, and she saw that it was calico pricked in the stack with pegs. She noticed this smell and of course she came and called me, and I got up and saw what it was. Then, as it happened, just at the time——

21,850. Did you go out to see what it was ?—Yes.

21,851. Did you examine it ?—As soon as I got up I examined it.

21,852. Tell us what you found there ?—I found the calico—I should say from 10 to 12 or 14 yards —pricked round the stack within some six to nine inches of the floor. Mr. Jackson has the calico at the town hall. It was pricked round the stack end. It came perhaps one-third of the way round each side of the stack and across one end (*describing the same*).

21,853. You say it was pegged in ?—Yes.

21,854. With wooden pegs ?—Yes, they were green pegs.

21,855. Did you look to see what kind of calico it was, or whether there was anything upon it ?—Yes, it was new ; it was saturated with naphtha and turpentine—I believe both.

21,856. (*Chairman.*) Did you ascertain that it was naphtha and turpentine ?—I could not.

21,857. But that was your belief ?—Yes.

21,858. (*Mr. Chance.*) Did you judge by the smell ? —Yes.

21,859. Was it wet or dry ?—Wet.

21,860. Did you smell it ?—Yes.

21,861. What did it smell like ?—The turpentine had the strongest smell, I think.

21,862. Did you smell turpentine then ?—Yes.

21,863. (*Chairman.*) Was it as if the thing had been saturated in turpentine ?—Yes.

21,864. (*Mr. Chance.*) Did you find anything else there ?—Yes, at the end of the stack at about the centre there were eleven boxes of common lucifer matches. Those matches were placed so as just to touch the calico. The calico was laid down so as to touch those matches.

21,865. But was the calico at the bottom of the stack ?—It was so as to touch the blades. Supposing a match got ignited, the blade must catch the calico.

21,866. Were the boxes put all together ?—Yes, just as if you had broken them and put them in a heap. I could count the boxes by the cases.

21,867. (*Chairman.*) You could count the cases then ?—Yes, they were pulled out in various ways and put all together.

21,868. Then the matches were all together loose from the boxes ?—Yes.

21,869. How far was this heap of matches from the calico ?—A few inches.

21,870. It was so placed that if the matches were lighted the calico would be lighted above them ?—Yes.

21,871. (*Mr. Chance.*) Did you find anything else there ?—Yes ; from those eleven boxes of matches some more calico had been saturated with naptha and turpentine, and there was, I think, some kind of bill papers or newspaper lapped round it. I should think it would be as thick as my wrist, if not thicker. That was perhaps four feet or four feet six inches, or it might be five feet long. This was laid down at the side of the stack end, and it came to those matches. Those matches were just on end to it. On the other end it came nearer to the corner of the stack, and in another place there was another box of matches. The

TWENTY-THIRD DAY.

J. Robinson.

3 July 1867.

little canvas and paper had been lighted by a match or matches, and it burnt I should think half a yard or perhaps two feet. I cannot say to a few inches.

21,872. (*Chairman.*) That is what you may call the fuse?—Yes, that was what it was intended for. I think it burnt about half a yard.

21,873. (*Mr. Chance.*) Was the place where it was lighted close to the plantation?—No. The place was the far corner from my house, pointing towards the plantation. It would be more than a hundred yards away from the plantation. It appeared to have burnt about a yard and then to have died out. You must be aware that I had taken this bank away a considerable time before and the clay had slipped down, and there was middling of grass there; there happened to be a bit of a drain there, and of course I attribute it to the wet. It was a foggy time. Sometimes I have thought that being dark they had missed saturating the calico just at that part.

21,874. (*Chairman.*) However, it stopped at that point?—Yes. Of course I was very much alarmed about it.

21,875. (*Mr. Chance.*) Did you find any bottles there?—Yes.

21,876. What were the bottles?—There were three bottles. I should think they would hold from a pint to a quart.

21,877. What did they contain? did you smell at them?—Yes; one contained naphtha and two contained turpentine, or *vice versâ*, I could not say which.

21,878. (*Chairman.*) There was either one of naphtha and two of turpentine, or two of naphtha and one of turpentine?—Yes; I daresay they would hold a quart each or three gills.

21,879. (*Mr. Chance.*) Were they empty?—Yes.

21,880. (*Chairman.*) How far were they away from the fuse?—It appeared as if they had carried away one bottle 40 yards, but the other was thrown out right away.

21,881. (*Mr. Chance.*) If they had not gone out it would have set the whole rick on fire, I suppose?—Yes.

21,882. (*Chairman.*) What was the value of the rick?—I think it cost me about 150*l*. I had the rick insured. Of course I was alarmed, and I sent for the police.

21,883. (*Mr. Chance.*) Where there any other ricks near there which might have been burnt?—No; there was only my stables.

21,884. How far were your stables from the rick?—Six or seven yards.

21,885. And if the rick had been set on fire the stables would have been in danger of being on fire too?—Yes.

21,886. Do you know how the wind was then?—No, I do not.

21,887. You do not know how it was blowing, whether it was from the rick to the stables?—No.

21,888. Was there anything in the stables?—Yes.

21,889. What?—Some straw and four or five horses, and I should have one or two cows. I might sometimes have three.

21,890. Were there any other buildings in connexion with the stables?—There was my carter's house adjoining it, and then there is a distance betwixt the stables and my house.

21,891. How far is it?—From the stack it would be 14 or 15 yards, I should think, but from the stables perhaps eight or 10 yards.

21,892. There would be 14 or 15 yards between the stack and your house, and 10 yards from the stable?—Yes; I cannot say to a few yards, but it would be about that.

21,893. Then supposing that the wind had been in that direction, would there have been any danger of your house being set on fire?—If it had been in the north-east no doubt it would have blown on to it.

21,894. What did you do after finding those things there?—I sent to Mr. Sills. He lived then below where I lived a considerable distance, at a place called School Street, and before he came Mr. Joseph Hodgkinson, of Intake, and Dr. Wilson were going past. Of course I beckoned them to come in, and I think Mr. Sills got there about the same time as they did.

21,895. Was a reward offered?—Yes, I sent to the fire insurance, or Mr. Sills went for them and they came and took possession; they and Mr. Sills together. Mr. Richardson, I think his name is.

21,896. Was a reward offered for finding out who had done it?—Yes.

21,897. Have you ever discovered who did it?—No.

21,898. Have you any reason for supposing that anybody had done it?—No, only the trade.

21,899. But you have no suspicion of anybody?—No; all I could trace was that it appeared they had run away across the planting, and across a turnip field. There were two feet marks and similar feet marks I thought to what I had noticed in my garden when the bottles exploded in my house.

21,900. Do you suppose that only one man had done it, then?—No, there would be two or three.

21,901. You said "two feet marks," you mean two sets of feet?—Yes, I saw two sets of feet.

21,902. You never heard anything more about it then?—No.

21,903. After that, in the year 1861, did you have more injury done to your property?—Yes.

21,904. What was that?—I had horses in a field, though I was away at the time, I had been a week at Cleethorpes with my wife and children, and on the Saturday morning, when my men went in for the horses they found one was dead.

21,905. How far is that field from the house?—It comes down to the house; my house is in the same field.

21,906. What was the cause of the death of the horse?—They did not know what to say about it. Of course they fetched the farrier and the knacker, that is the man who buys dead horses; the same one who bought the cow.

21,907. Can you tell me the cause of its death?—He had been picked with a small instrument in what we call the skirt, which you are aware is between the ribs and the hip. That is called the skirt, and the skin had gone over the hole, and he had bled inwards.

21,908. (*Chairman.*) But he had been pierced with an instrument from without, had he?—Yes.

21,909. (*Mr. Chance.*) Was that the injury from which he died?—Yes.

21,910. Was the horse quite well the night before?—Yes, for anything that I know he was.

21,911. Did you take any measures for finding out who did it?—No; I had the farrier's opinion, of course, and it was advertised. I am not aware whether I went to Mr. Jackson.

21,912. Did you ever hear anything about it?—No; Airey and Brayshaw and Sills generally used to come and arrange those matters for me.

21,913. Have you any suspicion who did it?—Only the trade. I am satisfied that it was the committee.

21,914. You had no private quarrel against anyone, had you?—No.

21,915. Do you remember in October a deputation coming to you?—Yes, in the October following that.

21,916. Was that in 1861?—Yes.

21,917. Who formed the deputation?—William Henry Owen and John Jarrett.

21,918. Who else?—There was no one else at that deputation.

21,919. You say that in 1861 William Henry Owen and John Jarrett called upon you?—Yes.

21,920. Were they members of the union?—Yes.

21,921. Were they members of the committee?—I am not aware of that.

21,922. What did they say to you?—They said, "Good morning;" I said, "What is your will this morning?" when I saw them at the door.

21,923. (*Chairman.*) How soon was this after the horse was hurt?—The horse was done in August, and I think this was in October. They said they were ashamed of their errand, but they had been deputed from the body to try to make peace with me. I could

TWENTY-THIRD DAY.

J. Robinson.

3 July 1867.

hardly say the answer, but it was something like, "What was the motive?" and they explained.

21,924. But that is very important; did you say, "What is your motive?"—I believe I was careless as to——

21,925. What did you say? did you say, "What was your motive for doing this?"—I said I wanted to be quiet and independent, and that if they would let me alone I should let them alone, or something of that kind.

21,926. What did they say to that?—They wished to make peace with me.

21,927. (*Mr. Chance.*) What did they say?—After us talking a little while, they said, "Let byegones be byegones."

21,928. Did they say that?—I believe they did, or "Let us forget our animosity."

21,929. (*Chairman.*) What did they say, it is very important?—I forget.

21,930. (*Mr. Chance.*) Just see if you can remember, because it is important to know the conversation; can you remember whether they said anything about byegones being byegones?—That I must forget and forgive; I do not remember the exact words; I do not wish to speak a falsehood.

21,931. What did you say to that?—I said I had no objection, if they would behave comfortably, but that I would not be tied to such sort of men as some of those that were in the union. We had a little talk about bits of matters, and they left me then.

21,932. Did they ask you if you would do anything?—They asked me if I would be agreeable to allow the men to join again. I said that on conditions I had no objections.

21,933. To let the men join what again?—The union. Then they left me a little while, not many days, and then they came again.

21,934. What did they say then?—They said that they had had a meeting, and that the trade were agreeable to take us in again, providing I would pay something for the mills for the grinding of the clay. I said no, I should not pay anything for any improvement that I could bring out. I considered I had a right to have the benefit of it, neither would I pay for a machine. I had some notion of a machine as well, and if I could not be in comfortably without paying for those things, I would not go in. Of course they said they would do what they could for me, and I believe they did the best they could for me with the trade; and then they left me.

21,935. Did anything more take place upon that occasion?—They had another meeting; at all events they came to me again.

21,936. How soon after?—In a very few days after. I cannot say exactly how soon; perhaps not more than a day or two after.

21,937. The same two men?—Yes.

21,938. What did they say?—They said all was made comfortable. They granted me all the privileges I asked for; but I said, "I do not feel satisfied, for we have been making arrangements at different times before, and you deviated from it then. If I have anything to do with the trade any more it will be with the understanding that we have an arbitrating party picked out. If you are agreeable do you pick six and let me pick six; I will come in on those conditions, and my men shall join it." I forget whether they left me then and came back again or not, but however either then they went away or came back again; I could not say; but they went amongst my men and lectured them, hoping that they would be good and invited them into the union.

21,939. Did they agree to your terms?—Yes the two, Owen and Jarrett agreed to my terms, but I would not be positive whether they went and had another meeting after that, but it was an understanding.

21,940. What condition did they make upon their entering into the union?—That they would take all what they called reasonable men into the unions such as we considered good brickmakers, on their paying their original entrance fee. That was 1*l.* 1*s.* 6*d.*

21,941. (*Chairman.*) Then they were not to pay up any arrears at all, but they were to begin as new members?—To begin as new members; I would not allow any arrears.

21,942. (*Mr. Chance.*) Did the men begin to go into the union?—There was a many of them that had not money to pay the 1*l.* 1*s.* 6*d.*, but some had, and they went in. They admitted a portion of them in that way. There were others that had not money to pay; of course they allowed them to keep on working subject to paying a halfpenny out of every shilling that they earned, and that was collected by one of the members each pay day. Perhaps if they had 25*s.*, they would only charge them 1*s.* or 24 halfpennies.

21,943. Did those men apply again to the union to take them in?—Yes, they applied again; sometimes one and sometimes the other, as they could get their money. Some of them paid it at two or three times.

21,944. (*Chairman.*) Were they admitted?—No.

21,945. (*Mr. Chance.*) Was any reason given why they should not be admitted?—Yes, from what I have heard my men say.

21,946. What was the reason?—All that they attributed it to was that they were Robinson's b—— and that they would not have them in, or something of that sort. That was what my man told me; I was not there to hear it.

21,947. (*Chairman.*) But they refused to admit them?—Yes.

21,948. (*Mr. Chance.*) Had you applied to them and told them that they ought to admit them?—No, I never bothered about it.

21,949. After that did a deputation again wait upon you?—Yes.

21,950. Do you remember how many men were admitted?—I do not remember; perhaps one-third of them.

21,951. And the remainder were not admitted?—No.

21,952. How many men should you have?—Perhaps from 30 to 40. There would not be more than 10 admitted, I think. They varied in number.

21,953. After this you say the deputation called upon you again?—Yes, they called a time or two I think in respect of moulds.

21,954. Who were the deputation?—I could not say who came after.

21,955. Were they the same men who called before?—No, not the first time after; I had like done with the affair.

21,956. But just answer this. Did a deputation call upon you again?—Yes, but it was a long time after.

21,957. How long was it after the time that you have just been telling us about that a deputation called upon you again?—It would be in 1865 I think.

21,958. (*Chairman.*) When was it that the men were admitted on that arrangement?—In 1861.

21,959. Between 1861 and 1865 how were you going on?—Very comfortably for a time.

21,960. Were you employing during that time union men or non-union men?—I was employing both.

21,961. Some of the men that had been admitted you were employing, and some that had not been admitted?—Yes.

21,962. And so you went on from 1861 to 1865, and was anything done to you?—No.

81,963. Was it not in 1862 that your horse was killed?—No, in 1861.

21,964. Therefore, from 1861, when the horse was killed, your men were admitted, and the trade tried to make peace with you, and you went on peaceably till 1865?—Yes.

21,965. (*Mr. Chance.*) What happened in 1865?—In 1865 they invited me to a meeting in respect of the master builders and master brickmakers, and such like as them. Of course, I do not want to be ill-natured, and I go.

21,966. Who invited you?—William Owen.

TWENTY-THIRD DAY.

J. Robinson.

3 July 1867.

21,967. William Owen came to ask you to attend a meeting ?—Yes.

21,968. And you went ?—Yes.

21,969. Where was it held ?—I think he took me. I do not know the name of the house, but it is in Snig Hill amongst the bricklayers there.

21,970. It was a meeting of the bricklayers, was it ?—Yes, I am not aware whether it was not where they had their union down in the "King's Head" yard,—the "Nag's Head" I think it is called. I have never been there but once or twice.

21,971. At their request ?—Yes.

21,972. What did they want you to meet them there for ?—To arrange in case they had disputes with master builders or contractors in various ways.

21,973. They wanted you to enter into union with them to protect yourself against the contractors and master builders ?—Yes, of course we had debates upon it, and it did not suit me.

21,974. What did they ask you to do ?—Supposing a master builder had some dispute with his bricklayers, they wished me to retain my bricks from supplying this builder.

21,975. (*Chairman.*) You were to refuse bricks to any master who did not comply with the terms of the trade ?—Yes.

21,976. You would not do it ?—I did not agree to that.

21,977. What happened ?—There was another meeting I think ; there were two or three.

21,978. Did it end in your refusing to come in to their terms ?—Yes.

21,979. (*Mr. Chance.*) How long afterwards was this other meeting ?—It was not long after. I could not say now when it was, perhaps it might be six weeks. I had orders to attend a meeting with the master brickmakers and the brickmakers' committee.

21,980. From whom had you orders ?—I have forgotten now.

21,981. (*Chairman.*) But did you go ?—I went. When we got there they sat a little while. William Owen ——

21,982. Never mind that; let us have it shortly. What was it about ?—He proposed a resolution that we were to pay 4*s.* 6*d.* for all the men working at the mills grinding clay.

21,983. If any person had a clay mill he was to pay 4*s.* 6*d.* a day for every person that he employed ?—Yes.

21,984. That was the resolution that they came to ? —Yes. He read this over to me, and I said it was very unfair to me, inasmuch as I had 11 men at work.

21,985. And did you refuse to agree to that ?—Yes. I said, "You will recollect, your agreement with me was to decide by arbitration, and I demand the arbitration now.

21,986. What did they say to that ? did they agree to your arbitration ?—No, not altogether, there were one or two ——

21,987. Did they ultimately agree to your arbitration ?—Oh no.

21,988. They refused your arbitration ?—Yes, and do to this day.

21,989. Did you agree to those terms ?—No.

21,990. Then you left them disagreeing ?—Yes.

21,991. (*Mr. Chance.*) What took place upon it ? —This was on the Thursday, and I believe it was to come into operation on the Monday ; but after that it might pass on a week, and then William Owen and two bricklayers (I forget the names of the other bricklayers who were with William Owen) came to see if I would agree to it, or rather there was another affair previous ——

21,992. (*Chairman.*) Never mind that. Did they come then to see if you would agree to their terms ? He began on the making of the bricks first, and I said I would not give it. One of the bricklayers said, "But there is something else first." Owen says, "Never mind, come on, come on," and leaves me to it. The next morning my men had notice to appear at the club house.

21,993. What, union men as well as non-union men ?—The union men.

21,994. Such men as belonged to the union were summoned to the trade meeting ?—Yes, and they were ordered out, I suppose.

21,995. Were they ordered to leave you ?—Yes.

21,996. And they left you ?—Yes.

21,997. (*Mr. Chance.*) How many left you ?—I have forgotten now.

21,998. Did all of them leave you ?—Not all the non-union men.

21,999. But the union men all left you ?—With the exception of the manager. The manager and his sons dared not go, because they were under a contract.

22,000. Did any of the non-union men leave you too ?—I think there were a few.

22,001. Do you remember whether they were to have anything during the time they were out ?—Decidedly, the union men were paid.

22,002. What were they paid ?—I think they told me 18*s.* a man per week, and I think 1*s.* 6*d.* for a wife and 1*s.* 6*d.* for each child.

22,003. How long did they remain out of work ?—Between a fortnight and three weeks. A portion of them they sent elsewhere to work.

22,004. Do you know, whether during that time they continued to receive the 18*s.* ?—Those that did not work elsewhere I believe did.

22,005. How long did they remain away from your work ?—In a fortnight and a few days there was a deputation waited upon me again from the committee.

22,006. These are the four names—Emanuel Elms, Francis Butt, William Elms, and Thomas Poole ; are those the four men who waited upon you ?—Yes.

22,007. What did they come to you for ?—They said they had altered their rules which they had disputed with me ; they thought if it would suit me they would do away with my paying 4*s.* 6*d.* to each man, provided I paid a halfpenny a thousand for grinding to the union. I said no ; I said I never would pay anything to the union no more. Of course they tried to argue with me ; they said it was very foolish of me. I daresay we were half an hour debating. After a good deal of debating one said, "Well, Mr. Robinson, "we shall not be hard with you, if you will only agree "to that, things will be blown over soon."

22,008. Did he make any other offer ?—He said, "You can pay when you like or do as you like ;" I said "What do you say ?"

22,009. Did they make any other proposal to you then ?—That was the proposition, that if I would only agree to that they should not bother me.

22,010. If you would agree to what ?—To pay a halfpenny a thousand.

22,011. Did you agree to that ?—Yes, I agreed to it because I was compelled ; my men were out. They said if I would agree to that there would be no bother afterwards.

22,012. What did they say ?—They said they would leave it to me ; I might pay when I minded, or as I minded.

22,013. (*Chairman.*) If they told you that they would leave it to you to pay as you had a mind, how were you forced to pay ?—I was not forced to pay ; I was obliged to do something to alleviate the position I was in.

22,014. How so ?—There were my men out ; they had sent different deputations to me ; almost every day when I went home my wife was pressing me to give in at any sacrifice. I said I would not, but a day or two previous to this my nephew's mother came ; she was left a widow. There were my relations coming and asking me to give in, and saying I should be shot or killed. I said I would not give in for such things unless they would decide by arbitration ; that they would not do ; but when they held out the inducement that I might pay and do as I liked, I said "Very well then, here goes !" and then I signed the paper.

22,015. You signed the paper to pay a halfpenny a thousand ?—Yes.

22,016. (*Mr. Chance.*) Haveyou ever paid it?—No.

22,017. Do you expect to be called upon to pay it? —From what they said I thought it would blow over and that I should never be bothered.

22,018. Since that have you had any further disputes with them?—I went on after that for something like eight months; I was applied to for this halfpenny.

22,019. (*Chairman.*) Now to what date have we got?—That would be in 1866; it is more than a year; it was just previous to the deputations of the trades unions having a regular conference at Mr. Broadhead's—a week or two previous to that.

22,020. I do not know when that was; was that in July 1866; we have heard of a conference at Mr. Broadhead's in July 1866, and you say that it was a little before that?—Yes.

22,021. (*Mr. Chance.*) You say that they applied to you then for the halfpenny?—Yes.

22,022. Who was it that applied to you?—I forget who it was that applied then.

22,023. Was it a member of the union?—Yes.

22,024. Was it one of those who had called upon you before?—Two of them had been about some business before, but I am sure my memory does not tell me who it was at that time.

22,025. Who was it?—I am certain it was Owen, he was one; there were three others I believe.

22,026. What did they say?—They said they had come for the halfpenny. I said, "What is your business?" They said I knew what their business was, that they had come for the halfpenny. I said, "You "are nice fellows! you consented to let me have it "tried by arbitration." They said they had nought to do with that and they left me.

22,027. (*Chairman.*) Did you pay them the halfpenny? did you say that you would pay or not?—Not then.

22,028. Did they ask you for it?—I told them I would not pay them.

22,029. And they left you?—Yes, I sent a word by one of my men that if they would let it stand over till that year had expired perhaps there would be something done then, because the trades would be amalgamated and perhaps there would be some alteration.

22,030. You meant the meeting at Broadhead's?—Yes, I meant if there was an arbitration picked out I would give in to what they would decide.

22,031. Did you send a man before the meeting of the trades unions at Broadhead's?—Yes, I sent one of my men to ask it to stand over till the end of the year to see if we could settle it.

22,032. (*Mr. Chance.*) Did they do so? did they let it stand over?—Yes.

22,033. After that had you any further communication with them?—Yes; at the expiration of the year a deputation waited upon me again.

22,034. Who were they?—I am at a loss to know who they were.

22,035. Was Owen one?—I think he was not at that time.

22,036. Was Stanley, Poole, or Elms there?—There would be Elms and Poole.

22,037. Was Elms one?—I cannot say? but they were all there at one time or another.

22,038. What did they come to you for?—For the halfpenny. I said I should not pay until they would let me have arbitration, because they had broken faith with me first before I broke with them the second. If they would allow me arbitration, which was agreed on before, I would settle it. I said, "You agreed with me for arbitration, therefore I "claim the arbitration." Of course they would not allow that; they asked me distinctly if I would pay. I said, "No, not till I have arbitration. If you let me "have a fair arbitration, I am decided by it either "for or against me, even if they charge more."

22,039. You refused to pay?—Yes.

22,040. What did they do?—They left me. I think it was the next day, or at all events within a very short time that they called my men out or persuaded them to go, both union and non-union men.

22,041. (*Chairman.*) They all left you?—Yes, with the exception of one or two. I have not paid no halfpennies.

22,042. All but one or two of your men left you? —Yes. I had had no communications with them except hearsay from here and there a man or two. A man who worked for me said that he had been threatened to be punched and I wanted to know who said that.

22,043. (*Mr. Chance.*) Who said that?—I forget his name.

22,044. How long did they remain out?—They are out yet, a portion of them.

22,045. They are out now?—Yes.

22,046. How many have come back again?—I could not say. A portion has come back.

22,047. About how many? have not the greater number come back?—Perhaps half.

22,048. Are they union men that have come back, or non-union men?—Both sorts.

22,049. Do you believe that they are kept out by the union?—Yes, I have every reason to believe so; they have told me so.

22,050. (*Chairman.*) They have told you that they were kept out by the union?—Yes, they were kept out four weeks. They only gave them pay four weeks; they told them that they must get work, anywhere but with me. They did not support them except in an odd case or two.

22,051. (*Mr. Chance.*) Have you had any communication with the union about it?—No.

22,052. (*Chairman.*) Have you been injured in your property at all since this?—No; except in this way—my foremen dare not work. They were eight weeks getting my bricks together, whereas they ought to be got together in two weeks. An old man had two sons, and they would not allow both to work with him; consequently it kept my work going on for eight weeks before they got down. During that time I set other men on. We are making bricks, but we had no men to burn. There are plenty of workmen that would burn for me, but they dare not.

22,053. (*Mr. Chance.*) Had those men been threatened that would work for you?—They said they dare not.

22,054. (*Chairman.*) You asked them and they said that they dare not work?—They said no.

22,055. On account of what?—On account of being shot or disabled.

22,056. They gave you that reason?—Yes.

22,057. (*Mr. Chance.*) Have they said so in as many words—that they were afraid of being shot?—They said they were frightened of being disabled.

22,058. They told you that they might be disabled? —Yes.

22,059. You have not been able to carry on your business to anything like the extent that you used to do?—No, not for some time. We have to go and burn ourselves. I am getting more men and going on with my work.

22,060. (*Chairman.*) When are you speaking of; you say they are out at the present time?—Yes, a portion of the union men and the non-union men.

22,061. At the present time you cannot carry on your business?—Yes, they have been quiet in consequence of this Commission being here.

22,062. Have you got all your men?—Yes, all I need.

22,063. Up to the time of this Commission you were not able to get your men?—Up to Christmas I was not.

22,064. Have you had them since Christmas?—Yes; first one came and then another after Christmas till I got what I wanted.

22,065. You think that the fact of this inquiry has enabled you to get men?—Yes, it has enabled me to carry on my business.

22,066. (*Mr. Chance.*) With regard to the non-union men, are they expected to pay a certain sum, though they do not belong to the union?—Yes, they

TWENTY-THIRD DAY.

J. Robinson.

3 July 1867.

are expected to pay a halfpenny out of every shilling. I have men who have worked with me the whole of the time.

22,067. (*Chairman.*) How much do the union men pay ?—6*d*. a man, and the non-union men pay a halfpenny out of every shilling.

22,068. (*Mr. Chance.*) If they do not pay a halfpenny in the shilling they are not allowed to work? —No.

22,069. The union men will not allow the non-union men to work unless they pay a halfpenny out of a shilling ?—No.

22,070. (*Chairman.*) They receive nothing from the contributions of the society if they are ill or out of work ?—No.

22,071. It is an arbitrary thing on the part of the union: they say, "Before you are allowed to work, you shall pay a halfpenny in the shilling" ?—Yes.

22,072. Although they do not belong to the union? —Yes, that is it.

22,073. (*Mr. Chance.*) Would they be allowed to go into the union, if they wished it ?—No; I have men working for me who have been with me eight or 10 years who have paid money to the union, and have not been allowed to join.

220,74. On what ground ?—Because they have been Robinson's b——s.

22,075. Because they have been Robinson's men ? —Yes, that is the explanation given out to me.

22,076. (*Chairman.*) Because they have been working for you and were obnoxious to the trade, they would not take them into the union ?—No.

22,077. (*Mr. Chance.*) They would allow them to work for you if they paid the halfpenny ?—Yes, until a union man is out of work, and then they will send that union man and turn the non-union man away.

22,078 (*Chairman.*) So that as long as the union men have plenty of work, they allow the non-union men to work for you ?—Yes.

22,079. And if they do work for you, they must pay a halfpenny in every shilling which they earn ?—Yes.

22,080. They pay, but they get no benefit from the union ?—Yes.

22,081. And if they have been in full work for you, and there is a union man who wants work, they put the union man upon you, and you must make room for him by displacing a non-union man ?—Yes.

22,082. (*Mr. Barstow.*) You have to dispose of the non-union men to make room for the union men ?— In one case, I have said to men, "You must go about your business."

22,083. (*Mr. Chance.*) Have you turned off non-union men for the purpose of giving the same work to union men ?—Yes, in one or two instances.

22,084. (*Chairman.*) That is not very kind to the non-union men if they have worked for you, for them to know that you have not stood to them but allowed them to be turned out ?—Some time back I said to men, "You can go to work at the mill." I did not turn them clean away.

22,085. (*Mr. Chance.*) Was not there a complaint at one time by the union that you had employed both non-union men and union men when you ought to have employed only union men ?—Yes, they have complained of that.

22,086. Was it more particularly in winter when there was less work to be done ?—Yes.

22,087. Was it a complaint against you by the union at any time ?—Yes.

22,088. (*Chairman.*) The brick trade is principally carried on in summer ?—My work is generally carried on all the year round.

22,089. The brick trade is generally carried on in summer ?—Yes.

22,090. The brickmakers can find work in the summer ?—Yes.

22,091. In the winter it is difficult to find employment ?—In many instances it is.

22,092. You carry on your work in such a way that you can employ the men both in winter and summer ? is that because you have a brickmaking machine ?— No, because I have a shed and machinery and mills to grind the clay. I can turn the clay to better account than by hand.

22,093. That is not a general thing in the trade ?— No.

22,094. You have a facility in winter which is not generally offered by brickmakers ?—Yes.

22,095. And the brickmakers, being union men and being out of work in the winter, then they want to come and work for you ?—Yes.

22,096. They do not care about you in the summer when they can get plenty of employment ?—Some of them.

22,097. But in the winter when they have not employment, they come and work for you and you have to turn off the non-union men ?—Yes.

22,098. (*Mr. Chance.*) As a general rule you have not turned them off ?—No.

22,099. It is only in one or two instances that you have done it ?—It is only in one or two instances.

22,100. It has been complained of by the union against you ?—Yes.

22,101. (*Mr. Barstow.*) You say that you employ machinery in your business ?—Yes.

22,102. What machinery do you employ ?—An 18-horse engine to grind my clay with a mill and millstones.

22,103. Is that what you call a pugging mill ?— No; it is called a mortar mill, generally.

22,104. Do you employ any other sort of machinery? —Only a press.

22,105. That is common is it not ?—Yes.

22,106. Have the members of the union ever objected to your employing machinery ?—Yes.

22,107. Who was that ?—I named it to Mr. Owen and Mr. Jarratt.

22,108. Have you ever had any machinery injured? —No.

22,109. What objection did Owen and Jarratt make ?—They did not sanction it; they neither said I must, nor must not do it.

22,110. They did not object ?—No, but I knew what it meant. I calculated what it meant.

22,111. What did they say ?—There was very little said in respect of that. I never had face to go into it.

22,112. They did not say anything, but you knew what they meant ?—Yes.

22,113. (*Chairman.*) I want to ask you a question as to the men who came to see you after you had the injury done to your house, horse, stack, and cows. I want to have a little more accurately what was stated by them; what did they say ? You said that they came to you and wanted byegones to be byegones; when was it ? Let us have the date fixed first ? —It was in 1861 I believe.

22,114. Do you recollect what time of the year it was ?—October 1861.

22,115. What had occurred to you before that ? what had been done to you ?—I had a cow's entrails cut out in 1859, and then an explosion in 1860. I had the stack nearly burnt in 1861, and I had the horse stabbed.

22,116. All that had happened to you ?—Yes.

22,117. All these things had happened to you, and after they had happened these two men, you say, came to your house and talked to you about them ?—Yes.

22,118. Tell me as near as you can what they said about what had happened to you ?—Yes.

22,119. What did they say ?—They said they were very sorry.

22,120. Sorry for what ?—They said they were sorry for what had been done to me and they were ashamed of their errand, for they had not a leg to stand on; they had had a meeting on my affair, and they could not find a fault against me and they were to try to arrange the matter with me the best way they could, and if I would make a statement of the

TWENTY THIRD DAY.

J. Robinson.

3 July 1867.

damage that had been done they would try to compensate me. I declined.

22,121. Did they at all allude to the damage which you had sustained?—Yes.

22,122. What did they say you had sustained?—They said if I would calculate what I had lost they would try to compensate me.

22,123. What do you mean by what you had lost? —I am not aware whether they meant all or what I had recently lost.

22,124. They said that if you would calculate what you had lost? what do you mean by "lost"?—The horse and the cow and the trouble that I had had.

22,125. Were the cow and horse mentioned?—I am not aware whether they were mentioned distinctly or not. I think they said if I would make calculations of what I had lost, they would compensate me.

22,126. Had you lost anything besides your trouble and your horse and cow?—No.

22,127. The only thing which you believe was done at that time was the injury to the horse and cow?—Yes.

22,128. Are you quite clear that you did not state at the time that that was the ground of complaint? the injury to the horse and cow? did not you say, "You have killed my horse and killed my cow." I think if I had lost a cow and a horse in that way I should have attributed it to some one?—I believe I did. I said the trade had done it.

22,129. Did you mention to them at the meeting that you thought the trade had done you that mischief?—I should say if there was anything said that I was satisfied they had done it.

22,130. Did you say to them that the trade had done you that mischief?—I should not say it in that way.

22,131. How would you say it?—I should say "You have used me very bad; there is no one used "so bad as I have been by the trade."

22,132. In what respect did you say that you had been badly used?—I meant having the blow up and the cow injured.

22,133. You mean that you said so?—No, they knowed without me saying it.

22,134. When you said that no person had been so badly used by the trade as you had, what did they say to that?—They repeated that they would compensate me.

22,135. Did you at allude to the several thousand bricks that you had had destroyed?—No, I think not.

22,136. What you had in your mind was the cow and the horse?—The serious thing to me was the explosion, that above all the other things was the serious affair to me.

22,137. That being a serious affair, do you recollect whether you did or did not mention it to them as being a serious affair?—Yes, I did.

22,138. Are you quite sure when you mentioned to them about the explosion, that in reference to it they said they would make you compensation?—I could not say whether they did at the time, but they did say so.

22,139. Are you quite sure that what they said about compensation was in reference to the injury which you had sustained by the blowing up, the killing the horse, and killing the cow?—Yes, I am sure of it.

22,140. You are sure that the compensation offered to you had reference to those subjects?—Yes.

22,141. When they offered you compensation for those injuries that you had sustained, what did you say?—I declined having anything to do with them.

22,142. Did not it occur to you that if they had been parties to it, and were coming to offer you compensation for an injury like that of blowing up your house, and putting your lives in danger, and damaging your horse and cow, you ought to have said that they had been guilty of felonious acts, and that they ought to be imprisoned?—No, I did not suspect the men who came to me, though I suspected the trade.

22,143. They were coming to act for somebody to make you compensation—Owen was the secretary of the society?—Not at that time.

22,144. We know that he was the secretary?—I was not aware of it.

22,145. Did not you say, "If you come and offer "to make me compensation you are a set of scoundrels, "and you ought to be taken up and punished"?—If I had known that Owen had been on the committee I should have said, "You are the guilty man to serve me so." I took him to be a particular friend of mine.

22,146. Why, if these people came to offer you compensation for the injury done to your cow and horse, and for blowing up your house, did not you then go to the police and say, "I have had men coming from the trade who have offered me compensation"?—I had been to the police in each case, but in this case I expected them to be as green of it as I was, thinking it was their motive to do good to me and their fellow-men.

22,147. We are wrong. Owen was not on the committee, Mr. Barstow thought he was?—I did not think he was.

22,148. On subsequent occasions you say they came to you and offered you compensation?—You mean before that.

22,149. Before that then?—No, no one came to me.

22,150. How many times did they come and offer you compensation?—I forget whether they had three or four interviews with me. It was named once or twice in the interviews, and I distinctly said I was independent of them.

22,151. It is not what you said, but what they said that I want to know, are you quite sure that the compensation which they offered you was in reference to the injury you had sustained in your house by being blown up, and the injury which you had sustained by your horse and cow being injured?—Yes.

22,152. What was the damage done to your house?—There was very little damage done to my house; it was the best room; my wife had put an oldish counterpane on the bed.

22,153. What was the damage done to the house?—About a sovereign, not more.

22,154. Now I want to know about the peril to your family; you slept in the adjoining room to where the thing was thrown in?—Yes.

22,155. Where were your daughters sleeping?—There were four rooms on a floor. I was sleeping on the one side—the room where my daughters were sleeping was through the door that opens next to it in the back room.

22,156. The one immediately beyond?—Yes.

22,157. You were sleeping in the front one, the room that was parallel to it?—Yes.

22,158. Your daughters were sleeping behind it?—Yes.

22,159. What separated the room in which your daughters slept from the room in which the explosion took place?—A $4\frac{1}{2}$-inch wall. At the top of the staircase there are three doors. (*The witness explained the position of the room to the Examiners.*)

22,160. Your four daughters and your son were all sleeping on the same floor?—Yes.

22,161. You stopped the explosion by putting your foot on the neck of the bottle?—The bottle had broken, or I could not have stopped the fuse.

22,162. There was powder about, and it went off like a squib? was there not a mark in the room where the bottle had dashed against the door?—Yes.

22,163. Was the bottle broken?—Yes.

22,164. Are you aware whether any people in your trade pay a sort of insurance to the union?—I do not understand you.

22,165. Are you aware whether the union will guarantee the brickmakers against injury to their property?—Yes, I believe they do.

22,166. Do you know anybody who has been

TWENTY-THIRD DAY.

J. Robinson.

3 July 1867.

guaranteed ?—No, but supposing I was all right at the trade, and I could show that they had done something to me in mistake they would compensate me.

22,167. Have you known of cases of that kind occurring where a man in the trade has had his bricks damaged and the trade has made up the damage done to him ?—I have known my own.

22,168. When you were a union man ?—Yes, it was before the limit of this inquiry.

22,169. You had injury done to you, and you applied to the trade ?—I said if they served me in that way because they could not agree amongst themselves I would not encourage the union. A deputation called on me and asked me if I would be compensated and be comfortable again. I said, "Yes, I have no objection, but why did they ratten me ;" they said it was a mistake, it was the fault of a former committee, and I received 7*l.*

22,170. You said "rattening ;" is the process of rattening adopted in the brickmaking trade, stamping on the bricks and so damaging them—is that what you call rattening ?—Yes, and spoiling tools.

22,171. (*Mr. Barstow.*) Do I understand that you received 7*l.* ?—Yes.

22,172. Who paid you the 7*l.* ?—There was a man called on me.

22,173. (*Chairman.*) Do you know of any case within 10 years of any person receiving a sum of money from the union in consequence of his bricks being destroyed, or his being rattened in any way ?—No.

22,174. You do not know any case ?—No, not within 10 years.

22,175. In this case there was an offer to compensate you ?—Yes.

22,176. Blowing a man's house up is not rattening, and killing his horse or his cow is not rattening ?—No.

22,177. (*Mr. Chance.*) Did you ever hear of putting pins and needles into bricks ?—They never did it to me.

22,178. Have you ever heard of it being done ?—Yes, I have heard of it different times.

22,179. (*Chairman.*) Is that a system of rattening ?—Yes.

22,180. (*Mr. Chance.*) Do you know of any case in which that occurred ?—I heard of the gasworks being served so, but it would be beyond 10 years.

22,181. We have had the secretary here, and he says that is the system of rattening which is adopted ?—Yes.

22,182. You know the contractor of the midland tunnel, I think, and there was the gasworks besides, you say ?—Yes, I recollect that being talked of.

22,183. Have they an amalgamated society of bricklayers and brickmakers ?—Yes.

22,184. Is each trade liable to be rattened in the same degree as the other ?—I do not know.

22,185. A bricklayer could hardly be rattened, could he ?—I am not aware that he could, but I have heard of a case.

22,186. How could you ratten a bricklayer ?—I heard a case in respect of Mr. Smith's house being built ; it was tarred over with tar.

22,187. How could they ratten a bricklayer ? I do not understand it ; a bricklayer is a man who buys bricks and puts them up and builds houses ?—He builds a respectable house with patent bricks.

22,188. How would you ratten him ?—I have not seen it.

22,189. How could it be done ?—I was informed that coal tar was brushed on the red bricks, and they were made black, and, it spoilt the appearance of the front.

22,190. If a man was building a house they would spoil his bricks by putting coal tar on them, and then he could not use his bricks ?—They would not appear to be red ; they would not be worse for wear.

22,191. He would be obliged to get fresh bricks ?—Yes.

22,192. (*Mr. Barstow.*) Supposing you were in dispute with the trade, would you have any difficulty in selling your bricks ?—Yes.

22,193. How would that be ?—By stopping the bricklayers from using my bricks.

22,194. How do they do that ?—They go to master builders and bricklayers and say they are not to use any of Robinson's bricks.

22,195. Do they picket your place ?—Yes, for five or six weeks there were three or four men picketing, and very few loads of bricks went out of my yard except they knew where they went to ; they went with them to the place.

22,196. They followed them ?—Yes.

22,197. Have you known any case where the trade have had a quarrel with a bricklayer, and in order to make him comply with the rules of the union they have rattened the brickmakers who were working for him ?—No.

22,198. We find in the grinding trade that it prevails, but you have never known a case of that kind ?—No.

The witness withdrew.

G. Robinson.

GEORGE ROBINSON sworn and examined.

22,199. (*Mr. Barstow.*) You are the nephew of the last witness, and you manage his business at Masbro' ?—Yes.

22,200. From 1862 to September, 1866, were you a member of the brickmakers' union ?—Yes.

22,201. Do you remember a dispute last year caused by the union wanting to compel you to pay a halfpenny per 1,000 ?—Yes, sir.

22,202. Did your men strike in consequence of that ?—Yes, there was a deputation sent up by the committee to our yard to tell us that there would be a meeting at the club room that night.

22,203. Did the men all strike ?—Yes.

22,204. Do you remember in December of last year being in your brickyard ?—Yes.

22,205. On the top of one of the coke ovens ?—Yes.

22,206. What did you see there ?—Me and my missus had been to market ; as we were returning I got into my brickyard. The coke ovens adjoins the same yard. When I got on the top of the coke ovens to go to my home there was a report.

22,207. There was a report of firearms ?—Yes ; I called out, "Holloa ! what is the matter ?"

22,208. Did you see the flash of the firearms ?—No.

22,209. Did you hear the whiz of a bullet ?—No, I did not hear the whiz of a bullet.

22,210. Where did the sound come from ?—From my left-hand side.

22,211. How far off was it ?—40 or 50 yards.

22,212. Do you know what sort of firearms it was ?—I do not.

22,213. (*Chairman.*) Was it a pistol, or what ?—A pistol or a revolver.

22,214. Was there more than one report ?—I heard one.

22,215. (*Mr. Barstow.*) You seemed to think that you were shot at ?—Yes ; a man jumped up by the ovens and said, if I went a yard or two further he would blow my brains out. I was attempting to go forward after the report went off.

22,216. That was not the man who fired the pistol ?—I cannot say who it was ; we saw three men 100 yards off.

22,217. You saw them going into the yard before you ?—We saw them going towards Bradgate.

22,218. As soon as you called out, some one addressed you ?—Yes ; as soon as I called out, a man jumped out and said he would blow my brains out if I stepped another yard further. I told him I had done nothing amiss. My missus screamed and ran to the nearest neighbour's.

22,219. Did this man come from the direction of the report?—Yes.

22,220. Was there any other person about but that man?—Not that I could see; I had been there beforehand.

22,221. What was your opinion as to who fired it?—I thought it must be one of the three; there were two lamps on the side of the road. These three men that we saw were 100 yards from us, and they seemed to be as if they were going to the bridge. As soon as I entered the yard and got on top of the ovens, there was a report. My missus says, "Oh! what is that?" I said, "Surely this man has not shot summat." I said, "Oh! what is the matter?" and a man jumped and said, if I went a few yards further he would blow my brains out.

22,222. How far was he from you?—About three yards.

22,223. Was it so dark that you could not see three yards?—Yes; it was very dark.

22,224. Did he hold out his hand as if he had anything in it?—I could perceive his arm, but I could not see anything in his hand.

22,225. Was his hand pointing towards you?—Yes, his hand pointed towards me, and his face, as he was talking, I could see the man's head above the ovens; when I saw him climb the ovens I ran.

22,226. I did not understand you to answer the question; did you see him point his hand towards you?—As he was climbing the walls I could see his arm and head.

22,227. Did you see his arm on the wall, or did he seem as if he was going to shoot at you?—I could not say whether he was intending to shoot at me.

22,228. He said, "If you go a step further I will blow your brains out?"—Yes.

22,229. You cannot say whether he had a pistol in his hand or whether he offered to blow your brains out?—I could not say that.

22,230. In fact, you did not stand still?—No; after my missus had left me I ran to the nearest neighbour.

22,231. Did he shoot at you?—No, not after the first report went off.

22,232. Did you go to the police?—Yes, I went to this neighbour and rattled him up, and asked him to take my missus into the house.

22,233. Did you go to the police?—Yes, I went to Rotherham and saw Serjeants Pilkington and Wade.

22,234. (*Mr. Chance.*) How far off were you when the shot was first fired?—Not about 50 yards.

22,235. That would be a very long distance for a man to shoot at you with a pistol?—I should not think it very far when I was on the top of the ovens and he was below.

22,236. It is a further distance than the length of this room?—I do not think that it was as long from where the men were.

22,237. If he had had a gun you would have seen it?—Yes; if he had had a gun I should have seen it.

22,238, Did you think that the men were tipsy?—I thought so at first. I did not take any notice of them.

22,239. Did you see the three men before you heard the report?—Yes.

22,240. Did the report seem to come from where the three men where?—We had to turn to the right hand in coming into our yard, and leave them to the left; when we got on to the top of the ovens it was quite dark, and the blaze dazzling before our eyes from the oven, we could not see anything below; when we got 50 yards into the yard opposite the old weigh-house, immediately a report went off; I had a child in my arms, and I cried out, "Holloa! what is the matter?" and as soon as I said that a man said if I went another yard further he would blow my brains out.

22,241. Did you suppose that that man was one of the three you had seen before?—I thought so.

22,242. How far was the spot where you saw this man from where you had seen the three?—Those three would be just about got to the place where the report came from.

22,243. How far was the place where you saw the one man who threatened to blow your brains out from the place where you first saw the man?—150 yards.

22,244. Could one of the three men have run that distance in the time?—Yes, because they were before us.

22,245. What space had you to go over in that time?—Only a matter of 100 yards; they were 100 yards before us, before we entered the yard.

22,246. Could not you see the men separate one from the other?—No; it is quite dark in our yard. We lost the men all at once.

22,247. Supposing the man had not said anything about blowing your brains out, should you have supposed that the shot had been fired at you, or amongst themselves?—I thought at first that one of them had shot the other, but when I made the expression, "Holloa! what is the matter?" and he said, "If you go any further I will blow your brains out," then we thought that he had fired at me.

22,248. It was that expression made by him that made you think that the shot had been fired at you in the first instance?—Yes.

22,249. If it had not been for that observation you would not have expected that it was shot at you?—No.

22,250. You had no actual reason to suppose that that one man was one of the three?—I had no reason except seeing the three before.

22,251. (*Mr. Barstow.*) Do you think that the man who said that he would blow your brains out was the same man who fired the pistol?—I cannot say, because I had not seen him before.

22,252. (*Mr. Chance.*) How long after this dispute was it that this firing took place?—The men were called out in September, and the firing took place on the 8th of December.

22,253. Had you had any disputes between those times with any members of the union?—No.

22,254. Nothing more?—No; nothing more.

The witness withdrew.

SAMUEL JOHNSON sworn and examined.

S. Johnson.

22,255. (*Chairman.*) What are you?—A fork grinder.

22,256. I am going to put some very serious questions to you, and before I put them I will tell you how you are placed. I am going to ask you whether you have committed a serious offence, and I can tell you if you have committed that offence, and make a clear disclosure that you have done so, and we are satisfied that you are telling the truth and not only telling the truth about it, but about all you know with respect to trades union matters, we can give you a certificate which will free you from any consequences, either criminal or civil of your own act or acts; and if you do not, and it should turn out that you are guilty of the offences imputed to you, you will be liable to be prosecuted. You may clear yourself by making a full disclosure, but if you do not disclose you will be liable to be prosecuted. Having told you that I am going to ask you some questions. You are a fork grinder?—Yes.

22,257. Are you a member of the union?—No.

22,258. Were you ever a member of the union?—Yes.

22,259. In February 1859 were you a member of the union?—A few weeks I was.

TWENTY-THIRD DAY

S. Johnson.

3 July 1867.

22,260. Did you know a man of the name of Roebuck ?—Yes.

22,261. Do you recollect a quantity of gunpowder being placed in his trough ?—I can recollect the day it was put in.

22,262. You recollect the day it was put in ?—Yes.

22,263. Where was he working ?—At Mr. Askham's at Broad Lane.

22,264. He worked in the hull immediately below you ?—Underneath ; he worked in the chamber. I worked in the garret.

22,265. He was a fork grinder ?—Yes.

22,266. So are you ?—Yes.

22,267. You were in the union and he was not ?—That is right.

22,268. Had you frequently before the morning, when he was blown up, gone to his door and called him a knobstick ?—No.

22,269. Mind ?—No.

22,270. Will you swear that ?—Yes.

22,271. Have you ever gone to his hull and said that he was a knobstick ?—No.

22,272. Have you ever called him a knobstick ?—No.

22,273. You swear that ?—Yes, I will swear that. I have told him to-day that he is a false man to himself for saying so.

22,274. You have heard what he said ?—Yes.

23,275. And you swear that you never went to his place and called him a knobstick ?—I never called him a knobstick.

22,276. Have you ever called him anything ?—I asked him whether he would rather have 2*s.* or 2*s.* 6*d.*

22,277. What did you mean by that ?—Whether he would have 2*s.* a gross or 2*s.* 6*d.* a gross.

22,278. What did you mean by asking that question ?—I do not know.

22,279. You know why you asked him that question. Why did you ask him whether he would rather have 2*s.* or 2*s.* 6*d.* ?—Our master said, " If he comes " in at 2*s.* you will have to have 2*s.* ; and if he has " 2*s.* 6*d.* you will have 2*s.* 6*d.*"

22,280. What do you mean by " coming in ?"—To work for 2*s.* or 2*s.* 6*d.*

22,281. Your master had said that if he came in at 2*s.* 6*d.* you should have 2*s.* 6*d.*, and if he got 2*s.* you should have 2*s.* ?—Yes.

22,282. Was he working at 2*s.* at that time ?—He was working at 2*s.*

22,283. You were very much annoyed at his working at 2*s.*, and you wanted him to get 2*s.* 6*d.*?—No.

22,284. It was with that object that you made that inquiry ?—Yes.

22,285. Then in point of fact he was preventing you from getting 6*d.* a gross more ?—No.

22,286. Yes, he was ?—It did in one way.

22,287. In every way ?—We were not union men.

22,288. But you were a union man ?—We throwed off not to be union men.

22,289. You were a union man ?—We throwed out.

22,290. At that time you belonged to the union ?—When we came in we did, but we throwed out.

22,291. At what time did you go to work that morning ?—Between half-past 8 and 9.

22,292. Who let you in to your work ?—I do not know.

22,293. Did a man of the name of Sharp let you in ?—A man in the time-house let me in.

22,294. A man in the time-house came to let you in ?—We came through the time-house.

22,295. When you got into your hull that morning were you not the first there ?—No.

22,296. Who was there ?—There was a lad there.

22,297. What was his name ?—Nobody about the place knew his name ; he went by the name of " Face ;" he was a little lad.

22,298. How old was he ?—13 or 14 years old.

22,299. And he was there ?—Ye.s

22,300. In order to get there he would have had to come through the time-room ?—The time-house ?

22,301. Yes.—We had all to come through the time-house.

22,302. If that boy went into that room that morning before you, he must have passed through the time-house to come there ?—He went through the time-house before me.

22,303. He could not have got in without going through the time-house ?—No, he could not get into the wheel without going through the time-house.

22,304. Sharp will speak about this ; do you swear that that boy was in before you ?—Yes, he was.

22,305. He was in before you ?—Yes, he was.

22,306. For whom did he work ?—They called him Samuel. I did not know what his other name was ; he did bolsters.

22,307. When you got up into your hull did you find that boy there ?—The boy was there and had kindled the fire.

22,308. What did you do in the hull when you got there ?—Whilst the time I was fetched out into the Askham's warehouse I never went down the steps any more.

22,309. And you swear that that boy was there first ?—Yes.

22,310. What time did you leave the place the night before ?—Between 5 and 6.

22,311. Were you the last there ?—No, I was not.

22,312. Whom did you leave in that hull ?—Four besides myself.

22,313. Give me their names ?—Henry Eastwood for one, William Browne's apprentice, and then Samuel, a bolster grinder, and there was his lad.

22,314. There were those four ?—Yes.

22,315. You left the four in the hull when you came away ?—Yes, there were those four and my own lad.

22,316. You left them all four in the hull when you came away the night before ?—Yes.

22,317. Are you sure about that ?—Yes.

22,318. There is no mistake about it ?—It is a long time since.

22,319. But you swear it ?—Yes.

22,320. Did you work with a boy ?—No.

22,321. What did you say about a lad ; who was he ?—I left him at the wheel.

22,322. What was your lad doing there if he did not work for you ?—He was grinding when I left him. Yes, my own lad worked for me.

22,323. The next morning you say the boy was there ?—Yes, first.

22,324. Did you go there alone the next morning ?—I went by myself ; my own lad stayed to bring something to eat for his dinner.

22,325. How did it happen that you wanted to go by yourself that morning ? why did not you go with your boy ?—I always went by myself, and the boy came after me.

22,326. Why did not your boy come along with you that morning ?—He stayed at home to bring something to eat with him.

22,327. Why should he stay at home to bring something to eat ? why should not he get your dinner ready and come along with you at the same time ?—In the morning ?

22,328. Yes.—He brought it with him and I used to go first.

22,329. Why did you go first there ? why did not you go with your son ? it is not true that he stayed behind to get victuals ?—He stayed to get something to eat. I went to get some shanks ready for the boy to grind afterwards.

22,330. How soon after you got there did your son come ?—Better than half an hour.

22,331. Did you see Roebuck that morning ?—No, I did not, not while I was fetched into the warehouse.

22,332. Did you see him go to the privy ?—No.

22,333. You swear that ?—Yes.

22,334. Could you see from your shop where you were working a man go out of his hull to the privy ?—No.

TWENTY-THIRD DAY.

S. Johnson.

3 July 1867.

22,335. You could not ?—No.

22,336. Do you mean that a man looking out from your door or your place could not see a man go down into the yard to the privy ?—No; you can go to the hull and look yourself. You cannot see him.

22,337. I do not mean whether you can see a man when he is in the privy ; but can you see a man going down from the hull when he crosses the yard to go to the privy ?—No.

22,338. You cannot see him ?—No.

22,339. You swear that when you are working you cannot see him ? but supposing that you are not working and looking out of your shop window, cannot you see into that yard ?—For about a yard you can. You can never see me looking out of the window.

22,340. On your oath did you see the man Roebuck go into the yard to the privy that morning ?—No.

22,341. You never did ?—No, I can take my dying oath on that.

22,342. Did you ever place any powder in his trough ?—No.

22,343. You swear that you did not ?—No.

22,344. Do you know who did ?—(*The witness hesitated.*) That is another question.

22,345. It is a question that you will answer; who did it ?—That is another question.

22,346. Who did it ?—I can tell you who did it.

22,347. You can ; then do so ?—The man that told me who did it is dead and gone ; but the man who did it is in the 82d Regiment—Thomas Yates, fork grinder. I was searched in Mr. Askham's warehouse over it the same morning, and I did not know while the next morning at 9 o'clock that there had been any powder done at all.

22,348. Who do you say was the man who did it ?—Thomas Yates.

22,349. How do you know that he did it ?—George Cowper, who is dead and gone, told me at the same time when I went with him that he did it. That is three years since.

22,350. George Cowper told you that Yates did it, and George Cowper told you this three years ago ?—Yes, about three years since.

22,351. George Cowper is dead ?—Yes.

22,352. Thomas Yates is in the East Indies ?—Yes, in the 82nd Regiment.

22,353. How did Cowper tell you this ?—He said, "Lad, thou wast very innocent of that Askham's "powder job." I said I wished I knew who did it; it was a very great shock to me. He said that Thomas Yates did it, and when they took him for a deserter he throwed his peg-whistle over the Ladies Bridge into the dyke.

22,354. What is a peg-whistle ?—What he had to whistle with to tell persons when there were folks about.

22,355. Had you known this man ?—I had seen him several times.

22,356. Where had you seen him ?—I had seen him working with George Cowper the last time I had seen him.

22,357. What was he ?—A fork grinder.

22,358. Was he a member of the union ?—Yes, he was.

22,359. Did he tell you why he had done it ?—No.

22,360. Where was he working at the time this was done ? — At Trafalgar Street with George Cowper.

22,361. He worked there at the time that this man had the powder put into his trough ?—Yes.

22,362. How far was that from your wheel ?—It would be half a mile off.

22,363. Had you ever seen him about the wheel ?—No.

22,364. Had you seen him that morning ?—No.

22,365. Had you seen him the night before ?—No.

22,366. If you heard three years ago that this man had done it, why did not you go to Mr. Askham and tell him like an honest man, "I have found who put "the gunpowder into that man's trough, and it is a "man out there." Why did not you tell him that ?—I thought nothing about going to tell him.

22,367. Why did not you go to Mr. Roebuck and tell him ?—Because I thought Mr. Roebuck knew.

22,368. Have you told this story to anybody before to-day ?—I told Mr. Roebuck to-day about it.

22,369. You say now that it was another man, and you knew it, and Cowper told you three years ago, and you have never told the story before to-day ; if the other man did it, how did he get in ?—I do not know how he got in.

22,370. He could not get in without going through the time-house ? — I do not know which way he got in.

22,371. It is very fine to tell a story about what a man did, who is in the East Indies ; but how could the man get in to do it ?—I do not know how he got in ; I know nought about it.

22,372. When Cowper, who is dead, told you this curious story, did not you ask him how he got in ?—No.

22,373. On your oath did not you do it yourself ?—No.

22,374. Is not this altogether a fiction of yours ?—No.

22,375. If this man comes from the East Indies and finds that you have been telling this story about him —— ?—He cannot bring me in at all.

22,376. Yes he can. Did you know that he was going to do it before he did it ?—No, I knew nothing at all about it.

22,377. Did you ever buy any powder ?—No.

22,378. Never ?—No.

22,379. Had you no powder at this very time in your possession ?—No.

22,380. Have you never bought any ?—No.

22,381. You swear that ?—Yes, not a halfpenny worth.

22,382. Had you ever any powder given to you about that time ?—No.

22,383. Had you ever any in your possession ?—No.

22,384. And you swear that you did not go down into that hull that morning ?—Yes, I will.

22,385. Can you explain this to me. You say that another man did it and you know who it was, can you say how he got in ?—No, I cannot say how he got in to this day.

22,386. Is it not an impossibility for any man to get in except through the time-house ?—We have all to go through the time-house.

22,387. And you have not only to go through to get in, but to come out ?—To come out and all.

22,388. If this man went in as you say, the man who keeps the time-house will be able to say whether it is true or not ?—Yes, he could.

22,389. The very morning that the powder was found of course the time-house man was applied to, to know who had been through ?—I do not know that, that is the first word I have heard of it.

22,390. You did not know that ?—No.

22,391. The time-house man is alive ?—I do not know.

22,392. Was his name Sharp ?—I do not know what his name was.

22,393. You do not know where he lives ?—No, he did live at Broad Lane, at the yard I expect.

22,394. You do not know where he lives now ?—No, I do not.

22,395. You cannot explain how the man went in ?—No.

22,396. Did not you tell Cowper it was a very curious story that he told you ?—Cowper told me it was Thomas Yates that did it.

22,397. Did not you say "But how did he do it? He "could not get in without going through the time-"house—how could he get in ?"—I did not say anything about the powder being put there.

22,398. You knew that any man who put the powder in the trough must have gone through the time-

TWENTY-THIRD DAY.

S. Johnson.

3 July 1867.

house to do it, and did not you tell him that he could not have done it unless Sharp knew. I caution you although this man is abroad. Did not you put it there yourself? now it is your only chance?—No.

22,399. Were you a party to it being put in?—No, I knew nothing about it being put in.

22,400. Look what a position you are putting yourself in, if Sharp comes and swears that a man never went through that time-house, who will believe your story?—I know nought about it.

22,401. You do know about it; you have told us that you know who did it?—No.

22,402. You say there is a dead man who told you all about it. You never told the owner and you never told the man who was attempted to be blown up, and I ask is not this altogether a fabrication, because you are found out?—No.

22,403. You had much better make a clean breast of it, I can do no more than caution you. I will give you a certificate if you will make a clean breast of it, and if you do not you will have to take the consequences of your own conduct. Again, I ask you, feeling the position you are placed in, did you know that he was going to put it there?—No.

22,404. When did you first know of it?—The next morning after it was done. I did not know that anybody had been hurting him at all.

22,405. Who was hurt?—William Mason and another.

22,406. Did this man Cowper tell you he had done some men?—No, he said he had put it into Roebuck's trough.

22,407. Did you know who did the other men?—No, Thomas Yates put it into Roebuck's trough.

22,408. What had Thomas Yates to do with it; why should he put it in?—I do not know.

22,409. Why should Thomas Yates put it in?—Because I expect he had been engaged to put it in.

22,410. Who had engaged him?—The trade I expect.

22,411. Were you ever engaged to do a thing of that kind?—No.

22,412. Have you done such a thing?—No, nor never would.

22,413. Why not?—Because I do not like to go and drink folks ale.

22,414. Is that the only objection?—No, I like to drink my own when I have any; I do not like to drink folks ale. I have my own to drink, then I know I am right; when I can pay for my own I know I am right. I do not like to have anybody's money but my own.

22,415. Did this man ever work at all in your hull?—No.

22,416. Did you ever see him about the place?—No.

22,417. Did you ever see any of the other men in your hull go to Roebuck's and tell him that he was a knobstick or anything of that kind?—No, never.

22,418. And you did not yourself?—No.

22,419. Did Roebuck go to you this morning and see you at work?—No.

22,420. (*Chairman.*) Let Mr. Roebuck stand forward.

22,421. (*To Mr. Roebuck.*) Is that the man you saw at work in the morning?—Yes.

22,422. Did he see you at the time you went up to see him in the hull?—No, I do not think he did.

22,423. You do not know that he saw you?—No.

22,424. Is that the man who has come to you frequently and called you a knobstick?—Yes, he called me so when I was working.

22,425. (*To Samuel Johnson.*) Now you hear what he says, and you see what a position you stand in; he swears that you have gone into his hull when he was at work and called him a knobstick?—I only spoke to him once, and I did not call him a knobstick then.

22,426. What did you call him?—I asked him whether he would have 2*s.* or 2*s.* 6*d.*; is that calling him a knobstick?

22,427. No; why did not you tell about this man?—I thought no more about it.

22,428. You were suspected of having done it, and at this very moment Mr. Roebuck believes that you did it?—He told me this morning, "I do believe thou art innocent now lad." I went and told him who had done it and everything, and he told me he believed me innocent.

T. Roebuck.

THOMAS ROEBUCK recalled and further examined.

22,429. (*Chairman.*) Do you know anything about the man whom Johnson has mentioned as the person who did this act and who has gone out with the 82nd regiment to India?—No.

22,430. Do you know of such a man?—I believe he was on the fork grinders committee at the same time.

22,431. You were told that he was?—Yes.

22,432. Had you ever seen him about your premises?—I did not know Yates personally at all. Cowper told me that he was on the committee; he never was suspected in the slightest.

22,433. Do you know where Sharp is?—He is somewhere in the town; I daresay I could get to know. He was timekeeper at the time; he is living; I saw him a short time since.

22,434. Would Sharp keep a book of the persons passing through?—No, but he would know.

22,435. Was his attention called to the fact? After you had found all this powder put in your trough was Sharp asked who had gone through his place?—Yes, he said he was the only grinder who had gone through; he told Mr. Askham so that very morning.

22,436. Can you tell me whether there was a boy that worked for Samuel?—No, I could see all over the hull and there was not a boy in at all; if there had been a boy in I could have seen him.

(*Witness to Johnson.*) He was there when I went in in the morning; if I knew where the lad was I would bring him forward. I do not know where Sam works or I could go there.

20,437. (*Chairman to Johnson.*) You hear what Roebuck says; you have still the opportunity of telling the truth?—I have told you the truth; I do not want to tell lies. I have not told you any lies.

22,438. You have kept the secret for three years?—If you ask me a lie I will not tell you one; I will tell you what I know, and lies I will not tell.

22,439. (*To Roebuck.*) Did you tell Johnson just now that you did not believe that he did it?—He told me Yates had done it, and I said if Yates had done it they could not both have done it.

22,440. Did you tell him that you believed his story?—No, I told him if Yates had done it he would be innocent.

22,441. (*To Johnson.*) Did you know this man Thomas Yates?—Yes.

22,442. Had Yates spoken to you at all about this?—No.

22,443. Had any of the fork grinders committee ever spoken to you?—No.

22,444. Who was the secretary at that time?—I do not know who was the secretary.

22,445. You were a fork grinder's union man, and you know who the secretary was?—I do not know.

22,446. Who was the secretary? do you recollect?—I do not know who was the secretary; I want to speak the truth.

22,447. Had anybody been to you from the trade asking you to do anything to this man Roebuck?—No.

22,448. Have they ever asked you to hurt any person then?—No, they have not.

22,449. Do you know how this person got in, whom you know about?—No, I do not.

22,450. How did you happen to be talking to Cowper about it?—I called for him. He said, "Lad, thou seemest very innocent of John Askham's affair." I said that I was innocent. I did not know till the next morning about folks being hurt with powder.

He said, "No, it was Yates that did the job." I said, "How do you know?" He says, "Ah!" and there was no more past.

22,451. (*Mr. Barstow to Roebuck.*) Did you look into Samuel the bolster grinder's hull?—Yes, he was in the top room.

22,452. There was no one there?—No.

22,453. Did you see whether his fire was lighted? —I do not think it was; when we are at the top of the ladder we cannot see the fireplace without going in. I did not look at the fireplace and I could not say whether it was in or not.

22,454. (*Chairman.*) Johnson says that a person cannot see another going into the yard, is that so?—They can see anyone if they look out of the window.

(*Witness Johnson.*) When they are working they cannot.

(*Witness Roebuck.*) I never said they could if they are working see the yard from the wheel.

(*Witness Johnson.*) If you stand looking at the window you cannot see who goes in and out of your hull then.

22,455. (*Mr. Barstow to Roebuck.*) Do you know any way in which a man could get into this wheel except through the time-house?—No, there is no other way, unless he climbed the windows.

22,456. Would it be a very difficult thing to do?—Yes, it would.

22,457. (*Chairman to Roebuck.*) I should very much like to see Sharp?—I will try to find him.

22,458. (*Chairman to Johnson.*) You have had your chance, if things turn out against you you must not blame us for it?—I have given you my evidence true.

The witness withdrew.

Mr. Thomas Thorpe sworn and examined.

T. Thorpe.

22,459. (*Chairman.*) You are managing clerk of Mr. Albert Smith, clerk of the county magistrates, and the borough magistrates of Sheffield?—Yes.

22,460. You have been in his service 36 years?—Yes.

22,461. It has been your office for the last 25 years to attend solely to the duty of assistant magistrate's clerk?—Yes.

22,462. Within 10 years from the time of the passing of the Trades Unions Commission Act, 1867, a great number of outrages had been brought before the police authorities in Sheffield?—Yes.

22,463. Have you seen a list of them?—I have.

22,464. By that list it appears there that are 166 rattening cases?—There are.

22,465. They have been brought before the police authorities?—Before the police authorities or the justices.

22,466. There are 20 cases of outrage?—Yes.

22,467. Twenty-two cases of threatening letters? —Yes; most of these have been written to the parties and brought to the police.

22,468. And 12 cases of intimidation?—Yes, about a dozen or more; but I do not find that there are any records of any dismissed cases of intimidation prior to November 1862.

22,469. The list which you have furnished us with is a complete list as far as you are aware of all the cases of rattenings, outrages, threatening letters, and intimidation?—It is so.

22,470. In some cases parties have beeen convicted, we are told?—Yes.

22,471. In others the cases have been merely inquired into by the police, and no evidence has been taken, so that the cases have dropped?—The great difficulty with the police was in getting evidence to support the cases.

22,472 And many have failed for want of evidence? —A great many.

22,473. Do you believe that there are a great many cases of rattening which never came before the magistrates and the police?—A great many.

22,474. Can you give me any reason why the parties in Sheffield did not go at once to the magistrates in rattening cases?—I can only say that they know the great difficulty there would be in making out a case, because all the parties were more or less connected with the unions.

22,475. Do you believe that there are many cases of outrage which have never been brought before the police or the magistrates?—I think not.

22,476. You think that cases of outrage are generally brought before the police?—Yes.

22,477. But in cases simply of rattening those are not brought before them at all?—No.

22,478. In cases of persons receiving a threatening letter, are those not commonly brought before the magistrates or police, or are they generally brought before them?—I have heard of some that have not been brought, but not so numerous as rattening cases.

22,479. There are a great many rattening cases which have never been brought before you?—That is properly taking away a man's tools or bands because he is deficient in his contribution or has offended the society.

22,480. With respect to outrages, I believe those are principally brought before you?—I believe they have been.

22,481. And threatening letters?—Yes.

22,482. And cases of intimidation?—Many of those have not come, I should think.

22,483. You have supplied us with a list of all those that have come within the knowledge of the authorities?—I have.

The witness withdrew.

William Owen recalled and further examined.

W. Owen.

22,484. (*Chairman.*) You falsified the books?—I tore the leaves out and burnt them.

22,485. (*Mr. Barstow.*) In October 1861, do you remember calling upon James Robinson in company with Jarrett?—I did, after being solicited.

22,486. (*Chairman.*) By whom?—I think it was our secretary.

22,487. (*Mr. Barstow.*) What is his name?—John Mawson, to the best of my recollection.

22,488. Were you an office bearer at this time?—No; I had not taken any part on any special occasion for eight years previous to that.

22,489. Why did you call upon Robinson?—I asked them the reason, and they said they thought I had more influence with him than any other man in the trade.

22,490. Were you a personal friend of his?—I had worked for him, and was on very friendly terms with him at the time.

22,491. What was the object of your having an interview with him?—The object was this: me and Mr. Jarrett were disgusted at the proceedings that were taken against Mr. Robinson; we did not know whether it arose from the union difficulties or not, but I adopted that account because Mr. Robinson was out of the union at the time.

22,492. What proceedings do you allude to?—I allude to those that Mr. Robinson and his own wife stated to me in his own house.

22,493. What were they? — Gunpowder thrown into his chamber window, and his horse's bowels ripped out, and a cow destroyed.

22,494. Was the object of your interview with him in reference to those?—My object was to effect a reconciliation between the trade and him.

22,495. You were aware at that time that Mr. Robinson was on bad terms with the trade?—He was on bad terms with them.

22,496. I will not take you all through the conversation, but did you desire Robinson to let byegones be byegones?—I never uttered such a thing.

22,497. Or any words to that effect?—No words to that effect were uttered by me.

TWENTY-THIRD DAY.

W. Owen.

3 July 1867.

22,498. Or by Jarrett in your presence?—He was with me.

22,499. Was anything of the sort said by Jarrett in your presence?—I cannot say; it is six years since the occurrence took place. Mr. Jarratt is in the hall here, and he will tell you if he heard them.

22,500. Did you offer to make Robinson compensation?—No such thing was mentioned.

22,501. Or did you attempt to effect a reconciliation? —I will be as concise as possible: I was chosen as the deputation to wait upon Mr. Robinson. I stated to Mr. Robinson the object of my visit. Emotion was shown on all sides when they came to relate the transactions that had taken place. I sympathised with him, and told him I would do all I could to effect a reconciliation between the two.

22,502. How did you propose to effect a reconciliation?—Not by offering him compensation, but by making them on more friendly terms, and taking his men within the pale of the society.

22,503. Did you offer that his men should be taken within the pale of the society?—That was all; no other inducement had been offered to him.

22,504. Had Robinson applied to have his men taken within the pale of the society?—No; we applied to him.

22,505. Did you think that Robinson, who had held out so long and suffered all the losses which he has described through the society would be reconciled by the offer to take his men into the society?—I thought so.

22,506. What induced you to think so?—I had no reason for thinking he would come in. I said I would make an effort to bring him in again.

22,507. You had no reason to think that you would succeed?—No; I did not think I should succeed when I went on the mission.

22,508. What induced the secretary to endeavour to reconcile Robinson to the union? do you know that? —No; they never stated their views on the subject to me.

22,509. They only asked you to call upon him?—They asked me to form one of a deputation to see Mr. Robinson.

22,510. To what do you attribute these different outrages which Mr. Robinson has told us of?—To rattenings by the union on account of his being out of the union; it is in consequence of his wanting to take advantage of the men when they was within the pale of the society.

22,511. You attribute it to his wanting to take advantage of the men when they were within the pale of the society?—Yes.

22,512. (*Chairman.*) You think that they having blown up his house and his having his cow and horse destroyed, was all owing to that?—Yes; I think it was nothing else.

22,513. That you have owned before?—Yes.

22,514. Have you any reason to know who did it? —Not the slightest.

22,515. You are to a certain extent candid; when you first went there you say that there was a good deal of feeling exhibited?—Yes; by all parties.

22,516. And Mrs. Robinson talked about her family being liable to be blown up?—Yes.

22,517. And then the horse and cow were killed?—Yes.

22,518. She told you all that?—Yes.

22,519. Did not you say that you were really very much ashamed of the whole business?—Yes, and I sympathised with them.

22,520. If you had nothing to do with it and the trade had nothing to do with it, it was of course no matter of shame to you?—I felt ashamed and disgusted at the proceedings taken against him if it were a trade matter, and I have reason to think it was a trade matter.

22,521. And you destroyed your books because you thought there were entries in them?—They were not destroyed by me; they were destroyed previous to me ever becoming secretary.

22,522. You had reason to know that there were entries in those books which would have shown who were the persons who had done it?—I have every reason to believe that it would have shown that monies had been paid for it, but it does not show who were the perpetrators of those deeds.

22,523. You have every reason to believe that the books, if they had existed, would have shown the money which had been given for these outrages?—Yes, I have every reason to believe that it would have to be accounted for.

22,524. (*Mr. Barstow.*) You mean that the books would have shown the money paid for the perpetration of these outrages?—Yes; men will not work for nothing.

22,525. (*Chairman.*) It is not our business to find out who did it, but have you suspicion at all who did it? —I have not the slightest. I cannot remember the names of all the men on the committee; they seem to have had the greatest feeling for Mr. Robinson.

22,526. I believe they do pay the money for the perpetration of the outrage, and then they exhibit a great deal of feeling?—Yes they do.

22,527. They exhibit feeling, and then offer a reward, and pass resolutions deeply sympathising?—There is no soft soap of that now amongst the brickmakers. They indulge in knocking each other in the head, as the "Telegraph" says, when they have no better pastime. I wish you could go a little more into Mr. Robinson's business. I wish to state before leaving this chair that I have heard Mr. Robinson state in this chair a great many falsehoods, and I should like to have them thoroughly sifted, but what I more particularly want to go into is in respect of his mill. It is said, and rumoured both in the papers and in the town, that he derived no benefit from paying a halfpenny a thousand for allowing him to grind by machinery. I deny that. We allowed Mr. Robinson to employ cheaper labour, but if he did employ our society labour then we asked him 4*s.* 6*d.* for 10 hours labour, and 3*s.* 6*d.* for 9 hours labour; every master in the town agreed to that but Mr. Robinson. Ultimately, at the finish, when he found that it was detrimental to his interest, he had an agreement drawn up, saying that there should be no deviation from this rule; he would coincide with those rules; he had an agreement drawn up, and I have that agreement endorsed with his name in my pocket now.

22,528. He said that he signed the agreement and refused to carry it out?—He would not carry it out.

22,529. There is no falsehood in that, because he admitted it; he said first that he wanted to have an arbitration, but subsequently he entered into an agreement which he signed, and then he would not carry out his agreement because you would not carry out the arbitration, and that is the way it stood. He said because you had been false to him he was false to you?—I believe I was one that was deputed.

22,530. You have been candid in showing that some of these rattenings have been done in a scandalous and disgraceful manner. I trust that some means will be adopted by a person of your respectability to prevent them?—They will not take place while I can raise a voice in the matter.

The witness withdrew.

(*Chairman.*) I believe there is no necessity to examine Mr. Jarrett, because the thing is clearly brought home to the union. We have a variety of matters to attend to which it is impossible for us to settle. We propose to adjourn from to-day to Saturday at 11 o'clock, but in the meantime we are anxious that persons shall come forward and give us any information they can to throw a light upon the subject-matter of the inquiry, and if they bring any cases before us between this and Saturday we shall be obliged. Our duty is to investigate every trade outrage connected with the unions either by combinations of masters or men, and if anyone has any information to give which comes within the scope of this inquiry, we hope that they will not hesitate to come forward and give it.

Adjourned to Saturday next at 11 o'clock.

TWENTY-FOURTH DAY.

Council Hall, Sheffield, Saturday, 6th July 1867.

PRESENT:

WILLIAM OVEREND, Esq., Q.C. | GEORGE CHANCE, Esq.
THOMAS IRWIN BARSTOW, Esq. | J. E. BARKER, Esq., Secretary.

WILLIAM OVEREND, ESQ., Q.C., IN THE CHAIR.

TWENTY-FOURTH DAY.

F. Jackson.

6 July 1867.

FREDERICK JACKSON sworn and examined.

22,531. (*Chairman.*) Are you the secretary of the Nail Makers' Union at Belper?—Yes, I am, if it deserves the name of a union.

22,532. Were you secretary of that union in the year 1861?—No.

22,533. Who was the secretary at that time?—I believe it was George Worthy.

22,534. Were you a member of the union at that time?—I expect I was.

22,535. Did you pay to the funds of the union?—Yes.

22,536. Were you on the committee of the union?—No.

22,537. But you were a person who contributed to the funds of the union at the time George Worthy was your secretary?—Yes.

22,538. Are you the secretary now, and do you produce the books of the union?—Yes.

22,539. Are they there?—Yes.

22,540. Are those all the books you have?—Yes.

22,541. Do they extend to the year 1861?—I really cannot say.

22,542. Give them to our secretary and he will look at them. (*The witness handed the books to Mr. Barker.*)

22,543. They are all the books you have?—Yes.

22,544. Do you believe there are any other books that have been destroyed?—I know there is one book, at least part of a book; when it was filled I took it to my house, and there were some of the leaves not filled up, and the children wanted some writing paper, and of course I took out some of them and they wrote on it, and it is destroyed.

22,545. What was that book?—It was a book similar to one of those, an account book.

22,546. Over what period of time did that account book extend?—I believe from Worthy's time downwards.

22,547. To your time?—Yes.

22,548. When did Worthy's time expire?—I really cannot mention the date.

22,549. Was it in 1861?—I should say it was.

22,550. When did you begin to be secretary?—I was temporarily appointed secretary as successor to Worthy.

22,551. When was that?—I do not know the date.

22,552. Was that three or four years ago?—More than three years.

22,553. It would be since 1861?—Yes.

22,554. During the period of 1861 when Worthy was secretary the account book has been destroyed?—Yes.

22,555. And by you?—I took it home and my children wrote in it.

22,556. Then you destroyed it?—They destroyed it, I did not destroy it; I was not aware at all it would ever have been required, or I would have taken care that it would not have been destroyed.

22,557. How was it that you allowed your children to write in that book?—It was not quite filled up and they wanted something to write in; I thought the book was of no use whatever and I allowed them to write in it.

22,558. Is this the book you allude to?—No.

22,559. What book is this?—I should say it is a book prior to that time.

22,560. It is May 1859?—It was one at the bottom of the box.

22,561. You see that that book is destroyed (*showing the book to the witness*)?—Yes.

22,562. Who destroyed it?—I cannot say; it is prior to my time.

22,563. When did you find that book in that condition?—I found it in that condition yesterday.

22,564. Is this book in the same condition in which it came to your hands?—Exactly.

22,565. When did it come into your hands?—I was not aware that in——

22,566. Answer the question; when did it come into your hands?—Yesterday.

22,567. From whom did you get it?—It was in the box.

22,568. Who kept the box?—I kept the keys of the box.

22,569. How long have you kept the keys of the box?—Since I have been secretary.

22,570. That is five years ago?—There are others who have been secretaries since then.

22,571. When did you begin to be secretary?—I cannot mention the date.

22,572. How long after the blow-up we are going to inquire into?—I cannot say; I know I succeeded Worthy.

22,573. How long after the blow-up at Thorpe Hesley did you become secretary?—I cannot say.

22,574. How long did Worthy continue secretary? up to the blow-up at Thorpe Hesley?—I cannot say.

22,575. How long do you believe he was?—I came here to speak the truth; I do not know.

22,576. How long did he remain secretary? until the blow-up at Thorpe Hesley?—Perhaps a year and perhaps more.

22,577. Do you believe he was more than a year?—Perhaps he was.

22,578. I do not know about perhaps; do you believe he was more than a year?—I cannot say that I can form an opinion.

22,579 What is your belief about it?—I really do not know what to say; I cannot form an opinion.

22,580. What is your belief, was he a year or more than a year?—I believe he was there a year.

22,581. Your belief is that he remained a year after the blow-up at Thorpe Hesley?—Yes.

22,582. After he ceased, you became secretary?—Temporarily.

22,583. At the time that you became secretary after this blow-up, was that book in the box?—I never remember seeing that book till yesterday.

22,584. Will you swear that you never saw it?—To the best of my recollection I never saw it.

22,585. You swear that you never saw it till then?—Yes.

22,586. You saw it then, and did you find it in that state, or have you mutilated it since?—It was exactly in that state when I found it; it has not been mutilated at all by me.

22,587. Did you inquire of anybody connected with your union how it happened to be in that state?—No, I made no inquiry of anybody.

22,588. Have you any knowledge at all of how it was done?—No.

22,589. Have you any knowledge why it was done? —No.

22,590. Do you know what entries were contained in this book before the leaves were cut out?—No.

22,591. Have you any notion why they were cut out?—No.

22,592. And upon your oath you do not know why it was cut out or who cut it out?—No.

22,593. Who cut it out?—I do not know.

22,594. You do not know why it was cut out, or what was cut out, or what was contained in it?—No.

22,595. You never found it so till yesterday?—No.

22,596. It was in this state when you found it?—Yes, it was.

22,597. It was kept in the box always?—Yes.

22,598. And you have the keys of it?—Yes; there were a lot of papers at the bottom of the box.

22,599. Do you in your union keep books of disbursements?—Yes.

22,600. Will you give me that book?—Yes.

22,601. Not the receipts but the payments?—Yes.

22,602. Fetch the book and point out the disbursements?—Yes.

22,603. Do you produce the book of your payments on behalf of the union?—Yes.

22,604. Which is the book?—This (*producing the same*).

22,605. Which is the earliest in date?—This (*handing the same to the Chairman*).

22,606. This is the earliest book of payments by the union?—Yes, that is all in my possession.

22,607. It begins in 1865 and continues down to the present date?—There was another secretary prior to that.

22,608. This begins in April 1865. Let us go by steps; where is the book containing the disbursements before 1865?—That was the book that I took home and the children wrote in it.

22,609. Was it a book as large as this?—It was just such another book.

22,610. And nearly full?—Yes, there were some of the leaves cut out, but it was nearly full.

22,611. At the time when you got it was it an entire book or were there leaves cut out of it?—Do you mean at the time I took it home?

22,612. At the time you got the books, when you got the book prior to these payments by the union, was the book a complete book or not?—Yes, I believe it was a complete book when I succeeded Worthy.

22,613. Was it a full book or not?—It was not full when I took it home; but I was only temporary and another man succeeded me. I believe another or more succeeded him.

22,614. That book you say was not full?—It was not full, when I took it home.

22,615. Did it become full during the time that you had it?—It was full when I succeeded Worthy.

22,616. What did you do with the book?—I took it home and the children wrote in it.

22,617. Do you mean to say that you, the secretary of the union, allowed your children to write in a book belonging to the union?—Yes, after it was filled up.

22,618. You said that it was not filled up; there were parts in it not filled up?—The leaves were partly filled up and carried forward.

22,619. And there were certain portions of it that were not quite filled up?—Yes.

22,620. Do you mean to say that it was a page like that (*showing the same to the witness*)?—Yes.

22,621. Have they written in the book as a book? —Yes.

22,622. They did not tear out part of the leaf first, but they wrote in the book as a book?—They had it as they liked; they wrote in the book as they liked.

22,623. Were there any leaves not written on in the book?—I dare say there might be some odd ones not written on.

22,624. Did not you keep your books in a box?—Yes, they are in a box.

22,625. Then what business had you, as the secretary of the union, having the charge and custody of the books, to allow them to be written in by your children?—I do not know that I had any business, but I thought the book was no use whatever.

22,626. You allowed the children to write in a book, and after they had written in it you destroyed it?—I did not destroy it.

22,627. What did you do with it?—I should say——

22,628. Do not tell us what you should say; tell us what you did?—It was left in the children's care and they did what they liked with it.

22,629. What has become of the book?—Part of the covers are in the house now.

22,630. The covers of the book you think are in your house?—I should say so.

22,631. You have no occasion to say so unless you know they are there.—I think I saw them some time ago.

22,632. When did you see them last?—Perhaps a month ago—perhaps six weeks ago.

22,633. A month or six weeks ago you saw the covers of the book; at that time were there any written entries in that book?—No.

22,634. There was nothing but th backs?—I believe the leather was torn off.

22,635. Was there anything inside?—No, nothing at all.

22,636. Who had torn out the leaves from that book?—I should say the children tore them out.

22,637. Will you swear that you did not tear them out?—Positively.

22,638. Is that the explanation which you give to us, that a book, the property of the union and not yours, was given by you to your children and they tore out the leaves of the book?—Yes.

22,639. It must have been taken out of the box?—Yes, it was taken out of the box.

22,640. Do you mean to say that you leave your union box open for the children to have access to it?—No; the box is at the public-house where the meetings are held.

22,641. How did the book get out of the box home to your house?—I took it.

22,642. For what purpose?—On purpose for the children to write in it.

22,643. And in point of fact it is destroyed?—Yes.

22,644. And you put it upon your children?—I must speak the truth.

22,645. However, the book is destroyed?—Yes.

22,646. If that book were here, would it contain any entries of payments in the year 1862?—I really cannot say.

22,647. Here we have 1855, 1856, and 1857?—Very likely it would.

22,648. Do not you know that it would?—No.

22,649. Do not you believe that it would contain entries of your payments in the year 1862?—Yes, I should not wonder.

22,650. Do not you believe that it would?—I really cannot say.

22,651. Yes, you can; you know how many entries you made in that year; do not you believe that it would contain entries of the year 1862 if it had been kept and shown?—It probably might have done so.

22,652. You believe it would?—I think it would.

22,653. Do you know that it would?—No, I do not know that it would.

22,654. Will you swear that it would not?—No, I will not swear that it would not.

22,655. Believing that it contained those entries, and knowing that it was of the greatest possible importance, have you not wilfully destroyed that book? —No.

22,656. Has any person destroyed it with your knowledge wilfully?—No.

22,657. Has it been destroyed in order that it might not be brought before us?—It has not.

TWENTY-FOURTH DAY.

F. Jackson.

6 July 1867.

22,658. Has it been destroyed because it contained entries that dare not face the light?—No; I never saw an entry that dare not face the light in that book.

22,659. Was there any entry in it of payment of any sum of money to any person for any improper purpose?—No, not one.

22,660. Was there any entry in that book of the payment of a sum of money to any person engaged in blowing up the shops at Thorpe Hesley?—No.

22,661. Have you examined it for that purpose?—No, I did not examine it for any purpose.

22,662. Then how can you swear so positively if you never examined it?—Certainly, I have looked it over.

22,663. You have looked it over?—Not for any particular purpose.

22,664. Have you looked it over to see what the entries were that were in it?—Yes.

22,665. Do you know whether there were entries in 1862 or not?—I cannot speak positively as to that.

22,666. You say that you have examined it?—Yes, but I have no recollection of it.

22,667. Did you know at the time that the Thorpe Hesley business took place that you were said to be implicated in it?—That I was?

22,668. No; that the union was?—It was said so.

22,669. Was not it said that they had hired a man and paid him for doing it?—It was said so.

22,670. And if they had paid them out of the funds of the society an entry of the payment ought to have appeared in this book; do not you know that?—No, I do not know that it ought to have been there, because I cannot say that that was the book; it was in the possession of the secretary at the time the job was done.

22,671. You say that you believe it was?—No, I do not believe it was; I just speak according to my belief.

22,672. I ask you if you believe it contained entries of 1862?—I do not know the year when the blow-up was.

22,673. As to the blow-up, it was in December 1861, on Christmas Eve. Having spoken to your belief that it contained entries from the year 1862, and you knowing that you were charged with this, your curiosity was never excited as to whether there was an entry of payment to anybody for any improper purpose during that period?—No, only this: those nailmakers were reckoned rather drunken kind of folks, and I looked it over to see what the expenses were with reference to ale and things of that kind, not with any improper motive.

22,674. You looked it over to see whether there was any improper entry of extravagance by your committee?—Yes; I casually looked it over.

22,675. Did you look it over for the purpose of ascertaining whether there was any payment to these men? It produced a great deal of excitement in the country. The men had been transported for 14 years. Did you look it over to see whether there was any payment by your union to these men for doing this wicked act?—No, I did not. I did not expect anything of the sort in the book.

22,676. Or for defending them?—No.

22,677. Do you know whether your union defended the men, when they were tried at York?—I believe there were collections for that purpose.

22,678. Was not the money paid out of the funds of the union for that purpose?—For defending them?

22,678a. Yes?—I believe there was.

22,679. If this book had been produced, the entries of those monies would have appeared in that book?—I do not think it would.

22,680. Why not?—I do not think they would.

22,681. Why not?—Because I never saw anything of the sort.

22,682. But why not? Why should not it appear if it was paid out of the funds of the union?—I do not know, I am sure.

22,683. But you must know it is a regular payment; it ought to have appeared in your books. Why should not it appear in your books?—It ought to have done.

22,684. Do you know whether it has appeared or not?—I never saw anything of the sort.

22,685. Will you swear that it was not there?—I will swear I never saw anything of the sort in the book.

22,686. Will you swear that it was not there?—I will swear I believe it was not there.

22,687. Will you swear that it was not there?—I should think it was not there.

22,688. Why should you think that it was not there?—If there had been any improper entries, would it have been likely they would have allowed other parties to come with the book in their possession with the improper entries in?

22,689. What other parties do you refer to?—Those who occupied the position prior to me.

22,690. You believe that amount of money was paid, and you think it an improper proceeding, do you?—Yes, if the money was paid it was very improper.

22,691. You think it was an improper proceeding, and would not be entered. Have you auditors?—I believe the book has never been audited since I have been secretary.

22,692. The books have never been audited?—Never, since I have been secretary.

22,693. You have contributions, have you not?—Occasionally.

22,694. And they are paid into your hands?—Not into my hands. I take account of them.

22,695. Into whose hands are they paid?—The treasurer for the time being.

22,696. Do you mean to tell me that there is a union in England in which monies are paid into the hands of an officer of a union, and that that officer's accounts are not audited by responsible men?—The accounts have never been audited during the time I have been secretary.

22,697. That is five or six years?—At intervals.

22,698. And during five or six years the property of this union has been at your mercy? if you are an honest or dishonest man, to use their funds as you please?—Thay have trusted me.

22,699. And you have had no auditor at all?—No, no auditor at all.

22,700. What is the number of members of the Nailmakers' Association?—There is not any number.

22,701. Do you mean to say that you have no persons belonging to it, or what?—No specified number.

22,702. What is the average number of persons contributing to the funds of your union?—It depends; sometimes more and sometimes less.

22,703. What is the average number?—I really cannot say.

22,704. What do you call your society? are there 300?—I should think so.

22,705. Are there 400 nailmakers contributing to your union?—No.

22,706. Are there upwards of 300?—There are not 300 contributing; only a part contributes.

22,707. Are there 300 members in your union?—No.

22,708. How many are there?—Sometimes there is no union.

22,709. Mr. Barstow has suggested that this is the state of things. There is only a union of men, and there is no regular union so as to contribute weekly?—No.

22,710. But there is a levy from time to time to work the union?—Yes.

22,711. And for what purposes do you make your levy?—If there is agitation against reduction, or for an advance, then there is a meeting called, and fresh officers are picked, or the old ones re-elected, and expenses put on for the time being.

22,712. You levy it always for particular purposes of that kind?—Yes.

TWENTY-FOURTH DAY.

F. Jackson.

6 July 1867.

22,713. Then you have not a general contribution of so much a week, or so much a score of nails, or anything of that kind?—No.

22,714. For this particular fund for defending these men it would be a levy?—Yes.

22,715. Had there been a levy before then for supporting the men who had been on strike for some time?—If there had been with regard to the Rotherham strike, it was prior to my time.

22,716. Do not you know that there was a strike? —Yes; there were levies put on, and the money was sent over to them.

22,717. The money was sent over to the men at Thorpe Hesley?—To Rotherham.

22,718. The Thorpe men would not go out to support the Rotherham men?—I think I understood some of them were at work.

22,719. The Thorpe Hesley men would not join the union?—At least part of them would not.

22,720. Part of them would not join the union when the Rotherham men were on strike?—Yes.

22,721. The contributions were sent to the Rotherham men to support them on strike?—Yes.

22,722. All these payments ought properly to have been entered in this book as payment on strike?—Yes, they are entered in a book, but they are not entered in the book that was destroyed.

22,723. Where is that book?—I do not know.

22,724. Is there no other person that you are aware of who has got any books besides the ones you produced?—No, I am not aware of any other books.

22,725. There is one book which you have destroyed, this book that you produce which is mutilated, and there is another book of which you say you do not know what has become of it; you do not produce the book containing the entries of the years 1861 and 1862?—I never recollect seeing anything.

22,726. But you do not produce them?—No, I do not produce them.

22,727. You swear on your oath that you did not destroy that book for the purpose of preventing the entries in that book being seen?—Yes, I will.

22,728. Will you swear that you did not get your children to do so?—I will.

22,729. I understand that there are no books of the period of 1861 or 1862 of payments or receipts?—I have never seen any.

22,730. Do you know what has become of them?—No.

22,731. Will you swear that you do not know what has been done with them?—I will.

22,732. Nor where they are?—No.

22,733. Will you swear that they are not in existence?—I cannot say that.

22,734. Will you swear that you do not know where they are?—I will swear that I do not know where they are.

22,735. Will you swear that it is not for the purpose of preventing our seeing them that they are not brought forward to-day?—Yes.

22,736. You will swear that?—To the best of my knowledge. If I had been aware that the book would have been required at any time, I would have taken every care of it; on my oath I should not have destroyed it, and it should have been brought up.

22,737. But the books have been destroyed?—Yes.

22,738. We have asked several secretaries, and they have confessed that rattening prevails in their trade. Does rattening prevail in your trade?—No.

22,739. Do you never ratten?—No, sir, I never have.

22,740. Has rattening ever been done by your trade?—Of course I can only speak for myself.

22,741. Yes, you can; you can speak for others.—It is reported that rattening has been done by cutting bellows and destroying them. It is supposed that things of that sort have been done.

22,742. It is reported that rattening has been done by your union, cutting bellows, and so on?—That is reported.

22,743. That is to say, that certain members of the union have authorized others, or authorized members of the union to cut bellows of persons who do not comply with the rules of the society?—Yes, that is the report.

22,744. Do you believe that report to be true?—I do not doubt that there is some truth in it.

22,745. Has bellows-cutting occurred in your time? —Yes, it has; at least I have heard say so.

22,746. Whose bellows have you heard have been cut in your time?—I heard a few weeks ago that a man named Cornelius Southall's bellows were cut some three or four months ago.

22,747. Where did he live?—He lived at Belper.

22,748. Do you know whether it was done by the authority of the union?—It certainly was not done with my knowledge or consent.

22,749. Was it done by the authority of the union? —I believe not.

22,750. Without going into that, you believe that cases of bellows-cutting have been done by the authority of the union?—It is possible; it might be so.

22,751. Do you believe that it is so?—Of course, if report is to be relied on at all——

22,752. Is it so talked of in your union?—Not in the union, but out of doors.

22,753. Is it said in your union?—No.

22,754. Have you any doubt about it in your own mind that the union have given money to persons for doing it?—If the union has employed any person for doing it they must have paid them. They would not run the risk of being caught without being paid.

22,755. Do you not believe that they have paid them?—Certainly, if they employed them they must have done so.

22,756. Do not you believe that they have employed them?—I believe they have.

22,757. You believe that they have employed them, and you believe that they have been paid for it. Is that a system which has been adopted for many years past in your union?—Yes, it has, for many years past.

22,758. Has there been any other system besides that of cutting bellows prevailing in your union? Has there been any system of putting cans of gunpowder into a man's shop or chimney?—I have never heard of anything besides the Thorpe Hesley affair.

22,759. Have you any reason to believe that it was done by the union?—I have no reason, except that I have heard the report.

22,760. Have you any reason to believe that it was done by the union?—No, I do not know that I have any reason to believe that it was done by the union.

22,761. Do you know a person of the name of Charles Webster?—Yes.

22,762. Was he a secretary at Belper?—I never knew him to be a secretary.

22,763. What kind of secretary did you know him to be?—A district secretary.

22,764. Was he the district secretary at Belper?—Yes; the district secretaries acted as committees at the time.

22,765. I do not follow you.—The town was divided into districts, and there was a secretary appointed to each district.

22,766. The district secretaries met together as a committee?—Yes.

22,767. Are you aware that any of these district secretaries have ever paid money for putting powder into a chimney?—No.

22,768. Are you aware that Charles Webster has paid any money for that purpose?—No.

22,769. Or any other secretary?—No.

22,770. Have you ever paid any yourself?—No, never.

22,771. Do you believe it to be true what you have heard stated?—I cannot say that. I do not know that it was true about the powder affair, but I do

TWENTY-FOURTH DAY.

F. Jackson.

6 July 1867.

believe that bellows-cutting and such like things as those have been done.

22,772. It is talked of in your union as having been done?—It is talked of out of doors.

22,773. And in your union too?—It is rather a delicate question to talk about.

22,774. It is no doubt a very delicate question; but still you do have delicate questions got up amongst you sometimes, and you talk about them?—They are not very prudent things to talk about before a meeting.

22,775. It is not a prudent thing to do them?—No.

22,776. Have those men who have paid their levies talked about them?—I have heard nailers talk about them, and others as well.

22,777. That bellows-cutting is a thing which the union adopted?—It was said so.

The witness withdrew.

JOHN HATTERSLEY sworn and examined.

J. Hattersley.

22,778. (*Chairman.*) You are a nailmaker, I believe?—Yes.

22,779. Living at Thorpe Hesley, near Sheffield? —Yes.

22,780. Are you a master nailmaker?—No, I work for a master.

22,781. Whom do you work for?—Mr. Favel, of Rotherham.

22,782. In the year 1859, had there been any dispute between you and the union as to your mode of working for Mr. Favel?—Yes.

22,783. What was the dispute?—It was Mr. Favel's foreman, and he lives at Rotherham. I did not think fit to join with the union or to have anything to do with them; they desired that I should.

22,784. Who did?—The union men. There was going to be a meeting, and they did not desire me to work if there was a strike, but to go along with them. Then I went and attended the meeting, and what I heard was going on I made known to my master; and then the week following there was another, and I attended it; then Mr. Favel made known to them that he knew what was going on at the meeting. They suspected it was me that had given information to him, and they desired then that I should not attend any meetings. They would not admit me. Ever since then I have not had anything to do with them. I have always worked, and never paid or had any correspondence with the men whatever. They thought I should make it known to the employers, and it would be against them.

22,785. After you had made known this at the union, were you subjected to any annoyance by the union men?—Yes, I was.

22,786. What was the annoyance to which you were subjected?—They never insulted me personally.

22,787. What did they do?—Sometimes there was a large stone came through my chamber window in the night when I was in bed; several times that occurred; it broke the window, and we were in danger of being hit by the stone in bed.

22,788. That has been done several times?—Yes, but who did it we did not know. Then after that I had my shop blown up.

22,789. When was that?—I believe it was somewhere about the 21st of December 1861.

22,790. Where was your shop? at Thorpe Hesley? —Yes.

22,791. Was it a nailmaker's shop?—Yes.

22,792. How was it blown up?—By gunpowder.

22,793. How was it blown up?—The roof was blown off.

22,794. Did you discover how the blowing-up had been effected?—They put a can of gunpowder in the shop, I believe. We did not know to be certain how they got it in, but we believe that they got a key and opened the door and put it inside and closed the door again. We could not perceive any other way that they could have done it.

22,795. But the roof was blown off?—Yes.

22,796. Were there any inhabitants living adjoining the shop?—There was another nailmaker's shop.

22,797. Were there any persons living there?—Yes, very near too.

22,798. Adjoining?—was it part of the same building or not?—There was about a yard between my shop and the next building.

22,799. Was there a space between?—Yes.

22,800. Who lived in the building?—Edward Shaw.

22,801. Was there much damage done to the shop? Yes, the roof was blown off and some of the windows damaged; the chimney was not blown down nor the stoves hurt.

22,802. Do you know at all why the stones were thrown into your chamber window?—No, I do not know why they were thrown in.

22,803. Had you any quarrel with anybody at the time?—No.

22,804. Had you any quarrel with anybody at the time that your shop was blown up?—No.

22,805. To whom do you attribute it?—I attribute it to the union; they might not have blown my shop up, but there were two other men working along with me; I had nothing to do with them, but having two other men and they continuing working, I suppose it was the union who blew it up, on account of these two men more than myself.

22,806. What were the names of these two men? Charles Butler and Butcher?—No; Joseph Hattersley, my brother, and George Walter.

22,807. Were they non-union men as well as yourself?—had they refused to join the union?—They had joined the union before, but they did not belong to it at the time.

22,808. Were some men prosecuted at the York March Assizes in 1862 for this offence?—Yes.

22,809. Who were prosecuted?—The two Watsons.

22,810. And a man called Tomlinson?—Yes.

22,811. And they were sentenced to 14 years' transportation?—Yes.

22,812. And I believe intercession was made for those men? they were supposed to have been wrongly convicted?—Yes.

22,813. They obtained a pardon and were liberated?—Yes.

22,814. Did Butcher work with you or not?—No, he worked in his own shop.

22,815. Where was his shop?—At Thorpe Hesley, the other end of the village.

22,816. He was a non-unionist also?—Yes.

22,817. The union which you were asked to join was the union of which the head-quarters were at Belper?—Yes, it was at the time; there was not any other union at Thorpe that I know of.

22,818. Do you remember at any time before this anything being done to your shop?—Yes; I was at work one morning very early, about 3 o'clock, when some person came and struck at me through the window with a large piece of wood; it did not hurt me, and I closed my window and went on with my work, and closed the door, and they went round the other side and threw large cinders at the door; I believe one weighed about 7 lbs. Then after that I continued to work, and they came and got this large piece of wood, and they knocked out the window to strike at me. They knocked the frame and the shutter altogether out while I was in the shop. That was one dark morning about 3 o'clock.

TWENTY-FOURTH DAY.

J. Hattersley.

6 July 1867.

22,819. At the time had you had any quarrel with the union?—No.

22,820. Were you a non-union man?—I said I have had no quarrel. It was just after I had been to this meeting and sent down the information to my employers. They had given me liberty to work, but still at the same time there would be some union men that would not like it, and very probably it would be some of those bad-disposed men.

22,821. Have you any notion who it was who did these acts in your shop at 3 o'clock in the morning?—No, I cannot say.

22,822. You do not know?—I dare not go out; I never saw one.

22,823. Do you know how many men did it?—I do not know; there might be one, two, three, or four.

22,824. Did you see anybody?—No; I dare not say out.

22,825. Have you any reason to suppose that any person had any private malice against you or not, or was it a trade matter?—I believe it was a trade matter; I had no quarrel with any one.

22,826. They never attempted to rob you or anything of that kind?—No.

22,827. Were you with Butcher at his place when he found something in his chimney a short time before you were blown up?—No.

22,828. Butcher is here, is he not?—Yes.

The witness withdrew.

C. Butcher.

CHARLES BUTCHER sworn and examined.

22,829. (*Mr. Barstow.*) Do you remember in 1859 being asked to join the union?—Yes.

22,830. Did you join the union?—No.

22,831. Do you recollect in 1861 something happening to you at 2 o'clock in the morning?—Yes; the shop was blown up.

22,832. What time of the year was it?—Rather near Christmas.

22,833. How was it done?—It was blown up by a can of gunpowder, as far as I could see.

22,834. Did you find any pieces of the can?—The shop was sought over some time after and the bottom of a can of gunpowder was found.

22,835. Do you remember Hattersley's shop being blown up?—Yes, it was the same night.

22,836. Do you live near Hattersley?—I live in the village; it is a small village.

22,837. To what do you attribute this?—I can give you my reason; the gentleman I was working for at the time had a party who thought fit to work for him and a party who thought fit not to work; some continued working.

22,838. You think that some of the parties who would not work blew your shop up?—I believe it was that. I do not know that I had any private malice against any one.

22,839. You think that it was the men who were not working?—Yes.

22,840. You cannot think of any one else who would be likely to do it?—No.

22,841. Do you ever remember anything thrown at your window?—No.

22,842. (*Chairman.*) Was that all that happened to you?—Before the shop was blown up, there was a can of powder found there.

22,843. How long before?—A few weeks. A few weeks before my shop was blown up, there was a can of gunpowder hung in my shop chimney.

22,844. Tell us all about it.—It was hung down the shop chimney; it was hung with a stick put into the chimney and let down towards the bottom of the chimney. I had a man working for me; he went there in the morning, and he had observed something being right across the chimney, and he examined the chimney, and found a can of powder hung down the chimney with a piece of fuse attached to it; he came to my house.

22,845. And you went in and found it as he described?—He had taken it out of the chimney, but I found it there. There was 1 lb. 2 oz. of gunpowder.

22,846. If the fuse had been lighted when you had made your fire up, what would have happened?—It must have gone off.

22,847. What would have been done when it went off?—A pitman told me that the very blast of the thing would have killed anybody.

22,848. Was it the same shop that was blown up?—Yes.

22,849. Was there any one living in the shop or near the shop, or was it part of one building?—No.

22,850. Is there any house near it?—There are two or three cottages.

22,851. It was a detached shop; it was separate from your other buildings?—Yes.

22,852. How far above the hearth was it in the chimney?—If it had been blown up it would have caught the fuse. The can might be about three quarters of a yard from the fire-place.

22,853. How high is the chimney?—About three or four yards.

The witness withdrew.

I. E. Watson.

ISAAC EMANUEL WATSON sworn and examined.

22,854. (*Chairman.*) Are you nailmaker?—Yes.

22,855. Do you live at Rotherham?—Yes.

22,856. In 1861 did you live at Chesterfield?—Yes.

22,857. Did you work in the same shop with Joseph Tomlinson?—Yes.

22,858. Were you in the union in 1861?—No.

22,859. Had you anything to do with the union?—I was not in the union; I did not pay any contributions, and neither did the others.

22,860. Do you recollect on the 21st of December going over to Thorpe Hesley?—I do.

22,861. Who went with you?—Joseph Tomlinson.

22,862. Who besides?—Samuel Proctor.

22,863. Did you go to the shop of John Hattersley?—Yes.

22,864. What did you do to him?—Put some powder down the chimney and lit the fuse.

22,865. What was the consequence?—We blew the roof off.

22,866. Did you go anywhere else the same night?—We went to Charles Butcher's shop.

22,867. What did you do to his shop?—We served it the same.

22,868. Did you put the powder into that shop?—Yes.

22,869. What was your reason for blowing up the shops of Hattersley and Butcher?—My reason for one thing was, we did not think they were doing right.

22,870. They were not doing right in what respect?—They were working for less than the Rotherham men.

22,871. What besides?—And another thing, we were engaged to do it.

22,872. Who engaged you?—That I never knew.

22,873. When you say that you were engaged what do you mean?—I received letters from the Belper postman, but no name.

22,874. What became of the letters?—I burned them because it said at the end of every letter "Burn as soon as read."

TWENTY-FOURTH DAY.

I. E. Watson.

6 July 1867.

22,875. What did the letter state?—It stated that a job wanted doing, and if we would do it we should be paid for it.

22,876. Who were the letters signed by? did they bear any signature?—There was no signature.

22,877. Did you know the handwriting?—I did not.

22,878. Did you know where they came from?—I knew they came from Belper, but no more.

22,879. Who were the parties that sent them?—I do not know.

22,880. You do not know?—No.

22,881. You say that you blew them up with powder?—Yes.

22,882. Where did you get the can of powder from?—I got one part of the powder at Chesterfield; I had a letter come to Chesterfield to me, telling me to meet a certain train, and I met it, and they said I should see a party there with a parcel. I went to the train, and I was looking for the party that I expected, and there was a gentleman put his head out of the window and said to me, "Will you get me a ticket for Whittington?" I took the money in my hand to do so, but then I turned back and said, "I beg your pardon, sir, but I am looking after a party." He said, "Is your name Watson?" and I said "Yes." He said, "Take this;" and he gave me a parcel, and there was six or eight pounds of powder in it—I cannot say which.

22,883. Who was that man who gave you the parcel?—I am not aware that I ever saw him before.

22,884. Do you know now who he was?—No, I do not.

22,885. You did not know then and do not know now?—No.

22,886. An unknown man gave you a packet of powder?—Yes.

22,887. When he gave the parcel to you did you speak to him about it?—No.

22,888. You never spoke to him about it?—No.

22,889. Having got the powder you say that you put cans down the chimney; where did you get the cans from?—I bought the cans for nail pots; the cans are what had been got previously for nail pots.

22,890. Where did you get them from?—I got them in the street below the Commercial Inn Yard at Chesterfield.

22,891. Do you know the name of the person who sold them to you?—No, I do not.

22,892. You put the powder into the cans?—I never saw it put in; I did not put it in; there was more powder than that.

22,893. Joseph Tomlinson and Samuel Proctor went with you to get the powder?—I believe Tomlinson got it. I did not see the powder put into the cans.

22,894. You saw the cans when they had the powder in?—Yes.

22,895. Who carried them?—I carried one and one of the others carried the other—I believe it was Tomlinson.

22,896. Were you then living at Chesterfield?—Yes; all three of us were.

22,897. How did you go from Chesterfield to Thorpe Hesley?—We came by train to Masbro' from Chesterfield, and then we walked from Masbro' to Thorpe Hesley.

22,898. Was that on the 21st of December?—Yes.

22,899. What time did you arrive at Thorpe Hesley?—Between 10 and 11 o'clock.

22,900. At night?—Yes.

22,901. And you did the thing in the two shops and then you came away again?—We came away another road.

22,902. Where is Tomlinson?—For anything I know, he is in London.

22,903. When was he in London?—I am not aware when he was in London.

22,904. Is he a nailmaker?—Yes, he is a nailmaker there.

22,905. Where is Samuel Proctor?—I have not seen him since we came from York.

22,906. You do not know what has become of him?—I do not.

22,907. Did you know the shop and the name of the people you were going to blow up before you got there?—I knew perfectly well all about them.

22,908. How did you know that?—I had been brought up about Thorpe Hesley.

22,909. You knew the shops, both of Hattersley and Butcher?—Yes.

22,910. Did the other men know the places, or did you show them?—Proctor did not know them, but Tomlinson did.

22,911. After you had blown them up you were told that you would be paid?—Yes.

22,912. And after you had blown them up what did you do? Did you write any letters to anybody to say that you had done it?—No.

22,913. What did you do?—We met the train, and there was no one there.

22,914. What train?—They were coming to pay the Rotherham men every week at that time on the Monday, and when there was no one in the train that we knew, I came to Rotherham from Chesterfield.

22,915. Was it the Monday afterwards?—Yes. I went into the Cutler's Arms; that was where they held their meetings. I looked round and said, "Show me the man from Belper." Whether they told him or not I do not know, but he motioned me out very soon, and he gave me some money.

22,916. Who was he?—I do not know; he was a stranger to me.

22,917. Do not you know that it was Charles Webster?—I do not know that it was Charles Webster, but I believe it was; I should not like to swear to him.

22,918. Would you know him again if you saw him?—I have seen him many a time at Belper, but I do not know that he is the same man.

22,919. You believe him to be the same man?—Yes, I believe him to be the same man.

22,920. What did he give you?—He gave me 2*l.*

22,921. Did he tell you what it was for?—No.

22,922. Did you tell him who you were?—He asked me if my name was Watson, and I said "Yes."

(*Mr. Webster was called in and pointed out to the witness.*)

22,923. Is that the man whom you believe paid you the money?—I believe it is, but I could not be sure.

22,924. You received how much?—2*l.*

22,925. Was that the sum which was agreed to be given?—No.

22,926. How much?—3*l.*

22,927. Was it mentioned in a letter which you have destroyed that 3*l.* should be given to you for your work?—Yes.

22,928. Did you ever get the 3*l.*?—Me and Tomlinson never did. Proctor went over to Belper.

22,929. Did he tell you that he had got it?—We never saw him; when he came back we were at Rotherham again.

22,930. You never got any more than the 2*l.*?—No.

22,931. You blew this up on the 21st of December?—Yes.

22,932. You were taken up for it?—Yes.

22,933. And tried for it?—Yes.

22,934. You and your brother?—Yes.

22,935. What was his name?—James Watson.

22,936. And you and Tomlinson were all tried for it?—Yes.

22,937. And all found guilty?—Yes.

22,938. You set up an alibi?—I did so.

22,939. You set up an alibi to show that you were not at Thorpe Hesley that night?—Yes.

22,940. And how many witnesses did you call?—15 or 16.

TWENTY-FOURTH DAY.

I. E. Watson.

6 July 1867.

22,941. And you knew when they all swore that you were not there that night that they swore falsely?—No; they were not all false.

22,942. How was it that they were not all false?—Because all those at Belper swore to my brother, and he was there; he was really at Belper.

22,943. But all those that swore to you?—There was never one swore to me but one woman.

22,944. And she swore falsely?—Yes.

22,945. And with respect to Proctor, how many swore to him?—None.

22,946. Only one person swore falsely?—There was only one that swore to me.

22,947. There were others who swore for an alibi to Tomlinson?—Yes.

22,948. How many swore to him?—Three or four.

22,949. And they all swore falsely?—Yes, all.

22,950. Are you sure that it was done falsely, or by mistake?—I believe it was a mistake.

22,951. They swore to Christmas Eve instead of Saturday?—Yes.

22,952. They fixed on the wrong night?—I believe it was so; we did not tell them different.

22,953. Some of the police swore to that; they did not commit perjury, but they swore to the wrong night; you knew that they were wrong when they gave their evidence?—Yes; but we did not tell them.

22,954. Some perjured themselves, others made a mistake, but there was a strong representation made for you, and you got off in consequence of the alibi that was set up; some people believed the alibi to be true, and that you had been improperly convicted, and you were set at large?—Yes.

22,955. You blew up these places and got the money?—Yes.

22,956. We have heard of a man finding a quantity of gunpowder in his workshop; did you put it there?—No.

22,957. Who did?—I do not know.

22,958. Had not you tried to blow him up before?—No; I did not want to blow him up then. When we were going to do it, I said, "Let us pass Charles Butcher's," but the others said he did not get the price for his work.

22,959. You did not want to do him?—No.

22,960. You wanted to do Hattersley?—I cared nothing about doing Hattersley.

22,961. You were perfectly indifferent whether you did it or not?—Well, I considered that he deserved it.

22,962. Then you know nothing about the can of powder being put into the man's shop?—I do not.

22,963. Do not you know who did it?—I do not.

22,964. Are you quite sure about that?—Yes.

22,965. You say that Tomlinson, you, and Proctor were the persons; are you sure that your brother was not one of the party?—My brother was never near it.

22,966. Have you ever been engaged in cutting any bellows?—I never cut a pair, and never saw a pair cut in my life.

22,967. Do you know of any person who did?—I believe I do.

22,968. Whom do you know?—Samuel Smith.

22,969. Who besides?—John Robertson.

22,970. Whose bellows did they cut?—Samuel Saunders'.

22,971. Where does he live?—At Belper.

22,972. We will not go into that. Are those all the offences which you have committed connected with trade matters within the last ten years?—Yes.

22,973. Do you know of any more committed by anybody else?—No.

22,974. You have said that you believed that man to be the person who paid you the money; are you not quite sure about it?—No, I cannot swear to that, but I believe he is the man.

22,975. Have you any doubt about it?—There is a little doubt, because I never saw the man before to my knowledge.

22,976. But he was the man who had come from Belper to pay the money?—Yes, it was the same man that came from Belper to pay the men that paid me.

22,977. Did you ever call upon him except for the work you had done at Thorpe Hesley?—No.

22,978. Did not you say anything as to why he did not pay you the whole of the 3*l.*?—No. He said we should have the other letter, and Proctor went over.

22,979. The man said you should have a letter, and Proctor went over?—Yes.

22,980. (*Mr. Chance.*) How did you do the blowing-up of the chimney?—We put the can of powder down the chimney.

22,981. How did you do that?—We hung the powder to a string, the fuse came out, and that way we lit it.

22,982. Did you swing it by a piece of wood from the top of the chimney?—No, a hoop.

22,983. How much did the chimney extend above the roof?—Perhaps three feet.

22,984. What was the length of the string that you hung the can to?—As nearly as I can tell it would be six feet down the chimney, three feet below the roof.

22,985. Did you endeavour to hang it as near the fire as possible?—No; we wanted no fire.

22,986. You lighted the fuse?—Yes; the fuse would be five or six yards long.

22,987. Did you ascertain whether there was anybody in the shop at the time or not?—We knew there was nobody in the shop; we never expected anybody in the shop when it was shut up at night.

22,988. (*Chairman.*) I suppose you did it very cleverly? which did you fire first?—Charley Butcher's.

22,989. And then the people in the village came to look at what had happened?—Well, we did not stay for that; I believe there were many.

22,990. And while they were looking at that you slipped off and fired the other?—We went a back road there.

22,990*a*. But you did one almost immediately after the other?—Yes, as soon as we could, but it was a quarter of a mile away.

The witness withdrew.

C. Webster.

CHARLES WEBSTER sworn and examined.

22,991. (*Chairman.*) Are you a nailmaker?—Yes.

22,991*a*. Were you secretary of the Nailmakers' Union in 1861?—No, I never was secretary.

22,992. Were you connected with the union in 1861?—I was on one committee, but I was not secretary.

22,993. Were you a district secretary?—Yes; we had the town divided into five districts.

22,994. You had one of the districts under your charge?—Yes, I had one to collect.

22,995. I believe the union had a quarrel with Mr. Favel about the prices he charged?—Yes, there was a kind of turn out.

22,996. He was paying less money than you thought was the proper sum to be received by the workmen?—Yes.

22,997. And there was a strike among the union men at Rotherham?—Yes.

22,998. And the men at Thorpe Hesley were working at the reduced prices against the rule of your union?—Yes, with the exception of one or so.

22,999. You supported the men on strike?—Yes.

23,000. Did you go over from Belper to Rotherham to pay the money to persons on strike?—Yes, I went in my turn; there were four went; sometimes one went and sometimes another.

23,001. Did you go to Rotherham the week after Hattersley's house was blown up?—I went over on the Monday before Christmas in 1861.

23,002. And you paid the men who were on strike?—Yes.

TWENTY-FOURTH DAY.

C. Webster.

6 July 1867.

23,003. Did the man who has just been examined as a witness come to you when you were in the public-house?—Yes.

23,004. Did you ask him if his name was Watson? —Yes; I did not know him. I do not know that I had ever seen him in my life.

23,005. Did you pay him 2*l.*?—I did.

23,006. For what did you pay him the 2*l.*?—They said they had done some work at Thorpe Hesley.

23,007. And you knew that these people had had their shops blown up?—I heard it that morning when I was in Rotherham.

23,008. And it was for that that you paid him the money?—Yes, I believe so.

23,009. He says that he had received some letters before he went there?—I never wrote him a letter. I never was secretary at all.

23,010. He says that he received some letters before he went over there; do you know who wrote the letters?—No, unless the secretary did.

23,011. Who was the secretary then?—George Worthy.

23,012. You do not know who wrote them?—No, nor what subject they were on; my dwelling was a mile or better from his.

23,013. Did you keep any book when you went over to Masbro' to pay the men their sums of money when they were on strike?—Yes.

23,014. Where is it?—I have not got it now. I had to give up my books and papers when I gave up being on the committee. It was merely the quantities paid. I paid them 8*s.* a week.

23,015. And you put down in your book that you paid to each man 8*s.* a week, the date, the name of the man, and the 8*s.*?—Yes.

23,016. How many men had you on strike then?—I cannot say; not a very great quantity; sometimes more and sometimes less.

23,017. Give me a notion of how many there were? —14 or 15 altogether.

23,018. Having paid such a large sum as 2*l.* for blowing up these places at Thorpe Hesley, you would, of course, enter in your book "paid to Emanuel Watson, 2*l.*"?—No, I do not believe I did.

23,019. Then what entry did you make;—I do not think it ever was entered.

23,020. Then you made no entry at all?—No.

23,021. Where did you get the money from?—The same as I got the other; they gave me so much money to pay.

23,022. Who gave you the money?—They collected it themselves.

23,023. Who gave you the money to pay?—The chairman.

23,024. What is his name?—James Bacon. We collected the money and took it altogether on Saturday night.

23,025. How much did he give you that Monday when you went to Masbro' to pay the men, do you recollect?—Somewhere between 8*l.* and 9*l.*; it is so long since I would not say. I cannot recollect.

23,026. You made an entry of the payment to the men on strike, but you made no entry to the man Watson?—No.

23,027. When you came back you had to account for the money that you had spent; what did you tell him about the 2*l.*?—I told him that I had paid it to Emanuel Watson.

23,028. Did you tell him what it was for?—Yes.

23,029. He would have the book; would he enter it or not?—I do not think it was ever entered.

23,030. Have you ever seen the books?—I have never seen the books. I have had nothing to do with them since early in 1862.

23,031. Do you know what became of the books at the end of 1861 and the beginning of 1862?—No: Worthy was the secretary at the time I left. I never went to a meeting afterwards.

23,032. Do you know what has become of those books at all?—No, I do not. I do not know whether they have new ones or not.

23,033. Had you any kind of audit in your club?—No, there were no auditors besides ourselves.

23,034. Did you pay anything to Tomlinson for this job?—No.

23,035. Nor to Proctor?—Nor to Proctor.

23,036. Did you see Proctor afterwards?—Yes, I saw him on the Thursday in Christmas week, the day following Christmas Day; I did not know him.

23,037. You saw him?—I saw him.

23,038. At the time when you paid Watson, did not you tell him that that was all the money you had, and that if he were to come over he would have the remainder?—No; he said that the 2*l.* was too little, and I said it was all I was ordered.

23,039. Then you got an order before you came off to pay the man?—Certainly, or I should not have paid it.

23,040. Who had given you the order?—The committee, as I called it, one among the other.

23,041. Did they say what you were to pay it for? —I was not aware what it would be.

23,042. What did they say to you?—They said there would be something done at Thorpe Hesley, and the party would come to me for some money.

23,043. Did the party come?—Yes.

23,044. Did they tell you that it would be Watson? They said it would be Emanuel Watson.

23,045. The party came and you gave him some money?—Yes.

23,046. And when you gave it him, he said that it would be too little?—Yes.

23,047. What did you say to him when he said that it was too little?—I said nothing.

23,048. Did you say anything about his coming over?—No, but Proctor did come over on the Thursday.

23,049. Have you ever paid anything else besides this to any other person?—No, not a penny.

23,050. Did you know that all these witnesses had gone over to York?—Yes.

23,051. And you knew that they had perjured themselves?—No, I did not.

23,052. You knew that Watson had done it on that night, and that those witnesses went to swear that he never was there?—All the witnesses that went from Belper went to swear on account of James Watson.

23,053. But with respect to Emanuel Watson; you knew that he had been there, because you had paid him the money?—Yes.

23,054. And you knew that he had called a witness to perjure himself?—I did not know that there was any witness for him.

23,055. Do you know anything about the expenses that were paid for these men; how much it cost?—Do you mean the trial?

23,056. Yes.—I cannot say.

23,057. But about how much did it cost?—A good bit.

23,058. How much did it cost for defending these men? there was the attorney and a lot of witnesses and counsel; how much do you think it cost?—40*l.* or 50*l.*

23,059. Was it a levy amongst your own union?—There was no particular union; it was a levy, and they collected the money to support the men when on strike.

23,060. Was not there a levy for the particular purpose of defending these men?—Yes, to defend these men.

23,061. Because they were so innocent?—I do not know that—I am not saying so.

23,062. (*Mr. Chance.*)—It would swallow up a large portion of the wages?—Yes.

23,063. (*Chairman.*) Did you get any contribution from any other union?—No, I believe not—not that I am aware of.

23,064. Did the sawmakers give you anything? —No, I think not—I believe not.

23,065. There was no contribution at all?—No.

23,066. There is an entry in their books very much

TWENTY-FOURTH DAY.

C. Webster.

6 July 1867.

like it?—Then they gave it to Rotherham or Thorpe, but it never came to Belper.

23,067. They may have given something to support the men on strike?—No.

23,068. But there is a curious entry to Thorpe Hesley?—The Sheffield men might pay something to Rotherham.

23,069. But not Thorpe Hesley?—No.

23,070. There is an entry in their books of a payment to Thorpe Hesley?—I did not know it.

The witness withdrew.

J. Chambers, Esq.

JOHN CHAMBERS, Esq., sworn and examined.

23,071. (*Chairman.*) You are a solicitor practising in this town?—Yes.

23,072. And you have been employed by the Association of Masters during this Inquiry?—I have.

23,073. You have obtained for us from the magistrates' clerk a list of the outrages which have been brought before the magistrates?—Yes.

23,074. Amongst them there is an outrage committed on July the 8th, 1861, upon Joseph Bolton?—Yes.

23,075. It is said here that a can of gunpowder was thrown through his dwelling-house window at Green Oak Toll Bar, at Totley, and that great damage was done to his house and furniture; have you made inquiries into that case to see whether it had anything to do with Trades Union?—I put myself in personal communication with Mr. Bolton, and he called upon me and told me that he did not think it had anything to do with trades unions; that he believed it was the result of private malice.

23,076. Did he state the persons whom he suspected had done it or not?—No; he named the person whom he thought had done it.

23,077. Is he connected with any trade?—Not in the least; not any connexion whatever with any trade union.

23,078. You had reason to believe that it was a matter connected with trades unions; but you find that it is the result of private malice?—Yes.

23,079. And on that you have brought no evidence before us?—No.

23,080. There is another case, namely, that of "Messrs. Craven, builders, Wicker," where a can of gunpowder was thrown into their premises on March the 19th, 1862; have you made inquiries respecting that?—Yes, and I believe that it was not connected with any trade union. Mr. Craven stated that there was no union in his trade.

23,081. There is a joiners' union? — But the outrage was not connected with them in any way, that is what he said.

23,082. He is the builder?—He has been summoned to come here.

23,083. Is there any other case that you are aware of in the town supposed to be in any way connected with trades unions which we have not investigated?—I am not aware of any other.

23,084. Do you believe that we have gone through all the cases which are supposed to be in any way connected with trades unions?—Yes with the admissions which were made by the secretaries, there are many cases of rattening.

23,085. We have not thought it necessary to go into them. With the exception of the rattening cases and letters of intimidation and so on, do you think that we have gone through all the cases?—In those cases we have prepared evidence to be brought before you.

23,086. But independently of those, are there any cases of outrage committed within the last 10 years? are you aware of any other besides those which we have already inquired into?—I am not.

23,087. You believe there are no more?—I believe there are not.

23,088. (*Chairman.*) There is the case of Bridges, which we are going into now; we shall have him before us, and we will ask him a few questions before we can say that we have got through our work.

The witness withdrew.

H. Bridges.

HENRY BRIDGES sworn and examined.

23,089. (*Mr. Chance.*) Do you keep a public-house?—Yes.

23,090. Were you formerly a brickmaker?—Yes.

23,091. Were you a brickmaker in the year 1861?—Yes.

23,092. Were you at that time a member of the Brickmakers' Union?—No.

23,093. Had you had any disputes with the union men at that time?—No; I do not know that I had had any disputes at all.

23,094. Do you remember one night in April 1861 having some bricks destroyed?—Yes.

23,095. How many?—There would be about 40,000 to 50,000, and a good many press bricks amongst them.

23,096. In what state were they?—The press bricks were all dried; they were in a shed; they took them and broke them.

23,097. Were they finished?—They were pressed and finished, and ready to go into the kiln.

23,098. How many pressed bricks had you?—About 25,000.

23,099. The remaining portion of the 40,000 were other kinds of bricks?—Yes; stock bricks.

23,100. What was the value of the bricks which were destroyed?—I thought about 40*l.* worth were destroyed, barrows and all things together.

23,101. Was that the loss of bricks, or the loss altogether?—Altogether, barrows, and press, and all?

23,102. What was the value of the bricks?—I am sure I cannot say. I reckoned it up in a lump sum about 40*l.*

23,103. Were the bricks destroyed altogether?—Yes.

23,104. Both the pressed bricks and the other bricks?—Yes.

23,105. At that time was anything else taken?—The barrows were broken.

23,106. How many?—Five or six barrows.

23,107. And the pressing machines?—Yes.

23,108. Were they destroyed?—Yes; my leather and other things were destroyed.

23,109. Was the value of the whole about 4*l.*?—Yes.

23,110. Would it have been the work of one or more men?—There might have been five or six came to do it; it would take a long while to break the pressed bricks.

23,111. How would they break them?—They would take them up and break them one on another.

23,112. Were you living anywhere near at the time?—About half a mile from there.

23,113. Was there any person living close by at the time that this took place?—No. Mr. Bradshaw's residence was the nearest.

23,114. Would anybody hear the breaking of the bricks?—Some men told me afterwards that they had heard it; but they did not take any notice, because sometimes we worked at night, and they thought that we were looking after the work.

23,115. After the things were destroyed, did you go to the committee of the Brickmakers' Union?—Yes; I went to see them on the Monday night following.

TWENTY-FOURTH DAY.

H. Bridges.

6 July 1867.

23,116. Whom did you see there?—John Baxter, and Frederick Peach, and Samuel Kay; there were seven or eight of them.

23,117. What did you say to them?—Baxter had been to my house the week before, and I believe he had had a few words with one of my men. I asked him what was the cause of my bricks being spoiled, and he told me he had been insulted by one of my men.

23,118. Did he mention the name of the man by whom he had been insulted?—It was a man called Poole, who was a member of the society.

23,119. Do you know whether he had been insulted by one of the men?—Yes; he sent a man across with his out-working money; the men who are not members pay a halfpenny in the shilling.

23,120. Answer my question. Do you know whether any of your men had insulted Baxter?—They had two or three words in the place, that was all. I asked Baxter, when he was going out, what was amiss, and he said, "If you want to know you must come to the committee."

23,121. When was that?—On the Saturday night before they spoiled my bricks.

23,122. I speak of when you went to the committee on the Monday night. Baxter said that one of your men had insulted him?—Yes.

23,123. Did he give that as the reason why your bricks had been destroyed?—Yes; and I said, "If my "men insult you, am I to stand the loss of having my "bricks spoiled?"

23,124. What did he say to that?—He did not say anything about it; he said there would be a general meeting on the Monday night following, and I could come then, and they would see what they could do.

23,125. Was that all that took place at this meeting?—Yes.

23,126. Did they decline to do anything for you?—Yes, they did not do anything for me.

23,127. Did you go to the general meeting?—No; they did not send to me and I did not go. They told my men that were working that they would not give me anything.

23,128. Some of your men went there?—Yes.

23,129. And they told you that they refused to give you anything?—Yes, they refused to give me anything.

23,130. Have you seen Baxter or any member of the committee since?—No, not to ask them about it.

23,131. You have never spoken to them about it?—No.

23,132. At the time that these bricks and property were destroyed you were not a member of the union?—No.

23,133. Had you been asked to pay anything as a non-union man?—They came about three or four months before; two men called upon me then.

23,134. Who were they?—Samuel Kay was one, the manager of Mr. White.

23,135. Was he a member of the union?—Yes.

23,136. Was he a member of the committee?—I do not know.

23,137. Was Samuel Kay a member of the committee?—I do not know whether he was then; he was at the time my bricks were spoiled.

23,138. What did they say to you?—They came and told me that I must pay them 1*s.* a week if I did any work in the yard. I told them I did not know; what bit of work I did would not be a deal, and I should not pay 1*s.* a week for it, and that was all the words that passed, and they went away.

23,139. Have you had any conversation about the same thing since that?—No, not a word.

23,140. Is it the usual thing for a non-union man to pay a certain sum to the union?—It is the usual thing for all men in regular work to pay a halfpenny out of every shilling to the club.

23,141. Is that for permission to work?—Yes; they do not receive any benefit out of the club.

23,142. They receive no benefit from the union?—No.

23,143. Did you refuse to pay this shilling a week?—Yes.

23,144. After your property was destroyed did you join the union?—Yes; a year or two years after, when they agreed to take all the masters in.

23,145. At this time were they working for only a certain number of masters?—There were many masters taken in at the same time; they would take them in to pay as half members.

23,146. Did you join the union then?—Yes, I paid 1*l.* 1*s.* 6*d.* I paid 4*d.* a week in summer and 2*d.* a week in the winter.

23,147. Did you join as one of the masters?—Yes.

23,148. What was the reason of your joining the union?—To keep quiet and peaceable, and to go on quietly if we could.

23,149. Would you have joined the union if you had not been afraid of your property being injured?—Of course I should not.

23,150. To what do you attribute the damage done to your bricks and wheelbarrows on that Saturday night?—I do not know.

23,151. What do you believe to be the cause?—I am sure I cannot say; I never had any idea; I have not now the least.

23,152. Had you any quarrel with any one?—No, not the least; every man had paid up his halfpenny, I believe.

23,153. Do you believe that it had been done because you refused to pay the 1*s.* a week?—I believe it was that; it could not be anything else.

23,154. Had you any quarrel with any one?—No, not at all. I never had any words with any of them.

23,155. Do you believe the reason given by Baxter was the reason why your property was destroyed?—I believe Baxter was the cause of it.

23,156. Do you believe that the damage was done because you had not paid the shilling a week?—I do not know what was the cause, whether it was the shilling a week or by him being insulted, but he said he had been insulted by one of my men; that was all I knew.

23,157. The property which was destroyed all belonged to you?—Yes; I told him it was very hard if I had to stand to my men insulting people when I had nothing to do with them.

23,158. What is your belief as to the cause of your property being destroyed?—I do not know any more than that I never had any words with one of them, and all the money was paid up except mine.

23,159. It might have been either one of two things—insulting Baxter by one of your men, or because you did not pay to the union?—It must have been one of them; there was naught else.

23,160. What, in your opinion, was it?—I do not know; it may have been both.

23,161. Have you ever had any conversation with Baxter about it since?—No, except the Monday night following.

23,162. Has he never given any other reason except being insulted by one of your men?—No; I have not spoken to him since about it.

23,163. Did you ever tell him that it was a trade affair?—I told him it was a trade affair; no doubt, if it was not, they would have paid me.

23,164. Why should they have paid you if they had not done it?—Because it is reckoned if the men pay out-working money we are to be protected.

23,165. You did not pay?—I did not, but my men did.

23,166. You refused to pay?—Yes.

23,167. Why should they pay if they had not done it?—There were none of the masters that paid at the time.

23,168. But would not they be more likely to have paid if they had done it?—If they had not done it the club would have paid.

23,169. Is that the rule?—Yes, that is the rule.

23,170. The rule is that if the men are paying and damage is done the union pays?—If the men pay out-

TWENTY-FOURTH DAY.

H. Bridges.

6 July 1867.

working money and there be any damage done to the bricks the club pay for it.

23,171. And all your men were paying regularly?—Yes.

23,172. Therefore you think that the union ought to have paid the money?—Yes; they ought to have done so.

23,173. And because they did not pay the money you believe that they did it?—Yes.

23,174. (*Mr. Barstow.*) What day of the week was it that the bricks were spoiled?—On the Saturday night.

23,175. On that day week John Baxter had a quarrel with one of your men?—Yes.

23,176. On the Saturday before?—Yes.

23,177. Which of your men was it?—It was Poole.

23,178. Do you know what the quarrel was about?—Simply about some out-working money.

23,179. The out-working money is a halfpenny in the shilling paid by the non-union men for leave to work?—Yes.

23,180. How did Baxter and Poole come to quarrel about the out-working money?—Poole sent Baxter some money by a little lad across the room.

23,181. Did Baxter say that the money was wrong?—Baxter says, "Is this all?" and Poole says, "Yes; what! do you want all the money a man earns?" Then he refused to have it, and sent it back again.

23,182. Baxter sent the money back?—Yes.

23,183. What followed on that?—I said to him, "Poole, you must go to the committee about it."

23,184. Baxter sent the money back and Poole received it?—Yes.

23,185. Did Poole say anything to Baxter when he took the money back?—No; there were one or two snappish words, and then Baxter went away.

23,186. Do you yourself know whether Poole had accounted rightly for what he gave him?—I do not know.

23,187. Do you know what it was?—No, I do not know what it was.

23,188. You told us the end of the quarrel between Poole and Baxter?—Yes.

23,189. What did you say? how were you concerned in it?—I asked Baxter what was up when he was going out of the room.

23,190. This took place in your house?—Yes.

23,191. What did he say to you?—He said if I wanted to know I must go to the committee. I said, "What am I to go to the committee for?"

23,192. You said what?—I said, "What should I go to the committee for? He said no more, but went away.

23,193. Did he tell you that Poole had been paying him too little?—No.

23,194. That was all he said, was it?—Yes. But I told Poole——

23,195. Stop a minute; what took place between you and Poole?—I told Poole that he might go to the committee and see about this, that we might have no bother.

23,196. You knew then that there was a quarrel between the committee and Poole?—Yes. This man and he had fallen out and had two or three words that night. There had never been naught before.

23,197. (*Chairman.*) It was a fall out about the amount that was to be paid to the trade?—Yes, he was working out then. He is a member now, but he was an out-worker then.

23,198. (*Mr. Barstow.*) When this property was destroyed did you apply to the police?—Yes.

23,199. Did any one come to you to examine?—Yes, one went down along with me right away to the place.

23,200. Was anything discovered?—No; they put two or three bricks on one side, and there were marks of nailed shoes and such like.

23,201. How many men do you say there were?—There would be five or six, I should say; there must be that quantity to do it.

23,202. You yourself had been asked to pay to the union at this time?—Yes, they had come before this and told me I must pay 1*s.* a week, but I thought it was too much.

23,203. And you declined to pay it?—Yes.

23,204. Since that you have joined the union, you tell us?—Yes.

23,205. Have you been disturbed in any way since that time?—Not in any way since that.

The witness withdrew.

H. H. Sugg, Esq.

HUBERT HENRI SUGG, Esq. sworn and examined.

23,206. (*Chairman.*) I believe you are a solicitor in this town?—Yes.

23,207. And you have been retained and have appeared during this inquiry for a Defence Committee? I have.

23,208. That committee representing the union men. How many unions do you represent?—I believe it is 41, embracing, I think, about 9,000 men.

23,209. Then most of the unions of Sheffield are represented by you?—Oh, yes.

23,210. Do you know of any that are not represented by you?—I do not know the name of any union that I do not now represent, although there are unions that I do not represent, certainly.

23,211. You represent most of the unions, or all of the unions in the purely Sheffield trade, do you not?—I should think I do.

23,212. And have they united together for the purpose of what is called this Defence Committee?—Yes.

23,213. I believe it is only fair to state that when the disclosures of Broadhead appeared, you excluded him altogether from it?—Mr. Broadhead was never a member of that Defence Committee.

23,214. But his union was one of the unions that appeared, was it not?—Yes, his union, in connexion with the other branches of the saw trade, were portions of the Defence Committee.

23,215. And although he had acted with you up to the time of those disclosures, immediately they took place, that ceased?—That ceased.

23,216. We have asked Mr. Chambers, who has appeared on behalf of a committee appointed by the masters, to bring forward cases either of rattening, outrage, or intimidation, or anything within the scope of our inquiry, which have been committed (as they say) by the unions, and they endeavour to trace them home to the unions. Now it is right to ask you, as representing all the unions of men in the town, whether you are aware of any case of outrage of any description committed by any combination of the masters of this town within a period of the last ten years?—I am only aware of that case which we have mentioned already, which has been taken into a court law.

23,217. Will you be kind enough to tell me the name of that case?—The case is against Mr. Glencross as the secretary, and the chairman of the File Manufacturers' Association, to recover damages.

23,218. By whom?—By one of the file cutters. There are about 50 or 60 I think, and it is brought by one of them.

23,219. One of the file cutters has brought an action against the chairman and secretary of the File Manufacturers' Association?—Yes.

23,220. What are their names?—George Glencross and Samuel Butcher.

23,221. What is Mr. Glencross?—He is the secretary.

TWENTY-FOURTH DAY.

H. H. Sugg, Esq.

6 July 1867.

23,222. And what is Mr. Butcher ?—He is the chairman, and he is a large manufacturer in Sheffield.

23,223. You say an action has been brought ?—Yes.

23,224. What is the action for ?—Well, it is to recover damages.

23,225. To recover damages for what ?—If you will excuse me, I would plead the privilege of attorney and client.

23,226. Then I think I must ask you the question in this way. You know the attorney has no privilege of his own; the only privilege that he has is the privilege of his client.—Exactly.

23,227. And whatever privilege the client has the attorney has, but he has no more. If, therefore, the person whom you represent were here, we should ask him the questions, and he must answer them. If you prefer that we should ask the question of your client, and will give us the name of the man, we will send for him and dispose of it in that way, by putting him into the box, rather than that there should be any kind of betrayal of confidence on your part. What is his name ?—I should like to mention one thing as regards the position of this matter: that supposing you inquire into this question, and the manufacturers, the two defendants, are called here, and the case is gone into, it would be in your power to grant them a certificate exempting them from all civil and criminal proceedings. If you granted a certificate of indemnity against such proceedings you would thereby destroy our damages.

23,228. I suppose we should. — That is just it. That is why I should not have power to do that.

23,229. You know this Act of Parliament under which we sit ?—I know it well.

23,230. I suppose the act was committed before the date of the passing of this Act ?—I am not sure of that.

23,231. This Act was passed on the 15th of April 1867, was it not ?—I really do not know the exact date.

23,232. Supposing the act to have been an act committed within the last ten years, we are ordered to inquire into it ?—Yes; and then you have the power to grant a certificate.

23,233. Then we have power to call the persons before us, and if they make a clean breast of it, to grant a certificate; and, I believe, we have nothing to do with the course of the action at law.—I only put that before the Court as regards my client's claim to damages.

23,234. There seems to be no reason why we should not know the nature of the action, because in our judgment it either may or may not come within the scope of the Act of Parliament. If you will tell me the nature of the action we shall be in a better position to judge of that. — I do not know that there is any harm in it. The action is brought to recover damages, I believe, in respect of the file masters having by some arrangement or agreement, or something of that kind, agreed amongst themselves not to employ any of the men who were in Messrs. Turton's employ, simply because they gave notice to leave at a certain time. The masters formed themselves into an association, and passed a resolution that none of the masters should employ these particular men.

23,235. Certain persons on a list ?—Yes, certain persons on a list.

23,236. Have you brought an action against them because they did not employ persons on a certain list ?—That is what it is. It is really an action for libel on the publication of the list.

23,237. Is that the only case that you know of ?—That is the only case that I know of.

23,238. Then the only case you are acquainted with is an action for libel, in which the masters have stated the names of certain persons on a list. I will take the opinion of my colleagues, but it strikes me that it does not come within the subject of our inquiry at all. Our business is to inquire into acts of intimidation; you can hardly call it that ?—No.

23,239. We have to inquire into acts of intimidation, outrage, or wrong. Have they published this list ?—Yes.

23,240. They published a list of the names of certain men whom they said they would not employ ?—Yes; they said, "We agree among ourselves not to do so." There is no intimidation about it, I presume, so far as actual interference with the person is concerned.

23,241. I do not give any opinion about your action. You may have very good ground of action for anything I know; we express no opinion at all about it, but I am satisfied (and I believe my colleagues, Mr. Barstow and Mr. Chance, are satisfied) that it is not a case either of intimidation, outrage, or wrong contemplated by the Act of Parliament; and that being so, I do not think there is anything for us to inquire into. You say you are acquainted with all the unions, and you know of nothing of the kind, but that one thing ?—Personally, I know nothing.

23,242. But do you believe there is anything ?—I have not been instructed in any case but that.

23,243. But are you aware of any other case ?—I am not aware of any other case personally.

The witness withdrew.

Mr. Sugg stated that witnesses were in attendance to corroborate the statements made by the witness Harriett Ann Morton on a previous occasion.

The *Chairman* stated that this was purely a collateral matter, and that it had better stop where it was, this Court not being a tribunal before which questions of perjury could be investigated.

Mr. William Christopher Gregory sworn and examined.

Mr. W. C. Gregory.

23,244. (*Chairman.*) You are a clerk, I believe, to Mr. Fretson ?—I am.

23,245. And I believe it has been your duty to investigate the cases that have been brought before us by the committee of manufacturers ?—It has.

23,246. And have you been to Messrs. Henry Craven, builders, in the Wicker, to ascertain about some powder having been thrown into their premises ?—Mr. John Craven called upon me at Mr. Fretson's office.

23,247. Did you go into the facts of that case ?—He did not give me any particulars of them. He merely informed me that in his opinion it had no connexion with any union. He stated that at that time there was no union in their trade, and that he had very good reason to believe that it was a case of private malice.

23,248. Mr. Craven is not here, I believe ?—He is not.

The witness withdrew after an interval of ten minutes.

TWENTY-FOURTH DAY.

Mr. J. Craven.

6 July 1867.

Mr. JOHN CRAVEN sworn and examined.

23,249. (*Chairman.*) Are you a builder, and do you carry on your business in the Wicker in Sheffield?—Yes.

23,250. In May 1862, was a can of gunpowder thrown into your premises?—Yes; I do not speak to the date.

23,251. But it was about that time, was it not?—Yes.

23,252. How was it thrown in?—I think it was pushed under the door. There was a cavity of a foot or more, perhaps, under the outer door. It was only a very rough sort of gate, and I think they would be able to push it underneath.

23,253. Did the powder explode?—In a very ineffectual manner.

23,254. Did it explode?—It did explode, but it did no harm.

23,255. Was it a can, then?—Yes, it was either a can or a breakfast bottle.

23,256. And you say it did no damage?—No, nothing whatever.

23,257. Do you know at what time it exploded?—It would be before six o'clock in the morning.

23,258. At that time was there any union in your trade?—Yes.

23,259. Were you a member of the union?—As employers we were.

23,260. I do not understand you. What do you mean by "as employers"?—The employers have an association.

23,261. You were in the union of employers?—Yes.

23,262. There is a union of masters as well as of men?—Yes.

23,263. You were in the masters' union?—Yes.

23,264. Had you men working for you who were in the union of the men?—Yes.

23,265. Had you men who were working for you who were not in the union?—I have no doubt of it.

23,266. Had you any complaint at all made to you at the time of your men working?—None whatever.

23,267. Had you any disagreement with the union at that time?—None.

23,268. Do you know whether any of your men had any disagreement with the union?—No; I am not aware that they had.

23,269. Have you any ground of suspicion as to why that can of powder was placed underneath your door?—Not the slightest.

23,270. Had you any private enemy that you know of?—None whatever that we knew of.

23,271. There was no forcing open of the door for purposes of plunder?—No.

23,272. Then to what do you attribute it?—We do not know, and never did know.

23,273. You mean to say that you had had no connexion whatever with any union dispute of any sort, either yourself or your men?—Not at that time.

23,274. Had there been any such dispute?—None.

23,275. Has there been since?—No.

23,276. Were you paying proper prices?—Yes; it is all day's work in our trade; they do not work by the piece.

23,277. But were you paying proper prices?—Yes, the top price in the town.

23,278. Had there been any complaint against you?—None at all.

23,279. Had there been no application from any secretary to alter your mode of business in any way?—None.

23,280. And upon your oath you do not believe that that was a trade business?—Upon my oath I would say we do not know anything at all about it.

23,281. Might it have been a trade business?—It might.

23,282. On what ground might it have been a trade business?—I don't know that there was any ground.

23,283. It was in 1862, was it not?—Yes.

23,284. Has it ever occurred since?—No.

23,285. There has never been any occurrence of the kind since?—No.

23,286. Have you experienced any annoyance of any kind since?—No; I am happy to state that we are very free from all interferences in our trade.

23,287. You do not know to what it was attributable?—No.

23,288. What quantity of gunpowder was put in?—I do not know.

23,289. What was the size of the can?—It would hold from a pint to three gills.

23,290. What kind of place was it that was blown up?—A sort of bottom shop under the carpenters' shop.

23,291. Was it a large place?—A large open place, nearly as big as this court.

23,292. Was there anything in the place?—Nothing but wood.

23,293. It might have set fire to the wood, might it not?—It might have done so.

23,294. Was there a large quantity of wood there?—Tons. It might have set fire to the whole place, and to our neighbours' also, but, fortunately, it did no damage, none whatever. It did not do a pennyworth of damage.

23,295–6. Had you any quarrel with any of the workmen?—No; we cannot form any idea. It might have been that they got at the wrong place, for anything we know. It might have been intended for somebody else, and might have been a mistake. We had that idea at the time.

23,297. Did you ever hear about that time of any other persons being in dispute with the employers or with the trade?—No; besides, our trade do not do that sort of thing, and never did, for the last 30 years that we have known the trade.

23,298. Have you ever heard of such a case?—Never.

23,299. Is there any rattening in your trade?—No; fair words is all we go to.

23,300. How far was the wood from the door of this place under which the powder was put?—Close up; but there happened to be a spare place with joiners' benches round, and the wood was ranged all about.

23,301. Close up to where the can exploded?—Yes.

23,302. (*Mr. Chance.*) Was the wood in planks?—Yes, and boards.

23,303. (*Chairman.*) Was it dry wood?—It was dry stuff of all thicknesses.

23,304. (*Mr. Chance.*) Were the planks piled one upon another?—They were end-way up.

23,305. Were there any shavings or small pieces of wood close by?—Mere dust and dirt; nothing like the larger joiners' shop. If it had been in the joiners' shop it would have set fire to it, because there is always abundance of shavings there.

23,306–7. Would a can of gunpowder exploding in that way set fire to boards of that kind?—Had there been loose accumulation enough to make a blaze it would, but I do not think that it would have set the boards on fire themselves, if there had been nothing but boards; but if there had been such refuse and shavings as there always are in a joiners' shop, it would undoubtedly have set fire to it.

23,308. There were shavings, were there?—It was mere dust.

23,309. Was it a kind of stuff that would have blazed?—No, it would have smouldered; it would have lasted a long time.

23,310. (*Chairman.*) Did it set something on fire?—I cannot say that it did absolutely. We found that it had left its mark, and that is all I can say.

23,311. But was the fire existing when you got there?—No, not at the time we got there.

TWENTY-FOURTH DAY.

Mr. J. Craven.

6 July 1867.

23,312. Had there been any fire burning there?—Just sufficient to say that there had been; there was a smell of fire. It was not managed well, whoever did it.

23,313. How so?—It would have done more mischief if it had been better managed.

23,314. Then you believe that the man who did it intended mischief?—I have no doubt about it; but whether it was intended for us or not we do not know. We could not form the slightest idea why they should do it, because it is a thing which is unknown in our trade.

23,315. Are you all, masters and men, on good terms?—We always have been so to the best of my belief.

23,316. Was there no quarrel between the masters and the men, or between the unions of the two branches?—No.

23,317. Are the masters' unions on good terms with the men's unions?—Yes.

23,318. There are no disputes at all?—No, only as they will arise with regard to questions of wages: the men want an advance, and the masters will not give it; but then it comes to a matter of argument between the masters and the men, and they meet and discuss it, but no mischief occurs; that is unknown in the trade.

23,319. Was there not Champion's case?—Yes.

23,320. What was that?—That was something that I do not know much about.

23,321. But what was it?—I knew that Champion shot Grayson.

23,322. That is a trifle, no doubt; but how did he shoot him?—I think it was with a pistol.

23,323. That is a trifle in Sheffield, is it?—It is no trifle, I am sorry to say.

23,324. Did that occur with reference to the trade?—I have reason to believe so.

23,325. Then why did you not tell me of it?—It is such an isolated case. We Sheffield builders never do take any harm at the hands of our men, or they from us.

23,326. But a man called Champion shot a man of the name of Grayson? when did that occur?—Well, I am sure it must be ten years ago, or more.

23,327. Was it more than ten years ago?—It was when the Duke of Norfolk's residence called "The Farm" was building.

23,328. Did that arise out of a trade matter?—Yes, I believe it did.

23,329. If that is within the ten years we ought to inquire into it.

Mr. Sugg stated that it was a private matter.

Mr. Chambers also stated that it was a private matter, a dispute between two workmen.

23,330. (*Chairman, to the witness.*) We are informed that it was the case of a non-unionist shooting the secretary of a union; was that so?—I believe so.

23,331. Do you know whether that was a trade matter, or what it was?—So far as I have heard the circumstance——

The *Chairman* inquired whether this affair occurred more than ten years ago.

Mr. Sugg replied that it occurred in the year 1858.

23,332. (*Mr. Barstow, to the witness.*) What became of Grayson, the man who was shot at?—He is resident at Sheffield now.

23,333. Was Grayson wounded?—Oh, yes; dangerously so.

23,334. (*Chairman.*) Were any proceedings taken upon it? was the man prosecuted?—Yes, he was.

23,335. What became of him?—I think he served some 18 months' imprisonment.

23,336. Can you describe that case to us?—So far as I know about it, Grayson was the secretary of the Operative Joiners' Union, and Champion was foreman for Mr. Fewsdale, the master carpenter. This circumstance did not occur in our employ. From some cause the union wished Champion, the foreman, to be removed; and Grayson being the secretary, we could only suppose that Champion naturally thought that the secretary had something to do with it, and knew something about it. He was not removed by his employer; and the upshot of it was that Champion came into the shop and shot at and wounded Grayson very seriously, and made an attempt to shoot another man, but was stopped in time.

23,337. The man that was to be removed thought that the union men had caused his removal?—Yes.

23,338. When you say that it was a trade matter, you mean that it arose out of some trade regulations; but do you know whether it was private malice, or what it was?—We have every reason to believe that the society wished Champion to be removed; or if the society did not wish it, the workmen in the employ of the same master did.

23,339. It did not arise out of any trade dispute?—We do not know that it did; certainly not. It might be just a shop affair.

23,340. It was not done for the purposes of the union, but a man who was angry at a step which was taken, thought that the secretary of the union was the cause of it and shot at him?—That is it.

23,341. There is no suggestion, is there, that this had been promoted by any trade union at all?—No.

The witness withdrew.

23,342. (*Chairman.*) Is there any person who can give us any information respecting any trade outrage or wrong of any sort connected either with the masters or with the men? because if there is, we shall be glad to be informed of it at once. We have now, I believe, finished our investigation of all the matters which have been brought before us; and we have inquired from everybody who could give us information whether there are within their knowledge any outrages or matters which would come within the scope of our inquiry, and we have received no answer. We have no further matters to investigate, but if any person can give us any information on these matters, we shall be very glad to receive it.

The Chairman paused, but no person came forward.

23,343. (*Chairman.*) No person giving us any information, I think the course which we shall now adopt will be this: in order that we may have an opportunity of granting certificates to such persons as have given evidence before us, and who have criminated themselves by their declarations, and who we think are entitled to receive certificates, we shall be glad to announce on Monday, to such persons as apply for certificates, to which of them we will grant such certificates. We think, therefore, of adjourning now until two o'clock on Monday, and then such persons as wish for certificates may make their applications. We shall not know, of course, until the persons apply, who they are who wish for certificates; but when they do apply, we shall immediately give them an answer whether they are or are not in our opinion entitled to the indemnity which they seek. Having made this announcement to them, then if they do get their certificates, they will receive them in a day or two, on application to Mr. Barker, our secretary. It will not be necessary that we should meet in open court for the purpose of giving the certificates, but we think it desirable that persons wishing to have certificates should apply to us for them in open court, and that we should publicly declare our decision. Perhaps it may not be agreeable to every individual to appear in person before us; but if any such person will depute an attorney to appear for him, we shall be glad to listen to such an application. We shall therefore adjourn now until Monday, in order then to receive the applications of such persons as are anxious to have certificates of indemnity.

Adjourned to Monday next, at 2 o'clock.

TWENTY-FIFTH DAY.

Council Hall, Sheffield, Monday, 8th July 1867.

PRESENT:

WILLIAM OVEREND, Esq., Q.C.
THOMAS IRWIN BARSTOW, Esq.
GEORGE CHANCE, Esq.
J. E. BARKER, Esq., Secretary.

TWENTY-FIFTH DAY.

WILLIAM OVEREND, Esq., Q.C., IN THE CHAIR.

Mr. W. Bragge.

8 July 1867.

Mr. WILLIAM BRAGGE sworn and examined.

23,344. (*Chairman.*) Are you the managing director of John Brown and Company, Limited?—I am.

23,345. In February and March of the present year did your men refuse to work at some reduced prices, at a reduction of 10 per cent.?—They did.

23,346. What clsss of men were they?—Puddlers.

23,347. In consequence of this did you bring various workmen from different parts of England and Scotland to supply their places?—We did.

23,348. Were the men whom you dismissed, and whose places you supplied, members of any union?—They were.

23,349. To what union did they belong?—To the Ironworkers Union I think it is called.

23,350. After you had dismissed those men and got other men in their places, did you notice whether the works which are in the neighbourhood of the railway station were picketed or not?—They were.

23,351. Did you hear of any cases of persons being at all assaulted or interfered with by the parties who were placed outside your works?—Several cases.

23,352. What was the kind of interference of which they complained?—In some cases of threatenings, and in other cases of actual punishment by beating.

23,353. In consequence of the treatment to which those men were exposed, what course of proceedings had you to adopt?—To protect the gates of the works by policemen, and to feed and lodge the men who had been brought from a distance, keeping them from Monday morning till Saturday night within the works.

23,354. And had you to lay down beds for them on your premises?—We had to put down beds, and to establish a commissariat.

23,355. How long did this state of things continue?—Not more than three weeks.

23,356. At the end of the three weeks did the men whom you employed give you notice to leave?—Some of them gave notice to leave during this period of anxiety and trouble, but they did not leave.

23,357. Did they continue with you, or did they leave you?—They did continue with us, and they have remained since.

23,358. Are any of the men here who have been assaulted?—They are.

23,359. Are the men whom you now employ unionists or non-unionists?—They are non-unionists.

23,360. Have you made it a rule that you will employ non-unionists only?—We have abstained from employing unionists.

23,361. On what ground?—On the ground of the coercion exercised by them when we employed them.

23,362. You have very large works, have you not?—Very large works.

23,363. What number of men do you employ?—Upwards of 3,000.

23,364. Do you find that you can obtain a sufficient number of men for your works without taking union men?—In the branch of which we are now speaking, viz., the ironworkers, we can, and we have done so.

23,365. What is the number of men that you employ in that branch?—Not fewer than from 800 to 1,000, but I cannot speak exactly.

23,366. Do you know whether Mr. Brown has been threatened, or have you yourself been threatened in any way?—Not in the slightest.

23,367. Are you aware whether Mr. Ellis has been threatened?—I think not in the slightest.

23,368. Nor have you been at all molested in any way?—Not in any way.

23,369. None of your principals (if I may use the expression) have been molested or threatened, but simply the men whom you brought from a distance to work for you?—Just so.

23,370. I think you stated that the cause of dispute war that the men would not take 10 per cent. discount?—A reduction in the prices paid.

23,371. You wished to reduce them 10 per cent. below the wages which they had up to that time been receiving?—Exactly so.

23,372. Your new men gave notice, you say, after they had been with you a fortnight or three weeks?—No, the new men did not give notice. Some of the old men who accepted the reduction gave notice owing to the pressure which was put upon them from outside.

23,373. Did those men leave?—No, they did not leave.

23,374. What was the reason why those men continued with you, they having given you notice?—The state of siege in which we had been had passed away, and they chose to remain. Their giving notice was a voluntary act on their part. We were glad for them to remain, and they withdrew the notice.

23,375. Have they been interfered with since, that you are aware of?—I am not aware of any interference since.

23,376. Is it your custom, when a man comes into your employment, to send to the place from which he has come to ascertain what is his character?—It is our custom.

23,377. Whether he is a union man or not?—Whether he is a union man or not.

23,378. If he is a union man is it your practice to engage him or not?—We should not do so now, though formerly we did.

The witness withdrew.

J. Dunhill.

JAMES DUNHILL sworn and examined.

23,379. (*Mr. Barstow.*) Are you a puddler?—Yes.

23,380. In February last were you working for John Brown and Company?—Yes.

23,381. Were you then a union man?—I have been, but I am not at present.

23,382. But were you a union man in February last?—No.

23,383. Do you remember the men leaving in February last?—Yes.

23,384. What was that for?—For a reduction of wages, I believe.

23,385. We have heard that it was in consequence of a reduction of 10 per cent. in the wages; was that so?—Yes.

TWENTY-FIFTH DAY.

J. Dunhill.

8 July 1867.

23,386. Were you warned by anyone to give over working ?—Well, I was not warned by anyone to give up working.

23,387. Did anyone speak to you to induce you to give over working ?—No.

23,388. Were you interfered with at all ?—Yes, I was interfered with.

23,389. At the time when you were working, before the men turned out, did anyone desire you to turn out ?—No.

23,390. When the men went out, did you continue in ?—Of course, I was ready for my situation when it was ready for me.

23,391. Then you mean, in short, that you remained in ?—Yes, of course.

23,392. After the men had gone out and struck, and left Messrs. Brown's employ, were you molested in any way ?—Yes, I was.

23,393. In what way were you molested ?—I was molested with a good hiding, or a bad one ; I don't know which to call it.

23,394. Did the men who were out abuse you or call you names ?—Yes.

23,395. Do you remember, about three weeks after the men were out being at a place called Towers' ?—Yes.

23,396. Were any of the men there who were working with you in your company at that time ?—There was only one that was with me.

23,397. What is his name ?—Edmund Higgatt.

23,398. What happened to you then ?—We called in and had two of gin apiece——

23,399. I do not want to know what you drank, but what happened to you ?—Of course I got struck.

23,400. Who struck you ?—James Harris.

23,401. Was James Harris alone, or were there any men with him ?—There was only one that I knew, but there were seven or eight besides, but I didn't know their names.

23,402. What is the name of the man whom you knew ?—Joseph Trowman.

23,403. Did they set upon you ?—Yes.

23,404. What did they do to you ?—They called me "a damned blackleg."

23,405. I asked you what they did to you ?—They only struck me ; that was all they did in that one house.

23,406. But did they strike you more than once, or did they only strike you once ?—They only struck me once ; they had not a chance to strike me any more.

23,407. How was that ?—Because I was rather quicker than them.

23,408. (*Chairman.*) You ran away ?—Yes, I did ; they had not a chance.

23,409. (*Mr. Barstow.*) Did you defend yourself ?—Yes, of course I did.

23,410. You struck them, I suppose ?—Well, of course I did my best.

23,411. What did they say to you ?—They called me a "blackleg," and said I was taking the bread out of their mouths.

23,412. What did you understand them to mean by calling you a "blackleg" ?—I expect they meant that I was doing work under price, but of course we had the price that we asked for.

23,413. Is a man who works under price called a "blackleg" ?—I suppose so. They say so. We had the price that we asked for before the turn out was.

23,414. Where did you go to after you left this place ?—We went down to the "Big Gun."

23,415. Did the men follow you ?—Yes.

23,416. I suppose you were drinking at the "Big Gun ?"—We had not the chance to drink.

23,417. They followed you immediately, did they ?—Yes.

23,418. Was Trowman there ?—Yes.

23,419. Did Trowman say anything ? — Yes, he said "Here is one of the b——, let us give it him now again."

23,420. What did they do to you ?—Of course they did the best they could for themselves, and we did the same.

23,421. (*Chairman.*) What did they do ?—They struck us several times.

23,422. You had a fight then, I suppose ?—Yes, it was a regular fight.

23,423. (*Mr. Barstow.*) There were only two of you ?—No, there were only two.

23,424. And how many of them were there ?—From seven to eight.

23,425. What were there names ?—I don't know only two of their names.

23,426. The seven or eight set upon you two, did they ?—Yes.

23,427. Were you much injured ?—I had a pair of black eyes and a cut face.

23,428. What did they strike you with ?—I am sure I cannot tell you for truth. I had not time to look what they struck me with.

23,429. But you could tell me whether it was with their fists, or whether it was with a stick, or what ?—They struck me several times with their fists.

23,430. You prosecuted them, did you not ?—Yes, I believe we did.

23,431. What was done to them ?—I believe they were bound over for six months.

23,432. Did you say before the magistrates what you have said to us ?—Yes, I believe I did.

23,433. And what do you say was done to them ?—They were bound over for six months, and one man, I think, was bound over in two cases ; he was bound in 50*l.* himself, and he had to find four sureties of 25*l.* each.

23,434. Nothing more was done than binding them over ?—No.

23,435. (*Mr. Chance.*) Are you sure that they began the row ?—Yes.

23,436. You did not say anything to them in the first instance ?—Not a word. We were the best friends in the world before.

23,437. (*Mr. Barstow.*) Did you ever apply to the the union in reference to this affair ?—No.

The witness withdrew.

EDMUND HIGGATT sworn and examined.

E. Higgatt.

23,438. (*Mr. Chance.*) Are you working for Messrs. Brown and Company ?—Yes.

23,439. Were you working for them when the union men went out ?—No.

23,440. When did you first begin to work for them ?—Five years ago, but I had left before the union men went out.

23,441. Then did you go to work for them after the union men went out ?—Yes.

23,442. Do you remember being at the "Big Gun" one Saturday night with Harris and Trowman ?—Yes.

23.443. Was the last witness, Dunhill, with you ?—Not that night.

23,444. Were there other men there besides Harris and Trowman ?—Yes, a many.

23,445. Were Harris and Trowman union men who had been working for Messrs. Brown and Company ?—No, they had left.

23,446. They had been working ?—Yes.

23,447. And they were union men ?—Yes. I was before I went till the time I came back, but still I was sent for back.

23,448. What took place when you were at the "Big Gun" ?—I went into the "Big gun" and had a glass of something to drink and Harris came up ; he was on the further side and I was close against the counter, and he said ; "There is that 'Snip' that has taken Joe Smith's job," that is a nickname, and then he came and struck me.

23,449. Where did he strike you ?—In the "Big Gun."

TWENTY-FIFTH DAY.

E. Higgatt.

8 July 1867.

23,450. But on what part of the body did he strike you?—On the face.

23,451. What with?—His fist of course.

23,452. Did any of the other men strike you?—They did not that night.

23,453. Who was Joe Smith?—A man that used to work there.

23,454. Was he one of the men who had left?—Yes, at that time.

23,455. Nothing more took place that night?—Not that night.

23,456. Did anything take place afterwards?—Yes, I went to the post office to send some money to Wolverhampton, and we went into Towers' and had something to drink.

23,457. Who was with you then?—There was Trowman and Harris in there.

23,458. Did you go in with Trowman?—No, I went in with Dunhill.

23,459. Were any other men there besides Harris and Trowman?—There were five or six, but we did not take any notice of any but those two.

23,460. What was done there?—I went to Trowman and asked him why he hit me, and I went to Harris and asked him why he had hit me on the Saturday night, and what I had done amiss.

23,461. Did you speak to them first, or did they speak to you?—Not on the Saturday night, I did first on the Monday, I asked them what I did amiss.

23,462. Well, what did they say?—I said, "Have I taken anybody's job." I said, "I was at John Brown's before you ever agreed for the price." I went to work at the price that they agreed for.

23,463. What did they say then?—He said he had hit me on Saturday night and he would hit me again, and so we got into a quarrel, but I cannot tell you which hit the other first, and after that I and Dunhill went down to the "Gun."

23,464. You had a fight then?—No, we did not fight, we were only wrestling with each other.

23,465. He did not hit you?—No. I do not think there were many blows exchanged.

23,466. Did the other man hit you at all?—No, not till we got down to the "Big Gun." It was same day that we went to the "Big Gun" and to "Towers'."

23,467. Now what took place at the "Big Gun"?—I said, "Dunhill, we can have a glass here and be quiet." We had not been in five minutes before six or seven of them came in. First was this Trowman, and then the other man set about me, and then I went to James Dunhill.

23,468. When you say the "other man," do you mean Harris?—Yes.

23,469. Had you said anything to him before they struck you?—I only asked him at Towers' what he hit me for, and naught to do but they came straight and set about me there.

23,470. Did you strike them again?—No, we got out of the road, we could not with six or seven of them kicking me.

23,471. Did they call you any names?—Only "blackleg."

23,472. What do they mean by that?—I suppose they meant my going in.

23,473. Were you much injured by the blows you received?—I played a fortnight.

23,474. Was that in consequence of the injuries which you had received there?—Well, I had a bad cold, but I cannot say it was the injuries. I had only a kick or two, but I played truant a fortnight.

23,475. I want to know what was the effect of the injuries which you received, could you have worked the next day after if you had not had a cold?—I could not, nor the next day after. I had only two days work for a fortnight.

23,476. How long did the injuries prevent you from working?—About nine days.

23,477. Where were you injured then?—In the shin and the ribs with the kicking.

23,478. Were any ribs broken?—No.

23,479. Did you have any doctor to you?—No, I did not go to a doctor.

23,480. How did those injuries keep you from working for nine days?—I could not turn over in bed.

23,481. (*Chairman.*) Do you know of any other person that was injured besides yourself?—Dunhill was.

23,482. And who besides?—Nobody that day but ourselves.

23,483. But at any other time do you know of any other workmen being injured?—No, I do not.

23,484. Did you communicate with the union about this. Did you go to the union and charge the union with having caused this to be done?—No, I did not.

The witness withdrew.

J. Skidmore.

JOHN SKIDMORE sworn and examined.

23,485. (*Chairman.*) Are you a puddler?—Yes.

23,486. About four months ago did you come to work for Messrs. Brown & Company?—Yes.

23,487. Where did you come from?—Garston, near Liverpool.

23,488. After you had been at work a fortnight or so did you see a man called Dimond in Blonk Street?—Yes.

23,489. I believe he used to work at Messrs. Brown's?—Yes.

23,490. And was he then on strike?—Yes.

23,491. What did he say to you?—As I was passing the door he made his appearance to me, and he says, "Halloa Jack, is that you," and I said, "Yes," and he said, "You are a fine beggar, you are. I did not think you were a man of that sort," I said, "For why?" he said, "For coming and filling up our places," I said, "I have not filled any man's place. "The work I have got is work that has been standing, "and it is fresh started." It had been started upwards of twelve months, and he caught hold of me by the collar, and while he had got hold of me 20 or 30 more of those hands came round and they abused me.

23,492. Did they abuse you by language or with blows?—In language.

23,493. What did they call you?—They called me a "blackleg."

23,494. Did they do anything else but abuse you by calling you a "blackleg"?—No.

23,495. You say there were 20 or 30?—Yes.

23,496. Of those union men?—Yes.

23,497. Did they never do anything to you at all?—No, they never did.

23,498. How was that?—I do not know. I expect they were afraid because I knew the biggest part of them.

23,499. All they did then was to call you a "blackleg"?—That was all.

23,500. Did they seize you by the collar?—Yes.

23,501. Have you ever been threatened by any of them?—Yes.

23,502. Who threatened you?—I did not know the persons. I was staying at Mr. Jenning's house, and the first morning that I was going to work as I was proceeding down Bower Street I overtook three men in the street, and they asked me if I knew a certain street and I said I did not, and I went on a little way further. Then they came and caught hold of me, and asked me where I was going, and if I was going to work; I said that was my business, and not theirs. Then they loosed me, and they followed me a little way further, and caught hold of me again and said if I did not tell them where I was going to work they would knock my b—— head off.

TWENTY-FIFTH DAY.

J. Skidmore.

8 July 1867.

23,503. What did they do then?—I told them I was not going to work at the trade.

23,504. What trade?—Puddling, but that I was going to work at the hammers. They asked me if I was certain, and I said, Yes, and then they loosed me and took to their heels.

23,505. Was there any strike of the hammer makers at that time?—No.

23,506. Merely of the puddlers?—Yes.

23,507. Have you ever been interfered with except on those two occasions?—No.

23,508. And have you continued to work for Mr. Brown?—Yes.

23,509. Did you apply to the union after you had been molested in this way?—No.

The witness withdrew.

THOMAS ROCK sworn and examined.

T. Rock.

23,510. (*Mr. Barstow.*) Are you a puddler?—Yes.

23,511. The week before Easter did you come here from Derby to work for Messrs. John Brown and Company?—Yes.

23,512. You went with the foreman and had supper at some public-house, did you not?—Yes.

23,513. After supper did you go into the street?—Yes.

23,514. Were there a large number of men in the street?—Yes.

23,515. What did they do?—They told me if I went to work I was doing wrong.

23,516. Did you try to get into the house again?—Yes.

23,517. Did you get in?—No.

23,518. Who prevented you?—The men that were there.

23,519. Where did they take you?—They took me to another public-house.

23,520. What did you do there?—They told me that if we would go back again they would pay our fare.

23,521. Did you sleep at the public-house?—Yes.

23,522. Who paid for your bed?—I do not know.

23,523. You did not?—No.

23,524. What happened to you the next day?—We had our breakfasts, and they sent me back home again.

23,525. And then what happened?—They sent me back home again.

23,526. Who sent you back?—The union, I suppose.

23,527. But who did?—I do not know who it was.

23,528. What men did?—The union men, I suppose.

23,529. But the union cannot have gone with you, some man must have paid for you?—The union men.

23,530. But did they go to the railway station with you?—Yes, they all went to the railway station the next day with me.

23,531. Did they all sleep in the house?—No.

23,532. Did you know any of them?—No.

23,533. You went back to Derby?—Yes.

23,534. Did you pay your own fare?—No.

23,535. So you got your bed and breakfast and railway fare paid for you?—Yes.

23,536. Did you know those men to be union men?—Yes.

23,537. How did you know that?—Because they took me to the union house.

23,538. That is your only reason is it?—Yes.

23,539. Why did you go back to Derby?—Because I was afraid to stop there.

The witness withdrew.

(*Chairman.*) We announced on Saturday that to-day we should be ready to declare to such persons as had given evidence before us, and who were anxious to have certificates, whether or not in our opinion they were entitled to receive them. If there is any person present who has given evidence before us, and who wishes to have a certificate, if he will apply to us either himself personally or by his attorney, we shall be glad now to announce whether or not in our opinion he is entitled to receive a certificate.

(*Mr. Sugg.*) I am instructed, sir, to make separate applications for certificates in several cases quite indepently of my character as representing the trades unions. I am instructed in the first place to apply for a certificate for Mr. Broadhead.

(*Chairman.*) We have considered Mr. Broadhead's case, and we think that he is entitled to a certificate, but at the same time we do not think that Mr. Broadhead is at all entitled to costs for appearing before us. We have laid down a principle for our guidance in this inquiry to which we intend to adhere throughout the whole of these cases, namely, that when a person has come forward and given us direct evidence, and has declared at once that he has been guilty of a serious offence, and we have had no reason to doubt that he has spoken the truth, we shall not only grant him a certificate but we shall also allow him the costs of appearing here; but in all cases where a witness who has appeared here has come forward and in the first instance committed deliberate perjury, and has then appeared a second time for the purpose of clearing himself from the consequences of such perjury, we shall decide that he is not entitled to any costs, even though he has eventually made full disclosures of all the facts within his knowledge. In this case we shall grant Broadhead a certificate, but we shall not allow any costs. With respect to the certificate itself of course we are anxious that it should appear on the face of the certificate for what the certificate is granted. We have accordingly drawn up a form of certificate which we have not yet finally settled, but we have been thinking over in each case what are the offences in respect of which a certificate is required, and we have endeavoured to specify those offences in each instance. In Mr. Broadhead's case, for instance, we have drawn up a number of offences for which we suppose he would claim the certificate. Are you prepared, Mr. Sugg, with a list of those offences in respect of which he would claim to be indemnified?

(*Mr. Sugg.*) No, sir, I am not. From what you hinted on Saturday I thought that that might be a matter for after consideration, but I can supply you with a list hereafter.

(*Chairman.*) Then without reading it over I may state that we have gone very carefully over the evidence, and have seen what are the crimes to which he has confessed himself to have been a party, and here is a list of them, and although perhaps in that list they are not described in the way in which they will be ultimately described in the certificate, yet they substantially appear here. We have thought it desirable to pursue this course, because we are anxious that everybody to whom a certificate has been promised should have a perfect protection, but a perfect protection only in respect of those offences of which he has admitted himself to be guilty. It is not a protection in respect of any offences which he has not admitted.

(*Mr. Sugg.*) It is only in respect of such offences as those on which they have been examined.

(*Chairman.*) It will only extend to offences in respect of which the person is examined. Therefore if you like to take this list (*handing a paper to Mr. Sugg*), it contains a list of the offences of which we believe Broadhead has confessed himself to be guilty. If you have any reason to think that that is not a perfect catalogue of his offences you can send in any suggestions you may desire to make to-morrow morning to Mr. Barker. I do not know whether my learned

TWENTY-FIFTH DAY.

8 July 1867.

colleagues will remain here over to-morrow, but I shall remain here for three or four days, and therefore I shall be able to make any additions or alterations that may appear desirable. This list has been very carefully made out by myself and my colleagues, Mr. Barstow and Mr. Chance, and I believe it contains a true catalogue of all the offences which Mr. Broadhead has admitted.

(*Mr. Sugg.*) I am much obliged to you, sir, on behalf of Mr. Broadhead for his certificate.

(*Chairman.*) You will see the way in which we have dealt with it. For instance Broadhead describes himself as having engaged Crookes to shoot Linley, or rather to shoot at Linley. Crookes shot at him, and it ultimately resulted in his death, and then afterwards Broadhead paid Crookes money for having done so. In that case therefore Broadhead was an accessory to murder, both before the fact and after the fact. That is easily described, but in addition to that we asked him this question: "Were you not a party to a great "many acts of rattening during the last 10 years?" He replied, "Yes, I was. I was a party to a great "number, and I paid money for many of them." But those cases were not specified, and the only way in which we can introduce them into the certificate is by speaking of them as "various acts of rattening "committed within a period of 10 years antecedent "to the date of the Act." That is the way in which we have done it so as to make the protection as perfect and complete as possible, because we have felt it to be our duty, having promised these men our protection, to make that protection as complete as it possibly can be made.

(*Mr. Sugg.*) The next case, sir, in which I have to apply for a certificate is the case of Mr. Thomas Smith, the secretary of the Saw Makers' Union.

(*Chairman.*) What is the offence which Mr. Smith has confessed?

(*Mr. Sugg.*) I believe it would be possible to implicate him by other evidence.

(*Chairman.*) But I want to know what offence Mr. Smith has confessed to?

(*Mr. Sugg.*) I do not know that it is necessary that a person should confess.

(*Chairman.*) Yes, he must; and Mr. Smith has confessed to nothing.

(*Mr. Sugg.*) Allow me to call your attention Sir to the words of the Act, "Any person examined as a "witness in an inquiry under this Act, who in the "opinion of the person or persons conducting the "inquiry makes a full and true disclosure touching "all the matters in respect of which he is examined "shall receive a certificate."

(*Mr. Barstow.*) Will you read on, Mr. Sugg?

(*Mr. Sugg.*) He "shall receive a certificate under "the hand of such person or persons stating that the "witness has upon his examination made a full and "true disclosure as aforesaid, and if any civil or "criminal proceedings be at any time thereafter "instituted against such witness in respect of any "matter touching which he has been so examined, "the tribunal before which such proceeding is "instituted shall, on the production and proof of "the certificate, stay the proceeding and may in its "discretion award to such witness any costs he may "have been put to by the institution of the proceed-"ing. Provided that no evidence taken under this "Act shall be admissable against any person in any "civil or criminal proceeding whatever." Therefore if a man has been examined upon the matter, I apprehend that that is quite sufficient to entitle him to a certificate.

(*Chairman.*) Clearly, if he has said anything in respect of which he is liable to either civil or criminal proceedings, he is entitled to a certificate. I do not recollect anything of the kind in Mr. Smith's case, but we shall be glad to consider his case.

(*Mr. Sugg.*) I was not here when he was examined, but I think you will find from his evidence that he confessed that he was an accessory after the fact to the New Hereford Street outrage.

(*Mr. Chance.*) Yes, inasmuch as though he did not pay the money he gave directions for the money to be paid in respect of that affair.

(*Mr. Sugg.*) Yes, he knew nothing beforehand about the actual offence that was committed but he afterwards, as secretary, paid out a certain sum of money towards the expenses.

(*Chairman.*) Then I think he ought to have his certificate. He shall have his certificate.

(*Mr. Sugg.*) The next application which I have to make is for a certificate for Mr. George Peace of Dore, who was engaged in one of those affairs.

(*Chairman.*) That will be granted.

(*Mr. Sugg.*) That, sir, ends my separate applications, and now I shall apply to you for certificates for various witnesses on behalf of the unions. The first application is with respect of two of the secretaries of the file trade, Cutts and Holland. I should not have applied for certificates in their cases but I see in the "Times" of to-day that a question has been raised before Mr. Justice Lush as to whether picketing is legal or illegal.

(*Chairman.*) I have not heard any such confession. Who is the man?

(*Mr. Sugg.*) Cutts confessed I think (if it is a confession) that picketing was a custom in their trade.

(*Chairman.*) Do you want a protection for that?

(*Mr. Sugg.*) I think so.

(*Chairman.*) We think that Cutts and Holland ought to have certificates.

(*Mr. Sugg.*) Then, sir, I come to the case of Robert Renshaw who confessed to the Acorn Street affair.

(*Chairman.*) That will be granted.

(*Mr. Sugg*) Then there are the cases of William Stanley, William Owen, and William Henry Owen in the brick trade. I think their evidence was partly as to the offences against Mr. Robinson.

(*Chairman.*) They gave evidence, but what did they say they had done?

(*Mr. Sugg.*) I do not know that they confessed to anything.

(*Chairman.*) There was the mutilation of the books but that is no offence. It may be a very wrong thing, but it is not an offence in law.

(*Mr. Sugg.*) I believe there was something more in Owen's case.

(*Mr. Chance.*) If I remember rightly Mr. Owen confessed to having cut out the leaves of the book but he did not confess to anything else. He was called directly after Mr. Stanley. At first he denied that he had cut out the leaves of the books but he afterwards confessed it.

(*Mr. Sugg.*) That remark of yours, sir, that if they do not confess any offence they do not get any certificate has rather affected my course of proceeding, certainly if they have admitted no offence they cannot be proceeded against and need no certificate, but if any offence might by implication be brought against any person he would need a certificate.

(*Chairman.*) Certainly, but if they do not confess any offence, and if they are not liable to be proceeded against either civilly or criminally in consequence of what they state before us they do not get any certificate. If we are taking too narrow a view of this, and if any person should hereafter be in jeopardy on that account I believe we should have full power to grant them a certificate on application. We are very anxious to carry out the spirit of the Act of Parliament, and to grant indemnity to every man who has come forward and confessed, and we shall be ready to grant such certificate at any time, if necessary.

(*Mr. Sugg.*) Then I will only ask for those certificates which are necessary.

(*Chairman.*) If you please. We are speaking in the most perfect confidence that we shall have power at any future time to grant a certificate, and I can assure you that we shall be quite disposed to do so in the case of every person who has made a full disclosure of all the facts within his knowledge.

(*Mr. Sugg.*) Then, sir, I come to the scissor trade,

and in connexion with that are the cases of William Fearnley, and Joseph Thompson, the secretary.

(*Chairman.*) We shall grant Fearnley a certificate, but Thompson's is a case in which we shall not grant one. We do not believe that he has made a full disclosure or a true statement.

(*Mr. Sugg.*) I am very sorry to hear that. Then I come to the case of the scythe trade. In the case of Michael Thompson, I believe you promised protection, though it was beyond the 10 years.

(*Chairman.*) We stopped that case, if you recollect.

(*Mr. Sugg.*) No, sir, we went into it with a promise from you that the man should be protected if it should be necessary, but we can deal with his case hereafter.

(*Chairman.*) Very well.

(*Mr. Sugg.*) That, sir, ends my list of cases.

(*Chairman.*) Is there any other person who wishes for a certificate? Does no person apply for a certificate for Crookes?

Henry Skidmore, the president of the Sawsmiths Association, came forward.

(*Mr. Barstow to Skidmore.*) Do you want a certificate?

(*Skidmore.*) I do.

The paper was handed to the applicant.

(*Mr. Barstow.*) Do you want one for anybody else?

(*Skidmore.*) No, sir.

Skidmore withdrew.

Thomas Barker, the secretary of the Saw-handle Makers Society, applied for a certificate.

(*Chairman to Barker.*) Here is your paper (*handing a paper to Barker*). In the course of a few days you will get the certificate properly signed.

Barker withdrew.

(*Chairman.*) Does any other person wish for a certificate?

(*Mr. Sugg.*) Thompson wishes to speak to you, sir.

(*Chairman.*) We have considered his case, and we do not believe what he has said. Does any person else wish for a certificate?

(*After a pause.*)

(*Chairman.*) Does not any person appear to ask for a certificate for Crookes? Mr. Jackson will perhaps take the certificates for Crookes and also for Hallam.

(*Mr. Jackson.*) Certainly, I will, sir.

The papers were handed to the chief constable.

(*Chairman.*) There may be a very good reason why they are not here, but we think they are entitled to their certificates, and Watson also.

The Court directed that it should be declared outside the Court that any person wishing for a certificate must now come forward and make application for it.

Samuel Crookes came forward.

(*Chairman to Crookes.*) We have granted you a certificate, and we hope that you have told us everything that you know about the matters in which you have been engaged. This paper is not your certificate, it is merely a list of offences of which you have admitted that you have been guilty. We wish you to look it over, and after having done so either by yourself or with the aid of any other person, a professional man or otherwise, if you see that there is anything else which ought to be inserted in the certificate you can communicate it to us through Mr. Barker, and when you have read it over, if you are satisfied with it, if you will go to Mr. Barker he will grant you a proper certificate signed by us which will be your protection hereafter. If you think that any alteration is required, and you inform us of it, we will consider it hereafter, and grant your application if we think it is desirable. We do this with a view of making these certificates as complete as possible.

(*Crookes.*) Thank you, sir, I am very much obliged to you. I am sure it is a truthful statement. I have stated all I know; it is all true.

(*Chairman.*) If we did not think so we should not grant you a certificate. In the first instance you did not reveal all that you knew.

(*Crookes.*) No, sir, I did not, but I begged your pardon on the second occasion.

(*Chairman.*) On the second occasion you did. I do not know whether you have been paid your expenses.

(*Crookes.*) No, sir, I have not.

(*Chairman.*) We shall order that you receive nothing for your expenses, because you did not come in the first instance and make a clear and full disclosure of all you knew. We act upon that principle throughout. If you had come at first and told the truth we should have given you your expenses, but as you did not do so we do not give you your expenses, although we do give you your certificate.

(*Crookes.*) Very good, sir.

Crookes withdrew.

George Shaw came forward.

(*Chairman to Shaw.*) You will have your certificate.

Shaw withdrew.

Charles Baxter came forward.

(*Chairman to Baxter.*) What do you want a certificate for?

(*Baxter.*) I took some bands, sir.

(*Chairman.*) It is for rattening then, is it?

(*Baxter.*) Yes, sir.

(*Chairman.*) Do you know the date?

(*Baxter.*) I do not.

(*Chairman.*) Whose bands were they?

(*Baxter.*) Messrs. Slack, Sellars, and Graysons.

(*Mr. Barstow.*) Were you one of their men?

(*Baxter.*) I do not work for them.

(*Chairman.*) You will get your certificate on application to Mr. Barker.

Baxter withdrew.

(*Mr. Sugg.*) I was nearly forgetting the case of Samuel Cutler. I am instructed by Mr. Cutler, sir, to apply to you for a certificate. He made a statement in connexion with the Acorn Street outrage.

(*Mr. Chance.*) He denied all knowledge of it. He never admitted anything. He cannot be prosecuted for that.

(*Mr. Sugg.*) That is very true, sir, but I think you will find that he was implicated.

(*Chairman.*) That may be. He has either made a full disclosure or he has not, but he certainly has not made a disclosure with regard to that offence.

(*Mr. Sugg.*) Well, I will look over the evidence, sir, and see how that is.

Joseph Copley came forward.

(*Chairman to Copley.*) You will have no costs either. You did not come in the first instance and tell all that you knew.

Copley withdrew.

William Fearnley came forward.

(*Chairman to Fearnley.*) You will have your certificate; Mr. Sugg has it.

Fearnley withdrew.

(*Chairman.*) Does any other person wish for a certificate?

(*Mr. Sugg.*) Mr. Cutler admitted, sir, that he went and made a bargain with Renshaw, and that he held the money that was to be paid for the commission of that offence, whatever it might be, which was then agreed upon; and the offence which was agreed upon, according to his own statement, was to have been the beating of this man, and not blowing him up; but that agreement ended in blowing up, instead of beating, and therefore he might possibly be implicated in the blowing up.

(*Mr. Chance.*) I think if you will look at the evidence, Mr. Sugg, you will find that he said that he gave the money back to Bayles because Renshaw had done that which he had no authority to do.

(*Mr. Sugg.*) I think, sir, that the evidence is so interlaced that Cutler might easily be brought in on

TWENTY-FIFTH DAY.

8 July 1867.

a criminal charge upon his own evidence. His own evidence goes to the effect that he positively went and made an arrangement with Renshaw for an illegal purpose at any rate.

(*Mr. Chance.*) To give him a thumping?

(*Mr. Sugg.*) Precisely.

(*Mr. Chance.*) And then he said that Renshaw did something which he did not authorize him to do, and then he said that he afterwards gave the money back to Bayles and that he would not have anything to do with it.

(*Mr. Sugg.*) Yes, sir.

(*Chairman.*) All that we could do would be to grant a certificate for the conspiracy to beat Wastnidge and Ripley. I should have no objection to give a certificate to that extent, but no further. Therefore if from any evidence it should appear afterwards that he is further implicated than he has admitted, he would be liable to proceedings.

(*Mr. Sugg.*) I should like to call your attention, sir, to the hardship upon witnesses coming and making disclosures of what they really knew. One comes forward and makes a disclosure of having committed a certain offence, and the person with whom he was associated comes forward also and says, "Yes, you " did so, you made an agreement with me, but I have " overstepped your authority." Another offence was thus committed, and consequently I submit the first person may be implicated.

(*Mr. Chance.*) There is no hardship in that, because if he did not do it he is not liable to be punished for the offence.

(*Mr. Sugg.*) But if he had not spoken at all he would not have been liable, that is where the hardship is.

(*Chairman.*) We have very great doubt about the truth of that story.

(*Mr. Barstow.*) I for one certainly do not believe it.

(*Mr. Sugg.*) I think it is confirmed by Renshaw more or less.

The Court deliberated.

(*Mr. Sugg.*) If you refuse Cutler, you do this; you let the principal out, and the presumed accessory gets in.

(*Chairman.*) The principal may be a very wicked man, a murderer even, but if he tells the truth he gets a certificate, while though an accessory may have committed a very small offence, if he does not tell the truth he does not get a certificate.

(*Mr. Sugg.*) Cutler's story is slightly confirmed by Renshaw.

(*Chairman.*) In Cutler's case we are very anxious to grant a certificate if we can, because we think it is our duty to protect all witnesses that come forward and give their evidence fairly, but we think it is a case which requires further consideration. We will discuss it together to-night, and if you apply to Mr. Barker to-morrow morning you will get an answer.

(*Mr. Sugg.*) I am very much obliged to you, sir.

(*Chairman.*) Is that all Mr. Sugg?

(*Mr. Sugg.*) That is all, sir.

(*Chairman.*) We have now discharged the duty which was imposed upon us by the Commissioners in London, when they appointed us to make investigations into the outrages in Sheffield and their connexion with the trades of Sheffield, and we cannot conclude our labours without offering our thanks to the Mayor and Town Council of this borough for the kind manner in which they have granted us this room to sit in, and for the assistance which they have in every way rendered to us. We are also exceedingly obliged to the Watch Committee for granting us the assistance of the various police officers who have been here to enforce order, to take our summonses, and to attend to other matters in furtherance of the objects of this inquiry. Both the Mayor and the Corporation, and the Watch Committee, have been of great service to us in enabling us to carry out this inquiry.

We think it also right to make an observation with regard to Mr. Barker our secretary, we feel that we are under very considerable obligations to him. He has discharged his duty in every way with the greatest possible ability, he has studied how he could best assist us in every possible way; and without his assistance I really do not know how we should have been enabled to carry on the important duties entrusted to us in connexion with this inquiry, or at all events with the expedition with which we have been able to conduct it. I believe that my learned colleagues as well as myself feel that we are under very great obligations to him and we believe that those obligations are shared by this town and by the country at large.

There is another gentleman to whom the Commissioners have been very considerably indebted, viz., the chief constable of this town. Throughout this inquiry he has shown great zeal, great discretion, and great intelligence; and in the whole of this matter he has afforded us the greatest possible assistance. We think that he is an officer of the greatest possible value, and we consider that Sheffield has not only cause to be proud of possessing such an officer, but that without such an officer the town of Sheffield which has been the subject of such lawless conduct for some time would be in considerable peril and jeopardy.

The gentleman whom we have employed to investigate the books of the various unions, Mr. Shrubsole, has also been very useful to us. He has done his duty very well, and his labours have very much facilitated our inquiries.

It is not our intention to make any allusion at all to the conclusions at which we may arrive with regard to the evidence which has been adduced before us. Our duty is first to the Commission in London. We have to make a report to the Commissioners; we are in process of making it now and when it is completed it will be laid before the Commissioners, and after that no doubt it will be printed and circulated so that the town will have ample opportunity of knowing what are the conclusions at which we have arrived. We think it would be improper on our part to make any observation whatever on the conclusion at which we have arrived, and we therefore purposely abstain from saying what are the effects which have been produced upon our minds by the evidence which we have heard.

I should say that we are not only obliged to the various officers of the town, and to the two gentlemen whose names I have mentioned, but also to the press for the manner in which the proceedings have been reported. We have had day by day the advantage of having the shorthand writer's notes in the press, and have thus had an opportunity of seeing everything which was done on each day. We have had great assistance from both the leading papers of the town in the way in which they have supported us in conducting this long and painful inquiry.

No doubt there have been very serious revelations and disclosures of terrible crimes in the course of these investigations, things which the country did not in any degree anticipate, and those revelations have certainly been felt to be a matter of very great disgrace to the town, but I trust that the effect of those revelations having been made will be the bringing about of a better state of things, and the putting of the unions in a better position, and that it will be the means of enabling the Commissioners in London to report to the Legislature in such a manner as to enable the Legislature themselves to provide suitable laws and regulations which will place the unions on a better footing than they have been on hitherto. At all events we may hope that it will put an end not merely to the crime of murder, but also to the various other crimes which it has been our painful duty to investigate. I believe (and I think my colleagues agree with me) that great good will be found to arise from this inquiry, and that, however painful the inquiry may have been, the result of this investigation will be great benefit to this town and to the country generally.

I think these are the only observations which it is right that we should make. As I said before we do not think it desirable that we should make any remarks on the results of the evidence. That we purposely abstain from doing, because in the first instance we must communicate our impressions to the Commissioners in London, and our observations on that subject will be confined to the report which we shall have to present to them.

(*Mr. Chambers.*) Your proceedings having now been concluded, if you will allow me, sir, I wish to offer my thanks for the courtesy and attention which I have received at the hands of yourself and your learned colleagues in this inquiry, and I may express my sorrow that the gentleman whom I have succeeded has been prevented by a serious affliction of Providence from conducting those labours which have devolved upon myself, and I am requested on his part, as also on the part of those gentlemen for whom I appear, to tender to you their thanks for the very diligent, skilful, and impartial manner in which you and your learned colleagues have conducted this inquiry. I shall not venture to make any further observation upon what you have said than to express a hope that your report will be followed by some useful act of legislation, which will confer a benefit not upon this town alone but upon the country generally, and I may venture to express an opinion that upon no class or body of men will a greater benefit be conferred by this inquiry than upon the working class themselves.

(*Mr. Sugg.*) On behalf of my clients, the trades unions, I can only most cordially endorse all that has been said by my friend Mr. Chambers. I quite believe with him that this Commission will be the means of purging the town of Sheffield and its neighbourhood from a great many crimes. I may also express the hope that it will be the means of reforming in a great degree the trades unions themselves, and that they will be from the date of this inquiry established upon a sounder and better basis altogether, and that this Commission will be the means of making trades unions what they ought to be, namely, unions for their own benefit, and for that alone. I may also mention that there are other matters with respect to trades into which you cannot inquire, but I hope that the trades unions will be called upon to appear before the Commission in London, and I trust that it will be mentioned by yourself, sir, to the Commissioners that some of the trades unions of Sheffield would like to appear before that Commission to explain their character and objects more fully than has been done up to the present time.

(*Chairman.*) Yes, but our duty was to ascertain whether and how far those outrages were connected with trades unions, and to that alone we have confined our investigations. We have now and then gone into certain other facts, but those we could not avoid. Of course the question of trades unions generally, so far as it does not affect the point at issue, is for the Commission in London, and we have therefore abstained from going into that question.

(*Mr. Sugg.*) I will only say in conclusion that I heartily endorse my friend's remarks, and that my clients, the trades unions, do not in the least regret the part they took in applying for the granting of this Commission.

(*Chairman.*) We now hereby close this inquiry.

INDEX OF WITNESSES.